THE OXFORD HANDBOOK OF

VIDEO GAME MUSIC AND SOUND

THE OXFORD HANDBOOK OF

VIDEO GAME MUSIC AND SOUND

Edited by

WILLIAM GIBBONS

and

MARK GRIMSHAW-AAGAARD

OXFORD
UNIVERSITY PRESS

OXFORD
UNIVERSITY PRESS

Oxford University Press is a department of the University of Oxford. It furthers the University's objective of excellence in research, scholarship, and education by publishing worldwide. Oxford is a registered trade mark of Oxford University Press in the UK and certain other countries.

Published in the United States of America by Oxford University Press
198 Madison Avenue, New York, NY 10016, United States of America.

Library of Congress Cataloging-in-Publication Data
Names: Gibbons, William (William James), 1981– editor. | Grimshaw-Aagaard, Mark, 1963 editor.
Title: The Oxford handbook of video game music and sound / edited by
William Gibbons and Mark Grimshaw-Aagaard.
Description: [1.] | New York : Oxford University Press, 2024. |
Series: Oxford handbooks series | Includes index.
Identifiers: LCCN 2023049384 (print) | LCCN 2023049385 (ebook) |
ISBN 9780197556160 (hardback) | ISBN 9780197556184 (epub) |
ISBN 9780197556191
Subjects: LCSH: Video game music—History and criticism. |
Video game music—Analysis, appreciation.
Classification: LCC ML3540.7 .O94 2024 (print) | LCC ML3540.7 (ebook) |
DDC 781.5/4—dc23/eng/20231025
LC record available at https://lccn.loc.gov/2023049384
LC ebook record available at https://lccn.loc.gov/2023049385

DOI: 10.1093/oxfordhb/9780197556160.001.0001

Printed by Sheridan Books, Inc., United States of America

Contents

SECTION 5 IDENTITY

SECTION 6 PRE-EXISTING MUSIC

SECTION 7 MUSICAL PERFORMANCE

SECTION 8 ACOUSTIC ECOLOGIES

List of Figures

List of Tables

Acknowledgments

We first wish to acknowledge the efforts of Oxford University Press commissioning editor Norm Hirschy and music editors Lauralee Yeary and Laura Santo who have helped shape this volume from its inception to the final manuscript. We are also grateful to their colleagues at OUP with whom we have not worked directly, but without whose behind-the-scenes work none of this would be possible. Thc many peer-reviewers of this project—both for thc proposal and for the manuscript—have also provided us with both support and meaningful feedback. This is a better volume because of their work.

Of course, this volume would not exist without the work of the dozens of colleagues and acquaintances who agreed to contribute chapters and stuck with us throughout the long process. We received the contract for this volume in March 2020, with no idea that in just a few days the world would change dramatically as a result of the COVID-19 pandemic. The efforts of each author to continue their research and writing despite the challenging circumstances are remarkable and gratefully acknowledged.

Contributors

David Arditi, Professor of Sociology, Department of Sociology and Anthropology, The University of Texas at Arlington

Sean Atkinson, Associate Professor of Music Theory and Director, School of Music, Texas Christian University

Michael L. Austin, Senior Lecturer in Music & Sound, Department of English and Creative Arts, Edge Hill University

William R. Ayers, Assistant Professor of Music Theory, School of Performing Arts, University of Central Florida

Gurminder Kaur Bhogal, Catherine Mills Davis Professor in Music, Department of Music, Wellesley College

Kevin R. Burke, Associate Professor of Music, School of Arts and Communication, Florida Institute of Technology

Jacob Collins, PhD Candidate in Musicology, Division of Music History, Theory, and Ethnomusicology, University of North Texas

KC Collins, Associate Professor, School of Information Technology, Carleton University

Karen M. Cook, Associate Professor of Music History, The Hartt School, University of Hartford

James Cook, ECA Director of Research Innovation, Senior Lecturer in Early Music, Reid School of Music, University of Edinburgh

James Deaville, Professor, School for Studies in Art & Culture: Music, Carleton University

Marc Duby, Professor Extraordinarius, Department of Art and Music, University of South Africa

Melanie Fritsch, Junior Professor for Media and Cultural Studies with a focus on Game Studies and related fields, Institute of Media and Cultural Studies, Heinrich Heine University Düsseldorf

Kate Galloway, Assistant Professor of Ethnomusicology, Games, and Sound Studies, Department of Arts and the interdisciplinary programs in Games and Simulation Arts and Sciences and Critical Game Design, Rensselaer Polytechnic Institute

Tom A. Garner, Senior Lecturer in Interactive Technologies, School of Creative Technologies, University of Portsmouth

William Gibbons, Dean, Crane School of Music, SUNY Potsdam

Nicolai Jørgensgaard Graakjær, Professor of Music and Sound in Market Communication, Department of Communication and Psychology, Aalborg University

Julianne Grasso, Assistant Professor of Music Theory, College of Music, Florida State University

Stefan Greenfield-Casas, Visiting Assistant Professor of Music Theory, Department of Music, University of Richmond

Mark Grimshaw-Aagaard, The Obel Professor of Music, Department of Communication and Psychology, Aalborg University

Elizabeth Hambleton, Audio Specialist, University Libraries, Texas State University

Iain Hart, independent scholar

Elizabeth Hunt, PhD Student, University of Liverpool

Stefan Höltgen, Assistant Professor, Department for Media Studies, University of Bonn

Andra Ivănescu, Senior Lecturer in Game Studies and Ludomusicology, Department of Arts and Humanities, Brunel University London

Michiel Kamp, Assistant Professor of Musicology, Department of Media and Culture Studies, Utrecht University

Bill Kapralos, Associate Professor, Game Development and Interactive Media program, Ontario Tech University

Neil Lerner, Professor and Chair, Department of Music, Davidson College

Stephanie Lind, Associate Professor, DAN School of Drama and Music, Queen's University

Enongo Lumumba-Kasongo, David S. Josephson Assistant Professor of Music, Brown University

Kate Mancey, PhD candidate, Department of Music, Harvard University

Brooke McCorkle Okazaki, Assistant Professor of Music, Carleton College

Phillip McIntyre, Professor of Communication and Media, School of Humanities, Creative Industries and Social Sciences, University of Newcastle, Australia

Elizabeth Medina-Gray, Associate Professor of Music Theory, School of Music, Theatre, and Dance, Ithaca College

James Millea, Lecturer in Popular Music and Media, Department of English and Creative Arts, Edge Hill University

William O'Hara, Associate Professor of Music Theory and Chair of Data Science, Sunderman Conservatory of Music, Gettysburg College

Costantino Oliva, Lecturer, Institute of Digital Games, University of Malta

Hyeonjin Park, PhD Candidate, Department of Musicology, University of California, Los Angeles

Fanny Rebillard, PhD Student, University of Liège, Liège Game Lab

Peter Smucker, Assistant Dean, School of Music, Stetson University

Tim Summers, Senior Lecturer in Music, Department of Music, Royal Holloway University of London

J. T. Velikovsky, independent scholar

Jonathan Weinel, Associate Professor in Video Games, School of Computing and Mathematical Science, Faculty of Engineering and Science, University of Greenwich

Denis Zlobin, Lead Audio Designer, Ubisoft RedLynx

About the Companion Website

www.oup.com/us/ohbvideogamemusic

Oxford has created a website to accompany *The Oxford Handbook of Video Game Music and Sound* in order to provide material that cannot be made available in a book, namely color images and audio and video files. The reader is encouraged to consult this resource in conjunction with the chapters. Examples available online are indicated in the text with Oxford's symbol ▶.

INTRODUCTION
A Hub World for Game Audio

WILLIAM GIBBONS AND
MARK GRIMSHAW-AAGAARD

FROM Princess Peach's castle in *Super Mario 64* (1996), to the titular god's House in *Hades* (2018), to the bustling cities of *World of Warcraft* (2004–), so-called hub worlds have become a staple of modern game design. Whether a starting point or a home base for between missions, these are spaces to which players return over and over, allowing developers to create a sense of familiarity and structure even in games that might otherwise be overwhelming. Hub worlds often provide additional in-game benefits, as well. For example, they could provide a safe space for players to communicate with one another, perhaps by trading items or sharing tips with newcomers. Or they might offer players the chance to improve themselves, whether by leveling up, gaining new skills, or purchasing equipment. Or perhaps a hub might simply provide a central location from which players can set off in any new direction they choose.

The Oxford Handbook of Video Game Music and Sound is intended to serve as a kind of scholarly hub world, as well—and for many of the same reasons. We intend for it to provide a convenient and comprehensible starting point for those just starting out in the discipline, full of tips and tricks to get newcomers up to speed on fundamental questions and primary methodologies. At the same time, we hope this handbook will spark an interest in new methodologies or approaches in veteran researchers, introducing new ways of exploring and analyzing game music and sound. Finally, although we anticipate that this volume will be primarily a nonlinear experience for readers—that is, not read from beginning to end—we have aimed to create sections that create meaningful structure and encourage dialogue between ideas.

Only a few years ago we would probably have begun this handbook with a defense of the study of video game music and sound, or at least a justification for why this topic merits such extensive treatment. Thankfully, that need has passed. The academic study of video game music and sound—sometimes broadly called "ludomusicology"—is now a well-established and thriving field, with numerous new publications and presentations adding to the body of knowledge each year. It is also a richly interdisciplinary field: video games (which we intentionally define broadly, including everything from arcade machines to console, mobile, and computer games) and their music and sound do not exist in a self-sustaining vacuum but, rather, have been and are influenced by other fields while also exerting their own pull on the wider world. For this reason, we have attempted in this volume to offer a cross section of approaches and methodologies drawn from various fields including, to name a few, sound studies, musicology, music theory, film studies, media studies, psychology, and library science with outstanding contributions from established scholars, younger scholars, and practitioners alike.

Handbook Structure and Chapter Summaries

Structure

The handbook comprises 47 chapters (excluding this Introduction) shared across 9 sections. It is always difficult to pigeonhole chapters into specific anthology sections, and the chapters in this handbook are no exception. In inviting contributions, we imposed no framework on the approach or contents of each chapter, allowing each contributor to deal with their topic in the manner they saw fit. A compounding factor is that many of the contributions are interdisciplinary. For example, the reader will come across chapters that deal with the perception of sound while proposing an analytical framework, or chapters that concern themselves with game audio technology but that also treat the methodology of traditional musicology. Consequently, the handbook structure groups chapters into sections based on our judgment of the main thrust of each chapter, but the reader should be aware that the section titles do not imply sole specificity as to the chapters' contents—in certain chapters, where appropriate, we have provided internal references to other handbook chapters that deal with similar subjects.

The opening section concerns itself in the main with broad disciplinary questions and issues of methodology. There are many ways to study and analyze the music and sound of video games, and several hurdles to overcome on the path to understanding. The five chapters in this section provide both useful questions for scholars to ask as well as a variety of proposed theoretical and methodological frameworks.

Section 2 contains seven chapters broadly dealing with the history and technology of video game music and sound. There are chapters tracing the antecedents of video game audio to the 19th century, the history of women composers in 1980s Japan, histories of early game console audio, programming audio with BASIC, and early game advertising, problems associated with the archiving of game audio, and discussions of the uses of video game audio technology for other audiovisual purposes.

The third section moves the handbook into the area of the perception and psychology of video game music and sound. Chapters range across specific topics, such as ambiguity and vagueness in video game sound or the promotion of altered states of consciousness, to more general topics, such as the psychological effects on the player of video game music or a framework for the design of video game sound according to psychology.

Section 4 comprises chapters on interactions across media. The roots of many aspects of video game music and sound can be traced to the practices and reception of cinema, and there is a widely acknowledged crossover between the two forms (composers, sound designers, music, and audio samples). However, cinema is far from alone in its reciprocal relationship with games. The section's chapters provide examples of some of the many interactions between these other media—extended reality, the music industry, and clubbing—and also explore new directions in cinema–game interactions.

Identity, broadly speaking, is the main topic of the fifth section—how the complex intersections of the identities of players, characters, composers, and developers are expressed in game sound and music. The chapters cover issues of sexual and gender identity, gamer-rap, hip-hop, and credibility across media, "exotic" music and Otherness in video games, indigenous-designed games and culture stereotyping, and ludomusical autobiography in single-developer video games.

Section 6 explores the use of pre-existing music in video games. Such music is often used for particular evocative effect or to tap into subcultures. Two of the chapters in Section 6 explore the use of popular music and connections to subculture and narrative, while a third deals with allusions to the supernatural and death through the use of American folk music. As in cinema, pre-existing music can be used for historical setting or to evoke particular moods in the game, and there are two chapters in this section covering the music used for games set during the European Renaissance and the use of Claude Debussy's music for the creation of atmosphere.

Not only are there some video games that are explicitly focused on the player's music performance, but also there is an increasing number of concert presentations of video game music, and so the issue of musical performance is the subject of Section 7. Some contributors explore the world of video game music concerts and transmediality, while the topic of the player's musicality is of interest to others.

Section 8 deals broadly with the topic of the acoustic ecologies of video games. There are chapters on the semiotics of musical communication in video games, environmental music, the sound of navigable narratives or walking simulators, the abstract representation of voices, and the use and simulation of spectator sounds in sports video games.

The final section contains chapters on the theory and practice of video game audio design in relation to notions of virtuality and reality and to the feeling of presence or immersion. Here are found design ideas on making sound effects unpleasant, the practicalities and wisdom of attempting to emulate reality with video game sound, and the role of music and sound in creating player immersion.

Chapter Summaries

To provide additional context for navigating this volume, in what follows we provide a brief overview of each chapter.

Section 1: Disciplinary Questions

Within the context of the development over the past decades of a new musicology that shifts the focus away from the autonomous work of art, Tim Summers opens the handbook by proposing 15 "awkward questions" for video game music scholars within the new field. As such a scholar himself, Summers poses the questions rhetorically as a means for self-reflection. With this approach, he highlights several questions and challenges of methodology within the new musicology that must be grappled with by video game music scholars.

On the back of 2020's The Game Awards recognition of that year's *Final Fantasy VII Remake* in the "Best Score and Music" category, William Gibbons explores the meaning of labels such as "the Beethoven of game music" applied to the composer Nobuo Uematsu. Gibbons is concerned with how our understanding not only of Uematsu but also of other game composers and their music is shaped by such labels; that this canonization of one composer risks overshadowing the relevance and importance of other video game music composers.

Sean Atkinson outlines three challenges faced when applying western music theory to the analysis of video game music: the theory was developed to analyze western art music; video game music is an art form that makes use of such art music but that also makes use of other musics; and the interactivity of video game music is a specific problem that must be accounted for. Regarding this last, and concentrating on the link to film music, Atkinson presents a ludo-cinematic continuum model that describes not the video game music itself but rather its function and use in the game. Thus, music with a more ludic function is more interactive and less choreographed compared to the scripted and choreographed cinematic function. In using the model to conduct a preliminary assessment of the music to be analyzed, Atkinson provides the means to determine the most appropriate analytical tools when it comes to the music itself.

Julianne Grasso's chapter provides a way to account for music in video games given that "humans naturally tend to narrativize" ludic challenges and the exploration and discovery of ludic spaces. Her aim is to show that, within the perception that musical loops and repetitions (particularly in early video games) promote a feeling of timelessness, the use of music implies narrative form and so enhances the narrativization of the play experience. Indeed, Grasso argues with the aid of case studies, music can be used to shape interactive play, and, in some cases, "the enacted narrative is fundamentally musical."

Phillip McIntyre and J. T. Velikovsky propose a systems-based approach to understanding creative practice in the production of music and sound in the video games industry. McIntyre and Velikovsky base their approach not on the Romantic view of creativity springing mysteriously from inspiration but on an evidence-based, rationalist view, traceable to Aristotle: creativity derives from a discoverable set of pre-existing conditions. Creative work in music and sound for video games arises from the interplay of three factors: structured knowledge of games and audio providing a symbol system to the agent; a judgment-based social organization; and the choice-making composer or sound designer as agent.

Section 2: History and Technology

Neil Lerner explores the roots of video game sound practices through an investigation of the sound of US pinball machines from the period 1871–1939. Lerner suggests that pinball and its predecessors always had sound as an element of play—for example, in pinball, sounds of the mechanical operation and of the ball's passage down the playfield—and this, along with the introduction of electromechanical sound-producing devices in 1934, provided invaluable lessons and resources to early 1970s video game sound designers that persist to this day.

James Deaville's chapter is an analysis of the sound, and especially music, of promotional material for the first video games and home consoles through to the Crash of 1983. Included for assessment are a number of Atari adverts but also adverts for the Magnavox Odyssey—the console's lack of audio being compensated for by the music of the commercials. In this and other cases, it was the music and sound of the audiovisual promotional material, Deaville argues, that were tasked with selling the product, but Deaville also shows that the soundtrack of the advertising kept pace with developments in the home-computer industry, stressing the opportunities for fun rather than work and featuring an increasing amount of narration, memorable jingles, and an emphasis on whole family enjoyment.

Kevin R. Burke provides a survey and assessment of the hardware and software that powered early video game sound and analyzes how the hardware limitations and innovative software led to specific compositional styles across platform developers. Throughout, Burke's focus is on the home consoles of the chiptune era, and he develops a "systematic" approach for the analysis of the audio hardware and software systems, systems which determine the challenges posed, and the possibilities afforded the games' composers.

Jonathan Weinel examines the use of video game engines for purposes other than gaming: specifically, how the software can be used for the purposes of visualizing music in scenarios such as audiovisual installations and concerts. The chapter outlines the early history of music visualization, music visualization's relationship to multimodal perception and synesthesia, and then shows how video game engines can be used for the visualization of music in pedagogical contexts far removed from game development education. Weinel identifies a new paradigm emerging where older means of visualizing music are reinvigorated with the interactive possibilities and mechanics offered by video game engines.

Brooke McCorkle Okazaki asks the question, "What did it mean to be a woman composer and sound designer [for video games] in 1980s Japan?" The question, triggered by a chance finding of a contemporary photograph of some of Capcom's female composers and sound designers, leads Okazaki to explore further issues regarding the politics, economy, and the social conditions for women in Japanese corporate culture of the time, and the subsequent visibility of these particular women's contributions to video games. The tale of the demise of this singular and short-lived instance of women's ability to find a *creative* space for their labor in Japan mirrors the all-too-common situation of women the world over—economic collapse in 1990s Japan, reproductive pressures, and the dominance of male composers and sound designers means that female contributions to video game music and sound risk being forgotten.

Fanny Rebillard discusses the issues surrounding the archiving of video game music. Rebillard identifies a number of problems, including those of changes in audio format and the loss of elements related to interactivity and graphics, and discusses how the resolving of these issues during the archiving process, especially through published soundtracks, can provide new perspectives on the wider place of game music. The organization of tracks in such archives is important, and Rebillard closes the chapter with some suggestions for published game music typologies.

Stefan Höltgen delves into the archives with a study of representative BASIC computer game program codes produced by a growing band of computer programming hobbyists from the 1970s to the 1990s. In contrast to other studies of game sound and music that typically provide aesthetic or functional categories, Höltgen's approach allows him to devise a distinct typography based on the sound–code connection. It is only by focusing on this connection, Höltgen argues, that the influence of the game platform's hardware and software specifications on the sounds' aesthetics can be fully appreciated.

Section 3: Perception and Psychology

Mark Grimshaw-Aagaard makes the case that focus should be placed on the study of ambiguity and vagueness in relation to video game sound design and analysis. In this, he proffers the opinion that ambiguity and vagueness should be used as video game sound design tools not least as an antidote to the dead end of deathly realism. Grimshaw-Aagaard begins his chapter with a brief survey of ambiguity in language and vagueness in the natural sciences, before he demonstrates how an understanding of our perception's ability to easily resolve and deal with these everyday facts of life can enhance video game sound design.

Tom A. Garner's chapter probes the "psychological relationship between player and video game," and highlights how, historically, game design parallels developments in understanding cognition and perception—there is increasing understanding of the integration between various systems while, at the same time, aspects of function and task are coming to the fore. Accordingly, Garner presents two arguments regarding video game sound. First, the conceptualization of such sounds best proceeds from their function; and, second, game designers should maximize their use of cutting-edge technology and experimental findings while still paying attention to a holistic view of the game system. In order to do so, and with the view that auditory perception is an emergent process, Garner provides a number of recommendations to game audio designers.

In an analysis of 3D action-adventure video games, William R. Ayers highlights the modular nature of their music. These musical modules require player input to be activated, and this is a part of the interactivity that games afford. But, as Ayers demonstrates, such musical interactivity and modularity is not unique to this genre of video games; these games continue a tradition of musical practice that can be traced back to the early years of silent film, where accompanists in the theater were provided not with complete scores but with cue categories or topics aligned with the film's scenes. These plot or mood topics formed the basis for the accompanist's selection of musical pieces; a practice of creating narrative pathways through films, and a practice that, as Ayers shows, is still extant in the use of interactive musical modules to support gameplay in 3D action-adventure games.

Jonathan Weinel explores aural aspects of the increasingly common representation in video games of an altered state of consciousness (ASC) such as intoxication, hallucination, and psychosis. He first outlines how ASCs, produced, for instance, by drug intake, form and shape our subjective experiences before suggesting how such experiences can be designed for video games. Weinel uses his own ASC audiovisual projects as a means to discuss the concept of "avatar-centered subjectivity": where the audiovisual design of first-person perspective (and thus first-person auditive) video games is based on a concept of the subjective perceptual experience of a player avatar. In this context, audio representing ASCs is disrupted in order to reflect the distorted aural experiences of the avatar.

Section 4: Interacting across Media

William O'Hara's chapter examines the use and transformation of sound and music in film-to-game adaptations, focusing on the format's rise in popularity during the 1980s. O'Hara contends that, rather than assessing the game's fidelity to the film, game adaptations are best viewed as a new form of media convergence. Using archival evidence, O'Hara sheds light on cross-media relationships during the adaptation process and uncovers cooperation and tension between different industries—changes and compromises had to be made in the games' audio design due to the exigencies of different technologies and narrative forms and the requirements of intellectual property law and advertising.

In his chapter, Tom A. Garner tracks the close association between video game sound design and effect and film sound. His particular focus is the new affordances of extended reality (XR) and what they offer game sound designers. Garner discusses the concepts "cinematic" and "cinematic sound" with regard to video games and highlights what he terms the "cinematic-interactive dichotomy" by asking how video games can be both cinematic *and* interactive. The chapter's argument is that XR technologies, in particular biosensing and the use of environmental data, offer both cinematic and interactive affordances to game sound designers, and thus game sound design using these technologies must perforce be integrative, not only within the cinematic-interactive dichotomy but also across other aspects of game production.

Jazz soundtracks in film-noir-inspired detective video games are the focus of Jacob Collins's chapter. The use of jazz in such games is leveraged by game developers to quickly convey framing information to players, a device adapted from the use of jazz in cinematic genres such as film noir and the later neo-noir, but, as Collins notes, such tropes and clichés can be problematic. The chapter demonstrates how jazz is used to frame these games in the noir genre, but Collins also shows how the use of jazz in game noir can all too often reinforce and play to the racist and misogynistic stereotypes that came to be associated with the music through its representation in early film noir.

David Arditi uses the term "unending consumption" to describe developments in early 21st-century capitalism whereby, rather than expanding the consumer base, an industry thrives by supplying the same consumer base with ever more goods. This shift in focus is used by Arditi to illustrate strategic changes in the music recording industry that took place in the early 2000s: a response to the revenue challenges posed by the video game industry by blurring the lines between gamer and music fan. Arditi explains this phenomenon by examining synchronization licenses and the later use of gaming platforms to live-stream music concerts. It is through this industry synergy, Arditi argues, that the recording industry has secured new means of revenue generation, enabling it to thrive in the new millennium.

Melanie Fritsch explains in her chapter that, despite media attention during the COVID-19 pandemic helping to highlight the release of video games depicting dance club culture—games often used by those unable to physically partake in clubbing—such depictions and the virtual experiences they bring with them are nothing new. Equally, discos and clubs have been used to market new games—a practice that can be traced back to at least the 1970s. Fritsch explores this overlooked relationship, showing the manifold ways in which game developers have explored and exploited club culture and social practices and suggesting that this naturally occurs because both forms provide experiential opportunities for staging "ludic possibility spaces."

Section 5: Identity

Using interviews with practitioners, while also drawing on personal experience, Enongo Lumumba-Kasongo explores the vibrant music subgenre of gamer-rap, focusing on the experiences of artists of color. As Lumumba-Kasongo uncovers, in the past decade, such artists had to navigate a path that risked either alienating non-Black audiences (due to the subgenre's proximity to nerd/geek rap) or undermining their credibility in the wider world of hip-hop. As gamer-rap becomes more mainstream, through lucrative deals with game studios and record labels, Lumumba-Kasongo sets out to bear witness to those artists who laid the foundation for this growth but have been largely ignored in academic scholarship and the nerd/geek rap scene.

Michael L. Austin begins his chapter with a history of sonic representations of sex and sexuality in erotic film and pornography, tracing the friction between such media and public morals and showing how the media borrowed musical tropes and clichés from mainstream media and used developments in technology to make the soundtrack hyperreal. Austin then turns his attention to sonic depictions of heterosexuality in mainstream video games such as *The Sims*, as well as a range of niche games, before focusing on sonic representations of homosexuality. Throughout, Austin shows how the use of music and sound supports the developing role of games as tools for constructively "enacting our real-life identity and personhood."

Kate Galloway tackles the topic of Indigenous video games and the newly important debates surrounding the use of audio and representation of Indigenous timbres and instrumentation in such games. Galloway uncovers a number of issues, such as the mislabeling of some games as Indigenous and the use of stereotypical sound design, which reinforce problematic and factually inaccurate perceptions of "primitive cultures disconnected from contemporary society." The chapter focuses on a number of recent Indigenous-made video games, and, in doing so, illustrates how Indigenous game designers use sound and music to re-present their histories more accurately, promoting and preserving Indigenous language and culture, while also presenting more equitable and speculative future scenarios.

Hyeonjin Park tackles the problem of Otherness in video game music—often the Orient as representing the Other. Specifically, the chapter analyzes received notions of authenticity and other discourses surrounding perceptions of the Gerudo and the desert in *The Legend of Zelda* series. For Park, the use of "exotic" music informs a relationship between the game world and the real world which illuminates "conversations about appropriation and (in)authenticity."

William Gibbons focuses on indie video game development, especially single-developer games, to uncover how the music factors into game design when the composer is also the person developing and structuring all other elements of the game. In particular, the chapter deals with the use of such games to present autobiographical narratives. Through three case studies, Gibbons explores how, and if, music plays a role in the construction of "ludomusical autobiography."

Section 6: Pre-Existing Music

Karen M. Cook uncovers the hidden Renaissance in video game music. It is Cook's contention that games set during, and thematically connected to, the European Renaissance (approximately 1400–1600) often make use of medieval and Baroque musical tropes. Such tropes might include a Gothic organ or harpsichord, counterpoint, drones, plainchant, and parallel fifths—all long fixed in the popular imagination as symbols of the distant historical or fantastical past. Moving past such tropes, Cook discusses musical referents more closely linked to the Renaissance itself, such as Renaissance musical works, recorders, lutes, and historically accurate styles. In so doing, Cook notes that such musical gestures solidify select historical people, events, and places (Leonardo da Vinci, the Reformation, Tudor England) as emblematic of the Renaissance writ large.

Gurminder Kaur Bhogal's chapter is an exploration of the influence or direct use of Claude Debussy's piano music: for instance, how his ethereal, "floating sounds," as found in works such as "Clair de Lune" have directed game designers' attentions toward the creation of Böhme's atmospheres in video games and the possibilities these atmospheres afford the player. For Bhogal, Debussy's music, and video game compositions drawing from it, is particularly effective in creating the virtual spaces players are invited to inhabit, where the atmospheres fashioned by the music can touch the player and make them feel.

James Millea focuses on the *Tony Hawk's Pro Skater* series of video games, its use of popular music, and how this transmediality between game culture and music culture shapes the series' "projection of authenticity." Millea critiques the vogue for viewing the music of video games through the lens of cinema—the ways in which popular music is used in the series have a markedly different genesis, that of music videos and television and other media depicting the culture of skateboarding. The transmediality of popular music and the series' games finds purchase in the skateboarding community through the creation of audio–visual relationships that are anything but cinematic.

Peter Smucker focuses on the use of American folk songs in video games and the effects of interpretations of these songs on the player experience. As Smucker shows, the specific use of Appalachian folk songs and other, freshly composed material can affect the player's social encounters and acceptance of a character's death during gameplay through their use of supernatural and religious tropes. By highlighting Southern Gothic features and Appalachian beliefs in music, Smucker offers the player new perspectives on the game character's life, death, and afterlife.

Andra Ivănescu's chapter examines the relevance of narrative theories to an understanding of music in video games. Ivănescu acknowledges the debates and criticism surrounding the relationships between narrative and the fields of musicology and game studies, while arguing that narrative theories can serve to enrich the field of ludomusicology. Concentrating on the use of popular music in games, Ivănescu shows that this use provides not only worthwhile ludic and musical experiences to players but also narrative experiences, and thus narrative, at least in the intersection between popular music and video games, is a productive field of inquiry for researchers.

Section 7: Musical Performance

Stefan Greenfield-Casas reviews the growing phenomenon of live concerts of video game music and asks if the experience of attending such concerts has an aesthetic effect on the concertgoer's memory of the experience of the game they have played. Greenfield-Casas's analysis is rooted in the game fans' experiences, and he constructs a theory of "ludic liveness" to argue that attendance at such concerts provokes experiences of replaying the games. Ultimately, video game music, remediated through live concerts, becomes ontologically validated in the real world.

Elizabeth Hunt's chapter focuses on the long-running concert series *Video Games Live* (VGL), which raises issues of gamification for both the audience and performers. Hunt argues that the VGL concerts subvert traditional concert codes by inciting the carnivalesque through gamification of the concert mechanics and through audience participation on stage. It is through such features that the audience member becomes a voluntary and active coproducer of the concert; this form of "participatory spectatorship" helps to break down the boundary between high art and low art erected, in part, by the traditional rules of orchestral concerts.

James Cook's chapter explores the growing phenomenon of the use of video game technologies and platforms to host "live" music concerts. Cook presents several brief case studies, each exploring the history or a particular dimension of musical performances within games. Thus, the chapter provides overviews of concerts in *Second Life* and *Fortnite*, as well as musical avatars such as Gorillaz and Hatsune Miku, and Cook's own experience of recording historical performances in reconstructed VR settings. Throughout, Cook expounds the view that such musical performances are examples of metalepsis; the events are a recontextualization of liveness and provide a "liminal space between the virtual and real world" into and out of which performers and audiences step.

Marc Duby uses J. J. Gibson's theories of ecological psychology and his concept of affordances to explore the links between electric guitar-playing and music video games such as *Guitar Hero* and *Rocksmith*. The chapter uses this framework to probe aspects of guitar heroism, networks of technology used to create signature sounds, and questions of authenticity and play in the chosen music video games. Throughout, Duby questions the valorization of the music played on actual instruments over the music produced by players of guitar games, suggesting instead that, while such games have in some cases inspired players to turn to real electric guitars, guitar games hold the promise of an "as yet unexplored musicality."

Stephanie Lind explores the phenomenon of rhythm games by wondering if players untrained in music theory have an intuitive awareness of the musical structures of the games and use this to predict dance moves and gestures. Through analyses of rhythm games like *Dance Revolution* and *Just Dance*, Lind highlights instances of kinesonic congruence (the synchronization of gesture with sound) in order to discover the role that repetition plays in these games. Lind concludes that nonmusical players have a visceral understanding of musical pattern and articulation, and that the kinesonic congruence the players experience aids in their perceptions of such patterns.

Costantino Oliva's chapter has its theoretical foundation in John Blacking's analysis of musical situations, whereby an intercultural understanding of music and musicality arises from an emphasis on the individual rather than the social. With this in mind, Oliva sets out to examine the musicality of the game player by focusing on the player's creative impulse and individual experience. Oliva shows that a variety of musical situations in video games challenge received elitist musical paradigms by facilitating a space of the expression of individual musicality and creative endeavor.

Section 8: Acoustic Ecologies

Elizabeth Hambleton explores the music and soundscapes of the paidic games she terms navigable narratives (also known as walking simulators). Navigable narratives are immersive "games without gameplay"; with no preset outcomes, they present artistic experiences, and the player is invited to discover and navigate their stories. Through four case studies, Hambleton analyzes the navigable narrative's music and sound, showing how composers create unique blends of the real and the imaginary to create the virtual worlds and use disembodied voices to interact with the player and the world, thereby prompting new experiences.

In a chapter on ambient ecologies of music in video games, Michiel Kamp argues for including nondynamic musical cues as part of the ecology of the game. Such music, unlike the dynamic music that is typically the subject of much academic discourse and media attention, provides no ludic signals about the gameplay state; it is an ambient cue that is "just there." Kamp argues that, far from being dismissed as mere background music, this ambient music is a key part of the ecology of the game, providing stability and persistence and a space within which to achieve the game's goals.

Iain Hart finds beauty in the mess of meanings that arises from interaction with video game music. Although music might be composed to communicate specific meanings to the player within gameplay, the inherent variability of human interaction may result in a failure to communicate those meanings as intended. And yet, miscommunications and missed communications still result in meaningful and semiotically relevant gameplay experiences. Hart suggests that the communication of meanings between player and game is the result of a negotiation that continues throughout gameplay, an ongoing conversation between the player and the composer about the meaning of musical signs.

Elizabeth Medina-Gray aims to provide a framework from which to analyze the abstract representation of voice in video games. Her focus is the use of vocal-like or dialogue sounds, having no linguistic meaning or comprehensible words and phrases and where the sound has noticeable technologically mediated qualities. The purpose is to allow for an exploration of the spaces at the intersection of the human and the mechanical, and, to this end, Medina-Gray makes use of both social semiotics and musical analysis of the sounds to suggest that players use imagination to uncover the human in such abstract representations.

Nicolai Jørgensgaard Graakjær's chapter deals with spectator sounds in sports video games, focusing on Electronic Arts' FIFA series and, specifically, *FIFA 19*. Graakjær shows how boundaries between the televised broadcast of football (i.e., soccer) matches and their video game versions have become increasingly porous—spectator sound effects traverse domains, from broadcast to game, and from game to broadcast, and reality becomes a construct in both mediums. Throughout, issues of audience and player expectation, perception, authenticity, realism, and reality in relation to the use of spectator sound effects lead Graakjær to conclude, referencing Baudrillard's concept of simulacra, that the resultant soundscapes embody "the generation by models of a real without origin or reality."

Section 9: Virtuality/Reality

KC Collins and Bill Kapralos investigate advances in spatial audio rendering for video game sound and discuss the pros and cons of the technology within the framework of realism. The authors first provide an overview of human localization of real-world sound, attempts to emulate these real-world conditions in virtual reality and video game audio technology, and the problems encountered in doing so. They then turn to the psychology of hearing—in particular, the role of attention and focus in our sound perception, and the importance of using sound design for emotion and expression. Collins and Kapralos argue that, in using sound as a "tool of realism" in video games, the artistic power of sound is lost: the belief that technological advances in spatial audio's emulation of the real world produces realism, or even hyperrealism, is misguided, and what often results is an anemic hyporealism that lacks the imagination both game and player require.

Similarly, an attack on the fetish of realism in video game sound design is the topic of Mark Grimshaw-Aagaard's chapter. In addition to discussing the lure of appeals to realism as a historical tool for marketing various forms of media—something still used today to market video games—he also differentiates realism from the related terms fidelity, authenticity, and verisimilitude. Establishing the distinct notions of realism of form and realism of content, Grimshaw-Aagaard argues that, in contrast to fidelity to, and authenticity of, sound source, it is the former that is most important for persuading a player of the game world's verisimilitude.

Kate Mancey uses the concepts of place illusion and plausibility illusion from the field of virtual reality to highlight the role of music in VR games. In particular, she is concerned with the perception of motion in music, a motion that, in the game's world, is independent of any changes in the player's head position. Using *Half-Life: Alyx* as an example, Mancey offers a methodology for analyzing motion in recorded sound and shows how music's independence of motion allows the player to imagine the presence of other entities beyond what can be seen.

The game audio designer Denis Zlobin uses his chapter to put forward the view that, rather than approach such design as the creation of sounds for video games, the designer should conceive of the role as creating video games via sound. To illustrate this, Zlobin uses the example of modulating player experience through the judicious use of intrinsically unpleasant sound effects. Zlobin proposes a framework for the evaluation, from various angles, of unpleasant sounds in video games then suggests how the audio designer can best create synergies with other areas of game development when seeking to use such sounds to serve the game.

In the handbook's final chapter, Mark Grimshaw-Aagaard highlights the importance of sound in the formation of presence in video games. Following some terminological clarification, the chapter outlines some of the debates on presence and immersion in the fields of virtual reality and video games using first-person perspective. Grimshaw-Aagaard provides a model of externality and self and uses this to show how sound waves from externality lead to the initial other-presences of a perceptual environment—it is against these other-presences that the self is defined and within this environment that the self is present.

The Companion Website

Oxford has created a website to accompany *The Oxford Handbook of Video Game Music and Sound* (www.oup.com/us/ohbvideogamemusic). Here, the reader will find many of the images in the book reproduced in color along with audiovisual examples.

SECTION 1

DISCIPLINARY QUESTIONS

CHAPTER 1

VIDEO GAME MUSICOLOGY IN PRACTICE

Fifteen Awkward Questions

TIM SUMMERS

DURING the latter years of my undergraduate music degree in the mid-2000s, I became aware of the possibility of undertaking academic research into video game music. I remember avidly describing the processes and methods that such study might entail with a postgraduate teaching assistant. We discussed several approaches, including how one might extract music data like MIDI directly from a game for analysis. "Ah," he said, his eyes widening, "so you could actually do OLD musicology with this kind of music!"

His reference to an "old" musicology alluded to a moment of methodological change in musicology. In the 1980s and 1990s, scholars such as Susan McClary (1991), Joseph Kerman (1985), Lawrence Kramer (1990), and others took a then-radical approach to scholarship that drew inspiration from literary studies. These scholars advocated for greater emphasis on interpretive methods, extensive use of critical theory, a broadening of repertoires, a shift away from the treatment of musical works as autonomous objects, and a critical understanding of both historiography and the tools of analysis. In short, this approach sought to counterbalance what they saw as inappropriate positivism and uncritical claims of objectivity within the discipline. The term "new musicology" began to coalesce around such perspectives, though it was not a movement with a specific manifesto. For some, the new musicology was a refreshing diversification of the tools and repertoires of musicology. For others, it represented a threatening emphasis on idiosyncratic interpretation, postmodern relativism, and a distraction from the work of analyzing and documenting a static history and fixed musical texts.

My postgraduate friend certainly had no objection to the new musicology (quite the opposite). Rather, he was surprised that a popular, relatively recently developed music, with pop-culture associations might so readily lend itself to traditional, even regressive, approaches. The rapid expansion of the repertoires of video game music and musicology occurred simultaneously. As game music scholars, we deal with a period of history that is well within living memory and with materials often found in (if not originating from) our own culture. Many critical issues of musicology initially arose when discussing music from another time and/or another place, beyond our personal experiences, or those of our contemporaries. Yet our cultural and temporal proximity to the materials does not eliminate important questions concerning musicology in practice.

Although video game musicology has now established itself as a fixture in the academic landscape, the field has yet to fully grapple with some methodological questions and challenges posed by the new musicology. In this chapter, I survey some critical sites of musicological study and discuss how video game music scholarship (re)frames these issues. The central aim of this chapter is to cultivate an awareness of the issues embedded in musical academic practices, so that researchers engaging with such methods and materials might work with thoughtful consideration of critical dimensions of musicological study.

One of the central aims of the new musicology was to cultivate critical self-awareness of the processes of musicology. In that spirit, I set here awkward questions to prompt such self-reflection in game musicology. These are not questions from me to others. These are questions I challenge myself to answer. I am keenly aware of the ways I have not met my own ambitions or failed to be sufficiently self-reflective. The questions are offered here in the spirit of communal improvement. I here use the deliberately mild term "awkward" because these questions are not meant to prohibit or even inhibit any approach, method, topic, or framework. Many of these questions may not have easy answers. My position is simply that, if we are to "do" musicology, we should be conscious of the results and meanings of that activity. When we create knowledge and understanding in the course of our academic activity, we have a responsibility to be mindful of what we do.

Critical Issues and Musicology

Denis Stevens's *Musicology: A Practical Guide* (1980) is designed to provide an overview of the discipline, introducing students to the "science" (as the dust jacket terms it) of musicology. Created just before the advent of the new musicology, it is endearingly untroubled by many of the critical and methodological developments that would soon arrive. It is also striking the degree to which Stevens (1980, 13) anchors his understanding of musicology in a definition presented some 95 years earlier by Guido Adler: "Dividing his subject in two sections—historical and systematic—Adler regards the first as a study of musical history, paleography, forms, theories, and instruments, and the second as an investigation of the laws of music as related to harmony, rhythm, and melody, along with musical psychology and aesthetics, pedagogics, and folklore."

The musicology of Adler and Stevens is one primarily concerned with explaining art works and aesthetics; describing musical developments (typically in a linear progression from the past to the present); and providing objective, dispassionate, and empirical explanations of musical phenomena. When Stevens calls his book a "practical guide," the practice he has in mind is using historical evidence to enable performances and editions that reflect history "as it was"—analytical work to demonstrate the underlying mechanics of music, and the documentation of historical facts.

In a public-facing talk, a colleague of mine recently described the work of musicology as "thinking critically about music" (Elphick 2021). This critical dimension, now seen (at least to some) as central to the definition of musicology, reframed much of the work of musicological scholarship. To see the influence of this disciplinary turn, one need only look at a modern counterpart to Stevens's book, *Musicology: The Key Concepts* (Beard and Gloag 2016). The contents page of this volume indicates that "key concepts" of musicology now encompass canon, class, disability, gender, historiography, politics, race, and so on. It would be inaccurate to claim that such themes and topics were absent from musicology prior to the 1980s, but the new centrality of such approaches to musicology illustrates the radical disciplinary changes. An important part of this new critical awareness is an understanding of how knowledge is constructed from the musical sources we use. As Leo Treitler (1989, 94) writes: "our categorical prejudgments effect not only the interpretation and assessment of art works but even those matters that we take to be open to 'objective,' 'scientific' treatment: the reading of art works and the attribution of authorship, chronology, and provenance."

In this sense, in J.P.E. Harper-Scott's (2018, 43) formulation, "history-writing is fictive, that is, as a form of writing, it recasts the past in narrative form. This does not mean, though, that history is fictional," but rather that history is created and fashioned. As such, the historian's relationship with the past is continually changing. These statements are cast in historical terms, but much the same holds for analytical and other kinds of music research.

It is not difficult to see how video game music might easily fall into older musicological patterns of thinking:

- Composers are often living, so authorial intention can be ascertained;
- Extraction of musical data allows access to a precision of musical content and instructions beyond even that of a written score's musical detail;
- Technological evolution provides a ready model for periodization and linear development;
- Much musical material is stylistically similar to western art music, allowing the application of existing techniques of analysis.

None of these activities are inherently negative or inappropriate, but unless applied critically and self-reflexively, they have the potential to inherit problematic dimensions of scholarship. We must remain aware of the sources and data we deal with, and how we make claims to knowledge as we undertake this fictive work of scholarship. How do we advance the central goals of the musicological project—that is, better understanding of game music and its cultural impact?

Sources

Q1. Which sources are you using, and what images or instances of the game work do they present?

Harper-Scott (2018), among others, characterizes music history post-1989 as one preoccupied (implicitly or explicitly) with the nature of the material it seeks to interrogate. He writes:

> What kind of historical object is music? Is it a "work," the product of creative labor, whose identity as a work can be fixed by its notation in a score; an autonomous object because it exists for its own internal compositional logic? Or is it some species of a sonic "event" discernible only in performance, with or without the notated trace. . . . If music is better understood as performance, then its essence is found in the social functions it discharges and supports; if it is a "work," then its disinterested and self-ruling inner workings are a form of cognition without representational concepts, which poses a potential danger to a social world it no longer flatters by imitation. (Harper-Scott 2018, 37)

In a polarized formulation, Harper-Scott alludes to one of the landmarks in new musicological thinking: the deconstruction of the understanding of a musical work as an inviolable entity. Lydia Goehr (1992) outlined the paradoxical nature of a musical work—an imaginary object, forged by an author (usually the composer), that exists beyond any single performance or score of a piece, but is nevertheless thought to be distinct, specific, and static. Older musicological practice often took the examination of such works as the primary object of enquiry; Adler (quoted in Mugglestone 1981, 9) wrote that "one must always, above all, retain the works of art themselves at the centre of investigation." The recognition of music's qualities as "event," however, has been a hallmark of modern musicological thinking.

As Harper-Scott (2018, 42) ultimately notes, "all music is partly work and partly performance." It may be tempting to view the video game source exclusively as a work: a self-contained cartridge, a surviving arcade cabinet, a dumped ROM, a recording of a complete playthrough of the game from beginning to end. But these sources still exhibit the tricky textuality of other kinds of musical sources. We should be careful not to assume that even a "complete" source like those listed above *is* the musical work in its totality. For instance, there may be divergent production runs of cartridges (e.g., the musical differences between earlier and later North American cartridges of *The Legend of Zelda: Ocarina of Time* [1998]), or the same code on different hardware (e.g., the different revisions of the SID chip, or the same MIDI data on different sound cards). The problems of the accuracy of emulation are well known, even if the information from a game has been downloaded accurately. The point here is not to critique oneself out of business with "what about?" criticisms (see Wegman 2012, 40), but to avoid being misled by the apparent definitiveness of these sources. A game encompasses different textual properties (like the gameplay, program/engine, music data, and so on), and itself sits alongside many other relevant sources, like interviews, liner notes, scores, reviews, ethnographies of production and consumption, and so on.

Q2. How does your work engage with issues of authorship, and the activity/power attributed to various agents in the game production? How do you negotiate between using composer/creator testimony and the trap of the intentional fallacy?

Video games present complicated images of musical authorship, which challenge received ideas of the solo composer that we inherit from the romantic image of musical composition. Even when there is only one named composer on a project, authorship is very often distributed across several agents, both in the production and enactment of game music. For instance, when audio director Lydia Andrew recounts her work on the *Assassin's Creed* franchise, it is clear that she had significant creative input on the games' musical directions (Andrew 2021, xxxiii–xxxv). Especially in earlier games, it is not uncommon for composers and sound designers to have their work unattributed. Hillegonda C. Reitveld and Andrew Lemon have documented how the work of the (mostly female) Capcom Sound Team was routinely left uncredited or attributed to pseudonyms shared between staff members (2021). As a result, uncovering the authorship of the sound of these games is tricky, even today.

Game directors and producers may also define specific aspects of the music of a game, from beyond the creative team. As composer Stephen Baysted testifies, marketing and corporate executives, too, may shape important components of the musical outcome (Baysted and Summers 2020).

Of course, one way to deal with these questions of authorship is to discuss and engage with the creative agents. This is certainly one of the advantages of scholarship that deals primarily with living composers. One must be careful, however, not to fall into the trap of the intentional fallacy,[1] and be wary of corporate interests that might inflect the testimony of creators.

Q3. How is the authorial agency of the player accounted for in your work? What is omitted from a single perspective on the musical source?

KC Collins (2013) has claimed that this distributed authorship is not simply a feature of the creative process of game music, but also how it is sounded in practice:

> Video games . . . alter the traditional relationships between creator and consumer, audience and performance. . . . If a player can create the overall soundscape through her game play or rearrange the music cues . . . is she not in some way the creator of the overall sound experience? If she is constantly "performing" sound by triggering the emitter of that sound . . . is she not also part performer? And if she is listening to the sounds as she plays (critical for some games), is she a listener/ [an] audience

> as well? . . . [T]here is considerably more overlap among [these roles] than in most other forms of music. (Collins 2013, 572–573)

Collins (2013, 573) notes that "most scholarship on music and sound design privileges a single perspective at any given time (usually that of the composer)," a situation she regards as inappropriate for the complexity of games. Of course, the musical agency of the player changes radically from context to context, sometimes even within the same game. There is not space here to interrogate that spectrum of possibilities in detail, but the point is clear—even if authorship can be solidly located in one composer, it does not follow that their control or musical ambition is fulfilled, given the indeterminacy introduced by the player.

Value and Canon

> Q4. Which examples have you chosen and why? How does your work engage with, reject, or configure assumed canonic values, even if it deals with well-known examples?

One reason why the critical interrogation of the work concept has been influential is that it is heavily bound up with issues of canon.[2] The canon of musical works is, according to Jim Samson (2001), "a list of composers or works assigned value and greatness by consensus . . . claims for ethical qualities and a universal status, occasionally cling to the term. . . . A canon, in other words, tends to promote the autonomy character, rather than the commodity character, of musical works."

The creation of a canon is bound up with the status afforded musical compositions. Concerning the creation of the classical canon, Lawrence Levine writes: "By the early decades of this [20th] century . . . the masterworks of the classic composers were to be performed in their entirety by highly trained musicians on programs free from the contamination of lesser works or lesser genres, free from the interferences of audience or performer, free from the distractions of the mundane; audiences were to approach the masters and their works with proper respect and proper seriousness, for aesthetic and spiritual elevation rather than mere entertainment was the goal" (Levine 1988, 146).

Indeed, this ethical-ideological dimension is deeply important. As William Weber has noted more than a decade after Levine: "Canonic ideology brought about the . . . ideologically articulated ranking of genres. . . . The ideology of the musical canon was manipulated to social and political ends from the very start: the classical music tradition never had social autonomy. Its authority was wielded chiefly as an assertion of cultural supremacy by the more learned publics within musical life over those less learned" (Weber 1999, 354). "The process of sacralization endowed the music it focused upon with unique aesthetic and spiritual properties that rendered it inviolate, exclusive, and eternal. This was not the ephemeral world of entertainment but something lasting, something permanent" (Levine 1988, 132).

Of course, canonization is not limited to classical music—it has been just as evident with the "great works" of popular music. And neither is it absent from game music. To a certain extent, as, William Gibbons (2018, 157–171; 2020a; chapter 2 this volume) has discussed, the canonization of game music has already been occurring in spaces outside academia, but, that is not to downplay the significance of musical research in reinforcing or combating canons, particularly when research work becomes the foundation for teaching or engagement with the broader public. Anne Desler (2013, 397) succinctly describes the relationship this way: "By making choices, whether in teaching or research, scholars negotiate relationships of authority and power, as authority and power are inherent both in the cultural capital represented by works of art and the possession of knowledge about them."

Criticism of canon-creation can be an easy target, not least when it may be an inevitable part of the evolution of a discipline. As a body of scholarship coalesces, it is perhaps unavoidable that, as scholarly texts build on each other, they will refer to the same examples. That said, the degree to which some games and composers have received such significant attention is striking. Few examples loom larger than the *Legend of Zelda* games, which have been the subject of many academic studies. At time of writing, the bibliography of game music scholarship hosted by the Society for the Study of Sound and Music in Games lists 22 entries that deal, to a greater or lesser extent, with *Zelda*. Of course, no scholar is guiltier of contributing to this imbalance than I, having written a monograph dedicated to *Ocarina of Time* (2021). Overrepresentation of certain musical genres, game types, and identities within the scholarly landscape is concerning, particularly when these materials become the foundation for education, and risk defining a scholarly domain that is more insular than outward-looking. It would be reductive to simply exhort scholars to stop discussing *Zelda*, and neither is it necessarily the case that frequently cited games work against agendas of inclusivity and accessibility: recurring examples can assist initiates in orienting themselves within a field of knowledge.

Though video game music scholarship is clearly developing its own academic canon (as Karen M. Cook [2020] and Hyeonjin Park [2020] have both highlighted), due to the textual instability noted above, it may be well placed to avoid the same degree of fetishization on a single image of the canonical work.[3] Similarly, the number of creative agents often involved in the music of a video game (composers, audio directors, music programmers, game directors, marketing representatives, and so on), can help to avoid the implication of a game score as the output of a single creative genius, even while we celebrate aesthetic successes.

Linear Histories

Q5. What narrative of history does your work present? How are technological factors and affordances presented without simplistic determinism? How might your history imply value, and is that intentional?

A further problem with the impulse to cast history as a series of works is the predisposition toward periodization and a linear understanding of video game history. James Newman writes:

> Both popular and scholarly accounts of game music history display a tendency to centre on the inevitability of technological progress or evolution. First, that there is an implied perfect or ideal state which this inexorable forward motion is heading towards. Second, that less advanced stages along this journey are characterized by limitations, which are progressively eradicated and rendered immaterial. Histories of early game music typically present an evolutionary narrative that is both teleological and demonstrably written from a backward-facing perspective in which the limitations are evident given the bounty of what is now known to have followed. (Newman 2021, 28)

The historical presentation that Newman describes is familiar to music historians who have been taught to be wary of periodization and teleological histories. Even in his introductory essay on music history aimed at those about to enter tertiary education, Jim Samson (2009, 10) warns his readers that "we should be careful anyway about assuming that music history describes a progression from simple to complex forms and materials."

Daniel Ross, writing in his book *Video Game Music* (2015), takes this teleological perspective to its most explicit metaphor—a race. In a section titled "Nobuo Uematsu—The Gamer's Richard Wagner," he writes:

> If composers such as [Koji] Kondo and [Koichi] Sugiyama were among the first to *take steps towards video game music being accepted* as seriously as film soundtracks or even classical music itself, then Uematsu was the *man who grabbed the baton and sprinted for the finish line.* Uematsu . . . composed his first *Final Fantasy* score in 1987 for game developers Square, and *changed video game music for ever.* The music still sounded lo-fi, the bleeps were still defiantly bleepy but the *music itself strived for the complexity and sensitivity of a full orchestral work.* Much like Richard Wagner did in his epic operas of the nineteenth century, Uematsu assigned different themes to characters in the games. (Ross 2015, 8–9; emphasis added)

Ross presents game music as a linear history of progress, one charted by the works of great individuals. Indeed, Ross locates Uematsu's value in how close his music comes to western classical music (here, Wagner). Even the compositional/analytical method of leitmotif (of which more later), is seen to be value laden. Uematsu's work is presented as "striving" to be released from the supposedly limited technology toward the "complexity and sensitivity" that (it is implied) orchestral music can produce, but to which Uematsu's chiptune only aspires.[4] Ross's writing is a particularly bald presentation of a theme prevalent in much commentary on game music, academic and otherwise.

Clearly, defining music by its limitations is problematic, and places focus on what is *not* possible, presenting the music as falling short of an unrealized ideal. It is particularly awkward when that ideal is presented as a music from a different cultural site (here, western classical music). That is not to say, of course, that we should not recognize the innovative techniques and approaches of composers. We can marvel at the way that the music for *Silver Surfer* on the NES (1989) shuffles parts across channels, implies more voices than the NES chip can accommodate, and develops striking acoustic effects, without having to see it as a compromised version of a never-realized ideal. A linear, teleological model of history implicitly devalues earlier music.

Q6. How might histories be alert to homogenizations from historical categorizations? How can the limits of shorthand terminology be made clear?

This techno-teleology of history often goes hand-in-hand with a periodization of video game music. I, among others, have relied on this model (see Summers 2017), and it is certainly an attractive framework given its ubiquity in casual game discourse. It is easy to discuss game history in terms of console generations, for example, as each subsequent set of dominant technology renders the former obsolete. As James Webster (2004, 49) notes, however, "[a] periodization is not true or false, but a reading, a way of making sense of complex data; periodizations serve the needs and desires of those who make and use them." Periodization is not always without use. Samson (2009, 17) does not dismiss periodization as a useful shorthand, but notes that we should be aware of its processes: "[P]eriodization is applied only when a period-defining theme has been identified. The whole process, then, is developmental or evolutionary, with the climax of the development represented as a kind of ideal, a 'point of perfection.'"

Aside from teleology, periodization also tends to ignore differences between musical materials. The ZX Spectrum and Commodore 64, both released in 1982, had radically different sound technologies, and both differed from the Famicom/NES (1983/1985). Even when discussing the same console or period, we must remain alert to the danger of painting a homogeneous picture; the musical aesthetics of the aforementioned *Silver Surfer* differ drastically from *Super Mario Bros.* (1985), released on the same console.

Analytical Approaches

Q7. How do your analytical approaches guide ways of hearing and interpreting the sonic materials? Do terms or frameworks need redefining or altering to respect the style/medium to which they are applied?

Q8. What musical features are emphasized in your analytical perspective? Which are ignored?

Q9. What values or perspectives are embedded in the methods you have chosen to use?

One exciting aspect of the development of game music scholarship has been the variety of analytical approaches applied to the musical materials of games. One of the contested and controversial threads of criticism of the new musicology was an attempt to recognize how tools of musical analysis are themselves value laden even if they appear to have the authority of objectivity (see Kerman 1980). An approach based on identifying leitmotifs (at least, in the conventional sense) is always going to privilege melodic qualities, while a Schenkerian approach will imply an organicist point of view. Transposing musical-analytical techniques from the repertoire for which they were designed to game music is not uncontested. In his volume *Studying Popular Music* (1990) Richard Middleton discusses the application of analytical techniques devised for classical music to popular musics. He writes: "it is not my intention to argue that musicology cannot understand popular music [but] that the bundle of methods, assumptions and ideologies which came to constitute 'mainstream musicology' in the later nineteenth and twentieth centuries renders it a less than useful resource in many ways" (104).

Middleton identifies terminology as a particular challenge:

> [T]erms are commonly ideologically loaded. "Dissonance" and "resolution" immediately suggest certain harmonic procedures, and a string of associated technical and emotional associations. "Motive" immediately suggests Beethovenian symphonic development technique. . . . "Accidental," "semitone," "third," "fifth," "dominant seventh," and so on, can hardly be used without producing images relating to the processes of functional-tonal music. . . . These connotations are ideological because they always involve selective, and often unconsciously formulated, conceptions of what music is. If this terminology is applied to other kinds of music, clearly the results will be problematic. (Middleton 1990, 104)

Likewise, Allan F. Moore (2001, 5) writes that "wholesale application of a conventional academic musicology [to rock] is both unwarranted and unhelpful. . . . [S]ince the techniques of such a discipline were developed for the analysis of European 'classical' tradition, their application towards a music (rock) that involves very different assumptions and practices leads to unsupportable conclusions."

The absolutism of Moore and Middleton's arguments are open to accusations of essentialism. Nevertheless, their central point remains compelling: terminology guides ways of thinking about (even hearing) music, and, as such, can be forces for misrepresenting or ignoring important aspects of the sonic materials. Moore and Middleton are specifically writing with mainstream pop/rock music in mind. The stylistic division between "classical" and "popular" music (as Moore and Middleton would conceive it) is not so clear-cut in the case of game music. Video game music operates over a huge stylistic range, including material close to classical art music repertoire (see, for example, Mark Sweeney's discussion of the stylistic affinity between 19th century symphonic art music and music for a modern RPG [Sweeney 2014]). On the one hand, this stylistic diversity might make the application of terminology and concepts from art music less problematic; on the other, it might disguise some of the critical challenges of this transposition.

Steven Reale (2021) has addressed this question directly. He writes, "the techniques and methodologies that underpin modern music theory are well suited to music frozen in time, but strain when asked to account for music that cannot be fixed in such a way" (Reale 2021, 218). Yet Reale successfully applies a set of theoretical lenses to game music (*Super Mario Galaxy* [2007] in particular). He uses thematic analysis, reductive analysis (in the general model of Schenker) and transformational theory (in the neo-Riemannian tradition) to derive observations. Crucially, though, such approaches should not be perceived as the default, expected, or only legitimate form of musical analysis for game music, in the way that they have come to dominate investigations of classical repertoire. These approaches may miss important qualities—as George Reid (2018, 282) notes, for instance, timbre is the most distinctive aspect of chiptune music, but much traditional musical analysis all but ignores this dimension of the music. A spectrographic analysis that analyzes the constituent harmonics of a tone, for instance is far better suited to analyzing timbre.

Any analytical lens will be limited in isolation. It is imperative that musicologists understand the embedded values of their tools and which dimensions of the sonic materials are obscured by that method, so they may ensure that the approaches are suited to the conclusions that are drawn. We should also be attuned to ideologies embedded within our analytical approaches and which may be implicitly perpetuated through their use (see Ewell 2020).

"The Listener"/"The Player"

Q10. How is your player position implicitly constructed by the scholarship? What assumptions underlie this construction? Are ranges of potential "players" encompassed, and, if so, how?

Once we begin to deal with the position of the "player" and/or "listener" in our discussions, we are confronted with the question of who this player/listener is. Game music scholarship has recently expended much effort on semiotic discussions of one kind or another (Hart 2014; Smith 2020). Along with topic theory (Atkinson 2019; Bradford 2020; Yee 2020), and theorizations that rely on player musical literacy (van Elferen 2016), we are asked to consider how our scholarship constructs the player. Where do their musical histories and interpretations lie? Are they able to recognize any musical reference, and decode any musical signifier that we can identify? Are their musical literacies bounded at all? Which audiences and whose perspectives do we have in mind?

This is a question raised in an exchange between Jonathan Godsall and William Gibbons. In his review of Gibbons's book on classical music in games, *Unlimited Replays*, Godsall notes "the range of understandings that individuals surely bring to classical music's interactions with games" (Godsall 2020, 114). In his response, Gibbons describes how his research questions

> assume the existence of a "player"—that is, I am typically concerned less with musical or ludic texts themselves than with how they are being interpreted. But who is this mysterious player? . . . I then had to choose a type of Model Player. . . . I might have chosen a naïve player, who would experience each text in a vacuum, with no intertextual, cultural, or historical context. . . . On the other hand, I could have assumed an ideal player, possessing an encyclopedic knowledge of all relevant contexts and intertextual references. . . . My solution was to attempt to capture a range of possible player experiences between these two extremes. (Gibbons 2020b, 116–117)

The process Gibbons describes here is one that occurs explicitly or implicitly, consciously or unconsciously, in most game scholarship.

> Q11. Whose experiences does your method aim to represent and why is that perspective valuable? How are the insights specifically useful, and/or do they represent the experiences beyond the individual?

A slightly different formulation of the "problem with players" (to use Gibbons's phrase) is discussed by Michiel Kamp. Kamp (2021, 162) starts from the question "What is it like to hear video game music while playing a game?" and then moves to consider the degree to which different approaches to the question "generalize from individual cases—or experiences." He continues: "Autoethnography focuses on the unique view of the experiencer, phenomenology on the essence of the act and hermeneutics on the idiosyncrasies of the object" (Kamp 2021, 162). In that sense, phenomenology tends toward generalizing across experiences and hermeneutics deals with the particular case. He situates autoethnography between these poles:

> Of course, my position as a gamer-cum-researcher is relatively idiosyncratic, but to what extent are all positions of gamers idiosyncratic? And to what extent is my position relevant at all to those interested in video game music? . . . Most methodologies of autoethnography to a degree argue that the method is not merely idiographic: my account does not just represent my own experience, but to some extent that of a larger group, and from there it can derive some of its value. This is where the autoethnographic method, that of systematic introspection, plays an important role. (Kamp 2021, 170)

Ethnography, though one step removed from the investigation of subjective experience that Kamp has in mind, also aims to draw insights from individuals, either specifically or as representatives of broader populations.

> Q12. How does your work respect the textuality of the event, and the performative/experiential qualities of the text?

An area of discussion where this question of individual perspective is particularly obvious is in work that emphasizes the experiential qualities of music. James A. Hepokowski (2013) and Harper-Scott (2021) both criticize approaches to musicology that set up false binaries of text/performance, knowledge/experience. Carolyn Abbate's writing on drastic/gnostic understanding of music (2004) privileges

> the spontaneity of the performance situation, the experience of *being there* (or of performing oneself). . . . Valued here are the bodily, the physical, the rapturous jouissance of the ephemeral instant . . . what is of value is not the work to be explicated "gnostically" through analysis and hermeneutics. . . . Instead, we have the opposite concept of "real music," a music that can only exist, "drastically," in the physicality of the evanescent moment of performance. (Hepokowki 2013, 34–36)

While this experiential quality of music was certainly ignored and underserved by traditional musicological methods, we should be wary of being guilty of similar essentialism in the opposite direction. As Harper-Scott (2021, 30–31) notes, drastic and gnostic are not opposites, and a binary perspective risks reinforcing mind–body duality (albeit with inverted values), downplaying cognition and encouraging submission to the scholar's experience as definitive.

Roger Moseley writes: "Both games and music are better conceived as drastic than gnostic . . . they are activities to be performed rather than texts to be deciphered" (Moseley 2016, 48). But perhaps we should seek to pursue a "both/and" rather than "either/or" agenda for such concepts. As Isabella van Elferen (2020, 111) puts it: "Ludomusicology can intervene in the gap between text and performance, and in the gap between real-life embodiment and virtual disembodiment. . . . Ludomusicology inhabits the gap between musical phenomenology and musical ontology." When van Elferen characterizes game musicology as inhabiting "gaps," she identifies it as mediating between unnecessary binary thinking (here the text/event duality). She is arguing that we can avoid being reductive to extremes.

Culture and Context

> Q13. How does your cultural context influence your scholarship? What perspectives and expertise do you bring to this research? Where are the limits of your cultural and disciplinary understanding, and how are those respected in the research?

One of the hallmarks of the new musicology was an insistence that music was not an abstract entity. Always sounding in innumerable frames of contextualization, such scholarship argued that understanding music in terms of human activity emphasized and added to the significance of musicological discussion, rather than detracting from it. Game music studies has begun the work of understanding its subject in terms of contextual cultural webs that both influence and are influenced by game music. Notable examples of these studies include Andra Ivănescu's (2018) discussion of class and music in *Beneath a Steel Sky*, Dana Plank's (2015, 2018) examination of both disability and geopolitics in game music, and Kiri Miller's (2007) investigations into race through the frame of music in games. Such issues of identity and contexts of creation and reception can easily serve as the main thrust of research projects. Beyond work that might specifically investigate contextual issues of game music, there are broader questions that are not limited to research that explicitly focuses on questions of context.

We should recognize that musicological research bears the legacy of its context, just as much as the materials it studies. This is not to suggest we should begin reductive or essentialist thinking about the relationship between the researcher and the subject. Yet it is wise to consider how one's own cultural location can inflect the scholarship produced. For instance, a great deal of scholarship on game music from Japan has been conducted by white, western scholars. It would be unhelpful and inappropriate to try to define who can/cannot research certain musics, and I am not suggesting that white westerners should not research Japanese game music. That said, it is useful for scholars to be mindful of how our professional, personal, and cultural (etc.) contexts illuminate and conceal aspects of the work we study. Of course, explicitly ethnographic studies have long foregrounded such issues, but these questions are not limited to methodologies allied to ethnography.

The discussion of the musicologist's perspective need not necessarily be explicitly presented to the reader, for this is a separate axis from the validity of the work, but rather, it involves a self-awareness of the way we encounter, discuss, and analyze the music. This is not a closing down of possibility, but an opening up in recognizing the value that a variety of disciplinary and cultural perspectives can bring to the subject matter. It may also foster collaborative and interdisciplinary multiauthor studies; video game music scholarship has tended to replicate the single-author model common in arts/humanities research.

Audiences and Education

> Q14. Who is the audience for this research, and how might the research format best reach the audiences and achieve the goals?

So far, I have primarily been concerned with the research process of game musicology. To conclude this chapter, I will briefly consider the purpose and impact of that research. Who are the audiences for our research? How might the presentation of the research best enable it to achieve its aims? The same underlying research or project can easily seek to engage different audiences, especially when it is presented in a variety of formats. While inroads have been made to engaging with both broader public audiences and with the professional industry, music academia has some way left to go in reaching these groups.[5]

At the very least, the intended audience and purpose for the scholarship can inflect aspects of its design and presentation. Game music presents an ideal venue for public musicology, given the ubiquity of games in modern, western popular youth culture. To effectively reach its audience, the musicological discussion should ensure it is accessible to the audience it addresses, not least through being mindful to explain concepts and technicalities as appropriate. This question of accessibility operates across disciplinary boundaries. If we aim to make our work more interdisciplinary, then we must ensure specialization does not become the insularity of musicologists simply talking only to themselves. My position is not to reject the importance of specialist terminology, particular expertise, technical discussion, and specialization—these discussions are essential for advancement of the subject area and research—but such specialist discourse need not be to the exclusion of other writing for broader audiences, too.

> Q15. What role (if any) does education and wider engagement play in your scholarship?

Education is closely allied to questions of audience and access. The integration of game music into school and university curricula should be undertaken with full awareness of the rich and complex questions it raises, and not simply as a token nod toward contemporary popular repertoire. To do that, however, musicological research must be presented in a way that facilitates translation to other contexts and for these other audiences.

References to game music have recently been introduced into syllabi of the United Kingdom's national qualifications (GCSEs/A-levels). Appropriately enough, this has prompted study/revision guides on the topic. James Manwaring (2018, 2019) and Simon Rushby (2018), among others, have designed such resources for school teachers and students. While recognizing the excellent clarity of language of these guides, and their commitment to utility, there are problematic aspects of their treatment of game music. There are some factual mistakes, game music history follows a teleological narrative, and the analysis is indistinguishable from the treatment of western classical programmatic music. It would be easy to nitpick at Rushby and Manwaring's efforts, but that would be churlish. A more productive activity is to consider how the communication and exchange of knowledge between academia and classroom education can be improved. Questions of formatting, language, and accessibility are all significant and will only improve though better dialogue with educationalists.

Conclusions

This chapter has aimed to raise awareness of key issues in the musicological scholarship of game music. I provide these questions for researchers to consider—they are not necessarily intended to be explicitly addressed in the scholarship. Indeed, not all these questions will apply to every project, and many are long-standing issues in musicological study broadly speaking. Part of my ambition is to ensure that, in our exuberance for this relatively new area of study, we do not ignore or dismiss these questions as inapplicable. I may also be fairly criticized here for not providing many concrete solutions to the questions I have posed. There are likely few definitive answers, and neither should there be one right way of doing music scholarship. As we continue to evolve as a discipline, by engaging with these "awkward questions," we can better advance our overall project of game musicology: understanding the meanings and experiences of game music.

Notes

1. That is, using the author's intention as the primary means of judging and interpreting the artwork.
2. As Dahlhaus (1983, 3–4) wrote, "the subject matter of music history is made up primarily, if not exclusively, of significant works of music. . . . The concept 'work,' and not 'event,' is the cornerstone of music history."
3. For an interesting counterpoint to this idea, see the argument by Julianne Grasso that suggests we can understand the music in a game as a "canonic" version of music later adapted and reconfigured through fan and extra-game rearrangement (Grasso 2020).
4. Ross is not primarily a musicologist by trade. That recognized, simply restricting the definition of musicology to only those employed as professional academics is reductive given the landscape of modern academic discourse. An author of a book on video game music presents themselves as an authority on the topic.
5. Outreach projects and musicology channels on YouTube have made significant efforts in music outreach (for example, 8-Bit Music Theory), while there have been examples of the involvement of professional game composers in academia (for example, Baysted 2016; Golding 2021; Krishnaswami 2020).

References

Abbate, Carolyn. 2004. "Music—Drastic or Gnostic?" *Critical Inquiry* 30 (3): 505–536.

Andrew, Lydia. 2021. "The Collaborative Art of Game Music." In *The Cambridge Companion to Video Game Music*, edited by Melanie Fritsch and Tim Summers, xxxiii–xxxvi. Cambridge: Cambridge University Press.

Atkinson, Sean. 2019. "Soaring through the Sky: Topics and Tropes in Video Game Music." *Music Theory Online* 25 (2).

Baysted, Stephen. 2016. "Palimpsest, Pragmatism and the Aesthetics of Genre Transformation." In *Ludomusicology: Approaches to Video Game Music*, edited by Michiel Kamp, Tim Summers, and Mark Sweeney, 152–171. Sheffield: Equinox.

Baysted, Stephen, and Tim Summers. 2020. "The Creative Process of Composing for Video Games." In *The Oxford Handbook of the Creative Process in Music*, edited by Nicolas Donin, n.p. New York: Oxford University Press.

Beard, David, and Kenneth Gloag, eds. 2016. *Musicology: The Key Concepts*. 2nd ed. London: Routledge.

Bradford, Wesley J. 2020. "Exploring the Narrative Implications of Emerging Topics in *The Legend of Zelda: Breath of the Wild.*" *Journal of Sound and Music in Games* 1 (4): 1–21.
Collins, Karen. 2013. "Implications of Interactivity." In *The Oxford Handbook of New Audiovisual Aesthetics*, edited by John Richardson, Claudia Gorbman, and Carol Vernallis, 572–584. New York: Oxford University Press.
Cook, Karen M. 2020. "Canon Anxiety?" *Journal of Sound and Music in Games* 1 (1): 95–99.
Dahlhaus, Carl. 1983. *Foundations of Music History*. Translated by J. B. Robinson. Cambridge: Cambridge University Press.
Desler, Anne. 2013. "History without Royalty? Queen and the Strata of the Popular Music Canon." *Popular Music* 32 (3): 385–405.
Elphick, Daniel. (a.k.a. Cult of Musicology.) 2021. "What Is Musicology?" YouTube, January 4, 2021. Accessed July 7, 2021. https://youtu.be/QYiBqXTPLAA.
Ewell, Philip. 2020. "Music Theory's White Racial Frame." *Music Theory Online* 26 (2). Accessed January 4, 2024. https://mtosmt.org/issues/mto.20.26.2/mto.20.26.2.ewell.html.
Gibbons, William. 2018. *Unlimited Replays: Video Games and Classical Music*. New York: Oxford University Press.
Gibbons, William. 2020a. "Rewritable Memory: Concerts, Canons, and Game Music History." *Journal of Sound and Music in Games* 1 (1): 75–81.
Gibbons, William. 2020b. "The Problem with Players: A Response to Jonathan Godsall." *Journal of Sound and Music in Games* 1 (1): 116–117.
Godsall, Jonathan. 2020. "*Unlimited Replays: Video Games and Classical Music*, by William Gibbons." *Journal of Sound and Music in Games* 1 (1): 113–115.
Goehr, Lydia. 1992. *The Imaginary Museum of Musical Works*. Oxford: Clarendon.
Golding, Dan. 2021. "Finding Untitled Goose Game's Dynamic Music in the World of Silent Cinema." *Journal of Sound and Music in Games* 2 (1): 1–16.
Grasso, Julianne. 2020. "On Canons as Music and Muse." *Journal of Sound and Music in Games* 1 (1): 82–86.
Harper-Scott, J. P. E. 2018. "How We Got Out of Music History, and How We Can Get Back into It." In *Theories of History*, edited by Michael J. Kelly and Arthur Rose, 37–59. London: Bloomsbury Academic.
Harper-Scott, J. P. E. 2021. *The Event of Music History*. Woodbridge: Boydell.
Hart, Iain. 2014. "Meaningful Play: Performativity, Interactivity and Semiotics in Video Game Music." *Musicology Australia* 36 (2): 273–290.
Hepokoski, James A. 2013. "Dahlhaus's Beethoven–Rossini Stildualismus: Lingering Legacies of the Text-Event Dichotomy." In *The Invention of Beethoven and Rossini*, edited by Nicholas Mathew and Benjamin Walton, 15–48. Cambridge: Cambridge University Press.
Ivănescu, Andra. 2018. "Beneath a Steel Sky: A Musical Characterisation of Class Structure." *Computer Games Journal* 7: 231–242.
Kamp, Michiel. 2021. "Autoethnography, Phenomenology and Hermeneutics." In *The Cambridge Companion to Video Game Music*, edited by Melanie Fritsch and Tim Summers, 159–175. Cambridge: Cambridge University Press.
Kerman, Joseph. 1980. "How We Got into Analysis, and How to Get Out." *Critical Inquiry* 7 (2): 311–331.
Kerman, Joseph. 1985. *Musicology*. London: Fontana.
Kramer, Lawrence. 1990. *Music as Cultural Practice*. Berkeley: University of California Press.
Krishnaswami, Ravi. 2020. "Playing Songwriter." *Journal of Sound and Music in Games* 1 (2): 68–83.

Levine, Lawrence. 1988. *Highbrow/Lowbrow*. Cambridge, MA: Harvard University Press.

Manwaring, James. 2018. "AQA AoS2: Computer Gaming Music." *Music Teacher*, November 2018, 8pp.

Manwaring, James. 2019. "Computer Gaming Music: Composition." *Music Teacher*, January 2019, 6pp.

McClary, Susan. 1991. *Feminine Endings*. Minneapolis: University of Minnesota Press.

Middleton, Richard. 1990. *Studying Popular Music*. Milton Keynes: Open University Press.

Miller, Kiri. 2007. "Jacking the Dial: Radio, Race, and Place in *Grand Theft Auto*." *Ethnomusicology* 51 (3): 402–438.

Moore, Allan F. 2001. *Rock: The Primary Text*. 2nd ed. Aldershot: Ashgate.

Moseley, Roger. 2016. *Keys to Play*. Oakland: University of California Press.

Mugglestone, Erica. 1981. "Guido Adler's 'The Scope, Method, and Aim of Musicology' (1885)." *Yearbook for Traditional Music* 13: 1–21.

Newman, James. 2021. "Before Red Book." In *The Cambridge Companion to Video Game Music*, edited by Melanie Fritsch and Tim Summers, 12–32. Cambridge: Cambridge University Press.

Park, Hyeonjin. 2020. "The Difficult, Uncomfortable, and Imperative Conversations Needed in Game Music and Sound Studies." *Journal of Sound and Music in Games* 1 (1): 87–94.

Plank, Dana. 2015. "'From Russia with Fun': *Tetris*, Korobeiniki and the Ludic Soviet." *Soundtrack* 8 (1–2): 7–24.

Plank, Dana. 2018. "Bodies in Play: Representations of Disability in 8- and 16-bit Video Game Soundscapes." PhD dissertation, Ohio State University.

Reale, Steven. 2021. "Analytical Traditions and Game Music." In *The Cambridge Companion to Video Game Music*, edited by Melanie Fritsch and Tim Summers, 193–219. Cambridge: Cambridge University Press.

Reid, George. 2018. "Chiptune: The Ludomusical Shaping of Identity." *Computer Games Journal* 7 (4): 279–290.

Rietveld, Hillegonda C., and Andrew Lemon. 2021. "Female Credit: Excavating Recognition for the Capcom Sound Team." In *The Cambridge Companion to Video Game Music*, edited by Melanie Fritsch and Tim Summers, 376–388. Cambridge: Cambridge University Press.

Ross, Daniel. 2015. *Video Game Music*. London: Elliott & Thompson.

Rushby, Simon. 2018. "AQA AoS3: Music for Media, Part 2—Michael Giacchino and Nobuo Uematsu." *Music Teacher*, October 2018, 10pp.

Samson, Jim. 2001. "Canon (iii)." *Grove Music Online*. Accessed June 26, 2021. https://www.oxfordmusiconline.com/grovemusic/view/10.1093/gmo/9781561592630.001.0001/omo-9781561592630-e-0000040598.

Samson, Jim. 2009. "Music History." In *An Introduction to Music Studies*, edited by J. P. E. Harper-Scott and Jim Samson, 7–24. Cambridge: Cambridge University Press.

Smith, Jeremy W. 2020. "'Wear People's Faces': Semiotic Awareness in Fan Adaptations of the Music from *The Legend of Zelda: Majora's Mask*." *Journal of Sound and Music in Games* 1 (4): 45–75.

Stevens, Denis. 1980. *Musicology: A Practical Guide*. London: Macdonald.

Summers, Tim. 2017. "Dimensions of Game Music History." In *The Routledge Companion to Screen Music and Sound*, edited by Miguel Mera, Ronald Sadoff, and Ben Winters, 139–152. New York: Routledge.

Summers, Tim. 2021. "*The Legend of Zelda: Ocarina of Time*"—*A Game Music Companion*. Bristol: Intellect.

Sweeney, Mark. 2014. "The Aesthetics of Videogame Music." PhD dissertation, University of Oxford.

Treitler, Leo. 1989. *Music and the Historical Imagination*. Cambridge, MA: Harvard University Press.

van Elferen, Isabella. 2016. "Analysing Game Musical Immersion." In *Ludomusicology: Approaches to Video Game Music*, edited by Michiel Kamp, Tim Summers, and Mark Sweeney, 32–52. Sheffield: Equinox.

van Elferen, Isabella. 2020. "Ludomusicology and the New Drastic." *Journal of Sound and Music in Games* 1 (1): 103–112.

Weber, William. 1999. "The History of Musical Canon." In *Rethinking Music*, edited by Nicholas Cook and Mark Everist, 336–355. Oxford: Oxford University Press.

Webster, James. 2004. "The Eighteenth Century as a Music-Historical Period?" *Eighteenth-Century Music* 1 (1): 47–60.

Wegman, Rob C. 2012. "Historical Musicology: Is It Still Possible?" In *The Cultural Study of Music*, 2nd ed., edited by Martin Clayton, Trevor Herbert, and Richard Middleton, 40–48. New York: Routledge.

Yee, Thomas B. 2020. "Battle Hymn of the God-Slayers: Troping Rock and Sacred Music Topics in Xenoblade Chronicles." *Journal of Sound and Music in Games* 1 (1): 2–19.

CHAPTER 2

ODE TO JOYSTICKS

Canonic Fantasies and the "Beethoven of Video Game Music"

WILLIAM GIBBONS

Introduction

Equal parts self-congratulatory spectacle and revenue-generating hype machine, The Game Awards celebrate the best video games released each year—the game industry's version of the Academy Awards. I was particularly excited for the 2020 Awards. It often takes a year or two for me to catch up on the latest games, but one of the very few advantages of a global pandemic was that I had the opportunity to play more than the usual number of new releases. Imagine my surprise, then, when amid a crowd of excellent new entries in the "Best Score and Music" category, the award went to a title I first played through 23 years ago. Well, sort of. The winner was *Final Fantasy VII Remake* (2020), a reimagining and expansion of the first part of the fan-favorite 1997 Japanese role-playing game (JRPG).[1] The multicomposer score is credited equally to Nobuo Uematsu, Masashi Mamauzu, and Mitsuto Suzuki, but it was Uematsu whose involvement drew the most critical attention and praise.

Although it surprised me at the time, in hindsight Uematsu's success at The Game Awards seems inevitable. One might even wonder about the fairness of including *Final Fantasy VII Remake* in this award category in the first place. New music, after all, could hardly compete with a soundtrack already ingrained in the musical memories of countless players—so familiar, so beloved, so . . . canonic.[2] In fact, I couldn't help but be reminded of another musical event of 2020: the celebrations of Ludwig van Beethoven's 250th anniversary.

Although muted by the COVID-19 pandemic, the classical music world was set to honor Beethoven's legacy through seemingly countless concerts, festivals, recordings, and articles throughout the year. This hullabaloo led several scholars and critics (including me) to suggest that devoting so much performance time to relatively few works by one already prominent composer might deter efforts to diversify the classical repertoire. As *San Francisco Chronicle* music critic Joshua Kosman put it, Beethoven "just takes up too much space" (Kosman 2020).

The Beethoven anniversary and *Final Fantasy VII Remake*'s Game Awards win reflect tendencies to situate a few works by a single composer as the core of a musical canon. And while the alignment of the two events is purely coincidental, it feels particularly appropriate given that the past few years have seen a marked tendency for journalists, marketers, musicians, and more to describe Uematsu as "the Beethoven of video game music." An article from the *San Francisco Classical Voice* offers a typical example:

> In case you are unaware, video games and video game music have come a long way since . . . *Donkey Kong*. It's a musical realm that has produced its own roster of superstar composers [including] Nobuo Uematsu's influential music for the highly successful *Final Fantasy* series. To the point that Uematsu has gained the title of "The Beethoven of video games music." (Farber 2019)

I believe this comparison warrants further exploration. What does it mean to repeatedly compare a composer—especially a composer of video game music—to Beethoven? And what does this comparison say about how musical canons are developing in the relatively young genre of game music? To begin teasing out answers to these questions, I briefly trace how Uematsu became "the Beethoven of game music," and then consider how that label shapes our understanding of the composer and his works.

The Beethoven of . . .

For better or worse, music history is replete with composers doomed to dwell in Beethoven's shadow.[3] In this section, however, I am concerned with one specific type of comparison: the identification of composers as "the Beethoven of" their particular musical domain. This linguistic device (a form of Vossian antonomasia, as it happens) helps quickly situate something or someone relatively unfamiliar by comparison to a better-known paragon.[4]

Mozart is a frequent paragon, for instance: the Norwegian chess prodigy Magnus Carlsen is often described as "the Mozart of chess," for example, while the Croatian athlete Dražen Petrovic is "the Mozart of basketball." These types of comparisons are even more common in classical music history. François-Adrien Boieldieu (1775–1834) was billed as "the French Mozart," Juan Crisóstomo Arriaga (1806–1826) as "the Spanish Mozart," and—most controversially today—Joseph Bologne (1745–1799) as "the Black Mozart." Bologne in particular highlights the central problem with this kind of Vossian antonomasia: it risks undermining the accomplishments of the "imitator" while reinforcing the supremacy of the "original."

Returning to Beethoven, consider just three examples of how the "Beethoven of . . ." trope comes into play. In 1822, the editor of one of the leading US music periodicals of the time labeled the idiosyncratic Bohemian-American composer Anthony Philip Heinrich (1781–1861) "the Beethoven of America"—a moniker endlessly repeated both in Heinrich's lifetime and in subsequent scholarship on the composer.[5] Likewise, biographical notes on the composer Fernando Sor (1778–1839) seldom fail to mention that the influential musicologist and critic François-Joseph Fétis once dubbed him "the Beethoven of the guitar"—though they never seem to provide any citations. Moving into the 20th century, the critic Paul Rosenfeld (1941) memorably billed Jean Sibelius (1865–1957) "the Beethoven of the North" in an otherwise lukewarm *New Republic* article.

Each of these comparisons can be traced to a single critic, whose judgment gets reused and recycled into a platitude. Someone had to be the first to make the comparison, of course, but the initial point of reference gets quickly dropped in favor of passive constructions—"often called," "described as," and so on. With Heinrich, for example, we know today that precisely one critic at one point in time referred to the composer as "the Beethoven of America," and that it was *not* a prevalent viewpoint in the 19th century. Yet we find technically true but misleading statements like "the man who became known as 'the Beethoven of America' . . . was born in Bohemia in 1781" (Gilliland 2015).

Uematsu's coronation as "the Beethoven of game music" followed a similar trajectory. In this case, the point of origin appears to be a 2013 article in an unlikely venue: the *Tampa Bay Times* (Fleming 2013). Although conveniently titled "The Beethoven of Video Games," the article isn't actually about Uematsu at all. Instead, the piece profiles Tommy Tallarico, a game composer now more famous for his role as impresario of the long-running *Video Games Live* series of concerts, in which a touring ensemble partners with local orchestras. As I have noted elsewhere (Gibbons 2018, 2020), Tallarico is keen to position video game music as the natural evolution of the classical canon, frequently singling Beethoven out as a model. A frequently cited Tallarico-ism is that "If Beethoven were around today he'd be a video game composer," for example, often in the same breath as he mentions Beethoven's impact on his own music (*NPR All Things Considered* 2008). One especially unsubtle *Los Angeles Times* article (Fleishman 2015) features a photo of a smiling Tallarico at home, leaning on a piano at eye level with a large bust of Beethoven.

In his *Tampa Bay Times* profile, Tallarico weighs in on Uematsu, whose music features prominently on *Video Games Live* concerts:

> If I had to pick one, what games [I] consider [to have] the best video game music, it's from the games *Final Fantasy*. . . . The scores are by a Japanese composer by the name of Nobuo Uematsu. He's kind of like the Beethoven or John Williams of the video game industry. His music is very classical.

This "very classical" idea invites further unpacking. At this point, however, we may simply note that Tallarico seems to be positioning Uematsu as a well-known figure in the industry—again using the "Beethoven of" construction to do some conceptual heavy lifting for audiences who may be unfamiliar with game music.

After the *Tampa Bay Times* article, the "Beethoven of game music" label becomes more and more frequent. Another key point in disseminating the term seems to be the ClassicFM Hall of Fame—an annual, user-determined list of the best classical works, which has in recent years included video game music (Gibbons 2018, 162–165). In 2013, Uematsu's *Final Fantasy* music peaked at #3 in the Hall of Fame, an achievement that can be attributed at least in part to UK-based PR executive Mark Robins, who repeatedly urged games journalists to vote for the *Final Fantasy VII* score for the Hall of Fame on the grounds that Uematsu is "gaming's Beethoven" (Bramwell 2014). The write-up on Uematsu in the 2013 ClassicFM Hall of Fame—released just a few months after Tallarico's profile—reinforces the connection further, noting in its opening line "sometimes referred to as the Beethoven of video games music, Japanese composer Nobuo Uematsu has made his career and reputation from his soundtracks to the *Final Fantasy* video games" (reprinted as ClassicFM 2019).

Things continued to spread from there. An indignant *Guardian* article noted in 2015 that "according to Classic FM, Uematsu is the 'Beethoven of video game music'" (Damman 2015), while in the same year the music news site CMUSE suggested he was being "hailed as a modern-day Beethoven" (Frey 2015). Uematsu's bio on Apple Music begins: "Often referred to as the Beethoven of video game music," and (as of December 2021) Wikipedia's page on Uematsu notes that he is "sometimes referred to as the Beethoven of video game music" (Wikipedia). The phrase appears just as frequently in marketing copy for "classical" performances of Uematsu's music. "Not much of a gamer?" asks a representative 2019 write-up for the touring Uematsu concert *Distant Worlds* concert. "The music alone is worth the trip. A living legend, composer Uematsu is widely known as the 'Beethoven of video games music' and has appeared in the top 20 of the annual ClassicFM Hall of Fame five times" (Lin 2019).

This brief bit of detective work suggests how Uematsu became the Beethoven of game music—but what does the comparison really *mean*? In purely musical terms, at least, I believe the answer is . . . "not much." A full stylistic comparison of Uematsu's and Beethoven's music is well beyond the scope of this chapter, but even a cursory examination of the two composers reveals wildly divergent approaches to musical content, style, and genre. Beethoven occupies a central position in the classical canon, while Uematsu's background is in prog rock—an influence prevalent throughout most of the *Final Fantasy* scores. He does not compose in forms typically associated with Beethoven, or with Western classical music in general (symphonies, concertos, sonatas, etc.). Neither does his music employ any of the celebrated hallmarks of Beethoven's compositional style (extended musical developments and codas, "germinal" motifs that expand into larger and larger structures, and so on). And although Uematsu does occasionally imitate historical musical styles, I am not aware of any *Final Fantasy* music that sonically resembles a work by Beethoven.[6] One might point to Uematsu's use of the full orchestra—synthesized or not—but that is a common element for game composers, especially for role-playing games.

In short, Uematsu's Beethovenian reputation isn't based on the music per se. Yet "the Beethoven of game music" holds true in other ways—meanings unintended, perhaps, by those repeating the phrase. In the subsequent sections I argue that to compare Uematsu to Beethoven invokes the transformation each composer has undergone into a "Hero" of their respective musical genres, how these two men have been positioned and constructed within their musical canons, and how groups of ardent supporters have shaped their legacies.

Uematsu Hero

Beethoven occupies a unique space in classical music. In a very real sense, in fact, to many people from avid aficionados to the most disinterested of bystanders, Beethoven *is* classical music—the embodiment of everything that makes music "classical" in the first place. Scott Burnham (1995) begins his book *Beethoven Hero* with "Beethoven. When asked to name the single most influential composer of the Western world, few would hesitate" (xiii). Beethoven's monolithic legacy rests largely on his so-called Heroic style, a few major works (mostly symphonies and concertos) that form a relatively small part of his total output. And yet this group of pieces has, in Burnham's words, become "the paradigm of Western compositional logic and of all the positive virtues that music can embody for humanity." Crucially, Burnham notes, this paradigm is not necessarily an intentional value judgment on the part of the listener, but is instead built into the core of classical music as a concept:

> This conviction has proved so strong that it no longer acts as an overt part of our musical consciousness; it is now simply a condition of the way we tend to engage the musical experience. The values of Beethoven's heroic style have become the values of music. (xiii)

Works that do not fit with our image of the heroic Beethoven—his numerous folk song settings, the idiosyncratic Eighth Symphony, or *Wellington's Victory*, for example—have been ignored, marginalized, or rationalized away. Indeed, Mark Evan Bonds (1996) made a compelling argument that the mythological image of Beethoven constructed after the composer's death (which Bonds calls "The Scowl") negatively impacts listeners today, making it difficult to understand his works that do not conform to the Heroic archetype.[7]

How did Beethoven and his Heroic style reach this exalted status? While any succinct response to that question is simplistic, the short answer is that he succeeded for the same reasons most successful people do: talent, luck, and great networking. As Tia DeNora (1997) summarizes in her landmark study *Beethoven and the Construction of Musical Genius*:

> Beethoven's claim to legitimate success and recognition became powerful because his exceptional abilities were accompanied by and interacted with a network of

> practices, musical-critical discourse, and music technology produced over time by Beethoven and his "support personnel"—his patrons and other musical assistants. *Beethoven succeeded because a complex network was constructed and oriented to the production and perception of his talent.* (187; emphasis mine)

In other words, Beethoven had a group of influential patrons and devotees both during his lifetime and afterward who systematically (1) established, and later reinforced, his reputation and legacy as a musical genius,; and (2) worked to (selectively) disseminate and popularize his music. These processes took place precisely as the musical canon was being constructed, and succeeded beyond any reasonable expectations. For many people, musicians and laypeople alike, Beethoven represents the pinnacle of musical genius—perhaps even of human accomplishment. In Peter Kivy's words (2011): "No image of genius in the history of the Western world is more familiar to the ordinary person than that of Beethoven" (119).[8] Much more than in musical terms, it is in this careful curation and ceaseless campaigning that Nobuo Uematsu might accurately be described as "the Beethoven of video game music."

Despite Uematu's extensive body of work—currently somewhere around 75 game scores—his reputation as a composer seems to rest almost exclusively on the *Final Fantasy* games, which make up less than a quarter of his output. Even then, only a few *Final Fantasy* games seem to make the cut: *FFVI* and *FFVII* undoubtedly for the core musical "masterworks," with perhaps *FFIV*, *FFVIII*, and *FFX* tied for third place. Even in those cases, a few tracks from each score seem to get most of the attention from fans, critics, arrangers, and scholars alike: the "Aria de Mezzo carattere" and "Dancing Mad" from *FFVI*, and "Aerith's Theme" and "One Winged Angel" from *FFVII*. As with Beethoven, then, Uematsu's reputation rests on a subset of a subset of a subset of his total output. This emphasis raises two major questions for me: (1) Why these particular scores and cues? and (2) What processes are at work to reinforce this repertoire?

The reasons for the emphasis on the *Final Fantasy* games at the expense of Uematsu's other scores is difficult to pinpoint, but name recognition surely plays a major role. *Final Fantasy* is a familiar franchise and an easy point of reference for critics, scholars, marketing professionals, and so on. If a symphony orchestra programs a work by Uematsu, for example, they are likely to choose music that they can reasonably expect potential audience members to recognize, at least by name. Furthermore, given the games' popularity, and the amount of musical repetition involved in playing a lengthy JRPG, audiences would be familiar with specific pieces of music, potentially having heard them hundreds or even thousands of times. (Gibbons and Grasso 2020) Even if some of his other scores share many musical similarities with his more popular *Final Fantasy* music—the JRPGs *Lost Odyssey* (2007) and *The Last Story* (2011), for example—they are less familiar and so are less likely to bring in audiences. This is especially true of the dozen or so soundtracks Uematsu composed prior to the first *Final Fantasy*, many of which remain unknown to North American audiences and, as recent research has shown, diverge sharply from the "*Final Fantasy* sound" with which Uematsu has become associated (Elkins 2022; Plank 2020).

That is not to say, however, that style is not an important element for the success of this specific repertoire. Although the *Final Fantasy* games are highly varied stylistically, the most popular soundtracks and cues, by and large, are those that veer closest to "classical" music traditions.[9] *FFVI*, for example, is an outlier in its overtly classical tone, probably as a result of its overall structure, which borrows heavily from opera both narratively and musically. Its extensive use of leitmotifs, for instance, suggests both Wagnerian opera and classic Hollywood film scoring practices, and Uematsu's musical language brings the string-heavy score in line with those practices (Thompson 2020).

The "Aria di Mezzo Carattere"—taken from an opera scene in *FFVI* that Tim Summers (2017) describes as "a significant touchstone in video game culture" (268)—strongly suggests the conventions of 19th-century opera. In his extended study of the scene, for example, William Cheng (2014) notes the "gentle arching contours, internal phrasal symmetries, steady harmonic rhythms . . . and consonant tonal language evoke the Italianate *cantilena* writing of Vincenzo Bellini, Gaetano Donizetti, and other early Romantics" (71). Likewise, the prominent organ and rapid neo-baroque figuration of the lengthy, final boss music "Dancing Mad" pays homage to J.S. Bach's organ works, as well as to the opening of Richard Strauss's tone poem *Also Sprach Zarathustra* (Kizzire 2022). In fact, Stefan Greenfield-Casas (2022) makes the case that "Dancing Mad" exists "as a kind of (neo-Romantic) 'work' "—that is, a "work" in the classical sense of a self-standing piece of music—owing to its "multimovement form, extended duration, and clever use of quotation (both intertextual and leitmotivic)." Both the Aria and "Dancing Mad" are structurally pivotal moments of *FFVI*, important set pieces with noteworthy music composed to match.

Although it does retain the leitmotiv structure of its predecessor, *Final Fantasy VII* is less explicit in its classical borrowings (Summers 2017, 161–165). Indeed, the soundtrack is especially diverse stylistically, from the industrial sound of "Shinra, Inc." to the bossa nova of "Costa del Sol." By far the two most celebrated cues from the game, however, are "Aerith's Theme" and "One Winged Angel" which adhere to more typically cinematic or classical models—or at least can be interpreted in that way.[10] Notably, both once again occur at pivotal points in the game. "Aerith's Theme" occurs immediately after the shocking death of a major character, while "One Winged Angel" accompanies the final boss fight. Their classical-ness, especially in contrast with much of the rest of the game's music, seems to emphasize the importance of these narrative points. Summers (2017) suggests as much with regard to "One Winged Angel":

> Alongside the synthesized orchestra, this bombastic piece of music includes a recorded choir singing snippets of text from the medieval Carmina Burana manuscript, interspersed with the name of the villain. The cue obviously takes influence from the *Rite of Spring* (Stravinsky) and Carl Orff's own *Carmina Burana*, and leaves the player in no doubt of the significance of this moment in the game's narrative. (167)

That is, the use of classical idioms here—as in "Dancing Mad" above—makes players aware that this is an important, decisive point in the narrative. The implication is that classical music imbues the gameplay with a sense of gravitas that other musical styles might not possess.

When Tommy Tallarico described Uematsu's music as "very classical," these are likely the pieces and styles he had in mind—we might call it Uematsu's Heroic style. The bulk of Uematsu's musical output, even for the *Final Fantasy* series, to be clear, is *not* composed in this style. Yet these Heroic pieces are nonetheless heavily represented in concert performances, as well as in journalistic sources, which frequently use terms like "epic" to describe the *Final Fantasy* music as a whole. Just as with Beethoven's scowling repertoire, music that doesn't match the expectation for *Final Fantasy*'s seriousness is cast aside or adapted. When concert performances feature Uematsu's non-Heroic works, for example, there are often arranged to be more classical. Consider, for example, the *Final Symphony* concert program from 2013, spearheaded by Thomas Böcker, creator of the long-running German *Game Concerts* series. Like a number of concert series, *Final Symphony* featured orchestral arrangements of music from *FFVI*, *FFVII*, and *FFX*, but here they were transformed into a "symphonic poem," "symphony," and "concerto," respectively. Such a symphonic metamorphosis has the effect of bringing more of the *Final Fantasy* music in line with works like "One Winged Angel" or "Dancing Mad"—more "classical," in other words. As I have argued elsewhere, this musical choice seems calculated to legitimize Uematsu's music to meet the expectations of "serious art" for a certain type of music patron (Gibbons 2018, 166–171; Greenfield-Casas 2022).

Programs like *Final Symphony* are where we return to DeNora's central premise, the network of supporters "constructed and oriented to the production and perception of his [Beethoven's] talent." The groundwork for Uematsu's reputation, and its reliance on his Heroic style, emerged from the work of a dedicated group of promoters, concert impresarios, journalists, and fans. We have already met some of these figures: Tommy Tallarico, Mark Robins, and Thomas Böcker. In the final section, I delve a bit more deeply into Uematsu's network, how it works, and the reasons for its success.

Dear Friends

Uematsu's transformation from prog-rocker-turned-game-composer-turned-prog-rocker into "the Beethoven of Game Music" is a process of canonization. As with Beethoven, however, it is not so much that Uematsu is being inducted into an existing musical canon, as that a canon is currently being constructed around him. This process unfolds in multiple ways, coinciding with the various types of canons.

Thus far I have mostly been concerned with the *performing canon*: the repertoire that appears on concerts, recordings, and the like. Orchestral game concerts are one prominent form of this performing canon, and one in which Uematsu's music plays a major—one might argue outsized—role. Popularly regarded as a pinnacle of music at its most "classical," orchestral concerts serve as a powerfully legitimizing force for game music, and, consequently, as a highly effective way of constructing canons (Gibbons 2020). It should come as no surprise, then, that Uematsu's legacy has benefited greatly from frequent orchestral performances over a long period of time, both in the form of one-off concerts and touring series, like *Final Symphony*, *Dear Friends: Music from Final Fantasy* (2004), or *Distant Worlds: Music from Final Fantasy* (2007–present). Indeed, Greenfield-Casas (2022) astutely suggests that the combination of venue (concert hall), instrumentation (western symphony), and frequent performance (repeatedly since 1989) "set the stage for Uematsu's music to not only explicitly garner cultural capital, but also to gather it at perhaps an accelerated rate." Despite their prominence in journalism and the public awareness, however, orchestral concerts are far from the only manifestation of game music's performing canon. Other arrangements and remixes of *Final Fantasy* music, for example, contribute significantly to Uematsu's reputation.

Consider two examples of remixes and arrangements of *Final Fantasy VII*, which, as I have already shown, occupies a particularly prominent position in Uematsu's output. The nerdcore artist Mega Ran (Raheem Jarbo) and producer Lost Perception released an album *BLACK MATERIA: Final Fantasy VII* (2011, "remastered" version 2016). This hip-hop album remixes tracks from *FFVII* with Mega Ran's new lyrics, interweaving his own lived experiences with the narrative of the game (Rogers 2018). As Mega Ran reveals in the introductory notes to the album, he "just wanted to give back to (FF7 creator Nobuo) Uematsu and co. for creating a masterpiece" (Mega Ran Music). While presenting the music in the form of hip-hop remixes subverts the "classical"-ness associated with Uematsu, it nonetheless cements his reputation as a "great composer"—in the same way that remixes of classical music in games playfully reinforce their status as "masterpieces" (Gibbons 2018, chap. 6).

The same is true of the five-disc album *MATERIA: Final Fantasy VII Remixed* (2015), the first of many musical remix projects released by The Materia Collective (abbreviated as "Materia"). This enormous undertaking brought together a wide range of many of the most prominent game music artists to celebrate the music of *FFVII* through contributions in disparate musical styles, from classical-style arrangements, to hard rock, to '80s-style synthpop, and (way) beyond. Materia, self-identified on their website as "game music record label, music publisher, and rights administrator," has grown into a multifaceted group under the leadership of executive producer and CEO Sebastian Wolf. Here even the name of the organization positions *Final Fantasy* at the core of their mission—materia is the substance from which magic is created in *FFVII*. The game's continued centrality in Materia's catalog resulted in the release of *One Beat Angel FFVII* (2020), another album of *FFVII* remixes created by the DJ and producer RoboRob (Robert Anderson), who specializes in EDM remixes of game music.

Finally, we might consider arrangements of *Final Fantasy* music posted to user-generated content sites. YouTube, for example, is replete with performances of this music, ranging from amateur contributions to professional undertakings. Violinist Taylor Davis, known for her YouTube covers of video game music, posted a violin and piano arrangement of "Aerith's Theme" from *FFVII* (performed with pianist Lara de

Wit) in 2016, which, as of July 2021, has around 1.4 million views (Davis 2016). Likewise, the Russian multi-instrumentalist Alina Gingertail's 2017 cover of *FFVII*'s battle music (Gingertail 2017) has around 1.2 million hits, the guitarist ToxicxEternity's heavy metal covers of various *FFVII* cues have accumulated hundreds of thousands of views, and so on.

Other user-generated sites show similar patterns. The online game-music community OverClocked Remix (OC Remix; ocremix.org), which Ryan Thompson (2021) succinctly describes as "one of the largest centres of organized fan activity surround game audio" (410) is a case in point. OC Remix allows users to submit remixes of game music, which are then evaluated by a panel for inclusion on the site. As of this writing, the 10 games with the most frequently remixed soundtracks include four *Final Fantasy* games: *FFVI* (#2), *FFVII* (#3), *FFIV* (#7), and *FFIX* (#8). The most frequently remixed title, *Chrono Trigger* (1995), also features music from Nobuo Uematsu, giving him the top three spots. Important moments in the growth of the OC ReMix community have been marked with releases of multiauthor remix albums, an effort in which *Final Fantasy* has played a critical role. In 2007 the site released *Voices of the Lifestream*, which, in Thompson's words, "established a new scale for what the community could do with their album format. *Voices* features a complete re-envisioning of every cue from *Final Fantasy VII*: in total, the album contains forty-five tracks from mor than forty artists across four discs"[11] (414). All this despite OC ReMix's avowed efforts to avoid "any notions of canon formation within the game audio community" (411).

Despite being less public facing than concerts and recordings, the scholarly and pedagogical canons—which I will loosely group into an "academic" category—are no less significant to building Uematsu's legacy. There is, quite simply, a disproportionate amount of research devoted to his music, nearly all of it centered on the *Final Fantasy* games. Likewise, although I admit to only anecdotal data here, I suspect that the *Final Fantasy* music plays a similarly outsized role in many of the increasingly common university courses devoted to game music.[12]

Owing to the series' "dominant position in game music culture" (Summers 2017, 158), *FFVII* receives approximately 18 pages of attention in Tim Summer's excellent text *Understanding Video Game Music*—the book's only extended case study of a single game. Sebastian Deken's (2021) volume on *FFVI* for Boss Fight Books—an accessible series devoted to landmark games and written for nonacademic audiences—is devoted entirely to Uematsu's music, rather than to a broader view on the game. And although Deken quickly dismisses Uematsu's Beethovenian heritage, the book's marketing leans into the connection, identifying *FFVI* as "the game that . . . launched Uematsu's reputation as the 'Beethoven of video game music.'" The first edited scholarly volume devoted to either a single game composer or a single game series draws together a distinguished group of scholars to explore Uematsu's *Final Fantasy* scores (Anatone 2022). And, lest I seem hypocritical, I am also conscious of my own contributions to this centralizing of Uematsu in the ludomusicological canon. Although I've tried to shy away from focusing unduly on Uematsu's works, I've made reference to the *Final Fantasy* games multiple times in my own writing, and 3 of 12 chapters in my coedited essay collection *Music in the Role-Playing Game* (Gibbons and Reale 2020) deal directly with Uematsu's music (two with *Final Fantasy*).

Conclusion

If scholars, performers, listeners, journalists, marketers, fans, and scholars can all agree that Uematsu is "the Beethoven of game music," what's the problem? At least for me, the problem is that canons can discourage us from asking important questions about history and about musical values. These questions are important for all of us, but they are particularly central to the musicological enterprise. Yet, as William Weber (1999) writes:

> If we are to understand the canon historically, we must become skeptical of it, and free ourselves from its authority, its ideology, and the whole manner of speech that surrounds it. Only by questioning this tradition can we understand either its musical or its social foundation. (337)

In other words, only by turning a critical eye toward how and why canons are constructed can we determine whose values are being represented. Meanwhile, the consequences of *not* engaging critically with musical canons have historically been dire. A final comparison to Beethoven's legacy, again from DeNora (1997):

> Mainstream musical history has . . . ensured a bias in favor of Beethoven's genius, an unacknowledged but nevertheless elaborate set of instructions for his appreciation. Because pro-Beethoven culture is so extensive, the experience of his music can be a very rich one. Yet to the extent that our attention to genius and its products . . . occurs from the perspective these cultures of appreciation provide, we are blinded to visions of how music history could have been otherwise. We close off from inquiry the issue of how and why some individuals, findings, and enterprises are celebrated over others, why some are perceived as exemplary and others not. (6)

We might just as easily substitute "Uematsu" for "Beethoven" in this passage, which I find troubling. It has taken decades or in some cases centuries for the classical music world to begin coming to grips with its own assumptions and biases—and the recent surge of interest in the music of silenced composers like Joseph Bologne, Clara Schumann, and Florence Price illustrates the rich rewards for doing so.

I do not mean to suggest that we should stop performing, analyzing, or enjoying Uematsu's music—yet at the same time we must be aware (or beware) of the impact of doing so. Taken individually, each performance can be a rewarding musical experience, and each piece of scholarship a thoughtful contribution to the field. But taken in totality, the privileging of a single composer (or a small group of composers) threatens to recreate classical music's "great master" rhetoric at the expense of a more complex and diverse picture of game music history. Hyeonjin Park (2020) has compellingly argued as much in an essay on the dangers of canonicity in game audio:

> We should continue to analyze and perform the music of composers such as Koji Kondo or Nobuo Uematsu, considering the vastness of their respective oeuvres and the numerous ways to approach them. I draw attention to these two composers because it would take little effort to have our field orbit around them. We should not get lost in the dozens of hours of music that these two composers wrote, especially knowing that the power structures of the gaming world focus on cisgender, white and Japanese, heterosexual, and male narratives. (89)

Even as Uematsu's star has continued to rise, histories are being (re)written in such a way as to make his fame inevitable and justifiable. Yet to make room for this monolithic legacy, other equally worthy stories have been minimized. For example, in a study of the mostly female Capcom Sound Team of the 1980s and 1990s, Andrew Lemon and Hillegonda C. Reitveld (2021) have noted that "female game composers have more often than not been *excripted* from game histories" (379)—that is, they have been omitted from the canon, their stories untold (see chapter 10 this volume for more on this).

With video game music, we have an opportunity to study—and if necessary, intervene in—the formation of a new musical canon. To uncritically accept Uematsu's central canonic position, and by the same token to accept the criterion of musical "greatness" that canonicity implies, would risk replicating the mistakes of the past. When all is said and done, canons are always fantasies—"a grand illusion," as Alex Ross (2014) writes of Beethoven, "generated by the erasure of a less desirable past." I am hopeful that we can change course and embrace a broader and more inclusive understanding of its game music history. Canons will always be fantasies, but they need not be final.

Notes

1. The other nominees for "Best Score and Music" in 2020 were *Doom Eternal* (Mick Gordon), *Hades* (Darren Korb), *Ori and the Will of the Wisps* (Gareth Coker), and *The Last of Us Part II* (Gustavo Santaolalla). The award is technically for "outstanding music, inclusive of score, original song and/or licensed soundtrack," but to date The Game Awards audio winners have all been for original scores.
2. In an extended case study of the music in the original *Final Fantasy VII*, Tim Summers (2020, 158–176) notes the particular emotional significance the music of *Final Fantasy VII* holds for many players, which he suggests emerges through Uematsu's canny navigation of both cinematic and ludic musical expectations.
3. On the "anxiety of influence" Beethoven created in the 19th century, see, for example, Bonds 1996.
4. This type of antonomasia is particularly common where brevity is key—titles, for example, or newspaper headlines. See, for example, Fischer and Jäschke 2020.
5. On Heinrich's background and legacy as "the Beethoven of America," see Shadle 2016, chap. 2.

6. In keeping with its Shakespearian tone, for example, the score for *Final Fantasy IX* frequently imitates musical styles from the European Renaissance (Kizzire 2014).
7. For an overview of the legacy and interpretation of Beethoven's "uncanonic" works, see also N. Cook 2003.
8. Kivy, it is worth noting, disagreed strongly with DeNora's assertions about the importance of Beethoven's network of supporters, favoring instead a less historically grounded view that the composer's success resulted from the transcendental genius of his works.
9. One could make a compelling argument that the instances of classicism in Uematsu's scores often stem from the overall musical influence of prog rock, which was in many cases itself influenced by classical works. In that sense, the classical aspects of, say, "Dancing Mad" is second-hand, filtered through groups like King Crimson, Renaissance, or Emerson, Lake & Palmer.
10. Uematsu himself regards "One Winged Angel" as more closely related to rock than classical music, or at the least an equal fusion of the two (Tate 2022).
11. The OC ReMix community has replicated this success with *Balance and Ruin* (a massive tribute to *FFVI*) and several other *Final Fantasy*–based albums.
12. *Pace* Karen Cook, who has argued that "Thus far in our field's existence, to the best of my ability to assess, we have not placed a significantly disproportionate amount of attention onto any single game, franchise, composer, or console, whether in publication or in public presentation." She continues, however, "With that said . . . at least in North American contexts, certain popular franchises and composers (Nobuo Uematsu for *Final Fantasy*, Koji Kondo for *Mario* and *Zelda*) do receive frequent mention . . . and . . . are often used as go-to examples for specialist and non-specialist audiences alike, for the sakes of familiarity, accessibility, and nostalgia" (K. Cook 2020, 97).

References

Anatone, Richard, ed. 2022. *The Music of Nobuo Uematsu for the "Final Fantasy" Series*. Bristol, UK: Intellect.

Bonds, Mark Evan. 1996. *After Beethoven: The Imperative of Originality in the Symphony*. Cambridge, MA: Harvard University Press.

Bramwell, Tom. 2014. "The PR Man Who Spams Games Journalists about Classical Music." *Eurogamer*, February 23, 2014. https://www.eurogamer.net/articles/2013-02-12-the-pr-man-who-spams-games-journalists-about-classical-music.

Burnham, Scott. 1995. *Beethoven Hero*. Princeton: Princeton University Press.

Cheng, William. 2014. *Sound Play: Video Games and the Musical Imagination*. Oxford: Oxford University Press.

ClassicFM. 2019. "Here's How Nobuo Uematsu Changed the Course of Classical Music with His *Final Fantasy* Score." June 10, 2019. https://www.classicfm.com/composers/uematsu/music/final-fantasy-soundtrack/.

Cook, Karen. 2020. "Canon Anxiety?" *Journal of Sound and Music in Games* 1:95–99.

Cook, Nicholas. 2003. "The Other Beethoven: Heroism, the Canon, and the Works for 1813–14." *19th Century Music* 27:3–24.

Damman, Guy. 2015. "Nobuo Uematsu: The Video Game Composer Shaking Up Classical Music." *Guardian*, April 7, 2015. https://www.theguardian.com/music/shortcuts/2015/apr/07/nobuo-uematsu-video-game-composer-shaking-classical-music.

Davis, Taylor. 2016. "*Final Fantasy VII*: Aeris's Theme (Violin & Piano Cover Duet Taylor Davis & Lara de Wit." YouTube, July 14, 2016. https://www.youtube.com/watch?v=LI7Wcl5y5Qs.

Dekan, Sebastian. 2021. *Final Fantasy VI*. Los Angeles: Boss Fight Books.

DeNora, Tia. 1997. *Beethoven and the Construction of Musical Genius: Musical Politics in Vienna, 1792–1803*. Berkeley: University of California Press.

Elkins, Alan. 2022. "Penultimate Fantasies: Compositional Precedents in Uematsu's Early Works." In *The Music of Nobuo Uematsu for the Final Fantasy Series*, edited by Richard Anatone, 181–205. Bristol, UK: Intellect.

Farber, Jim. 2019. "Game On: How Classical Music Helps Create the World of Online Role-Playing Games." *San Francisco Classical Voice*, September 28, 2019. https://www.sfcv.org/article/game-on-how-classical-music-helps-create-the-world-of-online-role-playing-games.

Fischer, Frank, and Robert Jäschke. 2020. "'The Michael Jordan of Greatness'—Extracting Vossian Antonomasia from Two Decades of *The New York Times*, 1987–2007." *Digital Scholarship in the Humanities* 35:34–42.

Fleishman, Jeffrey. 2015. "Video Game Music Comes to the Orchestra Concert Hall." *Los Angeles Times*, June 12, 2015. https://www.latimes.com/entertainment/herocomplex/la-ca-hc-video-games-music-20150614-story.html.

Fleming, John. 2013. "The Beethoven of Video Games." *Tampa Bay Times*, January 28, 2013. https://www.tampabay.com/archive/2013/01/27/the-beethoven-of-video-games/.

Frey, Angelica. 2015. "Video Game Music: Focus on Nobuo Uematsu." CMuse, March 21, 2015. https://www.cmuse.org/video-game-music-focus-on-nobuo-uematsu/.

Gibbons, William. 2018. *Unlimited Replays: Video Games and Classical Music*. Oxford: Oxford University Press.

Gibbons, William. 2020. "Rewritable Memory: Concerts, Canons, and Game Music History." *Journal of Sound and Music in Games* 1:75–81.

Gibbons, William, and Julianne Grasso. 2020. "'And So It Goes, On and On': Repetition in the Music of *Final Fantasy*." In *The Psychology of Final Fantasy: Surpassing the Limit Break*, edited by Anthony Bean, 43–60. Dallas: Leyline.

Gibbons, William, and Steven Reale, eds. 2020. *Music in the Role-Playing Game: Heroes and Harmonies*. New York: Routledge.

Gilliland, Norman. 2015. "Log Cabin Composer at the White House." Wisconsin Public Radio, October 15, 2015. Accessed December 29, 2021. https://www.wpr.org/log-cabin-composer-white-house.

Gingertail, Alina. 2017. "*Final Fantasy VII*—Let the Battles Begin/Those Who Fight (Gingertail Cover)." YouTube, May 18, 2017. Accessed December 29, 2021. https://www.youtube.com/watch?v=gmzzIsBK47I.

Greenfield-Casas, Stefan. 2022. "Uematsu's Postgame: The Music of *Final Fantasy* in the Concert Hall (and Beyond)." In *The Music of Nobuo Uematsu for the Final Fantasy Series*, edited by Richard Anatone, 291–311. Bristol, UK: Intellect.

Kivy, Peter. 2011. *The Possessor and the Possessed: Handel, Mozart, Beethoven, and the Idea of Musical Genius*. New Haven: Yale University Press.

Kizzire, Jessica. 2014. "'The Place I'll Return to Someday': Musical Nostalgia in *Final Fantasy IX*." In *Music in Video Games: Studying Play*, edited by K. J. Donnelly, William Gibbons, and Neil Lerner, 183–198. New York: Routledge.

Kizzire, Jessica. 2022. "Dancing Mad: Music and the Apotheosis of Villainy in *Final Fantasy*." In *The Music of Nobuo Uematsu for the Final Fantasy Series*, edited by Richard Anatone, 13–33. Bristol, UK: Intellect.

Kosman, Joshua. 2020. "It's Been 250 Years: Let's Come to Grips with Our Beethoven Fixation." *SF Chronicle Datebook*, January 29, 2020. Accessed December 29, 2021. https://datebook.sfchronicle.com/music/its-been-250-years-lets-come-to-grips-with-our-beethoven-fixation.

Lemon, Andrew, and Hillegonda C. Rietveld. 2021. "Female Credit: Excavating Recognition for the Capcom Sound Team." In *The Cambridge Companion to Video Game Music*, edited by Melanie Fritsch and Tim Summers, 376–388. Cambridge: Cambridge University Press.

Lin, Emilie. 2019. "Music from *Final Fantasy* Video Game in Concert." *CityScene Columbus*, May 30, 2019. Accessed December 29, 2021. https://www.cityscenecolumbus.com/arts-and-entertainment/weekendscene-weekend-rundown/music-from-final-fantasy-video-game-in-concert/.

Mega Ran Music. n.d. "BLACK MATERIA: *Final Fantasy VII*." Accessed December 29, 2021. https://megaranmusic.com/album/black-materia-final-fantasy-vii.

Moore, Andrea. 2019. "Commentary: Beethoven Was Born 250 Years Ago. To Celebrate, How About We Ban His Music for a Year?" *Chicago Tribune*, December 30, 2019. Accessed December 29, 2021. https://www.chicagotribune.com/opinion/commentary/ct-opinion-ban-beethoven-anniversary-20191230-ukklfgb25baaxcjjiddm3ud76y-story.html.

NPR All Things Considered. 2008. "The Evolution of Video Game Music." April 13, 2008. Accessed December 29, 2021. https://www.npr.org/templates/story/story.php?storyId=89565567.

Park, Hyeonjin. 2020. "The Difficult, Uncomfortable, and Imperative Conversations Needed in Game Music and Sound Studies." *Journal of Sound and Music in Games* 1:87–94.

Plank, Dana. 2020. "The Penultimate Fantasy: Nobuo Uematsu's Score for *Cleopatra no Ma Takara*." In *Music in the Role-Playing Game: Heroes and Harmonies*, edited by William Gibbons and Steven Reale, 76–96. New York: Routledge.

Rogers, Kate. 2018. "Rereading the Lifestream: Explorations of Identity and Society in Mega Ran's *Black Materia: Final Fantasy VII*." Paper presented at the 2018 North American Conference on Video Game Music, January 14, 2018.

Rosenfeld, Paul. 1941. "The Beethoven of the North." *New Republic* 104, no. 16 (April 21): 526–528.

Ross, Alex. 2014. "Deus ex Musica." *New Yorker*, October 13, 2014. Accessed December 29, 2021. https://www.newyorker.com/magazine/2014/10/20/deus-ex-musica.

Shadle, Douglas W. 2016. *Orchestrating the Nation: The Nineteenth-Century American Symphonic Enterprise*. Oxford: Oxford University Press.

Summers, Tim. 2016. *Understanding Video Game Music*. Cambridge: Cambridge University Press.

Summers, Tim. 2017. "Opera Scenes in Video Games: Hitmen, Divas and Wagner's Werewolves." *Cambridge Opera Journal* 29:253–286.

Tate, James S. 2022. "The Devil in the Detail: Analyzing Nobuo Uematsu's 'One-Winged Angel' from *Final Fantasy VII*." In *The Music of Nobuo Uematsu for the Final Fantasy Series*, edited by Richard Anatone, 34–66. Bristol, UK: Intellect.

Thompson, Ryan. 2021. "Game Music beyond the Games." In *The Cambridge Companion to Video Game Music*, edited by Tim Summers and Melanie Fritsch, 409–423. Cambridge: Cambridge University Press.

Thompson, Ryan. 2020. "Operatic Conventions and Expectations in *Final Fantasy VI*." In *Music in the Role-Playing Game: Heroes and Harmonies*, edited by William Gibbons and Steven Reale, 117–128. New York: Routledge.

Weber, William. 1999. "The History of Musical Canon." In *Rethinking Music*, edited by Nicholas Cook and Mark Everist, 336–355. Oxford: Oxford University Press.

Wikipedia. n.d. "Nobuo Uematsu." Accessed December 29, 2020. https://en.wikipedia.org/wiki/Nobuo_Uematsu.

CHAPTER 3

CROSSING THE LUDO-CINEMATIC CONTINUUM

Music-Theoretical Approaches to Video Game Music

SEAN ATKINSON

Introduction

The analysis of video game music through the lens of music theory presents several problems. One, music theory (narrowly considered here to mean music theory of the Western art music tradition) largely developed alongside the music it is designed to analyze. Western music's greatest voices in music theory and analysis also tended to be composers of that same music. Johann Fux, author of the 1725 treatise *Gradus ad Parnassum*, was himself a composer. Arnold Schoenberg, 200 years later, was just as much a music theorist of his own music as he was a composer. Though the separation between theorist and composer is greater today, composers such as Robert Morris continue to play a significant role in professional music theory circles in the United States. It is no wonder, then, that the tools of music theory are intimately tied and well suited to the analysis of music composed in the Western art music tradition. Two, video game music is a relatively new art form. While much of that music is diatonic and therefore *harmonically* compatible with music theory tools, video game music also draws on influences outside of the Western art music tradition. For example, composers of the music for Japanese role-playing games (JRPGs) often draw inspiration from rock music. Video game music does share a link with film music, which coincidentally brings me to the third and final challenge in applying music theory to video game music: video game music differs fundamentally from film music in that it is interactive. While many of the analytical mechanisms commonly applied to film music might hold true in video games, theorists must account for interactivity, especially when relating their analysis back to the game.[1]

Therein lies the thrust of what I will discuss in this chapter. Traditional tools of music theory are well suited to comment upon the descriptive function of video game music, just as in film music. But when the music adapts to the more ludic parts of a game (music tied up in the game's interactivity), theoretical tools often break down and become less useful in the context of the game itself. The difference between film-like music and game-like music is not a binary distinction; instead, the music often lies along a continuum, depicted in Figure 3.1. On the right of the figure lies game music with purely cinematic function. This is music that accompanies cutscenes in games, for example, in which the player has no control over how events unfold. On the left side of the continuum is ludic function, music that by its very nature is connected to a player's actions.[2] Music in a game can fall anywhere along this continuum and can continually shift positions over the course of a game.[3]

The difference between ludic and cinematic function is similar to the differences between game audio and film music described by Karen Collins. Collins (2008, 128) writes: "Although game audio typically maintains all of the functions found in film or television sound, there are also some distinct differences in the ways in which audio functions in games." Collins goes on to describe differences between the two musics as contingent to the *edit*: "[E]ither the film is cut (edited) to the music, or the music is edited to fit the cut" (128). This is one of the main ways that I distinguish between ludic and cinematic function. Music with a cinematic function is tightly edited to the events happening on screen, whereas music with a ludic function is typically less choreographed to the specific action of the game.

Part of the difference between functions also hinges on what Tim Summers (2016, 25) identifies as one of the most important differences between film music and game music: "The most obvious contrast between game music and music encountered in (and through) other media is the issue of interactivity. In most cases, the musical output of the game is dependent upon the player's engagement with the gameplay." In other words, the more the music is related to a player's active decision, the more ludic function it will embody.

In terms of music theory, where a particular example of music is located on the continuum should have vast implications as to the analytical approach taken with the music. For example, if a particular piece of music has a strong ludic function, analytical tools that examine the track as a unified whole might not be relevant to the music's use

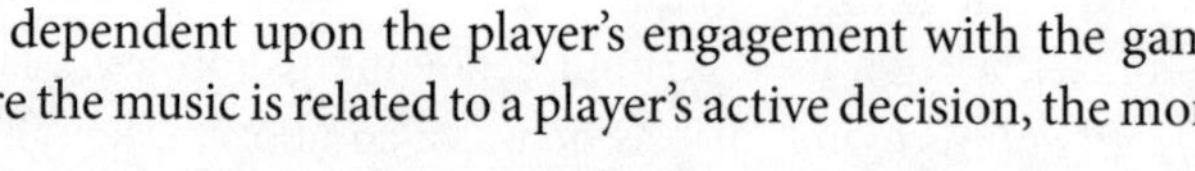

FIGURE 3.1 The ludo-cinematic continuum of video game music.

in gameplay. A particular cue in a game may be quite long on the soundtrack, but only sound in short segments during the game. The interactivity of a game also makes it hard if not impossible for the analyst to precisely align musical events with on-screen events. Music with a strong cinematic function, though, may benefit from more linear and holistic approaches, since the music will be heard in its complete form with the opportunity to precisely associate musical events with things happening in the narrative of the game. For the former, analyses that privilege shorter segments of music are preferable, and, for the latter, analytical tools such as formenlehre and linear analysis are more appropriate, as well as the vast resources available from the study of film music.

Admittedly, this continuum cannot fully account for all uses of music in video games. Games in which the music constantly reacts to player inputs would present a continually shifting soundtrack. Steven Reale (2014, 77–103) discusses the *BIT.TRIP* series of games as examples of these music games. In the *BIT.TRIP* games, successful gameplay actions are timed perfectly with the music and trigger additional musical sounds, so that the player is actively contributing to the music as the levels progress. The music in such games is clearly ludic since it connects closely to player input, yet the music is always in flux, suggesting the use of analytical methodologies more appropriate for indeterminate music. And in music/rhythm games, the music *is* the game, perhaps suggesting the clearest form of ludic musical function.

Where the continuum shines especially bright is in the genre of role-playing games. To demonstrate how function along this continuum can influence music analytical decisions, I will engage with three tracks from *Final Fantasy VII* (1997, PlayStation). The music for this game, composed by Nobuo Uematsu, is likely some of the best-known and most-loved video game music. William Gibbons (2018, 168–171) highlights this popularity, noting the presence of *Final Symphony*, a symphonic concert featuring arrangements of music from the entire *Final Fantasy* series (including *Final Fantasy VII*), on several different top classical music charts since 2015 (see also chapter 2 this volume). Uematsu's score for the original game is vast, containing over 100 individual tracks, including the final boss music "One-Winged Angel," a selection scored for synthesized full orchestra and prerecorded (not synthesized) voices. The breadth and depth of the soundtrack make it an ideal candidate to explore how the ludo-cinematic continuum can impact music-theoretical approaches to the music.[4]

To reiterate: the position of the music on the continuum is largely based on how the music is used in the game, not on the music itself. First, I will discuss *FFVII*'s victory theme (titled "Fanfare" on the official soundtrack), and how its appearance in the game lends it a particularly strong ludic rather than cinematic function. Next, the track "Steal the Tiny Bronco!" demonstrates a compelling example of cinematic function, as players have no control over the action on screen while the track plays, allowing the composer and the game designers to perfectly choreograph events on screen with the music. Finally, I will discuss an example that lies somewhere between the two with the track "Words Drowned by Fireworks," which appears once or twice during gameplay depending on player choices.

The Ludo-Cinematic Continuum

Ludic Function: "Fanfare" (*FFVII*'s Victory Theme)

Upon the completion of most battles in the *Final Fantasy* series, players are rewarded with the familiar victory fanfare. This fanfare, the first half of a short binary form, retains its characteristic melody between most installments of the game, making it one of the franchise's most recognizable musical cues. Adding to this recognition is the fact that players will fight hundreds, if not thousands of battles when playing the games in the series, likely making this the most heard, nonlooped music during gameplay. The opening two-measure fanfare constitutes the A section of this binary form, while a longer B section continues the cue and is repeated until the postbattle menus are cleared by the player. In terms of how this music functions during gameplay, it aligns most closely with ludic function rather than cinematic function. The music is triggered directly by player action (after a successful battle with an enemy) and reinforces a positive achievement in the game (the fanfare itself as a musical signification of victory).[5] Its duration can also be shortened by the player, adding another dimension of interactivity. After the fanfare, players will often exit the postbattle menus quickly, cutting the B section short.

From a purely analytical perspective, it is tempting to address the complete binary form of "Fanfare" as a single musical unit, and such an analysis does reveal an interesting connection to the other victory themes in the franchise that I discuss later. From a ludic perspective, however, this may not be the best approach, as many players will only hear the complete B section a handful of times, and some may never hear it at all beyond the first few seconds. Analyzing the whole track as a cohesive musical unit, while perhaps of analytical interest, does little to help explain the use of the music ludically.[6] Therefore, I will divide the analysis into two parts. The first considers just the fanfare, or A section, of the track and the ludic function this music has within the world of the game. The second analytical approach considers the entire track as a complete musical unit. Each approach is useful in its own way, but the former is more useful, considering how most players will experience the music. The latter, more holistic analysis, disregards the music's function in the game but provides an interesting comparison between variations of the victory theme in this game and with the victory themes of other games in the series.

The fanfare itself, shown in a piano reduction in Figure 3.2, has many of the musical hallmarks expected from a fanfare, including the heralding, regal triplets in the upper voices.[7] The lower, more flowing triplets are unexpected—a departure from the victory theme's treatment in previous *Final Fantasy* games. This unusual bass line appears to set up the following B section that will be discussed below. Nonetheless, the heralding call suggests a strong connection with the martial topic, reinforced by snare drum rolls (not shown here) during the fanfare. As mentioned above, the ludic function here is one of reward: a sonic reinforcement of the player's victory in battle. However, the fanfare's harmonies suggest a more complicated story.

FIGURE 3.2 Opening fanfare from "Fanfare," *Final Fantasy VII.*

FIGURE 3.3 Harmonic reduction of the "Fanfare" B section from *Final Fantasy VII.*

The opening C Major tonic moves to a D-flat add9 (flat-II), followed by B-flat major (flat-VII), moving to F minor (iv) and concluding on another D-flat add9 chord. This unusual harmonic progression, especially the ending on flat-II, signals to the player that this is not the end of the story. Yes, there is victory in the texture and style of the fanfare, but the open-ended harmonic progression leaves the player in search of a more complete closure. This lack of fulfillment may entice a player to continue listening to the rest of the track, yet players eager to continue the game will exit the postbattle menu as quickly as possible, leaving the harmonies unresolved. Over the course of a typical playthrough of the game, this could add up to several hundred incomplete auditions of the victory music.[8] Indeed, one could argue that the cumulative effect of that inconclusive ending foreshadows the game's somewhat ambiguous ending.[9]

Now, let's consider the track as complete unit. Figure 3.3 presents a harmonic reduction of the "Fanfare" B section. The theme's harmonies are slippery, shifting slightly one or two notes at a time. To begin, the first F-minor triad becomes an F-major triad when considering only the upper voices. The harmony is complicated by Uematsu's bass line, which falls to a D at the same time, creating a Dm7 harmony. In the context of F minor as a tonal center, this vi7 chord is not terribly out of keeping with common-practice harmony. Next, however, sees the reappearance of the F-minor triad in the upper voices paired with a D-flat in the bass, or a flat-VI7. Next, the F-minor triad becomes an E-augmented triad (or F-flat augmented as shown in the example). This motion preserves the half-step motion Uematsu has been using to transform the triads in the upper voices. Furthermore, the resulting harmony, with the added note G-flat in the lower voices, results in an F-flat augmented flat9. The harmony, as distantly related as it is from the tonic, borrows the function of a dominant in the resolution to the Fm7 that follows and begins the next phrase. The F-flat (or E) pushes up to F while the A-flat and C remain common tones. The G-flat then pushes down to F, reinforcing F as the tonic. Although subtle, this is the harmonic closure that is missing from the fanfare.

The harmonic cycle then repeats on the fifth harmony, but, after the Dm7, the progression steps up to an E-flatm7, followed by a final E-flatM7 before repeating to the beginning of the B section for the loop. This E-flatM7, or flat-VII7 in the context of F minor, serves the harmonic function of remaining open-ended and allowing for the return of the F-minor triad at the beginning of the progression.

As a whole, "Fanfare" presents several unusual and dissonant harmonies, which is a departure from the victory theme in previous installments in the series. Take, for example, the victory theme (also called "Fanfare" in the official soundtrack) from *Final Fantasy IV* (1991), which is representative of the victory themes in the first six games (see Figure 3.4). The opening fanfare shares the same melody, but after the initial tonic triad, moves to flat-VI, then to flat-VII, and back to I. The use of flat-VI and flat-VII harmonies, while perhaps unusual in a common-practice context, is commonly found in more popular genres, especially rock. And perhaps the most well-known victory theme in all of video game music, the *Super Mario Bros.* (1985) victory theme, heard when touching the flagpole at the end of a level, likewise features a prominent I, flat-VI, flat-VII, I progression. As such, this progression has come to have a strong association with victory in game music, and therefore has a clear ludic function. It also provides a more definitive conclusion to the fanfare itself.[10]

Compared to the games that came before it, *FFVII* saw substantial changes to the B section of the victory theme. In the *FFIV* version, the track carries on the regal style of the fanfare (the martial topic itself plays a larger role in the entire soundtrack for *FFIV*, owing to the pseudo-medieval setting). In contrast, the B section of *FFVII's* victory theme is more fluid, featuring running arpeggios in the lower parts and minimal percussion. Perhaps the lack of a significant martial topic lends to the setting of the game, which takes place in a futuristic setting.

Harmonically, however, the musical progressions of these disparate B sections appear to have the same tonal function, though achieved through different harmonic frameworks. The B section of the *FFIV* victory theme essentially oscillates back and forth between tonic and flat-VII, ultimately ending on a flat-VI harmony that propels

FIGURE 3.4 Opening fanfare from "Fanfare," *Final Fantasy IV*.

the loop of the B section music. But despite these similarities and differences in the B sections of the themes, does a harmonic and stylistic analysis help explain what is a predominantly ludic function of the music? Possibly, but given the fact that players will rarely encounter the B section of the victory theme, its connection back to the game is tenuous at best.

This is the heart of the issue that plagues music theory analysis of video game music. Should the analysis shed light on the music's use in the game, or should the analysis ignore the in-game use and treat it as a stand-alone entity? If the goal is the latter, then there is little that would separate the analysis of game music and any other music. But if the goal is the former, then care must be taken to understand the context of the music within the world of the game. I do not mean to suggest that one is inherently better (or worse) than the other, and there is certainly use in both approaches. But analyzing video game music outside of its original context is relatively unproblematic using conventional analytical tools. It is relatively simple for a music theorist to transcribe a track from a game and analyze it like music from any other genre. But unlike other formats and genres, the music in the context of a game may never sound to the player like it does in the soundtrack. A player may rarely or never hear the victory theme in its complete form, so what good does the harmonic analysis do for the player? When considering the context of video game music, establishing its function on the continuum suggests the kinds of analytical approaches that would be most appropriate.

Because of the track's brevity and consistent appearance after all victorious battles, its function is more squarely ludic than cinematic. Ludic-functioning music must be dealt with carefully, since analyzing out of context can lead to interpretations that do not coalesce with the way the music is used in game. Of course, it is valuable to analyze this music, from whatever lens music theory has to offer, but the application of those findings back to the game should be handled carefully.[11]

Cinematic Function: "Steal the Tiny Bronco!"

The brief cutscene in which the party steals the Tiny Bronco—a plane that the party hopes will enable them to cross the ocean—provides an excellent example of cinematic function in video game music. Through a series of prerendered cutscenes and in-game dialogue (which the player cannot control), the music can be directly synchronized with the on-screen action. The composer and the director have full control over the combined output, and the critical aspect of interactivity that helps distinguish video games from film is missing.

Because this music is synchronized to the visuals and will be heard in its entirety by the player, a full and complete analysis of the entire track will yield not only interesting analytical observations but also meaningful results in the context of the scene. My analysis of the music from this cutscene is split into several segments given the nature of the music, with different parts of the music analyzed using different methodologies.

The short cutscene (just over one minute in length) can be considered as its own dramatic mini arc in four distinct "acts." In Act I, the heroes successfully board the Tiny Bronco, take off, and begin to escape. Act II transitions to images of the heroes aboard the plane, triumphantly flying above the enemy forces and evading enemy gunfire. Act III begins when the plane's tail is hit, putting the fate of the plane and the heroes in jeopardy. The final act depicts the plane falling from the sky and crash-landing in the water.

As expected from music serving a more cinematic function, the action on screen is closely related to the action in the music. The voice-leading reduction shown in Figure 3.5 represents the music presented during Act I and contains three distinct motivic gestures. The first, annotated with the letter *a*, is a two-note motive that repeats throughout Act I. A detailed transcription of that motive is shown in Figure 3.6. The persistent back and forth between F-A and G-B dyads creates an oscillation that mimics the mechanical rotation of a plane's propeller. (This is a musical feature indicated by Erno Rapée as an example of "aëroplane" music for use in accompanying silent films.)[12]

The low brass, rising fourths, indicated with a *b* in Figure 3.5, are another cinematic reference to flight. Occurring twice, this motive is reminiscent of the brass ascending fifths at the beginning of *The Spirit of St. Louis* (1957), a film about Charles Lindberg's successful nonstop crossing of the Atlantic by plane. The ascending open intervals are strongly associated not only with military fanfare but also with the idea of soaring.[13] The Tiny Bronco is even visually similar to the *Spirit of St. Louis*: both are prop-driven planes with unenclosed cockpits.

The final motive, shown with the letter *c*, is music seemingly borrowed from *Final Fantasy IV*. The parallel sixths in the strings are a quotation, at the same pitch level, from

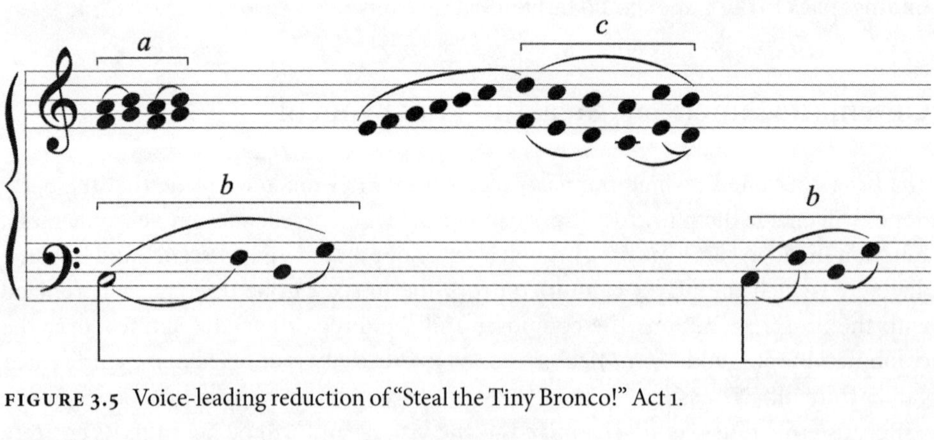

FIGURE 3.5 Voice-leading reduction of "Steal the Tiny Bronco!" Act 1.

FIGURE 3.6 Repeated motive from the beginning of "Steal the Tiny Bronco!"

FIGURE 3.7 Melodic and harmonic reduction of "Steal the Tiny Bronco!" Act 2.

a track called "The Red Wings." In *FFIV*, the Red Wings are a division of airships under the command of the game's main character, Cecil. This theme is closely associated with flight in that game, as well as with Cecil himself. It seems appropriate, then, that this first flight with the heroes of *Final Fantasy VII* should be accompanied by this motivic fragment.[14]

Act II is a quotation of the main theme from *Final Fantasy VII*, presented in a march style. Most often heard during the overworld sequences, this theme appears frequently throughout the game, including in the airship theme "The Highwind Takes to the Skies." But the march style used here, along with the faster tempo and snare drum accompaniment, transforms the theme into a heroic march. This is consistent with the way that the characters are depicted on screen, having successfully taken off in the Tiny Bronco and making their escape.

The harmonies accompanying the theme are similar to the harmonies that accompany the main theme elsewhere in the game, with one significant alteration at the end. The last note is harmonized with a polychord consisting of a B-flat-minor triad and an implied C-major triad (Figure 3.7). The cluster of notes creates a biting dissonance that occurs just as enemy gunfire hits the tail of the plane, bringing into doubt that the heroes will make a successful escape after all.

Act III—not illustrated here but best described rhythmically due to the nature of the music—features a faster tempo of 185 beats per minute and an irregular 5/4 meter. Rhythmic accents on beats one, three, and five further emphasize this irregularity, adding tension as the Tiny Bronco faces an imminent emergency landing. Visually, this is actually the most static part of the cutscene, with players only seeing brief dialogue between the characters on the plane. Crucially, that dialogue cannot be controlled by the player, allowing the next scene to remain in sync with the music. The frenetic pace of the music also helps to counter the visual stasis of the characters on screen.

The final act sees the descent of the Tiny Bronco into the water after it was damaged. The voice-leading sketch in Figure 3.8 shows a continuous, almost fully chromatic descent across three octaves, paralleling the descent of the plane on screen.

With this music, Uematsu takes the listener on a quick journey from the wonders of soaring through the sky, to a heroic escape, the panic of an emergency, and the descent of the plane into the water. All four musical pieces work together with the narrative arc to provide cinematic support for the actions on screen. By examining the track

FIGURE 3.8 Melodic reduction of "Steal the Tiny Bronco!" Act 4.

as a whole, we are able to best position the use of the music in the game due to the tight integration between the visual and audio domains.

Between Cinematic and Ludic Function: "Words Drowned by Fireworks"

"Words Drowned by Fireworks" lies somewhere in the middle of the continuum between ludic and cinematic function. The music is typically heard twice, in different dramatic circumstances, but since the player still has control of the dialogue during the times it is used, it lacks the tight integration with the visuals on screen experienced with "Steal the Tiny Bronco!" Before addressing more specifically the music as used in gameplay, I'll begin with an analysis of the music itself, this time focused on the melody, harmony, and texture.

A transcription of the music is provided in Figure 3.9. Note that the example as notated begins with measure four of the music when the melody begins. The first three measures introduce a harp that provides the harmonic support throughout the track. Also note the annotations in this reduction indicate which instruments are playing each part of the melody. Starting with bells, the harmonic context is fairly uncomplicated, largely staying within the context of D major, but once again following the harmonic conventions of popular music rather than Western classical music. For example, C Major (flat-VII) is used as a substitute for the dominant in measure five. This eventually leads to a deceptive motion from flat-VII to B minor (vi) in measure 17.

A flute then assumes the melodic duties in measure 21, and at the same time we can observe three important shifts. The first is the construction of the melody itself. During the previous section, the melody was fragmented into two-measure groups, themselves separated by extended periods of rest. Once the flute enters, the melodic phrasing becomes much longer and less fragmented. The second change is the rate at which harmonies change. The harmonic pacing increases from a chord change every four measures to a chord change every two measures. Such a shift in harmonic rhythm typically signals an upcoming cadence or otherwise strong conclusion to a phrase. In the last phrase, the harmonic rhythm increases again to a change every measure, ultimately leading to the final closure on D major before the track repeats. The final change here is one of register. The high tessitura of the bells is followed by the still high, yet lower

FIGURE 3.9 Melodic and harmonic reduction of "Words Drowned by Fireworks."

tessitura of the flute. This will then be followed by the still lower range of the oboe. All three of these shifts are potentially significant when addressing how the music is used in gameplay.

The first opportunity during gameplay a player has to hear "Words Drowned by Fireworks" is when protagonist Cloud goes on a date at the Gold Saucer amusement park. The party is there to retrieve an important item, but during some down time, Cloud and one of the characters go on a date. Either Tifa, Aerith, Yuffie, or Barret are chosen to go on this date based on dialogue choices that the player has made during the game up to this point.[15] The dates with the three female characters are largely the same, with no significant differences apart from dialogue changes appropriate to each character. For the purposes of this discussion, I will specifically reference the date with Aerith.[16]

As part of the date, Aerith decides she and Cloud should take a ride on a gondola, and it is during that ride that players hear "Words Drowned by Fireworks." The title of the track is appropriate here as well, given that a fireworks display is ongoing during the ride. The ride itself takes the couple high above the Gold Saucer, giving them views of the entire area. These are shown through a handful of short, prerendered cutscenes interspersed with dialogue inside the gondola. Cloud and Aerith's dialogue consists mainly of Aerith commenting on the sights during the ride and wanting to get to know Cloud better.

Despite the cutscenes, the function of the music leans slightly away from cinematic since the music and visuals on screen are not tightly integrated. A player lingering on a text box will affect the timing of the music with action on screen. As such, it acts here as a background to the events on screen, setting a mood more than directly reinforcing narrative events.

In the context of the date, the music—which begins melodically fragmented yet ends in a more cohesive phrase—might symbolize the tenuous relationship between Cloud and Aerith. This is the first time that Cloud and Aerith openly discuss their potential romantic feeling for each other. That communicative act perhaps begins the relationship, and this is symbolized musically by the tightening of the phrase structure as the track unfolds.

After the date, “Words Drowned by Fireworks” is heard one more time during the next part of the game—when Cait Sith, a remotely controlled robotic character, sacrifices himself for the team. Before doing so, and as the characters are saying goodbye, Aerith asks Cait Sith to read her fortune and the first thing she asks is how compatible her and Cloud are. It is at that moment that “Words Drowned by Fireworks” begins to play, instantly causing players to recall the date Cloud went on earlier at the Gold Saucer. It is important to note that no matter who Cloud goes with on the date at the Gold Saucer, Aerith is a required character at this point. Nothing about the interaction between her and Cait Sith changes as a result of the previous date. Therefore, a player might have very different reactions to this moment and the recurrence of the music here.

If Cloud went on the date with Aerith, this scene with Cait Sith seems somewhat expected as it appears that the game’s narrative is setting up a long-term relationship between Cloud and Aerith. But if Cloud went on a date with any of the other female characters, this moment might be embarrassing for Cloud, and by extension, for the player. The music would be a strong reminder of the date and the awkwardness of Aerith asking about their compatibility.

Yet a third way of perceiving this moment is possible. If players managed to manipulate the mechanics of the game in such a way that they go on the date with Barrett, “Words Drowned by Fireworks” is never heard during the date and will be heard here for the first time. With no musical associations with the date, the music takes on a fresh meaning in the context of Cait Sith’s sacrifice. In this context, the simple harmonies and increasingly unified phrase structure might now be related to Cait Sith.

Cait Sith is a complicated character in the game. He is a self-reported spy for Shinra, the evil cooperation that is at odds with the other characters for most of the game. Yet he remains a playable character through to the very end. He double-crosses the heroes on more than one occasion, but in this moment, he is willing to sacrifice himself so that the rest of the party can obtain the item they need to progress. Suddenly, the simplicity of the texture and the slow unification of phrase structure align with the narrative of Cait Sith’s character. He joins the team as an untrustworthy, double-crossing character who is distanced from the rest of the group (fragmented), but, at a critical moment, finds some sense of clarity (simple harmonies) and a team purpose (unification).

Such a bifurcated reading is entirely dependent on how and when players encounter “Words Drowned by Fireworks” for the first time. This imparts ludic function, since so much depends on player choice and interactivity. But at the same time, the music accompanies what are largely scripted scenes, lending it a certain degree of cinematic function. It therefore falls somewhere in the middle and acts as a great example of the variability and flexibility of music to function anywhere along the continuum.

Conclusion

The ludo-cinematic continuum is a useful way to determine which types of analytical tools and theoretical methodologies will be most appropriate for a given musical cue. As I mentioned briefly before, there are certain genres of games for which considering this continuum is less helpful. Music and rhythm games, for example, clearly have a ludic function, yet the music is experienced linearly. Most games in this genre also lack a cohesive narrative that would lend the music a cinematic function.

However, there are some aspects of other genres in which this kind of hyperludic usage can come into play. The ocarina from *The Legend of Zelda: Ocarina of Time* (1998) is a clear example. The melodies that a player performs on the virtual ocarina (via the Nintendo 64 controller) directly influence action in the game.[17] There is a similar moment in *Final Fantasy VII* that bears mentioning in this context. At some point during gameplay, the party has the option to visit the house where Tifa grew up. In her room is a piano, and, if Cloud approaches the instrument, the ability to play individual notes on the piano is granted. In this mode, button presses on the controller equate to the notes, represented on screen with solfege syllables. If a player inputs the melody of the main theme of *FFVII* (see Figure 3.7), Tifa is granted her final limit break for the game. This is an almost identical usage of a musical instrument for ludic function as that seen in *Ocarina of Time*, though on a much more limited scale.

Of course, music from a video game can always be analyzed outside the context of the game itself, and such analyses would largely mimic analyses of music that have no associated media component. This is a valuable way to approach the analysis of some video game music, given the popularity of video game music in classical music and streaming contexts. It also frees the analysis to explore aspects of the music that may be hidden or obscured in the context of the game, allowing for a more complete look at the composer's musical offering. Regardless of how the game music is approached, the intent of the analysis should be made clear in the beginning, as the context within a game will have significant consequences as to how the music should be analyzed.

Notes

1. This is an ongoing issue in the study of video game music. Multiple scholars have grappled with the inherent differences between static forms of media, in which the music and visual domains are fixed, and interactive forms, in which there is variability between action on screen and the music being heard. Most recently (and concurrently with the writing of this chapter), Steven Reale has written that the "idiomatic nature of storytelling has a substantial impact on the utility of the analytical tools used to study its music" (Reale 2021, 195). While Reale demonstrates that interactivity can influence the types of analytical tools used, I show that the context in which the music is heard (more cinematic, or static, versus more ludic, or interactive) heavily influences how the music should be interpreted.
2. Earcons, as described by Elizabeth Medina-Gray (2014, 192–209), might be thought of as the "textbook" example of music (or musical fragments) with a clear ludic function in a game.

3. The difference between storytelling and games, and the intersections between them, is a long-standing debate in game studies. Jesper Juul (2001), for example, contends that games are not narratives, primarily due to the interactive nature of the medium (games are often nonlinear and viewers have a different relationship with them). Juul does, however, concede that games can have narrative elements within them, allowing for the cinematic moments described in the continuum.
4. Because of its variety and sheer volume, the music of *Final Fantasy VII* is also used as a case study in Summers (2016). Indeed, the soundtrack features multiple styles, genres, and forms, making it an attractive option for music academics.
5. Raymond Monelle (2000) describes fanfares as representative of "traditional heroism," among other things, but this is often expanded to specifically reference the "victorious hero" in situations like this (19).
6. If a player were to linger on the menus that appear after a successful battle, they would hear that in this binary, the B section is the only unit that participates in the loop, ensuring that the fanfare itself it only heard once immediately after the battle is over.
7. Fanfares are often associated with the hunt and hero topics in music, however, the hero shines through in this example. According to Philip Tagg, the hunting horn, when mimicking the trumpet fanfare, can evoke a heroic and successful protagonist (Tagg 1979, 125–131).
8. The B section does provide a small sense of harmonic closure, but only at the very end of the track, something that few players will listen to but for a small handful of occasions.
9. After defeating Sephiroth, the final boss, players see a cutscene in which the last-ditch effort to save the planet is left unresolved. A postcredits scene depicts the planet 500 years later, which confirms that the planet was saved, but the fate of the characters, and all the other humans on the planet, remains unknown.
10. Summers describes this harmonic progression as the "Mario cadence" given the numerous times it appears in Koji Kondo's output (Summers 2021). Further, Frank Lehman describes the harmonic progression as having a close association with "heroism and hard-won triumph" (Lehman 2018, 199–200).
11. But this is not the entire story of the *Final Fantasy VII* victory theme. This game, like many in the series, features a number of minigames in which players perform certain tasks to help advance the plot. One such minigame is the Chocobo races that take place at the Gold Saucer. The Gold Saucer is an entertainment venue in the world of the game, and at one point in the story, Cloud, the main protagonist, must participate in and win several of these races. At the end of each race, players are presented with one of two altered versions of the victory theme. A win is followed by the victory theme as heard in the previous *Final Fantasy* games (see Figure 3.4). A loss, however, results in what the official soundtrack calls the "Tango of Tears," a minor-key reinterpretation of the victory theme that conveys the sadness and disappointment associated with losing the race.
12. Specifically, Rapée cites two examples from the Western musical canon as good examples of "aëroplane" music: the presto from the "Rondo Capriccioso" and the second movement from "Three Fantasies," both composed by Felix Mendelssohn. Both feature the same rapid alternation between pitches that sonically mimics the mechanical action of a propellor-driven plane (Rapée 1970).
13. I discuss the topic of soaring in more detail in Atkinson 2019.
14. This could also be a reference to the character of Cid in both games. Cid is an engineer in both *FFIV* and *FFVII*, and that character built the airships of the former and the Tiny Bronco in the latter.

15. The mechanics of how Cloud's date is chosen are largely hidden from the player, but it is based on choices that the player makes when interacting with these four characters throughout the game (Final Fantasy Wiki 2021).
16. The "date" with Barret is unlike the other three in that it is much shorter and uses different music. Barret's theme is heard during the gondola ride rather than "Words Drowned by Fireworks" heard during the other dates. This potentially has implications on how the track is perceived when it is heard later in the game.
17. Of particular note is Stephanie Lind's writing on the melodies presented by *Ocarina of Time* that must be performed by the player in order to advance the story or cause certain events to occur (Lind 2016).

References

Atkinson, Sean. 2019. "Soaring through the Sky: Topics and Tropes in Video Game Music." *Music Theory Online* 25, no. 2 (July). https://mtosmt.org/issues/mto.19.25.2/mto.19.25.2.atkinson.html.

Collins, Karen. 2008. *Game Sound: An Introduction to the History, Theory, and Practice of Video Game Music and Sound Design*. Cambridge, MA: MIT Press.

Final Fantasy Wiki. 2021. "Date Mechanics." Accessed June 27, 2021. https://finalfantasy.fandom.com/wiki/Date_mechanics.

Gibbons, William. 2018. *Unlimited Replays: Video Games and Classical Music*. New York: Oxford University Press.

Juul, Jesper. 2001. "Games Telling Stories?" *Game Studies: The International Journal of Computer Game Research* 1 (1). http://www.gamestudies.org/0101/juul-gts/.

Lind, Stephanie. 2016. "Active Interfaces and Thematic Events in *The Legend of Zelda: Ocarina of Time*." In *Music Video Games: Performance, Politics, and Play*, edited by Michael Austin, 83–106. New York: Bloomsbury.

Lehman, Frank. 2018. *Hollywood Harmony: Musical Wonder and the Sound of Cinema*. New York: Oxford University Press.

Medina-Gray, Elizabeth. 2014. "Modular Structure and Function in Early 21st-Century Video Game Music." PhD dissertation, Yale University.

Monelle, Raymond. 2000. *The Sense of Music*. Princeton: Princeton University Press.

Rapée, Erno. 1970. *Motion Picture Moods for Pianists and Organists*. New York: Arno Press.

Reale, Steven. 2014. "Transcribing Musical Worlds; or, is *L.A. Noire* a Music Game?" In *Music in Video Games: Studying Play*, edited by K. J. Donnelly, William Gibbons, and Neil Lerner, 77–103. New York: Routledge.

Reale, Steven. 2021. "Analytical Traditions and Game Music: *Super Mario Galaxy* as a Case Study." In *The Cambridge Companion to Video Game Music*, edited by Melanie Fritsch and Tim Summers, 193–219. Cambridge: Cambridge University Press.

Summers, Timothy. 2016. *Understanding Video Game Music*. Cambridge: Cambridge University Press.

Summers, Timothy. 2021. *The Legend of Zelda: A Game Music Companion*. Chicago: Intellect Books.

Tagg, Philip. 1979. *Kojak, 50 Seconds of Television Music: Toward the Analysis of Affect in Popular Music*. Göteborg: Musikvetenskapliga Institutionen.

CHAPTER 4

LUDOMUSICAL NARRATIVITY

Sound and Music as Structures of Play

JULIANNE GRASSO

INTRODUCTION

PLAY, in its sometimes-aimless pleasures, in the deceptive timelessness of playground hijinks (when teacher's whistle is a shock back to temporally regimented reality), is perhaps most easily understood spatially. Johan Huizinga's (1949) *magic circle* of play, in which actions and meanings are segmented away from "real" life, is a conceptual standby in game studies.[1] And after all, many video games are set within virtual worlds, whose ludic challenges dot landscapes both earthly and alien. Of course, it is the exploration and discovery of those spaces that make up the stuff of play, but humans naturally tend to narrativize such actions.[2] Consider one potential exchange between two people who play video games:

> PLAYER 1: "Did you ever play the first *Legend of Zelda* game?"
> PLAYER 2: "I started, but I kept dying in one of the dungeons, then got lost somewhere, and never finished."

In this exchange, the notion of "play" is understood as a beginning-to-end completion of *The Legend of Zelda* (Nintendo 1986). We might compare this conception of narrative to the act of reading a novel, in all the particular ways its plot is presented to us (flashbacks, various points of view, asides, and so on) rather than the content of the novel's story itself and the presumedly actual chronology of events. (This is a classic distinction in narratology of "discourse" versus "story.")[3] But such comparisons tend to fall short in capturing the special aspects of narrative in interactive media like games. To be sure, video games often contain stories (most *Zelda* titles, for instance, are built on an archetypal "hero's journey" paradigm) but *playing through* a story is a particular mode of engagement that differs from *reading* a story. It all perhaps comes closer to acting out a story (and it is no wonder that stage *plays* are so named). Still, video games, in their peculiar blend of interactivity, spectacle, virtuality, and challenge, present new horizons of narrativized experience. After all, no matter how invested you are in the story of a game, maybe you just kept dying somewhere, and were never able to finish.[4] Even if we conceive of play as existing in its own space, formalized games typically involve some species of time-bound structuring. Think of any game that is oriented by rounds, point maximums, time limits, and progressively difficult levels—let alone storytelling. Most video games, even while they may offer the spaces for untimed play, nevertheless also offer structures that provide some sense of beginnings, middles, and ends—the stuff of narrative experience.[5]

How could we account for music in these narrative paradigms of games? The stereotype of video game music—looping, repetitive cues (admittedly prevalent in relatively early games)—might seem to promote a sense of timelessness, or even spatial orientation. There is a sense that the music will continue forever, as long as you are present in this space. The goal of this chapter is not to prove that perception wrong, or suggest that our tendency toward narrativizing experiences eliminates other ways of understanding ludic spaces. Rather, I will explicate some of the ways that music (whether looping, linear, dynamic, or somewhere in between) nonetheless implicates narrative forms. Here, I will explore how music brings to bear both its own formal syntax as well as meanings packed with discursive potential. Together, these musical aspects intermingle with the syntactical and discursive structures of games as a means of narrativizing the play experience.

In a general sense, this approach is not at all new—my thoughts here certainly build from the work of other scholars who have analyzed music alongside narrativity in video games (Andra Ivănescu does so with popular music specifically [see chapter 31 this volume]). In her 2011 article exploring the nature of "diegesis" in video games, Isabella van Elferen argues for analysis that combines narratological and ludological approaches to music in video games in order to account for the ways music shapes experience. She outlines a vision of video game music that is essentially what she calls a "musical GPS" (gaming positioning system) that encompasses the myriad ways music can direct a player, within the game as a navigational space most obviously but also as a space of narrative worldbuilding and affective meaning-making. What this chapter offers perhaps operates prior to the emergence of van Elferen's musical GPS, in that it explores some of the mechanisms in music that narrativize player experience.

In describing musically structured play, this chapter will complicate the typical formal conceits of games that have preoccupied game studies: the *ludic* and the *narrative*, often understood in tandem as *ludonarrative*. I begin with a discussion of what typically defines ludic and narrative forms in games, and then move on to discuss how music can function among and beyond these forms. I will then analyze two cases that demonstrate paradigms of what I call *ludomusical narrativity*—how music shapes play within narrative paradigms. In *Final Fantasy III* (Square 1990), location-based musical cues change to communicate progress in the game. Furthermore, these changes can shape play in ways that correspond to narrative changes and invoke particular (and problematic) stereotypes. In *Journey* (thatgamecompany 2012), an aesthetically oriented platformer game, music can be understood to structure play, while its ludic and narrative aspects are instantiated relatively weakly. I suggest that difficulties in grappling with *Journey* as a game, per se, lie in the unexplored potential of music to be the primary structure of interactive play, and for play to activate an explicitly musical story.

The Play and Story Divide: Ludic "versus" Narrative

Narrative has been a contentious topic in games criticism, likely due to disagreements on what narrative means and its significance to play (and, for that matter, disagreements on what "play" means). When trying to reconcile game structures with narrative structures, some critics find games lacking as a medium for good storytelling.[6] If games, at their core, are about success and failure, points and items, competition and comradery, how can a well-designed narrative with fleshed-out characters fit into these interactive paradigms? Is storytelling through games even something worth pursuing?[7] After all, plenty of popular, fun games like the classic puzzler *Tetris* (Alexey Pajitnov 1984) don't really have stories. Nonetheless, the industry is also chock-full of story-oriented games, coming from big-budget, triple-A companies as well as small indie developers. Storytelling in video games is prevalent.

It is no wonder that in game and media studies the term "narrative" has most commonly referred to the literary sense of storytelling. Video games have been an interest of narratology for decades, posited as an exciting new medium for storytelling. Janet Murray's foundational text, *Hamlet on the Holodeck: The Future of Narrative in Cyberspace* (1997), finds exciting promise in interactive stories, particularly in the ways that a new medium for storytelling can open more possibilities for one of the claims of storytelling writ large: that it can reveal to us something fundamental about human nature.

In a 2016 update to the text, Murray doubles down on this potential:

> Storytelling is a constant of human society, allowing us to share meaning across the campfire, the proscenium stage, the printed page, or the glowing screen. As we increase our modes of engagement from listening, reading, and viewing to include navigating, enacting, and interacting, the future of narrative remains the same as it ever was: to deepen human understanding and widen our circles of connectedness. We need stories in every medium we can master, truth and fiction, ephemeral and enduring, unilinear and interactive, secret stories between lovers or family members, mass entertainments shared by millions. We need this creative practice for its own sake, but more than that, we need the process of continuously expanding our means of storytelling, because it allows us to expand our ability to know who we are and to collectively reimagine who we might become. (481)

Although Murray is not speaking exclusively of video games (her coinage, *cyberdrama*, is a broader term that includes other forms of computer-based or virtual realities that offer spaces for stories), these remarks reflect a desire to wield media such as video games to new expressive ends.[8] Literary scholar Marie-Laure Ryan's work on narrative across media has similarly reflected this ideal, focusing not only on how narrative is integrated in interactive media like video games but also on what these new forms of stories can tell us about storytelling writ large.[9] Indeed, much of the work on games from media scholars (alongside narrative approaches from game scholars) does not critique the idea of game stories but rather sees potential in a new medium.[10] (In fact, much of the work that *can* be considered critical of the idea of game stories dates from the 1990s and early 2000s, when the range of video games was relatively limited by technology and available platforms.)

It follows then that the infamous debate between so-called narratologists and ludologists is a scholarly war without much grounding in reality. Espen Aarseth (2013, 279), whose work has been foundational in video game studies and narrativity, explains as much in his definition of *ludology*: "Ludology has been erroneously contrasted with narratology (narrative theory), but since the 'ludologists' all used narrative theory in their approaches to games, this juxtaposition is misinformed and does not bear critical examination." Aarseth's narrative explanation is also a broad one that supersedes traditional storytelling, thereby encompassing the kinds of ludic considerations with which I opened this chapter.

Nevertheless, it seems that part of the basis for a ludology versus narratology debate lies not in scholarly identity or even methodological choice for game analysis. Rather, there seems to be a recognized fundamental difference, even incompatibility, between the formal properties of narrative and game, some of which will be summarized in the following section.[11] Meanwhile, in all of this hullabaloo, music is almost never considered as a formal component (at least by anyone who is not a music scholar) in games that are not categorized as music games, let alone as a potentially confounding feature that could entangle with ludic and narrative forms in meaningful ways.

The Ludonarrative Spectrum

Even beyond the scholarly realm, critics and designers alike have latched onto the notion that the gameness of games—the ludic—and the storyness of stories—the narrative—are opposing forces at play in the design of video games. For example, Aarseth (2012, 129–133) considers this ludonarrative spectrum to be enacted along four "ontic" dimensions that all games and all stories contain: (1) world, (2) objects, (3) agents, and (4) events. As summarized in Table 4.1, ludic elements in games privilege aspects of interactivity—explorable landscapes, usable objects, inhabitable avatars, agency over events, and embedded challenges. On the other side of this spectrum, narrative elements align more closely to filmic experiences, with the pacing of plot and character interactions mostly predetermined by designer.[12]

TABLE 4.1 A Comparative Table of Some Ludic and Narrative Elements in Video Games, Categorized via Espen Aarseth's Ontic Dimensions

	Ludic Elements	Narrative Elements
world	Explorable landscapes	Linear "corridor" design
objects	Usable, modifiable objects	Noninteractive objects
agents	Empty, inhabitable avatars	Designed, developed characters
events	Agency over events	Predesigned plot

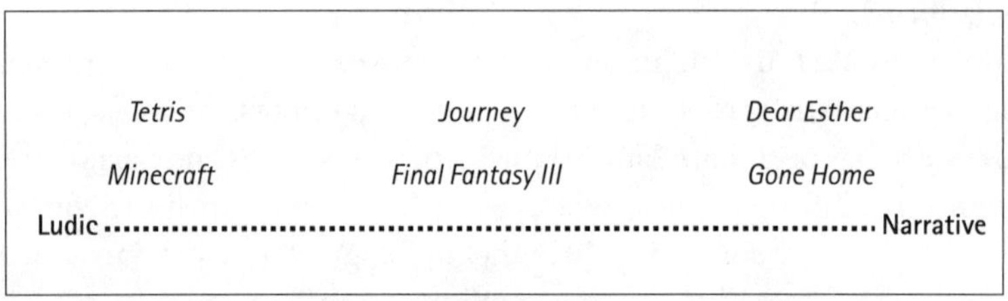

FIGURE 4.1 A sampling of video games plotted along the ludonarrative axis.

Placed on opposite ends of a spectrum, as shown in Figure 4.1, these ludic and narrative elements can be considered constitutive of the design of a game as a whole—this allows us to place games somewhere along this spectrum according to their overarching adherence to more ludic or more narrative elements. For example, abstract, "storyless" *Tetris* and open-ended sandbox game *Minecraft* (Mojang 2011) are examples that occupy the extreme ludic end of the spectrum: while these games might offer the potential for emergent narratives, the stories that arise are developed by players, not designers.[13] On the narrative end, games like *Dear Esther* (The Chinese Room 2012) and *Gone Home* (The Fullbright Company 2013) fall into the genre that Elizabeth Hambleton (2020, [see also chapter 38 this volume]) calls *navigable narratives*, involving a first-person perspective of moving through an area in order to uncover a prefabricated story world. This story is not itself directly influenced by the player and might only minimally incorporate the player's avatar as a distinct character. Other games, with their blend of interactive puzzles and predesigned story, including the cases described in this chapter, pepper the landscape in between.

A Note on Ludonarrative Dissonance

Overarching ludic and narrative design is usually privileged in games criticism; we can often see this in effect when games are, indeed, criticized on those terms. Perceived conflicts between the ludic and the narrative elements of a game give rise to a phenomenon known as *ludonarrative dissonance*, a term coined in 2007 by game designer Clint Hocking (2007). Ludonarrative dissonance describes the tension between, on the one hand, what we as game players are motivated to do by the rules of the game and, on the other, what the story tells us about the characters and world they inhabit.

A simple and common example of ludonarrative dissonance occurs in games in which the player adopts the role of some ostensibly strong, godlike character only to then begin the game wielding the controls poorly (such that this character runs into walls and falls off of buildings, for instance). Hocking warns game designers against elements of ludonarrative dissonance, explaining that ludonarrative dissonance negatively affects the player's ability to connect with the game; the interactive ludic elements do not make the player feel a part of whatever the narrative conceit is, and therefore the player will probably not enjoy the game in a neat ludonarrative wholeness that the video game medium should aspire to. In this critique of ludonarrative dissonance, we see the privileging of these two structuring elements, together considered essentially constitutive of play experiences. And, of course, it is common for me as a music scholar to read games criticism about player experience, engagement, and connection and find music oddly absent. To bring music into the picture where it is missing is not merely a fun heuristic exercise—it is also, I argue, a legitimate way of investigating how players get into a game, negotiate its ludic and narrative contracts, and come out magically unscathed. In arguing for the notion of a ludo*musical* narrativity, this chapter will contend that music can be considered operative within the conceptual space of the ludonarrative spectrum, and also function beyond it.

(Ludo)musical Narrativity

Music and narrative are old friends. Storytelling is one of the primary functions of music in cultures throughout the world and throughout history. Music is a core feature of established narrative multimedia like opera and ballet and was a part of film before recorded speech, accompanying film projections. An impulse toward narrativity is a structuring principle of much of music theoretical language—one need think only of the concepts of harmonic *progressions*, motivic *development*, and so on. What marks beginnings and ends? Is this theme a variation on a theme heard before? These are the kinds of questions that narrativize music in modern discourse. A review of all (or even some) of the ways music and narrative have worked together would be a tiresome exercise for both you and me. But music in the narrative structures of games is where things get stuck, largely due to the issues described in the preceding sections. We have been worried about the capacity for games to portray stories at all, let alone how *music* could shape these stories.

Nonetheless, there have been a number of formal accounts of music and narrative in video games. These approaches tend to focus on the role of the repeating musical theme, sometimes characterized as idée fixe (à la Berlioz), or leitmotif (à la Wagner). Themes or motives are analyzed as creating narrative coherence and providing meaningful resonances with other musical multimedia.[14] Part of the appeal of investigating musical themes is that it shows that music can solve ludic problems through narrativization—music can provide narrative depth to character and place, helping unite aspects of the story no matter what the player is (or is not) doing. A thematic analysis also gives us access to richer, more established musical traditions (particularly those of European classical music, the most thoroughly discussed in music analysis), thereby effecting a form of legitimization not just of the music but also of video games generally.

In the accounts of music that I take up in this chapter, I also follow those lines of thought, arguing that music offers narrativization functions, constraining aspects of play to linear, progress-based understandings. But I don't seek to leave the ludic behind. What I am calling *ludomusical narrativity* refers to the specific ways that music enacts what is understood under the rubrics of ludic and narrative, providing a musically specific formal structuring for play. After all, music is not only understood narratively. As much as we might describe musical progress and time, we also speak of musical space, motion, texture, motivic relationships, and even the quite ludic sense of competition between tonal areas. In other words, music is a powerful resource for many sorts of experiences, especially those which would transcend a ludic and narrative divide.

Reconciling the Ludic and the Narrative

In some ways, by focusing on music I am reconciling ludic and narrative, or at least offering a conceptual remapping for these structures. By observing how others have sought to reconcile ludic and narrative forms, we can see how music can help us do the same. For example, Henry Jenkins (2003) proposes a taxonomy for narrativity in video games that seeks to also capture ludic elements specific to games. He proposes four ways in which narratives can be mapped onto aspects of play, summarized here:

1. *Evocative spaces*. These are physical or virtual environments in games that "draw upon our previously existing narrative competencies" (123) to evoke aspects of story circling in our imaginations and memories. One example is the game *American McGee's Alice* (Rogue Entertainment 2000), drawn from (but not reenacting) Lewis Carroll's *Alice in Wonderland*. Similarly, games that license intellectual property from film franchises, but do not necessarily retell those stories, can fall into this category. *Star Wars: Battlefront* (Electronic Arts 2015) is a shooter that takes place on various planets in the *Star Wars* universe, incorporating familiar

characters like Luke Skywalker and Darth Vader without reenacting the stories of the films.

2. *Enacting stories.* Games that allow player agency in a story's events can be considered to allow for the *enacting* of those events. In *Final Fantasy III*, analyzed later in this chapter, fighting and defeating the enemy is as much a part of the game as it is an enacted element of the narrative. Jenkins relates this concept to improvisatory theater, which often includes a mix of basic structure and vocabulary with some degree of freedom. Several role-playing games and adventure games follow this model, particularly if games offer branching narratives that depend on player choice.
3. *Embedded narratives.* An embedded narrative is considered "less a temporal structure than a body of information" that is presented to the player. For Jenkins, the idea of an embedded narrative in games turns these games into "a kind of information space, a memory palace" (126). In this way, game designers guide players toward narrative understandings. *Myst* (Cyan 1993) is a classic example of an embedded narrative: players explore the world of Myst Island and solve puzzles to piece together character stories. *Journey*, analyzed later in this chapter, is another example of a story discovered through problem-solving and exploration. (Furthermore, we will see how music offers a way for designers to guide the player toward narrative understandings.)
4. *Emergent narratives.* These narratives are loosely structured by gameplay but not predesigned. They *emerge* through the player's acts of play. Simulation games often fall into this category. *The Sims* is an exemplar, in which control is left to players to construct the homes and characters and shape their paths (which are nonetheless limited to the capacities of the computer system).[15]

Each of Jenkins's four categories shares a concern with mappings between the ludic and the narrative, reflecting a desire to reconcile traditional narratives and game structures by thinking about how formal and aesthetic features of games can give rise to narrative experiences of play. These categories are also preoccupied with *spatial* storytelling. After all, the title of Jenkins's essay is "Game Design as Narrative Architecture"—he sees virtual environments as creating the potential for different kinds of narratives to exist.

Does music have a potential role in Jenkins's categories? For one, we could easily imagine how music borrowed from John Williams's scores for the *Star Wars* films would contribute to *evoking* narratives. The other categories seem to be more concerned with the processes of a story's presentation and the roles of players in those processes. As will become clear, music can both accompany and also constitute these processes, thereby enacting its own form of narrative.

Other scholars have seen potential in games to illuminate new kinds of narrative. Where Jenkins starts from the perspective of narrative and games as being separate, but mappable, concepts, Ian Bogost sees video game structures—particularly their *computational* architecture—as a new form of narrative with rhetorical implications. In *Persuasive Games* (2007), Bogost coins the term "procedural rhetoric" to describe the argumentative power of computational systems and the influence that video games can have on players as well as culture more broadly:

> *Procedurality* refers to a way of creating, explaining, or understanding processes. And processes define the way things work: the methods, techniques, and logics that drive the operation of systems, from mechanical systems like engines to organizational systems like high schools to conceptual systems like religious faith. *Rhetoric* refers to effective and persuasive expression. Procedural rhetoric, then, is a practice of using processes persuasively. More specifically, procedural rhetoric is the practice of persuading through processes in general and computational processes in particular. Just as verbal rhetoric is useful for both the orator and the audience, and just as written rhetoric is useful for both the writer and the reader, so procedural rhetoric is useful for both the programmer and the user, the game designer and the player. Procedural rhetoric is a technique for making arguments with computational systems and for unpacking computational arguments others have created. (2–3)

Games, he argues, have the power to alter attitudes through their interactivity as players become complicit in the unfolding of video games as computational procedures. An example of procedural rhetoric at work (or, at play) can be found in the web browser game *Thoughts & Prayers: The Game* (Everyday Arcade 2016) which renders the core mechanics of the game ("press T to think and P to pray") as ineffectual against a nationwide epidemic of mass shootings.[16] As players press T or P in efforts to prevent further shootings, the game's events remain unchanged, the system unresponsive. By embedding mechanics of failed efficacy in the game, the game uses procedural rhetoric to make an argument within the contentious gun control debate in the United States.

Music is undoubtedly a part of the proceduralism of video games—sound is deployed through computational procedures. But the potential rhetoric of music in video games is less clear—for most video games, music is not directly involved in the mechanics of play that Bogost focuses on. Most often, the effects of music are more subtle. The music in *Thoughts & Prayers* is high-octane rock that resembles the style of music often used in shoot-em-up game genres—games that feature *a lot* of gun violence. For those familiar with that genre of games, the music in *Thoughts & Prayers* takes on an extra layer of meaning as it evocatively shapes the image of the United States as a real-life shoot-em-up stage, perhaps enhancing the argument about the current state of affairs in US mass shootings.[17]

Musical features in combination with other game procedures can have a rhetorical effect that is not possible without music. In *Journey*, musical changes communicate not just something about the game, but about music itself. In this way, games can have a reciprocal exchange of meaning through procedural logic. But not all games have an immediately legible or predictable logic to their musical procedures. Music for a video game might be generated through generative procedures, as in the case of *Proteus* (Key and Kanaga 2013), which features a randomly generated world.

Each play instance of *Proteus*, then, is a new experience—to an extent. It is still computationally bound, and its randomness is limited. *Proteus* always looks and sounds like *Proteus*, particularly to those players who have played several instances of the game. It is thus possible to consider *Proteus* as an improvisation on the same core story world.

In what follows, I analyze cases from games that reflect short trajectories of play in which meaning develops through various forms of video game narrativity—progress, story, development, unfoldings of worlds, and music. I explore two games that are representative of two different eras of console technology, the 8-bit and the modern, thereby accounting for music in two paradigms: hard-cut loops, and the smoothly adaptive, cinematic style. *Final Fantasy III* (1990), in the former category, uses music to set affective bounds while gesturing toward a trajectory of narrative progress written into clear-cut musical changes. *Journey* (2012), maps musical progress onto player progress on a finer scale, more directly using notions of musical progression as narrative indicators. I argue for a ludomusical narrativity in both cases, in which play is structured by specifically musical forms of narrative that intersect with the game world in various ways.

Final Fantasy III: Basic Ludomusical Narrative Processes

Final Fantasy III, developed by Square in 1990 for the Famicom in Japan, features 8-bit graphics and music: five channels of sound generated from frequency modulation, the chiptune sound from which the still-prevalent beeps and "boops" characterization of video game music originates. Nobuo Uematsu composed for the game, which includes 43 unique musical tracks. In play, these tracks are activated across a turn-based adventure story, with a world of characters and monsters. One of these monsters is called Jinn (clearly borrowing from the mythological Jinn or "genie" from Arabian mythology). Jinn puts a curse on the town of Kazus, turning the townspeople into ghostly spirits (rendered as translucent outlines).[18] The party of characters is tasked with traveling to a cave, then finding and defeating Jinn in battle. Defeating Jinn will lift the curse of the town and restore the corporeality of its denizens.

This narrative sequence is accompanied by meaningful musical changes. Most notably, the difference between Kazus cursed and Kazus cured is shown visually but portrayed more evocatively by differences in the musical cues. Figure 4.2 shows the cue for Kazus under Jinn's curse. The music of the curse (a track translated as "Jinn, the Fire") begins sparsely, giving us not much more than a few notes at a slow tempo. The melody helps to situate things in D minor, but that E-flat is pervasive, feeling sometimes like a predominant Neapolitan, and other times just a chromatic upper neighbor that unsettles the tonic. The characteristic habanera rhythm is fully realized

FIGURE 4.2 "Jinn, the Fire" (*Final Fantasy III*). Three channels of sound are transcribed onto two staves.

by the seventh measure, under a melody and harmony seemingly stuck on Phrygian half-cadences. We could imagine that the unsettled D minor places the listener in a similarly unsettled state, while the habanera brings in connotations of Cuban or Spanish dance, perhaps even Bizet's famous habanera from *Carmen*.[19] Alongside the cursed town's visual appearance, however, "unsettled" is probably the most likely affective possibility from this music, and the player may proceed with caution in a place typically considered safe—towns in these kinds of video games are usually places for rest and regroup.

Once the player has gone off to the cave, found and defeated the Jinn to lift the curse, they can then return to the town with its curse lifted and hear music of a different sort (Figure 4.3). "Return of the Warrior" is a fanfare-like victory march in D major (happily the parallel major of the curse's D minor) with no chromatic uncertainties or lingering on half-cadences—instead it features a harmonic progression longer in scale, decidedly unstuck. Indeed, even the rhythmic framework of the bass stabilizes on strong beats, "resolving" the instability of the bass line in "Jinn, The Fire." Both affect and meaning seem straightforward: this is the music of a safe and happy return. (Spoiler alert: I will complicate this reading in just a few paragraphs.)

FIGURE 4.3 "Return of the Warrior" (*Final Fantasy III*).

Narrativizing the Ludic

The world of *Final Fantasy III* is organized such that the town of Kazus and the cave in which you go to fight the Jinn to remove the curse are two discrete locations on the overworld map. On this map, players can move characters between these locations freely. Players can also choose to explore other locations, though there are limitations to this freedom—players cannot access every part of the game at once. Nonetheless, this interactivity in exploration of space is *ludic*; it is an element of player agency. Figure 4.4 offers a basic visualization of this paradigm.

Now, add in music. Music narrativizes play simply through *changing* in a meaningful way: when the player completes their ludic task (beat the enemy Jinn in battle) and triggers a narrative event (curse is lifted), the music follows that change. The town of Kazus now occupies two points on a narrative timeline (Figure 4.5).

This is the connection between ludic and narrative that music can mediate, constraining ludic indeterminacy through clearly marked musical resolution. In fact, even if the player defeats Jinn, then stops playing and goes off and lives their life for 20 years, the music of this town will be the victory theme when she returns, emplacing her right back into the narrative structure of a game which otherwise invites ludic exploration. Of course, music is not the only thing that changes—the townspeople return to normal as well. But because townspeople are not immediately visible on screen upon entering the town, music is the first change encountered.

Indeed, music doesn't simply linearize play but also creates affective zones—spaces in which potentials for meaning and perception are shaped by these musical differences.[20]

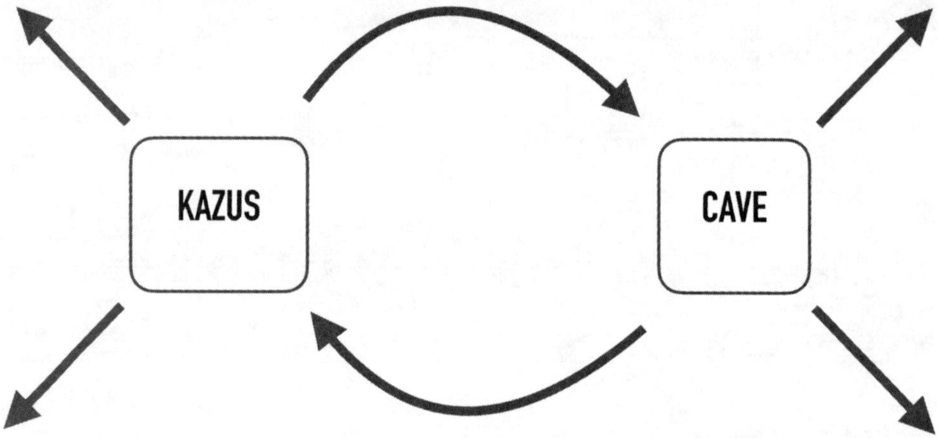

FIGURE 4.4 A diagram of the "ludic paradigm" between Kazus and Jinn's Cave in *Final Fantasy III*. Players are free to move between these locations, as well as other locations in the game world, in any order they choose.

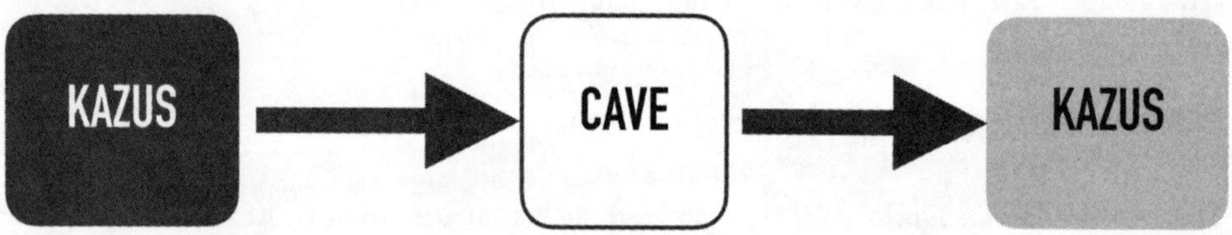

FIGURE 4.5 A diagram of the "narrative paradigm" between Kazus and the cave in *Final Fantasy III*. Musical changes (here as different shades) in Kazus after ludic progress in the Cave portray overarching narrative progress.

The musical changes in Kazus reshape that space: hearing the cursed habanera might evoke more apprehension (Is this town dangerous? Will I encounter enemies here?), while the victory march might evoke the kind of confidence that Kazus is now a safe town. This is the essence of ludomusical narrativity—the potential for music to shape ludic actions of play to fit narrative affects of story.

Procedural Exoticism

In a reciprocal fashion, playing this section of *Final Fantasy III* and triggering this musical change enacts a procedural argument about music itself. Danger and curse are signified by an approximation of Cuban dance music, and the return to "normal" is marked by its replacement with an approximation of a military march. And largely, my earlier comparison of the two tracks followed these associations, hearing D major and rhythms on strong beats as positive resolutions of D minor and syncopated rhythms that follow along with the game's narrative resolution. Embedded in this narrative are ideologies of music rooted in a long history of musical exoticism.[21] Here, the habanera of "Jinn, the Fire" stands in as a signifier of something dangerous, not to mention the specificities erased by the conflation of Cuban music and Arabian myth. "Return of the Warrior" is the "western," perhaps imperialist answer that sets the Jinn as an orientalist trope.[22] This is more than simply musical changes that accompany narrative changes; as in Bogost's concept of procedural rhetoric, playing the game executes the computational—and musical—processes that make an argument about cultural value. Music exoticism in video games and video game music has its own deep history, and this is just one example of myriad cases we could and should identify.[23] It is important to remember that these processes that shape gameplay experiences are not neutral, apolitical, or otherwise isolated from the "real" world outside the magic circle.

Journey: Ludomusical Narrativity and Aesthetics

The example from *Final Fantasy III* demonstrates how distinct musical change can communicate aspects of narrative and shape the play within the constraints of that narrative. This is a common paradigm in earlier games where the music consisted of static, looping tracks with little adaptability to game state. The technological capabilities of more recent gaming systems allow for more subtle musical changes that give the illusion of a continuous score that follows the player wherever they go and whatever they do. Such games offer fine-grained changes in music that make it difficult to identify sharp affective changes, but the basics of ludomusical narrativity remain the same: music shapes play into narrative understandings.

One example that illustrates this possibility is *Journey*, released in 2012 by thatgamecompany. It is categorized as much a platformer game as an art game, a burgeoning genre finding its footing with small, indie developers and aided by the increased openness of platforms like Steam over the more proprietary worlds of Sony, Nintendo, and Microsoft. Its music, composed by Austin Wintory, is rather cinematically styled, and adaptive to player movement over its world. Unlike the music of *Final Fantasy III*, Journey's score features subtler, fine-grained shifts.

The gameplay and story of *Journey* primarily involve movement through scenic but desolate landscapes and navigating a handful of obstacles on a path toward a mountain peak, along the way uncovering a story about a lost civilization (demonstrating Henry Jenkins's concept of embedded narrative). At each stage of *Journey*'s journey, more details are revealed about the circumstances of the world that lay before you: the well-trodden trope of an ancient, technologically advanced civilization that collapsed at the hands of its very own technologies. This story casts a characterful influence through the musical materials of Wintory's score: a mix of electronic sounds and symphonic

FIGURE 4.6 The main theme of *Journey*, as performed on cello in the track "Nascence."

FIGURE 4.7 Dorian hexachord collection in order of appearance in stage 3 of *Journey*.

instruments, with emphasis on cello and bass flute. These musical materials mesh well with *Journey*'s postapocalyptic landscape and a textless adventure that invites the player to explore the bounds of a world made mostly of beautiful landscapes with little explicitly told story.

Beyond its character, Wintory's score includes adaptive syntactical progressions, which link with player progress: when players find an object or uncover a new area, the music changes accordingly. This adaptability is certainly a staple of video game sound and music design. But rather than considering this feature solely as a feedback mechanism for player awareness, we might also consider the musical logic underlying these choices. What is a measure of musical progress?

I focus here on the third stage of *Journey*, considering the answer to this question as a matter of ludomusical narrativity. In sum, progress in the game is matched in the music through logics of musical activation. From the basis of a central theme for solo cello (shown in Figure 4.6), an accumulation of musical materials follows along with the player's progression through the level, cued to the literal activation of various physical elements of the landscape. General rhythmic activity and instrumentation also increase as the player progresses, as if activating hidden layers of musical spacetime.

As players begin stage 3, the starting soundscape establishes itself through sound effects, timbres, and pitches that blend in an ambient wash of sound. The glimpses of identifiable pitches seem to circulate around a Dorian hexachord that leans on F-sharp (Figure 4.7). Because the player has not yet done anything to progress through this landscape, this music effectively (and affectively) portrays a sense of beginning and possibility—and perhaps nothingness, a primordial wash of music. The rhythmless, modal sound—lacking in any particular direction temporally—portrays a sense of musical grounding over which any number of musical materials could emerge.

These musical associations are retroactively solidified as progress effects musical change. When the player approaches a floating piece of scarf-like cloth stuck in a device in the sand, they are expected to press a button that creates a kind of magical sonar that activates the power of this cloth. The cloth then animates with life, directing the player toward the next destination. The music also becomes animated, with increased rhythmic activity and recognizable motivic noodling in the flute (following the contour

FIGURE 4.8 The motivic contour activated through narrative activation, based on the main theme.

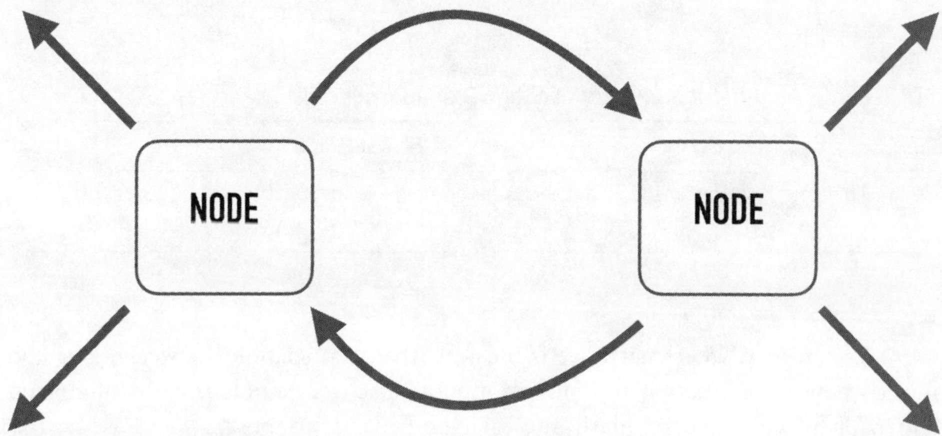

FIGURE 4.9 A diagram of the ludic paradigm in *Journey.* Players can go to any activation node they wish, in any order, and travel between each node freely.

of Figure 4.8). It is just a brief glance of the theme, a sign of life emerging from that F-sharp Dorian wash.

After activating a second node in this stage, the music reaches harmonic areas beyond the Dorian hexachord while also negating it—a D major chord "unlocks" tonal areas of the F-sharp minor theme, imbuing this music with both motivic and harmonic energy. Now, the ambient soundscape is turning into something we might follow along with—something with rhythm, with a harmonic progression, a sense of movement.

Journey's interactive world is premised on open, three-dimensional spatial exploration. For the most part, players are allowed to move around between activated and nonactivated nodes freely—there is no ludic or narrative consequence to lingering (Figure 4.9). But if we apply the logic of *Journey*'s musical progression, there indeed *are* consequences, at least musically. When players linger in an area for too long, the music will return to that original modal wash of sound—motivic noodling will fade, added instruments will recede to silence. These punitive measures of music (pun intended) encourage the player to move along, at least suggesting that they should. As a result, music narrativizes play through its own forms of progression connected to the ludic activation of these nodes (Figure 4.10).

Ludomusical narrative in *Journey* is not simply how music might shape play in relation to story. Rather, play unlocks a ludomusical narrativity, as players uncover a particularly musical story in the soundscapes of each stage. It follows Jenkins's *enacting*

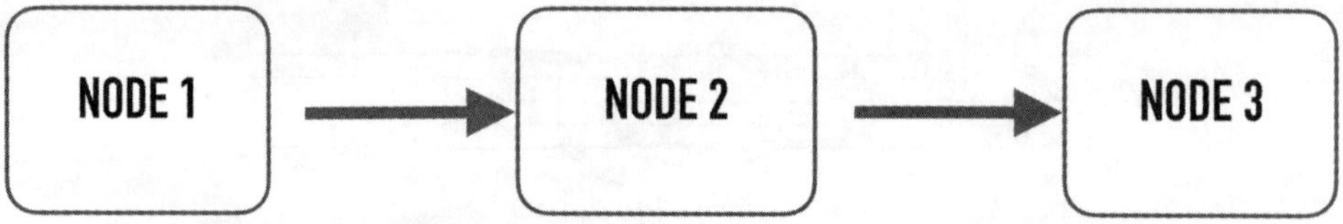

FIGURE 4.10 A diagram of the narrative paradigm in *Journey*. Through musical changes, players understand each activated node as one in a progressive sequence.

TABLE 4.2 Analytical Summary of Stage 3 of *Journey*

Basis	Stasis	Forward Paces
solo cello theme	modal hexachord; meterless wash of sound	motivic and tonal activation; increased rhythmic activity and instrumentation

narrative category, where narrative is musical. These associations between game and music—between animation and musical motion, discovery and harmonic fulfillment, and so forth—follow a particularly musical logic, laid out in Table 4.2.

As with *Final Fantasy III*, one could trace associative references for this sort of musical logic in *Journey*. Ludic progression that traces musical progression in "filling out" a musical scale (that is particularly western and European) draws on a tonal tradition that relies on sonic relationships in a system based on octave equivalence. Here, the connections to "real-world" cultures are not overt, particularly as ludic and narrative elements are more abstract in *Journey*. Nonetheless, the role of music here as an organizing structure is essentially connected with particular musical paradigms that rely on Western tonal understandings.

Side Story: *Journey* as an Art Game

Journey is sometimes categorized as an adventure game or platformer, but, in many descriptions, it is also considered an art game.[24] Scholars typically consider art games to be those whose ludic elements—the mechanics, goals, interactive challenges, and so on—are themselves artistically expressive in some way.[25] *Journey* seems to be considered an art game for its artful *aesthetics*, rather than its mechanics. In simple terms, *Journey* is a beautiful game, with beautiful visuals and beautiful sounds.[26] But this chapter relies on formal understandings of games, including formal understandings of music. Traditionally, the language used by game scholars to talk about structures in games rarely accounts for anything aesthetic, affective, or artful within those paradigms. But what if *Journey* is not steadfastly in the categories of video game *or* interactive story—and simply rather a work of art, as it is often characterized? As discussed above, much of the story that is activated by play is a musical story in musical terms. Might there be room in that story to account for its aesthetics?

One rather notable consideration is *Journey*'s multiplayer mode: players with internet access can access a network of concurrent *Journey* players, connecting with one randomly chosen anonymous companion at a time. Companions can only communicate through an undifferentiated "ping"—there is no text or voice chat included in the game. And while companions can guide and help one another, there is no task that absolutely requires cooperation—you are simply going through the journey with someone rather than by yourself. This minimalist approach to multiplayer keeps the game's landscape and soundscape in the fore of experience, and can be powerful: Katherine Isbister (2016) uses *Journey* as a case study in discussing the potential for emotional experiences in games, and Patrick Jagoda (2016, 73) has remarked that *Journey* offers affective experiences that "resist description and lead players to feelings of wonder, isolation, and even crying and tears." Such ability to resist description is the very ineffability that we often ascribe to art, which perhaps makes it difficult to analyze from traditional game studies approaches. But here, I would speculate that music coalesces feelings of togetherness through synchronizing musical progress with your progress *and* that of your partner, offering a kind of soundtrack to an otherwise silent companionship.[27] As players might aim to complete narrative nodes at the same time (or be in the same space when these narrative events happen), together they uncover the world as it seemingly unfolds through musical procedures.

Conclusion

Perhaps there is hope for the critics out there who find ludonarrative dissonance to be a problem. At the very least, considering music can offer alternative avenues for understanding how players experience and understand video games narratively. In the case of *Final Fantasy III*, I argued that music connects with narrative to shape ludic interactivity, framing play actions through a narrative lens. In *Journey*, I argued that, even while there is an *embedded* narrative of technology and apocalypse, the *enacted* narrative is fundamentally musical. In both examples, we might consider how the player's complicity in these ludomusical narratives is a persuasive argument for certain kinds of music meaning and syntax. Of course, these are just two of many possible angles to a *ludomusical narrativity* approach. In any case, what I hope these examples make clear is the value of music analysis within broader analyses of video games and play.

Acknowledgments

Various elements of this chapter, which also form the bulk of a chapter in the author's PhD dissertation, have been shared and discussed with colleagues whom the author would like to acknowledge here. Special thanks go to Amanda Shubert, Michiel Kamp, Andra Ivănescu, Jon Silpayamanant, Ryan Thompson, and Lawrence Zbikowski for their particularly helpful comments and conversations.

Notes

1. While he did indeed invoke the term in his text *Homo Ludens*, Huizinga did not himself focus particularly on "magic circle" as the definitive term for this play space. Nonetheless, the term has been a generative one within studies of digital media, particularly in the oft-referenced game-design text *Rules of Play: Game Design Fundamentals* (2003) by Katie Salen and Eric Zimmerman.
2. That humans could be fundamentally narrative creatures is a view that has been studied, observed, and argued across multiple disciplines. This chapter takes the simplest assumption that humans understand the world through a shared sense of basic narrative temporality, even though that temporality may be shaped by cultural, linguistic, and biological differences beyond the scope of this chapter. For more nuance on the human tendency to narrativize, see, for example, Meretoja (2014), Battersby (2006), and Margulis et al. (2019), the latter exploring this notion within music specifically.
3. The story/discourse rhetorical distinction was largely introduced by the literary theorist Gérard Genette (1980). For my discussion of the comparison between literary narrative and game narrative, see Grasso (2019).
4. One could extend this analogy to consider the concept of "difficulty" in reading texts. It is, of course, possible for the text to challenge us enough such that we get stuck and never finish, much like failing to complete a difficult dungeon in a game. Unlike reading difficulty in most literary texts, however, playing difficulty is a formal aspect of most video games that structures the playing experience accordingly.
5. Likely underrepresented in game studies are games with very little built-in story, as it is more difficult to adapt literary and narrative theories to these genres. For instance, sandbox games like *No Man's Sky* (Hello Games 2016) or simulation games like *The Sims* franchise (Electronic Arts) sometimes offer scenarios for winning, but the freedom to roam, design, and explore lends itself to Henry Jenkins's emergent narratives. And of course, slot machines, arcade games, and other kinds of pay-to-play games operate a bit differently. Given the design goal of having players return over and over again (with their wallets), the notion of "end" might never be realized in any way that resembles the kinds of games I discuss in this chapter.
6. For example, see Curiouser Institute (2019) and Guilherme (2019).
7. See Bogost (2017).
8. In an essay more specifically about games, Murray (2003, 10) says as much: "I would argue that we stop trying to assimilate the new artifacts to the old categories of print- or cinema-based story and board- or player-based game. We should instead think of the characteristics of stories and games and how these separable characteristics are being recombined and reinvented within the astonishingly plastic world of cyberspace."
9. Ryan points to media like film and games, showing how the concept of a story world as experienced phenomenologically should be central to narratology, particularly as it pertains to experiences within and beyond the narratives themselves. In other words, "[w]ithout the concept of the world, one cannot speak of narrative as a lived experience" (Ryan 2014, 43).
10. Patrick Jagoda (2018) explores some of these possibilities, alongside a discussion of the potential reciprocity of game studies and narrative theory.

11. For more discussion beyond the scope of this essay, see essays in Kapell (2015).
12. This compelling differentiation has been fruitful beyond games as well. See, for instance, Heidbrink (2013).
13. The developers of *Minecraft* would release *Minecraft: Story Mode* in 2015; it included a predesigned story.
14. See, for instance, Yu (2016), Brame (2011), or Thompson (2019).
15. Of course, narratives might emerge from any sort of game, and this does not even include the wide array of fan fiction that players might engage in.
16. *Thoughts & Prayers: The Game* can be accessed online at https://www.thoughtsandprayersthegame.com/.
17. To dig deep into the Roman origins of rhetoric, perhaps music is part of the *elocutio*, or style, of this argument.
18. The icon of what might appear to be a genie's lamp in the images of Kazus in this chapter are coincidental with the inclusion of a Jinn. Shops that sell healing potions often use the lamp as a symbol, likely derived originally from tabletop role-playing game *Dungeons and Dragons*. (Many thanks to Ryan Thompson for pointing me to the origins of this symbol.)
19. As William Gibbons (2018, 26) discusses, the use of the music (including the Habanera) from Bizet's *Carmen* in video games has been used to connote "Spanishness."
20. For more on my definition of affective zones, see Grasso (2020).
21. See *Grove Music Online*, s.v. "Orientalism," by Ralph Locke, last modified July 9, 2018, https://doi.org/10.1093/gmo/9781561592630.article.40604.
22. More resonances with *Carmen* might be found in the ways Bizet also encodes a kind of dangerous Otherness in music that accompanies the character of Carmen; it is a danger that is also eventually vanquished. See McClary (1992).
23. For a more in-depth discussion of musical exoticism in video games, focusing on an earlier Uematsu score, see Plank (2019).
24. See Stuart (2012) or Parker (2013).
25. See Sharp (2015).
26. This "simple" take here indeed sets aside a number of complexities around the relationship between art and aesthetics, but I invoke this connection here to point to one of many potential readings around *Journey*'s status as an art game. Furthermore, there has been plenty of resistance to the idea that games can be art. For Roger Ebert (2010), "game" and "art" are actually mutually exclusive categories.
27. Such an effect is perhaps akin to Claudia Gorbman's (1987, 68) category of "spectacle" music in film, which "punctuates a pause in narrative movement in order to externalize, make commentary on it, and bond the spectator not to the feelings of the characters but to his/her fellow spectators." The complication in video games, of course, is that players are in a state of actively embodying and enacting characters, but there is nonetheless a good deal of cinematic residue in the music of games like *Journey*.

References

Aarseth, Espen. 2012. "A Narrative Theory of Games." In *Proceedings of the International Conference on the Foundations of Digital Games*, 129–133. New York: ACM Press. https://doi.org/10.1145/2282338.

Aarseth, Espen. 2013. "Ludology." In *The Routledge Companion to Video Game Studies*, edited by Mark J. P. Wolf and Bernard Perron, 279–295. New York: Routledge.
Battersby, James L. 2006. "Narrativity, Self, and Self-Representation." *Narrative* 14 (1): 27–44.
Bogost, Ian. 2007. *Persuasive Games: The Expressive Power of Videogames*. Cambridge, MA: MIT Press.
Bogost, Ian. 2017. "Video Games Are Better Without Stories." *Atlantic*, April 25, 2017. https://www.theatlantic.com/technology/archive/2017/04/video-games-stories/524148/.
Brame, Jason. 2011. "Thematic Unity across a Video Game Series." *ACT: Zeitschrift für Musik und Performance* 2 (July). http://www.act.uni-bayreuth.de/de/archiv/2011-02/03_Brame_Thematic_Unity/index.html.
Curiouser Institute. 2019. "Video Game Stories (Are Not Really Stories)." November 19, 2019. https://www.curiouserinstitute.com/blog/curiouser/video-game-stories-are-not-really-stories.
Ebert, Roger. 2010. "Video Games Can Never Be Art." *Roger Ebert's Journal* (blog), April 16, 2010. https://www.rogerebert.com/rogers-journal/video-games-can-never-be-art.
Genette, Gérard. 1980. *Narrative Discourse: An Essay on Method*. Ithaca, NY: Cornell University Press.
Gibbons, William. 2018. *Unlimited Replays: Video Games and Classical Music*. New York: Oxford University Press.
Gorbman, Claudia. 1987. *Unheard Melodies: Narrative Film Music*. London; Bloomington: Indiana University Press.
Grasso, Julianne. 2019. "Music in the Time of Video Games: Spelunking *Final Fantasy IV*." In *Music in the Role-Playing Game: Heroes and Harmonies*, edited by William Gibbons and Steven Reale, 97–116. New York: Routledge.
Grasso, Julianne. 2020. "Video Game Music, Meaning, and the Possibilities of Play." PhD dissertation, University of Chicago.
Guilherme, Sterling. 2019. "Why Video Game Stories Are Bad." *Game Savvy*, March 30, 2019. https://gamesavvy.net/bad-video-game-stories/.
Hambleton, Elizabeth. 2020. "Gray Areas: Analyzing Navigable Narratives in the Not-So-Uncanny Valley between Soundwalks, Video Games, and Literary Computer Games." *Journal of Sound and Music in Games* 1, no. 1 (January): 20–43. https://doi.org/10.1525/jsmg.2020.1.1.20.
Heidbrink, Henriette. 2013. "1, 2, 3, 4 Futures—Ludic Forms in Narrative Films." *SubStance* 42 (1): 146–164.
Hocking, Clint. 2007. "Ludonarrative Dissonance in Bioshock." *Click Nothing: Design from a Long Time Ago*, October 7, 2007. https://clicknothing.typepad.com/click_nothing/2007/10/ludonarrative-d.html.
Huizinga, Johan. 1949. *Homo Ludens: A Study of the Play-Element in Culture*. Oxford: Routledge.
Isbister, Katherine. 2016. *How Games Move Us: Emotion by Design*. Cambridge, MA: MIT Press.
Jagoda, Patrick. 2016. *Network Aesthetics*. Chicago: University of Chicago Press.
Jagoda, Patrick. 2018. "Digital Games and Narrative." In *The Cambridge Companion to Narrative Theory*, edited by Matthew Garrett, 231–247. Cambridge: Cambridge University Press.
Jenkins, Henry. 2003. "Game Design as Narrative Architecture." In *First Person: New Media as Story, Performance, and Game*, edited by Pat Harrigan and Noah Wardrip-Fruin, 118–130. Cambridge, MA: MIT Press.

Kapell, Matthew Wilhelm, ed. 2015. *The Play versus Story Divide in Game Studies: Critical Essays*. Jefferson, NC: McFarland Books.

Margulis, Elizabeth Hellmuth, Patrick C. M. Wong, Rhimmon Simchy-Gross, and J. Devin McAuley. 2019. "What the Music Said: Narrative Listening across Cultures." *Palgrave Communications* 5 (1): 1–8. https://doi.org/10.1057/s41599-019-0363-1.

McClary, Susan. 1992. "Structures of Identity and Difference in *Carmen*." *Women: A Cultural Review* 3, no. 1 (June): 1–15. https://doi.org/10.1080/09574049208578099.

Meretoja, Hanna. 2014. "Narrative and Human Existence: Ontology, Epistemology, and Ethics." *New Literary History* 45 (1): 89–109. https://doi.org/10.1353/nlh.2014.0001.

Murray, Janet. (1997) 2016. *Hamlet on the Holodeck: The Future of Narrative in Cyberspace*. Cambridge, MA: MIT Press; New York: The Free Press. Citations refer to the Free Press edition.

Murray, Janet. 2003. "From Game Story to Cyber Drama." In *First Person: New Media as Story, Performance, and Game*, edited by Pat Harrigan and Noah Wardrip-Fruin, 2–11. Cambridge, MA, MIT Press.

Parker, Laura. 2013. "A Journey to Make Video Games into Art." *New Yorker*, August 2, 2013. https://www.newyorker.com/tech/annals-of-technology/a-journey-to-make-video-games-into-art.

Plank, Dana. 2019. "The Penultimate Fantasy: Nobuo Uematsu's Score for *Cleopatra no Ma Takara*." In *Music in the Role-Playing Game: Heroes and Harmonies*, edited by William Gibbons and Steven Reale, 79–96. New York: Routledge.

Ryan, Marie-Laure. 2014. "Story/Worlds/Media: Tuning the Instruments of a Media-Conscious Narratology." In *Storyworlds across Media: Toward a Media-Conscious Narratology*, edited by Marie-Laure Ryan and Jan-Noël Ton, 25–49. Lincoln: University of Nebraska Press.

Salen, Katie, and Eric Zimmerman. 2003. *Rules of Play: Game Design Fundamentals*. Cambridge, MA: MIT Press.

Sharp, John. 2015. *Works of Game: On the Aesthetics of Games and Art*. Cambridge, MA: MIT Press.

Stuart, Keith. 2012. "Is Journey a Game or a Piece of Interactive Art?" *Guardian*, March 15, 2012. https://www.theguardian.com/technology/gamesblog/2012/mar/15/journey-game-or-interactive-art.

Thompson, Ryan. 2019. "Operatic Conventions and Expectations in *Final Fantasy VI*." In *Music in the Role-Playing Game: Heroes and Harmonies*, edited by William Gibbons and Steven Reale, 117–128. New York: Routledge.

van Elferen, Isabella. 2011. "¡Un Forastero! Issues of Virtuality and Diegesis in Videogame Music." *Music and the Moving Image* 4 (2): 30–39. https://doi.org/10.5406/musimoviimag.4.2.0030.

Yu, Jason. 2016. "An Examination of Leitmotifs and Their Use to Shape Narrative in UNDERTALE." March 31, 2016. http://jasonyu.me/undertale-part-1/.

CHAPTER 5

A CREATIVE SYSTEM IN ACTION

Bringing Video Game Music and Sound into Being

PHILLIP MCINTYRE AND J. T. VELIKOVSKY

INTRODUCTION

THIS chapter examines the creative system, which we argue produces, or brings into being, video game music and sound. What we are about to demonstrate may run counter to the commonsense ideas many hold about creativity and their understanding of how it works, but with these research-based ideas of the creative system on board a sound practitioner's creative arsenal will expand pragmatically as they come to see their own industry practice from this vantage point. The scholarly work on creativity also points away from the commonsense point of view. We present evidence from the scholarship and from the lives of industry practitioners that the games industry fits this systems-based approach. However, before we elaborate on those claims, we first need to place the central concept of creativity within the context of evidence-based research rather than make assumptions about what it might be and how it works, as these assumptions may be based on specific, culturally located understandings of this phenomenon. As Keith Sawyer (2006, 18) asserts, "the scientific explanation of creativity has found that many of our beliefs about creativity are inaccurate or misleading. That's why I call them creativity myths. These creativity myths . . . are so widely believed that they sometimes seem obvious, common sense."

Margaret Boden (2004, 14), a British cognitive psychologist with a deep research interest in artificial intelligence, argues that western common-sense beliefs about creativity "are believed by many to be literally true. But they are rarely critically examined. They are not theories, so much as myths: imaginative constructions, whose function is to express the values, assuage the fears, and endorse the practices of the community that celebrates them." For Boden, there are two dominant conceptions that reside in the western public imagination. Both have underpinned early thinking about creativity. The first is the Inspirationist view and the second, later manifestation is called Romanticism.

The Background Literature

A brief look into the Greek classical tradition reveals a number of sources for western thinking on creativity. These include the idealist perceptions rendered by Plato and also the mythology surrounding the muse. Both formed the bedrock of the Inspirationist approach, which views creativity as "essentially mysterious, even superhuman or divine" (Boden 2004, 14). Romanticism developed later, in part as an outgrowth of this view, but pitted itself against the scientific rationalism of the European Enlightenment project. Romanticism's reaction to this project was to locate creativity in "a free wakeful play of the imagination" (Negus and Pickering 2004, 7) which eventually led to a belief that "creativity required a regression to a state of consciousness characterised by emotion and instinct, a fusion between self and world, and freedom from rationality and convention" (Sawyer 2006, 16). However, another tradition had also been set in train by Aristotle (1960), who declared in his *Metaphysics* that "whatever comes to be is generated by the agency of something, out of something, and comes to be something" (142). His work was thus "seminal to the rationalist as well as the naturalist tradition of interpretation" (Rothenberg and Hausman 1976, 28) since, for him, creative acts, "like other natural and human processes, are explicable in terms of antecedent conditions. It is important to emphasise that Aristotle, unlike Plato, views the resources with which the artist begins as both necessary and sufficient to account for all that is found in the created product" (28).

This Aristotelean perspective "stressed the conscious work required to bring a creative inspiration to completion" (Sawyer 2006, 15) and it set in motion, contrary to the Romantic view, a rationalist explanation for creativity. Both ways of seeing the world, the rationalist and the Romantic, resulted in what Peter Watson (2005, 610) has termed "the modern incoherence," where art and science are deemed to be incompatible rather than complementary. These sets of assumptions did not stop researchers from a wide variety of fields attempting to come to grips with what creativity might be and how it might work.[1] Summarizing the scale of this project, Dean Keith Simonton (2003, 304) noted that:

> Psychologists have tended to view creativity as an individual-level phenomenon. That is, they have tended to concentrate on the cognitive processes, personality traits, and developmental antecedents associated with individual creators. This focus follows naturally from the very nature of psychology as a scientific enterprise dedicated to understanding individual mind and behavior. Yet this tradition of "psychological reductionism" has also inspired an antithetical conception of creativity as an exclusively societal-level event. In the extreme form, that of a complete "sociocultural

> reductionism," the individual becomes a mere epiphenomenon without any causal significance whatsoever.

In 2010, Beth Hennessey and Teresa Amabile compiled a meta-analysis of this literature to see how far the research into creativity had come. They noted the now tacit agreement between creativity researchers around the world giving creativity an operational definition as follows: creativity is the bringing into being of novel objects or processes that are valued in at least one social setting (572). They declared that what was needed now was further "interdisciplinary research, based on a systems view of creativity that recognizes a variety of interrelated forces operating at multiple levels" (571). This conclusion was reinforced in 2017 when Hennessey published an updated overview. She stated that:

> There have long been at least a few voices calling for the reconceptualization of creativity from a systems perspective. But in 2010 when we published our review, this perspective was largely overshadowed by a decontextualized, even reductionist, approach. Researchers and theorists were doing all that they could to break down questions of creativity into the absolutely smallest components they could control and measure. An exploration of the most recent literature reveals that this situation may, in fact, be changing. A growing number of publications are now reflecting a systems perspective. (Hennessey 2017, 342)

Hennessey argued that "only with the adoption of a truly integrated systems perspective can researchers hope to ever understand the complexities of the creative process" (342) and cited the earlier research into creative systems by scholars such as Alfonso Montuori (2011) and especially Mihaly Csikszentmihalyi (1988, 1997, 2014). Csikszentmihalyi (1988, 338) had suggested that "perhaps even more than new research, what we need now is an effort to synthesize the various approaches of the past into an integrated theory." We suggest that this synthesis plays out in the systems model of creativity.

The Creative System in Action

It is not a surprise that "a complete scientific explanation of creativity would have to include detailed accounts of both psychological and social mechanisms" (Sawyer 2010, 368). Taking up this challenge, the idea of a creative system in action (McIntyre 2013; McIntyre, Fulton, and Paton 2016) synthesizes the sociological (Bourdieu 1977, 1993, 1996) with the psychological (Csikszentmihalyi 1988, 1997, 2014). It gives a comprehensive account of creativity and, from there, creative practice (Velikovsky 2016). To explain these ideas a little more fully, we note that Pierre Bourdieu's sociological account of creative practice can be set out as follows:

> It is the interplay between a *field of works* which presents possibilities of action to an individual who possesses the necessary *habitus*, partially composed of personal

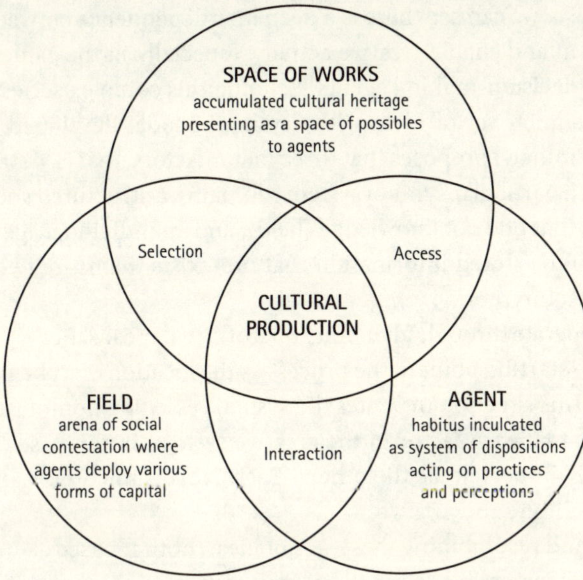

FIGURE 5.1 A representation of Pierre Bourdieu's interrelated ideas on cultural production (McIntyre 2021, 7).

> levels of *social, cultural, symbolic and economic capital* that then inclines them to act and react within particular structured and dynamic spaces called *fields*. These fields are arenas of production and circulation of goods, ideas and knowledges. They are populated by other *agents* who compete using various levels of the forms of capital pertinent to that field. Bourdieu suggests that it is the interplay between these various spheres of cultural production that makes practice possible. (McIntyre 2009, 7; see Figure 5.1)

This complex approach not only encompasses individual agents, in this case those who work in games audio, who draw on a unique but shared experience, but also entails "the set of social conditions of the production, circulation and consumption of symbolic goods" (Johnson 1993, 9), that is, the world in which game audio is produced and interacted with. Given the evidence supporting these ideas, some of which is presented below, it is no longer possible to either privilege individual creators *or* the sociocultural contexts within which they exist when accounting for creativity. We need to do both. We must account for "*all these things at the same time*" (9, italics in original).

It is the entwining of agency and structure, in essence their complementarity, that Bourdieu argued for. Agents, active choice-making entities, could be, dependent on scale, an individual, a group, or institution. As an example, they may be an individual audio-designer or the company they work for. These choice-making entities make decisions or choices—that is, take creative action—and are always defined by a complex set of social and cultural structures as these structures, which were thought to determine actions, provide instead the possibilities of action and the predisposition to take those actions. In this case, we can see there is a deep interdependence between the structures that both constrain and enable creative activity, especially in the games world, and the choices made by decision-making agents. Echoing this complex series of relationships is a remarkably similar set of ideas: "The systems model developed by psychologist Mihaly Csikszentmihalyi proposes that three major factors, that is, a structure of knowledge manifest in a particular symbol system (domain), a structured social organisation that understands that body of knowledge (field), and an individual agent (person) who makes changes to the stored information that pre-exists them, are necessary for creativity to occur" (McIntyre 2009, 7).

These factors operate through "dynamic links of circular causality" (Csikszentmihalyi 1988, 329) with no starting point to the process as the location of its beginning is "purely arbitrary" (329). This situation indicates the system's essential nonlinearity. What is important to note is that each factor in the creative system, in this case the audio-games systems, is equally important as the others. Each "affects the others and is affected by them in turn" (McIntyre 2009, 7).

By rethinking and recombining these sets of ideas, both focused at creativity and cultural production, it is possible to see that a dynamic creative system in action must account for a number of components. There is an *agent*, that is, a choice-making entity, whether that be at the scale of an individual, group, or institution, which is at one and the same time both enabled and constrained by a *field*. This field has a *constrabling* (simultaneously constraining and enabling) effect (Criticos 2021) on the agent as the field operates as a social organization where cooperation and competition, that is *coopetition*, using various forms of capital—social, cultural, symbolic, and economic—takes place. Both the agents and the field draw on, to varying degrees, the pre-existing work done to this point in time. This *domain* of knowledge thus contributes to the creation of novel and valued things (Runco and Jaeger 2012). Each of these parts of the system—in the case being argued here, the agent, field, and domain of game audio—are necessary but not sufficient, in and of themselves, to afford the possibility of creativity taking place (see Figure 5.2).

The creative system in action described briefly above, allows us to apply this complex set of ideas to the bringing into being—the creation—of the basic components of video game sound. This includes the creation of sound effects (SFX), dialogue, and music, whether they are analog recorded and/or digitally generated. Since nothing exists in a vacuum, we can claim the video games industry, like all systems (Capra and Luisi 2014), is locked inside a spatiotemporal context. It is into this contextualized world of audio that the professionals who design all the facets of games audio have stepped. Some came from the film world, some came from the audio world, and some developed their skills within the video game community itself. To produce what they do, all of them needed to be immersed in text, audio, and/or visual skills of various types as they went about bringing these games into being. In particular, those dealing with audio needed to be adept at producing quality SFX, voice, and music as they, and those around them, built the necessary soundscapes that continue to contribute so much to player immersion.

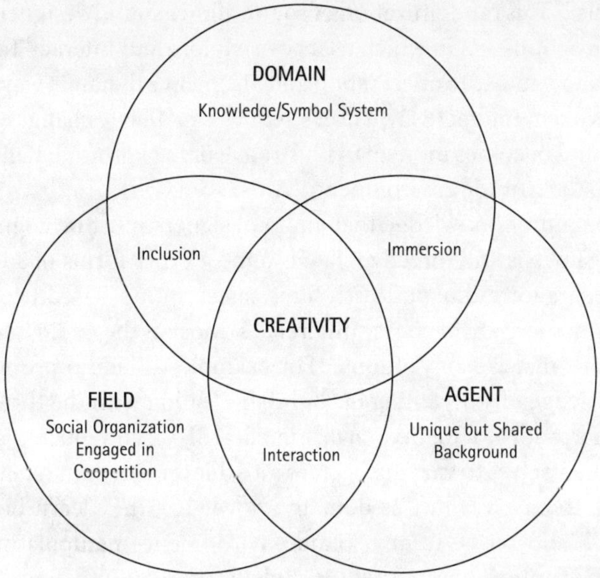

FIGURE 5.2 A reconfiguration of the systems model of creativity (McIntyre 2021, 8).

The Domain of Knowledge for Audio in Games

The domain of knowledge is a key element of the creative system in action. All the work that is housed in the domain presents the possibility of action for creative agents operating in the field of audio for games. The domain is a necessary—but not sufficient—part, by itself, of these creative systems: "The domain is the symbol system that the person and others working in the area utilise. It is the culture and conventions the person becomes immersed in. It includes all the work done to this point within that particular field and may be held within a person's idiosyncratic knowledge base or accessible from other sources within the field" (McIntyre 2012, 78).

A complex realm of technology and storytelling knowledge marks out the multipath interactivity involved in games. As Stanley Alten (2014) suggests, sound design for interactive media is not quite the same as for linear media, such as film. He notes that: "Creatively, an interactive sound designer is faced with decisions similar to those of a designer for linear media: consideration of the overall mood and tone of the production, the musical choices and styles to be used, and the types of sound effects to be incorporated. Implementing these creative decisions into an interactive production, however, presents different complexities and challenges" (376). Some of these, as Alten suggests, include the idea that users of a conventional production cannot explore at will. But with interactive sound design, audio is in a state of dynamic change as the user explores the game environment. Interactive sound design also affords an action possibility of having a variety of effects: "This randomization of sound allows sound designers to create more realistic sonic environments in which users can explore and interact. Interactive media and games also allow music to affect mood and pacing in a dynamic way. In linear media an underscore is fixed. Interactively, a user's actions can dictate changes in speed, pacing and style.... Sound becomes more than illustrative or background; it influences actions and choices with the gaming environment" (Alten 2014, 377).

While the domain of knowledge that audio designers must be cognizant of to produce audio for games is still directly related to most other forms of sound production whether that occurs for radio, podcasts, films, subscription-based television series, or music production, there are of course differences. Most of the audio knowledge has become traditional—that is, conventional. For example, all audio producers acquire at least some knowledge of storytelling in sound. In dealing with the three basic forms of audio—voice (narration), actuality (environmental SFX), and music—sound designers must immerse themselves to varying degrees into this knowledge system.

In immersing themselves in this domain knowledge, they learn how to effectively place voice, SFX, and music in any sound environment, manipulating at least three layers or planes of information. These include: (1) foreground sound, that is, sound which is designed to get one's prompt attention; (2) contextual sounds, that is, those sounds taking place in the vicinity of the foreground sound; and (3) the background field, which is the ambient soundscape against which the first two sound planes are contrasted (Schwartz cited in Truax 1999). In doing this they need to come to grips with what Rob Bridgett (2021) calls the "four basic food groups":

> sound (designed sound effects, ambiences, Foley etc.), music (both score and onscreen, or source music), dialogue (any voice-over from characters in the scene, or voice narration from characters offscreen or disembodied voice, as well as "Walla" crowds) and finally mix (not only the foreground and background choices, blending between those three food-groups at any particular moment, but any systemic or scripted mixing approaches that apply to the game such as static ducking, volume, panning, EQ and side-chaining, as well as moments of exaggerated perspective and distance etc). (Bridgett 2021, 10)

In manipulating these forms of audio and placing them in the various planes of information, sound designers for games must have some knowledge of acoustics; that is, the technicalities of audio and how it behaves, along with the fundamentals of producing human talent such as voice-over artists and musicians. They must also know about microphone types, placement, and usage and the characteristics of musical instruments, and must have some knowledge of sound synthesis and manipulation—that is, an ability to use and control the wide varieties of technologies used to manipulate audio that are increasingly available to them, including the massive variety of MIDI sound synthesis instruments and their peculiarities usually derived from the way they generate sound.

For SFX and Foley work there are choices to be made based on a knowledge of what works best and the circumstances it is to be used in. These choices include whether or not to use pre-recorded FX form libraries like Sonniss or Pixel Prospector, for example, which have large, royalty-free libraries of music and SFX samples. These are primarily used by indie games developers. Many experienced sound designers prefer to keep these as a library of last resort, however. In this case, the production of SFX may find the sound designer creating them in the studio, and/or recording them from the actual source, usually in the field with a Zoom H4N, for example. As stated by Akash Thakkar (2021), the sound designer for *Hyper Light Drifter* (2016) and *Infinifactory* (2015), the knowledge of how to design SFX "is a massively under-explored area for explosive improvements in game feel."

For those concentrating on creating music, there are similar domains of knowledge at play. For example, music can be obtained by having it composed and recorded from a particular piece, selecting it from a prerecorded music library, or by getting it from a commercial source. If it is to be recorded, which gives the sound designers much better control, sound designers, who are often their own composers (unless they are working on well-funded AAA games), must understand the characteristics of musical instruments and have some knowledge of sound synthesis and manipulation.

There are many other things sound designers need to know as they immerse themselves in the domain of knowledge. In terms of audio knowledge itself, this will likely encompass the physical behavior of sound, as well as its relationship to the psychobiological perception of certain stimuli. This includes the "objective behaviour of received sound [and] its subjective effect on those who hear it" (Alten 2014, xxix). Thus, they must gain some understanding of frequency and pitch, amplitude and loudness, wave shape, timbre and tonality, and the sound envelopes that provide the attack, decay, sustain, and release of sounds. They need to come to grips with the spatial relationship of binaural or stereo hearing, how direct, early, and reverberant sound behaves in a variety of environments—how absorption, diffraction, and diffusion affect this—and how to match acoustics to program material. In this case, they will also need to understand "spatial audio formats such as Ambisonic sound-field recordings or pre-designed and panned sound-fields" (Bridgett 2021, 11).

Each of these aspects of audio can be captured or manipulated using various microphones each with differing pick-up patterns and diaphragm types. They must learn about close or distant mic'ing, coincident and spaced mic'ing techniques, and such things as the proximity effect, signal-to-noise ratios, mic and line level, the impedance values of cable, and what these things may do to the sounds they are trying to record. They need to understand various mixers and surface controllers and how to automate them, as they optimize both analog and digital signals passing through this system. Frequency spectrum tools, graphic and parametric equalizers—as both outboard and plugins—as well as dynamic processors like compressors and limiters are conventional pieces of technology that provide sound designers a set of useful affordances (Gibson 1966) that *constrable* their actions (Criticos 2021). As well as things such as near field monitoring, and how this is coupled with studio monitoring systems working inside the dimensions of studio control rooms, they also need to know what sampling and quantizing is. They need to know Digital Audio Workstations and timecode to sync equipment, what jitter and latency is, and they also need to know the format requirements for the delivery of the audio products they come up with. And much more: "[An] audio developer, regardless of their place in the audio team, needs to be fluent with a number of software packages from multiple digital audio workstations to increasingly more sophisticated audio processors, sound design techniques, adaptive mix techniques, spatial audio, coding and procedural audio techniques" (Sinclair 2020, 6).

They must also know about system resources and work to these, adapting their work to the limitations of that shared system. In this case, such things as CPU, GPU, memory, the quality of various sound cards, file compression technologies, codecs, and standard file types for Mac, PC, or Linux all become important to understand to "record high quality digital sound, process it, and manipulate it in highly creative and advanced ways" (Alten 2014, 380).

For mixing, game-audio domain knowledge encompasses a working understanding of dynamic mixing systems and priority systems, so the system can "cull and control the amount of sounds being played back at any one time" (Bridgett 2021, 18). They will be confronted with choosing

> the most important element at any one time (a quite dynamic and complex problem when considering both the gameplay systems and the narrative contexts in which those systems are occurring). It helps if you think about game mixing as the "dynamic priority of what the player needs to hear," rather than "mixing" in any traditional film sound sense, because the mix of a game is about so much more than the relative volume of the sound categories of sounds—it includes the dynamic relationships between those categories. (Bridgett 2021, 18)

To be able achieve all of this, the sound designer/engineer/developer must, in addition to the extensive domain knowledge outlined briefly above, also immerse themselves in the field relevant to games.

The Structure of the Field of Games

A field is an arena of social cooperation and competition; that is, it is a space where necessary *coopetition* takes place. It is the place or space built around specific domain knowledge, in this case game audio as briefly outlined above, where networks of agents make decisions, not just about the technical aspects of game audio but also about who will get to work in this field, what is acceptable or good work, and, among many other decisions, who gets to advance their career in this field. It is a place where social, cultural, symbolic, and economic capital is traded. It has an immediate and direct effect in the creative system that brings novel games into being.

The structure of the field of games is as follows, as McIntyre and colleagues (2019) explain: developers make the game; publishers finance, market, and promote the game;

distributors are involved in the logistics of delivering the game to retailers or direct to consumers; the platform is the machinery, the console or format the game is played on; retailers sell the game to consumers or streaming services deliver the game direct to players; game critics critique the game; and, of course, there are the consumers (audience) themselves. For Williams and Srivastava (2014): "production takes place at the development stage in which games are conceived, created and programmed—the content. Games designed for one platform are often recoded at lower costs for another, a process known as 'porting' and recently made easier with the rise of Unity as a platform" (1).

As Lukefollows11 (2013) also explains, development generally occurs in one of three or four ways. However, first-party developers generally confine themselves to one platform. They are most often subsidiaries of game publishing companies, who may also be game console hardware manufacturers, such as Nintendo, Sony, or Microsoft, where most of their games are made internally. Financing is often unproblematic and the platform limitations are very well known to the developers. Second-party developers are generally owned independently of the platform, but games are made for the platform owners. In other words, the platform owners outsource the development of the game to an independent studio, who then makes the game exclusively for the platform or other company who funds the game. Third-party developers make games for multiple systems or platforms. They generally work for publishers who supply the financing. Both have input to the development of the game but, as elsewhere, whoever finances a production is the party who makes the final decisions. Independent developers are generally small firms who self-publish. They generally do not have the budgets of the prior categories. They do however get to make all the creative decisions with no financier establishing input. There have been successes here, however, as exampled by Mojang: "It started off as a two person company, Markus Persson and Jakob Porsér being the founders, with a third being brought in as a CEO at a later date, Carl Manneh. The game they produced was a huge success selling over 12 million copies and is still very popular to this day, that game was called *Minecraft*. Within a year the company grew to a size of twelve people to produce their second title named *Scrolls* and the company is still going strong" (Lukefollows11 2013, online).

According to Williams and Srivastava (2014), publishers, on the other hand, or subsidiaries of publishers "are the rights-holders for the games." They make several points:

- When the developer delivers the game, "the publisher is responsible for marketing the product's launch and the manufacturing process if there is a physical product. The manufacturing process is part of the licensing deal when making console games, and the major three manufacturers maintain strict control."
- This publishing sector has moved toward a concentrated oligopoly where there are "fewer and fewer publishers, which tends to mean less competition—and a tougher life for developers."
- Self-publishing has recently begun to develop as a force in the market but "the big publishers retain a lot of power in the industry" (1).

While the device manufacturers are also important, retailers sell a vast array of games primarily for entertainment purposes. Bypassing the retailers and the hard copy version of games are the streaming services, such as Stadia, Amazon Luna, GeForce Now, PlayStation Now, and Shadow (Greenwald 2021) as well as Steam.

Game development studios, the actual places where this all takes place which also exist within and across the hierarchy described above, as Velikovsky (2013) explains, are populated by various members of the field. The people who occupy these studios have a number of roles. Apart from human resources and admin—all necessary support workers inside this art world (Becker 1982)—a typical game development studio working on a AAA title may have around 50 people working full-time for two years or more, dependent on the contract and thus the budget. That team may include, on average, 2 producers, a project manager, 3 game designers, 4 level designers, 15 programmers, 15 artists, and 5 animators and, of course, a game narrative writer/designer. For the sound team there may be two in-house sound personnel who source and/or self-produce game SFX, and then program them into the game engine. This is the case for procedural audio, but, if samples or MIDI are used, then such files (SFX) exist external to the game engine which then calls them up. There will be a music composer on contract as well as voice talent hired. Of course, this example applies for games that have a considerable sound and music component and relates to game studios which can afford to keep all these staff on fulltime/in-house salaries. Often, however, much of the content, such as the game music, will be outsourced or created on short-term contracts (Velikovsky 2021) and, with indie games, these often require a single person to operate across a number of roles. Ryan Sims, sound designer at Sumo Digital, states that: "The role of a sound designer can vary greatly from company to company. At a first glance the main day to day responsibilities are usually to create sound effects needed for your project, which includes everything from recording footsteps to creating intricate ambiences to compel a desired mood or a hyper realistic weapon sound made by layering lots of sounds to create something new" (Sims cited in Staines 2017).

When a sound is designed, implementing it into the game presents a different set of challenges dependent on whether it is procedural or external to the game engine. However, the routines and the responsibilities a sound designer enacts vary from day to day. During preproduction, "sound designers will often spend a lot of time collaborating with colleagues in other departments, brainstorming and planning the overall shape a game's sound will take" (Staines 2017). Then when the game moves into production "the sound designer's role shifts to creating and implementing audio where it's required" (Staines 2017). Nick Laviers from Electronic Arts says that it was once the case that single programmers wrote games, including the graphics and sound, but specialist roles have emerged with clear distinction having developed between the creative and the technical: "Traditionally, your games sound person would be a musician who also had a great deal of mathematical skill, so that he could squeeze a lot of sound effects into a small amount of memory and probably write chip music as well. Nowadays, especially for us within EA Studios, it's splitting into two disciplines: there's the creative sound design side—the people generating the content—and then there's the technical sound design side, people who specialise in liaising with the programmers and actually making the sounds work in the game" (Laviers cited in Inglis 2002).

Chase Thompson, who has worked on game series like *Halo*, *Fable*, and *Star Wars*, concentrates all his efforts on implementation:

> In simple terms, my primary responsibilities are making sounds play in the game and building systems that help make the game sound better. Sometimes that involves actual sound implementation, like hooking up sounds to animations, effects, and other various game events. But most of the time I focus my energy on systems work. That includes designing, testing, and using systems that directly affect the way the game sounds—acoustic simulation, reverb, high dynamic range (HDR) audio mixing, and more. I also manage things like our data and content structure, our audio performance (how efficiently the game audio runs on the hardware), and the pipeline/workflow/implementation systems design that helps to make the work of implementing sounds more efficient. (Thompson cited in Bay 2021a)

While the roles and the nature of the tasks asked of sound designers vary across a project, we can see that fields are dynamic spaces which "denote arenas of production, circulation and appropriation of goods, services, knowledge, or status, and the competitive positions held by actors in their struggle to accumulate and monopolize . . . different kinds of capital" (Swartz 1997, 117). The use of capital in all its forms, within fields, is the pivot point around which power relationships resolve themselves within the field. However, this is not a simple process. Taking the actions of economic capital, "which is immediately and directly convertible into money" (Bourdieu 1986, 243), as a starting point, a salary or wage is crucial to continuing to be creative. As Csikszentmihalyi (1997, 333) asserts, "a huge number of talented and motivated artists, musicians, dancers, athletes, and singers give up pursuing their domains because it is so difficult to make a living in them." In support of this idea, extensive evidence indicates "creation is jeopardized when compensation is not available" (Levinson 2006, 64).

Most sound designers are not in salaried positions. They often work on a contract-to-contract basis dependent on the project. Jason Bay asserts that if an annual income is treated as a salary and averaged across the year, these "can start as low as USD$20,000 annually for entry-level audio positions. But they can grow to well over $100,000 per year for very senior audio engineers in lead positions" (Bay 2021b). These figures are likely to be "based on years of audio experience, areas of expertise, and whether there's a "manager" or "director" in the job title. The more experience you have, the more you're likely to get paid. However, there's also a difference in pay depending on what type of game project is being worked on. Audio engineers working for bigger studios and creating large, AAA-quality games can make significantly more than audio engineers working on smaller one-or two-person mobile teams, for example" (Bay 2021b).

While it is difficult to ascertain exactly what an audio budget might entail, as these vary across projects, Nathan Lovato's (2017) brief research reveals that different games and games studios allocate variable budgets, but they all tend to fall within an approximate range of between 5% and 10% of the total budget:

- "We set aside a little less than 10% of our budget on both the music and the sound design for *Lethis: Daring Discoverers*" @Triskell_Int
- "Same here, less than 10% on *Steredenn*" @pixelnest
- "It was 7% for *Drifting Lands*. In a perfect world, I would have liked to spend 20 to 25% to have full voice-overs and more soundtracks" @alkemigames
- "It was 5% of our total budget on the last project" @CheeseBurgames
- "For the OST and the voice-over, and some are direction from the actor, we allocated 5% of our budget on *Epistory*" @epistorygame
- "That was approximately 15% for us on *Wonder Boy: The Dragon's Trap*" @lizardcube.

Given these budgets, and their variability in terms of the actual numbers as opposed to percentages, gaining employment becomes a significant factor for most sound designers. However, there are no formal requirements for becoming a sound designer, although a strong background in audio production and engineering is obviously regarded favorably by most employers.

In terms of opportunities for new recruits to the game audio industry, Velikovsky (2021) suggests various annual game developer and games industry-related conferences exist which are appropriate places to advertise a CV or pitch skills and experience as a game audio professional. These include Game Connect Asia Pacific, E3 in the United States, the Game Developers Conference (also in the US), and GDC Europe. Many aspiring game audio professionals also place samples of their work online as a portfolio so that potential clients, game developers, can hear their work. One of the more popular game development sites is Gamasutra.com, now rebranded as Game Developer (gamedeveloper.com), with numerous articles on game audio, or sound and music in games. One possible way to break in as a game audio professional is to do the sound and/or music on an independent game, often gratis or for a minimal fee, and use that as an example of produced work to obtain future work. As Velikovsky (2021) points out, the book *Break Into the Game Industry: How to Get a Job Making Video Games* (Adams 2003) includes practical information on the skills required for entering the game audio field, as do sites like Game Industry Career Guide (Bay 2021a). In addition to developing skills through an immersion in the domain, successful games sound designers like Ryan Sim, Jaclyn Schumate, and James Magee "are unanimous in stressing the importance of making contacts in the industry" (Staines 2017). This situation highlights the importance to the creative system of social capital which is "made up of social obligations (connections), which is convertible, in certain conditions, into economic capital" (Bourdieu 1986, 243).

Similarly, symbolic capital (McIntyre 2012a, 74), which is the degree of accumulated prestige, celebrity, or honor one acquires, is also central to the operation of the field.

Awards do things for those who receive them. "Since their inception in 1998, the annual DICE awards are widely considered to be the equivalent of the Oscars in movies" (Velikovsky 2021, 6). Velikovsky also points out that, in Australasia, awards for Excellence in Audio as voted by the Game Developers Association of Australia (GDAA) for the Australian Game Developer Awards (AGDA) are bestowed at the annual Game Connect Asia Pacific (GCAP) conference. Likewise, the Game Audio Network Guild Awards (shortened to the G.A.N.G. Awards) is an award show that celebrates excellence in video game audio (*Game Audio Network Guild Awards* 2021).

These, and many other awards programs, not only provide avenues for the development of symbolic capital but also offer opportunities for advantageous commercial exploitation. For example, "The Game Awards was founded in 2014 by media entrepreneur Geoff Keighley, who also hosts and produces the program" (Keighley 2021). Keighley has been "a journalist, host, and producer of video game programming across multiple platforms, including print, television and digital" (Keighley 2021). His expertise, his domain knowledge, in this area was gained working for *Entertainment Weekly, Spike TV, G4*, and YouTube. His series of behind-the-scenes game development stories titled *The Final Hours* has been important in establishing his reputation. He also produces gamescom's *Opening Night Live* program. The awardees for Best Score and Music include Mick Gordon, Nobuo Uematsu, Masashi Hamauzu, and Mitsuot Suzuki as well as Darren Korb, and all have all profited from this boost to their reputation. Similarly for Best Audio Design, the winners in the 2020 Games Awards included id Software/Bethesda and also Sucker Punch/SIE. This last operating as Sucker Punch Production LLC, a production house that has been making games for 20 years, focusing on one title and one platform at a time, stating that "more than 2 million matches were played using online matchmaking" (Suckerpunch 2021) with players taking part in extensive online multiplayer games.

All of this requires a full team not only of game makers but also of financiers, admin staff, and marketers with promotional abilities as well as large contingent of support workers all relying for their income on the affordance provided by the structures of the field. The ability of game developers to continue to employ, contract, and hire games audio designers, and allow them the possibility of continuing to create games, is dependent on all of this.

Finally, for this section, it needs to be pointed out that a field cannot be simply equated to "the industry" and those employed there. Others, linked to but possibly lying outside "the industry," also have some effect on domain knowledge and how it is produced, used, and disseminated (Sawyer 2006), not the least of which are the game players themselves. Additionally, we can include grassroots communities, internet forums, and message boards, and so on, all populated by those who understand game audio knowledge—the domain—to a greater or lesser extent. These are not normally seen as part of an industry, as such, but still serve a critical role in the dissemination and organization of ideas about game sound and the shared experiences of its implementation. These entities, for example, are crucial for what music and audio (and software) is seen as good, bad, or indifferent by many working sound designers.

Choice-Making Agents

Sound designers rely on their knowledge of the field and their immersion in the domain to continue to create the work they do. They interact with a contingent of support workers, all relying for their income on the affordances provided by the structures of the games industry and its broader field. This industry's ability to continue to employ, contract, and hire game audio designers and allow them the possibility of continuing to create games, feeds directly into these sound designers' daily creative practice. Bourdieu "insists that practice is always informed by a sense of agency (the ability to understand and control our own actions), but that the possibilities of agency must be understood in terms of cultural trajectories, literacies and dispositions" (Schirato and Yell 1996, 148). As Johnson (1993) notes, Bourdieu suggests that the interplay between the two spheres of agency and structure makes practice possible, with the tool linking them being *habitus*:

> [Habitus is] a "feel for the game," a "practical sense" (*sens pratique*) that inclines agents to act and react in specific situations in a manner that is not always calculated and that is not simply a question of conscious obedience to rules. Rather, it is a set of dispositions which generates practices and perceptions. The habitus is the result of a long process of inculcation, beginning in early childhood, which becomes a "second sense" or a second nature. (Johnson 1993, 5)

"Habitus" is a term that deals with the way people like to be and accounts for their preferences, their tastes, values, desires, ideas, and the embedding in the narratives produced by family and the various social institutions they have interacted with across a lifetime. As a result, they are often predisposed to do things in ways that are unique to them but shared by many others. In other words, the social and cultural structures they are part of feed into their choice-making abilities or agency. Habitus can be seen in their personal narratives and life histories. Since agents, in this case individual sound designers, are an equally necessary but not sufficient component set, along with the fields and domains of the creative system we are discussing, it is necessary to exemplify these with a few cases of who those sound designers, those choice-making entities, are. Their unique histories and trajectories are a vital part of their contribution to the creative system of audio in games. Their individual habitus usually results from, as mentioned, a long process of inculcation which has often become second nature to them. In short, each agent brings their own personal background and story to the creative system.

For example, Peter Maguire is a senior sound designer, composer and discipline lead at Harmonix in the United States. His story is that he graduated from Oberlin Conservatory of Music and majored in what is called TIMARA (Technology In Music And Related Arts) developing the necessary habitus he would later use professionally. While at the Conservatory, his attention was on composition and synthesis, but he interned at Harmonix, becoming inculcated in the world of games, and began work on *FreQuency*. At the same time, he took on contracts to fulfill audio briefs for clients like Lexus and the Barbarian Group learning how the creative system worked as he went. Once he was hired full-time at Harmonix, he took on various roles including senior sound designer to lead producer. The games he worked on reflected his stage of professional development. These include *Amplitude*, *Guitar Hero*, *Rock Band*, *Fantasia: Music Evolved*, and *Rock Band VR*. He holds a teaching post at Berklee College of Music.

Also with a musical background, Jean-Luc Sinclair has found work as a producer, composer, and sound designer working in New York City since the early 2000s. His story gives a different route into the gaining of the habitus of a sound designer. He has produced pioneering work since the mid-1990s, along with musicians like Trent Reznor and the Scissor Sisters, and games companies like id Software and Royal Caribbean. He teaches at the Berklee College of Music on their Boston campus and also at New York University. He delivers classes on game audio, sound design, and software synthesis, writing on these topics in his book *Principles of Game Audio and Sound Design* (2020).

Industry biographies like these are replete with examples that illustrate their acquisition of habitus. It is the unique narratives and histories of those employed in the field that complete, along with the field and domain, the unity and complexity of the system and how habitus develops. Similarly, networking via the use of social capital figures large in these stories, and tales of low-paid or freebie internships abound. Chase Thompson, who worked on best-selling games such as *Halo*, *Fable*, and *Star Wars*, began his career as an audio implementer, after working in all areas of sound design and as an intern with Griptonite Games. In these internships, which can be viewed as either exploitative or replete with possibility (or both), he undertook a variety of tasks and "was often dropped into projects that were over my head" (Bay 2021a). This also points to the question of becoming skilled enough to attain what Csikszentmihalyi calls "flow" in the creative process. As Reed Larson suggests, "if the challenges of the activity are too great for a person's skills, anxiety takes over. . . . On the other hand if the challenges of an activity are too few for a person's skill or if one sees no way to make an activity challenging boredom takes over" (Larson cited in Csikszentmihalyi and Csikszentmihalyi 1988, 163–164).

However, once Thompson met those challenges, learning and gaining experience as he developed a sound designer's habitus, his work flowed effortlessly into a state where he was absorbed into his creative work, and he eventually achieved a balance between the perceived challenges of the activity and the skill he acquired. His actions followed smoothly from his thoughts. Finding his way like that "was great for me because I gained experience in a ton of different fields, and it helped me realize what my strengths and passions were" (Bay 2021a). Thompson "started taking on as many of those types of tasks as I could, and focused on improving the technical and implementation aspects of my areas of responsibility" (Bay 2021a). He eventually made the transition to a sound designer position with Microsoft Studios SoundLab, where he was "again dropped in over my head—but on even larger projects" (Bay 2021a). The set of challenges this presented gave him the impetus to go deeper into the technical/implementation aspects of game audio and he eventually spent time "on site at 343 Industries on *Halo 4*.

I worked primarily on voiceover for *Halo 4*" (Bay 2021a). At the same time, he took the opportunity

> to briefly help out on a number of different types of sounds—weapons, environments, cinematics, and more. . . . After having worked in those systems, I found a lot of areas for improvement in the systems design and audio implementation for *Halo*, and was eventually hired full time to work on Voice Over. In that role, I helped build a new, automated Voice Over implementation pipeline. After establishing that new system, I started working on designing implementation systems for other types of sounds, and eventually just naturally transitioned into a more comprehensive audio implementation role, rather than focusing on voice over exclusively. (Bay 2021a)

Jeff Seamster, the sound designer for *Bioshock Infinite*, as well as *Mortal Kombat vs. DC Universe* and *Blitz: The League II*, also illustrates an early and critical immersion in the domain of game sound:

> My two sisters and I used to record skits and fake radio spots when we were kids. Don't ask me why, this was just a thing we did. I went around with a tape deck recording and creating sound effects, then played them in the background on my dad's stereo while we recorded our shows. I made some interesting discoveries during that time, most of them accidental; Half-pressing the record button would run the tape at double speed allowing us to stretch normal recordings into big, booming effects when playing back at normal speed. I would also lug my recorder into our garage to get a bit of natural reverb when necessary. (cited in Hughes 2014)

Seamster took this early immersion into sound and eventually, after a lengthy series of contract positions, created the sound for *Mortal Kombat* and *Blitz: The League*. This led to his in-house position at Irrational Games, working there from 2009 onward.

These decision making agents—sound designers, composers, and implementers—have all made choices in their creative journey into the games industry; choices about the domain of knowledge and the field of games, that has allowed them to put their unique but shared contributions to good effect within this creative system at work.

Conclusion

We can see from the above, confirmation of the systems model in action. The three major factors of this creative system are all necessary to the system: (1) the structures of the domain knowledge of audio and games, which gives a choice-making agent access to the symbol system they will use in their creative work; (2) the structures of the field, that is the social organization that knows, uses, and makes judgments about that body of knowledge; and, of course, (3) the agent themselves, each of whom has made changes to the pre-existing store of information held in the domain. They are necessary, but are not sufficient, to allow creative (i.e., novel and valued) game audio activity to emerge.

These multiple factors operate in a nonlinear way through "dynamic links of circular causality" (Csikszentmihalyi 1988, 329). Each factor is of equal importance to the others as each "affects the others and is affected by them in turn" (329). To reiterate and understand more fully, we can say that this dynamic creative system in action accounts for the actions of an agent, an active choice-making entity, which may be—dependent on the scale of the system being looked at—an individual, a group, a company, or an institution. Agents in this system are thus, at one and the same time, *constrabled* (Criticos 2021), that is, both constrained and enabled, by the system. The field, as a major constituent factor of the system, works as a social organization, where cooperation and competition, that is *coopetition*, are used to deploy a variety of the forms of capital—social, cultural, symbolic, and economic—at play in the field. The field and agents draw, in a variety of ways, on the pre-existing work done to this point in time, which is held in the domain of game audio. This domain of knowledge contributes to the creation of novel and valued things by being the archive, canon, and catalyst for creative action.

Finally, we claim that all parts of the system—the agent, the field, and the domain—interact together, to afford the possibility of creative action. We conclude that it is the working of this creative system within the game industry which results in the emergence of multipath soundtracks for video games. This is how game audio comes into being.

Acknowledgments

Portions of this material were made possible through funding from an Australian Research Council grant, LP130100348 *Creativity and Cultural Production in the Hunter: An Applied Ethnographic Study of New Entrepreneurial Systems in the Creative Industries.* We acknowledge the assistance and insights generously offered to us by Isaac McIntyre, Australian editor for Dexerto.com.

Note

1. This research has been contributed to by researchers from disciplines such as philosophy (Paul and Kaufman 2014; Niu and Sternberg 2006), education (Bailin 1988), literary theory (Pope 2005), communication (McIntyre et al. 2016), cultural studies (McRobbie 2016), sociology (e.g., Wolff 1981; Zolberg 1990; Peterson 1976, 1982, 1985; Becker 1982; Bourdieu 1993), and psychology (e.g., Freud 1959; Bergquist 1999; Weisberg 1993; Greenfield 2008; Amabile 1983, 1996; Csikszentmihalyi 1988; Glăveanu 2014). Extensive summaries of this body of research are also extant (e.g., see Alexander 2003; Negus and Pickering 2004; Pope 2005; Sawyer 2006, 2011; McIntyre et al. 2018; and Thompson 2019).

References

Adams, Ernest W. 2003. *Break Into the Game Industry: How to Get a Job Making Video Games*. Emeryville, CA: McGraw-Hill/Osborne Media.

Alexander, Victoria. 2003. *Sociology of the Arts: Exploring Fine and Popular Forms*. Malden, MA: Blackwell.

Alten, Stanley. 2014. *Audio in Media*. 10th ed. Sydney: Wadsworth Cengage Learning.

Amabile, Teresa. 1983. *The Social Psychology of Creativity*. New York: Springer-Verlag.

Amabile, Teresa. 1996. *Creativity in Context*. Boulder, CO: Westview Press.

Aristotle. 1960. *Metaphysics*. Translated by R. Hope. Ann Arbor: Michigan University Press.

Bailin, Sharon. 1988. *Achieving Extraordinary Ends: An Essay on Creativity*. Dordrecht: Kluwer Academic Publishers.

Bay, Jason. 2021a. "How to Become a Video Game Audio Implementer: Game Industry Career Guide." Accessed July 15, 2021. https://www.gameindustrycareerguide.com/how-to-become-a-video-game-audio-implementer/.

Bay, Jason. 2021b. "Video Game Audio Engineer Salary for 2021: Game Industry Career Guide." Accessed July 15, 2021. https://www.gameindustrycareerguide.com/video-game-audio-engineer-salary/.

Becker, Howard. 1982. *Art Worlds*. Los Angeles: University of California Press.

Bergquist, Carlisle. 1999. "A Comparative View of Creativity Theories: Psychoanalytic, Behaviouristic and Humanistic." *Vantage Quest*. Accessed February 5, 2024. http://www.vantagequest.org/trees/comparative.htm.

Boden, M. 2004. *The Creative Mind: Myths and Mechanisms*. 2nd ed. London: Routledge.

Bourdieu, Pierre. 1977. *Outline of a Theory of Practice*. Cambridge: Cambridge University Press.

Bourdieu, Pierre. 1986. "The Forms of Capital." In *Handbook of Theory and Research for the Sociology of Education*, edited by John Richardson, 241–258. New York: Greenwood Press.

Bourdieu, Pierre. 1993. *The Field of Cultural Production*. New York: Columbia University Press.

Bourdieu, Pierre. 1996. *The Rules of Art: Genesis and Structure of the Literary Field*. Cambridge: Polity Press.

Bridgett, Rob. 2021. *Leading with Sound: Proactive Sound Practices in Video Game Development*. 1st ed. London: Routledge.

Capra, Fritjof, and Pier Luisi. 2014. *The Systems View of Life: A Unifying Vision*. Cambridge: Cambridge University Press.

Criticos, Harry. 2021. "The Constrabling Effect of Internet Radio." *Journal of Radio and Audio Media*. Accessed July 14, 2021. https://www.tandfonline.com/eprint/4RC6ZVW79HJYCXPTYJP9/full?target=10.1080/19376529.2021.1937629.

Csikszentmihalyi, Mihaly. 1988. "Society, Culture and Person: A Systems View of Creativity." In *The Nature of Creativity*, edited by Robert Sternberg, 325–338. New York: Cambridge University Press.

Csikszentmihalyi, Mihaly. 1997. *Creativity: Flow and the Psychology of Discovery and Invention*. New York: HarperCollins.

Csikszentmihalyi, Mihaly. 2014. *The Systems Model of Creativity: The Collected Works of Mihaly Csikszentmihalyi*. Dordrecht: Springer.

Csikszentmihalyi, Mihaly, and Isabella Csikszentmihalyi, eds. 1988. *Optimal Experience: Psychological Studies of Flow in Consciousness*. New York: Cambridge University Press.

Freud, Sigmund. 1959. "The Relation of the Poet to Daydreaming." In *Collected Papers*, Vol. 4, edited by Ernest Jones, 178–183. London: Hogarth.

Gibson, James. 1966. *The Senses Considered as Perceptual Systems*. Boston: Houghton Mifflin.

Glăveanu, Vlad. 2014. *Distributed Creativity: Thinking outside the Box of the Creative Individual*. New York: Springer.

Greenfield, Susan. 2008. "Creating Creative Brains." In *Creating Value: Between Commerce and Commons Conference*, June 25–27, 2008. Brisbane: Centre for Creative Industries and Innovation QUT. Accessed July 29, 2009. http://cultural-science.org/creatingvaluesusan1.html.

Greenwald, Will. 2021. "The Best Game Streaming Services for 2021: PCMag Australia." June 15, 2021. Accessed July 16, 2021. https://au.pcmag.com/game-streaming-services/86545/the-best-game-streaming-services-for-2021.

Hennessey, Beth. 2017. "Taking a Systems View of Creativity: On the Right Path toward Understanding." *Journal of Creative Behaviour* 51 (4): 341–344.

Hennessey, Beth, and Teresa Amabile. 2010. "Creativity." *Annual Review of Psychology* 61:569–598.

Hughes, Sam. 2014. "Interview with Irrational Games' Senior Sound Designer, Jeff Seamster: The Sound Architect." Accessed July 19, 2021. https://www.thesoundarchitect.co.uk/jeffseamster/.

Inglis, Sam. 2002. "Music & Sound Design for Video Games: Sound on Sound." Accessed July 14, 2021. https://www.soundonsound.com/techniques/music-sound-design-video-games.

Johnson, Randall, ed. 1993. "Editor's Introduction." In *The Field of Cultural Production*, by Pierre Bourdieu, 1–25. New York: Columbia University Press.

Keighley, Geoff. 2021. "About." thegameawards.com. Accessed July 18, 2021. https://thegameawards.com/about.

Levinson, Paul. 2006. "Electronic Watermarks: A High Profile for Intellectual Property in the Digital Age." In *Communication Theories: Critical Concepts in Media and Cultural Studies*, edited by Paul Cobley, 53–66. London: Routledge.

Lovato, Nathan. 2017. "Our 9 Sound Design Tips to Improve Your Game's Audio: Insight Hub: Game Analytics." Accessed July 16, 2021. https://gameanalytics.com/blog/9-sound-design-tips-to-improve-your-games-audio/.

Lukefollows11. 2013. "Organisational Structures in the Games Industry." *Lukefollows11.wordpress.com*. Accessed September 20, 2013. https://lukefollows11.wordpress.com/2013/09/20/organisational-structures-in-the-games-industry/.

McIntyre, Phillip. 2009. "Rethinking Communication, Creativity and Cultural Production: Outlining Issues for Media Practice." In *Communication, Creativity and Global Citizenship: Refereed Proceedings of the Australian and New Zealand Communications Association Annual Conference*, edited by Terry Flew, Brisbane, July 8–10. http://www.proceedings.anzca09.org.

McIntyre, Phillip. 2012. *Creativity and Cultural Production: Issues for Media Practice*. Basingstoke, UK: Palgrave Macmillan.

McIntyre, Phillip. 2013. "Creativity as a System in Action." In *Handbook of Creativity Research*, edited by Janet Chan and Kerry Thomas, 84–97. London: Edward Elgar.

McIntyre, Phillip. 2021. "Songwriting Practice and Production: The Past, Present and Future." *Songwriting Studies Journal* 1 (1): 5–26.

McIntyre, Phillip, Mark Balnaves, Susan Kerrigan, Evelyn King, and Claire Williams. 2019. "Creativity and Cultural Production in the Hunter: An Applied Ethnographic Study of New Entrepreneurial Systems in the Creative Industries." Accessed July 16, 2021. https://soci.newcastle.edu.au/hci/the-project/publications/.

McIntyre, Phillip, Janet Fulton, and Elizabeth Paton, eds. 2016. *The Creative System in Action: Understanding Cultural Production and Practice*. Basingstoke, UK: Palgrave MacMillan.

McIntyre, Phillip, Janet Fulton, Elizabeth Paton, Susan Kerrigan, and Michael Meany. 2018. *Educating for Creativity within Higher Education: Integration of Research with Media Practice*. Basingstoke, UK: Palgrave MacMillan.

McRobbie, Angela. 2016. *Be Creative: Making a Living in the New Culture Industries*. Cambridge: Polity Press.

Montuori, Alfonos. 2011. "Systems Approach." In *Encyclopedia of Creativity*, 2nd ed., edited by Mark Runco and Stephen Pritzker, 2: 414–421. London: Academic Press.

Negus, Keith, and Michael Pickering. 2004. *Creativity, Communication and Cultural Value*. London: Sage.

Newzoo. 2020. "Newzoo Global Games Market Report 2020: Newzoo.com." Accessed July 16, 2021. https://newzoo.com/insights/trend-reports/newzoo-global-games-market-report-2020-light-version/.

Niu, Weihai, and Robert Sternberg. 2006. "The Philosophical Roots of Western and Eastern Conceptions of Creativity." *Journal of Theoretical and Philosophical Psychology* 26:18–38.

Paul, Elliot, and Scott Kaufman. 2014. *The Philosophy of Creativity*. Oxford: Oxford University Press.

Peterson, Richard. 1976. *The Production of Culture*. Los Angeles: Sage.

Peterson, Richard. 1982. "Five Constraints on the Production of Culture: Law, Technology, Market, Organizational Structure and Occupational Careers." *Journal of Popular Culture* 17:143–153.

Peterson, Richard. 1985. "Six Constraints on the Production of Literary Works." *Poetics* 14:45–67.

Pope, Rob. 2005. *Creativity: Theory, History, Practice*. New York: Routledge.

Rothenberg, Albert, and Carl Hausman, eds. 1976. *The Creativity Question: A Reader*. Durham, NC: Duke University Press.

Runco, Mark, and Garrett Jaeger. 2012. "The Standard Definition of Creativity." *Creativity Research Journal* 24 (1): 92–96.

Sawyer, Keith. 2006. *Explaining Creativity: The Science of Human Innovation*. Oxford: Oxford University Press.

Sawyer, Keith. 2010. "Individual and Group Creativity." In *The Cambridge Handbook of Creativity*, edited by James Kaufman and Robert Sternberg, 366–380. Cambridge: Cambridge University Press.

Sawyer, Keith. 2012. *Explaining Creativity: The Science of Human Innovation*. 2nd ed. Oxford: Oxford University Press.

Schirato, Tony, and Susan Yell. 1996. *Communication and Cultural Literacy: An Introduction*. Sydney: Allen & Unwin.

Simonton, Dean Keith. 2003. "Creative Cultures, Nations and Civilisations: Strategies and Results." In *Group Creativity: Innovation through Collaboration*, edited by Paul Paulus and Bernard Nijstad, 304–325. Oxford: Oxford University Press.

Sinclair, Jean-Luc. 2020. *Principles of Game Audio and Sound Design: Sound Design and Audio Implementation for Interactive and Immersive Media*, 1st ed. New York: Focal Press.

Staines, Dan. 2017. "Unsung Heroes of the Games Industry: Sound Designers: IGN.com." Accessed July 15, 2021. https://www.ign.com/articles/2017/01/30/unsung-heroes-of-the-games-industry-sound-designers.

Suckerpunch. 2021. "News." suckerpunch.com. Accessed July 18, 2021. https://www.suckerpunch.com/category/news/.

Swartz, David. 1997. *Culture and Power: The Sociology of Pierre Bourdieu*. Chicago: University of Chicago Press.

Thakkar, Akash. 2018. *Maximizing Game Feel through Sound: A Composer/Sound Designer's Approach to Upgrading Your Game's Impact*. Los Angeles: Thakkar Audio, LLC.

Thakkar, Akash. 2021. "5 Minute Sound Designer: 4 Essential Techniques." akashthakkar.com. Accessed July 14, 2021. https://www.akashthakkar.com/videos.

Thompson, Paul. 2019. *Creativity in the Recording Studio: Alternative Takes*. Basingstoke, UK: Palgrave MacMillan.

Truax, Barry. 1999. *Handbook of Acoustic Ecology*. 2nd ed. Accessed December 27, 2021. http://www.sfu.ca/sonic-studio-webdav/handbook/index.htmlruax.

Velikovsky, Joe. 2013. "On Sound and Music in Games." Unpublished paper, University of Newcastle. September 11, 2013.

Velikovsky, Joe. 2016. "Communication, Creativity and Consilience in Cinema: A Comparative Study of the Top 20 Return-on-Investment (RoI) Movies and the Doxa of Screenwriting." PhD Thesis, University of Newcastle. Accessed July 12, 2021. http://hdl.handle.net/1959.13/1324018.

Velikovsky, Joe. 2021. "The Cultural Evolution of Aesthetics, Production Values & Sound Design in Videogame Audio." Unpublished paper, University of Newcastle, June 24, 2020.

Watson, Peter. 2005. *Ideas: A History from Fire to Freud*. London: Weidenfeld & Nicolson.

Weisberg, Robert. 1993. *Creativity: Beyond the Myth of Genius*. New York: W.H. Freeman and Co.

Wikipedia. 2021. "Game Audio Network Guild Awards." Accessed July 18, 2021. https://en.wikipedia.org/wiki/Game_Audio_Network_Guild_Awards.

Williams, Dmitri, and Jaideep Srivastava. 2014. "History and Structure of the Video Game Industry." ninjametrics. Accessed October 8, 2021. https://www.ninjametrics.com/tag/history-and-structure-of-video-game-industry/.

Wolff, Janet. 1981. *The Social Production of Art*. London: MacMillan.

Zolberg, Vera. 1990. *Constructing a Sociology of the Arts*. Cambridge: Cambridge University Press.

SECTION 2

HISTORY AND TECHNOLOGY

CHAPTER 6

A HISTORY OF EARLY US PINBALL SOUND, 1871–1939

NEIL LERNER

INTRODUCTION

THE term "video game" may appear to have an obvious definition, but it can actually be deceptively complicated to parse.[1] It is usually understood to mean some kind of amusement, possibly competitive but sometimes just for the sake of experiencing a simulation, that involves an interaction with a video screen that might be a dedicated video monitor, a television set, a tablet, a smart phone, or any other device in which the play of light signals something to our brains. Contained within the phrase, dulled, or perhaps completely erased because of its seemingly ubiquitous familiarity, is the Latin verb meaning "I see." While there have been some video games that partially or fully remove the visual element in favor of focusing on only the sound, most video games rely heavily on a player's ability to see. Yet to think of video games as a purely visual medium would be wildly inaccurate. Just as the early history of film began with a period of so-called silent film—directing attention away from the audio experience because most of their music was performed live at that particular moment and was thus ephemeral—so too do video games have an initial phase of lacking synchronized sounds as part of the gameplay. Melanie Fritsch (2013, 12) asserts that the first video games, from the 1950s and 1960s, were silent. Karen Collins (2008, 8) points to *Pong* (1972) as the moment when sound arrived with video games, though the far less successful but earlier coin-operated video game *Computer Space* (1971) did include white noise to represent rocket sounds and explosions.[2] Given *Pong*'s breakthrough success, it is reasonable to regard 1972 as the beginning of the sound era of video games, with earlier video games falling into what might be considered the genre's silent era.

Just as the young genre of film adopted many of its musical practices from the existing models of musical multimedia like melodrama, opera, pantomime, and program music, video games also drew from existing models for music and sound in coin-operated gaming contexts. Indeed, Julie Hubbert's (2011, 2) astute observation that the institutional practices of early film sound challenges "the assumption that the sound of film music was standardized or 'classicized' by Hollywood composers of the 1930s and 1940s" because composers like Max Steiner were drawing on "the culmination of three decades of silent film music experimentation," so too does the model for sound and music in video games of the 1970s parallel their being the culmination of nearly a century of prior experimentation in pinball sound and music. Pinball would have been the most dominant form of coin-operated amusements in the early 1970s. Video games incorporated a number of basic design principles from pinball, including the basic structure of the activity being something offering a limited number of chances in exchange for a coin, whether those chances were the number of balls in a game or the number of bases or lives in a game of *Space Invaders*. But creators of early video game sound and music could also learn from the lessons of pinball's several decades of prior existence, and thereby approach game sound as both a way to signal important information to a player (such as a scoring achievement or mastery of a certain game challenge) and as a way to draw players into the game by using sound in a ballyhoo fashion.

Pinball has always been a game that offered players not just visual input but also audible effects. From the initial thunk of a spring-driven plunger against a metal ball, sending it careening to the top of the playfield, to the calming almost ocean-like ambient sounds of the ball rolling down the playfield, pinball can be an experience for the ears as well as the eyes. As gravity pulls the ball down toward the drain (also known as the outhole), the ball creates sounds as it makes contact with elements such as bumpers, ramps, or spinners. In its earliest iterations, before pinball and in the era of the bagatelle, those playfield elements were usually just nails driven into the wood (the metal pins gave pinball its modern name) and perhaps a bell or two. When the electromechanical era of pinball began in late 1933, sounds from clicking solenoids and doorbell-like ringing elements entered into the mix. With the introduction of automated scoring, the clicking of scoring drums added another element that would become familiar, as would the chiming bell sounds that indicated different scoring achievements. One of the most beloved sounds from pinball machines in that era was the powerful thwack of a solenoid striking metal or the side of the cabinet, announcing to anyone within earshot that a free game had been won, while also indicating it even more powerfully to the player through the physical vibrations set off within the game's cabinet. As solid-state machines began to dominate the industry in the mid- to late-1970s, sound could now be synthesized and played through speakers. By the late twentieth and early twenty-first centuries, pinball sounds came to include synthesized and sampled sounds of increasingly higher definitions and elaborately tied to rapid changes in gameplay states.

Despite the remarkable outpouring of new research into video game music and sound over the past 15 years, music scholars have given relatively little attention to games from the important formative decade of the 1970s, or to earlier coin-operated but nonvideo games like pinball, whose corporate and manufacturing infrastructure was necessary for the emergence of the video game industry as it developed in the United States.[3] In her pioneering study of music in video games, Collins (2008) posits that the prehistory of video game music can be found in the sounds of much earlier mechanical coin-operated games like slot machines, bagatelle, and pinball. Collins (2016) develops this hypothesis further, tracing the history of various sounds, sounds she categorizes as voice, sound effects, and music, through electromechanical coin-operated machines. Collins's observations open up an important new chapter in the story of sound and music in video games, but there are still significant gaps and questions for even the most well documented part of this story. By exploring in some detail how pinball's sounds and music developed, from its origins in the 19th century and up to the beginning of pinball's electromechanical era in the mid-1930s, we can begin to piece together a clearer chronology of when these innovations occurred, who was responsible for them, and why they might have been added. In sharpening our understanding of the history of early pinball sounds, we can also begin to sharpen our understanding of how early video game sounds developed.

The Origins of Pinball Sounds in Bagatelle

Before there was pinball, there was bagatelle, a recreational activity dating back at least to the 17th century in Europe and thought to be an indoors adaptation of the outside activity of bowling on the green (Bueschel 1988, 14). The activity of bowling became an interior activity through reducing the size of the pins and pushing balls with a stick on a board instead of rolling balls along the ground. The basic principle of bagatelle was to project a ball with a stick (or cue) around a table set at an incline so that the ball would then roll down into various scoring areas. By the third quarter of the 19th century, bagatelle was common enough in the United States to be used as the setting for a famous political cartoon from the presidential campaign of 1864. Titled "A Little Game of Bagatelle, between Old Abe the Rail Splitter & Little Mac the Gunboat General," the cartoon features incumbent candidate Abraham Lincoln (holding a cue titled "Baltimore," the location of the Republican convention) and taking aim on what is called "The Union Board"; Democratic nominee McClellan sits to the side, holding a "Chicago" cue, referring to the location of the Democratic party's convention (see Figure 6.1).[4]

Bagatelle underwent an important transformation in the 1870s, making possible a new kind of play that eliminated the cue and instead used a novel technology to launch the ball up the board. Pinball historian Richard M. Bueschel (1988, 37) proclaims Montague Redgrave's invention of a spring-loaded ball shooter (or plunger) as "the single most significant patent in pinball history," explaining that the addition of the newly produced steel spiral spring—an important building block to a number of inventions from the late 1860s and 1870s, including the telephone, typewriter, electric light, gasoline engine, and even what he calls "the lowly paper clip"—brought an important new wrinkle of skill control to the game, one that has persisted throughout pinball's history. This game, known to

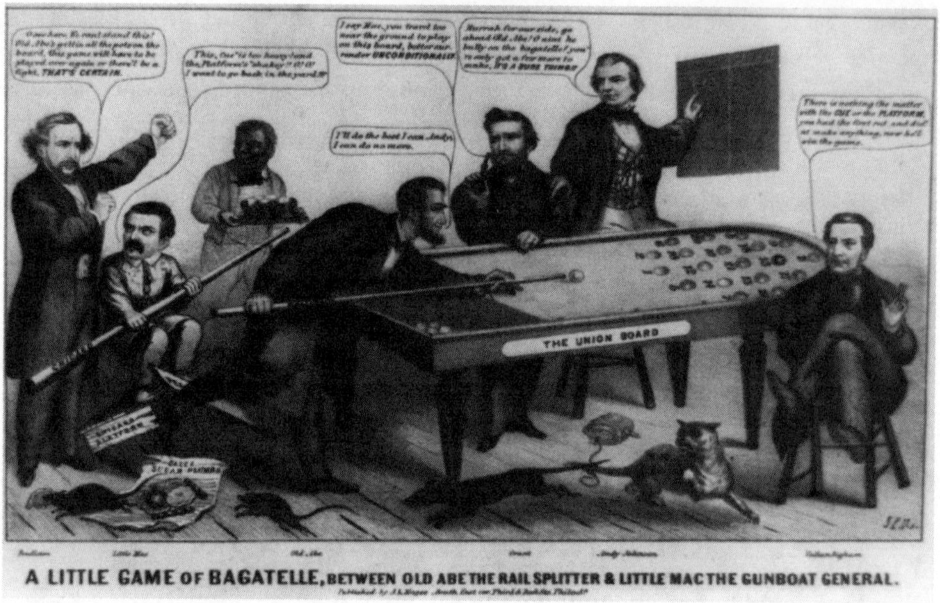

FIGURE 6.1 Political cartoon from 1864, "A Little Game of Bagatelle."

pinball historians by its patent title as *Improvements in Bagatelle* (1871), was completely mechanical in its design, utilizing the potential energy stored in the spring as a result of pulling back on the knob, and then relying on gravity and friction for the ball to make its way down to the bottom of the board and into various scoring pockets. In Figure 6.2, the diagram from Redgrave's patent application, the board contains two bells surrounded by thin nails (or pins) that demarcate different scoring regions (which in later games would be called "holes" or "pockets"). Even in this primordial Ur-pinball game, long before pinball even had bumpers or flippers, the sound of bells was one of its core features.

Additional evidence in the form of patent applications and advertising materials demonstrates the early and valued presence of bells in bagatelle boards. The 1876 game board shown in Figure 6.3 indicates three prominently placed bells, two along the top scoring area when 100 points and one in the more difficult middle part of the board to announce the scoring of 1,000 points. A games and sporting goods catalog from 1886 offered no fewer than six bagatelle tables for sale, ranging in price from $1 to the fanciest model, a $20 beast described as being "5 feet long, by 2 feet and 6 inches wide, covered with billiard cloth, rich black walnut frame, mounted with one silver and four brass bells, silver plate and screws, and suitable for the most handsomely furnished parlor or drawing-room."[5] The next most expensive board was $10.50 and featured one silver and the more modest number of only two brass bells. A patent from 1901 offered as a novel innovation the shifting of the bells from being situated directly on the board (thereby allowing the ball to directly strike the bell as the ball rolled downward) and instead moved the bell into a position hanging over the board and now only triggered when the ball went into a specially designed trap door (see Figure 6.4). The proliferation

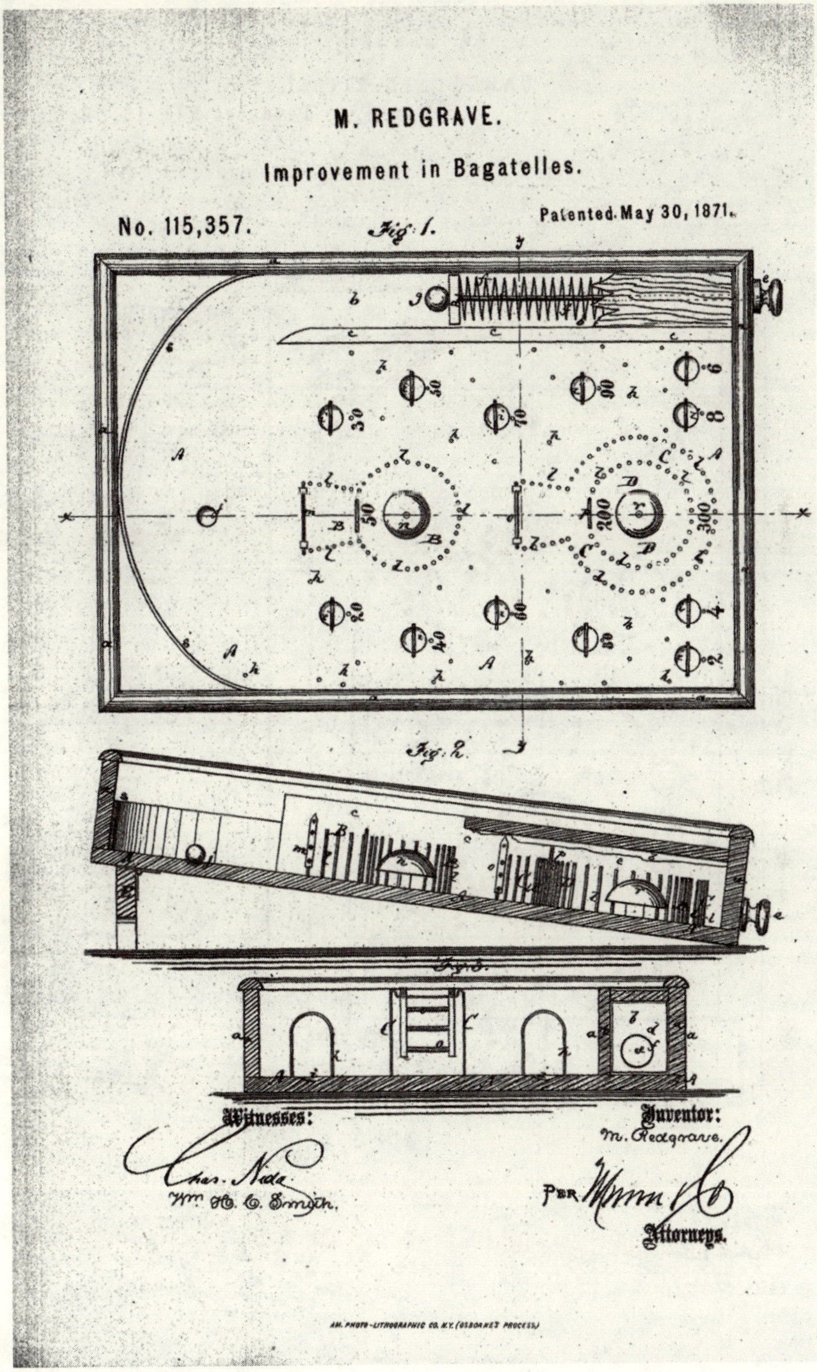

FIGURE 6.2 Redgrave's "Improvements in Bagatelles," showing the central placement of two bells (1871).

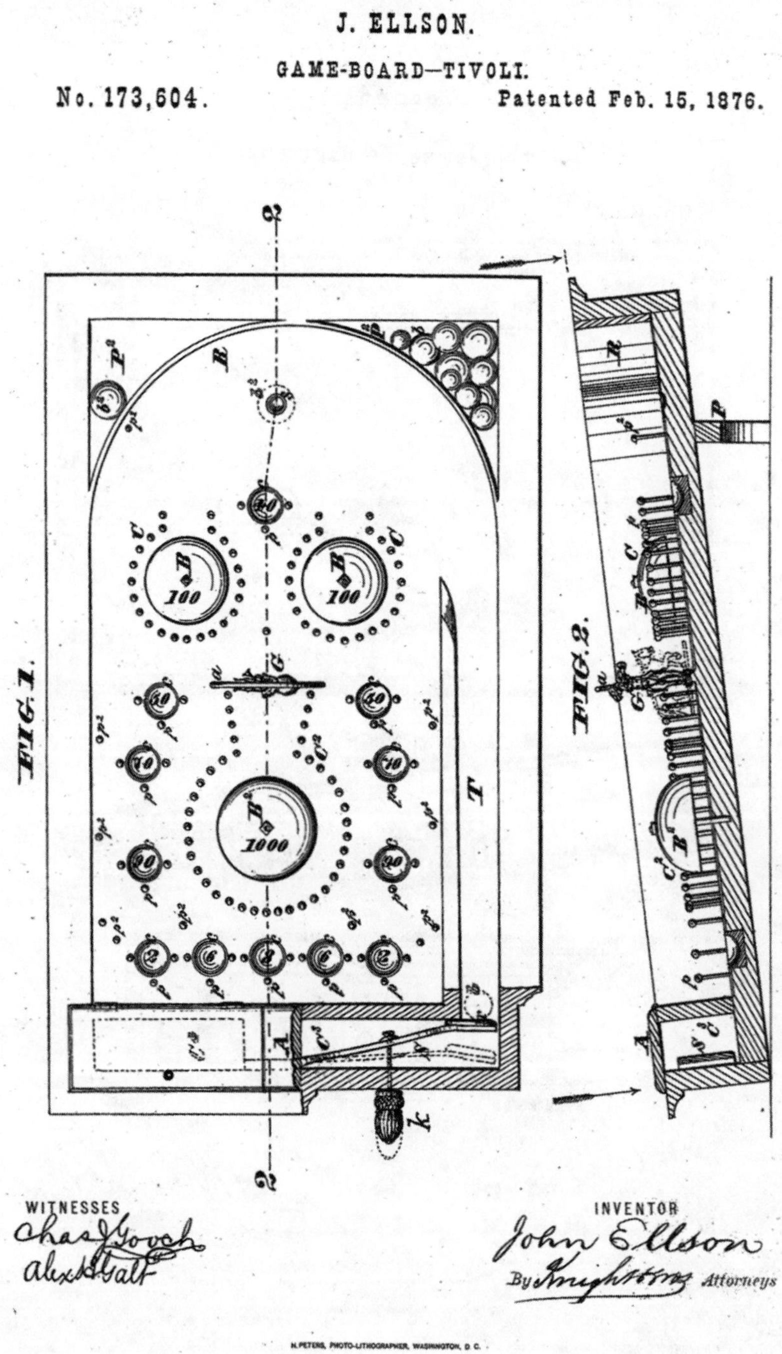

FIGURE 6.3 An 1876 patent showing the addition of bells to a bagatelle playfield; here, getting the ball in the top two pockets would score 100 points and ring a bell, while the more difficult to reach pocket in the middle would score 1,000 points and ring the bell.

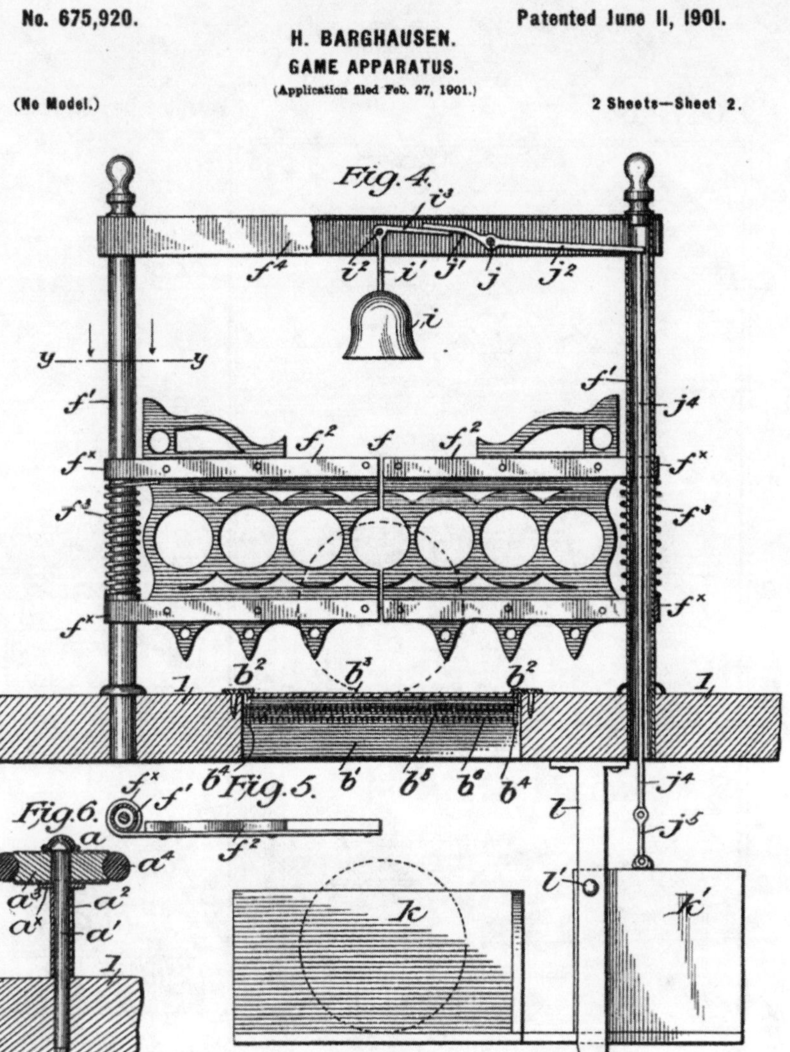

FIGURE 6.4 Patent for a 1901 design that placed a bell above, instead of on or below, the playfield.

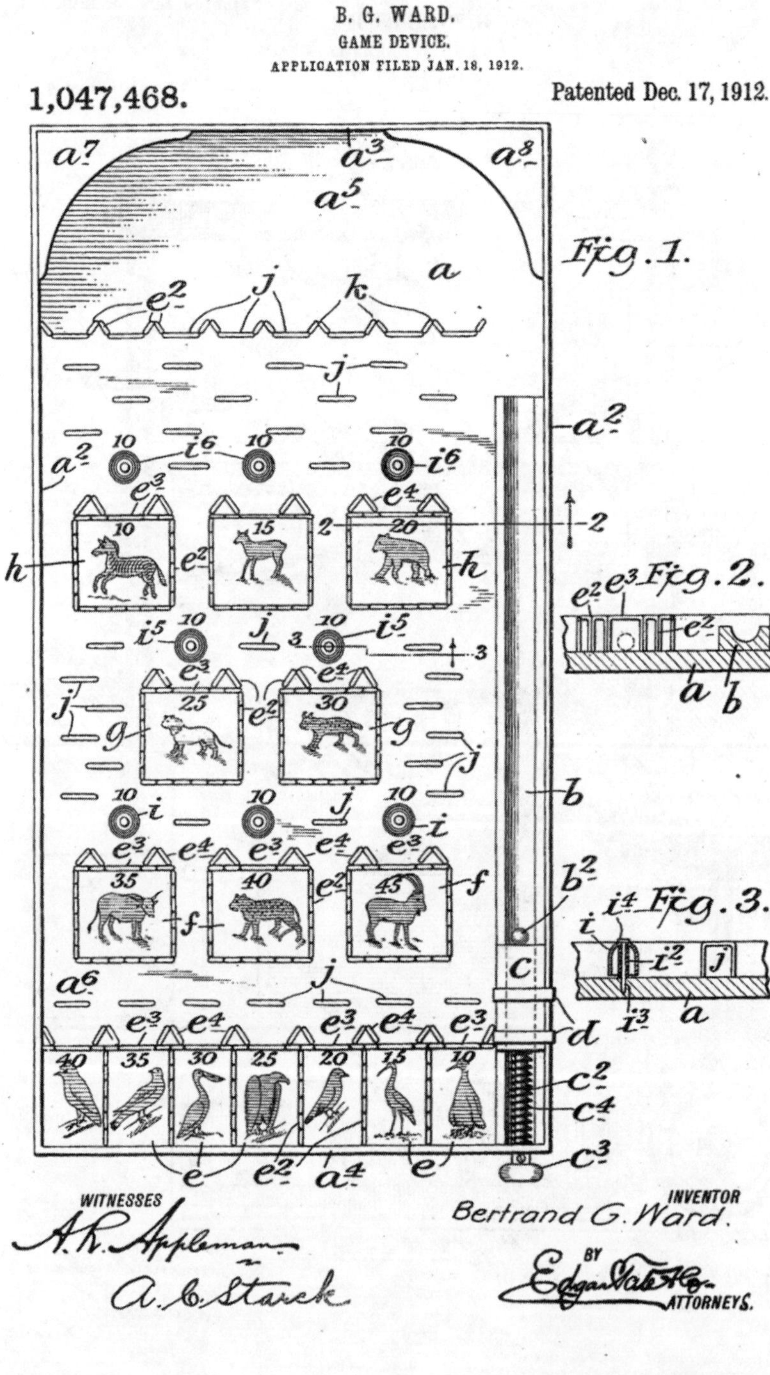

FIGURE 6.5 A 1912 patent for a bagatelle board with eight bells (each bell is indicated on the diagram with the letter "i").

of bells in bagatelle design can be seen in the 1912 patent that featured eight bells, each of them situated immediately above different scoring boxes (see Figure 6.5, wherein each bell is identified with the letter "i").

FROM BAGATELLE TO PINBALL

While many histories of pinball highlight the early 1930s as the moment when pinball emerged as a popular new entertainment in the United States—usually drawing attention to the highly relevant conditions of the Great Depression and the need for inexpensive diversions that could be played for a penny or a nickel—the basic concept of a coin-operated device that involved the projecting of balls around an inclined playfield was already in place in the early 1890s. Bueschel (1996, 9–10) points to an invention by Charles P. Young, of York, Pennsylvania, who in 1892 patented an invention called the *Coin Game Board*. Young's patent application took the pin-studded and glass-covered inclined playfield of bagatelle as prior art and argued its new innovation was its coin slot that allowed the game to be presented as a revenue-generating device. In 1901, Adolphe and Art Caille released a machine called *Log Cabin* that became one of the most successful games in this transitional moment between bagatelle and pinball. Like all games at this time, the player had limited control: flippers would not be added to pinball machines until after World War II, so these games only allowed player control in the form of how much force was applied to the initial shooting out of the ball or some sort of moving or shaking of the machine itself. Because the player had relatively little to do in the era before flippers, other elements of the game like sound could take on more important roles. Still, neither the *Coin Game Board* nor *Log Cabin* used bells, so the only sounds would have been the ones coming from engaging the ball plunger and the ball rolling down the playfield and occasionally striking the metal pins.

A major success occurred with the invention of Myrl Park, Earl Froom, and Arthur Paulin (Yohio Manufacturing Company, later to become Automatic Industries): a pinball game called *Whiffle* that appeared in the spring of 1931 (Bueschel 1988, 92). At this time, they were still not called "pin tables" or "pinball machines" but rather something with the word "marble" in it: marble board, marble game, or marble table, and a player obsessed with the game might be called a "marble-game maniac," like the character in William Saroyan's 1939 play *The Time of Your Life* (Bueschel 1988, 101).[6] Within a few days of the release of *Whiffle*, the In & Outdoors Games Company released another successful early game called *Whoopee* (Bueschel 1988, 94). Around this time, the Hercules Novelty Company released a marble game (*Roll-A-Ball*) that eschewed the usual five balls for the price of five cents and instead discounted the price to five balls for a penny (Bueschel 1988, 102). With these early successes, more companies jumped into the business and by the end of 1931, pinball's first major hit was released: D. Gottlieb & Company's *Baffle Ball*, the first pinball machine thought to have sold 50,000 or more units (Sharpe 1977, 33). Ray Maloney, who had begun his work in pinball as a distributor with David Gottlieb, left to create his own manufacturing company when he found the supply for *Baffle Ball* was unable to keep up with the demand. Maloney released a game in early 1932 called *Ballyhoo*, which took its name from a humor magazine of its time. That game would also soon go on to sell around 75,000 units and Maloney named his new company after it: Bally (Sharpe 1977, 34; Bueschel 1996, 27–28, 244).

Despite being named after the loud sounds, music, and shouting that were used in the era of the nickelodeon (and before) to draw in crowds, *Ballyhoo* was relatively undistinguished in terms of its own sound capabilities. Like *Baffle Ball*, and even *Whiffle* and *Whoopee* before it, it contained no bells as so many earlier bagatelle games had done. Bells, however, were not new to coin-operated amusements, having been used frequently with another coin-operated machine: the slot machine. Collins (2016) describes how catalogs for slot machines from the early 20th century sometimes marketed the important function of a bell ringing when a prize is won, thereby alerting operators of a winning jackpot but also if someone might have been cheating.[7] Bells had also been used in coin-operated shooting machines like *Rifle Range* (1929), advertised in *Automatic Age* with the heading "DING! Goes the bell, *another bullseye*!" with an image of a woman sitting with one foot on a stool, holding the game's gun and aiming it inside the machine.[8] Advertisements for new pinball machines in trade publications began to highlight bells as a selling feature as early as 1932. An ad for a game called *Bell Ball* (Reisinger Machine Works) says "it is thrilling—with the sound of the Bell doubling the score."[9] The Genco Manufacturing Company's 1934 game *Step Up* has an ad in *Billboard* that proclaims the game has "ALL the Features the players want: The 4-Note Musical Chime for a Real Thrill when the ball enters the Step Up hole" and, elsewhere, the ad has the words "with the 4 musical chimes" next to the icons of some musical notes just floating in space.[10] *Bell Ball* and *Step Up* were purely mechanical pinball machines, so the chiming sounds were created when balls propelled by gravity hit bells inside the machine and not through an electrical motor causing something to strike metal for the sound.[11] But the mechanical era of pinball was about to come to an electrifying end.

Pinball Adds Electricity: *Contact* and Sound in the Electromechanical Era

To the extent that sound gets mentioned in pinball histories—which is minimal—there is consensus that a monumental step forward in the use of sound in pinball occurred with Harry Williams's groundbreaking game, *Contact* (Pacific Amusement Manufacturing, 1933).[12] Lauded for being the first pinball machine with electromechanical elements—it had a solenoid running on direct current from a dry cell battery that would kick a ball out of a hole and into a higher scoring hole lower on the playfield when a second ball landed in the "contact" hole—*Contact* is important here for its inclusion of an electric bell that would be activated whenever the solenoid was triggered. There had been earlier games that used electricity for scoring lights. Harry Reed of Salem, Massachusetts, had created a Redgrave-like board that had lights to indicate scores with *Electric Bagatelle*, 1906 (Bueschel 1996, 11), and a 1931 game, *Electric Baseball* (Hercules Novelty Company) had an electric sound that John Goodbody, writing in the pages of

Automatic Age, described as possessing the "improvement" of "now hav[ing] a buzzer on the home run hole. This is a decided improvement and the storekeeper can now tell a home run without looking at the machine at all, if he is busy."[13] An October 1931 ad for *Electric Baseball* declares that "a buzzer rings every time the home run is made" and a June 1931 ad indicates that the buzzer was an add-on feature: "Buzzer for home run 50 cents extra."[14]

The story of how Williams came up with the idea of adding an electric bell is frequently told, but with some important differences. A 1960 profile about Williams in *True* magazine indicates that the bell was not initially present in the game and asserts that *Contact*'s "clattering solenoids and jangling electric bells had sounded the death knell of the mechanical pin game and every big-time company in Chicago knew it."[15] Roger Sharpe (1977) relied on personal interviews with Harry Williams when writing his book on pinball, and this telling of the story shares that the addition of the bell was a practical joke on his coworker, Fred McClellan.[16] While McClellan waited in the office for sales requests, other coworkers played the modified version of *Contact* (with the electric bell), and each time the bell in the game rang, McClellan ran to the phone to take an order, only to find no one on the line. After some of the other workers could no longer control their urge to laugh and the prank was revealed, one of them liked the bell so much that he tried an experiment with two machines. One machine had the original design without the bell, and the other one did have the bell. They set them up next to each other and discovered that the one with the bell "took in double the money of the other" (Sharpe 1977, 40). A nearly identical story is relayed in Natkin and Kirk's book, *All About Pinball*, also from 1977; it says the bell rang five or six times instead of four before McClellan figured out the ruse, and it also says that when the two versions were placed side by side, the one without the bell was played by "no one," a likely hyperbolic exaggeration.[17] A 1979 retelling of the incident changes the players of the bell-equipped *Contact* from other coworkers to Fred McClellan.[18]

Pinball historian Russ Jensen posted online his recollections of several conversations with Harry Williams in the early 1980s. Jensen writes that during a phone conversation on April 7, 1982, he asked Williams about the use of the tilt mechanism (another innovation for which Williams gets some credit) and the bells on *Contact*. Jensen then explains that Williams "said the first models had neither attachment, but that both were added somewhere during the first 100 games produced."[19] This detail is consistent with the patent Williams filed on December 18, 1933 (and not approved until March 9, 1937), which only puts forth the electrical solenoid action as the innovation here to pinball game designs.[20] (See Figure 6.6.) Bueschel adds one further wrinkle—that the idea for adding a sound in conjunction to the kick-out action of the solenoid was made by Bob Corbin—to the various anecdotes about *Contact*'s bell, relying on a 1993 profile on Jerry Inglis (in *RePlay Magazine*, April 1993) for this contrary explanation: "Harry put two solenoids onto a table spoon and invented the kick-out hole. Bob Corbin suggested putting a door buzzer onto it so each time the ball landed in there, it made a sound and popped back onto the playfield" (Bueschel 1997, 10).[21]

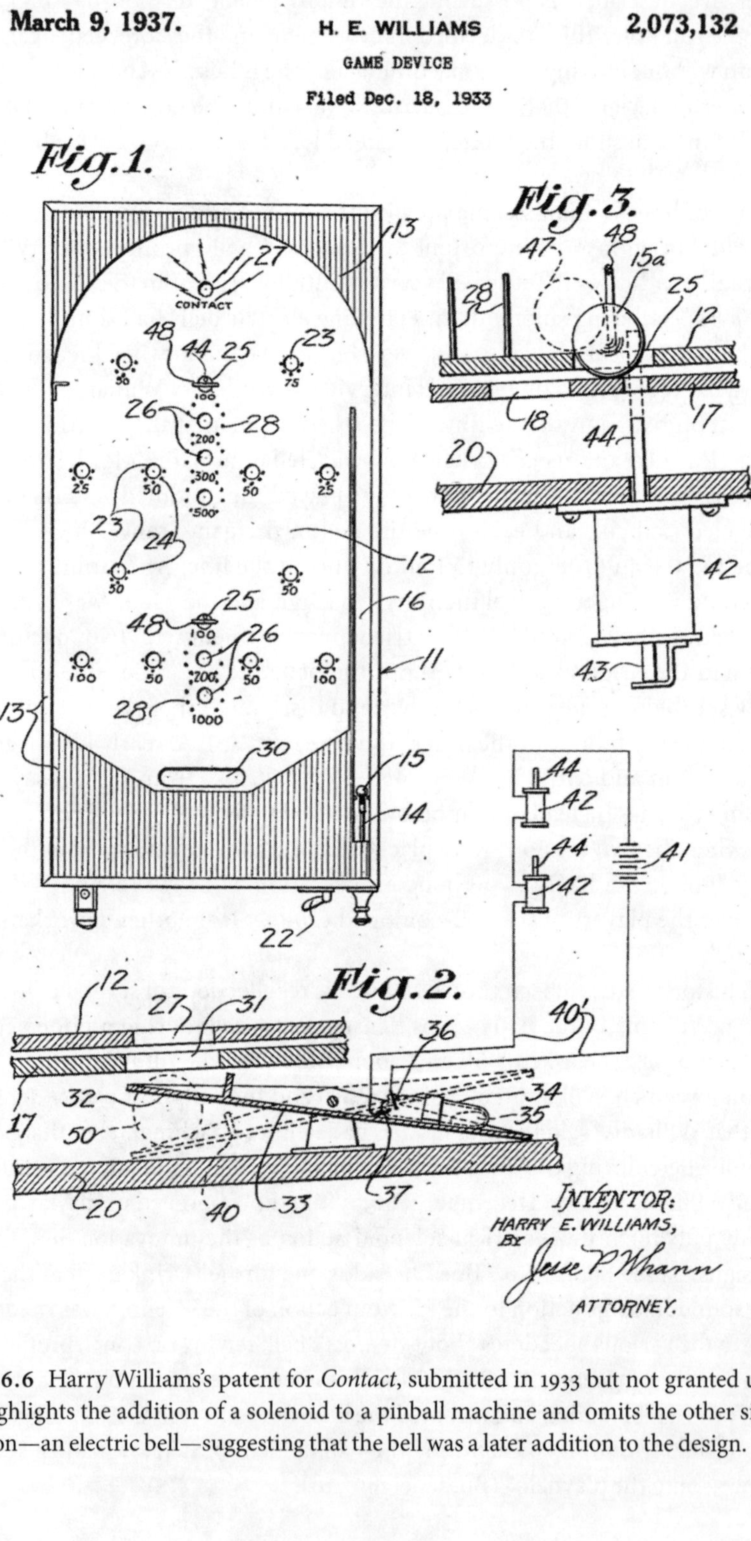

FIGURE 6.6 Harry Williams's patent for *Contact*, submitted in 1933 but not granted until 1937, which highlights the addition of a solenoid to a pinball machine and omits the other significant innovation—an electric bell—suggesting that the bell was a later addition to the design.

Responses to *Contact*'s Revolutionary Bell

Regardless of whether the idea to add the electric bell came after the prank on McClellen or from a suggestion of brother-in-law Bob Corbin, Williams's addition of an electric bell in *Contact* set the standard for nearly all future pinball games and would become the most common type of pinball sound for the next three decades with only a few attempts at other sound effects. Just as pinball manufacturers, for the most part, rushed in the mid-1930s to shift from purely mechanical to electromechanical machines, they also appear to have quickly added an electric bell or even other sound effects, making Williams's innovation one of the milestones in pinball history—arguably the most important change in pinball design prior to the introduction of the electromechanical flipper (in D. Gottlieb & Company's *Humpty Dumpty*, fall 1947). Writing in *Automatic Age* to pinball operators and exhibitors, and indicative of the industry-wide interest in bells, John D. Roberts observed that "players appear to get a bigger 'bang' out of ringing the bells than anything else, so let's give 'em what they want. The slogan should be bigger and more bells per pin game. What say?"[22]

Several new games appeared in 1934 that answered Roberts' plea and used bells. A June 1934 ad for *Contact* leads off with the new game's sound feature, announcing it as "a Bell Ringing—Ball Advancing Game—That Has Created a New Sport and Entertainment for Players—and a Great Source of BIG MONEY for Operators" while a lightning bolt aimed at the Contact hole states that "FIRST when the player puts the ball into this hole, the CONTACT BELL RINGS."[23] (See Figure 6.7.) A number of other games began to advertise themselves as also possessing this new bell-ringing feature.[24] The Daval Company's *American Beauty* (June 1934), a purely mechanical game that thereby lacked *Contact*'s electromechanical operation, nonetheless seems to be capitalizing on *Contact*'s appeal when it lists "Ten Superior *American Beauty* Features," with number nine being "PLAYER APPEAL: . . . Score Totalizer, Ball-O-Meter, and RINGING BELL and CATAPULT features actually hold the players spellbound."[25] Gottlieb's electromechanical game *Relay*, available in junior, senior, and deluxe versions, was advertised as including both bell and battery within its price of $28.[26] An August 1934 advertisement in *Coin Machine Review* promotes the Daval Manufacturing Company's *Big Bertha* as possessing a " 'Range Finder' hole with ringing bell action [that] presents a new style of marksmanship to pin game players" and a few lines later restates that the "bell rings when ball enters 'Range Finder' or 'Reserve' holes."[27] Gottlieb's *Flying Trapeze* (September 1934, though renamed "Senior" when a "Junior" version came out in December) tries to tantalize the potential purchaser by asking them to "hit the 'Allez-Opp' hole and see what happens! A bell rings!"[28]

Not everyone was happy about the wave of tintinnabular stimuli. In a 1934 column about how to make mechanical and electrical adaptations to machines, Leo Weinberg described a situation where a new machine, with a bell, was put into a hotel lobby and

FIGURE 6.7 A June 1934 ad for *Contact* (*Automatic Age*), leading off with its "bell ringing" as a key marketing feature.

that with each loud ring of the bell, "two or three bell boys [would] rush to the desk," mistakenly tricked by the pinball sounds into thinking they were being summoned to assist a patron.[29] He goes on to explain how to operate a machine without the bell by either removing the battery or, if the machine uses batteries for advancing balls, disconnecting the bell. Weinberg indicates that two machines with bells are the limit before the sound runs the risk of becoming a distraction to the operator: "[I]n a location where three or more bell equipped games are located, all being played, the merchant may become irritated at the constant bell ringing" (103). Writing to others in the pinball industry, John Goodbody complained about the sound quality of some of the bells ("jangling to the nerves") and shared that "in a number of cases [operators] have to mute the bells on their machines," worrying that a constant and unpleasant ringing sound might lead some operators not to want those machines in their spaces.[30]

Beyond Bells: Sound Innovations in the Electromechanical Era

Harry Williams's joke—the telephone-like bell ringing incorporated into a pinball game—launched a brief era of innovation into new sound effects that went through the decade. Electrically created sounds began to be used not only to enhance the player experience but also to aid exhibitors when trying to prevent cheating. As pinball still did not have flippers, the only way to influence the ball after launching it into the playfield was to physically nudge, jar, hit, or lift the machine (sometimes known as "gunching" or "english"). And because pinball machines at this time could offer payouts for successful games, there was increased incentive for cheaters. (Pinball would be criminalized in parts of the country because of its capabilities to be a gambling device akin to a slot machine, and it was not until the 1970s that the game lost its stigmatization and became known as an amusement device requiring skill and not just chance.) Harry Williams is credited with some of the important innovations that tried to prevent cheating, most importantly a way to disqualify the player for moving the game too much, or what would come to be known as tilting the game (Sharpe 1977, 25–28). Exhibit Supply Company's *Star Lite* (January, 1935) was among the first games to use a sound to indicate a tilt occurred, having one bell that sounded for scoring but also employing what one pinball restorer describes as an electrical "bell without a bell," suggesting the ringer unit alone would make a loud buzzing sound (and thus distinguishable from a bell that indicated scoring).[31]

Once pinball designers figured out how easily they could put what was a pre-existing technology in the form of an electric bell (the same technology had been around since the 19th century in doorbells and telephones), they began to experiment with sounds made when a solenoid made a striker hit something besides a resonant bell. The anti-tilt signal in *Star Lite* is one example of this kind of experimentation, but the breakthrough that introduced what is thought of as the first use of nonbell sound as an element of gameplay happened in July 1935 with the Rock-Ola Manufacturing Corporation's *Big Game*. Bueschel (as well as several other pinball historians) points to *Big Game* as being the introduction of "synthesized sound" (Bueschel 1997, 100). Marketing claimed that *Big Game* brought the player "for the first time, the heart-pounding thrill of sound effects," that it "lets you hear the staccato bark of rifle fire" and "the sharp report of a gun breaking through the stillness of night"; further, "at the very moment when the player hits a winner"—that is, gets the ball into the appropriate hole—"the entire playing field becomes alive with action" as "a clever new arrangement inside the machine magically reproduces the actual sound of gun shots" (emphases in original). The marketing department dipped into primitivistic hyperbole redolent of modernistic white supremacy when it promised that the game would draw "you irresistibly into all the mystery and all the adventures of the African jungle," making the game "so real and so lifelike . . . that you seem to hear the distant beat of native tom-toms and the eerie cries of wild beasts" (5). A game with a similar hunting theme, J. H. Keeney & Company's *Wild Cargo*, had appeared a few months before *Big Game*, but ads for it indicate that each "kill" (meaning getting a ball in a particular hole on the board) was accompanied by an electric bell while *Big Game* made a different sound by a "dashpot snapped by a magnet" (Bueschel 1997, 100).

David Rockola, founder of the company Rock-Ola, which would be best known for their jukeboxes, applied for a patent for *Big Game* on August 23, 1935, referring to it as a "hunter shooting game."[32] The innovation here was Rockola's pairing of a visible signal (a flashing light on the back cabinet) and an audible signal, which would be a sharply loud sound; together, the light flash and the sound at the same time were meant to simulate the sudden discharge of light and sound from firing a gun. Figure 6.8, an excerpt from Rockola's patent application, shows the figure that he explains in detail via prose. The principle is that when a ball lands in a certain hole, it will close an electrical circuit that quickly flashes a light and makes the gun sound. His step-by-step explanation of the particular actions connected to the sound generating apparatus are as follows: "The electromagnet 26 will thereupon attract the moving element or armature 42 and the arm 43 mounted thereon from full to dotted line position (Figure 6.5) forcing the solid element 47 mounted at the end 46 thereof against the strike plate 49 which is fastened to the bottom wall 48 of the cabinet 11. The bottom wall 48 being a form of a sound board, will thereby set up an audible alarm simulating the report of a gun."[33]

In September, 1935, *Automatic Age* devoted nearly two full pages to an entire story about Rock-Ola's *Big Game*'s sound effects, likening the coming of sound to "pin-game playing America . . . just as Warner Bros. brought the same idea to motion pictures and to a receptive world a few years ago."[34] Written in such effusively glowing terms that it might as well have come straight out of Rock-Ola's marketing and publicity department, it offers a history of the film industry in the 1920s when it said that "radio was keeping people home" and "high priced directors and 'yes-men' were fired" (95). Their story has a happy ending, though, as it touts the coming of sound to motion pictures and the film industry's subsequent financial and popular achievements as a result.

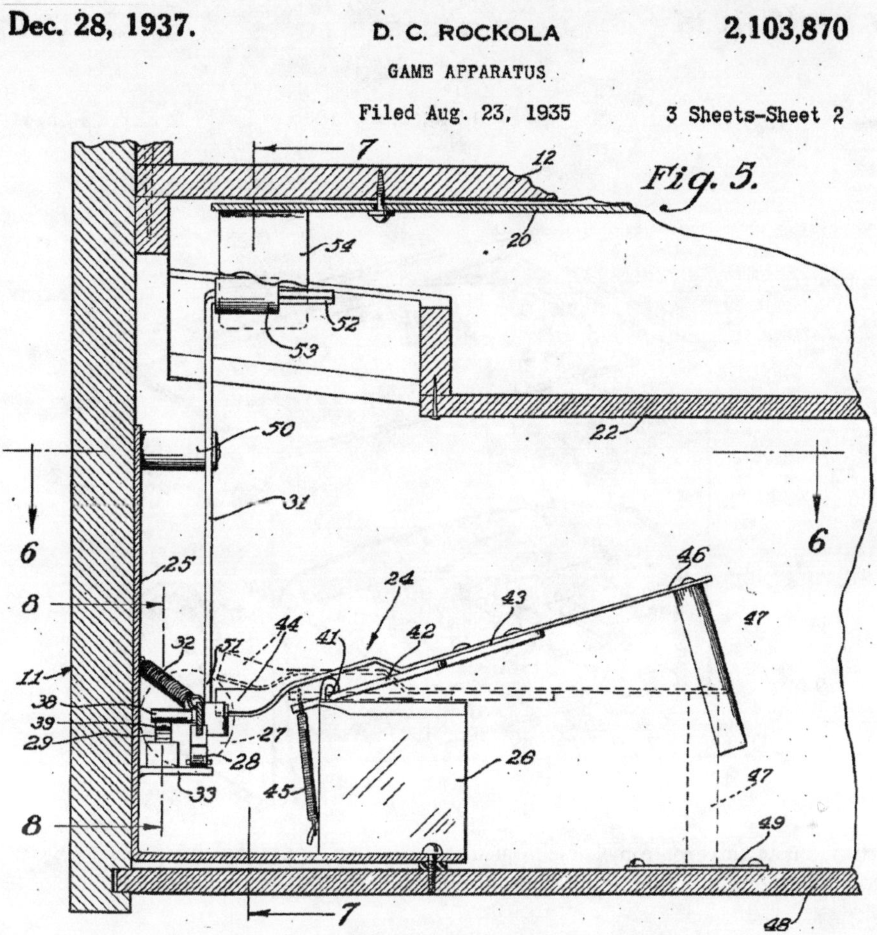

FIGURE 6.8 An excerpt from Rockola's patent application for *Big Game*, with a figure that illustrates what the prose describes: the synchronization of both a flashing light and a loud, sharp sound that was meant to simulate the sudden light and sound occurring with the discharge of a gun.

The essay ends with a prediction that sound effects in pinball machines would have the same positive results for the pinball industry: "Remembering all this—reflecting on what sound effects did to another industry devoted to the job of entertaining the public—Rock-Ola officials predict that sound effects will do much to stimulate public interest in pin games" (95).

Given all the excitement around the possibilities of pinball's new sound era, it comes as no surprise to find inventors attempting to expand the sound capabilities of a pinball machine. One such effort appears in Philip B. Corsello's patent, filed August 15, 1935, and granted April 12, 1938, for a talking pinball machine that could direct "various audible comments" at the players by having a phonograph playing apparatus inside a pinball cabinet that would get triggered by various events in the gameplay.[35] (See

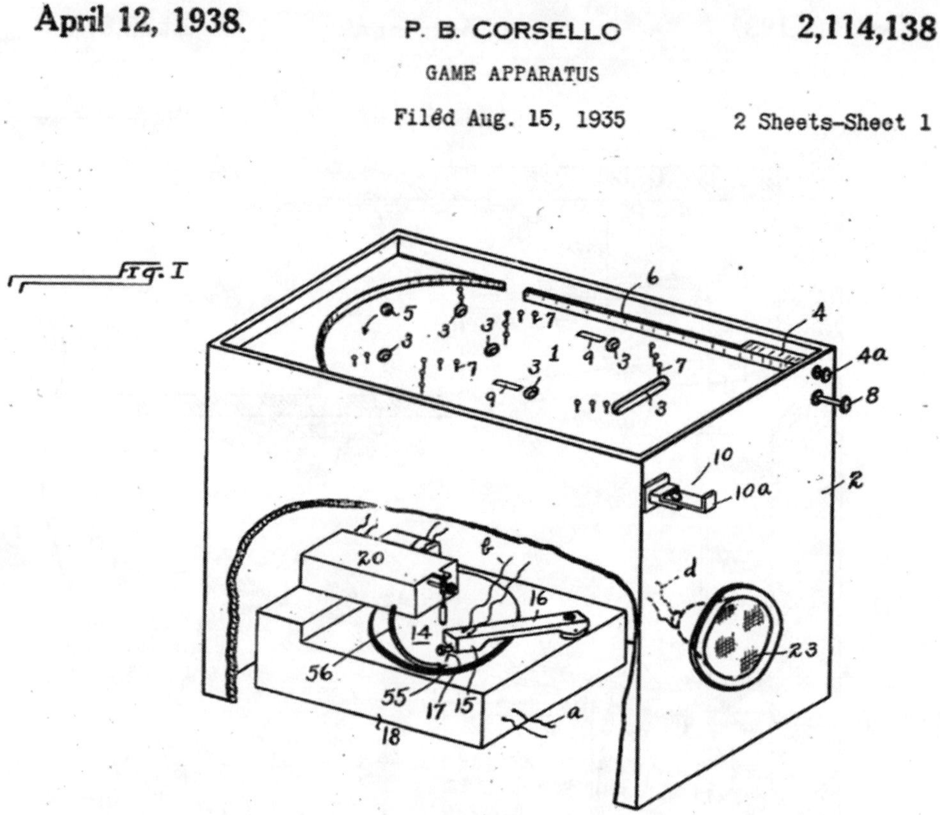

FIGURE 6.9 An excerpt from Corsello's patent application for a pinball machine equipped with a phonograph player that would give "various audible comments" to the player.

Figure 6.9.) Examples of the kinds of comments that might be heard, which are intended "to amuse the player by sounds," are described in the application as statements like "a very fine shot," "you have more luck than skill," and "robber, call the police," with the further claim that "upwards of 150 different comments may be recorded in the record and records of sound other than speech may be carried by the record."[36] Such a pinball machine would have had considerably more flexibility and diversity for adding sounds to a game than even video games would be able to do until the late 1970s and early 1980s. Commercially released pinball machines did not develop the capability to create vocal sounds until Williams's *Gorgar* (1979), which could speak only seven words ("Gorgar," "speaks," "beat," "you," "me," "hurt," and "got"), far less than the "upwards of 150 different comments" promised by Corsello. Collins (2016) has documented efforts to incorporate voice recordings into fortune telling machines and vending machines, like automatic cigar and cigarette machines, but says nothing about any games that used recorded voice. So far, I have been unable to find any evidence in any of the pinball histories that machines were constructed with Corsello's record-playing apparatus inside them. Even if a handful of such machines had been constructed, they almost certainly were not manufactured on a large scale. It is not apparent how the phonograph player inside the pinball machine would have been able to withstand what might have been considerable disruptions (and the skips and scratches made when the stylus went skidding over the phonograph) were players to apply the typical, much less atypical, nudging and pushing that the anti-tilt measures had been created to stop, and this limitation may be the reason why that technology was not viable until later in the 20th century.

Unfortunately, despite all the attention given to the exciting new world of sound pinball, there was actually fairly little innovation. Games would continue to be marketed on the basis of their new sound capabilities, but most of these sounds were variations on the gunshot simulations present in *Big Game*. Bally's *Prospector* (1935) offered a machine-gun sound effect and *Battle*, again by Bally and released in November, 1935, was promoted with the imperative commands to "see, hear and play BATTLE" (emphasis in original) and also had what one ad called "rat-tat-tat machine gun sound effects."[37] *Jumbo* (Bally, 1935) claimed its "curiosity-creating SOUND EFFECT draws players like a fire-alarm draws crowds" in one of its ads, while another ad describes *Jumbo*'s sound as a "BIG 'man-I-won-again' Sound Effect."[38] Ads for Rock-Ola's payout (i.e., similar to a slot machine) game *Alamo* (1936) mention but do not explain the game's "Battle of Alamo sound effects," though it's likely these were yet another variation on gunshot sounds.[39] A 1937 game by Stoner Manufacturing, *Latonia*, had a horse racing theme and was billed as having accompanying sound effects of "the clatter of horses' hoofs beating out a thrilling rat-a-tat."[40] The only other innovation to sound production in pinball games during the 1930s appears to have been new ways to cause bells to be sounded: Exhibit Supply's *Lightning* (August, 1938) used magnets underneath the playfield to create a rollover button that scored 1,000 points and rang a bell; and Bally's *Roller Derby* (October, 1939) would clang the bell for every 1,000 points scored (Bueschel 1988, 85, 89).

The sounds made by pinball machines were fairly well established and unchanging by the mid-1930s, with no significant additions until the introduction of multitone chime boxes in the late 1960s, which brought the utilized potential of various harmonies and the underutilized potential of playing simple familiar melodies. Further study remains to be done for the significant moment in the 1970s when pinball transitioned from electromechanical to solid state machines, which brought the possibility of the same kinds of electronically generated sounds that were being made by video games of the same era, as well as for the ways pinball music became vastly more sophisticated, with the ability to react to extremely rapid game actions and to reproduce more realistic sounds, in the final decades of the 20th century. But the breakthroughs in pinball sound up to the 1930s laid a crucial foundation for the soundscapes not only of pinball but also of video games, as the underlying idea of loud musical tones accompanying exciting moments of gameplay successes and of gun sounds accompanying the action of the (simulated) firing of a gun have persisted to the present.

Notes

1. A Mary Valentine-Andrew Cosman Research Fellowship supported my research at the Strong Museum of Play in Rochester, New York, where I am grateful for the assistance of Jon-Paul Dyson, Christopher Bensch, Beth Merkle, Julia Novakovic, Jeremy Saucier, and especially Martin Reinhardt, Arcade Conservation Technician at the Strong, who patiently helped me see the internal workings of the many machines in their collection. Thanks are due as well to Eric Keith and Josh Sacco of the Davidson College Department of Music, who helped me with recording equipment and video editing. I am especially grateful for the time shared by several creators from the pinball industry: Bob Baffy, Dan Forden, Eugene Jarvis, Brian Schmidt, and Roger Sharpe, each of whom granted me an interview or responded to my email queries.
2. On the inclusion of white noise sounds in *Computer Space*, see Lerner (2014, 321).
3. In addition to Collins (2008), Fritsch (2013), and Lerner (2014), see also Dittbrenner (2007).
4. From the Library of Congress's Prints & Photographs Online Catalogue, https://www.loc.gov/pictures/item/2008661662/ (accessed August 30, 2020). The cartoon draws attention to the questions of race surrounding this campaign through the drawing underneath the board of a dark dog whose tail is tied to a lighter colored cat whose name is given as "Miss Cegenation."
5. *Nineteenth Century Games* (1975, n.p.).
6. I learned of Saroyan's depiction of a marble-game addict in Sharpe (1977, 19). Saroyan's play, which won the Pulitzer Prize for Drama, was made into a poorly received film starring James Cagney in 1948. In the play, Willie, the marble maniac, finally beats the machine, at which point the stage instructions indicate that "the machine begins to make a special kind of noise . . . a bell rings loudly six times [then plays] a loud music-box version of the song 'America.'" I am aware of no games from 1939 that could have done what Saroyan describes; even the version depicted in the 1948 film seems to be constructed just for the film and contained several things, like flags shooting out of the machine along with the music, that would not be possible in pinball for several more decades. Bueschel (1996, 264) notes that Bally released a giant pinball machine, called *The Time of Your Life*, in conjunction with the film (for lobbies of select movie theaters), and indicates only six were made.
7. Collins (2016) details several examples of sound effects used in early electromechanical games, including a 1936 ad for the shooting game *Shoot-A-Lite*, which deployed an electronically controlled solenoid clapper that would strike a metal plate, thereby creating a loud bang that could serve not only to immerse the player but also to interest bystanders. See also *Automatic Age*, "Exhibit Introduces 'Shoot-A-Lite' Rifle Target Game," 13, no. 5 (December, 1936), 50.
8. *Automatic Age* 5, no. 8 (March, 1929), 24.
9. *Automatic Age* 8, no. 9 (April, 1932), 170.
10. *Automatic Age* 10, no. 12 (July 7, 1934), 73.
11. http://www.pinrepair.com/prewar/stepup.htm (accessed June 10, 2021). Its full explanation is as follows: "The chime sounds happen by balls hitting internal bells and the ball advancement is generated by the weight of balls on the trips. No electrical power is used in this game. Mechanical pinball."
12. See, for example, Bueschel (1988, 185; 1996, 245), Cahn (1960, 73), Rossignoli (2011, 94), Sharpe (1977, 40–43), Shalhoub (2002, 14–15), Smith (2020, 87), and Trapunski (1979, 26). Williams was one of the most important innovators in pinball design throughout the electromechanical era.

13. "Station S.M.A.C.," *Automatic Age* 7, no. 10 (May, 1931), 137.
14. *Automatic Age* 8, no. 3 (October, 1931), 10, and 7, no. 11 (June, 1931), 6.
15. J. P. Cahn, "Unguncheable Harry, King of the Pins," *True* (August, 1960), 54–55, 71–75.
16. Sharpe (1977, 40): Sharpe told me about his interviews with Williams as the source for his book in an email sent January 9, 2022.
17. Natkin and Kirk (1977, 86).
18. Trapunski (1979, 26).
19. https://pinballnirvana.com/forums/threads/a-visit-with-harry-williams.12048/ (accessed December 30, 2021).
20. U.S. Patent number 2,073,132.
21. Jerry Inglis was a friend and coworker of Williams from before he began to design pinball, and Bob Corbin was another coworker but also Williams's brother-in-law.
22. In the section titled "Pin Games with Action" in "News and Views from the Great Northwest," 10, no. 10 (May, 1934), 125–126.
23. *Automatic Age* 10, no. 11 (June, 1934), 94.
24. In the summer of 1934, the Genco Manufacturing Company released a game called *Step Up*, whose advertising emphasized musical notes. Ads like one in *Billboard* (July 7, 1934, p. 73) revealed a call-out with the words "with the 4 musical chimes," icons of musical notes, and the promise that the game has "ALL the Features the players want: The 4-Note Musical Chime for a Real Thrill when the ball enters the Step Up hole releases the balls that are in position to be advanced." Because this game is only mechanical, without any electrical components, the bells would have been activated by gravity as balls hit the bells that were inside the cabinet and underneath the playfield.
25. *Automatic Age* 10, no. 10 (May, 1934), 116.
26. *Automatic Age* 10, no. 11 (June, 1934), 37.
27. *Coin Machine Review* 7, no. 4 (August, 1934), 50.
28. *Automatic Age* 11, no. 2 (September, 1934), 18.
29. "Your Operating Equipment Requires Proper Care," *Automatic Age* 11, no. 2 (September, 1934), 105.
30. "Goodbody's Column," *Automatic Age* 11, no. 3 (October, 1934), 43, 45. His full rant roared as follows: "One word to manufacturers. Don't go 'bell-crazy!' We have had some games in here during the past few weeks, and the bells on the same are very irritating. Operators are reporting the fact that in a number of cases they have to mute the bells on their machines. A machine came out a few months ago that had some very musical chimes in it. I am wondering why these chimes cannot be substituted for some of the harsh bells that are now in machines? Can you imagine a druggist being in back of a partition trying to put up a very complicated prescription and having to listen to one of these bells every few minutes? It is enough to make any man want to have the machine out of the location. Now that we have bells on machines, I suggest that a manufacturer of bells be sought who can turn out a bell that is not jangling to the nerves." Goodbody's reference to "a machine [that] came out a few months ago that had some very musical chimes in it" might be to Genco's *Step Up*.
31. YouTuber Matt Walsh calls it a "bell without a bell" around the 4:35 mark in this video: https://www.youtube.com/watch?v=jmnzUkIYBok (accessed June 25, 2021). An *Automatic Age* ad in the April 1935 (11, no. 9) issue included *Star Lite's* "ringing bells" among its selling features (96). Designer Frank K. Maitland's patent for the game (U.S. Patent 2,096,348, granted October 19, 1937) does not mention either the scoring bell or the antitilt buzzer.

32. U.S. Patent 2,103,870, granted December 28, 1937.
33. Ibid., Page 2, right column, lines 54–63.
34. "Novel Sound Effects, A Feature of Rock-Ola's *Big Game*," 12, no. 2, (1935, 94).
35. U.S. Patent, 2,114,138.
36. Ibid., Page 2, right column, lines 61–62 and page 2, left column, lines 41–45.
37. *Prospector*'s sound effect is described as "a novel 'machine gun' sound effect device for announcing payout" in "Spectacular Campaign Introduces Bally's 'Prospector.'" *Automatic* Age 12, no. 1 (August, 1935), 132; *Billboard* (November 23, 1935), 82.
38. *Automatic Age* 12, no. 2 (September, 1935), 36, and *Billboard* (October 12, 1935), 82. In addition to its sounds, the visual elements of *Jumbo* were offered up as exemplary in a 1974 groundbreaking museum exhibition at the Dunlop Art Gallery of the Regina [Canada] Public Library. See Morgan (1974, 11), which explains that "games like *Jumbo* (1935) and *Skipper* (1937) exhibit a fine colour sense in their abstract design."
39. *Automatic Age* 12, no. 11 (June, 1936), 3–6. A website documenting the restoration of an *Alamo* machine makes the point that because this was a gambling machine, it and similar payout games were likely to have been destroyed in surprise police raids. In attempts to legitimize these gambling machines, some pinball manufacturers would attach vending functions like the optional addition of the "mint vendor" that Rock-Ola offered with *Alamo* and mentioned in the ad in *Automatic Age*.

    While the restoration focuses chiefly on the cabinet, playfield, and visual art, toward the end there is mention of what the restorer concludes was a missing bell, which he replaced with a telephone bell, though it might have been a variation on similar gun effects from that era that used a bell-striker hitting a metal plate instead of a bell for the gunshot effect. See https://www.aussiearcade.com/topic/66388-1930s-rock-ola-alamo-pinball-restoration/ (accessed December 31, 2021).
40. *Automatic Age* 13, no. 11 (June, 1937), 123. A later attempt to create the sound effect of horses galloping happens 42 years later in *Sharpshooter* (Game Plan Incorporated, 1979), an early solid-state machine designed by Roger Sharpe. The flyer for *Sharpshooter* draws attention to the "galloping spinner": "Return to those days of yesteryear with the incredible sounds of hoof beats in a power packed spinner that means points and access back to the top [of the playfield]." Other sounds indicated in the game's schematics include chimes, an explosion, a gunshot, a howl (meant to be that of a coyote), a ricochet, and a rattlesnake. I am grateful to Roger Sharpe for directing me to this game.

References

Bueschel, Richard M. 1988. *Illustrated Historical Guide to Pinball, Volume 1: Bagatelle to Baffle Ball, 1775–1931*. Wheat Ridge, CO: Hoflin Publishing.

Bueschel, Richard M. 1996. *Encyclopedia of Pinball: WHIFFLE to ROCKET, 1930–1933, Volume 1: The Origins of Pinball, Mechanical Marvels, Pinball Patent Wars, and Payouts*. N.p.: Silverball Amusements.

Bueschel, Richard M. 1997. *Encyclopedia of Pinball: CONTACT to BUMPER 1934–1936, Volume 2: Bells, Kickers, Lights and Buttons, Electricity Comes to Pinball, Ending the Patent Wars*. N.p.: Silverball Amusements.

Cahn, J. P. 1960. "Ungunchable Harry, King of the Pins." *True* (August, 1960): 54–55, 71–75.

Collins, Karen. 2008. *Game Sound: An Introduction to the History, Theory, and Practice of Video Game Music and Sound Design*. Cambridge, MA: MIT Press.

Collins, Karen. 2016. "Game Sound in the Mechanical Arcade: An Audio Archaeology." *Game Studies* 16 (1). Accessed April 6, 2021. http://gamestudies.org/1601/articles/collins.

Ditbrenner, Nils. 2007. *Soundchip-Musik: Computer- und Videospielmusik von 1977–1994*. Osnabrück, Germany: Osnabrück Verlag.

Fritsch, Melanie. 2013. "History of Video Game Music." In *Music and Game: Perspectives on a Popular Alliance*, edited by Peter Moormann, 11–40. Wiesbaden, Germany: Springer.

Goodbody, John. 1931. "Station S.M.A.C." *Automatic Age* 7, no.10 (May): 133, 135, 137.

Goodbody, John. 1934. "Goodbody's Column." *Automatic Age* 11, no. 3 (October): 43, 45, 47.

Hubbert, Julie. 2011. *Celluloid Symphonies: Texts and Contexts in Film Music History*. Berkeley: University of California Press.

Lerner, Neil. 2014. "The Origins of Musical Style in Video Games, 1977–1983." In *The Oxford Handbook of Film Music Studies*, edited by David Neumeyer, 319–348. New York: Oxford University Press.

Morgan, Wayne. 1974. *Tilt! Pinball Machines 1931–1958*. Conceived by Pat McCarthy. Regina, Canada: Dunlop Art Gallery.

Natkin, Bobbye Claire, and Steve Kirk. 1977. *All about Pinball*. New York: Grosset & Dunlap.

Nineteenth Century Games and Sporting Goods: Peck and Snyder 1886 Illustrated Catalog and Historical Introduction. 1975. Princeton: The Pyne Press.

Roberts, John D. 1934. "News and Views from the Great Northwest." *Automatic Age* 10, no.10 (May): 125–128.

Rossignoli, Marco. 2011. *The Complete Pinball Book: Collecting the Game and Its History*. 3rd ed. Atglen, PA: Schiffer Publishing.

Sharpe, Roger C. 1977. *Pinball!* New York: E. P. Dutton.

Shalhoub, Michael. 2002. *The Pinball Compendium, 1930s–1960s*. Atglen, PA: Schiffer Publishing.

Smith, Alexander. 2020. *They Create Worlds: The Story of the People and Companies That Shaped the Video Game Industry*. New York: CRC Press.

Trapunski, Edward. 1979. *Special When Lit: A Visual and Anecdotal History of Pinball*. Garden City, NY: Dolphin Books.

Ludography

Improvements in Bagatelle [Bagatelle board]. Montague Redgrave, 1871.

Coin Game Board [Coin operated bagatelle board]. Charles P. Young, 1892.

Log Cabin [Bagatelle board]. Caille Bros., 1901.

Electric Bagatelle [Bagatelle board]. Reed Fair Company, 1906.

Rifle Range [Mechanical gun game]. Fairchild Amusement Machine Corp., 1929.

Baffle Ball [Mechanical pinball machine]. D. Gottlieb & Company, 1931.

Electric Baseball [Electromechanical baseball game]. Hercules Novelty Company, 1931.

Roll-A-Ball [Mechanical pinball machine]. Hercules Game Company, 1931.

Whiffle Board [Mechanical pinball machine]. Automatic Industries, Incorporated, 1931.

Whoopee Game [Mechanical pinball machine]. In & Outdoors Games Company, 1931.

Ballyhoo [Mechanical pinball machine]. Bally Manufacturing Corporation, 1932.

Bell Ball [Mechanical pinball machine]. Reisinger Machine Works, 1932.

American Beauty [Mechanical pinball machine]. Daval Manufacturing Company, 1934.

Big Bertha [Electromechanical pinball machine]. Daval Manufacturing Company, 1934.

Contact [Electromechanical pinball machine]. Pacific Amusement Manufacturing, 1933.

Flying Trapeze [Electromechanical pinball machine]. D. Gottlieb & Company, 1934.

Relay [Electromechanical pinball machine]. D. Gottlieb & Company, 1934.
Step Up [Mechanical pinball machine]. Genco Manufacturing Company, 1934.
Battle [Electromechanical pinball machine]. Bally Manufacturing Corporation, 1935.
Big Game [Electromechanical pinball machine]. Rock-Ola Manufacturing Corporation, 1935.
Jumbo [Electromechanical pinball machine]. Bally Manufacturing Corporation, 1935.
Prospector [Electromechanical pinball machine]. Bally Manufacturing Corporation, 1935.
Star Lite [Electromechanical pinball machine]. Exhibit Supply Company, 1935.
Alamo [Electromechanical pinball machine]. Rock-Ola Manufacturing Corporation, 1936.
Shoot-A-Lite [Electromechanical shooting game]. Exhibit Supply Company, 1936.
Latonia [Electromechanical pinball machine]. Stoner Manufacturing Company, 1937.
Lightning [Electromechanical pinball machine]. Exhibit Supply Company, 1938.
Roller Derby [Electromechanical pinball machine]. Bally Manufacturing Corporation, 1939.
Humpty Dumpty [Electromechanical pinball machine]. D. Gottlieb & Company, 1947.
Gorgar [Solid state pinball machine]. Williams Electronics, Incorporated, 1979.
Sharpshooter [Solid state pinball machine]. Game Plan Incorporated, 1979.

Automatic Age citations

"Exhibit Introduces 'Shoot-A-Lite,' Rifle Target Game" 13, no. 5 (December, 1936), 50.
"Novel Sound Effects, A Feature of Rock-Ola's *Big Game*," 12, no. 2 (September, 1935), 94–95.
"Spectacular Campaign Introduces Bally's 'Prospector.'" *Automatic* Age 12, no. 1 (August, 1935), 132
Ad for *Rifle Range*. 5, no. 8 (March, 1929), 24.
Ad for *Bell Ball*. 8, no. 9 (April, 1932), 170.
Ad for *Step Up*. 10, no. 12 (July 7, 1934), 73.
Ad for *Electric Baseball*. 8, no. 3 (October, 1931), 10
Ad for *Electric Baseball*. 7, no. 11 (June, 1931), 6.
Ad for *Contact*. 10, no. 11 (June, 1934), 94.
Ad for *American Beauty*. 1, no. 10 (May, 1934), 116.
Ad for *Relay*. 10, no. 11 (June, 1934), 37.
Ad for *Flying Trapeze*. 11, no. 2 (September, 1934), 18.
Ad for *Star Lite*. 11, no. 9 (April, 1935), 96.
Ad for *Big Game*. 11, no. 12 (July, 1935), 4–5.
Ad for *Jumbo*. 12, no. 2 (September, 1935), 36
Ad for *Alamo*. 12, no. 11 (June, 1936), 3–6
Ad for *Latonia*. 13, no. 11 (June, 1937), 123.

Billboard citations

Ad for *Step Up*. (July 7, 1934), 73.
Ad for *Jumbo*. (October 12, 1935), 82
Ad for *Battle*. (November 23, 1935), 82.

Coin Machine Review citations

Ad for *Big Bertha*. 7, no. 4 (August, 1934), 50.

CHAPTER 7

SELLING PLAY THROUGH MUSIC AND SOUND

Audiovisual Promotion for Early Consoles, Home Computers, and Games to 1983

JAMES DEAVILLE

> The creation, form, and consumption of promotional material offers a unique insight into the workings of an increasingly competitive and lucrative industry.
>
> —Vollans et al. (2017)

INTRODUCTION

THE history of audiovisual advertising for video games[1] can be traced back to the earliest home console games for public consumption in the early 1970s that were promoted through television commercials.[2] These spots fall under broader marketing strategies for games that have encompassed trailers, print ads, radio spots, word-of-mouth, and "buzz generation" (Taynes-Ehle and Speedy 2017). Recent publications by specialists specifically looking at game trailers—in particular the 2017 special issue of *Kinephanos* dedicated to the "promotional context of video games"—have focused their attention on questions of paratextuality (Švelch 2017a, 2017b, 2020), persuasiveness (Taynes-Ehle and Speedy 2017), epistemology (Vollans 2017), national contexts (Fagundes Pase and Tietzmann 2017), historicity (Wright 2018), and marketing discourse (Therrien and Lefebvre 2017). While Vollans and colleagues' *Kinephanos* (2017), Švelch's dissertation (2017), and other histories of video game paratexts reference the earliest spots, none study the commercials in detail nor consider how their promotional messages for console games draw upon existing cinematic and televisual advertising discourses while introducing the new product.

There is more comprehensive work on the early audiovisual advertising in the literature from the history of technology and media history/media archaeology, such as Newman (2017) and Horton (2019). These and other scholars comprehensively study pre-Crash advertising—that is, dating from before the 1983 industry collapse—as a source for understanding both media culture in general and the emergence of console gaming in particular during a time of transition and growth for electronic entertainment.[3] Their work demystifies the origins of home console gaming while situating it within domestic discourses of the family and of household technologies. However, they treat the pre-1983 commercial spots for consoles and games like narratives consisting of moving images and dialogue, omitting consideration of background music (if any) and the sounds of play.

Of the literature that deals with pre-Crash console games, Švelch's dissertation from 2017 does consider music more expansively, identifying the paratextual qualities of licensed music and addressing how the music fits into the representational discourse surrounding games (115–116, 131–133). That said, Gibbons (2021) remains the only author to bring music centrally into the discussion of early audiovisual promotion for gaming: his discussion of Atari's advertising campaign "Have You Played Atari Today?" from the late 1970s and early 1980s serves as an important precedent for analyzing other console-based marketing from the era.

In this essay I extend Gibbons's assessment of Atari's significance to its parallel campaign for the home-computer 400 and 800 models, which, together with the game consoles, represent an important stage in the evolution of marketing for play. Key to the development of game promotion is its engagement with the audience through the immersive, visceral demonstration of game play. This element would prove fundamental for the emergence of game trailers in the 1990s, which augmented the cinematic trailer's sensory allures through its promise of interactivity via cut scenes and simulated game play. Indeed, all of the surveyed console and game spots leading up to and including the Atari ads featured some form of play, with sound and music fundamental to the advertised experience.

In pursuing such a trajectory, I investigate how the commercials' soundtracks contributed to the evolving promotional strategies of the game industry up to its collapse in 1983, at a time when television, consumers, and the games themselves underwent significant change. Beginning with the social and technological contexts for the rise of the home console, I first analyze a television commercial and promotional film for the Magnavox Odyssey system and observe how music compensates for the absence of game sounds. I then consider the developing soundscape of games in advertising spots during the transitional days of the later 1970s, when the basic sounds of *Pong* on the Atari VCS filled living rooms across North America, both as a game and in television commercials. The pre-Crash survey concludes with the rise of the home computer and the bifurcation of audiovisual promotions between gaming systems/games and personal computers, exemplified by the differing approaches to sound/music in spots for Atari's VCS/2600 consoles and 400/800 home computers.

Advertising Home Consoles and Video Games in the 1970s and Early 1980s

It stands to reason that the earliest commercials for console systems and games would use a platform and promotional tactics with which its audience would be familiar. Already "by 1964, 93 percent of all American households had television sets" (Tuckman 1991, 349), and so when, in 1966, Ralph Baer conceived of the home television set as a medium for the playing of games (Horton 2019, 76), its use for advertising them seemed only natural. After all, the public already had experience with games on television through the pre-Christmas spate of commercials that illustrated families engaging in good-natured board-game play, where children typically defeated their hapless parents in games involving motor skills. These scenarios readily transferred over to the early promotion of home consoles, for as Impellizeri (2019, 42) argues, "domestic harmony was the predominant theme of early video game marketing."

Whether depicted watching television programming or playing video games on the home TV set, the family circle was a trope that informed the audiovisual promotion of new domestic technologies, assuring consumers that "the products of modern technology . . . were comfortably accommodated within the hallowed circle" (Marchand 1985, 254). The stability of the family unit served as the initial advertising hook for the consumer of the early 1970s, at a time "when the middle-class suburban family faced significant social, cultural, and economic upheaval. Advertisers suggested that video games, by contrast, acted as a bulwark, reinforcing traditional family values" (Impellizeri 2019, 47).[4]

Such rhetoric behind the maintenance of the family circle was important, since video games threatened the traditional passive unidirectionality assigned to television consumption: in what amounted to a "medial polarity reversal, the player would produce the signals on the television, rather than receiving them from an external source" (Horton 2019, 76). Console technology also theoretically altered the configuration of domestic space, for unlike the bulky television, consoles could, relatively speaking, move more freely around the living room. Still, the typical commercial positions the console on an end table or similar piece of furniture in front of the TV set, with family members seated close to each other, facing the screen and manipulating joysticks.

Newman (2017, 73) aptly describes the domestic gaming experience as advertised in a commercial from the early 1970s: "It presents members of a 'typical' (white, middle-class, suburban) family engaged in sociable play around the console. The scenario is one of family togetherness." Over the course of the period under investigation, the emphasis in the advertising may remain on family, yet will shift from corporate console entertainment to individual benefits from work, study, and play on the home computer. Thus, in a 1981 promotional campaign for Atari 400 and 800 computers by Young & Rubicam, various half-minute spots emphasize how their technology can serve all members of the family in their personal needs for office work, school assignments, and entertainment (148–152).

Console and home-computer manufacturers and their advertising agencies strategically deployed music and sound from the beginning, albeit at first less professionally and consistently than by the early 1980s, when, for example, Atari purposively used its commercial hook/jingle "Have You Played Atari Today?" for marketing its products (Gibbons 2021). The challenge of "sounding" commercial messages for video games was to find an appropriate tone for the target consumer, one that made even educational programs seem like fun while avoiding trivializing the game or patronizing its users. Television advertisers could rely on game sounds to help sell the experience, which became a reality after the home version of *Pong* with its basic sounds was released in 1975.[5] The Magnavox Odyssey system did not feature any sound effects, which meant that its commercials' music had both to provide an exciting underscore for play and simulate the sounds of gameplay. The rise of home computers and their microprocessors in the late 1970s—the Atari VCS of 1977 led the way (Lowood 2009)—opened the floodgates for the more complex deployment of (music and) sounds, which "helped people to understand the game and give a gameplay depth" that the earliest visual elements could not (Kanitsakis 2020).

One other set of factors that influenced the sounds in audiovisual promotion for video games was the novelty and currency of the soundtrack. As we shall observe, Magnavox seemed particularly interested in musically conveying the cutting-edge qualities of their Odyssey product, which for them meant leaning heavily on the futuristic sounds of electronics and synthesizer, as modeled on the sonic realm of science-fiction television such as in the titles for *Outer Limits* or *Lost in Space* (Eng-Wilmot 2017). After all, already by the late 1970s the computer was widely considered the leading technology of the future (MacDonald et al. 1977),[6] so its electronic sounds seemed appropriate as sources for commercial soundtracks that traded in enabling the experience of alternate realities.

The Beginnings: Magnavox Odyssey (1972)

Game historians have already remarked on the system's titular debt to Stanley Kubrick's film *2001: A Space Odyssey* (1968), with its own reference to the Homeric myth of the Odyssey as a journey of exploration (Horton 2019). At the same time, the font Magnavox used for the word "Odyssey" was Moore Computer, "one of the most popular typefaces of the 1970s for futuristic electronics and science fiction entertainment" (Coles 2016).

The manufacturer clearly wished to position Odyssey as the "next evolution of the entertainment industry" (Gibbons 2021, 323).

Kate Willaert (2018, 2020) has established late 1972 as the best approximation for the date of the earliest Odyssey commercial. Fortunately, a copy of the untitled spot survives, the earliest known television commercial for a home video game system. Studying the 50-second ad[7] opens perspectives not only on the audio and visual practices of Magnavox in selling Odyssey's "total play and learning experience for all ages" but also on early 1970s ideals of domestic space and family interaction as afforded by the console and its games.

Since the first generation of Magnavox Odyssey consoles had no audio, the company's marketing was challenged to breathe sonic vitality into a game that was in essence silent. Their solution was for the commercials to rely on music to convey the excitement of gameplay, with a rhythmically synchronized percussive hit to simulate the sound of a ball/puck striking or being struck. The use of the simulated game sound assisted with immersing the consumer into the experience of play, which should translate into a purchase.

Here is the text of the 1972 Magnavox Odyssey television commercial voice-over: "This is Odyssey, the new electronic game simulator. You attach Odyssey to your television set in seconds to create a closed-circuit electronic playground. . . .[8] Odyssey is tennis, roulette, football and hockey, Analogic and geography. Odyssey comes complete with 12 electronic games and educational experiences. Many more are optionally available, like a shooting gallery, a prehistoric safari. Odyssey is an electronic teacher. Odyssey is a total play and learning experience for all ages. . . . Odyssey. . . . It's new. From Magnavox. Odyssey."[9]

The musical underscore falls into three sections that synchronize with text sections: A ["This is . . ."]—a simple, futuristic-sounding syncopated tune over a sustained synthesized tone that repeats three times;[10] B ["Odyssey is . . ."]—a busier call-and-answer idea that repeats; A[1] ["Many more . . ."]—a shortened return of the opening material that becomes cadential; B[1] ["Odyssey. . . . It's . . ."]—an abbreviated return of the B idea.[11] Although basic in its musical material, the commercial nevertheless draws on music to structure the narrative, to communicate the console's functions and values, and to simulate gameplay. If the slower, sci-fi-style A section provides product and set-up information, the livelier B section with its percussive hits viscerally conveys play while invoking the excitement of the game. The configuration of players is revealing, for it begins with father and mother, then focuses on the games themselves in the B section, and finally adds the two children—male and female—for the return of A. Before the visually and aurally stressed product logo at the end, we see all four family members at play, which underlines the central message of "fun for the whole family."

The 1972 Magnavox Odyssey ad presents tropes that will figure in other audiovisual promotion for home consoles during the early 1970s: the console furnishes entertainment for the entire family, represents the technology of the future, and its advertisement requires music and sound effects to convey the full experience of gameplay. While the ad may not have received much airplay,[12] it reflects the prevailing promotional discourse of the time surrounding domestic game consoles and their interactive potentials for amusement and—to a lesser extent—learning. The sophistication of the soundtrack's integration of narration, music, and sound effects will increase even as the consoles and games themselves begin to take the increasingly indispensable realm of audio to the next level.

Before proceeding to the emergence of Atari on the domestic market, however, one other audiovisual document from 1972 deserves mention. In that year Magnavox also produced and distributed a super-8 film to television dealers "in the Magi-Cartridge film-loop format, which could be viewed on special display devices in the dealer showroom" (Ausretrogamer 2015).[13] The five-minute promotional film offers consumers a detailed introduction to the system from set-up through play and learning within the family circle, emphasizing the pleasures afforded by interacting with the television through the console.[14] After a futuristic-sounding Magnavox logo, the film presents the narrative dilemma of a family confined to home but dissatisfied with television offerings, "while people who want television to do their thing entertain themselves with Odyssey." The film divides into five segments that introduce: (1) the family narrative (to 0:34), (2) set-up instructions (0:35–1:39), (3) the console hardware (1:40–3:05), (4) the console's basic games (3:05–4:05), and (5) further options (4:06–5:04). The music is stylistically congruent with the affective worlds of the unfolding scenes (Oakes and Abolhasani 2021), increasing in animation to the lively play of (4) with a banjo version of "Ain't We Got Fun." The tracks sound like library music of the era, albeit edited to fit the segment timings and alternating between orchestral (1), synthesizer (3 and 5), pop-combo (2), and Dixieland (4) stylings. The music invisibly supports the film's sales pitch (Tan et al. 2021), which clearly targets those consumers with the financial resources to invest in such modes of entertainment. That the film relies on nonstop narration and underscore rather than the sounds of gameplay and family interaction not only distinguishes it from the 50-second commercial but also highlights its function as an informational demo that addresses the Odyssey console's operation, features, and capabilities.

The Home Console: Atari's VCS, *Pong*, and *Space Invaders* (Later 1970s/Early 1980s)

With its three simple electronic tones, Atari's home version of *Pong* from 1975 predated the Magnavox corporation's "sonification" in its Odyssey2 game system. Lerner (2013, 321–322) details how *Pong* designer Al Alcorn came up with the sounds of the game, two B-flats one octave apart and a B natural. Summers (2017, 139) tempers a musical reading of the tones when he observes that "[t]his musical sound sits at the boundary between sound effect and music—undeniably pitched, but synchronized to the on-screen action in a way more similar to a sound effect." As Collins (2008, 20) notes, Atari released *Pong* on the Sears Tele-Games system, "which really brought gaming home to the masses."

In 1975, Atari actively promoted the adaptation of *Pong* as a game newly available for domestic play, producing a humorous, 30-second commercial in black-and-white that signaled *Pong*'s move from the arcade into the home.[15] In it, a man dressed like a Texas rancher calls out to missing family member "Doreen" (wife or daughter), who "plain forgot to come home." He offers a solution to her (unstated) addiction in the form of Atari's home version, concluding with the words "come on back home" (Impellizeri 2019, 51–52). To stress the impact of her absence on the home, the commercial's background reveals an apron-clad male figure (son?) engaging in domestic chores.

The commercial mobilizes ironic wit to speak to several concerns of the day surrounding video gaming, most obviously in reference to the arcade experience. Bringing Doreen home removes her from the dangers of the arcade and—by extension—the outside world, reinserting her into the safety and stability of the family circle (Huhtamo 2012, 32; see also Gibbons 2021, 324). The home also offers a possible antidote to the ad's subtext of addiction to gaming, through the salutary influence of domestic life (Newman 2017, 97–98). Still, as Newman points out from the tagline for another satirical Atari commercial, "anyone can get hooked," so that "even a woman—a mother—could be susceptible to the product's appeal" (73).

The ad's soundtrack is dominated by the voices of the rancher and the omniscient voice-over, both breaking the fourth wall through direct audience address. Although music is absent, we briefly hear and see *Pong* play in the transition between rancher and narrator (0:17–0:24). In such a short spot, those seven seconds represent a considerable investment of time that is dedicated to play through its action shot of the *Pong* screen with its octave tones sounding.

The success of *Pong* led to the proliferation of versions by other manufacturers: by 1976, "some seventy-five companies had launched a home version of Pong," according to Collins's count. Through the "*Pong* chip,"[16] its graphics were replicated and "the Pong sound was carried into hundreds of versions of the game" (Collins 2008, 20). A 30-second 1976 TV spot for the "Telstar" system by Coleco illustrates not only the similarities in ball-and-paddle gaming but also the shifts within the soundtracks of commercials.[17] The nondiegetic music of the Odyssey spots is absent, replaced by the ongoing sounds of play—here the focus is on the console's games rather than the context, although we see and hear the pleasure of a young couple engaging in gameplay. The octave tones become denser as all four games are displayed on one split screen, having the effect of a dynamic crescendo.

Atari's release of the Video Computer System (VCS) in October 1977—later rebranded as the Atari 2600—"was by far the most commercially and culturally successful home leisure product of the video game industry" (Newman 2017, 7), not least because its console was programmable. It featured no music but could provide an array of "rudimentary sound effects created with white noise" (Lerner 2013, 323). A 30-second television spot from December 1977 illustrates one trend in video game commercials, toward narrative content and recognizable faces.[18] George McCann and John Lawlor—well-known television personalities from the 1970s—act out a minidrama in a store, where customer McCann eagerly plays and wants to buy the VCS, but salesperson Lawlor informs another customer that they are sold out and tells George that the demonstrator belongs to him. Although the commercial lacks a musical score, the sounds of gameplay are featured, strategically at the beginning and then at two other points. However, the actors' voices dominate, with McCann's over-the-top enthusiasm and laughter contrasting with Lawlor's commanding voice-over. The use of familiar actors should not be confused with the early-1980s marketing strategy of celebrity endorsements, a down-to-earth William Shatner promoting the Commodore VIC-20, while the erudite George Plimpton spoke for Mattel's Intellivision products. And it should be noted that qualities of the invariably male voice-over—range, intensity, phrasing—contributed to the pitch on TV, whether the voice belonged to a celebrity or a nameless announcer.

Atari came out with its own celebrities in a 30-second spot from 1978 for its cartridges, with baseball luminary Pete Rose and soccer great Pelé respectively demonstrating the company's "Home Run" and "Air–Sea Battle" cartridges.[19] The ad strikes a humorous note: Pelé says that he has "quit soccer to play Atari" and both athletes are chided for not possessing the requisite skills. In a more clearly promotional voice-over, the commercial ends with the tagline, "Don't watch television tonight. Play it," thereby "defining Atari's identity in relation to TV and promising the transfer of television from a passive to an active medium" (Newman 2017, 67). Like other video game and console commercials from the later 1970s, here the (new) sounds of play fulfill the role that music and jingles will come to occupy in the early 1980s.

Not to be outmarketed by the competition, Magnavox aired commercials in the late 1970s that centered on the visuality and aurality of play through its Odyssey2 system "Continuous music" in a game. In a 25-second ad, without music except for the closing Magnavox soundmark, the continuous game sounds emanating from the television provide the underscore to a voice-over that lauds the many possibilities of play.[20] Half-minute spots for the Coleco Telstar (1976) and the Nintendo Color TV Game (1977) likewise foregrounded the game sound by featuring it at the outset and in the body of the spot, to foster an immersive engagement with the game among the television audience.

One of the most popular and influential games of the late 1970s and early 1980s was *Space Invaders*, which brought the hype created by *Star Wars* into the home through the Atari VCS console. As Newman suggests (2017, 184), "[i]t was no coincidence that *Space Invaders*' popularity coincided with the dominant presence in popular culture of *Star Wars*, in which warfare in a distant galaxy plays into boyhood ideals of courage in battle against a mortal enemy." Moreover, *Space Invaders* was the first video game to incorporate continuous music and not merely pitched sound effects: its four-note ostinato "increases in speed as the indefatigable aliens march ever-faster toward earth" (Summers 2017, 139). In doing so, the game's music possessed the potential of influencing the player's emotions, which opened the path for future developments in video game music (Schartmann 2013).

Of course, at the time Atari did not realize the game music's significance for posterity—its audiovisual promotion reflected console and game advertising of the period, which meant aiming at its target consumer: the suburban, middle-class, white family. In 1980 the television commercials for Atari still presented domestic scenes of multiplayer rather than single-player gaming, thereby reaffirming the case for video games as a means for family bonding as well as entertainment. Humorous takes on family play can be observed in two spots for *Space Invaders* from 1980–1981, with the sounds of gameplay dominating both 30-second commercials. In one we see and hear a boy using a joystick to play *Space Invaders* while his sister and father watch and his mother answers phone calls from three different girls who offer to babysit (but really want to play on their Atari system).[21] The game sounds, ringing phone, mother's voice, narrator's explanation, and cries from the boy and his sister creates a counterpoint of sounds that would render music meaningless and superfluous. The other ad likewise adopts a lighter tone in promoting Atari and its game, again showing a boy playing *Space Invaders* surrounded by family[22]—the father narrates their pleasure from the system yet disbelief in the game's invader premise, even as aliens noisily descend on the house. Both commercials end with a visual armada of flying Atari games and company logo accompanied by the musicalized sounds of gameplay; this is the closing for Atari spots until 1981.

Although music as such is lacking in the two *Space Invaders* spots, the listener-viewer might consider the game sounds as possessing musical qualities, whether in the rising or descending pitches of specific play actions or the rhythmic beat of the marching aliens. The second commercial makes the sound of the advancing foe's steps particularly prominent in the mix, perhaps to accentuate the irony of the aliens' apparent descent on the isolated house.[23]

From Home Console to Home Computer: Atari's VCS/2600 and 400/800 (Early 1980s)

The oversaturation of the market with games and systems, often hastily developed and produced, eventually led to the Crash of 1983. In the meantime, the glut of unsold games and consoles contributed to a surge in advertising for the larger companies such as Atari, Coleco, Activision, and Intellivision. The flood of audiovisual promotion would come to include 30-second minidramas as framing devices, custom-composed musical underscoring and trademark jingles, and well-compensated celebrity endorsements, which reflected the shift from selling game consoles to marketing home computers.

Newman (2017, 135–138) devotes considerable space to this transition, which began in earnest around 1977, when the home computer emerged as a consumer electronics product. He observes how opposing conceptions of value became intertwined in advertising discourses of the time, whether the device was intended for an adult or a child, as a tool or a toy: work (serious) or leisure (fun). As he notes for the toys Simon and Merlin introduced in 1978:[24] "The meanings of microchip technology in . . . spots for Simon and Merlin combine the power and novelty of the computer with the friendly competition of home play among family members, familiarizing and domesticating microprocessors while also selling the image of them as powerful thinking machines with the agency and identity conveyed by a personal pronoun" (137).

These dual attributes were not incompatible, since other domestic electronic devices like television and radio also possessed multiple overlapping uses: they could deliver into the home educational programming and news broadcasting as well as shows for pure entertainment. However, the home computer had the added feature of enabling work outside the office, which manufacturers may have regarded as a selling point, yet, for some social critics, raised a warning signal against the "home office" and the accompanying "threat to the development of relationship building skills" (Salem and Gratz 1983, 12).[25] Manufacturers tended to blunt such disapproval by mobilizing their marketing network to point out the domestic (and educational) uses of the home computer.

Given the market demand and industry competition, it is not surprising that television commercials for home consoles and computers from the early 1980s presented a more professional look and—importantly—sound than during the 1970s. They acquired narrative properties, often telling a 30-second ministory involving family and their use of the device. Soundtracks featured (male) voice-over for product information, dialogue of the characters, sounds of games and play, and musical underscoring.[26] Music tended to fall into two categories: either a consistently used brandmarking jingle or (library) tracks that were selected according to affect (Kupfer 2021). This musical component of the soundtrack varied even within the half-minute format, to match the shifting situations and moods presented on screen.

Atari was the industry leader, with, according to the *New York Times*, a "tremendous" advertising budget of over $100 million in 1982 (Pollack 1982). Thus, the firm could afford to hire powerhouse marketing firm Young & Rubicam in 1981 to promote the 8-bit 400 and 800 home computers, with the tagline "Atari Brings the Computer Age Home" (Newman 2017, 147–149). Its advertising hype of home-office applications notwithstanding, the most common use for the Atari computers was to play the company's video games, which the ads suggest can help to overcome the generational divide. While one spot exclusively featured daughter and mother interacting through the computer, the gender gap of early computing (fathers and sons) nevertheless persisted in Atari's marketing strategy throughout the 1980s.[27]

The resulting Atari commercials anticipated the marketing discourses surrounding game trailers as they would emerge in the 1990s. In both the pre-Crash advertising and the early trailers, music and sound converged within a unified narrative of 30 seconds that demonstrated the game's features and capabilities. It was with the advent of the World Wide Web in the mid-1990s that game promotion would shift from television-based advertising to online trailers, leading to the lengthening and proliferation of trailer texts and their differentiation according to purpose (e.g., reveal, game play, cinematic trailers).

Atari VCS/2600

Atari's campaign of 30-second television spots for the VCS/2600 home console system markedly differed from those for its 400 and 800 computer models. Gibbons (2021) has studied in detail the jingle "Have You Played Atari Today?" that the company undoubtedly commissioned for its effective campaign: this memorable eight-note tune "became almost synonymous with the company's golden age" (324). As Gibbons observes, the hook "is a clever way of positioning the product in viewers' minds" (325), by linking the consumer's activity (play) with the product (game). Gibbons focuses his analysis on a commercial from 1981,[28] which frames the console's best-selling games within a scenario of ever-increasing numbers and types of players around the same sofa, using a shot-reverse shot technique to alternate between the game and the expanding group of players, beginning with two boys. Here everyone gets to play a game through the joystick, the visuals cutting across gender and age barriers; the commercial conveys the message that "Atari's wholesome fun brings families, and even whole neighborhoods, together" (326).

The soundtrack consists of a (male) narrator identifying the games, the characteristic game sounds, the chaos of the crowd's jubilant cheers, and the musical score. The music is continuous and performed by a small ensemble of traditional instruments except for the last five seconds. Rising in pitch and volume as the crowd size grows, the melody gradually crystallizes into the jingle "Have You Played Atari Today?," which we first hear on the synthesizer (0:25) and then sung monophonically by a chorus (presumably the crowd), as the Atari logo appears and the words "Video Game System" are spelled out in Moore Computer font. This ending reminds the consumer that, although we have seen and heard the fun side of the games, they are the product of state-of-the-art technology, which explains the synthesized jingle and the futuristic font.

Gibbons addresses later iterations of the games pitch, each of his analyses focusing on a commercial for one of Atari's leading games: *Pac-Man*, *Breakout*, and *Berzerk*. In these and other spots from the advertising campaign (1981–1982), the music with lyrics is crucial to understanding what is occurring on screen, from the very opening.[29] Each of the commercials features a different scenario, but they all involve one or more people (family members or friends) seated on a sofa and playing a console game in the living room. The person who controls the joystick does vary from ad to ad: a sole adult male with wife and children as onlookers (*Breakout*),[30] two animatically presented young boys playing (*Pac-Man*),[31] one young boy with father advising and mother watching (*Super Breakout*),[32] a young girl with brother watching and mother joining play (*Yar's Revenge*),[33] and a boyfriend with his girlfriend, who, at the end, takes over and plays better than he did (*Defender*).[34] Their differences notwithstanding, these spots communicate two messages: playing games is fun and it brings people together—indeed, before the final statement of the jingle, the characters invariably enact some display of bonding.

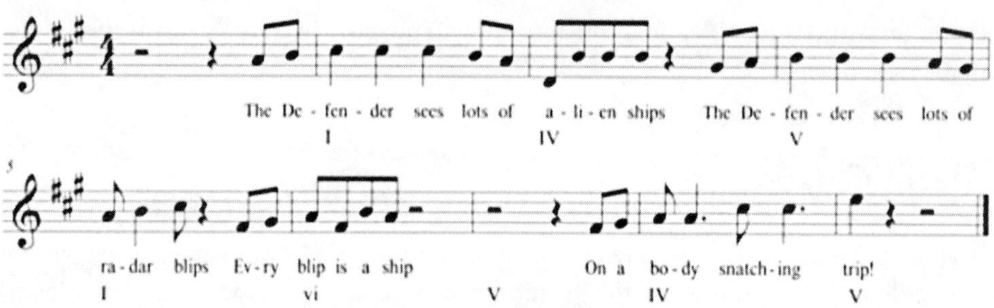

FIGURE 7.1 Opening of Atari VCS/2600 verse for *Defender* commercial.

In each scenario, music both structures and unifies the advertisement's narrative, creating the intertextuality between the commercials within the campaign. As Atari released new games, the company merely needed to create a new scenario and fashion a verse that fit the textual and musical pattern. Each commercial falls roughly into two halves: the first half sung, followed by a voice-over and then the jingle (the hook at the end—essentially a chorus). Using the commercial for *Defender* as a model, we hear the music beginning with a four-line verse (see Figure 7.1) that first poses two parallel statements about playing the game ("The Defender sees lots of alien ships / The Defender sees lots of radar blips"), after which the text presents two shorter lines of explanation ("Every blip is a ship / On a body-snatching trip"). The melody of the first two lines largely moves by step and is supported by a tonic-dominant-tonic harmony, while the second two lines linger on the subdominant before a closing dominant. This is followed by the antecedent and consequent phrases of the jingle tune ("And it's up to Defender to save them / Defender! A great Atari game"), the second line featuring different words from its use in the climactic hook at the end. The brief voice-over elaborates on the newness and popularity of the game, and then the consumer hears the synthesized and sung versions of the jingle.

This configuration repeats itself—with minor variations—for each of the Atari VCS commercials, regardless of who is depicted as playing (the lyrics vary according to the game on display). The familiarity of the pitch's formula should help to assure the consumer of the new product's quality while providing identification with the company through the recognizable advertisement itself (Oakes and Abolhasani 2021, 759). A further (intertextual) link is forged by using the same male vocalist for all but one of the spots, the exception being the *Breakout* ad: there we presume the wife is singing about the boy "deep inside of every man," waiting to break out (Gibbons 2021, 330).

Atari 400 and 800

In contrast, every early-1980s commercial for Atari's entries into the home computer market bears signs of individual crafting in their attempts to promote a distinct product, albeit potentially to the same consumers. Collectively, they adopt a lightly humorous approach to an important purchase decision, substituting the device's productive applications, flexibility, and technological sophistication for the overt ludic pleasure demonstrated in the company's console and game ads. Here, Atari emphasizes a home-office setting (and not a sofa) with computer, monitor, and appropriate chairs. Each 30-second ad presents a mildly dramatic story that could occur in any household in North America, whereby we experience the following scenarios: a boy explains to his younger brother how to use Atari software, including the programming aid Pilot and the game *Pac-Man*;[35] a father helps his son study French so he can greet the grandparents (and he can also play *Missile Command*);[36] a daughter "smartens up" her mother (and plays *Basketball*);[37] and a father "goes to work" at home but is caught by his son with *Space Invaders* on screen.[38]

The diversity of such plotlines does not mean that the campaign's spots lack the various intertextual features of the game ads; Young & Rubicam has devised a rough template that they redeployed throughout the campaign. This narrative arc presents the logo for Atari, a situation or problem (e.g., not knowing French or the names of state capitals), its solution through the computer, a game tie-in (with the obligatory stack of available programs), the resolution of the issue through Atari assistance (e.g., speaking to the grandparents in French or identifying a state capital), and a repeat of the logo. Through the unfolding ministory the consumer encounters characters who interact, speak, and—like the gamers—succeed, which underscores the product's domestic usefulness. The spoken and displayed tagline "Atari brings the computer age home" at the beginning and end of the commercials likewise conveys a sense of the microprocessor device's utility for work and learning at home.

The soundtracks also rely on an established pattern that stresses the sounds of speech over participant cheering, a nondiegetic musical score over the sounds of gameplay, and a spoken slogan over a sung jingle, all to help establish the important domestic productivity taking place through Atari intervention. At the outset the consumer should recognize both the visual Atari logo and the musical motive that identifies this campaign, consisting of flutes playing a descending fourth three times in quick sequence (and extended as needed). Such a motive can have a hailing function, and tends to front-load the promotional pitch in comparison with the game ads, since the resolutions to the home-computer scenarios typically evoke warm feelings that would not be well served by an energetic jingle. However, the commercials all feature a matching cadential figure at the end: a gently descending tetrachord over a vi–ii–V–I harmonic progression (see Figure 7.2).[39] That the melody and harmony resolve and "come home" in congruence with the graphic and spoken logo "We've Brought the Computer Age Home" is certainly

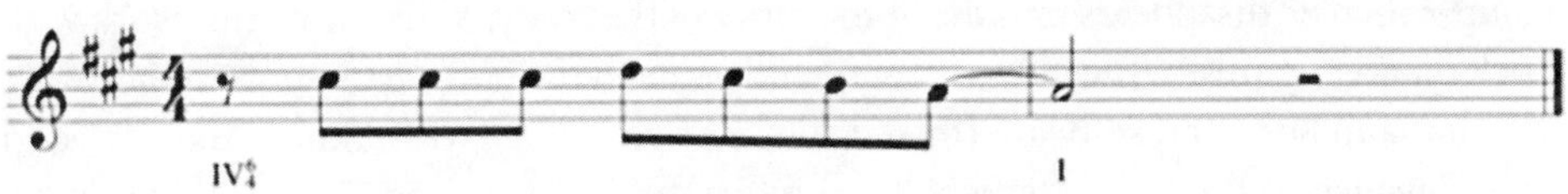

FIGURE 7.2 Cadential theme, Atari 400/800 home computers.

not a coincidence but a clever marketing tactic to underscore the "home" aspects of home computing.

Between the identifying motive at the beginning and the motto cadence at the end, the consumer encounters a wide palette of familiar musical tropes, commonly found in contemporaneous film and television.[40] Their selection and arrangement depend on the underlying premise of the particular ad, which leaves little doubt that the musical underscores were custom made for each ad, even if the process involved assembling library tracks. For example, after the opening of the conversational French commercial, we hear a synthesized version of "La Marseillaise" as we see the boy practice, which becomes an upbeat tune while someone loads and plays *Missile Command*. The melodic line sweetens and then drops out when the boy greets his grandparents in French, finally giving way to the closing cadential motto as the commercial ends. The ascending key sequence and the lively string accompaniment provide for musical forward motion and a sense of excited accomplishment, framed by the branding theme for Atari home computers.

The use of voice in these commercials also merits closer consideration. In comparison with the game/console ads, the actors speak and the voice-over is present in between moments of conversation. As a result, the audience may feel more immersed and invested in the minidramas while receiving information about the products and their versatility. Thus, in the spot about the device as a means to learn state capitals, the girl initially mischievously asks her mother—in vain—for a capital's name, accompanied by a puckish score. After we see the mother engaging with the computer under her daughter's guidance, the scenario repeats with her giving a correct answer, while the music sets a lyrical tone that seamlessly becomes the closing cadential figure.

The narrator is the same between all the 400- and 800-model commercials, which serves to brand the Atari home computer product while providing the specific advertising message with a positive and reassuring voice. He opens and closes the spot with a subtle yet noteworthy difference: at the beginning he narrates the words "Atari brings the computer age home," which by the end has become: "We've brought the computer age home," on top of graphic lettering. This shift is significant because it continues the work of identification and immersion, consumers being led to believe that they and Atari have introduced the latest technology into their domestic sphere.

One commercial for the Atari 800 from the Young & Rubicam campaign of 1981–1982 deserves special attention due to its complex narrative and elaborate musical treatment.[41] The spot entitled "Broker" ironizes the "home as a flexible space of work and play" (Newman 2017, 149–150) and as a liminal site for the negotiation of family roles. At the start, the father looks to be rushing off to work ("Gotta run, gotta go"), his wife saying "Have a nice day at the office" and his son harassing him with the query "late again?"; then he disappears into the home office of the study, where he begins work with stock market figures.[42] The video subsequently cuts to the obligatory shots of hardware (the 400 and 800) and software (mixed stacks of programs, with "Stock Analysis" and *Space Invaders* at the top), after which we return to the man, who sees the screen message "Stock Market Closed."[43] Craftily checking his surroundings and then smiling, he begins to play *Space Invaders*, only to have his son enter and say, "Market closed, Dad. Mind if I do my work?" Chagrined that he is caught, the father says, "No problem," but the spot ends with him looking annoyed (followed by the visual and audio tagline for Atari home computers).

The voice-over here functions outside the diegesis of the commercial—its extradiegetic sales pitch compels the consumer to make sense of the unfolding drama. After the opening tagline, it returns and synchronizes with on-screen action: "[visual: man leaving] With an Atari home computer, [man works in home office] you can easily work at home [hardware and software display] or open your home to a world of possibilities. In fact, the hardest part about [return to man] owning an Atari home computer [man inserts game cartridge] isn't how to use it but [son enters] who gets to use it [son dialogue, father responds]." On the surface this narrative layer affirms the computer's versatility as a device for work and education that can also run games (without ever mentioning "game"), but at another level it plays with the notion of the device's legitimacy for individual productive labor at home between family generations.

The score fully supports the unfolding story through an appropriately merry and energetic accompaniment of light orchestra with individual touches that suggest custom scoring. For example, as the man bustles down the stairs off to the "office," we hear the chugging bassoon underneath. When the son confronts him, the music responds with the readily recognizable muted-trumpet minor-third "wah-wah" of a deception unmasked.[44] The symbolic meanings associated with these and other details of scoring would be familiar to the television audience of the day through music for screen media, especially animation. Between the son's interruption and the close (right after the minor third), the string-dominated music becomes more lyrical—some might say wistful—which leads directly into the tone and style of the motto cadence. This degree of care in scoring is unusual for Atari's campaign and helps to distract from the underlying mercantile intentions, drawing attention to the interrelationships of the characters and what the home computer can do for them, much like the commercial with the boy learning French for his grandparents.

Conclusions

In the decade between 1972 and 1983, audiovisual promotion for consoles, home computers, and games made important progress in step with developments in these commodities and the industry that produced them. Music and sound were integral to the changes, and the advancements in the sounds of play carried over into the realm of advertising these consumer products. Thus, the music in television commercials was tasked with capturing the excitement of play for the earliest commercially viable home system, Magnavox Odyssey, which itself did not have audio capability. Nevertheless, it could be argued that, with the 30-second commercial from 1972 for Odyssey, the principle of the video game trailer was born, evolving through stages of promotion that ever more effectively highlighted the product's interactive use and usefulness.

As arcade games moved into consoles in living rooms of the early- and mid-1970s, commercials would present scenes of idealized consumer families—white, suburban, middle class—bonding over and through their new electronic toy. The sounds of games arising *from* the television set, initially the pitched tones of *Pong* and then the more complex soundscape of *Space Invaders*, came to mingle with the sounds of play ostensibly emanating from family members in pleasurable interaction *through* the game. Such a soundscape could have motivated purchase of the system and its game cartridges, in one case where a musical underscore might have distracted from the more decisive sounds of the game and play. At the same time (later 1970s), advertisers began introducing greater narrative substance into their spots for consoles and games, typically with a humorous or ironic twist to the pitch in keeping with the fun side of the devices—these spots largely relied on voice-over and enhanced game sounds to sell the product.

With the ever-increasing popularity of video games into the 1980s, commercials became more sophisticated in their storytelling and uses of sound and music. As a result, the rising star that was Atari exploited the possibilities for differentiated roles for sound and music in audiovisual promotion for game consoles and home computers, as revealed in commercials for the VCS/2600 consoles and the 400/800 computers. Both advertising campaigns strategically deployed music as the "ultimate hidden persuader" (Cook 2000, 122) and yet the nature and function of the scores significantly differed between the game and the computer spots.

While the booming market for video games ensured that all spots would feature at least one game, however briefly, Atari's promotion for the home computers mobilized a distinct strategy that focused on the device's usefulness for productive labor (as well as play). The tagline "Atari brings the computer age home"—the creation of advertising agency Young & Rubicam—aimed at selling the device's "interpretive flexibility . . . as a useful plaything, a toy with purpose" (Newman 2017, 149), a technology that could serve an adult for work and a child for learning while also providing them with entertainment. These commercials exploited music's capacity to track shifting affect in a series of lighthearted mini-dramas that highlight the home computer's versatility for a range of domestic situations.

In contrast, Atari's VCS/2600 ad campaign centered on the console's potential for playing video games, which we observe taking place in different social configurations, yet all on the home sofa. The company's game jingle "Have you played Atari today?"—positioned at the end of the spot—emphasizes the excitement of play through its lively tunefulness. The jingle's memorable words and melody may have only been heard in full in closing, however its musical material permeates earlier moments in the score as well. Here the spots present scenarios of family fun, with the music providing a repeating framework for lyrics that describe the experience of the specific game and lead directly into the closing jingle.

The strategic and effective use of music in these Atari ads reflects the maturation of promotional vehicles that needed to keep pace with the rapid development of the industry. The deployment of sound not immanent in the games themselves—the nondiegetic underscore—opened a range of expressive possibilities for audiovisual advertising that mirrored prevailing marketing discourses. Jingles and brand-related instrumental themes, differentiated musical styles according to product type, and the coordination of music with other soundtrack elements all signaled an advanced promotional practice in which music played a decisive role, anticipating the game trailer of the 1990s and beyond.

Notes

1. My special thanks extend to Will Gibbons (SUNY Potsdam), Tim Summers (Royal Holloway, University of London), and Chantal Lemire (University of Toronto) for their insights into aspects of the chapter.
2. Although the designations "commercial," "spot," and "ad" or "advertisement" have different connotations according to promotional medium, I use them interchangeably here, even as the primary and secondary literature do.
3. Regarding the Crash of 1983, considered a turning point in the industry, see above all Mirko Ernkvist's extended article "Down Many Times, but Still Playing the Game: Creative Destruction and Industry Crashes in the Early Video Game Industry 1971–1986" (2008).
4. For a recent discussion of promotion to families though commercials, see Winifred Phillips, "Music Genre and Games Genres" (chapter 5) in *A Composer's Guide to Game Music* (2014), which discusses a Wii ad from 2006 that clearly targets the domestic market (and uses a musical score instead of console sounds). She also observes how the music of Wii advertising differed between the campaign for industry and that for the consumer.
5. The game had only three sounds, those of the paddle and the wall being pitched one octave apart. For a comprehensive discussion of *Pong*, see Caprani (2014).
6. In one piece of its earliest marketing for Odyssey, the launch brochure, Magnavox called the console "The electronic game of the future." See Willaert (2020) for details of the company's print campaign.
7. "Magnavox Odyssey Commercial (1972)." https://www.youtube.com/watch?v=iCp-a90EP4c. Accessed December 3, 2021.
8. Ellipses here represent (slight) pauses in the narration, not omissions of text.
9. The full video can be screened at https://www.youtube.com/watch?v=JKar6QzUxPU.
10. Gibbons (2021, 323) specifically addresses this music's *2001*-like qualities, referencing Wendy Carlos' *Switched-On Bach* as a possible influence. It could also be said to bear some resemblance to the early titles for *The Twilight Zone* (1959–1964) as scored by Bernard Herrmann, especially through the music's congruence with the visual image of motion toward the stars.
11. Besides the narration and the musical underscore, the spot also features rather indistinct vocalizations from members of the family, ranging from "uh-oh" of the mother to the children's laughter.
12. As is typical for television advertising before the digital era, details for the dissemination of this spot are unknown.

13. In the decades prior to YouTube, super-8 Magi-Cartridge films were a relatively easy-to-use way for screening visual (but not audio) content, the consumer not being required to handle the film itself. See the entry "Technicolor Magi-Cartridge (early 1960s–early 1970s)" in the Museum of Obsolete Media (n.d.), at https://obsoletemedia.org/technicolor-magi-cartridge/.
14. "1972 Magnavox Odyssey Promotional Film." Accessed September 28, 2021. https://www.youtube.com/watch?v=jLGBtkKPj2U&t=1s.
15. "Atari 'Pong' 1976 Commercial." Accessed September 28, 2021. https://www.youtube.com/watch?v=yj1lz2Hj1mA.
16. Collins describes it as the "General Instruments chip that had been made available to any manufacturer" (Collins 2008, 20).
17. " 'Pong' Video Game Console." Accessed September 28, 2021. https://www.youtube.com/watch?v=uCqIkgFKHr4. The mislabeling is an error that several YouTube commentors identified.
18. "Atari 2600 Commercial December 17 1977." Accessed September 28, 2021. https://www.youtube.com/watch?v=YJNbhekKShI.
19. "Atari 1978 TV Commercial." Accessed September 28, 2021. https://www.youtube.com/watch?v=ZpqDNJKjznk.
20. "Magnavox Odyssey 2 1978 Commercial." Accessed September 28, 2021. https://www.youtube.com/watch?v=yrmUaagrh68&list=PLD3MboLuMLEoOVgQHoqgQhouMJAkNUGdh&index=20.
21. "Atari 2600—"We Don't Need a Babysitter" (Commercial, 1981)." Accessed September 28, 2021. https://www.youtube.com/watch?v=krGlnXY4HaY.
22. "Atari 'Space Invaders' 1980 TV Commercial." Accessed September 28, 2021. https://www.youtube.com/watch?v=ct_I2C_9Kf8.
23. The commercial takes pains to establish the house's location away from the city, opening with a nighttime outdoor shot and the sound of crickets. The narrator father begins with the statement, "Out here we entertain ourselves at home," which at once reinforces the family values promoted by Atari and rejects the culture represented by the urban arcade. The family's isolation also allows for the "invasion" to take place without the observation of neighbors.
24. Simon was an electronic game by Milton Bradley that tested memory, and Merlin was a handheld electronic device by Parker Brothers that supported six games.
25. See also Renfro (1982), who likewise critiques the concept of the "home office."
26. Intellivision was an exception: despite its considerable budget for advertising, Mattel seems to have preferred to allow spokesperson George Plimpton's mellifluous voice and upscale mid-Atlantic accent to dominate the soundtrack rather than incorporating music. The use of other celebrity spokespersons like Bill Cosby for Texas Instruments' TI-99 and Dick Cavett for Apple II likewise seems to have mitigated against the inclusion of musical underscoring.
27. Terry Britt comprehensively discusses the gender gap in computing magazines of the 1980s, using the analytical tool of discourse frames (2018). In the *Space Invaders* commercials discussed above, only the boy is shown as playing, despite the presence of the mother and the daughter on screen.
28. "Have You Played Atari Today?" Accessed September 28, 2021. https://www.youtube.com/watch?v=9vX2nHBploM.

29. The shared verse structure and melodic material suggests one agency was responsible for all the ads that use the "Have You Played Atari Today?" hook at the end.
30. "Atari 'Breakout' 1982 Video Game Commercial." Accessed September 28, 2021. https://www.youtube.com/watch?v=MmBmZkmIbOQ&list=PLD3MboLuMLEoOVgQHoqgQhouMJAkNUGdh&index=6.
31. "Atari 2600 1982 Commercial 'Pac-Man.'" Accessed September 28, 2021. https://www.youtube.com/watch?v=1FHkMqHx5xM.
32. "Atari 2600 Commercial: 'Super Breakout HQ.'" Accessed September 28, 2021. https://www.youtube.com/watch?v=ON5A2el_CuM.
33. "Atari 'Yar's Revenge' 1982 TV Commercial." Accessed September 28, 2021. https://www.youtube.com/watch?v=NSUx3_ByW1k.
34. "Atari 2600 Commercial: 'Defender' (July 4, 1982)." Accessed September 28, 2021. https://www.youtube.com/watch?v=ZEV7G2CqOTo.
35. "Atari 400/800 'Atari Brings the Computer Age Home' Commercial: 'Pac-Man' and 'Pilot.'" Accessed September 28, 2021. https://www.youtube.com/watch?v=iuZBtYsZQ54.
36. "Atari Home Computers 1981 Commercial Conversational French, 'Missile Command.'" Accessed September 28, 2021. https://www.youtube.com/watch?v=SXZN907qlWU.
37. "1981 Atari Computer Ad: States and Capitals / 'Basketball.'" Accessed September 28, 2021. https://www.youtube.com/watch?v=3pyNC07_pnA.
38. "1981 Atari Computer Ad: Stock Analysis / 'Space Invaders.'" Accessed September, 2021. https://www.youtube.com/watch?v=sjR07C4zGk4.
39. Any resemblance of this figure to the descending tetrachord in *Space Invaders* would appear to be coincidental.
40. On musical tropes and style topics, see above all Frank Lehman's introductory comments (2017, 502).
41. "1981 Atari Computer Ad: Stock Analysis / 'Space Invaders.'" Accessed September, 2021. https://www.youtube.com/watch?v=sjR07C4zGk4.
42. Newman (2017, 150) shrewdly observes that the broker is using his home computer screen to look at stock for Warner Communications, parent company of the conglomerate to which Atari belonged.
43. "Broker" collapses time in an interesting way, so that we are led to wonder how many hours he actually devoted to work, given that the ad ostensibly starts at the beginning of the workday.
44. The minor third has historically served as a sonic marker of failure or loss, from the playground and basketball court to film and television screens.

References

Ausretrogamer. 2015. "A 1972 Magnavox Odyssey Promo: I Like Them Cheesy." *Ausretrogamer*, January 2, 2015. Accessed December 3, 2021.https://ausretrogamer.com/a-1972-magnavox-odyssey-promo-i-like-them-cheesy/.

Britt, Terry L. 2018. "Home Computing's Halcyon Days: Discourse Frames in Computer Magazines in the Mid-1980s." *Journal of Magazine Media* 18, no. 2 (Spring): 1–18.

Caprani, Ole. 2014. "The PONG Game." Aarhus University—Department of Computer Science, Sound as Media, between Signal and Music—Introduction to Digital Audio.

Accessed December 3, 2021. http://web.archive.org/web/20180309023632/http://cs.au.dk/~dsound/DigitalAudio.dir/Greenfoot/Pong.dir/Pong.html.

Coles, Stephen. 2016. "Magnavox Odyssey Game Console, Logo, Packaging." *Fonts in Use*, December 15, 2016. Accessed December 3, 2021. https://fontsinuse.com/uses/15155/magnavox-odyssey-game-console-logo-packaging.

Collins, Karen. 2008. *Game Sound: An Introduction to the History, Theory and Practice of Video Game Music and Sound Design*. Cambridge, MA: MIT Press.

Cook, Nicholas. 2000. *Music: A Very Short Introduction*. New York: Oxford University Press.

Eng-Wilmot, Graham Lawrence. 2017. "Universal People: Audiovisual Experiments in Black Science Fiction, 1980–1986." PhD dissertation, University of California, Irvine.

Ernkvist, Mirko. 2008. "Down Many Times, but Still Playing the Game: Creative Destruction and Industry Crashes in the Early Video Game Industry 1971–1986." In *History of Insolvency and Bankruptcy: From an International Perspective*, edited by Karl Gratzer and Dieter Stiefel, 151–191. Huddinge, SE: Södertörns högskola.

Fagundes Pase, André, and Roberto Tietzmann. 2017. "Man's Best Enemy: The Role of Advertising during Atari's Launch in Brazil in 1983." *Kinephanos: Journal of Media Studies and Popular Culture* 7 (1): 74–105.

Gibbons, William. 2021. "'Have You Played Atari Today?': Music and Audience in an Early Video Game Advertising Campaign." In *The Oxford Handbook of Music and Advertising*, edited by James Deaville, Siu-Lan Tan, and Ronald Rodman, 322–333. New York: Oxford University Press.

Horton, Zachary. 2019. "A 'Total Play and Learning Experience': The Magnavox Odyssey's 1972 Dream of Media Convergence." *Continent* 8, no. 1 (September 17): 76–86.

Huhtamo, Erkki. 2012. "What's Victoria Got to Do with It: Toward an Archeology of Domestic Video Gaming." In *Before the Crash: Early Video Game History*, edited by Mark J. P. Wolf, 30–52. Detroit: Wayne State University Press.

Impellizeri, Kevin Donald. 2019. "The Multiplayer Game: User Home Video Games in the United States, 1971–1994." PhD dissertation, University of Delaware.

Kanitsakis, Stelios. 2020. "An Audio Research on the Gameplay Sounds of Atari's *Pong* and the Silence of Magnavox Odyssey's *Tennis*." Accessed December 3, 2021. https://stelioskanitsakis.medium.com/an-audio-comparison-between-the-sounds-of-ataris-pong-and-the-silence-of-magnavox-odyssey-s-83e6fac56653.

Kupfer, Peter. 2021. "Fitting Tunes: Selecting Music for Television Commercials." In *The Oxford Handbook of Music and Advertising*, edited by James Deaville, Siu-Lan Tan, and Ronald Rodman, 72–92. New York: Oxford University Press.

Lehman, Frank. 2017. "Methods and Challenges of Analyzing Screen Media." In *The Routledge Companion to Screen Music and Sound*, edited by Miguel Mera, Ron Sadoff, and Ben Winters, 497–526. New York: Routledge.

Lerner, Neil. 2013. "The Origins of Musical Style in Video Games, 1977–1983." In *The Oxford Handbook of Film Music Studies*, edited by David Neumeyer, 319–347. New York: Oxford University Press.

Lowood, Henry. 2009. "Videogames in Computer Space: The Complex History of *Pong*." *IEEE Annals of the History of Computing* 31, no. 3 (July–Sept.): 5–19.

MacDonald, Barry, Roderick Atkin, David Jenkins, and Stephen Kemmis. 1977. "Computer Assisted Learning: Its Educational Potential (UNCAL)." In *The National Development Programme in Computer Assisted Learning: Final Report of the Director*, edited by Richard Hooper, 1–32. London: The Council for Educational Technology. Accessed December 3,

2021. https://ueaeprints.uea.ac.uk/id/eprint/33872/1/MacDonald-1977-Computer_Assisted_Learning.pdf.
Marchand, Roland. 1985. *Advertising the American Dream: Making Way for Modernity, 1920–1940*. Berkeley: University of California Press.
Newman, Michael Z. 2017. *Atari Age: The Emergence of Video Games in America*. Cambridge, MA: MIT Press.
Oakes, Steve, and Morteza Abelhasani. 2021. "Musical Congruity in Advertising: Established and Emerging Themes." In *The Oxford Handbook of Music and Advertising*, edited by James Deaville, Siu-Lan Tan, and Ronald Rodman, 757–774. New York: Oxford University Press.
Phillips, Winifred. 2014. *A Composer's Guide to Game Music*. Cambridge, MA: MIT Press.
Pollack, Andrew. 1982. "The Game Turns Serious at Atari." *New York Times*, December 19, 1982.
Renfro, William L. 1982. "Second Thoughts on Moving the Office Home." *Futurist* 16, no. 3 (June): 43–48.
Schartmann, Andrew. 2013. *Maestro Mario: How Nintendo Transformed Videogame Music into an Art*. New York: Thought Catalog.
Salem, Philip J., and Robert D. Gratz. 1983. "High Technology and Social Devolution." In *Proceedings of the 1983 World Conference on Systems*, edited by Nagib Callaos. Caracas, Venezuela: The Foundation for the Investigation and Integration of Systems. Accessed December 31, 2023. https://www.academia.edu/4125557/High_Technology_and_Social_Devolution.
Summers, Tim. 2017. "Dimensions of Game Music History." In *The Routledge Companion to Screen Music and Sound*, edited by Miguel Mera, Ron Sadoff, and Ben Winters, 139–152. New York: Routledge.
Švelch, Jan. 2017a. "Exploring the Myth of the Representative Video Game Trailer." *Kinephanos: Journal of Media Studies and Popular Culture* 7 (1): 7–36.
Švelch, Jan. 2017b. "Paratexts to Non-Linear Media Texts: Paratextuality in Video Game Culture." PhD dissertation, University of Prague.
Švelch, Jan. 2020. "Paratextuality in Game Studies: A Theoretical Review and Citation Analysis." *Game Studies* 20, no. 2 (June). Accessed December 3, 2021. http://gamestudies.org/2002/articles/jan_svelch?fbclid=IwARopb1RvBRgtCss3jlab_T8PY_tgfryC3py4ZrXT_HxwDZmh5yoou3xjhzs.
Tan, Siu-Lan, Ron Rodman, and James Deaville. 2021. "Introduction: Music and Advertising: Production, Text, and Reception." In *The Oxford Handbook of Music and Advertising*, edited by James Deaville, Siu-Lan Tan, and Ron Rodman, 1–21. New York: Oxford University Press.
Taynes-Ehle, Zeynep, and Sara Speedy. 2017. "Quality of Video Game Trailers." *Kinephanos: Journal of Media Studies and Popular Culture* 7 (1): 246–273.
"Technicolor Magi-Cartridge (early 1960s–early 1970s)." n.d. Museum of Obsolete Media. Accessed December 3, 2021. https://obsoletemedia.org/technicolor-magi-cartridge/.
Therrien, Carl, and Isabelle Lefebvre. 2017. "Now You're Playing with Adverts: A Repertoire of Frames for the Historical Study of Game Culture through Marketing Discourse." *Kinephanos: Journal of Media Studies and Popular Culture* 7 (1): 37–73.
Tuckman, Gaye. 1991. "Sixteen—Pluralism and Disdain: American Culture Today." In *America at Century's End*, edited by Alan Wolfe, 340–358. Berkeley: University of California Press.
Vollans, Ed. 2017. "The Most Cinematic Game Yet." *Kinephanos: Journal of Media Studies and Popular Culture* 7 (1): 106–130.
Vollans, Ed, Stephanie Janes, Carl Therrien, and Dominic Arsenault. 2017. "'It's [Not Just] in the Game': The Promotional Context of Video Games." *Kinephanos: Journal of Media Studies and Popular Culture* 7 (1): 1–6.

Willaert, Kate. 2018. "Pixels in Print (Part 1): Advertising Computer Space—The First Arcade Video Game." Video Game History Foundation, April 10, 2018. Accessed December 3, 2021. https://gamehistory.org/first-arcade-game-advertisement-computer-space/.

Willaert, Kate. 2020. "Pixels in Print (Part 2): Advertising Odyssey—The First Home Video Game." Video Game History Foundation, March 20, 2020. Accessed December 3, 2021. https://gamehistory.org/magnavox-odyssey-advertisement-history/.

Wright, Esther. 2018. "On the Promotional Context of Historical Video Games." *Rethinking History* 22 (4): 598–608.

CHAPTER 8

HARD LIMITATIONS AND SOFT POSSIBILITIES

A "Systematic" History of Early Video Game Sound Technology

KEVIN R. BURKE

Introduction

This chapter presents an analytical approach to early video game sound that incorporates both the history of hardware limitations and the innovative software that shaped distinct styles among various developers. My use of the word "systematic" refers to the unique makeup of each gaming hardware. While many systems share similar sound components and forms of sound synthesis, the applications of the hardware are varied and diverse. I consider systematic composition in three configurations: idio-systematic—the software possibilities of the sound system's primary functions; meta-systematic—the sound system's functions that emulate or replicate operations that exist outside of the system; and cross-systematic—functions of the sound system that coordinate multiple sound sources. The range of gaming hardware reflected by this chapter includes four types of sound synthesis sources that I approach in detail: programmable sound generators (PSG); wavetable synthesis; frequency modulation (FM); and pulse-code modulation (PCM) samples paired with a digital signal processor (DSP). Musical examples from *Asterix* (NES), *Bloody Wolf* (Turbografx 16), *Verytex* (Sega Genesis), and *Chrono Trigger* (SNES) will serve as case studies, but the approach could apply to many other games and systems. At the end of the chapter, I provide appendices: a glossary of select terms; a summary of sound file formats; and a comprehensive list of sound chips, detailing some of their features and organized according to synthesis type.

A fetishism of retro gaming platforms is understandable. Game consoles, PCs, and arcade cabinets are tangible, visual icons to the past. Even when connected to a TV and the TV's speakers, it is the console that appears like a musical instrument. The analogy carries further when considering the physical and nonphysical components that contribute to musical sounds. As Thor Magnusson (2017) has recently argued, the widely adopted system of classifying musical instruments by Hornbostel and Sachs (1914) is insufficient for dealing with digital music technologies of the past few decades. Sound chips themselves do not emanate sound. And the same sound chip placed in two different systems may result in a different palette of possibilities due to other components in the hardware, such as processing units, clocking speeds, filters, and operational amplifiers (op amps). Furthermore, the capabilities of sound chips are realized only through programming, to execute what the chip was designed to be capable of (and perhaps more).

Certainly, modern gaming consoles have many hardware and software considerations worthy of discussion. But the focus of this chapter are the systems spanning the late 1970s, 1980s, and early 1990s, a soft *chiptune* era for video game music where sound architecture was more variable than that of other media (see also chapter 12 this volume for more on the game hardware and software of the period). While defining parameters for historical periods brings forth many issues that go beyond the scope of this chapter, I do adopt a few general criteria for how the term "chiptune" applies to the gaming systems considered in this chapter:

- Gaming hardware generates music from its own on-board components during gameplay
- Compression and/or sample bit rates are lower than that of Red Book Audio
- Chiptune is a natural result of the gaming hardware rather than a conscious throwback
- Reproduction (not recording) of the sound requires the actual gaming hardware or a convincing emulator.

While sound issues of retro gaming hardware represent only a small corner of ludomusicological inquiry, I hope this chapter will serve as a general guide for exploring how hardware and software interact in game composition and furnish the unique character and history of iconic game systems. When software possibilities guide inquiry, game systems serve as a springboard rather than as a container for innovative game music.

Methodology

While both traditional Western music notation and MIDI piano roll notation are generally valuable means of transcribing video game music, an unconventional application of their symbols and structures can uncover nuances attributed to the developer's approach to the gaming hardware. The music examples in this chapter all employ a modified form of Western music notation to highlight these key approaches:

- The number of (possible) audio channels (registers) employed
- The type of sound synthesis provided
- The coordination of multichannel effects for
  - Detuning
  - Echo (reverb)
  - Bi-timbrality
  - Stereo panning
- The distillation of multiple lines from within a single channel
- The adaption of sound chip function to emulate familiar music techniques

The Four Main Types of Sound Synthesis in Early Video Game Systems

Programmable Sound Generators

The limited number of audio channels on programmable sound generators inspired several creative approaches to expand polyphony and timbre complexity. The sound engineers at many game developers adopted similar meta-systematic techniques that borrowed or emulated the basic functionality of analog synthesizers. Examples include pulse-width modulation, chorusing, and arpeggios (arps). Some developers managed to shape a more unique sonic profile from other meta-systematic areas of inspiration, such as macros coding from computer programming and mix automation from the commercial music industry.

For the purposes of this chapter, I distinguish between generic and custom PSGs, as shown in the appendix. Generic PSGs include Texas Instruments's SN76489, found in the Sega Master System, ColecoVision, and a variety of personal computers, as well as General Instrument's AY-3-8910, found in early arcade cabinets, Mattel's Intellivision, and many personal computers. Custom PSGs include MOS's SID chip in the Commodore 64, Atari's TIA in the VCS (2600), and Ricoh's 2A03 in Nintendo's NES. The generic PSGs typically provide three to four audio channels of square waves (fixed duty cycle of 50%) with noise; however, the custom PSGs tend to offer further options from classic analog synthesizers, such as a triangle wave, a sawtooth wave, or variable pulse widths.

Although the general capabilities of the generic PSGs are very similar—three tone channels with noise—structural differences exist that inform idio-systematic approaches to music composition. For example, the first three channels of the SN76489 are fixed and can output only square waves, while any of the AY-38910's three channels can output sound from the square wave generator, the noise generator, or both simultaneously.[1]

Figure 8.1 is the opening measures to the "Game Over" track to *Asterix* (1993) for the Nintendo Entertainment System, composed by Alberto González. The score layout indicates all possible audio channels of the NES's audio processing unit (APU), including the two pulse wave channels, the triangle wave channel, the noise channel, and the (differential) pulse-code modulation (DPCM) sample channel—the latter is unused.[2]

A brief explanation of the graphics and notation: a symbol for the 25% duty cycle of the pulse wave is displayed above the first two staves—had the pulse width changed during the excerpt, an additional symbol would be shown at the point of the pulse width modulation. Both tremolo and rolled chord symbols are employed on the downbeats in the second pulse wave channel to illustrate a rapid, repeating arp of the chord. A single-channel, echo-like effect also occurs in the second pulse wave channel at the octave. Rather than using expressive dynamic markings to indicate the drop in volume of the echo, I have used smaller noteheads. The triangle wave channel carries two musical lines at once: the rapid, descending glissandi add body to the implied bass drum and snare drum shared with the noise channel, while the sustained tones form the foundation of a bass part. The switch to triangle noteheads for the downward glissandi helps distinguish the two musical parts within the single channel, as well as symbolize the triangle wave in its percussive role. The dotted line couples the parts of the triangle and noise channel that combine to form the snare and bass drum timbres. Finally, in the noise channel, beams and stems are suspended where a constant hi-hat pattern is implied by a rock drumbeat; the monophonic channel is unable to produce both drum sounds at the same time. Rather than trying to approximate the initial pitch of the noise channel's notes, the notation follows standard staff position for the implied snare drum, bass drum, and hi-hat.

From this technical transcription, one can glean some of the techniques González (both a composer and programmer) employed with his sound driver to extend the amount of polyphony and enhance the timbral variety from within the hardware

FIGURE 8.1 Measures 1–3 of "Game Over" from *Asterix* (1993) by Alberto González.

restrictions. Rapid-fire arps serve both as a percussive effect as well as an efficient means of providing harmonic accompaniment within a single voice. The technique was already prevalent among British and European composers in the late 1980s, often emulating the chord-strumming effect (Elkins 2017), and González made frequent use of them in his work for the ZX Spectrum prior to writing any music for the NES. The single-channel echo is far less common than the multichannel echo but was employed heavily by the game developer Konami for the NES after 1987 to feign reverb; however, González indicated that the octave echo was to give the articulation lift so it did not sound too static.[3] While the combination of downward pitch slides and noise for drum sounds is a regular occurrence in game soundtracks toward the end of the 8-bit era, the rapid toggle between the downward pitch slides and a sustained bass line within a single channel is far less common. González recalled observing the technique in Tim Follin's soundtrack to *Solstice* (1990), which he consulted in developing his own sound driver, and later adapted it to his own style of writing drum parts.

A comparison with the popular Simmons SDS electronic drum kit of the 1980s suggests a meta-systematic approach with this example. Bi-timbral drums are a clever application of the NES's custom triangle wave to add body to noise, with the rapidly descending glissando a compromise for the triangle wave's inability for volume attenuation.[4] The fading tone is therefore compressed in a similar fashion to a gated reverb following the drum hit. Figure 8.2 is a snapshot of the Simmons SDS 400 Brain. Included on the manual controls are the balance of tone and noise, the direction and speed of a glissandi on the tone, and an envelope for shaping the strength of the drum's attack and speed of the decay and release point. While the NES APU is hardly a substitute for the full capabilities of the SDS 400, the critical variables of building analog electronic drums are summoned through the capabilities of the NES.

Wavetable Synthesis

The term "wavetable synthesis" can apply to a wide range of possible applications and, historically, is frequently confused with sample-based synthesis. A detailed explanation of how the term originated in the late 1970s and how it evolved to encompass a variety of techniques is beyond the scope of this chapter; however, for the purposes of understanding video game sound design, it is helpful to distinguish between wavetable synthesis as a systematic structure and wavetable synthesis as a dynamic application.

As the name implies, the core structure is a table of predefined waveforms—a waveform table or wavetable—whether hardwired to a chip or loaded into RAM by software. The source of the waveforms could be data converted from recorded samples or simply data reflective of basic waveform shapes. Programs look up or reference waveforms for the oscillators to play from data pointers. Table-lookup oscillators are the primary form of wavetable synthesis one encounters in video game music, though the resulting sound possibilities can vary drastically from system to system.

FIGURE 8.2 Envelope, glissando, tone, and noise parameters on the Simmons SDS 400 Brain. Photo taken by author.

TABLE 8.1 A Comparison of the Most Common Wavetable Synthesis Platforms

Company	Chip/Platform	Channels	Length in Bytes	Bit Depth
Namco	WSG	3	32	4 (16 values)
Namco	N163	3	var.*	4 (16 values)
Konami	SCC	5	32	8 (256 values)
Nintendo	FDS	1	64	6 (64 values)
Nintendo	Gameboy	1	32	4 (16 values)
Nintendo	Virtual Boy	5	32	6 (64 values)
NEC	PCE/TG16	6	32	5 (32 values)

*Although the N163 is similar to the WSG in bit-depth.

Table 8.1 outlines the major parameter differences among the various wavetable sound chips/platforms: the number of waveform bytes, which reflect the length of a complete cycle; the bit-depth of the waveform, or the number of possible values for each byte; and the number of audio channels for waveform playback.

Waveforms become more refined—less stepped—with higher bit depth. Consider the convincing clarity of the bells chiming from the waveform channel of the Famicom Disk System (FDS), in the title track of the Japanese version of *The Legend of Zelda* (1986), for example, compared with the harsh chirps and honks of the Namco WSG in arcade classics like *Pac-Man* (1980) and *Galaga* (1981).

While custom waveforms provide greater timbral variety than the basic waveforms found in most PSGs, they remain as fixed waveforms in the structural sense. The more expressive aspect of wavetable synthesis is the dynamic modulation (or interpolation) of waveforms in a table. The timbral shifting of waveshapes reflects techniques pioneered and popularized by Wolfgang Palm for the PPG Wave Synthesizer. The result is dynamic instruments from quasi-periodic waveforms rather than fixed, periodic waveforms. Most video game systems from the 8- and 16-bit era did not make use of this technique, however, due to limitations in memory for the necessary programming, and to the absence of supporting components like a DSP that could minimize audible distortions from the periodic shifting of waveforms.

An excerpt from NEC's Turbografx-16 (the "PCE/TG16" in Table 8.1) will illustrate one of the few examples of this technique of waveform interpolation. The HuC6280 microprocessor includes an onboard sound generator capable of six channels of wavetable synthesis. Waveforms are built from 32 samples with 5-bit depth, which can be illustrated as values plotted on a 32x32 graph.[5] The waveform assigned to the bass instrument in the "Title Track" to Data East's *Bloody Wolf* (1989) will serve as an example (see Figure 8.3). The hexadecimal [hex] values for the 32 samples of the waveform are as follows:[6]

10 16 1D 1E 1D 16 11 10 11 16 1E 16 10 16 1D 1E

1E 1D 16 10 08 03 02 02 03 08 0C 0C 08 08 0C 10

And below are the values converted from hex to decimal:

16 22 29 30 29 22 17 16 17 22 30 22 16 22 29 30

30 29 22 16 08 03 02 02 03 08 12 12 08 08 12 16

Finally, the full, 32-byte sequence of 5-bit values, in decimal, are plotted in graph form in Figure 8.3.

By plotting the 32-byte sequence of sample values, one can visualize the periodic waveforms that form individual instruments in the game's soundtrack. However, the unique characteristics of waveform synthesis are more fully realized in quasi-periodic waveforms. While waveform modulation is a rare occurrence in the library of game soundtracks, its use highlights how sound engineers attempted to emulate the technology behind popular synthesizers of the 1980s with meta-systematic techniques.

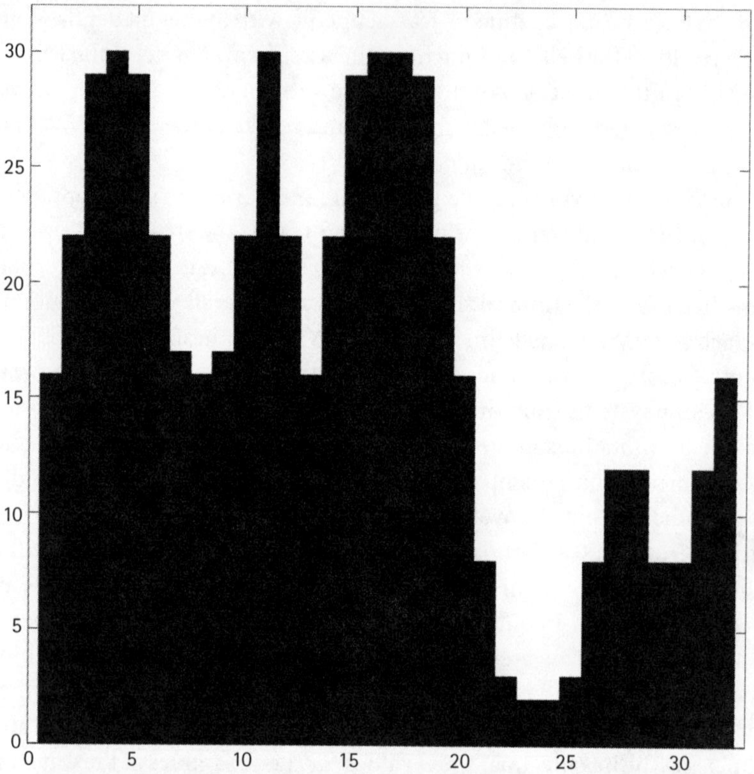

FIGURE 8.3 A graphical image of the bass waveform in the title track to *Bloody Wolf* (Data East, 1989).

Figure 8.4 presents the table of ten waveforms that render a modulating brass effect found throughout the soundtrack to *Bloody Wolf* (additional waveforms are in Figure 8.5). The cycle of waveform interpolation is varied, depending on the rhythmic duration of the note, and follows stages that are reminiscent of an ADSR envelope, that is, the rate of attack, decay, sustain, and release of the complete tone. The first waveform (A), which resembles a sawtooth wave, serves as an attack, and the final waveform (J), which resembles a sine wave, serves as a release point. The internal waveforms—shown with lowercase letters—will follow in sequence for the note's duration and skip directly to the final waveform just before the note's conclusion. See Figure 8.6. For the lead brass in measures 4–5, as an example, the dotted-quarter notes sweep through waveforms A–b–c–J, the quarter note through waveforms A–b–J, and the eighth note tied to the dotted half note through waveforms A–b–c–d–e–f–g–J.

As is typical of most game soundtracks employing wavetable synthesis, the remaining instruments in this example use a fixed waveform (bass, kick drum, tom toms) or the noise mode (snare), which can be enacted in the HuC6280's 5th and 6th channel.

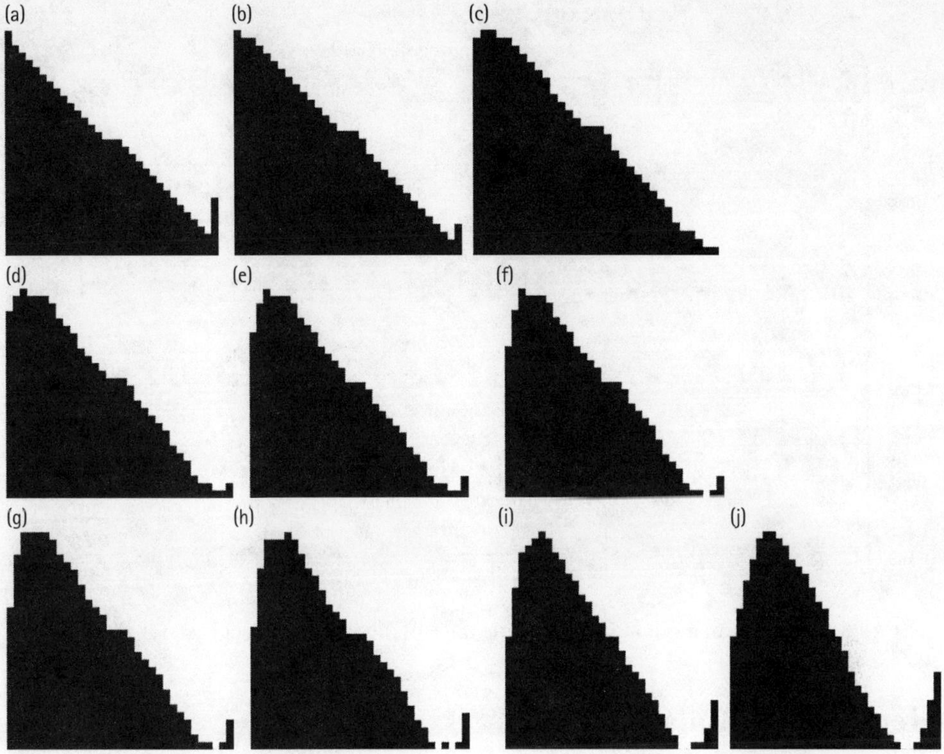

FIGURE 8.4 Graphical images of the modulating brass wavetable in *Bloody Wolf* (1989).

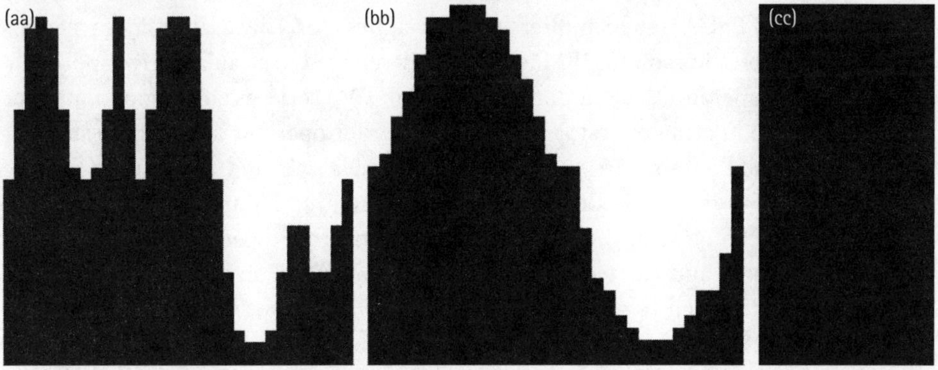

FIGURE 8.5 Additional Waveforms found in the Title Track to *Bloody Wolf* (Data East, 1989). (aa) Bass, (bb) Kick drum, (cc) Tom toms.

FIGURE 8.6 Waveform modulation in the title track of *Bloody Wolf* (Data East, 1989).

Frequency Modulation

Yamaha's phase modulation, marketed as *frequency modulation* (FM), was the most prevalent successor to PSGs in the 1980s as arcade boards, personal computers, and home consoles moved from the 8-bit to 16-bit eras. All dedicated FM sound chips from this era are Yamaha chips, though true frequency modulation itself was possible as a secondary function in some sound chips developed by other manufacturers. Unlike the subtractive approach to sound synthesis that is associated with analog synthesizers and PSGs, in which filters and envelopes chisel away at basic waveforms to shape more complex sounds, FM is frequently referred to as an additive approach. Oscillators (or "operators," as they are identified in FM) serve as either modulators or carriers. The modulating operator morphs the carrier operator at varying rates, according to defined parameters such as an ADSR envelope, and the resulting, more complex wave of the carrier is amplified. Most FM chips have four operators per audio channel, which can be arranged in various algorithms that determine their relationship as modulators and carriers, though two-operator and six-operator FM sound chips were also designed.

The appearance of FM in video game hardware coincides with Yamaha's introduction of the new form of synthesis to the music industry at large. In fact, Yamaha released an MSX standard personal computer for musicians in 1983, the CX5M, marketed as a music computer, which contained an FM sound unit module and could run software for creating and editing FM presets on the iconic DX7 keyboard.[7] Within a year, Atari launched the first arcade title to use Yamaha's FM technology, *Marble Madness* (1984), which contained the same 4-operator chip, the YM2151 (Operator Type-M, or OPM),

TABLE 8.2 A Comparison of the OPM, OPL, and OPN Families of Yamaha's FM Chips

OPM Family	OPL Family	OPN Family
4-operator FM	2-operator FM	4-operator FM + additional synthesis sources

found in the CX5M computer's FM sound module. The OPM became the most common FM chip for arcade boards developed by Sega, Konami, Data East, and others, in the second half of the 1980s.

Two other main families of FM sound chips played a large role in video game music as well: Operator Type-L, or OPL, and Operator Type-N, or OPN (Table 8.2). The YM2413 (OPLL), for example, appeared primarily for early personal computer sound cards and 8-bit home consoles, such as accessories for the MSX computer and for the Sega Master System in Japan.[8] The OPL family was a scaled-back form of FM that provided two, rather than four operators, per channel, and often with preset instrument patches hard-wired to the chip. The limited number of parameters for data input were therefore more manageable for 8-bit processors.

The OPN family of FM chips, on the other hand, maintained the use of four-operator FM synthesis, however, integrated additional audio functions to mitigate the cramped space within home consoles. The YM2612 (OPN2), for example, found in the Sega Mega Drive (Sega Genesis in North America), could change the function of the operators in channel six to play back 8-bit PCM samples. This feature makes sense, considering the vast space afforded by arcade cabinets where a discrete FM chip like the OPM could be paired with several specific PCM sample chips like the OKI MSM5205, forming a cross-systematic sound design. The OPN2 also included a special mode for the third audio channel, where the frequency of each of the four operators could be set independently. In addition to the timbral possibilities of dynamic changes to independent operators, the special mode also made it possible to expand the number of simultaneous tones in the harmony. Figure 8.7 illustrates how channel three mode can expand harmony by treating a single channel of four-operator FM synthesis like two channels of two-operator FM synthesis.

As in previous musical examples, I use technical music notation in Figure 8.7 to highlight systematic features of the overall sound design. The score layout indicates that the SN76489 PSG that was included as a legacy sound chip in Sega Genesis (for backward compatibility) is unused in the example, as well as the primary FM function (rather than PCM function) in the sixth channel of the YM2612 (OPN2).[9] The three FM instrument patches included in this excerpt are identified by the implied timbres—bells, brass, and slap bass—and a multichannel echo technique is indicated by the dotted line between channels one and two as well as the smaller note heads for the delayed echo at a lower volume.

The notation for channel three mode provides two pieces of information. The fundamental tones of two operators are shown with regular noteheads and the adjusted

FIGURE 8.7 Measures 4–7 of "The Void of Space" from *Verytex* (1991) by Hitoshi Sakimoto.

frequency of the other two operators are shown with diamond noteheads. The number in parentheses reflects the number of semitones above the fundamental instructed for the latter two operators, which results in dynamic harmonic intervals in the excerpt rather than a fixed harmonic interval. It is also important to note that the FM Brass instrument patch uses algorithm four, which uniquely configures the four operators into two pairs of modulators and carriers. Thus, when in channel three mode, each pair of modulators and carriers can carry a different frequency. Hitoshi Sakimoto, the composer of the track as well as the developer of the sound driver used in this game, therefore, forms sustained chords in just two channels, freeing up additional channels for multichannel echo and for the bi-timbral bass line in channels five and six.

Sample-Based Synthesis

I distinguish sample-based synthesis from general PCM playback, in that sample-based synthesis requires a DSP that reads and manipulates PCM samples for building complete, versatile instruments, rather than the basic playback of a fixed sample as found in early video game systems. Many PSGs and some of Yamaha's FM chips could play back PCM samples either in a separate audio channel or as an

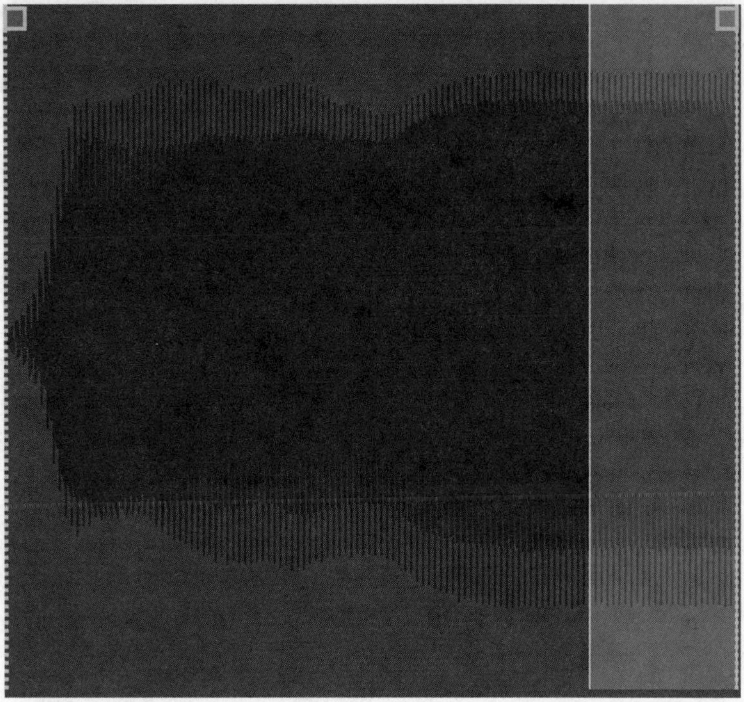

FIGURE 8.8 The loop region (to the right) of the oboe sample in *Chrono Trigger* (1995).

alternative application of one of the other audio channels. However, PCM as a form of sound synthesis requires further manipulation of the sample data to create fully functional instruments.

While playing samples at faster and lower speeds can adjust the frequency of the sample, the duration will be altered. PCM sound synthesis thus uses loop points to stretch out instrument sounds to save on memory and to create variable durations needed for dynamic musical lines. Figure 8.8 is a screenshot of the oboe sample used in the *Chrono Trigger* soundtrack, pulled from the SFC audio file with Plogue's Chipsynth SFC plugin. The sustain part of the sample, following the initial attack and decay, is highlighted to show the beginning and ending loop points. For the oboe to sustain notes of a long duration, the sample will loop the highlighted region, much like a flexible vamp, until it is time for the note's release. As is evident in the image of the waveform, there is no release point included in the sample. To save on memory, many samples were truncated. The DSP's ability to create volume envelopes for playing samples, means that many SNES music soundtracks use the DSP's envelope to create artificial release points for the termination of samples by allowing the sustain portion of the sample to loop as the volume is faded out to terminate the note. A high volume of recurring waveform data points can occur both from the process of compressing PCM data and from looping subsections of the sample. These recurrences (or aliases) of the signal can sometimes create audible, jarring distortions.[10]

The technological aspects of sample-based audio system like that found in the SNES have received far less attention in ludomusicological scholarship than those for systems with PSG- and FM-based audio. Karen Collins (2008), for example, frames an explanation of SNES audio by its similarities to sample-based wavetable synthesis and to hybrid approaches such as Roland's linear arithmetic (LA) synthesis. Dominic Arsenault's (2017) monograph on the SNES as a platform summarizes the basic architecture of the APU and notes how the possibility of diverse sample libraries took SNES game music composition in a variety of new stylistic directions.

In many ways, SNES audio is both simple and complicated. On the one hand, the notion of working with samples of real musical instruments, as opposed to imitating musical instruments with other forms of sound synthesis, is far less daunting. And with built-in tools for full stereo panning and special effects like reverb, the options seem to more closely resemble the full-palette range available to modern game composers. The challenges and innovations that encompass working with 8-bit systems and sound chips do not seem as relevant to the affordances the SNES audio technology provides. The basic understanding of PCM as a digital quantization of analog waveforms that, in turn, are read and converted to audible sound with a DAC, is straightforward. Several contemporaneous systems such as the Commodore Amiga, the Sega CD, and even Sony's PlayStation also employed PCM sample playback across multiple audio channels. Yet, SNES audio has a distinct character, so much so that companies such as Impact Soundworks and Plogue Art et Technologie have invested time and resources to create specialized VST plugins for musicians aiming to recreate the SNES sound. The core components that define SNES audio are the custom bit rate reduction (BRR), a form of adaptive differential pulse code modulation (ADPCM), and the settings of the SNES's DSP to produce effects such as reverb, frequency modulation, and equalization.

One structural difference that distinguishes the SNES from other contemporary systems that used PCM audio is the lack of a CD-ROM drive. Direct PCM data, or linear PCM, requires a significant amount of memory that CD-ROMs could spare. Even if pure Redbook audio was not used, there was still plenty of memory for PCM sample data in an uncompressed format. Differential PCM, as found on the NES and often simplified further by its 1-bit delta modulator, is a common form of PCM data compression that stores the differences in subsequent sample values rather than the actual quantized values. Difference values typically occupy a narrower range of values that can be expressed in fewer bits. Such compression relies on a considerable amount of repetition and predictability in the sample waveform data; otherwise, when the data is decompressed the final waveform will be significantly distorted. The SNES's form of compression, BRR, is a subset of DPCM known as adaptive DPCM, which allows the possible range of differential values to be adjusted in each subsequent block of waveform data. BRR further reduces the number of bits required to store the data, since the possible difference values can be adjusted as the waveform data progresses. The result is a compression ratio of nine bytes of BRR data for every 32 bytes of linear PCM data.

The echo effects enabled by the DSP form another defining characteristic of SNES audio. While echo-like effects were often added through both single and multichannel approaches to music tracks using PSG, Wavetable, and FM sound chips, as illustrated in the examples above, echoes were an integral, if perhaps necessary, component of all SNES audio. Echo was required at a minimum level to mask imperfections from the patchwork of sample BRR and loop points, much in the same way the Gaussian filter removes distortions from the extremities of the harmonic spectrum. A single echo is buffered for all samples, which is then mixed with the output of the original sample, at a timing delay that can be set between 0–240 ms in intervals of 16 ms. The DSP then permits a variety of effects for the echoes. Echo feedback creates a chain of subsequent echoes at varying intervals to create reverb. Additionally, eight coefficients (or taps) of finite impulse response (FIR) filters can gradually alter the sample during chains of echoes. The FIR filters were commonly used as a type of equalization, by attenuating the signal gain of the echoes at certain frequencies to create low-pass, high-bass, and band-pass filters, among others. Without the FIR filters enabled, the echoes would remain unaltered from the original sample.

While sampling capabilities of early video game audio technology are present in scholarship and historical guides, the sources of the samples are rarely discussed. Since industry samplers such as the Akai S612 and Roland S220 were capable of downsampling mic'ed audio sources for PCM data, a variety of sound modules and libraries popular in professional music studios were sourced. And for 16- and 32-bit era gaming hardware like the Super Nintendo Entertainment System that relied primarily on PCM sound architecture, samples from a diverse cocktail of modules could lend individual games a distinct sound palette.

The soundtrack to Square's *Chrono Trigger* (1995), for example, draws its particular sound set from a variety of sources: instrument manufacturer libraries from Roland, Korg, and Kurzweil; sampler manufacturer libraries from Akai, E-MU, and Fairlight; and third-party distribution CD-ROM collections from East West and Best Service.[11] It is worth noting that these sources were also popular in professional music-recording studios in the late 1980s and early 1990s, making timbres in many fourth- and fifth-generation game consoles not much different than contemporary pop music, save the varying sample rates. This transitional stage thus marks a time where video game music begins to sound less like a compromise or imitation of familiar instruments—it is still, though, distinguishable from other media, unlike much modern game music today.

While some game developers may have had in-house sound collections, such as instruments precoded into proprietary sound drivers, many with robust audio departments increasingly were equipped with a full menu of options. Photos of Sega of Japan's sound circa 1993, featured in Tokuma Shoten's *World of Phantasy Star* artbook (Highsmith), for example, provide evidence of sound module hardware like an Akai S1000 (1988) sampler as well as E-MU Proteus (1989) and Ensoniq SQ-R (1990)

FIGURE 8.9 Tokuhiko Uwabo with a variety of samplers and ROMplers in the Sega Studio.

ROMplers (see Figure 8.9). Likewise, third-party sound studios such as East West and Best Service released CD-ROMs of sample packs in file formats that could load on to some of the industry's most popular sampler units.

The analysis of video game soundtracks from PCM-based hardware that is paired with a DSP invites a different focus than those from PSG, FM, and wavetable sound chips. The DSP can produce effects such as reverb and echo within a single audio channel that would typically be coordinated across multiple channels in 8-bit-generation sound design. Furthermore, identifying familiar instrument timbres is also more realistic, given the common libraries of sample sources from the period.

The track "Corridors of Time" from *Chrono Trigger* illustrates the diverse sample sources that could contribute to a game's overall soundtrack palette. In the opening measures, an eclectic juxtaposition of "world instruments" enter, representing the sound libraries of market competitors: the gamelan, found on Korg's popular M1 Digital Workstation (1988–1995); the sitar, found on the Akai SL1058 disk for the Akai S1000 sampler; the tabla, found on the E-MU Emulator III Classic Series, Volume 2, CD-ROM; and the vocal *AHHs*, found on Peter Siedlaczek's Classical Choir CD-ROM library. Below, in Figure 8.10, I have provided a few measures from the track "Underground Sewer" to illustrate how sample sources may be identified as instruments in music examples. The sources provide a glimpse into the resources available to the audio department at Squaresoft during *Chrono Trigger*'s development. These conditions contrast with the conditions modern game composers share today, where they can work independently and remotely with vast libraries of digital samples at their fingertips.

FIGURE 8.10 Measures 9–12 of "Underground Sewer" from *Chrono Trigger* (Squaresoft 1995) expressed by the sample source.

Conclusion

The main examples discussed in this chapter focused on popular home consoles, where the interplay of software and hardware is most potent due to the limited architecture. The push to optimize audio capabilities from the constrained resources was the catalyst for idio-systematic and meta-systematic innovation. However, many of the same compositional approaches and sound parameters were also applied to games developed for personal computers and arcade boards, where a more open architecture is common. The expansive build of arcade sound boards typically resulted in more discrete sound chips. While companies endeavored to build arcade platforms that could be reused for multiple titles, development timetables (due to market pressure and to manufacturing and distribution logistics) did not always accommodate this. Thus, the audio mix could stem from multiple sound chips and forms of synthesis at the same time: cross-systematic.

The addition of sound expansion chips, sound cards, and other audio peripherals brings this additional layer to systematic sound design. In some cases, additions were developer-implemented into game cartridges, resulting in consistent playback for gamers; however, in other situations, the resulting audio could have dramatic variability due to elective factors. Consider the release of *Castlevania* (1993) for Sharp's X68000 personal computer. In addition to the X68000's built-in FM and PCM sound sources, MIDI protocol in the game ROM could also be routed to various desktop sound modules, such as Roland's MT-32 (1987), CM-64 (1989), and SC-55 (1991). In a similar vein, the music in *DOOM* (1993) will sound quite different between Gravis Ultrasound and Sound Blaster 16 sound cards.

In conclusion, I wish to stress the amount of archival work that has been enabled by an online community of enthusiastic fans. While this work allowed for retro video game emulation, the tools are also continually used and refined by chiptune artists, indie game composers, and other enthusiasts. While the active life of early video game systems was short-lived, the persistence of this fan labor illustrates that a rich and complex history of distinct timbres and compositional strategies remains to be uncovered. A detailed consideration of how individual game systems incorporated different types and variations of sound synthesis and how composers managed both hardware and software limitations, sheds light on the intersections with audio production in other media as well as on industry practices that have become standard today.

Glossary of Select Terms

Adaptive differential pulse code modulation (ADPCM): a form of compressing PCM sample data by recording difference values (rather than direct values) in adjustable blocks with fewer bit values.

Algorithm: the designated function and relationship of four or more operators in FM synthesis; the more operators the more algorithms that are possible.

Aliasing: an artifact of PCM data compression that can create audible distortions at regular intervals during the loop points of sustained samples.

Arp: the employment of an arpeggio as an effect, taking advantage of the CPU speed to cycle through a sequence of tones in fast repetition.

Attenuation: a reduction in the amplitude of a waveform.

Audio circuit: the arrangement of components that affect the audible output from a sound chip; these typically include fixed hi-pass and low-pass filters as well as operational amplifiers (op amps).

Bit depth: an indication of the number of possible values for representing a single point on a waveform; the higher the bit depth, the more closely the digital values can resemble an analog sound.

Byte (length): a group of eight bits that serves as the unit of measurement for the length of a waveform cycle or audio sample as a number of data points.

Digital signal processor (DSP): a controller for reading and manipulating PCM sample data in order to set loop points and add effects such as reverb.

Duty cycle: the rate or ratio of a pulse wave's "on" and "off" cycle.

Expansion audio: a term that describes additional sound sources combined with a console's otherwise fixed sound sources, usually included within a specific game cartridge rather than as a general peripheral to the gaming system.

Interpolation: a function applied to the values of a primary waveform to modulate to a secondary waveform in a uniform number of intermediary steps.

Loop point: defines which subregion of the PCM waveform data will be looped during playback to create longer durations.

Multichannel echo: a technique of feigning reverb by replicating the musical line of one audio channel in one or more additional audio channels with a slight time delay, often at a softer volume and detuned.

Operator: the oscillators that serve as either modulators or carriers in Yamaha's frequency modulation (FM).

Pulse code modulation (PCM): a representation of an analog sound source as a series of digital data.

Pulse width modulation (PWM): a dynamic change in the duty cycle of a pulse wave.

Rip: to extract targeted data from proprietary game software for purposes outside of the software's intended use.

ROMpler: a portmanteau of ROM and sampler that applies to MIDI-controlled sound units with a fixed library of instrument samples that are stored in ROM.

Single-channel echo: a technique of feigning reverb within a single channel with one or more subsequent repetitions of a musical tone at a lower volume and with a slight time delay.

Software-controlled sound generator (SSG): Yamaha's name for its licensed clones of generic PSG that were frequently integrated within its other sound chips.

Sound card: the destination for music protocol such as MIDI that is capable of producing sound.

Video Game Music Sound File Formats

AY: File format for ripped song data for General Instrument's PSG that was found on the ZX Spectrum, MSX, and Intellivision.

GBF: Game Boy Advance file format that derives from the PSF.

GBS: Game Boy Sound System file format for ripped soundtracks that can be played on an emulator.

HES: Hudson Entertainment Sound file format for ripped song data from the PC-Engine / Turbografx 16.

KSS: A multipurpose file format for the playback of music for MSX computers, including the AY-3-8910, the OPLL, and Konami's SCC expansion chip.

MOD: A general file format for tracker-based video game music that originated with the Commodore Amiga, which includes both sample data as well as data for patterns of notes and sequences.

NSF: Nintendo Sound Format. Unlike many other ripped video game music formats that just log data in a play state, the NSF file is a community-created container format for code ripped from games.

PSF: Portable Sound Format was created for ripping Playstation soundtracks, with variants created for ripping from other systems like the GBF Gameboy Advance Format.

SID: Sound Interface Device file format for the Commodore 64.

SPC: A dump of music and sound data sent to the SNES's S-SMP chip.

VGM: A broadly used format for logging music and sound data. It is most commonly used for Yamaha sound chips.

Sound Chips

Abbreviation Key

Ch	Number of channels
Op	Number of operators
Bit	The number of bits for waveform resolution
Byte	The length of the waveform expressed as a sequence of values
Rate	The number of sample values captured per second
A	Arcade Board
PC	Personal Computer
C	Console
G	(Game) Cartridge
H	Handheld
SC	Sound Card
P	Peripheral

Generic Programmable Sound Generators

Developer	Name	Ch	Selected Examples
General Instrument	AY-3-8910	3	Taito Z80 (A) Konami Scramble (A) Irem M27 (A) Bally Midway MCR-1 (A) Bally Midway MCR-2 (A) Capcom Z80 (A) Intellivision (C) Various MSX (PC) Amstrad CPC (PC) ZX Spectrum 128 (PC) Apple Mockingboard (SC)
Texas Instruments	SN76489	4	Sega SG-1000 (C) Coleco Vision (C) CreatiVision (C) Sega Master System (C) Sega Mega Drive/Genesis (C) Neo Geo Pocket (H) Neo Geo Pocket Color (H) Sega Pico (H) BBC Micro (PC) IBM PCjr (PC) Sharp MZ-800 (PC)
	SN76496	4	Sega Game Gear (H) Tandy 1000 (PC)

Custom Programmable Sound Generators

Developer	Name	Ch	Selected Examples
Atari	TIA	2	Atari VCS/2600 (C) Atari 7800 (C)
	POKEY	4	Atari 5200 (C) Atari 400/800 (PC) Atari XL (PC) Atari XE (PC)
Konami	VRC6	3	*Akumajō Densetsu* (G) *Mōryō Senki MADARA* (G) *Esper Dream II* (G)
MOS (Commodore)	VIC	4	Commodore VIC-1001 (PC) Commodore VIC-20 (PC)
	SID	3	Commodore 64 (PC) Commodore 128 (PC)
	TED	2	Commodore 16 (PC) Commodore Plus (PC)
Ricoh	2A03/2A07	5	Nintendo Famicom/NES (C)
Sharp	LR35902	4	Nintendo Game Boy (H) Nintendo Game Boy Color (H) Nintendo Game Boy Advance (H)

PSG Clones and Derivatives

Developer	Name (*Source*)	Selected Examples
Yamaha	YM2149 (*AY-3-8910*)	Atari ST (PC) Various MSX (PC)
Yamaha	YM3439 (*AY-3-8910*)	Atari Falcon (PC)
NCR	8496 (*SN76496*)	Tandy 1000 (PC)
Sega	Sega PSG (*SN76496*)	Sega Z80 (A) Sega Zaxxon (A) Sega System E (A) Sega Master System (C) Sega Mega Drive/Genesis (C)
Sunsoft	5B (*AY-3-8910*)	Sunsoft *Gimmick!* (G)
Toshiba	T7766A (*AY-3-8910*)	Various MSX (PC)

Wavetable Synthesis Chips

Developer	Name	Ch	Bit	Byte	Selected Examples
Atari	JERRY	16	16	128	Atari Jaguar (C)
Sharp	LR35902	1	4	32	Nintendo Game Boy (H) Nintendo Game Boy Color (H) Nintendo Game Boy Advance (H)
Ricoh	2C33	1	6	64	Nintendo Famicom Disk System (P)
Ensoniq	5503	8	8	var.	Apple IIgs (PC)
Hudson Soft	HuC6280	6	5	32	NEC PC-Engine/TurboGrafx-16 (C)
Konami	SCC	5	8	32	Various MSX Games (G)
Namco	WSG	3	4	32	Namco Pac-Man (A) Namco Galaga (A) Namco Pole Position (A)
	15XX	8	4	32	Namco Super Pac-Man (A)
	CUS30	8	4	32	Namco System 1 (A) Namco System 86 (A)
	N163	8	4	var.	Various Famicom Games (G)

Frequency Modulation Synthesis Chips

Developer	Name (Pedigree)	Ch	Op	Selected Examples
Yamaha	YM2151 (OPM)	8	4	Capcom CP System (A) Konami TMNT (A) Konami X-Men (A) Midway T-Unit (A) Sega X Board (A) Sega System 16 (A) Sega System 24 (A) Irem M72–M107 (A) Sharp X1 (PC) Sharp X68000 (PC) Yamaha SFG-01 (SC)
	YM2203 (OPN)	3	4	Various Taito Arcade Titles (A) Fujitsu FM-7 (PC) NEC PC-88 (PC) NEC PC-98 (PC)

Developer	Name (Pedigree)	Ch	Op	Selected Examples
				NEC PC6601 (PC) NEC PC6001 (PC)
	YM2608 (OPNA)	6	4	NEC PC-88 (PC) NEC PC-98 (PC)
	YM2610 (OPNB)	4	4	Various Taito Arcade Titles (A) SNK Neo Geo MVA (A) SNK Neo Geo AES (C)
	YM2612 (OPN2)	6	4	Fujitsu FM Towns (PC) Sega Mega Drive/Genesis (C)
	YM3438 (OPN2C)	6	4	Sega Mega Drive/Genesis 2/3 (C) Sega Nomad (H) Sega System 18 (A) Sega System 32 (A)
	YMF288 (OPN3)	6	4	NEC PC-98 (PC)
	YM3562 (OPL)	9	2	C64 Sound Expander (SC) Various Data East Arcade Titles (A) Various SNK Arcade Titles (A)
	YM3812 (OPL2)	9	2	AdLib MSC (SC) Covox Sound Master Plus (SC) Covox Sound Master II (SC) Creative Sound Blaster (SC)
	YMF262 (OPL3)	18	2	AdLib Gold 1000 (SC) Creative Sound Blaster Pro 2.0 (SC) Creative Sound Blaster 16 (SC)
	YM2413 (OPLL)	9	2	JP Sega Master System (C) Sega FM Sound Unit (P) MSX FM-PAC (SC) Various MSX 2+/Turbo R (PC)
	YM2164 (OPP)	8	4	Yamaha SFG-05 (SC) Yamaha FB-01 (P)
	YMF292 (SCSP)	32	6	Sega Saturn (C) Sega ST-V (A) Sega Model 2 (A) Sega Model 3 (A)
Konami	VRC7 (*YM2413*)	6	2	*Lagrange Point* (G)

Pulse Code Modulation Sampling

Developer	Name	Ch	Bit	Rate	Selected Examples
Atari	Jerry	16	16	44.1k	Atari Jaguar (C)
	SDMA	8	16	49.17k	Atari Falcon (PC)
Crystal	CS4231	32	16	44.1k	Gravis Ultrasound (SC)
QSound	DSP16A	16	16	24k	Capcom CP System II (A)
MOS (Commodore)	8364 Paula	4	16	28k	Commodore Amiga (PC)
Mitsumi	MM3205B	16	16	48k	Nintendo DS (H)
Namco	C140	24	12	42.78k	Namco System 2 (A) Namco System 21 (A)
	C219	16	12	42.78k	Namco NA-1 (A) Namco NA-2 (A)
	C352	32	16	42.67k	Namco System 22 (A) Namco System FL (A) Namco NB-1 (A) Namco NB-2 (A) Namco ND-1 (A) Namco System 11 (A) Namco System 12 (A) Namco System 23 (A)
National	LMC1992	4	8	50k	Atari ST (PC)
OKI	MSM5205	1	12	32k	Irem M-52 (A) Data East Z80 (A) Capcom 68000 (A) NEC PC Engine/TG16 CD-ROM (P)
	MSM6258	1	4	22k	Sharp X68000 (PC)
	MSM6295	4	12	32k	Capcom CP System (A) Midway T-Unit (A)
Ricoh	2A03/2A07	1	7	15.75k	Nintendo Famicom/NES (C)
	RF5C68	8	8	19.8k	Fujitsu FM Towns (PC) Sega System 18 (A) Sega System 32 (A)
	RF5C164	8	8	31.3k	Sega CD (P)
Sega	SegaPCM	16	8	31.25k	Sega Super Scalar (A) Sega OutRun (A) Sega X Board (A) Sega Y Board (A)

Developer	Name	Ch	Bit	Rate	Selected Examples
Sony	SPC700	8	16	32k	Super Famicom/SNES (C)
	SPU	24	16	44.1k	Sony Playstation (C)
	SPU2	48	16	48k	Sony Playstation 2 (C)
Roland	LA32	32	16	32k	Roland MT-32 (P)
	IC24	24	16	32k	Roland SC-55 (P)

Notes

1. A technical explanation is available in General Instrument Corporation (1979).
2. My discussion of the capabilities of the NES APU is brief in this chapter, as detailed accounts are already available: Altice (2015), McAlpine (2019), and Schartmann (2018).
3. Alberto González, correspondence with author, May–June 2022.
4. I make a more detailed comparison in Burke (2019).
5. The bit rate of each sample's depth offers insight into how closely the digital sequence approximates an analog waveform. Five bits results in 32 [i.e., 2 x 2 x 2 x 2 x 2] possible values, whereas an 8-bit sample would have the added refinement of 256 [i.e., 2 x 2 x 2 x 2 x 2 x 2 x 2 x 2] possible values within the same field.
6. I pulled the waveform data with the program NEZ Plug: nezplug.sourceforge.net.
7. A detailed discussion of the Yamaha CX5M, its features, and related variants is available at the MSX Resource Center: https://www.msx.org/wiki/Yamaha_CX5M.
8. Known as the Sega Mark III in Japan, before the name "Master System" was adopted for the release in the West. Later, a Japanese exclusive release of the Master System included the OPLL onboard.
9. Yamaha obtained a license to clone the AY-3-8910 PSG, which it named the YM2149 SSG and integrated into some of the OPN family of FM chips.
10. When the loop is repeated at regular intervals in order to extend the length of a note, the effect can resemble a tremolo.
11. Without explicit confirmation from a game developer or composer, it is difficult to verify the exact source used in game development. Many companies like Roland reused the same samples, albeit with slight modification, for multiple products. However, even with the variation caused by downsampling and compression, one can match a PCM sample to one that may have appeared on one or more products. A community forum for identifying sample sources in video game music maintains several spreadsheets, and its users corroborate findings with oscilloscopes and spectrographs, even applying relevant filters and sampling rate adjustments to software for verifying matches (Puglia 2012).

References

Altice, Nathan. 2015. *I Am Error: The Nintendo Family Computer / Entertainment System Platform*. Cambridge, MA: MIT Press.

Arsenault, Dominic. 2017. *Super Power, Spoony Bards, and Silverware: The Super Nintendo Entertainment System*. Cambridge, MA: MIT Press.

Burke, Kevin R. 2019. "Advancing the Chiptune Narrative: The Syndrum, TR-808, and SDS-V as Forebears of 8-Bit Drums." Paper presented at the North American Conference for Video Game Music. Hartford, CT.

Collins, Karen. 2008. *Game Sound: An Introduction to the History, Theory, and Practice of Video Game Music and Sound Design*. Cambridge, MA: MIT Press.

Elkins, Alan. 2017. "Too Many (Or Not Enough?) Notes: Contrasting Approaches in Polyphony and Texture in Japanese and American Nintendo Games." Paper presented at the North American Conference on Video Game Music. Austin, TX.

General Instrument Corporation. 1979. AY-3-8910/8912 Programmable Sound Generator Data Manual. Horsham, PA: General Instrument Corporation.

González, Alberto. 2009. "Interview with Alberto González (Composer)." Interview by Patrick Todd. Published on VGARC Video Game History. http://www.vgarc.org/vgarc-originals/interview-with-alberto-gonzalez/.

Highsmith, Alex (blackoak), trans. 1993. "Developer Interview." In *The World of Phantasy Star*, edited by Tokuma Shoten. Accessed January 14, 2024. https://shmuplations.com/phantasystar/.

Magnusson, Thor. 2017. "Musical Organics: A Heterarchical Approach to Digital Organology." *Journal of New Music Research* 46 (3): 286–303.

McAlpine, Kenneth B. 2019. *Bits and Pieces: A History of Chiptunes*. New York: Oxford University Press.

Puglia, Michael (AceK[ombat]). 2012. "The VGM/Others Instrument Source Thread." Halley's Comet Software Forum. https://hcs64.com/mboard/forum.php?showthread=24937.

Schartmann, Andrew. 2018. "Music of the Nintendo Entertainment System: Form, Technique, and Style." PhD Dissertation. Yale University.

Yamaha CX5M. MSX Resource Center. https://www.msx.org/wiki/Yamaha_CX5M.

CHAPTER 9

VISUALIZING MUSIC WITH VIDEO GAME TECHNOLOGIES

JONATHAN WEINEL

Introduction

An ethereal figure rendered in points of light levitates in a lotus position, while a pulsing techno beat throbs away as synthesizer pads wash over the mix. In the background, pyramids and other geometric shapes are rendered in neon particles, flickering in time to the music. The colors glow with each pulse from the drum machine. In the foreground, wireframe entities fly on-screen and are quickly destroyed by arcs of light emitting from the player, exploding like fireworks in glistening showers of dots. Each arc of light sounds an exquisite, plucked synthesizer note, forming a percussive layer in rhythmic synchronization and harmonic unity with the music. At once, shards of light explode from a cuboid entity and a spinning vortex transports us to another place, amid chiming sounds as the music swells with a rush of snares. Like a DJ dropping in the next track, the music transitions, and the scene changes. Now we are engulfed by organic creatures and morphing cubes, amid showers of light and sound that encircle, echoing harmonic fragments of sound, all building toward a glimmering, euphoric climax.

This is a description of *Rez Infinite* (Monstars 2017), an updated version of the video game *Rez* (United Game Artists 2001), which brings the classic title up to date with modern graphics and various other enhancements such as virtual reality (VR) support. Taking inspiration from the "visual music" paintings of Kandinsky (Gordan 2017), *Rez* adapted the form of an "on-rails shooter" game,[1] providing a psychedelic journey through retro-futuristic wireframe landscapes. Besides having a striking visual aesthetic, the game was innovative in the way it merged the mechanics of sound, music, and gameplay. In *Rez*, as the player fires shots at enemies, they trigger percussive hits and drum machine sounds, which are quantized in relation to the music, synchronizing sound effects with the music soundtrack and gameplay. In combination with the vibrations of the game pad, the game offers a multimodal experience, which can be understood as "synesthetic" through the interlinking of graphics, sounds, and interactivity in accordance with musical patterns and structures.[2]

Video game engines provide software frameworks for developing computer games. However, the use of these engines as tools for designing interactive 3D worlds is gradually becoming ubiquitous in areas beyond their immediate use-case in video game development. For instance, they are now used in areas such as digital art, film and TV, training simulations, architectural visualizations, and museum and heritage applications. The main reasons are related to cost, visual quality, the convenience of real-time rendering workflows, and their capabilities for developing for VR and augmented/mixed reality (AR/MR). Similarly, game engines also provide new opportunities for visualizing sound and music and are increasingly being used to generate live visuals projected at concerts, audiovisual installations, performances, and more (Weinel 2020a; Turchet, Hamilton, and Çamci 2021; chapter 34 this volume).

With the advent of COVID-19, this situation intensified, as many live music events were forced to reimagine themselves via live-streams or in virtual environments.[3] Here game engines often provide the toolkit for generating virtual concert arenas and spaces. For instance, electronic dance music megafestival *Tomorrowland* (2020) live-streamed all their concerts in virtual arenas that were made in the Unreal game engine (The Boolean 2020). DJs performing in front of green screens were superimposed over the elaborate, fictitious scenes of hedonistic revelry, in which computer-generated characters danced in front of elaborate digital stage sets and light shows. For human viewers, the scene would have been viewed over the internet, perhaps inducing bouts of jealously toward the surrealistic CGI automatons, who seemed to be having all the fun as they twerked away mechanically to big-name electronic dance music DJs like Tiesto.

From *Rez* to *Tomorrowland*, video game engines provide a variety of new ways to visualize and experience music. In this chapter I will discuss how these technologies are giving rise to new forms of music visualization.[4] First, I will provide a brief tour through a spectrum of work related to music visualization, from early visual-music paintings and films to the latest VJ performances, music video games, and VR experiences. Following this, I will discuss one of my own projects: *Cyberdream* (2019–2021), a VR music visualization, which takes the user on a psychedelic flight across synesthetic landscapes in which the user can "paint with sound" while listening to a soundtrack of 1990s-style rave music. Lastly, I will discuss a selection of student projects that explore sound design in the context of video game engines. These projects indicate new forms that may emerge when students studying programs not directly related to games development are brought into contact with these technologies. This will also provide some pedagogical insights that will be useful for educators wanting to support growth in this area. By tracing the trajectory of music visualizations from past to present, and observing nascent forms in this area, we shall see how a new paradigm of gamified music visualizations is gradually emerging. This paradigm is currently amorphous, as new possibilities are rapidly being explored by practitioners working in this area, but broadly consists of audiovisual projects created with game engines, which visualize music, yet may incorporate traces of the video games through aspects such as control systems, use of game characters or game-like virtual worlds. In this chapter I will indicate some of the new forms that are emerging in this area, while also discussing possible strategies for cultivating further innovation through education.

Music Visualizations

"Music visualizations" is a term that may often be associated with the visual plug-ins found in music players such as Winamp or iTunes, which generate colorful patterns of light that dance in correspondence with the frequency and amplitude of an input-audio signal. However, in this section I will take a somewhat broader view in order to consider a wider spectrum of practices in which visuals are produced in response to sound and music. While these may involve the use of generative methods and audio signal analysis, they may also be composed using artistic approaches of design. Using these approaches, it is possible to map and synchronize various aspects of sound to visual forms, either through automated, computational approaches; hand-made techniques; or approaches that fall somewhere between the two. By taking a broader view, it is my intention to highlight that each of these areas many suggest their own valid set of approaches, which may be informative for the design of new works.

In the early 20th century, the term "visual music" was coined in relation to the works of Kandinsky, whose paintings organize patterns and shapes into forms that interpret the structure of music. As discussed by Brougher and Mattis (2005), visual music is a field that would subsequently grow in the mid-20th century to include experimental animated films, such as pioneering works by Oskar Fischinger, Jordan Belson, John Whitney, and others. These works are characterized by meticulous hand-crafted animations in which abstract forms move across the screen in correspondence with music. Circles or squares may appear with their coordinates mapping to progressions in pitch; while visual textures may reflect qualities of sound; or the timing of visual events may be organized relative to musical divisions. These filmmakers used a range of techniques, such as hand-drawn animation, clips of kinetic sculptures, or early forms of computer graphics. In my own work (see Weinel 2021b), I have also been particularly interested in the visual music compositions of Harry Smith, whose works were conceptualized as representations of visual hallucinations that Smith saw while listening to jazz music under the influence of marijuana (Sitney 1965, 270). It is also of note, since here we are considering the progression of these artistic forms into new technological modalities, that visual music events such as the *Vortex Concerts* (1957–1959) explored the potential of planetariums for creating immersive spatial concerts with multiple projectors and loudspeakers,[5] pre-empting the fulldome[6] and VR experiences of today.

Running parallel to visual music in the 1960s and 1970s, psychedelic lightshows were another form in which visuals were designed to complement music. While visual music films were often meticulously composed via the crafting of fixed-media films, psychedelic light shows were usually spontaneous and ad-hoc, being formed live to provide the visuals for rock concerts of the time. As discussed in a recent interview, the Nova Express were one group who were active in providing these light shows in the United Kingdom, performing shows for Pink Floyd and others in the North of England during the late 1960s and 1970s (Weinel 2018b). In their work, liquids were mixed in concave glass dishes taken from clock-faces, above overhead projectors, stills were displayed via slide-projectors, while celluloid films beamed found imagery. These images would overlap with each other and the performing band members, causing sound and image to merge together into a synesthetic whole. These approaches were markedly improvisational, with multiple visual performers using their hands to mask the various projections, providing visual rhythms and textures to reflect musical patterns.

These psychedelic light shows were the forerunner of what would later become known as VJing (video jockeying) in the 1980s and 1990s (Faulkner 2006). In the era of music television (MTV), VJs would use hardware video mixing technologies to make cuts between different clips, providing visual montages of footage showing gyrating dancers or computer graphics animations. At nightclubs and festivals, these visuals provided a visual accompaniment for DJ performances. The style is epitomized by Humanoid's *Stakker Humanoid* (1988) music video, an intense and highly colorful stroboscopic visual montage drawn from footage that is also seen on two longer videos *The Evil Acid Baron Show* (Various Artists 1988) and *Eurotechno* (Stakker 1989). Long-form VJ mixes can also be found on various VHS tapes such as *Cyberdelia* (VR 1992); VR and Dr. Devious's *Dance in Cyberspace* (1992), and sequels; *Future Shock* (Various Artists 1993); the Studio!K7 *X-Mix* series (1993–1998); Hex's *Global Chaos* (1993); and Eat Static's *Intrusion* (1994). Many of these VJ mixes incorporate looping computer graphics animations. At this time, it was becoming more feasible to make computer animations with home computers such as PCs,[7] or the Commodore Amiga, which was also used for electronic dance music production (Weinel 2018a). Some VJ productions have stylistic connections with works produced within the demoscene, a computer subculture focusing on the production of real-time demos, which showcase graphical, musical, and coding skills (Polgár 2005). Many demoscene productions incorporate audio-reactive effects, and footage from Amiga demoscene discs can be spotted in many of visuals used in those VJ mixes on the VHS tapes mentioned above. Conversely, demoscene productions such as *Coma* by Rebels (1990), *Acid Collection* by The Outsider (n.d.), and *Music Compilation* by Random Access (n.d.), are among those that pay homage to acid house-style visuals and music—the influence clearly flows in both directions.

Music visualizers can be found as hardware or software devices. They use audio-reactivity, typically using frequency and amplitude properties of an audio signal to modulate visual images. Early hardware music visualizers such as the Atari Video Music receive an input audio signal, and output pulsing diamond patterns on a TV. Such devices were later replaced by software such as Jeff Minter's VLM, which was built into the hardware of video game consoles such as the Atari Jaguar CD, allowing the user to watch colorful patterns of sound and light generated in response to any piece of music (Bell 2019). While such approaches have been critiqued for not offering more tailored, specific visuals for individual pieces of music (Dannenberg 2005), clearly the utility of such approaches is their precision and flexibility, since they work with any audio signal and thus can be used with any piece or genre of music.

Also of relevance to our discussion here are Hex's innovative *Escape* (1991), *Anti Static* (1993), and *Head Crash* (1995) multimedia discs for the Philips CDi interactive system. These multimedia works blur the boundaries between visual music, music visualizations, VJ mixes, and demoscene productions, by providing a mixture of real-time graphics that incorporate generative elements, yet are specifically designed for a set of ambient and rave music tracks. The visualizations can run automatically, but also provide features that allow the user to control various parameters of the visuals, and choose the music track that will be played.

VJing practices extend into the 21st century, with technologies progressing with the times. Where, previously, video mixing required expensive hardware, low-cost home computers increasingly offered more power and became capable of real-time video mixing. Alongside this, software tools were created to facilitate VJ performance, such as Resolume or VDMX. Contemporary work in this area ranges from VJ mixes that provide the live visuals for nightclubs and festivals, to integrated audio-visual performances, in which the artist(s) create both sound and visuals. Examples of the latter type can be found at arts events such as *Splice Festival* (2016–2018) in London, however there are often no clear dividing lines between these areas. As explored in a panel discussion at London South Bank University (Rietveld et al. 2019), some VJs have their roots in club culture, while others may be inspired by visual music, experimental film, the demoscene, and other areas, broadly reflecting the diversity and cross-pollination of forms and genres that is often at play in contemporary art and music culture. With this in mind, modern VJ performances may incorporate carefully composed materials made with analog and/or digital techniques, real-time visuals generated through synthesis of graphics based on analysis of an audio signal, or real-time transformation of materials through manipulation of video filters using haptic interfaces and/or audio signal analysis leading to precomposed (fixed-media) or real-time works that are performed live.

As noted, video game engines provide interesting opportunities for artists wanting to create music visualizations, since they provide a readily accessible spatial toolkit with flexible possibilities for rendering 3D audiovisual environments.[8] Yet as may be observed via titles such as *Rez*, video game culture also comes with its own history of music visualizations, via commercial titles on various platforms. The design of *Rez* has been imitated or adapted by other games. For example, *Lost Future Omega* (Mebius 2018) is a recent indie example for Nintendo Switch that exhibits similar gameplay and audio-visual synchronization, while other shooting games such as *Beat Hazard* (Cold Beam Games 2010) offer a different approach by pairing arcade-style action with audio-reactive graphics.

The genre of "rhythm game," which includes popular titles such as *Dance Dance Revolution* (Konami 1998–2020), *Taiko no Tatsujin* (Namco 2001–2021), and *Guitar Hero* (Harmonix 2005–2015), challenges players to trigger buttons in synchronization with musical sequences, sometimes using nonstandard controllers such as dance-mats, drum-controllers, or guitar controllers, respectively. A recent adaptation of this format for VR, *Beat Saber* (Beat Games 2019) is a rhythm game that challenges the player to slash at colored blocks with a lightsaber in time with the music, and another variation of the rhythm game concept, *Audio Surf* (Fitterer 2008), challenges the user to control a vehicle as it races through a course structured on musical patterns. In a later variation of this idea, *Thumper* (Drool 2016) propels the player along courses at breakneck speeds, surrounded by spectral demonic forms, which are particularly effective in VR.

Lastly, though not games, there are virtual concert experiences made using game engines, sometimes for experience on a computer or VR. As already mentioned, the online edition of *Tomorrowland* used the Unreal game engine to provide concert footage of a virtual festival, with DJs superimposed, and the event live-streamed for ticket holders. Other online music festivals have taken slightly different approaches; for example, *Lost Horizon* provided a virtual festival site which players could walk around by using an avatar in VR (Kocay 2020). Meanwhile, the *Melody VR* (MelodyVR 2019) platform uses 360-degree concert footage to allow the user to experience videos of concerts from various angles.

In summary, this section has provided an outline of some of the main areas in the development of music visualizations to date. Of course, this is not an exhaustive account, but will be sufficient for our purposes here to illustrate key areas that are relevant to this field. Readers are encouraged to use this as a starting point for their own explorations, as closer inspection of individual artists and works will reveal many nuanced variations of what has been discussed here. Across those examples explored, we find various approaches whereby visual images are provided as a complement to music, but the approaches for doing this have been shaped by the evolution of technologies and audiovisual culture. As this occurs, earlier conceptual approaches may remain valid, and there is much to gain from applying these to generate works with newer immersive technologies, such as those provided by current video game engines. With this in mind, the next section will discuss *Cyberdream*, a piece made in Unity, which translates the aesthetic forms of 1990s VJing into the domain of VR.

Cyberdream

Cyberdream is VR music visualization that developed as a progression from my previous work in audiovisual performance under the alias Soundcat. Each Soundcat performance consisted of a DJ mix incorporating existing electronic dance music tracks, which were combined with a VJ mix of original visuals. The visuals were created using a variety of methods using analog and digital techniques including direct animation, where materials are hand-painted on 8mm film; geometric animations programmed in Processing (a programming language for visual design); 3D animations of abstract shapes; and stop-motion animation techniques (Weinel 2019b). These were used to create original music videos for each track, via live mixing in the studio with VDMX, and the individual music videos then provided the basis for the DJ/VJ sets, which were realized with Serato DJ Pro with a video plug-in.[9] The audiovisual content of these performances combined 1990s breakbeat hardcore music with retro-computer-graphics visuals, taking inspiration from psychedelic VJ mixes from this era (such as those discussed earlier), demoscene animations, and vaporwave.[10] Structurally, these performances provide transitions between tracks as the mix progresses in time, and each piece of music has a discrete set of corresponding visual materials. As I will discuss in this section, a similar aesthetic and structural approach was used in *Cyberdream*, translating the idea of a DJ/VJ performance into VR.

The first iteration of *Cyberdream* for Oculus GearVR provides an experience analogous to a DJ/VJ set, in which the user journeys through a series of 3D scenes set to a soundtrack of 1990s rave music and vaporwave (Weinel 2019a). Each scene was designed based on the visual language of these music genres, and has a corresponding music track, so that as the user moves through the various scenes, each offers a distinct audiovisual experience. The menu screen is a pastiche of a rave flier,[11] providing a looming face suspended over a retro-futuristic wireframe landscape, which is combined with original ambient-techno music. As the journey begins, the user flies above a bridge of oscillating tiles into a fractal pyramid, surrounded by strange sculptures and checkerboards. The next scene displays a 3D infinity pool suspended in a hazy pink sky, with broken mannequin heads floating lifelessly in the water, while a looping vaporwave track is heard in the background. The next track has a UK garage/grime beat and provides psychedelic spiral patterns, which oscillate in front of and behind the viewer, over a hand-painted background with various airbrush and paint textures rendered in purple and neon orange. Following this, a techno track is heard while flying through a sea of Windows 95 pop-ups that display messages like "work," "buy," "take selfies," and "like sponsored link." In the next scene, the visuals shift to a landscape of purple checkerboard mountains and rave music, while flickering pixel-art computer cursors rain from the sky. After this, the user finds themselves suspended above a sea of oscillating cubes, which change in size and color, producing wave effects above and below, while a vaporwave track is heard. In the next scene the user is suspended in a different room of oscillating cubes, while a more energetic track incorporating aspects of techno and vaporwave is heard. In the penultimate scene, more vaporwave sounds are heard, while pearlescent spheres move in Lissajous patterns. Finally, the user is plunged into a dark room with flickering arrows, while high-speed acid techno music is heard and a message reads "the future is lost, crash the system, back to the tribes." Overall, the experience provides a flight through a series of 3D audiovisual scenes, with a structure that is analogous to a DJ/VJ mix.

The second iteration of *Cyberdream* for Oculus Quest (Figure 9.1) built on and extended the GearVR version. Structurally, the piece continues to use the same 3D scenes as before, but the updated musical soundtrack focuses more significantly on original breakbeat hardcore compositions. These tracks were created using the Roland Cloud suite of virtual synthesizer plug-ins, which simulate classic synthesizers of the type commonly used in this style of music during the 1990s. In addition, this version uses the Wwise game audio middleware software to implement the sound design, improving the transitions between music tracks, and providing a more continuous sonic experience.

FIGURE 9.1 Jonathan Weinel's Cyberdream (2019–2020) project, featuring a journey through synesthetic environments, where the user can interactively paint with sound using audiovisual sound toys.

As one scene fades out and the next fades in, the music cross-fades in synchronization, in the style of a DJ mix. This is implemented with a "horizontal" music arrangement in Wwise,[12] so that moving between scenes triggers the introduction of a new track that comes in at the beginning of a bar and is matched with the same tempo.

Another addition which the Oculus Quest version of *Cyberdream* provides is the introduction of audiovisual sound toys (Weinel 2021c). As shown in Figure 9.1, these allow the user to project sounds and beams of light from their hands, where the look of the beams is related to the sound and vice versa. Three audiovisual sound toys are provided:

- Zig-Zag Toy shoots jagged orange beams and emits pulsing sounds, which are rhythmically synchronized with the soundtrack. This toy provides various pulse sequences, which the user can switch between using the primary and secondary triggers of the Oculus Touch controllers. Each time a pulse sound is emitted, the zig-zag arrangement of points on the beam changes. Sounds are spatially located to the left or right, depending on whether this toy is used with the left or right hand, and in situations where it is used in both, a temporal offset between the left and right pulses produces a satisfying thickening of the sound.
- Circle Toy projects linear blue-green beams, which rotate in a circular pattern, and sound asynchronous pulsing sounds, which are not synchronized with the background music. The user can adjust the rate at which the pulses of Circle Toy sound, and the speed and width of the circular rotations. For this toy, sounds emit from the end point of the beam, and pointing the beam in different directions allows spatial movement of these sounds in 3D audio.

- Streamer Toy emits yellow arcs of lighting from the hands, which fall away before the user and produce dissonant droning sounds. The movement of the arcs is related to gestural movements of the controllers, which continue to affect the coordinates of the beams as they fall away from the user. Sounds are spatialized from the tip of each lighting beam.

For all three sound toys, using the thumbstick on the Oculus Touch controller allows various filters and pitch-shifting effects to be applied in real time, where modifying the sound also produces corresponding changes to the visual appearance of the beams, by applying oscillating changes. The user can also switch between the various toys using the A and B buttons on the controllers. As before, the sound design of these features is also accomplished in Wwise, using various combinations of sound triggering and real-time parameter controls (RTPCs).

Informal feedback on *Cyberdream* has provided some positive indication that the approaches used work well for audiences. The project was shown at various events including: *Event Two*, an exhibition of computer art held at the Royal College of Art (London, July 15–17, 2019); *ACM Audio Mostly 2019* (University of Nottingham, September 18–20, 2019), where the demo received an award; and *SIGGRAPH Asia 2021* (Weinel 2021a). The piece exhibits several novel features that contribute toward our understanding of possible compositional methodologies in this area. First, it shows how a VR project can be organized to structurally resemble the form of a DJ or VJ mix, by incorporating a structure where the user flies through a series of 3D audiovisual scenes. Additionally, the design of the scenes themselves reflects what I refer to as a "symbolic" approach to music visualization, whereby iconic or representational visuals are designed in response to the visual language associated with the genres of music in question, as identified through associated cultural artifacts such as rave fliers, album artwork, or VJ performances (Weinel 2020b). This approach differs from those that base the design of the music visualization on analysis of audio signals, although such approaches could also be incorporated when using this method. A symbolic approach such as this makes sense for VR, because it allows for the construction of representational 3D spaces that are specifically related to the music. Lastly, the Oculus Quest version of the project incorporates interactivity via the inclusion of audiovisual sound toys, which allow the user to creatively paint with sound in a manner that interlocks with the rhythmic soundtrack. In this way, the macro structural form of the project resembles a DJ/VJ mix, while micro structural elements can be composed using the toys, and both forms are designed to merge together in terms of both sounds and visuals.

Student Projects

As part of courses in sound design that I have taught at London South Bank University and the University of Greenwich, I have supervised students working on a variety of projects using the Unity game engine. Some of these projects have been remarkably innovative, and they are interesting to consider for our discussion in this chapter. In this section I will therefore provide an overview of the projects produced by the students, and reflect on some pedagogical issues that arise on these courses. This will be informative for the purposes of this chapter, since the application of video game engines for visualizing music is quite a recent development, and bringing new minds to this area will support further innovation. Through appropriately designed courses, it is possible to bring students studying courses such as sound design, which are not primarily related to games development, into contact with game engine technologies. They can be encouraged to explore their use for creative projects that are not necessarily "video games" in the usual sense. The examples in this section will indicate the type of work that sound design students make in these contexts and will be revealing for educators keen to support the growth of work in this area.

At London South Bank University, from 2018–2020, Chris Holtum (2020) developed two audiovisual performances using video game engines, as part of his undergraduate degree. The first piece: *The Hill That Bleeds* (2019) was an interactive sound-art piece incorporating spatial audio and surrealist landscapes, with sonic sculptures that users can discover and explore. The second piece, *Simulacra* (2020), facilitates audiovisual performance, providing a linear narrative in which the composer travels between audiovisual landmarks inspired by surrealist art (Figure 9.2). Each landmark relates to a musical track and incorporates ambient and percussive layers of sonic material. The piece utilizes the game-audio middleware software FMOD to develop the audio interactions, which can be triggered and manipulated in live performances via a PlayStation 4 controller. Drawing on Holtum's interests in electronica and audiovisual performance,

FIGURE 9.2 Chris Holtum's audiovisual performance Simulacra (2020).

these pieces reflect interesting uses of Unity, FMOD, and game controllers as a means to facilitate audiovisual composition. In particular, *Simulacra* also points toward the use of a game engine as a vehicle for designing work that is performed by the composer, rather than by multiple players/users.

Together with the other works such as those discussed earlier in this chapter, Holtum's projects were among those used as examples for a third-year undergraduate module on sound design for games at the University of Greenwich, which I taught from 2019 to 2021. In the first semester, the students were first introduced to the Unity game engine. They learned how to create a 3D project using terrain tools, import third-party assets such as models, animations, and first-person perspective controllers, and implement sounds using spatial 3D audio. They then took part in a series of lectures and workshops addressing various areas of theory and practice in video game audio, leading to an analytical essay on video game audio, and a Wwise portfolio demonstrating interactive video game audio designs. In the second semester, the focus shifted back to Unity, as the students developed an independent sound design project using the video game engine. The students were encouraged not only to think about the video game engine as a tool for making games but to also consider how it might be used in other contexts for generating sonic art installations, music visualizations, or audiovisual performances. They were also introduced to the tools and workflows required for producing VR and augmented reality experiences with Unity and considerations for showcasing these works in exhibitions or performances.

In 2019–2020, teaching was predominantly carried out face-to-face, but shifted toward blended learning and online delivery toward the end of the course due to the COVID-19 pandemic. The student projects consisted of a mixture of game-like experiences and interactive artworks. These projects included: a psychological horror game set in a woodland campsite (Patricia Magyar); a science fiction horror experience set on a spaceship in outer space (Jack Bell-Hyland); and a journey across a postapocalyptic landscape (Eduard Fadgyas). Two other projects provided virtual music-festival experiences: one allowing the player to walk around an open-air rock festival which used stem-recordings of a rock band to provide 3D spatialization of the different instruments (Marek Fialka); and another provided multiple tents at an electronic dance music festival, complete with lighting and revelers wandering the site at dusk (Elliot Puffett). While the latter two pieces approximated the appearance of a real-world festival, Ashley Maclaughlin took a more experimental approach, developing his interests in psychedelic music by modeling a hallucinatory tropical island with giant mushrooms and abandoned military vehicles. This piece incorporated sonic sculptures as points of interest, which emitted sounds that were meticulously crafted using hardware synthesizers. Taking inspiration from the field of visual music, Mateo Monje Shefford's *Harmony of the Spheres* provided cosmic worlds with orbiting planets and abstract soundscapes responding to the movement of the player. Lastly, a visually striking VR piece by Daniela Zaharieva drew on vaporwave discourses, providing a surrealistic audiovisual journey through a *Euphoric Dystopia* (Figure 9.3).

In 2020–2021, the delivery of this course was predominantly online. However, this modality did not prevent the students from producing some outstanding projects.

FIGURE 9.3 Daniela Zaharieva's VR piece Euphoric Dystopia (2020).

Among these, Holly Bessell's *Blue Moon* utilized retro game aesthetics to provide a highly emotive, 2D side-scrolling platform game, based around the narrative of an astronaut stranded on a mysterious planet. Ethan Worts provided a virtual music festival on a desert landscape inspired by the *Burning Man* festival, complete with various art, sculptures, and live techno music, which he made by recording original jam sessions on hardware synths. Drawing on her interest in horror games such as the *Amnesia* series (Frictional Games 2010–2020), Jodie Clarke-Mattis's project created an *Astral Projection* visualization of Rose Hall, a historic Jamaican Georgian plantation house, providing a highly immersive, imaginative rendering of the haunted basement of this building reflecting the history of slavery at this site (Figure 9.4). Lastly, Tyler McIntosh built on his earlier work developing an affective computing (Picard 1997) software application, which uses machine learning to interpret emotion via input signals from a consumer-grade electroencephalograph (EEG) headset (McIntosh 2021). His game *Lundheim* adapted this system for a video game context with Unity and Wwise, to provide an interactive audiovisual narrative where the emotion of the user affects sounds, particle effects, and unlocks events (see Figure 9.5).

Across these projects we can identify several distinct types of work. Some projects were aligned with established video game genres, using these as a vehicle to develop the students' sound design skills in the context of work with interactive game engines. Several projects explored the notion of a virtual music festival or concert, which was rather timely in the context of the pandemic with many events moving online. These projects tended to focus on representing festivals as they might appear in the real world, while other projects utilizing sonic sculptures or other interactive audiovisual forms expanded on the opportunities video game engines provide for creating unreal audiovisual spaces. Only Holtum's work focused on the use of a game engine for creating a live

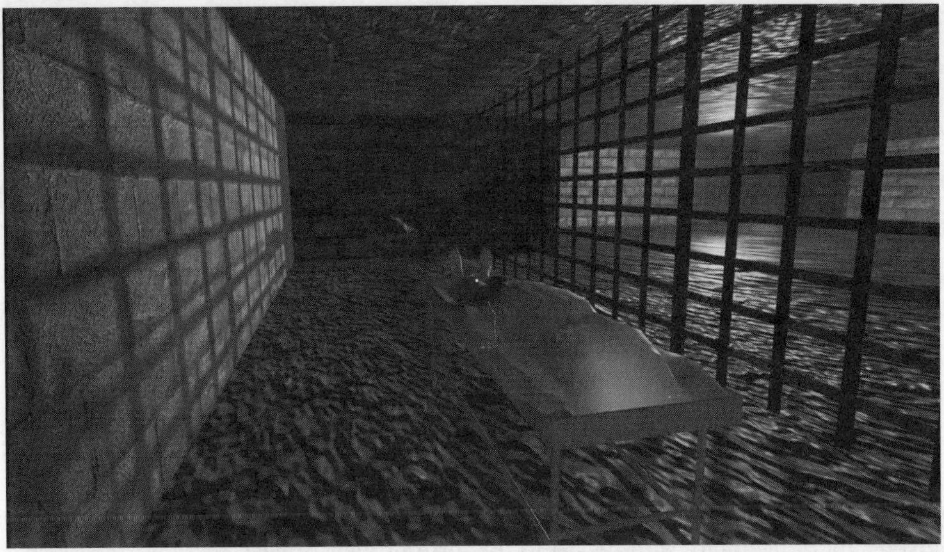

FIGURE 9.4 Jodie Clarke-Mattis's Astral Projection (2021), a haunted audiovisual interpretation of Rose Hall, Jamaica.

FIGURE 9.5 Tyler McIntosh's Lundheim (2021) project, which incorporates emotionally reactive sounds and visuals.

audiovisual performance, however this may have been shaped partly by the pandemic, since opportunities to present projects at gigs were limited.

In terms of pedagogy, the range of approaches that the students explored were related to the design of a fairly open-ended coursework brief, which gave the students scope to make a wide range of possible projects using the game engine. Students were encouraged to explore concepts that did not fit the usual mold of video games; to pursue ideas related to their individual creative practice with sound; and to build on the concepts of spatial audio, electroacoustic composition, and audiovisual composition, which they had explored earlier on in their studies. This approach is potentially also more inclusive, as it allows students to engage with highly individualized projects in areas of specific interest which they are likely to find more motivating to work on, which are not necessarily determined by any cultural biases the tutors may have. Of course, the students may still be influenced by the themes explored in the lectures and encouraged in particular directions, but the choice of project theme comes first and foremost from the student. This can also lead to innovative work as the students bring their own diverse interests and expertise and apply these to generate interesting game engine projects, which are not entirely "video games" or "music visualizations" but extend or expand our idea of these forms in ways that resist classification.

Of course, this work also comes with significant challenges. While the students were given a lot of flexibility with regard to the form of their project, there was a risk that they would need to work across too many areas to make a successful game project independently. This can be a common issue on video games courses, not least because students are now very used to seeing AAA (high profile, big budget) games on home video games consoles which are made by large teams and cost millions of dollars to produce. Exposure to AAA games may create expectations of detail and quality for some students that are difficult to produce independently. In the context of a sound design module, where the students do not have a strong background in other areas such as programming or 3D modeling, it was necessary to encourage a balanced approach, where sound design was to be the main focus. The students were allowed to utilize third-party 3D models and animations to assemble their projects, provided these were appropriately credited in the accompanying documentation. Some students were steered away from spending time working on overly ambitious features such as nonplayer characters with AI behaviors, or complex shooting mechanics, which might have been too demanding for the student and not left enough time to work on the sound design.

The intention was that this project would allow the students to develop competencies in working with game engines, thereby preparing them for future collaborative work, where aspects of programming, 3D modeling, and animation might be undertaken by other team members. Most students had fairly limited experience with programming prior to the course, so the coding aspects assumed no prior knowledge in C# or scripting, and the teaching focused on introducing techniques that would allow the student to provide simple forms of interactivity or to trigger sounds when entering particular areas of the virtual environment. Of course, in cases where the student had a stronger background in programming or was able to invest more time on improving their programming skills, more complex interactions were possible and they were better able to implement the game audio middleware tools. This highlights the importance of teaching coding skills to sound design students earlier on, since these skills give students much more flexibility in the work they can do and increases their employability in a highly competitive field.

Despite these challenges and the difficulties that all faced in the context of the pandemic, the module seems to have been successful based on feedback from the students, with many going on to postgraduate courses the following year or continuing to utilize video game engines and middleware tools in their subsequent work.[13]

Conclusion: An Emerging Paradigm

From visual music paintings and analog films to the latest VJ performances, video games, and VR experiences, through the course of this chapter we have seen how technologies have facilitated the evolution of music visualizations. Increasingly, game engines are appropriate tools for artists working in this field, since they provide flexible platforms that give convenient access to the latest graphics and spatial audio, while also allowing works to be realized for platforms such as VR. The spectrum of work in this area is broad, and we find many instances that build on developments from a multitude of fields, translating established aesthetic forms related to music visualization into the domain of video games. Here, we have seen how this can lead to many interesting projects such as interactive music visualizations, virtual music festivals, historic audiovisualizations, and audiovisual performances. These projects are frequently entwined with the design patterns and mechanics of traditional video games, as the characteristics, interfaces, and controllers of the medium are absorbed and repurposed. It seems this is rarely problematic for students working in this area, who are digital natives and have used video game technologies throughout most of their lives. Through this collective work, we can observe an emerging paradigm for music visualizations which not only harnesses the capabilities of game engine technologies but also transforms the concept of visualizing music into new gamified forms. This emergence is something that educators should cultivate and support, by designing courses that arm students with the necessary skills to work with code and video game engines in order for the students to realize their fantastic visions of interactive sound and music.

Notes

1. An *on-rails shooter* is a type of action video game where the player follows a predetermined movement path while shooting targets.
2. The phenomenon of synesthesia (Cytowic 1989) is described as a blurring of the sensory modalities, in which sounds may have a color, or colors may have a taste (for example). By linking graphics, sounds, and interactive features, *Rez* could be considered as exhibiting or representing synesthetic qualities in the form of a video game. These properties might also be described as "psychedelic," since psychedelic experiences precipitated by drugs such as LSD promote experiences of synesthesia, eliciting forms such as "sound-to-image" hallucinations, in which visual hallucinations manifest as associative impressions in response to sound (Bliss and Clark 1962).

3. Virtual concerts and music festivals have been discussed in various press. For example, Stubhub (2020) and Billboard (2020) provided summary lists of notable events; while Pollard (2020) gave journalistic commentary on various visual festivals and raves.
4. For the purposes of this chapter, the concepts of "visualizing music" and "music visualization" are considered interchangeable.
5. For more information, see the liner notes of *Highlights of Vortex: Electronic Experiments and Music* (Various Artists 1959).
6. "Fulldome" refers to a type of immersive hemispherical projection theater, which is often used in planetariums. See also Weinel (2018c, 131–133).
7. Autodesk Studio, a 3D computer animation program for PC, is credited as one of the visual production tools on the sleeve of *Future Shock* (Various Artists, 1993). Autodesk Studio is the forerunner of Autodesk 3ds Max, a popular 3D animation tool still that is still in use today.
8. For a further discussion of audiovisual performance with video game engines, see also Ciciliani, Lüneburg, and Pirchner (2021).
9. Earlier performances on a Mac laptop used the MixEmergency plugin, while at a later date Serato Video was used on a Windows 10 laptop.
10. Originating in the 2010s, "vaporwave" is an internet-born music genre and visual art style that mines the aesthetics of 1980s and 1990s corporate design, elevator music, and advertisements (Tanner 2016).
11. In particular, this scene provided a pastiche of the Fantazia New Year's Eve 1991–1992 event flier. For further examples of 1990s rave fliers, see also Savage (1996).
12. In this context, a *horizontal* interactive music system allows transitions to different sections of music on a timeline, as opposed to a *vertical* system, in which layers may be added or subtracted.
13. Several of the students whose work is discussed in this section went on to postgraduate study, where they have been able to build on the experienced gained working on the projects discussed in this section.

References

Beat Games. 2019. *Beat Saber*. VR Experience. Oculus Quest, Beat Games.

Bell, Eamonn. 2019. "Hacking Jeff Minter's Virtual Light Machine: Unpacking the Code and Community behind an Early Software-Based Music Visualizer." *Volume!* 16 (1). https://doi.org/10.4000/volume.7254.

Billboard. 2020. "Here Are All the Livestreams & Virtual Concerts to Watch during Coronavirus Crisis." *Billboard*, July 30, 2020. Accessed May 19, 2021. https://www.billboard.com/articles/columns/pop/9335531/coronavirus-quarantine-music-events-online-streams.

Bliss, Eugene L., and Lincoln D. Clark. 1962. "Visual Hallucinations." In *Hallucinations*, edited by L. J. West, 92–107. New York: Grune & Stratton.

Boolean, The. 2020. "Tomorrowland: A 2D Video Streaming Festival That Attracted Over 1 Million Viewers." *Boolean*, August 13, 2020. Accessed May 19, 2021. https://theboolean.io/2020/08/13/tomorrowland-a-2d-video-streaming-festival-that-attracted-over-1-million-viewers/.

Brougher, Kerry, and Olivia Mattis. 2005. *Visual Music: Synaesthesia in Art and Music since 1900*. London: Thames & Hudson.

Ciciliani, Marko, Barbara Lüneburg, and Andreas Pirchner. 2021. *Ludified: Artistic Research in Audiovisual Composition, Performance and Perception*. Berlin: The Green Box.
Cold Beam Games. 2010. *Beat Hazard*. Video Game. PC, Cold Beam Games.
Cytowic, Richard E. 1989. *Synesthesia: A Union of the Senses*. New York: Springer-Verlag.
Danneberg, Roger B. 2005. "Interactive Visual Music: A Personal Perspective." *Computer Music Journal* 29 (4). https://doi.org/10.1162/014892605775179964.
Drool. 2016. *Thumper*. Video Game. PC, Drool.
Eat Static. 1994. *Intrusion*. Video. VHS, Planet Dog.
Faulkner, Michael (D-Fuse). 2006. *VJ: Audio-Visual Art and VJ Culture*. London: Laurence King.
Fitterer, Dylan. 2008. *Audio Surf*. PC, Dylan Fitterer.
Frictional Games. 2010–2020. *Amnesia*. Video Game Series. Various platforms, Frictional Games.
Gordan, Lewis. 2017. "*Rez: Infinite:* How a Techno Street Parade Inspired Tetsuya Mizuguchi's Pioneering Music Video Game." *Fact Mag*, January 10, 2017. Accessed May 19, 2021. https://www.factmag.com/2017/01/10/rez-infinite-tetsuya-mizuguchi-interview/.
Harmonix. 2005–2015. *Guitar Hero*. Video Game Series. Various platforms, Harmonix.
Hex. 1991. *Escape*. Multimedia. CDi, Philips Media.
Hex. 1993. *Anti Static*. Multimedia. CDi, Philips Media.
Hex. 1993. *Global Chaos*. Video. VHS, Imagine Home Entertainment.
Hex. 1995. *Head Crash*. Multimedia. CDi, Philips Media.
Holtum, Christopher. 2020. "Simulacra: Using Game Development Software to Create Audio-Visual Performance Tools." *EVA London 2020 (Electronic Visualisation and the Arts)*, 100–103. https://doi.org/10.14236/ewic/EVA2020.17.
Humanoid. 1988. *Stakker Humanoid*. Video. Westside Records.
Kocay, Lisa. 2020. "Inside Lost Horizon: A Virtual Reality Music Festival." *Forbes*, June 1, 2020. Accessed May 19, 2021. https://www.forbes.com/sites/lisakocay/2020/06/30/lost-horizon-virtual-reality-music-festival.
Konami. 1998–2020. *Dance Dance Revolution*. Video Game Series. Various platforms, Konami.
McIntosh, Tyler. 2021. "Exploring the Relationship between Music and Emotions with Machine Learning." *EVA London 2021 (Electronic Visualisation and the Arts)*, 279–280.
Mebius. 2018. *Lost Future Omega*. Video Game. Nintendo Switch, Mebius.
MelodyVR. 2019. *MelodyVR*. VR Experience. Oculus Quest, MelodyVR.
Monstars. 2017. *Rez Infinite*. Video Game. PC, Enhance Games.
Namco. 2001–2021. *Taiko no Tatsujin*. Video Game Series. Various platforms, Namco.
Outsider, The. n.d. *Acid Collection #2*. Demoscene Production. Amiga OSC/ECS. Available via *Pouet*. Accessed May 19, 2021. https://www.pouet.net/prod.php?which=74563.
Picard, Rosalind W. 1997. *Affective Computing*. Cambridge, MA: MIT Press.
Polgár, Tamás. 2005. *Freax: A Brief History of the Computer Demoscene*. CSW-Verlag, Winnenden.
Pollard, Alexandra. 2020. "'My Neighbours Think I'm Losing It': From Livestreams to Virtual Reality Raves, How Musicians Are Coping without Touring." *Independent*, June 13, 2020. Accessed May 19, 2021. https://www.independent.co.uk/arts-entertainment/music/features/musicians-coronavirus-lockdown-livestreams-raves-phoebe-bridgers-rufus-wainwright-tim-burgess-a9561946.html.
Random Access. n.d. *Music Compilation*. Demoscene Production. Amiga OCS/ECS. Accessed May 19, 2021. http://arabuusimiehet.com/break/amiga/details.php?id=806.

Rebels. 1990. *Coma*. Demoscene production. Amiga OSC/ECS. Available via *Pouet*. Accessed May 19, 2021. http://www.pouet.net/prod.php?which=1650.

Rietveld, Hillegonda C., Christopher Thomas Allen, Laurie Bender, Mark Pilkington, and Jonathan Weinel. 2019. "VJ Panel: Immersive Visual Music." May 15, 2019. London South Bank University.

Savage, Jon. 1996. *Highflyers: Club Rave Party Art*. London: Booth-Clibborn.

Sitney, P. Adams. (1965) 2000. "Harry Smith Interview." In *Film Culture Reader*, edited by P. A. Sitney, 260–276. Reprint, New York: Cooper Square Press.

Stakker. 1989. *Eurotechno*. Video. VHS, Virgin Music Video.

Stubhub. 2020. "How to Enjoy Your Favourite Festivals in Summer 2020." *Stubhub*, June 10, 2020. Accessed May 19, 2021. https://www.stubhub.co.uk/magazine/virtual-festivals-summer-2020.

Studio!K7 (Producer). 1993–1998. *X-Mix*. Video Series. Studio!K7.

Tanner, Grafton. 2016. *Babbling Corpse: Vaporwave and the Commodification of Ghosts*. Alresford: Zero Books.

Turchet, Luca, Rob Hamilton, and Anil Çamci. 2021. "Music in Extended Realities." *IEEE Access* 9. https://doi.org/10.1109/ACCESS.2021.3052931.

United Game Artists. 2001. *Rez*. Video Game. Sega Dreamcast, Sega.

Various Artists. 1959. *Highlights of Vortex: Electronic Experiments and Music*. CD, Reissue, Smithsonian Folkways, 2004. Liner notes. Accessed May 19, 2021. https://folkways-media.si.edu/liner_notes/folkways/FW06301.pdf.

Various Artists. 1988. *The Evil Acid Baron Show*. Video. VHS, Polygram Music.

Various Artists. 1993. *Future Shock*. Video. VHS, Prism Leisure Video.

VR. 1992. *Cyberdelia*. Video. VHS, Prism Leisure Video.

VR and Dr. Devious. 1992. *Dance in Cyberspace*. Video. VHS, Prism Leisure Video.

Weinel, Jonathan. 2018a. "How Atari and Amiga Computers Shaped the Design of Rave Culture." *OUPblog*, April 5, 2018. Accessed August 12, 2020. https://blog.oup.com/2018/04/atari-amiga-computers-design-rave-culture/.

Weinel, Jonathan. 2018b. "Improvising with Light: Nova Express Psychedelic Light Show." *OUPblog*, December 14, 2018. Accessed July 29, 2020. https://blog.oup.com/2018/12/nova-express-psychedelic-light-show/.

Weinel, Jonathan. 2018c. *Inner Sound: Altered States of Consciousness in Electronic Music and Audio-Visual Media*. New York: Oxford University Press.

Weinel, Jonathan. 2019a. "Cyberdream VR: Visualizing Rave Music and Vaporwave in Virtual Reality." ACM Proceedings of Audio Mostly 2019, University of Nottingham, UK. https://doi.org/10.1145/3356590.3356637.

Weinel, Jonathan. 2019b. "Virtual Hallucinations: Projects in VJing, Virtual Reality and Cyberculture." *EVA London 2019 (Electronic Visualisation and the Arts)*, 293–301. https://doi.org/10.14236/ewic/EVA2019.57.

Weinel, Jonathan. 2020a. "Cyberdreams: Visualising Music in Extended Reality (XR)." In *Technology, Design and the Arts—Challenges and Opportunities*, edited by R. A. Earnshaw, S. Liggett, P. S. Excell, and D. Thalmann. Berlin: Springer. https://doi.org/10.1145/3478514.3487609.

Weinel, Jonathan. 2020b. "Visualising Rave Music in Virtual Reality: Symbolic and Interactive Approaches." *EVA London 2020 (Electronic Visualisation and the Arts)*, 78–84. https://doi.org/10.14236/ewic/EVA2020.13.

Weinel, Jonathan. 2019–2021. *Cyberdream*. Virtual Reality Experience. Prototype software application, Oculus Quest.

Weinel, Jonathan. 2021a. "Cyberdream: An Interactive Rave Music Visualisation." *SIGGRAPH Asia 2021*, Tokyo, Japan. https://doi.org/10.1145/3478514.3487609.

Weinel, Jonathan. 2021b. *Explosions in the Mind: Composing Psychedelic Sounds and Visualisations*. London: Palgrave Macmillan Studies in Sound.

Weinel, Jonathan. 2021c. "Synaesthetic Audio-Visual Sound Toys in Virtual Reality." ACM Proceedings of Audio Mostly 2021, Trento, Italy. https://doi.org/10.1145/3478384.3478400.

CHAPTER 10

ONNA NO JIDAI

Women and Video Game Sound in 1980s Japan

BROOKE MCCORKLE OKAZAKI

Introduction

A few years ago, while scrolling through my Twitter feed, a photograph caught my attention: it was a faded color image that originally appeared in conjunction with an article in *The Wire* about the video game music documentary *Diggin' in the Carts* (Dwyer 2017a). The image showed Japanese women who worked at Capcom in the 1980s, an era known in Japan for its unprecedented economic bounty. The photograph also captured shifts in political and social gender roles during the late 1980s zeitgeist dubbed *onna no jidai*, or "the era of women" (Kano 2016, 18–19). The 1987 photograph features five women who appear to be in their twenties relaxing during a meal at Capcom headquarters in Osaka (Dwyer 2017a). Fascinated, I began tracing the photograph's origins. The women in the photo—Kumi Yamaga, Manami Matsumae, Tamayo Kawamoto, Harumi Fujita, and Junko Tamiya—all worked for Capcom during the 1980s and into the early 1990s.[1] I soon discovered that the photograph had circulated on social media without the women's knowledge or permission (Matsumae 2021). It struck me that the image and how it was shared online illustrates broader structures of power that persist in music scholarship and gaming culture. Despite the large number of female participants and advances made in gender equality in both fields, gaming and music remain male-dominated in the popular imagination if not in actuality. This all led me to wonder: What did it mean to be a woman composer and sound designer in 1980s Japan? What did it mean to be a woman in the corporate world of video game development during that time? What did these women have in common, and how did they relate to the broader world of music making? How did their careers evolve after the burst of Japan's economic bubble and subsequent decades of economic stagnation in Japan? Using these questions as a starting point, I examine how a nexus of political, economic, and social conditions first made the existence of an all-women sound team at Capcom possible. Second, I explore how these conditions concealed Yamaga, Matsumae, Kawamoto, Fujita, and Tamiya's essential contributions to the world of video games, as exemplified in this chapter's appendix of games they worked on (see Appendix 1).[2]

Economics and Gender during Japan's Bubble Years

In 1980s Japan, the economy played a key role in bringing gender to the forefront of political discourse. The decade was a time of unprecedented prosperity in Japan. Following the conclusion of World War II, the country slowly rebuilt its economic infrastructure, concentrating on manufacturing and the service industry. Policies put in place in the 1960s enabled Japan's gross national product to expand the economy at a rate of 10% in 10 years, earning Japan praise as an "economic miracle" (Rhoads and McCorkle 2018, 106). As a result, manufacturing and business skyrocketed (much to the detriment of the environment), the economy rapidly expanded, and large companies flourished. This boom continued into the latter half of the 20th century, reaching a pinnacle of growth in the 1980s. In that decade, Japan's economy grew by 3% each year, and unemployment dropped to 2%—though in the end, such growth, known as the bubble era, was unsustainable (139). From the end of 1989 to the summer of 1992, Japan's Nikkei average plummeted 65%. Historian Andrew Gordon (2003, 291) observes: "the decade of the 1980s, in particular, was a remarkable moment of satisfaction and congratulation, unimaginable in the early postwar era and premature in retrospect."

The super abundance of the 1980s and its aftermath significantly impacted the role of women in the workplace. Because of the flourishing economy, women were hired in greater numbers in a wider variety of corporate positions. This hiring, in turn, led to broader discussions about gender equality. Yet, feminism was not just a political topic; as Japanese historian Ayako Kano (2016, 18–19) observes: "The *feminizumu* [feminism] boom in the 1980s was at once commercial, political, and academic in nature, as the era of women (*onna no jidai*) became a slogan for marketers as well as for activists and scholars." In other words, the feminist movement supported goals that Japanese companies shared with the government: increasing profits and growing the economy. In many ways, the concept echoed pre-1945 government policies that promoted women as creators of human beings that could serve as commodities—either as soldiers or factory workers (Ezawa 2011, 108). The practice of using women as centers of capitalist production continued well into the 21st century, with Prime Minister Abe Shinzō promoting "Womenomics," tapping into the country's "most under-utilized resource: Japanese women," under the guise of gender equality (Abe 2013).[3]

Japan's economic prosperity in the latter half of the 20th century directly affected women. In the immediate postwar years, the Allied occupation, led by the United States, crafted a Japanese constitution that included an equal rights clause for women

(McLelland 2012, 54–55). While women were ostensibly equal and free to pursue careers, social institutions and cultural pressures continued to encourage them to spend their time as mothers and homemakers. Nevertheless, the number of women pursuing higher education and careers continued to increase in the decades after World War II. For example, from 1955 to 1979, the number of women attending junior college multiplied eightfold and the number attending universities, sixfold (Hara and Fujimura-Fanselow 2011, 83). By the 1980s, the percentage of women pursuing higher education had vastly increased, and more women were joining companies with hopes of advancement. In the 1970s and 1980s, many artistically inclined young women born in the postwar years were actively following their dreams into arts and creative business areas previously inhabited by men only, such as writing manga, performing in a rock band, or becoming fashion designers (see Okazaki 2021, 2–3, 18–26; Shamoon 2012, 102–105, 120; Terada 2021, 235–236). The passing of the Working Woman's Welfare Act of 1972 and the ratification of the Convention on the Elimination of All Forms of Discrimination against Women (CEDAW) in 1980 laid the groundwork for future steps toward gender equality in the working world. By 1985, the Equal Employment Opportunity Law encouraged the hiring of women in all fields, including video game production.

These kinds of laws all sought to transform the extensive practice of occupational segregation by gender in Japan. As in other areas of employment, women at video game companies were initially relegated to positions as "office ladies" (often abbreviated OL)—clerical workers who were offered scant opportunities for promotion (Ezawa 2011, 109). However, by the middle of the 1980s, women were making headway in other roles. In a 1986 interview with *Beep! Magazine*, Ayako Mori related that she was among the first composers hired at Capcom (Okamoto et al. 1986). Likewise, women such as Yuki Ikeda, Hisako Takizawa, Reiko Oshida, Yuko Tataka, and Sanae Nito were all pioneers in the male-dominated field of video game design (Ikeda et al. 1990). Kanae Saeda, in corporate sales at Irem, was among the few women representatives in her section, and her gender was something of which she was certainly conscious. She shared: "It's rare to see women working in sales like this. There are merits: our demeanor is softer, and we're good listeners—in an interaction that might normally last only 10 minutes, we can stretch that out to an hour . . . but we also have to constantly stay vigilant about keeping those encounters as business-only, and not give those we work with the idea that we're romantically interested" (Ikeda et al. 1990).

Saeda's comments indicate that even as a woman breaking glass ceilings in the competitive realm of corporate sales, socially ingrained concepts of gender roles affected her approach to her job. Kaori Ikeda, who worked in promotions at Asmik, also observed a scarcity of women in the field and embraced the notion that women possess particular skills that could help companies attract young consumers: "There still aren't a lot of women in this line of work, so I think there's a lot of room for growth, and opportunity for a woman to bring her sensibilities to this job. For example, in advertising, in games for children, they're often wanting to use cute imagery. I'm especially interested in things like that. . . . If I had to guess, this industry is probably considered by most to be a 'men's only' industry, but women certainly have a right to enjoy it too, and I think there's plenty of opportunities for that" (Ikeda et al. 1990). Based on Ikeda and her contemporaries' assessments, it is apparent that despite being involved in various sectors of the video game industry, women workers frequently internalized gendered concepts of labor.

Furthermore, despite proclaimed policies like the Equal Employment Opportunity Law, prevalent discourse around an *onna no jidai* did not alleviate binarism and gender inequality. As Kano points out: "The basis of social policy in modern Japan is the assumption that all women are potential wives and mothers (and that all men are potential breadwinners and heads of households). . . . Japanese welfare and social policy enforces gender norms: it makes it easier for a girl to grow up to be a wife and mother, and makes it more difficult for her to reject those roles or to combine those roles with demanding careers" (Kano 2016, 8, 11).

In the 1980s, the women at the forefront of the *onna no jidai* era were entering the workforce and making spaces for themselves in the corporate realm, but they were not necessarily abandoning dreams of finding a partner and building a family. For many women of the postwar generation, figuring out how to maintain a career without "throwing away womanhood" (*onna wo suteru*) was (and remains) a tricky path.[4] As a result, due to a backlash against *onna no jidai* measures that supposedly contributed to social problems like higher rates of divorce and youth crime, the word *feminizumu* still carries a negative connotation in the 2020s (Kano 2016, 157).[5]

Japan, Women, and Video Game Music Scholarship

Until the 2020s, scholars of game music and culture had rarely championed women composers and sound designers of 1980s and 1990s Japan. This can be attributed in part to crediting practices, which Andrew Lemon and Hillegonda C. Rietveld (2021) outline in their collaborative research. Lemon and Rietveld primarily concentrate on how and why the Capcom Sound Team members were exscripted from game history for so long.[6] First, Capcom had a policy of requiring its creators to use gender neutral pseudonyms in their credits (Lemon and Rietveld 2021, 377). Part of this had to do with the cooperative approach to game music and sound; rarely was one individual solely responsible for a game's audio. As a result, crediting was a complex task simplified by team names and pseudonyms (Lemon and Rietveld 2021, 378; Dwyer 2017b).[7] Second, Lemon and Rietveld observe that sometimes companies replaced or rearranged arcade music by Japanese composers when the games were adapted for home consoles and overseas releases (Lemon and Rietveld 2021, 376).

Another crucial factor to consider is the predominance of English-language scholarship in the field of video game music studies. While Japanese-language scholarship on video games is growing, thanks to the foundation of Ritsumeikan University's Center for Game Studies and its English/Japanese journal *Replaying Japan*, the bulk of academic writing on video game music and sound is the purview of North American and European academics (Ritsumeikan University).[8] Part of this has to do with the organization of Japanese universities, very few of which have departments specifically devoted to the study of music. Instead, music-related courses are typically offered in a variety of departments and students interested in performing participate in extracurricular clubs. Music schools, on the other hand, tend to be conservatory models centered on performance, though some colleges developed degree tracks to include arts management and recording technology studies in the early 2000s (Tokyo University of the Fine Arts; Osaka University of Arts).[9] Partially as a result of these institutional structures and practices, academic studies of music and multimedia in popular culture are less common in Japan than in Canada, Europe, and the United States. Nonetheless, thanks to the establishment of the Ritsumeikan University's Center for Game Studies, as well as other groups such as Waseda University's Collaborative Research Center for Film and Theatre Arts and the Japan branch of the International Association for the Study of Popular Music (Waseda University; The Japanese Association for the Study of Popular Music), some headway in music and multimedia studies has been made.[10]

Finally, as Melanie Fritsch points out, the field of ludomusicology is relatively new and is therefore focused on developing tools and modes of analysis and interpretation rather than examining biographical backgrounds as well as broader social constructs such as gender and economics (Fritsch 2022, 179). Nonetheless, on the whole, ludomusicology embraces progressive research to a much greater degree than other related fields.[11] While such research is to be lauded, there are inherent dynamics at play. As William Gibbons (2020), Julianne Grasso (2020), Karen Cook (2020), and Hyeonjin Park (2020) explained in a colloquy appearing in the inaugural issues of *Journal of Sound and Music in Games*, a tendency to apply Romantic values of canonization to the new "repertoire" of video game music pervades the field of music studies. The lingering cult of Romanticism idealizes the individual genius rather than collective creativity, and ludomusicology perpetuates these nagging flaws of English-language music studies, with many scholars focusing on composers such as Koji Kondo and Nobuo Uematsu (see chapter 1 and chapter 2 this volume). Even the increased academic regard for Yoko Shimomura replicates the values of canonization and Romanticism to the detriment of work resulting from collective musical creativity.[12] As Fritsch (2022, 180) sums up, "the tendency in western media, documentaries, and scholarship to search for the one creative mastermind against the backdrop of aesthetic genius is still applied when studying games, instead of seeing their production as the collective process it usually is." No matter how hard we press against the practices of our academic fields, it is difficult to resist the allure of championing beloved artists; I replicate some of these practices here in this chapter by singling out members of the Capcom Sound Team. But while recognizing individual contributions, I also want to celebrate the process of creative collaboration. The 1980s Capcom Sound Team's cooperative approach models a progressive path forward for scholars in the humanities—a more general branch of study that itself has for too long valorized individual labor over collective artistry.

Gender and the Capcom Sound Team

The women of the Capcom Sound Team had a few things in common that afforded them the position and space to work on video games. First, all these women are of the same general age, born in the 1960s and coming of age in the 1980s during the bubble years when the *onna no jidai* was in full swing in the political and popular sphere. Second, they all had college educations, primarily at colleges of fine arts, though their training was rarely in composing in a western classical idiom. Matsumae, for example, graduated from the Osaka University of Arts in 1987, specializing in piano (Brave Wave 2017). Fujita had gone to design school and began composing as a hobby but was employed to pursue it professionally at SNK as a sound programmer before joining Capcom (Fujita 2015). Tamiya graduated from Osaka College of Music with a focus on performance (Tamiya 2014). Thanks to university connections, she joined Capcom in 1987.

The presence of women in creative positions at Capcom in turn generated a female space. For a short period of time, Capcom provided a unique atmosphere for young women in the creative public technosphere. The gathering of a prominent core of women at the company in turn made it attractive to other female applicants. In an interview with Matsumae, Alexandra Hall (2021) asked, "Many of the great composers at Capcom were female. Was it easier back then for women to make their mark in sound composition than in other areas of game development?" Matsumae provided an illuminating answer:

> When I joined Capcom, everyone in the sound team except Sakaguchi-san, the head of the department, was female. I wouldn't say it was easy for women to make their mark, but rather because everyone was female, inevitably they came to define the team. Unsurprisingly, there came a time when intense music created by men would become sought after, and many male composers joined the team after me. The vibe of the team slowly pulled away from being female dominated and the work of the women was compared to the men and vice versa. Both the men and women studied and polished their music, which resulted in a very wide range of music produced, a result that I think is still relevant to the company today. (Matsumae 2021)

Matsumae's nuanced observation points to the fact that she walks a fine line as someone still active in the music industry; as a freelancer, she must navigate questions without risking current or future employment. It's clear from the quote above, though, that the presence of other female members made it easier for women to work at Capcom, and therefore Capcom's team was attractive to this subset of applicants. This is evident in Matsumae's later comment: "When I joined the Capcom Sound Team, it was already filled with women, so I didn't think anything of it. I spent a lot of time with them outside of work as well, going on vacations together, attending the same swim schools, and so on. We did many things together" (Matsumae 2021). The many women participating in music and sound at Capcom inspired Yoko Shimomura, who began working at the company in 1988. She related: "When I joined Capcom originally . . . both of the top composers were women then. I heard them at the time, and they were talented and made great music. I felt that since the head staff were women, it was easier for other women to join the department" (Lemon and Rietveld 2019, 116). In short: representation mattered.

While Japan's corporate lifestyle is notoriously stressful, the work demands were doubly hard on female employees who hoped to build families (Nemoto 2013). Women in the game industry attested to this. Game designer Hisako Takizawa, active in the 1990s, said: "If you *really* love games, then that's one thing . . . but it's not the kind of job you should take if you want time to be in a relationship! They haven't gone so far as to make the women pull consecutive overnighters during crunch time, but you should be prepared for overtime and working on holidays" (Ikeda et al. 1990). Her colleague Ikeda Yuki commented: "It's harder than being a typical OL. A lot of the work requires a great deal of perseverance to see through. But knowing that, if you really love games, why not give it a shot?" (Ikeda et al. 1990). While these women were designers rather than music and sound creators, their reflections reveal the intense corporate culture in which the Capcom Sound Team functioned.

The Capcom Sound Team members' experiences echo those of Takizawa and Ikeda. For example, in an interview Kawamoto described her intense work schedule: "Usually, we would have around three months to complete a project. In addition, we would have around three projects running concurrently" (Kawamoto 2002). She also mentioned that working under the limitations of the PSG (programmable sound generator) chip at the time was very stressful. In a separate story, Kawamoto's coworker Matsumae described: "From the day I joined, I had to work overtime every day, which was a very tough experience. (Laughs.)" (Matsumae 2021). Later in the interview, she explained that the demanding Capcom schedule eventually drove her from the corporate world.[13] Fujita also faced harrowing experiences. In her interview with Chris Greening of Video Game Music Online, Fujita described her contributions to *Mega Man 3* and her departure from the project:

> For *Mega Man 3*, I composed the Gemini Man and Needle Man stages, as well as the Staff Roll. I had to drop out during the middle of development and leave the company to give birth to my child, so I ended up having Yasuaki Fujita take over for me. *Mega Man* is a hit series, so I was happy to have been involved in such a series. I wanted to see the project through to the end, but I was going to the hospital a lot during my pregnancy. I found it to be a regrettable retirement from the company. (Fujita 2015)

Greening failed to follow up this comment in the interview, and instead requested that Fujita share memories of other games on which she worked.[14] But Fujita's remark is worth closer consideration as it indicates that the employment demands made by the 1980s Capcom work culture were at odds with womanhood to the point that a pregnant female employee, even one as talented as Fujita, had no option but to depart the company and become a freelancer, even in 1991 (Fujita 2015). Yet this kind of atmosphere was not limited to Capcom. Fujita recalled her experience composing *Tomba!* (1997), a game produced by Whoopee Camp:

> For the first time in a while, I worked on this project together with producer Fujiwara-san, who I worked with at Capcom. I remember this being quite a tough project, with a lot of redos as the developers kept telling me about the imagery of the game. I also remember them asking me to get music back to them on the same day or even in the next two hours. That was quite tough. I remember giving birth to my second child while this game was in development. I took only a week off before getting back into it! (Fujita 2015)

Fujita's recollections make tangible the fact that despite moves to proclaim an *onna no jidai*, very little happened in the way of true change to help make it easier for women who become mothers to continue developing their careers.[15]

Leaving the Corporate World

Indeed, many of the Sound Team members' departures resulted from changes in their personal lives. In the context of corporate Japan, overseers assumed women would leave their positions upon marrying and having children. Kano (2016, 79) notes: "Nearly 70 percent of women leave their jobs by the time they give birth to their first child, and those who try to return to the workplace after giving birth find that it is hard to mesh motherhood and work." Even in the early 2000s, most women in companies received 12 months of maternity leave, and some took up to three years, ending when a child entered preschool. By that time, few were able to return to their prior positions and instead became part-time workers despite their college education (Ezawa 2011, 109–110). Therefore, female hires in Japan in the 1980s (and up through the present day) were frequently made as cost-saving, temporary hires. Gender discriminatory practices ensured that women would not become lifetime employees who would climb up the corporate ladder.

For Capcom and other companies, women could be used as temporary contributors to creative assignments with the assumption that they would leave the company and "retire" upon marriage—or if not then, then with the birth of children. Matsumae related: "I decided to get married and move to Tokyo. When I quit Capcom, I asked if I could work as a freelancer for them, but at the time, there were many composers in the company, so they couldn't accommodate my request! (laughs). . . . Women tend to quit working when they get married, so I imagine that's why some of them have retired from composing game music" (Matsumae 2021). In essence, Capcom took advantage of creative, young, single female production as a way of gaining an edge in the vibrant world of video game sound.

Once the exodus of female composers began, the atmosphere of the Sound Team changed; without other women with whom they could collaborate and build working relationships, it became more difficult for women to continue. This kind of soft power of minority representation plagues the global corporate world, and Japan was no exception. Likely, Capcom did not continue to hire young women as replacements particularly after the economic bubble burst. Instead, the corporate world prioritized male workers considered to be sole breadwinners rather than young, single women building careers (Nakano 2011, 263). When the economic bubble burst in the early 1990s, companies including Capcom subsequently adjusted their hiring policies to favor the promotion of men in leadership positions and creative roles. Women, especially as they "aged out" of the workforce around their thirties, were simply replaced with men, who were considered more stable and reliable, in that they would not need to leave work should a child be born, grow ill, or need help in school.

Matsumae's observations from the 2021 interview featured on the Kotaku website make it clear that despite the *onna no jidai* movement of the 1980s and the subsequent "Womenomics" of the Abe administration in the early 21st century, the gender gap continues. After the passing of the Equal Employment Opportunity Law, many companies created dual employment tracks: one for auxiliary work and one for career-focused work. As of 2007, among 123 companies that have separate "career" and "auxiliary work" tracks, female employees made up only 6% of the career track, a stark contrast to the European Union and the United States (Clark 2011).[16] Women also tended to be employed more as part-time rather than full-time workers. Not accounting for part-time laborers, women in Japan typically earned 69% of what men earned in 2008 (Nakano 2011, 258–260). While of course many women continue to maintain fruitful, successful careers after marriage and childrearing in Japan, the society, its companies, and its governmental policies do not make it easy. Even with programs like subsidized childcare, it is often difficult to acquire a space for one's child in the public daycare system.

Some of the former Capcom Sound Team members struck a balance by becoming freelancers. While freelancing as a woman was still relatively rare in the late 1980s and early 1990s, it did allow women to manage their own hours and to tailor their schedules to include fulfilling activities related to family life.[17] The flexibility that independent (indie) developers sometimes offered contributed to Matsumae's career trajectory. Indie developers and companies tend to have more equitable collaborations where people outside of the company can have significant input in the work. This is different from large companies, as Matsumae describes: "A large company means a large development team and an environment where it might take more time for people's opinions to be made known. Also, a large company tends to have many in-house composers, some of them famous in their own right, so unfortunately, I don't get many opportunities to work on their games" (Matsumae 2021). As a result, Matsumae and many of her former Capcom colleagues found fulfillment working in smaller, more independent contexts, while some seem to have left the music world completely.[18]

As for Fujita, she eventually departed from the game world around 2000 to pursue a career involved with stage music and musicals (Fujita 2011). Part of this has to do with vanishing professional ties to the gaming industry, and part with boredom at the repetition of game programming (Matsumae 2021). In addition to navigating a path with soundtrack releases and remasters and working on stage music, Fujita has occasionally come out of game composition retirement—for example, she worked on the smartphone game *Spidersaurs* (2019) by WayForward (Fujita 2023). In other words, like other women formerly of the Capcom Sound Team, she cultivated a path as a freelancer to balance a career with motherhood in the Japan of the post-bubble era and beyond.

Along with other composers including Matsumae and Shimomura, Fujita has collaborated with Brave Wave Productions, a company that specializes in releasing soundtrack recordings of video games on both CD and vinyl (Brave Wave). Brave Wave's highly sought-after releases of game soundtracks has helped bring recognition to Japanese female video game composers and sound designers in recent years. And as Lemon and Rietveld (2021, 378–379) point out, the musicians in this setup have some agency over the production and distribution of their music.[19] Thanks to the production and circulation of soundtrack recordings and to the popularity of video game music concerts, the 1980s Capcom Sound Team members are acquiring some long-overdue acknowledgment for their work.[20]

Onna no jidai Reboot

Women in the corporate world of 1980s Japan grappled with the binary bind, and the Capcom Sound Team was no exception.[21] Kano (2016, 124–125) opines: "In retrospect, the 1980s—the highpoint of Japan's economic powers—represented also the height of a very particular dichotomy for women: Did true liberation lie in pursuing lifelong careers and paid productive labor on a par with men, or in fully embracing the roles of housewife and reproductive laborer as women?" This question remains one with which women in Japan and around the world continue to wrestle. The members of the Capcom Sound Team eventually navigated their own paths, earning greater flexibility in fulfilling roles as parents and as working musicians.[22] By departing the corporate world, many Japanese female composers were free to find other outlets for creativity by forming their own companies or serving as freelancers. But as many of these women were no longer part of the official corporate ladder, the music of other, predominantly male, composers overshadowed their substantial contributions to video game music and sound.

In sum, the Capcom Sound Team of the 1980s was an unusual example of female creativity and labor in a Japanese corporate space. As such, the Capcom Sound Team seems to be a blip in the history of video game music. Political and economic factors provided certain affordances that made the formation of such a team possible at this specific time and place. Ironically, the same factors undermined female labor in the corporate sphere. Still, the 1980s Capcom Team is not unique as an example of the hidden creative labor of women, nor is the phenomenon of exscription of women limited to Japan. From female animators at Disney Studios to Black female mathematicians working at NASA in the

1960s, throughout the 20th century and across the globe the work of women in institutional settings has been concealed (Holt 2019; Shetterly 2016). Despite the creativity at the core of their work, labor by women has historically been deemed frivolous, repetitive, and unintellectual, whether the work is cross-stitching, coding, or composing for video games. The growing prominence of Shimomura as well as younger composers Manaka Kataoka and Atsuko Asahi of Nintendo combats the concealment of Japanese women's work in the world of video game sound and audio (Frank 2017; Park 2020). They and their predecessors' concerted and conscious efforts prove that the *onna no jidai* is here to stay.

Appendix 1: Timeline of Games and Composers

I have placed the Japanese titles first and the titles of the releases overseas in parentheses when applicable (Table 10.1). Often composers would provide arrangements as well.[23]

TABLE 10.1 Timeline of Games Scored by Female Capcom Team Members during the Bubble Years

Year	Game	Member	Role
1985	*Makaimura* (*Ghosts 'n Goblins*)	Fujita	sound effects
1985	*Exed Exes*	Kawamoto	composer
1985	*Senjō no ōkami* (*Commando*)	Kawamoto	composer
1985	*Gun.Smoke.*	Tamiya	sound
1986	*Rush and Crash* (*The Speed Rumbler*)	Fujita, Kawamoto	contributing composers
1987	*Top Secret* (*Bionic Commando*) (arcade version)	Fujita	composer
1987	*Tiger Road*	Fujita, Kawamoto, Tamiya	contributing composers
1987	*Higemaru Makaijima* (*Makai Island*)	Fujita	composer
1987	*Black Dragon* (*Black Tiger*)	Kawamoto	composer
1987	*Master Yōsuke Ide's Mahjong Battle*	Matsumae, Fujita	contributing composers
1987	*Rokkuman* (*Mega Man*)	Fujita	composer
1988	*1943: The Battle of Midway*	Fujita, Matsumae, Yamaga, Tamiya	contributing composers
1988	*Rokkuman 2: Dr. Wairī no Nazo* (*Mega Man 2*)	Fujita	with Takashi Tateishi
1988	*Dai Makaimura* (*Ghouls 'n Ghosts*)	Kawamoto	composer

TABLE 10.1 Continued

Year	Game	Member	Role
1988	*Hitler no Fukkatsu: Top Secret* (*Bionic Commando*) (NES version)	Fujita	composers
1989	*Final Fight*	Matsumae, Tamiya, Fujita, Shimomura	contributing composers
1989	*Tenchi wo kurau* (*Dynasty Wars*)	Matsumae	composer
1989	*Son Son 2*	Matsumae	composer
1989	*Area 88*	Matsumae	composer
1989	*Sweet Home*	Tamiya	composer
1989	*Strider*	Fujita, Tamiya	contributing composers
1989	*Willow*	Fujita	sound programming
1989	*Dokaben 2*	Tamiya	composer
1989	*Pumping World* (*Buster Bros.*)	Kawamoto	composer
1990	*Chip 'n Dale: Rescue Rangers*	Fujita	composer
1990	*Ningen heiki deddo fokkusu* (*Code Name: Viper*)	Tamiya, Fujita, Shimomura (possibly)	contributing composers
1990	*Reddo Arīmā Makaimura Gaiden* (*Gargoyle's Quest*)	Fujita, Shimomura	contributing composers
1990	*Rockman 3: Dr. Wily no Saigo!?* (*Mega Man 3*)	Fujita	in collaboration with Yasuaki Fujita
1990	*Adventure Quiz 2: Hatena no daibouken*	Matsumae, Tamiya	contributing composers
1990	*Senba no ōkami* (*MERCS*)	Matsumae	composer
1990	*Magic Sword*	Matsumae	composer
1990	*U.S. Navy* (*Carrier Air Wing*)	Matsumae	composer
1990	*Kuizu dono no yabō*	Matsumae	composer
1990	*Little Nemo: The Dream Master*	Tamiya	composer
1990	*Street Fighter 2010: The Final Fight*	Tamiya	music director
1991	*Street Fighter II*	Yoko Shimomura*	composer

NOTES

1. For clarity's sake I have placed Japanese surnames after given names, per English language customs. Translations from Japanese sources are my own except for those appearing on the shmupulations website.
2. As a white female academic working primarily in the United States, I recognize that I must vigilantly challenge the racist trap of white feminists pitying disenfranchised women in Asia or other parts of the globe. In this essay, I try to avoid scholastic imperialism by highlighting the ways Japanese economic and political structures impacted women's careers and by citing a diversity of authors and examples.

3. Abenomics, though indicative of neoliberal capitalist policies, did bring issues of gender equality to the forefront of political discourse, resulting in the 2015 Act on the Promotion of Female Participation and Career Advancement in the Workplace. Thank you to the external reviewer of this chapter for bringing this to my attention.
4. This concept of "throwing away womanhood" typically refers to older women giving up on trying to look feminine. The saying is so prevalent that it appeared in the popular Netflix show *Queer Eye Japan* (2019).
5. This is true to the degree that even all-female hard-core punk bands in Japan, such as Otoboke Beaver, rejected any whiff of the label until 2022 (St. Michel 2018; Yu 2022). Kano (2016, 155–160) provides greater detail on the antifeminist backlash.
6. The authors borrow the concept of exscription from Robert Walser, who used it regarding heavy metal (Walser 1993, 114–115).
7. The collaborative approach is true even of works now often attributed to solo composers. For example, while Shimomura is generally cited as the composer for *Street Fighter II*, she did not compose the Sagat theme (Dwyer 2017b).
8. Fritsch notes that because of the predominance of academics from the western hemisphere in ludomusicology, games and platforms that were most popular in those areas of the world (North America, the United Kingdom, and Europe) are overrepresented in studies (Fritsch 2022, 179).
9. For example, the oldest music school in Japan, which was subsumed into the Tokyo University for the Arts, now includes a musicology track and a musical creativity and the environment track that includes training in technology, arts management, and research.
10. Ritsumeikan's Center for Game Studies is noteworthy for being the only such research center in Japan, and it has the support of the government's Agency for Cultural Affairs. It has brought together scholars from a variety of countries and fields, including film, media, and music thanks to its international Replaying Japan conference along with its English/Japanese journal of the same name.
11. For example, immediately prior to the writing of this chapter, two other chapters on the Capcom Sound Team appeared in publication. See Fritsch (2022) and Lemon and Rietveld (2021).
12. Possibly the most well-known female game composer in the late 20th and early 21st centuries, Shimomura was, for a long time, exscripted from game sound history (Lemon and Rietveld 2021, 376). Shimomura has, however, enjoyed some degree of fame, even comparable to Nobuo Uematsu and Koji Kondo, thanks in part to her long career in the field and her involvement in high-profile games like *Street Fighter II* and *Kingdom Hearts*. Yet, part of Shimomura's early success with the former game had to do with her ability to create music that suited the hypermasculine arena of the fighting arcade game. In other words, she was able to write in a way that did not distract (that is, challenge) players' gendered expectations of gameplay and sound (Lemon and Rietveld 2019, 124).
13. It is difficult to imagine that the demanding work schedule was the only reason Matsumae left the corporate world. The institutionalized patriarchy of 1980s Japanese corporate life suggests that women in the workplace frequently experienced sexual harassment and microaggressions. While these issues pervade business life around the world up through the 21st century, this acknowledgment is especially relevant to the chapter's focus on women in 1980s corporate Japan.
14. It is possible that Greening's questions were predetermined because of translation complications and thus he was not able to adequately follow up.

15. This also speaks to Fujita's determination; while women in the United States frequently return to work after six weeks of maternity leave and some sooner, in Japan most women take at least six months to a year off, and sometimes up to three years.
16. According to reports, in 2011 women held 12% of managerial positions in the European Union and 40% in the United States. These numbers indicate that there is still much work to be done around the world in order to close the gender gap.
17. As mentioned earlier, in the early 1980s, Michiko Okazaki was among the first freelancers in the world of fashion design at the Wakoh Company.
18. Matsumae worked on the successful indie game *Shovel Knight* (2014). Later female video game music composers have also gone from working in-house to freelancing as their careers progressed. For example, both Michiko Naruke, known for her work on the *Wild Arms* series (1996–), and Yoko Shimomura left companies and went on to become successful freelancers (Collins 2019, 250, 383). Of course, freelancing is not limited to women. Many people, especially those in creative fields, find that the corporate lifestyle is not compatible with their personalities and goals. For example, Japanese male video game composer Testsuya Shibata, who worked on *Monster Hunter* (2004) and *Resident Evil* (1996) at Capcom starting in the late 1990s, eventually went freelance and started his own company (Collins 2019, 377–378). Hisayoshi Ogura who was at Taito from 1983 to 2007 also eventually went freelance (266–270). As a result of career decisions, information about some Capcom Sound Team members, such as Yamaga and Tamiya, is very sparse, as Melanie Fritsch (2022, 178) has pointed out. It would be worth pursuing personal interviews with these women if they are open to talking about their time at Capcom. However, it is also possible that, in leaving the field, they have decided to protect their privacy.
19. Furthermore, although Brave Wave is based in Shibuya, Tokyo, it is clearly marketed for overseas distribution as their website and social networking is in the English language. It is striking that all their merchandise for soundtrack CDs and vinyl prints sold out for American customers when I visited the site in August of 2021, indicating that demand is high for such material. One can, of course, purchase digital downloads. Brave Wave's Alexander Aniel, CEO, and Mohammed Taher, chairman, are also involved in video game music online.
20. Lemon and Rietveld (2021, 378–379, 388) make similar assessments. Future research, however, including personal interviews especially with Yamaga and Tamiya; music and sound analysis; archival and archeological research along the lines of Lemon and Rietveld's work; and broader histories of technology, culture, and gender, could be fruitful.
21. And of course, many women still contend with these issues today. A 2020 Global Gender Gap report by the World Economic forum ranked Japan 121st out of 153 countries regarding gender equality (Aulia and Kurniawaty 2021, 1).
22. In this sense, the paths the Capcom team took are like that taken by Okazaki in that, once leaving the company system, they were able to work freelance, select their jobs carefully, and determine their own hours. Of course, part of this has to do with the fact that they were not the sole breadwinners in the household, and, at the time, most families in Japan could get by on a single salary income. This kind of financial security is what allowed Matsumae and her colleagues, as well as Okazaki, to continue to work and remain creatively engaged in their fields.
23. This appendix requires more verification, but it gives an idea of the wide variety of projects the women of the Capcom Sound Team were involved in. I have included Shimomura given her continued presence in game music.

References

Abe, Shinzo. 2013. "Shinzo Abe: Unleashing the Power of 'Womenomics': Our Goal in Japan Is to Boost Women in the Workforce Significantly by 2020 and Reduce Pay Disparity." *Wall Street Journal*, September 25, 2013. http://ezproxy.carleton.edu/login?url=https://www-proquest-com.ezproxy.carleton.edu/newspapers/shinzo-abe-unleashing-power-womenomics-our-goal/docview/1436265566/se-2?accountid=9892.

Aulia, Bintang, and Kurniawaty Iskandar. 2021. "Towards Sustainable Society: Womenomics and Women Employment in Japan." *IOP Conference Series Earth and Environmental Science* 716 (1): 1–9. http://dx.doi.org.ezproxy.carleton.edu/10.1088/1755-1315/716/1/012103.

"Brave Wave Productions Announces THREE MOVEMENTS, the First Solo Album by *Mega Man* Composer Manami Matsumae." 2017. December 11, 2017. Accessed August 20, 2021. https://bravewave.net/news/2017/three-movements.

Clark, Nicola. 2011. "For Women in the Workplace, an 'Upgrade Problem.'" *New York Times*, January 26, 2011. Accessed July 5, 2022. https://www.nytimes.com/2011/01/27/world/europe/27iht-women27.html.

Collins, Karen. 2019. *The Beep Book: The History of Game Sound Interview from the Set of the Beep Movie*. Monee, IL: Ehtonal.

Cook, Karen. 2020. "Canon Anxiety?" *Journal of Music and Sound in Games* 1 (1): 95–99.

Dwyer, Nick. 2017a. "Nick Dwyer's Video Game Music Selection Looks to the Future." Interview by Sarah Drake. *Wire*, November 2017. Accessed August 2, 2021. https://www.thewire.co.uk/in-writing/interviews/diggin-in-the-carts-sara-drake-speaks-to-nick-dwyer.

Dwyer, Nick. 2017b. "Diggin' in the Carts." Season 2, episode 6. December 7, 2017. Accessed September 5, 2021. https://www.mixcloud.com/VGmix/2017-12-07-nick-dwyer-diggin-in-the-carts-season-2-episode-6-rbma-radio/.

Ezawa, Aya. 2011. "The Changing Patterns of Marriage and Motherhood." In *Transforming Japan: How Feminism and Diversity Are Making a Difference*, edited by Kumiko Fujimura-Fanselow, 105–120. New York: The Feminist Press.

Frank, Allegra. 2017. "The Unsung Women of Video Game Music." *Polygon*, March 24, 2017. Accessed August 25, 2021. https://www.polygon.com/2017/3/24/15049744/breath-of-the-wild-music-composer.

Fritsch, Melanie. 2022. "Heroines Unsung: The (Mostly) Untold Story of Female Japanese Game Music Composers." In *Women's Music for the Screen: Diverse Narratives in Sound*, edited by Felicity Wilcox, 177–191. New York: Routledge.

Fujita, Harumi. 2011. Interview. *STG Gameside*, no. 2. Accessed December 12, 2021. http://shmupulations.com/harumifujita.

Fujita, Harumi. 2015. "Harumi Fujita Interview: Ghosts, Goblins, and Gargoyles." Interview by Chris Greening. Translated by Alex Aniel. Video Game Music Online. Last modified December 5, 2015. Accessed August 15, 2021. http://www.vgmonline.net/harumifujitainterview/.

Fujita, Harumi. 2023. "Fujita Sound." Accessed August 13, 2021. https://fujitasound.wixsite.com/music.

Gibbons, William. 2020. "Rewritable Memory: Concerts, Canons, and Game Music History." *Journal of Music and Sound in Games* 1 (1): 75–81.

Gordon, Andrew. 2003. *A Modern History of Japan from Tokugawa Times to Present*. New York: Oxford University Press.

Grasso, Julianne. 2020. "On Canons as Music and Muse." *Journal of Music and Sound in Games* 1 (1): 82–86.

Hara, Kimi, and Kumiko Fujimura-Fanselow. 2011. "Educational Challenges Past and Present." In *Transforming Japan: How Feminism and Diversity Are Making a Difference*, edited by Kumiko Fujimura-Fanselow, 71–88. New York: The Feminist Press.

Holt, Nathalia. 2019. *The Queens of Animation: The Untold Story of the Women Who Transformed the World of Disney and Made Cinematic History*. New York: Little Brown and Company.

Ikeda, Yuki, Hisako Takizawa, Reiko Oshida, Yuko Tataka, Sanae Nito, Kanae Saeda, Kaori Ikeda, Meiko Wada, Manami Matsumae, Mari Yamaguchi, Yoko Shimomura, Minae Fujii, Yasuaki Fujita, Toshio Kajino, Yoshihiro Sakaguchi, Masaki Izumiya, and Isao Abe. 1990. "The Women of Game Design." *Beep! Megadrive*, October 1990. Accessed August 20, 2021. https://shmuplations.com/womenofgamedesign/.

"The Japanese Association for the Study of Popular Music." n.d. Accessed August 26, 2021, https://www.jaspm.jp/.

Kano, Ayako. 2016. *Japanese Feminist Debates: A Century of Contention on Sex, Love, and Labor*. Honolulu: University of Hawaii Press.

Kawamoto, Tamayo. 2002. "Moto Kapukon saundo chi-mu" (Capcom's Original Sound Team). Interview. https://web.archive.org/web/20030803073521/http://www.webcity.jp/gs/tsubo004.msp.

Lemon, Andrew, and Hillegonda C. Rietveld. 2019. "The *Street Fighter* Lady: Invisibility and Gender in Game Composition." *Transactions of the Digital Games Research Association* 5, no. 1 (December): 107–133.

Lemon, Andrew, and Hillegonda C. Rietveld. 2021. "Female Credit: Excavating Recognition for the Capcom Sound Team." In *The Cambridge Companion to Video Game Music*, edited by Melanie Fritsch and Tim Summers, 376–388. New York: Cambridge University Press.

Matsumae, Manami. 2021. "*Mega Man* Composer Manami Matsumae Doesn't Miss the 9–6 Grind." Interview by Alexandra Hall. *Kotaku*, May 3, 2021. Accessed August 5, 2021. https://kotaku.com/mega-man-composer-manami-matsumae-doesnt-miss-the-9-6-g-1846809139?utm_source=twitter&utm_medium=SocialMarketing&utm_campaign=dlvrit&utm_content=kotaku.

McLelland, Mark. 2012. *Love, Sex, and Democracy in Japan during the American Occupation*. New York: Palgrave Macmillan.

Nakano, Mami. 2011. "Employment and Poverty." Translated by Minata Hara. In *Transforming Japan: How Feminism and Diversity Are Making a* Difference, edited by Kumiko Fujimura-Fanselow, 257–267. New York: The Feminist Press.

Nemoto, Kumiko. 2013. "Long Working Hours and the Corporate Gender Divide in Japan." *Gender, Work, and Organization* 20, no. 5 (September): 512–527.

Okamoto, Yoshiki, Ayako Mori, Kenji Yoshida, Hiroshi Tsuji, and Kasatoshi Yoshino. 1986. "1986 Game Music Round Table Interview." *Beep! Magazine*, June, 1986. Accessed December 12, 2021. https://shmupulations.com/gamemusic1986/.

Okazaki, Brooke McCorkle. 2021. *Shonen Knife's* Happy Hour: *Food, Gender, Rock and Roll*. New York: Bloomsbury Academic.

Osaka University of Arts. n.d. "Musicology Department." Accessed August 27, 2021. https://www.osaka-geidai.ac.jp/en/departments/musicology.

Park, Hyeonjin. 2020. "The Difficult, Uncomfortable, and Imperative Conversations Needed in Game Music and Sound Studies." *Journal of Music and Sound in Games* 1 (1): 87–94.

Rhoads, Sean, and Brooke McCorkle. 2018. *Japan's Green Monsters: Environmental Commentary in Kaijū Cinema*. Jefferson, NC: McFarland & Company, Inc.

Ritsumeikan University. 2021. "Ritsumeikan Center for Game Studies." Accessed August 26, 2021. https://www.rcgs.jp/.

Shamoon, Deborah. 2012. *Passionate Friendship: The Aesthetics of Girl's Culture in Japan*. Honolulu: University of Hawaii Press.

Shetterly, Margot Lee. 2016. *Hidden Figures: The American Dream and the Untold Story of the Black Women Mathematicians Who Helped Win the Space Race*. New York: William Morrow.

St. Michel, Patrick. 2018. "I Can Only Speak My Own Truth: Otoboke Beaver Rocks Tunes Not Politics." *Japan Times*, April 11, 2018. https://www.japantimes.co.jp/culture/2018/04/10/music/can-speak-truth-otoboke-beaver-rocks-tunes-not-politics/.

Tamiya, Junko. 2014. "Junko Tamiya Interview: Creating Capcom's Incredible NES Scores." Interview by Alexander Brandon and Chris Greening. Translated by Alex Aniel. Video Game Music Online. Last modified May 19, 2014. Accessed August 15, 2021. http://www.vgmonline.net/junkotamiyainterview/.

Tokyo University of the Fine Arts. n.d. "Music." Accessed August 27, 2021.https://www.geidai.ac.jp/english/music/m_outline.

Terada, Naoko. 2021. *Mou hitotsu ifuku, homu-uea: ie de kiru apurerushi (Another Garment, Homewear: A History of Apparel to Wear at Home)*. Tokyo: Misuzu Publishing.

Walser, Robert. 1993. *Running with the Devil: Power, Gender, and Madness in Heavy Metal Music*. Middletown, CT: Wesleyan University Press.

Waseda University. n.d. "Collaborative Research Center for Film and Theatre Arts." Accessed August 26, 2021. https://www.waseda.jp/prj-kyodo-enpaku/.

Yu, Zhenzhen. 2022. "Otoboke Beaver, the Fierce and Funny Punk Band, Finds New Courage." National Public Radio, June 2, 2022. https://www.npr.org/2022/06/02/1102274080/otoboke-beaver-the-fierce-and-funny-punkband-finds-new-courage.

CHAPTER 11

SURVIVING THE GAME

Published Soundtracks as Archives

FANNY REBILLARD

Introduction

Video game sound is now acknowledged as a complex object, part of a delicate ecosystem where the creation of, and access to, audio archives and reliable sources still raises many questions. As the audio belongs to a ludic audiovisual whole, it is difficult to dissociate a game soundtrack from its original format: what is game sound without the game? How is extracted audio relevant for the industry and academia, and how can we regard these unplayable objects from a gaming perspective? Studying music out of its original context surely brings obvious challenges, starting with the loss of interactivity, visuals, and (often) original sound format. Despite these limitations, original soundtracks are an essential part of game sound's history, as they not only offer a sustainable trace of the original object but also provide new perspectives on the broader place of game music. In this chapter, I first explain the main archival issues hidden behind game sound as a sonic object linked to an impermanent media, as well as the broader upstream questions raised by the recording. As I will show, the physical releases of music, including (but not limited to) historical formats such as the CD and vinyl, both being still alive in the game music field, raise complex issues of music as an archive. I then address some useful basic typologies of game soundtracks, and demonstrate how they uncover different perceptions and representations of game music and sound as independent objects.

Recorded Sound, or the Biases of Unavoidable Loss

Game preservation and music archiving have more in common than one would initially imagine. First, the basic idea of their preservation raises technical questions about what they are and how they should be considered, used, and conveyed through historical, technological, and aesthetic lenses. In its original state, sound has no material form. It disappears after being heard, and without leaving a sustainable way to be heard again (whereas we can glance at a painting as many times as we want). Therefore, preserving it implies trapping it in some sort of out-of-context, intermediate physical state by using one or more additional layers of language or sign system such as (but not limited to) notation, analog recording, or digital recordings (Bachimont 2017, 29). In this sense—and it applies to some extent to music instruments and performance practice—an archived sound does not exist until it is technically deciphered, interpreted, or played. By nature, archives (especially recordings) disconnect sound from its original context of production.[1] Because sound is impermanent, a comparison is already easy to draw with the case of video game preservation: unless it is played, a game does not exist per se. Certainly, it can be frozen in time, "kept alive" through the original materials (consoles, cartridges, computers), emulation, copies/duplication, or alternative documentation (descriptive books, gameplay video recordings, etc.). But these are all fragile, and even if the physical vessel is preserved, the integrity of the data they hold is easily threatened (Guttenbrunner et al. 2010).

Without context and the technological knowledge that allows playback, these traces lack the essential interactive ludic and musical characteristics, which are ephemeral and, by definition, impossible to preserve. Published game soundtracks, like other recordings, also suffer from a more general lack of contextualization, which raises questions about their raison d'être. These interrogations share interesting similarities with studies on oral archiving and its complicated relationship with the notions of "aura" and "intangible cultural heritage." A comparison can also be drawn with popular mainstream music studies about the connection between the listener and published soundtracks through the materiality of the musical object, the media, and personal history it tells. Indeed, recording "shakes up the ontological status of oral music," which obtains its own "material reality and can therefore emancipate itself from its traditional environment" while "incorporating the effects of mass merchandising" (Fariji 2019). On the other hand, research in popular music and heritage points out that there is a "tension between music as a vibrant, intangible expression of contemporary culture and its heritagisation which tends toward replicating a more conventional 'bricks and mortar,' tangible approach" (Brandellero and Janssen, 2014). All these are especially important to fully understand how soundtracks change the way we look at game music and why they are important from a cultural perspective. To have a better knowledge and understanding of their story and structure would allow a different, critical approach of game soundtracks as a source of interest and study.

Archiving Orality: Music, Ethnomusicology, and the Intangible Cultural Heritage

Despite lacking many of the elements that characterize the live experience, recorded music became a major part of everyday life during the 20th century. From the first massive and fragile physical shells to today's streaming services, recordings have proven essential to the blooming and archiving of classical, popular, and traditional musics, to the point that recordings are now considered key resources for the ethnomusicological field (Gabry-Thienpont 2019). But taking music out of its frame compels us to consider it carefully: recordings can subvert the original material in both social and aesthetic ways, reflected and conveyed through their formal structure. Viewing recording through the lens of oral archives in Arabic cultures, Anis Fariji (2019) states that "in the oral tradition, musical form bears materiality only when it is deployed." Recording it therefore allows discarding the "community environment in which it is enclosed."[2] This adds an economic and social rupture to the way the music is consumed, practiced, and perceived by both creators and consumers outside of their circle of origin.

The lost interactivity and social bond between cultural groups and ceremonial practices, between musicians and audiences listening to a disc, is not so divorced from the issues we might encounter in game soundtracks, from a player/in-game experience perspective. Furthermore, the recording of oral traditions changes the relationship between musicians and music itself: because the final product is not the present performance but the disconnected future listening experience, the formal approach (in the sense of how the structure of a track is built) is evolving as well. Whether for technical reasons—lack of space on records, for example—or commercial reasons bound to how the music is consumed and appreciated, written, and improvised, Fariji points out that recordings vary according to new standards that are specific to the recordings fixed on a physical medium. For example, the length of breaks made during pieces in the traditional *maqām* are gradually reduced until these silent punctuations completely disappear over time. Some pieces become shorter, or the voice inflexions and melodic formulas are altered in a way that seems influenced by other types of music. Therefore, traditional songs evolve, become part of a broader culture—opposed to, or at least in many ways different from, the original.

On the western classical side of music as well as in US popular music, Mark Katz already observed the influence of recordings on instrumental practice and formal layout of the pieces, influencing violinists to make greater use of the vibrato, and jazzmen to shorten or write their solos in a way that fits the recordings' maximal length. Insisting on the many differences between live playing and recording, he explains: "How early jazz is understood, therefore, is often a function of its phonographic preservation, which in turn was for more than three decades subject to a severe and arbitrary time limitation." (Katz 2010, 86). Similar destructive interventions have been observed in other cultures that are not embraced by European classical notation. As William S. Gilbert (2020) explains about music belonging to religious practice or other contexts (e.g., shamanism in Korea or call and response in some American churches), dissociation is reductive for traditionally nonfixed forms. The distance from the source and original actors is also seen as dangerous, since those songs are part of a whole, transmitted "through both ritual and storytelling, which allows for the cultural histories to survive" (Gilbert 2020). His article presents itself more as a criticism of the philosopher Nelson Goodman's description of music as an allographic, therefore notated, sign system. But its emphasis on the difficulty of preserving unfixed, interactive music outside of traditional or day-to-day practice, and its description of music as a process more than a "stagnant, static and unchanging" art, is essential.

From this perspective, recorded music is often drifting away from the original performance, and can indeed be viewed as a kind of threat: recordings may tell the wrong story—or worse, no story at all. This narrative capacity has been interpreted through the specter of Walter Benjamin's aura; Fariji (2019), for example, argues that recording and mass consumption of oral performances cause a loss of the primary interactive component in a context where "transmission and performance are equally imbued with human presence," making the never-ending repetitions and contextual rewritings significant in the maintaining of culture. Although cultures of oral transmission are in some ways far removed from video game sound (game music being, for starters, part of an already "recorded," mechanical, and mass-produced media), its performative aspect, and the impossibility of its transmission in a satisfactory manner through recordings, allows the same biases to emerge. Because it is based on interactivity, game music cannot be precisely reproduced through a static recording. The loss of the live experience disrupts the musical organization linked to the game's interactive nature and the indivisible participatory role of the player.

Moreover, just as in the aforementioned oral cultures, game sound is tightly linked to practice and context: most of the music heard in games is deeply functional, and many cues depend on the player's actions in addition to what is seen on screen. Furthermore, just as some traditional oral systems often rely on improvisation and continuous rewriting, game soundtracks, especially the ones based on aleatory and generative systems, cannot be reduced to one recorded performance. On a larger scale, the original music structure of one game cannot be reproduced, the linear format of the recording narrowing it down to one interpretation. For example, although the soundtrack of *Wandersong* (2018) uses the same musical materials as in the game, it offers the listener only a snapshot of the possible rhythmic and melodic variations the player can cause the music to create. Just as concerts rewrite the memory of the game, Julianne Grasso has explained how game music "transforms from music designed for gameplay into music designed to remember gameplay" in these situations (Grasso 2020, 84)—the recorded album reproduces the overall musical narrative in a very different way, and builds its own, independent, game-influenced narration. Behind the idea that a recording is an accurate testimony of a past musical performance lies the reality of the recording as a fabricated memento, answering to legal or commercial purposes, or to the listener's expectation as an object of pleasure: "recorded sound is mediated sound" (Katz 2010, 2). Most of the players performances in *Wandersong* are offbeat, contain notes drifting away from the original melody, that would probably be judged as unfitting for a recording. Therefore, the bard's voice that can be heard in almost every track in-game is totally absent from the soundtrack. If recorded soundtracks can indeed be seen as a subversion of the original score, then that subversion raises relevant questions about how we can research these sources, and whether we should interpret them as recompositions, or new materials emerging with new purposes.

The notion of "intangible cultural heritage"[3] (ICH) allows identification of three major issues related to notating and editing music in the oral tradition: "the 'intangibility' of music caught up in the . . . heritagisation processes; the specific intersections between music, power dynamics and territory in this context; and lastly, the performative nature of the heritage constructions at play, conceived as operative fictions" (Broclain, Haug, and Patrix 2019). This approach—prioritizing the parts of music that are impossible to grasp—does not, however, close the door to physical traces that have been created, especially through editing and distribution. Indeed, "because industrial forms of music have long been integrated and due to the vast corpuses of records available, discographies can be a rich resource for reconsidering . . . the variety of human and nonhuman actors making up the community of a heritagised musical practice" (Broclain, Haug, and Patrix 2019, 9).

Video games have also been addressed from the ICH point of view. Their interactive form, strong presence in broad communities, and method of creation led them to be considered as potential tools to celebrate and help preserve fragile intangible heritages (Laiti et al. 2020). But, because games share common properties with oral cultures, concern regarding the lack of efficient ways to preserve games themselves is growing. Some researchers analyze games as digital archaeological sites, sharing the same definitions as physical ones (Reinhard 2017), while others suggest that they be considered as a legitimate part of the digital ICH (Caon 2020). Peritextual and epitextual approaches (Guay-Bélanger 2021) suggest the need to preserve both the practice and the culture of gaming, meaning that we must preserve more than the original game itself.

Embodying Memory: Legitimation as a Cultural Object

Recorded game soundtracks are not, by nature, complete and authentic representations of game soundtracks, but they belong to other circles of influence that supplement (if not replace) the original materials. Indeed, games are meant to be played, but they also exist and manifest themselves in different forms in our memories. The way we construct our representation of one game can easily be segmented into multiple points of view and influences, from the viewing of promotional materials to the feeling of interactive participation. Extracted music, remixes, amateur fan-made scores, and, of course, official soundtracks are part of these constructions made around a game. Once we acknowledge the fact that a distributed soundtrack is not, as Tim Summers (2016) discusses, a precise and specific representation of a game's relationship with sound, we can situate game soundtracks in the broader history of music, games, and game sound. Indeed, even though soundtracks seem disconnected from the game, "[g]ame players reflect and reminisce about their time playing the game with these recordings, which may come to stand for the game soundtrack in a concrete way" (Summers 2016, 47) Sometimes, a soundtrack can "escape" from the game and—in the hands of players and musicians—become a new version of itself, full of new musical, personal, or even social meanings (Smith 2020).

There is indeed no unique vision of an artwork, and the reminiscences we construct of that art are also important to archive. Soundtracks are questionable as sources to document the interactivity or even narrative of a game. They are, however, a good way to document how musical interactivity—and more generally game music and sound—are perceived. Indeed, I have already suggested that the recorded format alters the formal structure and cultural meaning of an in-game musical performance, removing the music from the authentic moment of gameplay. This loss of the performative, synchronized, nature of sound in favor of a new, adapted object which is only a projection of the original led to questioning (Fariji 2019) the aura of discs and other recordings.[4] Beyond Benjamin's notion that recordings and mass reproduction are diminishing the original work's aura, however, it is the relationship between aura and digital arts that presents the most interesting topic for study.

Aura has been discussed regarding the "infinite" reproducibility of digital media, its relationship with the material format, and the so-called uniqueness of a work of art. More so than a loss, changing how we access a piece of art creates a new, different aura, the value of which is not necessarily less than the original. From this perspective, the musical experience, and its reproducibility through recording instead of contextualized reenacting, is also prone to criticism: we have already seen that the fixation has been analyzed as a loss of aura. But if recordings discard the performance context—the cultural habits linked to the music, the presence of musicians, and the interaction between them and the audience—they nonetheless resonate through ears and communities. By adding a layer of complexity and bringing new modes of consumption and practice, recordings transform one sound into a different object that allows for a new kind of contextualization and fundamental historical documentation about music (Lambert and al-Akouri 2019). The musicians' and audiences' relationships to soundtrack recordings can be markers of how they want to remember a game and its music, as much as how they want it to be perceived by others. As Thoreau R. A. Bakker (2018, 29) writes in his thesis about aura and virtual objects, "aura is not simply about an 'original work' vs a reproduction, but about human beings' perception of, and access to, an artifact." Bakker uses the example of Wu Tang Clan's single copy of their album *Once Upon a Time in Shaolin* (2015) to demonstrate how the uniqueness of art as a product or a sensorial experience was biased, and that "there is such a thing as a digital 'original,' and that even a reproduction can possess one element of aura through human imposed scarcity." The production of one copy of the album has indeed been presented as a fight against standardization and reduction of the cultural value of music through mass production. The value of the album is here created by its backstory, and Bakker's analysis asserts that "the aura in this sense is synonymous with the exclusivity and prestige, rather than the experience with an original work of art or its reproduction" (27).

This attachment to an object or experience because of its rarity is one of many driving forces in the creation of what might become the last audio artifacts of some games. The increasing share of collector vinyl editions of game soundtracks—aside from the commercial aspect—is undoubtedly a manifestation of this aura of exclusivity and prestige. Even if collectors can be seen as the antithesis of art through the lens of consumerism, they are part of a dynamic that rejoins preservation focus and tries to embed gaming culture into a broader, more traditional frame. The impulse some game music enthusiasts feel to own a physical version of their favorite game's music, whatever be the price, has been described (along with the lack of official records from companies such as Nintendo) as one cause of the bootleg vinyl boom in the past decade (Ombler 2020). But this opposition between community and "authorized" archives of music has also been discussed as a virtuous circle that could benefit historical research. As Lauren Istvandity (2021) observes: "Music archives have the difficult job of trying to retain the material formats of an intangible cultural heritage prized for both its ephemeral performative forms and its physical commercial outputs. Both community and authorised archives play an important part in sustaining music heritage preservation activities," as their collaboration would reduce the risk of loss. Indeed, the lack of official media-preservation initiatives in many countries have led to a raised awareness in nonprofessional spheres regarding the importance of preserving game soundtracks (see chapter 12 of this volume on the archiving of BASIC code driving sound synthesis chips in early video games). The interest in game music as a way of nostalgically reenacting play connects to the performative nature of heritage through culture. Legitimation of defunct media products can be achieved through various actions taken by amateur communities to change the way they are viewed in retrospect. Publishing activity and materialization from "individual collectors to public institutions and private enterprises" play an important role in social legitimation, and shape what products are kept in the end (Brandellero et al. 2014). Attempts to gather stakeholders around archives started in 2017 in France. Since that time, the National Library (Bibliothèque nationale de France) now hosts annual meetings of academic researchers, game industry professionals, associations such as the Conservatoire National du Jeu Vidéo (CNJV) and the digital patrimony preservation institution MO5.COM, as well as online preservation groups (abandonware.fr) to discuss video game archiving (Forsans 2017).

Archives are never neutral. The choices made about what will be kept and organized will always condition both which stories are told in the future, and how those stories will be told. This is why these first steps are crucial to avoid any misconception: "[T]he diversity of actors in the field combine a variety of legitimizing discourses of popular music as heritage, ranging from personal and collective attachment and memory to commercial endeavours rebranding and canonising the musical pasts" (Brandellero et al. 2014, 220). Public attachment to physical objects through collector-driven practices and editors trying to pass on their versions of stories are manifestations of a will to "adopt more traditional formats of preservation, centered around material rather than immaterial culture." This led researchers such as Les Roberts (2014) to depict the notion of ICH as flawed and deeply political by nature, because "all heritage is intangible, in that meaning and values attached to objects and sites of memory are socially and culturally negotiated."

From a player's perspective, a soundtrack is a lot more than a mere sound extraction, and some publishers are inclined to promote their games beyond the "mere entertainment" image.[5] Published soundtracks are an important step to openly claim, by putting it in different, permanent contexts, that game sound is something to be remembered. "Material culture plays a critical part in the empowerment of individuals—the power of choice has to be mastered in such a way that individuals choose in a fashion that makes 'cultural sense' both to themselves and to others" (Bennett and Rogers 2015, 3). CDs and vinyl records can be played and displayed in libraries that are not specific to gaming. They are a few among many physical traces (such as clubs and concert halls, instruments and portable players, ticket stubs and autographs) that Roberts (2014) identifies as ways to (re)enact and give a body to sound souvenirs, since "by definition, music is intangible, as indeed are people's musical memories" (271). These extensions illustrate both the changing nature of the audience's engagement with music and of an adaptive process to allow the private and public revival of it. They are valuable traces. This can be linked to William Gibbons's (2018) study on the relationship between games and classical music: to some extent, published game music is a way to compare with "higher" standards. Gibbons observed how pre-existing music was gamified or used in games to insinuate a more noble role from narrative, educative, or cultural perspectives. Conversely, published game soundtracks, just like concerts, will often "de-gamify" game music to connect it to another renowned musical tradition (the concert hall, the recording) and to "reinforce its claim to artistic merit by association" (Gibbons 2018, 17). It is also a way to make game music more visible, to make it look more authentic in the eyes of other medias, to give it more prestige by putting it in spaces that are imbued with a more traditional aura: radios, music stores, press, charts, and so on.

Video Game Original Soundtracks: Typologies

Now that we have seen how published soundtracks are complex but historically important, we can move on to the next question: how do soundtracks—physically reproduced sounds—manifest their connection to the game itself? Various answers can be found just by looking at how soundtrack albums are produced and organized. Taking sound out of a game is often not a simple process: it implies costs, material and technical knowledge, and sometimes archaeological work.[6] As we will now see, even if there are exceptions, published soundtracks reveal a lot about how music (and sometimes sound design) is viewed in relation to games. Different typologies can be identified, depending on observations as simple as the track order or the portion of the game's soundtrack included in the final product.

What Does the Soundtrack Say? Oriented Approaches

Angelo Orcalli (2013) explains in his critical approach of audiovisual sources that since music can never be archived as a whole, its preservation can follow different approaches. He identified five of these approaches that are useful for the analysis of game soundtracks: conservative, documentary, sociological, reconstructive, and aesthetic. These five approaches are neither restricted nor closed; instead, they can intersect with one another to create hybrid points of view about the representation of video game music. Depending on the point of view and primary objectives, preservation of sound can, for example, be "conservative" in that it is trying to be as close to the original as possible—a facsimile. Most of the soundtracks discussed here can be included in this very straightforward approach, so it is important to ask questions about, among other issues, the quality of a recording. A soundtrack made with a bad emulator, for example, will be very different from the original, and some game soundtracks have suffered severe quality loss during extraction.

The documentary approach focuses on the logical connections between multiple elements and aims to explain, if not reproduce, the technological context. In the case of a game soundtrack, it is important to link the music to the original game or its technical history. These connections can be as simple as tracks' names that relate music and scenes or music and characters, for example. Linking musicians' names to tracks is also an important part of the publishing process, though it is far from being systematic: many of the official *Legend of Zelda* games soundtracks (such as *The Wind Waker* [2003]) do not provide detailed credits. Only the most recent games, such as *Breath of the Wild* (2017) and the Switch remake of *Link's Awakening* (2019), come with track-by-track lists of composers and arrangers showing the evolution of attention to these details. Some games go so far as to document, for example, the relationship between the game and the music. The Nintendo 3DS *Pokémon Omega Ruby & Alpha Sapphire Super Music Complete* six-CD set contained a booklet with interviews and detailed "scores" explaining how to use musical tiles to reproduce some songs in the game.

The reconstructive approach is more inclined to create an ideal version of a piece, by acknowledging that there cannot be one real authentic reproduction of it. The choice here is to consider intellectual and material elements to match the author's original intent as closely as possible. Although documentation and interviews are essential to recontextualize the recordings, editions based on this approach can go farther by embracing how the music, as originally conceived, differed from the in-game version. Interesting examples of this approach can be found in some of Hitoshi Sakimoto's works. The soundtracks for *Final Fantasy Tactics Advance* (2003) and *ASH: Archaic Sealed Heat* (2007) each contain two discs. The first one contains original tracks as heard in-game, and the second contains the original "full sound" or "internal sound source" version. This differentiation also helps us better understand the music-creation processes for Game Boy Advance and Nintendo DS, revealing more information about the tools and sound banks used by composers, as well as how the integration was destructive for the original samples.

The sociological approach aims to reproduce, with as much historical accuracy as possible, the original *context* of listening. It is by far the most difficult (if not impossible) approach to achieve through a fixed soundtrack, as recreating the context would mean playing the original game. Apart from the soundtracks that extensively document the game in the booklets through interviews, stories, trivia, or even screenshots and sprite prints (as the Pokémon games' soundtracks do), a few composers tried to give to the listener a more authentic in-game feeling by adding sound effects and voices. In the context of published music, these additions could be considered invasive. But in soundtracks and remixes like *Valkyrie Profile Voice Mix Arrange*, *Star Ocean Till the End of Time Voice Mix Album* by Motoi Sakuraba, or the *Persona 3 Portable Voice Mix Arrange* by Shinji Hosoe and Nobuyoshi Sano, the music is mixed with repeated voice samples from the original games. This is a way not only to include musical or cinematic scene memories but also to trigger the reminiscence of in-game battles and dialogues by reproducing the dramatic tension and evolution of the fight with short iconic cues used by characters, making a very different use of voice than in dramas.

Finally, the aesthetic approach is considered the least appropriate for archiving. It regroups productions that deliberately differ from the original. As aesthetic changes can cover a wide range of parameters, this category can extend to every marketed soundtrack: the simple act of cutting a loop to make it fit into a linear track can be seen as deviant. But most of the time, the aesthetic approach will be used to categorize remixes, reorchestrations, or tracks that were cleaned and enhanced using modern technologies to obtain a "better" (though different) sound, more fitting for today's quality standards. Though sometimes criticized for drifting too far from the original, reinterpretations are nonetheless important in documenting public reception, status, and the expectations regarding video game music. Furthermore, not all aesthetic-oriented projects reject the original's properties. Many official soundtracks mix previous approaches with this one to offer different perspectives on one game. Some preservation projects also fully acknowledge the rewriting as part of the process and consider it as a proof of historical interest and the artistic respect that they use to document and enrich the original. Following those paths, we could mention *Génération Delphine—A Synthwave Tribute to Delphine Software* that recently unveiled its roadmap in France (Verdin 2021). Presented as a tribute and preservation project around the games published by the former development studio Delphine Software International (with a focus on works of the late composer Jean Baudlot), Génération Delphine will contain both remastered soundtracks—restored from the Amiga and Atari ST versions—and "symphonic" reorchestrations closer to a cinematic style (Gechter 2021). The project will be freely available online, but concept albums containing synthwave remixes will be commercialized. The whole project will be deposited to the French main game-preservation association (MO5.COM), as well as to the French National Library (BnF) for historical documentation and preservation.

Interactivity and Soundtrack Structure: A Short Typology

In this section, I propose a simplified typology of officially published game soundtrack albums. These albums lay the foundations for multiple ways of looking at soundtracks that may seem commonplace today but are far from being obvious. What can or should be included in a game soundtrack has indeed been standardized through multiple lenses that change the listener's perception. During my research, I identified two main characteristics that are essential for published soundtrack analysis: the "completion level" they achieve—in how far they go to present the "full" game soundtrack—and the tracklist organization. Each of these two main categories can be divided into multiple subcategories.

Completion Level

What we usually see as a "complete" game soundtrack is variable. Soundtracks aiming to reproduce a full version of a game's music did not in fact exist per se before the second half of the 1980s, dating to the emergence of famous adventure games and RPGs. Two important milestones are the compilation of original and arranged music from the first two *Final Fantasy* games released in 1988, and a similar collection of music from the *Dragon Quest* series released in 1986. The latter soundtrack sold 260,000 copies and contributed to the defense of game music as a legitimate way to initiate children to classical music in Japan (Yamakami and Barbosa 2015). Even the first *Legend of Zelda* games did not have extracted soundtracks and were instead promoted through remixes and albums shared with other games (for example, *Nazo no Murasamejo / The Legend of Zelda: The Hyrule Fantasy Original Soundtrack Orchestra Version* from 1986). Once official soundtracks—that is, music taken directly from games—become more common, we can identify three soundtrack completion levels: "partial," "complete," and "additional content."

Partial soundtracks are probably the most widespread type, as they are often used for promotional purposes. They can be found in press-kits or collector editions of games that come with small cardboard cases and soundtracks containing best-of and limited tracks selections of favorite music. *The Witcher 3: Wild Hunt* soundtrack presents a typical example, as its music was released in many different, incomplete versions. Similar goodies were found, notably on the Nintendo Club, where track selections from games such as *Animal Crossing: Let's Go to the City* and *Baten Kaitos: Eternal Wing and the Lost Ocean* could be exchanged for points. Incomplete soundtracks can also be sold officially. In cases like the *Silent Hill* series soundtracks, most of the ambient tracks are missing, which can imply that some tracks are removed because they are considered less interesting than others, and not fit for out-of-context listening.[7] In other situations, partial soundtracks are released for copyright reasons, the best example being *Tales of the Abyss*, and the difference in the tracks written by composer Motoi Sakuraba in the second edition of the original soundtrack from 2009 and the ones composed by Motoo Fujiwara in his album from 2006.

Complete soundtracks are mostly made available through unofficial channels—fan communities and sharing through YouTube and other streaming platforms. They are also important when officially published, as they spread very different points of view on what is "complete," and how the numerous variations of one track are organized. Many soundtracks will use only one variant of each track or may publish an independent album as a collector or limited bonus. The *NieR: Automata Original Soundtrack Hacking*

Tracks album, for example, contains 8-bit variations that are not in the official orchestral oriented soundtrack. But some soundtracks attempt to present as many variables as possible. There are two common ways of organizing these pieces. In the first, each version can be the subject of a dedicated track, as is usually the case in *Pokémon* games—*Diamond & Pearl*'s soundtrack uses one track for each day or night version of outdoor music, for instance, and *Black & White*'s soundtrack includes a track for every seasonal arrangement, while only using the version with percussion.[8] In the second type, different versions of a theme can be compiled into a single track. This is the case in most of the *Zelda* games, as with *Breath of the Wild*'s soundtrack mixing day and night versions of towns' music, as well as the five steps of the exploration of the Divine Beasts. This second mode of soundtrack design, though logical from a narrative and musical point of view, can be misleading in analysis, because it can create musical sequences that would never be heard in the actual game.[9]

The place of sound effects in the complete soundtrack category is also worth exploring. Indeed, not all "complete" soundtracks reserve a place for these fundamental game sounds, yet some publishers and composers do put significant emphasis on highlighting nonmusical sound. Sound effects can be either assembled in one track (as in the 1996 soundtrack of *Panzer Dragoon II Zwei*, for example) or put in separate, individually named tracks (as is the case in the five volumes of *The Square Enix Sound Effect Collection*). Though it can seem like an afterthought, the presence of sound effects is an important feature that reveals the historical importance sound design occupies in game sound history and the significance of sound to a game's soundtrack and identity. From this perspective, they are seen either as valuable additions from an aesthetic point of view or as indivisible parts of one complete memory of the gameplay experience. The fact that each of the 151 first-generation Pokémon cries occupy more than one dedicated CD in the *Red and Green Super Music Collection*, for example, is revealing.

Finally, soundtracks that contain additional content include a wide range of possibilities. Some include content that is not directly from the game, such as music from trailers (e.g., *Breath of the Wild*) or unused tracks. In other cases, composers include "Beta versions" of their music, as Yasunori Mitsuda did with some of his work before the orchestral recordings of *Xenoblade Chronicles 2*, or—as we saw earlier—alternative versions of the tracks. But other cases go beyond the game, by adding completely new material: the first Japanese edition of *Silent Hill 4: The Room* soundtrack is made of two discs, the second one being made of entirely new compositions from Akira Yamaoka, accompanying a narrator telling a horror story unseen in the game. Though drifting away from the strict definition of an original soundtrack, this last category is important either to include games in another creative or artistic process or to give further information about how a game's music was discussed and created.

Track List Organization

The track list organization is one other key piece of information about a game's music that helps identify it as a distinct archive. Indeed, the order in which tracks are presented says a lot about how music outside of a game is considered and embodied from a formal and structural point of view. Much could be said about the representation of loops, for example: most soundtracks usually follow a pattern of repeating a loop two times before ending on a fade-out. However, there are some exceptions, in which loops end on conclusive cadences, or include extensions of the original tracks: in some of *Ace Attorney*'s soundtracks, for instance, the tracks include endings that are not heard in the game. In terms of track order, the most common follows the game's (ideal) narration—that is, the order players would likely encounter the music in the game—but other types of organizational structures appeared over time, such as orders based on tracks function or original sources.

Chronological order is not always an accurate representation of the player's actual experience, but this structure aims to offer the most logical chaining of tracks from a narrative perspective, whether it is following the game's story at large, or the chaining of smaller events, in the same way as some concerts follows a canonical idea of a game's narrative (Grasso 2020). This organizational method is much like one would find in a film soundtrack and mimics the player's perspective in narrative-focused genres like role-playing games and adventure games. But chronological order also raises question about musical narrative in other genres that rely more on the levels' organization, or on different levels of gameplay-related tension. Some soundtracks such as *Super Mario World*'s (which includes arrangements but also most of the original music since the first *Mario* game) first present all map tracks, then the different types of level music. But these tracks also take into account smaller events that happen during the exploration and have an impact on the music. The percussive instruments that begin playing when the player rides the dinosaur Yoshi, for example, will not enter before the second half of the track in the original soundtrack, and reflect this type of smaller narrative.

A functional track order can be seen as an alternative to the chronological order when it is not quite fitting the type of the game. This type of organization is particularly common in games where the player's choices can completely change the list and the order of the tracks they will hear through their journey. Some massively multiplayer online role-playing games, such as *Final Fantasy XI*, fall into this category: the tracks are organized by environments, character species, and cinematic scenes. But some more traditional games use this organization as well, as is the case for the *Xenoblade Chronicles*' soundtrack, which dedicates one CD to cinematic scenes, another to characters and ambient themes, and a third to battle and locations tracks.[10] This organizational approach demonstrates an intention of highlighting how music functions in a game, as well as how the development team and composers may have approached the soundtrack.

Finally, ordering tracks based on their origin source is perhaps the least common method and relies on exterior parameters that cannot be properly seen in the game. The most obvious example would be *Grand Theft Auto V*'s soundtrack. In this case, the three albums draw a clear distinction between "original music" that was commissioned from famous bands, the "original score" composed by musicians directly affiliated to the game or the series, and "the soundtrack" made with pre-existing tracks whose copyrights have been negotiated for the occasion. Something similar is found in *Dawn of Mana*'s original soundtrack, whose first CD contains only pieces that come from other titles of the iconic series. The second CD presents the new compositions in chronological order. Still other soundtracks also order the tracks based on stylistic choices, or more arbitrary visions bound to the game's scenario: the *Star Ocean 3: Till the End of Time* soundtrack makes a clear distinction between orchestral and progressive rock tracks between its two volumes. With a different point of view, *Valkyrie Profile 2*'s soundtrack symbolically switches between the heroine's opposed personalities by separating calm and dynamic tracks on two albums each dedicated to these characters.

Conclusion

Caught between artistic views and commercial purposes, personal attachment to a memory and collective celebration of history, official game soundtracks are part of a wide galaxy. In this regard, they need to be relocated not only with respect to the games they represent but also with respect to other important elements that space precludes me from fully listing in this chapter.[11] As subjective representations of games, soundtracks have a lot to tell, and some deeper research is necessary on the disc-publishing houses, their relationships with game studios, and how soundtracks are constructed in response to the players' and listeners' preferences and local practices. Since soundtracks have been published for a long time now, their influence on game music recognition and the relationship they have with game development's history is worth studying.

Notes

1. Decontextualization of sound is already a significant topic, from an aesthetic point of view, which uses a lot of theoretical approaches in cultural studies, especially cinema and video games. Notions such as schizophonia or acousmatic sound (Miller 2011) are not the focus of this chapter but are nonetheless important, as their existence causes similar preservation issues in electroacoustic music (Vincent, Bonardi, and Bachimont 2011) and video games (Rebillard 2018).
2. Translated from French by the author.
3. ICH is a concept defined as a way "to recognize the equal significance of [a] cultural heritage that does not take tangible forms as buildings and sites, but plays a significant role in maintaining cultural traditions and cultural identity. [. . .] Different from this dominant view of cultural heritage, the concept of intangible cultural heritage emphasizes the value of oral traditions, ritual practices, and traditional performing arts forms, which would otherwise be neglected by the western framework." (Li 2013, 1)
4. Tightly bound to the idea of presence, therefore uniqueness and authenticity of a work of art, the notion of "aura" discussed by Benjamin includes the social rituals bound to the original (for example, its location, or the religious rituals attached to it). In the modern industrial era, "mechanical reproduction emancipates the work of art from its parasitical dependence on ritual," reversing its function and questioning its identity and its potential use as a political tool (Benjamin 1969, 6).

5. From a commercial point of view, the relationship between games and popular music as potential mutual audience influencers has been acknowledged and studied, as seen in Holly Tessler's (2008) essay about EA and other game publishers' strategy to enter the music market and be promoted by popular artists. But soundtrack publishing goes much farther back, with roots in the 1980s in Japan and labels such as G.M.O. Records, founded in 1985 by Harusomi Hosono from the Yellow Magic Orchestra. More recently, the promotional use of orchestras and famous recording studios (e.g., *Final Fantasy XV* soundtrack recording in Abbey Road Studios) as well as small documentaries about game music creation during the development process (*Everybody's Gone to the Rapture*) shows a growing interest from game companies toward this type of communication.
6. As we learned through the experience of the French label Wayô Records, technical recovery can lead to cancellation of a soundtrack publishing project, because no viable copies of a game's music or files were found (Rebillard 2018, 91).
7. Apart from the aesthetic choices, one other reason for these selections is the format limitation, as most CDs followed the Red Book audio standard, which allows a maximum of 80 minutes of audio to be burned on a CD, or 99 tracks. This standard makes most games' soundtracks in their original state nonsuitable for edition and undoubtedly influenced their making.
8. There is a difference in-game between the moments when the player is steady (without percussion), and the ones when they are walking or running that have added rhythmic accompaniment. This detail must have been seen as too anecdotal to be included in a soundtrack that already contains four CDs.
9. Some people have, for example, assumed, while listening to Outset Island's theme from *The Wind Waker* soundtrack, that it cites both Aryll's and the Deku village's theme one after the other. However, this mashup is only heard in the soundtrack: the real Outset Island's theme actually plays either one or the other (Aryll's citation being replaced by the Deku village's one after the character is kidnapped). In the same way, Uroboros's battle theme from *Bravely Default Flying Fairy* is constructed as a linear buildup of all three phases of the battle, which uses more complex evolving loop accumulations through the fight.
10. One interesting exception occurs in this soundtrack, as the last battle theme is not with the others but placed at the end of the character tracks: as the music symbolizes a fight against one specific character, the choice to put it in this category illustrates how the role assigned to music can be cross-sectional or even contradictory when trying to dissociate narrative and gameplay points of view.
11. The legal challenges at stake and the differences between physical and dematerialized versions are a massive part of original soundtrack studying. For example, the song "Reset" composed by the Japanese artist JUN vanished from the last re-editions and remasters of the game *Okami*. This retrieval likely happened for copyright reasons, as none of the dematerialized versions of the original soundtrack contains the song. The only trace left of it is in the PlayStation 2 version of the game, and in the 2006 physical release of the original soundtrack, the later editions of both the game and the soundtrack being incomplete. These alterations of game music bring new challenges on music and game sound impermanence. They remind us of the need to reconstruct history from multiple sources and to thoroughly contextualize every aspect of it.

References

Bachimont, Bruno. 2017. *Patrimoine et numérique: Technique et politique de la mémoire*. France: INA.

Bakker, R. A. Thoreau. 2018. "Objects in the Age of Virtual Reproduction: Aura and the Elusive Third Axis." MD dissertation, OCAD University.

Benjamin, Walter. 1969. *The Work of Art in the Age of Mechanical Reproduction*. Translated by Harry Zohn. New York: Schocken Books.

Bennett, Andy, and Ian Rogers. 2015. "Popular Music and Materiality: Memorabilia and Memory Traces." *Popular Music and Society*, no. 39, 28–42.

Brandellero, Amanda, and Susanne Janssen. 2014. "Popular Music as Cultural Heritage: Scoping Out the Field of Practice." *International Journal of Heritage Studies* 20 (3): 224–240.

Brandellero, Amanda, Susanne Janssen, Sara Cohen, and Les Roberts. 2014. "Popular Music Heritage, Cultural Memory and Cultural Identity." *International Journal of Heritage Studies* 20 (3): 219–223.

Broclain, Elsa, Benoît Haug, and Pénélope Patrix. 2019. "Introduction. Musique: Patrimoine immatériel?" *Transposition* 8. https://doi.org/10.4000/transposition.4121.

Caon, Maurizio. 2020. "Designing Systems for the Digital Immortality of Intangible Cultural Heritage." In *Human Interaction and Emerging Technologies. IHIET 2019. Advances in Intelligent Systems and Computing*, edited by Ahram, Tareq et al., 1018: 783–789. Springer, Cham. https://doi.org/10.1007/978-3-030-25629-6_122.

Fariji, Anis. 2019. "Le disque, agent d'une subversion intégrale de la musique de tradition orale." *Annales islamologiques* 53:25–48.

Forsans, Emmanuel. 2017. "Colloque sur la conservation du patrimoine vidéoludique—Quels enjeux? Quels acteurs?" *AFJV*, November 17, 2017. https://www.afjv.com/news/8238_colloque-sur-la-conservation-du-patrimoine-videoludique.htm.

Gabry-Thienpont, Séverine. 2019. "#Turāṯ." *Annales islamologiques* 53:3–24.

Gechter, Frédéric. 2021. "Génération Delphine—Découvrez l'immense hommage Synthwave dédié à Delphine Software!" Rom-game.fr, June 22, 2021. https://www.rom-game.fr/news/4541.html.

Gibbons, William. 2018. *Unlimited Replays: Video Games and Classical Music*. New York: Oxford University Press.

Gilbert, William S. 2020. "A Critique of Nelson Goodman's Aesthetics: Music as Process." *PANDION: The Osprey Journal of Research and Ideas* 1 (2020). https://digitalcommons.unf.edu/pandion_unf/vol1/iss1/6

Grasso, Julianne. 2020. "On Canon as Music and Muse." *Journal of Sound and Music in Games* 1:82–86.

Guay-Bélanger, Dany. 2021. "Assembling Auras: Towards a Methodology for the Preservation and Study of Video Games as Cultural Heritage Artefacts." *Games and Culture* 17 (5): 1–20.

Guttenbrunner, Mark, Christoph Becker, and Andreas Rauber. 2010. "Keeping the Game Alive: Evaluating Strategies for the Preservation of Console Video Games." *International Journal of Digital Curation* 5:64–90. http://www.ijdc.net/article/view/147.

Istvandity, Lauren. 2021. "How Does Music Heritage Get Lost? Examining Cultural Heritage Loss in Community and Authorised Music Archives." *International Journal of Heritage Studies* 27:331–343.

Katz, Mark. 2010. *Capturing Sound: How Technology Has Changed Music*. Berkeley and Los Angeles: University of California Press.

Laiti, Outi, Sabine Harrer, Satu Uusiautti, and Annakaisa Kultima. 2020. "Sustaining Intangible Heritage through Video Game Storytelling—The Case of the Sami Game Jam." *International Journal of Heritage Studies* 27 (27): 296–311.

Lambert, Jean, and Rafik al-Akouri. 2019. "Patrimonialisation 'sauvage' et archéologie industrielle de la musique yéménite: Les premiers enregistrements commerciaux à Aden (1935–1960)." *Annales islamologiques* 53:49–94.

Li, Mai. 2013. "Traditional Music as 'Intangible Cultural Heritage' in the Postmodern World." MM thesis, University of Texas, 2013.

Miller, Kiri. 2011. *Playing Along: Digital Games, YouTube, and Virtual Performance*. New York: Oxford University Press.

Ombler, Matt. 2020. "Are Bootleg Game Soundtracks Damaging the Industry?" *gamesindustry.biz*, May 6, 2020. https://www.gamesindustry.biz/articles/2020-05-06-are-bootleg-video-game-soundtracks-damaging-the-industry.

Orcalli, Angelo. 2013. "Traces sonores du XXè siècle, pour une critique des sources audiovisuelles." In *Portraits polychromes (Hors série thématique) / Musique et technologie—Préserver, archiver, reproduire*, edited by Daniel Teruggi, 33–74. Paris: INA, 2013.

Rebillard, Fanny. 2018. "Les enjeux de l'archivage du son dans les jeux video." MD dissertation, ENSSIB.

Reinhard, Andrew. 2017. *Video Games as Archaeological Sites: The Interactive Past: Archaeology, Heritage, and Video Games*. New York: Berghahn.

Roberts, Les. 2014. "Talkin bout My Generation: Popular Music and the Culture of Heritage." *International Journal of Heritage Studies* 20:262–280.

Smith, Jeremy W. 2020. "'Wear People's Faces': Semiotic Awareness in Fan Adaptations of the Music from *The Legend of Zelda: Majora's Mask*." *Journal of Sound and Music in Games* 1:45–55.

Summers, Tim. 2016. *Understanding Video Game Music*. Cambridge: Cambridge University Press.

Tessler, Holly. 2008. "The New MTV? Electronic Arts and 'Playing' Music." In *From "Pac-Man" to Pop Music: Interactive Audio in Games and New Media*, edited by Karen Collins, 13–25. UK: Ashgate.

Verdin, Guillaume. 2021. "Génération Delphine, un bel hommage musical en preparation." *mag.MO5.com*, June 26, 2021. https://mag.mo5.com/actu/201602/generation-delphine-un-bel-hommage-musical-en-preparation/.

Vincent, Antoine, Bruno Bachimont, and Alain Bonardi. 2011. "Préservation de la musique avec dispositif électronique: L'intérêt des processus de production sonore." In *Actes des 17ès Journées d'Informatique Musicale (JIM 2011)*, 71–76. Saint-Etienne: Université Jean Monnet, 2011. https://hal.archives-ouvertes.fr/hal-01107051.

Yamakami, Yôhei, and Mathieu Barbosa. 2015. "Formation et développement des cultures autour de la 'Geemu ongaku' (1980–1990)." *Kinephanos* 5 (1). https://www.kinephanos.ca/2015/geemu-ongaku/.

Soundtrack References

Akumajo Dracula Best Music Collections BOX, Konami Digital Entertainment Co., Ltd., 2010, https://vgmdb.net/album/17063

All Sounds of Final Fantasy I • II, Polystar Co., Ltd., 1988, https://vgmdb.net/album/41

ASH: Archaic Sealed Heat Original Soundtrack, Aniplex, 2007, https://vgmdb.net/album/4598

Baten Kaitos: Eternal Wings and the Lost Ocean Soundtrack, Nintendo of Europe, 2003, https://vgmdb.net/album/8207
Bravely Default Flying Fairy Original Soundtrack, Square Enix Co., Ltd., 2012, https://vgmdb.net/album/33726
Castlevania Akatsuki no Minuet & Akumajo Dracula Sougetsu no Juujika Original Soundtrack, Konami Co., Ltd., 2006, https://vgmdb.net/album/5225
Final Fantasy Tactics Advance Original Soundtrack, DigiCube, 2003, https://vgmdb.net/album/17
Final Fantasy XI Original Soundtrack, DigiCube, 2002, https://vgmdb.net/album/9
Gyakuten Saiban 5 Original Soundtrack, SULEPUTER, 2013, https://vgmdb.net/album/40637
Gyakuten Saiban 6 Original Soundtrack, SULEPUTER, 2016, https://vgmdb.net/album/58263
The Legend of Zelda—Takt of Wind—Original Sound Tracks, Scitron Digital Contents, 2003, https://vgmdb.net/album/418
The Legend of Zelda: Breath of the Wild Original Soundtrack, Columbia, 2018, https://vgmdb.net/album/75831
The Legend of Zelda: Link's Awakening Original Soundtrack, Columbia, 2020, https://vgmdb.net/album/96462
The Music of Grand Theft Auto V [Limited Edition], Mass Appeal Records, Rockstar Games, 2014, https://vgmdb.net/album/49022
Machi e Ikou yo Doubutsu no Mori ~Mori no Ongakukai~, Aniplex, 2009, https://vgmdb.net/album/11919
Nazo no Murasamejo / The Legend of Zelda: The Hyrule Fantasy Original Soundtrack Orchestra Version, Toshiba EMI Ltd., 1986, https://vgmdb.net/album/5400
NieR:Automata Original Soundtrack Hacking Tracks, Square Enix Co., Ltd., 2017, https://vgmdb.net/album/66118
NieR:Automata Original Soundtrack, Square Enix Co., Ltd., 2017, https://vgmdb.net/album/65091
Nintendo 3DS Pokémon Omega Ruby & Alpha Sapphire Super Music Complete, The Pokémon Company, 2014, https://vgmdb.net/album/48057
Nintendo DS Pokémon Black・White Super Music Collection, Media Factory, Inc., 2010, https://vgmdb.net/album/20831
Nintendo DS Pokémon Diamond & Pearl Super Music Collection, Media Factory, Inc., 2006, https://vgmdb.net/album/3945
Okami Original Soundtrack, SULEPUTER, 2006, https://vgmdb.net/album/2411
Panzer Dragoon II Zwei Original Soundtrack, PolyGram K.K., 1996, https://vgmdb.net/album/1033
Persona3 Portable Voice Mix Arrange, Team Entertainment, 2010, https://vgmdb.net/album/20916
Pokémon Red·Green Super Music Collection, The Pokémon Company, 2016, https://vgmdb.net/album/57107
Seiken Densetsu 4 Original Soundtrack—Sanctuary—, Square Enix Co., Ltd., 2007, https://vgmdb.net/album/3950
Silent Hill 2 Original Soundtrack, Konami of Europe, 2001, https://vgmdb.net/album/8019
Silent Hill 4—The Room—Original Soundtracks, Konami Media Entertainment, Inc., 2004, https://vgmdb.net/album/1081
Song for Tales of the Abyss Motoo Fujiwara, Toy's Factory, 2006, https://vgmdb.net/album/8240

Square Enix Sound Effect Collection, Square Enix Co., Ltd., 2011, https://vgmdb.net/album/26911

Star Ocean Till the End of Time Original Soundtrack, Vol.1, Team Entertainment, 2003, https://vgmdb.net/album/2986

Star Ocean Till the End of Time Original Soundtrack, Vol.2, TEAM Entertainment, 2003, https://vgmdb.net/album/2987

Star Ocean Till the End of Time Voice Mix Album, Team Entertainment, 2003, https://vgmdb.net/album/1031

Tales of the Abyss Original Sound Track, Lantis, 2009, https://vgmdb.net/album/11766

Valkyrie Profile 2—Silmeria—Original Soundtrack Vol.1 Alicia Side, TEAM Entertainment, 2006, https://vgmdb.net/album/1259

Valkyrie Profile 2—Silmeria—Original Soundtrack Vol.2 Silmeria Side, TEAM Entertainment, 2006, https://vgmdb.net/album/1260

Valkyrie Profile Voice Mix Arrange, first smile, 2000, https://vgmdb.net/album/1258

The Witcher 3: Wild Hunt, CD Projekt RED, 2015, https://vgmdb.net/album/54638

Xenoblade2 Original Soundtrack [Type B], Procyon Studio Co., Ltd., 2018, https://vgmdb.net/album/75751

CHAPTER 12

SYMBOLIC MUSIC AND ALGORITHMIC COMPOSING

Computer Archaeological Perspectives on BASIC Game Sounds

STEFAN HÖLTGEN

Introduction

When home computers emerged in the late 1970s,[1] not only did the market for professional computer games[2] begin to bloom but also a new hobby—almost a cultural movement—arose: computer programming. The small machines from Atari, Commodore, Amstrad, Sinclair, and dozens of other manufacturers were mostly equipped with a dialect of the easy-to-learn programming language BASIC (Beginner's All-purpose Symbolic Instruction Code). If the users wanted to use their computer, in most cases they first had to learn the basics of this programming language. Manuals included with the computers, secondary literature, magazines, computer clubs, and likeminded users all provided help in this process. Within twenty years (between 1975 and 1995), a distinct subculture emerged from this hobby. Their achievements have been archived in paper-based and software publications—but mostly in (private) gray literature and on data-storage media with never-published homebrew programs. This archive awaits a systematic exploration.

In this chapter I discuss a selection of BASIC computer game codes from the archive. These programs show the (predominantly autodidactically gained) programming and technological skills of those private hobbyists programming BASIC games. After I have introduced the syntax and some dialects of the BASIC programming language, I will briefly discuss a handful of BASIC game listings, published in computer magazines,[3] with regard to their manner of sound programming. From this, I devise a new typology of sounds and music in games to extend existing classifications of computer game audio output with regard to the sound-code connection (see chapter 8 this volume for an analysis of game sound from the period). This typology may help to classify vintage computer games in considering their very different specifications (compared with modern systems). Previous classifications of vintage (and modern) computer games only focused on aesthetic categories and did not consider the game platform's specifications, which had a crucial influence of the games' sound aesthetics but can only be analyzed by examining the codes and hardware features of the game and its platform.

BASIC Culture

From computer historiographies, we know that computer games are much older than the computer game industry. Actually, the invention of computers is accompanied by game development either because the concept of computing coincides with the concept of gaming in general[4] or because computer games have often been used for testing and even inventing new computer hardware.[5] When minicomputers[6] came to small businesses, universities, and schools in the 1960s, game programming was not long in coming. This was triggered and accompanied by secondary literature about those computers: in 1969 David H. Ahl published his first edition of *101 BASIC Computer Games* with PDP-BASIC games contributed by hobbyists.

Steven Levy characterizes the transition phase from sporadic game hacking of the early 1970s to the phenomenal enlargement of the programming movement in the late 1970s (Levy 1984, 313–331) as a follow-up of the hacker movement that started 20 years earlier. Their credo was: "You can create art and beauty on a computer" (30)—where the "can" can be understood as a consequence of their demand to get "access to computers" (30) to acquire an understanding of that technology "hands-on" (7). The 1970s machines from Apple, Radio Shack, Commodore, and, later on, Sharp, Atari, and Texas Instruments, became the manifestations of these ideas because of their small RAM, slow mass storage units and hard-to-expand architectures. Software for these machines was either "professional" (and therefore expensive) or had to be self-made (home-brewed) by their users—which opened the creative path to the systems.

The first generation of home computers was equipped with only sparse sound and graphic capabilities and interfaces for game controllers. But the machines of the second generation from Atari, Amstrad, Commodore, and the MSX computers featured all the technologies that made them proper gaming systems. In particular, they used dedicated chips for graphics and sound generation in order to reduce the processing load on their CPUs. This was the crucial technological step to make computers versatile audiovisual gaming systems. The first to develop such a special processor was Atari, which, in 1978, updated their 1976 TIA (television interface adaptor) chip for their home computer models 400 and 800. Atari's competitors used self-made custom chips (like Commodore with the SID and VIC) or standard components (like MSX or Amstrad that implemented the AY-3-8910 in their computers).

Paperware

Unlike today's microcomputers, the early home-computer systems were mostly incompatible with each other. The reason software from a Commodore computer could not be loaded onto an Atari computer was their different data-storage formats and interfaces. Even if the systems used the same CPUs, they did not "understand" each other's software because of the diverse custom chips that handled the input, output, and processing of data differently—especially when it came to sound and graphic operations. Some computers featured built-in speakers, others output sound through standard audio jacks, mixed their audio signal to the TV signal, or provided separate pins for the audio signal within their monitor sockets. The sound capabilities varied depending on the sound-generator chips (Höltgen 2018) and the specification (frequencies, number of voices, sound shaping, filters, noise generators, etc.).

This diversity of hardware architectures and the sheer number of different home computer systems in the mid-1980s led many specific user groups to build local and national networks, clubs, or loosely organized groups to share ideas and programs but mostly games. A more systematically organized connection became possible via secondary literature about the systems. Home computers and related books, magazines, and zines mutually influenced each other's development during the first half of the 1970s: the first home computers were provided as kits with DIY magazines. Afterward, these magazines also provided supplies in the form of peripherals and software. Their articles either reported about new professional solutions or documented the self-made developments of their readers and users: soldering courses, instructions for rebuilding and repairing hardware, as well as programming courses and program code as type-in listings. The latter occupied much space in such magazines (Figure 12.1).

FIGURE 12.1 Selection of computer magazines with BASIC listings (Photo: Stefan Höltgen).

With an increasing number of home-computer systems coming to the market, the number of specialized magazines and books rose in equal measure. Their authors were not always professionals with a background in computer science or technology journalism but hobbyists who published fanzines, magazines, or computer books themselves. Publishers saw the opportunity behind the movement and established new book series and topics. Such publications helped to accelerate the self-teaching of the (mostly young) computer users and sometimes made them authors themselves. Submissions were mostly provided as type-in listings written in BASIC, assembly, or (less often) in other high-level languages (Pascal, Forth, Logo). This text type was a characteristic of magazines from that time that cannot be found in IT magazines of later generations. The specific mélange of articles from the editors (reviews, reports, interviews) and the readers (classifieds and program listings) cultivated an attractive resource for information and networking for computer users.

Those magazines were always accompanied by advice literature from which computer users of any level could gain information about their systems that the (mostly comprehensive and didactically superb [cf. Lucaßen and Höltgen 2014]) manuals did not provide. The topics ranged from guides for ready-made software, collections with type-in listings, technical instructions for repairing, building, and extending hardware, to teaching books for programming languages and how-to guides for programming specific software of different genres. Most of those books were concerned with computer games—they provided either complete type-in game listings or routines to implement into one's own programs (e.g., for game sound) (Figure 12.2).

FIGURE 12.2 Selection of home computer books with game program listings (Photo: Stefan Höltgen).

Programming Wetware

Program listings as a specific text type fill a strange position between *program codes within the computer* and *printed discourses* in magazines. They have to be read by human readers who then must literally type them into their computer so that the computer can read and execute them afterward. The typists find themselves in the role of a medieval book copyist:[7] they do not read and understand the program listing hermeneutically like common text but transfer it—just like a media channel—from one storage medium (paper) to another (the computer RAM and later-on the magnetic mass storage). They obviously resemble John Searle's translator from the "Chinese room" (Searle 1994) who need not understand a foreign language to translate it; having said this, they actually gain a rudimentary understanding of the code and its structure even if they do not know the programming language (Busjahn, Schulte, and Busjahn 2011). Moreover, typos occur that lead to a break (down) or an unexpected behavior of the computer. Therefore, meticulous rereading and comparing of the text source and the input code will be necessary.

As mentioned earlier, most type-in programs were provided in BASIC. This language's didactic paradigms make it possible to gain an understanding of the code by reading it—even if the used dialect differs greatly from the original ideas of the BASIC inventors (cf. Höltgen and Ernst 2014). An initial reading of the code helps to apprehend the structure and syntax of it and to avoid or find errors/typos. The reader mentally computes the algorithms in advance—in anticipation of their later execution from the computer. Programming tricks and useful algorithms can be learned this way, or they can be copied/converted for the user's own programming projects. The interpreting comprehension of the program code puts the programmer in a kind of machine state—as described by Alan Turing in 1936 when he wrote about paper machines (Turing 1936, 249).

This mental operation inevitably fails when the code addresses the hardware directly to execute time-critical machine functions. As will be seen later, this particularly happens with sound routines. Even today, most hobby programmers do not understand the black box BASIC close enough to know what their computer does when a BASIC command is executed.[8] Behind each command, function, or operation is a whole library of interconnected machine language routines that translate the high-level language BASIC into instructions which the computer can execute. This translation (*interpretation*) resembles a second, now machine-like transcription, that runs through the BASIC program in real time, recognizes structures like loops and conditional jumps, organizes variables and addresses into memory tables and, of course, executes the instructions. This happens at an incomprehensibly high speed so the programmers get the impression of a real-time execution of their code.

BASIC Dialects and Sound Programming

Because of its aforementioned use in home computers, the vast amount of literature, and the user groups that formed around it, BASIC has the largest cultural history of all programming languages: no other programming language had been learned and used by so many people. This was possible because of a combination of the (economic) decisions to neither patent nor license BASIC and the didactical design of the language. Hence, BASIC could even be used by small computer manufacturers to build low-cost systems with an easy-to-learn, built-in language.

BASIC was invented in 1964 at Dartmouth College in the United States by Thomas E. Kurtz and John G. Kemeny. Their goal was to develop a programming language for teaching students from the arts and humanities that was comprehensive and could be learned quickly. This is why BASIC does not have features that many other programming languages have (e.g., different data types) and supported interactive programming from the beginning. To achieve this, Kurtz and Kemeny simultaneously developed a time-sharing operating system (Dartmouth Time Sharing System, cf. Rankin 2018, 66–105). This allowed them to attach many terminals to just one computer and to provide hands-on programming courses to large learning groups. By using time-sharing, it appeared to every participant that they used the computer exclusively to run their BASIC program even when other students did the same simultaneously. This might have led to an imperceptible slow-down of the system, but it remained undetected by the users since the language did not feature time-critical functions back then.

Soon after the publication of BASIC, schools offered programming courses to their pupils by using the time-sharing system via a telephone connection to Dartmouth's computer center (cf. Rankin 2018, 68). When other colleges with different computer technology adopted the idea of programming classes for BASIC, the translator program (compiler) had to be reprogrammed for their systems. So BASIC versions for Hewlett-Packard, Digital Equipment Corporation, and other minicomputer manufacturers were developed—with different features and syntactic extensions. When Bill Gates and two of his fellow students at Harvard University learned about BASIC, they came up with the idea to adapt it for the recently available microcomputers. Since they lacked memory and data storage capacity, BASIC had to be redesigned as an interpreter language. That decelerated the execution of BASIC programs noticeably (when each programming instruction had to be translated "on the fly" by the interpreter) but retained the interactive programming philosophy. Gates and his colleagues founded the Micro-Soft[9] company in 1976 that would develop dozens of BASIC dialects for different microcomputer systems over the next two decades.

Basic BASIC

To help readers comprehend the game listings discussed in the third section of this chapter, I will outline some fundamental aspects of BASIC syntax and its use in home computers.

Even if BASIC was a didactically planned programming language for nontechnology students, it always retained somewhat machine-orientated[10] features that resemble the assembly programming language and machine-language programs and algorithms: for example, the imperative programming style where the computer executes programs as a series of operations. BASIC still shares this feature with other programming languages, but it is also the reason for its syntactical structure. Translating a BASIC command, the interpreter tries to find:

1. a keyword (an executable instruction), or
2. a line number (that can be used for later execution of the code), or
3. a variable name (to allocate data).

If none of these possibilities is detected,[11] the interpreter produces an error message in English (Höltgen and Ernst 2014, 23) and thus comprehensible for the learner. A short example demonstrates the structure of a BASIC program:

```
10 CLS: REM Clear Screen
20 PRINT A$;
30 GOTO 20
```

After starting the program with `RUN`, it erases the screen and prints endlessly, and juxtaposed, the content of the (not yet declared) variable `A$`.

The line numbers (10, 20, 30) structure the program linearly in an increasing order. If the distance between the line numbers is big enough, more lines of code can be inserted later—like the missing declaration for the variable:

```
15 LET A$="Hello, World! "
```

Line numbers not only provide the program structure but also serve as "labels." They can be jumped to from anywhere in the program. Line 30 shows how this works. With `GOTO 20`, a jump back to line 20 is performed so this program line will be executed again and again and again.

The command `CLS` in line 10 is a typical Microsoft BASIC instruction but can be found in other dialects as well. Sometimes commands with similar functions have different codes (in Commodore BASIC 3.5/7, the screen-clear operation is named `SCNCLR`) or surrogate functions can be used (for Commodore 64: `PRINT CHR$(147)` and for Atari, `GRAPHICS 0` provides the same operation).

The command `REM` (REMark) allows the programmer to leave a comment that would be ignored by the BASIC interpreter. The colon makes it possible to put more than one instruction into one program line. This helps to save space on the screen but makes the program listing hard(er) to read—especially if complete algorithms are put into one line.[12] The `CLS` command does not need or have arguments. `PRINT` allows additional information about what and how to print: either data in the form of numbers, variables (like `A$`), or strings and specific control characters such as where to place the cursor for the next `PRINT` command. Here, the semicolon causes the next output to be immediately to the right of the former. Otherwise, it would have been printed one line below.

To give the `PRINT` command the content of the variable `A$`, it has to be defined previously. Line 15 conducts this assignment with `LET A$=...`, where the `LET` command is optional in most BASIC dialects because it only shows that "=" does not mean a mathematical equality but the operation of assigning a variable. String variables (such as words and phrases) are identifiable by the post-positioned "$" sign—without it, it would be treated as a numerical variable.

The forced structuring of BASIC programs, with line numbers that serve as labels/ branch targets, resembles the machine-orientated assembly language:

```
C000  INC $D408

C003  JMP $C000
```

Here, the hexadecimal numbers (C000 and C003) are memory addresses where the instructions `INC` (to increment the content of the address D408) and `JMP` (jump back to the address C000) are stored. Both programming languages have a similar structure. This similarity did lead to criticism regarding the programming didactics[13] but facilitated the "jump" from BASIC to assembly language for programmers. Knowledge of assembly language of a specific platform[14] was inevitable for programming time-critical routines (e.g., for music generation).

The growth of the home computer market through the emergence of new manufacturers and their systems continuously produced new BASIC dialects. The new dialects enabled the use of new technologies that were built in the machines—especially new graphic and sound capabilities. The language was supposed to make them accessible to the home computer users. For this, BASIC had been extended with system-specific commands and functions. If such functions could not be addressed with BASIC, users could use machine-orientated "tricks" or load alternative BASIC dialects that provided such functions.[15]

The next subsections show sound programming for four different home computers and their built-in BASIC dialects. This helps to comprehend the BASIC games of the third section and gives a first insight into the time-critical aspects of sound programming with BASIC.[16]

Atari-BASIC

Shortly after Atari introduced their computer gaming console VCS, the company entered the home computer market. In 1979 they released their models 400 and 800 (followed by the XL and XE systems in the early 1980s) that used a similar hardware architecture as the VCS: special processors for graphic (GTIA) and sound (POKEY). Just like in the VCS, the software could be loaded via ROM cartridges. Atari-BASIC was one of these titles put on an 8 KB cartridge. A printed manual showed the users some details of the language and how to use it.

POKEY not only generates the sounds but also serves as an interface controller (POtentiometer & KEYboard controller). It provides four channels for monophonic sound that can be activated independently and can be merged in a mix mode. 256 pitches (between 125 Hz and 32 kHz) can be generated with 16 volume steps. A white-noise generator is available, too. Some of these sound parameters can be controlled with the Atari-BASIC `SOUND` command (Atari 1983, 5):

```
SOUND A, B, C, D
```

A indicates the sound channel (0–3), B holds the pitch (0–255), C is a parameter for "distortions" (0–14, only the even numbers), and D sets the volume level (0–15). Figure 12.3 shows the pitch distribution on a piano keyboard with three octaves.

```
FOR I=0 TO 255:SOUND 0,I,10,15:NEXT I:END
```

These commands produce a run-through of all pitches that can be activated from BASIC on channel 0 with the volume set to 15. With END, the sound output is stopped.

```
FOR I=0 TO 255:SOUND 0,I,10,15:SOUND 1,I,8,10:NEXT I:END
```

Here the commands activate two channels (0, 1) simultaneously with two different volumes (15, 10) and two different "distortions."

The "distortion" parameter (C) can be set to 0, 2, 4, 6, 8, 10, 12, or 14, but only 10 produces "clean" (undistorted) sounds. Any other value distorts the output in a different way:

> Distortion as used here is not equivalent to the standard interpretation. For example, "intermodulation distortion" and "harmonic distortion" are quality criteria specified for high-fidelity stereo systems. These types of distortion refer to waveform degeneration, where the shape of the wave is slightly changed due to error in the electronic circuitry. The computer's distortion does not alter waves (they are always square waves), but rather deletes selected pulses from the waveform. This technique is not adequately characterized by the word "distortion." A more descriptive and appropriate term for these distortion methods is "noise." (Crawford et al. 1982, 46f.)

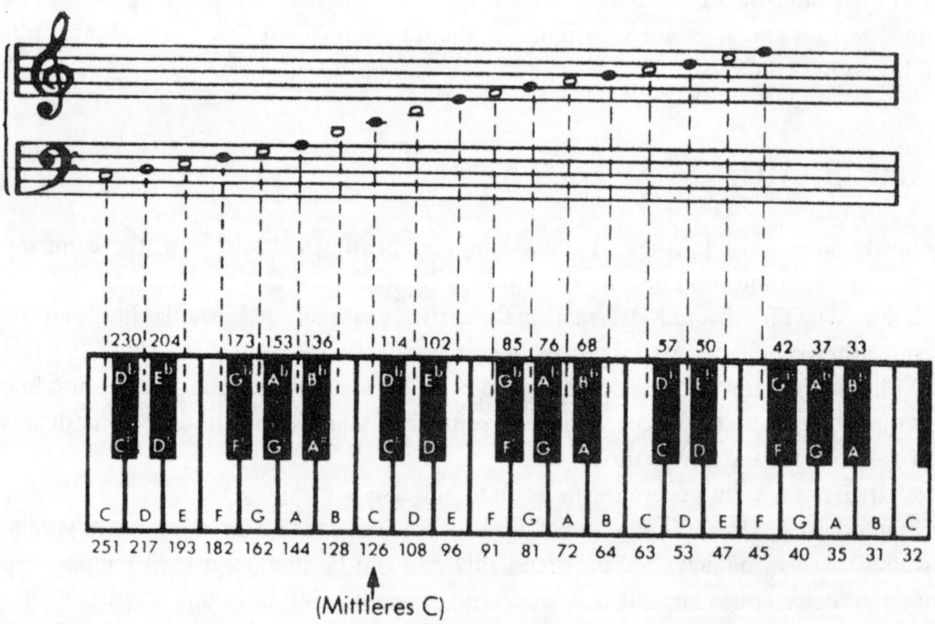

FIGURE 12.3 Relation of a piano keyboard to the Atari BASIC SOUND command (Credit: Atari 1984: 56).

Mixing the BASIC's channels is only possible by using the POKE command to address POKEY's registers directly. This is also the only way to generate more accurate frequencies than with only 256 steps. The audio control registers (AUDC1 to AUDC4) and the audio frequency registers (AUDF1 to AUDf4) of the POKEY chip control these parameters. To program filters, channel mix modes, and changes in the frequency range, the AUDCTL register can be changed (with up to 1.79 MHz changing speed) the same way by using bit masking (Crawford et al. 1982, 90).

Locomotive-BASIC

Amstrad's Colour Personal Computer (CPC) was widespread because of the company's license model: Amstrad cooperated with different electronic resellers across Europe. In Germany, Schneider sold the home computer models CPC 464, CPC 664, and CPC 6128 with their own company label. The computers were sold with either a built-in cassette recorder (464) or 3-inch disk drives (664, 6128) and 64 (464, 664) or 128 KB (6128) of RAM. They were equipped with a green or a color monitor. Sound was emitted by a little built-in mono speaker. Besides this, the computers featured a standard audio jack where the three sound channels could be put out in pseudo stereo (voice 1 on the right, voice 2 on the left, and voice 3 on the left and right channel).

For its programmable sound generator, the CPCs used the AY-3-8912 (a variant of the AY-3-8910) from General Instrument. This sound chip was published as early as 1978 and was put in many home computers and arcade games. It featured three voices, each with 1024 pitches and 16 volume levels. All voices could be modulated by one envelope demodulator. A built-in random number generator produced noises that could be mixed to each voice.

The CPC's Locomotive-BASIC is one of the most extensive dialects of any home computer from that era. It provides four commands to generate and shape sounds: SOUND activates one or more voices with specified parameters, ENT defines a tone envelope, ENV defines a volume envelope (Spital et al. 1985, 3, 21–24), and RELEASE starts a "channel rendez-vous" (Spital et al. 1985, 3, 65).

```
SOUND <channel status>, <tone period>, <duration>, <volume>,
<volume envelope>, <tone envelope>, <noise>
```

With the "channel status" the programmer can choose one of three voices or define a "rendez-vous" (8, 16, 32) to activate a voice in dependency with another activated voice. "Noise" adds a noise with the period 0–32 to the defined voice. Both envelope parameters have to be defined in advance by two specific instructions:

```
ENT <envelope number>[,<envelope section>][,<envelope section>]
[,<envelope section>][,<envelope section>][,<envelope section>]

ENV <envelope number>[,<envelope section>][,<envelope section>]
[,<envelope section>][,<envelope section>][,<envelope section>]
```

Each of the 15 possible tone envelopes (ENT) may be complemented with two or three parameters: <number of steps>, <step size>, and <pause time> or <tone period> and <pause time>. Additionally, each of the five volume envelopes (ENV) can be defined with either three parameters (<number of steps>, <step size>, and <pause time>) or two parameters (<hardware envelope> and <envelope period>).

This BASIC program shows the usage of the aforementioned instructions:

```
10 ENV 1,100,1,3:REM VOLUME ENVELOPE 1

20 ENT 1,100,5,3:REM TONE ENVELOPE 1

30 SOUND 1,142,300,15,1,1,5:REM CHANNEL 1, PITCH 142, DURATION 300
```

In lines 10 and 20 the envelope for voice 1 is shaped. Line 30 plays the concert pitch a (440 Hz) in volume 15 with the length of 300 milliseconds. This sound is transformed by the envelope curves (1, 1) and is enriched by a noise with an interval of 5.

RELEASE is used to activate a queue of sounds:

```
RELEASE <channels>
```

Here the <channel> parameter names the voices to be activated and/or mixed—either one (1, 2, 4), two (3, 5, 6), or all three voices (7) can be released.

Locomotive-BASIC provides a software interrupt (cf. Höltgen 2020) to play sounds in between other program instructions. The commands EVERY and AFTER can be used to regularly jump to a sound playback routine periodically:

```
10 AFTER 250 GOSUB 100

20 PRINT X;:X=X+1:GOTO 20

100 SOUND 1,142,300,15

110 RETURN
```

Five seconds after the program has started the interpreter jumps to the subroutine in line 100 to play a sound and return to the main program afterward. The value of AFTER is a multiple of a 50th of a second (Spital et al. 1985, 3, 4).

```
10 EVERY 100 GOSUB 100

20 PRINT X;:X=X+1:GOTO 20

100 SOUND 1,20

110 RETURN
```

Line 10 presets the program to jump to the subroutine in line 100 every 2 seconds (the parameter defines a multiple of a 50th of a second, cf. Spital et al. 1985, 3, 27).

Both commands' timings are provided by the interpreter's software timer. With this, it is possible to play background music with Locomotive-BASIC. The slight delays that can be heard when the sound subroutines are jumped give a hint of the fundamental timing problems with BASIC sounds.

Commodore-BASIC

The third BASIC dialect I want to introduce is widely known from its implementation in the Commodore 64 computer. This BASIC dialect contains only 34 commands and 26 functions which is poor in comparison to those of other home computers.[17] The C64's sound processor (SID, Sound Interface Device) belongs to the most complex PSGs that can be found in home computers. It provides three voices, a noise generator, four wave forms (square, sawtooth, triangle, and noise), ring modulation, amplitude modulation, analog filters, and even an audio input to loop external sounds through. Unfortunately, none of these features are accessible in the Commodore-BASIC.

The computer's manual and a wide range of secondary literature try to compensate for this by explaining how the SID is programmed machine-oriented with `POKE` and `PEEK` (cf. CBM 1982, 152–154, 160–162).[18] Just like POKEY, the SID chip can be activated and provided with sound parameters through its internal registers. These registers are located within the address range from 54272 to 54300 (cf. CBM 1982, 161f.).[19] To activate a voice (e.g., voice 1) the programmer has to define its volume first:

```
10 POKE 54296,15: REM VOLUME 15 ON VOICE 1
```

Afterward a 16-bit note value (divided in a high byte and a low byte part) has to be set:

```
20 POKE 54273,57:POKE 54272,172: REM STANDARD A ON VOICE 1
```

Now the sound envelopes can be set:

```
30 POKE 54277,105: REM ATTACK 1 SECOND, DECAY = 750 MILLISECONDS

40 POKE 54278,252: REM SUSTAIN = 10, RELEASE = 2.4 SECONDS
```

Finally, a wave form has to be chosen which starts playing the sound:

```
50 POKE 54276,33: REM SAW TOOTH FOR VOICE 1
```

To program a lasting tone, a waiting loop can be programmed:

```
60 FOR I=0 TO 1000: NEXT I
```

The sound is switched off by just setting a new wave form for the channel:

```
70 POKE 54276,34: REM SQUARE WAVE FOR CHANNEL 1
```

Nick Montfort developed the following BASIC one-liner[20] to show how random the settings of these sound parameters sound. For this he used the RND pseudo random number generator to poke random numbers into random SID addresses:

```
10 POKE 54272+RND(1)*25,RND(1)*256:GOTO 10
```

Sinclair-BASIC

While Commodore-BASIC V2.0 lacked any sound commands to program the multiple functions of the SID chip, the situation with Sinclair's ZX Spectrum is the opposite: its BASIC provides a command to activate the computer's built-in speaker but the Spectrum does not contain a sound chip. Instead of this, the Z80 CPU controls the sound output.[21] Because of this, the Spectrum provides just one voice with only square waves of a single amplitude (volume). The benefit of this technology is a very wide range of generatable frequencies (from 0 to 437.5 KHz). Even if frequencies above 20 kHz are not audible, this can be used for high-frequency pitch changes to create polyphonic sound impressions. Therefore, the ZX Spectrum is widely known as a 1-bit music (Troise 2020) generator. Unfortunately, this feature cannot be used with BASIC.

In the Sinclair-BASIC, the BEEP command is used to play sound. It only requires two parameters: the duration (given in seconds) and the pitch (given as notes with half steps) (see Figure 12.4):

```
BEEP 0.5,9
```

This plays half a second of standard A. To put a pause in between different `BEEP`s, the `PAUSE` command can be used. Pauses can be set in 50th second steps (which is derived from the machine's video frequency and is therefore an interrupt-dependent parameter):

```
BEEP 1,6:PAUSE 50:BEEP 2,7:PAUSE 25:BEEP 1,6
```

The sounds programmed in Sinclair-BASIC (Figure 12.4) are only monophonic since the CPU can only generate one square wave at a time on the specific output port. Only by programming machine language can the ZX Spectrum play pseudo-polyphonic sounds.

While the BEEP command is executed, any interrupt signals of the ZX spectrum's CPU are suspended to avoid an interrupt of the sound output. This leads to a stop of the BASIC program execution while sound is played. Because of this, any playback sound or background music playing while a BASIC program is executing is impossible.

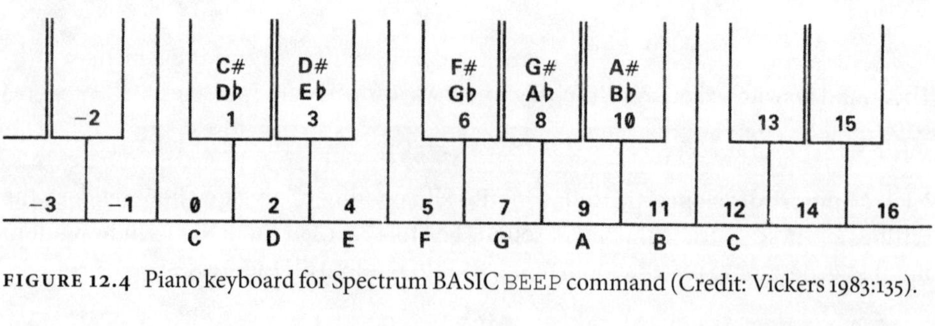

FIGURE 12.4 Piano keyboard for Spectrum BASIC `BEEP` command (Credit: Vickers 1983:135).

BASIC Games with Sound

After this short introduction into the sound-generating possibilities of the four systems, and their activation through BASIC programming, I will discuss some different applications that make use of BASIC programmed sounds. For this, video games programmed by hobbyists have been chosen from different historic computer magazines as type-in listings. The sound programming and usage in these games differs greatly in complexity and usage.

Many BASIC games do not provide sound for different reasons: either the specified platform does not generate sound regularly[22] or a game listing is provided for different platforms, so specific features (like graphics and sound) have to be avoided for maximum compatibility (e.g., Isaaman and Tyler 1982). Also, many games and game genres do not need sound output to be playable—even if they could be enriched aesthetically by adding sounds.

Time Critical Sounds: ZX Spectrum

The German home computer magazine *HC—Mein Home-Computer*, published between the end of 1983 and 1986, addressed users of different computer platforms—as one can see from the BASIC listings contained in the magazine. Starting from the very first issue, programs for Sinclair ZX Spectrum were released. Issue 12/1983 contains a game program with only 33 BASIC lines called *Hinterhalt* (Ambush) as a type-in.[23]*Hinterhalt* (Figure 12.5a) is a strategy game with random elements. The players have to steer their avatar through an area in which traps are hidden that only show up when she walks by. She must not step on those traps otherwise a falling sound can be heard [405–420],[24] the game is over and can be restarted by pressing Enter. The aim of the game is to walk as many steps as possible before falling into a trap, and the program counts the steps the player walks. The sound output gives an aural feedback that the game has been lost or has ended. Since this is the final part of the game, and no other routines have to be executed, it can last longer than the other sounds.

The following issue of *HC—Mein Heim-Computer* (1/1984) features another BASIC game listing for the ZX Spectrum called *Vier gewinnt* (Connect Four) (Figure 12.5b). The source code contains more BASIC lines than *Hinterhalt* and implements a two-player version of the famous grid game (cf. Allen 2010). The computer only monitors the rules and the course of the game. *Vier gewinnt* provides sounds for different situations: a sound of 1/20th of a second is played any time a player moves her disk above the grid [198]; another sound with the length of 3/10th of a second is played if she cannot put her disk into a chosen column [204]; an algorithmically produced glissando rings while a disk is falling down a column [221]; and a short melody (F. J. Ricket's "The Colonel Bogey

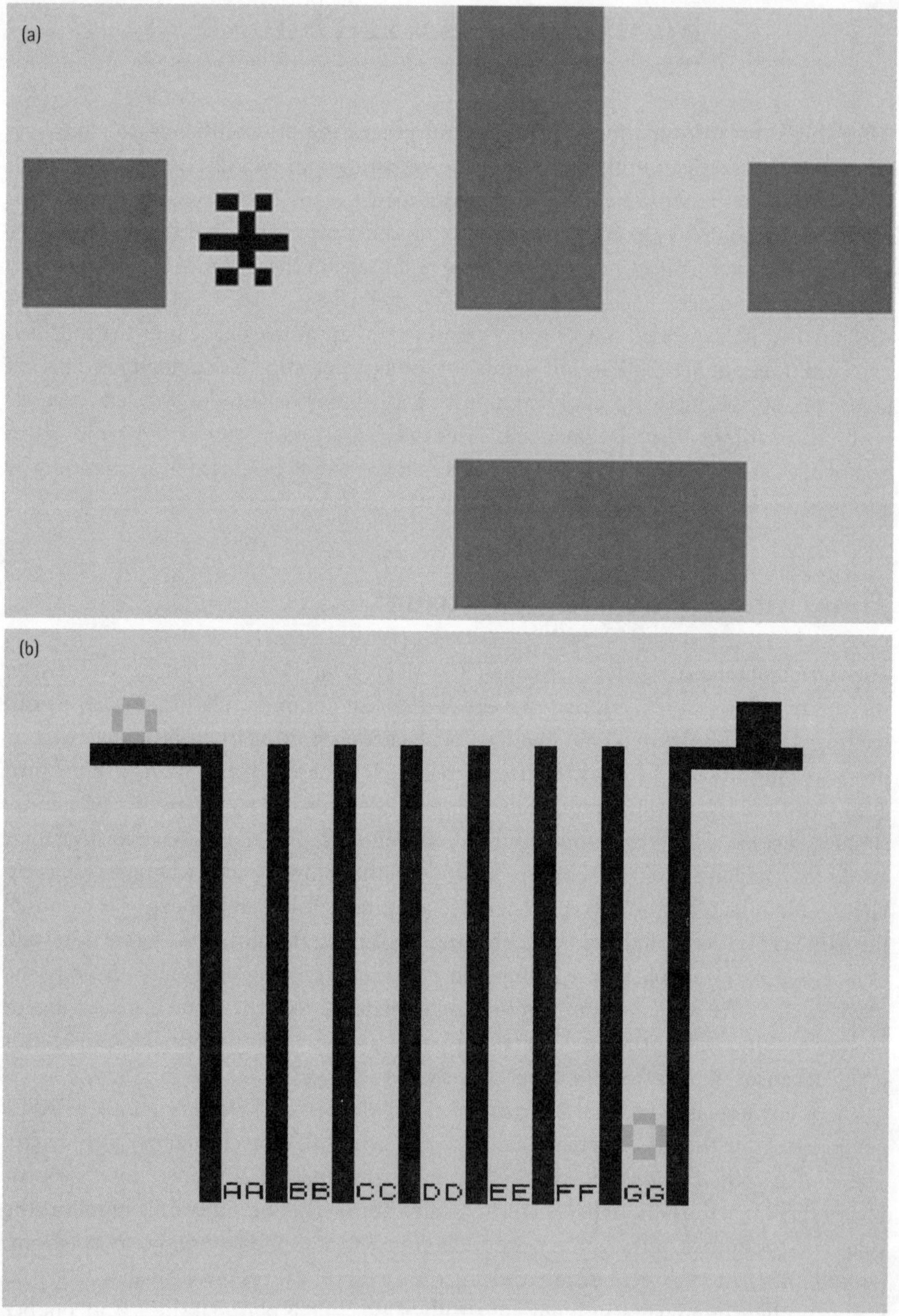

FIGURE 12.5 (a and b) *Hinterhalt* (code edited and commented by Hartig [1983]) and *Vier gewinnt* (code edited and commented by br [1984]) (Screenshots: Stefan Höltgen).

March" from the movie *The Bridge on the River Kwai*) is played if one of the players has won the game [265]:

```
256 BEEP 0.3,13: BEEP 0.6,10: PAUSE 25: BEEP 0.3,10: BEEP
0.3,11: BEEP 0,3,13: BEEP 0.6,22: BEEP 0.6,22: BEEP 0.6,18
```

The duration of the sounds that are played during the course of the match is way below one second. This allows to give a sound feedback of the players actions while not interrupting the game for too long. As in *Hinterhalt*, a more complex sound output is only possible at the end of a match because of the BEEP command's implementation.

The usage of sound in both games is very typical for ZX Spectrum BASIC games. Its duration and complexity are shaped by considerations about if and how long the game can be interrupted for sound playback. Since the BASIC interpreter works very slowly and the BEEP command does not provide more than two sound parameters, the computer cannot play back any more complex sounds—not to mention 1-bit music. For this, machine-language routines have to be used.

Versatile Programming: Amstrad CPC

Horror Caves (Figure 12.6a) for the Amstrad CPC is a BASIC game with 280 BASIC lines that is a lot more complex than the former examples for the ZX Spectrum. It belongs to the genre of action games players have to dig for iron ore deep in the mines of the Pyrenees. There, the avatar is constantly chased and attacked by ghosts; it can only escape by running through the labyrinth-like caves. Simultaneously, the air supply decreases and this creates time pressure. On reaching a specific score, the air supply can be stocked up again.

The game provides an artificial intelligent opponent and an increasing difficulty. The BASIC listing is well structured (as opposed to the ZX Spectrum programs) and the different program parts provide comments from the author so that the user can easily manipulate the code (as suggested in the introductory text). The magazine text supports this by listing the specific variable names used in the program.

Sound output can be heard in different parts of the game:

- when the title credits are shown, a kind of scratching sound is played [2260]

The first channel is activated continuously (every 1/100th second) with 1244 Hz and paused for 2/100th seconds.

- After the title screen graphics are completed, a two-part musical tune is played (the refrain from "Itsy Bitsy Teenie Weenie Yellow Polka Dot Bikini"). It can be stopped by pressing a key, and then the game starts. [2380–2590]

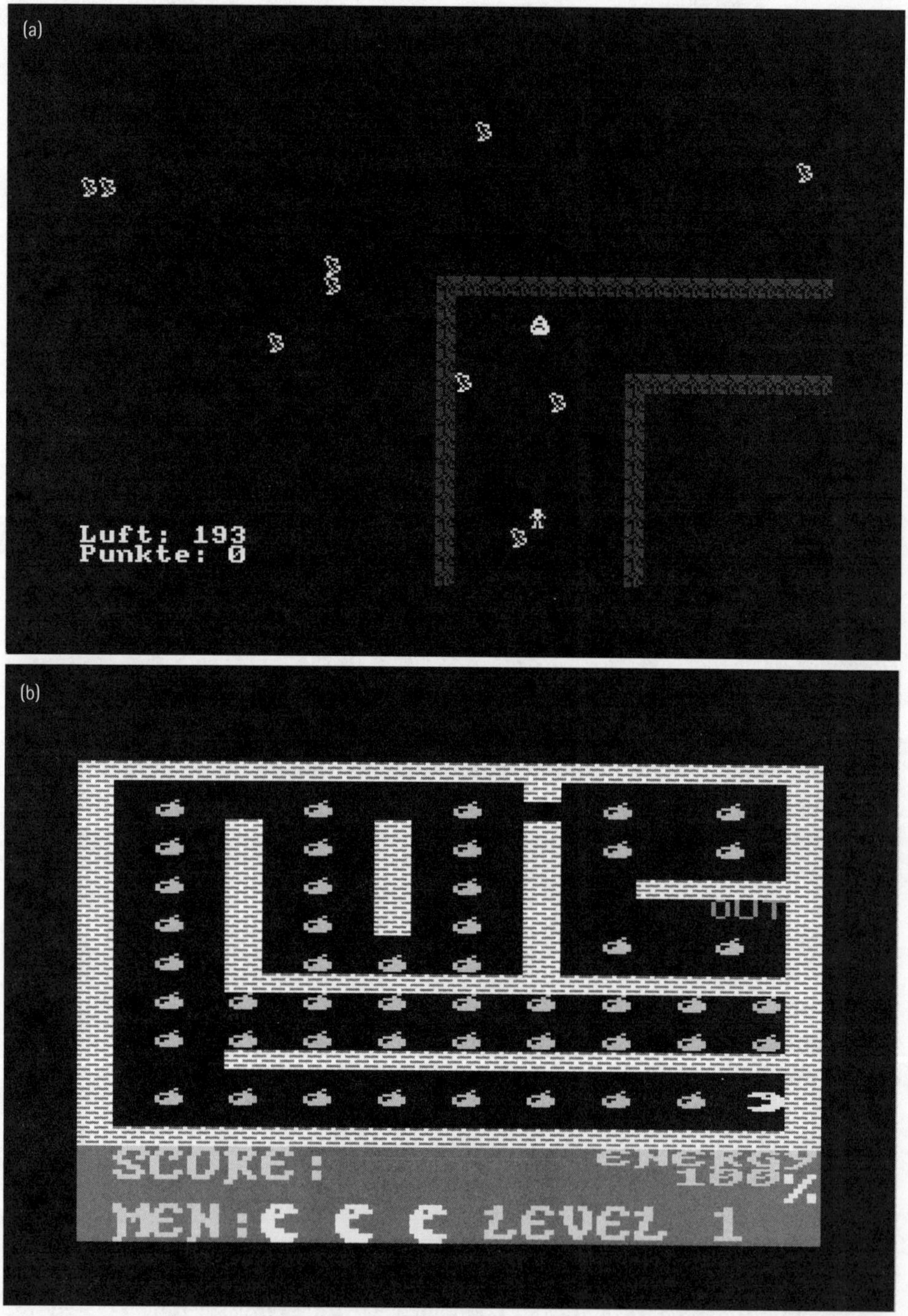

FIGURE 12.6 (a and b) *Horror Caves* (code edited and commented by bez [1985]) and *Pak Caverns* (Screenshots: Stefan Höltgen).

This complex tune is built from parameters for the channel, tone period, and duration that are read from a DATA table [2500–2590]. They are read within a loop (98 iterations) and played by the `SOUND` command. When the playback is finished, it starts all over again until a key is pressed.

- one sound (1/10th second) that is played when ore is collected [2670]
- one sound (half a second) that is played when a ghost is touched [910]
- a sound sequence (1/25th seconds) that is played when the air supply is low [980]

These sound outputs are likewise short and can only be heard when the gameplay can be paused for a short while (ore collecting, ghost hitting). The warning sound is even shorter and can be played in between the avatar's steps. At no point is the software timer from Locomotive-BASIC used for sound playback.

Craig Mitchell's *Pak Caverns* (Figure 12.6b), printed in a 1985 issue of the *Amstrad Computer User* magazine, consists of two parts: a loader program and a main program (which is loaded from the former). The loader program presents the game instructions, the graphics, and machine-code routines. The main program provides the game algorithms that use the previously loaded graphics and sound data. The aim of the game is to steer the avatar through a labyrinth to collect (eat) apples, and, in so doing, the snake-like avatar gets longer. It will not stop crawling and must neither touch the walls nor its own body in order to avoid losing a life. *Pak Caverns* uses a variety of sounds; only some of them (that are different from those of *Horror Caves*) are discussed here.

Again, the title melody (from Scott Joplin's "Maple Leaf Rag") is deposited in DATA lines and played back from the loader program [2060–2430]. The sound parameters are stored in a three-dimensional array, the envelopes are prepared [400–530] and then the sound is played while other game data are processed in the background; for this, the command `EVERY 5 GOSUB 500` [170] is used. After starting the "main program," a second melody is played ("Enola Gay" by OMD) that repeats until the game starts. As with the previous sounds, it is stored in DATA lines [1250–1540 and 2060–2430] and played back from an array.

The game program plays short melodies and sound sequences when a level is finished [2780], when a new high score is reached [5840–6130], when a life is lost [2580, 2600], or when the game is over [5290–5330]. These sound outputs are similar to those discussed above: they are either very short (so they do not interrupt the game play) or are played during standby times (e.g., while entering the next level).

Machine-language routines (prepared in the loader program) are only used for fast screen setup (level backgrounds, characters). Sound is only provided by game algorithms or played back from data tables.

Backgrounds: Atari-BASIC

The game for Atari computers uses a special, hybrid technology to play sounds. *The Castle* (Figure 12.7) was published by Thomas Fischermann in issue 7 of *HC—Mein Home-Computer* in 1985 (Fischermann 1985). The player controls a knight who throws stones from a castle wall to prevent enemies from climbing up eight ladders. If one of them reaches the top of the wall, the game is lost. The stones have to be fetched one by one from the left or the right end of the wall, carried to the top of a specific ladder and thrown onto an enemy. If the gamer fends off all enemies, the process repeats in the next level—only faster than before.

The Castle uses multiple sound-programming techniques. Again, a title theme is played while the start screen is depicted [1810]. The arrival [1390], and any movement of the avatar [160] and the enemies [1210, 1250], is accompanied by short sounds; also, the fetching [200] and the throwing [330] of a stone—the latter presented as a short glissando. Reaching a level's end [1140–1480] and losing a life (when an enemy reaches the top of the wall) [1560] are also accentuated acoustically. These sounds are either programmed with specific parameters or generated by loops. Good structuring of the BASIC code (with inverted headlines within the listing and the listed program structure and variable table in the introductory text) make finding and manipulating sound operations easy.

The most prominent feature of *The Castle* is its continuously played background music.[25] This is realized by a machine language routine integrated within the BASIC

FIGURE 12.7 *The Castle* (Screenshot: Stefan Höltgen).

code [950–1010]. The DATA codes contain the playback program and musical data (notes, timing information, etc.). Both are implemented with a BASIC loader [950] that `POKE`s the read data into the computer's memory starting with address 1536 (hexadecimal: 0600). To call this routine periodically, an interrupt register (cf. Höltgen 2020) of the operating system's timer routine is manipulated [960]. For this purpose, the 16-bit address 0600[26] is transferred to the memory addresses 550 and 551.

To make the sound appear dynamically (in tandem with the game play), some parameters have to be changed from time to time by the BASIC program. The sound must be silenced if a level is finished, and this takes place in lines [1440] and [1560] by setting the timer to 0 and switching off the sound channels 2 and 3. Additionally, the game tempo has to be increased after a level is finished, mirrored in speeding up the musical tempo. This raises the player's stress levels (cf. Höltgen 2016b). To achieve this, the predefined parameter within the music data table (memory location 1577, hexadecimal 629) can be manipulated. In the beginning, it is set to 6 [960] and will be reduced anytime a level is won [1530].

Even if the sound appears to be emitted while the game is played, both processes cannot be executed at the same time but must alternate. The execution of the BASIC game is interrupted by the machine-language program periodically in microtemporal intervals to play back the sound. The sound playback is also interrupted continuously to execute the next BASIC instruction and so on. The fact that these interrupt processes happen within microseconds creates the impression of simultaneousness. This effect cannot be achieved with BASIC but only with machine language.

Allround Sound: Commodore 64

Other computers use BASIC games with interrupt-controlled music playback too. The text adventure *SPION III* (Goebbels 1986) for the Commodore 64 plays Johann Sebastian Bach's *Nun ruhen alle Wälder* with three (instrumental) voices as an endless loop. This is based on a similar programming technique to *The Castle*.

The last example to discuss does not belong to the historical type-in games but to the retro-computing genre of "BASIC Tenliner" programs. Those are programs that consist of a maximum of ten BASIC lines (or less) and are mostly demo programs or games. This kind of programming art demands the most intimate knowledge of the platform and virtuosity in BASIC programming. Tenliner programs must not use machine code, all algorithms have to be implemented in BASIC (only addressing graphic and sound chips by `POKE` is allowed if no other way exists—like with the C64). Particularly when programming graphics and sound, the programmer has to find ways of saving memory, for example, with algorithmic methods (cf. Braguinski 2018, 71; Höltgen 2021, 37).

Remember (Figure 12.8) is a BASIC Tenliner game programmed in 2017 by "Drazil." It is an adaptation of the well-known *Simon* game, where the player has to remember a growing series of sounds and colors to reproduce it in the correct sequence. The programmer Guido Bonerz managed to implement that game with only nine BASIC lines.

FIGURE 12.8 *Remember* (Screenshot: Stefan Höltgen).

For this, he uses very elaborate programming tricks that make his code nearly unreadable. But because the C64 uses specific memory addresses that are reserved for the sound chip's registers, the code can be comprehended by identifying them and their variable names:

- All sound output is generated in line [9]. The parameters for the first and the second voice are defined there: wave form, envelopes (attack and hold), and the frequencies.
- This sound routine is called by `GOSUB 9` from the lines [5], [6], and [7]. In those lines, the needed parameters for the waveform (F), the frequency (S), and the duration (P) are set.
- The frequencies played in [9] are stored in a 16-bit array that is generated from the DATA list entries 9 to 16 [1]. This is conducted in [2] with the `READ` instruction, which stores the values in array NL() (low byte of the frequency) and NH() (high byte of the frequency). The 4 low bytes and 4 high bytes are combined to 16 different frequencies from the program.

```
9 SI=54272: POKE 54296,15: POKE SI+5,20: POKE SI+12,20:
POKE SI+6,200: POKE SI+13,255: POKE SI+0,NL(S): POKE SI+1,NH(S):
```

```
POKE SI+2,200: POKE SI+3,0: POKE SI+4,F: FOR T=1 TO P: NEXT:
POKE SI+4,0: RETURN
```

Depending on the sound (start or end melody, correct or false input), the variable `S` is used to choose one out of 16 frequencies, modified by a specific waveform and envelope. Any sound played in *Remember* is generated algorithmically, even if the frequencies are tightly defined.

This example shows how BASIC can be programmed with great virtuosity, when, for example, it comes to sound programming and only one routine is used to define and generate sounds where other programs use different programming techniques for the same purpose. Inventing such routines can be understood as "gaming a system" (Zimmerman 2009, 25; Fritsch 2018, 70–75) and playing/tinkering around with the syntax of BASIC programs and the possibilities of the interpreter becomes a kind of gamification of programming.

Finally, I will compare the sounds of the aforementioned programs and their sound programming to provide an overview of the BASIC sound programming techniques. This will lead to a new kind of classification of computer-game sounds.

Sounds in BASIC Games

Researchers classify sounds in computer games into very different categories. This has changed through the history of game studies. First, sounds were differentiated by their connection to the game plot as diegetic (the sound is related to the game play, e. g., shooting or explosion sounds) and nondiegetic (sounds that do not relate to the game play, e.g., title or background melodies) (Jørgensen 2007, 6). This categorization was criticized for its origin in film studies—video and computer games are quite a different media type and need a dedicated terminology (Jørgensen 2010). Thus, sounds were then categorized, for example, according to whether they are related to specific technical or virtual interfaces (Jorgensen 2010, 91–93). Such ideas can be conveyed to BASIC games as well.

A look beneath the games' aesthetic surfaces at their codes, their programming languages, and hardware platforms with their very different ways of generating sounds, facilitates different approaches to classification. For this, the different sound-programming techniques, the timings (of sound generation and the game play), and the technical possibilities of the specific platforms and how they are programmed/addressed with/from BASIC can be distinguished. In doing so, the different aesthetic features of sound categories (diegetic, interface-related, etc.) can be coupled to their technical disposition. In particular, early computer games provide aesthetics that are ruled by the technical (im)possibilities of the platforms, programming languages (BASIC dialects), and coding skills of their authors. Sounds have to be programmed efficiently with due regard to the other game program algorithms that also jostle for the little processing, memory, and time available in the home computers.

TABLE 12.1 Sound Categories in BASIC Games

	Occasionally			Permanent	
	Very short (< 0.5 Sec.)	Short (0.5–1 Sec.)	Long (> 1 Sec.)	Opening/end credits	Background
BASIC coded	Vier gewinnt Pak Caverns The Castle	Vier gewinnt The Castle	Hinterhalt Vier gewinnt The Castle	Horror Caves	
playback from DATA	Horror Caves	Horror Caves		Horror Caves	
playback from array		Pak Caverns Remember	Pak Caverns Remember	Pak Caverns	
algorithmically generated		Remember	Remember	The Castle	
machine language					Spion III The Castle

Vintage video and computer games cannot be analyzed regardless of their technical (im)possibilities. With modern gaming systems, nearly any aesthetic seems to be possible, so the interpretation of game sounds and other aesthetic features does not need to focus on whether the platform is not able to produce that specific output or not.[27] When video and computer games first emerged, the situation was quite different: the aesthetics had to follow the platform's specifications tightly. Viewed from today, these specifications not only define the "quality" of the graphic and sound output but also provide clues as to the platform's technology and their creative uses. Programmers of such systems either dealt with the limits of their home computers or tried to shift them to gain new aesthetics by "hacking" their machines. This can be observed by a look into their programming codes. Thus, analyzing the sound programming techniques of hobbyist video and computer games provides an insight into the individual's and communities' thinking and handling of technology. The categorization of BASIC game sounds (Table 12.1) is also a categorization of different ways of handling the machines—from programming according to the instructions given by the manuals to inventing new ways of sound generation by "gaming the system."

Conclusion

The archive of BASIC computer games is huge. Six decades of professional and hobbyist programmers have written innumerable games for dozens of home computer platforms. Some of them were published in books, printed magazines, or disk magazines—most of them are awaiting discovery in paper and data-storage archives. Focusing on sound programming shows what kind of knowledge can be recovered from such programs: they speak about their platforms and programming languages but most of all about the culture and praxis of hobby programming.

The programming language BASIC is wide open for research on such topics because of its simple structure and its significance for books and magazines of the home-computer era. BASIC listings in books and magazines have a similar status for the history of computer game music as musical notation for the history of music: they provide an explicit formal language for re-enacting a musical performance. A look at the program listings shows the algorithmic entanglement of sound generation with the other game codes and shows that in principle any computer game music is "diegetic" when the game is only available as printed code. As a printed listing it shows its internal connections (its "algorithmic coherence") to the other sections of the game code. On this analytical basis, another categorization of the sound-gameplay dependency is required.

Unlike music played by humans, the digital playback of programmed compositions is not altered by the idiosyncrasies of the musician but is only interpreted by a machine—a BASIC interpreter. Here, the only influences are the electrical and physical variations/oscillations of the hardware platform (as the musical instruments). Only they are able to modify the sound output (even if this usually cannot be heard). Such re-enactments demand real and operative platforms. Particularly in the case of sounds, no software emulation of a system can achieve the authenticity of the original platform's performance. Sound hardware cannot be emulated in a lossless manner by software; the microtemporal interaction between the system's hardware, the programming language and the specific program code can only be performed authentically if a system clock generator orchestrates the processes between hardware and software rhythmically.

Notes

1. Thanks to Chiara Rochlitz for copyediting this chapter.
2. Throughout, for platform reasons, I retain the label "computer game" as opposed to "video game" where I refer to video games produced on and for the home computer market using BASIC programming. Also, there is a technological and epistemological reason to distinguish between video games and computer games, as Claus Pias (2017, 313) showed.
3. To follow this discussion, a look into the source codes is unavoidable. To make this possible, the source codes and program image files can be downloaded as a ZIP file: http://txt3.de/basicsound1 (Only *Remember* is not presented there, since the author published the code and the executable file in his GitHub repository.)
4. Claus Pias writes: "that the world of the (digital) computer is itself already a game world" (2017, 11) because computers always simulate which can be understood as mimicry (Caillois 1960, 19) of real-world processes.
5. The computer scientist Alexander Reinefeld (2006) calls game programming "the drosophila of computer development" (252, my translation).

6. Minicomputers are computing systems that used semiconductor circuits but did not yet use high-integrated CPU chips. They were mostly used from the early 1960s to the mid-1970s (when the microcomputers emerged). The term "mini" refers to their small size in comparison to the mainframe computers that filled whole rooms whereas most minis were the size of a refrigerator.
7. This association stems from my student Philip Zumpe. It is true even if those typists were BASIC programmers because you cannot get the idea of a program, or even of one of its algorithms, by linearly reading and typing it into the computer. So, the comparison is valid because the medieval copyists did not need to know the whole content of the book in advance to copy it properly. (Cf. Searle 1994.)
8. With ROM listings (e.g., Brückmann, Englisch, and Gerits 1985), the users can gain insight into the detailed operations of the BASIC interpreter and operating system.
9. Later, Microsoft.
10. Here I only address the nonstructured dialects from the period 1975–1985. Later BASIC dialects moved away from such properties that were accused of being "anti-algorithmic and machine-orientated" (Höltgen 2016a, 145).
11. For option 1, this could mean that the instruction was misspelled; for option 2, this could mean the line number is out of the possible range; and, for option 3, this could mean a false variable name (with either a wrong data type or a reserved keyword) had been chosen.
12. So-called *BASIC One-Liner* is a program genre that carries this principle to the extreme: Complete programs are put into only one BASIC line—containing loops and conditional branching. It needs highly skilled BASIC and system knowledge to reach this level of this programming art (cf. Lucaßen et al. 2014; Saukas and Digital Prawn 2014).
13. Especially as a programming language used by children and taught in schools, a more "structural" programming style was preferred that could be used independently from a specific hardware platform. BASIC afforded neither: because of its GOTO statements, code is highly unstructured, and the possible uses of POKE and other commands (which addressed the hardware directly) led to many different versions of BASIC—each for a specific platform.
14. Assembly languages and the machine languages they denote not only differ from microprocessor to microprocessor (with different instruction sets) but also from one system architecture to another: the memory locations for the program code, how custom chips (for graphics, sound, and I/O) are addressed, where the BASIC interpreter resides in the memory, and so forth. All these differ from platform to platform. To program assembly language, not only the language and syntax has to be known but specific knowledge of the programmed platform's architecture as well. The example shows a program for a MOS 6510 processor in the Commodore 64 that changes the screen frame color continuously by changing the specific register content of the VIC-II graphic chip.
15. To extend the C64 with specific commands for graphics and sound that the built-in dialect lacked, for example, Simons' BASIC could be used (cf. Smith 1983, 6.1–6.19 and 11.1–11.11).
16. All programming examples can be tested with these online emulators:

    Atari 800: http://rtro.de/atari8-emu
    Commodore 64: http://rtro.de/c64-emu
    Amstrad CPC 6128: http://rtro.de/cpc-emu
    Sinclair ZX Spectrum: http://rtro.de/zxspec-emu

17. For comparison: Locomotive-BASIC version 1.1 for the Amstrad CPC 6128 provides 105 commands and 55 functions (http://txt3.de/basicsound2).
18. The manual's appendix shows a piano keyboard program as a type-in listing to learn about the BASIC programming of SID sounds (CBM 1982, 147).
19. The technology where peripheral addresses are placed under RAM addresses is called memory-mapped I/O, and is used by most computers whose CPUs lack dedicated I/O ports.
20. http://txt3.de/basicsound3
21. Later models of the ZX Spectrum (starting in 1985) used the programmable sound generator GI AY-3-8912.
22. Even home computers without dedicated sound capabilities have been hacked to play sounds in rather exotic ways (cf. Höltgen 2018).
23. Thanks to Spyros Konitopoulos and Uwe Geiken (both members of the "BASIC on the ZX Spectrum" Facebook group) who helped with the Spectrum type-ins and generating TAP image files of the programs.
24. Numbers and ranges given in square brackets reference the BASIC lines from the original listings (cf. endnote 3).
25. Many thanks to the Atari hacker Thomas Schulz (2016) for helping me analyze the assembly program and its call routines.
26. The 16-bit number is calculated from the content of address 551 multiplied by 256 and added to the content of address 550 (256*0 + 6) in reverse order (Little Endian).
27. Even modern computers format their video and audio outputs depending on their hardware specifications. But since these platforms feature fast CPUs, mass storage, and built-in memory with high capacities they are *seemingly* able to produce any possible aesthetic output. But this only appears to be so to the human sensory system. The microscopic pixelation of images and the microtemporal interrupts of sounds are qualitatively the same as in early home computers. The structure of digitalization, algorithmization, and serial processing has not changed in digital computers since their debut.

References

Allen, James D. 2010. *The Complete Book of CONNECT 4: History, Strategy, Puzzles*. New York: Puzzle Wright Press.

Atari. 1983. *Atari BASIC*. Sunnyvale: Atari Inc.

bez. 1985. "*Horror Caves*. Dieses Spiel bringt Ihnen den absoluten HORROR!!!" *Computronic*, no. 3–4, 71–75.

br. 1984. "Vier gewinnt." *HC—Mein Home-Computer*, no. 1 (January): 37–38.

Braguinski, Nikita. 2018. *RANDOM: Die Archäologie elektronischer Spielzeugklänge*. Bochum: Projekt.

Brückmann, Rolf, Lothar Englisch, and Klaus Gerits, 1985. *CPC 464 Intern. Mit kommentiertem ROM-Listing*. Düsseldorf: Data Becker.

Busjahn, Teresa, Carsten Schulte, and Andreas Busjahn, 2011. "Analysis of Code Reading to Gain More Insight in Program Comprehension." *Koli Calling. ACM*, 1–9. https://doi.org/10.1145/2094131.2094133.

Caillois, Roger. 1960. *Die Spiele und die Menschen. Maske und Rausch*. Stuttgart: Durt E. Schwab.

CBM. 1982. *Commodore 64 MicroComputer User Manual.* Carmel: Commodore Business Machines, Inc. & Howard W. Sams & Co., Inc.

Crawford, Chris, Lane Winner, Jim Cox, Amy Chen, Jim Dunion, Kathleen Pitta, and Bob Fraser. 1982. *De Re Atari: Anno Domini MCMLXXXI.* Atari Program Exchange. http://txt3.de/basicsound13.

Fischermann, Thomas. 1985. "The Castle." *HC—Mein Home-Computer*, no. 7 (July): 82–85.

Fritsch, Melanie. 2018. *Performing Bytes*: Musikperformances der Computerspielkultur. Würzburg: Königshausen & Neumann.

GI. 1979. *AY-3-9810/9812 Programmable Sound Generator Data Manual.* General Instruments. http://txt3.de/basicsound8.

Goebbels, Steffen/dm. 1986. "Spion II—Die Jagd nach der Bombe." *64'er Sonderheft Abenteuerspiele*, no. 4, 134–141.

Hartig, Jochen. 1983. "Hinterhalt." *HC—Mein Home-Computer*, no. 12 (December): 43.

Höltgen, Stefan. 2014. "BASIC-Spiele und ihre Geschichte. Das kann ich auch programmieren! Ein Kurzinterview mit Yoda Zhang, dem, Programmierer von Gulp!" *Retro, Sonderheft BASIC*, 20–22.

Höltgen, Stefan. 2016a. "GO BACK GOTO: Ein kurzer Überblick über die Entfernung der Schulinformatik von den Computern." *Grundlagenstudien aus Kybernetik und Geisteswissenschaften* 57, no. 3 (September): 141–152. http://txt3.de/basicsound9.

Höltgen, Stefan. 2016b. "Time Invaders: Zeit(ge)schichten in Computer(spiele)n." In *Time to Play: Zeit und Computerspiel*, edited by Stefan Höltgen and Jan-Claas van Treeck, 51–69. Glückstadt: VWH.

Höltgen, Stefan. 2018. "Play That Pokey Music: Computer Archaeological Gaming with Vintage Sound Chips." *Computer Games Journal* 7, no. 4 (December): 213–230. https://doi.org/10.1007/s40869-018-0068-5, http://txt3.de/basicsound10.

Höltgen, Stefan. 2020. "Das magische Panoptikum. Technologien der Überwachung zum Zwecke des Spiels—Eine computerarchäologische Analyse." In *Überwachung und Kontrolle im Computerspiel. PAIDIA-Sonderausgabe*, edited by Martin Henning and Marcel Schellong, 124–155. Glückstadt: VWH. http://txt3.de/basicsound11.

Höltgen, Stefan. 2021. "Little Data: Fraktale Bildkompression; Von einer netzhistorischen Miszelle zum medienstrukturellen Bruch." In *Jahrbuch Archiv für Mediengeschichte 19: "Kleine Formen,"* edited by Friedrich Balke, Bernhard Siegert, and Joseph Vogl, 27–41. Berlin: Verlag Vorwerk 8.

Höltgen, Stefan, and Wolfgang Ernst. 2014. "Programmieren in BASIC: Zehn Bemerkungen zu einer verfemten Programmiersprache." *Retro*, no. 29, 16–23.

Isaaman, Daniel, and Jenny Tyler. 1982. *Computer Space Games.* London: Usborn.

Jørgensen, Kristine. 2007. *A Comprehensive Study of Sound in Computer Games: How Audio Affects Player Action.* Lewiston/Queenston/Lampeter: Edwin Mellen Press.

Jørgensen, Kristine. 2010. "Time for New Terminology? Diegetic and Non-Diegetic Sounds in Computer Games Revisited." In *Game Sound Technology and Player Interaction: Concepts and Developments*, edited by Mark Grimshaw, 78–97. Hershey; New York: Information Science Reference.

Levy, Steven. 2981. *Hackers: Heroes of the Computer Revolution.* New York: Doubleday.

Lucaßen, Carsten, and Stefan Höltgen. 2014. "BASIC-Handbücher von Homecomputern: Die längst fällige, vergleichende Rezension." *Retro, Sonderheft BASIC*, 13–15.

Lucaßen, Carsten, Ingolf Ihrig, Torsten Othmer, and Stefan Höltgen. 2014. "Einzeiler; BASIC-Spiele und Demos für verschiedene Systeme." *Retro, Sonderheft BASIC*, 13–15.

Mitchell, Craig. 1986. "Pak Caverns." *Amstrad Computer User*, no. 1 (January): 53–54, 56, 79–80.

Pias, Claus. 2017. *Computer—Game—Worlds*. Zürich/Berlin: Diaphanes.

Rankin, Joy Lisi. 2018. *A People's History of Computing in the United States*. Cambridge, MA: Harvard University Press.

Reinefeld, Alexander. 2006. "Entwicklung der Spielbaum-Suchverfahren: Von Zuses Schachhirn zum modernen Schachcomputer." In *Informatik. Aktuelle Themen im historischen Kontext*, edited by Wolfgang Reisig and Johann-Christoph Freytag, 241–273. Berlin/Heidelberg: Springer.

Saukas, Einar, and Digital Prawn. 2014. "Kreativer Missbrauch Oneliner-Programmiertechniken in Sinclair-BASIC." *Retro, Sonderheft BASIC*, 16–17.

Schliesser, Jörg, and bn. 1986 "Duell der Geister." *Happy Computer*, no. 9 (September): 60–64.

Schulz, Thomas. 2016. "To Be (Just) in Time: Die Kunst zeitkritischer Programmierung von Spielen in Maschinensprache." In *Time to Play: Zeit und Computerspiel*, edited by Stefan Höltgen and Jan Claas van Treeck, 120–143. Glückstadt: VWH.

Searle, John R. 1994. "Geist, Gehirn, Programm." In *Künstliche Intelligenz. Philosophische Probleme*, edited by Walther Ch. Zimmerli and Stefan Wolf, 232–266. Stuttgart: Reclam.

Smith, Michael G. 1983. *Simons' Basic: 114 Additional Programming Commands*. Frankfurt a. M.: Commodore.

Spital, I., R. Perry, W. Poel, and C. Lawson. 1985. *Amstrad CPC 6128 User Instruction*. Brentwood: AMSOFT. http://txt3.de/basicsound12.

Troise, Blake. 2020. "The 1-Bit Instrument: The Fundamentals of 1-Bit Synthesis, Their Implementational Implications, and Instrumental Possibilities." *Journal of Sound and Music in Games* 1 (1): 44–74.

Turing, Alan M. 1936. "On Computable Numbers, with an Application to the Entscheidungsproblem." *Proceedings of the London Mathematical Society* (Series 2), no. 42, 230–265.

Vickers, Steven. 1983. *Sinclair ZX Spectrum. BASIC Programming*. 2nd ed. Cambridge: Sinclair Research.

Zimmerman, Eric. 2009. "Gaming Literacy: Game Design as a Model for Literacy in the Twenty-First Century." In *The Video Game Theory Reader 2*, edited by Bernard Perron and Mark J. P. Wolf, 23–32. New York/London: Routledge.

SECTION 3

PERCEPTION AND PSYCHOLOGY

CHAPTER 13

AMBIGUITY AND VAGUENESS IN VIDEO GAME SOUND

MARK GRIMSHAW-AAGAARD

Introduction

The problem with ambiguity is that its meaning is difficult to pin down. This could have serious and potentially harmful consequences, according to the Stoics, because the use (or misuse) of ambiguity has ethical and moral implications for the welfare of the persons involved (Atherton 1993, 132–133). The eradication of ambiguity is one of the purposes of a language's rules of syntax and grammar,[1] and so, for the Stoics, ambiguity was a part of a discussion of dialectics, dealing "with the σημαινόμενα [signified] of linguistic items [because] ambiguity is by definition a linguistic phenomenon" (132–133). Indeed, this categorization of ambiguity has been maintained in the modern era, in English at least, as demonstrated by the word's definition in the *Oxford English Dictionary*: "([O]f language) having more than one meaning—unclear because not distinguishing between alternatives."

And yet, despite the best efforts of language teachers, grammarians, and lexicographers to strangle it at birth, ambiguity not only persists and thrives as a tool for mischievous, iconoclastic, or even dishonest politicians, diplomats, comedians, authors, playwrights, and poets[2] it is also applied to nonlinguistic areas too. In the field that concerns this chapter—video game sound—ambiguity is an ill-defined tool for description and a tool for design, although I reserve judgment on whether its use has potentially harmful consequences. It is also a means for the player to engage with the video game world. Sound as a perception is multimodal (even speech exhibits this), and the ultimate percept, and any meaning ascribed to it, depends on other modalities, such as vision, so how sound is ambiguous, and how to utilize such ambiguity, is a lot more difficult to pin down than its written-down variety.

As I note elsewhere (Grimshaw-Aagaard 2019, 106), vagueness is also generally viewed negatively, especially in the natural sciences. One might even say that the purpose of the natural sciences is to eradicate vagueness through precision and measurement systems. And yet, vagueness is wonderfully resistant to such purpose, and persists even in the building blocks of the natural sciences[3]—including those branches concerned with sound and hearing (acoustics and psychoacoustics).[4]

The metaphorical descriptors we employ in both everyday and professional usage are equally characterized by vagueness (see Grimshaw-Aagaard 2019; Walther-Hansen 2019). Instrumental tone, for example, is often characterized by such metaphors. Who, having learned to play a wind instrument, has not been pleaded with by a patient (hopefully!) music teacher to develop a warm, round tone? At what point, though, does a cold sound become a warm sound, and, if a sound is not round (whatever *that* precisely means) is it shapeless, spiky, angular, or even square? Like ambiguity, vagueness is a fact of (human) life, and rather than attempt to root them out in video game sound design through, for instance, the pursuit of realism (see chapter 43 and chapter 44 this volume for more on realism), the possibilities they offer to enhance player experience and presence in the game should instead be welcomed with open arms.

One final introductory note: I am aware of the perils that might arise in transferring concepts and terminology from one domain to another that is significantly different. One should bear in mind that the concepts and terminology were devised for a specific domain (in the case of ambiguity, linguistics), and so do not easily transfer to the other. A case in point is the use of film sound analysis tools for the analysis of video game sound, a fine example being the concept of *diegesis* as applied to cinema and film sound. At first sight, there is much in common between the two audiovisual mediums, and it might seem a simple task to adapt Chion's (1994, 73) definition of nondiegetic sound in cinema—"sound whose supposed sound source is not only absent from the image but is also external to the story world"—to video game sound. Thus, a video game music track, the volume of which is typically independently (to the sound FX) controllable by the player, might be deemed nondiegetic while the sound FX of the game would be classified as diegetic. The problem with video games, though, is the much greater degree of interactivity in comparison to film and the consequently nonlinear nature of most video games. Thus, in many cases the music changes according to the actions of the player (an early example is the accelerando of *Space Invaders*' [Taito 1978] simple theme). Where the player takes on the role of a diegetic character, there are many sound FX that are ambiguous in their diegesis: is the "humiliation!" sound effect of *Quake III Arena* (id Software 1999) intended for the player only, and thus nondiegetic, or is it for the character, and thus diegetic (indeed, through presence, *is* the player the character)? Such issues in conceptual transfer have led several video game sound theorists to adapt the terminology of diegesis (see Grimshaw 2008; Jørgensen 2009, for example) or eschew it altogether (see also chapter 45 this volume). Such adaptation may well be necessary in the case of ambiguity and vagueness when investigating their applicability to video game sound, but it remains necessary to first ascertain the use of concepts as defined in other fields because there, broadly speaking, is where they first arose.

In what follows, I base my thinking on the framework I describe in chapter 47 this volume. I direct the reader there for a full presentation but, briefly, the framework models presence and provides definitions of terminology, some of which I use here such as *potential*, *self*, and *externality*, of which *salient externality* provides the sensable potential that is available to the self with which to perceptually model that externality. This model is an *environment*, populated with percepts fashioned through sensation and cognition, in which artifacts from externality have *other-presence* (to the self) and in which the self can become present, providing a means to act within and upon externality. The *world* is the self's long-term memory, which, through cognition, aids in modeling salient externality, and which is constantly supplemented through the self's *reality* (the current experience of the model environment).

In this chapter, I concentrate on ambiguity and vagueness in video game sound FX rather than music or dialogue (see also chapter 46 this volume for more on ambiguity and fear). It is not my intention to provide a thorough accounting of ambiguity and vagueness regarding video game sound, nor does space provide for it. Instead, I provide a preliminary framework for such accounting by turning to the concepts of ambiguity, as applied in linguistics, and the problem of vagueness when it comes to measurement and categories in the natural sciences and everyday usage. I begin with a brief note on ambivalence, explaining why I discard it as a focus of my discussion here. I then summarize some of the important and, to my mind, relevant thinking on ambiguity and vagueness, before discussing the relationship between the two concepts. I close by applying the concepts and terminology previously brought to light to video game sound, as a means both to analyze sound and as a design tool for sound.

A Brief Note on Ambivalence

Perhaps even more so than with vagueness, ambiguity is often confused with ambivalence. It is a mistake to do so, because, fundamentally, ambivalence is about coexisting contradiction, which ambiguity is not. An ambivalent statement displays its contradiction proudly on its sleeve, and a good example of this is the oxymoron. Horn (2006) provides several examples, including: *make haste slowly*, *living death*, *cruel kindness*, and *true lies*. Another example of ambivalence which Horn provides that is not oxymoronic, but is no less contradictory for it, is Zerlina's response to Don Giovanni (in the 1787 eponymous opera by Mozart): "Vorrei e non vorrei."

A statement such as: "I am ambivalent about politics" might betray a cavalier insouciance about events on which one's life floats, but it would be wrong to suggest that lack of concern is a defining characteristic of ambivalence. Zerlina's utterance (roughly, "I want to and I don't want to") betrays the flux of contrasting emotions she finds herself experiencing, and the concerned indecision she feels, between moral forbearance and lustful desire; choosing between one or the other would have all-too-clear consequences whatever the choice. Like ambiguity, ambivalence also has its comic uses. Horn gives the classic example of "military intelligence," which, falling on the right ears, would be oxymoronic. And, here, the ambivalent statement, in the right context, can also show ambiguity as in the statement: "The decision to invade Iraq was based on military intelligence."[5]

Thus, while ambivalence is not ambiguity, and can be distinguished by its all-too apparent inherent contradiction, it can provide the basis for ambiguity. There is also little vagueness per se about ambivalence until one begins to unnecessarily unpack the ambivalent statement in the hunt for vagueness: I could question what is "military" and, particularly, how "intelligence" is defined, but, while I might indeed uncover a certain vagueness, this does not elucidate further the ambivalence.

What Is Ambiguity?

There is neither space nor good reason in this chapter to fully elaborate the conceptions and uses of ambiguity found in linguistics. I leave it to others more expert in this area than I and direct the interested reader to the excellent and amusing overview found in the *Stanford Encyclopedia of Philosophy* (Sennett 2011) and its related article on vagueness (Sorensen 1997). What I provide here is a summary of some (but not all) of the main types of linguistic ambiguity as a means to then test their efficacy in the field of video game sound. I should stress (a) that the vast majority of recent work on ambiguity relates to language;[6] (b) that linguistic ambiguity research tends to concentrate on the written word—the disambiguating effects of speech patterns and, especially, gestures are often overlooked; and (c) that much of the recent work on linguistic ambiguity relates to the English language—ambiguities found there are not necessarily transferrable to other languages, even those that are closely related.[7]

Sennett (2011) identifies several forms of linguistic ambiguity, of which I think three are generalizable enough to be worth investigating for their potential when discussing video game sound. In all cases, the ambiguity can arise through different potential meanings, and it is this multiplicity of potential meaning that is defining of ambiguity. First, *lexical ambiguity* arises from the existence of homographs, homophones, and homonyms, which can take several forms:[8] words that are spelled the same but pronounced differently (homograph); words that are pronounced the same but spelled differently (homophone); and words identical in spelling and pronunciation but having different meanings (homonym).[9] An example of the first type of potential cause of lexical ambiguity, the homograph, would be the word *axes*, a noun which can have different meanings depending on its pronunciation. The written word lacks the explicit pronunciation that speech provides: to write *he drew the axes on the paper* is potentially ambiguous when written but not when spoken, in which case, assuming correct pronunciation, the meaning is clear as either axes relating to mechanical rotations or a Cartesian graph (for example) or axes as tools or weapons. The strict homophones—words spelled differently but pronounced the same—are perhaps the more common causes of lexical ambiguity in speech, and, at first sight, perhaps of most interest in the context of video game sound. In English, *to*, *too*, and *two* are homophones, and, while there is no lexical ambiguity when written as *I want you to*, *I want you too*, or *I want you two*, they can cause confusion when spoken. To speak the phrase *I want you two* could be understood variously as: *I want you to (do that)*; *I want you too (as you want me)*; or *I want you two (the both of you)*. Finally, the homonym can be exemplified by the word *duck*: the written or spoken phrase *duck down* (which, coincidentally, uses two homonyms) can mean either an instruction to take cover or the soft underfeathers of a duck so beloved of duvet manufacturers.[10] Metaphors deserve a special, if brief, mention. The phrase *he kicked the bucket* is similar to a homonym but is an entire phrase that is ambiguous between literal (he applied his foot with some force to the pail) or metaphorical (he died).

Second, *syntactical ambiguity* can derive from word order and grammar. Sennett (2011) gives several examples including *the chicken is ready to eat*. I prefer to use the example of *the dog is ready to eat*, because, to my European sensibilities, it shows the importance of context—she might well be shocked by the outcome of uttering that phrase were Paris Hilton to travel to the Korean peninsula with a pair of pampered Pomeranians stashed in her clutch purse. Pronouns, in English certainly, can be a cause of syntactical ambiguity as noted in an earlier endnote. Articles, too, can introduce such ambiguity as in the phrase *everyone loves to play the piano* (pianos generally or that specific one there, over in the corner?).

Third, *pragmatic ambiguity* relates to the precise meanings of actions, in particular those actions prescribed by verbs. There is the old joke *how does my dog smell?*[11] but, developing the example given above, I could introduce pragmatic ambiguity in addition to the syntactical ambiguity, as in *everyone can play the piano*. Here, "can" might refer to a utopian wish, what is allowed,[12] or to the abilities possessed by those in the room. Another form of pragmatic ambiguity is presuppositional ambiguity in which the reader or listener is left to infer a pre-existing state or context and in so doing resolve the ambiguity (correctly or not). The lexically ambiguous homophone "too" can equally well provide this form of ambiguity, as in the phrase *I love you too*. Bach (1982, 593) identifies four different meanings, the resolution of each of which depends on different presuppositions. The meaning of *I love you too*, said by Jack to Jill, depends on a variety of prior knowledge: like Jill loves him; that Jack also loves someone else; like Bill, he also loves Jill; and Jack is in a love-hate relationship with Jill (a resolution of ambiguity that uncovers an ambivalence). From such presuppositional ambiguity, relationships flourish or flounder.

WHAT IS VAGUENESS?

"Vagueness" is often confused with, or incorrectly interchangeably used as, "ambiguity." Additionally, Sorensen (1997) notes:

> Vagueness is standardly defined as the possession of borderline cases. For example, "tall" is vague because a man who is 1.8 meters in height is neither clearly tall nor

> clearly non-tall. No amount of conceptual analysis or empirical investigation can settle whether a 1.8 meter man is tall. Borderline cases are inquiry resistant. . . . [Indeed, the] inquiry resistance typically recurses. For, in addition to the unclarity of the borderline case, there is normally unclarity as to where the unclarity begins. . . . Consequently, "borderline case" has borderline cases. This higher order vagueness seems to show that "vague" is vague. (Sorenson 1997)

One might add to this example of male human height that even the choice of measurement unit potentially adds further vagueness: 1.8 m might well be an agreed-on standard for tallness in continental Europe,[13] but this equates to 5'10.8661" in those countries doggedly sticking to imperial measures such as post-Brexit Britain. Perhaps the British prefer the neater and easier-to-remember border of 6'00", but this equates to 1.8288 m.[14]

The understanding of time is especially vague and subject to a variety of susceptible-to-vagueness measurements. If you cannot decide, to the satisfaction of all, just at what point dawn can be said to have occurred or started, the definition of "dawn" can be said to be vague—there is a zone between night and day comprising further borderline cases of predawn, dawn, and postdawn, and no argument will conclusively resolve the matter. You might, in an effort to try to resolve the vagueness, impose all sorts of natural or artificial thresholds: the first sight of the sun; a certain luminance expressed in lux; the revelation of the dawn chorus; 06:00 hours; and so forth. Yet such attempts will always be confounded by many factors including astronomical effects on sunrise, atmospheric conditions, or a lack of birds in the vicinity. And scientific attempts to measure the earth and its place in the solar system will always, in this regard at least, be undermined by the exigencies of life and a lack of precision: summertime or wintertime; decisions as to which side of the International Date Line one's Pacific Island nation should lie; is 06:00 hours equivalent to 05:59.9999 hours or 06:00.0001 hours; by my watch or yours? What all these factors, and the many others I have not listed, exhibit is that the border between night and day is not at all clear. In being vague, not only does the border between night and day have borderline cases (*perhaps it's dawn, perhaps it's not—let's wait another five, maybe ten minutes to be sure*) but the threshold's definition itself is plagued by borderline cases (which measurement do we take? do three birds a chorus make or nine? religious observance or workday requirements? and so on).

The question of vagueness arises from attempts to categorize; that is, categorical statements that *he is tall* or *dawn has started* possess an inherent vagueness because of the existence of borderline cases (uncertainty), and because the choice of "tall" (as opposed to "short") or "has started" (instead of "has not started") rests on an assessment made against a threshold that itself is open to question regarding its position on a continuum and/or its precision.

One must also bear in mind that standards and thresholds change through time. A case in point is the definition of the meter: defined during the period of the French Revolution (as one ten-millionth of the earth's quarter meridian passing through Paris from the North Pole to the Equator[15]) and proudly standardized and cast as a platinum rod a few years later, the meter provided the measure of all things metric for almost

200 years (despite the original rod being replaced several times with ever-more accurate versions). In 1960, the meter was defined anew based on the wavelength of light emitted from a krypton-86 atom, and, in 1983, further redefined as the length of the path that light in a vacuum travels over the period 1/299,792,458 secs. (see Alder [2004] for an engaging and illuminating history of the meter).[16]

Regarding the adage that, if it cannot be measured, it does not exist, one could take the nihilistic view that no one thing can actually be accurately measured (because there is no such thing as an accurate measurement), and, if it cannot be accurately measured, it cannot be measured at all: ergo, no things exist. This view, however, would neither be very pragmatic nor sufficient to allow action and all the busy life that springs from that. The essentiality of existential pragmatism is something I return to later. Suffice to say that, though vagueness is omnipresent and inescapable, ambiguity is not (precisely because species, including humans, are essentially existentially pragmatic).

The Relationship between Ambiguity and Vagueness

Where precision and accuracy might be viewed as the bone fides of a rational, scientific mode of inquiry—the product of a misguided and obsessive desire to compartmentalize and categorize and carve up externality into bite-size, manipulable units—our everyday experience of externality is one of vagueness and ambiguity; externality is ready-to-hand rather than present-at-hand (see Heidegger 1962). Other than in the artificial and scaffolded confines of research institutions and textbooks, we do not normally describe a sound with physics and acoustics terminology. It would seem very strange, in describing it to a friend, to list all the acoustic parameters of the small waterfall I am listening to while I write this: the variable fundamental frequency, the constantly changing amplitude envelope of the complex waveform, the frequency and amplitude envelopes of the sound wave's overtones, which overtones are present, how the sound wave's partials interact with the material space of externality, *that* resultant complex waveform and so on, and so on, and so on. Were it even possible to precisely so describe the sound wave (and I would argue that, even in a laboratory setting, with all the technology one could wish for at one's disposal, or with the most beautiful and exacting mathematical formulae,[17] it simply is not possible to replicate *exactly* in some other form the complexity and variation of this naturally occurring waveform over time), my friend would have drifted off to sleep long before I finished or would have wandered away, preferring instead to talk to a wall. Far better, and more economical in time and for ensuring continued friendship, to, with just a few words, paint an impressionistic daub that adequately describes the sound of the waterfall and its effect on me, allowing my friend's experience and imagination to fill in the gaps (Grimshaw-Aagaard 2019): a pleasant, watery tinkling in the background. Alternatively, I could just say "waterfall" and, with that metonym, have done with it.

This utilitarian vagueness is fundamental to the formation of percepts in my environment, which formation and constant re-forming operates under time pressure. Humans (and our antecedents) would have stood no chance were we to have evolved to take our time, in a present-to-hand manner, to model and assess salient externality, nor would the saber-toothed tiger have allowed it. It is enough, and often more conducive to life, to be able to assess something quickly as long or short, large or small, distant or near, safe or threatening without recourse each time to a tape measure. This is what I mean by essential existential pragmatism. Our sensory apparatuses are significant aids to this end: the overwhelming nature of externality is dramatically reduced and made manageable by the inability of sensory apparatuses (of whatever species) to sense potential beyond those that sensory thresholds and horizons allow to be sensed (see von Uexküll 1992; Campbell 1974; Walther-Hansen and Grimshaw-Aagaard 2020).

Ambiguity, too, provides the means to other-presence for the percepts of my environment. Where vagueness is resistant to resolution, ambiguity can be resolved (Sennett 2011). In fact, it invites resolution, as in ascribing one meaning from two or more possibilities. This resolution might not be the correct one within a particular frame of reference—as in the case of the McGurk Effect, where the resolution is incorrect within the terms of reference provided by acoustics—and the first resolution might be corrected as a wider context of meaning unveils itself, but a resolution *is* quickly and efficiently sought for. A percept is vague, were I to attempt to describe it, but it is the result of an often multimodally aided resolution of ambiguity.

A sound wave travels from a loudspeaker in a stereo system to my ears. In combination with a probably different sound wave from the other loudspeaker, I might, according to acoustics and psychoacoustics, localize the apparent sound wave source on one or the other loudspeaker or perhaps somewhere in-between. Yet, in the context of a first-person perspective video game, this does not make sense. My world, from which my cognition directs the construction of my environment, leads me to suppose that the sound wave source is somewhere within the game—perhaps that flash of light appearing like a muzzle explosion in the top right quadrant of my computer monitor. In the context of the first-person shooter I am playing, I localize the sound perception within my environment on the perception of a flash of light, and this, with an experienced understanding of the context leads to the percept in my environment of an enemy lurking in the bushes ahead and to the right who is firing at me. The environment's dynamic nature requires an inquisitive self to assess salient externality's potential. That the percept is fundamentally multimodal (the actualization of sound waves and light waves) aids in a faster resolution of the ambiguity of meaning—designing a video game for sighted players where one primary modality such as vision is severely restricted and providing only audio, can deny efficient production of other-presence, leading to an unsettling experience, and this is a favorite trick of survival-horror video game designers.

The main difference, then, between ambiguity and vagueness is one of resolution: indeed, ambiguity *begs* to be resolved, while vagueness cannot be fully resolved, and the inherent vagueness of its thresholds is itself often infinitely recursive. Vagueness *can* in some cases be somewhat resolved by recourse to comparison, but this simply shifts the onus of vagueness from the thing under discussion to the vague threshold and vague characteristic(s) through which we attempt to categorize the thing. For example, I and others might well describe myself as tall, and this might well be generally accepted as true if the threshold for tallness is agreed at 1.8 m (or even 1.8288 m), but can I be thought of as tall either by myself or others if the threshold shifts to 2 m or I am surrounded by giants? Suddenly, I am now short.

The resolution of ambiguity comes with the use of information extraneous to the ambiguity. In language, this information is what is already known—that is, what has been written or said before (if it pertains to the ambiguity in question)—what comes immediately after, or general knowledge of the context beyond the specific writing. Thus, *we've just been for a long walk in the park and the dog is now ready to eat* offers the possibility of correct resolution,[18] *he kicked the bucket at an early age, succumbing to tuberculosis just before his twentieth birthday* is unambiguous (assuming knowledge of the metaphor), while *everyone can play the piano like Liszt* is a little more specific (if wishful thinking). Speech, especially with sight of the speaker or the surrounding area, can add further information to resolve the ambiguity: *duck down* in a war zone is obviously a command; with a softening of my eyes, the correct and wisest meaning of *I love you too* is conveyed; and resolution is somewhat achieved in the case of the statement *everyone can play the piano* if I point to the piano in the corner. Of course, I could change the words or add clarifying words—*he drew the Viking axes on the paper*—but then there is no potential ambiguity to begin with.

Ambiguity and Vagueness in Video Game Sound

I start with the assertion that externality is inherently meaningless—it requires an inquisitive self to provide meaning to it. Thus, there is no meaning in a sound wave, but there *is* meaning in sound (sound is a perception whereas the sound wave is simply potential in externality—see Grimshaw and Garner 2015). This is true also for the potential provided by a video game, the one significant difference to our everyday externality being complexity—a video game is limited for many reasons (mainly technical) in what it can provide, and so its externality is less complex.[19] The inquisitive self, or, as Heidegger (1962) would put it, the concerned being of *Dasein*, forms meaningless externality into meaningful environment through the construction of interlinked percepts. These percepts are fashioned multimodally (even the sound of an unseen footstep behind me might, from my experience, be the percept of a foot in an army boot taking a step on gravel—so taking in the visual modality) from unimodal perceptions arising from the conjoined actualization of potential as sensation and the cognitive use of the self's memory store, its world. This innate inquisitiveness or concern drives the meaning-making that is the basis for the weaving of percepts into a workable environment: the environment is sense made of externality, the locus of the self's presence and the other-presence of salient externality's artifacts.

Remembering that ambiguity requires resolution while vagueness resists it, I am now at a point where I can make a preliminary analysis of video game sound through these lenses. Taking a typical first-person shooter (FPS) game as an exemplar, my salient externality is one of multiple sound waves and light waves that, in themselves, have no meaning. In this age of multimedia, and after millennia of exposure to pictorial representation (the fundamentals, at least, of which are part of the self's world), it is very difficult to escape its perceptual conventions. Thus, while playing, I am able to form image perceptions from the light waves from the monitor, because, the coloring of the pixels is so arranged by the game engine as to present light and shade, conformation to artistic perspective, gestalt foreground and background, outlines of shapes that move across the screen, and so forth, and these, through perceptual conventions indelibly imprinted on my world, become buildings, trees, weapons, characters, and so on in the self's environment. It is thus that the light waves are transformed into meaning.

Waiting to receive these images are sound perceptions (see chapter 47 this volume on presence for the argument that sound perceptions are formed before image perceptions from the same event). Once again, convention plays a role in ascribing meaning to sound waves, as do the experience and knowledge stored in the self's world—a particular sound wave's amplitude envelope thus denotes an explosion of some type that, through the knowledge that I am playing an FPS game (of which I have experience), might be narrowed down to the firing of a gun, or the continual high pitched sound wave I sense might become the perception of twittering (ultimately, a percept of birds). Equally, more modern listening conventions allow me to overcome Schafer's (1994, 88–91) notion of schizophonia, so that the sound waves emanating from my loudspeakers are, through an act of ventriloquism (cf., Chion's [1994, 62–63] *synchresis*), sourced on the patterns of light issuing from the monitor.

In terms of vagueness, then, the percepts so formed are, like all percepts, vague. I could not possibly detail all the features of the gun percept (image and sound perception as one) I experience, nor would I wish to, because I must act in the moment and make decisions on which my character's life depends. It is enough that the percept is gun-like, and that allows me to be present in my environment and to act within and on the externality of the game. The essential existential pragmatism that characterizes life exists even within the safe confines of the game.

The percepts are ambiguous too. It might seem strange to claim that the meaninglessness of externality becomes an ambiguous percept, but the ambiguity is not devoid of meaning; the ambiguous percept simply has multiple potential meanings. Within the game's externality, is it an event that is far from or nearby to my character? Which of the many guns available in the game might it be? Does it represent a danger, or is the percept resolved to a teammate firing in support?[20] The resolution of ambiguity comes from comparison to other percepts arising from the game. If I have another percept of a teammate just by me, and possibly the percept of a muzzle flash (from the perception of a bright light and knowledge of what it might represent), then the ambiguity can be resolved in that direction by merging the percepts into one (teammate firing), in another direction if I have the near-simultaneous percepts of a grunt from my character and decreasing health status displayed on the screen.

None of this is to suggest that sound designers can willy-nilly supply any audio file and trust that players will ascribe (the correct) meaning to it. Rather, I suggest that sound designers need not pursue realism and authenticity to the nth degree, providing, instead, audio files that are close enough in form to the source they represent while still requiring an active inquisitiveness from the player's self. The obvious does not engage query and, indeed can provoke boredom with deleterious consequences for presence.

While my focus here is on sound FX in video games, briefly, it is easy enough at first glance to apply the framework of linguistic ambiguity outlined above to music. Taking music as developed in the European tradition, such music has a grammar and syntax as language does, the rules of which, as with language, can be pushed and stretched into ambiguity. Many of Debussy's compositions (e.g., "Nuages" 1899) display a lexical ambiguity in the context of functional harmony. Syntactical ambiguity might be provided for by chord inversion (although, such tonal ambiguity might be grouped with musical lexical ambiguity). Cross-rhythms and -meter and devices such as interrupted cadences bear clear parallels to the workings of pragmatic ambiguity in language. In merely drawing some prima facie parallels, I will not take this further: ambiguity in music is a large and specialized topic (see, for example, Thomson 1983; Cross 2005) and my focus is elsewhere. But finally, I should mention that it can often be difficult to determine the diegesis of music heard in films and video games. A favorite example is the Rommel level in the first-person shooter *Urban Terror* (2000–2022), in which the player hears Edith Piaf's song "Tu Es Partout." Is it nondiegetic or diegetic? Once it is determined that the music emanates from a gramophone in a bombed-out building, it can be determined as diegetic, the music being used as a scene-setting sound effect.

Finding parallels to linguistic ambiguity in sound FX is more difficult, because sound FX as a class lacks a (thoroughly defined) grammar and syntax to be played with. This is perhaps because, in a clear difference to language and music, which can be viewed as somewhat self-standing, sound FX require the explicit multimodal context in which to be interpreted. This is even the case for a sequence of sound FX alone, such as Andrew Sach's *The Revenge* (1978) which was presented as "[a] play for radio without words"[21]—in the expectation of a narrative (it is a radio play), the listener knits the sound FX together within that framework. Video games, typically, have the advantage of vision: expectations arise from experience of the genre or even prior playing of the game in question, in addition to any narrative there might be. Thus, at first sight, the ambiguity of sound perceptions formed from sound FX is one of lexical ambiguity, in which the inherent ambiguity of a sound perception is resolved into one percept within the environment and one meaning (general though it might be) as the image is sensed and perceived and fused to the sound.

As a lexical ambiguity, the perception of a video game sound effect might be classed as a homophone (spelled differently but pronounced the same). In spoken language, for any one word, pronunciation is never the same (e.g., regional variations), and so there is a certain vagueness, as there is no one precise pronunciation (as with other modes of vagueness—is one short or tall?), the pronunciation need only be close enough to a hazy, unexpressed standard. So too with sound FX, where pronunciation might be equated to form or structure of the sound wave (length, amplitude envelope, frequency envelope, and so on). As a homophone, the sound effect must be close enough in its sounding to be matched to knowledge in the self's world (memory), but the content of the form (its spelling) can be substantially different (its frequency spectra, for example). I do not suggest that the sound effect's spelling can be radically different—as with linguistic homophones (e.g., "to," "too," "two"), there must be enough similarity for the pronunciation to be executed effectively. This is how Foley sound design works its magic, and why so many sources can be used for the sound of footsteps on snow or a gun. In terms of vagueness, there is no one, archetypal definition of a gun sound effect (though we all recognize it when we hear it). Narrowing down to a recording of, for instance, a Franchi SPAS-12 shotgun—as all sound waves from any one source are affected by the medium, various surroundings, and signal processing used for effect in cinema and video games, there is still no one, archetypal sound wave of the Franchi SPAS-12. The vagueness is supremely resistant to resolution.

The homophone is the most easily identifiable and useful ambiguity in sound FX design.[22] Bearing in mind my previous admonition against wholesale transfer of terminology and concepts from one domain of knowledge to another, it is more difficult, if not ill advised, to attempt to describe sound FX as either syntactically or pragmatically ambiguous. Regarding syntactical ambiguity, a sound designer might reverse the order of the three sound FX *tank engine starting*, *tank engine ticking over*, *tank engine revving as it moves off* to *tank engine revving as it moves off*, *tank engine ticking over*, *tank engine starting*, but, in the context of the game (its images and action [*tank starts up then drives away*]), while syntactically ambiguous (like a change in word order), it would be nonsensical so is unlikely to be used. Pragmatic ambiguity in sound FX can be found in the example I gave earlier (*an enemy firing at me or a teammate supporting me?*) and can be resolved. Because pragmatic ambiguity relies on ambiguity of the verb or action described, it might perhaps have its greatest use in humor—the recording of a duck quacking applied to a shotgun firing in an FPS game, for example.

Concluding Thoughts

What I have offered here is an initial attempt to provide a means to analyze video game sound, and thoughts on how to design such sound, through the twin lenses of ambiguity and vagueness. As stated earlier, I have not set out to provide an all-encompassing framework for this. For example, it might well be that the inclusion of the inherent physiological vagueness of our hearing would be worthwhile—such as the role of just noticeable difference (in the inner ear) in discriminating between two different frequencies—but I think this is probably more relevant to a discussion of music than sound FX. What I hope I have provided is a start to a wider discussion on the importance of ambiguity and vagueness in video game sound design. This has importance in the modeling of the game's externality as a workable environment in the consciousness of the player—percepts in the environment are vague but utilitarian, enabling the player to function in the game world, and arise in the environment through the efficient sifting of externality's inherent meaninglessness into resolvable ambiguities.

On a final note, I should like to mention an inherent Achilles heel in all ambiguity not least in ambiguous sound FX in video games. One of my favorite examples (spoiler alert) of an ambiguous sound effect is one found in *Left 4 Dead* (2008). Those new to the game, on first hearing this wonderful example, might well assume it represents not danger but the crying of a young girl and, being the noble hero that they are, will rush to this pitiful creature's aid. Little do they realize that the pathetic crying is a cunning trap set by the witch, one of the game's more powerful and initially difficult-to-overcome enemies, luring the innocent player into her deadly embrace. This shows the power of ambiguity to mislead and sow confusion but also its weakness—all this power is lost forever as the ambiguity is resolved in a vicious spatter of blood, and the sound effect, from that point on, takes on a different meaning. Once bitten, twice shy.

Notes

1. Indeed, one of the tasks for editors of handbooks such as this is to root out all ambiguity of phrasing and meaning in contributors' chapters. In this, we hope we have been successful.
2. All such and similar professions are dishonest in one sense, hence the Stoics' concern.
3. Despite its powerfully used claims for precision, accuracy, and, indeed, truth, the dirty secret of the natural sciences is that its foundations, its measurements, and classifications, are fundamentally vague.
4. See Grimshaw-Aagaard (2019, 107–108) for a brief critique of the American National Standards (Accredited Standards Committee S1, Acoustics 2013) definitions of "reverberation room" and "live room."
5. That the decision was also based on intelligence from other services only demonstrates further the humorous ambiguity of the ambivalence. Further, suggesting that the "intelligence was faulty" would be an oxymoronic form of ambivalence. See (Russell 2002) for the role of military and CIA intelligence in political decisions to go to war.
6. It is, of course, a term that is common currency in other fields of research such as psychology, artificial intelligence, statistics—anywhere where the meaning or categorization of something, given the context, is doubtful or potentially multiple. Ambiguity of categorization is more properly vagueness, such as, for example, when an AI-driven technology like a self-driving car must make a decision as to whether an object on the road ahead is a danger or not.
7. For example, the syntactical ambiguity of the English phrase *he loves his mother* does not exist in Danish because Danish syntax forces one meaning or the other—*han elsker sin mor* (his own mother) or *han elsker hans mor* (some other male's mother). In this case, the possessive pronouns (*sin* and *hans*—both translated as *his* in English) provide the disambiguation and are syntactically required to clarify the semantics of the phrase. It would not make sense to state *han elsker sin mor* about Mads while pointing at (an unrelated) Søren's mother. Perhaps this syntactic rigor is why Danish, at least me as a native English speaker, seems to have less opportunity for humor.

8. There are other forms that exist, such as words with variant spellings but the same meaning as found across differences in US/UK English (e.g., color/colour), but there is not necessarily ambiguity to be found. There is, of course, only one correct way to spell whisky.
9. There is a fair bit of confusion, even in dictionaries, about the precise meaning of the three terms and the differences between them. For example, Merriam-Webster gives the following definition for homonym: "[A] word that is spelled *and* pronounced like another word but is different in meaning" (my italics). The entry then proceeds to confound the issue with contradictory examples which suggest that homophones and homographs are all instances of homonyms, the respective examples given being *their* and *there* (pronounced the same *but* spelled differently) and *lead* (the spelling of several lexical entries whose meanings depend upon different pronunciations and/or context—one a verb, one a noun or adjective denoting position, and one a noun denoting the metal) (https://www.merriam-webster.com/dictionary/homonym, accessed November 19, 2021.)
10. Stretching the imagination just a little, there is a third meaning which comes from the laconic command to a hunting dog to go fetch that duck which has just been shot down.
11. My dog smells with his nose of course!
12. Strict English would avoid the ambiguity with the word "may" replacing "can."
13. Of this, I have no idea, but, since I am above the threshold, the supposition suits me. It is more likely that qualitative statements of height differ from country to country and are modified by factors such as age, gender, national nutrition standards and changes in public health, and so on.
14. If, on the basis of this, one were to claim that post-Brexit Britain is a nation of pygmies, then this would be understandable if not a little unfair (both ambiguities are entirely intentional).
15. As this standard was chosen *prior* to the physical production of a meter and subsequent measuring tools based on it, when the circumference of the earth came to be measured, it was found that the meter was not in fact a meter by that definition.
16. One can only imagine the despair of those setting the definition that they had to come up with one that was as close as possible to the previous definition. Thus the 1/299,792,458 secs. rather than the neater and easier to remember 1/300,000,000 secs. Imagine the chaos in international measurement if the latter had been chosen in 1983! One begins to understand why Alice's adventures could only ever have been written by a mathematician, as it is all too easy to disappear down a rabbit hole when discussing the vagueness and vagarity of measurement.
17. The mathematical definition of an overtone (defined as a sine wave component of a complex waveform) is $y(t) = A\sin(2\pi ft + \varphi)$ (taken from https://en.wikipedia.org/wiki/Sine_wave, accessed November 23, 2021). A complex waveform, such as a waterfall, has many, many such overtones, each varying over time.
18. The glimmer of a possibility. There is still the chance of a gastronomic misunderstanding—perhaps the dog has been roasting to perfection during our walk.
19. I might also add that even a video game striving for emulation of another externality (a racing game, for example) can only ever be a simulation not least because video games are severely limited in the modalities they can provide (no smell of petrol fumes, for instance).
20. In this, I must trust the intentions and accuracy of that teammate.

21. See https://genome.ch.bbc.co.uk/731c3868560546f1ab8369520c0297fe (accessed November 29, 2021). *The Revenge* can be heard at https://soundcloud.com/bronaanorb/andrew-sachs-the-revenge (accessed November 29, 2021).
22. I might even claim that the homophone *enables* sound design.

References

Accredited Standards Committee S1, Acoustics. 2013. *Acoustic Terminology: ANSI/ASA S1.1-2013*. ANSI. Melville, NY: Acoustical Society of America.

Alder, Ken. 2004. *The Measure of All Things: The Seven-Year Odyssey and Hidden Error That Transformed the World*. London: Abacus.

Atherton, Catherine. 1993. *The Stoics on Ambiguity*. Cambridge Classical Studies. Cambridge: Cambridge University Press.

Bach, Kent. 1982. "Semantic Nonspecificity and Mixed Quantifiers." *Linguistics and Philosophy* 4 (4): 593–605.

Campbell, Donald T. 1974. "Evolutionary Epistemology." In *The Philosophy of Karl Popper*, edited by Paul Arthur Schilpp, 413–463. La Salle, IL: Open Court.

Chion, Michel. 1994. *Audio-Vision: Sound on Screen*. Edited and translated by Claudia Gorbman. New York: Columbia University Press.

Cross, Ian. 2005. "Music and Meaning, Ambiguity and Emotion." In *Musical Communication*, edited by Dorothy Miell, Raymond MacDonald, and David J. Hargreaves, 27–34. New York: Oxford University Press.

Grimshaw, Mark. 2008. *The Acoustic Ecology of the First-Person Shooter: The Player Experience of Sound in the First-Person Shooter Computer Game*. Saarbrücken: Verlag Dr. Mueller.

Grimshaw, Mark, and Tom Alexander Garner. 2015. *Sonic Virtuality: Sound as Emergent Perception*. New York: Oxford University Press.

Grimshaw-Aagaard, Mark. 2019. "The Necessity of Vagueness and Ambiguity to the Imagining of Sound." In *The Oxford Handbook of Sound and Imagination*, edited by Mark Grimshaw-Aagaard, Mads Walther-Hansen, and Martin Knakkergaard, 105–113. New York: Oxford University Press.

Heidegger, Martin. 1962. *Being and Time*. Translated by John Macquarrie and Edward Robinson. Oxford: Blackwell.

Horn, Laurence R. 2006. "Contradiction." In *Stanford Encyclopedia of Philosophy*. Accessed November 16, 2021. https://plato.stanford.edu/entries/contradiction/.

Jørgensen, Kristine. 2009. *A Comprehensive Study of Sound in Computer Games: How Audio Affects Player Action*. Queenston: Edwin Mellen Press.

Left 4 Dead. 2008. Video Game. Valve.

Quake III Arena. 1999. Video Game. Activision.

Russell, Richard L. 2002. "CIA's Strategic Intelligence in Iraq." *Political Science Quarterly* 117 (2): 191–207. https://dx.doi.org/https://doi.org/10.2307/798180.

Sachs, Andrew. 1978. *The Revenge*. United Kingdom: BBC Radio 3.

Schafer, R. Murray. 1994. *The Soundscape: Our Sonic Environment and the Tuning of the World*. Rochester, VT: Destiny Books.

Sennett, Adam. 2011. "Ambiguity." *Stanford Encyclopedia of Philosophy*. Accessed October, 27, 2021. https://plato.stanford.edu/entries/ambiguity/.

Sorensen, Roy. 1997. "Vagueness." *Stanford Encyclopedia of Philosophy*. Accessed October 27. 2021. https://plato.stanford.edu/entries/vagueness/.

Space Invaders. 1978. Video Game. Taito.

Thomson, William. 1983. "Functional Ambiguity in Musical Structures." *Music Perception: An Interdisciplinary Journal* 1 (1): 3–27.

Urban Terror. 2000–2022. Video Game. Silicon Ice.

von Uexküll, Jakob. 1992. "A Stroll through the Worlds of Animals and Men: A Picture Book of Invisible Worlds." *Semiotica* 89 (4): 319–391.

Walther-Hansen, Mads. 2019. "Sound Quality, Language, and Cognitive Metaphors." In *The Oxford Handbook of Sound and Imagination*, edited by Mark Grimshaw-Aagaard, Mads Walther-Hansen, and Martin Knakkergaard, 459–472. New York: Oxford University Press.

Walther-Hansen, Mads, and Mark Grimshaw-Aagaard. 2020. "Don't Extend! Reduce! The Sound Approach to Reality." In *Proceedings of the 15th International Conference on Audio Mostly*, 8–15. https://dl.acm.org/doi/proceedings/10.1145/3411109.

CHAPTER 14

A FUNCTIONAL APPROACH TO THE PSYCHOLOGY OF VIDEO GAME SOUND

TOM A. GARNER

> At first, Stanley assumed he had broken the map, until he heard this narration and realized it was a part of the game's design all along. He then praised the game for its insightful and witty commentary into the nature of video game structure and its examination of structural narrative tropes.
>
> —The Narrator. *The Stanley Parable*. 2011

Introduction

Understanding the psychological relationship between player and video game is the key to good design. However, the components of this relationship do not exist in isolation. Even tracing back to the relative simplicity of the 8-bit era, games were the result of multiple interrelating elements: sound effects, music, graphics, physical interaction, motion, and language. Modern games add further complexity. They layer system on system, with dynamic organization structures. They integrate artificial intelligence, adaptive components, and procedural generation technologies. They may even extend beyond their traditional closed-system boundaries to interact in real time with all kinds of data, potentially moving us toward a model of "system as codesigner." In parallel, academic study of cognition and perception is also increasingly engaging with more integrated, holistic perspectives. Theories of embodied cognition, emergent perception, and user-centered design are finding increasing support from empirical studies and realizing notable successes in practical applications. Furthermore, our understanding of the sensory against the perceptual, top-down processes against bottom-up processes, cognitive state against affective state, and the modalities of experience, is all changing in that such distinctions are now being questioned, despite being long-established. Yet, as many of these lines continue to blur, new lines appear to be forming, based largely on function and task.

I present two central arguments within this chapter. The first is that the nature of video game sound is best-characterized and structured in terms of sound-function, and that this is in alignment with developments in contemporary thought on auditory perception and on cognitive psychology more broadly. The second is that the march of time consistently provides advances in wider technological, theoretical, and cultural contextual factors that can enable new functions of video game sound to emerge, but also more experimental functions to eventually become mainstream. This implies that innovative designers should seek not only to conceptualize video game sound in terms of function but also to expand and push the boundaries of more experimental functions while, crucially, not losing sight of how such designs will integrate into the broader game model.

To discuss the above arguments, the chapter begins with a potted history of game sound, structured by function, tracing key developments from the arcades of the 1970s to the gaming systems of the present day. Following from that, notable developments and prominent theories of auditory perception are reviewed to consider the potential impact of translating such understanding to game sound design. The chapter then closes with a set of recommendations for designers in an effort to elucidate the practical applications of an emergent perspective of auditory perception to game sound design.

The Functions of Sound Throughout the History of Games

From the Top: Player-Action, Feedback, Perceptual Gaps, Immersion, and Fun

When we trace the history of video game landmarks, sound first features at landmark title number three, *Computer Space* (Nutting Associates 1971). While its predecessors *Tennis for Two* and *Spacewar!* (see Graetz 1981) were of the short-lived silent era of video games and accessible only to a limited few, *Computer Space* featured rudimentary sound to complement the graphics and gameplay.[1] Watching the action play out on the screen, it is decidedly difficult at first to ascertain precisely what all of the sounds in *Computer Space* represent. A delightfully crunchy explosion sound can be clearly associated with when the player's vessel or enemy vessels are destroyed. A burst of white noise reliably occurs when the play activates the thrusters of their 16-pixel craft. A high-pitched repeating beep is revealed to represent the single-axis rotational movement of the player's vessel. Another, lower-pitched repeating beep is also present, but its purpose is very difficult to realize. After careful listening it seemingly indicates that the player has launched a pixel-sized missile. Answers on a postcard if you know better.

Despite the limitations in its effectiveness (highly understandable considering the relative lack of sophistication of the underlying technology of the time), *Computer Space* directly demonstrates at least four discrete functions of video game sound. The first is confirmation, or reinforcement, of player-action (the white-noise burst emitted each time the player activates their ship's thrusters). The second is feedback, namely an auditory signifier of a response in the game's state, relevant to the player's actions (the explosion sounds when player/enemy craft are destroyed). The third is perhaps one of the more intriguing, particularly when considering the psychology of sound design for games: filling perceptual gaps. In *Computer Space* the graphical representation of the thrusters is a single line of no more than four pixels, positioned at the base of the craft. While the white-noise burst may not be perceived as the most high-fidelity auditory depiction of a spacecraft thruster, it does present a richer representation than the graphics, thereby helping to fill a potential perceptual gap in the player's understanding. Finally, the sound in *Computer Space* facilitates the perceptual effect of presence by way of immersion. Both presence and immersion are somewhat magnets for semantic argument (see chapter 47 this volume), but the key assertion here is that the use of quite literally any sound within a game stimulates immersion. As Grimshaw (2008, 119) observes, sound "has a real volume and dimensionality that is a 3-dimensional representation of the 2-dimensional representation of the 3-dimensional world of the game." Where the visuals are perceptually located at the screen, game sound reaches out to fill the player's space, thereby immersing them in sound and creating a tacit, sensory bridge to engage presence by drawing the player into the world of the game.

Moving on to landmark title number four, we can observe that *Pong* (Atari 1972) commonly enjoys misattributed status as the first example of video game sound,[2] or, at the very least, accidentally misleading attribution.[3] This is slightly dubious when you observe how *Pong*'s usage of sound is arguably even more rudimentary than its predecessor; consisting of a single tone beep when the pixel-ball hits a player's paddle, a discernibly lower, single-tone beep when the ball hits either vertical edges of the screen, and a quick buzzer, emitted when the ball hits a horizontal edge and constitutes a point being scored (though the harsh tone arguably sounds far more disapproving of the loser, than approving of the winner). In these instances, the purpose of video game sound is reducible to exclusively diegetic audio, meaning sounds that are *of* the world of the game itself. This equally restricts the function of the sound quite substantially to that of reinforcing interaction by way of auditory feedback. Three of the four individual sound effects present in *Computer Space* are directly responsive to the three available forms of player input (rotation, forward momentum, and firing a weapon), with the fourth reflecting the only two individual indicators of success/failure (destroying an enemy and being destroyed). Likewise, the function of *Pong*'s sound effects is exclusively to reinforce the player's perception of interaction; as confirmation of player action (contact between player's paddle and the ball) and success (scoring/conceding a goal).

It is also worth briefly mentioning the value of sound simply as inherently fun within toy play activity. As infants, the vast majority of us will have experienced sound-augmented toy play as we (and likely also our family and friends together) made gleeful "neeeows" as the toy car in our hands turned a sharp corner (see Deák et al. 2018, for example). Using sound makes play more fun and this fact was not lost on video game designers.

Once More with Feeling: Emotion, Instruction and Mood

Subsequent video game titles continued to innovate, both creatively and technologically, but the landmarks with regard to sound proceeded with two specific titles: *Gunfight* (Taito 1975) and the immortalized *Space Invaders* (Taito 1978). Both games introduced nondiegetic musical content, and with it, the function of evoking player-arousal. Of these titles, *Gunfight* pioneered noncontinuous musical content, specifically the epitomal phrase of Chopin's *Piano Sonata No. 2* (the "Funeral March"), which plays when either the player or their adversary is defeated in the duel.[4] *Space Invaders* took us one step further, introducing players to continuous music. Although decidedly simple, the repeating four-note descending sequence along a minor scale remains an exceptionally pure example of affective function, through the single added feature of a steadily increasing tempo.[5] Few will be wholly unfamiliar with the gameplay of *Space Invaders*, but for the exceptions to the rule, the premise is that a little pixel-tank must fend off five rows of pixelated aliens, moving together horizontally until they reach the edge of the play area, at which point they all descend vertically by one row. The player must destroy all the invading aliens, lest one of them reach the bottom row, at which point the game is over. For each row that the aliens advance, their overall movement speed increases. The music reflects this sequence of events and the increases in speed with an accompanying increase in tempo. The closer the invading aliens, the quicker the tempo and, crucially, the greater the perceived urgency. This simple four-note sequence is deceptively multilayered, servicing two discrete functions of game sound. Alongside its potential for eliciting player-arousal, it also functions as a communication of temporal aspects of play: the pacing of the game in this particular instance.

The sound design within both *Gunfight* and *Space Invaders* utilizes highly comparable techniques to fulfill the same functions of interaction reinforcement and feedback that were also observed in *Computer Space* and *Pong*. Nothing is removed, but the use of nondiegetic, musical content adds the layer evoking arousal. *Gunfight* utilizes a musical theme that is both widely recognizable and commonly interpreted as a representation of death. By doing so, the game sonically enriches the feedback to the player. Beyond simply notifying them of their avatar's state, it characterizes that state for the function of evoking an affective response. *Space Invaders* utilizes its continuous musical content for the same purpose, choosing gradual acceleration in tempo to evoke arousal through the process of rhythmic entrainment (see Trost et al. 2017). It is worth noting however, that the function of evoking arousal is not the exclusive domain of music, with sound effects also demonstrating that capability. This is evidenced in the mid-1970s arcade title *Death Race* (Exidy 1976), a game with the, some may say, unsavory title of being the first thematically controversial video game. In *Death Race*, the player is tasked with running their pixelated vehicle into as many flailing pixelated pedestrians as possible within the allotted time limit. Most notable in this interaction is the very particular sound emitted whenever a pedestrian is hit. The tone is a sudden, high-pitched beep with a sharp, downward pitch bend before the release, effectively capturing as much of the sonic quality of a human scream as was possible with the technology of the time.[6] While the primary function of the sound may have been to feedback a response to player action, there was undoubtedly a secondary function of emphasizing the affective aspect of the real-world action being represented. It is worth noting that it has taken scientific inquiry several decades from the release of *Death Race* to even begin conducting empirical testing on the connection between continuous music and positive player-affect, though initial studies are returning results that favor this hypothesis (Klimmt et al. 2019).

In the years that quickly followed, the number of video games produced substantially expanded and landmarks subsequently moved from being embodied by individual titles, to specific hardware platforms (individual console and personal computer systems). Within this period, arguably the most significant landmark event came in the form of a specific console, the Magnavox Odyssey 2 (1978). To be precise, an expansion module for the console called *The Voice*. Plugged directly into the Odyssey 2's cartridge port, *The Voice* afforded the console greatly enhanced computational resource to enrich the timbral breadth and depth of the audio. More importantly, *The Voice* facilitated speech synthesis, enabling textual information to be communicated to the player as audible language. The timbre of the voice synthesis was so low in fidelity and human-like timbral depth, that actually comprehending the speech was a challenge in and of itself.[7] Despite this limitation, *The Voice* presented players with a sixth distinct function of game sound: instruction. Through text, games were of course already capable of delivering instruction, but with sound as the modality of delivery, games were now endowed with the powerful feature of multimodal layering. As a theoretical perspective, particularly within digital interaction literature, multimodal layering is a decidedly younger topic of study when compared to the Magnavox Odyssey 2, and its meaning is conceptually similar but not identical to the functionality of *The Voice*. Broadly speaking, multimodal layering examines interactive technologies' representational, semiotic, activity and functional properties as they are engaged across the different sensory modalities of the user (see Schnaider et al. 2020). As of the end of 2021, very little has been published considering multimodal layering in video game design, particularly in terms of games without an explicit learning purpose (serious games). As such, the concept has yet to be robustly applied to video game sound design. However, even at this initial stage there is arguably overlap between this concept and the added functionality that voice synthesis was offering players all those years ago. Text inescapably consumed screen space when presenting character dialogue or instructional information, consequently limiting the amount of graphical content that could be simultaneously displayed. As a multimodal layer however, games were now able to utilize auditory content to present what had previously been text-based, without consuming a single pixel. Games could now, more effectively, realize multiple functions in a single moment.

In the years that followed, continuous musical content with more overt compositional features such as phrasing, theme, and variation began to appear. *Rally-X* (Ito et al.

1980) is typically cited as the progenitor in this instance, boasting a credited composer in Toshio Kai, and a discernible riff[8] that designated a transition from mere sound with musicality in games to clear music in games. The presence of more crafted composition in game music expanded the functionality of game sound even further, supporting prior functions in feedback (see *Donkey Kong* [Miyamoto et al. 1981] as one of Nintendo's earliest masterclasses in player infantilization and infuriation with distinct musical stings to honor their successes, and deeply taunt their failures[9]), evoking player arousal and communicating temporal aspects of play, but now additionally functioning as an indicator of atmosphere and mood. The majority of game music compositions across the early 1980s began reflecting the thematic content and genre of their titles. Casual platformers such as *Frogger*[10] (Konami 1981), with bright color palettes and a younger target audience, commonly featured up-beat, major-arpeggiated musical phrases full of vigor and bounce. In contrast, science fiction shooters such as *I, Robot*[11] (Theurer and Dawe 1984), with a more serious narrative and wider demographics, featured more ominous and droning, minor pentatonic phrasing.

The Business of Art and the Art of Business: Aesthetics, Branding and Realism

As we progress into the mid-1980s, more experienced composers were being increasingly commissioned to score video game music, leading to the next discrete function of video game sound: presenting additional aesthetic and artistic value. The forerunner of this function is both subjective and subject to debate, though at the very least a good example of this function can be observed in *Super Mario Bros.* (Miyamoto 1985), the score being composed and produced by Koji Kondo. While drawing a causal link may be inappropriate, it is worth noting that historical reviews of chiptune music commonly date back to the same time as *Super Mario Bros.*'s initial release (Driscoll and Diaz 2009; McAlpine 2018). Identifying specific scores over others as of artistic value in their own right may be unreasonable, but there is a general consensus that this particular period in video game history marks the point at which video game music demonstrated the potential to be an aesthetic peer to the graphics and the gameplay.[12]

Original compositions able to garner appreciation for adding aesthetic and artistic value to a game were also likely to have the potential for establishing or reinforcing brand identity by way of sonic branding. The term "sonic branding" did not appear within literature until the early 2000s. Its first significant appearance as a subject of study was in *Sonic Branding* (2003), where author Daniel Jackson begins with the observation that while the term was new, its application was not. We could go as far back as the 1890s, during which time the first slot machine forerunners were manufactured, the whirrs of their spinning reels and the avalanching metallic clinks of their jackpot payouts both being hugely attracting sonic signatures of the device and of the experience. Although something of a world away from the contemporary business of video games, various development and publishing companies of the 1980s, not to forget console and computing manufacturers, had clear strategies for building their brand with sound. Indeed, every home console from the 1982 Vectrex to the 2020 PlayStation 5 came equipped with a distinct audio cue emitted upon start up, while personal computers picked up on the notion in the early 1990s with Microsoft's Windows 3.1.[13] For the games themselves, music was arguably a very powerful tool in establishing sonic branding. The distinct, now iconic musical characteristics of Koji Kondo's themes for *Super Mario Bros.* saw both variations and reproductions used for numerous subsequent titles in the series. Of course, Mario himself contributed to sonic branding through nonmusical audio, from his characterful vocalizations to his equally distinct jump-sound, both of which saw only minor tweaks as the series progressed.

While nonmusical video game sound would most certainly contribute to the functions of establishing atmosphere and providing additional aesthetic value, the heavy constraints of computing resources, particularly those afforded to sound, were unable to advance in timbral richness and sonic detail at the same pace as compositional techniques. This of course would not be a permanent state of affairs and a subsequent technological development would see nonmusical sound present powerful new functions. The technical details of video game sound are minimized here, with excellent texts on the subject already well established (see Collins 2008). This aids us in keeping the focus on functionality. That said, it would be unhelpful to begin discussion on the following game sound functions without a little light technical backstory. Across the 8-bit and 16-bit eras, sound was largely produced by way of programmable sound generators (PSGs; controlled arrays of mostly sine wave oscillators, through assembly language), subtractive synthesis (an extension of PSG, integrating filters that subtract frequencies from the basic oscillator output to further shape the sound), frequency modulation (a more additive process where multiple sine waves are combined and processed through an envelope generator to produce the final waveform), or wavetable synthesis (uses digital samples of physical instruments in favor of building synthetic sounds from basic oscillator waveforms). Against this backdrop, *Dragon's Lair* (Bluth and Dyer 1983) was significantly ahead of its time, eschewing the ubiquitous cartridge in favor of the laserdisc, thereby boasting prerendered graphics and sound.[14] While the musical score is largely synthetic in character, save for a few percussive elements, the ambient, character, event, and impact sounds throughout serve a further function: promotion of perceived realism. Benefiting most probably from the hyperreal, stylized sounds of animated fantasy films, *Dragon's Lair* reproduced audio fidelity comparable with, in some instances, the real world or, in others, the fantastic experience of cinema.

The limitations of the laserdisc in context of the broader hardware characteristics and games development processes of the time, relegated the medium and its sonic functions to a short-lived experimental format while the cartridge retained its mainstream position. However, it was not forgotten as a forerunner. The technology would of course eventually become mainstream in the mid-1990s with the advent and proliferation of 32-bit, CD-ROM games systems. At this moment in time, the disc format was now in far greater alignment with wider technologies and development processes. Compact discs had become the dominant format for music recordings and would still not peak until the early 2000s (High Resolution Audio 2021), while digital audio workstations had matured in ease of use, affordability, and availability (Levine 2019). This empowered sound designers and composers to produce richer game dialogue, music, ambiences, and effects as the new standard of video game sound. The impact of this new landscape was a substantial number of sound designers and studios across the world who were carefully considering how this technology could now be leveraged to provide new sound functions to enrich the overall quality of the games being produced.

Spatialization, Modeling, Personalization, and Expressive Narrative

Just as *Dragon's Lair* pioneered the sound function of perceived realism in the early 1980s before it became more commonplace a decade later, a subsequent game of the 1990s would introduce the functions of directing player's spatial attention, which would also not become standardized until the following decade. The use of audio spatialization technology in video games first appeared in 16-bit home consoles and some PC builds, the notable forerunning adopter of which was the Super Nintendo Entertainment System (SNES) build of *Jurassic Park* (Ocean Software 1993). The SNES itself is often lauded for being sonically ahead of its time in its usage of the Sony SPC700, a revolutionary sound module that made surround sound possible, if experimental, and was responsible for introducing to video games stereophonic sound and digital signal processing (DSP) effects. The audio of *Jurassic Park* exploited the SPC700 and was mastered in tandem with an early Dolby Pro Logic system that facilitated quadraphonic sound, albeit if the user possessed the right equipment plus some significant ingenuity (Elmore 2019). Most players, however, were limited to reproducing the audio in stereo, which was itself still seen as highly cutting edge. Importantly, a degree of spatialization was still retained, most noticeably in the first-person perspective sections of gameplay. As the player bids to evade hordes of velociraptors,[15] the creatures' various shrieks provide a nonvisual cue as to their relative position, directing the player's attention to points in the virtual space where unseen threats were located, thereby enabling the player to evade these threats more effectively.

In addition to the spatialization function it pioneered, the SPC700 module also facilitated one further function by way of its array of DSP effects. As Collins (2008) explains, the introduction of DSP enabled developers to apply effects that included echo, reverberation, chorus, compression, time stretching, and high/low-pass filtering. Of these, the combination of filtering and reverberation in particular presented opportunities for characterizing the material and physical properties of the game's diegetic world. Singular ambient, character, and event sounds could now be modified to better represent the locale. A hammer impacting on a shield could now sound significantly different in, for instance, a dungeon as opposed to a meadow. This can be observed in games such as *Final Fantasy VI* (Square 1994), in which the various event sounds triggered as the player explores the mines possess a distinct echo.[16]

The sheer volume of video games titles being released across the 1990s makes it particularly difficult to identify a single originator of a particular sound function, though this particular period in video game history arguably saw the proliferation of two further sound functions: environmental contextualization (or scene setting) and expressive narrative. As Grimshaw and colleagues (2013) observe, sound is a powerful asset in establishing a game world's mise-en-scène, at once imbuing a virtual world with structural, aesthetic, thematic, historical, and temporal character. With regard to scene setting, the capability to embed pre-produced audio into games allowed sound designers an unprecedented opportunity to capture real-world sound sources, presenting audio that far outstripped the fidelity, richness, and perceived realism of its graphical counterpart. A real-time rendering (or even prerendered) visual depiction of a bird on a 32-bit system ranged from distinctly unreal at best, to little more than a digital cardboard cut-out at worst. By comparison, an audio sample of birdsong was, to most listeners, quite simply the sound of birdsong. Admittedly, this is a slightly unfair comparison, as we are considering a computer-generated or synthetic visual artifact against a capture and reproduction of a real source for the audio artifact. That said, captured video (e.g., FMV) would, in most instances, still be of a lesser fidelity to an audio equivalent, or require a substantially greater amount of computing resource to utilize while also being much more difficult to cut between or layer. This made audio samples the clear winner over the visual equivalent, and the result was a significant new potential to represent far greater depth, complexity, interplay, and dynamics than was possible through graphics alone. *Resident Evil* (Capcom 1996) stands as a strong example of the era in terms of auditory scene setting. As the player navigates the dining room of the game's eponymous mansion, a grandfather clock steadily ticks away. With this sound there is little need to present an animation of the pendulum swing. Later, as the player explores the gardens, a persistent cricket chirp with an occasional wolf howl help to sonically flood the space, providing a sense of motion and environmental character with just a single, looping sample;[17] and without a single graphical correlate.

The communication of embedded narrative, whether by dialogue, monologue, or narration, was until this point, predominantly realized graphically by way of text. Synthesized or sampled audio may have been able to present single utterances, words, or short sentences, but not extended narrative. CD-ROM technology however, provided the opportunity to represent narrative by way of voice-acted, recorded, and embedded sound. As Collins (2008) points out, CD-ROMs were limited to 72 minutes of uncompressed audio, meaning sound designers still needed to carefully consider efficient selections and length of samples to conserve disc space. During this time, game genre dramatically determined how such resources were allocated, with point-and-click adventure titles, predominantly popular on personal computers, heavily exploiting the available audio resources, and even limiting graphical complexity and scale, to present substantial quantities of voice-acted speech in service of the expressive narrative function of sound. The developers of *Loom* (Lucasfilm Games) would even go so far as to produce their game in both its 1990 original 3.5 floppy disk medium and then subsequently on CD-ROM in 1992, so that voice-acted speech could be presented. This proved a controversial decision as the trade-off was to cut a significant portion of the dialogue (Gibbons and Reale 2019). In both *Loom* and many of the adventure games that followed, the quantity of speech provides a clear distinction from that offered by the Magnavox Odyssey2 and its voice synthesizer module, but another key feature is emotional expression. While the tones of *The Voice* now epitomize the robotic voice trope, the capture of real human voices endowed games such as *Loom* with characterful and evocative speech.

As the 32-bit generation of home consoles progressed, increasingly sophisticated audio compression techniques steadily began lifting this restriction on sampled audio and this gradual shift can be observed in titles that include the *Tomb Raider* series, of which five individual titles all ran on Sony's PlayStation (now PSX). As the series progresses, there is a distinct increase in the amount of voice-acted dialogue, as we move from the original *Tomb Raider* (Core Design 1996) to *Tomb Raider Chronicles* (Core Design 2000), evidencing that although narrative function of audio was of a lower priority, utilizing sound over text to present narrative was at the very least, desirable.

As the new millennium dawned, the transition from fifth to sixth generation of home consoles made official a particular function of video game sound that had arguably been present in some form from the very beginning: individualized auditory player-experience. Playing video games with an independent source of music was commonplace in home console usage and video arcades alike. Savvy PC-gamers quickly realized the potential to use software media players to enable listening of digital audio from the hard drive while running games via the CD-ROM. For those in the know, *The Sims* (Maxis 2000) would enable players to use custom sound files that would play through their sim's radio or hi-fi by locating the right folder in the installation directory and swapping out the original audio files, while *Black and White* (Lionhead Studios 2001) represented the first game to explicitly support custom soundtracks with a decidedly *un*hidden game interface. An array of sixth-generation titles facilitated a common custom soundtrack functionality in which music downloaded to the console hard drive would replace the original soundtrack of the game, while games that did not support this functionality could still be played with custom music in a manner akin to the earlier PC media player method.

To Sum Up

With all of the above functions, there are of course other instances that may have originated earlier or in a more meaningful way at a later date. Individualized auditory player-experience could alternatively be traced back to the introduction of in-game audio settings, while the more recent technological advances in digital signal processing have facilitated far more detailed and physically accurate simulated acoustic environments. As Stevens and Raybould (2013) discuss, auditory environmental modeling in modern audio engines now comprises increasingly realistic occlusion (the effect of an object muffling a direct soundwave and its reflections when positioned between the source and the listener), obstruction (a partial-muffling effect where only the direct soundwave is obscured), geometric extraction (a deadening effect where the material properties of the environment absorb the soundwave so only the direct soundwave with no reflections reach the listener), and geometric reflection (essentially the reverse of extraction, in which the modeled properties of the space add reflections to the direct soundwave) effects. However, what is important to observe in this historical review is that earlier-established functions enjoy higher status in game sound design. They are more likely to be viewed as priority functions across a wider range of titles, while more recent, less refined, or integrated functions are more likely to be viewed as desirable or decorative, or even dismissed as niche or experimental. Therefore, although the earlier functions should most certainly not be forsaken, innovative game sound design should strive to further explore ways in which the later functions could be expanded and refined while considering the possibility that discrete new functions may be waiting to be discovered.

Table 14.1 summarizes the functions for a more at-a-glance view.

TABLE 14.1 Summary of Game Sound Functions with Notable Game Title Instances

Function	Original/Key Game Instance (year)
Confirmation/reinforcement of player-action	*Computer Space* (1971)
Feedback response to player action	
Feedback response to changes in game state	
Filling perceptual gaps	
Emphasize presence by way of immersion	
Promotion of toy-play	
Evoking player-arousal	*Space Invaders* (1978)
Communicating temporal aspects	
Establish an atmosphere/mood	*Frogger* (1981)
Presenting instruction	*Nimble Numbers Ned* (1982)
Promoting perceived realism	*Dragon's Lair* (1983)
Adding aesthetic/artistic value	*Super Mario Bros.* (1985)
Brand identity/sonic branding	
Expressive narrative/storytelling	*Loom* (1992)
Directing player's spatial attention	*Jurassic Park* (1993)
Material and physical characterization of the virtual space	*Final Fantasy VI* (1994)
Environmental contextualization/scene setting	*Resident Evil* (1996)
Facilitate individualized player-experience	*The Sims* (2000)

Key Theories and Positions in Cognitive Psychology and Auditory Perception

The Resurgence of the Figure-Ground Theory

In 1934, from the Psychological Laboratory, Cambridge, P. E. Vernon authored one of the earliest treatises on the subject of auditory perception. Vernon's work would explore the application of Gestalt psychology, considering the relevance of the figure-ground principle and discussing so-called definite and indefinite modes of listening. Also notable for pointing out the limitations of the literature's reliance on musical sound to explain auditory perception, Vernon took issue with the assertion that it should be possible to explain audition with complete physical analysis of the soundwave, as he believed that the underlying principle that all sound is conveyed to the listener by way of a soundwave was not entirely true. Part of Vernon's opposition was drawn from his observations that partials of a sound could vary significantly, yet still be identified by a listener as the same sound. He also posited that the physical properties of a soundwave were sensitive to the environment and would always be different between points of transmission and transduction, with the acoustic environment and the physiological properties of the pinnae and middle ear identified as key factors in understanding sound as a perceptual artefact. Vernon (1934, 24) posits that "a melody is determined, not by its separate component notes, but by the pitch and temporal relations between the notes," referring to figure-ground perception that explains how we cannot perceive individual elements within the world, even if our attention is on them (i.e., we have designated them as *figure*). Vernon elucidates this with a visual analogy, describing Ruben's figure-ground vase illusion (see Figure 14.1), in which the figure of the vase is an emergent perception arising from the ground of the faces (or potentially the reverse). For sound, pitch is analogous to space, as we cannot close off the periphery of sensory experience, and tempo to time, as our memory gives us no choice but to experience any given moment in the context of that which preceded it.

Moving closer to present day, Grimshaw and Garner (2015) review historical and contemporary thought on auditory perception with an emphasis on holistic interpretation to contextualize our relationship with sound in embodied, ecological, psychological, and ontological terms. The work presents sound as an emergent perception; an actualized singularity resulting from a precise, and complex, arrangement of circumstance. In place of the vase illusion, Grimshaw and Garner utilize the Kanizsa Triangle illusion (Figure 14.2), demonstrating a comparable gestalt principle, but emphasizing how the ground in this instance is formed of a much greater number of precisely arranged elements than that which is implied by Ruben's vase.

FIGURE 14.1 The Figure-ground vase illusion.

Source: Figure-ground vase image. CC0 (https://www.iconspng.com/image/93739/rubins-vase#, accessed July 5, 2021).

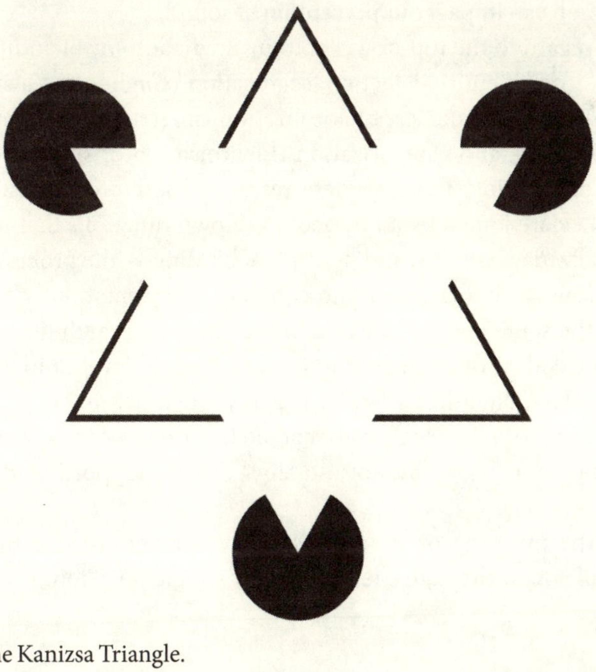

FIGURE 14.2 The Kanizsa Triangle.

Source: Fibonacci. Kanizsa Triangle. CC BY- SA 3.0 (https://commons.wikimedia.org/w/index.php?curid= 1788 215, accessed July 5, 2021).

In most recent instances of the literature, the contemporary study of perception now visibly favors the field of neuroscience, within which *predictive coding* is asserted by Denham and Winkler (2020) to be the dominant framework, highly applicable to auditory perception. Advocates of predictive coding posit that the brain perpetually updates a bespoke mental model of ourselves and of the environment, encompassing our sensation, perception, understanding, and sense of meaning; and that this model is itself a significant modulator of all sensory experience. This presents clear echoes of both Vernon's (1934) application of figure-ground theory to auditory perception and Grimshaw and Garner's (2015) theory of sounds as emergent perception, in which the mental model and the sensory input (soundwave) are both elements of the ground, through which the figure of auditory perception (*a sound*) emerges.

Blurred Lines

Over the previous decade, researchers have increasingly questioned the extent to which previously drawn lines between perception and sensation, between top-down and bottom-up processing, and between audition and the other modalities, genuinely represent the architecture of neural processing (Kondo et al. 2017). One key line of inquiry within the field is that of cross-modality. As explained in depth by Rosenblum and colleagues (2017), research is increasingly supporting the notion of the *supramodal brain*, a theory of cortical architecture that suggests the structure of the brain derived more from function and task, than from sensory modality. The implication here being that we have largely underestimated both the effect auditory stimuli can have on our perception and response to other modalities of input, but equally the extent to which nonauditory stimuli can impact our perception of sound.

With specific regard to the top-down/bottom-up dichotomy of auditory perception, Lotto and Holt (2010) identify detection, segregation (singling out a specific auditory source or stream from a soundscape), localization (inferring a position of the source, relative to the listener), and categorization (identification of source) as the four primary processes of listening. In subsequent research, these processes are certainly not dismissed, but they are joined by additional top-down functions that include selective attention, generalized awareness, and perceptual binding—"the process of merging individual bits of sensory information into coherent representations" (Stevenson 2015). Within broadly the same period, however, trends in the research literature also reveal a back-to-basics trend, with a renewed interest in the low-level fundamentals of auditory perception. Here, pitch in particular is garnering much interest. A recent review article by Oxenham (2018) has suggested that pitch is a significantly important factor in a listener's capacity to segregate auditory streams, thereby supporting identification and localization.

Deciphering the meaning of sound has led researchers to question our perceptual placement of sound through the deceptively simple question: *where is sound?* As

O'Callaghan (2011) observes, three competing positions have been proposed: distal (sound is located at the source); medial (sound is located at the soundwave between source and listener); and proximal (sound is located at the listener). In a review by Casati (2020), additional aspatial theories of sound are presented that, broadly, posit that the location of sound is not inherent to the physical soundwave and is instead a percept. Such a view arguably resonates with predictive coding and suggests that the question *where is sound?* is flexible and is determined by the individual listener's unique ground.

From the literature, including much of that which is discussed above, theories of sound are markedly moving toward more holistic, comprehensive models that seek to explain auditory perception and our human interactions with sound as multilayered, integrated, multisensory, embodied, and environmentally situated. Of course, such a perspective is something of a monolith; inaccessible and difficult to translate into viable recommendations for video game sound design. That said, while these theories start from a position of acknowledging the complexity and holistic nature of sound, they do not preclude us from focusing back on more granular elements and processes. Further reinforcing Rosenblum and colleagues' (2017) supramodal brain notion, numerous studies have supported the idea that the organization of the brain is best conceptualized as distinction-via-task-feature (Dizeux et al. 2019; Hahn et al. 2018; Wang et al. 2019). In other words, the functions elicited by a task correlate significantly to the structure of cognition, with potential effects on perception and action.

Auditory Function and Applications to Video Game Sound

Returning to 1934, P. E. Vernon's work provides us with an early taxonomy of auditory perception, dichotomized in terms of indefinite and definite listening. The former of these terms is depicted as more passive, nonattentive interaction with sonic stimuli, its occurrence characterized by the presence of up to seven discrete features: reflexive bodily response; general euphoria; stimulation of thought processes unrelated to the sound; generalized affective interpretations of the sound; evocation of dramatic imagery; lapsing awareness of the sound, balancing on the "margin of consciousness" (129); or *mere* awareness of the presence of a stimulus but with no further response. By contrast, definite listening would be present if one of more of the following were observed: kinesthetic bodily response; synesthetic response; visualizations of entities or processes relevant to the stimulus; explicit vocalization of objective properties of the sound; specialized affective interpretation; evocation of auditory imagery; or direct intellectual, technical, or theoretical analysis. Vernon's taxonomy can itself be traced back to the Victorian writings of Edmund Gurney, and his observation that "the conditions of satisfaction in colour or tone are totally irrelevant to our perception of particular forms or melodies as beautiful" (Gurney 1881, 38). For Gurney, the physiological aesthetics evoked through tonality, and which would become associated with indefinite listening, were entirely removed from any appreciation of matters of musical form such as melody, harmony, and structure, drawn from what would become definite listening.

Many years later, and much of Vernon's thinking is retained. Tuuri and Eerola (2012) identify a set of distinct modes of listening across three broad divisions: experiential; denotative; and reflective. Experiential modes are immediate and preattentive. They include reflexive (autonomic physical/physiological responses), kinesthetic (preattentive response to the position, orientation, and/or movement of a source), and connotative (free-association imagery response) listening. Denotative modes are directly relevant to attention and identification of a sound source (causal listening), its affective characteristics or denoted purpose (empathetic and functional listening respectively), or its contextual meaning (semantic listening). Lastly, reflective modes are postattentive and considered. They include reduced (focusing on discrete physical properties of a sound) and critical (evaluating the effectiveness of a sound in context) listening. Subsequent research has considered the more reflective modes of listening in a professional practice context (Bijsterveld 2008), asserting several further discrete processes, namely: synthetic (general acoustic impressions of a soundscape); analytic (specific acoustic properties or features of an individual sound or soundscape at a limited point in time); and interactive listening (acoustic changes directly attributable to an intended action by the listener). Further expansion of these modes can be drawn from Grimshaw and Schott (2007) who add navigational listening, plus an array of related functions that could be collectively termed spatiotemporal listening: choraplast (spatial characteristics of a physical space); topoplast (spatial characteristics of a virtual paraspace); chronoplast (short-term temporal characteristics of a space); and aionoplast (long-term temporal characteristics [epochs/historical eras]).

Figure 14.3 is an initial attempt at pulling these seemingly disparate but, in truth, highly interconnected elements together. When considering the video game sound functions against the modes of listening, we can observe that video game sound predominantly resonates, and has the longest established history, with the denotative listening modes; the functions of identification of object, event, and environment being critical means of facilitating interaction. Reflexive modes feature with heightened prominence in game genres that require them for either bespoke mechanics (interactive music games for instance) or experiential qualities (survival horror games). Reflective modes arguably remain the least applied in video games, with only a very short list of titles utilizing reduced listening (see *The Witness* [Thekla, Inc. 2016] for one of the few instances) and only the highly experimental exploring critical listening (see *Phonopath*[18]).

One further gap relates to the embodiment of auditory perception, specifically the importance of the body. Material and physical characterization of the virtual space is

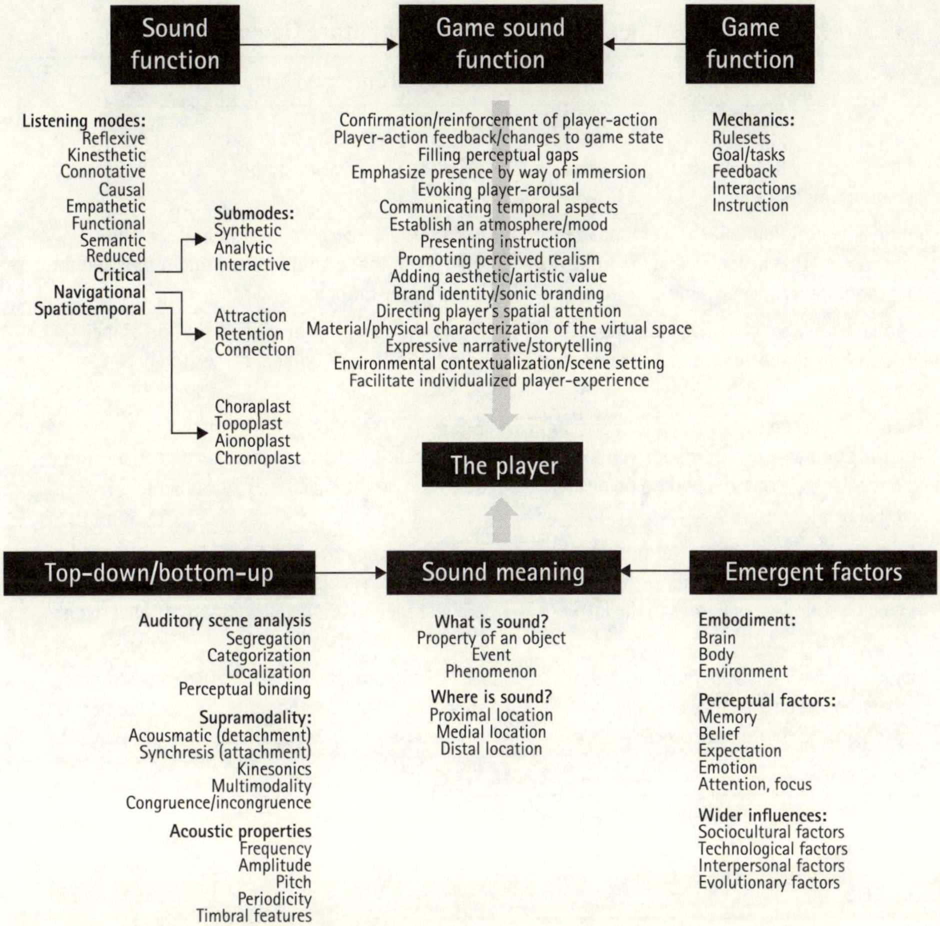

FIGURE 14.3 Theoretical framework of video game sound by function.

concerned with the environmental contribution to embodied experience but neglects the human body, particularly its bidirectional relationship with game sound. Therefore, more development is needed in designs that seek to influence game sound through physiological and kinesthetic interactions.

Bringing this chapter to a close, the overarching recommendations drawn from the above discussion are to evoke as wide a range of listening functions as possible to add cognitive and affective breadth and depth to the experience. Table 14.2 outlines recommended aims for future video game sound design. The functional outcome examples given do vary in their innovative quality, but the argument in those instances is that these more established outcomes instead need to be championed and more consistently embedded in the game design process.

TABLE 14.2 Summary of Recommended Aims for Future Game Sound Design

Aim	Functional Outcome Example
Consider the supramodal brain; structure game sound by task type and associated listening function.	E.g., prioritize clarity when presenting instruction; heighten presence via emphatic spatialization; etc.
Emphasize multimodality and emphasize game design that accommodates sound, not just sound that reflects game design.	E.g., craft an environmental soundscape first, then using that soundscape as the foundation for building the graphical environment.
Emphasis on more attentive listening processes to support more innovative game experiences.	E.g., make identification/interpretation of meaning from sound a core gameplay mechanic.
Encourage placement considered prioritization of sound across proximal, distal, and medial locations, depending on desired gameplay effect.	E.g., raise in the mix the environmental sounds that are emphatic of the acoustic space (medial) when attention on the space is a priority.
Consider the bidirectional relationship between the body and sound, with the former not being simply a responder to the latter.	E.g., explore new ways in which the player-character's physiological state might by affecting not just their hearing, but their attentional focus on certain sounds.
Reflect the notion that perception is best understood as an interplay between both top-down and bottom-up processes.	E.g., require the player to deconstruct a complex soundscape into components, or make connections between seemingly separate sounds to establish a 'big picture'

Notes

1. *Computer Space* (1971) gameplay capture: https://www.youtube.com/watch?v=YR7gmVpw6Io. Accessed July 5, 2021.
2. https://bdcampbell.net/music/. Accessed July 5, 2021.
3. https://www.monitoraudio.com/en/blog/the-evolution-of-video-game-sound/. Accessed July 5, 2021.
4. *Gun Fight* (1975) gameplay capture: https://www.youtube.com/watch?v=xYaoG6KGayk. Accessed July 5, 2021.
5. *Space Invaders* (1978) gameplay capture: https://www.youtube.com/watch?v=uGjgxwiemms. Accessed July 5, 2021.
6. *Death Race* (1976) gameplay capture: https://www.youtube.com/watch?v=aBBtt72aJLA. Accessed July 5, 2021.
7. For anyone curious about the sound of The Voice: https://www.youtube.com/watch?v=rKZDRgAFMHs. Accessed July 5, 2021.
8. *Rally-X* (1980) gameplay capture: https://www.youtube.com/watch?v=YAnLEVcb8sc. Accessed July 5, 2021.
9. *Donkey Kong* (1981) gameplay capture: https://www.youtube.com/watch?v=Pp2aMs38ERY. Accessed July 5, 2021.

10. *Frogger* (1982) gameplay capture: https://www.youtube.com/watch?v=WNrz9_Fe-Us. Accessed July 5, 2021.
11. *I, Robot* (1984) gameplay capture: https://www.youtube.com/watch?v=vln2TLQIzt4. Accessed July 5, 2021.
12. And yes, 1981's *Pacman Fever* by Buckner and Garcia did exist, and it predates *Super Mario Bros*. Now let us never speak of it again.
13. Not to be mean, but the Windows 3.1 start-up sound was rubbish. Windows 95 however takes us elder millennials back to our childhoods: https://www.youtube.com/watch?v=miZHa7ZC6Zo.
14. *Dragon's Lair* (1983) gameplay capture: https://www.youtube.com/watch?v=P3XNQjaoH7I.
15. *Jurassic Park* (1993). SNES build. Gameplay capture: https://www.youtube.com/watch?v=BwPoIS1UYDg. Accessed July 5, 2021.
16. *Final Fantasy* VI (1994) gameplay capture: https://www.youtube.com/watch?v=iGNskqYu2_o. Accessed July 5, 2021.
17. *Resident Evil* (1996) gameplay capture: https://www.youtube.com/watch?v=moW4wLlZnHk. Accessed July 5, 2021.
18. Phonopath website: http://phonopath.com/about.htm. Accessed July 5, 2021.

References

Bijsterveld, Karin. 2008. *Mechanical Sound: Technology, Culture, and Public Problems of Noise in the Twentieth Century*. Cambridge, MA: MIT press.

Bluth, Don, and Rick Dyer. 1983. *Dragon's Lair*. Video Game. El Cajon, CA: Cinematronics.

Collins, Karen. 2008. *Game Sound: An Introduction to the History, Theory, and Practice of Video Game Music and Sound Design*. Cambridge, MA: MIT Press.

Core Design. 1996. *Tomb Raider*. Video Game. Eidos Interactive.

Core Design. 2000. *Tomb Raider Chronicles*. Video Game. Eidos Interactive.

Deák, Gedeon. O., Anna. M. Krasno, Hector Jasso, and Jochen Triesch. 2018. "What Leads to Shared Attention? Maternal Cues and Infant Responses during Object Play." *Infancy* 23 (1): 4–28.

Denham, Susan L., and István Winkler. 2020. "Predictive Coding in Auditory Perception: Challenges and Unresolved Questions." *European Journal of Neuroscience* 51 (5): 1151–1160.

Dizeux, Alexandre, Marc Gesnik, Harry Ahnine, Kevin Blaize, Fabrice Arcizet, Serge Picaud, José-Alain Sahel, Thomas Deffieux, Pierre Pouget, and Mickael Tanter. 2019. "Functional Ultrasound Imaging of the Brain Reveals Propagation of Task-Related Brain Activity in Behaving Primates." *Nature Communications* 10 (1): 1–9.

Driscoll, Kevin, and Joshua Diaz. 2009. "Endless Loop: A Brief History of Chiptunes." *Transformative Works and Cultures* 2 (1). Accessed December 26, 2023. https://doi.org/10.3983/twc.2009.096.

Elmore, Andrew. 2019. "Did You Know These Retro Game Consoles are Capable of Surround Sound?" *Medium.com*. Accessed January 9, 2024. https://medium.com/@AndrewElmore/did-you-know-these-retro-game-consoles-are-capable-of-surround-sound-70336b760252.

Exidy. 1976. *Death Race*. Video Game.

Gibbons, William, and Steven Reale, eds. 2019. *Music in the Role-Playing Game: Heroes and Harmonies*. Oxfordshire: Routledge.

Graetz, Martin, 1981. "The Origin of *Spacewar*." *Creative Computing* 7 (8): 56–67.

Grimshaw, Mark. 2008. "Sound and Immersion in the First-Person Shooter." *International Journal of Intelligent Games and Simulation* 5 (1): 119–124.

Grimshaw, Mark, and Tom Garner. 2015. *Sonic Virtuality: Sound as Emergent Perception*. New York: Oxford University Press.

Grimshaw, M. N., and Gareth Schott. 2007. "Situating Gaming as a Sonic Experience: The Acoustic Ecology of First-Person Shooters." *Situated Play*. Digital Games Research Association (DiGRA). Accessed December 26, 2023. http://www.digra.org/digital-library/publications/situating-gaming-as-a-sonic-experience-the-acoustic-ecology-of-first-person-shooters/.

Grimshaw, Mark, Siu-Lan Tan, and Scott D. Lipscomb. 2013. "Playing with Sound: The Role of Music and Sound Effects in Gaming." In *Psychology of Music in Multimedia*, edited by Siu-Lan Tan, Annabel J. Cohen, Scott D. Lipscomb, and Roger A. Kendall, 289–314. New York: Oxford University Press.

Gurney, Edmund. 1881. "The Power of Sound." *Musical Times and Singing Circular* 22 (544): 38–39. Musical Times Publications Ltd.

Hahn, Andreas, Gregor Gryglewski, Lukas Nics, Lucas Rischka, Sebastian Ganger, Helen Sigurdardottir, and Chrysoula Vraka. 2018. "Task-Relevant Brain Networks Identified with Simultaneous Pet/Mr Imaging of Metabolism and Connectivity." *Brain Structure and Function* 223 (3): 1369–1378.

High Resolution Audio. 2021. "The Rise and Fall of the Compact Disc." Accessed July 7, 2021. https://www.hiresaudio.online/the-rise-and-fall-of-the-compact-disc/.

Ito, Hirohito, Kazuo Kurosu, Kouichi Tashiro, and Toshio Kai. 1980. *Rally-X*. Video Game. Namco.

Jackson, Daniel. 2003. *Sonic Branding: An Essential Guide to the Art and Science of Sonic Branding*. Basel: Springer.

Klimmt, Christoph, Daniel Possler, Nicolas May, Hendrik Auge, Louisa Wanjek, and Anna-Lena Wolf. 2019. "Effects of Soundtrack Music on the Video Game Experience." *Media Psychology* 22 (5): 689–713.

Konami. 1981. *Frogger*. Video Game.

Kondo, Hirohito M., Anouk M. van Loon, Jun-Ichiro Kawahara, and Brian C. J. Moore. 2017. "Auditory and Visual Scene Analysis: An Overview." *Philosophical Transactions of the Royal Society B: Biological Sciences* 372 (1714): 20160099.

Levine, Mike. 2019. "The History of the DAW." Yamaha Music USA. Accessed July 7, 2021. https://hub.yamaha.com/proaudio/pa-history/the-history-of-the-daw/.

Lionhead Studios. 2001. *Black and White*. Video Game. Electronic Arts.

Lotto, Andrew, and Lori Holt. 2011. "Psychology of Auditory Perception." *Wiley Interdisciplinary Reviews: Cognitive Science* 2 (5): 479–489.

Lucasfilm Games. 1990. *Loom*. Video Game.

McAlpine, K. B. 2018. *Bits and Pieces: A History of Chiptunes*. New York: Oxford University Press.

Miyamoto, S. 1985. *Super MarioBros*. Video Game. Nintendo.

Miyamoto, S., G. Yokoi, Y. Kaneoka. 1981. *Donkey Kong*. Video Game. Nintendo.

O'Callaghan, C. 2011. "Lessons from Beyond Vision (Sounds and Audition)." *Philosophical Studies* 153 (1): 143–160.

Ocean Software. 1993. *Jurassic Park*. Video Game. Ocean Software.

Oxenham, Andrew. 2018. "How We Hear: The Perception and Neural Coding of Sound." *Annual Review of Psychology* 69:27–50.

Rosenblum, Lawrence D., James W. Dias, and Josh Dorsi. 2017. "The Supramodal Brain: Implications for Auditory Perception." *Journal of Cognitive Psychology* 29 (1): 65–87.

Schnaider, Karoline, Limin Gu, and Oscar Rantatalo. 2020. "Understanding Technology Use through Multimodal Layers: A Research Review." *International Journal of Information and Learning Technology* 37 (5): 375–387.

Square. 1994. *Final Fantasy VI*. Video Game.

Stevens, Richard, and Dave Raybould. 2013. *The Game Audio Tutorial: A Practical Guide to Creating and Implementing Sound and Music for Interactive Games*. Oxford: Taylor and Francis.

Stevenson, Ryan. 2015. "Perceptual Binding." Sensory Perception Research. Accessed July 12, 2021. https://sensorylab.ca/research/90-2/.

Theurer, Dave, and Rusty Dawe. 1984. *I, Robot*. Video Game. Atari, Inc.

Thekla, Inc. 2016. *The Witness*. Video Game.

Trost, W. Johanna, Carolina Labbé, and Didier Grandjean. 2017. "Rhythmic Entrainment as a Musical Affect Induction Mechanism." *Neuropsychologia* 96:96–110.

Tuuri, Kai, and Tuomas Eerola. 2012. "Formulating a Revised Taxonomy for Modes of Listening." *Journal of New Music Research* 41 (2): 137–152.

Vernon, Philip. 1934. "Auditory Perception: I. The Gestalt Approach." *British Journal of Psychology* 25 (2): 123.

Wang, Aria Y., Leila Wehbe, and Michael Tarr. 2019. "Neural Taskonomy: Inferring the Similarity of Task-Derived Representations from Brain Activity." *Advances in Neural Information Processing Systems* 32:15501–15511.

CHAPTER 15

HOW VIDEO GAME MUSIC PLAYS US

Musical Topics, Modularity, and Compulsion Loops

WILLIAM R. AYERS

Introduction

In many action-adventure games, players must shift between two distinct forms of gameplay: exploration and combat. The combined term *action-adventure game* emphasizes the dual focus of this genre, indicating that a player character will take on different roles through the course of the narrative. The *Batman: Arkham* series of games, for example, requires Batman not only to investigate mysteries and survey his surroundings but also to engage enemies in both random encounters and coordinated combat segments. Many composers view this switching between different forms of gameplay as an opportunity for musical enhancement, supplying new tracks or layers to accompany battle sequences that can then dissipate when combat ceases. Describing these "opposing gameplay states," Winifred Phillips (2014, 42) notes that music can serve a crucial ludic function:

> In this situation, music can help to quickly identify the current state of gameplay. For example, a player may be attempting to stealthily avoid a confrontation with a group of nearby enemies. Suddenly, the enemies spot the intruder, and the musical score kicks into an anxious, high-energy mode. Even if the player hadn't yet noticed the change of circumstances, the music can be relied on to quickly announce that stealth has failed and the time has come to fight.

These dynamic musical effects allow composers to "manipulate the intensity of an interactive musical composition" so that it can "react to the shifting nature of gameplay" (200), but they also "provide the player with all the information needed to mentally adjust from one gameplay type to another" (43). Tim Summers (2016, 117) corroborates this idea: "Many games use this communicative medium to tell the player information about the gameplay progression in such a way that interacting with, and listening to, the music of the game can be a significant part of the complex process of playing the game."

In this sense, games and their accompanying soundtracks are not just responsive but also manipulative. This statement is not meant to be taken in a negative sense, though the potential for negative manipulation is absolutely possible in video games. Rather, video games and their music have the ability to influence player sensibilities and actions; they can compel players to feel and behave in ways that promote perpetual gameplay interactions, consistent narrative progression, and a continued sense of immersion or flow, a concept set out by Csikszentmihalyi and Csikszentmihalyi (1988) and furthered in video game scholarship. Game designers, aware of this potential, "set up situations aimed at bringing certain kinds of actions and impulses to the fore" (Isbister 2016, 64). The alternation between exploration and combat gameplay is a simple and common example of how this influence plays out. By exploring a virtual game world, players can obtain new equipment, weapons, or information that will help them take on higher-level enemies. With the rewards obtained from combat (currency, experience points, etc.), players can purchase upgraded items from in-game vendors, unlock advanced abilities and perks, and even access new parts of world maps, leading to future enemy engagements and exploration opportunities. Games can use incremental and cyclical rewards to launch players into an exploration-combat gameplay loop in which they feel compelled to push forward to the next challenge.

This persistent feeling, a compulsion to continue to the next gameplay task, can appear in numerous situations. Allen Kwan (2016, 157) notes a similar gameplay loop in the *Metroid* series: "Initially powerless, the player must find ways to give Samus the ability to access new passages, which in turn unlocks new areas where they can find new abilities. This loop repeats itself until the player has unlocked access to the entire game world and can challenge every single enemy in the game on even terms." Kwan refers to these cyclical reward systems as "compulsion loops" (44), a term (used regularly in the game industry) that acknowledges the manipulative intent of game designers: to keep players dependent on, and devoted to, playing their games. In a discussion of mobile games with developers Paul Murphy and Patrick Moberg, writer Lev Grossman (2015, 56) correlates the idea of a compulsion loop with that of a "Skinnerian motivational trap that keeps players in a state similar to addiction," comparing the mobile video game player to a "lab rat [looking for a] bump of dopamine."[1] These loops can be simple in structure and diverse in their application; Jesper Juul (2013, 76) recognizes a "positive feedback loop" in games as disparate as *FarmVille* and *Counter-Strike*, both of which capitalize on extended player engagement. The habitual behaviors that video games promote with their reward systems can send players bouncing from one gameplay state to the next, searching for items that will only allow them to return to the previous gameplay state but also injecting them with a sense of achievement and progression in the process.

Since music is structured around these changes in gameplay—as Phillips notes, music reacts to game states but also incites actions—it may also play a role in this compulsive behavior.[2] By telling players when it is appropriate to fight or explore, to sneak or flee, music reinforces underlying game structures that influence our play. While we play video games, game music is simultaneously playing us; it is exploiting our desire to succeed at game tasks, leading us along, telling us what we are meant to do. Since video game music both reacts to gameplay situations and connects those situations to real-world scenarios through musical semiosis, a theory to examine its manipulative abilities must account for both its dynamic and referential qualities. To examine the effects of this influence, I will consider the intersection of two different methods that have recently been used to analyze video game music, namely topic theory (Summers 2012, 2016; Ayers 2015; Atkinson 2019) and modularity (Medina-Gray 2014a, 2014b, 2017, 2019). A musical topic is a "familiar style type with easily recognizable musical features" (Hatten 2014, 514 emphasis removed), such as *singing style* or *minuet*, names that are meant to evoke dances, genres, or other categories of musical ideas. However, a topic "only becomes topical when it is imported, without losing its identity, into different contexts" (514 emphasis removed). Topics (or *topoi*) allow listeners to immediately recognize musical evocations and take part in (or at least comprehend) their semiotic references and meaning. When used in the context of dynamic video game music, topics often align with musical modules, "fixed pieces or segments of music [that] are triggered and modified in real time to yield the soundtrack for any given gameplay session" (Medina-Gray 2014a, 3–4). The modularity of video game music can channel the expressive musical content inherent in media scoring. By coordinating music's ability to both respond to game statuses and evoke semiotic meaning, this chapter will demonstrate that video game music can reinforce and instigate the actions, compulsions, desires, and goal orientations that result from standard gameplay loops and situations (see also chapter 18 this volume).

I will begin by considering a forerunner to the practices of dynamic video game music, the application of musical topics in the modular accompaniments of early 20th-century silent films. Previous studies by Neil Lerner (2014a, 2014b) have taken a similar starting position to examine scoring practices in early video games; I will use the design of silent film music to set up a discussion of modern video game scoring, specifically in the game *Batman: Arkham Origins* (2013).[3] By coordinating the concepts of modularity and topics to examine how video game music can lead players to specific gameplay behaviors, this chapter provides a point of difference with how music works in film, displaying the critical functional roles that game music can serve.

Silent Films and the Path to Musical Topics in Video Games

Studies on video game music can draw insight from studies on film music due to the shared characteristics of these media formats—most films and video games employ visual projections and stereophonic sound to imitate a spatial reality and enhance its perception. Yet there are significant differences between how films and video games operate, especially with regard to music. Summers (2016, 143–145) comments on how the "superficial" similarities of film and game media require game music to comply with certain practices in film music while still functioning in a ludic context:

> Game music is challenged to negotiate a balance between two factors—the particular demands of the video game medium, and the players' interpretive framework and expectations for moving-image media that they have learnt from film and television. . . . On one hand the unaltered direct replication of film music is neither technically possible nor suitable; on the other, media consumers have been primed by the film music model and it serves as a foundational part of the media music literacy of players.

To accomplish this delicate balance, composers of game music can replicate familiar styles and types of music that are commonly used in films and adapt them to accompany appropriate gameplay sections. Summers notes that "the deployment of musical topoi [can] serve to contextualize the ludic mechanics of the game" (145).

Originating in the work of Leonard Ratner, topics are "characteristic figures [that serve as] subjects for musical discourse" (Ratner 1980, 9 emphasis removed). The "subjects" in topic theory can be either "intra-musical—elements of the language of music—or extra-musical—taken from other media of expression" (Ratner 1991, 615); topics can refer to previous musical practices, as when a composer cites the rhythms of a *bourrée* (see Mirka 2014, 270), or they can use elements that call to mind cultural associations, as when horn calls remind listeners of the sound of nobles at the hunt (see Monelle 2006). While topics have largely been used to describe a sense of musical dialogue and interaction in concert works of the 18th century, they may also be used in works of later centuries and other media formats to guide narrative listening, to serve as formal delineations, or simply to express "affects or ideas readily comprehensible to contemporary listeners" (Dickensheets 2012, 99). The subjects of topic theory are easily recognizable in film media from the early 20th century onward; as Tobias Plebuch (2012, 78) writes, they "are not secret messages for the initiates [but are meant to be] obvious" to common listeners and viewers.

Video game music can take advantage of this familiarity to present topical content to players just as films and concert works present this content to viewers and listeners, but games draw on another (historical) aspect of film music: the modular design of early film scores, and in particular the compiled scores used to accompany many silent films in the 1910s and 1920s. A brief consideration of silent film music through the lenses of topic theory and modularity will help to focus the analytical inquiry into video game music that follows.

As defined by Rodney Sauer (1998–1999, 55–56), compiled film scores were "assembled from previously written music [and were] remarkably efficient," since they allowed for the reuse of existing pieces in the repertoire of a movie theater pianist, organist, or orchestra. Film music catalogs (dating back at least to 1914) listed pieces of music that could be used to accompany films and provided some information about the process; Lyle C. True's *How and What to Play for Moving Pictures* (1914), for instance, includes an expansive list of pieces, many of them familiar 19th-century works that had been used to accompany live theater, organized by descriptive categories indicating general moods or styles: dramatic, romantic, characteristic dances, marches, hunting, and pastoral, among others (4–12). These categories resonate with (and at times replicate) the topics associated with 18th- and 19th-century music, but they occasionally overlap with the emotional effects that film music organizers wish to bestow on their listeners: agitated, plaintive, and so forth.

To use these catalogs, theater musicians would refer to a film's cue sheet—a listing of recommended music to accompany each scene (Sauer 1998–1999, 56). Cue sheets could offer general ideas or recommend specific pieces. As Simon Trezise (2019, 10) has noted: "Some of the first cue sheets gave advice on *melos* but nothing specific." As an example, Trezise uses Thomas Edison's 1909 feature *'Tis Now the Very Witching Time of Night*, which indicates only the moods for given scenes, *hurry* or *march*, styles that were "familiar from [19th-century] melodrama and would have indicated a vast repertoire of suitable music" (11). Later cue sheets would include incipits of desired pieces, descriptions of onscreen action, and timings to permit more accurate accompaniment. Sauer (1998–1999, 56) mentions that "music directors were expected to maintain a library of music, and either use the music suggested on the cue sheet or substitute similar pieces from their collections." Appropriate pieces could easily be found by examining True's catalog or other similar listings, but to use the cue sheet's specific suggestions, theaters would need to have the pieces on hand to accommodate the short preparation time (generally only a few days between receiving the information and performing the compiled score).

To facilitate faster preparation, a number of musicians working in and around picture houses published collections of pieces (either newly composed or drawn from existing repertoires) that followed a catalog system similar to that used by True. Some of the earliest collections were produced by the Sam Fox Publishing Company, which primarily promoted music by John Stepan Zamecnik written specifically to accompany moving pictures but not tied to any specific production. Other collections used pieces already in the accompanimental repertoire, such as Erno Rapée's 1924 "rapid-reference collection" called *Motion Picture Moods*. Pianists or organists using such a collection would only need to flip to the appropriate section (organized by stylistic categories) and play a fitting piece. Table 15.1 lists all the categories in Rapée's *Motion Picture Moods*, including the quick-reference categories listed to the side of each page of music in the collection. Comparing this figure to similar lists of topics from Kofi Agawu (1991, 30; 2009, 43–44) and Janice Dickensheets (2012) for 18th- and 19th-century music, one can see some noticeable similarities and some striking differences. For instance, styles such as *hunting* and *pastoral* are retained through changes of centuries and media, but cultural styles based around the representation of some countries or peoples (e.g., Turkish music listed by Agawu) have given way to new forms of exoticism (e.g., *oriental* music and a multitude of *national* styles listed by Rapée). Additionally, technological advances in the

TABLE 15.1 Topical Cue Categories from Erno Rapée's *Motion Picture Moods* (1924)

aëroplane	funeral	misterioso	pulsating
band	grotesque	monotony	quietude and purity
battle	gruesome	music-box (chimes)	race (chase)
birds	horror	national (bugle calls)	railroad
chatter	humorous	neutral	religioso
children	hunting	orgies	sadness
dances	impatience	oriental	sea and storm
doll	joyfulness or happiness	parties	sinister
festival	love-themes	passion	wedding
fire-fighting	lullabies	pastorale	western

nineteenth and twentieth centuries promote new topical categories (e.g., *aëroplane* and *railroad*) since they are often depicted in film. Some of these new categories eventually led to common topics in video game music discourse, such as Sean Atkinson's *soaring* topic (2019) or Wesley Bradford's *mechanistic* topic (2020). Most importantly, while specific references may change, there is a similarity in the form and degree of semiotic representations between earlier practices and those of 20th-century film.

Like video game music, the music of silent films evokes ideas and affects for its listeners to absorb and provides a vehicle for emotional responses to onscreen action. As Claudia Gorbman (1987, 84) writes in her discussion of connotative cueing: "Narrative film music 'anchors' the image in meaning. It expresses moods and connotations which, in conjunction with the images and other sounds, aid in interpreting narrative events. . . . Soundtrack music reinforces what is (usually) already signified by dialogue, gestures, lighting, color, tempo of figure movement and editing, and so forth." Theater musicians enhance the effects of cinematic action by supplying topical references in a modular format, choosing segments of music in particular styles to accompany battle sequences, mysterious creeping, or moments of triumph. These musical cues offer powerful suggestions to listeners, leading them to fight, sneak, or cheer (at least internally). As the following section will show, the modular structure and manipulative intent of silent film soundtracks are direct precursors to similar concepts in video game music.

Manipulative Musical Modules in *Batman: Arkham Origins*

The tradition of using topical cue categories continues in modern film and video game scores. For example, a number of Christopher Drake's cues for *Batman: Arkham Origins*

(2013) carry the expressive marking *misterioso*, employing the name of a popular cue category to accompany exploration (as in "Open World 6 Explo") or other types of surreptitious behavior and sneaking (e.g., the "Execution Room" cutscene in Blackgate Penitentiary at the opening of the game, a sequence that the player character secretly witnesses).[4] The style used in these cues (sometimes spelled *mysterioso*) aligns quite well with the typical codes for the Batman character himself, as it is often associated with music for stealth and horror (see the "Misterioso" from Zamecnik 1919). Along these same mysterious lines, Matthew David Young (2013, 102) uses the term *ombra* to capture both Batman's mysterious qualities and the supernatural associations the character projects. The "restless motion" of the *ombra* topic, as described by Clive McClelland (2014, 282–283), allows a "portentous or mysterious atmosphere."

Historically, the *misterioso* of silent film produces a "Mickey-Mousing" effect, replicating the quietly sneaking footsteps of a figure wishing to remain hidden. See, for instance, the melody of eighth notes broken up by rests in Zamecnik's cue "Mysterious - Burglar Music," given in Figure 15.1. Notably, Lerner (2014a, 15–18) uses Zamecnik's music to align the *misterioso* topic with the "Underground" theme from the original *Super Mario Bros.* The sneaking pattern in the cue of Figure 15.1 is accentuated by some distinctive chromatic elements; the opening arpeggiation of the tonic G minor (briefly broken up by the note E-flat, scale-degree six) is followed by C-sharp on the downbeat of measure two, recalling Scott Murphy's m2M transformation, motion from a given minor triad to the major triad a whole step above, in this case G minor to A major. Murphy (2014, 488) associates this progression with a "general experience of suspense or mystery," highlighting the connection of this cue to its topical category. Further, the cadence on the fully diminished seventh chord in measure four prompts a connection to McClelland's (2014, 282) description of the *ombra*, diminished sevenths being the primary harmonic marker for this topic.

Ultimately, the *misterioso* and the *ombra* achieve the same stylistic goals, reinforcing ideas of the supernatural and mysteriousness. This aesthetic is unmistakable in the music of Batman media leading all the way back to the 1943 serial, but the style is most memorably asserted in the 1989 *Batman* film, a work overflowing with references to macabre aesthetics, assisted by the "dark style" of Tim Burton and the equally tragic score by Danny Elfman (Young 2013, 124). K. J. Donnelly (1998, 147) considers both the filmic topics in Elfman's main theme and the thematic relations to the title character, writing: "The theme for Batman himself codes the Gothic at its opening, with deep strings and

FIGURE 15.1 Opening measures of John Stepan Zamecnik's "Mysterious—Burglar Music," *Sam Fox Moving Picture Music, Vol. 1* (1914).

brass, and then the martial, where it leads to a pounding march with snare drum and brass punctuation. It functions directly as a fanfare for Batman, announcing his presence while being associated solidly with both film and character." Donnelly extracts three primary characteristics from this theme. The term "Gothic" recalls the ideals of Romantic horror fiction, closely associating this concept with the *misterioso/ombra*. The theme's emphasis on scale-degree six in its opening ascent and the m2M harmonic shift (B minor to C-sharp major) that occurs just after this opening mimic Zamecnik's "Mysterious" cue from Figure 15.1. Combined with the dark orchestration (the "deep strings and brass" mentioned by Donnelly), these items solidify a connection to the *ombra* style. The terms "martial" and "march" indicate a shift in focus from the masked or hidden style of the *ombra* toward a more active style associated with the military and battle. Finally, the brass "fanfare" in this theme punctuates the active martial section, but suggestions of this fanfare proclamation underlie the entire theme, projecting the primary character's arrival and his heroic status. Young uses these thematic elements analytically in his study of the film, claiming them as topics that are in dialogue throughout the work.

The characteristics that Donnelly mentions also saturate the varying musical textures of *Arkham Origins*, but these stylistic references now act as individual modules in a dynamic and coordinated musical system. A handful of orchestral *misteriosos* accompany the open-world sections in the game; the persistent *ombra* theme, representing Donnelly's "Gothic" quality, permeates the entire score, but is most prominent in those sections where the player character is simply exploring the three-dimensional world. Consider Figure 15.2, a reduction of an exploration track in *Arkham Origins*. The score is highly chromatic, and the harmonies progress nonfunctionally, continually shifting between minor chords. The resulting sound could potentially represent a restrained version of what Dickensheets (2012, 118–122) called the *demonic* style in reference to supernatural evocations in 19th-century music. The tritonal root shifting between minor chords provides the "demonic" sound of the diminished-seventh interval between successive harmonies. The orchestration of the cue with high tremolo strings offers a mysterious contrast to the slow harmonic progression. All these aspects combine to generate the mysterious aesthetic that players can experience in this module; the unpredictable harmonic movement and the slightly stringent (but glistening) timbre generate a constant sense of unease, motivating players to keep moving. The track subtly encourages continued engagement with the game world.

The track in Figure 15.2 continues through combat sections at a lower dynamic level as a new, active track takes center stage. Figure 15.3 displays the persistent rhythmic bass line of the track that supplements the music of Figure 15.2 to signal a combat state. This new combat layer generally aligns with the harmonies of the exploration layer, but a slight alteration of F-sharp to F-natural in measures 30 and 32 diverges from the original harmonic progression. To avoid any modular disjunction (à la Medina-Gray) when these elements play together, the volume of the combat track is raised and that of the exploration track lowered to such a degree at the midpoint of these examples that their interference is unnoticeable. The combat module enters immediately when an enemy

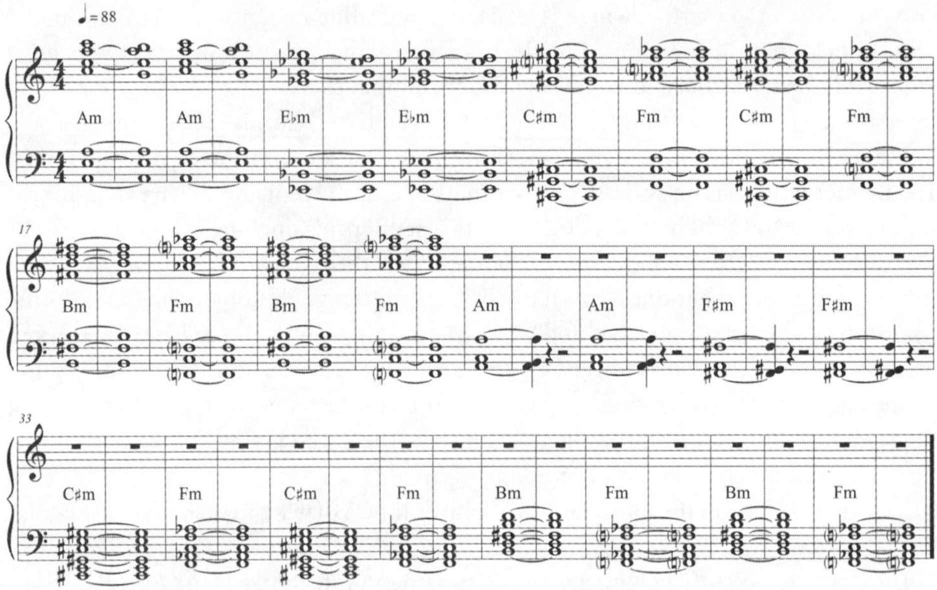

FIGURE 15.2 Harmonic reduction of Christopher Drake's cue "Open World 5 Explo," *Batman: Arkham Origins* (2013).

recognizes the player character, warning the player that battle is about to begin. This repetitive rhythmic action is directly linked to the *march* of the *military* style used in the eighteenth and nineteenth centuries. Dense orchestration and louder dynamics indicate action and presence, reinforcing the gameplay state and providing a clear contrast with the passive and hidden style of the *misterioso/ombra*. Silent film music similarly saw combat as an opportunity for driving rhythm; Rapée uses two rhythmically active movements from Beethoven piano sonatas for his *battle* category: the third movement ("Presto agitato") from Piano Sonata No. 14 in C-sharp minor, op. 27, no. 2, and the opening movement (minus the extended slow introduction) of Piano Sonata No. 8 in C minor, op. 13. Similar to the combat module from *Arkham Origins*, the rhythmic action is constant and unrelenting; all of these cues are meant to keep the player/listener engaged and in a heightened state of awareness.

Since the topical references in these figures are produced by different modules, which are triggered by gameplay, the progression from the *misterioso/ombra* in exploration states to the *military/march* of combat states is completely dependent on player actions and can happen at any point in the examples. Additionally, these tracks are used only in the open-world sections of the game; this combat track is used for random encounters with enemies, not for designed battle scenarios. It is incorporated whenever the combat state activates, whenever Batman happens upon an enemy that recognizes him as a threat, but the track dissipates when all enemies have been defeated—or in the subversive case in which Batman chooses to flee the area instead of responding to the invitation of the battle music, the track dissipates when the enemies are no longer aware of

FIGURE 15.3 Combat bass line that accompanies Christopher Drake's cue "Open World 5 Explo," *Batman: Arkham Origins* (2013).

the player character's presence.[5] As tensions subside after a given battle, the player must prepare to continue exploring the game world, so the exploration track returns to full volume, reinstituting the mysterious aesthetic. The music aligns with the narrative trajectory, responding to changes in gameplay state, but it can also be viewed as a guiding influence, informing the player of the appropriate gameplay mode and persuading them to take part.

Players can continue exploring the open world, encountering enemies, defeating them, moving on, exploring, fighting, winning, and so on. By constantly regressing back to the exploration state and its accompanying *misterioso/ombra* after combat segments, players can easily fall into a gameplay loop that is supported and enhanced by a musical soundtrack. At certain points in a game, players may even seek out these quick changes of gameplay and music, scouring the game world until the *military* style soundtrack returns, informing them that enemy engagements (and potential level gains and item enhancements) are imminent. Grinding for upgrades can come with its own repetitive underscore.

Promoting this compulsion loop may be the easiest way for game designers to keep players engaged, but there are other possible gameplay (and musical) outcomes that can occur at the conclusion of combat to keep players on their toes. Figure 15.4 displays some of these possibilities. While there is no marker for success after the combat track in Figure 15.3 fades away (other than the return of the exploration track at full volume), more choreographed sections of gameplay include an additional musical module after the player character defeats the enemies in an area. Victory modules in video games represent an achievement and often carry some topical markers of a *fanfare*. Each victory stinger in *Arkham Origins* employs a sustained tonic note, or at least a sustained pitch center, with a brighter orchestral tone, but the rhythmic characteristics of the *fanfare* are subdued due to the pervasive *ombra* aesthetic surrounding the Batman character. Additionally, the formal placement of video game "fanfares" at the *conclusion* of combat

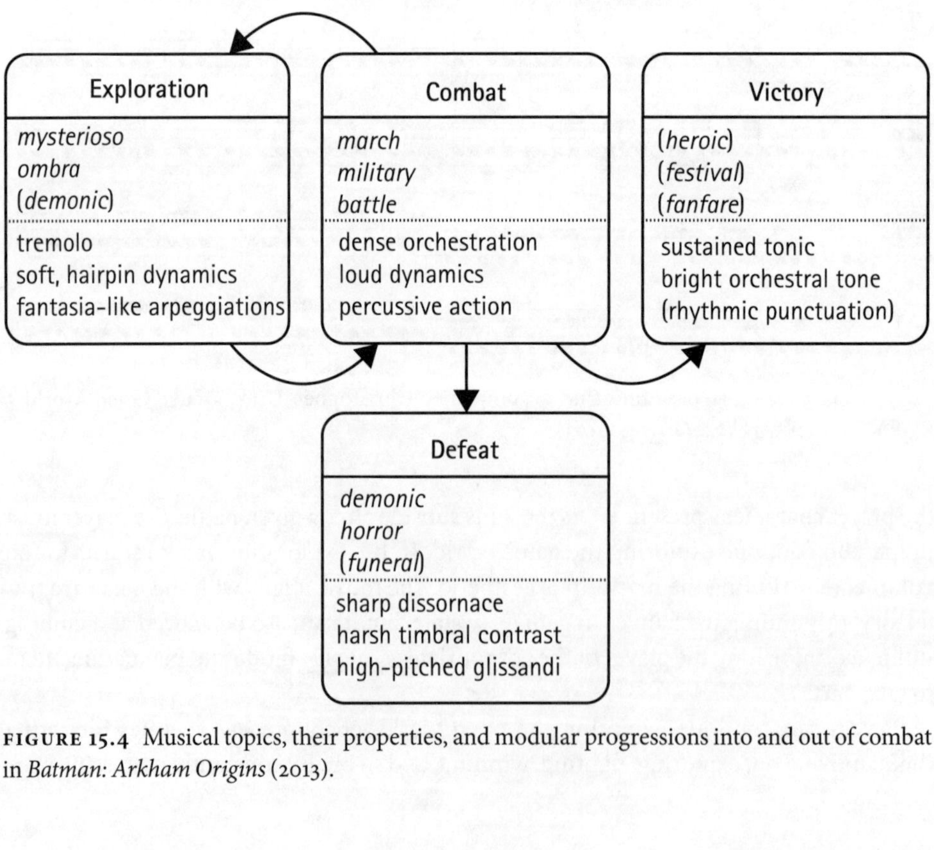

FIGURE 15.4 Musical topics, their properties, and modular progressions into and out of combat in *Batman: Arkham Origins* (2013).

music goes against their typical formal associations. William Caplin (2005, 117) notes that the fanfare is often used as a formal beginning or a proclamation but allows for the possibility of an ending fanfare, or a "fanfare *peroratio*" as Agawu (1991, 18) would say. While a victory cue may occur at the end of a musical structure, it may alternatively be viewed as *leading into* the following section of gameplay (whether the next situation is accompanied by music or not), heralding the victory of the player character.

Victory modules typically encourage players to consider their controlled character as the hero of the story at the end of combat segments, promoting a sense of accomplishment with an additional musical cue. Comparing the victory modules of *Arkham Origins* with the 19th-century *heroic* style that Dickensheets explores in connection with Beethoven, however, produces some conflicting results. She writes: "Used frequently to signify victory, it is most often delivered in a powerful major key. Its fanfare figures often encompass the entire orchestra and are frequently accompanied by timpani and trumpet . . . in an expansive show of heroism" (Dickensheets 2012, 118). Additionally, Agawu (1991, 48) notes that the "fanfare is essentially a rhythmicized arpeggio, which makes it a particularly mobile topic." For the "fanfares" of *Arkham Origins*, the major key is absent, and the rhythmic activity is attenuated. While the victory modules deliver on some elements of the heroic style, such as the focus on a single pitch center and the employment of a powerfully resonant chord, it is important to note that these chords would not typically be associated with the classical *fanfare* topic. While in dialogue with other victory motives in video games, the victories of *Arkham Origins* must yield to the mysterious, supernatural qualities of the primary character. A fantastical fanfare like those used in early *Final Fantasy* or *Legend of Zelda* iterations, while perhaps aligning well with the grandiose *festival* themes from silent film practice, would seem as out of place in *Arkham Origins* as using a rhythmically subdued minor sonority to proclaim victory in a high fantasy setting. Further, the sense of realism in modern iterations of the Batman character calls less for celebration of victory and more for concentration on the duty of a tragic hero.

To consider how these victory modules arise, we can examine an extended section of gameplay, summarized in Figure 15.5. In an early part of the game, Batman infiltrates the Sionis Industries Steel Mill, which has been taken over by a group of hostiles. When the enemies recognize Batman, a coordinated combat segment begins, complete with a percussive, mechanical combat track. Notably, this track continues between two separate waves of enemies, signaling to the player that this combat section is not complete; only the final victory tag, a resonant D minor harmony, fully orchestrated, offers relief from the situation as a marker of success. With the music shifting from a rhythmically active combat module to a static victory module, players can recognize the change in gameplay state, from heightened interaction to more relaxed. At times, the soundtrack for *Arkham Origins* encourages continued combat engagement; in other cases, it promotes player achievements. Thus, the victory cue that concludes this section of gameplay *must* provide a differentiation with the previous combat music, since a continued rhythmic effect in the victory fanfare might imply a continued combat situation. While other video game settings can rely on a shift from a minor-key combat theme to a major-key victory

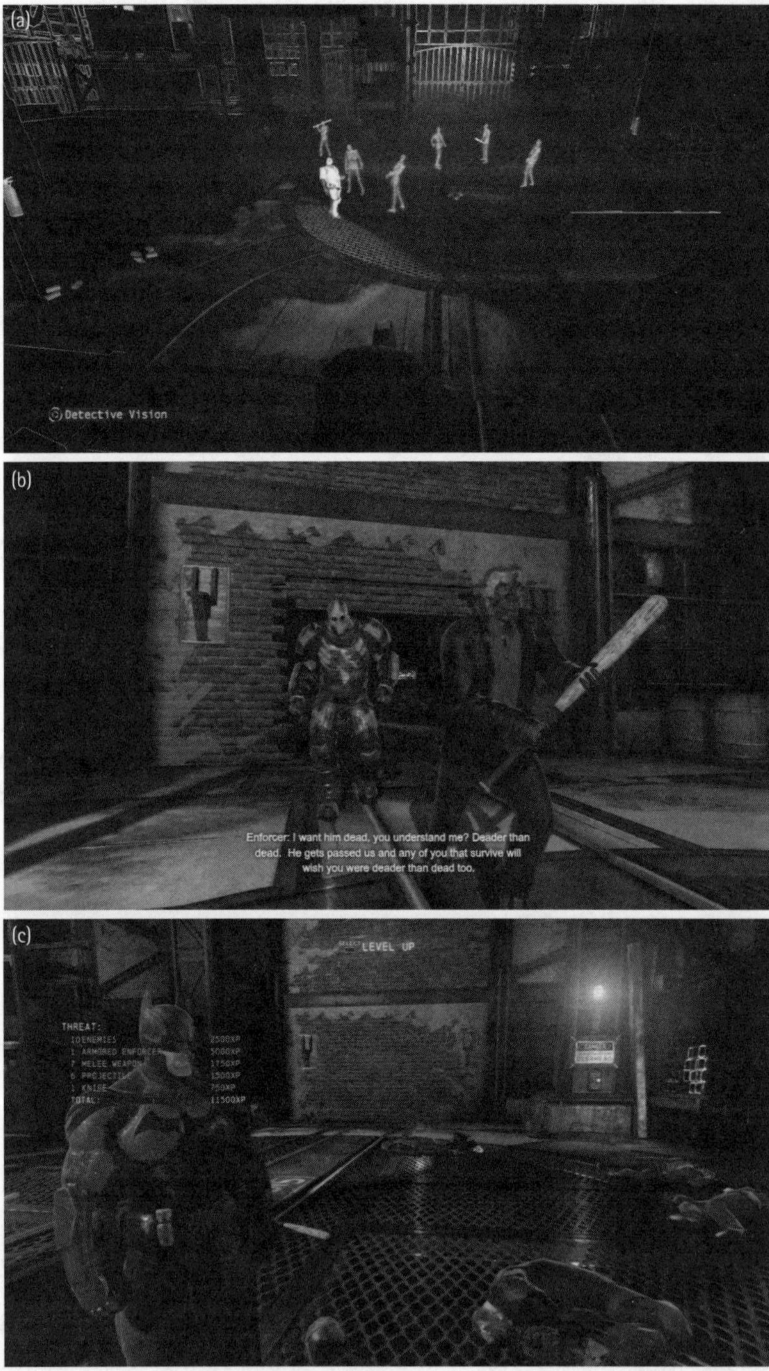

FIGURE 15.5 Series of screenshots from the Sionis Industries Steel Mill in *Batman: Arkham Origins* (2013).

theme to indicate changes of gameplay state, *Arkham Origins* must rely on a change in rhythmic activity.

In direct opposition to these victory modules, depictions of failure after combat sequences provide a musical outcome that halts the narrative progression. The defeat modules in *Arkham Origins*, triggered after combat failure and indicating the death of the player character, are relentless with sharp dissonance and harsh timbral contrast with the preceding combat modules. By employing high-pitched string glissandi, these cues reference an extreme element of the *demonic* style. While some death themes in films and video games can lend themselves to *funereal* marches and a sense of loss or grief for onscreen characters, the themes of *Arkham Origins* tend toward depicting the horror of death. In many ways, this drastic style of scoring video game death is quite fitting for the medium. While a player may momentarily feel a sense of loss for the characters they are controlling, they are quickly reminded that the loss is not permanent; their character can reappear in the game world, perhaps with only minor consequences for the failure. Some games, however, take this as an opportunity to scold the player. For example, after a defeat module plays in *Arkham Origins*, the face of a familiar enemy appears on screen to mock the character's demise in the previous round of combat. In Figure 15.6, the Joker speaks directly to the camera, giving the impression that the visual depiction has changed from a third-person perspective to a first-person perspective. The mockery can be experienced through the eyes of the main character as Batman sees his archenemy towering over him, but the message could also be interpreted as a directed taunting of the player. The harsh musical cue can similarly be viewed as a punishment for the failure, a psychological consequence in place of a gameplay consequence. The music urges the player to avoid failure in the future to escape the grating sounds of a horrible death.

FIGURE 15.6 The Joker speaks to the camera to taunt the player in defeat.

Conclusion

Music's ability to instill a sense of success or failure demonstrates the significant control that video games exert over our emotions and actions. This type of encoding implies that the medium generates new and characteristic topical styles, extending the "universe of topic" described by Agawu beyond the realm of static or passive media formats. Though game music can draw on the history of film music, its future lies in a sincere consideration of interactivity and what it means for musical signification. Examining the musical ramifications of situations unique to video games will surely lead to further topical outcomes that are similarly potent. For instance, music associated with video game bosses (Yee 2020) or level grinding (Armstrong 2021) or any number of other distinctive circumstances can yield new topics or tropes, add new levels of semiotic referencing, and expand the ability of video game music (and musical media in general) to communicate ideas.

With these expanded abilities, it is likely that video games will become more manipulative than they already are. Their influence over player actions grows deeper with every new entry in a series, every novel gameplay mechanic, and every soundtrack with more engaging and dynamic music. As players, we may nominally have control over gameplay choices, but we often allow games and their music to take control over us, to guide us on the right path. We trust games to tell us what to do, to inform us of whether we succeeded, and (if we didn't) how we should do better next time. Game music (and its modular design and topical signifiers) can drive our compulsions to continue, complete, and succeed; each time we do these things, we are more likely to give ourselves over to game music's desires the next time around.

Notes

1. Research conducted by Aviv Weinstein and Michel Lejoyeux (2015) indicates that the release of dopamine associated with the playing of video games is similar in magnitude to that associated with the use of drugs or alcohol. Further, Joshua Krook (2017) writes that video game companies use the same tactics as casinos and that some have even hired psychologists to ensure that consumers are continually engaged and invested in (or addicted to) playing their games.
2. In this sense, video games are similar to electronic gambling machines, which use sound effects "for a variety of feedback and reward systems" (Collins et al. 2011, 8).
3. Elements of this research were presented at the 2015 Society for Music Theory Annual Meeting and at the 2015 North American Conference on Video Game Music.
4. Here, I must thank orchestrator Patrick Russ and composer Christopher Drake for allowing me access to the scores for this work.
5. While video game music may afford certain interactions (Grimshaw 2007; Kamp 2014; Grasso 2020), these encoded invitations to act in a given way must also be interpreted by players, potentially leading to situations of misunderstanding and confusion. As noted by

Adrienne Shaw (2017, 597), whose research extends the work of Stuart Hall (1980) into the realm of interactive media, scholars can examine "what uses (and users) are encoded into the design of interactive objects/texts" but must also "look at how they are then decoded or what emergent uses we see when they are in the hands of users themselves."

References

Agawu, Victor Kofi. 1991. *Playing with Signs: A Semiotic Interpretation of Classic Music*. Princeton: Princeton University Press.

Agawu, Victor Kofi. 2009. *Music as Discourse: Semiotic Adventures in Romantic Music*. Oxford: Oxford University Press.

Armstrong, Stephen. 2021. "Sounding the Grind: Musicospatial Stasis in JRPG Battle Themes." *Journal of Sound and Music in Games* 2 (2): 1–21.

Atkinson, Sean E. 2019. "Soaring through the Sky: Topics and Tropes in Video Game Music." *Music Theory Online* 25 (2). https://doi.org/10.30535/mto.25.2.1.

Ayers, William. 2015. "Analyzing Narrative in Video Game Music: Topic Theory and Modular Design." Paper presented at the Society for Music Theory Annual Meeting, St. Louis, MO, October 31, and at the North American Conference on Video Game Music, Texas Christian University, Fort Worth, TX, January 17, 2015.

Bradford, Wesley J. 2020. "Exploring the Narrative Implications of Emerging Topics in *The Legend of Zelda: Breath of the Wild*." *Journal of Sound and Music in Games* 1 (4): 1–21.

Caplin, William E. 2005. "On the Relation of Musical *Topoi* to Formal Function." *Eighteenth-Century Music* 2 (1): 113–124.

Collins, Karen, Holly Tessler, Kevin Harrigan, Michael J. Dixon, and Jonathan Fugelsang. 2011. "Sound in Electronic Gambling Machines: A Review of the Literature and Its Relevance to Game Sound." In *Game Sound Technology and Player Interaction: Concepts and Developments*, edited by Mark Grimshaw, 1–21. Hershey, PA: Information Science Reference.

Csikszentmihalyi, Mihaly, and Isabella Selega Csikszentmihalyi, eds. 1988. *Optimal Experience: Psychological Studies of Flow in Consciousness*. Cambridge: Cambridge University Press.

Dickensheets, Janice. 2012. "The Topical Vocabulary of the Nineteenth Century." *Journal of Musicological Research* 31:97–137.

Donnelly, Kevin J. 1998. "The Classical Film Score Forever? *Batman*, *Batman Returns* and Post-Classical Film Music." In *Contemporary Hollywood Cinema*, edited by Steve Neale and Murray Smith, 142–155. New York: Routledge.

Gorbman, Claudia. 1987. *Unheard Melodies: Narrative Film Music*. Bloomington: Indiana University Press.

Grasso, Julianne M. 2020. "Video Game Music, Meaning, and the Possibilities of Play." PhD dissertation, University of Chicago.

Grimshaw, Mark. 2007. "The Acoustic Ecology of the First-Person Shooter." PhD dissertation, University of Waikato.

Grossman, Lev. 2015. "Video Games in the Age of Cell Phones." *Time*, June 22, 2015.

Hall, Stuart. 1980. "Encoding/Decoding." In *Culture, Media, Language*, edited by Stuart Hall, Dorothy Hobson, Andrew Lowe, and Paul Willis, 128–138. London: Routledge.

Hatten, Robert. 2014. "The Troping of Topics in Mozart's Instrumental Works." In *The Oxford Handbook of Topic Theory*, edited by Danuta Mirka, 514–536. Oxford: Oxford University Press.

Isbister, Katherine. 2016. *How Games Move Us: Emotion by Design*. Cambridge, MA: MIT Press.

Juul, Jesper. 2013. *The Art of Failure: An Essay on the Pain of Playing Video Games*. Cambridge, MA: MIT Press.

Kamp, Michiel. 2014. "Musical Ecologies in Video Games." *Philosophy and Technology* 27 (2): 235–249.

Krook, Joshua. 2017. "The Business of Addiction: How the Video Gaming Industry Is Evolving to Be Like the Casino Industry." *Conversation*, September 12, 2017. https://theconversation.com/the-business-of-addiction-how-the-video-gaming-industry-is-evolving-to-be-like-the-casino-industry-83361.

Kwan, Allen. 2016. "Authored Agency: Exploring the Language and Grammar of Video Games." PhD dissertation, University of Guelph.

Lerner, Neil. 2014a. "Mario's Dynamic Leaps: Musical Innovations (and the Specter of Early Cinema) in *Donkey Kong* and *Super Mario Bros.*" In *Music in Video Games: Studying Play*, edited by K .J. Donnelly, William Gibbons, and Neil Lerner, 1–29. New York: Routledge.

Lerner, Neil. 2014b. "The Origins of Musical Style in Video Games." In *The Oxford Handbook of Film Music Studies*, edited by David Neumeyer, 319–347. Oxford: Oxford University Press.

McClelland, Clive. 2014. "*Ombra* and *Tempesta*." In *The Oxford Handbook of Topic Theory*, edited by Danuta Mirka, 279–300. Oxford: Oxford University Press.

Medina-Gray, Elizabeth. 2014a. "Modular Structure and Function in Early 21st-Century Video Game Music." PhD dissertation, Yale University.

Medina-Gray, Elizabeth. 2014b. "Meaningful Modular Combinations: Simultaneous Harp and Environmental Music in Two *Legend of Zelda* Games." In *Music in Video Games: Studying Play*, edited by K. J. Donnelly, William Gibbons, and Neil Lerner, 104–121. New York: Routledge.

Medina-Gray, Elizabeth. 2017. "Musical Dreams and Nightmares: An Analysis of Flower." In *The Routledge Companion to Screen Music and Sound*, edited by Miguel Mera, Ronald Sadoff, and Ben Winters, 562–576. New York: Routledge.

Medina-Gray, Elizabeth. 2019. "Analyzing Modular Smoothness in Video Game Music." *Music Theory Online* 25 (3). https://doi.org/10.30535/mto.25.3.2.

Mirka, Danuta. 2014. "Topics and Meter." In *The Oxford Handbook of Topic Theory*, edited by Danuta Mirka, 357–380. Oxford: Oxford University Press.

Monelle, Raymond. 2006. *The Musical Topic: Hunt, Military and Pastoral*. Bloomington: Indiana University Press.

Murphy, Scott. 2014. "Transformational Theory and the Analysis of Film Music." In *The Oxford Handbook of Film Music Studies*, edited by David Neumeyer, 471–499. Oxford: Oxford University Press.

Phillips, Winifred. 2014. *A Composer's Guide to Game Music*. Cambridge, MA: MIT Press.

Plebuch, Tobias. 2012 "Mysteriosos Demystified: Topical Strategies within and beyond the Silent Cinema." *Journal of Film Music* 5 (1–2): 77–92.

Rapée, Erno, ed. 1924. *Motion Picture Moods*. New York: G. Schirmer Inc.

Ratner, Leonard G. 1980. *Classic Music: Expression, Form, and Style*. New York: Schirmer Books.

Ratner, Leonard G. 1991. "Topical Content in Mozart's Keyboard Sonatas." *Early Music* 19 (4): 615–619.

Sauer, Rodney. 1998–1999. "Photoplay Music: A Reusable Repertory for Silent Film Scoring, 1914–1929." *American Music Research Center Journal* 8–9: 55–76.

Shaw, Adrienne. 2017. "Encoding and Decoding Affordances: Stuart Hall and Interactive Media Technologies." *Media, Culture and Society* 39 (4): 592–602.

Summers, Tim. 2012. "Epic Texturing in the First-Person Shooter: The Aesthetics of Video Game Music." *The Soundtrack* 5 (2): 131–151.

Summers, Tim. 2016. *Understanding Video Game Music*. Cambridge: Cambridge University Press.

Trezise, Simon. 2019. "Historical Introduction." In *Music and Sound in Silent Film: From the Nickelodeon to The Artist*, edited by Ruth Barton and Simon Trezise, 1–21. New York: Routledge.

True, Lyle C. 1914. *How and What to Play for Moving Pictures*. San Francisco: Music Supply Co.

Weinstein, Aviv, and Michel Lejoyeux. 2015. "New Developments on the Neurobiological and Pharmaco-Genetic Mechanisms Underlying Internet and Videogame Addiction." *American Journal on Addictions* 24 (2): 117–125.

Yee, Thomas B. 2020. "Battle Hymn of the God-Slayers: Troping Rock and Sacred Music Topics in *Xenoblade Chronicles*." *Journal of Sound and Music in Games* 1 (1): 2–19.

Young, Matthew David. 2013. "Musical Topics in the Comic Book Superhero Film Genre." PhD dissertation, University of Texas at Austin.

Zamecnik, John Stepan. 1914. *Sam Fox Moving Picture Music, Vol. 1*. Cleveland: Sam Fox Publishing Company.

Zamecnik, John Stepan. 1919. *Sam Fox Photoplay Edition, Vol. 1*. Cleveland: Sam Fox Publishing Company.

CHAPTER 16

AUDITORY HALLUCINATIONS AND ALTERED STATES OF CONSCIOUSNESS IN VIDEO GAMES

JONATHAN WEINEL

Introduction

We Happy Few (Compulsion Games 2016) is an action-adventure, survival horror game set in an alternate swinging-sixties dystopia, where society is addicted to a hallucinogenic drug called Joy, which keeps them blissfully unaware and under control. In the *Lightbearer* downloadable content, you take on the character of Nick Lightbearer, a faded rock star. After taking some pills he finds in the bathroom, suddenly your character is shrunk, in a humorous scene reminiscent of *Alice's Adventures in Wonderland* (Carroll [1865–1871] 1993). From a first-person perspective, your character must explore bookcases, dashing across cupboards and kitchen countertops that glow with an eerie luminescence, while psychedelic sonic atmospheres and echoing sitars are heard in the background. Later, the drugs wear off and Nick is returned to his normal size—yet he cannot resist plucking a purple pill from a bowl: "I'll quit some other, less stressful day . . ." Suddenly, he has four arms and is propelled into a blinding white light. Now, he must navigate a hallucinatory version of the corridor, where the walls and carpets seem to breathe, as color hues shift from purple to an ominous red. On the soundtrack we hear the familiar sitars again, as his voice echoes into space like one of the more out-there, effects-laden parts of The Jimi Hendrix Experience's *Electric Ladyland* (1968) LP. Droning sounds and looping noises intensify, as the doors of the corridor the protagonist is in become terrifying jaws of flame. As Nick heads down the staircase, we hear descending choral notes as his vision blurs, the sound warping in pitch like a broken turntable. With a visual flicker, suddenly the corridor becomes a blood-red river, before the protagonist is plunged into darkness, finding himself traveling though mirrors surrounded by spectral faces and whispering voices. Finally, a melting corridor with Bridget Riley–style op-art wallpaper sucks him into a flaming meat grinder amid rising tones and laughter. The chaos fades to black. Nick wakes the next day with a severe headache—"no more purples!"

This fantastical scene from *We Happy Few* seems to take inspiration in equal parts from Terry Gilliam's *Fear and Loathing in Las Vegas* (1998) and Stanley Kubrick's *The Shining* (1980). Yet while these films incorporate cinematic representations of hallucinations, in *We Happy Few* these are experienced interactively. The player is in control of the protagonist, seeing what he sees, and hearing what he hears as he experiences a drug-induced altered state of consciousness (ASC) from a first-person perspective. The sequence is interactive and uses a variety of visual and sonic techniques to represent these experiences. Graphical effects and postprocessing change the way the game looks, while background music and digital signal processing (DSP) effects such as echo and reverb are applied to the dialogue. These are used in combination with various scripted events and musical materials to provide a narrative sequence that is visually striking and sonically detailed, ultimately giving the player an exotic, narrative experience which contributes toward narrative development.

Sequences like this one, which depict states of intoxication, hallucination, or psychosis, have become increasingly common in video games over the last few decades. In this chapter, I shall explore the design and function of these sequences by drawing together existing research and examples in this area. First, I will outline how ASCs may shape subjective experience in various ways, focusing in particular on sensory aspects of these experiences. This will allow us to consider how these may provide a practical basis for the design of corresponding sequences in video games. Following this, I will provide an overview of existing games that represent hallucinations, allowing us to see what techniques are used already. Next, I discuss several of my own projects that represent auditory hallucinations and ASCs in sound and video games. This discussion will provide the necessary backdrop through which we can then consider the concept of "avatar-centered subjectivity," whereby the design of graphics, sounds, and controls are modified to represent the subjective experience of a player avatar from a first-person perspective. Through an exploration of examples and the concept of avatar-centered subjectivity, I will provide the conceptual tools that readers need to understand how ASCs can be effectively represented in games, allowing them to undertake their own analyses and practical work in this specialist area of sound design and games development.

Auditory Hallucinations and Altered States of Consciousness

The term "ASC" was popularized in the 1960s (Ludwig 1969) and describes a variety of nonordinary perceptual states, including states of dream, meditation, trance, intoxication, psychosis, and hypnosis. ASCs can be induced with or without the use of drugs, eliciting a variety of effects. For example, dreaming is something we often experience naturally during sleep, and may result in various visual and auditory sensations. Dreams have been characterized by Hobson (2003) as being reminiscent of hallucinating while asleep. On the thresholds of sleep, it is also possible to experience hypnogogic hallucinations, as in episodes of sleep paralysis, where one may perceive a suffocating being or "old hag" sitting on the chest (Hufford 1989). Meditation involves various techniques for promoting relaxed focus of attention, with the aim of increasing awareness. Meanwhile, trance states may occur in various ritualistic contexts, where extreme stimulation of the senses through music, dance, and/or the spraying of liquids can induce ASCs through sensory overload. States of intoxication may be precipitated by ingesting plants such as the peyote cactus, or psilocybin mushrooms. Alternatively, or drugs such as LSD (lysergic acid diethylamide) or alcohol may also induce ASCs. The form of ASC produced can vary significantly depending on the substance in question. For example, psychedelic drugs such as LSD or psilocybin mushrooms may induce visual and auditory hallucinations, or distortions to time perception. In contrast, alcohol may impair the function of the nervous system or produce blurred vision. Hallucinations can also occur in other contexts, for example, psychosis is a symptom of mental illness, during which a person may experience visual or auditory hallucinations. Lastly, hypnosis may involve sensory reduction under instruction and can result in relaxation.

When considering the form of ASCs, it is important to acknowledge that there are many possible types. Of course, these are also subjective experiences and may vary not only between individuals but even between instances in different contexts. Even so, it is usually possible to identify some common features of ASCs, which we can then use as a basis for designs that represent these experiences. To find these commonalties, we can look at existing studies that may include reports describing the experiences of participants during ASCs. For example, Klüver's (1971) work on the effects of the psychedelic drug mescaline showed that it may often produce "form constants": tunnels, spirals, lattices, or cobwebs. In Klüver's study, participants would see visual hallucinations of these patterns in the earlier stages of hallucination, while these would later be replaced by more fully formed impressions. Similarly, studies have shown that psychedelic hallucinations may also precipitate auditory hallucinations, in which the participant hears sounds that do not have an immediate external, acoustic basis in the surrounding acoustic environment (Weinel, Cunningham, and Griffiths 2014). These auditory hallucinations may consist of noises, voices, or music. By looking at qualitative descriptions of these experiences, it is possible to draw up a list of features that one may use as a basis for design when representing states of hallucination in video games.

ASCs can be understood as temporal states of significant deviation from a commonly accepted normal waking consciousness (accepting the limitations of such a definition). When considering how these experiences may unfold in time, it can be helpful to think of consciousness as a continuous experience where various aspects may dynamically increase or decrease in intensity over time. Models, such as Hobson's (2003) "state-space" concept of consciousness, reflect this approach. State-space describes how brain activity may involve high or low levels of *activation*, focus on sources of sensory *inputs*, or utilize different *modes*, in which events may be committed to memory or forgotten to varying degrees. This model aims to describe how aspects of consciousness may change throughout the day, as an individual moves from normal-waking consciousness, to dreamless and dreaming sleep states. As these transitions occur, the intensity of brain activity may change; attention may shift from the external surrounding environment toward internal visions; and events may be recollected or forgotten.

Along similar lines, Rouget's (1985) discussion of trance draws on the idea of consciousness as a continuum, highlighting how stimulation or reduction of the senses may elicit high- or low-energy states. From this perspective, ASCs could be considered to reflect heightened emotional states with varying degrees of intensity. Rouget based his discussion on Fischer's (1971) cartography of ecstatic and meditative states, which describes consciousness as a continuum ranging from *ergotropic* states of energy expenditure to *trophotropic* states of energy conservation. In contemporary work within the field of affective computing, Russell's (1980) circumplex model of affect, is a similar model that describes affective states according to *valence* and *arousal*, where arousal indicates the energetic or activation level of the individual, while valence describes whether the experience is pleasant or unpleasant. Though these models are reductive, they can be useful in computer systems, as they allow aspects of consciousness or emotions to be conveniently captured and parameterized.

In summary, the term "ASC" encompasses many forms of experience such as dreams, meditations, trances, hallucinations, states of intoxication, psychosis, and hypnosis. These states can be precipitated through various means and may result in multiple changes to the perceptual experience of an individual. If we are interested in representing a particular ASC in a video game, we can look at experiential reports or other research data in order to identify typical features and commonalities which can then be used as a basis for design. For example, if looking at psychedelic ASCs, we might identify features such as visual patterns of hallucination, auditory hallucinations, or distortions to time perception. Having identified key features, we can use them as a basis for the design of changes to graphics, sound, and other aspects of interactivity in a game, such as the player control system. When implementing these features, it is useful to see ASCs as dynamic processes in a constant state of flux, so we should consider using parametric values to reflect a changing intensity of these effects over time. In the next two sections, we will look at some existing representations of ASCs in video games, some of which do precisely this.

ASCs in Video Games

ASCs can be found in many titles throughout the history of video games. An early example can be found in the adventure game *Fantasy World Dizzy* (Oliver Twins 1989), where Dizzy finds a bottle of liquor which the player can choose to use. Doing so causes Dizzy to roll around drunkenly for a short time, putting him at increased risk of falling into the jaws of a hundred crocodiles, or rolling into some flames and turning into a fried egg. Here, 2D sprites are used to reflect Dizzy's intoxication, as we see him rolling around on-screen, while a temporary, automated disruption to the player controls allows the player to experience this interactively. As with many of the examples we will discuss in this section, the representation of intoxication provides a means through which to develop the narrative involvement of the player, but it also affects their kinesthetic and ludic experience.[1]

Some similarities can be observed in the combat racing game *Death Rally* (Remedy Entertainment 1996), in which the player can collect a magic mushroom which causes a rippling distortion effect on-screen, making it hard to control the vehicle, while an amusing "wow, man" voice is heard on the soundtrack. Along similar lines, the *Grand Theft Auto* series includes many representations of intoxication, such as in *Grand Theft Auto: Vice City* (Rockstar North 2002) where, on one mission, the player must drive a military vehicle while drunk on alcoholic fumes. Player controls are disrupted, with a swaying camera view and visual trail effects suggesting impairment to the motor skills and sight of the player.[2] Sound is used to communicate the experiences of the characters through slurred speech and dialogue in which they describe their experiences. As before, both scenes serve a kinesthetic function, disrupting the player's experience of control, and this also has ludic implications since it makes it harder to win the level. At the same time, they are aesthetically appealing, and support narrative development.

While sequences of intoxication reflect temporary impairment, other games incorporate power-up items which lend the player special abilities and may reflect a temporary ASC for the game character. In *Sonic the Hedgehog* (Sonic Team 1991), the player can collect speed boots that allow Sonic to move more quickly for a short period of time. This temporary change is signified in sound via an acceleration of the music. This increases the player's sense of urgency and reflects a temporary state of high arousal through sound.[3] Although the speed boots are not framed as a drug, elsewhere in *Duke Nukem 3D* (3D Realms 1996) the collectable steroids provide a similar effect, giving the Duke a temporary speed boost, while audio is used to reflect a temporary, high-energy state via a rapid heartbeat sound. Along similar lines, berserker power-ups such as the quad damage found in *Quake* (id Software 1996) give a temporary boost to the damage inflicted on enemies by the player's weapons. The effects of the quad damage are drug-like, as we can see in the image displaying the player's face in the graphical user interface (GUI), which contorts as if in a frenzy, while a heightened state of arousal is also signified via a flickering blue light around the player. In terms of audio, a distorted sound effect is heard upon collecting the quad damage, which sounds each time the player fires a weapon, underscoring the sense of aggression and urgency.

Psychotic hallucinations are perhaps the most common type of ASC used in contemporary games. A notable early instance can be found in *Max Payne* (Remedy Entertainment 2001), in which the protagonist is drugged and finds himself wandering through hallucinatory corridors, which are strangely distorted and drip with blood, while surrealistic echoing voices and cries are heard in the background. Here the function is primarily a narrative one, as the sequence provides a means through which to uncover memories from Max's past, which help us to understand his psychological experience, and past traumas, which are pivotal to the storyline. From a technical point of view, in these scenes the hallucinations are realized through the design of specific game levels, which resemble distorted scenes from Max's past, via the use of elongated rooms and textures. Sound has an important role, with vocal dialogue and looping cries being triggered throughout and processed with digital signal processing (DSP) effects, such as filters, echoes, and reverbs, so that we hear fragments of events from Max's past as sonically distant and blurred.

Hallucinations like these are also found in various other titles, and often serve a similar function. For example, *Silent Hill* (Konami 1999), *F.E.A.R.* (Monolith 2005), and *Batman: Arkham Asylum* (Rocksteady Studios 2009) are just three examples that use hallucinations as one of the means to develop horror atmospheres and narratives.[4] More recently, in *Hellblade: Senua's Sacrifice* (Ninja Theory 2017) psychosis is pervasive in the game via representations of visual and auditory hallucinations. From the outset, your character experiences auditory hallucinations, as she hears voices which give the player an insight into her troubled, conflicting thoughts and motivations. When experienced through headphones, binaural audio techniques are used to bring the spatial perception of these as close as possible to the listener. In this case, the sound designers did not rely solely on existing tropes for representing hallucinations, instead consulting experts and groups who experience auditory hallucinations to base the dialogue and audio on actual reports and lived experiences (VentureBeat 2017).

Psychedelic drugs are also represented in a growing number of video games. For example, *Far Cry 3* (Ubisoft Montreal 2012), *Grand Theft Auto V* (Rockstar North 2013), and *We Happy Few* (Compulsion Games 2016) are all games in which your character can take virtual drugs. In these examples, post-processing, shaders, or visual effects are used, sometimes in combination with 3D animations and scripted events, to suggest the visual experience of hallucinations. In first-person perspective games such as *We Happy Few*, a camera is used to suggest the eye-view of the player, and this can be used to communicate the visual distortions that would be subjectively perceived by the player's character while on drugs. While third-person perspective games do not use a camera to suggest the eye-view of the player avatar, in games such as *Grand Theft Auto V* visual filters are similarly applied to the main camera in the scene during sequences where the player character is on drugs. During these sequences, sound is used to reflect intoxicated states, through the triggering of materials suggesting auditory hallucinations, while DSP effects warp and distort those sound sources within the scene. Atmospheric musical sounds such as ambiences or drones may also be utilized. In each of these examples, time-varying parameters are used to vary the intensity of effects and bring sounds suggesting hallucination in and out of the mix.

As we move into the domain of virtual reality, which has seen a resurgence in recent years via technologies such as the Oculus Quest, we find a variety of experiences that incorporate ASCs. Various applications, such as *Guided Meditation VR* (Cubicle

Ninjas 2016), provide virtual meditation experiences. These do not represent ASCs, but rather aim to induce them by submerging the user into computer-generated locations such as tropical islands, forests, and clifftops. Here, audio is used to generate relaxing soundscapes with sounds of nature, while a spoken-word guided meditation instructs the user. These applications could have benefits for training people to meditate, although it must be said that it is not necessary to wear a VR headset to practice meditation, and placing the individual in a virtual environment could potentially be distracting. Even so, there are other interesting examples in this field, such as *Soundself* (Andromeda Entertainment 2020), which varies this concept by instructing the user to use their voice to create droning sounds which propel them through psychedelic visualizations of sound. Here, sound from the user is captured from a microphone and transformed with DSP effects by the application. Along similar lines, *Ayahuasca* (Kounen 2019) is perhaps the most elaborate ASC experience in VR to date. Beginning in front of a shaman, the user gradually sees various geometric patterns that engulf the visual field, sending the viewer on a journey through tunnels of snakes and geometric patterns which are modeled on the form and progression of an ASC induced by the Amazonian hallucinogenic brew ayahuasca. In this case the soundtrack is based on transformations of a shamanic vocal song and rainforest ambiences.[5]

This section has outlined various representations of ASCs in games which reflect different types of ASCs and purposes. Of course, there are also instances where games may integrate more than one of these. For example, *Cyberpunk 2077* (CD Projekt RED 2020) includes various scenes in which the player's character can choose whether to drink alcohol while in a bar. If the player chooses to do so, visual filters are applied which blur and distort the camera, reflecting intoxication. However, the game also features recurring digital hallucination sequences, which are narratively related to a malfunctioning computer chip in the protagonist's brain. In these scenes, the character of Johnny Silverhand appears as an apparition to provide exposition. Here, the player-character's hallucinatory state is communicated through various glitch visual effects and sounds, sometimes in combination with DSP effects such as echo and reverb, as Johnny Silverhand flickers in and out of visibility. The alcohol scenes are relatively trivial, a minor novelty, which serve to add variety to the dialogue sequences and reinforce a sense of the player's agency in decision-making. The Johnny Silverhand scenes, however, are pivotal to the main storyline of the game; they are the means through which it is able to give the player a sense of consciousness hacking, thereby bringing to life an essential trope of the cyberpunk genre.[6]

Projects and Approaches

In my practice-led research in sound design, electronic music, and audiovisual composition, I have explored a variety of approaches for representing ASCs such as psychedelic hallucinations. For instance, in the field of electroacoustic music, I investigated approaches for composing sonic artworks based on altered states of consciousness (Weinel 2016). Here the methodology used can be summarized as follows:

1. Sounds are designed based on typical ASC features;
2. These are then organized into structures based on the typical progression of an ASC in time.

Using this approach, I composed works such as *Nausea* (2011), which incorporates sounds based on the typical features of hallucinations (Weinel 2013). For instance: droning sounds were used to indicate distortions to time-perception, where a single moment seems to last longer than usual; rotating percussive sounds, which orbit the listener spatially, were used to indicate the tunnel formations described in Klüver's (1971) work; and transformations of whispering voices suggested encounters with hallucinated beings. These materials were then organized into structures that were analogous to the form of a hallucination as it occurs in time, where there is a gradual onset of the experience which gradually builds in intensity until reaching a plateau before the effects wear off and eventually terminate.

Translating these approaches into the field of video games, the *Quake Delirium* (2010) project was a real-time modification, adapting the PC version of the first-person shooter game *Quake* (id Software 1996) to represent a delirious or hallucinatory experience (Weinel 2011). This was technically accomplished using a bespoke Max/MSP patch, in combination with QuakeC scripts, which allowed data to be sent to the game to manipulate graphical and game parameters while also triggering a real-time soundtrack. Visually, the project automates camera properties such as field-of-vision, gamma, a red hue effect, a red/blue stereoscopic effect, and a drunk mode, thereby applying multiple distortions to suggest hallucinations (Figure 16.1). The project also modifies the game speed, slowing down the game at points to indicate distortions to time perception. Each property is automated individually with predesigned envelopes, and these are also used to modify parameters of sound and DSP effects on an electroacoustic soundtrack which is generated in real time using the techniques described above. In summary, *Quake Delirium* has a design where graphics and sounds are modified to represent an ASC experience, and these effects are automated to provide dynamic changes in intensity over time.

In subsequent development of this work, *Psych Dome* (2013) was a project that used Max/MSP (a programming language for sound) and Processing (a programming language for visual art) to generate real-time sounds and graphics based on features of hallucination (Weinel et al. 2015). The project was sited in a mobile fulldome[7] and used a consumer-grade electroencephalograph (EEG) headset to modulate aspects of the audiovisualization, thereby linking the brainwaves of the user to the experience generated. Visually, the project provides a sequence of animations displaying funnels of dots and vortex patterns, which are based on visual patterns of hallucinations

FIGURE 16.1 *Quake Delirium* (2010) represented an ASC by automating various graphical and game parameters, while also providing a corresponding soundtrack.

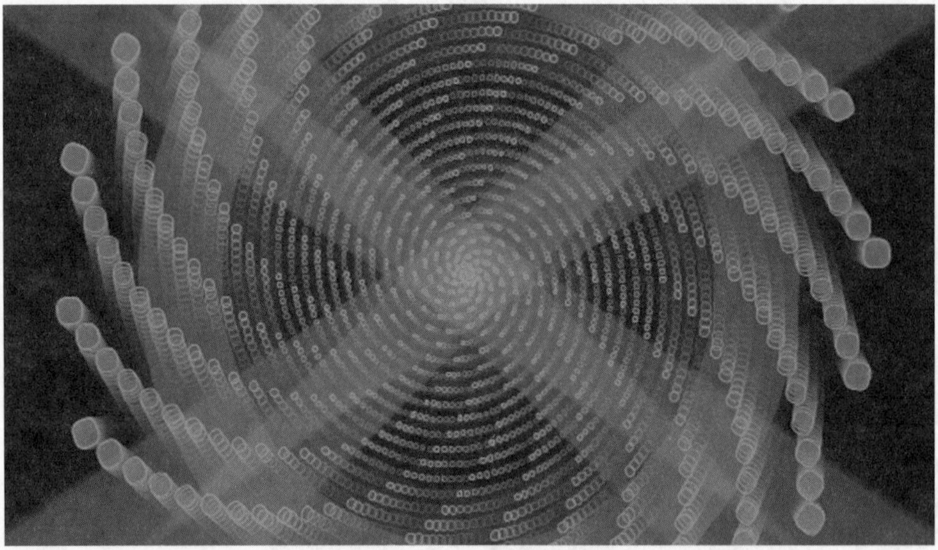

FIGURE 16.2 *Psych Dome* (2013) provided an EEG-driven audiovisualization based on ASCs inside a mobile fulldome.

(Figure 16.2). These utilize input signals from the EEG headset, which change the colors and shapes of the patterns. In correspondence with this, the Max/MSP patch generates various electronic sounds, such as percussive patterns which rotate spatially. By linking brain activity to the generation of sounds and visuals based on ASCs, the project provides users with a passive (Zander et al. 2010) connection to the experience generated.[8] This system was also applied to *Quake Delirium* via the *Quake Delirium EEG* project, which similarly used input signals from the EEG headset to dynamically affect various parameters, rather than using preset automations.

In a later project, colleagues and I carried out further investigations of approaches to designing sounds based on auditory hallucinations as described in accounts of intoxication from a database of reports (Weinel, Cunningham, and Griffiths 2014). This project produced a classification system which identified varying degrees of auditory hallucination described by participants, ranging from low-intensity experiences where only mild distortions were perceived, to high-intensity ones where noises, voices, or music were heard that did not have an acoustic basis in the immediate surrounding environment. Our team then used these classifications and descriptions to design sounds and short electroacoustic compositions based on the reports, thereby demonstrating practical techniques for designing sounds based on auditory hallucinations.

This investigation also provided the basis for a subsequent project in Unity, *ASC Sim* (2017), where three prototype mechanisms were designed to represent specific aspects of auditory hallucinations in real time (Weinel and Cunningham 2017). The first mechanism focused on changes to auditory attention, as described in situations where participants undergoing ASCs found they became completely absorbed by the sounds of specific objects in their surroundings. In *ASC Sim*, this phenomenon was represented by first identifying the object that the player is paying attention to, based on the direction they are looking in, and then adjusting the amplitude of sound-emitting objects in the scene so that only the object being attended to can be heard. The second mechanism looked at the idea of enhanced sonic experiences, where participants described sounds as more detailed or interesting than usual during an ASC. This was represented by mixing across multiple sound sources, thereby changing the sounds of objects to relatively more bright or dull versions by filtering the frequency spectrum. Lastly, the third mechanism explored disruptions to aural perception of space, as described by participants who experienced sounds as closer or more distant than usual during ASCs. This was simulated in Unity by automating the movement of sounds in oscillating patterns around the objects with which they were associated, so that sounds are heard from different localizations than one would expect.

In this section it is also of relevant to note two final year projects by undergraduate students whom I supervised in 2021–2022 at the University of Greenwich, which explored ways to represent ASCs in Unity. Each project provided three interactive game sequences using first-person perspective, which explored the design of various illusory mechanisms that were created through combinations of scripting, level design, visual postprocessing effects, and sound. Max Hegarty's project included a "stagger effect" that disrupted the player experience of control; time-varying visual blurring effects; illusory effects that moved the player in and out of environments such as distorted corridors; woodland areas where rows of trees scrolled infinity forward; and an MC Escher–inspired environment with impossible staircases for the player to navigate (Figure 16.3). Daisy Bain's project provided a forest environment where the player

FIGURE 16.3 Max Hegarty's game demo provided various interactive ASC sequences exploring optical illusions.

FIGURE 16.4 Daisy Bain's game demo explored the design of time-varying effects by using curve fields to modulate parameters of graphics and sounds in real-time.

could collect hallucinogenic plants that elicit various ASC effects (Figure 16.4), which were generated by automating visual postprocessing effects such as bloom, camera lens distortions, color grading; and real-time DSP effects such as echo, which were applied to sounds such as hallucinated voices. Both projects were made in Unity and made use of scripting techniques such as "curve fields"[9] to design time-varying changes to parameters.

This series of projects demonstrates various ways in which sounds can be designed, transformed, and organized based on concepts of auditory hallucinations and ASCs. Some of the techniques explored in these projects are similar to those utilized by commercial video games discussed in the previous section. For instance, representing intoxicated states by animating parameters of graphics and sounds is a technique that is now commonly used to represent ASCs in commercial games. However, the projects described in this section also indicate some approaches that are less well trodden, such as the design of mechanisms to reflect more nuanced, highly specific descriptions of auditory hallucinations; or the exploration of specific approaches such as the design of optical illusions. In the current form these are prototypes, but an extension of this work could bring these various approaches together to provide a comprehensive system, such as a plugin for a game engine, which would allow various ASCs to be conveniently implemented in games.

Avatar-Centered Subjectivity

From the various examples from commercial video games and research projects discussed in this chapter, we can identify a common conceptual approach, whereby graphics, sounds, or controls are modified to represent the subjective perception of a player character. Note that, in typical first-person perspective video games, a virtual camera approximates what the player avatar sees, while sound is used to provide a listening point in 3D space, which is used to calculate the levels of sound sources in the surrounding environment. This approach replicates the sensory inputs that the player avatar would receive and transmits these to the player via a display and loudspeakers (or headphones). This allows the player to see and hear the sensory inputs that the avatar would receive from the game world in any given situation. However, for the projects discussed, sounds and graphics are also modified to represent the subjective visual or aural impressions of the avatar. Controls and movement can also be disrupted, to give impressions of disorientation or impaired motor skills. I refer to this approach as "avatar-centered subjectivity" since a concept of the subjective experience of the player avatar is used to inform the design of graphics, sounds, and controls.

While a more in-depth discussion of this concept has been provided elsewhere (Weinel and Cunningham 2019), here it will be useful to offer a concise summary of how this concept can be used:

1. A concept of an avatar's cognition, emotion, or state of consciousness is first acquired;
2. This is then used to generate or modify graphics, sounds, and controls, to represent what the avatar experiences, taking into consideration subjective phenomena.

This is a useful extension to the concept of first-person perspective commonly used in video games, since it allows for the communication of phenomena such as auditory hallucinations and other perceptual changes which filter the avatar's interaction with the environment. As explored through the examples discussed earlier, this may allow us to gain a better comprehension of the conscious state that (conceptually) the avatar is in, which supports character development and sophisticated game narratives.

While this chapter has focused on auditory hallucinations and ASCs, it is worth commenting on the broader implications of avatar-centered subjectivity since it can also be applied in other contexts. For example, this approach has also been used in empathic virtual reality experiences such as the *Autism TMI Virtual Reality Experience* (National Autistic Society 2016) which represents the sensory experience of a child with autism with the aim of raising social awareness of autism (Weinel, Cunningham, and Pickles 2018). Other recent video games have also sought to represent different forms of sensory experience, for instance *Perception* (Deep End Games 2017) and *Blind* (Tiny Bull Studios 2018) are two games that seek to represent the experiences of visually impaired protagonists, and these can also be understood as examples of avatar-centered subjectivity.

It is worth noting some limitations to this concept. Most obviously, avatar-centered subjectivity as described here relies on the interactive audiovisual interfaces used by games, and this limits the possibilities for communicating other aspects of sensory experience, emotion, or cognition. Graphics may be used to suggest visual distortions or hallucinations, while sound may be used to reflect changes to aural perception such as auditory hallucinations. The timing of a game or the player's feeling of control can also be adjusted or modified, as in those examples that slow down game speed or disrupt player control inputs. However, commercial game interfaces do not communicate smell, and though other senses such as touch can be indicated though vibrating controllers, these are relatively limited tools of communication. Of course, ASCs also cause various other changes to thought patterns and emotions which are more difficult to communicate through the systems provided. The examples discussed often use dialogue, so the avatar may describe what they are thinking or feeling, while affective states may be suggested through emotive music on the soundtrack. There are strategies available, then, but I must acknowledge that avatar-centered subjectivity is reductive, and emphasizes sound, image, and control.

More positively, there could be interesting ways to extend avatar-centered subjectivity in the near future. For example, olfactory and taste technologies, eye tracking, biofeedback devices, and haptic controllers that use robotics to provide resistance or a sense of weight, are all in development and might eventually be available in commercial video games. In the previous section I discussed the use of biofeedback technology (consumer-grade EEG), as a means to enhance projects that represent ASCs, by providing a passive connection between the brain activity of the user and the generated experience. As Williams (2021) notes, the successful use of these technologies presents various challenges, and there are important ethical factors that require careful consideration before they are used more widely. Nonetheless, it may soon be possible to do more to fill in the gaps and create even richer representations based on the concept of avatar-centered subjectivity.

Conclusion

Over the past few decades, video games have rapidly grown to become a dominant force in popular culture that transcends geographic and social boundaries. Through this rapid expansion, and the economic backing it has attracted, we have seen a drive toward cinematic designs in games, which strive for increasingly photorealistic visual styles. These games require worlds that are more rich, detailed, and expansive than ever before, and, within these worlds, storylines, characters, and interactions that are nuanced and sophisticated. It is in this context that representations of auditory hallucinations and ASCs provide a means to enrich games by giving us deeper insights into the psychological states of game characters. As we have seen through the examples discussed throughout this chapter, graphics, sounds, and controls, are the main tools that developers have to communicate avatar-centered subjectivity. Sound in particular can be used to provide materials that communicate features of auditory hallucinations and ASCs, thereby representing subjective experiences such as hearing voices, which do have an acoustic basis in the immediate environment that the game engine represents. Both these sounds and those which are related to sound sources in the game world, can also be dynamically modulated in time, in order to represent temporal forms of sensory derangement that are typical of hallucinations and intoxicated states. Filtering techniques can suggest heightening or dulling of the senses, while DSP effects or disruption to the spatial localization of sounds relative to their associated object in the game world, may allow us to design aural experiences that are suggestive of ASCs. These designs can be usefully understood as examples of avatar-centered subjectivity, and this concept will provide a vital means through which to analyze and design audio for the next generation of video games.

Notes

1. The discussion in this section draws upon Calleja's (2011) theory of player involvement, which describes kinesthetic, spatial, shared, narrative, affective, and ludic dimensions.
2. The description here refers to the PlayStation 2 version of *Grand Theft Auto: Vice City* (Rockstar North 2002), which has differences from the PC version. For a further discussion of representations of alcohol in video games, see also Smucker (2018).
3. For a further discussion of correspondences between affective states and musical features, see Gabrielsson and Lindstrom (2012).
4. For a further discussion of auditory hallucinations in horror games, see also Demarque and Lima (2013).

5. For related work in the field of electroacoustic composition, see Gary Kendall's *Ikaro* (2009–2010).
6. For example, digital hallucinations and consciousness hacking are also featured in other cyberpunk works, such as William Gibson's novel *Neuromancer* ([1984] 1995) and the film *Johnny Mnemonic* (Longo 1995).
7. Fulldome is a type of immersive, 360-degrees projection theater.
8. For a further discussion of biofeedback and psychophysiological approaches to sound and music in games see also Williams (2021).
9. Curve fields provide a convenience means in Unity create programmable animation curves that can be defined with a graphical user interface. For more information, please refer to the Scripting Reference available on the Unity website (https://docs.unity3d.com/ScriptReference/EditorGUILayout.CurveField.html).

References

3D Realms. 1996. *Duke Nukem 3D*. MS-DOS, GT Interactive Software.
Andromeda Entertainment. 2020. *Soundself: A Technodelic*. VR Experience. PC, Andromeda Entertainment.
Calleja, Gordan. 2011. *In-Game: From Immersion to Incorporation*. Cambridge, MA: MIT Press.
Carroll, Lewis. [1865–1871] 1993. *Alice's Adventures in Wonderland and through the Looking-Glass*. Reprint, Ware: Wordsworth Editions.
CD Projekt RED. 2020. *Cyberpunk 2077*. Video Game. PC, CD Projekt.
Compulsion Games. 2016. *We Happy Few*. Video Game. PC, Gearbox.
Cubicle Ninjas. 2016. *Guided Meditation VR*. Microsoft Windows, Oculus Rift.
Demarque, Thainá Cristina, and Edirlei Soares de Lima. 2013. "Auditory Hallucination: Audiological Perspective for Horror Games." In *SBC—Proceedings of SBGames 2013*, 19–26. São Paulo, Brazil.
Fischer, Roland. 1971. "A Cartography of the Ecstatic and Meditative States." *Science* 174 (4012): 897–904.
Gabrielsson, Alf, and Erik Lindström. 2012. "The Role of Structure in the Musical Expression of Emotions." In *Handbook of Music and Emotion: Theory, Research, Applications*, edited by Patrik N. Juslin and John A. Sloboda, 367–400. Oxford: Oxford University.
Gibson, William. [1984] 1995. *Neuromancer*. Reprint, London: Harper Voyager.
Gilliam, Terry. 1998. *Fear and Loathing in Las Vegas*. Feature Film. Universal Pictures.
Hobson, John Allan. 2003. *The Dream Drugstore*. Cambridge, MA: MIT Press.
Hufford, David J. 1989. *The Terror That Comes in the Night: An Experience-Centered Study of Supernatural Assault Traditions*. Philadelphia: University of Pennsylvania Press.
id Software. 1996. *Quake*. MS- DOS, GT Interactive.
Jimi Hendrix Experience, The. 1968. *Electric Ladyland*. 2xLP, Polydor.
Kendall, Gary. 2009–2010. *Ikaro*. Electroacoustic Composition. Accessed May 27, 2021. http://garykendall.net/compositions-files/Ikaro.html.
Klüver, Heinrich. 1971. *Mescal and Mechanisms of Hallucinations*. Chicago: University of Chicago Press.
Kounen, Jan, dir. 2019. *Ayahuasca: Kosmik Journey*. VR Application. PC, Atlas V.
Kubrick, Stanley. 1980. *The Shining*. Warner Bros.
Longo, Robert. 1995. *Johnny Mnemonic*. Feature Film. TriStar Pictures.

Ludwig, Arnold M. 1969. "Altered States of Consciousness." In *Altered States of Consciousness: A Book of Readings*, edited by Charles T. Tart, 9–22. New York: John Wiley & Sons.

National Autistic Society. 2016. *Autism TMI Virtual Reality Experience*. Virtual Reality Experience. VR Cardboard.

Ninja Theory. 2017. *Hellblade: Seanu's Sacrifice*. Video Game. PC, Ninja Theory.

Oliver Twins. 1989. *Fantasy World Dizzy*. Atari ST, Codemasters.

Remedy Entertainment. 1996. *Death Rally*. MS-DOS, GT Interactive.

Remedy Entertainment. 2001. *Max Payne*. Sony PlayStation 2, Rockstar Games.

Rockstar North. 2002. *Grand Theft Auto: Vice City*. Sony PlayStation 2, Rockstar Games.

Rockstar North. 2013. *Grand Theft Auto V*. Sony PlayStation 3, Rockstar Games.

Rocksteady Studios. 2009. *Batman: Arkham Asylum*. Sony PlayStation 3, Eidos Interactive.

Rouget, Gibert. 1985. *Music and Trance: A Theory of the Relations between Music and Possession*. Chicago: University of Chicago Press.

Russell, James A. 1980. "A Circumplex Model of Affect." *Journal of Personality and Social Psychology* 39 (6): 1161–1178.

Sonic Team. 1991. *Sonic the Hedgehog*. Video Game. Sega Mega Drive, Sega.

Smucker, Pete. 2018. "Gaming Sober, Playing Drunk: Sound Effects of Alcohol in Video Games." *Computer Games Journal* 7: 291–311. https://doi.org/10.1007/s40869-018-0069-4.

The Deep End Games. 2017. *Perception*. Video Game. PC, Feardemic.

Tiny Bull Studios. 2018. *Blind*. PC, Fellow Traveller.

Ubisoft Montreal. 2012. *Far Cry 3*. Video Game. Sony PlayStation 3, Ubisoft.

VentureBeat. 2017. "Hellblade: Senua's Sacrifice Documentary." YouTube. Accessed May 27, 2021. https://youtu.be/s8mLbnaZn6o.

Weinel, Jonathan. 2011. "*Quake Delirium*: Remixing Psychedelic Video Games." *Sonic Ideas/Ideas Sónicas* 3 (2): 22–29.

Weinel, Jonathan. 2013. "Nausea: An Approach to Sonic Arts Composition Based on ASC." In *Proceedings of the Fifth International Conference on Internet Technologies and Applications 2013*. Wrexham Glyndŵr University, UK.

Weinel, Jonathan. 2016. "Entoptic Phenomena in Audio: Categories of Psychedelic Electroacoustic Composition." *Contemporary Music Review* 35 (2): 202–223.

Weinel, Jonathan, and Stuart Cunningham. 2017. "Simulating Auditory Hallucinations in a Video Game: Three Prototype Mechanisms." In *ACM Proceedings of Audio Mostly 2017*. London: Queen Mary University of London. https://doi.org/10.1145/3123514.3123532.

Weinel, Jonathan, and Stuart Cunningham. 2019. "Designing Game Audio Based on Avatar-Centred Subjectivity." In *Foundations in Sound Design for Interactive Media*, edited by M. Filimowicz, 59–77. Abington: Routledge.

Weinel, Jonathan, Stuart Cunningham, and Darryl Griffiths. 2014. "Sound through the Rabbit Hole: Sound Design Based on Reports of Auditory Hallucination." In *ACM Proceedings of Audio Mostly 2014*. Aalborg: Aalborg University. https://doi.org/10.1145/2636879.2636883.

Weinel, Jonathan, Stuart Cunningham, and Jennifer Pickles. 2018. "Deep Subjectivity and Empathy in Virtual Reality: A Case Study on the Autism TMI Virtual Reality Experience." In *New Foundations in Third Wave Human-Computer Interaction: Vol.1—Technologies*, edited by M. Filimowicz, 183–203. Berlin: Springer.

Weinel, Jonathan, Stuart Cunningham, Nathan Roberts, Shaun Roberts, and Darryl Griffiths. 2015. "EEG as a Controller for Psychedelic Visual Music in an Immersive Dome Environment." *Sonic Ideas/Ideas Sónicas* 7 (14): 81–92.

Williams, D. 2021. "Psychophysiological Approaches to Sound and Music in Games." In *The Cambridge Companion to Video Game Music*, edited by M. Fritsch and T. Summers, 302–318. Cambridge: Cambridge University Press. https://doi.org/10.1017/9781108670289.019.

Zander, Thorsten O., Christian Kothe, Sabine Jatzev, and Matti Gaertner. 2010. "Enhancing HumanComputer Interaction with Input from Active and Passive BrainComputer Interfaces." In *Brain–Computer Interfaces*, edited by D. Tan, and A. Nijholt, 181–199. Human–Computer Interaction Series. London: Springer.

SECTION 4

INTERACTING ACROSS MEDIA

CHAPTER 17

MUSIC AND SOUND IN EARLY FILM-TO-GAME ADAPTATIONS

WILLIAM O'HARA

Introduction

THE opening sequence of a 1993 episode of *The Simpsons* (1989–present) finds two main characters in a video arcade. The camera moves across the noisy panorama and settles on a boy playing an arcade cabinet called *My Dinner with André*—a parodic adaptation of the 1981 film of the same name, which stars André Gregory and Wallace Shawn as thinly fictionalized versions of themselves and takes place almost entirely at a single booth in an upscale café. In the film, the two converse about their lives, about working in the theater, about society, and about the nature of reality and experience. The player in this imagined adaptation—which is drawn in a slightly pixelated style, with the telltale scanlines of a cathode-ray tube—seems to assume the role of Wallace Shawn. As André takes a sip of espresso and pauses in his musings over expressing the inexpressible, the camera pans down to reveal that the player may respond by pointing a joystick at one of three options painted on the arcade cabinet in bold yellow: TRENCHANT INSIGHT, BON MOT, or "TELL ME MORE."[1]

This vignette can be read in several ways, and probing it reveals the precarious critical and ontological status of film-to-game adaptations at an important moment in their history. On the surface, it is a throwaway gag that relies on the viewer's knowledge of established characters to fill a few seconds before the episode's action begins: a nerdy minor character is drawn to the most subdued and cerebral game imaginable, in stark contrast to the violent game that Bart Simpson plays at the adjacent cabinet. In this capacity, the joke is also a commentary on the movie itself—a film in which virtually nothing happens besides an extended conversation—and its ill-suitedness to the video game format. While narrative games have become common in the decades since the episode was made, two men nibbling on roasted quail and discussing the fascist undertones of esoteric performance art would be unusual material for a video game even today.

If taken a bit more seriously, however, the joke carries additional subtext. At the time this episode aired, video games based on movies were ascendant. The first mainstream adaptation games appeared in the early 1980s, and the genre grew steadily in popularity over the coming years, becoming widespread by the time of this 1993 episode. Most Hollywood blockbusters of the era boasted a tie-in game, and sometimes several. Along with a touch of self-awareness—*The Simpsons* was itself the subject of two game adaptations in 1991—the series' many arcade sequences happily present parody adaptations in frequent sight gags, responding to the ubiquity of the format at the time in comic book or magazine advertisements, filling the endcaps of the local video rental store, or advertised within the pages of any magazine or comic book. And much like real film-to-game adaptations in their early, graphically abstract forms, recognizable movie titles provide the audience with a ready-made frame of reference (Aldred 2012, 94–98): a viewer can easily imagine what a game based on a familiar title might be like. Finally, hinging as it does on the tongue-in-cheek juxtaposition of art house cinema with coin-operated amusement, the joke dramatizes the position of aesthetic inferiority from which games (and games based on movies in particular) have often struggled to rise.

Such tensions between media are a central concern of the discipline of adaptation studies. While critics have often been interested in analyzing or critiquing the translation of literature (to take one common example) to the silver screen, contemporary scholars of adaptation generally argue that transmedia adaptations ought to be regarded as works in themselves, rather than pale imitations of their source material (see Leitsch 2007, 2008; Hutcheon 2006). Video games adapted from movies are not immune to the former critique, as the *André* joke humorously dramatizes, and as numerous negative reviews attest. But regarded from another perspective, video game adaptations might be seen to encourage the latter style of reading. Given the need to transform a fixed, linear narrative into a flexible one, the need to offer choice and interaction, and (in more recent decades) the expectation that games ought to provide much more than 90 minutes of entertainment, one would be hard-pressed to say that many tie-in video games are true adaptations of a source work at all; instead, they are loosely related works that refer to an original. Rather than evaluating them purely by their degree of fidelity, we might productively regard game adaptations as an important form of *media convergence*, which Henry Jenkins (2006, 2–3) describes as "the flow of content across multiple media platforms, the cooperation between multiple media industries, and the migratory behavior of media audiences who will go almost anywhere in search of the kinds of entertainment experiences they want." Adaptations are thus useful as cultural texts that help to shed light on the relationships between media, and the interactions between large media entities: film studios, game development companies, auteur directors, programmers, and engineers.

This chapter explores the role music and sound played in early film-to-game adaptations, with a particular interest in the production process. It covers the birth and early growth of the genre in the 1980s, in two important formats: early home video game consoles, and coin-operated arcade games. The former format accounts for the birth of the genre and offers its earliest prominent examples, but the latter format—with more sophisticated technology and greater audiovisual flexibility—serves as the core of this essay though a pair of case studies covering sound and music development in two Atari arcade adaptations from the mid-1980s. I will investigate how *Star Wars* (1983) and *Return of the Jedi* (1984) used cutting-edge voice synthesis technology (and how the former title was effectively a test vehicle for Atari's adoption of that new technology); how the development team corresponded with Lucasfilm to acquire audiovisual reference materials and align the gameplay with the narratives of the films; and how sound and music were used in both the gameplay and the advertising campaigns that promoted the games.

These case studies combine traditional archival work, carried out in the Atari Coin-Op Division Corporate Records collection at the Strong Museum of Play in Rochester, New York, with extensive research in digital archives, including the Internet Archive (www.archive.org), various videogame enthusiast websites, and even the personal website of a former Atari engineer. Alongside the official documents held in the Strong's Brian Sutton-Smith Library—which include internal memos, weekly project updates, design documents, cost estimates, and more—the diligent documentation of fan-driven websites has been essential in finding examples, collating release dates, and tracking versions, while the Internet Archive has made these games available for all to play and study in virtual form. Studying the production process behind these games reveals that they are far more than translations of narrative, image, and sound from one medium to another; rather, their production is nonlinear, following numerous paths from concept to playable game. They are collaborations between engineers and executives, between game developers and marketers, and they are shaped by the forces of technology, intellectual property, advertising, and storytelling. As we will see, music was one of the most important and vivid ties between a game and its source film. Understanding how sound and music were approached at the origins of the film adaptation genre better prepares us to understand how it has functioned throughout the format's four-decade history.

Understanding Game Adaptations

As Kevin Flanagan (2017, 441–442) has argued, the history of video games is in many ways a history of adaptation. Many of the earliest games, such as *Tennis for Two* (1958) and *Pong* (1972) were digital versions of existing sports, while other games appropriated hardware intended for business or research purposes.[2] As video arcade games became well established in the 1970s, early home consoles gained a foothold in large part by adapting coin-operated games for the home, with early devices such as the Magnavox Odyssey relying almost entirely on the pioneering arcade hit *Pong*, and successor consoles like the Atari VCS and the ColecoVision building their libraries around well-known games like *Asteroids* (1980), *Missile Command* (1981), and *Centipede* (1981).

One of the most important cross-media relationships in the history of video games is their relationship to cinema, and their entwinement with popular Hollywood franchises.

Much as early cinema sought to model itself on the prestige of the opera house,[3] early game developers and marketers looked to the silver screen for both narrative inspiration and for tropes and techniques that could be repurposed. As Neil Lerner (2013) has shown, early game sound design was heavily indebted to tropes that originated in silent film scores and cartoons, such as brief invocations of familiar tunes like Chopin's "Funeral March" (from the B-flat minor piano sonata) and "Taps" to indicate that the player character has died, or "Ta-Ra-Ra Boom-De-Ay" to indicate success. These early applications of music were pragmatic, meant to help make games legible to their players. "Early game melodies were not only familiar," writes Lerner, "but they possessed narrative functions similar to those same melodies as they had been used in early cinema accompaniment" (331).[4] These references were also expedient from the standpoint of game development: early design teams were very small, and programmers often had to take on sound design tasks themselves—even if they were not necessarily trained musicians (Gibbons 2009, 41). They turned to notated, public-domain music that offered ready-made cultural and narrative associations, happily deploying clichés from cartoons and early sound film to help make their games legible for players.

Connections to film soon became explicit rather than indirect and metaphorical: as the so-called golden age of video games reached maturity, game development companies turned their attention to transmedia opportunities, licensing games from major Hollywood studios like Warner Bros., Paramount, Lucasfilm, and Universal. After several fits and starts, the concept of the film adaptation game began to reshape the game industry in the early 1980s as a flood of adaptations arrived. "Once upon a time, excellence in books, comic strips, radio shows and other forms of American popular culture would be recognized by adaptation into a motion picture," begins a 1982 article in *Electronic Fun* magazine. "Times have changed and it looks as though the hottest new translation medium is the video game" (Hulse 1982, 22). This cross-pollination was mutual: as Judd Ethan Ruggill (2009, 109) notes, games and game-based aesthetics began to appear prominently in Hollywood films such as *Tron* (1982), *WarGames* (1983), and *The Last Starfighter* (1984) around the same time. The entertainment industry's infatuation with cinematic games burned hot, and in some ways quickly burned out, before settling into the form it would take over the next few decades. The lower-quality titles within the flood of adaptation games are often held up—whether fairly or not—as a primary factor in the video game industry's severe post-1983 contraction (Ruggill 2009, 109; Aldred 2012, 91).

Beginnings: Adaptations on the Atari VCS

Video games based on films began inauspiciously in the mid-1970s, with a series of unlicensed titles that were adapted from hit movies without their studios' consent. First came *Shark Jaws* (1975), a game clearly based on Steven Spielberg's *Jaws* and released under a false company name to protect its actual creator (Atari) from liability. The second was *Death Race* (1976), developed by Exidy and inspired by—though not affiliated with—*Death Race 2000* (1975).[5] The first prominent home tie-in, *Superman* (1979, for Atari's VCS console)[6] arrived in 1979, already the product of corporate synergy: Warner Communications had purchased Atari in 1976, and the company was eager to create a game to promote its 1978 *Superman* film.[7] After the game's tepid reception, however, it would be several years before another tie-in adaptation was attempted (Aldred 2012, 93). The format did not hit its stride until 1982, a year that saw adaptations of several prominent blockbuster films: *Raiders of the Lost Ark*, *Alien*, *The Empire Strikes Back*, and—infamously—*E.T. The Extra Terrestrial*. Most of these adaptations were for the Atari VCS, which was at the time the most popular home console; a few were also available for competing consoles like Mattel's Intellivision and ColecoVision. "Where do you look for dramatic new game ideas?" asks a 1982 article in Atari's own enthusiast magazine, *Atari Age*. "If you're Atari, you turn to the top creative teams in filmmaking . . . and form partnerships to develop tomorrow's breakthrough video game concepts" (Atari 1982, 7). Numerous other game magazines reported on the trend as well: *Blip*, *Videogaming Illustrated*, *Vidiot*, and *Electronic Fun* all ran cover stories with titles like "Video Games Go Hollywood" and "Hollywood Video Game Explosion."[8]

Jessica Aldred (2012, 96–101) has analyzed the difficulties and the affordances of representing prominent film characters in the rudimentary graphics of the Atari VCS. The use of humanlike avatars was rare at the time—rather than attempt to render humans, game developers were more likely to omit the player's avatar entirely in favor of a first-person or fixed third-person perspective, or to let the player be represented by a vehicle or an object. Film adaptation games, however, often invoked their star characters directly, in highly abstracted forms. For Aldred, this representational gap between the film or the game's cover art, and what was actually shown on the television screen—the player did not control Harrison Ford, they controlled a stick figure wearing a squared-off fedora—left imaginative space for the player to relate to the hero as they saw fit. The player's relationship to a pixelated Indiana Jones or E.T. was carefully described in marketing copy, and instruction manuals often explicitly situated the player as either controlling the action from the outside—the player "helps" E.T., for instance—or fully embodying the hero.

Musical cues in the earliest adaptation games functioned in much the same way. Just as early console graphics were limited in their representational capacity, so too were the sonic capabilities of those early consoles highly constrained. The Atari VCS, for instance, had only two sound channels at its disposal, controlled by a programmable sound generator that derived its frequencies through an idiosyncratic division of the fundamental pitch, yielding an incomplete gamut with notable tuning problems (Collins 2006). For this reason compromises often had to be made, and musical scores were often monophonic, since harmony was difficult to achieve with an incomplete gamut: one voice might lack the notes present in the other, or needed to harmonize with it. Even a simplified theme can be powerful, however; as Mark Richards (2016, 1) notes, cinematic main title themes have a tendency to "become part of a film's entire identity," serving as

FIGURE 17.1 Theme from *Raiders of the Lost Ark* (Atari VCS, 1982).

one of the most recognizable signifiers of a given movie; in turn, the musical theme is identified almost entirely with the movie from which it came. Given these games' visual and ludic abstraction, and the anxiety over faithfully representing beloved characters in a few dozen pixels, it is clear that music also played a prominent role in tying early film-to-game adaptations to their source material. "Put this cartridge into your VCS, turn it on, and listen—it's the theme song from *Raiders!*" begins a write-up of *Raiders of the Lost Ark* in *Atari Age* magazine (Atari 1982, 7). After the cover art, hearing a recognizable main title theme was one of the first and most compelling ties to a franchise—even if that theme was heard in drastically reduced form.[9]

The opening screen of *Raiders*—which lacks even the game's title, depicting only a small figure wearing Indiana Jones's fedora—features a four-measure loop of composer John Williams's title theme ("Raiders' March") from the film, which has been rendered in 3/4 time for the game, as opposed to the 4/4 original. As shown in Figure 17.1, the distinctive dotted rhythms of each pickup beat have been smoothed out into straight eighth notes, and the end of the theme has a simplified (and lower) contour, presumably due to the limitations of the VCS's programmable sound generator. In the absence of a true title screen, this theme serves as the cartridge's primary identification.

Other Atari VCS adaptations treat their themes in similar ways. *Star Wars: The Empire Strikes Back* (1982) begins with the fanfare from the films' opening title. No music plays during the game itself, however; outside of the flourish, its soundtrack consists entirely of white noise of various timbres, representing laser shots, explosions, and crashes. And while *E.T.: The Extra Terrestrial* is notorious for the role it played in the "Great Video Game Crash" of 1983, the game's presentation of Williams's famous "Flying Theme" serves as a model for incorporating a recognizable soundtrack.[10] So too does *Halloween* (1983), which seems to be the first game to incorporate polyphony in its rendition of a movie theme. The film's haunting 5/4 piano motif is rendered with a bass line, although as Figure 17.2 demonstrates, the two-voice limitation renders the final sonority as an uncharacteristic (and almost comical) major chord. Faced with the choice between the two notes in the film soundtrack's sixth measure (and perhaps forced to take the higher note by the console's limited gamut), the sound programmer ended the line on A#. Because the Atari's higher voice also does not follow the change of harmony in m. 5, the bass's A# fills in the F#—C# perfect fifth, creating a surprising major chord.

In this format, recognizable movie themes became a sonic signature for an adaptation game. Due to the technical limitations, music did not loop throughout a game.[11] Instead, like the blocky outline of Indiana Jones's fedora, a few measures of music would set the

FIGURE 17.2 Themes from (a) the film *Halloween* (1978), and (b) the Atari VCS cartridge *Halloween* (1983).

stage for the action to come. In many cases, it also served as a reward (much like "Ta-Ra-Ra Boom-De-Ay" did in 1977's *Circus*). As a preview of Atari's *The Empire Strikes Back* notes: "If the player wins, he or she is rewarded by invincibility through the Force—and two electronic refrains of the *Star Wars* theme."[12]

Not every movie tie-in game incorporated music from its source film's soundtrack. For example, *Alien* (1982), an Atari VCS adaptation of the 1979 film, closely resembles the arcade hit *Pac-Man* (Namco, 1980) in both its gameplay and its sound design. A blocky figure (presumably Ellen Ripley) flees through a square, single-screen maze from three pastel-colored aliens (reminiscent of *Pac-Man*'s ghosts), attempting to pick up every dot on the screen without being caught in the creatures' disproportionately large jaws. The game does not incorporate any music from Jerry Goldsmith's influential (though admittedly less than tuneful) score; instead, its sound design is virtually indistinguishable from *Pac-Man*, from the siren-like noise that accompanies the player's movement, to the shift in tone when the player picks up a starburst to turn the tables on the aliens. It could be argued that *Alien* is not so much an adaptation of the film, but rather an imitation of

Pac-Man with the name of a movie attached, and the lack of music is yet more evidence of its failure in that respect.

Adapting *Star Wars* for the Arcade

While corporate synergy and the emergence of multimedia entertainment conglomerates played a significant role in the birth of film adaptation games, not all adaptations began as product-promotional tie-ins; others acquired their promotional licenses after development had already begun.[13] For instance, Atari's well-known arcade game *Star Wars* (1983), which came several years after the movie it adapted (1977), began with a memo circulated in late 1979. In it, Atari engineer Jed Margolin proposed a game entitled "First-Person Space War." As corporate documents held by the Strong Museum of Play reveal, the game was to be made with vector graphics (three dimensional wireframes, along the lines of Atari's *Battlezone*, which was then nearing completion under the similar working title "First-Person Tank"). Margolis envisioned the player in the cockpit of a starfighter, facing off against either computer opponents or another player in a linked cabinet. "A tie-in with one of the space movies such as *Star Wars II* might be desirable," Margolin noted near the end of his proposal.[14]

Margolin's notes indicate that while he hoped the game could be attached to an upcoming movie (*The Empire Strikes Back*, here referred to as a generic *Star Wars* sequel), this was at the time speculative; the license would help promote the game, rather than vice versa (indeed, company documents indicate that Atari would pay a licensing fee to use any theme that might be attached to the game).[15] The project was developed for nearly three years under the working title *Warp Speed* until the middle of 1982, when Atari finally acquired the license that Margolin had hoped for: a wide-ranging contract with Lucasfilm to create games based on the *Star Wars* license.[16] Comments from project director Mike Hally imply that the existing *Warp Speed* project—characterized as "a two-year-old space game research project," which memos indicate was lying fallow[17]—benefited from this new contract; the deal was not motivated by the in-progress game, but rather the game's status within the company was resurrected by the new collaboration. The refreshed, reimagined game progressed quickly, and appeared in 1983, six years after the original film. A follow-up arcade title adapted *Return of the Jedi* a year later, and a conversion kit appeared in 1985, allowing arcade operators to turn their *Star Wars* cabinets into a new game based on *The Empire Strikes Back*.[18]

In the early 1980s, arcade cabinets—which were built from scratch for each game, or at least customized from previous models based on the needs of each title—had the potential to deliver more sophisticated hardware designs than early home consoles, which were restricted to very few sound channels and a limited range of timbres (Guins 2015, 9–15). Arcade game designers thus had much broader sonic palettes with which to work, and, as we will see, they were able to quickly incorporate new technologies into their games, rather than being limited by the capabilities of consoles that might have been developed years before. At the same time, coin-op developers were beholden to both production costs and logistics; numerous Atari documents indicate the per unit price associated with every aspect of hardware, and innovative designs had to be balanced against potential profit. Developers were likewise beholden to the conventions of arcade game design, since their customers were not players but arcade operators who had certain expectations about the consumption patterns their games should encourage. Both of the *Star Wars* games studied in this chapter follow a "three-stage" model: each chapter presents a novel challenge to the player, and these cycles repeat at increasingly higher difficulty levels, until the player stops putting coins in. Both were subjected to focus groups during their development and compared against competing cabinets in "field tests" before their full commercial release.

Despite its origins, *Star Wars* thoroughly integrates sound and music from its source film, and this audible reference was an important part of its appeal. One advertising flyer proclaims, "*Star Wars* features 'random' music. A song will be repeated no more than once every 7 minutes, in stereo. And the music is taken from the original *Star Wars* soundtrack."[19] Unfortunately, this seems to be an exaggeration, in two respects. First, the music of *Star Wars* is anything but random. The game is underscored by a series of short, recognizable fragments of John Williams's soundtrack. Each theme lasts less than 10 seconds, and contrary to the claim of "randomness," they occur in precisely the same order, each time, separated by several seconds of silence (see Table 17.1). There are even clear narrative correlations: the transition from the first stage to the second, for instance, is underscored by the battle music that accompanies a squadron of X-Wings

TABLE 17.1 Soundtrack Excerpts in *Star Wars* Arcade Game (see Lehman 2022)

Theme	Appearance in Game	Source from Film
"Main Theme," A-section	Game start	Opening logo and title crawl
"Main Theme," embellished	During gameplay, first stage	Simplified version of main title credits, B-section
Fragment from end credits: Modification of Main Theme B-section, leading to final fanfare	During gameplay, first stage	Final credits [2:03:16]
"Force Theme," imitative and intensifying	Transition to second stage (skimming surface of the Death Star)	X-Wings flying down to the surface of the Death Star [1:46:17]
Rebel fanfare	During gameplay, third stage (Death Star Trench)	*Millennium Falcon* being pulled into the Death Star's hangar [1:05:24]
Death Star explosion	End of game—victory	Immediately post–Death Star explosion [1:57:20]
"Force Theme," march version	End credits / high scores / attract mode	Medal Ceremony

turning downward to attack the Death Star in the film.[20] Next, regarding the length of time: there *is* some degree of adaptive variability in the game, in the sense that if a player takes longer to clear a given wave of enemies, they might hear a few more themes. It is also possible to miss the pivotal shot in the Death Star trench at the end of the game, which causes the trench sequence simply to start over—as clear a dramatization as any that early video games treated narrative differently than films. But even the slowest playthrough of *Star Wars* takes only about three minutes.[21] The claim of "seven minutes" between repetitions seems only tenuously to be true, perhaps if one takes into account the "attract" mode and the game's high-score screen.

While the music may lack somewhat compared to the advertising campaign's promises, the selection of dialogue reproduced from the movie is impressive for 1983. *Star Wars* was one of several Atari cabinets to use the Texas Instruments TMS5220 Sound Chip, which allowed developers to employ digitized speech by encoding it and resynthesizing it as needed, thereby avoiding both the prohibitive costs and immense circuit board space that would have been required to store recordings.[22] An additional set of documents reveals how Atari's experiments with then-emerging voice synthesis technology coincided with the development of *Star Wars*, and how the game was one of the first cabinets to use it. In 2001, Jed Margolin—the engineer who had originally proposed *Star Wars*—posted an archive of his internal Atari email, or "VAX Mail," to his website.[23] A long-running 1982 discussion of the details of the TMS5220 and other voice synthesis chips reveals Margolin's important role in assessing potential voice synthesis technologies, and pioneering their use in *Star Wars*. In early April, Margolin canvassed Atari's engineers about their interest in using synthesized speech for their current projects; while four engineers expressed interest and a series of meetings ensued, only *Star Wars* pursued the Texas Instruments voice system in earnest, as the team began working that summer to convert their experimental space game into a blockbuster license.[24]

Margolin's early memos show that instead of purchasing the premade "vocabulary lists" offered by Texas Instruments, Atari purchased a workstation called a PASS, which allowed them to digitize their own speech samples for reproduction by the TMS-5220. The device cost the company $25,000 (roughly equivalent to $79,500 in 2024).[25] A company-wide VAXmail from 1984 details the system's operation: "[The] TI PASS system analyzes the speech and allows the user to edit it, frame by frame. The system typically makes a number of pitch errors, amplitude errors, and filter parameter errors, which have to be cleaned up by hand. It's a fairly slow process, and requires some intuitive feel for linguistics and why we perceive certain phonemes the way we do, etc."[26] A 1983 magazine article describes the collaborative process that went into creating the game's script. "Hally and [sound designer Earl] Vickers pored over the movie script, looking for appropriate pieces of dialogue to use in the game. They indicated their choices to Lucasfilm, who then lifted those pieces off the soundtrack and sent them to the labs for digitization" (Williams 1983, 25). As one memo describes the results, "the sound quality is a little unnatural but preserves some of the speaker's identity and expression."[27] Through this grainy synthesis, Obi-Wan Kenobi (Alec Guinness) advises the player to "Use the Force, Luke"; Darth Vader (James Earl Jones) growls menacingly,

"I have you now." The dialogue reacts to events in the game: being hit by an enemy will sometimes cause Luke Skywalker (Mark Hamill) to say, "I'm hit but not bad; Artoo, see what you can do with it." Should the player make it to the end of the game, they will hear Han Solo (Harrison Ford) give the "all clear" to take the shot that will destroy the Death Star: an achievement that will be greeted with another appropriately timed flourish from the film's soundtrack.

Star Wars was extremely well received. In their unsigned review, *Computer & Video Games* magazine wrote: "[T]he force of the powerful new video game assaults the imagination visually with graphic simulation and special features that include music and dialogue created from the movie."[28] In a later column on arcade games adapted from films, the magazine described it as having "great graphics and even better sounds," while *TV Gamer* described it as "the best non-laser [disc] game to come out of 1983." *Video Games* magazine called it "one of the best video games ever produced," and praised the game's music, sound, and particularly speech, which it compared favorably with 1983's other voice-chipped games, *Sinistar* and *Star Trek*.[29]

By early 1984, *Star Wars: The Arcade Game* had been ported to numerous home console systems and computers.[30] In these versions, the gameplay is generally identical to the arcade versions, but the graphics and sound are noticeably simplified, throwing into sharp relief the audiovisual differences between arcade- and home-based games of the time. The soundtracks are particularly spartan when compared to the original arcade cabinet: voices from the film are entirely absent, and there is no music save for a single iteration of the *Star Wars* fanfare at the beginning of the game. In that sense, these console ports deploy the film's main title music as a brief acoustic signifier, exactly as the made-for-console adaptations discussed above did. On the Commodore 64, this theme is presented in two voices (melody and bass, as in the arcade version), while on Atari VCS and ColecoVision it is monophonic. The VCS represents laser blasts and explosions with two different timbres of white noise, while the Commodore and ColecoVision each mimic laser sounds with their waveform generators.

Star Wars also signaled an important shift in the division of game development labor with regard to sound design. On his website, former Atari engineer Jed Margolin tells the story of how the expansion of the *Star Wars* development team led to changes in sound production throughout Atari:

> At some point Rick [Moncrief, director of Margolin's group at Atari] hired Earl Vickers to do sounds and speech development. Up until then, the game programmers were responsible for sounds, which they generally hated doing, so usually the programmers would use Pokey sounds that had already been developed. That's why, for many years, Atari's games sounded alike. The other game groups decided that having someone just do sounds was a good idea, so Earl became the nucleus of a completely separate Sound Group that did sounds for all of the games.[31]

While it would be short-sighted to attribute an industry-wide shift to a single game—particularly on the strength of an anecdote related by one of that game's designers and chief advocates—Vickers's sound-specific role on this and subsequent titles offers useful context for the rapidly increasing ambition of game soundtracks in the mid-1980s.

Working with a Film Studio: *Return of the Jedi* (1984)

In a 1983 interview, project leader Mike Hally recalled the process of working with Lucasfilm to ensure that all elements of the *Star Wars* arcade adaptation were faithful to the film: "They were excited with our ideas, but they're very protective of what they call the "*Star Wars* Universe," Hally explains. This means that all ideas, concepts, characters, and storylines presented in the film must be preserved in any licensed products" (cited in Williams 1983, 24).

The Strong Museum's archives hold very little information about the discussions that went on between Atari and Lucasfilm during the development of *Star Wars*. However, the interactions between the two companies during the development of the game's sequel, *Return of the Jedi* (1984), are well documented.[32] So too is the process of sound development and programming, and the incorporation of more digitized speech into the game. While documents concerning the development of *Star Wars* shed light on Atari's exploration of new technology, *Return of the Jedi* offers even greater insight on the collaborative processes of licensed game design and the communication between developer and licensor.

Atari's coin-op division was eager to capitalize on the success of *Star Wars*. They turned their attention quickly toward a sequel, though they looked to the franchise's most recent installment to do so, adapting *Return of the Jedi* (1983) rather than *The Empire Strikes Back* (1980), which they would not adapt until 1985. *Return of the Jedi* features an isometric view (angled, from the top down) rather than first-person perspective, and it uses filled, sprite-based graphics rather than line-based vectors. Like its *Star Wars* adaptation, Atari's *Return of the Jedi* featured three "waves" based on scenes from the film. The player first controls Leia for a speeder bike chase in the forest. Then, a combined second wave intercuts between Chewbacca in his commandeered Imperial walker and Lando Calrissian flying toward the Death Star in the *Millennium Falcon*; and a final wave in which Lando blows up the Death Star and then escapes from its tunnels. Marketing copy focuses especially on the "split wave" feature in the second section of the game, which mimics the cinematic intercutting between the action on the surface and out in space.[33] The many speech samples from the film not only tie the game to the film but also serve an important purpose in the game's design. A few seconds before each shift in perspective, the player hears a line of dialogue from either Han, Leia, or Lando, warning them that the perspective is about to shift.

Documents from October 1983 and March 1984 list the sound effects that were planned, including distinct engine sounds for the game's numerous vehicles, as well as scrapes and impact noises that would represent different surfaces (trees, metal, etc.).[34] The developers were clearly committed to reproducing the varied soundscape of the movie as closely as possible, rather than relying on generic laser and explosion sounds. The game would run on four Atari "POKEY" sound chips (referred to as "quad pokeys" in memos, see chapter 12 this volume for further details of the chip's operation), which provide two sound channels each, and one TMS5220 voice chip—the same sound hardware *Star Wars* had used. The developers imagined a rich soundscape based on dozens of sounds and speech samples from the film, and there was concern that there were not enough channels—a familiar challenge facing audio programmers in the 1980s. One issue was the idea of using continuous engine noises, including distinct engine drones for the three or more speeder bikes that might be on screen at once. Combined with music, which was originally planned to occupy six channels of audio (or *twelve* stereo tracks, an almost unheard-of bandwidth), there were not many channels left for other sound effects such as laser blasts and explosions.

In the end, several compromises seem to have been struck to balance the variety of sounds needed with the capabilities of the hardware. In the opening sequence, for example, the speeder bikes are represented by a general backdrop of white noise. Each enemy speeder makes a sound representing its acceleration as it appears and joins the chase, but other than that, the engine noises are not tied to specific objects in-game. The game's music was eventually scored for three voices, generally with a melodic voice, harmony or counterpoint for it, and a bass line. The developers also mostly restricted music to the beginning and end of each level, with the exception of playing the "Imperial March" in three voices as the player flees the exploding Death Star at the end of the game. Presumably, this was possible because there are no enemies in that sequence (and thus no engine noises or shots).

Throughout the development process, Atari's team was in frequent contact with Lucasfilm. Their correspondence indicates the scope of the game's sonic ambitions, with long lists of quotations and detailed, unique sound effects. Atari made their first soundtrack requests in September 1983, asking for 42 lines of dialogue on 1/4-inch reel-to-reel tape, ranging from plot-critical exposition to exclamations from supporting characters.[35] After their initial request, Atari would repeatedly ask for more sound and music. While the Strong Museum only holds Atari's side of the correspondence, it seems that concerns must have been raised at Lucasfilm about sharing so much footage: a January 1984 letter pleads for more tapes from *Jedi*, promising that none of the sounds will see personal use, and that direct audio quotes are essential to "increase the game player's interest and fantasy about living in the *Star Wars* experience."[36] In March 1984 Atari wrote again, mentioning 18 lines of dialogue that were reproduced poorly on the tapes that Lucasfilm had previously sent, and also requesting 14 *new* lines.[37]

An internal memo from March 1984 lists the progress on the game's sound production, noting the rough condition of many sounds: the *Falcon* sound is "all wrong," while numerous sound effects "need work" or are "too soft."[38] The *Star Wars* theme, the memo notes, needs to be shortened by half, and numerous sounds based on the film were still missing from the game, despite plans for a field test in only a few days. Atari was also concerned with securing the rights to reproduce John Williams's music: every status update from April to July of 1984 proclaims, "Still do not have rights to use music . . . 'not to worry.'" All this evidence points to a working method in which placeholder sounds were used, before being filled in—at times—with samples from the films. It also chronicles a gradual reduction in ambition, as the great majority of dialogue samples requested here were cut from the final game. Pruning ideas back from the initial stages of development is not unusual, and these documents offers a fascinating glimpse at the team's brainstorming process.

From the 1980s to Today: The Rise and Fall of Video Game Adaptations

Taken together, the console and arcade games surveyed in this chapter offer a vivid picture of the early days of cinematic adaptation games. From the early console examples such as *Raiders of the Lost Ark* and *E.T.* to the technically sophisticated arcade cabinets of *Star Wars* and *Return of the Jedi*, adaptation soundtracks went from simple auditory indices pointing toward a film's heroic main theme, to complex compositions in music, sound, and dialogue that, as one Atari memo puts it, supports "the player's interest and fantasy about living in the *Star Wars* experience."[39]

As computing technology advanced, game developers continued to pursue the techniques and metaphors of cinema. The short-lived, mid-1980s genre of LaserDisc games used video to recreate the aesthetic of Saturday morning cartoons (*Dragon's Lair*, 1983), or incorporate film scenes directly into their arcade adaptations (*Firefox*, 1984).[40] Beginning in the early 1990s, PC games incorporated recorded voices, live orchestral soundtracks, and fully rendered animations or live video "cutscenes"; console games followed as soon as their storage media would allow, and the close relationship between video games and cinema is now firmly cemented.[41] Far from the suggestive cueing of *Raiders of the Lost Ark*'s brief, looping introduction, the influence of cinema on gaming's audiovisual content has in large part become a broad generic background underlying many—though not nearly all—large-scale narrative games.

At the peak of adaptations' popularity in the mid-2000s, *most* box office hits boasted video game tie-ins.[42] Since 2010, however, mainstream game adaptations have slowly begun to decline, and it is no longer a given that a major Hollywood blockbuster will be translated into videogame form. Numerous lamentations over the decline of the format in the popular and trade presses have blamed the cost of licensing deals with film studios; the short development periods imposed on developers by Hollywood production timelines; and the rise of online-oriented multiplayer games, which have made narrative-driven experiences a less-certain prospect. Journalist Chris Kohler has proposed that video game developers have become better at crafting cinematic experiences, and that prominent game franchises (such as *Call of Duty* or *Assassin's*

Creed) have built up the name recognition—and thus the marketing force—of major film properties.[43] Another factor may be the rise of mobile gaming, as film studios and game developers shift resources from time- and labor-intensive console games toward simpler adaptations for smart phone.

The "convergence" described by Henry Jenkins and others continues in more forms than ever, from smart phones to streaming video platforms, and it would be surprising if games did not continue to play an important role in transmedia franchises. As the medium of the cinematic adaptation game enters a new era with unknown prospects and potentially new formats, it is worth keeping its origins in mind. As this chapter has shown, such projects are often even more complicated than they seem, a collective creative endeavor with numerous lines of communication, many sources of pressure, and many developmental roads not taken. And archives like those consulted here—both traditional collections of paper and digital records, and contemporary digital archives maintained by not-for-profit, volunteer, or enthusiast curators—can help us to tell many more behind-the-scenes stories about the design of film-to-game adaptations, and about sound and music development in particular. Those stores should inspire us to look at these games as works unto themselves rather than aesthetic aberrations, and to search for the value, creativity, and cultural relevance that can be found in them. As we see from *Star Wars*, for example, adaptation games can be ideal vehicles for experimentation and innovation, with the production values of Hollywood inspiring Atari's engineers to test out new ways of rendering space in three dimensions and to explore how new technology could bring the sound of cinema into the arcade. And with the sometimes-quixotic sonic ambitions of *Return of the Jedi* now firmly within the technical capabilities of contemporary video game designers, we are well equipped to understand how the process of adapting blockbuster film into a successful game has changed during the past four decades—and the ways it has hardly changed at all.

Notes

1. In this respect, the fictional game is almost certainly modeled on LaserDisc games such as *Dragon's Lair* (1983), which featured animated video on a LaserDisc player within the cabinet. Players interacted with the game by making choices when prompted, and branching narratives and outcomes could be represented based on those choices. See Perron (2017, 137–134).
2. *Spacewar* (1962), for instance, was made by MIT graduate students on a mainframe computer meant for nuclear research and was inspired by the science fiction novels that several of its creators often read (Brand 1972).
3. See Gibbons (2018, 50–71). On early silent film adaptations of opera as a gesture toward prestige, see Marks (2005, 71–76), Altman (2004, 251), and Grover-Friedlander (2005, 19–21). On the cultural implications of opera in video games, see Cheng (2014, 167–171).
4. Zach Whalen (2004) also argues for the indebtedness of video games to early cartoon techniques such as "Mickey Mousing" (the cartoon-like synchronization of music with on-screen actions).

5. For more on these titles see Collins (2008, 108–110); and Monfort and Bogost (2009, 125–126).
6. VCS, or "Video Computer System," was the original name of Atari's 1978 console. It was later renamed the Atari 2600 to fit the naming convention inaugurated by its successor, the Atari 5200 (released in 1982). In this chapter, I will follow the common scholarly practice of referring to the system by its original name.
7. On Warner's acquisition of Atari, see Goldberg and Vendel (2012, 200–207); and Fleury (2019, 100–125). On *Superman*, see Fleury (2019, 162–198). On corporate synergy and the emergence of film adaptations, see *Blip* (June 1983, 3) and *Videogaming Illustrated* (December 1982, 13).
8. See *Blip* (June 1983, 2–4); and *Electronic Fun* (November 1982, 10–15).
9. Gibbons (2018, 59–62) makes a similar argument about *Sorcerer's Apprentice* (1983), an Atari VCS adaptation of a sequence from Disney's *Fantasia* (1951): "[b]ecause the game's narrative differs so greatly from the original story—and because it lacks the lavish visuals of Disney's animation—sound is central to bridging the gap between *Fantasia* and *Sorcerer's Apprentice*."
10. On the pitch and tuning limitations of the Atari VCS, see Collins (2006). For a full transcription and comparison between John Williams's original score and the Atari VCS version, see Schartmann (2018).
11. Collins (2008, 19) notes that, even once this became technically feasible with consoles like ColecoVision, continuously looping background music did not become common in videogames until 1984.
12. "Eye On: What's New in Hardware, Software, the Industry!" *Videogaming Illustrated* (August 1982, 10).
13. Archival documents quoted in this section and the next two are from *Atari Coin-Op Division Corporate Records* collection (hereafter *ACDCR*), held at the Strong Museum of Play's Brian Sutton-Smith Library and Archives. They are identified by the boxes and folder numbers containing the records for each game. Atari had separated the operations of its coin-op and home entertainment divisions in 1978; see Goldberg and Vendel (2012, 362).
14. Memo, Jed Margolin to distribution list, November 14, 1979. Records for *Star Wars* are held in *ACDCR*, Box 4, Folders 30–34.
15. Production Status Report (PSR), *Star Wars*, August 6, 1982.
16. The details of this contract are not publicly documented, but Jamie Williams's November 1983 "Behind the Scenes" article in *Video Games* describes an arrangement involving games based on each of the three *Star Wars* films (p. 24), while *Atari Age* (September/October 1983, 7) announced the partnership with Lucasfilm alongside a similar relationship with the Children's Television Workshop.
17. See *Star Wars* PSRs, *ACDCR* boxes 4/31 and 4/34. Weekly project updates began on June 20, 1980 and indicate a hiatus from January through April of 1981. The second half of 1981 is missing from the archive, but later updates indicate a "restart" date of Jan 11, 1982.
18. These games would later be the basis of several updated collections produced by Sega, including *Star Wars Arcade* (1993) for the 32X console, and the arcade cabinet *Star Wars Trilogy Arcade* (1998).
19. *Star Wars* advertising flyer, 1983. *ACDCR*, Box 4/30.
20. It is possible that in the advanced stages of the game, the music is truly random. Atari documents refer to a case in which a player managed a five-hour play session on a single

credit, leading engineers to discuss the randomly generated level structures that a player might encounter after their 20th round.

21. Numerous Atari memos confirm an average of three-minute playtimes for both *Star Wars* and *Return of the Jedi*. See, for instance, an *ROTJ* Field Test Summary from August 24, 1984 (ACDCR, Box 3/34).
22. Chips like the TMS-5220 relied on *linear predictive coding* to encode information about phonemes and resonance, rather than actually recording sound. "If all we did was a straight digitization of speech," noted Mike Hally, "then for the amount of speech we used in *Star Wars* we would have needed a printed circuit board measuring 11 1/2" by 19" just to store it! The speech integrated circuit we used is 1/28th in size and basically one memory chip which together replaced that entire board." See Williams (1983, 25).
23. The VAX-11/780 was a supercomputer used by engineers and developers at Atari, which included an internal, company-wide precursor to email. Margolin's personal archive of other people's messages and his own memos can be found at http://www.jedmargolin.com/vmail/vmail.htm and http://atariemailarchive.org.
24. Jed Margolin, "Speech Synthesis Meeting," April 2, 1982; and "TI Speech Development System," April 26, 1982 (http://www.jedmargolin.com/vmail/Stat82.txt).
25. See Jed Margolin, "Speech Status," March 19, 1982; and "Speech Synthesis Status," Sept. 20, 1982 (http://www.jedmargolin.com/vmail/Stat82.txt).
26. Atari VAXmail, "Sound Chips," January 19, 1984. http://atariemailarchive.org/thread/sound-chips-20.
27. Jed Margolin, "Sound Chips." Another message in the same thread indicates a gendered component to the system's accuracy, noting that its default 8 kHz sampling rate is ideal for men's voices, but not women's. The note recommends several settings that should be changed in order to facilitate 10 kHz sampling for women's voices; these are resource-intensive workarounds that indicate a degree of gender bias in the design of the system. See "TI Speech Option, Yamaha & Pokey Clock rates," March 21, 1984.
28. "Now the Force Is With You!" *Computer and Video Games* (October 1983, 30).
29. "Arcade Action," *Computer and Video Games* (April 1984, 27); "Games from the Movies," *Blip* (May 1984, 14); "Reviews: Star Wars," *Video Games* (October 1983, 55).
30. Flanagan (2017, 448) notes that videogame ports are characterized by their adaptation to the "technological, aesthetic, and cultural constraints" of a new platform.
31. Jed Margolin, "The Secret Life of Vector Generators" (2001, 52). http://www.jmargolin.com/vgens/vgens.pdf.
32. Documents related to *Return of the Jedi* are held in *ACDCR*, Boxes 3/34 and 4/1.
33. *Return of the Jedi* marketing document, May 25, 1984.
34. "Jedi Sounds," handwritten note, October 2, 1983.
35. Letter from Dennis Harper (Atari) to Rita Dodson ATTN: Gary Summers (Lucasfilm), September 15, 1983.
36. Letter from Dennis Harper (Atari) to Susan Leahy (Lucasfilm), January 3, 1984.
37. Letter from Dennis Harper (Atari) to Katherine Gruhn (Lucasfilm), December 5, 1983.
38. "Jedi Sounds," memo from Chris Downend to Cindy Petroka, March 3, 1984. It is unclear whether the sound effects for *Return of the Jedi* came directly from Lucasfilm, or whether they were created by Atari. In an interview, Earl Vickers mentions having to create his own sound effects for *Star Wars* (see Williams 1983, 25), and the sounds in *Jedi* generally do not resemble those from the film, indicating they may also have been created in-house.
39. Letter from Dennis Harper (Atari) to Susan Leahy (Lucasfilm), January 3, 1984.

40. On LaserDisc games, see Robert Alan Brookey (2010, 7–9).
41. See Collins (2008, 95–97 and 108–111) and Cheng (2014, 59–63).
42. Brookey (2010, 4–5) writes that seven of the top-ten grossing films in each of the years 2005, 2006, and 2007 were accompanied by game adaptations, and describes the lack of a video game companion to Christopher Nolan's *The Dark Knight* (2008) as "the exception that proves the rule."
43. Kohler, "Why Games Based on Movies Disappeared."

References

Aldred, Jessica. 2012. "A Question of Character: Transmediation, Abstraction, and Identification in Early Games Licensed from Movies." In *Before the Crash: Early Video Game History*, edited by Mark J. P. Wolf, 90–104. Detroit: Wayne State University Press.

Altice, Nathan. 2015. *I Am Error: The Nintendo Family Computer / Entertainment System Platform*. Cambridge, MA: MIT Press.

Altman, Rick. 2004. *Silent Film Sound*. New York: Columbia University Press.

Atari. 1982. "New Cartridge Report." *Atari Age*, November/December 1982: 7.

Brookey, Robert Alan. 2010. *Hollywood Gamers: Digital Convergence in the Film and Video Game Industries*. Bloomington and Indianapolis: Indiana University Press.

Cheng, William. 2014. *Sound Play: Video Games and the Musical Imagination*. New York: Oxford University Press.

Collins, Karen. 2006. "Flat Twos and the Musical Aesthetic of the Atari VCS." *Popular Musicology Online* 1. http://www.popular-musicology-online.com/issues/01/collins-01.html.

Collins, Karen. 2008. *Game Sound: An Introduction to the History, Theory, and Practice of Video Game Music and Sound Design*. Cambridge, MA: MIT Press.

Flanagan, Kevin. 2017. "Videogame Adaptations." In *The Oxford Handbook of Adaptation Studies*, edited by Thomas Leitch, 441–456. New York: Oxford University Press.

Fleury, James Bernard. 2019. "*Space Invaders*: Warner Bros. and the History of Hollywood in the Video Game Industry." PhD dissertation, UCLA.

Flint, Richard. 2020. "What Happened to Video Games Based on Movies?" *Escapist Magazine*, March 24, 2020. https://onlysp.escapistmagazine.com/what-happened-to-video-games-based-on-movies/.

Gibbons, William. 2009. "Blip, Bloop, Bach? Some Uses of Classical Music on the Nintendo Entertainment System." *Music and the Moving Image* 2 (1): 40–52.

Gibbons, William. 2018. *Unlimited Replays: Video Games and Classical Music*. New York: Oxford University Press.

Gorbman, Claudia. 1987. *Unheard Melodies: Narrative Film Music*. Bloomington and Indianapolis: Indiana University Press.

Guins, Raiford. 2015. "Beyond the Bezel: Coin-Op Arcade Video Game Cabinets as Design History." *Journal of Design History* 28 (4): 1–22.

Guins, Raiford, and Henry Lowood. 2020. "Atari's *Army Battlezone* Project: An Interview with Mike Querio." *ROMChip: A Journal of Game Histories* 2(1). https://romchip.org/index.php/romchip-journal/article/view/108.

Grover-Friedlander, Michal. 2005. *Vocal Apparitions: The Attraction of Cinema to Opera*. Princeton: Princeton University Press.

Hulse, Ed. 1982. "Games Go Hollywood." *Electronic Fun*, November 1982: 22–27, 97.

Hutcheon, Linda. 2006. *A Theory of Adaptation*. New York and London: Routledge.
Jenkins, Henry. 2006. *Convergence Culture: Where Old and New Media Collide*. New York and London: New York University Press.
Kohler, Chris. 2013. "Why Games Based on Movies Disappeared (and Why They're Coming Back)." *Wired*, February 15, 2013. https://www.wired.com/2013/02/movie-games/.
Lehman, Frank. 2022. "Complete Catalog of the Themes of *Star Wars*." Accessed February 1, 2022. www.franklehman.com/starwars.
Leitch, Thomas. 2007. *Film Adaptation and Its Discontents: From "Gone with the Wind" to "The Passion of the Christ."* Baltimore: Johns Hopkins University Press.
Leitch, Thomas. 2008. "Adaptation Studies at a Crossroads." *Adaptation* 1 (1): 63–77.
Lerner, Neil. 2013. "The Origins of Musical Style in Video Games, 1977–1983." In *The Oxford Handbook of Film Music Studies*, edited by David Neumeyer, 319–347. New York: Oxford University Press.
Marks, Martin. 2005. *Music in the Silent Film: Contexts and Case Studies, 1895–1924*. New York: Oxford University Press.
Monfort, Nick, and Ian Bogost. 2009. *Racing the Beam: The Atari Video Computer System*. Cambridge, MA: MIT Press.
Perron, Bernard. 2017. "Genre Profile: Interactive Movies." In *The Video Game Explosion: A History from "PONG to PlayStation and Beyond*, edited by Mark J. P. Wolf, 127–134. Westport, CT: Greenwood Press.
Richards, Mark. 2016. "Film Music Themes: Analysis and Corpus Study." *Music Theory Online* 22 (1). https://mtosmt.org/issues/mto.16.22.1/mto.16.22.1.richards.html.
Ruggill, Judd Ethan. 2009. "Convergence: Always Already, Already." *Cinema Journal* 48 (3): 105–110.
Schartmann, Andrew. 2018. "Music as Problem Solving: Transcribing Tunes for the Atari 2600." January 14, 2018. Paper presented at the North American Conference on Video Game Music, University of Michigan.
Whalen, Zach. 2004. "Play Along: An Approach to Videogame Music." *Game Studies* 4(1). http://www.gamestudies.org/0401/whalen/.
Williams, Jamie. 1983. "The Making of *Star Wars*, the Video Game: Behind the Scenes at Atari Coin-Op." *Video Games* 2 (2): 23–27.

CHAPTER 18

SOUND, EXTENDED REALITY, AND THE CINEMATIC-INTERACTIVE DICHOTOMY

TOM A. GARNER

Shadow and light are two sides of the same coin. One cannot exist without the other.

—Princess Zelda. *The Legend of Zelda: Twilight Princess* (2006)

Introduction

VIDEO game sound has always been technically, emotively, and aesthetically connected to cinema (see also chapter 15 this volume). This connectivity between sound in motion pictures and in video games has increased significantly since the advent of the CD-ROM and preproduced sound content that could deliver anything from high-fidelity speech to a complete symphonic orchestral performance. Contemporary virtual reality (VR) has equally widespread associations with both gaming—due to the marketing for commercial head-mounted displays focusing heavily on games applications—and cinema, with 360° film technology now firmly established, particularly among experimental filmmakers. More broadly, extended reality (XR) presents VR gaming with a wide array of novel technological affordances that have significant potential to disrupt how we experience games as both cinematic and interactive entities. The aim of this chapter is to consider these new affordances and their relevance to video game sound design.

Of the Cinema

The term "cinematic" is broadly accepted to mean being *of* the cinema. To be cinematic is to possess features and qualities derived from cinema, but also to evoke affective sensations akin to the broad user-experience of watching a film. The features are the most straightforward to delineate, predominantly comprising narrative, costume, props, acting, speech, cinematography, lighting, environment, mise-en-scène, visual effects, and, of course, musical scoring and sound design. To incorporate one or more of these features into a work, irrespective of execution and impact, may still be described as cinematic. "Cinematic quality" is a little more ambiguous, though efforts to build a taxonomy of cinematic quality can be observed in the academic literature. Mills (2013) identifies four key markers of cinematic quality: evidence of experimentation and innovative design; more physically accurate special effects and cutting-edge computer-generated imagery; richer texturing of audiovisual elements; and greater consideration of temporal aspects of the content, including pacing and, in particular, a focus on lingering scenes that facilitate audience-reflection.

When we discuss the cinematic quality of something outside of cinema itself, the top-level structure is a bidirectional relationship between this artifact and the cinema as two discrete entities, in which both elements influence the other in some way. Researchers have examined this relationship across multiple matters, including cartography (Caquard and Taylor 2009), geographical landscape (Lukinbeal 2005), and even the teaching of mathematics (Ibrahim 2021). More correlational associations have also found general acceptance, arguably due to their consistency. A good example is the link between cinematic quality and big budgets. It has been suggested that mainstream cinema, now largely represented by major studio films, incurs, for each film, an average of $65 million in production costs (Mueller 2020), supporting the assertion that being cinematic is synonymous with being expensive (Newman 2013).

Although speaking specifically with regard to the composition of a film's score, Davis (2010) identifies four functions denoting cinematic quality that can be translated to wider contexts. The first function is physicality, describing content that accentuates and reinforces the physical properties of objects or events within the diegetic world. The second function is structure, referring to content that bridges gaps, smooths continuity breaks, and, more broadly, brings multiple components and layers together to create a perceptually unified diegetic world. The third function is direction, denoting content that emphasizes specific elements, drawing a viewer's attention toward them (and potentially away from other elements) to better guide the viewer through the narrative of the diegetic world in a way that best reflects the intention of the designer(s). The final function is affect: to enhance the overall potential to be emotionally evocative, potentially through reinforcement but alternatively as a means of tonal counterbalancing.

Cinematic Video Games

In both video games and more broadly, embodying a cinematic quality is for many, synonymous with "good." Globally, video-game marketing departments have made persistent usage of the term "cinematic" as a part of their lexicon for shifting more units, capitalizing on this synonymous relationship with "good" and the wider associations between cinematic quality and greater player anticipation, by way of theoretical mediators such as enhanced prestige or authenticity (Wright 2017). More explicit piggybacking of a particular film may present a further explanation for this presumed connection in players' anticipated quality of a game. As King and Krzywinska (2002, 149) suggest, "[t]he 'immediate' thrill produced by direct engagement in the interactive experience is often based on a sense of 'hypermediacy,' of awareness that the world 'occupied' virtually is akin to that of another form of representation." That said, although such mechanisms may be present, the extent to which players actually assume being cinematic is equal to being good is highly questionable. In 2015, u/andy3471 asked Reddit the question: *what does the term "cinematic game" refer to?* They promptly received 120 responses.[1] Recurring words and phrases within these responses included: action-packed, unique set pieces, spectacle, over-the-top, scripted, storytelling, explosions, cutscenes, quick time events, atmosphere, dialogue-heavy, linear, character interaction, camera effects (depth of field, tilt-shift, film grain), sequence of events, forced perspective, exposition, high production value, and directorial control. These terms generally emphasize features and design techniques that are inspired by cinema being adapted and integrated into a video game format. More opinionated keywords and phrases included: marketing buzzword, masking technical inadequacies, and go buy something fun, though it is worth noting that overall judgment on cinematic games was generally balanced, diplomatic, and contextualized, with commentators largely accounting for personal taste and the specifics of how and when cinematic features are executed; an important notion that we shall return to later.

Taking in an equally general overview of video game studies literature, "cinematic" is not too dissimilar in its understanding. In fact, articles often present instances in which, to become more cinematic, a game feature is adapted from a form that is more supportive of interactivity (*of* the game), to one which is more *of* the cinema. Examples of this include altering the camera (Galvane et al. 2014) from action-based (continuous first-person, third-person, isometric, etc., perspectives that facilitate clearer feedback to support play) to cinematic (cutting between shots, close-ups, over-the-shoulder, long shots, etc.). It can also include manipulating the lighting by selecting expressive lighting (compositions that may reflect a scene's dramatic characterization, emphasize an affective state of the narrative, directly or indirectly influence character's feelings and behaviors, etc.) over more consistent and brighter lighting that, again, prioritizes clarity of feedback to support interaction (El-Nasr and Horswill 2003). It may alternatively shun more overt and consistent character animation in favor of more nuanced expressions, once again prioritizing the communication of narrative and affect over interactivity and reliable player feedback (Maraffi and Jhala 2011).

Gamez (2019) posits that cinematic games are effectively a genre in their own right, due to the features and qualities shared between them. While this is a fair assessment, it creates a multilayering effect when we consider how the titles that repeatedly adorn online compilations of cinematic games (see Carnevale 2019; LeBlanc 2019) commonly evoke a specific, well-established film genre. The *Uncharted* series (Naughty Dog 2007–2017) epitomizes the action-adventure, while *The Last of Us* (Naughty Dog 2014) is a thoroughbred zombie-horror, *Red Dead Redemption* (Rockstar San Diego 2010) is unquestioningly a western, and *Detroit: Become Human* (Quantic Dream 2018) is thoroughly consistent with the science fiction thriller. *L.A. Noire* (Team Bondi 2011) initially appears to be one of the least inventively titled games in history (the result of hammering together the genre [film noir] and the direct film influence [*L.A. Confidential*]) until you appreciate the exchange of "noir" for "noire" is a subtle comment on the gender assignment in its cinematic usage. This minor adaptation aside, the game exudes characteristics of the film genre that inspired it (see chapter 19 this volume).

From the above, a general impression of a distinct dichotomy is consistently reinforced. Cinematic qualities appear separate, even in opposition to, interactive qualities of a game. Ultimately, we are making our way toward the more specific question of how video game sound fits into this dichotomy. First, a little groundwork as we consider the meaning of cinematic sound and the broader historical tussle that has existed throughout the history of video games, between their often contradictory requirement to be both cinematic and interactive.

Cinematic Sound

To the question of what makes sound cinematic, literature broadly echoes qualities described above. For Jacobs (2017), cinematic sound is that which possesses substantial immersive quality, physically surrounding the listener and obscuring the actual points of mechanical reproduction so that the sound feels everywhere. Alternatively, Bridgett (2007) asserts that cinematic sound is that which evokes a perception of artistic craft in its production. We can summarize cinematic sound at its most fundamental as sound utilized in a motion picture, because it appears as one of the core features of the cinema itself. At the more qualitative level, cinematic sound is that which supports the qualities broadly associated with being cinematic: experimental and innovative design; accurate representation of certain real-world entities; built of cutting-edge technology and technique; reflective of large budgets; rich multilayered textures; encouragement of audience-reflection; and direction of audience-attention, cognition, and emotion.

To support the collective effort to present a cinematic quality is one further perspective on cinematic sound; As Ward and Leung (2008, 81) remind us, "[t]o be cinematic is to combine [sound, visuals, and story] in ways that make the impact of the resulting experience larger than the sum of its parts." That said, writers on the subject have put more focus on sound, beyond it being simply a piece of the cinematic puzzle. Theorists such as Stilwell (2001) respectfully bemoaned the persistent marginalization of sound within cinema, asserting that the general understanding of cinematic sound has barely evolved from the three-part-function description: speech provides narrative, sound effects direct attention, and music evokes emotion. Despite this issue being raised over 20 years ago, there arguably remains some truth to it as a continuing contemporary problem.

For Chion (1994), cinematic sound is *vococentric* (prioritization of the voice above other forms of sound), though more recent considerations of the cinematic soundscape have begun to question the extent to which this remains true in more recent motion pictures (Chattopadhyay 2012). Indeed, Stilwell's turn-of-the-century frustration with the wider acceptance of an overly simplistic model of cinematic sound has found further critical reinforcement and suggestions for progress. As Pauletto (2012) observes, sound effects, ambiences, vocalization, and music rarely appear in isolation. For instance, the design of the soundscape in the background, from its place in the mix to its spatial, temporal, or timbral features, will undoubtedly have a perceptual bearing on the received sound of a dialogue positioned within the foreground. Pauletto also points to a growing awareness in the potential to utilize production techniques traditionally associated with one form of cinematic sound on another; specifically, the use of more nonnaturalistic (hyperreal or unreal) digital signal processing effects on speech, blurring the lines between both application of technique and the previously demarcated functions of speech, ambience, effects, and music.

In a conceptual review of sound within Indian cinema, Chattopadhyay (2012) delineates cinematic sound by function, identifying three classes: sound as observation (establishing a scene, the material and physical environment, and identification of objects and events within), sound as emotion (communicating affective content, evoking specific emotive responses, encouraging empathy and identification with character, etc.), and sound as cognition (presenting nonauditory information concerning the narrative in an auditory form). Chattopadhyay states that these functions demand different, perhaps contradictory, features or qualities of sound design, with sound as observation largely realized through accurate capture and representation of real-world spaces and sound objects while sound as emotion encourages nonnaturalistic, modulated, and hyperreal designs. An alternative, but still function-focused, model of cinematic sound is put forward by Ward and Leuen (2008) as the four key cinematic functions of sound: hierarchically positioning emotional truth (affect across different periods of time, establishing acute emotion feeding into mood, then into overall affective characterization or energy); point of view (emphasizing priority visual elements within a scene); storytelling; and physical experience (embodied, tactile considerations).

One notable trend across the literature on cinematic sound is arguably one of integration and emergence; a collaboration of multiple interconnected elements, and the space between the notes as a received sense of cinematic quality emerges in the perceptual foreground. Just as a cinematic quality in sound design must avoid siloing of the commonly drawn distinctions of sound type (speech, ambience, music, effect) and be considerate of how the qualities of one can impact on another, cinematic quality in general must avoid siloing of the common cinematic features (sound, narrative, lighting, acting, etc.) and appreciate the integrative effects as these features are brought together into a singular artifact.

The Cinematic-Interactive Dichotomy

To be cinematic is to provide a crafted, directed, and precise experience that takes the audience on a predetermined journey. To be interactive is to facilitate agency, provide the opportunity to disrupt events, and to make the audience an active component of the unfolding narrative. How then, can a video game be both cinematic and interactive? This question is at the heart of the cinematic-interactive dichotomy. This dichotomy is well represented broadly within video games by the humble cutscene, a prescripted sequence commonly presumed to dictate the absence of player-agency and the presence of curated exposition. In an examination of cutscenes, Witchayapakorn (2021) observes several positions on their value. Here, the most negative judgment is that cutscenes present an undesirable interruption and undermining of gameplay. In defense of cutscenes, proponents have asserted that they can act as a player-reward, provide opportunities to take a break from gameplay action and provide space to engage cognitively, strategically, and empathetically with the game. This section commences with a very brief review of how video games have historically managed the cinematic-interactive dichotomy in terms of broad design, then closes with a more focused consideration of video game sound and its relevance, power, and responsibility in helping video game design balance and, more importantly, bridge the cinematic-interactive dichotomy.

The Historical Tussle

Tracing the history of video games back to the commonly accepted year of origin, 1971, we can observe that crossover between games and cinematic media, albeit television at this point, was present from the very beginning. In the same year, the influential title *Computer Space* (Bushnell and Dabney 1971) was released, along with the less remembered *Star Trek* (Mayfield et al. 1971), a text-based adventure game tie-in to the 1960s television series. Around the same time, televised representations of computer-generated worlds began to appear, as in *World on a Wire* (Fassbinder 1973). In terms of the basic features that may define a cinematic quality with regard to video games in the 1980s, elements such as rich narrative, visual effects, and an original musical score were all arguably present across the early second and third home console generations (see the Atari 2600 and Nintendo Entertainment System respectively as epitomic examples), but their relatively low fidelity discouraged associations with cinematic quality. The rare exceptions came in titles such as *Dragon's Lair* (Bluth and Dyer 1983), a progenitor of the now-infamous "quick time event." Here the popularized trade-off of the cinematic-interactive dichotomy was undeniably overt. Audiovisual fidelity was perceptually comparable to that of motion pictures it was emulating, but with player-interaction limited to specific button presses, required at very precise moments to proceed.

By the fifth generation (arguably dominated by the Nintendo 64 and Sony PlayStation home consoles, but also seeing significant consumer popularity in PC gaming via Windows and DOS), video games broadly utilized a divide-and-conquer strategy, within which the cinematic-interactive dichotomy arguably reached its most pronounced. Here, cinematic became a noun rather than an adjective, referring to noninteractive cutscenes that provided exposition and characterization and established both setting and situation before returning to a distinctly demarcated gameplay section. Certain titles, such as *The 7th Guest* (Trilobyte 1993) and the infamous *Night Trap* (1992) would further reinforce this differentiation with the use of full-motion video (FMV) cutscenes, featuring live action and prerendered visuals far more qualitatively comparable to film than the real-time rendered graphics and synthesized audio of the more interactive portions of the game. At this point in time, genre became a significant determiner of cinematic approach. While action-oriented genres, including first person shooters and platformers, largely rejected any cinematic approach that undermined the gameplay in any perceptible way, narrative-driven genres such as point-and-click adventures were built on a clear prioritization of cinematic quality, where interactivity was still present, but the mechanics specifically served the storyline, characterization, and aesthetic of the game.

Creating a clear line between cinematic and interactive components of a game arguably served the industry well for several years. Players were responsive to the benefits of cinematics that included: a break from gameplay while advancing the overall experience; an audiovisual reward for successfully completing a discrete section of the game; a means of transitioning more smoothly between different locales; and a means of more vividly and emotively representing the outcomes of their choices, successes, and failures (Salen and Zimmerman 2004). However, toward the end of the decade, a relatively small number of titles evidenced some distaste for the cinematic-interactive dichotomy by presenting a more integrated alternative. *Half-Life* (Valve 1998) represents a particularly well remembered instance of this integration. Here, traditional cutscenes were replaced with a series of sequenced in-game animations, cleverly exploiting established limitations of first-person shooter interactivity to preserve player agency but ensure they could not intervene in the narrative. Opening scenes delivered initial exposition through dialogue between nonplayer characters (NPCs) and one-way conversations between NPCs and the player-character, Dr. Gordon Freeman. In these sections of gameplay, the player has no weapon, head-up display, or melee functionality, effectively minimizing the player's expectation for intervention. In later scenes, despite Dr. Freeman acquiring an increasingly expanding arsenal of weapons, animated interactions between NPCs are either interruptible but nonessential for driving the narrative forward or made noninterruptible by means of world design. For example, the repeated use of bullet-proof glass and locked doors between corridors and rooms enables the player to observe a preset animation and offers a clear diegetic rationale for why they cannot intervene.

Half-Life eschewed cinematic camera angles, cutting between shots, and of course negated much opportunity for character expression in deciding to feature a mute protagonist. However, the experience of *Half-Life* is arguably still highly cinematic. The approach to exposition described above was highly experimental and innovative for the time, despite being a mainstream title. Additionally, the avoidance of any cuts between gameplay sections demonstrated in *Half-Life* is highly comparable to so-called one shot cinema: methods of shooting an entire film from a single camera without cutting (see *Blindsone* [Novotny 2018]) or using film editing to create that impression (see *1917* [Mendes 2019]).

Looking to more recent video games, some of the titles cited earlier in this chapter exemplify various approaches to reconciling the cinematic-interactive dichotomy. Were we to place these titles on a cinematic-interactive continuum, *L.A. Noire* (Team Bondi 2011) would arguably be the most centered. The gameplay intersperses several decidedly different interaction mechanics with varying degrees of player agency in an effort to create an overall sense of balance between cinematic and interactive quality. Players drive across 1940s Los Angeles with a largely standard control mechanism in which they are free to control their vehicle. Comparable to other driving games, they can decide on the ideal route to their destination or take a detour should their whim demand it. Firefights utilize established combat mechanics, emphasizing agency in action sequences, while more investigative moments such as crime scene analysis and suspect interrogation are markedly limited to constrained movement and multiple-choice mechanics. *Detroit: Become Human* (Quantic Dream 2018) leans more toward the cinematic edge of the spectrum. The game also commonly features investigatory mechanics that enable free player-movement (though decidedly limited in pacing and range of movements) but become largely preset animations when the player interacts with an object of interest. Moments of character dialogue also utilize a multiple-choice mechanic. *The Last of Us* (Naughty Dog 2014) remains a cinematic game but pushes more toward the interactive side of the continuum, largely attempting to hide its cinematics in plain sight. More exposition-heavy elements do mitigate player agency, but are relatively brief, commonly avoid more jarring transitions to cinematic camera angles, and often provide a narrative rationale, such as in the opening moments where the player-character is the passenger in a car as it crosses town, presenting the setting, while the driver and another passenger offer additional exposition and characterization through dialogue. The game also encourages stealth tactics to reach objectives, giving the opportunity for more lengthy and uninterrupted exposition from NPCs as the player bides their time in the shadows. In addition, all of the above titles heavily feature traditional cutscenes where the player's physical agency is entirely negated, though modern real-time rendering technology has progressed to the extent that these cutscenes are no-longer required to be prerendered or FMV to evoke cinematic quality, and they therefore can at least provide an audiovisual continuity that somewhat supports the perceptual blurring of the lines between cinematic and interactive beats within the game.

While the above examples may give the impression that contemporary game design favors careful balancing of the cinematic-interactive dichotomy, it should be observed that many titles have opted to reinforce distinctions between these elements. Interactive film has become a recognized video game genre with titles such as *Her Story* (Barlow 2016) reinvigorating the use of FMV to present cinematic quality, though integrative strategies still persist in such instances. *Her Story* curates its FMV content within a narratively consistent, emulated computer operating system and database, in which the player runs queries to navigate between clips, reads text files, and tags the video content with comments. Here, the interaction may be constrained, but these constraints feel appropriate in the wider thematic context of the game.

As we trace the line of video game development, there is a distinct trajectory toward reconciling of the cinematic-interactive dichotomy by way of more integrative approaches. Developers may choose to instill an array of cinematic qualities within their game, but there is evidence of a generally acute awareness of the pitfalls of negating player-agency through impeding interactivity. The solution may be to compartmentalize sections of game experience into discrete, cinematically dominant and interactively dominant sections. It may be to make the interaction mechanisms consistent with the diegetic world, or such that they more subtly constrain player action, allowing cinematic content to play out without disruption while the player retains a sense of agency. One further solution that is more visible in recent big-budget studio games is to put the responsibility for finding the "cinematic sweet spot" on the player. This is a binary option in most cases, such as in *Fallout 4* (2015), where the player can disable the "dialogue camera," allowing them to remain in full control of their avatar rather than dialogue being presented from a fixed, face-on perspective. Another example can be observed in *Ghost of Tsushima* (Sucker Punch Productions 2020), which offers players the option of a monochromatic "Kurosawa filter" as an homage to the samurai dramas of Akira Kurosawa. So far, I have considered the cinematic-interactive dichotomy and the various approaches to it largely in more overarching terms of presentation and interaction design, but what is the role of sound in this equation? The next section focuses on this aspect.

Cinematic-Interactive Dichotomy in Video Game Sound

Cinematic game sound broadly restates the qualities of cinematic sound detailed earlier in this chapter, qualities that include: the potential to stimulate cognition and evoke emotion, textural complexity, and contribution to mise-en-scène beyond the confines of the visual frame. Cinematic game sound may equally reflect immersive quality, enveloping the listener with the potential to directly affect physiological state. It may also imply care and expertise in its craft, contribute to perceived realism through naturalistic quality or conversely be decidedly unreal, depending on its function in the moment. As Collins (2016) observes, the sonic aesthetic of cinema and video games, particularly big-budget (so called triple-A, or AAA) games, have become increasingly similar. Games studios and publishers assume players will reliably associate cinematic with realistic, with the latter itself presumed to be a hallmark of user-experience quality. The progression from text-based dialogue systems, prominent in role-playing games, to expressive voice-acted speech has been asserted to have inherently afforded an enhanced cinematic game experience (Barton 2019). Ambient soundscapes, sound objects, and events have been shown to reveal the diegetic world of a video game, bringing a player out of being themselves playing a game, and into a new fictionalized role and situation (Jørgensen 2006). Indeed, there is arguably truth to the assertion that simply by being present, sound adds a significant layer of cinematic quality, due to the origins of sound design itself being very much *of* the cinema.

This is not to say that video game sound has reached a cinematic peak. Republished in 2017, Bridgett (2008) observes that subtlety and silence are two cinematic qualities that video games have yet to fully realize. Arguments could be made that there are exceptions to this rule, particularly in contemporary horror titles, and the past decade has seen notable increases in cinematic usage of both subtlety and silence. That said, video game sound continues to favor clarity of received meaning, emphasizing support of interaction over cinematics.

Of course, the fundamental difference between cinema and video games is the crux of the cinematic-interactive dichotomy: interactivity. In game music, this dichotomy is most apparent in the tussle between a score that is highly responsive, both temporally and characteristically, to the actions of the player and the fluctuating state of the game world, and a score that retains the musicality (structure, flow, melodic phrasing, recapitulation, and development, etc.) that audiences are more likely to associate with cinematic music. Various sound effects suffer from issues with repetition and complex interaction. Rapidly repeating a sample of a single gunshot from an automatic rifle is acoustically very different to an actual burst of automatic fire, as it does not account for the nuance between shots due to slight variances in the mechanical interaction. Capturing a wide range of samples for alternate durations of fire may produce the more cinematic sound but would struggle to be flexible enough to support FPS gameplay. Conversely, purely synthesized effects will maximize temporal flexibility and synchronicity while also offering better responsiveness to alternate environmental and situational circumstances. With synthesis, a far greater array of weapons could be built into the game, each with its own signature acoustic profile, and without requiring a huge sample library. The trade-off comes in the form of a loss of perceived naturalistic authenticity, as synthesized audio broadly lacks the timbral richness of its sample-based counterpart. Lastly, speech suffers from a similar dilemma. Voice-acted samples of human speech offer unparalleled richness, timbral authenticity, nuance, and expression but prerecorded content can only be responsive to player-action if interactivity is constrained. Multiple choice dialogue tree systems can facilitate sample-based character dialogue, but the potential for exponential growth in responses requires the tree to be heavily pruned lest the game include hundreds of hours of prerecorded voice content. Alternatively, a text-based or synthetic speech dialogue system facilitates much greater responsiveness to the extent that, combined with an artificial intelligence (bot) system, multiple choice could be replaced with free-text fields to give the player far greater control over how they converse with a nonplayer character, but at the cost of losing all the highly desirable qualities of sampled human speech.

An Integrated Approach

Considering the early history of games studies research, Girina (2015) points out that the notion of a conflict between ludology and narratology became incorrectly entwined with video game theories that were attempting to make sense of the respective differences between cinema and games. Of course, drawing such lines of distinction moves us away from more holistic analysis that favors an integrated approach.

The last 10 years have seen increasing attention paid to the question of whether a separation in design approach between cinematic and interactive is actually helpful. For instance, Habel and Kooyman (2014) explain how careful game design can manipulate player-agency across more of a spatiotemporal gradient, than a binary distinction, to enable more cinematic content to be introduced without presenting a disruptive culling of agency for the player. The authors reference the survival horror title *Dead Space* (EA Redwood Shores 2008). In this example, spatial manipulation includes placing the player in a constrained, claustrophobic space such as a ventilation shaft, thereby severely limiting their range and speed of motion but with diegetic validity and retained physical agency. Conversely, temporal manipulation can be seen in events where the player's avatar is momentarily pounced on by an enemy, triggering a short, preset animation sequence. This reduces agency but only for a very brief period and, as with the spatial example, is consistent with the narrative of the game. These sequences are also avoidable, meaning the cinematic animation additionally provides direct feedback on the player's performance, as such events represent a failure of the player to adequately dispatch of the attacking hordes before they get too close. Similarly, Witchayapakorn (2021) asserts that even if a cutscene were to temporarily limit user-controller input, this does not remove the opportunity for interactivity. Instead, the cutscene could require cognitive or empathetic engagement as part of a problem-solving mechanic, thereby facilitating the cinematic potential of the cutscene while mitigating the undermining of player-agency.

The key position advocated by an integrated approach is that it recognizes games are not films, just as cinematic qualities are not equal to interactive qualities, but that the gaps between these elements can be bridged with good design. Specifically, good design that utilizes an understanding of the affordances of a medium to identify appropriate techniques that at the very least, enhance either cinematic or interactive affordance without compromising the other, but potentially uncover little gems of design that contribute to both. This brings us to extended reality, the unique affordances it presents, and the meaning of these affordances for the cinematic-interactive dichotomy and good game sound design.

Connecting Affordance, the Cinematic-Interactive Dichotomy and XR Game Sound

A Quick Primer on Extended Reality and Its Affordances

The term "extended reality" first appeared within academic literature in the mid-1990s, where the term found usage in theoretical physics and referred to the notion of our universe (or plane of existence) being connected to an infinite sequence of *extended* parent realities in an ever-continuing linear sequence of birth, death, and universal renewal (Ne'eman 1996). Across the array of classifications and abbreviations, extended reality (XR) conceptually predates its technological forms by many years, to the point it could be asserted that the ideas underpinning XR have been present from the moment humanity embraced representation and imagination. In commonly accepted terms, Milgram and Kishino's (1994) taxonomy of mixed reality remains the standard-bearer for delineating elements within XR. These elements are by no means perfectly distinguishable, with attempts to classify them suffering from limitations and exceptions. That said, a good starting position is to consider the extent to which the user and the system interact with the physical and the virtual aspects of the singular experience. By this measure, virtual reality (VR) is that which places a greater emphasis on virtual content, though neither user nor system can be entirely immersed in the virtual. The system is largely closed and defined virtually in fixed programming code, externally responsive only to physical user input. The user is immersed in virtual audiovisual content, with natural light and external sounds obscured by the hardware. Of course, they still require a physical surface to stand on, physical controllers to interact with, and physical air to breathe, but the perceptual focal point is the virtual world. Augmented reality (AR) inverts this relationship, placing greater emphasis on physical content. An effective AR system is typically open to physical inputs, both from the player and the wider physical environment. It may be responsive to visual images, external soundscapes, electromagnetic fields, infrared light, or even the composition of particles in the air. The user may interact with virtual elements (technology interface, auditory or visual overlays, etc.) but the perceptual focal point is the physical world.

While Milgram and Kishino's (1994) taxonomy presents "mixed reality" as an umbrella term, encapsulating virtual and augmented reality, the more contemporary user-experience of XR encourages some light restructuring, in line with the measure of delineation described above. As is illustrated in Figure 18.1 (above), XR-type is a classifier that delineates the underlying systems of VR, AR, and AV (augmented virtuality). As presented in Figure 18.2 (below), XR-type can alternatively be structured factorially rather than on a linear continuum. Here VR and AR are diagonally positioned, as they are both consistent across both system and user-experience in being either virtually or

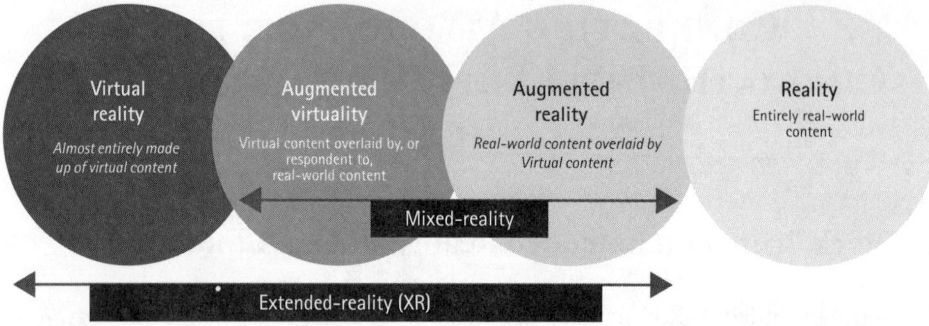

FIGURE 18.1 Modified version of Milgram and Kishino's (1994) continuum of mixed reality.

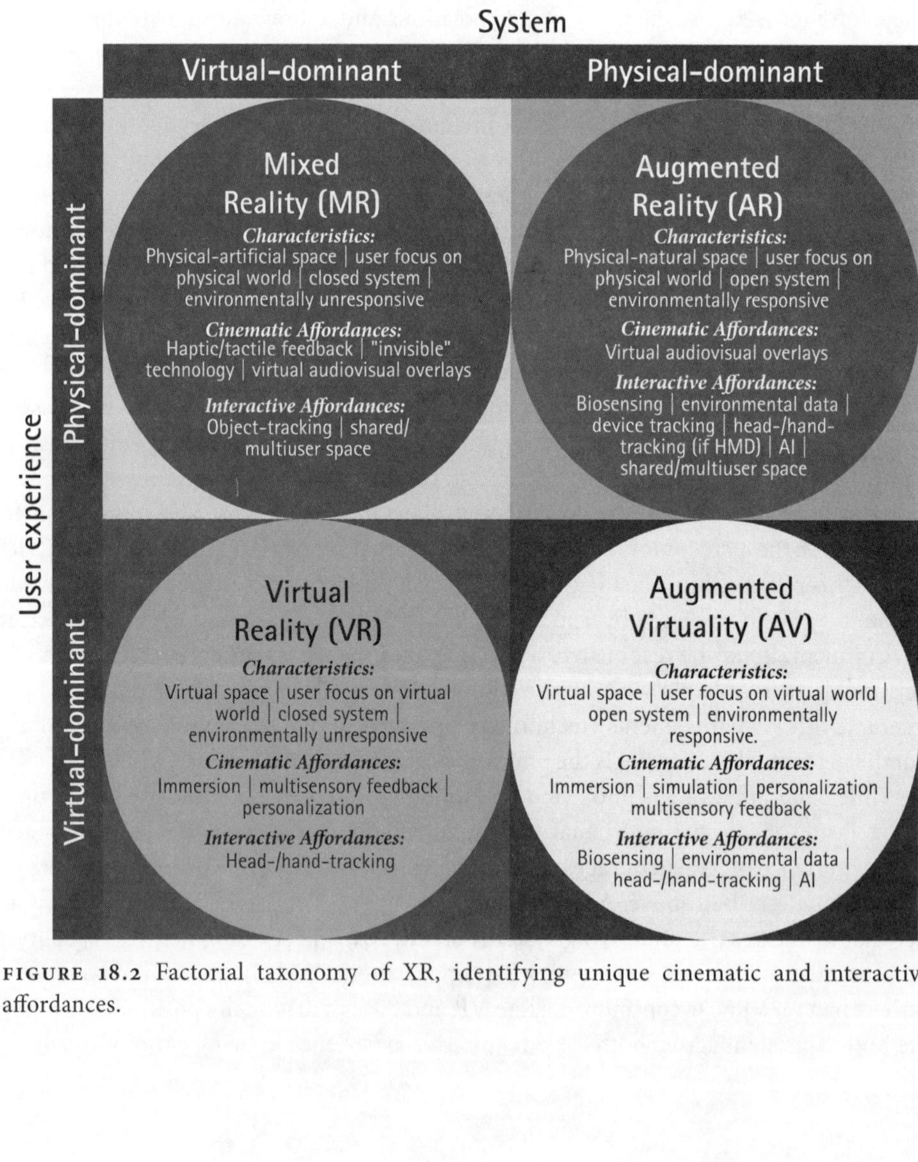

FIGURE 18.2 Factorial taxonomy of XR, identifying unique cinematic and interactive affordances.

physically dominant. Positioned in the opposing diagonal line are augmented virtuality and mixed reality. Augmented virtuality (AV) utilizes broadly similar technological and design features to VR. However, the system is not closed but rather responsive to external physical input, comparable in the system sense to AR. Mixed reality inverts this arrangement, commonly describing physical installations and props that perceptually immerse the user in a physical space, while the virtual content (holographic displays, virtual soundscapes, etc.) reflects a more closed system.

The affordances of XR, and the majority of its component technologies, remain frustratingly unestablished, particular outside of literature within closely related fields of study. An early, though still recent, effort by Steffen and colleagues (2019) to formalize such affordances into an accessible framework distinguishes four broad quadrants of affordance all in relation to the physical world: enhancement of positive aspects, diminishing of negative aspects, recreation of existing aspects, and creation of new aspects that do not yet exist. The enhancement quadrant includes individual affordances such as evoking empathy, filtering and enhanced presentation of data, and benefits to communication. Diminishing negative aspects includes reducing physical and emotional risk, for example, training simulations of extremely hazardous or stressful environments. Recreation incorporates key affordances such as reduced resource cost (due to flexible, reusable content) and enabling users with certain physical disabilities, while the creation quadrant describes "depictions of the non-existent [and the capability to] overcome space-time linearity" (Steffen et al. 2019, 721). The difficulty with these affordances, and definitions of XR more broadly, is that they do not distinguish the new technologies associated by the wider public to epitomize XR (namely the head-mounted display), from other digital technologies that include video games and traditional flatscreen/mouse/keyboard human-computer interfaces. Furthermore, there appears to be a fundamental disconnect between the technological capabilities of contemporary XR devices and the affordances with which XR is becoming increasingly associated.

Focusing on the technology, VR is synonymous with enhanced user-presence (Bouvier et al. 2008), realized predominantly by the singular technological affordance of a tracked audiovisual display. Using a head-mounted display (HMD), 6DOF (degrees of freedom) tracking of the user's head, combined with the rendering of the three-dimensional world displayed at the eye and responsive to their position and orientation, centralizes the user within the virtual space and facilitates a naturalistic viewing interaction much more closely comparable to real-world viewing than that the flat-screen and controller or mouse/keyboard interfaces offer. By way of tracked hand controllers, users can now engage their whole body (though predominantly their upper body) to interact with virtual objects. They can look underneath objects (a surprisingly engaging interaction), reach out and "pick up" objects, open and close doors, slide drawers, pull levers, and push buttons. Conversely, AR brings real-time environmental sensing to the table by way of integrating numerous hardware and software technologies into a singular application. The hardware could be anything from simple microphones and cameras to biosensors (monitors of electrodermal activity, respiration rate, heart rate variability, etc.) and global positioning data, while software could include (but is certainly not limited to) speech-to-text processing, image recognition, and facial coding. Augmented virtuality effectively combines the technological affordances of both VR and AR, while mixed reality presents similar affordances to VR (though through different means) with additional haptic feedback, provided by way of the user being able to directly interact with various discrete, physical objects.

How Does XR Affect the Cinematic-Interactive Problem of Video Game Sound?

Although this may be subject to change, as of mid-2021, mixed and augmented reality platforms largely eschew video game applications in favor of installation-based experiences and training. VR is of course the most established XR platform for video games, suggesting that understanding the relevance of VR affordances on the cinematic-interactive dichotomy is the priority. However, there are grounds for positing that the additional affordances of augmented virtuality (AV) are also important to consider if we are to be open to likely future technological developments. It is also worth noting that, although its usage within commercial applications is limited, existing consumer-level VR technology is already supportive of certain affordances of AV. Therefore, the focus here will be on the cinematic and interactive affordances of both VR and AV. Illustrated in Figure 18.2 (below), VR technology presents head and hand tracking as its key interactive affordances, with immersion, enhanced multisensory feedback, and potential for personalization its primary cinematic affordances. AV builds on these affordances with the addition of biosensing (measurement of physiological state, interpretation of cognitive and affective state), environmental data acquisition and artificial intelligence processing as additional interactive affordances, with the capacity for enhanced simulation the more exclusive cinematic affordance.

To broadly answer the titular question of the ways in which XR affects the cinematic-interactive problem of video game sound, the effect of XR affordances is to inherently widen the gap between cinematic and interactive qualities. However, there are some caveats within that observation and some opportunities for sound designers to exploit particular affordances as a means to bridging the gap. Head and hand tracking add a significant degree of granularity to user-interaction and camera control. Gone is the possibility of having the player press "A" to open a door, triggering a carefully crafted sequence in which the door is very slowly opened, gently yet persistently creaking as the tension steadily rises before the unknown on the other side is finally revealed. If the player wishes to grab the handle and blunder in, they are free to do so. In which case, our lovingly crafted gradual creaking sound is now entirely inappropriate. Likewise, if the player drops an object on the floor, the force with which they do so is now a variable, causing what was previously a physically accurate sample to no longer correspond effectively to the interaction with which it is associated. While this adds significant additional challenge to game sound designers wishing to retain cinematic quality, head/hand-tracking conversely contributes to the cinematic affordance of personalization, as the player's physicality is drawn into the virtual world with far greater depth than is possible through a traditional game interface.[2] However, while presence is generally regarded as a positive aspect of user-experience, perceptually drawing the player closer into the virtual world, it consequently enhances player-sensitivity to anything that fractures the established consistency and realism. Effectively, our player is greatly encouraged to "play"—to explore their new interactive affordances and test their limits and responsiveness while, in the same moment, presenting immersive audiovisual feedback that greatly exposes any inconsistencies or errors.

Encompassing numerous potential measures, biosensing presents a glut of interactive opportunities. However, what is particularly notable here is that, with biosensing, the interactive and cinematic affordances can be, in some instances, far greater in alignment. For example, voice detection and speech analysis represent a widening effect if used to conduct conversations with NPCs. Just as immersion exposes limitations of interactivity, the affordance to a player of using their own voice emphasizes the constraints of a multiple-choice conversation mechanic; the train of thought being "*if I can use my own voice to talk, why can I not use my own words?*" However, voice detection functionality can extend beyond conversation and may instead drive more subtle gameplay interactions that enhance cinematic potential. A good example of this already present in a mainstream video game is *Alien: Isolation* (Creative Assembly 2014), in which the use of an external microphone facilitates decibel-level measurement that enables NPCs to respond to the physical voice of the player. This can dramatically emphasize cinematic tension as the player literally holds their breath as they hide in a locker, waiting for the Xenomorph to pass by, but it can also enhance interactive affordance by enabling players to use their voice strategically to distract or draw out enemies.

By way of connection to the cinematic affordance of simulation, environmental data transcends the dichotomy, and presents the affordance as a particularly powerful tool in XR game design. Offline (not real-time) environmental data, in tandem with AI processing, has already proved exceptionally popular in *Microsoft Flight Simulator* (Asobo Studio 2020) where global topography data presented a cinematic simulation of Earth where, should the mood take you, you are free to virtually fly over your own home. However, the use of online environmental data in real time, by way of continually updating data sets or through more localized environmental sensors within an AV or video game context, remains largely unexplored, while the offline systems predominantly connect the data to visual facets of the virtual world, making online environmental data to drive auditory systems within AV/video games effectively untouched.

Other biosensing methods such as eye-tracking, facial electromyography and electroencephalography have seen usage as direct user-control methods, but when utilized in this way, have realized little positive feedback from either players or researchers (Gorzkowski and Sarwas 2019). This is largely due to them suffering from poor accuracy and reliability, particularly when compared to a traditional game controller or mouse/keyboard interface (invasiveness is also a significant factor, with eye-tracking, electrodermal activity and camera-based facial analysis far more likely to feature in future systems due to being either noncontact or light-touch). When considering cinematic and interactive affordances, the negative response to these limitations becomes doubly understandable, as use of biosensing in this way arguably contributes to neither cinematic nor interactive affordance. That said, as with voice detection, measures of bodily state have been recognized in academic literature as possessing substantial potential when utilized in more indirect, ambient contexts (Mandryk and Nacke 2016). Auditory biofeedback systems include the use of electrodermal activity to determine affective arousal and thresholds to signify a high arousal state that triggers an auditory blunting effect in which all diegetic sound in the game becomes muffled. The key factor here is whether the biosensing affordances are being exploited for means of direct user-control or as a more indirect and diffused means of influencing the virtual world. With the latter, biosensing can contribute to the cinematic affordance of personalization without severely impacting on immersion, so long as the technology and its execution is perceptually invisible.

Closing Thoughts

XR technology presents game sound designers with new challenges, from greater player-expectations for realism, responsiveness, and consistency, to the relatively uncharted waters of biosensing and environmental datasets that represent wholly new game mechanics and therefore require new approaches to auditory reinforcement. The fundamental value of XR technology is built on both cinematic and interactive affordances, meaning a divide-and-conquer approach will rarely satisfy an audience. Consequently, an integrative sound design strategy becomes essential. This strategy must demonstrate an awareness of how an affordance can be effectively realized, without compromising another. When constructing an individual sound or soundscape, designers should seek to explore combinatory approaches that construct sounds through both synthetic and sampled components, with an awareness of where (and in what way) cinematic or interactive quality takes priority. Lastly, to be cinematic is to consider each component of the whole artifact in relation to every other component, meaning sound designers cannot work in isolation. Instead, game sound designers must be ready to adopt a multilevel approach and work closely and consistently with other production teams. It is a tightrope walk: when everything is so interconnected, there is always the possibility of tweaking one element only for it to impact another seemingly disparate element. Quantum entanglement has entered the realm of video game sound design. I didn't say at any point that this would be easy.

Notes

1. https://www.reddit.com/r/Games/comments/2wrjl8/what_does_a_game_being_marketed_at_cinematic/.
2. It is worth noting that much of this discussion is dependent on the VR hardware being suitably supportive of audio. While some commercial headsets do incorporate reasonable quality over-head earphones, many have opted for smaller speakers integrated into the body of the headset; an approach that significantly limits auditory immersion and could have notable effects on player presence.

References

Asobo Studio. 2020. *Microsoft Flight Simulator*. Video Game. Xbox Game Studios.

Barlow, Sam. 2016. *Her Story*. Video Game.

Barton, Matt, and Shane Stacks. 2019. *Dungeons and Desktops: The History of Computer Role-Playing Games*. Boca Raton, FL: CRC Press.

Bethesda Game Studios. 2015. *Fallout 4*. Video Game. Bethesda Softworks.

Bluth, D. and R. Dyer. 1983. *Dragon's Lair*. Video Game. El Cajon, CA: Cinematronics.

Bouvier, Patrice, François De Sorbier, Pascal Chaudeyrac, and Venceslas Biri. 2008. "Cross-Benefits between Virtual Reality and Games." In *International Conference and Industry Symposium on Computer Games, Animation, Multimedia, IPTV, Edutainment and Security* (CGAT'08). April 2008. http://dx.doi.org/10.5176/978-981-08-8227-3_cgat08-26.

Bridgett, Rob. 2007. "Post-Production Sound: A New Production Model for Interactive Media." *Soundtrack* 1 (1): 29–39.

Bridgett, Rob. 2017. "Dynamic Range: Subtlety and Silence in Video Game Sound." In *From Pac-Man to Pop Music: Interactive Audio in Games and New Media*, edited by K. Collins, 127–133. Oxfordshire: Routledge.

Bushnell, Nolan, and Ted Dabney. 1971. *Computer Space*. Video Game. Nutting Associates.

Carnevale, Robert. 2019. "The 17 Best Cinematic Video Games." *Tom's Guide*. https://www.tomsguide.com/uk/round-up/best-cinematic-video-games.

Caquard, Sébastien, and D. R. Fraser Taylor. 2009. "What Is Cinematic Cartography?" *Cartographic Journal* 46 (1): 5–8.

Chattopadhyay, Budhaditya. 2012. "The Cinematic Soundscape: Conceptualising the Use of Sound in Indian Films." *SoundEffects-An Interdisciplinary Journal of Sound and Sound Experience* 2 (2): 65–78.

Chion, Michel, 1994. *Audio-Vision: Sound on Screen*. Translated by Claudia Gorbman. New York: Columbia University Press.

Collins, Karen. 2016. "Game Sound in the Mechanical Arcades: An Audio Archaeology." *Game Studies* 16 (1). Accessed December 26, 2023. https://gamestudies.org/1601/articles/collins.

Creative Assembly. 2014. *Alien Isolation*. Video Game. Sega.

Davis, Richard. 2010. *Complete Guide to Film Scoring: The Art and Business of Writing Music for Movies and TV*. Milwaukee: Hal Leonard Corporation.

EA Redwood Shores. 2008. *Dead Space*. Video Game. Electronic Arts.

El-Nasr, Magy Seif, and Ian Horswill, 2003. "Expressive Lighting for Interactive Entertainment." In *2003 IEEE International Conference on Multimedia and Expo. ICME'03. Proceedings* 1:1–425.

Fassbinder, Rainer Werner. 1973. *World on a Wire*. Television Serial. Janus Films.

Galvane, Quentin, Rémi Ronfard, Marc Christie, and Nicolas Szilas. 2014. "Narrative-Driven Camera Control for Cinematic Replay of Computer Games." In *Proceedings of the Seventh International Conference on Motion in Games*. 109–117. https://dl.acm.org/doi/10.1145/2668064.2668104.

Gamez, A. 2019. "The Art of Cinematic Video Games and the Varying Degrees of Convention Put into Them to be a Sort of 'Interactive Movie'". *Medium.com*. Accessed December 30, 2023. https://medium.com/@jhska/the-art-of-cinematic-video-games-and-the-varying-degrees-of-convention-put-into-them-to-be-a-sort-5e456d13d19.

Girina, Ivan, 2015. "Cinematic Games: The Aesthetic Influence of Cinema on Video Games." Doctoral dissertation, University of Warwick.

Gorzkowski, Szymon, and Grzegorz Sarwas. 2019. "Exploitation of EMG Signals for Video Game Control." In *2019 20th International Carpathian Control Conference*. 1–6. https://doi.org/10.1109/CarpathianCC.2019.8765983.

Habel, Chad, and Ben Kooyman. 2014. "Agency Mechanics: Gameplay Design in Survival Horror Video Games." *Digital Creativity* 25 (1): 1–14.

Ibrahim, Moustafa. 2021. "Cinematic Approach for Teaching Mathematics." Available at SSRN 3874446.

Jacobs, Bryce. 2017. "Interview with Bryce Jacobs." Sound Architect. http://www.thesoundarchitect.co.uk/brycejacobs/.

Jørgensen, Kristine. 2006. "On the Functional Aspects of Computer Game Audio." *Audio-Mostly '06*, October 11–12, 2006. Piteå, Sweden.

King, G., and Krzywinska, T. (eds). 2002. *Screenplay: Cinema/Videogames/Interfaces*. New York: Wallflower Press.

LeBlanc, Wesley. 2019. "10 Video Games That Are Basically Already Movies." *Twin Infinite*. https://twinfinite.net/2019/05/10-video-games-that-are-basically-already-movies/.

Lukinbeal, Chris. 2005. "Cinematic Landscapes." *Journal of Cultural Geography* 23 (1): 3–22.

Mandryk, Regan L., and Lennart E. Nacke. 2016. "Biometrics in Gaming and Entertainment Technologies." In *Biometrics in a Data Driven World*, edited by Sinjini Mitra and Mikhail Gofman, 215–248. Boca Raton: Chapman and Hall/CRC.

Maraffi, Chris Topher, and Arnav Jhal. 2011. "Performatology: A Procedural Acting Approach for Interactive Drama in Cinematic Games." In *International Conference on Interactive Digital Storytelling*, 322–325. Berlin, Heidelberg: Springer. Accessed December 23, 2023. https://link.springer.com/chapter/10.1007/978-3-642-25289-1_39.

Mayfield, Mike, David Ahl, and Bob Leedom. 1971. *Star Trek*. Video Game.

Mendes, Sam., dir. 2019. *1917*. Universal Pictures Worldwide.

Milgram, Paul, and Fumio Kishino. 1994. "A Taxonomy of Mixed Reality Visual Displays." *IEICE Transactions on Information and Systems* 77 (12): 1321–1329.

Mills, Brett. 2013. "What Does It Mean to Call Television 'Cinematic'?" *Television Aesthetics and Style*, 57–66.

Mueller, Annie. 2020. "Why Movies Cost So Much to Make." *Investopedia*. https://www.investopedia.com/financial-edge/0611/why-movies-cost-so-much-to-make.aspx.

Naughty Dog. 2007–2017. *Uncharted* (series). Video Game. Sony Interactive Entertainment.

Naughty Dog. 2014. *The Last of Us*. Video Game. Sony Interactive Entertainment.

Ne'eman, Yuval. 1996. "Inflationary Cosmogony, Copernican Relevelling and Extended Reality." In *Symposium-International Astronomical Union*, edited by M. Kafatos and Y. Kondo, 168: 559–562. Cambridge: Cambridge University Press.

Newman, Rich. 2013. *Cinematic Game Secrets for Creative Directors and Producers: Inspired Techniques from Industry Legends*. Milton Park: Taylor & Francis.

Novotny, Tuva, dir. 2018. *Blindsone*. Nordisk Film.

Pauletto, Sandra. 2012. "The Sound Design of Cinematic Voices." *New Soundtrack* 2 (2): 127–142.

Quantic Dream. 2018. *Detroit: Become Human*. Video Game. Sony Interactive Entertainment.

Rockstar San Diego. 2010. *Red Dead Redemption*. Video Game. Rockstar Games.

Salen, Katie, and Eric Zimmerman. 2004. *Rules of Play: Game Design Fundamentals*. Cambridge, MA: MIT Press.

Steffen, Jacob, James Gaskin, Thomas Meservy, Jeffrey Jenkins, and Wolman Iopa. 2019. "Framework of Affordances for Virtual Reality and Augmented Reality." *Journal of Management Information Systems* 36 (3): 683–729.

Stilwell, Robynn. 2001. "Sound and Empathy: Subjectivity, Gender and the Cinematic Soundscape." In *Film Music: Critical Approaches*, edited by Kevin J. Donnelly, 167–87. Edinburgh: Edinburgh University Press.

Sucker Punch Productions. 2020. *Ghost of Tsushima*. Video Game. Sony Interactive Entertainment.

Team Bondi. 2011. *L.A. Noire*. Video Game. Rockstar Games.

Trilobyte. 1993. *The 7th Guest*. Video Game. Virgin Interactive Entertainment.

Valve. 1998. *Half-Life*. Video Game. Sierra Studios.

Ward, Mark, and Linda Leung. 2008. "Beyond the Visual: Applying Cinematic Sound Design to the Online Environment." In *Digital Experience Design: Ideas, Industries, Interaction*, edited by Linda Leung, 81–91. Bristol: Intellect.

Witchayapakorn, Korphong. 2021. "Cut-Scene, a Re-Conceptualization of." *Journal of Human Sciences* 22 (1): 86–107.

Wright, E. 2017. "Marketing Authenticity: Rockstar Games and the Use of Cinema in Video Game Promotion." *Kinephanos: Journal of Media Studies and Popular Culture* 7 (1): 131–164.

CHAPTER 19

GAME NOIR

The Functions of Jazz in the Detective Adventure Video Game

JACOB COLLINS

Introduction

The scene opens with a shot of a disheveled bookshelf which quickly pans toward a glass door. "721 | John Blacksad | Private Detective," it reads. A cool jazz combo sounds offscreen. Brushes swirl around a snare drum. A walking bass line meanders up and down the chord changes while a piano joins in with a soft comping pattern. Finally, a muted trumpet plays a soft, improvised-sounding solo. A voice-over cuts in from an unseen narrator: "Sometimes when I walk into my office, I get the sense that I'm walking among the ruins of a lost civilization. Not because of the reigning disorder, but because it feels like the remains of the civilized person I used to be." The camera pans to our protagonist, John Blacksad—an anthropomorphic cat clad in dress pants, a white button-up shirt, and a tie—sitting casually on the side of his desk, floor length trench coat on a coatrack just offscreen. In the room, the camera pans past a desk cluttered with loose papers and a half-empty bottle of tequila before resting on a close-up of Blacksad's face as he takes a long drag of a cigarette. He lets the smoke waft slowly between him and the camera. This opening scene references many classic aspects of film noir, such as a postwar urban setting, a tough-guy private eye with ambiguous morals, and most importantly, a jazz soundtrack. However, this is not a movie, but a video game: *Blacksad: Under the Skin* (2019)—one of a long line of adventure games that cast the player in the role of a noir detective.

This chapter explores the role that jazz (or jazz-influenced) soundtracks play in the film-noir-inspired detective adventure game. Film noir, from its inception in the early 1940s, was based around recurring tropes, including smoking; drinking; shadows; a trench-coat-wearing detective; a crime in which that detective faces his own morals as a major obstacle; and female archetypes such as the damsel in distress and femme fatale. In addition to detective narratives, urban settings are also a crucial aspect of noir media, and the soundscape of the city permeates the genre (Wager 2017, 1–19). Musically, classic film noir (made roughly between 1941 and 1958) features a symphonic score with the occasional bit of diegetic jazz when nightclubs, gambling dens, or immoral behaviors were depicted on-screen; but as later films, known as neonoir, expanded the genre, filmmakers began to use jazz to represent all urban environments, eventually creating what David Butler (2002, 166–171) calls "a retrospective illusion of . . . an entire film era" in which neonoir films use jazz to evoke classic noir visual archetypes, causing the public to associate jazz with the smoke, crime, sexual themes, and other classic noir visual elements without any of the sonic realism of classic noir itself. Among other examples, Butler cites *Taxi Driver* (1976) and its use of jazz to depict the city as a whole rather than its specifically crime-infested locales as an expansion of the genre. This aural phenomenon, known to fans as "crime jazz," was solidified on film and television, forging the future relationship between jazz, criminality, and the detective (see also Adinolfi 2008). As Andra Ivănescu (2019, 29–31, 40–51) points out, video games often comment on the media they emulate through hypermediacy, putting the player in a position where they are aware (perhaps only tacitly) that they are essentially immersed in a playable movie. It is therefore not surprising that developers would invoke these specific visual, narrative, and musical tropes when creating neonoir-inspired video games.

By oversaturating detective adventure video games with jazz, developers are able to quickly communicate vital information to the player regarding setting, gameplay, and narrative expectations. But in so doing, I argue, they also invoke what Phil Ford (2008, 112–118) terms "jazz exotica"—the broad use of jazz to portray Otherness, often in the form of racist and sexist stereotypes—which in turn fosters a problematic nostalgia for an imagined past. I begin by explaining how jazz signifies and subverts common tropes used in game noir, such as urban settings and the femme fatale. I then offer observations about some common ways that game designers use jazz and its distinct traits—such as form, instrumentation, and harmony—to fill some established roles of audio in video games, which aid in communicating information to the player. By establishing characteristics of an "ideal type" of game noir, I hope to draw attention to the ways that jazz is most commonly used within these games, some of the troubling associations that these uses can sometimes reinforce, and some of the ways games subvert these associations.[1]

Setting the Scene: Jazz as Archetype

Music in game noir is, first and foremost, tasked with communicating the imagined soundscape to the player. Take, for example, *Déjà Vu* (1985) for the Nintendo Entertainment System (NES), an early noir-inspired detective adventure game. Since the NES had smaller memory capabilities than modern consoles, its games often relied on familiar musical signifiers to trigger an instant aural cue for the player to understand the setting. In the case of *Déjà Vu*, relatively few unique musical themes accompany the various areas of the game. Whenever the protagonist, Ace, does move into a new area, however, the underscore transitions to a different loop, giving the player a sense of change. The game features many "immoral" urban locales in which noir films traditionally feature jazz, such as a bar and a casino, yet the all-jazz soundtrack prevents them from standing out. Visually, most building's walls are often peeling, cobwebs abound in unused corners, and the entire landscape seems to be in disrepair. The game's various jazz-influenced musical cues, such as the "Peoria Streets" theme, act as a counterpart to the visuals—a type of sonic wallpaper that aurally associates the soundscape with disrepair. The player is thus given the sense that it is not the bar or casino that is the crime scene, but the whole city. Such musical cues are clearly derived from neonoir film tropes, but their implication is complicated. As Wager (2017) points out, the association between jazz and immorality in film noir stems from racist fears of Black male hypersexuality (see also Butler 2002, 29–60; Jeremy Barham 2017; and Krin Gabbard 1996).[2] While no Black bodies exist in *Déjà Vu*, in an effort to gain quick and easy associations for the player, the game propagates a conflation of crime, jazz, and urban space, and thereby feeds into stereotypes of Otherness, even if unintentionally.

Another example is the game I mentioned in the introduction: *Blacksad: Under the Skin*. The main character, John Blacksad, fits all the film-noir archetypes (with the notable exception of being an anthropomorphic cat). He is a hard-boiled private detective sporting 1940s business attire and a trench coat, and he is a war veteran battling his own internal demons. Throughout the game, *Blacksad* represents the posh neighborhoods and dark alleys of New York City by using nondiegetic jazz, reminiscent of films such as Miles Davis's score for *Ascenseur pour l'échafaud* (1958). A slow swing beat accompanied by string bass underscores most gameplay, with occasional interjections from a muted trumpet or saxophone. Different background tracks accompany different areas, although without connections to specific location types (bars, lounges, etc.) as in classic film noir. Much like *Déjà Vu*, *Blacksad* uses jazz to represent the city, but *Blacksad*'s city shows a diversity of dark and happy spaces, which despite aural unity, demonstrate a more nuanced take on urban-living in the 1950s. This sense of location is grounded using a diegetic radio. When investigating at a diner, Blacksad can focus on the in-game radio, which then plays similar crime jazz to what the player hears nondiegetically in the background, creating connection between what the player hears and what Blacksad hears. The creators of *Blacksad* drew on the visual aesthetic of classic film noir—citing Humphrey Bogart as Sam Spade as inspiration—but explicitly use crime jazz to show it.[3] In this sense, the visual and aural aspects of *Blacksad* and other game noir both immerse the player in Blacksad the character's reality as if it were a noir film onscreen and demonstrate the deliberate attempt to comment on noir media through its use of crime jazz. One standout moment in the game is how it intentionally addresses race. In the comic series which the game is based on, Blacksad deals with a group called the Arctic Nation, which is a group of white supremacist anthropomorphic animals. In the context of the game, Blacksad deals with small examples of racism, especially when interviewing fellow Black animals like himself, but his identity as a Black cat seems to act as a reclamation of the identity of the detective. In classic noir, the detective is always white, unless there is an example I am unaware of. By placing a Black body (1) as the protagonist, and (2) outside of the club, the game inverts established stereotypes about Blackness in noir media. The game itself is not shy about making racial commentary, but with a small shift, such as changing the identity of the protagonist, the player then reinterprets Blackness and the cityscape outside of this stereotype. Additionally, by using jazz to represent this nuanced depiction of the city, the developers seem to complicate the stereotype of an evil cityscape like the one presented in *Déjà Vu*. These items combined disrupt the racism within the established stereotype, especially when compared to other games.

Grim Fandango (1996, remastered 2018) also plays with the archetypes of film noir. Protagonist Manny Calavera's dimly lit office building is an idea borrowed straight from film noir. The game reinforces the narrative connections between jazz and the skyscraper and, by extension, the connection between jazz and the urban environment with scenes such as this. During Manny's travels, he enters a poetry club called the Blue Casket (likely a reference to the Blue Parrot from the 1942 film *Casablanca*). Upon entering, the player sees a dimly lit room with blue neon lights adorning the space. Patrons are sitting around small tables enjoying their drinks. The music instantly shifts from a cool/symphonic jazz style to a more intimate jazz combo—a track called "Blue Casket Bop." It sounds as if there are only four instruments in the combo: drums, bass, piano, and saxophone. As the title suggests, the angular saxophone lines and bold harmonic patterns indicate something more akin to contemporary bebop or modern jazz. Overall, this scene combines a 1940s club visual aesthetic with bebop, which may have been truer to contemporary 1940s jazz clubs than film noir. Another big portion of the game is its ties to Mexican folklore, such as Manny's resemblance to a *calaca* figure used to celebrate Day of the Dead, the parade commemorating DOTD, and the setting of the Land of the Dead. These specific stylized areas, such as the parade, feature music appropriate for those locations as opposed to jazz, which not only highlights the importance of music as a setting signifier but the tendency of games to modify strict noir tropes in interesting ways as well.

Femme Fatale Reinterpreted

Apart from the cityscape, various common character tropes or associations with film noir exist in game noir. While not every film contains every trope or archetype, these tropes identify a common pool from which games noir draw. In particular, video games frequently play with the femme fatale trope, challenging the perceived monolith of female roles in film noir.

The widely accepted stereotype of a femme fatale is that she is overtly sexual and manipulates men to get what she wants. She frequents bars, clubs, and other seedy establishments, and betrays the detective. However, in the end, she usually gets punished for her misdeeds. Both Wager (2017, 12–13) and Ian Brookes (2017, 67–68) acknowledge how power struggles between men and women—in terms of traditional gender roles during World War II and the postwar period—manifest in sexual tension onscreen that often resolves itself by letting the femme fatale succumb as an evil antgonist for daring to push past societal norms. Yet Wager also proposes that a pure good/evil binary is not an acceptable methodology to analyze the complexities of female characters within classic noir. To allow for some freedom of female expression, Wager redefines the categories of women in noir as (1) the "femme fatale," who facilitates her own demise, and (2) the *femme attrapée*, who is trapped by the patriarchy (12–13). Julie Grossman (2009, 5) further suggests that the femme fatale is not an object to be affected by masculinity (somewhat similar to Wager's thinking) but instead functions as her own narrative apart from the male protagonist. Grossman continues: "In some sense defining the women in exceptional noir films who are not really femme fatales begs the issue [of the identity or traits of the archetypal femme fatale], since the comparison relies on *a prioi* 'femme fatale' which is drawn from the many films that, read closely, reveal the absence of a 'femme fatale': she exists as an effect of problems in the culture, not as a thing in herself" (40). Grossman's analysis suggests that the "femme fatale" concept may too be an "imagined" relic of the past, much like the complete jazz score Butler analyzes. I do not mean to suggest the archetypal traits are nonexistent, but understanding the context around the role she fills is essential for analysis. These tropes have been filtered through early uses of jazz as sexual metaphor, which have been filtered through various films, which is in turn reinterpreted in game noir (see Butler 2002, 62; and Wager 2017, 8).

Though the femme fatale is as amorphous a character as the noir genre itself, some trends emerge—such as the femme fatale as a jazz singer or chanteuse. This role carries overtly sexual connotations and is aptly parodied in many films, such as the over-the-the top portrayal of Jessica Rabbit in *Who Framed Roger Rabbit* (1988). In games, however, those connotations are frequently subverted or otherwise obscured in service of a different narrative purpose. Building on Andra Ivănescu's (2015) in-depth discussion of Elsa Lichtmann in *L.A. Noire* (2011), I wish to add examples to this stereotype of femme fatale as a jazz singer/chanteuse. Broadly speaking, Ivănescu asserts that Lichtmann, a German jazz singer, represents a type of Otherness, which, accompanied by her performance with Black musicians, puts her in a position to foreshadow detective Cole Phelps's tragic end. This position is supported by lyrical analysis of Lichtmann's diegetic songs and the dichotomy of her onstage/offstage treatment (48–58)—both of which point to aspects of objectification. More importantly, this creates a link to the "hyperreality" of neonoir and the imagined past as discussed by both Butler and Ivănescu by playing up the traits of this imagined a priori femme fatale as a jazz singer for the player to easily understand. However, unlike the stereotyped femme fatale, Lichtmann does not meet her own demise. Lichtmann is clearly straddling the line between being a victim of abuse offstage, while using song as a vehicle for social commentary/mobility onstage, which fits into Grossman's (2009) problematized view of the femme fatale (5, 40, 60, 141–142). *Grim Fandango* offers another example of the chanteuse. The player first encounters the game's femme fatale in a club, the Blue Casket. Olivia Ofrenda, the club owner, wears a trench coat and a beret in a manner more akin to a slam poet than a detective or jazz singer—though she speaks in a deep, seductive voice between long drags from a cigarette like one might see from a chanteuse. When Ofrenda first appears, she emerges from a back closet with a man who is not her boyfriend. She confidently leans against the door frame as if challenging Manny to rat her out. Her real boyfriend, a mob boss, provides access to the finer things in life, and Ofrenda uses her charm to get what she wants outside of that. Later in the game, Ofrenda reappears to aid Manny on his quest to root out the afterlife travel embezzlement. Ofrenda double-crosses him, and, like the stereotyped femme fatale, she is punished for her transgressions: she is "sprouted" (the only way to kill someone in the afterlife) by one of Manny's allies.

Bebop-esque jazz accompanies Ofrenda in the club—a departure from the type of jazz expected in noir media—which suggest a level of sophistication. The patrons are slam poetry connoisseurs, mirroring bebop's more modern focus on a niche audience of practitioners and status as high art. The audience promptly boos and hisses when Manny approaches the microphone and recites a poem, which is constructed by the player who selects the various phrases. But when Ofrenda saunters over to the microphone and repeats the exact same poem, the audience applauds. Manny—who admittedly is not the best or luckiest detective to begin with—is in *Ofrenda's* world, not vice versa. It is *her* club. She calls the shots in *her* relationships, and she pulls the strings in *her* own destiny. Arguably, bebop's status and sophistication parallels Ofrenda's while simultaneously underscoring her sexuality via the club environment. When Ofrenda reveals her true colors later in the game, the sexual metaphor is no longer relevant, and jazz represents the crime motif instead. Still, she ultimately receives the traditional femme fatale punishment, despite her autonomy, which complicates the trope by utilizing some aspects and subverting others.

A different expression of this stereotype appears in the VR game *The Secret of Retropolis* (2021), which takes place in a posthumanity future that evokes a 1940s-style American city. The player steps into the shoes of robot detective Philip Log, who fits the drinking, smoking, trench coat wearing stereotype of a hard-boiled detective. Log receives a job from Jenny Montage, a famous robot actress and singer, to find her missing Sapphire nucleus—her power source stolen by her boyfriend, Senator Meric. While Montage's autonomy as a person (robot) is controlled by patriarchal forces, at no point does she try to betray the detective for her own gain—yet she still succumbs in the end (unless the player intervenes). But up until that choice, Montage is somewhat an equal partner to the success of the story; she distracts Meric with her singing at The Blue Screen club, while Log sleuths around, and even saves him from Meric just when all hope is lost. In this case, jazz and the club are repurposed to serve these new goals—from objectification to a useful tool. Ultimately, Montage's depiction shows that some games are willing to give the femme fatale a chance to reclaim her autonomy and become an agent of success in the story rather than a strict object of the trope's patriarchal anxieties.

Ludic Functions of Jazz in Game Noir

Although jazz helps situate the detective adventure video game within the context of film noir history, the uniquely interactive nature of video games as a medium requires adapting and reimagining jazz in ways not required in cinema. A player-driven narrative necessitates the use of audio clues to direct or encourage actions to progress the story. That is not to say that video game music does not fill other linear film-style roles, such as cueing a cutscene or providing transition material between scenes. However, the cues that underscore actions in film noir must now *motivate* story-progressing actions on the player's part in a video game (see Collins 2008, 125–128).

Video games are predicated on a dynamic relationship between the player and the game. The indeterminate nature of this relationship necessitates a creative approach with communication—both visually and aurally—to create a cohesive and immersive game world. But what does "immersive" mean? Tim Summers (2016, 58) adopts the view that immersion is a "progressive experience that includes suppression of all surroundings (spatial, audio-visual, and temporal perception)." Collins (2008, 134) further proposes an "imaginative immersion," in which the player has "a chance to use her imagination, empathize with the characters, or just enjoy the fantasy of the game" (see also Summers 2016, 59). Both definitions indicate that an immersive game includes audio that reacts to player input, builds up the game world, and communicates essential information to the player (see also chapter 47 this volume).

One useful tool for analyzing immersion offered by Summers is "texturing," which can be described as using music to fill in or flesh out the visuals of a game to enhance its narrative (see Summers 2016, 58–63; and William Gibbons 2018, 74–78). I borrow this term to highlight specific narrative-driven elements of game noir, as opposed to the larger connection between game noir and film noir aesthetics. These individual narrative-driven elements are derived from what Collins (2008, 4) describes as "dynamic audio." She uses the term to encompass both interactive and adaptive audio, defining it as audio that "reacts both to changes in the gameplay environment, and/or to actions taken by the player" (4).

The specific types of interaction required of game music depend heavily on genre. Video games typically have two genres: one based on narrative content (in this case, detective noir) and the other based on gameplay (in this case, adventure games). As William Gibbons (2020, 414) argues, music can be helpful in navigating both, as each gameplay tradition has expectations of its own. That is to say, the detective audio tropes must coexist with the action/adventure ones that the player expects. Music, then, also provides a few essential functions for gameplay: patterns that reflect either right or wrong choices, clue indicators, or even character interactions that reveal narrative information.

Narrative Cueing

The detective adventure video game often uses jazz-inflected interactive crime-jazz-style musical cues to guide the player toward finding a clue, making an accusation, and advancing the story. Steven Reale (2014) presents a multitude of important points of how audio cues function in the detective adventure game through his analysis of *L.A. Noire* as a music game. In particular, Reale highlights the branching score—where player choice affects the path which the score takes—that occurs whenever Phelps interviews someone (97–105). He also highlights the tones that sound when Phelps interacts with a clue. *L.A. Noire* appears to be the most detailed game I studied in which this happens, but similar gestures occur elsewhere as well.

Blacksad best emulates *L.A. Noire*'s use of jazz-influenced harmonies as a plot signifier. Blacksad, the detective, can ponder clues in his head. The interface is a tool for the player to simulate Blacksad's thoughts, as this menu suspends both time and audio. Whenever the player selects two or more clues to combine into a deduction, the game responds in one of two ways. If the clues result in a successful deduction, the player hears an ascending F# half-diminished arpeggio beginning on an A played on piano. If the combination does not make a deduction, the player hears a lone F# from the piano. Although sound design in *Blacksad* can underscore specific moments, generally these musical events are less scripted and often happen by chance.

Similarly, in one section of the VR game *Madrid Noir* (2021), the player must find the trench-coat-wearing detective hidden in a dark street. When the player highlights the detective onscreen, players hear a minor-major 7th chord (a minor chord with a major 7th on top) on a vibraphone, indicating that the detective has been located. He quickly disappears, forcing the player to repeat the process several times, until the next cutscene triggers. The vibraphone fits the crime jazz aesthetic. The dynamics of the cue often vary, which can blend with the background music by chance, depending on the timing of the player's actions with respect to the timing of the chaotic looping background music. One possible result is a barely audible cue against a loud portion of the loop hiding the player's success, which might induce the feeling that the player needs to look more thoroughly.

Dynamic Elements

Aside from narrative cueing, interactive or dynamic music can be crucial to maintaining a sense of player immersion in the detective adventure game—a sense, in other words, that the player is starring in a film noir they can control. Composers use a range of techniques to create these effects. The first I would like to discuss is the most basic: looping, or the composition of music that can be infinitely repeated based on the game's needs (see Collins 2008, 140–141 and Summers 2016, 21–25). Most games contain some form of looping, which is essential because the amount of time players spend completing tasks is highly variable. Looping presents some challenges in the case of jazz and the detective adventure genre. How do detective adventure games cope with keeping the background music interesting and unobtrusive when the "level" spans an indeterminate amount of time compared to games with more linear levels? And how do game noirs adapt complex jazz elements such as traditional formal structures and improvisation to looped formats? This section offers a few answers to these questions.

Previously mentioned *Déjà Vu* has the least complex soundscape of these case studies, which is understandable given its release date and the technological limitations of the NES console. Jazz forms are ideal for this type of short repetition, with most lasting less than thirty-two measures. For example, the very first location theme in *Déjà Vu* is "Joe's Bar"—a simple AABA form tune with each section lasting 4 bars, totaling 12. In *Déjà Vu*, each location's loop cuts out immediately when the player moves to a new location, but the introduction of a new area's loop can soften this transition. For example, when the player leaves the bar, "Peoria Streets Theme" begins with a drum intro that is not repeated on subsequent loops. The result is a "smoothing" effect in that "Joe's Bar" will always transition to the drum intro of "Peoria's Street Theme" (in that particular transition), so there is no conflicting harmonic material. This theme repeats endlessly every time the player visits Joe's Bar, as do the similar loops for each in-game location. With a total of five location-based tracks of similar length (all the game's music excluding the title screen, end credits, and game-over tracks) *Déjà Vu* has minimal adaptability to player response other than having different location themes. These short loops distinguish each location by being technically different, but still maintain a simple jazz combo–like texture with similar melodic and harmonic content. Though the limited amount of music may eventually be grating to the player, the frequency at which the player moves between these locations reduces listener fatigue (see Julianne Grasso 2020, 97–102).

In *Sam and Max Save the World* (2006), after the cut from the title screen to the office, the music immediately transitions to a prelude to the main office theme. The prelude, which coincides with a cutscene, contains all the nonmelodic material from the office loop—drums, bass, piano, vibes, and organ—with stingers, short chords that interject to punctuate a moment, from muted and unmuted trumpets. This transition serves two purposes. First, background music without a melody is quieter and more invisible, foregrounding the dialogue of the cutscene. Second, it allows a bit of narrative cueing in the form of jazz nostalgia. This prelude transitions almost seamlessly from the prerendered cutscene into the actual gameplay when the usual office loop begins. The form of the office loop is AABA, and each section is 8 measures, with an additional 8-measure introduction, totaling 40 measures per repetition. This initial repetition of just the melody with the rhythm section (drums, bass, piano) and no improvised solos is called the "head" or chorus, which is derived from song form in Tin Pan Alley songs (see John Covach 2005, 66–69 for a detailed reference). The loop begins with the A section (minus the melody). When the ensemble enters with the head, both the saxophone and muted trumpet trade the melody through each repetition of the A section. In the B section, the piano plays the melody with flute accompaniment. In the final A section, the trumpet enters with the melody while the saxophone plays a countermelody.

After one time through the head, the saxophone and trumpet take turns playing improvised solos over the form. To be clear, although the solos were likely improvised at the time of recording, they repeat identically in the game. Under normal circumstances, the intro A with no melody would not be repeated, making a 32-bar AABA form; but in this case, the intro A section is repeated during the solo section. The saxophone takes the first half of the chorus (the first three As), the trumpet takes the second half, and both instruments solo on the last A section. Collins offers some insight to the use of (micro/meso/macro) loops as a manner of what appears to be loop management in this case (see Collins 2007, 211–212). In this example, the head plus solo section is the macroloop. Each macroloop is composed of one mesoloop repeated twice with solos over the second time. The head, or song form is the base mesoloop that the entire structure revolves around, and the solos provide an additional layer on top of the head. The major difference is that *Sam and Max* utilizes a more complex composition strategy than *Déjà Vu* by using expanded jazz forms and layering solos on top of loops to create a longer module, much as a live jazz combo would in a club. Notably, the instruments are acoustic as opposed to MIDI, which hinders (if not foregoes entirely) the use of smart software to employ adaptive samples.

Grim Fandango takes this approach and alters it even further. There are still loops tied to each game area, but here each loop shifts fluidly back and forth between various styles, forms, and instrumentation.[4] I would argue that this approach serves two purposes: (1) it masks the looping nature of the music, and (2) it allows for potential smoothness or seamless transitions between different game areas, which was a large consideration for LucasArts games (see also Willem Strenk 2013, 81–92; Summers 2016, 72–77; and Collins 2008, 51–57). The first is the most self-explanatory. For example, the theme that plays in Manny's office, features an almost constant hi-hat rhythm with a clarinet lead. At some points, the clarinet is accompanied by strings playing long notes and the hi-hat drops out. At other times, a string bass accompanies the hi-hat and clarinet. The beginning of each loop functions as a cue to the player's location and breaks up some of the redundancy of either location's loop from dominating the entire time the player explores the large area. These open forms with fluctuating instrumentation and rhythm demonstrate the fluid shift from symphonic music to jazz that the score often makes. From my playthroughs, this loop plays straight through as written until interrupted by moving into another area. The second point is more nuanced, which aids in its invisibility. Some of the loops for different areas have sections within them that connect with other adjacent parts of the map, much like a puzzle piece. Granted, these interactions can make a smooth aural transition but can just as easily conflict with one another, as each loop restarts when you enter a new area. Elizabeth Medina-Gray (2014, 114–116) applies the idea of smoothness and disjunction here.[5] Often, loop modules of adjacent map areas will contain either similar instrumentations, melodic/harmonic content, and/or tempos, which allows for seamless transitions to happen. The opposite can occur accidentally or intentionally. Equally important are Collins's (2008, 142–147) observations about branching pathways. There are multiple ways to go about finding the next location or clue, and the player can travel through many different areas within the same location. Each area has its own loop module, so each path the player takes results in a unique branching score.

In the second act, for example, Manny can follow several paths after leaving his newly acquired club. The path to the left leads to a central bridge location on the harbor with several more branching paths. The music that underscores this section is like the type described above: a hi-hat accompanies a baritone saxophone playing free, improvisatory licks. A bass clarinet enters with longer notes interspersed with similar licks and takes over the lead from the saxophone. If the player takes one path to the north, the scene shifts to the docks. The loop in this area begins with a long bass clarinet note. In my tests, I found that walking into the center of the path, briefly pondering which path to take, then choosing the north path, results in a seamless transition from bass clarinet note to bass clarinet note. The loops also have similar textures and harmonic content, which aids in smoothness. Any faster or slower movement causes the loop to be in a different spot and creates an abrupt change from saxophone to bass clarinet. From that point, the player can make their way to the harbor, which has similar instrumentation, harmonic, and melodic content, but the game adds traditional harbor sounds such as ship horns, bells, and faint bird sounds into the mix to create a more complex environmental sound that blends with the jazz score. Each playthrough will ultimately yield different results, giving players different "cinematic" transitional moments each time.

However, there are some necessities for hard cuts in these loops. For example, when the player enters the Blue Casket club, the audio cuts directly to the "Blue Casket Bop." The club is situated in the middle of surrounding areas with relatively subdued audio, so there is no chance for audio to match in a "smooth" fashion. These hard cuts bring attention to the change of scenery. I mentioned earlier that an all-jazz score can soften the distinction between these stereotyped locales. While *Grim Fandango* isolates specific jazz tunes to certain locations like the Blue Casket, it still uses a mostly jazz score outside of the club (see also Collins 2008, 131–133).[6] By switching from symphonic jazz to bebop instantly, the player experiences different sensations and picks up different connotations about this new location, like classic noir. This is a more extreme example of *Sam and Max* having different themes associated with each locale because each hard cut seems intentional due to the stark differences between the surrounding areas.

Another way the detective adventure game creates a cohesive game world is through its modeling of specific detective milieu to communicate information. Previously, I addressed the diegetic use of jazz to give a sense of place in classic film noir, such as visible jazz combos or onscreen radios that layer on top of dialogue. Games noirs use similar tactics, although the traditional diegetic/nondiegetic relationship of music is often "ill-suited" for games (see Collins 2008, 121–127). Often, an onscreen (or implied onscreen) radio will increase or decrease in volume to serve dialogue or break temporal restrictions the game places on other aspects of the game world.

One common strategy for achieving the necessary volume change without creating a rupture in the narrative illusion is a subtle shift from nondiegetic to diegetic musical sources. By placing the music source onscreen, it allows the player to reason with the decreased volume in an organic fashion, increasing the invisibility of the music and immersion in the game. The opening few minutes of *Grim Fandango* utilizes this technique. As soon as Manny leaves his office and walks down the hall toward his boss' office, the music shifts to a grainy radio playing a track called "Mr. Frustration Man," a 1920s/30s-style swing jazz (as opposed to the cool or modern jazz in the rest of the game). It is an especially stark shift from the symphonic jazz associated with Manny's office. There are a few items onscreen that could be the audio source, but it is not immediately clear. This implied diegetic audio source is significantly quieter than the normal background music. This shift, clear or implied, is important for the same reason as the onscreen radio in *Blacksad*; it grounds the player's aural experience in the character's experience. Creating a singular point from which the music resonates also draws the player to important places in the environment, such as Eva's desk in this case; she is an invaluable distributor of plot information in this section, and this location-based layer portrays that. When the player speaks to Eva, the radio volume decreases in deference to the dialogue.

To revisit the diner scene from *Blacksad*, its deliberate layering and diegetic shift via the radio demonstrates a similar technique albeit a different function to the radio in *Grim Fandango*. When Blacksad speaks to Mary in the diner, he can use his cat senses, which disrupt time and suspend all audio, much like the act of combining clues and making deductions. The camera shifts to a first-person view, and the player is free to look around and discover clues in the environment. A white arrow points to a clue when the player is relatively close, and the arrow turns into a complete circle when the player places the cursor directly on a clue. When the player "sees" the clue, it triggers a "whoosh" sound, and Blacksad narrates his observations. However, the radio in the diner presents a unique approach to clue discovery. Before the player selects the radio, there are visible waves emanating from it, indicating sound, and the songs on the radio slowly increase in volume with a slight crackle. When discovered, the radio breaks the suspension of time, and both Blacksad and the player hear what is playing in real time. All the clues disrupt the silence and give way to a Blacksad voiceover. This one does not, which entices player interaction. When the jazz begins to play, the temporal freeze breaks, and the radio becomes the only window into the outside world. The concept of "jazz radio" has been discussed in the *Bioshock* franchise by William Gibbons (2014), both as a narrative signifier and a ludic element to motivate player interaction. The radio seems to be an important element not only in those game noir that emulate the milieu of classic noir but to adjacent neonoir-inspired series as well—especially regarding jazz.

Conclusion

The games discussed in this chapter reflect a small number of noir-inspired games that exist. The genre of neonoir films created polyvalent interpretations of the noir genre, making it nearly impossible to say anything definitive about these films and the games they inspired. However, a few notable trends emerge. As I have shown, games use the narrow visual aesthetic of the classic noir detective and crime jazz to communicate narrative and ludic information to the player. In doing so, games must strike a balance between using this imagined past of a neonoir-esque all-jazz score to connote classic noir tropes instantly to the player and using music to motivate actions to progress the story in established ways similar to other video games outside the genre.

An all-jazz score may have softened the racist practice of tying jazz to crime-infested locations or the overtly misogynistic associations of sexuality and the club with the femme fatale, but are these associations still inherent in the detective adventure video game despite attempts to subvert tropes and stereotypes? Does an all-jazz score truly soften these associations by diluting their meanings to urban spaces in general? As I have shown, these interpretations are complicated. In the case of *Déjà Vu*, I argue that it does engage in racist stereotype for the sake of that easy connotation for the player. In *Blacksad*, the developers obscure the racist stereotypes of these tropes by changing the race of the protagonist and by making the cityscape a mix of crime-infested and safe areas, shedding the perception that the city as a whole is crime-ridden. How each game addresses the role of the femme fatale is similarly problematic. *L.A. Noire* does not shy away from Lichtmann being abused and restricted by patriarchal forces, but in the end, she presumably lives a normal life, while the protagonist perishes for his transgressions. Conversely in *Grim Fandango*, Ofrenda maintains almost full control of her situation, even over men, yet still causes her own demise. *The Secret of Retropolis* offers a reclamation of autonomy by the femme fatale, allowing her to become a required agent of success in the story. Importantly, she does not *have* to die at the end either. While yes, this is still the male protagonist's choice, it shows that developers are eager to explore deliberate subversions of these problematic tropes. I think there are many ways games can portray these stereotypes, and *Blacksad*, *Grim Fandango*, and *The Secret of Retropolis* offer a few promising explorations of how developers can use jazz and these established archetypes to reclaim some power taken from them. While no example is perfect, it offers a window into how challenging these archetypes can lead to a more complex and interesting story, and as a result, change what jazz represents in that context. We should not underestimate the meaningful interaction that enacting these subversive interpretations of stereotypes can have on the player. In short, I think being aware of these pitfalls are important, but game noir is a medium which has nearly unlimited potential for reclamation and subversion.

These observations represent a narrow slice of game noir. Many of these approaches will require exploring genres of music outside of jazz and potentially exploring different relationships between cultures. *Blacksad*, for example, was developed by a Spanish company, Microids, but was still set in the United States. Many reinterpretations of an American genre can vary wildly based on country of development. Furthermore, games such as *Max Payne* (2001) and *Heavy Rain* (2010) are a few prime examples of the game noir genre that do not use jazz as an aural signifier and have many twists on traditional archetypes—the former is also a third-person shooter, and the latter has the protagonist/detective as a 20th-century victim's father trying to save his son rather than a war-hardened 1940s detective. I think the way these archetypes unfold in these games is compelling to explore, but it is important to recognize how the genre developed using classic noir and jazz to communicate information to the player. While I limited my study to jazz and neonoir interpretations of classic noir tropes, it seems clear that expanding beyond those two items is a next step for understanding game noir.

Notes

1. While my focus is on games that use jazz to portray specifically classic noir visual archetypes, many games outside of my parameters draw on similar ideas. While some games try to emulate classic noir as much as possible, they rarely forego the all jazz soundtrack. A notable exception, *L.A. Noire* (2011), follows the classic noir tradition of reserving jazz for these immoral spaces like the club and is an outlier in terms of what a typical game noir is—if such a definition can ever truly exist. Games also compound this issue at times by doing the opposite and foregoing the jazz soundtrack altogether while maintaining a noir detective narrative. *Max Payne* (2001) is a good example of this phenomenon.
2. Each of these sources contains quality discussion on Black male masculinity. What I highlight is a well-covered and complex topic.
3. Jason Frye, "*Blacksad: Under the Skin* Developers Talk about Music and Animations in Latest Trailer," *Pure PlayStation*, September 13, 2019. https://pureplaystation.com/blacksad-under-the-skin-developers-talk-about-music-and-animations-in-latest-trailer/2019/09/.
4. In the original 1999 version, this is completely due to the dynamic layering of the iMuse system. In the Remastered version, I am unsure of how the effect was recreated, but in my observations, the game recreated the effects of iMuse in good faith.
5. See also Matt Arnold, "iMUSE and the Future of MIDI in Game Audio," matarnoldaudio, June 18, 2018. http://matarnoldaudio.com/adaptive-music/imuse-and-the-future-of-midi-in-game-audio/.
6. Collins discusses a similar premise to this in that game audio either grounds the player in the game reality or builds up the illusion by creating these specific soundscapes for specific areas, especially in *Grim Fandango*.

References

Adinolfi, Francesco. 2008. *Mondo Exotica: Sounds, Visions, Obsessions of the Cocktail Generation*. Edited and translated by Karen Pinkus with Jason Vivrette. Durham, NC: Duke University Press.

Barham, Jeremy. 2017. "Birth and Death of the Cool: The Glorious Afflictions of Jazz Onscreen." In *The Routledge Companion to Screen Music and Sound*, edited by Miguel Mera, Ronald Sadoff, and Ben Winters, 375–387. New York: Routledge.

Butler, David. 2002. *Jazz Noir: Listening to Music from "Phantom Lady" to "The Last Seduction."* Westport, CT: Praeger.

Brookes, Ian. 2017. *Film Noir: A Critical Introduction*. New York: Bloomsbury Academic.

Collins, Karen. 2007. "In the Loop: Creativity and Constraint in 8-bit Video Game Audio." *Twentieth Century Music* 4: 209–227.

Collins, Karen. 2008. *Game Sound: An Introduction to the Theory and Practice of Video Game Music and Sound Design*. Cambridge, MA: MIT Press.

Covach, John. 2005. "Form in Rock Music: A Primer." In *Engaging Music Analysis*, edited by Deborah Stein, 65–71. Oxford: Oxford University Press.

Ford, Phil. 2008. "Jazz Exotica and the Naked City." *Journal of Musicological Research* 27 (2): 113–133.

Gabbard, Krin. 1996. *Jammin' at the Margins: Jazz and the American Cinema*. Chicago: University of Chicago Press.

Gibbons, William. 2014. "Wrap Your Troubles in Dreams: Popular Music, Narrative, and Dystopia in Bioshock." *Game Studies: The International Journal of Computer Game Research* 11, no. 3 (December). http://gamestudies.org/1103/articles/gibbons.

Gibbons, William. 2018. *Unlimited Replays: Video Games and Classical Music*. New York: Oxford University Press.

Gibbons, William. 2020. "Music, Genre, and Nationality in the Postmillennial Fantasy Role-Playing Game." In *Music in the Role-Playing Game: Heroes and Harmonies*, edited by William Gibbons and Steven Reale, 9–20. New York: Routledge.

Grasso, Julianne. 2020. "Music in the Time of Video Games: Spelunking *Final Fantasy IV*." In *Music in the Role-Playing Game: Heroes and Harmonies*, edited by William Gibbons and Steven Reale, 97–116. New York: Routledge.

Grossman, Julie. 2009. *Rethinking the Femme Fatale in Film Noir: Ready for Her Close Up*. New York: Palgrave Macmillan.

Ivănescu, Andra. 2015. "Torched Song: The Hyperreal and the Music of *L.A. Noire*." *Soundtrack* 8, no. 1–2: 41–56.

Ivănescu, Andra. 2019. *Popular Music in the Nostalgia Video Game*. Wiesbaden: Springer.

Medina-Gray, Elizabeth. 2014. "Meaningful Modular Combinations: Simultaneous Harp and Environmental Music in Two *Legend of Zelda* Games." In *Music in Video Games*, edited by K. J. Donnelly, William Gibbons, and Neil Lerner, 104–121. New York: Routledge.

Reale, Steven Beverburg. 2014. "Transcribing Musical Worlds; or, Is *L.A. Noire* a Music Game?" In *Music in Video Games*, edited by K. J. Donnelly, William Gibbons, and Neil Lerner, 77–103. New York: Routledge.

Summers, Tim. 2016. *Understanding Video Game Music*. Cambridge: Cambridge University Press.

Strank, Willem. 2013. "The Legacy of iMuse: Interactive Video Game Music in the 1990s." In *Music and Game: Perspectives on a Popular Alliance*, edited by Peter Moorman, 81–92. Wiesbaden: Springer.

Wager, Jans B. 2017. *Jazz and Cocktails: Rethinking Race and the Sound of Film Noir*. Austin: University of Texas Press.

CHAPTER 20

SYNERGY AND SYNCS

Record Labels, Video Games, and Unending Consumption

DAVID ARDITI

INTRODUCTION

AT the turn of the 21st century, the recording industry was in turmoil. Outwardly, record labels and the Recording Industry Association of America (RIAA) sold the idea that piracy on file-sharing networks caused a massive decline in recorded music sales. The RIAA then used this piracy panic narrative to tighten control over intellectual property and access to consumers through new public policies (Arditi 2020). However, in the International Federation of Phonographic Industries (IFPI) yearly reports on the state of the music industry, a different story emerged about why the recording industry could be struggling. In 2002, the IFPI's *Recording Industry in Numbers* (RIN) report points to the problems of "Competing for consumers' attention in this environment has become more critical for the music industry" especially with regard to "increased competition from a revived gaming industry and DVD video" (IFPI 2002). In the following year, the IFPI goes on to state the problem is not just competition for consumers: "Sales have been affected by competition from newer forms of entertainment, particularly DVD and video games which saw strong growth in 2002. This has reduced the amount of retail space available to CDs and cut into consumer spending on music" (IFPI 2003). Video games had become such a vital part of entertainment consumption that the music industry viewed them as a direct threat to music's position in popular culture. As a result, record labels conducted a concerted effort to incorporate music into video games through synchronization licenses (syncs) and synergistic activities.

By the 2004 RIN, the IFPI pushed the idea to make music ubiquitous in everyday life, they called it "lifestyle music" in which "consumers are becoming exposed to music via film, television, games and mobile devices" (IFPI 2004, 3). In this report on the state of the music industry, the IFPI had a section dedicated to competing with other parts of the entertainment industry. The IFPI states that "though these sectors continue to compete for 'share of wallet,' music is a key component in the finished products or services offered in each of these segments—something music companies have been successfully exploiting in terms of strategic licensing" (IFPI 2004, 17). Notice their use of the word "exploit" here, which suggests not purely ethical intentions. Furthermore, they point to their strategy "to promote synergy between games and the music soundtracks for them, more and more opportunities are emerging from the sector for the promotion and marketing of music and artists" (IFPI 2004, 18). By the 2010 report, the IFPI provides information about the growth of video games, reports opportunities, and discusses constraints as if the two industries are one and the same (IFPI 2010).

Fast-forward over a decade, and one video game executive declared that the power of video games is bigger than MTV (Ombler 2018). Not only do video games provide opportunities for sync licenses but music placement in video games also helps to drive recorded music consumption. After Activision and Neversoft released the popular *Guitar Hero: Aerosmith* (2008), Aerosmith saw a 40% increase in consumption of their catalog (Ambrosino 2014). These are synergistic moves between record labels and video game publishers. Musicians make money from the appearances in video games, but also earn more revenue from their music as video game players become familiarized with artists' music. President of music at EA Games, Steve Schnur states: "We knew that video games could become what MTV and commercial radio had once been in the 80s and 90s. Any given song in *FIFA 19*—whether it's a new track by an established act or the debut of an unknown artist—will be heard around the world nearly 1bn times" (Ombler 2018). Instead of competing, the video game industry and recording industry have developed a symbiotic relationship. Increasingly, video games drive gamers directly to streaming music services. For instance, "*Beat Fever* is a mobile game helping to generate better engagement between players and musicians: players tap along to their favorite music and are then invited to stream the tracks in full on platforms like Spotify and Apple Music" (Ombler 2018).

Taking things a step further, Warner Music Group made an eight-figure investment in the online gaming platform Roblox (Aswad 2021). According to Warner Music Group's chief digital officer, Oana Ruxandra, "everything is going toward gaming, and we want to make sure we're capturing value within it. It's the future of entertainment" (Singleton 2021). The main value Ruxandra sees in the game is utilizing Roblox to live-stream concerts to fans, but this is not the only value derived from investing in the platform. Steve Cooper, Warner's CEO, continues: "On track to be a several hundred-billion-dollar market by 2025, gaming is among the fastest-growing sectors of digital media, and we've positioned ourselves to forge meaningful partnerships within the gaming community" (Singleton 2021). Record companies are less concerned with selling recorded music than making revenue. At the same time, music companies are developing video games. Writing for *Billboard*, Tatiana Cirisano (2020) details how "online job postings show that Sony Music is hiring its own team of game developers, and Epic Records is partnering with professional esports organization FaZe Clan to create a soundtrack to the upcoming film *The FaZe Clan Universe*, among a growing list of other music industry players making moves in the gaming space." Yes, Warner Music Group anticipates profits from having its artists perform concerts on Roblox, but this massive investment in games is also in keeping with the capital investment-driven focus music companies have taken over the past decade.

These changes happen as part of a broader strategy of the current phase of capitalism, which I term "unending consumption" (Arditi 2021, 2018). During the 20th century, as consumption of consumer goods became saturated, companies turned to expansion of the means of consumption. In other words, companies survived by selling more goods to the *same* consumers instead of trying to locate new consumers. For instance, the recording industry developed as gramophone producers recognized they could only sell so many gramophones, so they began to emphasize the production of music to sell records to be played on gramophones. With music's turn to digital, the emphasis shifted from selling physical goods to licensing content. Streaming music creates the technological apparatus for unending consumption because users pay a fee to access music. In the video game industry, having a *Pac-Man* arcade console in every home would limit consumption, but creating the Atari 2600 allowed gamers to play *Pac-Man* and other games. Instead of buying a single game, video game consoles allow game producers to sell multiple games to one gamer, a model Nick Dyer-Witheford and Greg de Peuter call the "razor-blade model" (Dyer-Witheford and Peuter 2009). As more platforms move to streaming and subscription models, gamers can now pay a monthly fee to play unlimited games. Subscriptions allow the revenue to be constant and consistent, and therefore unending. Record labels deploy synergy and syncs in video games to expand the means of consumption. Unending consumption allows media industries to perpetually generate revenue.

In this essay, I argue that the major record labels strategically employ synergy and syncs to create unending consumption by enticing gamers to become music fans and vice versa. First, I explain the basics of synchronization licenses. These licenses allow record labels and music publishers to generate revenue through their use in video games. Next, I look at the first wave of popular music in video games, which uses sync licenses to play prerecorded music in games. Finally, I explore the second wave of popular music in videos, where there is an increasing phenomenon of concerts in live music.

Synchronization Licenses

A synchronization (sync) license refers to "the right to use music, as the contracts often put it, 'in timed relation to visual images'" (Hull, Hutchison, and Strasser 2011, 136). Technically, there are two separate licenses we refer to as syncs: synchronization licenses and master-use licenses. Synchronization licenses cover the composition of the recording and go to the publishing rights holders (i.e., the songwriter) (Klein, Moss, and Edwards 2015). Master-use licenses are issued for the use of recordings of specific songs in “audiovisual projects” (Gordon 2008, 9). These are for the specific performance/recording of the song used. For example, if a video game producer wanted to use Whitney Houston’s cover of “I Will Always Love You,” Dolly Parton (as songwriter) would have to issue a synchronization license, and Whitney Houston’s estate would issue the master-use license. While only the former is a synchronization license, most people in the recording industry use the term sync to refer to both licenses/rights because in both cases the licenses are required to synchronize music with video. Video game producers hire music supervisors whose job it is to find music for games and clear the licenses. These licenses can vary from a few thousand dollars to multimillion-dollar contracts; in some cases, artists even license their music free for perceived promotional purposes. Even though sync licenses are far more costly than producing music specifically for a game, the use of popular music in video games creates cultural synergy that develops a music fan’s affinity with the game and the gamer’s affinity with music.

In 2003, the IFPI remarked that the “value of music licensing is not currently measured and is excluded from current music sales reports. This may need to change in the future as mobile phones and video games use recorded music as an integral part of their offering” (IFPI 2003, 3). Up to this point, the recording industry did not see a reason to track sync licenses. It was a small part of recording industry and music publishing revenue. Rock musicians were notoriously reluctant to lend their music to advertising for risk of being labeled as a “sell-out” (Klein, Meier, and Powers 2017), so through the 1990s there was not a big emphasis by record labels of all sizes to try to exploit copyrights in videos. “What is most striking about the activities associated with selling out—musicians advertising products, angling for mainstream success, or partnering with companies—is that they are no longer exceptional or even noteworthy” (Klein, Meier, and Powers 2017). Selling out is not something that most musicians, especially those signed to big corporate labels, concern themselves with because it is just another source of income. By 2020, Goldman Sachs estimates sync licenses in “a movie, TV programme, TV advert, video game, toy and novelty item and account for c.20% of music publishing revenue” (Yang et al. 2020). In other words, songwriters can earn one-fifth of their income through sync licenses—and the current trajectory of the music industry suggests this percentage will only increase.

As more musicians become amenable to linking their music to third-party video, the revenue for these syncs keeps increasing. “Synchs for desirable tunes can command anywhere from $100,000 to about $1 million on the publishing side, with a like amount to the labels if an artist’s original master recording is used” (Parisi 2019). While these high-dollar amounts are for Super Bowl commercials, video games provide comparable revenue for prominent song placements.

Having a sync license is not the only revenue generated from having a song in a video game, however. If people hear a song in a video game, they may like the song and decide to stream it or buy an album. In this way, music and video games create synergy because the performance of music in a video game can generate interest in an artist’s music and vice versa; a music fan may purchase a video game because their favorite artist’s music is in the game. Chris Rigopulos, vice president of Harmonix, explains the potential impact of licensing music in video games: "All our music partners recognize that videogames are a growth area for them, which is particularly important, given some of the challenges with other areas of their business. *Rock Band* and *Dance Central* are promotional opportunities for artists. We're putting their music and name in front of millions of people. The deal terms and money are important to everybody, but it's really not as important as you'd think" (Thomsen 2011). In the streaming era, there is often a strong correlation between the release of a game and streams of the game's soundtrack.

While sync licenses have existed since filmmakers began placing music in films, their deployment has increased in video games over the past 20 years. There are two waves of sync licenses in music. The first wave emphasized deploying recorded music in video games. The second wave uses sync licenses in live music in the form of virtual concerts and Twitch performances. Today, these waves work concurrently to deploy synchronization licenses.

Recorded Music in Video Games

Dance Dance Revolution (*DDR*) was released in 1999, and, by 2001, every time I entered an arcade, I could hear the strange rhythm of people tapping their feet on the floor. While the popular rhythm and dance game did not include American pop stars at first, *DDR* demonstrated that licensing music in video games is profitable. Around the same time, *Tony Hawk's Pro Skater* featured the band Goldfinger—notice the choices for licensed music closely align with the culture associated with the video games because Goldfinder was associated with skateboard culture. By the mid-2000s, licensing music in video games became common place.

The release of *Guitar Hero* (2005) changed the relationship between popular music and video games as popular music went from a part of the experience to the main feature of the game. Following *DDR*, *Guitar Hero* was a music rhythm game that allowed players to play popular music by bands such as The Red Hot Chili Peppers, Stevie Ray Vaughn, and The Donnas using guitar-shaped game controllers. *Rock Band* (2008) expanded the game genre by adding drums, microphones, bass guitar, and keyboards. Together, the two music rhythm games "spearheaded an explosion of music-based games that generated more than $1.4 billion for the year [2008]" (Bruno 2011). The popularity of the game spurred competitions. I will never forget walking through a student center while I worked on my PhD and saw a *Guitar Hero* competition as about 100 students gathered to watch several people battle it out. Furthermore, these games inspired many gamers to purchase guitars contributing to a $30 million increase in fretted-instrument sales in 2007 (Buskirk 2008). In effect, *Guitar Hero* contributed to income in three industries: recorded music, video games, and instrument manufacture (see Dozal 2016; Arditi 2016). This is the core of unending consumption which convinces the same consumers to purchase more, often of what they already have.

Another early adopter of music synchronization licenses is the popular *Grand Theft Auto* (*GTA*) franchise by Rockstar Games. While *GTA* has had a radio since the first release of the game in 1997, *GTA: Vice City* (2003) was the first to license popular music extensively. The music for earlier *GTA* games tended to be written for the game, but in *Vice City*, producers licensed over 100 songs to recreate the feel of the 1980s including music from Michael Jackson, REO Speedwagon, Hall & Oates, and Herbie Hancock. *Vice City* became a boom for 1980s music acts' deep catalogs. Ever since, *GTA* and popular music sync licenses have become intertwined with the biggest licenses coming out with the release of *Grand Theft Auto V* (*GTAV*, 2013).

Upon release, *GTAV* sold more than 10 million units in the first day, grossing $800 million dollars, and in the first three days brought in over $1 billion (Morrell 2013). This was the single largest selling entertainment commodity in that length of time. The vast amount of licensed music in the game matches the enormous size of this audience. Producers licensed 241 songs across 17 radio stations (Corriea 2013). Rockstar Games originally aimed to include 900 tracks on the game but ended up with 241 songs. However, there is no information available on how much Rockstar spent on licensing music. With artists from Snoop Dogg to Elton John, Rhianna, and Queen, the game makers must have spent a significant portion of the estimated $135 million budget on music.

Since sync licenses must be obtained for both the sound recording and the composition, the 241 tracks on *Grand Theft Auto* result in 482 separate licenses for both synchronizations and master-use. As a result, it is conceivable that Rockstar games spent over $10 million on licensing for *GTAV*. Some video games, especially *Rock Band* and *Guitar Hero*, have found ways to reduce license costs by paying for the synchronization license and commissioning their own recordings of existing songs—this means bypassing the fees associated with master-use licenses from expensive popular recording artists. To do this, *Guitar Hero* and *Rock Band* list the name of the song, but the artist listed is something along the lines of "Neversoft." These cover songs sound remarkably similar to the originals and players do not really miss anything from their being covers. In these instances, the band did not agree to the syncs for the video game, but the songwriter did. Therefore, a cover band performed the song popularized by another artist, but the songwriter received payment anyway. This is a product of how licenses work differently for publishing and recordings. The owner of a master recording can restrict where the song gets played, but the publishing rights holder can still decide to agree to a license. However, *GTAV* did not cut corners because all *GTAV*'s music comes from original master, sound recordings.

While the synchronization licenses alone served as an increase to the recording industry's revenue, the synergy with music in *GTAV* went two steps further. First, video games can serve as an important way to launch new recording artists. Record labels and music publishers have in-house employees dedicated to getting their artists' music in video games (Knopper 2020). *GTAV* included plenty of unknown artists. But it also convinced established artists to record or release songs specifically for the game, which totaled 162 of the 241 tracks. Therefore, the game itself moves from a licensing platform to a distribution platform. Furthermore, Rockstar has been updating the music for the game, including new radio stations designed to introduce players to new music (Mamo 2020; Bain 2021). Second, Rockstar games released a three-volume audio soundtrack on iTunes and Spotify. Each volume is available on iTunes for $9.99 or the whole set for $24.99. This causes *GTAV* fanatics to provide even more revenue to the recording industry.

The biggest impact of video game music on the recording industry has likely been through boosting catalog sales. The popularity of *Rock Band* and *Guitar Hero* acted as a catalyst for music sales where "artists found that sales of tracks included in the games would skyrocket in the weeks following a title's release" (Bruno 2011). The most successful example of an artist's catalog boost is probably *Guitar Hero: Aerosmith*, which sold more than 4 million copies by 2015 (Ambrosino 2014). Furthermore, as previously mentioned, Aerosmith's album sales increased 40% in the few weeks after the game's release (Quan 2008). In fact, *Guitar Hero: Aerosmith* is the single largest contributor to the band members' net worth (Ambrosino 2015). "Drawing the attention of the much greater number of occasional record buyers to one track begins another virtuous circle of sales, chart position, airplay and more sales" (Rutter 2011, 178). The streams of an artist following a video game release increases their chart position, which causes more people to stream their music. "Nielsen Soundscan tracked sixty-two of the seventy featured songs on *Guitar Hero III* and found that sales increased on all of them following the release of the game" (185). Popular music in video games contributes to unending consumption because it allows labels and publishers to keep developing new sources of revenue without necessarily creating new products.

While syncs in the first wave of video game syncs increased revenue for artists, labels, songwriters, and publishers, it did not change the recording and performance of music. As video games adapt to the streaming era, the second wave of popular music in video games could be the harbinger of greater changes in music production, distribution, and consumption.

Live Music in Video Games

As governments worldwide closed down gatherings of 10 or more people to deal with the COVID-19 pandemic, few industries were hit as hard as the live concert industry. Overnight, live music went from a multibillion-dollar industry to an industry existentially challenged by concerns about the safety of gathering in large crowds, potentially forever (Brooks 2020). As a result, musicians and their fans turned online to listen to music and create community at live-streamed events. Video games influenced the move to present concerts online through live-streaming video games and the popular platform Twitch. While video game platforms have streamed live concerts for close to two decades, the second wave of game concerts turned into a tsunami as musicians explored new ways to reach fans during the pandemic.

Video games increasingly create their own worlds from massively multiplayer online role-playing games (MMORPGs) like *World of Warcraft* (2004–) to Battle Royale games like *Fortnite* (2017–). Whereas offline games on game systems in the 1990s presented static, never-changing game worlds, digital networks facilitate constant updates to video games. With streaming technology, servers permit online games to exist in an ever-changing world (Arditi 2021). Each time a gamer logs on to these games, they may experience a different gaming environment without updating their software. Since online games are wildly popular, Billboard states "games—which offer a built-in, enormous, youthful audience eager to pony up real cash for virtual merchandise—are the future of the live-music business" (Cirisano 2020). While I think the sentiment of some commentators is overblown (MIDiA Research founder Mark Mulligan exclaims: "Games are the new venues of tomorrow" [cited in Cirisano 2020]), video game concerts have a definite cultural and economic impact.

Unlike most other online video games, *Second Life* (2003–) is an open virtual world that lacks an objective. Users navigate the online world using an avatar and they can choose to chat, play games, start a business, etc. This created a perfect platform to host concerts (see also chapter 34 this volume). IONn 2006, "Suzanne Vega and Duran Duran, respectively, became the first two major recording acts to perform live concerts inside *Second Life*, which at the time had around 400,000 members" (Cirisano 2020). Though Suzanne Vega and Duran Duran are big name acts, *Second Life* developed the capacity to host anyone playing music on the platform. The game has a list of music venues and procedures for how to play a concert in the virtual world. However, the aging demographic of *Second Life* users does not open itself to a robust concert platform in 2021.

Since its launch in 2017, Epic Games' *Fortnite* has become one of the biggest video games in the world. As of May 2020, *Fortnite* had over 350 million registered accounts (Statt 2020). While Epic Games does not release information on the number of concurrent players, the gaming company did announce that "in April alone, players logged 3.2 billion hours of *Fortnite*" (Statt 2020). Both the size and youthful demographics of Fortnite make it a perfect platform for concerts. Furthermore, Epic launched a new mode for the video game that does not involve guns or building called "party royale." Much like *Second Life*, party royale mode allows users to walk around a city and interact with each other without necessarily competing in anything (Webster 2020). This is an exciting development, especially for the games' demographics. Aside from the pandemic, people under 18 have an increasingly difficult time going to concerts with parents becoming more protective. These online game environments allow adolescents to experience aspects of concert life without leaving home.

Before the development of party royale mode, the first concert in *Fortnite* was by Marshmello during which Epic Games suspended the use of weapons for the duration of the 10-minute concert (Statt 2019). Epic Games reported that the event had 10.7 million viewers log on for the concert and, at the time of writing, there are almost 60 million views on Marshmello's YouTube page.[1] Following Marshmello's *Fortnite* concert, his song "Check This Out" realized a 24,000% increase on streaming platforms (Cirisano 2020). *Fortnite* offers the opportunity for music fans to experience concerts, interact with their friends, be a part of something, and buy merchandise (more on this below). Marshmello's concert demonstrated that *Fortnite* could be the perfect platform for unending consumption by introducing game players to new music and music fans to games.

Following the successful Marshmello concert, *Fortnite* decided to go even bigger. Travis Scott held a five-show in-game concert residency, beginning April 23, 2020, in *Fortnite*'s new party royale mode (D'Anastasio 2020).

> The initial event drew 12.3 million concurrent players at its peak, and a staggering 27.7 million unique players from around the globe joined across five total airings of "Astronomical," over the course of three days and multiple time zones. Including repeat viewers, fans showed up for the event a total of 45.8 million times—and that may not count another 73 million views logged by the official YouTube version, and millions more on gaming-focused livestreaming platform Twitch, where Nielsen SuperData estimates the premiere's official stream reached a peak average-minute audience of 2.3 million viewers. (Twitch does not release exact viewer numbers.) (Cirisano 2020)

The data on Travis Scott's concerts are mind-blowing when seen from the view of an executive in either the video game industry or the music industry. No concert has ever had 12.3 million fans in one place. While live events like the Super Bowl have larger audiences, there is no mechanism for social interaction, as they work on an older broadcast model. People logged on to watch the show at the same time to be a part of something. Following the show, people continued to watch it on YouTube because it was discussed so much.[2]

But how does a free-to-play video game make money from a concert? The problem is there is not a direct correlation between viewers of the concert and revenue. *Fortnite* makes money by selling skins and weapons in the game. Travis Scott's foray into the video game space is significant not just for the scope of the concert, but also for his ability to sell merchandise. First, *Fortnite* sold Travis Scott skins, clothing, emotes (i.e., dance moves), and more in the run-up to and following the concert. Epic Games announced the concert on April 20 alongside an announcement for in-game merch (merchandise) available April 21 to prepare for the sequence of shows April 23–25, 2020 (Fortnite 2021). Furthermore, the *Fortnite* store included these items for a limited time. The effect was that gamers and Travis Scott fans made in-game purchases ahead of the concert lest they be without the ability to score the merch. Second, Travis Scott sold real-world merchandise to commemorate the *Fortnite* concert, from t-shirts to keyboard wrist pads (Grobe 2020). Travis Scott and *Fortnite* proved to be a synergistic team capable of driving gamer/fans into hyperconsumption. This is the ideal of unending consumption: a seemingly free concert (i.e., no price for admission) drives consumers to spend more than they otherwise would have in late April 2020.

The next contributor to the video game concert model is *Minecraft*. While *Minecraft* (2011–) began holding concerts in 2016, these were small affairs limited by server space for a select few (Fingas 2016). Following the onset of the pandemic, however, *Minecraft* also made a move into virtual space by increasing the number of music festivals on the game platform. On April 25, 2021 (at the same time as Travis Scott's "Astronomical" concert), Minecraft hosted its first music festival, called Block by Blockwest. The brainchild of an indie band, Courier Club, the music festival inundated the server with 100,000 fans trying to join the show (Shafer 2020). Concerts in *Minecraft* have a do-it-yourself feel to them—users build stages/venues and host the performances on servers. A notable difference between *Minecraft* and *Fortnite* is that *Minecraft* requires money to purchase the game, as well as a monthly fee to play online. When *Minecraft* decides to pay musicians for concerts (most are free concerts set-up by the bands themselves), they likely do so as part of their marketing budget. The idea is to entice a musician's audience to purchase and/or subscribe to *Minecraft*. Then hopefully the fans will become regular players and maintain their subscription. An underlying goal of unending consumption is to maintain subscribers to a service, even when subscribers never use the service.

As I discussed in the introduction, Warner Music Group invested heavily in Roblox to develop a concert stage in the digital platform. Roblox is uniquely positioned to host concerts because it is more of a platform than other games—the entire game is a series of games that users create in an open universe. In a way, Roblox is similar to *Second Life* in that it creates a metaverse—"a simulated world which allows its denizens to live as whoever they designed their avatars to be, in a shared reality which is always on and beyond the control of any one user" (Cross 2021). Users create an avatar and move among different games/scenarios built by other users, and users can decide whether or not to charge to use their games. Roblox users can create their own concert games within the platform. While Warner made headlines investing in Roblox, Sony Music has been actively creating concerts on the platform and recently signed an agreement with the platform (Broadwell 2021). In fact, Sony-affiliated artist Lil Nas X held a concert on Roblox that was attended by 30 million users on November 13 and 14, 2020. Then another Sony artist, Zara Larsson, launched her latest album in a game version of her home that allowed users to explore her house (Broadwell 2021). However, not much has been released about the revenue for artists. How much did Roblox pay them? Was the value of their having the concert a promotional tool for Roblox? Regardless of how much money artists make, these deals and concerts demonstrate the music industry's interest in video game concerts.

But can more traditional video games in less-open worlds also incorporate concerts? "EA, a company that's no stranger to the commercial power of music within video games, says it has plans of its own, too. Virtual concerts would be a natural fit for existing EA titles such as Madden NFL if they could be incorporated as halftime shows" (Ombler 2020). As of July 2021, EA Sports had no publicized plans to have a Madden NFL Super Bowl halftime show, but the idea must remain tantalizing for the company. If they pick the right musician(s), they could exponentially increase the game's reach. For instance, there may be little connection between Madden NFL gamers and fans of the South Korean boy band BTS—BTS fans have demonstrated an appetite to purchase *anything* BTS-related because their fans (aka the BTS Army) focus on consuming everything BTS. If EA Sports were to include a BTS concert within the game, they would undoubtedly sell more copies of the game (Ewe 2021). Through synergy, the music and video game industries expand consumption by targeting fans who may not otherwise be interested in a given product.

Over the past decade, Twitch has been one of the leading innovators in video games. In my ethnographic work, I met several musicians who have performed on Twitch. These intimate concerts allow fans to interact with a musician, tip them, and make song requests. However, aside from some of these musicians being Twitch gamers too, they do not have a direct link to games. Arguably, these musicians need to acquire synchronization licenses from the publisher of songs if they are not the songwriter, but if they play live, they do not need master-use licenses. While this may be outside the scope of popular music in video games, there have been some innovative uses of the platform. For instance, Post Malone played a concert for *Pokémon* to mark the brand's 25th anniversary. The *Pokémon* concert streamed live on Twitch and YouTube Live. The 13-minute show happened on February 27, 2021, with an avatar of Post Malone embedded in a virtual game world alongside Pikachu and other Pokémon. This created synergy between Pokémon and Post Malone as "a showcase of the vast world of Pokémon while also appealing to your casual listener of the Hot 100" (Stedman 2021). The cross-branding synergy of *Pokémon* has always been strong with video games, card games, television, and movies, but adding popular music to the mix increases the game's cultural reach. By playing recordings of Post Malone's songs this again differs from other concerts in the need to acquire sync licenses. While Post Malone's own music may have been licensed free of charge, he also covered Hootie & the Blowfish's "Only Wanna Be with You," which would require at least a synchronization license from the songwriter.

While sync rights are not clear in the second wave of popular music in video games, they are a part of these events. Most of the "live" events are prerecorded music set to a video and made live at a given time. These concerts demonstrate that the close relationship between video games and popular music will only increase in the future as people become accustomed to viewing concerts through video games.

Conclusion

When record label executives scrambled to reckon with a new media ecology in the early 2000s, they recognized the existential threat the recording industry faced through the growing competition with video games for entertainment dollars. The strategy record executives took to negotiate competition was one of unending consumption. Instead of competing for those entertainment dollars, record executives developed ways to divide the pie with video game companies. The two main tools the recording industry used to incorporate revenue were syncs and synergy. By using sync licenses, record labels and song publishers ensured popular music would remain relevant in video games. Through synergy, record labels created new opportunities for revenue around their artists.

Two consecutive waves marked distinct strategies for including popular music in video games. First, video games licensed popular music to be included in the game. Second, video game producers began using streaming technology to include concerts in their games. These waves built on each other. As the recording industry develops new ways to exploit their copyrights (and their artists), video games will be an important part of the strategy to increase the consumption of recorded music.

Notes

1. https://www.youtube.com/channel/UCEdvpU2pFRCVqU6yIPyTpMQ.
2. https://youtu.be/wYeFAlVC8qU.

References

Ambrosino, Brandon. 2014. "Aerosmith Made More Money from *Guitar Hero* than from Any One of Its Albums." *Vox*, July 11, 2014. https://www.vox.com/2014/7/11/5890237/aerosmith-made-more-money-from-guitar-hero-than-from-any-one-of-its-albums.

Arditi, David. 2016. "Virtual Jam: A Critical Analysis of Virtual Music Game Environments." In *Music Video Games: Performance, Politics, and Play*, edited by Michael Austin, 177–194. New York: Bloomsbury Academic.

Arditi, David. 2018. "Digital Subscriptions: The Unending Consumption of Music in the Digital Era." *Popular Music and Society* 41 (3): 302–318. https://doi.org/10.1080/03007766.2016.1264101.

Arditi, David. 2020. *ITake-Over: The Recording Industry in the Streaming Era*. 2nd ed. Lanham, MD: Lexington Books.

Arditi, David. 2021. *Streaming Culture: Subscription Platforms and the Unending Consumption of Culture*. SocietyNow. New Milford, CT: Emerald Publishing Limited.

Aswad, Jem. 2021. "Warner Music Makes 'Eight-Figure' Investment in Gaming Platform Roblox." *Variety*, January 7, 2021. https://variety.com/2021/digital/news/warner-music-investment-gaming-roblox-1234880693/.

Bain, Katie. 2021. "Label Look: How Monstercat's Gaming Partnerships Have Helped Its Acts Thrive through the Pandemic." *Billboard*, March 4, 2021. https://www.billboard.com/articles/news/dance/9525922/monstercat-gaming-partnerships-label-look/.

Broadwell, Josh. 2021. "Roblox Signs Agreement with Sony Music to Create 'Innovative Music Experiences' in the Metaverse." *GameDaily.Biz* (blog), July 12, 2021. https://gamedaily.biz/article/2099/roblox-signs-agreement-with-sony-music-to-create-innovative-music-experiences-in-the-metaverse.

Brooks, Dave. 2020. "The Year That Broke the Business." *Billboard*, December 19, 2020.

Bruno, Antony. 2011. "Fade to Black." *Billboard*, February 19, 2011.

Buskirk, Eliot Van. 2008. "*Guitar Hero*: Gateway Drug to Six-String Bliss." *Wired*, April 28, 2008. https://www.wired.com/2008/04/guitar-gateway/.

Cirisano, Tatiana. 2020. "Game On: What Travis Scott Is Teaching Music Stars about the World's Biggest New (Virtual) Stage." *Billboard*, July 24, 2020. https://www.billboard.com/articles/business/9422287/travis-scott-fortnite-billboard-cover-story-interview-2020.

Corriea, Alexa Ray. 2013. "The Accidental Excellence of *GTA 5*'s Soundscape." *Polygon*, October 3, 2013. http://www.polygon.com/2013/10/3/4795292/the-accidental-excellence-of-gta-5s-soundscape.

Cross, Tristan. 2021. "Roblox Wants to Build the Metaverse: Can It?" *Wired UK*, April 7, 2021. https://www.wired.co.uk/article/roblox-metaverse.

D'Anastasio, Cecilia. 2020. "Games Like *Fortnite* Are Today's 'Third Places.'" *Wired*, April 29, 2020. https://www.wired.com/story/fortnite-travis-scott-party-royale-third-place/.

Dozal, Mario. 2016. "Consumerism Hero: The 'Selling Out' of *Guitar Hero* and *Rock Band*." In *Music Video Games: Performance, Politics, and Play*, edited by Michael Austin, 127–152. New York: Bloomsbury Academic.

Dyer-Witheford, Nick, and Greig de Peuter. 2009. *Games of Empire: Global Capitalism and Video Games*. Minneapolis: University of Minnesota Press.

Ewe, Koh. 2021. "The Wildest Ways People Are Preserving Their McDonald's BTS Meals." *Vice.com*, June 22, 2021. https://www.vice.com/en/article/jg8j47/mcdonalds-bts-meal-packaging-viral-kpop.

Fingas, J. 2016. "*Minecraft* Gets Its First Live Concert." *Engadget* (blog), March 23, 2016. https://www.engadget.com/2016-03-23-minecraft-live-concert.html.

"*Fortnite* and Travis Scott Present: Astronomical." n.d. Fortnite. Accessed July 14, 2021. https://www.epicgames.com/fortnite/en-US/news/astronomical.

Gordon, Steve. 2008. *The Future of the Music Business: How to Succeed with the New Digital Technologies*. 2nd ed. Winona, MN: Hal Leonard Music Pro Guides. Music Pro Guides.

Grobe, Max. 2020. "Travis Scott's *Fortnite* Merch Is Meant for Gamers." Highsnobiety. 2020. https://www.highsnobiety.com/p/travis-scott-fortnite-merch/.

Hull, Geoffrey P., Thomas W. Hutchison, and Richard Strasser. 2011. *The Music Business and Recording Industry: Delivering Music in the 21st Century*. 3rd ed. New York: Routledge.

IFPI. 2002. "Recording Industry in Numbers." International Federation of the Phonographic Industry.

IFPI. 2003. "Recording Industry in Numbers." International Federation of the Phonographic Industry.

IFPI. 2004. "Recording Industry in Numbers." International Federation of the Phonographic Industry.

IFPI. 2010. "Recording Industry in Numbers." International Federation of the Phonographic Industry.

Klein, Bethany, Leslie M. Meier, and Devon Powers. 2017. "Selling Out: Musicians, Autonomy, and Compromise in the Digital Age." *Popular Music and Society* 40 (2): 222–238. https://doi.org/10.1080/03007766.2015.1120101.

Klein, Bethany, Giles Moss, and Lee Edwards. 2015. *Understanding Copyright: Intellectual Property in the Digital Age*. Los Angeles: SAGE.

Knopper, Steve. 2020. "Gaming's Top Synch Players." *Billboard*, July 24, 2020. http://www.billboard.com/articles/deep-dive/gaming-musics-next-big-play/9423572/gamings-top-synch-players.

Lisa Yang, Heath P. Terry, Piyush Mubayi, and Heather Bellini. 2020. "Music in the Air: The Show Must Go On." Market Analysis. New York: Goldman Sachs. https://www.goldmansachs.com/insights/pages/infographics/music-in-the-air-2020/report.pdf.

Mamo, Heran. 2020. "*Grand Theft Auto* Announces New Radio Stations Hosted by Julian Casablancas & Joy Orbison." *Billboard*, December 10, 2020. https://www.billboard.com/articles/news/9497924/grand-theft-auto-new-radio-stations-julian-casablancas-joy-orbison/.

Millard, Drew. 2011. "Flashback." *Billboard*, November 12, 2011.

Morrell, Alex. 2013. "Carl Icahn's Bet on *Grand Theft Auto V* Paying Off as Sales Top $1 Billion." *Forbes*, September 23, 2013. http://www.forbes.com/sites/alexmorrell/2013/09/23/carl-icahns-bet-on-grand-theft-auto-v-paying-off-as-sales-top-1-billion/.

Ombler, Mat. 2018. "'Bigger Than MTV': How Video Games Are Helping the Music Industry Thrive." *Guardian*, August 22, 2018. http://www.theguardian.com/games/2018/aug/22/video-games-music-industry.

Ombler, Mat. 2020. "Are Video Games the Future of Live Music?" *GamesIndustry.Biz* (blog), June 10, 2020. https://www.gamesindustry.biz/articles/2020-06-10-are-video-games-the-future-of-live-music.

Parisi, Paula. 2019. "Super Bowl Synch Report: Dylan, Queen Push Sony/ATV ahead of Publisher Pack as Brands Place Fewer Ads." *Billboard*, February 4, 2019. https://www.billboard.com/articles/business/8496277/super-bowl-2019-synch-publishers-commercials-ads-music-soundtrack.

Quan, Denise. 2008. "Is *Guitar Hero* Saving Rock 'n' Roll?" CNN.com, August 20, 2008. https://www.cnn.com/2008/SHOWBIZ/Music/08/20/videol.games.music/.

Rutter, Paul. 2011. *The Music Industry Handbook*. 1st ed. Media Practice. New York: Routledge.

Shafer, Ellise. 2020. "More Than a Game, *Minecraft* Music Festival Is a Blockbuster." *Variety*, May 13, 2020. https://variety.com/2020/music/news/all-about-minecraft-music-festivals-1234598970/.

Singleton, Micah. 2021. "Roblox Raises $520M from Warner Music Group and Others." *Billboard*, January 6, 2021. https://www.billboard.com/articles/business/tech/9507991/roblox-warner-music-group-gaming-investment/.

Statt, Nick. 2019. "*Fortnite*'s Marshmello Concert Was a Bizarre and Exciting Glimpse of the Future." *Verge*, February 2, 2019. https://www.theverge.com/2019/2/2/18208223/fortnite-epic-games-marshmello-concert-exciting-bizarre-future-music.

Statt, Nick. 2020. "*Fortnite* Is Now One of the Biggest Games Ever with 350 Million Players." *Verge*, May 6, 2020. https://www.theverge.com/2020/5/6/21249497/fortnite-350-million-registered-players-hours-played-april.

Stedman, Alex. 2021. "Post Malone Pays Tribute to the Wide World of *Pokémon* in P25 Music Virtual Concert." *Variety*, February 28, 2021. https://variety.com/2021/music/news/post-malone-pokemon-concert-p25-music-1234917182/.

Thomsen, Michael. 2011. "Licensed to Ill." *Billboard*, November 12, 2011.

Webster, Andrew. 2020. "*Fortnite*'s New Experimental Mode Is about Partying, Not Fighting." *Verge*, April 29, 2020. https://www.theverge.com/2020/4/29/21241414/fortnite-party-royale-ltm-mode.

CHAPTER 21

PLAYGROUND DISCO

Playing with Clubs and Aspects of Club Culture in Digital Games

MELANIE FRITSCH

Introduction

In early 2021, clubs in many parts of the world were still closed due to the COVID-19 pandemic that had fully hit in 2020 and brought some forms of social and cultural life to a complete halt. Against this backdrop, many game reviewers across different media breathed a happy sigh when a new game was released on January 20, 2021 on a broad range of platforms: *Hitman 3* (IO Interactive). In the shoes of professional assassin Agent 47, the player's path leads them to Berlin and into a nightclub called Club Hölle. As, for example, Peter Kirn (2021) writes: "Crowds of people, bright lights piercing the darkness, techno bouncing against cavernous industrial concrete—oddly the game *Hitman 3* is a refuge for people who miss clubbing."

While *Hitman 3* seems to have hit a nerve by offering at least a reflection of what many people were missing so dearly at the time of the game's release, depicting a club in a game is nothing out of the ordinary. On the contrary, clubs, as well as aspects of club and rave culture, appear in multifarious forms and functions in the world of gaming well before COVID-19 happened: in an expansion pack for *GTA IV* entitled *Grand Theft Auto: The Ballad of Gay Tony* (Rockstar North, 2009), players are put in the shoes of Luis Fernando Lopez to help out nightclub owner "Gay" Tony Prince with all kinds of criminal troubles and shady nightlife business. In DJ games such as *beatmania* (Konami, 1997), *DJ Hero* (Activision, 2009), or *Fuser* (NCSoft, 2020) the DJ as a music cultural figure as well as the action of spinning the turntables are the pivot of the game experience. Since the early 2000s, online games and virtual worlds such as *Second Life* (see, e.g., Harvey 2015) hosted virtual concerts and clubs. In *Minecraft* (Mojang Studios, 2011), for example, Club Matryoshka opened its virtual doors in July 2019 (see Celera 2019) with the goal to put local artists from Manila and the Philippines center stage, as one of the founders, Jorge Wieneke (DJ similarobjects), states in an interview with Arte (see Arte TRACKS 2020, 5:09).

Conversely, clubs and festivals have been used to market games or gaming equipment: on May 15, 1978, visitors to the legendary Studio 54 in New York witnessed a four-foot diameter, saucer-shaped object appearing above the club's dance floor, its four giant buttons flashing with the music booming through the room (see Knoblauch 2016, 30; Edwards 2000). This alien object was an enlarged version of the electronic musical toy "SIMON" produced by the company Milton Bradley. The event had been orchestrated on the occasion of the toy's launch for promotional purposes (see Knoblauch 2016, 30). In the mid-1990s, Sony sponsored big festivals such as the Lollapalooza or the installation of gaming rooms in British clubs such as the "Ministry of Sound" in London with the goal of marketing their new PlayStation to an audience of young adults neglected by other game publishers in those spaces where this specific target group spent their leisure time (see, e.g., Stuart and Boxer 2014). Additionally, a racing game named *Wipeout* (Sony Computer Entertainment, 1995) was produced, including renowned acts such as Orbital, The Chemical Brothers, Underworld, and Leftfield.

Looking just at these few, but also very different, examples from several decades, it is surprising that the topic of games, music, club culture and their manifold interrelationships and mutual influences has not yet been widely addressed in ludomusicological discourse.[1] In this chapter, though, I will limit myself to investigating depictions of clubs[2] and aspects of club culture for ludic engagement presented to players in digital games. My goal is to shed light on the topic that centers around the idea of both clubs and games as designed material bases to stage ludic possibility spaces[3] that can be entered and used by clubbers/players to realize specific experience projects,[4] such as a wished for party, or the gaming experience, as advertised either on promotional material such as a party invitation or by a games' marketing assets. I approach this topic by first outlining the perspective on clubs as ludic possibility spaces as applied in this chapter. Second, I investigate the depiction of clubs and aspects of club culture in games and music games against that backdrop by looking at a range of examples.

Designing the Party: Curating Possibility Spaces and Bodies in Clubs

According to Madison Moore (2013), clubs are consciously curated spaces, in which nightlife is staged in a certain way and then promoted via several channels to attract a specific target audience that is thought capable of realizing the organizer's idea of nightlife in the form of an envisioned "social sculpture":

> By social sculpture, I mean the trajectory a party takes from a thought or idea to an actual situation that bodies can tangibly experience. This is, in other words,

> everything that goes into making the party *real.* To reach that point, a number of things need to happen: hosts, a venue, a DJ, the décor, the dress code, performers and the door person; all of this needs to be decided beforehand. . . . In my view, a party is always about how bodies have activated and responded to those sculptural propositions. (65, italics in original)

These "sculptural propositions," I suggest, cannot be chosen by the organizer at liberty, but must match stylistic codes following the respective musical genre's social practices in order to create a coherent context and opportunities for engagement for the participants who in turn successfully realize the envisioned party. The term "social practices" as used here is rooted in the work of music semiotician Gino Stefani, revised and summarized by Stefan Strötgen (2014, 134) as "meanings which emerge through the ways music is used and engaged with in social contexts and have to be learned" (my translation).[5] These meanings are shaped by discourses about music that emerge between social groups, individuals, and institutions (130). These meaning-generation processes then influence the codes and subsequent expressions of a musical culture: "Social practices thus lead to cultural norms that shape our idea of what music is, and how music is or should be dealt with in given contexts" (133, my translation).[6] The "sculptural propositions" Moore describes must therefore match the social practices of the music that is played in the given context of staging a party in order to be both decodable and acceptable (or meaningful, more generally) for the audience members, as their active participation in and playful exploration of the social sculpture are at the same time key to realizing the intended party successfully. When, for example, promoting a "'90s rave," this will arouse expectations not only regarding the sounding music but also the kind of venue, décor, dress code, hair styles, dancing styles, the other party guests, and so forth that shape the entire party experience that, when engaged with or staged in what is interpreted as the "wrong" way can ruin it. In other words, if expectations are not matched and the sculptural propositions that are to be realized during the party cannot be read by participants as "'90s rave," the audience is likely to be disappointed, which can result in an unsuccessful party experience.

What kind of party audiences attend is further related to their preferences and desired experience projects. As Sarah Thornton (1995, 15, italics original) highlights: "Club cultures are *taste cultures*. Club crowds generally congregate on the basis of their shared taste in music, their consumption of common media and, most importantly, their preference for people with similar tastes to themselves." Clubs are therefore also exclusive spaces. Besides enforcing security and compliance with club rules, general social rules, and local laws (e.g., no smoking)—plus identifying potential troublemakers in advance—bouncers and/or a doorperson are positioned at a club's entrance to ensure that only the "right" people get in. Therefore, Moore (2013, 70) also proposes that, besides party organization as curatorial practice, "nightclub doors are sites of curation." But complete uniformity is not desirable, because "a party loses its steam when the crowd is too monolithic. No matter how much I prefer transgressive dress up parties, every attendee does not need to be in a look because too much sameness actually makes things boring and destroys the element of surprise" (72).

So, to have a chance of entering, beyond general social and local rules one further needs to know the respective codes, correct behaviors, and styles (hair, clothing) based on the music's social practices as an additional, socially negotiated rule system. This rule system also includes that clubgoers are constantly challenged to strive for variation and find creative ways to express their unique take on the stylistic codes of the musical culture they wish to participate in. In other words, the social and cultural practices emerging in these spaces and forming what has come to be understood as club culture in general, or a specific club's culture as well as the music-related codes, are constantly being socially (re)negotiated between clubgoers, club owners, and managers as well as other staff and surrounding societies (e.g., by local laws). This creates a broad set of demands and opportunities: one has the freedom, but also the requirement, to express oneself creatively and playfully in a curated space—one which replaces (or at least loosens) general social constraints with its own and constantly renegotiated rulesets, and which is explicitly dedicated to leisure while also demanding creative labor beforehand in order to be entered. Subsequently, Moore (2013, 62, italics original) summarizes: "A party is a loosely scripted work of art, and when we understand the party as an aesthetic proposition, nightlife becomes a cultural form, a unique relational space of *creation* and *curation*."

A party, therefore, can be interpreted as a form of social and embodied game that is realized in a phenomenologically perceptible way when partygoers/players set it into motion in the provided and curated possibility space of the club, following the contextual rules (such as social rules, laws) as well as the community's self-imposed rules and "guided by a system of representation that has its own rules for 'what things mean'" (Salen and Zimmerman 2004, 366). It is vital, though, that the rule-system combined of all the aspects mentioned above is still "loosely scripted" as Moore writes, thereby leaving room for creative play within the frame of and with the rules in order to still allow for an "element of surprise." The subsequent emerging experiences in the ludic possibility spaces of clubs and game worlds, I suggest, are then brought into being and explored through play in the sense of Salen and Zimmerman as "**free movement within a more rigid structure**" (304, bold in original) of rules and rulesets that are at work on several levels. The term "game world" as used here refers to "the *performative space* in which all actions induced by the game take place, including those in front of the screen" (Fritsch 2014, 170, italics original). As with (digital) games, the party would not come into existence without the active, competent, and bodily engagement of participants.

In summary: clubs offer curated and exclusive possibility spaces to a changing community of like-minded people sharing the same (musical) taste. The bodies of party participants are needed to realize the party, and, at the same time a main site of creative labor and curation, both by themselves but also by door and invitation policies. To remain part of this community it is vital to keep up with the pace and stay on top of styles, social practices, and codes and to comply with the constantly (re)negotiated rulesets while at the same time using them as opportunity for creative play (or misbehavior) through and with their own curated bodies.

Clubs and Aspects of Club Culture in Games

In digital games, players can slip into several roles, be it as a club owner or manager, a DJ, a clubgoer or someone who enters a club, but for another purpose than dancing or being at leisure, for instance, when fulfilling a quest. Subsequently, players are invited to playfully interact with different aspects of a club cultural experience as previously outlined, depending on the overall intended gameplay experience as offered by the designers through the staging of the game. In the following section I start out by looking at some examples and highlight the functions the club or aspects of club culture fulfill in the respective configuration.

Creative Curation and Labor to Leisure: Club Management Games

While not a genre in its own right, club management games have in common that players are put in the shoes of club owners or managers. A typical example is the PC-title *Disco Tycoon* (Astragon, 2010).[7] The game allows players to choose between 20 different scenarios or free play. To start, players get a basic location, a fixed basic budget, and five days' time. The club needs to be furnished and equipped, the supply of food and beverages needs to be taken care of. Staff must be hired and tasked, and the player can run publicity campaigns and special events such as a Happy Hour, Ladies night, or a foam party to attract clubgoers. Players also need to decide on opening and closing hours—and, of course, which music genres are played. They (and the NPC[8] clubbers with them) can either listen to their own music or select between Dance/House, Techno, '70s, Pop, or Rock. Additionally, finances must be kept in mind, such as the upkeep of the club, or the pricing of entrance, food, and beverages. If the player runs low on money, they may take out a loan, reduce staff, or sell interior items. All of this happens without time limits during the day mode, but, while in night mode, the club is (hopefully) filled with happy party people. Still, the food and drink supply must be monitored, the room temperature can be regulated via an AC, and the fog machines, laser lights, spotlights, and flashlights can be either set on automatic or switched on and off to keep the guests happy. Finally, the player must address incidents, such as neighbors calling the police because of the music being too loud. As is common in such simulation games, time can be brought to a complete halt (e.g., for thinking about the next steps) or sped up (e.g., to see how the decisions made play out). After each night, statistics are provided to see how the club fares. A similar game, *Disco Simulator*, was scheduled to be published on Steam in 2021 by Games Incubator (see Games Incubator 2021). The trailer promised even more detailed customization and micromanagement options: equipment and interior could be designed by players from scratch, or they could actively curate clubgoers themselves at the entrance and decide, checking one by one based on their stats, whom to grant access to. As the Devlog on the game's Steam page reveals, players would further be able to step into the shoes of DJs by offering them a music-mixing console in the game, which opens up a music game option.

In both *Disco Tycoon* and *Disco Simulator*, the main goal is to successfully establish and maintain a club by making NPC clubbers happy, earn more in-game currency, and unlock more items and upgrades. When not catering to their NPC audiences' needs, the club will fail. This gameplay experience can simply be understood as an economy simulation with the main task to optimize specific metrics with a side dish of decoration and more or less fine-grained customization options. Following Moore, though, this gameplay experience can also be understood as an act of curation: the focus lies not on the final "social sculpture," the emerging party (that can be sped up to see the results), but on the prior act of "setting the stage" by choosing and arranging "sculptural propositions." Subsequently, the experience project that is to be explored by players is not the emerging party, but the act of curation. Gameplay enjoyment, then, derives from curational creative labor in the form of optimization and decoration. As Thornton (1995, 13–14, italics original) describes when investigating club culture, she found herself in the role of an outsider by the fact that she was "*working* in a cultural space in which everyone else (except the DJs, door and bar staff, and perhaps the odd journalist) was at their *leisure*. Not only did I have intents and purposes that were alien to the rest of the crowd, but also for the most part I tried to maintain an analytical frame of mind that is truly anathema to the 'lose yourself [*sic*] and 'let the rhythm take control' ethos of clubs and raves." Similarly, while players still might enjoy the music, they are also not at leisure when playing such games, but rather tasked to stay alert to their NPC audiences' needs and creative and curational labor.

Another angle regarding the aspects of labor and leisure can be observed in *Nightclub Empire—Idle Disco Tycoon*, which was in early access on the GooglePlay Store (RSGapps—Idle Tycoon Games) at the time of writing in early 2021. Players manage up to nine clubs and upgrade their interior. While this sounds stressful, unlike the other two games, such so-called idle games "reduce gameplay to a single repetitive interaction or even automate gameplay, making player input optional" (Deterding 2016, 1). This happens by simply clicking or tapping on the phone, thereby buying items (often by using in-game currency that is bought for real money or acquired by watching adverts), or by just waiting for new items and rewards to be unlocked after a certain cooldown time. Also, in *Nightclub Empire*, tasks are reduced to simple one-click actions such as "Hire a DJ" or "Upgrade facility X." The game experience is therefore not about club managing in the form of optimization and creative curation that the other two games try to meticulously simulate. Edward Castronova (2021, 38–39) suggests that such idle games "take advantage of a surprising fact about human play: people like to watch machines as they run. . . . An idle game is not about winning or losing: it lets you win, and the only question is how rapidly you do so." In that regard, the game seems to reverse the labor aspect of managing a club back into an effortless leisure-time action that can be performed in any kind of idle moment during the day. That way, the idle game also subjects players to rhythms, though it is the rhythm of the "machine" they have set in motion by picking up the game and letting it play-out mostly by itself, producing virtual income that can quickly go up to immense numbers. Second, it is the rhythm of their own everyday lives, in which they can always find a brief moment to adjust the machine with effortless clicks to set a new and more effective loop in motion. That way, instead of a challenging (micro)management experience, this game offers a "just let go" aspect, but in the form of tiny leisure bubbles fitted into one's everyday rhythms, while at the same time giving players a feeling of continuous success, immense productivity, and control as the club's manager, even in these brief moments when they watch the virtual "social sculpture" in motion in the form of a never-ending party.

Sex, Thugs, and Drugs: Clubs as In-Game Location

Like the club management games described above, the *Grand Theft Auto: After Hours* DLC (Rockstar North, 2018) in *Grand Theft Auto Online* allows players to purchase and manage a nightclub (see, e.g., Green 2019, further information can also be found via GTA Wiki: "Nightclubs.") But, in order to profitably run the club, it is necessary to be the owner of additional businesses such as "organic produce" (weed production), "South American Imports" (coke) or "Printing & Copying" (document forgery). The nature of these businesses is consequently related to the overall narrative in the GTA game series, thereby pointing toward a trope that permeates digital game history: clubs serve as hideout for gangsters and are spaces in which violence occurs or/and criminal business is conducted. For example, in *Spider-Man: Mysterio's Menace* (Activision, 2001) hostages are held by the gangster Hammerhead in the unnamed nightclub.[9] The player in the role of Spider-Man must swing, hit, and kick their way through the main dancefloor, as well as the many weapon-stuffed backrooms of the building, and beat up mobsters in order to free the hostages. In *Mass Effect 3* (Electronic Arts, 2012) the club and bar Purgatory, at Citadel space station, serves not only as a leisure-time space for all kinds of intergalactic citizens but also as base of operation for the shady NPC character Aria T'Loak.[10] Starting out as an exotic dancer in the Afterlife Club on space station Omega, Aria killed its owner and took over not only the club but eventually the entire station. After losing control over Omega again, she fled to Citadel and entered it as an illegal immigrant. In a cutscene during the story of *Mass Effect 3*, players meet Aria in the Purgatory club when she has just been detected by an official immigration officer and is asked to comply with immigration processes. Annoyed, she calls a high-ranking official (the Asari councilor), who immediately gives her clearance (see Mass Effect Wiki, section "Mass Effect 3"). Again, the club is used as a hideout, but in this case for someone depicted as powerful and socially high-ranking enough to openly pull strings to protect and conduct illegal activity on Citadel.

Another common function of clubs or bars with a dance floor is to serve as flirting and pick-up spots such as in *Leisure Suit Larry in the Land of the Lounge Lizards* (Sierra

On-Line, 1987) or *Codename: ICEMAN* (Sierra On-Line, 1989),[11] both featuring scenes during which the player, in the shoes of the male hero, seduces a woman after dancing with her. In the 1982 Arcade game *Disco No. 1* (developed by Data East), the entire gameplay is centered around this topic. The player slips into the shoes of an unnamed guy in a roller skate disco. As the play guide (see Museum of the Game) explains, the main task is to encircle and thereby draw a square around pink female figures ("disco girls") or female figures wearing skirts ("beauty queens") to score points. The bigger the square, the more points awarded. Running into them causes the avatar's head becoming red, signifying embarrassment. At the same time, one has to avoid brawny figures in blue suits and hats (named "ruffians") because they beat up the player's avatar when running into them, as well as another figure with a broom (a "witch"), that appears after gameplay has already gone on for a while—most likely to cause the player to fail and spend another coin for another round. While the exaggerated depiction of flirting and violence in these examples points toward parody or a humorous undertone, the violence, crime, and sex tropes can also be intertwined in a more serious manner: in the action-adventure game *Heavy Rain* (Sonic Computer Entertainment, 2010) the player can enter the Blue Lagoon club in the role of the female character Madison Paige. To enter the VIP lounge of the criminal club owner Paco Mendez, and get the information needed, she has to make herself look seductive (by ripping her skirt shorter and putting on more make-up) and is even forced to perform a striptease for Paco. This example further points to another narrative function of clubs as exclusive spaces not everyone is allowed to enter, in which players can either meet special characters of interest or/and gather intel. To succeed, one usually must get past bouncers into the club and/or sneak into VIP areas to have a conversation with the club owner, club manager, the bartender, or any other special character. Like taverns in fantasy settings, in these cases, clubs fulfill a special narrative function and offer respective opportunities for interactions: gathering information, finding specific (oftentimes shady or otherwise morally questionable) characters, and fulfilling tasks or quests to follow the storyline. The rite (and right) of passage to enter these separate spaces can be usefully staged in games as the challenge of "doing it right" without knowing how exactly "right" is defined or what exactly is going on behind the closed door creating what Moore (2013, 69) interprets, regarding the door policies of Studio 54, as follows: "[T]he door scene at Studio functions as a site of intensified energy. By intensified energy, I mean that the aura of the space proposes potentiality and possibility." This "potentiality and possibility" therefore inspires fantasies of the yet undisclosed possibility space beyond and presents an interesting challenge to overcome both in a digital game but also in real life.

This kind of staging is influenced by tropes, depictions of clubs and their visitors, and ways of storytelling both in earlier games but also in other audiovisual media forms such as movies, TV series, and literature. Further, these attributions of a demimonde, or even a criminal, but at the same time vibrant, exclusive, and glitzy world filled with lowlife thugs as well as powerful underground puppet masters, tickles the imagination but also allows for (sometimes otherwise impossible) fantasies to thrive and be played out within these curated and closed possibility spaces.

Playground Disco: The Rave Experience in Music Games

Following the above and, from his point of view, monodimensional depiction of clubs in digital games, in his article entitled "How Come All Nightclubs in Video Games Are Full of Strippers and Aliens?" journalist Josh Baines (2016) draws the conclusion that: "The problem with gaming's take on clubbing is simple: it's an experience that really can't be replicated in anything other than, well, lived experience. Even as games get more and more sophisticated. . . . [T]here are things that games simply cannot do, no matter how prettily they try. Clubbing is one of them." In the realm of music games, though, the idea of transporting at least aspects of the experience of clubbing or the rave as a part of the core gameplay by making use of the game medium itself as a possibility space has already been addressed in several ways.

Curated Communities and Embodied Experiences

Reminiscent of Moore's (2013, 62, italics original) definition—"[a] party is a loosely scripted work of art, and when we understand the party as an aesthetic proposition, nightlife becomes a cultural form, a unique relational space of *creation* and *curation*"—the Facebook social game *Nightclub City* (Booyah, 2010) provides an interesting approach in terms of social practices and how unwritten rules are set into motion and create an apparently meaningful game experience to a huge number of players. As with many of the social games featured on the platform around 2010, the title was multiplayer and according to the still-available sources,[12] seemed to have acquired quite a large user base. The game itself is not playable anymore, and gameplay can only be reconstructed in the form of remaining YouTube videos as well as the game's trailer.[13] Users could open and customize their own virtual nightclub, personalize a DJ Avatar, sell drinks, and invite celebrities (such as Vanilla Rice, Celine Dijon, or Puff Baddy) thereby increasing the reputation of their club (see Mayer-Flores 2010). Over time their club could grow, more people could visit, and they could invite their Facebook friends to virtually hang out (see, e.g., Southpaw n.d.) When progressing through the game, the time a DJ set could be played also increased from 15 minutes in the beginning to 5 or 6 hours, until up to 12 hours on very high levels (Mayer-Flores 2010; for a—supposedly incomplete—song list, see David 2010). According to an article on gamesindustry.biz, this aspect of listening to DJ sets, thereby exploring new music by up-and-coming artists, was the core idea of the game: "Since its soft launch in April 2010, more than 4.5 million monthly active players have joined the party in Nightclub City to promote emerging real-world musicians. Artists currently involved in the game have seen more than a 1000 percent increase in 'Likes' on their Facebook fan pages" (GamesIndustry International 2010). In August 2010, this approach of marketing musicians through the game was underlined by announcing the Drop the Bass challenge, which the developer Boyaah initiated in collaboration with Indaba Music (for further information on the company see, e.g., Ehrlich 2010; Ong 2018) and Ableton Live and involved the game's community. Artists could submit their music during a time span of four weeks using "tools provided by Indaba Music . . . for inclusion in Booyah's Nightclub City. Once submitted, a panel of Booyah, Indaba and Ableton employees will choose a select number of songs, and Nightclub City players will vote for their top ten favorites tracks. Ten chosen winners will then have a featured set in Nightclub City showcasing their musical creations" (MGAceman 2010). In January 2011, the resulting soundtrack was released under the title *Drop the Bass: Original Music from Nightclub City*:[14] "Around 1,000 songs were submitted to be include [sic] on the soundtrack (and in the game), and the 10 on the album were the big winners. The album can be purchased for $10 on iTunes and on the Indaba Music web site" (Goad 2011).

Though created and initiated mainly for the purpose of marketing, *Nightclub City* managed to provide a virtual possibility space curated by the players, in which they not only could experience a club simulation built around the social practices of dance music at the time but also could discover new music together with like-minded people via the Facebook platform. That way, the game added another dimension to the emerging "social sculpture" in the form of a virtual party: it managed to build a vivid and active community that was held together by "their shared taste in music, their consumption of common media and, most importantly, their preference for people with similar tastes to themselves" (Thornton 1995, 15) plus their shared knowledge of the provided context of clubbing or, more generally, contemporary commercial electronic music as a culture. This is also underlined by other promotional events in the game referring to game and electronic music culture as symbolic frameworks. Following a marketing campaign initiated in December 2010 for the *TRON: Legacy* movie in cooperation with Disney, the development company stated in January 2011 in their blog section:

> Players were able to fully immerse themselves in the TRON world by moving their virtual Club to TRON City, where they were able to unlock TRON-themed items, such as a lightcycle or special DJ booth, as well as costumes that turn Nightclub City avatars into TRON "programs." . . . The TRON Soundtrack was added as a playlist within the game, allowing users to rock out to the scintillating sounds of famed-duo, Daft Punk, creating an even more immersive environment in Nightclub City. (Booyah 2011)

I would argue that this social aspect was essential to the success of the game.

While *Nightclub City* focused on the social aspect of a fluid community (and tried to capitalize on that), other game designers aim to recreate the embodied experience of music in the form of dancing. VR titles such as *Disco Time 80s VR* (Indiecode Games, 2017) and *Personal Disco VR* (Dual Heights Software, 2017) try to model this aspect by allowing players to dance with virtual partners on a virtual dancefloor. Browsing Steam user reviews[15] on both games offers a mixed or somewhat positive tendency, revealing that some users get bored after a while as there was not much to do except dancing, find their dance partners' avatars creepy, or criticize clunky technological execution and complain about the lack of multiplayer options, while others applaud the general idea of VR discos, find it amusing for a while, or enjoy being able to dance or relax in a virtual club room with their own music in *Personal Disco VR* (which allowed the integration of YouTube videos). All in all, the approach of both games to transport players in a virtual club environment seems to be lacking something: while apparently offering a sufficient bodily experience (dancing) both games fell short for some reviewers on other vital aspects of club culture as a shared social experience and the feeling of belonging to a community (as offered by *Nightclub City*), which is expressed, for example, in the demand for multiplayer options. The criticism regarding the avatars being creepy, ugly, or not convincing enough points toward the questions regarding the role of these other bodies. Following Moore (2013, 65), the VR party might have failed in becoming real by not becoming tangible with regard to the actual presence of other bodies, as "a party is always about how bodies have activated and responded to those sculptural propositions." Also, dance scholar Gabriele Klein (2001, 173, my translation) states that especially the rave depends on the physical presence of other bodies, as ravers dance "outwards, the gaze and the posture of the upper body orientated towards the dancers, from whom they expect to draw 'a lot of energy.' "[16] Referring to Ben Malbon, Moore (2013, 69) further highlights, in his analysis of Studio 54's door policies, that clubgoers' bodies are themselves subjected to curation as part of the sculptural propositions: "As clubgoers approached the door as a stylized, heightened version of themselves, doormen curated the right people from the crowd as a way to produce a site of belonging where bodies from diverse backgrounds could intersect intimately in a way that might not be possible outside of the club context. . . . A tight door policy thus creates a site of curated bodies, where the curation relates to the specificity of what a given person will contribute to the party in order to sustain its energy." For the reviewers complaining about them, the avatar bodies in these cases were apparently not sufficient to keep up the virtual party energy.

This aspect of the body being at the center of the experience is essential to club cultures also beyond Studio 54, as Klein (2001) points out regarding rave culture. Techno offered an escapist experience in the form of a "world of sensual pleasure and delight worth diving into" (Klein 2001, 171, my translation).[17] Featuring simple monotonous rhythms and deep, pounding basslines, techno pervades the room and the bodies and causes them to vibrate in rhythm with the machine sound (see Klein 2001, 174). That way, the music is designed to fully envelop the bodies and transport them into another sensory realm: "In this context, the dancing body can no longer be adequately described with the category of the human body, instead, it is a body expanding into technology, a body that 'contains' technology in the form of music, light and drugs. The 'raving body' can thus only be grasped in terms that characterize precisely this novel interplay of mind, body and technology" (174, my translation).[18] Dancing, and subsequently the body in combination with the music, venue, and the other ravers, is the core element of the techno experience to create the "social sculpture" in the form of a separate playful world of pleasure, but the party always depends on people's bodies submitting to it as "a party is always about how bodies have activated and responded to those sculptural propositions" (Moore 2013, 65).

The Microsoft Kinect game *Child of Eden* (Ubisoft, 2011) addresses most of these aspects by creating what I have elsewhere called a musical culture-based gameplay gestalt that aims at translating the social practices of a musical style "directly into a diegetic environment, narrative and gameplay, culminating finally in the creation of a distinct gameworld" (Fritsch 2014, 173).[19] The game was designed by Tetsuya Mizuguchi, who also created the predecessor *Rez* (Sega, 2001), which functions in a similar way. Mizuguchi reportedly was inspired to create *Rez* while visiting the 1997 Zurich Street Parade and watching a dancing techno crowd from a balcony: "This DJ is playing, and 100,000 people are moving with the music. The sound changed, and the movement changed. . . . In my mind, I recalled Kandinsky. And I thought, wow—this is a digital Kandinsky. If he was around now, what kind of a new game, what kind of an experience, would he make?" (Mizuguchi cited in Robinson 2015).

Like its predecessor, *Child of Eden* is a rail shooter music game. Its electronic dance music is performed by the Genki Rockets, a visual and musical project created by Mizuguchi himself and music producer Kenji Tamai (Johnson 2011, 12). The protagonist is the 17-year-old virtual singer Lumi. The game's narrative also turns on Lumi, the first human born in outer space, on September 11, 2019. She expresses her dreams and feelings about the unfamiliar Earth in songs and sends them to people on Earth. After her death, and alongside the "collective knowledge" of humanity, her songs, memories, and data were archived in the Internet, now known as Eden. The game starts when researchers in the 23rd century recreate her persona in Eden as a data body: but, as she awakens, a virus attack occurs. The player's task is to save Lumi and Eden from the viruses during five stages called Matrix, Evolution, Beauty, Passion, and Journey (for further information on the game see GiantBomb, "Child of Eden").

Mizuguchi's company Q Entertainment developed a special peripheral device, a corset with four vibrating controllers to let players feel the music, but it was never released (see Robinson 2011). Nevertheless, players embody the music in another way by enacting social practices of EDM as a dance culture that are represented both in the game's narrative as well as in the interaction design. Disconnected from an Earth that Lumi does not know, she creates her own environment through the medium of her songs to connect with humans on Earth. Players, conversely, interact with her songs, as the game is a musical railshooter with the goal of saving Lumi and Eden and purifying Eden from the attacking viruses. The game provides the player with no avatar in the diegetic world, only a crosshair can be controlled by movements of the player's arms. During play, players furthermore collect purple Euphoria items. When they have collected enough, they can throw both arms up in the air thereby spending all Euphoria and cleaning all viruses visible on screen, like a dance crowd during a party's climactic moments. When playing with the Kinect peripheral, players therefore use their own bodies to realize the party as a separate possibility space of pleasure in their own living room, through the interaction design which creates a form of dance that lets them dive into the beautifully depicted, colorful and technoid diegetic environment on screen. Through the interaction pattern, as well the game's narrative, players dissolve into the game world, the performative playground created by the game's EDM soundtrack thereby becoming themselves a body that "expands into technology" and enacts many aspects of the distinct philosophy and social practices of 1990s European techno and EDM culture that inspired Mizuguchi. That way, the game design can be understood as a form of "sculptural propositions" that allows players who are familiar with EDM's social practices to be transported into a separate world of EDM by acting them out via their own bodies when playing the game.

Conclusions

This cursory overview has demonstrated that the ways clubs and club culture are depicted in games are not as one-dimensional as criticized by Baines. Beyond using clubs as a location for specific narrative purposes or stereotypical interactions following tropes also known from other media forms, game developers have engaged with several aspects of club culture and its music's social practices in many ways within game design and game narratives: the act of curating a playful space in which the "social sculpture" of the party can unfold; issues of work and leisure time experiences; club culture as taste culture; secluded separate spaces of possibility in which new experiences can be made; and the body as a site of playful performances.

Certainly, there are many more avenues and aspects to explore, which could not be addressed in this chapter for reasons of space. Recent developments and advances of club culture into gaming spaces, such as the opening of the previously mentioned Club Matryoshka and similar virtual venues that were explored during the pandemic years, show that interrogating the intersections between games, music, and club culture will become a more prominent topic. Conversely, gaming also trickles into clubs beyond mere marketing endeavors: On May 15, 2022, *NeuroXcape: The Role Play Game* took place in a Barcelona-based venue. As the website (LaCapella 2022) advertises:

> *NEUROXCAPE: the Role Play Game* is a fantasy sci-fi work that operates as an abstraction of our behaviour on social media, grouping types or patterns of online behaviour into fantastical clans or systems. It is an expanded collective performance project, a work of fiction that takes the form of an urban fantasy (science fiction + medieval fantasy) live-action role playing game (LARP) that uses the context of leisure as a scenario in the form of a club (physical and virtual). . . . It will take place in the physical world (Chapel Club) and the virtual realm (internet and Club Cooee) in an event that five groups of participants and their avatars will be invited to take part in: a quest to imagine a multiple collective environment, new mental and social spaces.

The event was created by NeuroDungeon, an artistic and electronic music collective initiated by the artists Kaverna, Bartolomé, and Y€$Si Perse. Such projects invite an exploration through the lens I have offered here, namely of an understanding of both clubs and games as designed material bases to stage ludic possibility spaces which can be entered and used by clubbers/players to realize specific experience projects.

Notes

1. Some exceptions are Joanna Demers's (2006) reflections on the use of electronic dance music in the dancing game *Dance Dance Revolution* (Konami, 1998) and Rob Gallagher's (2017) insights into the emergence of grime and its ties to gaming. More recently, Hillegonda Rietveld (2021) has provided an overview on the topic of the rise of home computers and music production, and Sara Bowden (2021) has analyzed *Strobophagia|Rave Horror* (Green Tile Digital, 2020). Connections between gaming and electronic music have generally been pointed at in studies of chipmusic and tracker music (see, for example, McAlpine 2019, 125–169). Most material to date, though, has been unearthed by journalistic investigation (see, for example, Lovett 2015; Ombler 2018).
2. Historical predecessors as well as other clubs such as any kind of sex or strip club, or gambling casinos will be excluded, as worthwhile as an examination of these certainly would be.
3. The idea of specifically the 1990s rave as a liminal playground, enabling spontaneous performances and the specific features of Techno as sounding phenomenon, was first presented in Adamowsky (2000, 113–165).
4. I am building on the concept "subjektives Erlebnisprojekt" as discussed in Zumbansen (2008, 62).
5. Social practices refer to "*zu erlernende Bedeutungen, die durch die Art der Nutzung von und Auseinandersetzung mit Musik in gesellschaftlichen Kontexten entstehen*" (original italics). The full discussion of the concept can be found in Strötgen (2014, 129–134).
6. "Soziale Praxen führen also zu kulturellen Normen, die unsere Vorstellung davon prägen, was Musik ist und wie mit Musik in bestimmten Zusammenhängen umgegangen wird oder umgegangen werden soll."
7. Information on the game and gameplay footage can be found via https://sandboxgamesdb.com/games/disco-tycoon/. See also deluxe.mp4. 2010. *Disco Tycoon Gameplay*. YouTube video, 4:34. Accessed December 2, 2021. https://www.youtube.com/watch?v=KB8J5MmEI6E.
8. NPC is the abbreviation for Nonplayable Character and refers to characters that are not controlled by players.
9. I'd like to thank user @RedheadDyke for pointing me toward this example on Twitter.
10. More information and the full background story of the character can be found at the Mass Effect Wiki: "Aria T'Loak."
11. I'd like to thank Filippo Beck Peccoz and user @Cow_Palace for pointing me toward these examples on Twitter.
12. Besides some press coverage and walkthrough (see, e.g., Mayer-Flores 2010) or Reddit discussions, one can also find an abandoned Twitter account as well as the abandoned game page on Facebook (see https://www.facebook.com/nightclubcity/) with the last entries from 2011, under which people in 2021 are still asking the company to bring the game back. The fanbase having liked the page was at the time of writing still over 600,000 users.

13. See BooyahUnplugged. 2010. *"Nightclub City": The Best Game Ever*. YouTube video, 1:41. https://www.youtube.com/watch?v=gooqFknON9A (accessed December 2, 2021).
14. The list of winners can be found on the Indaba website via Wayback Machine (Indaba 2010).
15. By mid-2021, *Disco Time 80s VR* has received 62 and *Personal Disco VR* has received 34 user reviews on Steam. I assessed reviews in both English and German. It would be interesting, though, to see whether reviews in other languages might reveal other views on the aesthetic appeal of the games, and whether different or similar views were expressed by audiences from different cultural contexts, for example, regarding the acceptance of virtual dancing partners.
16. Ravers dance "nach 'außen,' den Blick und die Haltung des Oberkörpers auf die Tanzenden gerichtet, von denen sie sich 'a lot of energy' versprechen."
17. Techno would provide a "Welt der Sinneslust und des Vergnügens, in die sich das Abtauchen lohnt."
18. "Der tanzende Körper läßt sich hier nicht mehr mit der Kategorie des humanen Körpers angemessen beschreiben, sondern ist ein in Technologie expandierender Körper, ein Körper' der in Form von Musik, Licht und Drogen Technologie 'enthält.' Der 'ravende Körper' läßt sich demnach nur in Begriffen fassen, die genau dieses neuartige Zusammenspiel von Geist, Körper und Technologie kennzeichnen."
19. The concept of a music-based gameplay gestalt is developed from Craig Lindley's work (see Lindley 2002). A complete analysis of *Child of Eden* as a realization of rave culture and techno philosophy in game form can be found in Fritsch (2018, 198–216).

References

Adamowsky, Natascha. 2000. *Spielfiguren in virtuellen Welten*. Frankfurt am Main: Campus-Verlag.

Arte TRACKS. 2020. "Virtuelle Partys: Wie auf Minecraft, Fortnite und IMVU gefeiert wird." October 12, 2020. Television reportage. Accessed December 2, 2021. https://www.youtube.com/watch?v=-rPVHUB7gg4.

Baines, Josh. 2016. "How Come All Nightclubs in Video Games Are Full of Strippers and Aliens?" *VICE*, June 27, 2016. Accessed June 30, 2022. https://www.vice.com/en/article/53ez7n/how-come-all-nightclubs-in-video-games-are-full-of-strippers-and-aliens.

Booyah. 2011. "Booyah Drives Huge Brand Awareness for Disney's *TRON*." Booyah Press release, January 21, 2011. Accessed June 30, 2022. https://web.archive.org/web/20110303170743/http://www.booyah.com/booyah/2011/01/booyah-drives-huge-brand-awareness-for-disneys-tron.html.

Bowden, Sara. 2021. "Thank You for Dying: Sound Affects and Musical Disorientations in Strobophagia." Presented at Ludo2021—Tenth European Conference on Video Game Music and Sound, Online, April 23–25, 2021.

Castranova, Edward. 2021. *Life Is a Game: What Game Design Says about the Human Condition*. New York: Bloomsbury Academic.

Celera, Lex. 2019. "Inside Club Matryoshka, an Exclusive Club Found in a Minecraft Server." *VICE*, August 23, 2019. Accessed June 30, 2022. https://www.vice.com/en/article/7x5vdg/inside-club-matryoshka-an-exclusive-club-found-in-a-minecraft-server.

Club Transmediale. 2021. "Club Matryoshka x CTM. Virtual Minecraft World Remains Open until 28 February 2021." CTM Festival. Accessed June 30, 2022. https://www.ctm-festival.de/festival-2021/programme/features/club-matryoshka-x-ctm.

David. 2010. "The *Nightclub City* Songs List." NightClub City Secrets, June 22, 2010. Accessed 30 June, 2022. https://web.archive.org/web/20110120203337/http://www.nightclubcitysecretsx.com/nightclubcitytips/nightclubcitysonglist/.

Demers, Joanna. 2006. "Dancing Machines: *Dance Dance Revolution*, Cybernetic Dance, and Musical Taste." *Popular Music* 25, no. 3 (October): 401–414.

Deterding, Sebastian. 2016. "Progress Wars: Idle Games and the Demarcation of 'Real' Games." Proceedings of 1st International Joint Conference of DiGRA and FDG. http://www.digra.org/wp-content/uploads/digital-library/paper_267.pdf.

Dual Heights Software. n.d. *Personal Disco VR*. Accessed May 15, 2021. https://store.steampowered.com/app/618350/Personal_Disco_VR/.

Ehrlich, Brenna. 2010. "New Marketplace Helps Musicians Find Opportunities." *Mashable*, November 2010. https://mashable.com/archive/indaba-marketplace.

Edwards, Owen. 2006. "The Not-So-Simple Simon Proved the Young Were Swifter Than the Old." *Smithsonian Magazine*, September 2006. Accessed July 15, 2021. https://www.smithsonianmag.com/smithsonian-institution/not-so-simple-simon-proved-young-were-swifter-than-old-180953561/.

Fritsch, Melanie. 2014. "Worlds of Music: Strategies for Creating Music-Based Experiences in Video Games." In *The Oxford Handbook of Interactive Audio*, edited by Karen Collins, Holly Tessler, and Bill Kapralos, 167–177. New York: Oxford University Press.

Fritsch, Melanie. 2018. *Performing Bytes: Musikperformances der Computerspielkultur*. Würzburg: Königshausen und Neumann.

Gallagher, Rob. 2017. "'All the Other Players Want to Look at My Pad': Grime, Gaming, and Digital Identity." *GAME: The Italian Journal of Game Studies* 6, "Hear the Music, Play the Game. Music and Game Design: Interplays and Perspectives," edited by Hillegonda Rietveld and Marco Carbone: 13–29.

Games Incubator. n.d. *Disco Simulator*. Accessed July 15, 2021. https://store.steampowered.com/app/1226970/Disco_Simulator/.

GamesIndustry International. 2010. "*Nightclub City*: Uniting Music Lovers and Helping Them to Connect Directly with 'Hot New Artists.'" Gamesindustry.biz, July 14, 2010. Accessed June 30, 2022. https://www.gamesindustry.biz/articles/nightclub-city-uniting-music-lovers-and-helping-them-to-connect-directly-with--hot-new-artists.

GiantBomb. n.d. *Child of Eden*. Accessed July 15, 2021. https://www.giantbomb.com/child-of-eden/3030-31716/.

Goad, Libe. 2011. "First-Ever Facebook Game Soundtrack Released." AOL, January 24, 2011. Accessed June 30, 2022. https://www.aol.com/2011/01/24/first-ever-facebook-game-soundtrack-released/?guccounter=1.

Green, Jake. 2019. "*GTA After Hours* Nightclubs Guide—Names, Locations, Prices, Best Nightclub." *USGamer*, March 25, 2019. Accessed June 30, 2022. https://www.usgamer.net/articles/30-07-2018-gta-after-hours-nightclubs-guide-names-locations-prices.

GTA Wiki. n.d. "*Grand Theft Auto: The Ballad of Gay Tony*." Accessed June 6, 2021. https://gta.fandom.com/wiki/The_Ballad_of_Gay_Tony.

GTA Wiki. n.d. "Nightclubs." Accessed July 20, 2021. https://gta.fandom.com/wiki/Nightclubs.

Harvey, Trevor S. 2015. "Virtual Worlds: An Ethnomusicological Perspective." In *The Oxford Handbook of Virtuality*, edited by Mark Grimshaw, 378–391. New York: Oxford University Press.

Indaba. 2010. "Drop the Bass: *Nightclub City* Original Song Contest: Get Your Music into the Hot Facebook Game and Be Heard by Millions." Announcement. Archive.org snapshot, December 14, 2010. Accessed June 30, 2022. https://web.archive.org/web/20101214003645/http://www.indabamusic.com/opportunities/nightclubcity.

Indiecode Games. n.d. *Disco Time 80s VR*. Accessed May 20, 2021. https://store.steampowered.com/app/649880/Disco_Time_80s_VR/.

IO Interactive. n.d. *Hitman III*. Accessed August 4, 2021. https://hitman.com/global/.

Johnson, Jason. 2011. "Say Hi to Lumi." *Kill Screen. Games. Play. Life.* 1 (5): 8–14.

Kirn, Peter. 2021. "Tour the Berlin-Style Hölle Techno Club in *Hitman 3*." *CDM*, February 3, 2021. Accessed June 30, 2022. https://cdm.link/2021/02/tour-the-berlin-style-holle-techno-club-in-hitman-3/.

Klein, Gabriele. 2001. "Urban Story Telling: Tanz und Popkultur." In *Techno-Soziologie: Erkundungen einer Jugendkultur*, edited by Ronald Hitzler, 161–176. Opladen: Leske + Budrich.

Knoblauch, William. 2016. "SIMON: The Prelude to Modern Music Video Games." In *Music Video Games: Performance, Politics, and Play*, edited by Michael Austin, 25–42. New York: Bloomsbury Academic Press.

LaCapella. 2022. "NeuroXcape: the Role Play Game (Chaüel Club)." Event announcement. Accessed August 4, 2021. https://www.lacapella.barcelona/en/neuroxcape-role-play-game-chapel-club.

Lindley, Craig A. 2002. "The Gameplay Gestalt, Narrative, and Interactive Storytelling." In *Computer Games and Digital Cultures Conference Proceedings*, edited by Frans Mäyrä, 203–215. Tampere: Tampere University Press. http://www.digra.org/wp-content/uploads/digital-library/05164.54179.pdf.

Lovett, Ben. 2016. "Gamers' Groove: Dance Music in Video Games." *Defected*, October 14, 2015. https://defected.com/news/post/gamers-groove-dance-music-video-games.

Mass Effect Wiki. n.d. " Aria T'Loak." Accessed June 6, 2021. https://masseffect.fandom.com/wiki/Aria_T%27Loak#Mass_Effect_3.

Mayer-Flores, Jam. 2010. "*Nightclub City* Walkthrough." *GameZebo*, May 5, 2010. https://www.gamezebo.com/walkthroughs/nightclub-city-walkthrough/.

McAlpine, Kenneth B. 2019. *Bits and Pieces: A History of Chiptunes*. New York: Oxford University Press.

MGAceman. 2010. "Drop The Bass in *Nightclub City*." *Mental Gamers*, August 27, 2010. Accessed June 30, 2022. https://mentalgamers.com/1443/drop-the-bass-in-nightclub-city/.

Moore, Madison. 2013. "Looks: Studio 54 and the Production of Fabulous Nightlife." *Dancecult: Journal of Electronic Dance Music Culture* 5 (1): 61–74. https://doi.org/10.12801/1947-5403.2013.05.01.04.

Museum of the Game. n.d. "*Disco No. 1*." Accessed May 5, 2021. https://www.arcade-museum.com/game_detail.php?game_id=7593.

Ombler, Mat. 2018. "Video Games and Club Music Have Always Been Intertwined." *Noisey UK*, republished on *VICE*, October 29, 2018. Accessed June 30, 2022. https://www.vice.com/en/article/a3pb45/video-games-club-music-history.

Ong, Jennifer. 2018. "Splice Acquires Indaba Music, Online Music Community That Pioneered Remix Contests & Created the Rubber Tracks Sample Library. Indaba's Founder, Dan Zaccagnino and CEO, JJ Rosen Join the Splice Executive Team." Businesswire. Press release. February 26, 2018. Accessed June 30, 2022. https://www.businesswire.com/news/home/20180226006083/en/Splice-Acquires-Indaba-Music-Online-Music-Community-That-Pioneered-Remix-Contests-Created-the-Rubber-Tracks-Sample-Library.

Rietveld, Hillegonda. 2021. “Digital Muse: Game Culture Enters the Dancefloor” Presented at Ludo2021 Tenth European Conference on Video Game Music and Sound, Online, April 23–25, 2021.

Robinson, Martin. 2011. “ ‘Kapow! 11: *Child of Eden* Has Corset Peripheral. Though You Can’t Play It . . . Yet.” *IGN*, April 10, 2011 (updated June 29, 2016). Accessed June 30, 2022. http://www.ign.com/articles/2011/04/10/kapow-11-child-of-eden-has-corset-peripheral.

Robinson, Martin. 2015. “In Media Rez: The Return of Tetsuya Mizuguchi: From *Sega Rally* to *Child of Eden*, the Past, Present and Future of the Influential Designer.” *Eurogamer*, February 8, 2015. Accessed June 30, 2022. https://www.eurogamer.net/articles/2015-02-08-in-media-rez-the-return-of-tetsuya-mizuguchi.

Salen, Katie, and Eric Zimmerman. 2004. *Rules of Play: Game Design Fundamentals*. Cambridge, MA: MIT Press.

Southpaw. n.d. “*Nightclub City* on Facebook.” Nocturnal. Accessed June 30, 2022. https://www.nocturnal.asia/omfg/games/nightclub-city-on-facebook-2/.

Strötgen, Stefan. 2014. *Markenmusik*. Würzburg: Königshausen und Neumann.

Stuart, Keith, and Steve Boxer. 2014. “Level Up: How PlayStation Infiltrated Youth Culture.” *Guardian*, December 3, 2014. Accessed June 30, 2022. https://www.theguardian.com/technology/2014/dec/03/how-playstation-infiltrated-youth-culture.

Swink, Steve. 2009. *Game Feel: A Game Designer’s Guide to Virtual Sensation*. London/NewYork: CRC Press.

The Sandbox Games Database. n.d. “Disco Tycoon.” Accessed June 6, 2021. https://sandboxgamesdb.com/games/disco-tycoon/.

Thornton, Sarah. 1995. *Club Cultures: Music, Media and Subcultural Capital*. Cambridge: Polity Press.

Twitch. “Club Matryoshka.” Accessed January 21, 2021. https://www.twitch.tv/clubmatryoshka.

Yopko, Nick. 2020. “SAN HOLO, TNGHT, 100 GECS, MORE TO PLAY MINECRAFT BENEFIT FESTIVAL FOR THE OKRA PROJECT ‘LAVAPALOOZA.’ The Digital Festival Will Be Benefitting the Okra Project’s Battle against Food Insecurity in the Black Trans Community.” *EDM.com*, August 9, 2020. Accessed June 30, 2022. https://edm.com/events/san-holo-tnght-minecraft-festival-okra-project-lavapalooza.

Zumbansen, Lars. 2008. *Dynamische Erlebniswelten: Ästhetische Orientierungen in phantastischen Bildschirmspielen*. Munich: kopaed.

Ludography

beatmania (game series), Konami, Arcade, 1997.

Child of Eden, Ubisoft, Xbox 360 / PlayStation 3, 2011.

Codename: ICEMAN, Sierra Entertainment, Amiga et al., 1989.

Dance Dance Revolution, Konami, Arcade, 1998.

DJ Hero, Activision, PlayStation 2 et al., 2009.

Disco No. 1, Data East, Arcade, 1982.

Disco Simulator, Games Incubator, PC, tbp.

Disco Time 80s VR, Indiecode Games, PC, 2017.

Disco Tycoon, Astragon, PC, 2010 (rereleased in 2014 as *Disco Manager* by UIG).

Fuser, NCSoft, PlayStation 4 et al., 2020.

Grand Theft Auto: After Hours, Rockstar North, 2018. DLC for *GTA 5 Online*, PlayStation 4 et al., 2013.

Grand Theft Auto: The Ballad of Gay Tony, Rockstar North, 2009. Expansion pack for *Grand Theft Auto IV*, PlayStation 3 et al., 2008.
Heavy Rain, Sonic Computer Entertainment, PlayStation 3 et al., 2010.
Hitman 3, IO Interactive, Playstation 5 et al., 2021.
Leisure Suit Larry in the Land of the Lounge Lizards, Sierra On-Line, Amiga et al., 1987.
Mass Effect 3, Electronic Arts, Xbox 360 et al., 2012.
Minecraft, Mojang Studios, Windows, 2011.
Nightclub City, Booyah, Facebook, 2010.
Nightclub Empire—Idle Disco Tycoon, Android, tbp (Beta version available).
Personal Disco VR, Dual Heights Software, PC, 2017.
Rez, Sega, Dreamcast et al., 2001.
Spider-Man: Mysterio's Menace, Activision, Game Boy Advance, 2001.
Strobophagia | Rave Horror, Green Tile Digital, PC, 2020s.
Wipeout, Sony Computer Entertainment, PlayStation et al., 1995.

SECTION 5

IDENTITY

CHAPTER 22

BEYOND NERDCORE

Hip-Hop, Race, and the Business of Gamer-Rap

ENONGO LUMUMBA-KASONGO

Introduction

Throughout much of hip-hop's 50-year history, video games have served as rich source material for lyrics, beats, music videos, and styles of dress. Although casual fans of hip-hop music may be unfamiliar with DJ Jazzy Jeff & The Fresh Prince's single "Human Video Game" (1988) they can likely recite from memory the couplet delivered by the late rap icon Notorious B.I.G. on his rags-to-riches single "Juicy" (1994): "Super Nintendo, Sega Genesis / When I was dead broke, man, I couldn't picture this." And, within hip-hop's visual culture, the music video for "Sock It to Me" (1997) by Missy Elliott represents a pioneering moment in the merging of video game iconography with hip-hop sensibilities. Dreamt up by the visionary director Harold "Hype" Williams, the video follows the rap songstress and the track's featured guests, the rappers Da Brat and Lil' Kim, as they traverse the galaxy in costumes modeled after the bulbous armor donned by Capcom character Mega Man. Regarding the fresh appeal of the video's costuming, the record executive Sylvia Rhone remarked: "No one's really used that Japanimation kind of thing, and I want to take this video and try to sell the concept of these characters—which are played by Missy, Lil' Kim, and Brat. . . . Black folks haven't moved into that genre" (cited in Als 1997).

In the years since Biggie celebrated his acquisition of the premier game consoles of the early 1990s and Hype Williams paid homage to the aesthetics of the "Blue Bomber"[1] via Missy, Da Brat, and Lil' Kim, several popular hip-hop artists have emerged as active players across a range of new video game spaces. Whether as guests on video game soundtracks, voice-over actors, characters in game franchises, online streamers, game publishers, and even game designers, rappers of the past 25 years have found new ways to innovate alongside and within the increasingly ubiquitous world of gaming.[2] It should come as no surprise that one of the biggest concert events of 2020, a year that summarily destroyed the possibility of live performance for all touring musicians due to the global pandemic caused by COVID-19, was a virtual set by the rapper Travis Scott within the wildly popular game *Fortnite* (2017), an experience that drew more than 45.8 million views in-game, and 73 million views on the video-streaming site YouTube (Cirisano 2020).

The braiding together of hip-hop music and culture with the tastes of a vibrant video gaming public over the past 25 years has also led to new sonic possibilities for the actual form and substance of contemporary rap music. Traditionally artists who have drawn heavily on video game aesthetics and stories to form the basis of their artistic identities, lyrical content, and instrumental tracks have predominantly operated within DIY and underground musicking scenes, to mixed commercial and critical success (Sewell 2015, 227). Loosely categorized under the banner of "nerdcore," video-game-inspired rap music cohered as a recognizable subgenre around the 2010s out of internet rap forums that emerged earlier in the decade, and was often celebrated by its predominantly white, male listenership for its rejection of dominant tropes found within commercial rap music and culture (Kendall 2011; Ronald 2012; Sewell 2015). Yet, with recent developments like the 2019 announcement of *Lost Rings*, a Columbia Records imprint with an artist roster primarily composed of black women gamer-rappers and -singers, it seems that the mainstream musical landscape may actually become the latest frontier for video game focused hip-hop artists to flourish (Brown 2019). It remains unclear how much these kinds of efforts will be supported in earnest by record executives trying to capitalize on the moment, or whether these opportunities actually represent viable pathways for independent and underground gamer-rap artists to gain broader cultural relevancy and financial success. In either case, however, they raise many interesting provocations, namely: what have been the creative and cultural challenges faced by gamer-rap artists in translating their work for the different communities they wish to speak to through their music? And what are the affordances of working within such a space?

Drawing on personal interviews with a range of gamer-rap artists, my own experience performing as SAMMUS, a rapper and producer who frequently operates within video game music scenes, as well as scholarship in the fields of hip-hop studies and critical game studies, this chapter will examine the vibrant world of gamer-rap as it has been shaped by the artists on the ground.[3] In particular, the chapter will focus on the stories of Black and Brown gamer-rap artists, most of whom have been excluded from scholarly analyses of nerdcore, chiptune, and geek music scenes.[4] These artists in many ways seem uniquely poised to weather the instability of the music industry, given the existence of a ready-made audience of gamers across the globe. Yet, as this chapter reveals, their proximity to other nerd/geek rap scenes can also cause feelings of alienation among non-Black audiences, and even risk their credibility among respected hip-hop heads and publications. Furthermore, their reliance on video games as source material can position these artists as targets for audiences within their desired fandom who are unfamiliar with, or antagonistic toward, their experiences of the world. Only through strategies like framing their work alongside—and at times against—other self-proclaimed nerd/

geek rappers, have gamer-rappers of color been able to persist despite these challenges. As the creative and monetary potentialities of the gamer-rap space continue to grow, whether through lucrative partnerships with blockbuster game studios or distribution deals with major record labels, it is important to call attention to artists who have laid the foundation for other underrepresented groups. Doing so not only enriches the record with regard to the diversity of people interfacing with video games but it also resists the mechanisms of erasure that so often accompany a subgenre's propagation from the niche to the mainstream.

On Hip-Hop and Video Games

Within ludomusicology, Michael Austin has written compellingly about the social and video games that have developed around mixtapes and other music curation and sharing practices (2015), as well as the politics of hip-hop's representations within games (2018). And, in game studies discourses, several scholars have also called attention to the racialized and gendered performance of what Miles White (2011, 22) calls the "hip-hop body" and its crystallization around the centuries-long racist trope of Black masculinity as the embodiment of hyperviolence, hypersexuality, and criminality in game series like *Grand Theft Auto* (Miller 2008), and *NBA 2K* (Gray 2016) among others. Further, the recuperative efforts of the game scholars TreaAndrea Russworm and Samantha Blackmon (2020) to collect the oral histories of Black women and girls as gamers and present their experiences as a kind of "mixtape" invites hip-hop feminism into view as a useful frame for engaging with critical game studies discourses about race, gender, and representation. Kiri Miller's (2017) ethnographic project on intimate dance games like the *Dance Central* and *Just Dance* franchises asks readers to consider the player's relationship to the performance of racialized bodies in dance games that are largely powered by the choreographic repertoires and labor of Black and Brown women and queer performers. Still, for all of their important contributions, none of these works focuses on the intersection of Black expressive culture and video game aesthetics as it has been imagined by Black and Brown rappers and producers themselves. This chapter thus offers a new perspective on the ways that underrepresented groups contribute to gaming cultures and discourses.

The Politics of Gamer-Rap and Nerdcore

Before reflecting on the ways that Black and Brown artists move within the video game hip-hop ecosystem, it is important to clarify some of the language and naming conventions that I will use in this chapter. To honor the perspectives of my interviewees, I also frequently use terms like "geek," "nerd," and "nerd/geek" interchangeably, as a set of identities that loosely refers to individuals who are deeply passionate and knowledgeable about esoteric or technical subject matter and who may present outwardly as socially awkward or unfashionable or maintain some combination of the two.[5]

In regard to the musical conventions at the heart of this chapter's inquiry, I have devised the term "gamer-rap" to emphasize the deep interplay to be found in this subgenre between artists' identities as hip-hop artists and as gamers. This is in contrast to the kinds of one-off, game-themed rap songs and instrumentals dropped by hip-hop artists whose catalogs generally do not reflect a deeper engagement with video game aesthetics and storylines.[6] The term "nerdcore" is more recognizable as a label to describe gamer-rap, but I resist using it here as a synonym for "gamer-rap," in part because it refers to rap music that covers a broad range of traditional nerd/geek topics including comic books, video games, science fiction, anime, and technology. Lumping these forms of hip-hop music together overlooks the nuances of how gamer-rap artists enjoy a particular relationship with the actual music of different video game soundtracks like, for instance, the way that hip-hop beats and video game music share a core mechanic of looping.

Additionally, uncritical use of the term "nerdcore" flattens the complex experiences of gamer-rap artists, who represent a diverse range of cultural and musical styles, and instead it prioritizes the sonic interventions made by a group of rappers and producers in the early 2000s who developed nerdcore to center the nerd/geek archetypes echoed by their lived experiences. According to artists like MC Frontalot, who coined the term in his song "Nerdcore Hiphop" (2000), the nerdcore community has emerged on- and offline as an important site for many geek- and nerd-identified artists and fans to participate in a cultural form that has traditionally prioritized voices from the margins, while rejecting the conventions of coolness commonly associated with the hip-hop body, and, by extension, modern heteronormative western masculinity (Sewell 2015). In his work on hip-hop, race, and the performance of masculinity, Miles White (2011, 23) notes: "For white adolescent males coming to terms with issues of masculinity and identity, the image of the swaggering black male in hip-hop videos is an appealing figure that has become iconic of an authentic and desirable representation of masculinity to be emulated." Instead, many early nerdcore artists—who tended to be white, technically inclined, male, and middle class—leaned into their perceived status as social outcasts, rapping about topics like hacking, data encryption, and, in the words of MC Frontalot, "the defeat of coolness in general" (cited in Sewell 2015, 223).[7]

In recent years, a new generation of self-described nerdcore artists has proliferated online, particularly on YouTube, where the streaming success of their polished, often pop-inflected rap songs about anime and video games suggests a shift from the decidedly anticool, antiestablishment messaging espoused by earlier artists in the subgenre.[8] And although several artists of color have also taken on the nerdcore label and productively complicated long-held perceptions in the scene about the meaning of nerd and geek identities, the early associations of nerdcore with the performance of "hyperwhiteness" (Bucholtz 2001, cited in Ronald 2012, 50) have meant that the label remains fraught for certain gamer-rappers and -producers, myself included. The music discussed in this chapter will therefore only be referred to as nerdcore if the distinction is directly relevant to the argument, or the artist behind said work uses that label to describe their work.

Finally, any referrals to an artist as a gamer-rapper or -producer in this chapter should not imply that the entirety of their catalog or even their musical identity is solely based around being a gamer; only that some significant portion of their work reflects this relationship. Each of the individuals interviewed for this chapter has released music that would likely not be considered gamer-rap by their fans or by the artists themselves.

Gamer-Rap Origin Stories

In his memoir *Dream Master*, gamer-rap trailblazer Mega Ran (Raheem Jarbo), formerly known as Random, discusses much of his early identity formation alongside parallel developments in hip-hop artistry and the video games industry beginning in the late 1980s. For example, after an anecdote about his decision to trade all of his Nintendo games with a classmate for a copy of the game *Mega Man 3* (1990) in middle school, he notes having similar feelings of anticipation for the release of Public Enemy's *Apocalypse 91 . . . The Enemy Strikes Black* (1991) around the same period in his life (Jarbo 2021, 40–41). In regard to his relationships with other gamers and hip-hop heads, he writes that popular fighting games like *Street Fighter II* (1994) and *Mortal Kombat* (1992) often indirectly strengthened his relationship to the music, through hours-long gaming sessions with his high-school friends (who would soon become members of his first rap crew) played to a soundtrack of rap rebels like Redman, Das EFX, and the Beastie Boys (48–49). And in regard to his appreciation for the musicality of video game tracks as valuable compositions in their own right, he shares that his creation of mixtapes, using his portable "Kidcorder" cassette recorder to capture the biggest radio and television rap hits, soon led him to consider the possibilities of relistening to the loops in the games he was playing, noting: "*Mega Man 2*'s music was unlike anything I had ever heard. . . . I realized the music continued to play when you hit pause, and it gave me a crazy idea. . . . I used the Kid-Corder to capture music from the game" (35). This early experiment resulted in his creation of a mixtape that reflected his dual musical interests, with one side committed to popular rap tracks of the time and the other to his DIY video game sound recordings: "While I switched between Takashi Tateishi's sparse, yet lush, eight-bit melodies of *Mega Man 2* and Hank Shocklee and the Bomb Squad's hard-hitting funk-laced soundscapes of Public Enemy tracks, something clicked. Hip-hop and video games became the soundtrack to my forty-five minute bus rides, and later, my life" (36).

His decision to eventually use video games as source material for his beats and rhymes is perhaps best summed up in the final bars of his song "Dream Master (2010)," in which he raps his origin story over a beat that samples and loops the stage transition jingle in the Nintendo game *Little Nemo: The Dream Master* (1990):

> So he thought back to childhood
> And how he survived in such a wild hood
> Then he realized, they didn't hate him
> And whatever didn't break him, that's what made him
> So he decided to combine his love for the games and raps
> Open his soul up and let 'em in
> Then he chopped up some 8 bit sounds, put it down
> Now Random is now known as Mega Ran

These vignettes, which chart Mega Ran's path from avid gamer and hip-hop head to gamer-rapper, in many ways reflect the journey of several artists born in or just after what Bakari Kitwana (2002) calls the "hip-hop generation." This nomenclature refers to Black children who were born in, or emigrated to, the United States between 1965 and 1984, the first generation to have come of age with the backdrop of hip-hop actively shaping their lives (although certainly many non-Black people born during this period were profoundly shaped by hip-hop music and culture). The earliest musical memories of frequent Mega Ran collaborator K-Murdock (Kyle Murdock)—a gamer-producer, sound designer, and professor from Washington, DC—were also marked by the sights and sounds of early console games and hip-hop's golden age, although these interests drew him more toward the technical side of music production. It was, in fact, a recognition of the artist behind the instrumental loops in one of his favorite Sega Genesis games that enabled him to begin exploring video game composition with the same passion he felt for his favorite hip-hop beats:

> The moment it resonated to me as far as video game music [being] dope, it was when I played *Streets of Rage* back in '91 and '92. I had never noticed but on the press-start screen, the title screen, at the bottom it said "Music copyright by Yuzo Kushiro." I was like "Woah!" I had never seen that before, where you feature the person who's the game composer. And then I started paying attention in the same way I would listen to and buy CDs and read the liner notes, like who engineered this, who produced this, for hip-hop. . . . Anything he did, I had to have. . . . And I really liked the music that he did in *Streets of Rage* because I was like this dude is in Japan but he was obviously making music that sounded like New Jack Swing. . . . I remember playing *Super Adventure Island* (1992) [also scored by Kushiro]. And when you [paused] it, the music would keep playing. I remember I would just sometimes start the game at my favorite level and just pause it and clean my room. It was dope.[9]

Like Mega Ran, K-Murdock's hip-hop-trained ear drew him to the function of the loop, even providing him with a frame for understanding the familiar compositional style of

FIGURE 22.1 A press photo of Mega Ran wearing a number of gold-spray-painted video game controllers around his neck in a style similar to how many rappers don layers of gold chain necklaces (Doench, 2015).

the *Streets of Rage* soundtrack as a version of the then popular hip-hop and R&B "New Jack Swing" production style—marked by its swung percussive elements and prominent "bap" snare sound. And when discussing his process for devising the beats on *Forever Famicom* (2010), a collaborative video game-themed album with Mega Ran (Figure 22.1), he names the flexible quality of hip-hop artistry as the foundation for his approach to sample selection even when working with music from Nintendo and Super Nintendo games: "It's just hip-hop. Hip-hop samples jazz . . . soul and funk. So, the stuff I was sampling was either video games or like progressive rock."[10]

For other artists within gamer-rap, their identities as gamers long preceded their relationships to hip-hop as listeners and as artists. CreateLadyJ (Jonae Townsend), a gamer-rapper and -producer based in the Washington, DC, metropolitan area, and a recording studio owner and engineer, describes growing up as a third-generation gamer, citing her grandmother and mother as her biggest game-play cheerleaders:

> My mom was always playing games, my grandmother played games. They were . . . just like, "No, you're not getting the Sega Genesis until you play Atari. You know where

> games come from?" We played and the first day I was like, "Okay . . ."And then eventually, I loved it. And eventually, she got me a Sega. And it literally became one of those things where I was bonding with my family playing games.[11]

She also credits her mother for her general love of music, through constant exposure to a range of R&B luminaries, but her desire to make hip-hop emerged when she was a teenager, after she watched the film *8 Mile* (2002) starring the rapper Eminem. As she began crafting her voice within hip-hop, she instinctually incorporated themes and samples from her favorite video games into her work. Some of her earliest attempts involved rapping over the pop-rock and chiptune-driven soundtrack for the PlayStation 3/Xbox 360 game *Scott Pilgrim V. The World* (2010), composed by the band Anamanaguchi. She realized that there was a wider community of similar artists worth tapping into only after a high school friend told her that what she appeared to be making was nerdcore hip-hop. She has since released two nerdcore concept albums that detail storylines and sample music from the role-playing games *Final Fantasy XIII* (2009) and *Kingdom Hearts* (2002).

In my own experiences growing up in the small, mostly white town of Ithaca, New York, several years before hip-hop emerged as the dominant form of popular music, I was not exposed to rap music beyond what I watched on MTV and what was passed down through my older brother by way of CD trades and purchases. I played games regularly as a child on our home consoles, and developed an early interest in music production after becoming enamored with Masato Nakamura's work on the soundtrack of *Sonic the Hedgehog 2* (1992). Although I was never formally trained, by my junior year of high school I was using the digital audio workstation Reason to compose synth-heavy video game inspired beats on my brother's laptop with the hopes of one day creating music for a video game. Occasionally, to produce dance and progressive-rock influenced synth tracks, I turned to the PlayStation game and compositional tool *MTV Music Generator* (1999), a game that has been credited by Mega Ran (Jarbo 2021, 49, 100–101) and other hip-hop producers, like Grammy-recipient Sounwave, as an early beatmaking tool (Phillips 2017).

After I developed an interest in sample-based rap production in high school, I began sampling tracks from my favorite childhood video game soundtracks, downloaded from the peer-to-peer file sharing platform LimeWire, and dragged into the digital audio workstation GarageBand for easy splicing and mixing. Like the pioneering beatmakers of the hip-hop generation who first sampled soul and funk records from the 1960s and 1970s, I recognized the practice of sampling as a time-travel mechanism through which I could pay tribute to the musical loops that had, in many ways, informed my musical identity. Similarly, each of the artists interviewed has produced work that relies on the so-called retro, sawtooth-wave-sounding game compositions for Nintendo and the Sega Genesis; they each also picked up on nostalgia as a driving force for their desires to rap and produce in this style. As K-Murdock notes in regard to his production decisions in *Forever Famicom*: "People were like, why did you sample *Secret of Mana* (1993) and *Chrono Trigger*? And I was like, because those are the games I played, so it was kind of like me walking back in my childhood to a degree."[12] When I started rapping in 2010, I too returned to those early games as the inspiration for my moniker—lifted from the character Samus Aran from the Nintendo game *Metroid* (1987)—as well as for much of my subject matter.

Navigating Fans and Fandoms in Gamer-Rap

These kinds of origin stories represent the typical journey into the gamer-rap orbit for artists across a range of cultural and musical backgrounds. In the case of nerdcore hip-hop, the musicologist Amanda Sewell (2015, 223) notes that most of the rappers in the scene got their start simply because "they wanted to rap, they wanted to rap about familiar topics, and the topics familiar to them were nerdy." But these stories take on a special significance when the artists in question are Black and Brown, particularly if they are women, nonbinary, and/or queer. Certainly, for many white rappers within the gamer-rap space, their lyrical content reflects real experiences of ostracization, alienation, and even ridicule as it relates to their social status as nerds and geeks (Sewell 2015; Kendall 2011). When Susan Cole, a 2016 contestant on the gameshow *Jeopardy*, explained that her favorite kind of music, nerdcore, involved rappers waxing philosophical about "video games, science fiction, [and] having a hard time meeting romantic partners," the host, the late Alex Trebek, flippantly replied by calling these artists, "Losers, in other words" (Jarbo 2021, 193–194).[13] But the stakes of navigating the world as a geek or nerd of color—visible and/or audible particularly one who identifies as queer, trans, and/or a woman—can be vastly different. And, within the universe of gamer-rap, that difference often means triangulating between, on the one hand, the desire to creatively participate in a fandom in a meaningful way and build community with others who share their identities, and, on the other, the pressure to present their experiences to audiences that are ignorant or openly hostile to their realities.

One common refrain that emerged from the interviewees was the challenge they each frequently faced in dealing with audiences who didn't share their love and understandings of hip-hop culture and Black cultural experiences more generally. When reflecting on the dissonance between the realities of being a Black man in America, and his audience's appreciation for his more light-hearted game content, Mega Ran notes:

> I have the hardest time balancing what I do as Mega Ran with who I am as Raheem. I get the amazing opportunity to provide an escape to my listeners and concert-goers, with whimsical rhymes about robots and spaceships. I also get to enter spaces where not many African-American males are, and to share my world with people who have no idea of my background or lifestyle. . . . You'll hear me use dialect that I use with my friends on the block, even when I talk about things like video games. I want people

> to know that they are listening to a Black man when they hear me. The worst thing I hear is, "I don't really see color when I look at you." That means you don't see my experience. (Jarbo 2021, 168)

Working within the gamer-rap space offers Mega Ran the opportunity to explore the fantastic and otherworldly in his music while directly challenging perceptions about the experiences of Black men that are commonly held by people who may never have listened otherwise. But these opportunities also come with dehumanizing consequences, such as, in this case, the erasure of his Black identity by fans who do not know how or refuse to interface with issues of race and racism. And for Shubzilla (Shiboo Blalack), a Seattle-based gamer-rapper whose work includes concept albums about *Donkey Kong Country 2* (1995) and the *Castlevania* series, she found that this kind of ignorance also informs many nerdcore fans' negative attitudes toward hip-hop music and culture more broadly, particularly when she first began visiting nerdcore internet forums: "I felt like for people that are supposed to be rapping, they weren't giving respect to the culture. Because [in the forums] it was just all like, 'Oh, I don't like rap, but I can do nerdcore.' And to me, it's so fucking disrespectful, given how hip-hop was birthed."[14] Originally drawn to hip-hop through her love of dance, Shubzilla eventually turned to rapping in 2010 once the physical demands of professional dance began to wear on her body, and because rapping allowed her to move beyond choreographed routines and share her own unique vision. As a queer, Filipina rapper, she notes that she has spent much of her career figuring out how to share her experiences in a subgenre virtually absent of voices from Asian American and Pacific Islanders (AAPI)[15] without taking up space and opportunities for black gamer-rappers and -producers:

> So once I took a step back, I thought to myself, how else can I participate in this culture, in this movement in a way that is not invasive? . . . I thought about writing because that was something that I was always good at. And I also didn't see folks that looked like me. And you know, I get that Asian Pacific Islanders, we are guests to this culture and this movement, so I wanted to make sure that I did not overstep when I was speaking what I was speaking, and when I was in spaces that are made for Black and Latino folks. It's something I still navigate to this day. I don't want to talk over anybody.[16]

According to Sewell (2015, 228), most nerdcore artists maintain a respectful and often reverential relationship with other forms of hip-hop: "Nerdcore artists frequently express gratitude toward their hip-hop influences and insist that they take their parent genre seriously." However, this claim is certainly up for debate, and has in fact remained an active contention at the heart of many critiques of the form (Kendall 2011, 518–519). The reality of my own experience and those of the Black and Brown gamer-rap artists documented here has been that oftentimes non-Black listeners, and even some artists within gamer-rap, remain woefully disconnected from and disrespectful to the genre that has informed their favorite artists. Like Mega Ran, I have frequently been the recipient of backhanded "compliments" that either seek to erase my identity as a Black woman, or imply that what I make is somehow distinct from and more valuable than hip-hop because it often centers the game-related cultural cues with which my listeners are familiar. These claims not only devalue the creative innovations behind other forms of rap music that are less legible to certain nerdcore audiences but also disrespect the hip-hop artistry of MCs like Del Tha Funky Homosapien, and Jean Grae, who have both meaningfully engaged video game sounds and storylines in their work, without necessarily referring to their music using the language of gamer-rap or nerdcore.[17] In response to the question of whether the term "nerdcore" is unhelpful for understanding her work, Jean Grae noted in a 2012 interview: "Just let it be what it is, let people enjoy it. I looked at Complex Magazine, and the headline was, 'South African Nerd Rapper.' I wrote back to them and said, 'That has to be the funniest thing I've seen all day! What now makes me a nerd rapper?' " (cited in Walker 2012).

Beyond these issues of erasure, other interviewees also expressed concerns about having to field negative interactions with video game fandoms in regard to their creative choices with the source material. It is perhaps unsurprising that these issues would emerge as particularly salient for gamer-rap artists from underrepresented groups, given that the world of gaming has long been a hostile and dismissive space for participants who are Black and Brown, women, queer, and trans whether they're entering as casual gamers, cosplayers, commentators, game developers, streamers, e-sports competitors, or, in this case, musical artists.[18] According to Eglash (2002) the complicated nature of nerd/geek identities means that, although many of the white, educated, middle-class men who identify as geeks and nerds occupy a socially marginalized position, their race, class, and gender positionality nonetheless affords them the power to gatekeep others from certain forms of social or technocultural access. Geek and nerd cultures have become so synonymous with the policing of "canonical" characters' appearances and stories that the popular term "nerd rage" has come in part to describe the vitriol exhibited by nerds/geeks for any perceived infraction against their fandom by "outsiders." Within the vocal cross section of bigots and online trolls who also identify as nerds/geeks, these "infractions" need only take the form of feminist critiques of popular video game properties, or calls for greater diversity in the games industry, to unleash torrents of targeted abuse and threats in the manner exemplified by the misogyny-fueled Gamergate campaign of 2014 (Gray et al. 2017).

CreateLadyJ certainly felt the pressures of managing an aggressive fandom when she decided to release an album based on the popular RPG *Kingdom Hearts* in 2020. Although she calls the project a success, she notes that many fans of the *Kingdom Hearts* franchise were vocal online about their distaste for the album, citing her engagement with so-called sensitive themes and trap style beats:

> Nobody's done the hip-hop *Kingdom Hearts* anything and because of that, it . . . caused a lot of controversy. A lot of people were like, "This is Disney! It's *Kingdom*

> *Hearts*. What is this? This is trap *Kingdom Hearts*?" I got a lot of hate [and] a lot of love. . . . The characters in [the game] are kids and there's this innocent undertone and I definitely trapped it up, grunged it up. Had some really, really sensitive topics in it. So yeah, it shook people up. That is the bad part of using solely the fandom to [market a project] because they will attack you.

In particular, the listeners' "concerns" about the association of trap production with the "innocence" of the childlike *Kingdom Hearts* characters, echo deeper historical anxieties about aural miscegenation (Douglas 2004, 88–99), given trap music's origins from Southern Black drug and hustle cultures (Bowen 2021, 6), which are in turn deeply interwoven with the Black strip club and other sites of the "Black Ratchet Imagination" (Stallings 2013). Heard through the "listening ear" (Stoever 2016)—a set of racialized listening practices that associate coded concepts like noisiness and rawness with the sound and therefore essence of Blackness as it has been constructed by the white imaginary—trap interpolations of the *Kingdom Hearts* soundtrack and storyline can only be understood as disruptive and dangerous in nature.

In my experience of creating *Another M* (2014), a concept album based on the classic Nintendo game *Metroid* (Figure 22.2), I anticipated receiving similar feedback given my use of trap drums to frame the looped sample of Hirokazu Tanaka's "Item Obtainment Jingle" in my lead single "Power-Ups." I said as much in a written reflection about the process of creating the album, where I framed these anxieties around possibly receiving "judgment from hip-hop purists about my use of a trap-style beat" (Lumumba-Kasongo 2015). And though I thankfully did not receive any direct backlash for either the song or the album, the experiences of CreateLadyJ and myself reveal how the gamer-rap space can still largely *feel* unsafe for aural invocations of Blackness that may be illegible for many self-identified geeks and nerds. These debates about the musicality and meaning of trap music of course extend far beyond the edges of gamer-rap, but they are in some cases more pronounced here than they might appear in other spaces because so many well-known artists in the gamer-rap adjacent space of nerdcore have traded on parodying or directly taking aim at the aestheticized Black "failure to uplift" (Stallings 2013, 136)[19] that is often prioritized in trap music and gangsta rap among other popular hip-hop musical forms.[20]

Strategies for Sustainability in Gamer-Rap

The world of gamer-rap can often place artists in problematic situations, but it has also emerged as a lucrative space for many black and brown gamer-rap artists. For most gamer-rappers, myself included, generating buzz in the game-rap space can mean being invited to perform at major game-centered events, such as: San Diego

FIGURE 22.2 The album cover for my concept album about the video game *Metroid*, which features a Black interpretation of the game's typically white, blond main character Samus (Eng-Goetz, 2013).

and New York Comic-Con; PAX East, West, and South; and the Music and Gaming Festival (MAGFest) in National Harbor, MD, the last of which boasted attendance of 24,000+ at the most recent event in January 2020, prior to temporarily shutting down operations due to COVID-19.[21] And these artists enjoy a certain amount of creative freedom that comes with being able to center their identities as gamers in their work. When discussing his first foray into sampling, Mega Ran notes how conscious he was about the stigma associated with playing games among his high school peers: "I sampled tons of video games with my beats, but I didn't dare let anyone know. I thought they'd laugh me out of the room" (Jarbo 2021, 97). And for K-Murdock, this discomfort manifested in dishonesty with friends about the kind of games he secretly enjoyed playing:

> I'm totally a geek. Was I comfortable with saying that? No. I can think back [to] when I was in middle school or high school and everyone in my neighborhood, we'd play games. But when I went home, I would be like, "Y'all I'm going back to the crib to play *Madden*." . . . I was going to the crib to play *Shining Force*! Of course, when my buddies came over I was like switching the game. I'd put Madden in. Until you find somebody, like a friend of yours that you thought would judge you, be like, "Yo, I know that game." And you're like, "What you know that game too? You're a nerd too?"[22]

Even as he began to experiment with sampling video game soundtracks, K-Murdock still expressed reticence to lean into the video game rap space, particularly because he had already found some success as one-half of the underground hip-hop duo Panacea. Although the group was on hiatus when he began working with Mega Ran on their *Forever Famicom* project, the idea of pivoting to work more fully in nerdcore-adjacent spaces felt uncomfortable until he embarked on a successful 2011 tour with Mega Ran, and subsequently had a conversation with a friend that changed his perspective about the gamer-rap space: "[He asked] 'Why are you running away from this? Whatever this video game stuff is, it's obvious people like the stuff you're doing. People support you, it's been able to do stuff that Panacea never did, like, you even went to Japan and the UK,' like I was promised when I was signed and the label never delivered."[23] For K-Murdock, being plugged into a community of listeners who had already formed deep emotional connections with the music being sampled, some of whom had also loved his work in Panacea, afforded him access to a financial and creative lifestyle that was simply unavailable to him in the world of underground rap.

Since 2011, Mega Ran has sustained himself as a full-time artist, and K-Murdock has continued to tour and work in the area of sound design; during my last two years of graduate school I was able to fully support myself through the income I generated as a touring gamer-rapper. Given these benefits, many gamer-rap artists have thus developed innovative strategies for operating within and alongside the gamer-rap space, in ways that allow them to be legible to all of the different communities they represent. Chief among these strategies has been adopting a flexible approach to naming their work. For Mega Ran, the nerdcore label has been a valuable if contentious one, as he recognizes that employing it can oftentimes damage his credibility with notable hip-hop publications and commentators:

> Very few hip-hop people wanted to touch "nerdcore" because of the negative stigma surrounding it. The term nerdcore conjured up images of white middle-class guys who were inspired by Eminem and wrote songs of angst and fire, while working at well-paying jobs and treating the struggle of the nerd as if it were the worst form of persecution next to racism, sexism, and homophobia. (Jarbo 2021, 137)

Although he still refers to parts of his catalog as nerdcore and regularly tours with other prominent nerdcore rappers like MC Frontalot and MC Lars, he also describes his sound as "bits and rhymes" as a play on the phrase "beats and rhymes," as well as "chip-hop," framings that are less burdened by the cultural politics of nerdcore, but that also call attention to the specific instrumentation and retro style of the production.

In my own case, I have opted to use "Afrofuturism" as the framing for my *Metroid*-themed concept album *Another M*, and I have dubbed my work that relies less heavily on video game tropes "Black-girl-nerd-rap." Coined by cultural critic Mark Dery (1994) in an essay titled "Black to the Future," "Afrofuturism" initially served as a useful frame for linking literary works that engage the histories, hopes, and legacies of African Americans through a technocultural lens. And while Dery was primarily interested in the works of Black speculative fiction writers like Octavia Butler and Samuel Delany, several artists and scholars have since widened the Afrofuturist frame to also describe a range of sonic interventions that explore the Black liberatory capacities of nonlinear and speculative storytelling including the (retroactively labeled) work of the avant-garde jazz icon Sun Ra or the free jazz/noise/rap oeuvre of multidisciplinary sound artist Moor Mother. In *Another M*, I am similarly harnessing unique narrative forms by repurposing the visual and sonic iconography of the game *Metroid*, in a way that invites more Black women and girls into the speculative and fantastic worlds of gaming. For example, in the chorus of my song "Mae Jemison" (2014), I move from describing myself via *Metroid*'s protagonist, Samus, as "the fifth element mixed with Mae Jemison," which draws a connection between myself, the alien heroine Leeloo from the film *The Fifth Element* (1997), and my lifelong hero, Dr. Mae Jemison, the first Black woman to travel into space. Paired with hip-hop beats that I produced using samples from the 8-bit soundtrack of *Metroid*, the lyrics of each song on *Another M* layer references from across spacetime to present a possibility of multiversal sonority for those rendered silent by hegemonic myths that limit who can inhabit and shape other worlds and future spaces. Calling *Another M* an Afrofuturist project thus situates my work within a long, radical tradition of black speculative sonic practices in a way that the nerdcore label simply cannot. Much the same can be said for my coinage of "Black-girl-nerd-rap," which I adopted so that listeners would have to interface with the fact of my Black womanhood as an entry point for engaging with the nerd/geek content in my music.

Yet even with all of these considerations about how I want my music to be categorized, I still make use of other peoples' association of my music with the nerdcore subgenre—tagging my music on Bandcamp, Soundcloud, and YouTube with the "nerdcore" tag, for example, or performing as part of the Official Nerdcore Showcase several times at the South by Southwest festival (SXSW). I have found that strategizing in this way has led to greater legibility among the different audiences I am seeking to engage, whether they see themselves as Black feminists, gamers, hip-hop heads, activists, punks, nerds, and/or geeks. And in the case of highly competitive events like SXSW, which require lesser-known acts to submit an application, flagging my music as nerdcore often ensures greater likelihood that I will be selected to participate than if I applied under the broader umbrella of indie hip-hop.

Sustainability for Black and Brown artists in the gamer-rap space has also been contingent on coalition-building and strategically organizing to increase the presence of their voices in these spaces. When Shubzilla first started recording and sharing music in online nerdcore forums, she made a point of trying to find other women in the space, particularly women of color, to build connections in a space that she found to be quite unforgiving:

> [A]t the time, I believe I was the only Asian Pacific Islander, especially woman, who was in that space. And I remember it being very isolating. And I felt very alone. . . . Especially women of color, anytime I encountered one of our sisters, I would make sure they knew that (1.0) I was around and (2) if they needed anything, that I was there, whether it was an ear to hear, plug-in event, hit me up. You're in town hit me up, you have a place to stay, you have food to eat, you know, you have transportation.[24]

I, in fact, met Shubzilla through an online nerdcore forum in 2013, and she has since hosted me on several occasions and invited me to perform as part of a woman-centered geek convention in Seattle called GeekGirlCon, which she cofounded in 2011. With a similar strength-in-numbers mentality, in 2014 Mega Ran enlisted a group of self-proclaimed geeky and nerdy visual and musical artists, athletes, and scholars to form the Nerdy People of Color Collective (NPC Collective). Drawing on the common gaming acronym for "nonplayable character" (characters that are unusable and therefore typically relegated to supporting roles), the NPC Collective has produced events, organized panels at conventions, and successfully pushed for greater diversity in the make-up of gamer-rap and nerdcore artists who are invited to perform at major events like SXSW, PAX, MAGFest, and Comic-Con. Had SXSW not been canceled due to COVID-19, the 2020 Official Nerdcore Showcase would have featured a lineup with 9 out of the tw12elve acts led by Black and Brown artists—more than twice the number in 2015, when I first performed at the showcase. Thanks to the efforts of groups like the NPC Collective and the rap group Wreck the System (led by CreateLadyJ), gamer-rap and nerdcore scenes are finally beginning to reflect the diversity of people who play and work in games.

Conclusion

This chapter has examined gamer-rap as it has been shaped by the Black and Brown artists whose voices have largely been absent from scholarly accounts of both video game music and nerd/geek music scenes more broadly. For these artists, working within gamer-rap and nerdcore spaces affords them the opportunity to freely express themselves as nerds/geeks and to be intimately connected with fans in ways that are often unusual and difficult to facilitate in the broader world of indie hip-hop. For example, when representatives from the game developer Capcom learned that Mega Ran was sampling music from their games for his beats, they shared that they were fans of the work, offering him an interview and a license to use their music in other songs rather than pursuing litigation to protect their intellectual property (Jarbo 2021, 131–132). This outcome is largely unimaginable in the broader world of indie hip-hop. But, as this chapter has revealed, these opportunities also come with many challenges, including having to interface with ignorant and harmful listeners, demanding fandoms, and deep experiences of alienation, in addition to the ever-present risk of being boxed in as an artist. To the last point, hopefully what I have also unearthed in this chapter is the need for more capacious and porous understandings of the labels that bisect different Black and Brown identities—whether those labels are gamer, geek, or nerd. I think of CreateLadyJ, who identifies as queer and calls herself "alternative Black" or "alt-Black" to account for her strong connection with punk music and culture, which she hopes will show up in whatever she releases next, as well as the recent conversations in pop culture about the so-called rise of the "blerd"—the Black nerd—in popular consciousness through highly visible figures like Misha Green and Jordan Peele (Bradley 2021). This space at the intersection of gaming and hip-hop culture seems a particularly ripe place to deepen this discourse.

Notes

1. "Blue Bomber" is a popular nickname for the Capcom character Mega Man. See ("Mega Man II" 1989, 9).
2. For a quick breakdown of the intersections between hip-hop culture and video games, see (Alexander 2019, 1:58–11:38), a talk given by game developer Shawn Alexander at the Game Developers of Color Expo in 2019. See Austin (2018) for additional perspectives on hip-hop's representation within video games.
3. I want to thank each of my interviewees Mega Ran, K-Murdock, CreateLadyJ, and Shubzilla, without whom this project would not have been possible. These artists of course do not represent an exhaustive list of notable Black and Brown gamer-rap artists and were selected based on their range of skill sets, identities, and cultural backgrounds.
4. For histories of nerdcore, see Kendall (2011), Ronald (2012), and Sewell (2015); for histories of chiptunes, see Paul (2014) and McAlpine (2018).
5. Nerd and geek identities have long been the subject of study among scholars at the intersections of technology, gender, and race. As it relates to the relationship between nerd and geek identities, scholars and cultural critics differ on whether it is necessary to distinguish between the two. Like Eglash (2002), I believe that "nerd" and "geek" are essentially interchangeable, and their usage is a matter of personal preference. Other scholars of race and/or gender, and technology have found it useful to parse out distinctions between the two identities as a way to better understand the nuances of how racial and gender constructs emerge across different kinds of technocultures. See (Ciciora 2009; Eglash 2002, 61n1; Dunbar-Hester 2014, 32; Kendall 1999, 264) for perspectives on the sociocultural distinctions between nerds and geeks.
6. Popular examples of one-off game-themed songs include "Game Over" (2004), the hit single from the rapper Lil' Flip, which samples the theme song from *Ms. Pac-Man* (1981) or more recently, "Chun-Li" (2018) by the international rap star Nicki Minaj, which positions the rapper as battling her haters in a manner akin to the iconic character of the same name from the popular *Street Fighter* franchise.

7. MC Frontalot further leans into his identity as a nerd through his regular performance attire, which includes a pocket protector, tucked-in shirt, tie, and thick glasses; see (Kendall 2011, 507; Sewell 2015, 223).
8. Since 2010, self-described "Nerdcore/Anime Rapper and Producer" Rustage has amassed over 1.2 million YouTube subscribers and 520 + million overall channel views according to Social Blade, a site that tracks and aggregates social media statistics such as viewership and engagement. Other artists in the video game and anime rap space on YouTube with sizable online followings include Fabvl (665k subscribers), Shwabadi (157k subscribers), and Shao Dow (30k subscribers).
9. Kyle Murdock, interview by author, June 22, 2021.
10. Kyle Murdock, interview by author, June 22, 2021.
11. Jonae Townsend, interview by author, June 20, 2021.
12. Kyle Murdock, interview by author, June 22, 2021.
13. This statement by Alex Trebek initiated a playful rap "beef" with a variety of nerd/geek rappers that received coverage in national publications like *TMZ*.
14. Shiboo Blalack, interview by author, June 23, 2021.
15. Other AAPI rappers in gamer-rap include the lawyer and former rapper Adam WarRock as well as LEX the Lexicon Artist.
16. Shiboo Blalack, interview by author, June 23, 2021.
17. In 2000 Del Tha Funky Homosapien released "Proto Culture," a track about his love of video games, featuring Khaos Unique, which samples a track from the fighting game *Darkstalkers* (1994). In an interview with Red Bull Music Academy, he also credits the *Mega Man X* series with giving him the idea to release an Afrofuturist concept album titled *Deltron 3030* (1999) alongside Kid Koala and Dan the Automator (Red Bull Music Academy 2014). Jean Grae has used the language and iconography of games in her songs and music videos, perhaps most notably on her track "Kill Screen" (2013), which refers to a screen that prevents a player from progressing. For more on her identity as a gamer see (Walker 2012). The rapper and producer Charles Hamilton is another example of a well-known MC who has detailed a deep connection with video games in his music.
18. Thanks in large part to the work of scholars at the intersections of feminist media studies, critical race studies, and critical game studies, there exists a wealth of scholarship that documents and draws connections between the frequent swells of sexism, racism, and homophobia that have become so endemic to game culture and internet life more broadly. Although not an exhaustive list, see Consalvo (2012), Gray (2014), Gray et al. (2017), and Nakamura (2012, 2014) for perspectives on the toxicity of game culture, and in some cases strategies for combatting these acts of hate.
19. Stallings draws on Halberstam's (2011) conceptualization of failure to theorize the "Black Ratchet Imagination" and the productive possibilities that exist within its failure to engage the performance of Black respectability.
20. For examples of nerdcore artists who have parodied and/or critiqued elements of hip-hop music and culture, see Kendall (2011, 511–519) and Sewell (2015, 227–228). Also see "The Rappist" (2007) by Schaffer the Darklord for one of the more direct examples of a nerdcore rapper articulating the ways that nerdcore is distinct from hip-hop.
21. The number of attendees at MAGFest 2020 was pulled from the MAGFest website: https://super.magfest.org/what-is-magfest.
22. Kyle Murdock, interview by author, June 22, 2021.
23. Kyle Murdock, interview by author, June 22, 2021.
24. Shiboo Blalack, interview by author, June 23, 2021.

References

Alexander, Shawn. 2019. “Hip Hop and Video Games.” Game Devs of Color Expo. September 9. Panel discussion, 51:44. https://youtu.be/LveQUbRj7LU.

Als, Hilton. 1997. “Missy Elliott’s Hip-Hop.” *New Yorker*, October 20, 1997. https://www.newyorker.com/magazine/1997/10/20/ the-new-negro.

Austin, Michael L. 2015. “From Mixtapes to Multiplayers: Sharing Musical Taste through Video Games.” *Soundtrack* 8 (1–2): 77–88.

Austin, Michael L. 2018. “‘Playas’ and Players: Play at the Intersection of Hip Hop and Video Game Cultures.” In *The Oxford Handbook of Hip Hop Music*, edited by Justin Burton and Jason Oakes. New York: Oxford University Press. https://doi.org/10.1093/oxfordhb/9780190281090.013.55.

Bowen, Sesali. 2021. *Bad Fat Black Girl: Notes from a Trap Feminist*. New York: Amistad.

Bradley, Adam. 2021. “The Black Nerds Redefining Culture.” *New York Times*, March 24, 2021. https://www.nytimes.com/2021/03/24/t-magazine/black-nerds-culture.html.

Brown, Harley. 2019. “Lost Rings Is the Record Label Prioritizing Women Gamers of Color.” *Fader*, September 11, 2019. https://www.thefader.com/2019/09/11/lost-rings-is-the-record-label-prioritizing-women-gamers-of-color.

Bucholtz, Mary. 2001. “The Whiteness of Nerds: Superstandard English and Racial Markedness.” *Journal of Linguistic Anthropology* 11 (1): 84–100.

Ciciora, Phil. 2009. “Geeks May Be Chic but Negative Nerd Stereotypes Still Exist, Professor Says.” *Illinois News Bureau*, March 3, 2009. https://news.illinois.edu/view/6367/206011.

Cirisano, Tatiana. 2020. “Game On: What Travis Scott Is Teaching Music Stars about the World’s Biggest New (Virtual) Stage.” *Billboard*, July 25, 2020. https://www.billboard.com/articles/business/9422287/travis-scott-fortnite-billboard-cover-story-interview-2020.

Consalvo, Mia. 2012. “Confronting Toxic Gamer Culture: A Challenge for Feminist Game Studies Scholars.” *Ada: A Journal of Gender, New Media, and Technology* 1. https://adanewmedia.org/2012/11/issue1-consalvo/.

Dery, Mark. 1994. “Black to the Future: Interviews with Samuel R. Delany, Greg Tate, and Tricia Rose.” In *Flame Wars: The Discourse of Cyber Culture*, edited by Mark Dery, 179–222. Durham, NC: Duke University Press.

Douglas, Susan. 2004. *Listening In: Radio and the American Imagination*. Minneapolis: University of Minnesota Press.

Eglash, Ron. 2002. “Race, Sex, and Nerds: From Black Geeks to Asian American Hipsters.” *Social Text* 71: 49–64.

Gray, Kishonna L. 2014. *Race, Gender, and Deviance in Xbox Live: Theoretical Perspectives from the Virtual Margins*. New York: Routledge.

Gray, Kishonna L. 2016. “Living Da Dream More Like a Nightmare.” *Not Your Mama’s Gamer*, March 22, 2016. https://www.nymgamer.com/?p=13266.

Gray, Kishonna L., Bertan Buyukozturk, and Zachary G. Hill. 2017. “Blurring the Boundaries: Using Gamergate to Examine “Real” and Symbolic Violence against Women in Contemporary Gaming Culture.” *Sociology Compass* 11 (3). https://doi.org/10.1111/soc4.12458.

Dunbar-Hester, Christina. 2014. *Low Power to the People: Pirates, Protest, and Politics in FM Radio Activism*. Cambridge, MA: MIT Press.

Halberstam, Jack. 2011. *The Queer Art of Failure*. Durham, NC: Duke University Press.

Jarbo, Raheem. 2021. *Dream Master: A Memoir.* Bloomington, IN: AuthorHouse.

Kendall, Lori. 1999. “Nerd Nation: Images of Nerds in US Popular Culture.” *International Journal of Cultural Studies* 2 (2): 260–283.

Kendall, Lori. 2011. "'White and Nerdy:' Computers, Race, and the Nerd Stereotype." *Journal of Popular Culture* 44 (3): 505–524.

Kitwana, Bakari. 2002. *The Hip Hop Generation: Young Blacks and the Crisis in African American Culture*. New York: Basic*Civitas* Books.

Lumumba-Kasongo, Enongo. 2015. "On Samus, Writing Reflexively, and Finding My Voice." *Mary Sue*, August 26, 2015. http://www.themarysue.com/samus-and-finding-my-voice/.

McAlpine, Kenneth. 2018. *Bits and Pieces: A History of Chiptunes*. New York: Oxford University Press.

"Mega Man II." 1989. *Nintendo Power*, July/August 1989.

Miller, Kiri. 2008. "The Accidental Carjack: Ethnography, Gameworld Tourism, and *Grand Theft Auto*." *Game Studies* 8 (1). http://gamestudies.org/0801/articles/miller.

Miller, Kiri. 2017. *Playable Bodies: Dance Games and Intimate Media*. New York: Oxford University Press.

Nakamura, Lisa. 2012. "Queer Female of Color: The Highest Difficulty Setting There Is? Gaming Rhetoric as Gender Capital." *Ada: Journal of Gender, New Media, and Technology* 1. https://adanewmedia.org/2012/11/issue1-nakamura/.

Nakamura, Lisa. 2014. "Gender and Race Online." In *Society and the Internet: How Networks of Information and Communication Are Changing Our Lives*, edited by Mark Graham and William H. Dutton, 81–98. Oxford: Oxford University Press.

Paul, Leonard. 2014. "For the Love of Chiptune." In *The Oxford Handbook of Interactive Audio*, edited by Karen Collins, Bill Kapralos, and Holly Tessler, 507–530. New York: Oxford University Press.

Phillips, Yoh. 2017. "How a Playstation Music-Making Game Inspired a Generation of Producers." *DJBooth*, May 19, 2017. https://djbooth.net/features/2017-05-19-mtv-music-generator-history.

Red Bull Music Academy. 2014. "Deltron 3030: An Oral History." Accessed May 19, 2021. https://daily.redbullmusicacademy.com/2014/08/deltron-3030-oral-history.

Ronald, Jessica E. 2012. "Alternative Performances of Race in Hip-Hop Music: Nerdcore Counterculture." Master's thesis. University of Illinois.

Russworm, TreaAndrea M., and Samantha Blackmon. 2020. "Replaying Video Game History as a Mixtape of Black Feminist Thought." *Feminist Media Histories* 6, no. 1 (Winter): 93–118.

Schaffer the Darklord. 2007. "The Rappist," July 27, 2007. Music video, 6:18. https://www.youtube.com/watch?v=tB4sTc5ZYEc.

Sewell, Amanda. 2015. "Nerdcore Hip-Hop." In *The Cambridge Companion to Hip Hop*, edited by Justin A. Williams, 223–231. Cambridge: Cambridge University Press.

Stallings, LaMonda H. "Hip Hop and the Black Ratchet Imagination." *Palimpsest: A Journal on Women, Gender, and the Black International* 2:135–139.

Stoever, Jennifer L. 2016. *The Sonic Color Line: Race and the Cultural Politics of Listening*. New York: New York University Press.

Walker, John. 2012. "Gaming Made Me: Jean Grae." *Rock Paper Shotgun*, September 11, 2012. https://www.rockpapershotgun.com/gaming-made-me-jean-grae.

White, Miles. 2011. *From Jim Crow to Jay-Z: Race, Rap, and the Performance of Masculinity*. Urbana: University of Illinois Press.

CHAPTER 23

PRESS START TO (FORE)PLAY

Sex and Sexuality in Game Music

MICHAEL L. AUSTIN

Looking For, and Finding, Sex and Sexuality in Games

Nearly as long as there has been published media, there has been sexual content in that media. "Great art is always flanked by its dark sisters, blasphemy and pornography" (Paglia 1990, 24–25)—and of course, sex sells—but, at least in the United States, censorship and moral panic often follow not far behind. Led by Senators Joe Lieberman (D-CT) and Herb Kohl (D-WI), the US Congress held hearings in late 1993 to address public concerns about violence and other adult themes found in video games, which ultimately led major developers in the industry to form the Entertainment Software Ratings Board (ESRB) to self-regulate the mature content found in published titles. The games in question included *Mortal Kombat* (Midway 1992) for its gruesome depictions of violence, and *Night Trap* (Sega 1992) for its sexual content and exploitative depiction of women. But instances of sex and sexuality can vary widely in video games, and when designing games with sexually themed content, game designers must juggle a number of ethical and aesthetic issues regarding narrative and social context, the politics of representation, and morality. Furthermore, because sex is often not a silent activity, designers must consider the sounds of sex and sexuality along with the visual elements; according to the game designer and scholar Brenda Brathwaite (2007), sex is "an incredibly immersive experience that affects all the senses deeply. Games that hope to fully simulate this experience must affect as many senses as they possibly can to recreate a sexy aesthetic" (4). In this chapter, I consider some ways in which sex and sexuality are represented sonically within video games, tracing auditory tropes used in video games back to their roots in film and pornography. Then, taking male homosexuality as an example, I discuss the possible means through which sexuality may be subtly or overtly represented in video games through voice acting, sound effects, and musical content.

To begin a discussion about the myriad ways in which sexuality can and has been represented in video games, it is important to understand and appreciate the fact that it is difficult to even agree on a single definition of sexuality. Essentialist definitions of sexuality prioritize physicality and external experience over any other possible emotional or psychosocial variables; not only do such definitions propose that anyone who does not experience physical intercourse (or at least physical urges of a sexual nature) does not have a sexuality, these interpretations are also ableist, suggesting that those who experience paralysis of the lower body, and those who experience some developmental disabilities must, by default, be labeled asexual. As we have come to understand it over the past few decades, *sex* (or the physical and physiological differences between males, females, and those who are intersex, that is, possessing both male and female sex characteristics) is not only a physical construct but also a social one, manifested as a status assigned to a person at birth based on their sex characteristics, namely, their genitalia. We understand this social status assigned to us at birth based on our perceived sex as our *gender*, which either becomes more and more a part of our identity as we mature, becomes rejected by a person if their sex and the gender with which they more closely identify are incongruous, or becomes blended to various degrees with other gender identities to match a person's realization of their own identity. Not only do we perform our gender identity, the cognitive and emotional understanding of our *sexual orientation* is understood through examining a combination of our desires and attractions, behaviors, self-expression, and relationships with others—so much so that our *sexual orientation identity* is often both internalized and viewed externally as a defining feature of our overall identity.[1] So, while it may be tempting to define sexuality based solely on sexual attraction and the sexual or romantic experiences a person may have with others (or not, in the case of those who identify as asexual), sexuality is expressed in a very wide variety of ways that extend well beyond intercourse, some of which help us to form our identities and communities.

Hearing the Roots of Mediated Sex and Sexuality in Film

In 1915, the US Supreme Court ruled in *Mutual Film Corp v. Industrial Commission of Ohio* that the First Amendment right to free speech did not extend to film. Subsequently, films with risqué material released throughout the late 1910s and 1920s drew the ire of politicians and the public. But rather than allowing government entities to determine what was and was not allowed in film, which would likely cause problems for national distribution should various states adopt different acceptability limits, former Postmaster General William H. Hays was hired as founding president of the Motion

Picture Producers and Distributors of America (MPPDA), an organization formed to develop a code by which the industry would regulate itself. Hays formed a committee and developed a set of recommendations in 1927 called "Don'ts and Be Carefuls" which listed topics or tropes that should be handled with caution, if not left out altogether, such as profanity, nudity, drugs, sexual perversion and venereal diseases, white slavery and interracial relationships, rape or attempted rape, men and women together in bed, extramarital sex or adultery, excessive or lustful kissing, and so on. The Hays Code remained the system that governed film content until it was abandoned in 1968 with the introduction of the Motion Picture Association of America's (MPAA, now called the Motion Picture Association) rating system.

Although sex depicted in art and printed pornography had existed for centuries, sexuality on film first took the form of heterosexual romance between two cisgender individuals, expressed through flirtatious and romantic actions, such as holding hands and kissing, and various types of relationships, *viz.* courtships and marriages; in fact, Thomas Edison filmed the first on-screen kiss in 1896, but even then, such overt public displays of affection were frowned upon. Once recorded dialogue was introduced, possibilities for romantic expression expanded greatly—so long as conversations remained within the bounds of the Hays Code. Verbally mentioning genital sex acts would not be allowed—even as a weakened dysphemistic insult, such as "screw you"—until well into the 1960s.

In instances where on-screen kisses begin to reach the limit of censors' notions of excess or lustfulness, directors and editors employed what the film scholar Linda Williams (2008, 38) calls *osculum interruptum*, or fade-outs, scene changes, or tilting the camera to another focal point in the same shot. Music proved to be a useful sonic version of this tool, at once serving as a relief valve, a privacy screen, a metaphorical stand-in, and a sonic bridge for filmmakers who wanted to imply that more physical romance was taking place, even when they could not display it visually or aurally on screen. Kisses in Code-era films were briefly bathed in light before an *interruptum* and were often accompanied by swells of nondiegetic orchestral music, sonically providing audiences with the titillation the unseen physicality would have provided, completing the unseen kisses or alluding to other types of more physical contact. Even after the Code and well into today's contemporary filmmaking practices, the bodily sounds, moans, and so forth that accompany sex acts are often drowned out with music. In other words, throughout the Golden Age of Hollywood, music represents sex or intimate romance by *replacing or implying* it. In old Hollywood films, kisses are often accompanied by symphonic flourishes as the camera focuses elsewhere or the screen fades to black. In Alfred Hitchcock's *To Catch a Thief* (1955), for example, the nondiegetic orchestra swells as Grace Kelly and Cary Grant's kiss is covered aurally by music and visually by fireworks, a heavy-handed metaphor implying that other romantic activities were to follow.

Due to the inability to access the necessary sound-recording and syncing equipment without studio support, however, films of a more pornographic nature (that is, films with the primary objective to sexually stimulate the audience) remained primarily silent into the 1960s. Williams (2008, 88) describes these films as "excruciatingly silent" and performed and shot to achieve "maximum visibility." However, *Playboy* magazine and other male-oriented periodicals informed men living in bachelor pads of "what music to listen to, clothes to wear, alcohol to drink, and furniture to buy in order to participate in a hip version of professional-class taste culture," so one could reasonably imagine hearing the jazz, lounge music, exotica, or blue comedy albums prescribed by *Playboy* magazine played in the background in high fidelity while these films played on film projectors with no sonic fidelity at all (Sewell 2011, 4).

In 1965, Super 8 film was introduced, allowing home movies—and pornography—to be recorded much more easily. The ability to record with sound without the support of professional filmmakers or studios arrived in 1973, when Super 8 film started to include a magnetic strip on the side of the film. However, the filmmaking process was not democratized overnight. Super 8 film still had to be processed, and since they could not take their films to a nearby photo development store for processing, pornographers had to develop their own film at home. Percussive tracks, such as bongo-heavy exotica music and funk music often associated with pornography of that era, seemed to be best at withstanding the chemicals and cutting, splicing, dubbing, and other forms of manipulation involved in the editing process, as they "tended to best survive any warping or projection glitches" (Bieschke 2015, para 10).

The popularity of the grindhouse exploitation film in the 1960s and 1970s gave rise to the sexploitation film, creating a public audience for softcore, low-budget independent films, in what is known as the "Golden Age of Porn." The soundtracks for these films were often copied from other films or lifted from popular records and used without permission; directors would use this copyrighted music with a sense of impunity, betting on the fact that the copyright holders would be too embarrassed to pursue legal action. "Ennio Morricone was the big one" recounts William Margold, prominent adult film director of the time. "There was something about his soundtrack work that was just so visceral, but also could be very funky. If you ran most of the adult films from the '70s through a program, most of the music would come up Morricone. We thought he would get that we were giving him a whole new audience. Either that or he would too embarrassed to go after us" (Bieschke 2015, para. 20). The gay film historian Evan Purchall explains how the soundtracks for gay pornography were purloined in much the same way:

> There was a lot of money being put into [straight porns of the 1970s]. . . . A lot of people seeing them. So the filmmakers would use library tracks or private musicians to compose original scores. The gay side was like Poverty Row, and very low-budget. The filmmakers knew that people would never admit to seeing these movies, so they had no problem stealing whatever music they wanted. You'll hear The Beatles, Pink Floyd, a lot of disco, even Steve Reich. (cited in Caporale 2020, para. 13)

As the boundaries between sexploitation and Blaxploitation became more blurred, so too did the boundaries between popular film and pornography. Leading funk musicians contributed tracks to Blaxploitation films, which were often marketed for their explicitness; for example, director Melvin van Peebles advertised *Sweet Sweetback's Baadasssss Song* (1971), as having been "rated X by an all-white jury" (cited in Koven 2010, 14–15). Additionally, White Americans would grow to associate funk music with sex, thanks in part to sexually themed songs such as James Brown's "Get Up (I Feel Like Being A) Sex Machine" and funk's relatively explicit lyrics. Funk music was used so widely that it has become a sort of synecdoche for all pornographic music, where "Bow-chicka-wow-wow" (or variations thereof) is still used as onomatopoetic shorthand for nearly any adult-themed content.[2] In an interview about his memoir, *Confessions of an Ivy League Pornographer*, Sam Benjamin describes the music of 1970s pornography:

> 70's porn music sounds like a high-school band performing a soundtrack to a disco musical that should have never existed—so bad, it's bad. If you took the worst genre in the history of contemporary American music (funk-disco—narrowly edging out big-pants trance for sheer lack of imagination) and paid a group of mustachioed degenerates sixty bucks apiece to "jam" for a couple of hours so you could give your badly-lit, badly-shot, ill-conceived, glorified stag film the non-diegetic musical punch it didn't need in the first place, you'd end up with typical 70's porn music. And yes, that's exactly what happened. (Allen 2009, para. 4)

The soundtracks of adult films in each following decade added genres to match the musical tastes of adults coming of age at that time: rock, easy listening and sultry smooth jazz played on an alto or soprano saxophone, and synth pop in the 1980s. Once "hardcore" pornography was effectively legalized in 1987, "harder" genres, such as hip-hop, metal, and house music became dominant in porn soundtracks in the late 1980s, 1990s, and 2000s. Describing the music of 1980s pornography as colorfully as he does music of the preceding decade, Benjamin continues:

> 80's porn music reeks of repetition, stupidity, loneliness, unoriginality, and unrelenting sadness—and that's a great thing. 80's soundtracks actually speak to the visceral experience of masturbation itself: it's like the dull, throbbing death-beat of your heart in your head as you forsake real life and real partners for yet another unhealthy, scared wank. 70's porn music is busy; conversely, 80's porn music is solitary. The advent of the analog synth meant that one lonely loser could score your whole movie for you. (Allen 2009, para. 8)

Of course, the ability to make music with synthesizers and drum machines would help to eliminate the need for a band of musicians to perform a pornographic film's score, ostensibly making it possible for a single person to write, perform, and record the music, mirroring the shift from watching pornographic film with a group of people in public theaters and stag parties as in previous decades to more private viewing at home on VHS tapes and cable TV.

Technological advancements and the ability to easily edit film and its accompanying soundtrack have made sexuality on film more hyperreal than ever before. Eric Warner, sound editor for porn studio Kink.com, explains that he records with a single camera microphone, and even it picks up too much sound. "A lot of my job as sound editor is actually removing sounds," such as director's instructions and natural sounds that viewers may not find sexy. During postproduction, Warner adds "natural" sounds to make the scene more vivid: "skin slaps, gasps, moans, fabric rustling, palms rubbing down a face" (Bieschke 2015, para. 36). And as filmmaking and editing technology has developed to allow pornographers to easily produce sexually explicit content, the need for large production teams was reduced. With the advent of videotape, studios could churn out more content more quickly and cheaply, and distribution via the internet has only made this process even faster. Likewise, the growing libraries of stock music available online has greatly reduced the need for composers to write bespoke music for films to which people arguably pay little attention, especially once videotape, and now the internet, returned watching pornography to a primarily at-home activity. And with the advent of software such as Final Cut and iMovie, the proliferation of adult-themed YouTube-style sites online that make porn simple—and often free—to access, and a resurgence in the popularity of amateur content, usually distributed online through websites such as pornhub.com and onlyfans.com, the budget for studio-produced pornography continues to shrink.

And because romance and sex have been among the primary plot points of much of the media we consume, these musical techniques from erotic film and pornography developed into metaphors, tropes, and clichés we now associate with love and love-making. For example, the saxophone has become closely associated with sex and sensuality in contemporary media, likely beginning from its use in playing jazz and R&B music in burlesque houses and brothels, to the saxophones of film noir that accompanied various femmes fatales who walked into the offices of grizzled detectives looking for assistance, and later through its use in pornographic films in the 1970s–1990s. Smooth jazz and pop songs that heavily feature saxophone, such as Wham!'s "Careless Whisper" (1984) have become cliché tropes in and of themselves. From Jessica Rabbit's leitmotif in *Who Framed Roger Rabbit?* (1988), to the music that accompanies Flynn Rider's "smolder" in *Tangled* (2010), sultry saxophone licks have become aural shorthand for "sex" and "sexy" (or at least incredibly flirty).

It is worth noting that music's connection to dance also intertwines the aural with amorous, romantic, and/or sexually charged movement to various degrees of public acceptability, depending on the culture, era, and a very wide range of contexts. Coming-of-age religious ceremonies and ritualistic initiations into adulthood, courtly dances, high school sock hops, wedding dances, twerking, burlesque, exotic dance, and other forms of live adult entertainment all involve music and thus potentially lead observers and participants to draw referential connections to types and genres of music and to other expressions of our identity beyond (or at the intersection of) our sexuality, such as gender, race, class, (dis)ability, and so on. For example, electric guitar riffs that mimic stereotypical 1980s glam rock music are used in the TV program *Scrubs* (2001–2010) any time the show's protagonist, JD, meets an attractive woman, capitalizing on the fact that the genre is stereotypically associated with exotic dancing, strip clubs, and music video vixens.[3]

(Sonic) Representations of Sex and Sexuality in Video Games

Although it is important to understand how sex and sexuality are represented through music in various media (outlined above through the history of mainstream and pornographic film and spilling over into TV and animation), video games differ in that they are not passively experienced. Instead, the interaction inherent to video games can potentially render sex and sexuality as performative, with the player dictating if and when sex and sexuality are implicitly or explicitly expressed, seen, *and heard* on screen. In her groundbreaking essay on the study of sexuality in video games, Mia Consalvo (2003) discusses how the fact that human beings manipulate characters to perform actions within a game also implies the ability to imply a gender and sexual orientation to their avatar: "How a player's input alters or reinforces what is presented in the game—how static representations become dynamic—becomes much more complicated, especially as more queer readings arise, and the heterosexuality implied in the games either fails to matter/materialize, or can be subverted in interesting ways" (173). These "static" representations refer to the default genders and sexualities found within in-game relationships in most video games, and in most games that feature romantic or sexual content, a monogamous heterosexual relationship between a cisgender pair of characters is the *only* option. Thus, video games provide us with seemingly countless examples of what Adrienne Rich (1980) calls "compulsory heterosexuality," referring to the fact that heterosexuality is not only the most common form of sexuality but it is considered to be the default; a person is presumed to be straight until they claim another sexuality or act in a way that suggests otherwise, while other sexualities are ignored, devalued, criminalized, or otherwise punished. Further, compulsory heterosexuality leads society to socialize us to prioritize social relationships with the opposite sex in the hope that they develop into heteronormative romantic relationships which ideally lead to child-bearing sexual relationships within the context of patriarchal marriage (Rich 1980). Under compulsory heterosexuality, women are conditioned by society to be the objects of male desire, and men are conditioned to desire them, so, then, default heterosexuality is often the only option.[4]

Until recently, heterosexuality was also default and compulsory for video game players, and the narrative of many games centered around brave male avatars saving princesses, defending the honor of their (female) love interest, or winning (or buying or taking by force) the admiration and affection of female NPCs throughout the game. Some more recent games that give players the illusion of being able to choose other sexualities; however, their narratives still center around heterosexual relationships. The game scholar Casey Hart (2015, 158) calls these options a "false-choice," noting that while "players believe they have choices in how to pursue sex or relationships within games, the game dynamics limit these choices and their outcomes." Even though "gender preference" became available in *The Sims 2*, which determined a Sim's sexuality based on a players actions (namely, the gender of the other characters with which they most often flirt), the game's mechanics are shaped by player's action, thus limiting a player's romantic and/or sexual prospects. And because heterosexuality is foregrounded as default, some players may not even know homosexuality or bisexuality is an option within the early games in *The Sims* series, since player action is often required to trigger the option and is rarely the default option. The transgender game designer Anna Anthropy describes this phenomenon in an interview with an unnamed staff writer for the *San Francisco Examiner*, describing the ways in which some games offer variations to the sexual norm require players to "opt in," remarking, "As queer people, we can watch [game characters] roll around with a dude if you press the 'gay button.' . . . But we shouldn't trust corporations with images that represent our lives" (San Francisco Examiner 2013, para. 4). However, the fact that video game sexuality relies on a "choice" could potentially lead players to mistakenly conflate in-game choices to real-life sexualities and believe that sexuality is essentially a "preference" and that deviations from "normal" heterosexuality are the result of a choice, so having protagonists within video games with a wide variety of sexual identities that are the default option and on which the game's narrative is based is important.

The Sims and Sex: A Case Study in Sonic Representations of Sex in Video Games

The sonification of sex acts has a long history in video games, reaching back into the infancy of console gaming in the 1970s and 1980s—despite the fact that the audio capabilities of these often puerile and absurd games were quite limiting. However, even though sound accompanied in-game action, many of the adult games of this era were relatively music-less. For example, in *X-Man* (Universal Gamex 1983) for the Atari 2600, if a player was able to get their character—the vague, boxy semblance of a man with a not-so-vague erection—through a Pac-Man-esque maze to a door in its center while avoiding teeth, crabs, and scissors (all of which presumably can inflict harm to his penis), the player is rewarded with an opportunity to simulate sex. By moving the joystick back and forth with increasing speed, they can raise a "Sexual Excitement Meter" and help the "Sexy Blonde" on screen reach climax.[5] A simple, singular pulse wave can be heard with each thrust (i.e., joystick movement), perhaps symbolizing the squeaking of a moving bed, and an ascending, pulse wave chromatic scale indicates the increasing level of sexual satisfaction. At the moment of orgasm, the game characters flash various colors to an eruption of white noise (another reference to Hitchcock's fireworks, albeit a less obvious one). Unlike the passive sexual interaction of *The Sims*, *X-Man* players are actively controlling the sexual activity and the accompanying sound effects are heard in real time as a form of sonic feedback to indicate success within the game. *Beat 'Em and Eat 'Em* (American Multiple Industries 1992) has similar mechanics to *Space Invaders* (Taito 1976), but rather than moving a laser cannon across the bottom of the

FIGURE 23.1 Modified "Charge" Bugle Call in *Custer's Revenge* (1982) (in-game sound approximately one half-step lower than written).
Upon reaching the other side, he rapes a racist caricature of a native woman tied to a pole to the sound of the Tommy Walker's "Charge" fanfare often heard at sporting events.

FIGURE 23.2 Tommy Walker's "Charge" fanfare.

screen to avoid bullets from spaceships, players move naked women in order to catch semen in their mouths as it falls from a man masturbating on a rooftop; after a rising sequence of tones to indicate an orgasm, players only hear singular pulse wave tones to signify a successful catch or higher tones when drops of ejaculate hit the ground. *Custer's Revenge* (American Multiple Industries 1982) is a sinister, adult-themed side-scroller for the Atari 2600 from the same era, in which the titular character (George Custer, the leader of the American cavalry during the Battle of Little Bighorn of 1876) charges naked across the screen at the sound of a modified version of the official military "Charge" bugle call played by pulse waves while avoiding arrows raining down from the sky (sonically represented by 8-bit drum beats; see Figures 23.1 and 23.2).[6]

Leisure Suit Larry in the Land of the Lounge Lizards (Sierra On-Line 1987) is relatively silent except for occasional sound effect, but players hear 8-bit renditions of "99 Bottles of Beer" in a corner store and "Love Me Tender," played in homage to Elvis Presley in a wedding chapel scene. And when the player wins the entire game by helping Larry loses his virginity to a woman in a hot tub, John Phillip Sousa's "Stars and Stripes Forever" (1896) can be heard, but no sex can be seen.

As video game technology developed, 8-bit music and sound effects were replaced with 16-bit audio files, and thus, the sounds of sex and sexy music in games became more realistic—enabling easier references to musical tropes from mainstream film and pornography. For example, in Brian Eno and Cliff Martinez's procedural score for *Spore* (Electronic Arts 2008), the music itself seems to reproduce, replicating itself and evolving over time as the player progresses through each stage of the game. But rather than using the same original ambient-electronic music for the mating ritual of the game's creatures, the game's developers opted to use pre-existing, nonprocedural light orchestral easy listening/lounge music from the 1950s and early 1960s. Players travel to nearby nests hoping to attract a mate, using a mating call if necessary. Once they find an attracted mate, they court by shaking their bottoms at each other as lounge music plays. The four possible pieces that play, "Après Ski" by Frank Chacksfield, "Spring Love" by Robin Cree, "The Lovers" by Roy Marsh, and "5th Avenue" by Ray Denny, can all be found on a stock music library album by West One Music called "Lounge: 60s and 70s Easy Listening" (WOM034), released in 2004.[7] Although Chacksfield's contribution is the only song of the four that seems to have existed in the 1960s, all seem to rely on the Space Age bachelor trope, where this music functions as mood music to encourage a sexual encounter that ultimately results in an egg.

Sonified sex acts can also appear as part of a game's mechanics at times when sex acts are traded as currency for in-game advantages or presented as a reward. For example, when players engage in sex within *Mass Effect* (Microsoft Game Studios 2007), they earn an achievement trophy called "Paramour," earning them points and increasing their online ranking. Likewise, games in the *Fable* series award players trophies and achievement points for having sex with individuals or multiple characters at a time by hosting an orgy and for watching others have sex. In *Grand Theft Auto: San Andreas* (2005), players can engage in side quests between larger missions, some of which include CJ, the game's protagonist, taking various women on dates to earn a better reputation with each one in exchange for benefits, such as the ability to use her car, and depending on her occupation, receiving awards and special abilities from the encounter. If the date goes well, in addition to these rewards, and once he has earned enough relationship points, CJ gets invited into a girlfriend's house for some "coffee," which is code for sex. If the player chooses to take her up on her offer and goes inside for sex, under normal circumstances, CJ goes inside while the game designers provide an *osculum interruptum* and do not show the sex act visually, but they leave the sounds of sex for the player to hear—although these sounds are muffled since the player views the scene from an outside perspective. However, the controversial "hot coffee" mod to the game allowed players to accompany CJ into the house and see, as well as hear, him engaging in intercourse.

Sex within *The Sims* games is almost entirely a sonic experience, as *osculum interruptum* is employed by game designers who moved all intercourse under the bed covers. Players who purchased the "Livin' Large" expansion pack (called "Livin' It Up" in Europe) for the original *The Sims* game, or those with the deluxe edition, could have sex if they purchased the "Vibromatic Heart Bed," which could be activated by depositing in-game currency. Once two sims undress and get under the blankets, sounds of amorous Simlish (the fictional gibberish language spoken by the game's characters), laughing, barking, and purring can be heard. Similarly, sims can have sex in a heart-shaped hot tub, but the intercourse takes place underwater, and as one might expect, the vocalizations take on a gurgling quality. Sex in *The Sims 2* is a markedly louder affair. If cinematics is enabled, sex is initiated by selecting the appropriate menu option: a cut-scene plays where the screen is narrowed to a wide screen perspective and funk music begins to play—a tongue-in-cheek homage to 1970s erotic films. One character then squeezes the buttocks of the other, causing an absurd squeaky toy sound and the recipient of the squeeze to shout "Woo hoo!," an exclamation used throughout *The Sims* series as coded language to refer to intercourse. The amorous vocalizations and laughter become much more maniacal. The camera quickly cuts away from the action, and players can hear various other noises depending on the environment, such as rocking bedpost noises or splashing water. Near the end of the encounter, the green jewel that floats over playable characters' heads ejaculates sparks from its tip (a nod of sorts to Hitchcock's fireworks mentioned previously), accompanied by cartoonish noises. Sex sounds in *The Sims 3* are more subdued, represented sonically with vocalizations and harp arpeggios. In *The Sims 4*, intercourse is accompanied by 1960s-style easy listening orchestral music, while the game's characters moan and laugh, and, depending on location, incidental banging and other environmental noises caused by sex can be heard. In the "Vacation" expansion pack, the same music plays, but it is modified to match the locations of various expansion packs, such as using Japanese instruments for the hot springs in the "Snowy Escape" expansion pack, Hawaiian instruments in the "Island Living" pack, and so on. For the "Vampires" expansion pack, the music is rearranged in a minor key and features pipe organ, accordion, and otherwise stereotypically "scary" instrumentation.[8]

Sounding Gay: A Case Study in Sonic Representations of Sexuality in Video Games

Working with definitions that center primarily around genitalia and their use, one would be hard-pressed to find examples of sexuality in video games without focusing exclusively on the visual and sonic cues indicating that in-game characters are engaging in sensual acts on-screen. And because this definition regards sexuality as experiential, body oriented, and genitally oriented, it would be impossible to know their level of arousal without visual or aural indications of their corporeal reactions. Subtle sonic indicators of sexuality within a video game would ultimately take a back seat to visual simulations of intercourse and its associated dialog and sound effects. But that does not necessarily mean that the sonic representation of sexuality is impossible. The remainder of this chapter serves as a case study that focuses on the representation of homosexuality in video games through music and sound, focusing on voice acting and musical genre as key indicators of same-sex attraction to men and homosexual eroticism.

In his 2014 documentary film *Do I Sound Gay?*, director David Thorpe examines the stereotypes surrounding the speech patterns of gay men, investigating what it means to have a "gay voice" or to "sound gay." While the vocal stereotypes explored in the film seem to be a fixture in popular culture, they remain a subject for derision and a trigger for bullying and harassment, often causing gay men to internalize homophobia and resort to hypermasculine sonic expressions of their identity. These vocal stereotypes, along with other sonic markers of male homosexuality, are often exploited in the aural representations of LGBTQIA+ characters in video games. Clichéd, and/or hackneyed voice acting, for example, or stereotypically "gay" music, such as disco, EDM, or dance music, serve as sonic shorthand for the gay community. Here, I consider the presence or absence of these vocal and musical stereotypes and tropes in video games with overtly gay themes, such as *Coming Out on Top* (Obscurasoft 2014), *Dream Daddy: A Dad Dating Simulator* (Game Grumps 2017), and various games by experimental game designer Robert Yang. I further discuss their value as camp and as vehicles for positive and/or political representations of gay men in video games.

In 1994, Rudolph Gaudio became one of the first of many linguists to search for differing pitch properties in the vocal utterances of gay and straight men. He found that although people could correctly identify the sexuality of the speaker, the identification did not correlate with pitch—indicating that other factors such as phonetics and speech patterns also play a role. And such an assumption about the speaker's sexuality overlooks variations present in non-English speakers, and even in subgroups of gay English speakers. Furthermore, gay men often stretch their own voices beyond their physical acoustical qualities to speak at a lower pitch in order to meet cultural expectations of masculinity, often in an attempt to fit in or conceal their sexual identity; nevertheless, high voices and falsetto singing are still prominent tropes in the sonic representation of gay men.

In *The Queen's Throat: Opera, Homosexuality, and the Mystery of Desire*, Wayne Koestenbaum (1993) admits to having "always feared the falsetto: voice of the bogeyman, voice of the unregenerate fag; voice of horror and loss and castration; floating voice, vanishing voice. With a grimace I remember freak pop singer Tiny Tim tiptoeing through the tulips with his ukulele" (165). This, of course, is not true for every listener or singer, and many popular musicians, such as Marvin Gaye, Justin Timberlake, Justin Bieber, and Adam Levine sing in the falsetto register without appearing to general audiences as either freakish or feminine. However, as with drag, BDSM, and other subversive expressions of identity prevalent in the gay community, strategic identities and their public performance or expression have long been important sites of political action and gay liberation and affected effeminacy and camp are tools to express these identities. The musicologist and media studies scholar Edward Miller writes:

> In dance music, openly gay singer Sylvester in the 70s, and later Jimmy Somerville, used the falsetto voice to express not only passion but also political freedom. Their voices exhibited a way of moving beyond restraints, and traditional definitions of masculinity. But make no mistake, their voices expressed lust and had nothing to do with tiptoeing through tulips. Instead their falsetto iterated a kind of affirming cruising on the dance floor. Sylvester sounded "mighty real" in his falsetto, and Somerville articulated a pride in his identity through his vocal choices. (Miller 2003, para. 13)

An excellent example of falsetto as feminizing can be found in the theme song of the game *Dream Daddy: A Dad Dating Simulator*. Inspired by the Tumblr page "DILFs of Disneyland," this narrative game invites players to assume a male avatar and meet other single dads in the neighborhood to which he and his daughter have recently moved. The theme song is composed by the electronic musician Will Wiesenfield, known by the stage name Baths. The theme song is tongue-in-cheek, and purposefully sounds both dreamy and cheesy—as if it were a parody of an early 1990s doll commercial. When asked about the creative process, Baths even tweeted that he "couldn't stop laughing and fucked up so many takes." The lilt of the word "Daddy" at the end of the opening phrase is both provocative and dripping with camp. The background music within the game shares a similarly saccharine aesthetic, both in the chiptune songs and pizzicato string ditties that accompany some of the more quotidian events in the game and in the electric piano pads that can be heard during dates and in other romantic scenes.

Interestingly, *Dream Daddy* is primarily text-based, with very little recorded dialogue beyond various vocalizations (such as "Huh?," "Hmm.," and "Oh!"); however, each dateable daddy offers verbal feedback at the end of each date that can potentially give players a little more insight to their personalities and gender expressions. For example, Craig "Fitness Dad" Cahn is an old college friend of the player and can be heard saying things such as "Nice!" "That was an amazing date!" and "That was a gold-medal performance for sure!"—all of which can be heard as being particularly masculine. The same is true for the date responses from Mat, Robert, and other characters with cis-masculine appearances, and even some daddies, such as Joseph, whose pink shirt and preppy sweater tied around his neck can be read as a little more stereotypically effeminate. Conversely, Damien "Goth Dad" Bloodmarch exudes much more camp and stereotypically gay traits, most notably in his obsession with the Victorian Era and his campy vampiric clothing. His speech is also both hyperarticulated and precise, and very sibilant, which are stereotypical speech patterns of gay men, and he uses slang terminology associated with gay culture (which itself comes from the Black and Latino Ballroom scene); this can be heard clearly at the end of a successful date when Damien says, "Are you familiar with the works of Corey Feldman? He simply *slayed* in The Lost Boys."

Coming Out on Top (Obscurasoft 2014), a similar dating simulator—although admittedly, one much more focused on sex—takes the opposite approach. There is an obvious hypermasculine aesthetic echoed throughout the visuals and narrative of the game—a masculine character uses a dating app to seek out dates and sex at masculine places (such as the gym, football field, wrestling ring, etc.), almost exclusively with other masculine characters. Unlike *Dream Daddy*, which allows for a wide variety of body types and shapes (even, notably, allowing for trans-male avatars), the menu for *Coming Out on Top* only features one customization option, called "Hair and Beards," which allows you to specify which characters have facial and body hair (or not). The music of *Coming Out on Top* also plays into hypermasculine tropes, such as using electric guitar-heavy blues music in the bar scene to represent the fact that characters are not meeting in a typical gay nightclub with flashing lights and dance music, but instead, in what looks more like a cigar lounge decorated almost completely in wood and leather. When the player brings men back to their bedroom at the end of a date, or for a hookup, they hear funk music playing to signal that sex is imminent. The theme music, which plays automatically when a player opens the title screen, is the 1990s queercore band Pansy Division's "Luv, Luv, Luv" (1998), which helps the game's designers cash in on what could be viewed as the hypermasculine and antisaccharine aesthetic of punk music.

Reminding players that "sound is important" as they begin to play many of his gay-themed experimental games, Robert Yang places the hypermasculine representational politics of American gay culture at the forefront of the player's attention both visually and sonically. *The Tearoom* (2017), a historical nickname once used by gay men to refer to public restrooms that were used for sex, is set in a highway rest stop in Mansfield, Ohio, the site of a notorious police sting operation in the summer of 1962. Based on the sociological research of Laud Humphrey, published in his book *Tearoom Trade: Impersonal Sex in Public Places* (1970), the game highlights the injustices perpetrated by local police departments of the time, which would set up sting operations to entrap gay men and imprison them under antiquated sodomy laws. As a protest for having his previous games banned from Twitch, Yang created this cruising simulator, replacing the penises of any male companions with guns (which, for some reason, are more palatable and less offensive to mainstream game designers and publishers). Although four of their tracks are used throughout the game, the only music that can really be heard during gameplay is "God Dammit Bill," a song by a Vancouver-based band called The Lonesome Billies, whose sound is reminiscent of the honkytonk, western roadhouse music of the 1960s and 1970s and in a style similar to Johnny Cash, Hank Williams, and other especially masculine performers of this genre.

Players hear the song throughout gameplay, first as diegetic music playing from what sounds like small radio or public address system. But as the player kneels next to a urinal to take the bait of the undercover officer, the music becomes nondiegetic and much more audible, and players can much more clearly understand the song's lyrics, in which the singer shares his disappointment with his friend, who keeps falling off the proverbial wagon, not for lack of trying, but because the struggle is futile and the wagon has "got no wheels." In his artist statement about the game, Yang discusses how he was keen to include music by The Lonesome Billies in this game, both because country music was somewhat underrepresented in video games and because their music in particular evoked a 1970s "outlaw country" aesthetic that he argues "has some rural working class roots (unlike 2015-era 'bro country') while also feeling a little pop and punk" (Yang 2017).

Yang's *Rinse and Repeat* (2015) is a shower fantasy simulator in which players are asked to wash another man in a public shower. The character being washed is rendered visually and sonically as hypermasculine, with a hairy, muscular body, and is inexplicably wearing aviator sunglasses into the shower (perhaps to make the encounter more anonymous). Throughout the interaction, this character interjects phrases such as "Yo Pal!," "Man!," "Work that shit . . .," and "fuck yes" with especially macho inflection. Once the washing is completed, the player's performance is rated with phrases such as, "That was great, guy," "You did real good, bro," and "I love your touch, pal," with especially stilted voice acting that seems poorly executed on purpose, with the masculine colloquial vocatives/hailnames seemingly added as an unnatural afterthought. Yang discusses the absurdity of this speech when discussing updates to the game in 2018:

> I'm glad I didn't invest any time into naturalizing the hunk's robotic speech patterns; I enjoy the dissonance between his robotic performance of masculinity versus his absurd muscular body. Today, his performance reminds me of the stereotypical hunky gay Instagram guy ("instagay") who seems to live inside their own video game, and in many respects, this game is about how you must never actually attempt to consummate your online thirst. (Yang 2018)

At the climax of the interaction, players hear a deluge of water, created by Yang by mixing together several tracks of someone drowning he collected from FreeSound.org, symbolically drowning the object of desire in expectations he is unable to meet. The player suddenly snaps back to reality, and the once confident man you have been washing timidly and apologetically mumbles, "dude, I can't do this anymore, sorry," and walks away, leaving the player to look down at the avatar's own body, which is noticeably different in both fitness level and race from the hunk's body.

According to Yang, *Rinse and Repeat* is a study in the erotic possibilities fluid dynamics simulation design, inspired by the music video for avant-rap duo Boody and Leıf's "Soda" (2013), in which "two hunks spray themselves with gushing fluids [soda], suggestively shooting up from the bottom of the frame" (Yang 2015). The dreamy, synth-pop music that players hear during this fantasy simulation is "Vyvanse," by the Toronto-based band Grounders, and the lyrics—"Making me believe . . . Show him, show him joy / Finally sensing"—speak directly to the sensuality of the game's mechanics and objectives.

Conclusion

Games can be a powerful tool for enacting our real-life identity and personhood; as the game scholar James Paul Gee (2003) argues, "games recruit identities and encourage identity work and reflection on identities" (49). The same can be said of the games discussed above when taken at face value, as is the case with games in *The Sims* series, where sexual identities are chosen and/or enacted by a player, or critiqued through satire or farce, as is the case in Robert Yang's games. And as we have seen in games such as *Custer's Revenge* or *Grand Theft Auto: San Andreas*, video games can also serve as a perverted version of Lisa Nakamura's "identity tourism," where players can enact rape fantasies without having to deal with any of the real-life consequences.[9] And as time progresses, the representational politics surrounding various identities in games—and the relationship these identities share with game audiences—are playing a progressively larger role in the way players understand and appreciate a game's narrative, mechanics, and reception. Although sex and sexuality can be especially private parts of our identity, finding ways for players to explore them though video games and other interactive media in constructive and healthy ways grows increasingly important, as do the ways in which game developers sonically represent these sexual identities and activities.

Notes

1. See Horowitz and Newcomb (2001) and Savin-Williams (2011).
2. This trope features heavily in an Axe Body Spray advertising campaign launched in March 2007.

3. This connection comes as no surprise since music plays a central role in both the aesthetic and raison d'être of strip clubs. As journalist Susan Shepherd points out:

   > Strip clubs literally can't exist without music. Because without it, there is nothing for strippers to strip to. From hair tossing to twerking, the soundtrack is what powers the moves that make a striptease work. The exotic dancers of the '80s inspired and were inspired by hair metal, creating pop culture iconography with a much wider reach thanks to MTV: "Girls, Girls, Girls," "Cherry Pie," "Pour Some Sugar On Me": this was specifically stripper-identified pop music gone very much mainstream. (Shephard 2013, para. 1)

4. The game scholar Meghan Blythe Adams explains:

   > While the compulsory is a requirement that can be resisted, the compulsive heterosexuality of the game is impossible to avoid without exiting the game entirely, making games unique spaces in which player actions can be not merely privileged to varying degrees but literally unavailable as an option altogether. . . . Every potential choice the player can make is limited by what the game designers see fit to include in the game. It is this submission to the game in order to play it that makes the proscribed heterosexuality of the classic game compulsive rather than compulsory. (Adams 2015, 42)

5. The text from the instruction booklet for *X-Man*, in which gameplay is described, can be found online: https://atariage.com/manual_html_page.php?SoftwareLabelID=601. Accessed January 3, 2022.
6. Somewhat ironically, this bugle call is also used to signify "Man Overboard."
7. The game's producers give these songs new titles for the game: "You and Me Are Perfect Together," "Let's End This On a High Note," "Sweet Love to the Lady," and "At the End of a Long Day" respectively.
8. It should be noted that in most games in *The Sims* series, Simlish murmurings among the couple always seem to indicate through inflection that a request for consent is made and consent being given, that sex is occurring, and postcoital aftercare and emotional nurturing is offered.
9. See Nakamura (2005).

References

Adams, Meghan Blythe. 2015. "Renegade Sex: Compulsory Sexuality and Charmed Magic Circles in the Mass Effect Series." *Loading . . . The Journal of the Canadian Game Studies Association* 9 (14): 40–54.

Allen, Mark. 2009. "Why 70's Porn Music Was Never 'Classic,' Why 80's Porn Music Is Far Superior (Even Though It's Much Worse), and the Disingenuous Lie of the 'Bow-Chicka-Bow-Wow' Phrase." *WFMU's Beware of the Blog*, June 22, 2009. https://blog.wfmu.org/freeform/2009/06/how-dare-you-other-bloggers-look-at-the-title-of-my-post-here-in-the-typepad-program-before-it-goes-.html.

Bieschke, Marke. 2015. "Sex Tracks and Porno Grooves: An Intro to Erotic Film Music." Red Bull Music Academy. https://web.archive.org/web/20190329165756/http://daily.redbullmusicacademy.com/specials/2015-porn-soundtracks-feature.

Brathwaite, Brenda. 2007. *Sex in Video Games*. Boston: Charles River Media.

Caporale, Micco. 2020. "The Funky Tale of How 'Bow-Chicka-Wow-Wow' Came to Mean 'It's Doin' It Time.'" *Mel Magazine*, July 12, 2020. https://melmagazine.com/en-us/story/the-funky-tale-of-how-bow-chicka-wow-wow-came-to-mean-its-doin-it-time.

Collins, Rebecca, Steven Martino, Marc Elliott, and Angela Miu. 2011. "Relationships between Adolescent Sexual Outcomes and Exposure to Sex in Media: Robustness to Propensity-Based Analysis." *Developmental Psychology* 47:585–591.

Consalvo, Mia. 2003. "Hot Dates and Fairy-Tale Romances: Studying Sexuality in Video Games." In *The Video Game Theory Reader*, edited by Mark J. P. Wolf and Bernard Perron, 193–216. New York: Routledge.

Gaudio, Rudolf Pell. 1994. "Sounding Gay: Pitch Properties in the Speech of Gay and Straight Men." *American Speech* 69:30–57.

Harper, Davis. 2014. "The Timeless Art of Porno Music." *Vice*, April 4, 2014. https://www.vice.com/en/article/69vp3r/the-timeless-art-of-porno-music.

Hart, Casey. 2015. "Sexual Favors: Using Casual Sex as Currency within Video Games." In *Rated M for Mature: Sex and Sexuality in Video Games*, edited by Matthew Wysocki and Evan W. Lauteria, 147–160. New York: Bloomsbury Academic Press.

Horowitz, Janna L., and Michael D. Newcomb. 2001. "A Multidimensional Approach to Homosexual Identity." *Journal of Homosexuality* 42:1–19.

Humphreys, Laud. 1970. *Tearoom Trade: Impersonal Sex in Public Places*. London: Duckworth.

Koestenbaum, Wayne. 1994. *The Queen's Throat: Opera, Homosexuality, and the Mystery of Desire*. New York: Poseidon Press.

Koven, Mikel J. 2010. *Blaxploitation Films*. Harpenden: Oldcastle Books.

Miller, Edward D. 2003. "The Nonsensical Truth of the Falsetto Voice: Listening to Sigur Rós." *Popular Musicology Online* 2. http://www.popular-musicology-online.com/issues/02/miller.html.

Nakamura, Lisa. 2005. "Race In/For Cyberspace: Identity Tourism and Racial Passing on the Internet." Works and Days 13 (1–2): 181–193.

Padgett, Esra Soraya. 2019. "Tracing Porn Soundtracks from the Inga Films to Pornhub." *Cultured Magazine*, June 21, 2019. https://www.culturedmag.com/article/2019/06/21/porn-soundtracks.

Paglia, Camille. 1990. *Sexual Personae: Art and Decadence from Nefertiti to Emily Dickinson*. New Haven: Yale University Press.

Rich, Adrienne. 1980. "Compulsory Heterosexuality and Lesbian Existence." *Signs: Journal of Women in Culture and Society* 5 (4): 631–660.

San Francisco Examiner. 2013. "At San Francisco Convention, Gay Gamers Are Diversifying the Industry." August 5, 2013. https://www.sfexaminer.com/news/at-san-francisco-convention-gay-gamers-are-diversifying-the-industry/?oid=2535082.

Savin-WIlliams, Ritch C. 2011. "Identity Development among Sexual-Minority Youth." In *Handbook of Identity Theory and Research*, Vol. 1–2, edited by Seth J. Schwartz, Koen Luyckx, and Vivian L. Vignoles, 671–689. New York: Springer Science + Business Media.

Sewell, Jessica Ellen. 2011. "Power, Sex, and Furniture: Masculinity and the Bachelor Pad in 1950s–60s America." *Occasional Papers for the School of Social Science—The Institute for Advanced Study* 43. https://www.ias.edu/sites/default/files/sss/papers/paper43.pdf.

Shepard, Susan. 2013. "Taking the Boom Out of the Boom-Boom Room: Why Are Strip Clubs Banning Rap?" Complex, December 4, 2013. https://www.complex.com/music/2013/12/strip-clubs-ban-on-rap.

Sprankle, Eric L., and Christian M. End. 2009. "The Effects of Censored and Uncensored Sexually Explicit Music on Sexual Attitudes and Perceptions of Sexual Activity." *Journal of Media Psychology: Theories, Methods, and Applications* 21:60–68.

Taylor, T. L. 2009. "The Assemblage of Play." *Games and Culture* 4 (4): 331–339.

Williams, Linda. 2008. *Screening Sex*. Durham, NC: Duke University Press.

Wright, Chrysalis L., and Michelle Craske. 2015. "Music's Influence on Risky Sexual Behaviors: Examining the Cultivation Theory." *Media Psychology Review* 9 (1). https://mprcenter.org/review/musics-influence-on-risky-sexual-behaviors-examining-the-cultivation-theory/.

Wright, Chrysalis, and Erum Qureshi. 2015. "The Relationship between Sexual Content in Music and Dating and Sexual Behaviors of Emerging Adults." *Howard Journal of Communications* 26 (3): 227–253.

Yang, Robert. 2015. "Rinse and Repeat as Cup Runneth Over." *Radiator Design Blog*, September 17, 2015. https://www.blog.radiator.debacle.us/2015/09/rinse-and-repeat.html.

Yang, Robert. 2017. "The Tearoom as a Record of Risky Business." *Radiator Design Blog*, June 29, 2017. https://www.blog.radiator.debacle.us/2017/06/the-tearoom-as-record-of-risky-business.html.

Yang, Robert. 2018. "Rinse and Repeat HD Remastered, and Three Years of Reflections and Thwarted Plans." *Radiator Design Blog*, November 19, 2018. https://www.blog.radiator.debacle.us/2018/11/remastered-on-rinse-and-repeat-hd-and.html.

Ludography

Baity, Sean. 2000. *The Sims*. Redwood City, CA: Electronic Arts. Windows/Mac OS X.

Baity, Sean.2004. *The Sims 2*. Redwood City, CA: Electronic Arts. Windows/MacOS/Game Boy Advance/GameCube/Nintendo DS, PlayStation 2/Xbox.

Baity, Sean. 2009. *The Sims 3*. Redwood City, CA: Electronic Arts. Windows/MacOS/PlayStation 3/Xbox 360/Nintendo DS/Wii/Nintendo 3DS.

Boon, Ed, and John Tobias. 1992. *Mortal Kombat*. Chicago: Midway Manufacturing. Arcade.

Houser, Dan, James Worrall, and DJ Pooh. 2005. *Grand Theft Auto: San Andreas*. New York: Rockstar Games. PlaySation 2.

Karpyshyn, Drew. 2007. *Mass Effect*. Redmond, WA: Microsoft Game Studios. Xbox 360.

Lowe, Al, et al. 1987. *Leisure Suit Larry in the Land of the Lounge Lizards*. Los Angeles: Sierra On-Line, Inc. MS-dOS/Amiga/Apple II/Apple Macintosh/Atari ST/Tandy Color Computer 3

McDonell, Terry. 1992. *Night Trap*. Irvine, CA: Sega. Sega CD.

Mystique. 1992. *Beat 'Em and Eat 'Em*, from the "Mystique Presents Swedish Erotica" series. Northridge, CA: American Multiple Industries. Atari 2600.

Mystique. 1982. *Custer's Revenge*, from the "Mystique Presents Swedish Erotica" series. Northridge, CA: American Multiple Industries. Atari 2600.

Nishikado, Tomohiro. 1976. *Space Invaders*. Tokyo: Taito Corp. Arcade/Atari 2600.

Obscura. 2014. *Coming Out on Top*. Eureka, CA: Obscurasoft. Windows/MacOS/Linux.

Roberts, Alan. 1983. *X-Man*. Los Angeles: Universal Gamex Corp. Atari 2600.

Shaw, Vernon, and Leighton Gray. 2017. *Dream Daddy: A Dad Dating Simulator*. Los Angeles: Game Grumps. Windows/macOS.

Von Mayrhauser, Danielle. 2014. *The Sims 4*. Redwood City, CA: Electronic Arts. Windows/MacOS/PlaStation4/Xbox One.

Wright, Will, et al. 2008. *Spore*. Redwood City, CA: Electronic Arts. Windows/Mac OS X.

Yang, Robert. 2015. *Rinse and Repeat*. Robert Yang. Windows/Mac OS X/Linux.

Yang, Robert. 2017. *The Tearoom*. Robert Yang. Windows/Mac OS X/Linux.

CHAPTER 24

INDIGENOUS-DESIGNED PIXELS, CIRCUITS, AND GAME MUSIC AND SOUND

KATE GALLOWAY

INTRODUCTION

WHEN I typed the phrase "Indigenous video games" into my Google search box in May 2021, my top hits included *Custer's Revenge* (1982), *This Land Is My Land* (2019), *Never Alone* (2014), *Mulaka* (2018), and *Thunderbird Strike* (2017). Only two of these hits are actually Indigenous-designed games (*Thunderbird Strike* and *Never Alone*), and one other involved a cultural consultant (*Mulaka*). Yet, this group of games—which includes the controversial and appropriative *Custer's Revenge* and *This Land Is My Land*—are homogeneously and inaccurately referred to as "Indigenous games" simply because they include Indigenous peoples as characters. This naming practice or mode of labeling by the industry erases issues of inequity, representation, sovereignty, and ways of being that we hear and see (or do not) in these games and in the broader video game industry (see LaPensée, Laiti, and Longboat 2021).[1] In recent years, however, Indigenous game developers are connecting with broader audiences in increasingly accessible ways and gaining access to new skills through specialized online workshops and tutorials that are held free-of-charge.

In 2021, the game company Gameloft redesigned the contentious educational game *Oregon Trail* for Apple Arcade, including more accurate depictions of Native Americans and 19th-century Native American life, and adjusting previous characters and storylines to eliminate harmful stereotypes and historical inaccuracies. Gameloft's redesign also involved writing new storylines and introducing playable Native American characters. T. K. Tallie (2021), a historian of colonialism, race, and indigeneity, writes of the new version, "Indigenous North Americans are no longer background characters in what was, upon reflection, a wildly solipsistic game. In historically accurate clothing, fully playable, and realized Indigenous characters respond to settlers as equals, have full dialogue, and even their own game play scenarios." Because Gameloft Brisbane creative director Jarrad Trudgen was aware there were inaccuracies in the sound design, story, visual design, and gameplay that he as a "white, middle-class Australian" would not perceive immediately as harmful and in immediate need of redesign, he sought out the culturally specific expertise he lacked and hired three Indigenous historians to consult on the redesign: Dr. Margaret Huettl, a historian at the University of Nebraska who has Lac Courte Oreilles tribal ancestors; Dr. Willy Bauer at the University of Nevada, Las Vegas, who is a citizen of the Round Valley Reservation in northern California; and Dr. Katrina Phillips, an enrolled member of the Red Cliff Band of Lake Superior Ojibwe at Macalester College (King 2021; Gershon 2021; Tallie 2021).

Trudgen's Indigenous consultant team quickly identified how *Oregon Trail*'s instrumental timbres (e.g., heavy use of flute and drums) reinforce problematic and factually flawed stereotypes of Indigenous representation as primitive societies disconnected from contemporary society (King 2021). On the flipside, when the Cook Inlet Tribal Council worked with E-Line Media/Upper One Games in the development of *Never Alone*, the cultural ambassadors for that project similarly chose not to use drums, throat singing, or archival field recordings of Iñupiat music because these soundscapes did not signify contemporary Indigenous life, and instead perpetuated the very stereotypes the project sought to repair and distance itself from. In these instances, the developers for the *Oregon Trail* reparative redesign and *Never Alone* productively attend to what the Dakota historian Philip Deloria (2004) calls the politics of "unexpectedness" in each of their respective contexts. This move was necessary, considering lingering cultural stereotypes and the deeply troubled politics of recognition where it is often the case that non-Indigenous people in positions of authority are problematically given the authorization to decide who counts as an Indigenous person and what makes Indigenous cultural production Indigenous. These stereotypes and inequitable industry power structures have direct implications for how Indigenous media arts are perceived and understood by both Indigenous and settler-descendant audiences in the 21st century. Pushing back against harmful stereotypes and challenging the status quo also means eliminating elements of gameplay that are popular with a particular demographic of players. While bows and arrows are popular weapons of choice across the contemporary game landscape (e.g., *Tomb Raider* series [1996–present], *The Last of Us* [2013]), they were omitted from the *Oregon Trail* redesign because of their historical inaccuracy. The consultants highlighted that Native American trappers at that time on the Oregon Trail would use a rifle, and a popular combat game mechanic was not more important than eliminating an outdated stereotype from the game.

This chapter explores Indigenous-made video games, such as *Terra Nova* (Maize Longboat [Kanien'kehá:ka] and Ray Caplin [Mi'gmaq], 2019), *Thunderbird Strike* (Elizabeth LaPensée [Anishinaabe], 2017), and *Hill Agency: PURITY/decay* (Meagan Byrne [Âpihtawikosisân-Métis], 2023), that push back against extractive and colonialist modes of cultural exchange. These games use sound in processes of cultural and artistic expression, self-determination, cultural sovereignty, Indigenous futurism, experiences rooted in human–nonhuman relationships, and Indigenous communities' resistance through gaming culture (LaPensée, Laiti, and Longboat 2021). All of these designers and their respective games explore how video games create narratives that explore the medium's potential to convey their specific message. In *Indians in Unexpected Places*, Philip Deloria (2014, 4) writes that the custom of imagining Indigenous peoples in terms of "primitivism, technological incompetence, physical distance, and cultural difference" has remained "familiar currency in contemporary dealings with Native people." Redressing this conventional narrative, Deloria describes Indigenous peoples engaged in activities in everyday life—singing opera, driving cars, acting in Hollywood—that conflict with the expectations of non-Indigenous people in settler societies. While these games are developed for an Indigenous audience and designed with those communities' worldviews, stories, and aesthetics in mind, these Indigenous game developers also intend their games to extend beyond that demographic. I use these case studies to sketch out some of the approaches taken by Indigenous artists in engaging digital media to adapt and retell stories from their communities and develop new stories that serve the needs of their communities to promote and preserve their stories, languages, and cultures.

Thunderbird Strike

Thunderbird Strike continues the scholar and game designer LaPensée's activist work of decolonizing the game industry and addressing embodied knowledge of the land—turning in this instance to the extractive resource industry.[2] The extractive industries are a product and tool of settler-colonialism and capitalism. The game was developed in support from the Arrowhead Regional Arts Council, O k'inādās Residency, The Banff Musicians in Residence Program, and Terri-Aur(i)al Imprints Exchange. Environmental humanities scholars and activist artists refer to serious environmental challenges as "wicked problems," which are those where the solutions are likely to be complex and require input from diverse perspectives (Rockström et al. 2009; Wilson 2016). These issues include addressing the current global biodiversity crisis, meeting the food and energy security needs of an ever-growing human population, confronting the water scarcity problem that impacts all life on Earth, and the destructive legacy of the extractive industry that is complexly embedded in the socioeconomic livelihoods of many who are precariously dependent on these industries (Koh et al. 2004; Schmidhuber and Tubiello 2007; Vörösmarty et al. 2000).

Thunderbird Strike was created to raise awareness concerning Enbridge's Line 5 oil pipeline. A multiplatform 2D side-scroller in three levels, users play thunderbird flying from the Tar Sands in Alberta to the Straits of Mackinac in the Great Lakes protecting Turtle Island. As the thunderbird, a traditional figure in Indigenous storytelling, the player recharges in the clouds and calls down searing lightning upon mining company infrastructure (e.g., buildings, pipelines, trucks, and machinery) of the settler-colonial-capitalist extractive industry that threatens the lands and waters. Players can also strike lightning at the bones of caribou, wolves, and buffalo, bringing them back to life. Line 5, which has leaked multiple reported times since its construction in 1953, runs through Indigenous lands and under the Great Lakes. Although only intended to last until 2003, Line 5 continues to transfer approximately 540,000 barrels of Alberta tar sands and crude oil per day. As a game designed to promote activism, its message is that it is not a matter of *when* pipelines will spill, because they already have. It is an Indigenous worldview of ecological harm that traces climate change and forms of environmental violence back through the damaging legacy of settler colonialism and extraction, which decimated Indigenous lands and transformed existing ecologies (see further Attebery 2020). *Thunderbird Strike* is a game about how we need to be careful moving forward in our protection of waters and lands continually traumatized by the extractive industry. It weaves together Anishinaabe narratives, telling their stories of extraction, with a game mechanic that gives points to players who participate in the destruction of fossil-fuel infrastructures while also rejuvenating animals and humans impacted by extractivism.

Each level is introduced with a cutscene that situates the player in the level environment: the tar sands as dump trucks transport supplies, outside the oil refineries where anti-extractivism protesters march, and battling the snake/actual pipeline that is slowly leaking along the bottom of the Great Lakes water system. The player witnesses the extension of the pipeline across the map of the Great Lakes in the cutscenes that connect these three levels. Even though the player has successfully destroyed oil industry infrastructure, absorbed the power of anti-extractivism protesters, and brought back to life the nonhuman animals whose habitats were displaced and toxically poisoned by the oil industry they cannot stop the pipeline.

Flying as the thunderbird, the player travels across the tar sands, industrial sites, and oil refineries. A distorted, gravelly, masculine-coded voice-over interjects with commands that indicate to the player that they must fly into the clouds to power-up in order to destroy and restore with the power of lightning (e.g., "gather lightening" and "electrified"). This voice is modeled after those in the early combat games of the late 1980s and early 1990s, such as *Street Fighter* (1987) and *Mortal Kombat* (1992) where the voice-over announces each successful hit and opponent defeat. The semimusical qualities of these vocals, specifically their timbre, aligns with the timbral character of the vocals in industrial music.[3] In *Thunderbird Strike* composer and sound artist Casey Koyczan (Tłı̨chǫ Dene) indigenizes and repurposes this iconic vocal utterance, its texture, and the cultural reference it signifies to players by using it to announce instances of successful industrial destruction ("fatal strike") as well as restorative hits that bring animals back to life ("activation") and the significance of community support when the thunderbird absorbs the power of the anti-extractivism protesters in level two (Figure 24.1 and Figure 24.2). This voice-over style might initially sound out of place; however, these brief vocal interjections highlight early on in the game that a hit that is destructive and a hit that is restorative are equally heroic and forms of successful gameplay.

LaPensée designs games with pan-Indigenous creative teams in the belief that to ethically engage in Indigenous stories and cultural content and follow protocol, it is

FIGURE 24.1 Before and after as the Thunderbird destroys a dump truck in Level 1.

FIGURE 24.2 Before and after as the Thunderbird restores a caribou in Level 1.

necessary to place Indigenous people in roles on the design team, and not solely as cultural consultants (Turner et. al 2020). In the development of *Thunderbird Strike*, she collaborated with Koyczan, a Tlicho Dene interdisciplinary artist and musician from Yellowknife who works across electronica, hip-hop, and metal/industrial. Koyczan's practice began in visual and installation art before moving into immersive media art in virtual reality (VR) and game development. Koyczan takes his stage name from the Tlicho word for "bushman," a legendary spirit of the woods in the Northwest Territories, which serves as a reminder to respect the land, water, and all their inhabitants. Koyczan contributed the original music for the soundtrack, sound effects, and voice acting. Sound effects included those produced by the Thunderbird character, as well as other sounds from the environment, while, for the voice-over work, Koyczan took inspiration from both the *Street Fighter* series of games and the vocal performances that characterize 1980s WWF wrestling matches he would often encounter on television growing up in Yellowknife (Cabin Radio NWT). The subject matter of *Thunderbird Strike* motivated Koyczan to collaborate on the game "because he also cares deeply about informing people of Indigenous perspectives on resource extraction" (LaPensée 2018b, 30). While working on the music and sound for *Thunderbird Strike* Koyczan came to realize that each team member's community-specific perspective on Indigenous land rights and the extractive industries informed game development since these are issues that systemically and unevenly impact all Indigenous people, even though the game is told from an Anishinaabe perspective about a specific pipeline (Turner et al. 2020). Koyczan's other work, such as the VR/360/XR work *City Tipi* (work in progress, 2019–) and the multimedia installation piece *Emotive Ascension* (2013) have also explored issues of Indigenous futurity, and more specifically Tłı̨chǫ futurity in his solo project, and a range of interactive digital storytelling techniques rooted in cultural, spiritual, and ceremonial practices. Inspired by Dene Nahjo's Urban Hide-Tanning Camp, *City Tipi*, Koyczan presents a vision of a Tipi in the middle of a city intersection, using VR/360/XR to reimagine the place of Indigenous communities and tradition in urban environments, while in *Emotive Ascension*, more-than-human trees reclaim architectural space through olfactory engagement, audio, and their physical presence that challenges the colonial and sterile histories of the gallery space. His process is grounded in culture, environmentalism, and technology—and while his work does not always include all three of these elements in equal parts, there is a mixture of these topics in everything he produces (Turner et al. 2020).

The industrial sector, which includes the extractive industries, serves as both the subject matter and the aesthetic foundation. Koyczan's use of instrumentation choices, harsh timbres, throbbing bass and drum layers, and postproduction that introduces delay, reverb, and distortion, sonify the industrial complex of the extractive industries implicated in the gameplay and narrative. Koyczan's music and sound design is atmosphere-driven, and his sound work in *Thunderbird Strike* is informed by personally witnessing mining and toxins buried in the Northwest Territories. The dense layers and loops of instrumental and vocal effects evoke the layers of the earth that extend below and beyond its surface—that archive of past stories, sounds, lived experiences of the land, and the stratified trauma and ecological harm that lies out of the visible and audible range. In *Thunderbird Strike*, Koyczan employs electric guitar prepared with distortion and delay for both the game's score and for the thunderbird's sound effects, developing interconnections between the diegetic sonic environment of in-game action and the nondiegetic score of the levels and cutscenes. Koyczan's choice of electronic guitar, timbral references to industrial music, and electroacoustic digital sonic-processing effects, illustrates how game sound can be Indigenous without reproducing stereotypes, and what the varied nature of Indigenous game sound can sound like. As LaPensée and Koyczan explained in a panel on Indigenous game design for Pax Online 2020, musical references to popular culture in the form of guitar power chords and effects pedals are not incompatible with the stories of the thunderbird woven through the game (Turner et al. 2020).

Sampling, layering, and forms of removal and replacement, like processes of extraction, are aesthetic practices used in the composition of the music as well as other design features in *Thunderbird Strike* to refigure and reclaim extractivism. Extraction and sampling is also used to embed local place-based knowledge into games. As in previous titles such as *Honour Water* (2016) (see LaPensée 2017a, 2018a, 2018b), LaPensée's art style is generated from digitized, hand-drawn line art layered with magnified textures modified from photos of water, soil, rocks, oil, birch bark, beads, and other materials that come from places along the pipeline.[4] These materials are connected to an Indigenous knowledge of the land that LaPensée personally gathered. The textures in this scene from level one, "Tar Sands," are tires from the large mining trucks; in the final pipeline snake battle, the water textures are of actual waters impacted by pipeline leaks and spills (Figure 24.3). LaPensée relates land and Indigenous worldviews within the game mechanics themselves through vital choices in level, character, and narrative development. The side-scrolling movement progresses opposite to the expected convention in side-scroller games—moving from right to left instead of left to right, which reflects an Anishinaabeg worldview. The game also does not dictate that you take either a destructive or a restorative approach. You can sabotage the infrastructure or the industry or undo the historical damage of extractivism through the revival of people and animals. In a game industry where many video games demand that we kill to win or advance, *Thunderbird Strike*'s interspecies relations stand out in stark relief. It resists not simply through destruction—players are rewarded for revitalizing living nonhuman creatures.

FIGURE 24.3 Gameplay screenshot from final battle with pipeline snake from *Thunderbird Strike*.

Hill Agency: PURITY/decay

Hill Agency: PURITY/decay is a 3D, third-person, narrative-driven detective game featuring a black-and-white noir style where you play as the private investigator Meygeen Hill, who is hired to solve a murder case that reveals social divisions between the poor and the upper class.[5] By making choices that shape the direction of your investigation and solving puzzles, "the heart of *Hill Agency* is discovery through investigation" (Achimogames 2021). This "discovery through investigation" style of gameplay takes the form of interviewing and evidence-finding. As Meygeen Hill, the player is equipped with a notebook, which they use to record and keep track of the people they meet and interview, the objects and evidence they find, and the testimonies they gather during their investigation. Players succeed in the game through analysis and deduction rather than combat, which is not even present in the game. *Hill Agency* is set in the thriving and vibrant Indigenous metropolis of Akâmaskiy in a distant speculative future in the year 2762 where the oppressive legacies of settler colonialism have been dismantled and diligently repaired.

Developed and released by Meagan Byrne (Âpihtawikosisân, Ontario Métis)—owner and lead narrative designer at Achimostawinan Games, Canada's first Indigenous-owned and operated indie Indigenous game company—and in partnership with animator Tara Miller, the creative and cultural direction of *Hill Agency: PURITY/decay* was grounded in featuring an entirely Indigenous cast that was set in a period in the future rather than in a static past (see Figure 24.4). The design and development team is also majority Indigenous, and of those Indigenous team members, the majority are Métis or Cree, so that the game is in part informed by individual backgrounds and worldviews that speak from those two nations (Byrne 2020). As Byrne writes in *Hill Agency*'s promotional materials:

> The year is 2762 and you're, [*sic*] Meygeen Hill, a tough as nails P.I. working in the slums of one of the last major cities in North America. Life is all missing kids and cheating spouses until a dame barges in from the Risen-City and changes your life. Her sister has been murdered and the cops are useless. It's up to you to find out who the real murderer is. Murdered sisters, mind wiping drugs and flying palaces, this case goes way farther than the banks of this one detective's little slum in this indigenous cybernoir. A narrative detective game in the spirit of *Oxenfree* and *The Shiva* that lets you solve who did it.
>
> (Achimogames 2021)

Achimostawinan Games is dedicated to developing Indigenous games for an Indigenous audience (and the world) while also helping Indigenous artists and communities develop interactive and digital content. At Achimostawinan Games, "we strive to create stories that speak to you. After all, Achimostawinan means, 'Tell us a story' in Cree. We believe in crafting original Indigenous stories for everyone" (Achimogames 2020).

FIGURE 24.4 Screenshots illustrating the cyber noir style of *Hill Agency: PURITY/decay* from Summer of Gaming 2022 trailer.

I include *Hill Agency* as a case study in this chapter because it deals directly with a contentious question posed to many Indigenous artists: What makes your work Indigenous? In a talk for Dirty Rectangles in Toronto, Byrne directly addressed this question: "It's Indigenous because I am Indigenous" (Byrne 2020). However, not all of her work is Indigenous, she asserts—even when she, a Métis designer, produces it. She has been involved in a number of game development projects as the only Indigenous person on the team and although her background and worldview frames her design (e.g., advocating for the removal of colonialist content), her presence on the team does not make it an

Indigenous game. In her portfolio of work, Byrne vocally frames what is and is not an Indigenous work, as defined by her personal politics and experience of Indigeneity.

Throughout the development and release of *Hill Agency*, Byrne was asked what made her game Indigenous, because to non-Indigenous players and reviewers it did not appear to feature the cultural characteristics that they (as settler outsiders) expected of Indigenous cultural works.[6] This is a question that "asks for performance," Byrne (2020) explains. That is, it did not contain the stereotypes of Indigenous culture and communities which settler popular culture had conditioned them to associate with indigeneity. What is authentic Indigenous creation has been "curated" by non-Indigenous people, Byrne explains in her critical game design, and only recently have Indigenous people been able to be their own curators. "Your idea of what is 'authentically' Indigenous has been curated to you by a non-Indigenous person or if they are an Indigenous person, most likely they are not Indigenous to that community or that nation that they are curating" and they perpetuate the same ideas of what is and is not Indigenous (2020). Inspired by LaPensée's critical game design activism, Byrne continues the call to stop asking Indigenous arts to perform a particular kind of indigeneity and challenges the expectation that Indigenous art contain cultural tropes that are equally recognizable by specific Indigenous communities, the global pan-Indigenous population, *and* non-Indigenous people (Byrne and LaPensée 2020; LaPensée 2018a, 2018b).

In an interview for the podcast *NomadCast*, Byrne revealed that her design team asked themselves: "What would an Indigenous futurism on the cusp of total freedom from colonialism look like?" (*NomadCast*).[7] The game also contains content that is not for all players even though anyone can play the game. *Hill Agency* is an intentional layering of cultural references, containing cultural references that service the broadest demographic of players, as well as "Easter eggs" for Cree players. While some of the game is designed for both Indigenous and non-Indigenous players, other parts are designed to resonate with Indigenous players and, in some instances, specifically those who are Cree and Anishinaabe.[8] Who Byrne designs for also extends to language. Increasingly, her games use Cree language as much as possible to participate in language reclamation work, increasing the number of native Indigenous language speakers and to normalize engaging in everyday conversation in one's Indigenous language.[9] Growing up on detective novels and pulp fiction, it is not surprising that Byrne included several stylistic features of the visual novel in *Hill Agency*, such as the inclusion of narrative-shaping multiple-choice questions that require player interaction, and well-paced dialogue that generates character development necessary for reading people and solving the case.

As one of the few non-Indigenous members of the creative team, the composer and jazz musician Colin Lloyd is transparent with the fact that he was exploring new territory and scoring the experience and stories of his pan-Indigenous collaborators who had firsthand experience with the material and subject matter of the game (email with the author). What makes the combination of the synthesizer-driven electronic music of cyberpunk with the acoustic smoky jazz arrangements of film noir in Lloyd's soundtrack Indigenous are the ways these music genre references are re-contextualized and re-sounded in a futuristic dystopian world where Indigenous people and the planet rebuild and thrive after the non-Indigenous majority have fled in the face of crisis and disaster. By taking the iconic soundscapes and scoring of cyberpunk and film noir and making them their own using processes of adaptation and remediation, Achimostawinan Games is indigenizing these musical references and tropes. Lloyd recalled a residency talk promoting the game in the early days of development where Byrne made a quick humorous, yet critical interjection as Lloyd explained his compositional process. She half-jokingly said to him, "You will not be putting drums in there" (Lloyd, personal correspondence with author, February 3, 2022). The omission of the drum or any instrument or digital sound postproduction effect that might sound like a drum is a deliberate aesthetic choice to challenge and eschew the sonic stereotypes of indigeneity perpetuated in media and expressive culture produced by settler creatives. The goal was to compose in the most respectful way possible, to avoid cultural appropriation at all costs, and to listen to the game sound and music from multiple auditory perspectives, taking into consideration that the game would be used by individual players from different cultural backgrounds and communities.

For Byrne, the experience of working on these games just "feels different" when they are being made from a culturally specific perspective and with members from the same Indigenous nation. This is because the team members do not have to explain and unpack the cultural references and aesthetic decisions that they are making, but when they do have to, they are speaking in a creative space where their lived cultural knowledge is valued as an authoritative source. Here, Byrne is referencing the conflicting North American Indigenous (relaxing) versus non-Indigenous (stressful and ominous) experiences of Lisa Jackson's *Biidaaban: First Light* (2018), an immersive virtual reality experience in Anishinaabe language that depicts a postapocalyptic Toronto that has become overgrown and re-wilded by nature (Turner et al. 2020; Johnson 2018). *Hill Agency* is an Indigenous game because it features Indigenous characters, addresses Indigenous issues that deliberately don't speak to the experiences of non-Indigenous people, and is set in an Indigenous community. It is also Indigenous because Byrne identifies *Hill Agency* as an Indigenous game.

Terra Nova

Designed and developed by an Indigenous-led team based in Montreal, *Terra Nova* tells an alternative story of first contact set in the distant future, after an environmental catastrophe has flooded the Earth. This devastating ecological event split human society into two groups: one that remained on Earth and learned how to survive in their postapocalyptic reality while combining their collective efforts to rebuild, but not replicate, the past; and another group who decided to leave Earth and colonize another habitable planet that can support human life. The decisions of this latter offshoot of Earth's human population directly reflects the narrative of space colonization broadly encountered across audiovisual popular culture, including AAA and indie games.

Maize Longboat is Kanien'kehá:ka from Six Nations of the Grand River, and French Canadian of Finnish descent, and was raised on the traditional, ancestral, and unceded territory of the Squamish Nation near Vancouver, British Columbia. Longboat first became invested in Indigenous-designed and Indigenous-determined video games following his first encounter with the "animal-like" character of Tauren from *World of Warcraft*, an Indigenous-inspired video game character who was loosely based on Native American culture in stereotypical ways (Muzyka 2019). He was fascinated with how Indigenous culture and video games intersect and wanted to explore these intersections through practice-based research in game design. Longboat's work in critical game design and Indigenous-determined digital storytelling is part of a broader movement in Indigenous digital media that is promoting media creation by Indigenous creators who are actively repairing the damage inflicted by negative stereotypes and representations of Indigenous people and culture by non-Indigenous creators. This includes teaching Indigenous youth about digital media creation, so that they can critically engage with the representational practices across new media while also becoming creators of the digital media and games they are actively consuming.

Terra Nova is Longboat's thesis project from his graduate work at Concordia University, where he used the institutional resources of the settler-descendant university system to amplify the voices and culture of Indigenous peoples in game culture.[10] Following his master's degree, he became the associate director of the SKINS Workshops organized by the Initiative for Indigenous Futures based at Concordia University, where he teaches Indigenous youth how to use digital storytelling to adapt stories from their community into experimental digital media, such as video games. Speaking with Kyle Muzyka for the Indigenous-focused Canadian radio program *Unreserved*,[11] Longboat said: "I wanted to tell a story of first contact, but I didn't really want to do it in a historically framed kind of manner. I wanted to create something new and something that had the possibility for many different outcomes of that contact" (Muzyka 2019).

Terra Nova is a two-player, co-operative platformer. Players take the roles of Terra, an Elder Earthborn land keeper who is an Indigenous-coded character, and Nova, a youthful Starborn inventor who is a settler-coded character (Figure 24.5). The game's narrative explores what first contact between Indigenous and settler peoples might look like thousands of years in the future. Unlike many other co-op games, which allow for both single-player and two-player modes (such as *Never Alone*), *Terra Nova* requires two simultaneous players at all times. The interactive storytelling within the game is unique, telling different stories for each character that eventually intertwine as gameplay progresses. The split-screen, two-player design of *Terra Nova*—Terra on the left-hand side and Nova on the right-hand side—allows for two worlds and stories to separately unfold until the characters meet each other later in the game and converge (Figure 24.6). Each player is thrust into gameplay immediately, without a cutscene or opening context to provide backstory on who you are, where you are, and what you must set out to achieve in this game world. Without this backstory the player must explore, look and listen to things in the game world, and talk to nonplayer characters (NPCs) to figure out the purpose of their character and their identity. Play is a mode of information gathering

FIGURE 24.5 Split screen of Terra and Nova at the opening of the game.

and grounding the character in their environment in the game. The story that Terra and Nova are both a part of unfolds as each of the players start co-exploring the game world with their respective character.

Thursday Night Live, a livestream series and talk show centered on Digital Art that launched during the COVID-19 pandemic, live streamed a playthrough of *Terra Nova* with Longboat, who answered viewer questions and provided critical commentary (MacKenzie 2020). Hosts Cat Bluemke and Jonathan Carroll also engaged Longboat in discussion addressing the process of the game's creation and the practice of making interactive digital art. The element of interactivity, Longboat observed, is one of the prominent features of video games that make them an effective medium for digital storytelling for many Indigenous young people, including himself. The player as viewer and listener of the artwork has some degree of control over how they experience the artwork. The artwork also requires the player to participate and engage with it in order to experience the work and progress further in the narrative. The player embodies the characters and the story as they use the controller to move their character through the game world environment and understand it, interact with characters, and become a part of the narrative and message.

Minutes into the game, Terra is alerted that there is something alarming and suspicious in the sky, and the player must head to the lookout in her town to investigate the situation. Once she arrives, her mentee Luna draws her attention to the "bright new star in the sky" that was noticeable to Terra's naked eye. Luna first noticed the bright star shining over the lowlands as soon as she woke up and sent for Terra right away because they were late for settlement training (school). On the right-hand side of the screen,

FIGURE 24.6 Single screen before (top) and after (bottom) Terra and Nova make first contact.

Nova is in their space vehicle, red lights throbbing and alarms buzzing, alerting Nova and the rest of the on-ship crew that after many years searching outer space for a new habitable planet they have finally found one that will sustain human life. That planet just happens to be the Earth they left behind years ago. As Terra looks through the telescope and observes the starship crashing into the territory, both players see and hear Nova experience the crash firsthand from within the laboring vehicle. Before taking action and exploring what just fell into their territory, Luna reminds Terra of their role in this unexpected moment of outside contact. Luna explains: "It's important that our community has a say in what we do about whatever just fell into this territory. You're one of them! The Leaders are the people who make collaborative decisions about what happens in our community." Meanwhile, Nova (who is initially introduced to us as #8222) has exited the starcraft and is tasked with testing the environment for certain ecological and physiological requirements to sustain human life and monitoring for potential threat and conflict from living things indigenous to this planet. Nova emerges from the starcraft into a lush, green wooded area replete with an animate biophonic soundscape. As Nova begins to explore the ecology of what they believe to be a newly "discovered" territory, the player is asked if Nova wants to clean-up some of the debris from the crash. Even from this early stage in the game the player is asked if Nova and their community want to approach first contact and the process of colonization differently this time by taking responsibility for the immediate and gradual environmental trauma left in their wake and participate in the rehabilitation process.

Games can communicate meaning not just through the text-based narratives that they tell, but also through the aesthetics of the interactions, and the transitions between the different game world environments. In *Terra Nova* meaning communicated through mechanics and design is conveyed to the players through the presence of simultaneously left and right side-scroller motion—the player who plays as Terra scrolls right while the player who plays as Nova scrolls left—and the dynamic sound design that provides the players with sonic clues that Terra and Nova are exploring the same world and their in-game and ancestral storylines are interconnected. The sonic environments of these opening split screen scenes of gameplay feature deliberately contrasting sonic environments that situate the two players and their playable characters in their respective physical environments, setting players up for the surprising moment when Terra and Nova meet and the two communities of the Earth that once existed reunite. The colonizer discovers that they are also the colonized. In many other split-screen multiplayer games, players can look over into the split screen windows of other players in hopes of catching a glimpse of information that will give them an advantage. In *Terra Nova*, however, as players look and listen to the other screen they may begin to notice similarities between their respective visual and sonic environments; a common bird call, a similar terrain and landscape contour, and shared species of plants. Approximately 40 minutes into gameplay, Nova reaches the above-ground opening of the abandoned below-ground sewer system once used by the pre-apocalypse human society and comes face to face with Terra. The split screen becomes a single screen as the text on the screen reads: "A peculiar alien creature emerges from the brush." Is the alien Terra or Nova? The interactive dialogue system in this moment engages both players in a series of back-and-forth questions: What is your name? Who are your people/What are you?[12] The dramatic moment in the game is the moment of first contact between Terra and Nova when the players' split screens converge into a single screen containing the gameplay for both characters, and we realize that their game world was the same one all along.

The soundscape design and dialogue system provide environmental feedback that informs players how Terra and Nova relate to their world and figure into its ecology. In the starship, elevators make noises and airlock doors hiss when opening or closing. Interactive dialogue also provides feedback for players as they navigate between choices. Terra and Nova even have a set of unique vocalization sounds that play when they confirm interactions with the NPCs and objects in the world.[13] The distinctive individual sounding voices of Terra and Nova connect their voice to their material body on the split-screen that produces it while also enhancing the co-players' sense of identification with their respective avatars. The use of avatar-specific vocalizations for Terra and Nova without having them speak their dialogue was a way to help players connect with the characters and their personalities. This sound design approach to avatar dialogue also helped to manage the game's scope and kept the narrative dialogue fluid during the iteration process. This intentional sound design activates a listening space where players listen to the experiences of first contact from both Indigenous and settler perspectives.

"I am human. This planet is known as Earth. You and your people are unannounced visitors to this territory," Terra says to Nova in the game when they first make contact on Earth following the crash of Nova's starship. Nova is not sure where their community originates from because starships are the only places they have ever known; however, there are legends of a former planet that they were forced to leave because of its uncertain ecological future. Over the course of their conversation, Terra and Nova come to a shared understanding and decide to work together toward a common goal, thus rejecting models of first contact based in colonialist narratives of overcoming and overpowering the "Other." And who *is* the "Other"—is it the Starborn or the Leaders? They are now in contact with each other, merged, and in relation to each other. They can never go back to before because of this moment of contact, and it is up to them to decide how each of their communities move forward. How do they choose to engage in relations, and what is the nature of those relations now that their histories are entangled? Working together to locate the other Starborn following the crash, Terra and Nova work together to understand their respective communities' relationship to Earth and locate the crash site of Nova's starcraft. Longboat is not alone in grappling with such questions and envisioning possible alternatives and futures. These questions resonate with those asked by Dylan Robinson in his discussion of settler-Indigenous encounters and collaboration in *Hungry Listening* (2020, 113–146).

In the opening minutes of *Terra Nova* the initial soundscape features heard on either side of the split screen are soft, textural, ambient tones that signal to the players the game takes place in the not so distant future and that the Earthborn and Starborn worlds are not so different from each other. Before the players have the opportunity to become immersed in this shared soundscape, Terra's sonic environment dramatically shifts to a sonorous soundscape of re-wilded nature while Nova's cybernetic starcraft sonic environment bleeps, bloops, and buzzes with the sounds of settler space exploration technologies.[14] The elevator in the starcraft, for instance, was intended by sound designer Beatrix Moersch to sound like an ever-increasing revolution of incessant sonic and mechanical tension, and to reference the sonic palette widely used in science fiction sound design. The Earthborn village environment is filled with sounds of people carrying out everyday activities and tasks, animals, and wind blowing high above the ground. In contrast, the Starborn starship environment has beeps and boops of the vessel's various robots and space instruments as they communicate. The use of subtitles and the absence of voice acting is an aesthetic choice that ensures that the game does not perpetuate primitivist representations of Indigenous vocality, and as players read the text either as Terra or Nova they can more directly identify with that character's experience of first contact and the role that they play.

Sound connects the spaces that the split screen divides even when players are unaware the characters occupy the same game world following the starship's crash landing. Longboat outlines the sound design mechanics developed by his collaborator Beatrix Moersch as such:

> With the help of a custom left-right audio listener system developed by Moersch, the game's Sound Designer, the unique soundtracks from both environments and player perspectives blends seamlessly together without becoming incoherent. This effect is achieved using the Unity engine by manipulating the listener component of each respective player and splitting each into left and right stereo feeds. This system is active throughout the split-screen portion of the game to tie together the contrasted split visuals of each player using sound. Whether the game is played using speakers or with two pairs of headphones connected to an audio splitter, players experience overlapping sounds from both Earthborn and Starborn perspectives. (Longboat 2019b, 34)

The soundscape of re-wilded Earth is lush, overgrown, and sonorous—the Earth restored to its natural uncultivated state. Vines and greenery grow over and consume the built architecture of pre-apocalyptic Earth, illustrating not only the resilience but also the survivance of nonhuman Nature. "Survivance" is a term developed by Gerald Viznor (2008) that pushes beyond the narrative of resilience, an ability to survive and rebuild to where you were before the trauma. Survivance is the ability to survive and rebuild, becoming something better than before. The humans in Longboat's narrative of first contact and the nonhuman nature players experience on postapocalyptic Earth are models of survivance in the face of traumatic environmental disaster.

Longboat didn't want the game to have any competitive element. It is about encountering an alien for the first time, from both sides of the split screen. The form of the game communicates a great deal about what a speculative future first contact could be from Longboat's point of view. Terra and Nova experience the story of first contact together, but that moment of contact when the split-screen becomes one screen and the realization of the ancestral connections between their human communities is central to Longboat's alternative retelling of first contact, one where the two communities learn from each other and come to understand their shared ancestry from a time before environmental catastrophe on Earth. The game audio is a key narrative component that foreshadows Longboat's Indigenous reimagining of first contact. Long before Terra and Nova make first contact on screen, the player listens to the incremental confluence of their respective soundscapes as the physical distance between these two characters decreases (e.g., the sonorous re-wilded nature of foliage and animal life in Terra's Earth bleeds into Nova's experience of Earth as Nova explores further away from the starcraft crash site before eventually meeting Terra).

This game design feature contrasts with other games that use cooperative play that players might be more familiar with, where the two characters move side by side in the same window or directly help each other advance and succeed in the game. Longboat's design instead references the split-screen cooperative system of games like *Brothers: A Tale of Two Sons* (2013), where each joystick controls one of the two brothers, or like *Never Alone*, in which the player(s) (whether in single-player or co-op mode) must alternate and toggle between the playable characters because they each have a distinctive skill set that is required to solve the puzzles and advance in the game. Narratives of first contact are complex, but they are not always framed that way. Video games are an active medium where Longboat can communicate a complex narrative of colonialism and first contact.

Conclusion

Indigenous traditions are often misinterpreted as something static or conventional, and the game audio in these three case studies reinforce the Indigenous narratives of Indigenous futurity that imagine the possible futures (see Deloria et al. 2018; Gartner 2015; Lewis 2016, 2014). Discussions of game audio are also inseparable from issues of representation, sovereignty, decolonial and anticolonial initiatives in critical game design, and Indigenous activism (LaPensée, Laiti, and Longboat 2021). In her discussion of digital storytelling by Indigenous creators, Candace Hopkins writes, "Storytellers in indigenous communities are continually embracing new materials and technologies, including video and digital media. I would suggest that this shift does not threaten storytelling traditions in these communities but is merely a continuation of what aboriginal people have been doing from time immemorial: making things our own" (Hopkins 2006, 324). Each of the games, and their Indigenous design teams that I have discussed, uses the affordances of digital storytelling, game mechanic design, animation and visual art, and game sound design to engage with and contribute to critical conversations about what it means to be Indigenous and what it means to be a settler within new, speculative-future scenarios to imagine something more positive and equitable for all involved.

Notes

1. Run by Indigenous game designers Meagan Byrne and Elizabeth LaPensée, the site Indigenous Game Devs showcases and supports Indigenous/Native video games and their creators, including their Indigenous Interactive Media and Video Game Database. This community and outreach resource can be found at https://www.indigenousgamedevs.com/.
2. For an overview of environmental humanities scholarship that explores both literal extraction and cultural approaches to extraction, see Junka-Aikio and Cortes-Severino (2017).

3. For more on the semimusical qualities of characters' voices and dialogue in games, see Medina-Gray (2021).
4. For example, in *A Short Hike* (2019), referencing colors were derived from searching for full nature photos of the Canadian Shield and sampling directly from them, which helped Adam Robinson-Yu define the color palette and landscape textures for the game. Like LaPensée, he drew on references from a landscape that he is intimately familiar with.
5. As of writing, the game was released for purchase on Steam and itch.io and a free downloadable game jam prototype of *Hill Agency* for Windows and macOS was available at https://byrneout.itch.io/purity-decay.
6. The question "What makes your game Indigenous?" is also not the same as asking a designer what Nation they are from, who on your team is Indigenous, which communities are you accountable to when Indigenous and non-Indigenous players encounter a game that visually and audibly reads as Indigenous. These questions, Byrne explains, are why Indigenous creators like herself "are always asking who on your team is Indigenous and what is their Nation because essentially we're asking is who are you, where are you from, and who are you responsible for. Who gets to call you out when you do something wrong?" (Byrne 2020).
7. NomadCast, August 2020 Episode, https://open.spotify.com/episode/4Stc9kyOLatG5wRtzgvQmx.
8. Here I am also referencing Dylan Robinson's (2020) clear directive in *Hungry Listening* for settler readers to stop reading and skip ahead to a specific section because what follows is exclusively for his Indigenous readers. He expects his readers to follow the different protocols for reading that he lays out and ethically engage with his words. They will know if they have violated his clear request and that is on them. I have not included the page in *Hungry Listening* where Robinson instructs his settler-readers to cede space to Indigenous readers, trusting settler-readers to not read the passages that were not written for them. This is a moment of anticolonial academic writing that each reader should discover on their own without knowing in advance which page or section Robinson's directive will be encountered.
9. For further scholarship addressing the intersections of Indigenous language learning, storytelling, and songwriting, see Jacobsen (2017).
10. *Terra Nova* received funding through support from Aboriginal Territories in Cyberspace (AbTeC), the Initiative for Indigenous Futures (IIF), the Hexagram Network, and the Social Sciences and Humanities Research Council (SSHRC) and, from these sources, Longboat was able to hire a full design team to augment his game development skills as he set out to design and develop his first game. *Terra Nova* was the winner of "Best Emerging Digital or Interactive Work" at the imagiNATIVE Film & Media Festival in 2019. Longboat's MA research-creation (a term used in the Canadian academic system to refer to practice-based research) thesis project examined Indigenous video games and development and design practices through the production of *Terra Nova*.
11. Hosted by Falen Johnson (Mohawk and Tuscarora [Bear Clan] from Six Nations Grand River Territory).
12. Longboat's dialogue system gives the players the appearance that the choices they make among the dialogue options presented will impact where the narrative of *Terra Nova*, that is only an illusion. If you replay the game and make new choices the players will realize that all dialogue options result in the same narrative outcome. While it was Longboat's original plan to create a choose-your-own-adventure style narrative structure with branching

narrative trees and side quests, time and design constraints did not make that possible for the current iteration of the game (MacKenzie Art Gallery 2020).

13. For more on the relationships among character voices, dialogue, and player immersion in games, see Medina-Gray (2021), Grimshaw (2011), Jørgensen (2009), Stockburger (2010), Ward (2010).
14. For further scholarship on Indigenous cyberspace and cyberpunk, see Lenhardt (2019) and Todd (1996).

References

Achimostawinan Games. n.d. *Hill Agency: PURITY/*decay. https://byrneout.itch.io/purity-decay.

Achimostawinan Games. 2020. https://achimogames.ca/our-games/hill-agency-purity-decay/.

Attebery, Stina. 2020. "Oil, Water, Lightning: Indigenous Posthumanism and Energy Futures in Elizabeth LaPensée's *Thunderbird Strike*." *American Quarterly* 72 (3): 697–717.

Beer, Molly C. 2020. "The Next Chapter of Indigenous Representation in Video Games." *Polygon*, February 20, 2020. Accessed February 12, 2022. https://www.polygon.com/features/2020/2/25/21150973/indigenous-representation-in-video-games.

Byrne, Meagan. 2020. "Extended Meagan @ Dirty Rectangles." YouTube, August 13, 2020 [25:31]. Accessed October 1, 2021. https://www.youtube.com/watch?v=YXBDRYkrArc.

Byrne, Meagan, and Elizabeth LaPensée. 2020. *Night of the Indigenous Devs Proceedings 2019*. Pittsburgh: Carnegie Mellon University. https://doi.org/10.1184/R1/13247339.v1.

Cabin Radio NWT. 2018. "*Thunderbird Strike*: Interview with Casey Koyczan." January 11, 2018. Accessed October 5, 2021. https://cabinradio.ca/4919/video/controversial-video-game-voiced-by-yellowknife-performer/.

Deloria, Philip. 2004. *Indians in Unexpected Places*. Lawrence: University Press of Kansas.

Deloria, Philip J., K. Tsianina Lomawaima, Bryan McKinley Jones Brayboy, Mark N. Trahant, Loren Ghiglione, Douglas Medin, and Ned Blackhawk. 2018. "Unfolding Futures: Indigenous Ways of Knowing for the Twenty-First Century." *Daedalus* 147 (2): 6–16.

Gaertner, David. 2015. "Indigenous in Cyberspace: CyberPowWow, God's Lake Narrows, and the Contours of Online Indigenous Territory." *American Indian Culture and Research Journal* 39 (4): 55–78.

Gershon, Livia. 2021. "New *Oregon Trail* Game Revisits Westward Expansion from Native Perspective." *Smithsonian Magazine*, May 17, 2021. Accessed October 10, 2021. https://www.smithsonianmag.com/smart-news/new-oregon-trail-game-features-playable-native-american-characters-180977744/.

Grimshaw, Mark. 2011. "Sound and Player Immersion in Digital Games." In *The Oxford Handbook of Sound Studies*, edited by Trevor Pinch and Karin Bijsterveld, 347–366. Oxford: Oxford University Press.

Hopkins, Candice. 2006. "Making Things Our Own: The Indigenous Aesthetic in Digital Storytelling." *Leonardo* 39 (4): 341–344.

Jacobsen, Kristina M. 2017. *The Sound of Navajo Country: Music, Language, and Diné Belonging*. Chapel Hill: University of North Carolina Press.

Johnson, Rhiannon. 2018. "Anishinaabe Artist's New VR Experience Takes an Indigenous Futurist Look at Toronto." CBC News, April 14, 2018. Accessed June 15, 2021. https://www.cbc.ca/news/indigenous/lisa-jackson-biidaaban-vr-future-toronto-1.4619041.

Jørgensen, Kristine. 2009. *A Comprehensive Study of Sound in Computer Games: How Audio Affects Player Action*. Lewiston, NY: Edwin Mellen Press.

Junka-Aikio, Laura, and Catalina Cortes-Severino, eds. 2017. "Special Issue: Cultural Studies of Extraction." *Cultural Studies* 31 (2–3): 175–447.

Kinder, Jordan B. 2021. "Gaming Extractivism: Indigenous Resurgence, Unjust Infrastructures, and the Politics of Play in Elizabeth LaPensée's *Thunderbird Strike*." *Canadian Journal of Communication* 46 (2): 247–269.

King, Anna. 2021. "A New Spin on a Classic Video Game Gives Native Americans Better Representation." *NPR All Things Considered*, May 12, 2021. Accessed September 20, 2021. https://www.npr.org/2021/05/12/996007048/no-bows-and-arrows-and-no-broken-english-on-the-updated-oregon-trail.

Koh, Lian Pin, Robert R. Dunn, Navjot S. Sodhi, Robert K. Colwell, Heather C. Proctor, and Vincent S. Smith. 2004. "Species Coextinctions and the Biodiversity Crisis." *Science* 305 (5690): 1632–1634.

LaPensée, Elizabeth. 2016. "Games as Enduring Presence." *Public* 27 (54): 178–186.

LaPensée, Elizabeth. 2017a. *Thunderbird Strike*. https://www.thunderbirdstrike.com/.

LaPensée, Elizabeth. 2017b. "Transformations and Remembrances in the Digital Game *We Sing for Healing*." *Transmotion* 3 (1): 89–108.

LaPensée, Elizabeth. 2018a. "Self-Determination in Indigenous Games." In *Routledge Companion to Media Studies and Digital Humanities*, edited by Jentery Sayers, 128–137. New York: Routledge.

LaPensée, Elizabeth. 2018b. "*Thunderbird Strike*: Survivance in/of an Indie Indigenous Game." *Video Game Art Reader* 2 (1): 28–37.

LaPensée, Elizabeth A., Outi Laiti, and Maize Longboat. 2021. "Towards Sovereign Games." *Games and Culture*. https://doi.org/10.1177/15554120211029195.

Lenhardt, Corinna. 2019. "Indigenous Futurisms." In *The Routledge Companion to Cyberpunk Culture*, edited by Anna McFarlane, Lars Schmeink, and Graham Murphy, 344–352. New York: Routledge.

Lempert, William. 2014. "Decolonizing Encounters of the Third Kind: Alternative Futuring in Native Science Fiction Film." *Visual Anthropology Review* 30 (2): 164–176.

Lewis, Jason Edward. 2014. "A Better Dance and Better Prayers: Systems, Structures, and the Future Imaginary in Aboriginal New Media." In *Coded Territories: Tracing Indigenous Pathways in New Media Art*, edited by Steve Loft and Kerry Swanson, 48–77. Calgary: University of Calgary Press.

Lewis, Jason Edward. 2016. "Preparations for a Haunting: Notes towards an Indigenous Future Imaginary." In *The Participatory Condition in the Digital Age*, edited by Darin Barney et al., 229–249. Minneapolis: University of Minnesota Press.

Longboat, Maize. 2019a. "*Terra Nova*." Master's Thesis, Concordia University.

Longboat, Maize. 2019b. "*Terra Nova*: Enacting Videogame Development through Indigenous-Led Creation." Master's Thesis, Concordia University.

MacKenzie Art Gallery. 2020. "Let's Play *Terra Nova* with Maize Longboat." YouTube, June 18, 2020 [1:31:56]. Video. Accessed September 10, 2021. https://www.youtube.com/watch?v=PCc97TG5uOE&t=773s.

Medina-Gray, Elizabeth. 2021. "Music, Sound Effects and Dialogue in Video Games." In *The Cambridge Companion to Video Game Music*, edited by Melanie Fritsch and Tim Summers, 176–192. Cambridge: Cambridge University Press.

Muzyka, Kyle. 2019. "Telling the Story of First Contact . . . with a Futuristic Video Game." CBC Unreserved, March 8, 2019. Accessed September 20, 2021. https://www.cbc.ca/radio/unreserved/looking-towards-the-future-indigenous-futurism-in-literature-music-film-and-fashion-1.5036479/telling-the-story-of-first-contact-with-a-futuristic-video-game-1.5047127.

Nash, Curtis. 2016. "Cultural Appropriation, Postcolonial Fetishism, and Indigenous-Settler Relations in Blizzard Entertainment's *World of Warcraft*." MA thesis, University of Guelph.

Perea, Jessica Bissett. 2021. *Sound Relations: Native Ways of Doing Music History in Alaska*. Oxford: Oxford University Press.

Perea, Jessica Bissett, and Gabriel Solis. 2019. "Asking the Indigeneity Question of American Music Studies." *Journal of the Society for American Music* 13 (4): 401–410.

Robinson, Dylan. 2020. *Hungry Listening: Resonant Theory for Indigenous Sound Studies*. Minneapolis: University of Minnesota Press.

Rockström, Johan, Will Steffen, Kevin Noone, Åsa Persson, F. Stuart Chapin III, Eric F. Lambin, Timothy M. Lenton, et al. 2009. "A Safe Operating Space for Humanity." *Nature* 461 (7263): 472.

Roetman, Sheena. 2016. "Arcade Aboriginal: Indigenous Storytelling Takes a New, Compelling Shape in Video Games." *Native Peoples Magazine* (March/April): 46–49.

Schmidhuber, Josef, and Francesco N. Tubiello. 2007. "Global Food Security under Climate Change." *Proceedings of the National Academy of Sciences* 104 (50): 19703–19708.

Stockburger, Axel. 2010. "The Play of the Voice: The Role of the Voice in Contemporary Video and Computer Games." In *Voice: Vocal Aesthetics in Digital Arts and Media*, edited by Norie Neumark, Ross Gibson, and Theo van Leeuwen, 281–299. Cambridge, MA: MIT Press.

Tallie, T. J. 2021. "On Nostalgia and Colonialism on the New *Oregon Trail*." *Hyperallergic*, May 16, 2021. Accessed February 10, 2022. https://hyperallergic.com/645727/on-nostalgia-and-colonialism-on-the-new-oregon-trail/.

Todd, Loretta. 1996. "Aboriginal Narratives in Cyberspace." In *Immersed in Technology: Art and Virtual Environments*, edited by Mary Anne Moser and Douglas MacLeod, 179–194. Cambridge, MA: MIT Press.

Turner, Allen, et al. 2020. "Indigenous Game Design of Turtle Island: Panel with Allen Turner, Elizabeth LaPensée, Meagan Byrne, and Casey Koyczan." PAX Online 2020, October 19, 2020. Accessed June 1, 2021. Panel Session Archived at https://www.youtube.com/watch?v=k39A8FdjoUY.

Vizenor, Gerald. 2008. *Survivance: Narratives of Native Presence*. Lincoln: University of Nebraska Press.

Vörösmarty, Charles J., Pamela Green, Joseph Salisbury, and Richard B. Lammers. 2000. "Global Water Resources: Vulnerability from Climate Change and Population Growth." *Science* 289 (5477): 284–288.

Ward, Mark. 2010. "Voice, Videogames, and the Technologies of Immersion." In *Voice: Vocal Aesthetics in Digital Arts and Media*, edited by Norie Neumark, Ross Gibson, and Theo van Leeuwen, 267–279. Cambridge, MA: MIT Press.

Wilson, Edward O. 2016. *Half-Earth: Our Planet's Fight for Life*. New York: W.W. Norton.

CHAPTER 25

LISTENING TO THE GERUDO AND THE DESERT IN *THE LEGEND OF ZELDA* SERIES

HYEONJIN PARK

INTRODUCTION

UPON finding out that he cannot take his horse with him to the Gerudo Desert, Link boards his animal companion at the stable—a place of rest—before returning to the path that leads to a vast region unknown to him. Across the kingdom, some Hylians have expressed wariness of the area. Some have also shared sexual fantasies of its inhabitants, the Gerudo, describing what sounded like an exotic harem. The wind whispers as Link steps out into the desert. As the day passes and the sun's rays become stronger, though, his expression changes to exhaustion. He desperately looks for any signs of life to save him from the dangers of this heat and, eventually, spots an oasis, Kara Kara Bazaar. The cooler temperature and familiar musical texture of the piano bring relief, and he rests before continuing his trek across the dry environment. As Link nears Gerudo Town, the player hears a change in music to a dulcimer carrying an ornamented melody. He slows in front of the entrance to the town, seeing two towering Gerudo glaring at him, unsure of what to do next.

I begin this chapter with a brief description of what it was like to encounter the Gerudo Desert for the first time in Nintendo's *The Legend of Zelda: Breath of the Wild* (2017, hereafter *BotW*).[1] While our reactions may have differed, something many players have in common is our audiovisual experience, from the towering rock formations before the Gerudo Desert to the "exotic" music that begins to play as you near Gerudo Town.[2] This musical topic is not unfamiliar to us, as it appears in various manners in other video games that also feature regions such as the desert. These musical pieces all stand out due to existing musical representations evoking Otherness—the so-called Orient—that establish this environment as different from the rest. As Dana Plank (2020, 78) points out, we "*perceive* and *receive* certain markers of difference from normative musical practices;

therefore, musical exoticism must rely on codified devices and gestures to be intelligible as such" (emphasis original). These sonic markers carried over from western art music traditions play a large role in establishing the stereotypes of how the desert should sound in screen media. Game music is doubly prone to enforcing these stereotypes, due to Hollywood further grounding these markers as "authentic" representations.

Numerous games use the desert as a backdrop, whether it be for a level, a dungeon, or a region. They may even take place solely in this environment. Some readers may wonder why I chose to focus on *The Legend of Zelda* series, considering how many options I had. It is not to say that the series is more "problematic" than other games, or that other games are less interesting. I choose to analyze these games due to my love for them and, more importantly, an interest in the relationship between identity and environment to non-western art music traditions. More specifically, I analyze the Gerudo women and the desert through the lens of Orientalism and their ties to alterity, following Meyda Yeğenoğlu's argument (1998, 26) that "the Orient and its women are not two distinct enterprises, but rather are interwoven aspects of the same gesture."

The goal of this chapter is twofold: first, I wish to demonstrate the ways we can conduct close analyses of environmental music by analyzing the Gerudo and Lanayru Deserts in *Twilight Princess* (2006, *TP*) and *Skyward Sword* (2011, *SS*), respectively; second, I want to consider further nuances of this environment when the Gerudo are included in these analyses by exploring the music of the Gerudo Valley and Gerudo Desert in *Ocarina of Time* (1998, *OoT*) and *BotW*, respectively. Ultimately, I wish to show how heavily coded music and sound actually are. Music does not exist in a void, nor can we analyze music by itself. It is crucial that we take care in navigating what we hear because of existing discourses surrounding the ways we understand such music.

Video Games and Musical Otherness

As I have previously mentioned, game music is rife with stereotypical depictions of the desert, relying on the audience's preexisting knowledge of musical Otherness and its "authenticity" to construct an imaginative world of audiovisuals, much of which was and still is influenced by Hollywood. In this section, I will briefly draw attention to particular examples in order to provide some context of the kinds of musical coding that occur in video games.

One of game composers' greatest sources of inspiration for deserts is the Arab world, particularly thinking of the Sahara as well as other similar regions in North Africa and West Asia. When it comes to a game's visual design, the architecture and/or cultural icons further establish its supposed authenticity. For example, thatgamecompany's *Journey* (2012) shows the influences of Islamic architecture to complement the game's desert setting (Figure 25.1). In an interview, *Journey*'s creative director, Jenova Chen, mentioned how he and the art director, Matt Nava, picked the art and architecture style, stating that they did not want "extremely Western, like Greek or Roman ruins" nor

FIGURE 25.1 Architecture in *Journey*. Screenshots captured by author.

something "extremely Eastern, like Chinese or Japanese" and, so, opted for something "in between [which] became the Middle East" (2012).

Musically, composers make numerous gestures to the aforementioned regions' music traditions, such as instrumentation (e.g., a zither or an oud, and percussive instruments such as a doumbek and tambourine), ornamentation, and musical scales (most notably, the double harmonic major scale with the use of augmented seconds). Games such as *Banjo-Kazooie* (1997) and *Super Mario 64* (1996) feature deserts, valleys, and canyons that have Arab-inspired music to depict a supposedly authentic experience of the region, further grounded by the visuals (Figure 25.2).[3] Designers and composers are also

FIGURE 25.2 *Banjo-Kazooie* (top) and *Super Mario 64* (bottom). Screenshots captured by author.

inspired by other desert regions of the world, though less so than those found in the Arab world. Games such as *Paper Mario* (2000) and *Super Mario Odyssey* (2017) offer an alternate land and soundscape from ones that are usually Arab-inspired (Figure 25.3). In these particular examples, audience may recognize audiovisual designs inspired by Mexican culture, often mixing in other elements from other Latin American cultures.

This borrowing runs into the question of whether this is appreciation, appropriation, or (in)authentic. Frankly, this is a conversation that is not only outside the scope of this chapter but also unproductive. I say this not because I find the debate frivolous (quite

FIGURE 25.3 *Paper Mario* (top) and *Super Mario Odyssey* (bottom). Screenshots captured by author.

the contrary); rather, it does not address how and why music and sound function this way. Shin Aoki (2017, 945) expresses the concern of "being bound by the spirit of political correctness and lacking insight into realities." I am interested in the "realities" Aoki highlights, which *are* often anything but politically correct. It is by understanding these "real" experiences that we can further elucidate such phenomena to then approach questions related to representation.

This also runs into the "us" versus "them" debate, which is not as clear cut as one may believe. As Timothy D. Taylor (2007, 7) notes, "People in different historical situations have ways of constructing their Others in different ways." In other words, "us" and "them" will never be static. We generally understand this to be the more binary "East" versus "West" situation, one that Edward Said explores in his foundational work, *Orientalism*, and notes that this geographical distinction is imaginative and "arbitrary" (1979, 54). However, consider that most of my earlier examples and the games I focus on are primarily from Nintendo, a Japanese company. Where does Japan's positionality fall in all of this? How do they construct their Others, especially when they themselves have been depicted as Other? There are no easy answers to any of these issues I have brought up, and I do not have any intentions of promising to give (or have) any by the end of this chapter. I merely make these points to acknowledge the complications of the topics that I will cover.

The Ghosts of the Gerudo

I begin my analysis with *SS*'s Lanayru Desert. This may seem to be an unusual decision, considering the only mention of the Gerudo is a dragonfly of the same name native to the area. However, a subtle yet significant connection exists between the Gerudo women and the Lanayru Desert. *SS* is the next main installment in the series after *TP*. Those who have played *TP* will remember the name "Lanayru" from one of the provinces of the earlier title, which is where Lake Hylia and Zora's Domain are located.[4] Considering this reference, the Lanayru Desert comes as a shock. Even for those who have not played the aforementioned game, they may still express shock when Fi, Link's companion in *SS*, reports that the once lush area "changed dramatically as climate forces rapidly turned it into a desert." This drastic transformation creates a shift in emotion, one from shock to wistfulness. This can either be because players may recall their adventures in the Lanayru Province in *TP* and/or, in the context of *SS*, from learning about a once advanced civilization having disappeared from a now dry expanse.

While there are visual aesthetics to consider and their relationship to the music in the Lanayru Desert, we must also consider the depiction of time and its affect on the audiovisuals. *SS* takes place long before Hyrule came to be, evoking the ancient past to the player and, perhaps, nostalgia for what once was. The peritext of the game, particularly its prologue, depict what occurred long before the creation of Skyloft, making the Lanayru Desert carry an air of an even earlier era further established by the remnants of structures.

On YouTube uploads of the music heard in the *SS* Lanayru Desert, users have commented how it suited the moment as they draw from extramusical materials which, in this case, is the series' lore and the Lanayru Desert landscape. One user commented that the music "feels very holy and mystical," while another wrote how the composers "have truly captured the essence of time's depth and continual forward motion, which deserts show great evidence of."[5] Both of these comments reflect on the concept of an ancient time and the mysteries that it holds. This reverance of the desert is not an unfamiliar one, as Irene Chien (2017, 132) points out that the environment evokes "a locus of enchantment and spiritual renewal that counters the exhaustions of . . . modernity." Furthermore, the Lanayru Desert evokes "the 'double temporality' that governs the mythic image of the [environment]: 'It is both the place of origin and the utopian prospect of the future, always fleeting beyond the present' " (Mitchell 2000, quoted in Chien, 143–144). "Double temporality" is twofold in *SS*. The game harkens to an ancient past found in the desert while also looking toward the future. The series reveals on its official timeline that *SS is* the ancient past, and players have been playing these games out of chronological order.[6] All desert music and soundscapes that they have heard up to this point were from the future—sounds of what could be.

Continuing this concept of the past, the Lanayru Desert broadly gestures to pre-Columbian aesthetics. Visually, the Lanayru Mines in particular feature architectural elements that seem to be inspired by Inca art, such as the semicircle patterns atop the conveyer belts that are similar to Inca masks. The geometric shapes and colors are an invocation of the "ancient." Moreover, turquoise is prominent in this area, whether it be in the designs or when the Timeshift Stones are activated (Figure 25.4). They harken back to the cultural significance of this gemstone in Aztec culture.

Musically, a wind instrument carries a mysterious yet peaceful melody. I suggest that this instrument is an ocarina for a few reasons: (1) similar timbres; (2) its prevalence in pre-Columbian cultures; and (3) its nod to *OoT*, in which the instrument plays a crucial role, which, relatedly, the main theme of *SS* is "Zelda's Lullaby" (a playable melody in *OoT*) backward. In doing so, there is a double musical coding that is the series' history as well as our own. As Tim Summers (2020, 37) writes, such connections "accumulate meaning and [tie] together the franchise." Ambient synths, not dissimilar to chanting,

FIGURE 25.4 The Lanayru Mines (left) and an active Timeshift Stone (right). Screenshot on left captured by author. Image on right from Zelda Wiki.

are heard in the musical texture to create the "holy and mystical" musicscape that seem to echo an untouchable past. Another prominent part of the music is the slow and steady rhythm of drums and rattles that underly the melody, as well as a stringed instrument that further contributes to the mysterious atmosphere. Finally, the absence of a conventional resolution of the melody instills a wariness of the endless dangers found in the desert.

The audiovisual aesthetics of the Lanayru Desert come together to create an aura of mystery, a temporal "veil . . . through which Western fantasies of penetration into the mysteries of the Orient and access to the interiority of the other are fantasmatically achieved" (Yeğenoğlu 1998, 39). In this case, the Orient is the Lanayru Desert. While the Gerudo are not present in *SS*, they have ghostly presences that can be heard in the music, foreshadowing the eventual existence of their race after the events of the game. The Gerudo, much like the Lanayru Desert, are "enigmatic, mysterious, concealing a secret behind [their] veil[s]" (73). Even though a different race inhabited the area, the Gerudo's voices can be heard everywhere due to their deep connections to the desert from prior titles, an impenetrable enigma due to their physical absences.

There is a similar experience in the Gerudo Desert of *TP*, where there are no Gerudo women to be found except their ghostly presences.[7] Their absence makes the desert of *TP* all the more haunting, their presences unseen but felt. The visuals support this by showing a desert that covers a vast expanse, most of the surface being overrun with monstrous enemies. Furthermore, the game's gloomy aesthetics heighten this haunting as the land is shrouded in darkness. This establishes the common assumption that the desert is a barren wasteland, often followed by the decision to make the environment hostile and mysterious. Once again, the way music and extramusical materials interact with the concept of time is worth exploring, as it makes similar in-game and meta references also found in *SS*. The audiovisuals play with the idea of the ancient, although, in this case, inspiration emerges from other geographic regions and time periods: the Arabo-Islamic world and ancient civilizations such as Rome and Egypt. When Link and Midna make their way to the Gerudo Desert toward their destination, the Arbiter's Grounds, the player can see towering, ornate pillars, their designs similar to the minarets found on or adjacent to mosques (Figure 25.5).

Outside of the Arbiter's Grounds, players find ruins of columns, walls, and scaffolds partially buried in sand, all of which are reminiscent of what may have been structures such as the Great Pyramid of Giza or the Colosseum. The columns found inside and outside the Arbiter's Grounds are a hybrid of Greco-Roman and Egyptian architecture. From fluted Doric columns to simply decorated columns all made from stone; these decrepit structures evoke a sense of what used to be. Inside, the columns feature visibly ornate designs that often complement the inscribed walls not unlike the ones found inside the pyramids (Figure 25.6). These aesthetic decisions are meant to fill the player with awe and fear, as the desert is "a sign of both ancient origins and apocalyptic futures" (Chien 2017, 132). *TP* explores this in great depth, the Gerudo Desert serving as a particularly apt location to understand this haunting spatial and temporal blur. The visuals uphold the liminal space that is the past *and* future, but the blurring I speak of happens in the music leading up to Arbiter's Grounds.

FIGURE 25.5 The minarets that surround the Arbiter's Grounds. Screenshot captured by author.

The music constructs the emotional experience that helps establish the desert's history and what lies within. In this case, this is the Arbiter's Grounds, which has a different, more ambient music playing in the background rather than what is heard in the desert. However, the music of the Arbiter's Grounds only seems eerie and otherworldly *because* of the Gerudo Desert's theme. The series' lore and the desert's history intertwine in a way that adds nuance to the entire region, which come together when the player first enters the Gerudo Desert. The desert's theme confirms the player is somewhere that is more than just mysterious. It is a frightening unknown that is evoked by gesturing toward varying music traditions and the musical past to truly Other this region.

In the Gerudo Desert's theme, there is a prominent, percussive texture composed of what sounds like a shaker and a doumbek, the latter being an important part of many North African and West Asian music traditions. There is also occasional ornamentation from a guitar for additional accents in the rhythm. This use of guitar is curious, as it gestures more to the Andalusian region. However, this is not entirely random for two reasons: (1) fans of the series will recall the use of the guitar from the theme of Gerudo Valley in *OoT* which features a prominent and "exotic" melodic line for this instrument; and (2) the aesthetic influences of when the region was under Muslim rule signify a historically cultural and temporal Other.

Overlaying this percussive texture are two distinct sections to this theme. One section carries a melody led by what sounds like a reed instrument. The other, which I want to draw particular attention to, is a melody led by chant. This returns to the idea of evoking a "holy and mystical" atmosphere like the Lanayru Desert in *SS* by including a religious-sounding chant. In doing so, this can go two directions for Othering: it either sounds

FIGURE 25.6 Outside the Arbiter's Grounds (top left) and the interior (top right and bottom). Screenshots captured by author.

reminiscent of Gregorian chants or, perhaps to fit the rest of the audiovisual aesthetics, Islamic chant.[8] Players will also immediately recognize this chant to be a variation of the overworld theme heard in Hyrule Field.

Whether the musical inspiration is from the past or the Arabo-Islamic world (or both), its association with a ruined desert emphasizes the region's distance from the rest of Hyrule: an uncivilized region with "primitive desert dweller[s] governed by mystic religion rather than secular reason" (Chien 2017, 132). It is the land of the desolate Other, especially so when one remembers that the Arbiter's Grounds served as the place of punishment for Hyrule's worst criminals. Furthermore, the variation on the overworld theme suggests Hyrule's powerful presence in the region—perhaps an imperialist one—and their need to conquer this threatening Other, spatially and musically.

There is no way to know whether the composers would have used the same music had the Gerudo been present in *TP*. However, the music enforces the need to distance the desert from the rest of Hyrule, especially considering its history in-game. This distancing also removes the Gerudo from the rest of Hyrule figuratively and literally: in the figurative sense that their presence is heard through the music that is so often affiliated to the

Other, much like them; and, in the literal sense, their removal from the game itself, existing as ghostly figures instead.

It is crucial to mention this haunting due to players' prior knowledge of past titles in *The Legend of Zelda* series—specifically *OoT*—that established the affiliation of the Gerudo to this arid environment. The removal of the Gerudo in *TP* creates an incongruous experience of the desert as the player recalls their existence and now must consider a grim future where they might not have survived. The music serves as a connection between the Gerudo and the desert, with subtle elements such as the guitar and the chanting to confirm their status of Otherness. This connects to the musical past of *OoT* which also features similar musical elements heard in this environment.[9] *TP* presents a darker—even heartbreaking—perspective of the desert through its violent history and overwhelming presence of monsters that Link must defeat. As a result, the music is a reminder of the Other, but it also haunts.

A Gerudo with Many Qualities

I now formally introduce the Gerudo, who are a race almost entirely made up of women.[10] They are generally wary of anyone who is not of their race. They are especially suspicious of men, who, as one Gerudo in *BotW* explains, are "strictly forbidden" from entering within their walls. The many inhabitants of Hyrule—mostly Hylians—whom the player encounters reciprocate this wariness, encouraging them to perceive the Gerudo in a similar fashion. The representation of the Gerudo is "interwoven by sexual imageries, unconscious fantasies, desires, fears, and dreams," and they are inextricably linked to their environment that carries its own history of Otherness (Yeğenoğlu 1998, 26). It is not a coincidence that they are isolated from the rest of Hyrule, the desert appearing on the corner of maps in these games. In doing so, it establishes the point that "[they] had to be ideologically distanced," and these maps were "a mode of containment as well as a mode of representation, a way of putting Others and their Elsewheres in view while keeping them safely at a distance" (Taylor 2007, 26).

The Gerudo are recognized by their red hair, pointed noses and, most prominently, their darker skin. Hylians, on the other hand, carry traits that are similar to indigenous Northern Europeans, from their fair skin to blonde-to-brown hair. From their clothes to their weapons, the Gerudo are meant to depict filmic stereotypes of Arab women and, in the case of *BotW*, Amazons (Figure 25.7).[11] In almost all their appearances in the series, they are found in the desert and heavily affiliated with the environment by in-game characters and fans alike.[12] The Gerudo are depicted as thieves in earlier games, though in *BotW*, there is a shift to depict them as merchants.[13]

While the Gerudo are depicted as fierce warriors in all their appearances in the series, they are also in a peculiar position of being made up of one gender in an isolated space—almost like a harem. They are grounded in the historic feminization of the Orient when considering their (theoretically) impenetrable living spaces, their garments, and their

FIGURE 25.7 Nabooru in *Ocarina of Time 3D* (2011) (left) and Urbosa in *BotW* (right). Screenshots captured by author.

interest in pursuing boyfriends outside of their dwellings.[14] Yet, they also pose a danger because they subvert expectations of the conventional, feminine depictions of the Other in the fear they instill vis-à-vis physical violence.

As I have noted, both the desert and the Gerudo are depicted as "enigmatic [and] mysterious" (Yeğenoğlu 1998, 73). They are as "fascinating" as they are "frightening" to men, who as *voe* ("man" in the Gerudo language), cannot penetrate the metaphorical veil.[15] In doing so, this results in a monstrous depiction of the Gerudo and the desert—in the case of the latter, quite literally with all of its enemies. As women, the Gerudo become the monstrous feminine with the power to "sustain life or end it" (Pennington 2020, 285). The Gerudo sustain life by helping Link, yet also end it with their (supposed) hostility, making them far more complex than they let on, much like the environment they reside in.

I have presented some context of who the Gerudo are not only for readers who are unfamiliar with the series but also because extramusical material plays a role in constructing their Otherness in Hyrule. Analyzing the Lanayru Desert and Gerudo Desert in *SS* and *TP*, respectively, shows that the music takes particular care to depict these environments as different from the rest of Hyrule; that this is a place of danger and mystery. Furthermore, the knowledge that players already have of the Gerudo while playing these games further establishes the connection they make between the women and the environment. I now shift my focus to *OoT* and *BotW*, in which the music associated with the Gerudo explores, complicates, and even disrupts the construction of difference.

Hearing the Gerudo and the Desert

I begin this section with an analysis of the Gerudo Valley from *OoT*, the game, I would argue, that creates the model of how the Gerudo and the desert should sound for the franchise.[16] Comments across forums and videos express their adoration of the region's theme, ranging from arguments that this is the best theme not only in the game but also in the series to exclamations of cultural pride from Spanish and Mexican users. It is not lost on players that the music is hybridized, either, as they poke fun at its multicultural nature on YouTube.[17]

The pride that some users feel is not without merit, nor are their observations of musical hybridity. There are clear influences of flamenco and mariachi in the Gerudo Valley's theme, styles which are heavily coded to stand out from the rest of the game's music with their flair and "exotic" elements. It is a curious pairing, and even more so when considering how the Gerudo are presented in the game, wearing stereotypical Arab-inspired clothes while wielding scimitars. The combination of these audiovisual elements creates a discordant experience that makes the region and its people noticeably different from everything and everyone else.

The familiar Hyrule Field disappears as Link enters the unfamiliar Gerudo Valley on his steed Epona. A conventionally western orchestra also fades away to be replaced by acoustic guitars and bass, as well as accented clapping that mimics the bulería, followed by a trumpet line akin to mariachi overlaying this rhythmic pattern (Park 2015, 68–71).[18] The music follows the visuals to establish the Otherness of the Gerudo and the desert in *OoT*.

Gender is another layer to consider when approaching these music traditions in relation to the desert and the Gerudo. Flamenco and mariachi are also gendered in ways that have influenced our cultural imaginations of these two music traditions. Music positions the desert and the Gerudo to slip past the gender binary in such a way that it complicates what we see on screen. Indeed, music is still taking part in Othering, but it also disrupts and challenges the visuals that sexualize and emphasize femininity in a way that calls for further investigation of the sociocultural components surrounding environments and peoples.[19]

There is a tendency to connect flamenco to femininity because of the stereotypes that arose from non-Spanish composers' depictions (e.g., Georges Bizet's *Carmen*), playing a large role in what Joaquina Labajo (2003, 67) describes as "the flowering of an exotic gendered language of gestures and attitudes" toward the music tradition. The clapping rhythms heard in the Gerudo Valley embody flamenco, coaxing the listener to dance along. The gendering of flamenco has a complex history, and I want to draw particular attention to the Roma women and their significant contributions to the genre, with myths surrounding them, such as being primitive, exotic, and having mystical powers (68–69). This is not unlike the mythology of the desert.

To further complicate this depiction, there are dances and modes of expression traditionally associated with men that women have co-opted, contributing to the gender construction of flamenco. This leads to "not only a practice full of sexual meanings, but also a display of athleticism performed according to compelling theatrical rules . . . asserting in this way their power and authority and simultaneously evoking their oriental roots and Indian origin in order to satisfy the desire for exoticism of their masculine audience" (76). In relation to the Gerudo, their beauty entrances Hylian men, further emphasized by the stereotypically feminine rhythms in a strictly women-only space. Yet, these rhythms also have ties to stereotypical masculinity that enforce the Gerudo's power. To further establish this, the history of the guitar in flamenco has been perceived to be "a virtue in a man's hands and a defect in the hands of a woman" (77). The Gerudo Valley's theme has a virtuosic-like guitar that occasionally carries the melody which co-opts a historically masculine practice to suggest the Gerudo as "the image of the powerful female flamenco dancer [that] might tie into the notion of feminine authority" (Summers 2020, 159). How does this compare, then, with the moments where we hear mariachi-inspired trumpets?

The use of mariachi, as Mary-Lee Mulholland (2013) notes, is an oft-perceived masculine (more specifically, macho) genre. Alongside flamenco, this leads to a fascinating play on gender. At surface level, to hear mariachi in relation to the desert and the Gerudo troubles notions of the feminine due to this affiliation to a traditionally male occupation. Furthermore, instruments that are traditionally attributed to male mariachis such as the trumpet (or the shared instrument with flamenco, the guitar) seem to position the Gerudo as less feminine (369). As a result, this emphasizes the Gerudo's known fierceness in relation to this aura of masculinity in the melody when the trumpet plays.

Digging deeper, the Gerudo exist in a similar space as do female mariachis, where they are "transgressing the boundaries and representations of normative feminine constructs" (Mulholland 2013, 370). There is some relief in this liberating affirmation in relation to masculinity; however, it is complicated by the historical and musical depictions of the desert that lock the Gerudo into the feminine Other—one of inaccessible beauty and danger, in particular—which is a twofold problem when considering the ways in which women *and* men who have been Othered are perceived as threats for reasons ranging from promiscuity to terrorism.

There are numerous layers to the ways in which gender and Otherness function in the Gerudo Valley's theme. They work to complicate the Gerudo's positionality, especially in relation to the desert, and "slip into the in-between spaces of normative identity constructs" (Mulholland (2013, 360). The stereotypical feminine depictions of flamenco make the Gerudo dangerously alluring and mysterious, much like the desert they inhabit. Yet, the co-optation of the masculinity of flamenco by female performers is more liberating and gives the Gerudo agency over themselves. On the other hand, while the stereotypical masculine depictions of mariachi make the Gerudo seem fierce and powerful, they are at odds with the ways in which flamenco functions in this theme. With the inclusion of the desert, Latin America—specifically Mexico—and its connection to the desert plays a role when we hear mariachi. Flamenco is an outlier, though Andalusia's proximity to the desert may also play a role in its inclusion in this theme. Koji Kondo, the composer of *OoT*, "does not claim any authenticity of representing a musical tradition," but there is a sense of uneasiness with "the use of a Spanish-Mexican musical fusion to accompany a group of people known in the game as 'the noble thieves of the desert' " (Summers 2020, 159). Such music, ultimately, serves to play with Otherness and gender in ways that complicate what we hear.

BotW continues to complicate the Otherness of the Gerudo and the environment. However, this complication is also taking into consideration that the reception of the game's music was mixed, some of the less-than-positive comments expressing disappointment that there was a more minimalist approach to the music. Even for me, it came as a surprise (a pleasant one, though) when I first heard the thin musical texture of a piano. This was especially the case when I entered the desert, half-expecting something more exciting that followed the traditions of past musical depictions of this environment. Despite the qualms that some players have expressed, there were plenty of others who found the music stunning in its own way, appreciating little details woven into various cues, such as "Zelda's Lullaby" while Link is riding his horse during the day or hearing unique cues while playing. For example, when temperatures fluctuate during the day and night in the Gerudo Desert, the music follows suit to warn the player to dress Link in appropriate gear that would keep him from taking damage from heat exhaustion or freezing. The music that plays when it is hot, for many, evokes a sense of "slowly dying in the middle of the desert" or how it "makes [them] feel dehydrated."[20]

One notable detail in *BotW* is that, unlike the other games I have analyzed, the standard overworld music plays in the desert, even if only briefly. This serves to connect the desert to the rest of Hyrule, musically depicting the region as less hostile and suggesting closer relations with other races. The music unites them with the rest of the kingdom, perhaps an acknowledgment of the needed alliance across all races to defeat a greater evil threatening their world. The desert remains a hostile place, considering the music that primarily plays is one that alerts the player of danger, but there are, in fact, musical moments that avoid a complete Othering of the Gerudo.

First, I want to briefly consider the music heard at Kara Kara Bazaar, which serves as a locational and musical transition between the Gerudo Desert and Gerudo Town. The bazaar is a literal oasis that serves as a place of rest before reaching Gerudo Town. The location's music serves a similar purpose, the use of the piano evoking elements of the overworld theme that keeps the desert tied to the rest of Hyrule. It emphasizes its hybridized position due to the inclusion of the dulcimer, which is crucial in its relation to the Gerudo as it makes a prominent appearance in Gerudo Town's own theme.

Even before the player reaches the walls of Gerudo Town during the day, they hear a steady rhythm from a dulcimer, before a higher-pitched dulcimer enters with an ornamented melody.[21] The dulcimer establishes itself as a representation of the Gerudo,

FIGURE 25.8 B section of Gerudo Town's theme played by two shinobue. Transcription by author.

woven into the musical blanket that represents the various races in Hyrule, all of which are connected by the piano.[22] Despite this form of representation, there is still an element of Othering, whether it be the auxiliary percussion that is reminiscent of prior desert themes in the series or an entirely new melody unlike the Zora, Gorons, and Rito (who, in their own ways, are also the Other due to their non-Hylian appearances).[23] The most noticeable form of Othering is in the B section of Gerudo Town's theme when the shinobue take over the melody, with open fourths playing throughout that are reminiscent of the Oriental riff (Figure 25.8).

Unlike my prior examples, I argue that this theme is an autoexoticism that asserts its "Gerudoness": that is, "not only by differentiating itself from an 'Other' but by being differentiated by the Other" (Iwabuchi 1994, 51). I draw attention to this because, thinking outside of the game, it reflects Japanese composers' use of instrumentation that is evocative of Japanese sound, even the dulcimer's similarity to the koto, to depict the Otherness of the Gerudo. It is Japan's complicity in the exoticized view that comes from what Noriko Manabe (2013, 36) considers "the West's persistent perception of Japan as a perpetual other." When it comes to the melody and structure of the theme, however, they are "basic signifiers of chinoiserie"—an imitation of an imagining—despite the self-referential musical elements (Waseda 2004, 149).

The Gerudo are aware and accepting of their difference from the rest of Hyrule. They worship the Seven Heroines instead of the goddess Hylia, whose statue is "found, forgotten, in a back alley" (Thorpe 2018a, 139). They function as an autonomous nation with their own distinct customs—prohibiting men from entering, for example. Even within the desert itself, they differentiate themselves by building walls around their city and establish authority over their surroundings, particularly by controlling the source of the water. There is ownership in their difference, however, and this can even be heard musically. Manabe (2013, 38) notes that in Japanese traditional music, "performers need not be in synchronisation with each other—nor be in perfect tune with one another." The music of Gerudo Town is freer, whether it be the shinobue playing harsher articulations than expected or the dulcimer at night less in-sync with the synths. In other words, there is a "preference for imperfections" (39), even if subtle, that differentiates the Gerudo from the rest of Hyrule.

There is a complication in the Gerudo's positionality as women in an enclosed space in the desert. Autoexoticism can establish their uniqueness, but it is still trapped in the space of their Othering. It is especially so when looking at femininity Orientalized; a femininity that is veiled, excessively sexualized, and subject to the western male gaze. I would argue that there is an even stronger desire to understand and sexualize the Gerudo in *BotW* than in any other game in the series, with Hylian men openly sharing their dreams of entering Gerudo Town or becoming flustered when Link disguises himself as a Gerudo woman and approaches them (Figure 25.9). Even Link is complicit in the male gaze by pretending to be a Gerudo woman, "determined to have access to this 'hidden' space" to the point that he "uses every single means that is available," even if it is for the sake of the greater good (Yeğenoğlu 1998, 74).

Musically, the intricate ornamentation heard throughout Gerudo Town's theme retains the Gerudo's status as Other. It matches the unique designs of the Gerudo women's clothes, their elaborate hairstyles, and bejeweled weaponry that reflect the exotic imagery and fantasies that lie in the seemingly impenetrable desert. They are reminiscent of what is not only heard in *TP*'s desert theme but also numerous other games that feature such ornamentation when representing the desert. As much as the Gerudo and the music establish themselves as their own, being a historically feminine and racial Other in an environment that is also the Other keeps them at a safe distance.

Conclusion

The Gerudo and the desert in *The Legend of Zelda* are musically complex and call for us to listen carefully to how we code them. There are multiple extramusical layers to consider that inform the way we hear them and, more broadly, music in relation to peoples and environments. We can analyze the music of the desert itself, which is rich in content as demonstrated in *SS* and *TP*. However, we can also consider its relationship to its people—in this case, the Gerudo—and reapproach the music to explore other components such as identity and its ties to the social, cultural, and historical, as demonstrated in *OoT* and *BotW*. Even in *SS* and *TP*, the Gerudo still leave a musical impression despite their absences when one considers the narratives, musics, and myths surrounding the games.

FIGURE 25.9 Hylian men sharing their thoughts on the Gerudo and their city with Link dressed in Gerudo clothing (top) and in regular clothing (bottom). Screenshots captured by author.

Looking broadly at the field, I contemplate how we can consider these complexities in game musics and sounds. Crucially, we must listen to the conversation that is happening between the game world and the real world (or the world outside of games), as the latter greatly informs the construction of the former's universe. Our interactions with the texts and musics surrounding the object of study lead to intriguing insights on how and why we hear characters and environments the way we do. When we put these elements in dialogue with one another, we move past superficial conversations about appropriation and (in)authenticity to, instead, focus on nuances that affect players' experiences and imaginations.

Acknowledgments

I thank Jordan Hugh Sam, Clayton McKee, and Ross Mitchell for their help and support as I worked out my ideas for this chapter. I also thank Toru Momii for generously sending me articles on self-Orientalism, as well as helping me identify instruments in Gerudo Town's theme.

Notes

1. I will be referring to *The Legend of Zelda* titles by their subtitles and abbreviating them after they are first introduced.
2. It is important to address the way we use certain words, such as "exotic." Timothy D. Taylor (2007, 209) points out the problematic use of "exoticism," stating that it is a "stylistic label; it does not explain anything in and of itself. Instead, it obscures." He goes on to mention that the use of this term "can impede the deeper historical, cultural, and social analysis," and calls for musicologists to pay attention to this. It is my hope to carefully navigate this term. I acknowledge that there are discourses to take into consideration, though, unfortunately, they are outside the scope of this chapter.
3. The track titles and regional names are "Gobi's Valley" and "Lethal Lava Land," respectively.
4. The Zora are a humanoid race in the series who inhabit aquatic environments. They have fish- and amphibian-like physical traits.
5. The first comment was from user whostolecarlosrox, while the second comment was from user Curse Counter. A quick look through the comments will show other users using words such as "ancient" to describe this music. See GilvaSunner, "Lanayru Desert—The Legend of Zelda: Skyward Sword," YouTube, November 23, 2011, video, 3:39, https://www.youtube.com/watch?v=oLfAcKnDYWQ.
6. In *Hyrule Encyclopedia* (Thorpe 2018b), an updated timeline from *Hyrule Historia* (2013) begins with the genesis of what eventually becomes Skyloft in *SS*. The timeline continues until it splits into three branches from *OoT*: (1) the hero is defeated, (2) the hero is triumphant and Ganondorf is stopped (the "child" timeline), and (3) the hero is triumphant and Ganondorf is sealed away (the "adult" timeline) (2018b, 10). In *Creating a Champion* (Thorpe 2018a), *BotW* takes place so far ahead in the future that everything before the 2017 title has faded to myth.
7. Players have come up with theories as to why the Gerudo are not present during the events of the game, despite the inference that they existed. A compelling theory made by a Reddit user was how in *OoT*, the Gerudo lived in the Gerudo Valley and largely avoided the desert. The user drew connections between the desert's locations in the two games, pointing out that in *TP*, only the desert is explored and not the valley, suggesting that the Gerudo went into hiding there. (See u/oberyns_python, "Gerudo in Twilight Princess," r/truezelda, Reddit, November 29, 2019, https://www.reddit.com/r/truezelda/comments/e3c2ri/gerudo_in_twilight_princess/.) *Hyrule Encyclopedia*, published over a decade after the release of the game, stated that the Gerudo were driven out of the desert (Thorpe 2018b, 45), debunking any player's theory of their demise. However, this is not to say that Nintendo's explanations have greater value than fan theories, considering fans' contributions to building the mythology of the series.
8. Players may remember the controversy surrounding the music heard in the Fire Temple in *OoT* which also featured a chant that sounded like Islamic chant.

9. Chanting is technically heard in the Fire Temple which is in Death Mountain. While this is neither the desert nor related to the Gerudo, I believe this is still worth considering due to the similar reference to unbearable heat and its geographic and musical distance from the rest of Hyrule. There is also the Spirit Temple, which *is* in the desert, and has a mystical sound coming from ambient synths in its cue.
10. Every hundred years, a male Gerudo is born, who ends up being the main antagonist of the series. It would be interesting to further explore his positionality, though this is outside the scope of the chapter.
11. *OoT 3D* (2011) is the remastered version of *OoT* for the handheld console, Nintendo 3DS. The screenshot of Urbosa is from the downloadable content pack, *The Champions' Ballad* (2017).
12. The only title that features Gerudo who are *not* in the desert is *Majora's Mask* (2000, *MM*). Instead, they are in a pirate fortress by the sea in the Great Bay region.
13. A passing Hylian man in *BotW* comments that he heard rumors of thieves living in Gerudo, suggesting that there is still wariness of the Gerudo, even thousands of years after they were last seen.
14. In *OoT*, there is a gossip stone that points out the Gerudo sometimes visit Hyrule Castle Town to find boyfriends. Similarly, in *BotW*, some of the Gerudo mention their interest in finding (male) partners (Thorpe 2018a, 139). There is even a side quest to help a Hylian find a wife, who ends up being a Gerudo.
15. In *OoT*, one of the carpenters saved in the Gerudo Fortress comments: "The Gerudo are beautiful and brave. . . . They are just so fascinating!" In *MM*, a fisherman remarks that they are "so frightening, they could scare a crying baby into silence."
16. While the valley (where they are based) is not technically the desert, the fact that the player can hear the theme in the actual desert links the two areas, establishing that relationship between the people and the environment.
17. See Nintendo-Reuploads, "Gerudo Valley—The Legend of Zelda: Ocarina of Time," YouTube, August 9, 2019, video, 2:55, https://www.youtube.com/watch?v=ohEYvdMoF2g.
18. See also Summers's analysis of the clapping pattern in "Gerudo Valley" (2020, 158).
19. I want to acknowledge that this is an essentialist approach to gender which, while problematic, still holds a power over our musically coded cultural imagination.
20. The first comment was from user dcepticonn, while the second comment was from user Awful Waffle. See Yara, "Field (Desert)—The Legend of Zelda: Breath of the Wild | Extended Music," YouTube, November 27, 2018, video, 30:04, https://www.youtube.com/watch?v=5CFAkat-tTs.
21. If Link reaches Gerudo Town at night, rather than the lower-pitched dulcimer, the theme begins with synths before the dulcimer enters with the melody.
22. The unity of these instruments is clearest when the player completes the side quest to bring villagers into Tarrey Town.
23. The themes of Zora's Domain and Goron City are variations of *OoT*'s. Rito Village is a variation of Dragon Roost Island's theme in *Wind Waker* (2003).

References

Aoki, Shin. 2017. "Singing Exoticism: A Historical Anthropology of the G.I. Songs 'China Night' and 'Japanese Rumba.'" *Journal of American History* 103, no. 4 (March): 943–955.

Chen, Jenova. 2012. "Game Designer Jenova Chen on the Art behind His *Journey*." Interview by Kevin Ohannessian. *Fast Company*, March 12, 2012.

Chien, Irene. 2017. "*Journey* into the Techno-Primitive Desert." In *Gaming Representation: Race, Gender, and Sexuality in Video Games*, edited by Jennifer Malkowski and TreAndrea M. Russworm, 129–146. Bloomington: Indiana University Press.

Iwabuchi, Koichi. 1994. "Complicit Exoticism: Japan and Its Other." *Journal of Media and Cultural Studies* 8 (2): 49–82.

Labajo, Joaquina. 2003. "Body and Voice: The Construction of Gender in Flamenco." In *Music and Gender: Perspectives from the Mediterranean*, edited by Tullia Magrini, 67–86. Chicago: University of Chicago Press.

Manabe, Noriko. 2013. "Representing Japan: 'National' Style among Japanese Hip-Hop DJs." *Popular Music* 32, no. 1 (January): 35–50.

Mulholland, Mary-Lee. 2013. "A Beautiful Thing: Mariachi and Femininity in Jalisco, Mexico." *Anthropologica* 55 (2): 359–72.

Park, Hyeonjin. 2015. "Melodies of Distant Realms: World Music in the Context of Video Games." BA thesis, Mount Holyoke College.

Pennington, Rosemary. 2020. "Monstrously Feminine: Orientalism Embodied in 2017's *The Mummy*." *Journal of Communication Inquiry* 44, no. 3 (July): 279–96.

Plank, Dana. 2020. "The Penultimate Fantasy: Nobuo Uematsu's Score for *Cleopatra no Ma Takara*." In *Music in the Role-Playing Game: Heroes and Harmonies*, edited by William Gibbons and Steven Reale, 76–96. New York: Routledge.

Said, Edward W. 1979. *Orientalism*. New York: Vintage Books.

Summers, Tim. 2020. *"The Legend of Zelda: Ocarina of Time": A Game Music Companion*. Bristol, UK: Intellect.

Taylor, Timothy D. 2007. *Beyond Exoticism: Western Music and the World*. Durham, NC: Duke University Press.

Thorpe, Patrick. 2013. *"The Legend of Zelda": Hyrule Historia*. Translated by Michael Gombos, Takahiro Moriki, Heidi Plechl, Kumar Sivasubramanian, Aria Tanner, and John Tomas. Milwaukie, OR: Dark Horse Books.

Thorpe, Patrick, ed. 2018a. *"The Legend of Zelda: Breath of the Wild"—Creating a Champion*. Translated by Keaton C. White. Milwaukie, OR: Dark Horse Books.

Thorpe, Patrick. 2018b. *"The Legend of Zelda": Hyrule Encyclopedia*. Translated by Keaton C. White. Milwaukie, OR: Dark Horse Books.

Waseda, Minako. 2004. "Looking Both Ways: GI Songs and Musical Exoticism in Post–World War II Japan." *Yearbook for Traditional Music* 36 (1): 144–164.

Yeğenoğlu, Meyda. 1998. *Colonial Fantasies: Towards a Feminist Reading of Orientalism*. New York: Cambridge University Press.

CHAPTER 26

LUDOMUSICAL AUTOBIOGRAPHY AND THE INDIE COMPOSER-DEVELOPER

WILLIAM GIBBONS

Introduction: Going Solo

The rise of independent developers is one of the postmillennial game industry's great success stories—perhaps even, in the words of game scholar Jesper Juul (2019, 1), "one of the most interesting and important events in the history of video games." Indie games collectively present a compelling underdog story, conjuring images of solo developers and small teams as metaphorical Davids against the Goliaths of major studios.[1] Part of that narrative, at least, is true: after decades of market domination by ever-expanding studios with ever-expanding budgets, indie games began to gain mainstream traction late in the first decade of the 2000s.[2] There are several reasons for the sudden success of indie games. Digital distribution models, including Valve's Steam platform (est. 2003), Sony's PlayStation Network (est. 2006), and Apple's App Store (est. 2008), enabled small developers to reach exponentially larger audiences than had previously been possible. At the same time, the widespread availability of development tools like inexpensive (or free) software, internet tutorials, modding communities, and even university game design curricula reduced the once-prohibitive barriers to entry.

As my Steam library can attest, the result is a cornucopia of independent titles ranging from text-based interactive fiction to innovative puzzle games, to 80-hour role-playing games that rival the latest major studio releases. This dazzling variety highlights the complex, contradictory nature of indie games as a genre. Indeed, what exactly makes a game "indie" at all is anything but clear—which is perhaps the point. In a study of LGBTQ experiences in indie games, for example, Bo Ruberg

(2021) makes a compelling argument that "[r]ather than being a distinct category of videogames or game production, indie is best understood as an imaginary: a set of dominant narratives about what independent games are, who develops them and how, and what makes these games meaningful." In this conception, "indie" is more an aspect of identity rather than a set of shared characteristics. While I agree—and will return to this point later—there are nonetheless several recurring conceptual and stylistic features of that indie identity.

As with so-called indie music, the term "indie" can have economic meaning for game development—that is, games created without funding (and the accompanying interference) from major studios. But it also carries aesthetic connotations of a shared artistic sensibility that rests outside the mainstream or may even be aggressively antimainstream.[3] We might consider, then, the discourse and practices of indie games. They often, although not always, eschew cutting-edge graphics in favor of a retro, pixelated art style. They can take experimental approaches to gameplay, art, or narrative. Or they can deal with more challenging subject material that larger studios would avoid.

The size of the studios—scrappy groups as opposed to monolithic AAA companies—is also a frequent marker of indie status, even if the data reveals a more complicated picture. As Paolo Ruffino (2021) summarizes, "[i]ndependence is no longer a marginal or alternative mode of production (if it ever was); instead, it is the most common type of organization within the videogame industry."[4] Despite the realities, however, perceptions linger that the smaller the studio, the more "indie" it is understood to be. Indie developer Eric Barone, for example, was quoted in a 2019 article as saying: "The larger your team is, the more difficult it is to maintain a strong, singular vision. . . . Part of what makes games like *Stardew Valley* ([2016] just me) or *Hollow Knight* ([2017] two-man team) successful is that you can 'feel' the personal touch in the game" (Schwerin 2019). Thus, while most independent games are produced by teams of like-minded developers, there is a special place reserved in the indie ethos for works that are the product of a single creator. As with "auteur" films (a flawed and controversial term), games created by these solo developers (or "solo devs") are often celebrated as manifestations of a designer's personal vision, untainted by commercial ambitions or corporate interference.

In her influential book *Rise of the Videogame Zinesters*, author and developer Anna Anthropy (2012, 103) outlines a set of artistic and ethical imperatives for single-developer games:

> Books are written by single authors or by author-editor teams. Visual art is typically made by an individual artist. It makes sense for creators to be close to their work and to own their work completely, and that's something that the big teams that big-budget games demand can't have. When an individual or pair is solely responsible for a work you can watch an individual style develop: you can trace themes, both mechanical and otherwise, across a creator's work. . . . And being able (or learning to) identify the individual style, and growth, of individual authors leads to better criticism and a critical understanding of games. Not to mention, like I said, more personal games, more relevant games, more games with something to say. I want a world where everyone is capable of sitting down at a computer and making a game by herself. This is not to

> say that all games need to be made that way, but as a paradigm, I think the individual author has more to offer us than the team, especially at a time when videogames are so seemingly creatively bankrupt.

These values are at the core of the single-developer mythology. Outsourcing programming, level design, script writing, or art direction, for example, would likely challenge the perception of a single authorial voice.

Music, however, seems to be outside, or at the boundary of, the expected responsibilities for solo developers. Anthropy's own short guide to creating indie games includes sound effects ("Task 5: Make Some Noise"), but not music. Her best-known game, the highly personal and autobiographical *Dys4ia* (2012), includes music by another composer (Liz Ryerson). Other solo devs have done likewise, supplementing their vision with outside musical assistance. Indeed, some of the most highly celebrated post-millennial indie games follow this solo-dev-except-music paradigm, including *Spelunky* (2008), *VVVVVV* (2010), *Thomas Was Alone* (2012), *Dust: An Elysian Tale* (2012), *Boot Hill Heroes* (2013), *The First Tree* (2018), and *Song of Iron* (2021).

For another group of developers—a group I call composer-developers—the music constitutes an essential part of the design process. Consider Jason Rohrer, for example, whose game *Passage* (2007) is in the permanent collection of the MOMA, and who, in 2016, was the first developer to have a solo show of their games in an art gallery. In an interview with Juul, Rohrer identified music as a key component of his artistic vision. Being a solo developer, Rohrer notes, "helps make the end product a very personal thing. I'm not only making the game I'm also making the website, coming up with a PR plan, and doing tech support. And recording the music and writing the music and everything. So when the end user interfaces with this product, they are getting a very personal person-to-person thing" (quoted in Juul 2019, 14).

Some of these composer-developers have achieved some measure of fame (and financial success) from their works. Barone's massively successful RPG-sim *Stardew Valley*, for example, has sold over 10 million copies and gave its creator a net worth well over 30 million USD (Nunneley 2020). Likewise, Toby Fox, composer-developer of the RPG *Undertale*, has achieved considerable musical success in addition to game sales. The chiptune score for the game has been re-released in a variety of formats and cover albums, and a live concert in 2020 for the game's fifth anniversary drew a large (virtual) audience (Hernandez 2020). Many others, however, have created games with more localized scope—often released for free (or pay-what-you-can), and/or geared toward a more niche audience seeking experimental or self-consciously artistic experiences. (See Table 26.1 for a selective list of composer-developers since 2004.)

These composer-developers raise several questions for the field of ludomusicology. Does music function differently in games when the composer is structuring all elements of the game? Or what happens when the music is composed prior to, or concurrent with, level design rather than afterward, as it typically works with mainstream games? This chapter is far too brief to delve too deeply into these questions, but I will start to address one issue exclusive to solo developer games. As Anna Anthropy suggests, one

TABLE 26.1 Selected Composer–Developers and Their Games since 2000

Game Title	Initial Release Year	Developer
Cave Story	2004	Daisuke Amaya
Passage	2007	Jason Rohrer
Calamity Annie	2008	Anna Anthropy
Gravitation	2008	Jason Rohrer
To the Moon	2011	Kan Gao
Inside a Star-Filled Sky	2011	Jason Rohrer
Polymer	2012	Whitaker Trebella
Anodyne	2013	Melos Han-Tani/Marina Kittaka
Problem Attic	2013	Liz Ryerson
Kero Blaster	2014	Daisuke Amaya
Papers, Please	2014	Lucas Pope
Lisa: The Painful	2014	Austin Jorgensen
Undertale	2015	Toby Fox
Piloteer	2015	Whitaker Trebella
Axiom Verge	2015	Thomas Happ
Consumed Orient	2016	Melos Han Tani
Even the Ocean	2016	Melos Han Tani/Marina Kittaka
Stardew Valley	2016	Eric Barone
LiEat	2016	Miwashiba (nom de plume)
OneShot	2016	Nightmargin (Casey Gu), Eliza Velasquez, and Michael Shirt
Finding Paradise	2017	Kan Gao
Atchafalaya Arcade	2017	Tamara Duplantis
Rakuen	2017	Laura Shigihara
All Our Asias	2018	Melos Han-Tani
Iconoclasts	2018	Joakim Sandberg
ESC	2018	Lena Raine
Return of the Obra Dinn	2018	Lucas Pope
For Today, I Breathe Again	2019	Tamara Duplantis
Baba Is You	2019	Arvi Teikari

benefit to the single developer model is the ability to weave more unfiltered, personal narratives into game design. In recent years particularly, the result has been a proliferation of introspective, autobiographical (and semiautobiographical) games. Through three case studies, I will consider if, and how, music factors into the autobiographical nature of solo-developer games—asking how, in other words, these developers express their unique identities through what we might call "ludomusical autobiography." Before turning to these case studies, however, I will offer a brief overview of autobiographical indie games as a recent trend.

Indie Games and Autobiography

As scholar and novelist Christopher B. Patterson (who writes fiction and criticism under the name Kawika Guillermo) has noted, solo devs "are creating games that overlap with literary genres of autobiography and testimonial" (Guillermo 2018). At the same time, however, he continues, "these 'personal games' . . . do not signal a turn to autobiography so much as they push the boundaries of what personal writing is. All of these games rely more on impression than literal realism . . . virtually none of the *biography* is within these autobiographies. Instead, life stories are told through interaction, so that players experience the moods, the emotions, the swings, and the frustrations of others." The result is a kind of hybrid narrative structure in which the player and author to some extent overlap.

Exactly how autobiographical these games are can range widely. For my purposes, I am defining "autobiographical" as broadly as possible, encompassing games along a spectrum from those with implied autobiographical elements—say, characters that share significant life experiences or identity markers with the developer(s)—to those that reveal their creators' lives with overt, even voyeuristic transparency. For example, the interactive fiction game *Depression Quest* (2013), written by Zoë Quinn and Patrick Lindsey, draws on the writers' experiences living with depression while not being overtly autobiographical. *Cibele* (2015), by contrast, uses a combination of live-action video, simulated chat spaces, and an in-game online game (MMO) to trace a budding internet-to-real-world romance based on the life of developer Nina Freeman. Freeman includes highly personal documents in the game, including photos, creative writing, and actual chat transcripts—and she portrays herself in the game's video portions. As one reviewer noted, the game puts the player in the position of "invading her privacy because it gets so intimate. Freeman lets you get a glimpse into her life that most people would hide under lock and key, which is admirable—but at the same time, it makes me feel voyeuristic" (Wallace 2015).

Many autobiographical games are not particularly joyful, or even enjoyable, experiences. Indeed, *Depression Quest* and the equally poignant *Actual Sunlight* (2015) attempt to convey the struggle of living with long-term depression by putting the player into intensely frustrating no-win situations, subverting all standard heroic game archetypes. Will O'Neill, the developer of *Actual Sunlight*, identifies closely with the game's depressed protagonist, Evan: "I am that person in *Actual Sunlight*. The apartment is modeled very closely after my own. Even things I softly allude to are things that were going on in Toronto at the time" (quoted in Smith 2015). The medium provided O'Neill with a unique mode of expression tied to his own experiences: "Once I understood that a lot of what I wanted to write about was video games and having your life revolve around them, that's when it felt right to do it as a game. . . . All of a sudden I'm not just a loser addicted to games. I'm a game developer with something to say" (quoted in Smith 2015).

Some autobiographical games even deal directly with intense, traumatic experiences such as abuse or loss. *That Dragon, Cancer* (2016), sometimes described as an "empathy simulator" for its tendency to draw intense emotions from players, is a particularly well-known example.[5] Numinous Games, the small team that developed the title, included lead designer Ryan Green and writer Amy Green; the game movingly depicts their young son Joel's protracted illness and eventual death from cancer. The game expressed not only the Greens' grief but their identity as devout Christians, which is at the core of the game's concept and design. As *Wired* editor Jason Tanz (2016) writes in a longform story on the game and its meaning: "The questions *That Dragon, Cancer* is asking . . . are the kind of spiritual and existential quandaries that have haunted humanity since Job."

Indeed, each game I have mentioned in this section expresses the unique identity of its creator(s) through autobiographical game design. The goal in these games (as with other forms of autobiography) is not only artistic self-reflection from the developers but also to engender a sense of empathy from the player—in other words, they are not simply an expression of identity, but also an opportunity to help others better understand aspects of that identity. None of the games I have mentioned in this section were created by composer-developers. Yet game music has significant capacity for creating and expressing identity for creators and players alike. In a study of game music and identity, Chris Tonelli (2021, 341–342) synthesizes how players perceive aspects of in-game characters' identity from the music, and likewise how they may understand or project aspects of their own identity partially from the music:

> music is a tool that commonly helps us negotiate feelings that we register and then expand into a sense of self-understanding, a sense that feeling this way matters, it is part of who we are. Conversely, music can emotionally configure us in ways we know we prefer not to be configured. . . . Certain game music can configure us emotionally in ways where we become the versions of ourselves we most identify with, while other game music fails to affect us in that way.

By extension, we might assume that composer-developers would be singularly equipped not only to express their own identities musically in games but also to use music as a tool to help players better understand those expressions of identity. In the brief case studies that follow, I explore the role of music in three postmillennial solo-dev games, each of which contains autobiographical elements. I do so in the hope that we might begin to better understand how composer-developers incorporate music in their game design—and how their music fits into the narrative of solo dev games as autobiographical expressions of identity.

Case Study 1: Jason Rohrer, *Gravitation* (2008)

Jason Rohrer's *Passage* (2007) and *Gravitation* (2008) are touchstone examples of game design as self-reflexive artistic expression. Each game positions Rohrer himself as the protagonist of his own adventure. *Passage* is a five-minute reflection on time, life, and the inevitability of death, while the almost equally brief *Gravitation* explores his deeply personal challenge of balancing an active creative existence with a rewarding home life.

In his short book *Works of Game: On the Aesthetics of Games and Art*, John Sharp (2015) devotes several pages to Rohrer's autobiographical games. He writes:

> For players used to the products of the commercial game industry, Rohrer's two video games confront expectations in so many ways—low-fidelity, two-dimensional graphics; short play sessions; lack of typical game goals; simple game mechanics; and mundane subject matter closer to their own lives than those of elves or zombies. . . . Rohrer's autobiographical videogames distilled life and experience down to a form that allowed others to see into it and reflect back on their own lives. (55–56)

At no point does Sharp mention that Rohrer also composed the music for these games. Actually, he doesn't mention the music at all. Yet Rohrer's sparse soundtracks reinforce his games' themes in subtle but effective ways.

This emphasis on music comes as no surprise, given that Rohrer is also an active musician—he cofounded the record label APN in 1995, and has completed several audio-based art projects in addition to his games. Indeed, Rohrer's first game, the 2D-shooter *Transcend* (2005), includes a musical gameplay mechanic fundamental to its design. In his words, "As you play through a level, you are simultaneously assembling an abstract visual collage and arranging a unique piece of music. Transcend merges video games with pure art—it can be viewed either as a game or as a multimedia sculpture" (Rohrer n.d.).[6]

Blending game mechanics with music design carries forward into Rohrer's other games, as well. In a *Critical Inquiry* interview with the game scholar Patrick Jagoda, Rohrer expands on his approach to creating music for his games:

> I'm working in an interactive medium, so I want all aspects of my games to be interactive. Most games have interactive graphics and underlying systems, but they have static or minimally dynamic music. I've tried to make games where the music was an important interactive component. You actively build the music in *Transcend*, *Between* [2008], and *Sleep is Death* [2010]. The music is directly tied to the protagonist's mood in *Gravitation*. And in *Cultivation* [2007] and *Inside a Star-filled Sky* [2011], the music is procedurally generated in real-time by the gamestate. . . . I don't think as carefully about the design of my musical systems as I do about the design of my game mechanics, and music is always the very last thing that I add to a game, but making some kind of interactive music that fits into my game is automatic for me. Looking at the almost-finished game, I ask, "How can music be interactive here?" (Jagoda 2011)

Rohrer's note that "music is directly tied to the protagonist's mood in *Gravitation*" is intriguing from the point of view of identity and autobiography, because Rohrer *is* the protagonist of *Gravitation*. In this game, players directly control an authorial persona—an avatar of Rohrer himself placed into the game world.[7]

Rohrer has not been coy about *Gravitation*'s autobiographical nature. In his artist's statement, he writes:

> One night, while lying in bed, the idea hit me: I needed to make a game about this process that I was going through. About success, and creative leaps, and mania, and mood cycles, and the aftermath. . . . I was also observing how my moods and creative endeavors affected my family, which was knee-deep in big changes at the time. Mez, my first child, was almost 5 (my baby was growing up), and we were on the verge of having our second child. I knew that our relationship with Mez would never be quite the same—the end of "just the three of us," which had been incredibly sweet. As it turns out, our new baby, Ayza, was born just three days after I started working on *Gravitation*. . . . Lest I trivialize the suffering of someone with a truly debilitating disorder, I want to make it clear that I've never experienced clinical mania or depression. My moods are much more gentle than that, and they don't interfere with my life in a significant way, but I still find the bipolar model useful when I try to understand myself. For me, what I call "mania" involves an excited feeling, fast talking, mental racing, and an onslaught of creativity. At the peak of this mood, it can feel a bit like my brain is on fire. . . . The mechanics themselves are relatively simple, but the emergent behavior harbors a lot of texture. Know that there are no "accidents" in this game design. Everything you notice about the game, and every subtle interaction that you experience, is intentionally packed with meaning. *Gravitation* explores how a particular corner of my life feels, as only a game can. (Rohrer 2008)

As with some of Rohrer's other titles, the game mechanics thus become a central part of its content. And, in this case, the fundamental game mechanics provide a very clear message about the highs and lows of his own creative life.

Even if *Gravitation* does not fit cleanly into any genre, its fundamental game mechanics are reminiscent of a 1980s-style platformer. Players must jump and maneuver the playable character along a largely vertical game space, collecting blue stars and returning them to the forge at the bottom right of the map—pulling starry ideas from the sky and transforming them into work product. Initially, however, the visual space is limited, and the player cannot jump and so cannot reach the stars. To get enough energy to reach the platforms, players must first interact with a child in the lower left-hand corner—an avatar of Rohrer's son Mez—by tossing a ball back and forth. Once that interaction provides sufficient energy, the protagonist begins to sparkle, the screen expands to reveal platforms, and players can briefly reach the stars. The energy eventually subsides and must be recharged through interaction with Mez. And so on, for the full eight-minute playtime of the game—at least until Mez disappears, and there is no longer any way to recharge. Players can try again for a higher score, or they can ignore the stars and play with Mez instead, but there's no "happy" ending to the game.

The symbolism is clear: you can't have it all. To achieve professional success (shooting for the stars, literally), our digital Rohrer must ignore his family—the very thing that provides him with the necessary energy to continue his efforts. Do that long enough, and you miss out on their lives. They leave, and you might not even notice. And you get no prize for the most stars, no endgame beyond the act of hoarding or associated bragging rights—so what was it all for in the first place?

The visuals to the game are intentionally limited, almost to the point of abstraction. Although the avatar does sparkle when entering a "manic" state (suggesting the "brain on fire" sensation Rohrer mentions), it is otherwise difficult to ascribe a particular mental state to the character—which is where the music comes in. As with the visuals, Rohrer opted for a retro approach suggesting an 8-bit musical aesthetic while also evoking electronic dance music styles (a common approach in chiptune composition). When digital Rohrer is in a "low energy" state, the music consists of only basic elements: a slow four-measure bassline; a sparse, staccato melody; and a reedy inner voice. As his energy increases, the entire scope seems to change. The visible area expands to reveal more of the map, the color palette deepens—and the music adds additional layers, starting with drums, then an agile countermelody, and it gradually increases in complexity until it is bursting at the seams. As the energy state drops, the layers drop out until it returns to its original state.

Although Rohrer implies that this level of interactivity is uncommon, this type of layering has a long history in games, particularly where it enhances relatively sparse graphical textures. Tim Summers (2016, 190) describes it as "dynamizing the ludic action," offering an example of the snowboarding games *SSX Tricky* (2001) and *SSX 3* (2003), in which the electronic dance music soundtrack is layered in such a way that it reflects the player's actions. In *Gravitation*, this dynamizing is a crucial part of conveying the protagonist's mental state. And intriguingly, since the protagonist's mental state *is* Rohrer's mental state, the music in essence tells us how it feels to be him—conveying in a sonic, almost intimate way the choice between pursuing the exciting "manic" music or settling for the basic tracks. And much like the pursuit of accolades, the music here encourages players to take a certain path (especially on a first playthrough); creating awkward silences or minimizing musical input is a common technique to encourage players toward particular ludic goals—even, as I have argued, if the player knows those goals are morally questionable (Gibbons 2014; see also chapter 40 this volume).

Rohrer thus creates a siren song, drawn from his own lived experiences, to help players empathize with his struggle—to help place them in a situation where they must choose between doing what the game tells you to do and complete the ludic objectives (collect all the stars, do whatever it takes to succeed) or fighting against those impulses and refusing to play the game (forget collecting stars and enjoy your life). As with many autobiographical games, Rohrer provides no answers. Instead, he uses his own experiences—including musical—to create space for players to reflect on his choices, and by extension our own. What would we do in his (digital) shoes?

Case Study 2: Melos Han-Tani, *All Our Asias* (2018)

Melos Han-Tani (formerly Sean Han Tani) is best known as part of Analgesic Productions, the two-person indie studio responsible for philosophical titles including the action-adventure games *Anodyne* (2013) and its sequel *Anodyne 2: Return to Dust* (2019). Several other solo-dev games, however—including *A High Fiber, Japanese Empire Cereal* (2014), *Hiroshima 2016* (2016), *Consumed Orient* (2016), and most extensively *All Our Asias*—have explored questions of racial, ethnic, and cultural identity. These are deeply personal questions for Han-Tani. From the biographical note in the art book for *All Our Asias*: "Melos is Chicago-Suburb-American, Taiwanese-American, Japanese-American, and Irish-American. He is interested in work that analyzes notions of race in America and how it relates to the rest of the world, especially Asia" (Han-Tani 2018, 157). This type of autoethnographic exploration is uncommon in games, especially with Asian American developers. As Patterson (2020a, 78) notes, "Asian North American game developers and designers—the vast majority of whom do not represent Asian bodies in their games—remain unrecognizable to scholars, bloggers, and even players."

All Our Asias is Han-Tani's longest game to date devoted to the exploration of Asian and Asian American identity, and was an opportunity to investigate challenging questions surrounding his racial and ethnic background.[8] Featuring low-poly graphics that intentionally harken back to the PlayStation 1 era of the 1990s, *All Our Asias* tells a science-fiction story of Yuito, a young man who enters the memories of his estranged, dying father in the hope of gaining a kind of mutual understanding. Through those memories, Yuito experiences the racism his father faced as an immigrant and gains some understanding of the infinite complexities of Asian identity. In his words: "My motivation for the story was that there exist very few games touching on or discussing the topics All Our Asias does. I wanted to use the story of AOA as a way to reflect on how I developed an understanding of race as well as the complex term 'Asian'" (Han-Tani 2018, 149).

Here, the expression of identity—the autobiographical aspect of the game—is, as with *Gravitation*, somewhat abstracted. In an interview with Christopher Patterson, Han-Tani reveals that the game is personal, and in a sense autobiographical:

> C: All Our Asias is a game about memory, immigration and race, which you wrote the story for. Was the game personal for you?
>
> M: I based the protagonist, Yuito, off of a future projection of myself if I had "branched" in a different direction at a past point in my life. The Chicago locations are places I've been to often, but there's not much directly autobiographical, though various aspects are based on my experience. (Patterson 2020)

Though not based on direct experiences, the game's protagonist is a "road not taken" projection of Han-Tani himself, which reflects aspects of his experiences as an Asian American in Chicago. Moreover, as with *Gravitation*, the creator places himself into the context of the game as an author surrogate: in this case, as "The Storyteller" who sets the stage for the game.

Like Rohrer, although Han-Tani's games have attracted considerable attention—not least for their exploration of Asian and Asian American identities—his music seldom enters into the discussion. That omission is surprising, because, in addition to his game design, Han-Tani is an accomplished composer. Indeed, he changed his name from

"Sean" to "Melos" in reference to his "lifetime of being around music-making, analysis, or creation, and its influence on [his] work/approach to making stuff" (Han-Tani 2020).[9] From 2016 to 2019, he taught game music composition (as well as game design) at the School of the Art Institute of Chicago. Though most of his music is for games, Han-Tani has also released one independent album of instrumental tracks, which he created using the computer program Ableton Live in a very similar style to his soundtracks. Although no songs have lyrics or other overtly political content, the album—titled *Model Minority No More* (2015)—is nonetheless explicitly devoted to issues pertaining to Han-Tani's lived experience as an Asian American.[10] From the album's page on bandcamp.com: "The order of the tracks constructs a light narrative of the process for me of realizing how my interests/skills/personality have been shaped due to being a racial minority, and dealing with the aftermath and the ambiguity of deciding what to do once you realize these things and your place in society."[11] At this point, it would seem, Han-Tani embraced the potential for music to express both sociopolitical content and markers of personal identity.

In that context, I would suggest that we might understand the soundtrack to *All Our Asias* as a musical reflection of the game's narrative. That is, we may view it as an attempt to reconcile or synthesize multiple aspects of Asian American—or "Asian/American," to follow David Palumbo-Liu's (1999) linguistic representation of the opposition—identities. I confess that when I first played the game, I was surprised by the absence of obvious, even stereotypical, musical markers of Japaneseness. Instead, my perception was that the soundtrack sounded like "standard video game music" from the late 1990s or early 2000s—the era evoked by the game's graphics, as well. Missing in my assessment, however, was that much of the prominent game music of that era *was* Japanese; we just tend not to perceive it as a nonwestern product. Han-Tani's companion book to *All Our Asias*, which explores his creative process in some detail, contains descriptions of each cue from the game's soundtrack, including what he perceived to be the primary musical influences (see Table 26.2).

From *Shin Megami Tensei*, to *Final Fantasy*, *Phantasy Star Online*, and *Golden Sun*, the soundscape draws heavily on the works of Japanese video game composers—especially Japanese role-playing game series popular during the first decade of the twenty-first century. At the same time, Han-Tani admits significant influence from the Japanese progressive-rock musician Susumu Hirasawa (who has also contributed to several anime soundtracks). Han-Tani seems keen to demonstrate the impact of a range of Japanese musical influences on his own style—and while these make sense as stylistic influences in the context of an atmospheric video game, they also suggest his own exposure to "Asian" musics through games and popular music. Notably, these game soundtracks are also media that American audiences consume as localized products, which in many cases obscure their Japaneseness to appeal more broadly to North American audiences (see Gibbons 2021). This music and their games—even video games more broadly—are "Asiatic products" (Patterson 2020, 58), but culturally divorced from that context and

TABLE 26.2 Musical Influences on *All Our Asias*

Track	Title	Mentioned References
1	Title Screen	Susumu Hirasawa, *Landscapes* (1994)
3	Yuito and His Mother	"Royal Road" chord progression (common in Japanese pop)
6	Advent Station	Hideaki Kobayashi and Fumie Jumatani, "Image of Hero" from *Phantasy Star Online* soundtrack (2000)
7	Crossroads of the Mind	Motoi Sakuraba, soundtracks to *Golden Sun* games (2001–2010)
10	The Club Manager	"trailer from a Hollywood disaster movie . . . you know, those low, uninventive and dramatic horn sounds"
12	Interworld 55	SNES instruments; Masashi Hamauzu and Nobuo Uematsu, "Thunder Plains" and "Mi'hen Highroad" from *Final Fantasy X* soundtrack (2001)
13	Faster, Faster!	Susumu Hirasawa, "Byakkoya" (2006)
14	Grey Space	Various composers, *Shin Megami Tensei* game series
17	How Will He Live?	Ryota Kozuka, Kenichi Tsuchiya, and Toshiki Konishi, "Tokyo," from *Shin Megami Tensei IV* soundtrack (2013); "Love, So Estranged," Rocketship (2014)
20	Help Them Out	Various composers, "Ellinia" from *Maple Story* soundtrack (2003)
22	Proposal Hearing	Kenji Yamamoto, "Sanctuary Fortress" and "Torvus Bog" from *Metroid Prime 2: Echoes* soundtrack (2004)

rendered palatable to western audiences. As Mia Consalvo (2016) notes, many avid consumers of 1980s and 1990s Japanese games were unaware the games originated in Japan.

By evoking these particular soundtracks, *All Our Asias* suggests the complex cultural dynamic—Asian, American, Asian American, and Asian/American—that affects not only protagonist Yuito but also video games, their music, and in this case, the game's creator. By the end of the game, Yuito has embraced a highly pluralistic understanding of his own identity, and it is clearly Han-Tani's intention that the game encourages such a reading. As critic Kyle Bradford (2018) wrote of his own experience with *All Our Asias*:

> Defining your identity is a tricky thing. . . . Our places within such generalizations like race can complicate things even further, making us question what it means to be part of something so varied and diverse. In All Our Asias, I found a meditation on intersectionality that helped me come to terms with something I had been struggling with for a long time. Perhaps even my entire life. While understanding the identities of ourselves and others can often be difficult, the game's title helps put things into perspective, at least for me. *All Our Asias*—it's inclusive. It's ours, even if we don't recognize it to be.

Case Study 3: Tamara Duplantis, *Atchafalaya Arcade* (2017)

Tamara Duplantis is a multimedia sound artist and game developer originally from Louisiana, and now based in California. Duplantis's games typically defy categorization—indeed, "game" may not even be the right word, since she draws influence from multiple arts in search of a contemplative ludomusical experiences. One frequent medium of choice is the Nintendo Game Boy, a popular 1990s handheld platform; several of her games are available on actual "homebrew" Game Boy cartridges or are playable through Game Boy emulators.

By 2017, Nintendo's handheld Game Boy console had been outdated for decades, but Duplantis's choice of medium is not entirely surprising. Indeed, the Game Boy has a long history as a musical instrument and has enjoyed an extended lifespan as a popular technology for chiptune composers. The Game Boy Camera add-on contained a program called *Trippy-H* (1998), which allowed the Game Boy to function as a fairly limited music sequencer, and almost immediately thereafter individual users and music collectives began expanding the Game Boy's musical possibilities through fan-developed programs like Nanoloop (1998) and Little Sound DJ (2000) (McAlpine 2019, 180–188). Today, the Game Boy remains a staple of the chiptune artist community around the world—at once a synthesizer, sequencer, and instrument for live performance (Pasdzierny 2013).

In terms of purely musical content, most of Duplantis's games fall squarely into line with indie and retro-gaming trends toward procedural audio generation, a DIY visual and musical aesthetic, and a focus on mechanics as opposed to narrative content.[12] What sets these ludomusical experiences apart from the pack is the frequent self-reflexive, autobiographical elements of several of her games. *For Today, I Breathe Again* (2019), for example, is a deeply moving interactive poem that explores her own experiences with domestic violence.

Atchafalaya Arcade (2017) is far more playful in tone, but still explores her own lived experiences in a meaningful way.[13] In her words, it is "a homebrew audiovisual performance game for the Game Boy handheld console. Inspired by fond memories of the Louisiana wetlands, Atchafalaya Arcade allows you to improvise chaotic chiptune music on a series of newly designed Game Boy instruments while creating images of abstract bayou pixelscapes" (Duplantis n.d.). Players select one of three newly created digital "instruments" (timbres): Mosshboard ("The Mossy Drum Machine"), Bayoulens ("The Harmonious Riverside"), or Oakordion ("The Mellifluous Evergreen"). Once the game begins, the player can then control a few musical elements, depending on which instrument is selected; during play, an abstracted landscape is procedurally generated by the player's musical choices. When players switch between instruments, they must also click to progress line by line through pastoral poetry depicting the beauty of the Louisiana landscape. Pressing one of the Game Boy's two buttons progresses the text in English, while pressing the other advances the text in Cajun French.

Playing *Atchafalaya Arcade* is a contemplative experience. It is also, I argue, deeply nostalgic for specific chronological (childhood in the 1990s) and geographical (the landscape of rural Louisiana) settings drawn from Duplantis's own experience and heritage. This personal nostalgia shapes the entire design of the game: its medium, title, content, and gameplay. In the materials provided for *Atchafalaya Arcade* to IndieCade (an annual juried festival of indie games), Duplantis notes that the game was "inspired by fond memories of playing games in the backseat of my parents' car, traveling to grandma's house through the Louisiana wetlands" (*Atchafalaya Arcade* n.d.).[14] This explanation, connected to her unique childhood experiences, neatly identifies three threads of childhood nostalgia: (1) family/cultural heritage; (2) the natural landscape; and (3) (retro) video games.

Duplantis's Louisiana heritage is a prominent aspect of her artistic identity. She publishes under the name "Tambalaya," for instance—a portmanteau of "Tammy" and "jambalaya" (a quintessential American Cajun/Creole food). Likewise, the three instruments in *Atchafalaya Arcade* are portmanteaus of nature and a traditional Cajun instrument: Mosshboard (moss + washboard); Bayoulens (bayou + violins); and Oakordion (oak + accordion). Especially given Duplantis's obvious affection for wordplay, the title *Atchafalaya Arcade* also bears consideration. The first word is fairly straightforward: the Atchafalaya River runs through Louisiana and is a site of such importance to the area's Cajun/Creole population that, in 2006, the Atchafalaya basin was designated a National Heritage Area. "Deep in America's South," the area's website reads, "there is a rich and mysterious country filled with twisting bayous, backwater lakes, vast marshes and the nation's largest river swamp. . . . It is among the most cultural rich and ecologically varied regions in the United States, home to the widely recognized Cajun culture as well as a diverse population of European, African, Caribbean and Native-American descent" (atchafalaya.org).

"Arcade," however, contains multiple levels of meaning. Most obviously it seems to refer to video-game arcades—the now largely defunct public spaces where groups would gather to pay games in the 1980s and 1990s (not coincidentally, also the Game Boy era). It also suggests "Arcadia"—the utopian place of unparalleled natural beauty depicted by the ancient poets Theocritus and Virgil, and by countless in the millennia since. It was the natural beauty of the North American wilderness that led Europeans to name the New French colony "*Acadie*," or "Acadia," in reference to this Arcadian paradise—a name that followed displaced Acadians when they settled Louisiana in what is now known as the "Acadiana" region and became known as "Cajuns."[15] Thus the title *Atchafalaya Arcade* simultaneously suggests the Acadian/Cajun ethnic group, video game culture of the 1990s, and the pastoral ideal of coexistence with natural beauty.

Finally, the choice of the Game Boy (and its soundscape) as a medium feels particularly apt for a game about childhood nostalgia. Duplantis specifically identified playing games in the backseat of her parents' car—probably something akin to a Game Boy—as part of the inspiration for *Atchafalaya Arcade*. As I noted above, through its prominence in chiptune culture, the Game Boy has also in some sense become emblematic of a bygone era of digital musicianship. McAlpine (2019, 256–257) calls chiptune "the sound of childhood," a timbre that creates "a direct link to a time in all our lives when life was simpler; a time before we get ground down by the pressures of life"

We can read *Atchafalaya Arcade* as a threefold expression of nostalgia for a particular childhood moment: it is a handheld 1990s-style video game *about* Cajun/Creole cultural identity and the natural landscape that surrounds that culture, rooted in the composer-developer's very specific memories of *playing* 1990s handheld games while immersed in that culture and place. With a remarkable economy of means, the gameplay of *Atchafalaya Arcade* abstractly recreates the soundscape (chiptunes), visual landscape (procedurally generated visuals), and cultural context (poetry and instruments) of that specific childhood experience. Moreover, through this ludomusical immersion, it allows other players a window onto all these aspects of her childhood—a multisensory abstract autobiography through interactive art.[16]

Conclusions

The three case studies in this chapter each explore how the music of indie composer-developers can express their creators' identities in the context of video games with autobiographical elements. I want to be careful not to suggest that *all* music by composer-developers is autobiographical or, indeed, that their creations should always be read as expressions of personal identity. Yet the artistic possibilities of solo-dev games present unique opportunities for the study of digital autobiography, and, more broadly, for the relationship between music and game design, and the future of multimedia interactive artforms. It is my hope that in broaching these complex topics here, I encourage scholars of game sound and music to continue exploring the aesthetic and musical questions endemic to independent and solo-dev games, and to consider what artistic voices are privileged (or silenced) through focusing on major studio and franchise games.

Notes

1. I will use the term "indie game" interchangeably with "independent game" throughout.
2. John Sharp (2016, 261–262) identifies nine factors that "created the conditions from which the indie phenomenon emerged: indie focused game websites, indie-operated download websites, digital distribution services, independent game studios, Internet-based communication challenges, a focus on experimentation, academic game programs and research groups, indie game festivals and conferences, and increased media attention." For a more in-depth survey of indie game history, see Juul (2019, 57–124).
3. As Wendy Fonarrow (2006, 25) notes regarding British indie rock, "Although indie has no exact definition, the discourse and practices around the multiple descriptions of indie detail a set of principles that reveal the values and issues at stake for the community."
4. For a more data-driven overview of perceptions of indie game identity, see Periera (2021).

5. The lengthy development of *That Dragon, Cancer* is documented in the film *Thank You for Playing* (2016).
6. *Transcend* is available for free from SourceForge at http://transcend.sourceforge.net/.
7. *Gravitation* is available for free from SourceForge at http://hcsoftware.sourceforge.net/gravitation/.
8. *All Our Asias* is available for free via itch.io at https://han-tani.itch.io/aoa or via the Steam Store.
9. Han-Tani added the hyphen at the same time (i.e., "Sean Han Tani" became "Melos Han-Tani"). His name appears both with and without the hyphen in various venues, but I have elected to maintain his own preferred spelling unless directly quoting another source.
10. In further experimentation with his name as an expression of identity, *Model Minority No More* was released under the name "Sean Han-Tani-Chen-Hogan."
11. https://htch.bandcamp.com/album/model-minority-no-more-5-2015-solo-album.
12. D'Errico (2015, 197), for example, argues that indie games frequently use procedural music generation for both aesthetic reasons and "as a technical strategy for generating content despite limited production resources."
13. *Atchafalaya Arcade* is available for free via itch.io at https://tambalaya.itch.io/atchafalaya-arcade.
14. Notably, Duplantis's grandmother also provided the Cajun French translations for the game's text.
15. "Acadian" and "Cajun" are both terms still applied to the ethnic group containing descendants of these displaced settlers.
16. Or, in the words of one critic, *Atchafalaya Arcade* provides a "dreamy, lo-fi" experience "that lets you explore another person's experience of Louisiana swamps through musical experimentation" (Gach 2017).

References

Anthropy, Anna. 2012. *Rise of the Video Game Zinesters: How Freaks, Normals, Amateurs, Artists, Dreamers, Dropouts, Queers, Housewives, and People Like You Are Taking Back an Art Form*. New York: Seven Stories Press.

"Atchafalaya Arcade." n.d. Accessed December 23, 2021. https://indiecade.fandom.com/wiki/Atchafalaya_Arcade.

Benedetti, Winda. 2008. "When Has a Video Game Ever Made You Cry?" CBS News, October 15, 2008. Accessed December 23, 2021. https://www.nbcnews.com/id/wbna27188395#.UToWhxxxoyo.

Bradford, Kyle. 2018. "The Game That Made Me Question What It Means to Be Me." *Unwinnable Monthly*, March 28, 2018. Accessed December 23, 2021. https://unwinnable.com/2018/05/28/the-game-that-made-me-question-what-it-means-to-be-me/.

Consalvo, Mia. 2016. *Atari to Zelda: Japan's Video Games in Global Contexts*. Cambridge, MA: MIT Press.

D'Errico, Michael. 2015. "Worlds of Sound: Indie Games, Proceduralism, and the Aesthetics of Emergence." *Music, Sound and the Moving Image* 9: 191–206.

Duplantis, Tamara. n.d. "Atchafalaya Arcade." Itch.io. Accessed December 23, 2021. https://tambalaya.itch.io/atchafalaya-arcade.

Fonarrow, Wendy. 2006. *Empire of Dirt: The Aesthetics and Rituals of British Indie Music*. Middletown, CT: Wesleyan University Press.

Gach, Ethan. "'Atchafalaya Arcade' Turns Old Nintendo Hardware into a Miniature Electronic Orchestra." *Kotaku*, October 8, 2017. Accessed December 23, 2021. https://kotaku.com/atchafalaya-arcade-turns-old-nintendo-hardware-into-a-m-1819261341.

Gibbons, William. 2014. "Wandering Tonalities: Silence, Sound, and Morality in *Shadow of the Colossus*." In *Music in Video Games: Studying Play*, edited by K. J. Donnelly, William Gibbons, and Neil Lerner, 122–137. New York: Routledge.

Gibbons, William. 2021. "Open Worlds: Globalization, Localization, and Video Game Music." In *The Cambridge Companion to Video Game Music*, edited by Melanie Fritsch and Tim Summers, 359–375. Cambridge: Cambridge University Press.

Guillermo, Kawika. 2018. "Can You Live in a Video Game? Autobiography & Living the Author in Video Games." *Medium*, April 18, 2018. Accessed December 23, 2021. https://medium.com/anomalyblog/playing-the-author-video-game-autobiographies-46367939c70a.

Han-Tani, Melos. 2018. *Game Design Works Volume 1: "All Our Asias."* Self-published.

Han-Tani, Melos. 2020. "New Name!" *ambient-melodic: Melos Han-Tani's Blog*, January 13, 2020. Accessed December 23, 2021. https://meloshantani.wordpress.com/2020/01/13/new-name/.

Hernandez, Patricia. 2020. "Undertale's Surprise Concert Got the Internet in Its Feelings." *Polygon*, September 16, 2020. Accessed December 23, 2021. https://www.polygon.com/2020/9/16/21439939/undertale-anniversary-toby-fox-orchestra-fandom-music-megalovania.

Jagoda, Patrick. 2011. "Between: An Interview with Jason Rohrer." *Critical Inquiry*, May 2011. Accessed December 23, 2021. https://criticalinquiry.uchicago.edu/the_jason_rohrer_interview/.

Juul, Jesper. 2019. *Handmade Pixels: Independent Video Games and the Quest for Authenticity*. Cambridge, MA: MIT Press.

McAlpine, Kenneth B. 2019. *Bits and Pieces: A History of Chiptunes*. Oxford: Oxford University Press.

Nunneley, Stephany. 2020. "*Stardew Valley* Has Sold over 10 Million Copies Worldwide." *VG24/7*, January 23, 2020. Accessed December 23, 2021. https://www.vg247.com/authors/stephany-nunneley.

Palumbo-Liu, David. 1999. *Asian/American: Historical Crossings of a Racial Frontier*. Stanford: Stanford University Press.

Patterson, Christopher B. 2020a. *Open World Empire: Race, Erotics, and the Global Rise of Video Games*. New York: New York University Press.

Patterson, Christopher B. 2020b. "Interview: Melos Han Tani." *First Person Scholar*, February 5, 2020. Accessed December 23, 2021. http://www.firstpersonscholar.com/interview-melos-han-tani/.

Pasdzierny, Matthias. 2013. "Geeks on Stage? Investigations in the World of (Live) Chipmusic." In *Music and Game: Perspectives on a Popular Alliance*, edited by Peter Moormann, 171–190. Wiesbaden: Springer.

Periera, Leônidas Soares. 2021. "The Elusive 'Indieness': Measuring the Defining Characteristics of Indie Games." *Loading . . . The Journal of the Canadian Game Studies Association* 14:48–69.

Ruberg, Bonnie. 2021. "Queering Indie: How LGBTQ Experiences Challenge Dominant Narratives of Independent Games." In *Independent Videogames: Cultures, Networks, Techniques and Politics*, edited by Paolo Ruffino, 43–57. New York: Routledge.

Ruffino, Paolo. 2021. "After Independence." In *Independent Videogames: Cultures, Networks, Techniques and Politics*, edited by Paolo Ruffino, 1–25. New York: Routledge.

Schwerin, Mac. 2019. "The New Auteurs of Gaming." *Outline*, March 19, 2019. https://theoutline.com/post/7220/indie-game-auteurs-stardew-valley-hollow-knight-golf-story.

Sharp, John. 2016. "Independent Games." In *Debugging Game History: A Critical Lexicon*, edited by Henry Lowood and Raiford Guins, 259–267. Cambridge, MA: MIT Press.

Sharp, John. 2015. *Works of Game: On the Aesthetics of Games and Art*. Cambridge, MA: MIT Press.

Smith, Ed. 2015. "*Actual Sunlight* Might Be the Most Painfully Real Video Game You'll Ever Play." *Vice*, August 11, 2015. https://www.vice.com/en/article/4wbn9d/actual-sunlight-might-be-the-most-painfully-real-video-game-youll-ever-play-000.

Rohrer, Jason. n.d. "*Transcend*: A Video Game by Jason Rohrer." SourceForge. http://transcend.sourceforge.net/.

Rohrer, Jason. 2008. "A Note about *Gravitation*." SourceForge. http://hcsoftware.sourceforge.net/gravitation/statement.html.

Tanz, Jason. 2016. "A Father, A Dying Son, and the Quest to Make the Most Profound Videogame Ever." *Wired*, January 2016. https://www.wired.com/2016/01/that-dragon-cancer/.

Tonelli, Chris. 2021. "Game Music and Identity." In *The Cambridge Companion to Video Game Music*, edited by Melanie Fritsch and Tim Summers, 327–342. Cambridge: Cambridge University Press.

Wallace, Kimberly. 2015. "*Cibele*: The Complexities of Love in the 21st Century." *Game Informer*, November 2, 2015. https://www.gameinformer.com/games/cibele/b/pc/archive/2015/11/02/cibele-review-game-informer.aspx.

Werning, Stefan. 2017. "The Persona in Autobiographical Game-Making as Playful Performance of the Self." *Persona Studies* 3:28–42.

SECTION 6

PRE-EXISTING MUSIC

CHAPTER 27

HEARING THE RENAISSANCE IN VIDEO GAMES

KAREN M. COOK

INTRODUCTION

IN both scholarly fare and popular consensus, "the Renaissance" typically signals a rebirth of culture—a rise in intellectual and artistic endeavor, political and economic revitalization, global exploration, religious reform, and scientific inquiry, much of which is attributed to a renewed interest in Greco-Roman antiquity—and, as a period, is often assigned the oversimplified dating of 1400–1600 (Brotton 2006; Le Goff 2015).[1] But, sandwiched between a Middle Ages that overextends its reach and a precocious Baroque that is already a symbol of the medieval past in popular imagination, the Renaissance fades into the background like an unfortunately placed chameleon.[2]

Perhaps because of these conflicts in historiographical positioning, or the overwhelming presence of the medieval in the public imagination, even with regard to things otherwise noted as Renaissance, it is challenging to answer the rhetorical yet intriguing question posed recently by James Cook, Alexander Kolassa, and Adam Whittaker (2018): "[I]s there such a concept as 'renaissanceism'?" Scholars such as James Cook (2018), Daniela Fountain (2018), and Kendra Preston Leonard (2016) have explored how various Renaissance premises have been musically illustrated in film and television. However, such attention has yet to be turned toward video games—perhaps because comparatively few games bear a chronological, geographical, or thematic connection to the Renaissance. A quick search for the term "medieval" in the popular game platform Steam, for example, receives over 2,500 hits, with over 1,700 games tagged "medieval," but there is no "Renaissance" tag, and such a search reveals only 61 games, many of which use the term in other ways. But rather than this paucity acting as an analytical stumbling block, it instead allows for a fairly thorough corpus study of how video games sonically depict the Renaissance.

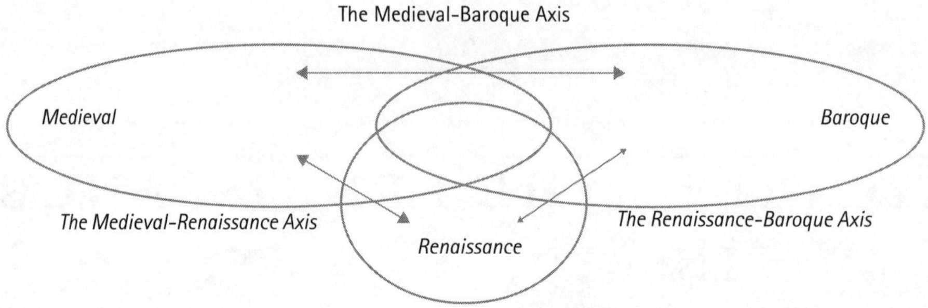

FIGURE 27.1 Axes of interaction between Medieval, Renaissance, and Baroque tropes.

In this chapter, I focus on games that are largely set between 1400 and 1600, the dates typically assigned to the European Renaissance period (hereafter "the Renaissance").[3] The games must also have some sort of geographical or thematic connection to the Renaissance—regardless of whether they aspire toward historical specificity or where the games themselves were developed. (See Appendix A.) I then evaluate the musical cues and contexts in these games along several axes: the medieval-Baroque axis by which Baroque musical cues have come to symbolize medievalism, and the medieval-Renaissance and Renaissance-Baroque axes by which musical cues belonging to these periods overlap with one another (see Figure 27.1). I attempt here to peel back the portion of the umbrella under which the Renaissance hides and shed light on both how the period is represented in game music and what its music is used to represent. I thus offer this chapter as a prolegomenon toward a future understanding of "Renaissance-ism."[4]

The Medieval-Baroque Axis

Musical signs of medievalism occur in all sorts of modern media and can be traced back through film, opera, and western "classical" music traditions. The timbres of church bells, lute, harp, recorder, bagpipe, horn, ceremonial trumpet, frame drums, tambourine, and monkish voices are all medievalist symbols.[5] So too are open fourths and fifths, parallel motion, drones, and imitating plainchant or organum. Medieval dances are frequent cues; these often use thin textures and modal melodies, compound or triple meter, perfect intervals, and some sort of frame drum. More modern literary, operatic, and cinematic tropes include epic film scoring, military-style percussion, brass fanfares and horn calls, the Gothic pipe organ, Baroque counterpoint, and wordless vocal passages (see Haines 2014; Cook 2017, 2018, 2019). While most of these vocal and instrumental timbres listed above were present in the European Middle Ages (hereafter "the Middle Ages" or "medieval"), the kinds of harpsichord and organ heard in video games were not. Instead of the smaller portative organ or the late 14th-century clavicembalum, it is almost always their later Baroque incarnations that are heard in game music.[6]

As I have discussed elsewhere (Cook 2019), the pipe organ inherited its now common medievalist overtones through Gothic novels and silent films (see van Elferen 2012a, 2012b). William Gibbons (2018) has also drawn specific connections between Baroque counterpoint and game music. He notes that consoles such as the Nintendo Entertainment System (NES) had the ability to render three pitched voices (two square-wave channels and one triangle-wave channel); Baroque trio sonatas or contrapuntal keyboard works are often voiced similarly and are in the public domain, thus providing early game designers with music that could be readily (and freely) programmed or emulated. Moreover, Baroque counterpoint relies on repetitive harmonic and melodic patterns that work well when game music needs to repeat without growing stagnant; Dana Plank (2019) notes at least fourteen 8-bit video games that use the Toccata and Fugue in D Minor, for example. Since so many early games using quasi-Baroque counterpoint had medievalist themes of castles, kings, quests, and labyrinths, the sounds and styles of Baroque keyboard music became ingrained in video game depictions of the medieval.[7]

In Renaissance-oriented games, a Gothic pipe organ is often associated with religious scenarios. Playing humorously on Gothic tropes of eeriness, ghostliness, and death, a pipe organ imitates the opening notes of the "Dies Irae" chant near the end of *Hamlet, or the Last Game without MMORPG Features, Shaders and Product Placement* (aka *Hamlet!*, 2010). An implied organ plays a chant-like melody over a drone in the church of St. Greavsie in *Touché: The Adventures of the Fifth Musketeer* (1995), while in the game's monastery, the same organ plays another chant-like melody, occasionally in parallel fifths. "L'Organo del Duomo" and "Jeu d'Orgue" from *Painters Guild* (2015) remind of a Bach chorale, while the organ alongside what sounds like an ethereal choir in "Sakral" from *The Guild* (2002) sounds loosely like a Bach cantata. And themes similar to the Toccata and Fugue in D minor occur in the short "Prayer" theme from *Castlevania III: Dracula's Curse* (1990) and "Amen" from *Medieval II: Total War* (2006).

Certain tracks clearly use a harpsichord in the kinds of Baroque counterpoint that Gibbons describes, even when technological constraints permit different compositional strategies.[8] A harpsichord-like timbre is heard upon time-traveling to meet Joan of Arc in "October 1428, French Castle Town" from *Time Twist: Rekishi no Katasumi de . . .* (1991), and in the NES version of *Mario's Time Machine* (1993) during the 1602 Shakespeare quest. Whereas the organ often appears in tracks associated with religion, the contrapuntal harpsichord most frequently symbolizes royalty or eliteness, complementing Gibbons's (2009) observation that Bach's music reinforces notions of importance and authority in games such as *Battle of Olympus* (1988) and Sid Meier's *Pirates!* (1991).

The Medieval-Renaissance Axis

The line between medieval and Renaissance is porous, and much of the popular depiction of the Renaissance relies heavily on medievalist tropes. The collapsing of the

Renaissance into the medieval(ist) in popular culture, at least in the United States, is perhaps most apparent in the Renaissance faire. A hodgepodge of handmade wares, period costumery, turkey legs, jesters and musicians, knights and queens, sword-fighting, and jousting, the Renaissance faire is a symbol of both 1960s counterculture and the "white and nerdy" contingent (Rubin 2014, 246). As Elizabeth Emery (2015) observes, many of the most recognizable components of a Renaissance faire are just as central to a diner's experience at the theme restaurant Medieval Times. Moreover, faire originator Phyllis Patterson envisioned something "modeled on the open-air festivals of medieval Europe," but called it a Renaissance faire to avoid negative connotations associated with the medieval period's perceived approach to human rights (Rubin 2014, 24–25). Musically, a Renaissance faire is a veritable smorgasbord; William Byrd rubs elbows with The Byrds, belly dancers, bagpipers, or a Viking rock group.

In many video games that chronologically progress from the medieval period to the Renaissance, the musical signs skew toward the medievalist. Take *Age of Empires II: The Age of Kings* (1999), for example, in which the player controls their chosen civilization from the "Dark Ages" through the Renaissance-like "Imperial Age." Its menu theme uses many of the aforementioned medievalisms, especially slow modal melodies, drones, mixed choirs singing on open vowels, persistent military-style drums, brassy blasts, and cinematic epicness. Several tracks use medievalisms to create a sense of the distant past. "Tazer," for example, features what sounds like a harp, later a hammered dulcimer or psaltery, playing a modal melody in octaves against a plucked drone moving in fifths. Similarly, the opening of "Voodoodoodoo" consists of two flutes or recorders occasionally moving in perfect intervals. Lastly, in "I Will Beat on Your Behind," a bell's low peal precedes a Gothic organ and voices entering on wordless "oohs." These tracks thus add medievalist signifiers to those in the menu theme, namely prominent perfect intervals and medievalist vocal and instrumental timbres.

Similar styles occur in *Medieval: Total War* (2002) and *Medieval II: Total War*, both of which stretch from the Middle Ages into the 15th and 16th centuries respectively. Both games use epic cinematic scoring and the timbral choices listed earlier. In *Medieval: Total War*'s dance-like "Winning Theme," what sounds like a hurdy-gurdy provides an ornamented drone accompaniment for a jaunty melody on a bagpipe or crumhorn-like instrument, with snare and hand drums. "Amen," in *Medieval II*, uses a Gothic organ alongside low-voiced men singing snippets of plainchant before harmonizing in parallel intervals, and a boy's treble voice repeatedly sings "Alleluia." Such medievalisms are not restricted to games set in the early Renaissance but perpetuate throughout almost all the games in this study, regardless of their chronological setting.

Epic cinematic scoring, with its brassy fanfares, insistent percussion, military-style rhythms, lush orchestral strings, pealing bells, and grunting male voices or bombastic *Carmina Burana*-esque mixed choirs, occur most often in title themes and in games that include battle, as in *Bladestorm: The Hundred Years' War* (2007), *Lionheart: Legacy of the Crusader* (2003), and *Kingdom Come: Deliverance* (2018). The main theme for *Touché* is a heroic fanfare full of implied brass, snares, and cymbals, while that for *Anno 1602 A.D.* (2000) is even more martial and insistent. Battle themes emphasize brass and military percussion, as in *Expeditions: Conquistador* (2013), to which *Europa Universalis IV* (2013) adds wordless voices atop sweeping strings. In other games where battle is not prominent, however, this style of writing occurs much less frequently.

Such scoring also occurs alongside other medievalizing cues, most commonly parallel perfect intervals or perfect intervals at cadence points. *Europa Universalis III* (2007) is set between 1453 and 1789, yet its title theme uses epic scoring alongside recorders and voices moving in parallel fifths and octaves. Similarly, *Europa Universalis IV*'s track "De Hominis Dignitate" begins with strings droning on parallel fifths before segueing to a more heroic style. In contrast, "Bonfire" from *Anno 1503* symbolizes a rustic past via recorders playing in parallel fifths against a low-pitched frame drum. Open fifths at cadences or parallel perfect intervals also occur sporadically throughout *Touché* and *The Guild 2* (2006).

Medieval-style dances are often associated with taverns or food and drink. In *Kingdom Come: Deliverance*, for example, "Rattay Feasts" and "Beer and Women" feature a modal recorder melody over bowed strings playing open fifths in parallel motion; the strings also take turns doubling the melody at the fifth against tambourines, finger cymbals, and frame drums.

But in scenarios involving a religious theme, area, or person, the predominant musical cue is the male voice singing something reminiscent of plainchant, often alongside other medievalizing cues such as parallel fifths, drones, or church bells, as in "Monastery" and "Monumental Cathedral" from *Anno 1404* (2009) or "Mönchgesang" from *The Guild*. Moreover, such religious medievalizing cues often permeate the aforementioned sounds of battle; despite taking place on the Caribbean seas, many of the battle themes for *Pirates!* include the low peal of a town or church bell, and the melodic contour of "Pirate Hunter Battle 2" is similar to the "Dies Irae." I will return to these observations later.

Semiotically speaking, these signs are not inherently or exclusively medievalist; as Iain Hart (2021 and chapter 40 this volume) reminds us, no sign, musical or otherwise, can ever be truly fixed in meaning, and thus musical signs are always contingent on cultural literacy and context. The musical timbres, styles, and compositional choices listed above are best interpreted as medievalist when used in conjunction with visual, narrative, or thematic contexts that are also medievalist. In this vein, using existing medieval compositions would be an obvious medievalism, if their contexts reinforce such an understanding. But in vague or anachronous contexts, they might well contribute to other readings. For example, most of the Renaissance-period works in *Europa Universalis II* (2001) are dances for recorder, gamba, lute, and percussion, instruments that also accompany some of the secular songs. But nestled among these works is one early 13th-century monophonic estampie, performed on what sounds like a flute doubled by oboe and plucked psaltery. Similarly, *Four Last Things* (2017), a point-and-click game that combines Renaissance art with Monty Python-esque humor, relies almost exclusively on Renaissance and Baroque music, but includes a few monophonic medieval dances. While musically distinct from the rest of the soundtrack, they fit much better with the game's Renaissance theme than does Gabriel Fauré's Barcarolle No. 1 (slyly noted in the game as "slightly out of place") or Erik Satie's *Gymnopédies*. Without additional medievalizing cues such as parallel fifths, these dances might not appear distinct from the other Renaissance tracks, contributing instead to a generic sense of the past or even to an overarchingly Renaissance-ist interpretation. Conversely, the medievalist connotations that some musical cues have in the popular imagination might be too strong for the narrative or visual contexts of the games to completely redirect, if that is even a goal. This holds true especially if either the cues or the game contexts are equally plausible as medievalist or Renaissance-ist, like the Renaissance faire mentioned earlier.

The prime example is liturgical plainchant in Latin, or music composed to allude to that genre; it often symbolizes the medieval, despite plainchant being a living musical practice in postmedieval periods. This complicates a purely medievalist reading of plainchant or chant-like music in games clearly set in the Renaissance or later. Take *Pirates!*, which is set in the 16th- through 18th-century Caribbean. The player can visit a Jesuit mission, reflecting the active role the Catholic Church played in colonizing the Americas; its primary theme includes a heavy church bell ringing behind a male voice and a group of men responsorially performing plainchant. *Mission 1545* (2017) features young protagonist Willa attempting to save her friend, the Dominican Brother Joseph, from execution by Henry VIII. Throughout the game, low men's voices sing snippets of plainchant or open vowels against the occasional peal of a bell. In contrast, women's voices repeatedly sing the word "Kyrie" in a more modernist style when Willa enters the Tower of London's chapel. In *Assassin's Creed II* (2009), the protagonist Ezio Auditore is sent to kill a priest chanting on top of the Duomo during the Bonfire of the Vanities. As I discuss elsewhere (Cook 2023) for *Assassin's Creed*, and which applies to *Pirates!* and *Mission 1545*, these examples of plainchant are historically appropriate for their in-game time and place, but they also connect Catholicism specifically, and religion more generally, to a medievalist sense of past-ness and history.

The Renaissance-Baroque Axis

Just as the boundary between the medieval and Renaissance is nebulous, so too is that between the Renaissance and Baroque. These historical periods share a vast number of instrumental timbres and, of course, the human voice. As I showed earlier, Baroque characteristics such as the Gothic organ, the harpsichord, and contrapuntal writing are firmly attached to medievalism in popular imagination, and might appear as medievalizing factors in otherwise Renaissance-oriented media. But this study also reveals that a number of other Baroque (and occasionally later) musical elements appear regularly as symbols of the Renaissance.

It is impossible to tackle this discussion without further acknowledging J.S. Bach's long shadow. Bach-like counterpoint, and allusions to or quotations of the Toccata and Fugue in D Minor attributed to him, have already been described as medievalisms. However, other pieces by Bach appear in every Renaissance-themed game that borrows Baroque music, but in ways that support an interpretation of the game context as Renaissance-ist. Perhaps most obvious is the soundtrack for the Renaissance era in Sid Meier's *Civilization IV* (2005), which comprises instrumental music by well-known composers of the Baroque, Classical, and Romantic periods: Bach, Wolfgang Amadeus Mozart, and Ludwig van Beethoven. It consists (with the exception of movements from Bach's cello suites) entirely of movements from large-ensemble symphonies or concerti, including one from Bach's Violin Concerto and several from his Brandenburg Concertos and the Concerto for Two Violins. *Four Last Things* and *The Procession to Calvary* (2020) are both pastiches set in the Renaissance, although they frequently and humorously refer to other time periods. Movements of Bach's cello suites appear in both games, while his first violin sonata appears in the former, along with Louis Clérambeault's Suite du Deuxième Ton for organ. The latter is a bit more varied, including Bach's keyboard concerto in D Major, the Prelude and Fugue in A Minor, and the Brandenburg Concerto no. 2, and pieces by Vivaldi, Handel, Kuhnau, and François Couperin, the last uniquely a vocal work. Lastly and chronologically latest, movements of the Brandenburg Concertos also appear in *Anno 1602*, alongside Bach's Air "On a G String" from the Orchestral Suite no. 3 in D Major and the Bach-Gounod "Ave Maria." This array of works informs about which Baroque or Bach-like musical characteristics are plausibly perceived as Renaissance-ist: small chamber orchestras comprising strings, flutes, recorders, and harpsichord continuo; solo harpsichord; and fugal works or the cello suites that have a sense of perpetual motion, to borrow a phrase from Jessica Kizzire (2014, 194).

As I mentioned earlier, William Gibbons (2014) notes that Bach's music often heightens a sense of authority or nobility in video games. For many games in this study, tracks composed in the style of Bach or using the Baroque characteristics I just outlined appear in scenarios involving royalty or other elite scientific, artistic, governmental, or (rarely) religious figures or places, an observation that both bolsters and extends Gibbons's observations. Of these, the harpsichord timbre is the most pervasive stylistic cue, perhaps due to its deep associations with both the Renaissance and Baroque periods (Fountain 2018, 51). Frequent arpeggiation or even an Alberti bass in the keyboard's left hand creates the sense of perpetual motion Kizzire associates with Baroque style; in *Mario's Time Machine Deluxe* (1996), it is heard when meeting Michelangelo in Florence in 1503. So do tonal scalar passages, especially in the left hand, as happens in the chorale-like central section of "San Marco" from *Painters Guild*, in which the player controls a prestigious art academy in the Italian Renaissance. A sense of forward propulsion is also created by melodic or harmonic sequences, as in "Doge's Palace" in *Anno 1503*.

The tracks for the governors in *Pirates!* (2004) all consist of solo harpsichord. The overall style and tonality of the track for the British governor sound like something from the American colonial period, with hints of William Byrd's virginal works; the same could be said of the theme for the Dutch governor. Those for the French and Spanish governors, however, have more in common with later styles; the Spanish theme sounds like a stereotypical pasodoble, while the French theme is reminiscent of "Sobre las Olas" ("Over the Waves") by Juventino Rosas or the Tin-Pan Alley song "Take Me Out to the Ball Game."

The harpsichord is a prominent part of chamber ensembles in tracks associated with royalty. A stately string ensemble is joined by a continuo harpsichord, oboe, and full choir, similar to a Bach cantata, in "Banquet for His Majesty" from *Anno 1404*. Relatedly, an active harpsichord accompanies what sound like a flute or recorder, oboe, and possibly bassoon, akin to a Baroque trio sonata, in "Rondo" from *Anno 1503*. Simpler, tuneful melodies with similar orchestration, as in Bach's Air "On a G String" or portions of the Brandenburg Concertos, occur in tracks such as "Royal Palace" from *Uncharted Waters: New Horizons* (1994). But the regular phrasing and overall tonality of "Eine Kleine Court Musik" from *Europa Universalis III*, plus the title's obvious reference, point even later toward Mozart and the Classical period. Numerous other instances of the harpsichord, as throughout *The Secrets of Da Vinci: The Forbidden Manuscript* (2006) or at the theater or Aldgate brewery in *Mission 1545*, act as generally historicizing cues since they lack characteristics specific to either the Renaissance or the Baroque periods. Note, though, that these less overtly Baroque themes are not associated with royalty or elite figures; even in the first example, Da Vinci is already deceased.

Because the harpsichord was also prominent in the Renaissance, it appears in themes that include other Renaissance instruments or have characteristics such as Renaissance dance-like rhythms. For example, the harpsichord plays both tune and accompaniment in "Kings Court" from *Europa Universalis IV*, then shifts to a largely chordal accompaniment for recorder, tambourine, and later, gamba. The instrumental timbres, limited ornamentation, and pavane-like feel point more toward the Renaissance. This track is somewhat of an anomaly, though, for in contrast to the demonstrable link between Baroque styles and nobility, more Renaissance-ist harpsichord tracks are almost entirely associated with taverns. For example, the harpsichord plays a dignified duple-meter piece that sounds like a Renaissance pavane in "Daytime in the Tavern" in *Bladestorm: The Hundred Years' War*. Similarly, the tavern theme in *Touché* is a jaunty tune in compound meter in which what sounds like a harpsichord accompanies synthesized instruments: winds, possibly a guitar, and a frame drum, all of which also indicates the Renaissance.

Renaissance-ism?

Thus far, my aims in this chapter have been to identify musical cues that are medieval(ist) or Baroque in origin, and to ascertain how and why they are used in games otherwise connected to the Renaissance. Given that many of these cues have substantial similarity with those that pertain directly to the Renaissance, I have also attempted to show how they might be distinguished from one another, in both musical style and narrative function. I revisit these observations in this section, where I identify musical cues that have demonstrable origins in the Renaissance period or that specifically emulate Renaissance musical styles and establish how they are used within these games.

Perhaps the most obvious musical cue is the borrowing of actual Renaissance-period music. The theme for the Henry VIII retro simulator game *Fit for a King* (2019) is "Pastime with Good Company," written by the king himself around 1513. The song is rendered in full 8-bit style with a harpsichord-like timbre, thus alluding both to the actual Renaissance period and to the keyboard styles so prominently used in 1980s video game soundtracks (see Gibbons 2018). "Greensleeves," often attributed to Henry VIII, was first printed in various versions in the 1580s, becoming popular enough to be named in Shakespeare's *The Merry Wives of Windsor* (1597–1602). A lush modern orchestration of its later hymn version "What Child Is This?" appears in *Anno 1602*, while "Greensleeves to a Ground," published by John Walsh in *The Division Flute* (1706), is heard in *The Procession to Calvary*. Despite the late date, the familiarity of the tune and the recorder and harpsichord timbres in the latter likely still read as Renaissance-ist to many player-listeners.

In *Anno 1503*, a recorder consort performs "Belle qui tiens ma vie," published by Thoinot Arbeau in *Orchésographie* (1589). This pavane is popular among modern performers of Renaissance music, since Arbeau printed it in four-voice arrangement with percussion and full text (Pittaway 2017). Its reputation evidently precedes it, for in the game, the pavane is simply called "Renaissance." Instrumental dances for lute are also popular choices. Hans Neusidler's 1536 lute passamezzo "Wascha mesa" occurs during the Johannes Gutenberg case in *Carmen Sandiego's Great Chase through Time* (1997). *The Procession to Calvary* features a lute pavane by William Byrd, while *Four Last Things* includes a sinister lutenist offering to play Robert Johnson's "The Witches Dance" and John Dowland's galliard "Can She Excuse My Wrongs." The latter two games also include an intabulation of Orlando di Lasso's "Von morgens fruh," a lute fantasia by Dowland, and Francesco da Milano's lute fantasia no. 58. But other instruments also appear: trumpets and trombones or sackbuts in Giovanni Cavaccio's Canzona "La Forest"; what sounds like a recorder consort in Thomas Morley's "Though Philomela Lost Her Love"; and what sounds like a shawm with percussion in Giorgio Mainerio's "Ungarescha."

Littered throughout both games are visual references to instruments, even when their associated music is actually sounded by something different. For example, in *The Procession to Calvary*, a group of men playing shawms, cornettos, and sackbuts perform a selection from Richard Wagner's *Siegfried*, and in another scene, the game itself mentions that the musician in question is performing a Scarlatti sonata "on a harp that sounds suspiciously like a guitar."

Renaissance vocal music, both sacred and secular, also appears in these two games. *Four Last Things* uses Claudio Monteverdi's "Tirsi e Clori" for a scene involving a pie-eating contest and a blind portrait painter, while in *The Procession to Calvary*, the protagonist must successfully sing "Lasciatemi Morire" from Monteverdi's lost opera *L'Arianna*. And as the protagonist in *Four Last Things* enters the Church of Heavenly Peter, the player hears a setting of the motet *Adoramus te, Christe* by Palestrina.

Civilization IV includes quite a lot of Renaissance music; however, as I have discussed above and at length elsewhere (Cook 2014), the game designers did not always accurately align musical periods with game eras. Just as the soundtrack for the Renaissance era is composed of music by Bach, Beethoven, and Mozart, real-world Renaissance music—three plainchants and sixteen compositions from the 15th and 16th centuries—constitute the soundtrack for the game's Medieval era. These works run the gamut from instrumental dances and one of Diego Ortiz's recercadas to vocal works, all but one of which (Josquin des Prez's "El Grillo") are longer sacred pieces, including John Sheppard's 22-minute motet *Media Vita*. About the only musical cues to the medieval in this era's soundtrack, through a lens of historical accuracy or of medievalist expectation, are the examples of plainchant. In timbre, harmonic approach, and musical style, the rest of the works point solidly toward the Renaissance, even as they also read as premodern, early, or old.

Most of the games in this study, however, do not interpolate pre-existing Renaissance music. Instead, they contain music newly composed in Renaissance styles or that imitate particular Renaissance works. Of the latter, the turn-based strategy game *Machiavelli: The Prince* (1995) is an interesting case, for its menu theme strongly evokes works found in the Buxheimer Orgelbuch ("Benedicite," "Christus surrexit") and the Lochamer Liederbuch ("En avois"). Although those works are not likely to be familiar to many players, the theme's overall modality, triple meter, light syncopation, occasionally thinner harmonic approach, and implied keyboard timbre would certainly read as appropriately "early" for a game set in the early 16th century.

"Greensleeves" is much better known, both as a Tudor-period work and a generically Renaissance or even "ancient" tune. The song itself is incorporated into several games, as I noted above, but its compound meter, galliard-like rhythmic inflections, minor modality, and occasional chromatic alteration at cadences are emulated in tracks like "Highland Wanderer" from *Europa Universalis III*, "Herdsman" from *Anno 1503*, "Building Tavern 1" from *The Guild 2*, and the entire soundtrack to the short online platformer game *Romeo Wherefore Art Thou* (2010).

In addition to imitating previously composed works, these tracks often use Renaissance dance rhythms, in particular those of the pavane and galliard. The latter contains the dotted rhythm gesture in "Greensleeves" and, as with the aforementioned emulations of that song, is often connected to pastoral scenes, working-class people, or taverns, as in "We are Peasants" in *Anno 1404*. The pavane, conversely, is a slower, statelier dance in duple meter and is more frequently associated with nobility or elite figures. As I mentioned, the harpsichord-based "Kings Court" from *Europa Universalis IV* is pavane-like, and in *Mario's Time Machine Deluxe*, the theme that plays for Joan of Arc in 1429 Orléans also seems like an ornamented pavane with overtones of a royal fanfare. Certain chronological and geographical situations, namely Elizabethan England and Renaissance Italy, are musically treated as though they were themselves elite: "Royal Pavan" from *Carmen Sandiego's Great Chase through Time* plays when visiting Shakespeare, and the theme for the Italians, which plays during game set-up in *Age of Empires II*, sounds like a Renaissance pavane for plucked strings and percussion.

In other tracks without overt connections to a particular Renaissance dance, instrumental (or vocal) timbre, stylistic considerations such as compound meter and ornamentation, and a fuller harmonic approach that leans away from a medievalist emphasis on parallel and perfect intervals can convey a sense of Renaissance-ness. Harps, lutes, flutes and recorders, gambas, percussion, bagpipes, organs, bells, and of course the human voice were present in both the Middle Ages and the Renaissance, and the harpsichord gained popularity into the Baroque. All might act as aural cues for the Renaissance if used in Renaissance scenarios, as I demonstrated for the two examples of plainchant in *Mission 1545* and *Assassin's Creed II*, or if they occur in conjunction with any of the other stylistic elements I just defined, as with several of the previously described harpsichord-based tracks.

The harp and lute are connected with a wide range of Renaissance scenarios, events, and peoples; as such, their timbres can be considered general historicizing cues. Both are used in dance-like tunes such as the moderately paced triple-meter "Simple Song" in *Rise of Nations* (2003), or in more sedate, sometimes free-form works throughout games such as *Painters Guild, Mission 1545, Uncharted Waters: New Horizons, Kingdom Come: Deliverance, Aspectus: Rinascimento Chronicles* (2011), and *Gold and Glory* (2000). The lute is also strongly connected to both Elizabethan England and Renaissance Italy (Fountain 2018), as evidenced by its role in games such as *Elsinore* (2019), *The Guild* and *The Guild 2, The Secrets of Da Vinci: The Forbidden Manuscript, The House of Da Vinci* (2017), and its sequel *The House of Da Vinci 2* (2019). Ailbhe Warde-Brown (2021, 44–45) has also observed that the version of "Ezio's Family" that appears in *Assassin's Creed II* symbolizes Renaissance Italy to the player via its lute-like guitar accompaniment, its allusion to plainchant, and its *prima* and *seconda pratica* styles of writing.

A recorder consort, however, is generally associated with pastoral, rural, or isolated scenarios, as in *Expeditions: Conquistador* (2013). The same can be said of a single recorder alongside a lute or guitar, perhaps with gamba, which can be heard playing folksy tunes throughout the point-and-click game *Elsinore*, in John Fox's "Upon the Greenwood Bough" in *Carmen Sandiego's Great Chase through Time*, or in "Among the Poor" in *Europa Universalis IV*, where it furthers a connection between rural scenarios and lower-class peoples.

Two other Renaissance-ist musical signifiers warrant deeper exploration. The first is the preponderance of madrigal-type pieces in these games. In *Assassin's Creed: Revolutions*, for example, singing lutenists often run up to Ezio, blocking him from moving forward until he has thrown them a coin. The music they perform tends toward the unsophisticated, perhaps mildly raunchy, and is sung in heavily accented English. Later, Ezio must disguise himself as one of these lute-wielding minstrels; in fact, he ends up using his lute to assassinate his final target (Cook forthcoming). Shakespearean song styles occur repeatedly throughout *Elsinore*. But the most overt, if tongue-in-cheek, reference to the English madrigal tradition is found in the comedy narrative game *Astrologaster* (2019), in which the 16th-century astrologer-physician Simon Forman must consult the stars to diagnose a bevy of local inquirers (or querents). As each patient approaches Forman's home, a custom madrigal introduces them and their problem, often in humorous or mocking fashion. These newly composed pieces are similar to secular songs by Thomas Morley or William Byrd. I also note that, for some of the more religious querents, the work is more like an English anthem by Thomas Tallis, though not necessarily divested of its humor. While many of these works are performed by an a cappella mixed choir, others of them, including as the main theme, are accompanied by appropriate Renaissance instruments such as harpsichord, recorder, crumhorn, gamba, lute, and hand percussion.

The other musical cue is the flamenco-esque guitar. Lidia López Gómez (2021) has discussed flamenco style as a stereotype for all things Spanish in video games, regardless of chronological or geographical location, and her observation holds true in several Renaissance-oriented games. A flamenco-esque guitar is heard in themes related to sailing to the Americas in *Carmen Sandiego's Great Chase through Time*, for the quest to find Ferdinand Magellan's steering wheel in 1520 in the NES version of *Mario's Time Machine*, and frequently in games depicting the Spanish presence in the Caribbean or the Americas, such as *Pirates!* or *Expeditions: Conquistador*. A less overtly flamenco-esque guitar, but one that still has some stereotypically Spanish inflections, is heard in similar games such as *Windward* (2015), *Voyage Century Online* (2006), and *Rise of Nations* (2003). While the guitar and other plucked string instruments have a long history in the Iberian Peninsula and were popular during the Renaissance period, flamenco as a genre emerged only in the later 18th century and its earlier origins are still debated. This musical trope, then, while commonly used in Renaissance-oriented games, is used to convey a sense of Spanishness first, and only secondarily a sense of historicity.

Conclusion

Listening to the Renaissance in video games involves a range of musical signs, including those with apparent connections to the medieval, Renaissance, or Baroque musical periods; medievalist musical practices; and a host of other cinematic, modernist, minimalist, and popular musical styles. But listening to Renaissance—or rather Renaissance-ist—signs reveals several intriguing patterns.

First, what do we now know about how the popular imagination might perceive, or be expected to perceive, the Renaissance? From the games themselves, we can see that the "Renaissance" as a period is most overtly aligned with particular historical people, places, events, and cultural phenomena, as follows:

- Italy, Florence, Rome; Leonardo da Vinci, Michelangelo, Machiavelli; cardinals, doges, and popes; art, science, technology
- England, Henry VIII, Queen Elizabeth I, Shakespeare and his plays
- Sailing to and colonizing the Americas, Spanish conquistadors, pirates
- The Reformation; Johannes Gutenberg and the printing press
- France; Joan of Arc

The musical signs that appear throughout the soundtracks all reinforce this popular perception of the Renaissance. First and foremost, the musical features in these games act alongside other visual and narrative cues as generally historicizing elements. Regardless of how closely they approach historical musical styles, the themes I have discussed all symbolize on some level the distant past or a premodern time, just as the vast majority of these games seek not historical accuracy but a broader sense of believability.

They also tell us a fair bit about *where* this distant past is believed to have occurred. Each of the games chosen for this study already had geographical connections to western Europe or to the Americas during the period of colonization, so naturally those areas will be reflected in the musical cues. But the musical cues also reinforce the association of the Renaissance with western Europe, or western European people in the Americas, in some of the more globally oriented games. Furthermore, particular regions are often treated with an extra degree of musical specificity. I noted above that flamenco-style guitar playing is always associated with Spanish or Iberian scenarios, English madrigals appear in Tudor-period games, Palestrina and Monteverdi are heard in Italian locales, and a German lute dance represents the birth of the printing press in Mainz.

Even beyond that kind of specific historical association, Italy and England are often distinguished further through Renaissance-ist musical signs. Consider, for example, the themes for individual civilizations in *Age of Empires II*. Given the game's chronological span from the "Dark Ages" through its own version of the Renaissance, it is not surprising that the civilization themes draw on medievalist cues. Unsurprisingly, the Spanish theme is composed for lute or guitar, though not in a later flamenco style. The Celtic theme makes anachronistic, if medievalist, use of thick bagpipes and a military snare. The Frankish theme is a short medievalist dance with limited harmonic accompaniment and a jagged rhythmic contour. But the theme for the Britons straddles the line between medieval and Renaissance symbolism: what sounds like a recorder and violin or fiddle play a short modal theme in compound meter overtop a lute or guitar on perfect fifths, while frame drum and tambourine keep the beat. As the lute takes over the theme, the harmonic accompaniment becomes richer, acting like a countermelody moving in thirds; this fuller approach to harmony leans more to the Renaissance side of the spectrum. The theme for the Italians also begins with what seems like a sparser harp or lute, changing to a more arpeggiated, chordal texture and fuller harmonic approach as the theme continues. Their Renaissance-ist textural and harmonic approaches distinguish these two civilizations from their more medievalist neighbors.

This Renaissance-ist reinforcement of certain geographical locations often goes hand in hand with special musical treatment of certain historical figures. As I described earlier, a Baroque or Renaissance-style harpsichord and a stately pavane often occur in scenarios involving royalty, nobility, or other kinds of elite personae. Note again the musical treatment of the governors in *Pirates!* (2004), Joan of Arc in *Mario's Time Machine Deluxe*, or the Doge in *Anno 1503*. But even in games with multiple such figures, certain ones receive heightened Renaissance-ist treatment. In the Super Nintendo version of *Mario's Time Machine* (1994), characters such as Joan of Arc, Leonardo da Vinci, and the Medicis are met with cartoonish or rockabilly type themes, but Shakespeare and Queen Elizabeth are portrayed by the Mario theme arranged for Renaissance or Baroque harpsichord. In *Mario's Time Machine Deluxe*, all the Renaissance locations and figures use a generally Renaissance-ist musical approach, but once again, Shakespeare and Queen

Elizabeth are further distinguished, here by a fanfare. In *Zoda's Revenge: StarTropics II* (1994), the soundtrack for Italy uses a tango or habanera rhythm underneath a tuneful melodic line, but the theme for Leonardo da Vinci includes something more akin to a Baroque harpsichord. And in *Carmen Sandiego's Great Chase through Time*, Queen Elizabeth and Shakespeare are denoted by a pavane, Leonardo Da Vinci by a lute dance, and Johannes Gutenberg by an actual Renaissance German lute work.

These games thus illuminate a public-facing understanding of the Renaissance as a time of exploration and cultural contact, scientific investigation and technological innovation, taverns and dancing, royalty and social hierarchy, strategy and intrigue, religious turmoil, and, yes, battle. But my analysis of their musical cues further refines this image; more overtly Renaissance-ist music is used to support all of the above aspects of the Renaissance *except* the last two. Throughout these games, scenarios involving battle, violence, or death have musically medievalist cues, namely epic cinematic scoring, military percussion and brass, allusions to the "Dies Irae" chant, and plainchant-like or Orff-inspired vocal passages, as I described earlier. Unlike in more explicitly medievalist games, religion is not as visible here, despite the religious turmoil of the Reformation; when it is present, though, it too is most often characterized through medievalist musical signs including plainchant, organ, and bells.

In his study of early modern medievalism, Mike Rodman Jones (2016, 89–90) observes that "the popular understanding of medieval and early modern culture (usually still termed 'Renaissance' in non-academic discourse) remains entrenched, and shaped partly by tacit assumptions about secularism and individualism that characterise some branches of early modern studies, particularly the study of Shakespeare." I have shown here that the musical cues used in these games betray exactly these tacit assumptions: that the Renaissance was a more secular and scientifically minded period in which religion was outdated, intelligence and strategy were superior to the mass barbarisms of medieval battle, and a handful of influential individuals reshaped the world.

APPENDIX A

GAMES WITH THEMATIC, GEOGRAPHIC, AND/OR CHRONOLOGICAL CONNECTIONS TO THE EUROPEAN RENAISSANCE

NB: This is a thorough but not exhaustive list. Not all these games are discussed in this chapter; some are text-only games, with no or little sound, while others have been discontinued or were unavailable for review.

- *Age of Empires II: The Age of Kings* (Microsoft/Konami, 1999)
- *Age of Empires II: Definitive Edition* (Xbox Game Studios, 2019)
- *Age of Empires III* (Microsoft, 2005)
- *Anno 1404* (aka Dawn of Discovery; Ubisoft, 2009)

- *Anno 1503: The New World* (aka *1503 A.D.: The New World*; Sunflowers Interactive/EA Games/ Ubisoft, 2003)
- *Anno 1602: Creation of a New World* (aka *1602 A.D.*; Sunflowers Interactive/GT Interactive/ Ubisoft, 2000)
- *Apothecarium: The Renaissance of Evil* (Icestone, 2019)
- *ARTé: Mecenas* (Triseum, 2016)
- *Assassin's Creed II* (Ubisoft, 2009)
- *Assassin's Creed: Brotherhood* (Ubisoft, 2010)
- *Assassin's Creed: Revelations* (Ubisoft, 2011)
- *Aspectus: Rinascimento Chronicles* (DGform, 2011)
- *Astrologaster* (Nyamyam, 2009)
- *Bladestorm: The Hundred Years' War* (Koei, 2007)
- *Call to Power II* (Activision, 2000)
- *Carmen Sandiego's Great Chase Through Time* (aka *Where in Time Is Carmen Sandiego?*; Broderbund, 1997)
- *Castlevania III: Dracula's Curse* (Konami, 1990)
- *Civilization: Call to Power* (Activision, 1999)
- *Crusader Kings* (Strategy First/Paradox Interactive, 2004)
- *Crusader Kings II* (Paradox Interactive, 2012)
- *Crusader Kings III* (Paradox Interactive, 2020)
- *Daikoukai Jidai III: Costa del Sol* (Koei, 1996)
- *Daikoukai Jidai Gaiden* (Koei, 1997)
- *Daikoukai Jidai IV: Porto Estado* (Koei, 1999)
- *Die Kathedrale* (Software 2000, 1991)
- *Elsinore* (Golden Glitch, 2019)
- *Europa Universalis* (Strategy First, 2001)
- *Europa Universalis II* (Strategy First, 2001)
- *Europa Universalis III* (Paradox Interactive, 2007)
- *Europa Universalis IV* (Paradox Interactive, 2013)
- *Expeditions: Conquistador* (BitComposer, 2013)
- *Fit for a King* (Kitfox Games, 2019)
- *Four Last Things* (Joe Richardson, 2017)
- *Gold and Glory* (Revolution Software, 2000)
- *The Guild* (aka *Europa 1400: The Guild*; JoWooD Productions, 2002)
- *The Guild 2* (JoWooD Productions/Aspyr, 2006)
- *Hamlet, or the Last Game without MMORPG Features, Shaders and Product Placement* (aka *Hamlet!*; Denis Galanin, 2010)
- *Henry VIII: Dressed to Kill* (Historic Royal Palaces, 2011?)
- *The House in Fata Morgana* (MangaGamer, 2016)
- *The House of Da Vinci* (Blue Brain Games, 2017)
- *The House of Da Vinci 2* (Blue Brain Games, 2019)
- *Jerusalem: The Three Roads to the Holy Land* (Cryo Interactive, 2002)

- *The Journeyman Project 2: Buried in Time* (Sanctuary Woods, 1995)
- *Kingdom Come: Deliverance* (Deep Silver/Warhorse Studios, 2018)
- *Knights of the Cross* (Cenega, 2002)
- *Lionhearted: Legacy of the Crusader* (Black Isle Studios, 2003)
- *Lupus in Fabula* (Spitoufs, 2017)
- *Machiavelli: The Prince* (MicroProse, 1995)
- *The Magician's Workshop* (Choice of Games, 2019)
- *Malediction* (FIEA, 2019)
- *Mario's Time Machine* (The Software Toolworks, 1993/1994)
- *Mario's Time Machine Deluxe* (The Software Toolworks, 1996)
- *Medieval: Total War* (Activision, 2002)
- *Medieval II: Total War* (Sega/Feral Interactive, 2006)
- *Merchant Prince* (QQP, 1994)
- *Merchant Prince II* (Take-Two Interactive, 2001)
- *Mission 1545* (City Quests Games, 2016)
- *Mount & Blade: With Fire and Sword* (Paradox Interactive/1C Company, 2011)
- *Painters Guild* (Lucas Molina, 2015)
- *Port Royale: Gold, Power and Pirates* (Tri-Synergy, 2002)
- *Port Royale 2* (Tri-Synergy, 2004)
- *Port Royale 3: Pirates and Merchants* (Kalypso Media, 2012)
- *The Procession to Calvary* (Joe Richardson, 2020)
- *Rise of Nations* (Microsoft Game Studios, 2003)
- *Rise of Venice* (Kalypso Media, 2013)
- *Romeo Wherefore Art Thou* (Shakespeare Country, 2010)
- *Santa Paravia en Fiumaccio* (George Blank, 1978)
- *Santa Paravia en Fiumaccio* (Keypunch Software, 1988)
- *The Secrets of Da Vinci: The Forbidden Manuscript* (Tri-Synergy, 2006)
- *Shadow of Memories* (Konami, 2001)
- *Sid Meier's Civilization* (MicroProse, 1991)
- *Sid Meier's Civilization II* (MicroProse, 1996)
- *Sid Meier's Civilization III* (Infogrames, 2001)
- *Sid Meier's Civilization IV* (2K Games/Aspyr, 2005)
- *Sid Meier's Civilization V* (2K Games/Aspyr, 2010)
- *Sid Meier's Civilization VI* (2K Games, 2016)
- *Sid Meier's Colonization* (MicroProse, 1994)
- *Sid Meier's Pirates!* (Ultra Games, 1991)
- *Sid Meier's Pirates! Gold* (MicroProse, 1993)
- *Sid Meier's Pirates!* (Atari/2K Games, 2004)
- *Teenage Mutant Ninja Turtles: Turtles in Time* (Konami, 1991/1992)
- *The Tudors* (Merscom, 2009)
- *To Be or Not to Be* (Tin Man Games, 2015)

- *Touché: The Adventures of the Fifth Musketeer* (Clipper Software, 1995)
- *Uncharted Waters* (Koei, 1991/1992)
- *Uncharted Waters: New Horizons* (Koei, 1994)
- *Uncharted Waters Online* (Koei, 2005)
- *Vespers* (Jason Devlin, 2015)
- *Voyage Century Online* (IGG Inc./Snail Games, 2006)
- *War of the Roses* (Paradox Interactive, 2012)
- *Where in Time Is Carmen Sandiego?* (Broderbund, 1989)
- *Windward* (Tasharen Entertainment, 2015)
- *Zoda's Revenge: StarTropics II* (Nintendo, 1994)

Notes

1. I thank Samantha Bassler, Krissie England, Adam Knight Gilbert, William Gibbons, Julianne Grasso, Dana Plank, and Ryan Thompson, and an anonymous reviewer, for their support and helpful insights into this chapter as it developed.
2. This blurriness is exacerbated further by the very term's disappearance in the historian's vernacular in favor of viewing the later 15th century onward as the "early modern" period. While historiographical constructions of the European Renaissance in academic thought are fascinating and deserving of critical treatment, this chapter is more concerned with how the Renaissance is perceived and presented in the popular imagination (see Sturtevant 2018). Additionally, I acknowledge my western and particularly American positioning, and my references to popular culture and imagination pertain most to the United States, although many of the games discussed in this chapter were developed in other areas of the world.
3. I specify the European Renaissance here (and, below, the European Middle Ages) not only to distinguish from the Harlem Renaissance but also to acknowledge that this periodization is a western phenomenon and does not apply to other global locations, traditions, and histories.
4. It is beyond the scope of this chapter, however, to assess every game that might make use of historical Renaissance music or music written in Renaissance styles if those games do not have any other chronological or geographical connection to the Renaissance (see Hart [2021]).
5. I refer to these interchangeably as timbres or as the instruments themselves, although in many video games the sounds are synthesized and an association with a particular instrument can be subjective, in which case I have attempted to clarify how I have chosen to interpret the timbre.
6. In popular imagination, the harpsichord is also closely aligned with the English virginal school of the later Renaissance period.
7. James Cook (2021) has even recently suggested that this trope has since moved outward from video games into other kinds of screen media.
8. Although *Final Fantasy IX* (2000) is outside the purview of this study due to its subject matter, Jessica Kizzire (2014) notes that the Baroque harpsichord plays heavily into the construction of a medievalist past in its score.

References

Brotton, Jerry. 2006. *The Renaissance: A Very Short Introduction*. New York: Oxford University Press.

Bull, Marcus. 2005. *Thinking Medieval: An Introduction to the Study of the Middle Ages*. New York: Palgrave Macmillan.

Cook, James. 2018. "Representing Renaissance Rome: Beyond Anachronism in Showtime's *The Borgias* (2011)." In *Recomposing the Past: Representations of Early Music on Stage and Screen*, edited by James Cook, Alexander Kolassa, and Adam Whittaker, 17–31. New York: Routledge.

Cook, James. 2021. "Game Music and History." In *The Cambridge Companion to Video Game Music*, edited by Melanie Fritsch and Tim Summers, 343–358. New York: Cambridge University Press.

Cook, James, and Karen M. Cook. 2018. "Medievalism and Music." In *Oxford Bibliographies in Music*, edited by Bruce Gustafson. New York: Oxford University Press. https://doi.org/10.1093/obo/9780199757824-0241.

Cook, James, Alexander Kolassa, and Adam Whittaker. 2018. "Introduction: Understanding the Present through the Past and the Past through the Present." In *Recomposing the Past: Representations of Early Music on Stage and Screen*, edited by James Cook, Alexander Kolassa, and Adam Whittaker, 1–14. New York: Routledge.

Cook, Karen M. 2014. "Music, History, and Progress in Sid Meier's *Civilization IV*." In *Music in Video Games: Studying Play*, edited by Neil Lerner, K. J. Donnelly, and William Gibbons, 166–182. Routledge Music and Screen Media Series. New York: Routledge.

Cook, Karen M. 2017. "Beyond the Grave: The 'Dies Irae' in Video Game Music." *Sounding Out!* (blog), December 18, 2017. https://soundstudiesblog.com/2017/12/18/beyond-the-grave-the-dies-irae-in-video-game-music/.

Cook, Karen M. 2018. "Beyond (the) Halo: Chant in Video Games." In *Studies in Medievalism*, edited by Karl Fugelso, xxvii, 183–200. Suffolk, UK: Boydell & Brewer.

Cook, Karen M. 2019. "Medievalism and Emotions in Video Game Music." *Postmedieval* 10 (December 1): 482–497.

Cook, Karen M. 2020. "Gaming the Medievalist World in Harry Potter." In *The Oxford Handbook of Music and Medievalism*, edited by Kirsten Yri and Stephen Meyer, 750–763. New York: Oxford University Press.

Cook, Karen M. 2023. "Assassin's Creed II: Ezio Trilogy." In *The Museum of Renaissance Music: A History in 100 Exhibits*, edited by Vincenzo Borghetti and Tim Shephard, 438–441. Turnhout: Brepols.

Elferen, Isabella van. 2012. *Gothic Music: The Sounds of the Uncanny*. Cardiff: University of Wales Press.

Elferen, Isabella van. 2012. "The Gothic Bach." *Understanding Bach* 7:9–20.

Emery, Elizabeth. 2015. "Medieval Times: Tournaments and Jousting in Twenty-First Century North America." In *Medieval Afterlives in Contemporary Culture*, edited by Gail Ashton, 67–77. New York: Bloomsbury Publishing.

Fitch, Fabrice. 2020. *Renaissance Polyphony*. Cambridge Introductions to Music. Cambridge, UK: Cambridge University Press.

Fountain, Daniela. 2018. "'Frame Not My Lute': The Musical Tudor Court on the Big Screen." In *Recomposing the Past: Representations of Early Music on Stage and Screen*, edited by James Cook, Alexander Kolassa, and Adam Whittaker, 51–62. New York: Routledge.

Gibbons, William. 2009. "Blip, Bloop, Bach? Some Uses of Classical Music on the Nintendo Entertainment System." *Music and the Moving Image* 2, no. 1 (April 15): 40–52.

Gibbons, William. 2018. "Little Harmonic Labyrinths: Baroque Musical Style on the Nintendo Entertainment System." In *Recomposing the Past: Representations of Early Music on Stage and Screen*, edited by James Cook, Alexander Kolassa, and Adam Whittaker, 139–152. New York: Routledge.

Haines, John. 2014. *Music in Films on the Middle Ages: Authenticity vs. Fantasy*. Routledge Research in Music 7. New York: Routledge.

Hart, Iain. 2021. "Semiotics in Game Music." In *The Cambridge Companion to Video Game Music*, edited by Melanie Fritsch and Tim Summers, 220–237. Cambridge, UK: Cambridge University Press.

Hong, Sun-ha. 2015. "When Life Mattered: The Politics of the Real in Video Games' Reappropriation of History, Myth, and Ritual." *Games and Culture* 10, no. 1 (2015): 35–56.

Jones, Mike Rodman. 2016. "Early Modern Medievalism." In *The Cambridge Companion to Medievalism*, edited by Louise D'Arcens, 89–102. Cambridge, UK: Cambridge University Press.

Kizzire, Jessica. 2014. "'The Place I'll Return to Someday': Musical Nostalgia in *Final Fantasy IX*." In *Music in Video Games*, edited by Neil Lerner, K. J. Donnelly, and William Gibbons, 183–198. Routledge Music and Screen Media Series. New York: Routledge.

Le Goff, Jacques. 2015. *Must We Divide History into Periods?* Translated by Malcolm DeBevoise. New York: Columbia University Press.

Leech-Wilkinson, Daniel. 2002. *The Modern Invention of Medieval Music: Scholarship, Ideology, Performance*. New York: Cambridge University Press.

Leonard, Kendra Preston. 2016. "The Past Is a Foreign Country: World Musics Signifying History in/and Elizabethan Drama." *Borrowers and Lenders: The Journal of Shakespeare and Appropriation* 11 (1). http://www.borrowers.uga.edu/783573/show.

Leonard, Kendra Preston. 2014. "The Use of Early Modern Music in Film Scoring for Elizabeth I." In *Gender and Song in Early Modern England*, edited by Leslie C. Dunn and Katherine R. Larson, 169–183. Women and Gender in the Early Modern World. Burlington, VT: Ashgate.

Meyer, Stephen C., and Kirsten Yri, eds. 2020. *The Oxford Handbook of Music and Medievalism*. New York: Oxford University Press.

Owens, Jessie Ann. 1990. "Music Historiography and the Definition of 'Renaissance.'" *Notes*, Second Series, 47, no. 2 (December 1): 305–330.

Pittaway, Ian. 2017. "The Pavan, the Priest and the Pseudonym: 'Belle Qui Tiens Ma Vie' and Arbeau's 'Orchésographie' (1589)." *Early Music Muse* (blog), March 9, 2017. https://earlymusicmuse.com/orchesographie/.

Plank, Dana. 2019. "From the Concert Hall to the Console: Three 8-Bit Translations of the Toccata and Fugue in D Minor." *Bach* 50, no. 1 (2019): 32–62.

Rubin, Rachel Lee. 2014. *Well Met: Renaissance Faires and the American Counterculture*. New York: New York University Press.

Sturtevant, Paul B. 2018. *The Middle Ages in Popular Imagination: Memory, Film and Medievalism*. New York: Bloomsbury Publishing.

Upton, Elizabeth Randall. 2016. "Coconut Clops and Motorcycle Fanfare: What Sounds Medieval?" *Sounding Out!* (blog), September 19, 2016. https://soundstudiesblog.com/2016/09/19/coconut-clops-and-motorcycle-fanfare-what-sounds-medieval/.

Warde-Brown, Ailbhe. 2021. "Waltzing on Rooftops and Cobblestones: Sonic Immersion through Spatiotemporal Involvement in the *Assassin's Creed* Series." *Journal of Sound and Music in Games* 2, no. 3, 34–55.

CHAPTER 28

CLAUDE DEBUSSY'S PIANO MUSIC AND THE EVOCATION OF ATMOSPHERE AND HUMOR IN VIDEO GAMES

GURMINDER KAUR BHOGAL

Introduction

This chapter explores how two central aspects of Claude Debussy's unique pianistic style have been used to enrich the ludic experience: his "serious" cultivation of atmospheric sound, on the one hand, and his "playful" characterization of musical humor, on the other hand. The atmospheric quality of the French composer's style has been observed since the earliest reception of his music, when some listeners and critics sought to make sense of his modernist innovations by drawing parallels with the contemporaneous impressionist art of Claude Monet. Just as Monet strove to capture the changing aura of light in his pursuit of *l'enveloppe* (a hazy atmosphere), Debussy similarly aimed to evoke nature's mystery and beauty through the portrayal of an ephemeral sound—one that is barely there, yet palpable in its intensity. Film directors and video game designers have readily explored this quality within visual contexts, although scholars are only beginning to fully interrogate the ludic contributions of atmospheric music and sound in video games.

The composition that music scholars tend to identify with Debussy's atmospheric soundscape is his opera of 1902, *Pelléas et Mélisande*. In contrast, this chapter examines how video game composers and sound designers continue to draw on his short piano piece "Clair de Lune," from *Suite Bergamasque* (1890–1905), in ushering ludic attention toward the atmospheric dimension. Although Debussy himself had little regard for it, no other piece of classical music can compete with "Clair de Lune" when it comes to facilitating a player's entry into an otherworldly domain, whether an inner realm of dreaming and moody introspection or, following a more literal reading of the title's allusion to moonlight, the habitation of outer space and a proximity to the moon itself. This short and simple piano composition continues to enjoy significant cultural cachet across all domains of popular culture (Bhogal 2018, 11–53).

A striking counterpart to the hazy timbres and diaphanous textures that characterize Debussy's atmospheric sonic worlds can be heard in his cultivation of a humoristic style: short motifs, incisive syncopated rhythms, chromatic harmonies, and unusual timbres come together within a discontinuous flow to underscore his allusions to musical wit. The humor behind these techniques reflects the composer's ever playful sensibility as he experiments with nontraditional musical gestures and sonic effects to subvert musical norms. The source for some of his musical material in African American danced performances of the cakewalk in Paris during 1902 and 1903 reveals the composer's wide-ranging musical tastes and his active participation in a cultural movement where elite, white French artists appropriated African American corporeal and sonic vocabularies to invigorate their own modes of expression. For his part, Debussy's reimaginings of ragtime and the cakewalk were placed alongside allusions to popular songs heard at the circus, music halls, and cabaret cafés of Paris. Even as the incorporation of classical music confers prestige and cultural capital in video games, as William Gibbons (2018, 52) explains, I explore how prestige and capital can also run the risk of erasing markers of race and consider how composers and sound design teams might work toward acknowledging the full histories and contexts of pre-existing music even as it is adapted and recomposed for the purposes of game play.[1]

This chapter studies a handful of Debussy's piano compositions across diverse genres of video games. I will first show how Debussy's ethereal sounds have the potential to evoke a striking atmosphere, as well as a sonic backdrop, for intimate moments within narratives that explore fantastical spaces and otherworldly realms. Just as "Clair de Lune" serves as a sonic mood for *Rain* (2013), and a haven for introspection in *The Evil Within* (2014), the final movement of *Suite Bergamasque*, the "Passepied," offers a space for contemplation in Batman's decision to play this movement when he says he needs "to focus" in *Batman: The Telltale Series* (2016–2017). Next, I will show how Debussy's music is used to heighten a sense of contrast between opposing states, thereby enhancing the level of thrill and unpredictability that accompanies interactive play. While contributing to the evocation of atmosphere, Debussy's floating sounds emphasize sensorial dissonance between the realms of space and earth in *Adr1ft* (2016), reality and the supernatural in *The Evil Within*, and love and loneliness in *Rain*. Finally, I examine how the formal, rhythmic, motivic, harmonic, and timbral innovations of Debussy's *Préludes* (Books 1 and 2, 1909–1913) are used in *Untitled Goose Game* (2019) to heighten the player's experience of bucolic humor. A pursuit of dynamic music foregrounds an unusual interplay between silence, ambient noise, and compositional rearrangement to reveal an ideal mode of ludic scoring whose "balanced approach" is recently held up by Rob Bridgett (2021, 115) as a model for new composition in video games.[2]

I am not alone in observing how the "serious" and "lighter" aspects of Debussy's compositional style coexist in his piano music; and how these two qualities are well suited to gameplay given how efficiently (and subtly) they are able to evoke and sustain a mood, even within a short timeframe. During the initial phase of my research for this chapter, I was delighted to discover improvisations and recordings by the German pianist Benyamin Nuss, who was among the first classically trained pianists to perform and record his own transcriptions of video game music.[3] Nuss is an ardent performer of French piano music, and perhaps it is no coincidence that pieces by Ravel, Debussy, and Poulenc find themselves on the same program as Nuss's transcriptions of video game scores by Nobuo Uematsu and Masashi Hamauzu (see Figure 28.1). (Other Japanese video game composers whose music Nuss has arranged for piano include Masayoshi Soken, Hideki Sakamoto, and Shiro Hamaguchi.)

In my conversations with Nuss and his piano duo partner, Cathy Yang, both emphasized broad stylistic connections between the work of these composers and the French piano school, especially with regard to the creation of atmospheric timbres, a textural privileging of decorative motifs, and an emphasis on lyrical fragments of melody. The limited scope of this chapter prevents me from examining some fascinating alignments between the atmospheric intensity of Debussy's and Ravel's pianistic styles and Japanese evocations of mood, affect, and emotion in video game music as reflected in the music of the above-mentioned composers and others including Takashi Yoshimatsu, but I hope others may want to interrogate sources of influence. Indeed, the video game journalist Emma Kent recently made a similar plea as she drew on music by Debussy and Ravel to argue, "when games lean into this focus on mood and atmosphere, they can unlock something quite powerful."[4]

At the turn of the 20th century, these composers were among the generation of French artists deeply inspired by Japanese art whose unique aesthetics and style brought about a widespread and dramatic transformation of sound, color, and movement across the arts. *Japonisme*, as this cultural movement was called, swept through all of Paris. As I heard the music of Uematsu, Hamauzu, Soken, Sakamoto, and Hamaguchi in Nuss and Yang's recital at Wellesley College in 2019, I couldn't help but marvel at how the bold visual strokes and decorative subtlety that Debussy and Ravel had absorbed from Japanese art and had used as the basis of their vibrant pianistic tableaux, had been reabsorbed into the fantastical worlds of epic Japanese games. To my ears, the symbiotic flow of ideas is nowhere more apparent than in Uematsu's "If You Open Your Heart" (*Final Fantasy VII* [1997]) where he clearly pays tribute to Debussy's *Rêverie* (1891). The lilting figuration of the opening arpeggiated accompaniment gently carries the dreamy introspection of Debussy's piece into Uematsu's score and, in so doing, allows the Japanese composer to cast his sweeping soundscapes through a uniquely French sonic lens. My chapter begins to explore these kinds of cultural and historical connections, but I hope further study will shed light on how the transnational dynamics that propel game production and marketing have significant analogs in aspects of game scoring and sound design.[5]

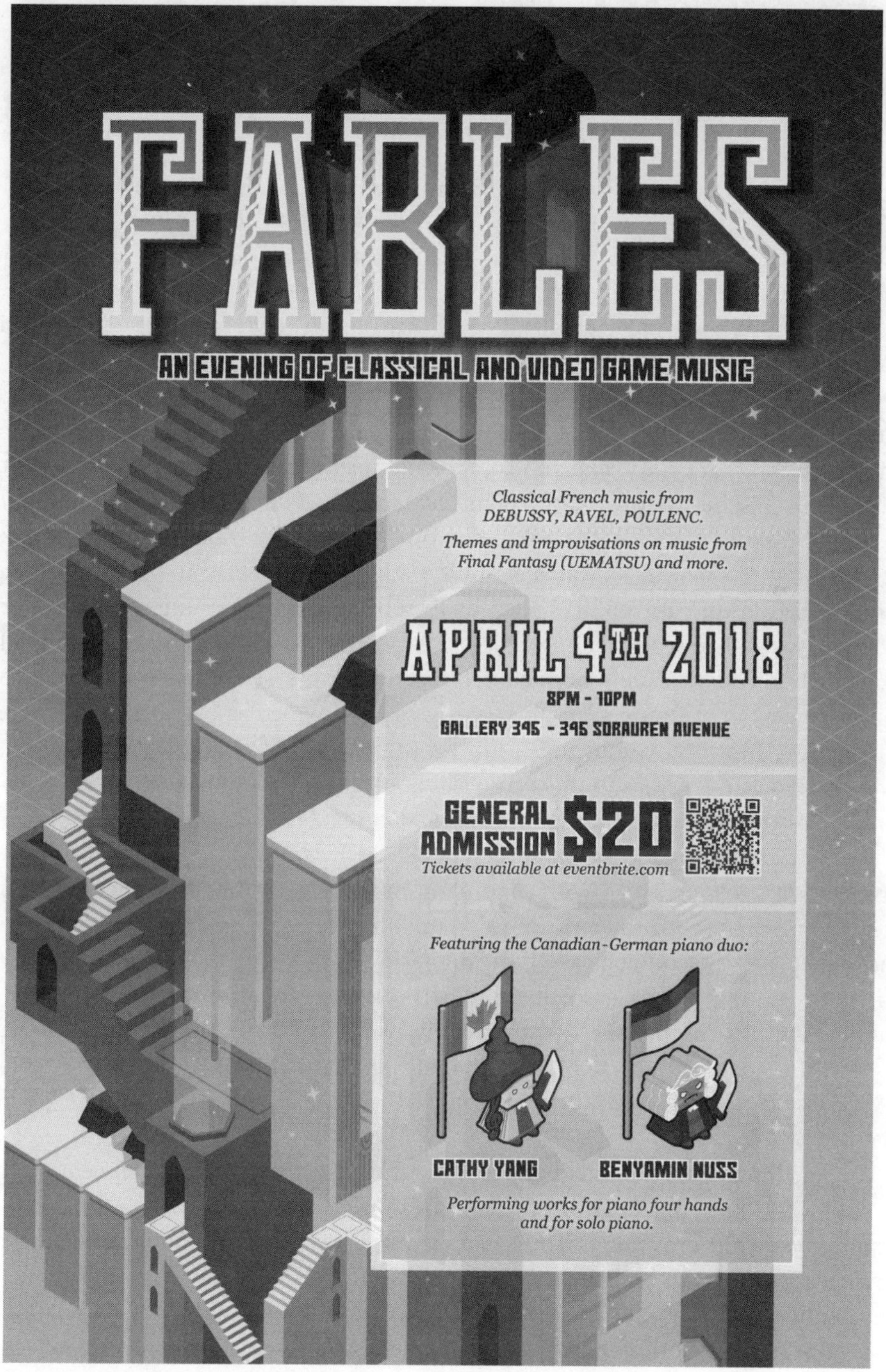

FIGURE 28.1 Poster for the *Fables* concert by Cathy Yang and Benyamin Nuss © Jess Leung (alittlejess.com).

Feeling the Atmosphere with "Clair de Lune"

> You do me a great honour by calling me a pupil of Claude Monet
> —Debussy to Emile Vuillermoz (Debussy 1987, 313)[6]

There are many reasons why a composition like "Clair de Lune" is frequently used in trailers, opening and closing credits, as well as in specific levels and episodes of gameplay. The most practical among these has to do with ease of availability: this music is in the public domain and thus readily included in digital music libraries accessed by composers and sound designers. It is there for the taking whether it is to be used in its original form as an evocative piano composition or in an arrangement (to which this piece has been subject across a range of musical styles and idioms since its inception).[7]

As I have explored elsewhere, another reason for the unceasing popularity of "Clair de Lune" has to do with its status as sonic cliché (Bhogal 2018, 51–53). Even though some composers circumvent this piece by turning to other lesser-known piano works by Debussy (such as Dan Golding's choice of the *Préludes* for *Untitled Goose Game*), I argue that its status as sonic cliché confers a certain expressive clout especially when it comes to generating atmosphere and evoking a mood aligned with longstanding themes of romance, heartbreak, loneliness, introspection, and dreaming. Furthermore, the strength of "Clair de Lune's" status as cliché is doubled with every new occurrence, given how each iteration builds on the histories and contexts of previous versions, thereby contributing to a monumental palimpsest of "Clairs de Lunes," if we might imagine such a thing. Tim Summers's (2016, 60) concept of "musical texturing" is also helpful for understanding the unique role of "Clair de Lune" in video games: "even where graphics and gameplay are technologically limited, music can use general musical signs and/or references to other media and cultural touchstones that are already well-established to enhance the game experience." Summers draws on the intertextuality of Johann Strauss II's *The Blue Danube* waltz, but "Clair de Lune" similarly thrives on a web of interconnected associations in "creating depth, implied detail and rounded context . . . for gameplay activity."[8]

Part of this piece's continued appeal has to do with its constant reinvention; the most effective rearrangements reconceive the music in ways that continue to foster its associations with romantic, moonlit nights, and a melancholic mood, while allowing new creative elements to build on these topics in offering an original interpretation. Reinvention is the key to longevity, as Danny Konstantinovic also notes in relation to two indie games that offer novel remixes of Debussy's piece: Andrew Jeremy's "Moon Bright" from *Coffee Talk* (2020) and Daniel Olsén's "Clair de Lune" from *Sayonara Wild Hearts* (2019). He pleads, "2020 should be full of games that cover Clair De Lune. Put it in Cyberpunk 2077. Make KK Slider sing it in Animal Crossing: New Horizon, you cowards. Put it straight into my veins" (Konstantinovic 2020).[9]

Jeremy and Olsén both offer striking electronic adaptations of Debussy's music. In Olsén's *Sayonara Wild Hearts* (described by the Swedish game design company, Simogo, as a "pop-album video game"), a vivid digital reimagining of pianistic timbres allows the music to shift the player's attention to a supernatural realm immediately after the opening credits.[10] The opening narration is accompanied by "Clair de Lune" as the premise for the game is laid out:

> Long ago a harmonious universe existed beyond ours and three divine arcana watched over it. But one night a cursed arcanum intersected the astral highways and along with her star-crossed allies they stole all harmony and hid it in their vile hearts. Before the divine trio started to fade, they created a heroine from the shards of a broken heart and hoped that one day she would be strong enough to save their world.

A bejeweled magical butterfly appears to the heroine in her dreams and leads her into a vibrant pink-hued nocturnal landscape where she must collect hearts to restore the harmony of the universe. Even if "Clair de Lune" was a convenient practical option, it is also an effective expressive choice that clearly signals the key themes of this game: heartbreak and hope. Isabella van Elferen (2016, 37) explains that game music need not be (and should not be) too complicated because the ludic framework requires easily recognizable and interpretable sonic cues: "Literacy in a game music's interpretation should be easy to acquire: because of music's crucial role in gaming interaction, the sonic cues that the player gets must be immediately recognizable and interpretable. Game musical literacy's contribution to immersion, thus, must be characterized by an almost clichéd audio-visual intertextuality."[11] In this respect, the (near universal) literacy of "Clair de Lune" provides players with a focal point for emotional contact, and one that retains a strong potential for immersive play.

The reimagining of "Clair de Lune" in the intimate setting of *Coffee Talk* is similarly compelling. A late-night coffee shop is, of course, a perfect space for Debussy's piece where it functions as background music (literally, coffee-shop music) to set the mood for late-night banter between humans and other fantasy creatures. "Clair de Lune" is another obvious and effective choice for this game given how it invites what I call a distracted mode of listening (also described by Gregor Herzfeld [2013, 151] as a "superficial . . . sense of hearing").[12] I have explored how this mode of engagement appeals to ludic contexts where "Clair de Lune" appears to sit "just as comfortably in the background as in the foreground of our listening experiences, and often at the same time" (Bhogal 2018, 2). In this regard, the affective quality of Debussy's music is vastly different from the music of other classical composers.

Tim Summers (2018) and William Gibbons (2009, 2018) have both examined how music by composers including Wagner, Bach, and Tchaikovsky operates within video games.[13] While elements of gameplay and visual markers enforce that this music is acknowledged and heard as classical (in the popular meaning, thereby asserting its status as high art), Debussy's atmospheric compositions are instead content to whisper soothing sounds in the background. Their striking evocations of mood and affect and inherently decorative characteristics (which willingly occupy the periphery of our aesthetic experience) render them ideal for game play. Unlike other types of classical music, the Debussy sound articulates a strong presence without asking, in Lawrence Kramer's words, "to be listened to" directly (cited in Gibbons 2018, 17). Given their frequent use of this piece, composers and sound designers are undoubtedly aware of how Debussy's music rests on the periphery of the player's auditory perception, oscillating between background and foreground spaces to heighten the player's affective experience of game play, but without drawing attention to its mysterious and impactful workings on their imagination and mood.

How does a piece like "Clair de Lune" evoke atmosphere and mood? There are three ways to answer this question. The first requires "listening to music as atmosphere [which] means not paying attention to sophisticated structural devices" (Herzfeld 2013, 151). Thus, in adopting Herzfeld's atmospheric attitude, I point to the minimalist, muted gestures of the opening measures and the languid, gossamer, and utterly nonchalant unfolding of chains of thirds whose narcissistic lingering defies the notated meter of 9/8. The consonances are sweet, but rhythmic fluidity renders the dissonances even sweeter, one might even say bittersweet, in keeping with the melancholic aura of Paul Verlaine's poem, "Clair de Lune," the literary source for Debussy's composition.[14] As the entire opening phrase tumbles from a high to a resonantly warm, deep register at the downbeat of measure nine, the sweeping arabesque contour promises to trace another luxurious arc with the return of the opening thirds. Debussy draws on the simple technique of repetition to draws us deeper into the world of our dreams.

Second, in answering this question from a historical perspective, I draw stylistic connections between "Clair de Lune" and a contemporaneous work for which Debussy similarly held little regard: *Printemps* (1887), an orchestral piece whose opening shares some melodic and structural resemblances with "Clair de Lune." *Printemps* was negatively criticized by the Académie des Beaux-Arts for its "vague impressionism" while the "dreamy atmosphere" of the first movement raised particular concern; the Académie expected better of the composer who had just won the revered composition prize, the Prix de Rome (Vallas 1973, 42).[15] The rest is history. The label of impressionism has stuck, and as much as Debussy tried to separate his music from this category—calling those who used this term "imbeciles"—he ultimately failed in his cause as indicated by the continued association of the composer with this painterly style (to the present day).[16] What was it about the connection between the two Claudes (Debussy and Monet) that sealed their artistic alliance for life through this single, whimsical label?

A third way of thinking about how atmosphere emanates from "Clair de Lune" calls on theories of atmosphere to help illuminate commonalities in their common pursuit of an ephemeral, yet palpable, presence of light and sound. While working on *Printemps*, Debussy wrote to his friend Emile Baron of his aim to recreate "as many sensations as possible."[17] This goal finds a striking parallel in Monet's pursuit of *l'enveloppe*, a term he used to describe the atmosphere that surrounded objects and whose faint presence had the potential to stimulate sensory perception. Monet remarked in 1895: "To me the motif itself is an insignificant factor; what I want to reproduce is what lies between the motif and me" (cited in House 1986, 29).[18] Monet's attention to the space of the in-between has an analogue in Debussy's sound famously characterized by Jacques Rivière as a "delicious halo": Debussy's music allows "shimmering rays [to] emerge; there is a center and around it a vaporous trembling, the floating of a thousand vague harmonies; we stand in the midst of a flight of sounds; they depart from us and dissipate into all our senses, forming around us a delicate vapor which is constantly in the process of vanishing" (cited in Bullard 1971, 270–271).[19] Rivière highlights the sonic attributes that speak to Debussy's privileging of atmosphere: its otherworldliness, fragility, evanescence, ambiguity, and ability to stimulate sensory perception.

Rivière's definition of the Debussy sound finds an intellectual companion in Gernot Böhme's extensive theories of atmosphere, which extend Monet's notion of *l'enveloppe*, and provides a way of thinking about how atmosphere emanates from "Clair de Lune" in ludic environments. Böhme's observations give us a sense of how Debussy's sonic atmospheres articulate presence and how this kind of delineation might be felt as expressive during play. First, Böhme reminds us that atmosphere is an indeterminate, intermediate dynamic space that pours out into the gap between subject and object, and whose presence is felt primarily through the body. Second, Böhme notes how atmosphere is suffused with emotional power; it is a spatial carrier of moods and feelings that can engulf and transform the body, allowing us to experience atmosphere through a state of affective resonance; Böhme (2017a, 118) explains, "one is *tuned* by an atmosphere."[20]

Atmospheric games constitute an important category that breaks with stereotypes of video games as offering solely fast-paced, action-oriented opportunities for sensory overload. To be sure, sensory activation is a primary goal of atmospheric play where a heightening of a player's sense of place, mood, and bodily sensation results in an intense, almost hyperawareness of self; what Böhme sees as *retunement* of the self (2017a, 20). Across a range of genres, composers and sound designers have turned to "Clair de Lune" to enable a fully engaged sensorial ludic experience where music encourages players to become more attuned to who they are and *how* they feel (literally) as acute attention is given to perceived connections between sensorial and emotional feedback initiated by music.

Following Böhme, the ludic contexts that I now explore focus on how atmosphere pours out into an intermediate space where emotions are felt, and memories are made; Böhme's (2017b, 2) point, that "you can enter an atmosphere and you can be surprisingly caught by an atmosphere . . . atmospheres are not beings like things; they are nothing without a subject feeling them," explains why "Clair de Lune" depends on the willingness of the player to receive Debussy's sonorities as a catalyst for evoking moods and feelings.[21] Sean Fenty's (2008, 23) description of nostalgia is especially pertinent to understanding Debussy's enigmatic sonic atmospheres, given how they traverse the space "between the two worlds of the real and the game world—of being on the threshold."[22] Nestled in the realm of the in-between, the nonintrusive sounds and textures of Debussy's music can only start to resound and act on a player's imagination if there is a willingness to claim them as something that is felt and cherished.

Cultivating Atmosphere in Survival Horror and Adventure-/Space-Themed Games

How does Debussy's piano music contribute to a type of play that is attentive to atmospheric mood? Herzfeld (2013, 151) explains that the "atmospheric attitude" is built around music whose "codified emotional contents"—read: romance, melancholy, and introspection for "Clair de Lune"—function to steer and "dominate the sense of hearing and its affective responses." Debussy's music is used to evoke an intense, expressive atmosphere that delineates space and heightens affect in the adventure/stealth game *Rain*. Since the storyline for *Rain* is ultimately about a longing for companionship, it seems fitting that "Clair de Lune" should feature as the soundtrack for the trailer where it satiates "the *trailer ear*" (as described by James Deaville) given how the music is elevated "to a formal element," which demands "an intensified mode of listening" (Deaville 2017, 241).[23] This music is also central to critical entry and exit points (the opening and closing chapters) and appears intermittently throughout the game to reinforce and sustain its trademark melancholic mood.

In tandem, the visual setting assumes a distinctly impressionistic aura given the muted strokes of grays, shades of black, and tints of white, whose hazy intermingling seems to waft directly out of an impressionistic depiction of mist, fog, and rain as seen in the paintings of J.M.W. Turner and J.A.M. Whistler; the watercolor-styled animation at the opening and closing also frames the distinctly French painterly aura of the game (Figure 28.2). Perhaps it is the pseudo-Parisian setting of *Rain* that leads the player to

FIGURE 28.2 Screenshot from *Rain*.

feel an acutely synesthetic ludic experience where the cool colors of the visual palette are intensified by the sound of thick, wet raindrops, and the sensation of being touched by escaping steam from sidewalk vents and gutters while being drenched by the rain. Beyond a literal correspondence of rain with meteorological atmosphere, rain assumes an expressive structural role in this game since it delineates the faint, bodily forms of the central characters, a young boy and girl, who are only visible when they are being rained on. Unfortunately, visibility also makes them prey for the invisible beasts that chase them throughout the game, preventing the boy and girl from being together until the very end.

The unassuming quality of "Clair de Lune's" opening thirds seem even more self-effacing within the context of *Rain*, where they emerge from the pitter patter of raindrops as water pours into the environment (to invoke Böhme's imagery). By providing sonic atmosphere, "Clair de Lune" mediates the lonely, gray space that engulfs the player upon entering the game and which surrounds the characters. Debussy's music does three things for the player in this game. First, "Clair de Lune" functions as a signifier of emotion by tapping into the long-standing association of this piece with melancholy and loneliness. Second, this piece deepens the player's cultural knowledge of the game's environment by suggesting a pseudo-French backdrop. Third, by tapping into this piece's long-standing historical and cultural significance at key entry/exit points, the composer Yugo Kanno prefaces his own musical attempts to evoke atmosphere by channeling the techniques of his musical model: the bare textures and plaintive melodies of his piano score grow directly out of Debussy's composition, allowing Kanno to acknowledge the creative source for his atmospheric sound, while presenting his own compositional work as a natural extension of Debussy's soundworld.[24]

Kanno's techniques are especially striking in the closing episode, where he overlays "Clair de Lune" with his original song, "A Tale Only the Rain Knows." This compositional strategy enacts a palimpsestic process of layering as does the animation whose synchronized timing against a complete iteration of Debussy's piece lifts the player's attention away from the melancholic grayness of the supernatural realm up toward a watercolor-styled, multihued rainbow (much like Verlaine, whose poem similarly draws the reader's attention up toward the tall fountains and the moon in the final stanza). Drawing from Debussy's "Clair de Lune" and his multiple sources (the poetry of Verlaine and the paintings of Jean-Antoine Watteau), the designers of *Rain* experiment with a slower, meditative pace that requires the player to *feel* sensorial interplay between sound, sight, and bodily sensation as mediated through the atmospheric intensity of Debussy's composition.[25] For example, one review, while describing *Rain* as "beautiful, lyrical, and extraordinary deep in feelings," also mentions how Debussy's composition is able "to touch us and make us part of its own rain."[26] The symbiosis between Debussy's piece and the affective experience of playing *Rain* gives the impression that they were made for other.

Herzfeld (2013, 50) reminds us how role-playing games and first-person shooters also "depend heavily on the success of the atmospheric setting." "Clair de Lune" assumes a different kind of atmospheric function in *The Evil Within* (2014), a third-person survival horror game. In *Rain*, this piece saturated the environment as it poured into the space between the player and the virtual realm, but in *The Evil Within* "Clair de Lune" is confined within a discrete space: "Safe House" locations containing a gleaming mirror. The peaceful music beckons the player's avatar, Detective Sebastian Castellanos, to look toward the mirror as he takes a break from killing zombie-like creatures. In comparison to the chilling wails and sounds of weapons that accompany Castellanos through the game, "Clair de Lune" provides sonic comfort. The composer, Masafumi Takada, highlights this piece's atmospheric role through acousmatic means. Castellanos hears the piece whenever he is close to a Safe House, the music becoming louder as he approaches the source of sound; Riviere's definition of the Debussy sound as "a vaporous trembling" seems to have found its physical correlate in the shimmering appearance of the mirror. Van Elferen (2016, 40) explains that the acousmatic approach is "especially powerful in survival horror games" which depend on the "affective importance" of music "to move players' emotions."

In the context of *The Evil Within*, the Debussy sound is indeed magical, given how it allows Castellanos to teleport to a safe haven. The use of "Clair de Lune" achieves two goals in this game. The first is practical in that the meditative quality of this piece offers the player an opportunity to take a brief break from the intense pace of the game. The designers draw on long-standing characterizations of this piece as peaceful and restorative by offering the player a chance to reflect on their play while literally recharging their avatar's batteries; at these moments, the game play switches to a different register as indicated by the calming arrangement of "Clair de Lune" for violin and piano. An eeriness is retained since the music is manipulated to sound as though it comes from an old, scratched LP.

Second, even within the genre of survival horror, it is striking that, *over any other piece of music*, it is "Clair de Lune" that compels the listener to look inward in pondering questions concerning their identity and existence in this game. The dazzling mirror makes visible the fantastical space from which the soothing sounds of "Clair de Lune" beckon the player through sensory overload of sound and sight; as Castellanos gazes at his reflection, he enters the deep recesses of his troubled mind, which bring to the fore questions of whether his battle takes place in the real world or in the fantastical realm of his nightmares. This piece has a similarly meditative role in a piano room, where the character Ruben Victoriano's memories seem to be triggered by this music. In these ways, *The Evil Within* deliberately exploits "Clair de Lune's" status as sonic cliché toward expressive ends, thereby ascribing positive value to music that some might feel is incapable of carrying expressive weight because of its overuse.

Indeed, overuse is the primary reason why the composer for *Batman: The Telltale Series*, Jared Emerson-Johnson, actively avoided "Clair de Lune." In an interview with me in 2018, he mentioned that his decision to use "Passepied," the final movement of *Suite Bergamasque*, was largely driven by a desire to introduce lesser-known pieces to players. Having heard a recording whose slow tempo emphasized the delicate and introspective quality of this movement, he felt that "Passepied" would work perfectly for a moment of the game where Bruce Wayne retreats to the Batcave and seeks out music to help him focus on solving a mystery. While it is tempting to hear the left-hand eighth notes as mirroring the whirring motion of his mind, this movement also functions atmospherically given how its sound issues from the horn of the record player and reverberates through the Batcave as the player roams freely, looking at objects and trying to solve the mystery of Gotham City's decline. As with *The Evil Within*, it is significant that diegetic uses of "Clair de Lune" often point to the physical object of the record player as the source of atmosphere during these episodes of game play.

Emerson-Johnson explained that, in choosing "Passepied" for the intimate space of the Batcave, he wanted to show Bruce listening to music that reflects his personal taste; even if Bruce chooses the jazz or ambient music options, he ends up playing "Passepied" at Alfred's request. The privacy of this moment makes for jarring contrast later in the game when Joker torments Bruce by playing the same piece (also on his record player) during dinner, thereby mocking Batman and everything Bruce Wayne stands for. This grotesque inversion leads the player to wonder how Joker could have known about the significance of this music for Bruce. What is considered highbrow in the Batcave—Bruce says, "you can't go wrong with the classics"—loses its cachet when heard in Joker's underground realm. The soothing and stimulating role of Debussy's music in the Batcave is thus subverted when it comes to accompany Joker's acts of violence and provocation. Although Debussy's music resounds in an "anempathetic" way in this episode (to use Michel Chion's term [1994, 8]), the player's memory imbues its diegetic presence with an emotional significance that motivates their efforts to remove Batman from physical and psychological harm.[27]

Turning now to a different genre of games altogether, those set in space, I will explore how "Clair de Lune" orients the player's attention toward the sensory field, in particular, a drastically altered experience of bodily sensation. Unsurprisingly, the piece's titular reference to moonlight renders it suitable for trailers and opening sequences the seek to signal the player's immersion in another world from the outset. It is because Debussy's title is so deeply ingrained in the cultural imagination that the recent game, *Claire de Lune* (2021), is able to dispense entirely with his music, relying instead on a punning title to signal otherworldliness and the loneliness of a father and his daughter (Claire) who try to find one another on a distant planet.

Other games draw on Debussy's ethereal music to shape the player's experience of time and corporeal sensation as we see in *Adrıft* (2016). The commercial trailer uses "Clair de Lune" in its original version for piano to heighten the effects of virtual reality as a lone female astronaut (Commander Alex Oshima) drifts through space amid the wreckage of a space station.[28] Critical reviews of the game describe its strong points in terms that relate to Debussy's prefacing music: the game offers "strong atmosphere," "a sense of weightlessness," "an excuse to gently float around in a beautifully ruined space station."[29] Interestingly, "Clair de Lune's" overriding associations with serenity and dreaming direct the player's attention to aspects of visual space and texture; as noted by Stephany Nunneley: "Adrıft is rather gorgeous on its own. But when you combine such loveliness with Claude Debussy's tranquil Clair de Lune, you'd assume the game would be a pleasant, relaxing experience. But you'd be wrong" (2016).[30] While the slow tempo of Debussy's music accompanies beautiful views of Earth and a nauseatingly real experience of being able to see objects from unusual viewpoints—given the ability to rotate 360 degrees in a gravity-less environment—it detracts from this clichéd function by exacerbating the dissonance between soothing sound and otherworldly sensation. In the opening sequence, the long, drawn-out silences between Debussy's punctuating musical gestures provide gaps that endanger "the fragile sense of immersion," to use Gibbons's phrase (2014, 124).[31] However, this deliberate tactic uses the intermittent presence/absence of piano music as a means to elevate the visual dimension and draw attention to an embodied ludic experience where the player is invited to experience the strangeness of Oshima's corporeal sensations as her body floats through space and around her space station.

Prey: Mooncrash (2018) builds on these topical associations, although here the atmospheric contribution of the music is exaggerated through effects of digital distortion. The arrangement of "Clair de Lune" by Ben Crossbones relies on an array of digital techniques whose masterful intermingling with the ambient sounds of moving around the space station create a surreal distortion that contributes to the player's sense of disorientation as they explore their unfamiliar surroundings. The bodily sensations that we feel through "Clair de Lune" in *Adrıft* and *Prey: Mooncrash* invoke Lisa Coulthard's notion of "affective intensity." This idea is particularly suitable for understanding how Debussy's music functions in "space games," where atmospheric music is not involved in establishing an emotional connection between the player and their actions (as we saw with *Rain* and *Batman*) but, rather, the establishment of a "corporeal and psychological experience," which is mediated by atmospheric phenomena. She explains, "we are invited to *feel* the impact, not just *feel for* a character, and sound is key to this subjective and affective implication." These instances show how "Clair de Lune" is especially effective in establishing "affective intensity" in games about space (2017, 58).[32]

These examples show how Debussy's music can inflect the act of play without being intrusive. The atmospheric quality of his sound presents itself as an ideal companion for gameplay given how it leaves "some open space for the player's performance," as described by Herzfeld (2013, 154). As revealed through reviews on *Metacritic* and fan comments on various platforms, some players have experienced Debussy's compositions as enhancing their sense of immersion. While drawing attention to how Debussy's music extends into the digital realm, I also highlight his importance as a composer of atmospheric sound that inhabits the realm of the in-between, a seemingly empty space that is alive with sensory and affective potential.

Humoristic Rethinking of Game Audio

The dreamy soundscape of "Clair de Lune" presents a strikingly different style and mood in comparison with Debussy's attempts at pianistic humor. Scholars often point to his unexpected interweaving of Wagner's famous "Tristan chord" within the jovial context of "Golliwog's Cakewalk" (*Children's Corner*, 1908) as an example of his subtle musical wit and penchant for musical parody. Through the use of musical quotation, the composer no doubt enjoyed the opportunity to mock the highbrow status of this operatic gesture within the lowbrow musical setting of a short piano piece that strives to capture the idiosyncratic rhythms, motifs, and harmonies of the cakewalk (a type of dance in which African American slaves created a parody, through music, song, dance, and comedy, of their white plantation owners).[33] Debussy heard the cakewalk performed by two American troupes composed of African American and white performers ("Les Elks") and an all-female African American group ("Florida Creole Girls") in 1902 and 1903. The composer eagerly consumed and perpetuated these examples of racial stereotyping by filtering what he saw and heard through his imagination into a handful of piano pieces including "Minstrels" (*Préludes*, Book 1), which was used in the first trailer for *Untitled Goose Game* in 2017 (Figure 28.3) and whose music now appears in the game itself.[34] In tandem with the visual design, Debussy's cakewalk-inspired music (which the composer marked *nerveux et avec humour* [agitated and humorous]) charmed the viewers of the first trailer and continues to delight players many of whom enjoy the "playful piano music" and the "light, jazzy soundtrack" of the game (Lee 2019; Wilde 2019).[35]

Dan Golding, composer of *Untitled Goose Game*'s score, has written extensively about his compositional technique and the development of this game, not to mention his deliberate efforts to avoid musical cliché: "perhaps the less said about the many uses—or abuses—of "Clair de Lune" from the *Suite bergamasque* in films, television, and trailers, the better" (2021, 5).[36] In this regard, the selection of "Les collines d'Anacapri" (Book 1) for the official 2019 trailer is certainly an original and unexpected choice (as was

FIGURE 28.3 Screenshot from *Untitled Goose Game*.

"Minstrels" for the first trailer).[37] Unlike "Clair de Lune," few players are likely to have encountered Debussy's *Préludes* beforehand. Also unlike "Clair de Lune" is the fragmentary and discontinuous quality of the music, which is characterized by abrupt snippets of melody, incisive rhythmic motifs, patterned figuration, and constantly changing tempi in "Les collines d'Anacapri"; "Minstrels," meanwhile, includes musical effects that allude to the instruments and playing styles of early 20th-century minstrel bands, as well as a reference to the sentimental style of contemporaneous music-hall ballads (this is the diegetic music that comes from the radio in the 2017 trailer).[38] "Clair de Lune" sustains a single, meditative, uninterrupted mood whereas the frantic 16th figuration of "Les collines d'Anacapri" with which Golding opens the official trailer—he omits the prelude's entire opening section, mm. 1–12—feels skittish and disorienting (much like the "victims" of the rogue goose). Debussy's oscillating figuration maps perfectly on to the determined waddling of the goose. What better way to orient the player's attention toward the mischievous antics of a goose than through this simple mickey-mousing technique as Golding describes it?

Golding explains how his adaptation of Debussy's *Préludes* to the ludic context allows them to function both as external sound—akin to mickey mousing—*and* as internal sound, since the music responds directly to the player's actions.[39] His compositional design is unusual for the purposes of gameplay because it retains silence as a key expressive "audio" feature that works alongside two additional states at which the game operates: a high-energy performance (what we might expect to hear at a recital, for instance) and low-energy performances, which Golding (2021, 11) describes as, "quite dramatic and unconventional interpretations of Debussy's music, including changes in tempo, articulation, note velocity, dynamics and dynamic range, sometimes the register of notes, and, very rarely, the notes themselves." In order for the music and storyline to create an interactive sense of humor, Golding undertook an extensive "deconstruction" of Debussy's *Préludes* to create "stems" that would correspond to the three "musical moods for the game: silence, low energy, and high energy, the goal being to divide the stems into short enough units "that convincingly respond to the player's actions" (12). Each play elicits segments of Debussy's compositions in a random order depending on the player's motivations and how much mischief they want to create. It is the subtle layering of these stems with ambient sounds created and recorded by Em Halberstadt—the goose "honk," pitter patter of webbed feet, natural sound of birdsong, breaking tea-cups and vases, and much more—that facilitate an especially fun ludic experience (Andersen 2019).[40] Indeed, *Esquire* magazine declared it so in 2019 with an article headline that read: "*Untitled Goose Game* Is the Most Joyful Video Game of the Year" (Nero 2019).[41]

As much as I relish the interactive, ludic situation for which Debussy's *Préludes* have been reimagined, I also wonder whether moments such as these offer valuable opportunities to alert players, composers, audio designers, and the entire development and production team to the rich historical and cultural contexts of pre-existing music (regardless of idiom). On the part of composers and developers, how might their attitudes toward using Debussy's *Préludes* for ludic purposes be shaped by a knowledge of early 20th-century performances by minstrel bands and the music-hall/cabaret scene that gave rise to the pop song heard in the official trailer 30 seconds in (Debussy asks the pianist to play this melody *avec la liberté d'une chanson populaire* ["with the freedom of a popular song"])? For players, might this historical and cultural awareness bring a different intention toward interactive play given how Debussy's appropriation and adaptation of the cakewalk intermingled with other sources of popular music from the circus, music hall, and cabaret clubs, as well as his own avant-garde pianistic gestures?

Intertextuality is at the heart of the ludic encounter, and as game scoring continues to evolve with the kind of subtlety heard in *Untitled Goose Game* it is worth reflecting on how developers and players can work together to create an enriched experience of game play that keeps creative networks and their sources of influence in clear sight. This is especially pertinent for a game like *Untitled Goose Game*, where the algorithmic arrangement of stems results in a unique sonic experience for each player, thereby opening up the possibility for players to emerge as cocreators.[42] Of course, such an effort would require a different pace of engagement for designers and players—I recall Stephen Baystead's (2017, 329) complaint about "crushingly compressed timescales . . . and procedural protocols"—but surely this goal is worth contemplating given the potential of video games for personal and social transformation.[43]

On a personal level, games are often the first place where players encounter classical music and, quite often, establish a life-long (nostalgic) attachment to certain compositions and their original ludic contexts. For many of us, video games are among those media (including film and animation) that have sparked deep affection for classical music. As seen in fan comments across platforms, players are often eager to know more about the composers of their favorite soundtracks and approaches to audio design. On a broader scale, the eye-opening insights of *Woke Gaming: Digital Challenges to Oppression and Social Justice*, a collection of essays edited by Kishonna Gray and David Leonard (2018), speak to the perpetuation of injustices surrounding race and gender in video games and the industry.[44] Inclusive gaming communities are eager to dismantle stereotypes and inequities, and context-sensitive attitudes toward the development of game content are critical to this endeavor. More and more, *games have the potential to inform and reform.*

Feeling Sound

One of the most exciting features of *Untitled Goose Game* is the expressive role that it affords silence, which is a defining quality of atmosphere, and whose expressive capacity is highlighted through its juxtaposition against other shades of music (more energetic/less energetic) to create a broad-ranging sonic experience. This technique subverts the "wall-to-wall" tendency that Rob Bridgett (2021, 115) observes in most games while offering players an opportunity to create a nuanced sound palette.[45] Pockets of silence allow players to develop a heightened state of attention toward their environment. As we have seen across a range of ludic contexts and genres, the sonic dimension is not only manifest in the "nuts and bolts" of what is heard—the melodies, rhythms, harmonies, motifs, and so on. Pieces like "Clair de Lune" and "Passepied," and movements from Debussy's *Préludes*, show how his compositions, in particular, but not only, have the potential to pour out into the atmosphere (to invoke Böhme). The question of how music, especially, can take on an expressive atmospheric function is explained by Böhme's (2017a, 51) perception of sound as "energetic or material emanations by which things fill a space and thereby evidence their presence." In video games, players are asked to inhabit virtual spaces and it is by paying attention to their bodily presence within these spaces that the atmospheres of games (whether survival horrors like *The Evil Within* or something much more meditative like *Rain*) are able to touch them.

Video games thrive on the relationships that players establish with their virtual environments. By asking players to attune themselves to their specific surroundings, ludic dimensions demand a porous mindset; Böhme explains, to perceive atmospheres "takes time and openness, and we must allow ourselves to be involved and touched by them" (2017a, 120). I hope that my attention to the expressive role played by Debussy's music across a variety of games will spark further discussion on the topic of "what games do" while contributing to conversations about "how games can make us feel."

Notes

1. Gibbons (2018).
2. See Bridgett (2021, 115).
3. See http://www.benyaminnuss.com (last accessed June 2, 2021).
4. See Kent (2021).
5. On this topic see Gibbons (2021).
6. Lesure and Nichols (1987, 313). Letter from Debussy to Emile Vuillermoz, January 25, 1916.
7. For more on this topic, see Bhogal (2018, 11–53).
8. Summers (2016, 60).
9. Konstantinovic (2020).
10. https://simogo.com/work/sayonara-wild-hearts/. Also see https://danielolsen.net/?project=sayonara-wild-hearts (last accessed June 2, 2021).
11. Van Elferen (2016, 37).
12. Herzfeld (2013, 151).
13. See, for example, Summers (2018) and Gibbons (2009, 2018).
14. See Paul Verlaine, "Clair de Lune" (from *Fêtes galantes*, 1869).
15. Vallas (1973, 42). For the original report by the Permanent Secretary of the Académie des Beaux-Arts from 1887 see *Les arts français* 16 (1918), 92.
16. Lesure and Nichols (1987, 188). Letter from Debussy to Jacques Durand, March 1908.
17. Lesure and Nichols (1987, 20). Letter from Debussy to Emile Baron, February 9, 1887.
18. Cited in House (1986, 29).
19. Rivière (1913), cited in Bullard (1971, 1:270–271).
20. Böhme (2017a, 118). Also see Böhme (2017b) and Griffero (2016).
21. Böhme (2017b, 2).
22. Fenty (2008, 23).

23. Deaville (2017, 241).
24. For a more detailed discussion of Kanno's score, see Bhogal (2018, 50).
25. For a range of reviews, see https://www.metacritic.com/game/playstation-3/rain/critic-reviews (last accessed June 2, 2021).
26. See *Meristation*, October 1, 2013.
27. Chion (1994, 8).
28. See https://www.youtube.com/watch?v=aKiBnRMMfpU (last accessed June 2, 2021).
29. See Stapleton (2018), McElroy (2016), and Orland (2016).
30. Nunneley (2016).
31. Gibbons (2014, 124).
32. Lisa Coulthard (2017, 58).
33. For more on this topic, see Deaville (2014) and Caddy (2007).
34. https://www.youtube.com/watch?v=wQknBJo4aBQ (last accessed June 2, 2021).
35. Lee (2019) and Wilde (2019).
36. Golding (2021, 5).
37. https://www.youtube.com/watch?v=9LL2AtHo1gk&list=RDCMUCGIY_O-8vW4rfX98KlMkvRg&start_radio=1&t=17s (last accessed June 2, 2021).
38. Also see the discussion of "Minstrels" by Paul Roberts (1996, 218–220).
39. Golding (2021, 6).
40. Andersen (2019).
41. Nero (2019).
42. On the topic of participatory culture, see Miller (2012).
43. See Baystead (2017, 329).
44. Gray and Leonard (2018).
45. Bridgett (2021, 115).

References

Andersen, Asbjoern. 2019. "Behind the Charming Sound Design—and Glorious Honks—for *Untitled Goose Game*." *A Sound Effect*, October 10, 2019. Accessed June 2, 2021. https://www.asoundeffect.com/untitled-goose-game-sound/.

Baystead, Stephen. 2017. "Simulation: Squaring the Immersion, Realism, and Gameplay Circle." In *The Routledge Companion to Screen Music and Sound*, edited by Miguel Mera, Ronald Sadoff, and Ben Winters, 328–337. New York: Routledge.

Bhogal, Gurminder. 2018. *Claude Debussy's "Clair de Lune."* New York: Oxford University Press.

Böhme, Gernot. 2017a. *Atmospheric Architectures: The Aesthetics of Felt Spaces*, edited and translated by Anna Christina Engels-Schwarzpaul. London: Bloomsbury.

Böhme, Gernot. 2017b. *The Aesthetics of Atmospheres*, edited by Jean-Paul Thibaud. New York: Routledge.

Bridgett, Rob. 2021. "'Less Music, Now! New Contextual Approaches to Video Game Scoring." In *The Cambridge Companion to Video Game Music*, edited by Melanie Fritsch and Tim Summers, 110–119. New York: Cambridge University Press.

Bullard, Truman C. 1971. "The First Performance of Igor Stravinsky's 'Sacre du Printemps.'" PhD dissertation, University of Rochester (Eastman School of Music). 2 Vols.

Caddy, Davinia. 2007. "Parisian Cake Walks." *19th-Century Music* 30, no. 3 (Spring): 288–317.

Chion, Michel. 1994. *Audio-Vision: Sound on Screen*. Translated by Claudia Gorbman. New York: Columbia University Press.

Coulthard, Lisa. 2017. "Affect, Intensities, and Empathy: Sound and Contemporary Screen Violence." In *The Routledge Companion to Screen Music and Sound*, edited by Miguel Mera, Ronald Sadoff, and Ben Winters, 50–60. New York: Routledge.

Deaville, James. 2014. "Debussy's Cakewalk: Race, Modernism and Music in Early Twentieth-Century Paris." *Revue musicale OICRM* 2, no. 1 (2014): 20–39.

Deaville, James. 2017. "Trailer or Leader? The Role of Music and Sound in Cinematic Previews." In *The Routledge Companion to Screen Music and Sound*, edited by Miguel Mera, Ronald Sadoff, and Ben Winters, 240–254. New York: Routledge.

van Elferen, Isabella. 2016. "Analysing Game Musical Immersion: the ALI Model." In *Ludomusicology: Approaches to Video Game Music*, edited by Michiel Kamp, Tim Summers, and Mark Sweeney, 32–52. Bristol, CT: Equinox.

Fenty, Sean. 2008. "Why Old School Is 'Cool': A Brief Analysis of Classic Video Game Nostalgia." In *Playing the Past: History and Nostalgia in Video Games*, edited by Zach Whalen and Laurie N. Taylor, 19–31. Nashville: Vanderbilt University Press.

Gibbons, William. 2009. "Blip, Bloop, Bach? Some Uses of Classical Music on the Nintendo Entertainment System." *Music and the Moving Image* 2, no. 1 (Spring): 40–52.

Gibbons, William. 2014. "Wandering Tonalities: Silence, Sound, and Morality in *Shadow of the Colossus*." In *Music in Video Games: Studying Play*, edited by K. J. Donnelly, William Gibbons, and Neil Lerner, 122–137. New York: Routledge.

Gibbons, William. 2018. *Unlimited Replays: Video Games and Classical Music*. New York: Oxford University Press.

Gibbons, William. 2021. "Open Worlds: Globalization, Localization and Video Game Music." In *The Cambridge Companion to Video Game Music*, edited by Melanie Fritsch and Tim Summers, 359–375. New York: Cambridge University Press.

Golding, Dan. 2021. "Finding 'Untitled Goose Game's Dynamic Music in the World of Silent Cinema." *Journal of Sound and Music in Games* 2, no. 1 (2021): 1–16.

Gray, Kishonna L., and David J. Leonard, eds. 2018. *Woke Gaming: Digital Challenges to Oppression and Social Justice*. Seattle: University of Washington Press.

Griffero, Tonino. 2016. *Atmospheres: Aesthetics of Emotional Spaces*. New York: Routledge.

Herzfeld, Gregor. 2013. Atmospheres at Play: Aesthetical Considerations of Game Music." In *Music and Game Perspectives on a Popular Alliance*, edited by Peter Moorman, 147–157. Wiesbaden, Germany: Springer.

House, John. 1986. *Monet: Nature into Art*. New Haven, CT: Yale University Press.

Kent, Emma. 2021. "What Debussy Can Tell Us about Mood in Games: Drawing Parallel (Octaves)." *Music Week*, March 15, 2021. Accessed June 2, 2021. https://www.eurogamer.net/articles/2021-03-10-music-week-what-debussy-can-tell-us-about-mood-in-games.

Konstantinovic, Danny. 2020. "Please Never Stop Remixing 'Clair De Lune.'" *Medium*, February 7, 2020. Accessed June 2, 2021. https://medium.com/@DannyKonstantinovic/please-never-stop-remixing-clair-de-lune-e8bd2b16340e.

Lee, Dami. 2019. "How *Untitled Goose Game* Adapted Debussy for Its Dynamic Soundtrack." *Verge*, September 23, 2019. Accessed June 2, 2021. https://www.theverge.com/2019/9/23/20879792/untitled-goose-game-nintendo-switch-debussy.

Lesure, Francois, and Roger Nichols, eds. *Debussy Letters*, translated by Roger Nichols. Cambridge, MA: Harvard University Press.

McElroy, Justin. 2016. "Adrift Review." *Polygon*, March 31, 2016. Accessed June 2, 2021. http://www.polygon.com/2016/3/31/11334468/adrift-review-adr1ft-pc-oculus-rift-vr.

Miller, Kiri. 2012. *Playing Along: Digital Games, YouTube, and Virtual Performance*. New York: Oxford University Press.

Nero, Dom. 2019. "*Untitled Goose Game* Is the Most Joyful Video Game of the Year." Esquire, October 10, 2019. Accessed June 2, 2021. https://www.esquire.com/lifestyle/a29416107/untitled-goose-game-video-game-review/.

Nunneley, Stephany. 2016. "*Adr1ft* and 'Clair de Lune' Make the Perfect Pair in This New Trailer." *VG247*, February 20, 2016. https://www.vg247.com/adr1ft-and-clair-de-lune-make-the-perfect-pair-in-this-new-trailer

Orland, Kyle. 2016. "*Adr1ft Review*: It's Lonely Out in Space." *Arstechnica*, March 28, 2016. Accessed June 2, 2021. http://arstechnica.com/gaming/2016/03/adr1ft-review-its-lonely-out-in-space-embargo-10am-monday-328/.

Rivière, Jacques. 1913. "Le Sacre du Printemps." *La Nouvelle Revue Française* (November): 706–730.

Roberts, Paul. 1996. *Images: The Piano Music of Claude Debussy*. Portland, OR: Amadeus.

Stapleton, Dan. "*Adr1ft* Review." *IGN*, November 24, 2018. Accessed June 2, 2021. http://www.ign.com/articles/2016/03/28/adr1ft-review.

Summers, Tim. 2016. *Understanding Video Game Music*. Cambridge: Cambridge University Press.

Summers, Tim. 2018. "Opera Scenes in Video Games: Hitmen, Divas and Wagner's Werewolves." *Cambridge Opera Journal* 29, no. 3 (2018): 253–286.

Vallas, Léon. 1973. *Claude Debussy: His Life and Works*, translated by Maire O'Brien and Grace O'Brien. New York: Dover.

Wilde, Thomas. 2019. "Honk: Why *Untitled Goose Game* Has Become One of the Most Unexpected Success Stories in Gaming." *GeekWire*, October 1, 2019. Accessed June 2, 2021. https://www.geekwire.com/2019/honk-untitled-goose-game-become-one-unexpected-success-stories-gaming/.

CHAPTER 29

POP SHOVE-IT, POP MUSIC

Tunes, Tricks, and Transmediality in Tony Hawk's Pro Skater

JAMES MILLEA

Introduction: Pop Shove-It, Pop Music

Watch this, then get off your couch and go skate.

—*Tony Hawk's Pro Skater* (1999)

In September of 2020, Activision released *Tony Hawk's Pro Skater 1 + 2*. A remaster of the first two installments (1999, 2000) in what was a highly successful skateboarding video game series, there was a large and wide-ranging marketing campaign rolled out. A website was created, multiple social media accounts established, performances of some of the new songs and artists on the game soundtrack recorded live (Noisey 2020), and several trailers and clips dropped throughout the year in the buildup to and beyond the actual release of the game itself. Among these varied supporting materials was a behind-the-scenes series of interviews with the roster of real-life skateboarders who featured as playable characters in the game (Neo Gamer 2020). In talking-head-style exchanges, cut with clips from the original and the remake, the skaters spoke about their love of the games, highlighting the effect that *Tony Hawk's Pro Skater* has had on each of their lives. Interestingly, although each of the skaters spoke about the games in a similar fashion, two interviewees stood out among the roster: veteran Rodney Mullen and relative newcomer Lizzie Armanto.

Rodney Mullen, born in the late 1960s in Florida, is one of the founding fathers of skateboarding. Some have even gone as far as to call him the "Godfather of Street Skating" (TED n.d.). Among a plethora of accolades and awards, he has been credited with inventing many of the sport's fundamental tricks, including the "Ollie" and the "kick-flip" (Mullen 2021). In his monologue, Mullen talks about skateboarding and history. He argues that because the sport is a "rogue" form, it "doesn't have a long history," per se. At the very least, it did not have one when the video game first appeared. He contends that, because those involved with the franchise "did things right," the *Tony Hawk's Pro Skater* games were and continue to be "so representative of: 'this is our history'" and therefore have an "important place in skateboarding" as a sport and as a community (Neo Gamer 2020). While Mullen was a 33-year-old professional skateboarder whom many understood to be a pinnacle figure in the sport when the first game was released in 1999, Lizzie Armanto would have been just six at the time. Although the Finnish American had featured in other games in the *Tony Hawk's* series and was a highly decorated skateboarder in her own right, having won an X Games gold medal in 2013 (X Games n.d.), she joined the roster of names in the remakes from a decidedly different position to that of Mullen. She is of a new generation of skaters, a generation that grew up with this series of games as a constituent part of their skateboarding experience. In her interview, Armanto is a little more to the point. She argues, among other things, that "this game remains true to skateboarding culture" (Neo Gamer 2020).

While Armanto refers to culture and Mullen to history, they both speak to the authenticity, albeit projected or perceived, of *Tony Hawk's Pro Skater*. Mullen suggests that the games, having been diligent in their representation of the culture, have become an important part of the relatively short history of the form. Armanto, 27 years younger than Mullen and standing at a completely different point in the sport's history, sees this set of games as a faithful reflection of this community and sport. As a new flag-bearer of skater culture, Armanto's endorsement of a remaster 22 years after its original release qualifies Mullen's point. These games are a clear echo of a culture and were intended to be. Interestingly, that projection of authenticity, as attested to by Mullen and Armanto, has meant one thing for skaters and another for scholars. For those who skate it has meant both being able to try out new tricks and runs in a virtual environment and, maybe more importantly, having their sport and community monumentalized in a unique and lasting fashion. For video game scholars it has meant the creation of a fascinating relationship between audio and image. More specifically, through its projection of authenticity, and the transmediality that shapes that projection, the *Tony Hawk's Pro Skater* video game series has created a unique platform for the role of popular music in video games.

In investigating the role of sound and music in any media, researchers and practitioners often look to a form's predecessors to find a potential map for its construction and its explorations. As demonstrated in David Schroeder's *Cinema's Illusions, Opera's Allure: The Operatic Impulse in Film* (2002), scholars in particular have drawn on the staged melodrama of opera as a way to create a blueprint of the purpose and possibilities of sound and music in narrative film. Like Karen Collins (2008) points out, "Games are not Films! but . . ." (5), with their own use of traditional orchestral instruments, cutscenes, and musical motifs, studies in the soundtracks and sound design of video games have taken a similar approach. The cinematic soundtrack is at the very least the framework against which the sound and music of this newer form is most often read (see Collins 2008; Whalen 2013; Gibbons 2014; Lerner 2014; Summer 2016). And yet, such an approach does not quite fit the model of popular music in *Tony Hawk's*

Pro Skater. The short history that Mullen talks of and the skateboarding culture that Armanto references are shaped by a decidedly different media lineage. The use of popular music in these games comes from the sport's manifestation in skate tapes, music television, and music videos, where popular music has had a different role and purpose (see also chapter 42 this volume). From a cinematic perspective, popular music in video games tends to be used with a particularly delicate touch, and its presence is regularly justified through the onscreen diegesis. In *Tony Hawk's Pro Skater*, this music abounds freely across the images, at times paying little attention to any sense of narrative or game states. Punk, hip hop, ska, and rock play out noisily alongside the images of street and vert[1] skating, making the game's audio central to *Tony Hawk's Pro Skater* in a different way.

This chapter explores popular music's role in creating the experience of *Tony Hawk's Pro Skater*, focusing specifically on the first two games in the series and then the more narrative-based *Tony Hawk's Underground* (2003). It contends that, by the end of the 1990s, skateboarding had become a highly mediated activity, a transmedial sport, a culture that unfolded "across multiple media platforms, with each new text making a distinctive and valuable contribution to the whole" (Perrott, Vernallis, and Rogers 2020, 15). Skateboarding culture and history came to be defined by the world created across skate tapes, music videos, and MTV, and in this mediation, popular music became a central component to the world of the sport and community onscreen. As these musical aesthetics found their way into *Tony Hawk's Pro Skater* and the games that followed, they brought with them a distinct construction of the video game soundtrack that has altered the purpose and possibilities of popular music across the medium.

From 720° to the 900°: The History of Skateboarding Video Games

While *Tony Hawk's Pro Skater* is the watershed moment in skateboarding video games, it was not the foundation of the genre. The first skateboarding video game of note was Atari's *720°* (1986), an arcade game named after a rotational trick that Tony Hawk had pulled off for the first time in 1985 (McMahon 2020). Released the following year, the game challenges riders to perform tricks and jumps, gaining enough points to "compete in all the city's skateparks and ultimately win the world skateboarding champion title" (SurferToday 2020). Dodging "street traffic, BMX riders, street gangs, and frisbee throwers," players "collect money, buy skate gear, and cruise around in a closed environment or neighbourhood" (SurferToday 2020). When the game's timer expired, a swarm of angry bees arrive and kill the onscreen skater. So began a decade-long experimentation with the genre, with a number of attempts at skateboarding video games emerging from various different avenues. A year after *720°*, Absolute Entertainment released *Skate Boardin'* for the Atari 2600, the brainchild of Activision cofounder David Crane.

Other companies followed suit throughout the rest of the decade with Epyx's *California Games* (1987) and *California Games II* (1989) and Electronic Arts' *Skate or Die!* (1987) and follow-up *Skate or Die 2: The Search for Double Trouble* (1990). 1988 saw the release of *Town and Country Designs: Wood and Water Rage* for the Nintendo Entertainment Systems (NES), a game named after the Hawaii-based surf shop and surfboard manufacturer. Uniquely, the game features Town and Country Designs' mascots as playable characters (McMahon 2020).

While the end of the 1980s was filled with various iterations of the skateboarding video game, it was not until well after the middle of the next decade that we saw the genre settle, both in terms of gameplay and soundtracking. Especially notable is Sega's arcade title *Top Skater* (1997), which, upon release, featured a built-in skateboard controller that players manipulated to perform the necessary stunts. A slalom-style game, *Top Skater* can be best understood now as a "spiritual predecessor to the Japanese giant's coming *Crazy Taxi*" (1999) (McMahon 2020). After the title sequence, which features the playable characters warming up and cuts from the game itself, players choose their character. As players move through the course, they have two objectives: collect time and use that time to achieve the highest score possible through tricks and jumps. The most interesting aspect of *Top Skater*, however, is its soundtrack. Across the title sequence and throughout the game, players hear a collection of pre-existing songs by Pennywise, a punk band from California. Taken from the group's back catalog and accompanied by a voice-over narrating the tricks onscreen, the punk songs start with no specific correlation to the player's actions or game's states and continue until the end of gameplay.

In terms of home consoles, in the middle of the 1990s Sony developed and published *ESPN Extreme Games* (1995), with follow ups *2Xtreme* (1996) and *3Xtreme* (1999). In this series, skateboarding is just one of several extreme sports featured. EA's *Street Sk8er* (or *Street Skater*), released in 1998, was a clear blueprint for *Tony Hawk's Pro Skater*, particularly in terms of the Sony platform. In *Street Sk8er*, players are offered more choices than in other games, including different game modes, locations, characters, and skateboards. While aspects of the game are based on a slalom model, *Street Sk8er* moves closer to mediated depictions of real-life street and vert skating, with the characters spending large parts of their time sliding on metal bars, skating on quarter pipes or half pipes, and using discernibly city-like locations to perform their tricks. Like *Top Skater*, music plays a central role in *Street Sk8er*. The game opens with a montage of the characters performing various stunts, with the names of the key tricks and locations superimposed over an intermittent black screen, and all to the sounds of Toskiyuki Kakuta's original punk/trance composition (IMDb "Toshiyuki Kakuta" n.d.). We also hear Kakuta's music over the game's replays and in *Street Sk8er*'s nondescript locations—the bowl, half pipe, and big air. The game does feature a collection of popular songs—punk, or alternative music from the likes of The Pietasters, H2O, Less Than Jake, and Plastilina Mosh (IMDb "Street Sk8ter: Soundtrack" n.d.). Interestingly, this popular music appears in the game's specific city locations—Los Angeles, Tokyo, and New York. Again, like *Top Skater*, these songs start with no specific correlation to the player's actions or game's states. Narratively independent and sonically prominent because of their use of vocals and lyrics, these songs play out across the images, across the game play, in what could be conceived as an audiovisual counterpoint. This is in contrast to other games released in the same year, such as *MediEvil* (1998), *Spyro, the Dragon* (1998), *Star Wars: Rogue Squadron* (1998), and, most applicably, *1080° Snowboarding* (1998), a slalom-style snowboarding game that uses original compositions that draw on popular music aesthetics without taking specifically from the canon of popular music.

Just as in *Street Sk8er*, *Tony Hawk's Pro Skater*, or *Tony Hawk's Skateboarding* depending on where the game was released, opens with a videographic montage. As Tony Hawk completes the "Loop of Death," landing on the far side of the 360° ramp in which a skateboarder turns completely upside down, the game's titles materialize across his success. To the sounds of "Police Truck" (1980) by the Dead Kennedys, originally a B-side to the band's single "Holiday in Cambodia," players are introduced to the collection of real-life vert and street skaters who feature as playable characters in the game through cuts of various skate tapes.[2] Each skater gets a few seconds of screen time, performing various tricks across different locations that were captured with varying camera shots, angles, and lenses. Switching from the loading screen to the main menu, which is scored by Brian Bright's hip hop-esque title music (IMDb "Brian Bright" n.d.), *Tony Hawk's Pro Skater* offers players a number of options, including a choice of skateboard, trucks, and wheels. Alongside some credible sound design, with the expected sounds of the skateboard accompanied by an applauding audience in competition sections of the game, *Tony Hawk's Pro Skater* also features a collection of popular music, generally defined as a mix of alternative, ska, and punk, including artists like Goldfinger, Speedealer, Primus, and the aforementioned Dead Kennedys (IMDb "Tony Hawk's Pro Skater: Soundtrack" n.d.).

In these details, *Tony Hawk's Pro Skater* is little different from those games that came before. It is, in the simplest sense, the next step forward in the genre. It presents skateboarding in video games just like the decade or so of titles that preceded it. It has a collection of skate characters, allows for the altering of equipment, has levels that include both street and vert scenarios, and the soundtrack features either popular music that is discernibly punk, ska, hip hop, or alternative rock or original music that echoes those same musical aesthetics. And yet, because of its transmediality, *Tony Hawk's Pro Skater* is decidedly different, a difference that makes it an important node not just in skateboarding video games but also in understanding the role of popular music in video games generally.

The Influence of Media: Transmediality and Popular Music in Video Games

Transmedia, in a contemporary sense, emerged in the early 1990s in the work of Marsha Kinder, "who explored children's consumption of media, suggesting that young consumers move cheerfully between different kinds of media while simultaneously remaining engaged with a consistent storyworld throughout" (Harvey 2017, 15). Henry Jenkins later defined the term "transmedia storytelling" as a narrative that "unfolds across multiple media platforms, with each new text making a distinctive and valuable contribution to the whole" (Jenkins cited in Elleström 2019, 6). In 2006, Jenkins coined the term "convergence culture" to address the "technological paradigm shift impacting every aspect of global life" and distinguished between three "synergic tendencies that encompass media convergence": "the cross-over of old and new media, technological convergence, and economic convergence (the case of franchises)" (Kudláč 2019, 197). Rather than narratives carried across media, recent scholarship in the area has focused on Jenkins's idea of world making, or "the development of storyworlds across media texts" (Ryan and Thon cited in Fleury 2021, 167). Matthew Freeman has, for instance, defined transmedia storytelling "as a set of industry 'strategies for holding fictional storyworlds together across multiple media and for pointing audiences across those media'" (cited in Fleury 2021, 167–168). As James Fleury (2021, 167–168) notes, this definition leaves room for an "emergent approach" that can "better respond to creative developments and market trends while also encouraging closer engagement with the audience, permitting, for instance, fan contributions to media franchises." Fleury also makes an important distinction between multimedia and transmedia. The former, he argues, involves texts that "adapt shared material (e.g., a novelization or tie-in videogame that retells a film's story)" whereas the latter delivers "different material so that the totality of a franchise presents an overarching story" (168–169). There are, therefore, a number of elements understood to be central to the idea of transmedia, including "narrative continuity," "canonical world-building," and the centrality of fans reading and elaborating of storyworlds across diverse media platforms (Perrott, Vernallis, and Rogers 2020, 15). It is in this sense that Perrott, Vernallis, and Rogers's (2020, 3) use of the synonyms "cross," "traverse," or "through" in their edited collection on transmedia film directors is so obviously appropriate. So, what about the transmediality of video games?

Martin Kudláč (2019, 192–193) argues that, throughout their short history, "video games appeared in a myriad of different versions [whether] as text-based games, emulating choose-your-own-adventure books, arcade games, or video games capitalizing variously on the audio-visual potential of the medium," something which made them hard to "pin-down." Just as cinema had integrated the traditions of "theatre, art, literature and music" so too were video games able to provide a "convergent platform in which [these] previous forms [were] absorbed" (192). Kudláč points out that the hybrid nature of the media's sources, of the influences of video games, has led to a "theoretical schism dividing the academic community into two camps" (193). The first of these camps, Kudláč notes, is based on the ludic tradition which considers video games as "a rule-based formal system with a variable and quantifiable outcome, where different outcomes are assigned different values, the player exerts effort in order to influence the outcome, the player feels attached to the outcome, and the consequences of the activity are optional and negotiable" (Juul cited in Kudláč 2019, 193). The second camp draws on theories derived from "literary and cultural studies," in which "video games were regarded as texts, particularly narrative texts" (193). It is in this latter context that we find the traditional understanding of popular music in video games, itself an echo of the role of the music in narrative cinema.

Those cinematic musical influences that Kudláč mentions above can be mapped primarily from the world of opera and specifically to the impact of Richard Wagner, who, Max Steiner argued, would have been "the number one film composer" if he had lived into the 20th century (cited in Thomas 1973, 122). Early film composers, and eventually scholars, drew on operatic and Wagnerian techniques like the leitmotif, a musical theme that represents "a person, an object, an event, a personal quality, or perhaps even an emotion" (Schroeder 2002, 75); the setting of a film's title sequence as a kind of overture, "a self-contained piece of music" that helps to prepare "the audience for what will follow" (85); and the idea of Gesamtkunstwerk, in which the "forms and elements of a text should all be mutually reinforcing (Flinn 1992, 34), something which, for cinema, has meant that the sound and music of a film should be "inaudible" so as to evade "the conscious awareness of the audience" and appeal, instead, "directly to their sensory backgrounds" (Rogers 2013, 154). When the classical scoring practices of the 1930s and 1940s returned in the mainstream cinematic soundtracks of the 1970s—such as in the scores of John Williams for *The Poseidon Adventure* (1972), *The Towering Inferno* (1974), *Jaws* (1975), and *Star Wars* (1977) as these techniques suited the narrative format for the modern blockbuster (Davison 2004, 3)—so too returned this understanding of sound and music in film. Popular and previously composed music is therefore often seen in opposition to these values. This music can be "louder" and more noticeable than the compositions of John Williams, Thomas Newman, or Anne Dudley. Popular music is something that can find its way into "the conscious awareness of the audience" (Rogers 2013, 154), moving from the inaudible to the audible. Anahid Kassabian (2001, 3) outlines as much in her discussion of compiled scores, which she contends can "bring the immediate threat of history" for an audience. Carrying external associations, the use of popular or previously composed music can pull on threads from outside the film screen and then create a "fair bit of mobility within it" (3), which can disrupt, challenge, or simply alter the film's primary narrative track.

In his discussion of the role of popular music in *Bioshock* (2007), William Gibbons (2010) details various ways in which popular music has featured in video games since the early 1990s, when "CD- and later DVD-based games first allowed soundtracks to include popular tracks precisely as they would sound on a CD." As with cinema, Gibbons details the complication of this relationship: popular music lacks the flexibility needed to "rapidly switch between multiple layers or transition to different music depending on a player's actions." To change popular songs to correspond to a player's actions, as adaptive music might, is "essentially impossible" (2010). Gibbons points to games with narratological and ludological solutions, however. In the case of the latter, games use popular music as their central premise, such as in *Guitar Hero* (2005) or *Rock Band* (2007), or to "mask" what Gibbons calls the "boring" elements of a game (2010), such as in the use of Jimi Hendrix's "All Along the Watchtower" (1968) over the title menu in 2016's *Mafia III*. Popular music is either the very premise of the gameplay or outside of it completely. Even in sports games like EA's *FIFA* or *NHL* series or 2K Sports's *NBA* series, which would be most comparable in terms of their general lack of narrative and focus on gameplay to the early *Tony Hawk*'s games, popular music still only features across title sequences and menu screens. It is for this reason that scholars like Holly Tessler talk about the potential cross-promotion of popular music and video games, or the consideration of video games as the "new MTV" (2008).

In the case of the former, the narratological purposes, Gibbons points to popular music that works with the story or within the storyworld. In the most recent installments in the *Grand Theft Auto* (*GTA*) series, for instance, Kiri Miller (2012) argues that the use of popular music at particular venues or on car "radio stations not only increase the verisimilitude and immersive qualities of each game world but also encourage players to associate particular music with particular characters and places" (55). In *GTA*, popular music does not contribute to the narrative directly but to the narrative world generally. In connection with the linear narrative of games, popular music features in either cutscenes or moments of cinematic spectacle, as in the use of Gary Jules's cover of "Mad World" (2001) in *Gears of War 3* (2011), or, as in Gibbons's (2010) examination of *Bioshock*, through the "incorporating [of] specific popular songs at key moments throughout the game, while the player is controlling the action." The use of music in semistructured moments of narrative gameplay allows for the inclusion of structured popular songs that would otherwise be troublesome for the game's players, just as it would be for cinema's audience. For most video games, therefore, including popular music is a delicate balancing act that has not strayed too far from the approaches, inclinations, and creative intent of cinematic practitioners and scholars alike. And yet, the use of popular music in cinema has seen recent developments, with transmediality at the center of that change.

In Perrott, Vernallis, and Rogers's collection on transmedia filmmakers, the editors collate chapters that attempt to explore the work of directors who "seem intoxicated by the possibilities" of the media swirl that defines modern culture and art. Although "scholars like David Bordwell, Jeff Smith and Carol Vernallis began noting that directors and practitioners were producing work across multiple media" over 20 years ago, a current batch of filmmakers, which in this case includes Wes Anderson, Michael Bay, and David Lynch, among others, have found their styles resonate across "theme parks, restaurants, museum exhibitions, speakers, furniture, wallpaper and diamonds, as well as fashion, opera stagings, commercials, virtual reality and streaming television" (Perrott, Vernallis, and Rogers 2020, 1–2). At the heart of this ability to move across media with a continued authorial stamp, the editors argue, are "intensified audiovisual aesthetics," approaches to sound and music that are particular and distinctive (Perrott, Vernallis, and Rogers 2020, 3). All the directors and practitioners in this collection are, what Claudia Gorbman calls "auteurs mélomanes": "music-loving directors [who] treat music . . . as a key thematic element and a marker of authorial style [and] seek novel realisations of the soundtrack in relation to the image" (cited in Perrott, Vernallis, and Rogers 2020, 3). In contrast, the media swirl in the skateboarding video games at the center of this chapter is one that seems to balance between ludic and narrative intentions. Where the transmediality of the filmmakers in Perrott, Vernallis, and Rogers's collection is defined by an authorial stamp which manifests an idiosyncratic structuring of sound and image across multiple media, in *Tony Hawk's Pro Skater* this becomes an authentic projection of culture that reshapes the relationship between sound and image so as to echo a storyworld constructed not of fantasy characters but of mediated skaters and tricks.

Like most sports, "skating is in large part understood through media" (Sharp 2013, 162). In this next and final section, I chart that media history, highlighting how the authenticity that Armanto and Mullen mentioned in the opening has engendered a transmedial text in *Tony Hawk's Pro Skater* that has disrupted the normative structures of video game sound and music.

Reading Tunes and Tricks in *Tony Hawk's Pro Skater*

By 1999, skateboarding had become a culture expressed and shaped across multiple media. Over many births and deaths, and particularly since the start of its modern era in the 1980s, skateboarding had come to exist across print magazines, professional and do-it-yourself (DIY) skate tapes, television, and music videos. As John Sharp notes, in particular, "the importance of magazines and videos on skating's culture and practice cannot be overlooked" (2013, 161).

Skateboarding germinated in print media across two opposing magazines, *Thrasher* and *Transworld Skateboarding*.[3] First published in 1981, *Thrasher* embraced "an all-in skater lifestyle," defined by the "skater as punk-tinged outsider," while *Transworld Skateboarding*, first published two years later, "placed emphasis on skating as a more reputable, sophisticated sport" (161). Sharp contends that, between the two, "everything a young skater needed to know about the latest tricks and the skater way of life were laid out in print," including the culture's slang, music, and sense of humor. When a new trick was developed, "it would receive a spread in one (or both) of the magazines that provided some insight into how the trick could be reproduced" (161). Photographer and filmmaker Spike Jonze highlights the bridge between print and audiovisual media in skateboarding culture. In 1991, he and others developed *Dirt*, a general interest magazine for teen boys. Having been employed at other small BMX and skateboarding magazines, the team focused on skateboarding "as a cultural marker" (Yochim 2010, 60). At the same time, Jonze was directing skateboarding videos, a platform that was "even more important to spreading the sport and culture of skateboarding" because it "codified skater culture—the fashion, the slang, the music, and the attitude" (Sharp 2013, 161). Jonze's *Video Days*, also released in 1991 for *Blind Skateboarding*, is of note here. With the sport at a crossroads, "with fresh styles, new companies and young pros pushing past the old brands and tired heroes," Jonze captured "the unique talents of a seminal group of skaters at a critical time in the history of modern skateboarding" (Transworld 2018). Like the video games already mentioned, *Video Days* featured a raft of popular music, including War's "Low Rider" (1975), Black Flag's "My War" (1984), and Dinosaur Jr's "Just Like Heaven" (1987) (IMDb "Video Days" n.d.). Like Jonze, skateboarding's transition to video toward the end of the 20th century was long lasting.

Founded by Stacy Peralta and George Powell in the late 1970s, Powell-Peralta, a board and wheel manufacturer, began producing videos of their sponsored pro-skaters. Eventually, the company found out that the videos were themselves a huge hit among the skating community and so they began to make these videos for sale. By the late 1980s, Sharp argues, "all the skate equipment companies were producing videos, making them the primary vehicle for spreading the minutia of the ever-growing repertoire of tricks" (2013, 161). These videos were not "how-to videos, 'greatest hit' compilations, or taped coverage of skateboarding contests," they were, rather, "videos produced by niche skateboarding companies to highlight the skills and lifestyles of skateboarders" (Yochim 2010, 140). Although that meant that there were often idiosyncratic elements in each, there were also those characteristics that stayed the same throughout, such as skaters skating "through numerous public and private spaces throughout the 'developed' world: parking lots, city parks, loading docks, city sidewalks, and skate parks" (140). Similarities existed also in the aesthetics of the videos, how they were shot and what they sounded like. Emily Yochim notes that skate videos use a "variety of lenses and film formats, multiple camera angles, and jump-cut and continuous editing," creating montages that "operate to define each skateboarder's—and company's—sense of 'style,'" which loosely refers to his or her identity and attitude toward skateboarding or the world at large (140). There was also a concurrent relationship in these videos between skateboarding and certain musical genres, particularly punk and metal, that were signified not only by the choice of music but also in the skater's choice of clothes, which included "bandanas, black clothes and band t-shirts" (Willing, Green, and Pavlidis 2020, 838). Music dictated the length of individual tapes or portion of tapes too, with 30- to 60-minute videos often being spliced into individual skater montages that lasted the length of one or two pieces of popular music (Yochim 2010, 168). The skater's tricks, abilities, strengths, and personality were expected to shine within this one- or two-song window.

Although skate tapes were produced by various arms of the skateboarding industry and were often promotional materials for specific products, they were widely regarded by skateboarders as authentic. Yochim (2010, 140) argues that this is because skate videos were understood as a platform that allowed enough space for individual skateboarder's various identities within a set formula. It is this that signified "authenticity for the audience." Skateboarding videos work "to define skateboarding culture; they tell skateboarders who they are" (141). And so, while skateboarding was finding its way onto television at the same time, through animated characters skating in *Teenage Mutant Ninja Turtles* (1987) or *The Simpsons* (1989) and in live sports with ESPN's *The Extreme Games* (1995) (Yochim 2010, 58–59, 62), video held, and continues to hold, a position of authority within the community.

This position of authority meant that these professional skate tapes shaped other parts of the culture's mediation. In the immediate sense, amateur skateboarders produced their "own short versions of skate video identities" that echoed these tapes. Their "sponsor-me tapes" developed in "dialogue with skate videos" and operated "to define individual skateboarders and claim individual skaters' identity and place within the larger skateboarding culture and community" (Yochim 2010, 140–141). Skate tapes shaped the culture's migration to music videos, too. The American punk/hip hop group Beastie Boys are a particularly salient example. In the music video for the group's first single, "Hold It Now, Hit It" from their album *Licensed to Ill* (1986), we see the trio, Adam "MCA" Yauch, Michael "Mike D" Diamond, and Adam "Ad-Rock" Horovitz, arrive in shot on two bicycles and a skateboard which stay in shot throughout the rest of the video. Images and clips of skateboarding feature prominently in the music videos for later releases too, including "Looking Down the Barrel of a Gun" (1989), "Time for Livin'" (1992), and "Pass the Mic" (1992). At times, these music videos are somewhat indistinguishable from the skate tapes mentioned above, not just because of the use of skaters in vert and street skating scenarios but also because of the visual structuring of the work. Like the skate tapes that Yochim details, these music videos used a "variety of lenses and film formats, multiple camera angles, and jump-cut and continuous editing," creating montages that placed the band and the video's peripheral characters in "parking lots, city parks, loading docks, city sidewalks, and skate parks" (Yochim 2010, 140). Released as a double-single with "Hey Ladies" from their second studio album, *Paul's Boutique* (1989), the music video for "Shake Your Rump" is noteworthy here also. The video is primarily of the three bandmates performing to three static cameras on a rooftop with each using fisheye or pinhole lenses, staples of those variety of film lenses and film formats that Yochim describes. And yet, there is not a skateboard, ramp, or trick throughout the video.

These same aesthetics of skateboarding video tapes found their way into the *Tony Hawk's Pro Skater* series through two specific avenues. The first is the inclusion of skate tapes and skate tape-like clips at various points throughout the games. As mentioned, *Tony Hawk's Pro Skater* opens with a video montage, highlighting to the player the various real-life skaters that feature in the game. *Tony Hawk's Pro Skater 2* (2000), released for Sony's PlayStation, follows the same formula. Opening this time to the sound of Rage Against the Machine's "Guerrilla Radio" (1999), the game shows clips of the extended list of real-life skaters. Just as skate tapes, music videos, and the first game in the series, the opening montage of *Tony Hawk's Pro Skater 2* utilizes multiple camera angles, a variety of lenses, various film formats, and jump-cuts with the camera focused on the skaters' lower halves, detailing the various tricks performed in both street and vert scenarios. After the player completes the game, winning the third and final competition, they unlock a special character, which in this case is the superhero Spider-Man, and a special skate tape. This tape, unlike the game's introduction, is of "slam scenes," which Yochim (2010, 140) defines as "images of the skateboarders failing" and something which is a composite element of a considerable portion of skate tapes. The second line of migration was through the inclusion of real-life skaters and, in particular, the game's titular figure, Tony Hawk.

On its return to the spotlight in 1986, skateboarding featured in *Sports Illustrated*, with Hawk at the center of the sport's contemporary rebirth (Yochim 2010, 56). In his spread in this major American sports magazine, Hawk positioned himself between the skateboarding's two pillars of print, *Thrasher* and *Transworld Skateboarding*, arguing that he sat "right between" the pair. The magazine's emphasis of Hawk's "punk hunk look" furthered this (57). It argued that while the skater came across as "articulate, sensitive, [and] unswayed by others" his knees were also "bloodied and scarred by cement" (57). Hawk was also the lead protagonist in skateboarding's move to television too. An extreme sports[4] competition now held twice a year, organized, recorded, and presented by ESPN, the X Games started in Providence and Newport, Rhode Island, in 1995. The winter games were added two years later (National Geographic n.d.). Primarily a vert skater, Hawk's style and abilities suited the event-like nature of television, as he performed big tricks on big ramps. In 1999, he landed "the 900," a trick so called because of the degrees of rotation that a skater spins around, essentially two and a half turns. Performing the trick during the X Games Best Trick competition in San Francisco, the 900 was skateboarding's holy grail at the time (Spratt 2020). The moment came with its own added drama. The other skaters in the competition stopped their participation, instead choosing to leave Hawk to continue to try the trick over and over. Landing the 900 on his tenth attempt, and well after his allotted time, Tony Hawk further crystallized his decade-long role in skateboarding and, more importantly, the mediation of that culture (Spratt 2020).

In landing this trick on television, Hawk became a skateboarding superstar mediated both in print and in audiovisual media. When *Tony Hawk's Pro Skater* was then released in 1999, the inclusion of skate tapes and real-life skateboarders like Hawk, although pixelated, as playable characters drew on this specific history. The use of these aesthetics, direct and indirect, echoed a sense of authenticity that connected this video game to the mediated world of skateboarding. These games became a part of the storyworld of skateboarding, reflecting and adding to the narrative of the sport, of the community, of the culture. In echoing this media visually, the sound and music of print magazines, skate tapes, and music videos have also come to shape the soundtracks of these skateboarding video games.

Tony Hawk's Underground (2003) was released for the Sony PlayStation 2, Microsoft's Xbox, and Nintendo's GameCube. Much of the game's structure is the same as its predecessors. It still opens with a video montage, littered with prominent skateboarders landing tricks to the sounds of hip hop group Jurassic 5's "A Day at the Races" (2002); it features leading skate brands and customizable board elements; it allows the player to travel the world, skating both street and vert in a number of locations; and it has skateboard-centric missions and tasks within each level. Many of those elements had also changed or, upon closer inspection, had at least developed. In particular, *Tony Hawk's Underground* now featured a narrative that had a much greater impact on the game. This is not to say that the previous games did not have some elements of story or narrative—*Tony Hawk's Pro Skater 4* (2002) has, for instance, a career mode that is not restricted by time and has goals that are instead set by characters within the gameplay—but rather that the narrative in this version was an overarching one that dictated the development of the gameplay throughout.

As the name might suggest, *Tony Hawk's Underground* centers on the idea of the player building a character in game and then going on to try to establish a skateboarding career as themselves, from a humble amateur making connections in their local New Jersey neighborhood to landing both major tricks and endorsements around the world. The story meant an increase in dialogue, nondiegetic voiceovers, and sound effects, but just as in the games that had gone before, it still featured a prominent use of popular music tracks throughout, with a far larger collection of songs than the other games in the series up to that point (IMDb "Tony Hawk's Underground" n.d.).

In the game's menus, Bright's work is now replaced with music taken from the game's longlist of popular songs. These play out as the player sets up the game. As they start, the game's narrative opens with the bedroom radio playing Jurassic 5's "A Day at the Races," echoing the opening video montage. The player's character is hurriedly ushered outside by their friend and initial game guide. The song continues to play in the background until the character gets to the first of the in-game tutorials. After this a blanket of popular music plays openly across the screen whenever the game's character is skating, with the same popular music often bleeding into the player's interaction with characters in game. This includes sections where the player steps off their board, a first in this game, to move between spaces, platforms, or ramps and continue their skating. Almost as if it is emanating from the process itself, as if the sound of feet-on-board and wheel-on-ground or the mere thought of skating produces these very sounds, in these moments in *Tony Hawk's Underground*, punk, hip hop, and alternative music play across the images, paying little attention to other aspects of game state or location. While the charge against the early *Tony Hawk*'s games could be that their lack of a central narrative means that they are freer to use popular music—acknowledging therefore its ability to disrupt—such a detraction falls short in a game like this because of the centrality of an overarching storyline. And yet, this would be to miss the point.

While ludic and narrative concerns are important in this medium generally, these games and their use of popular music are centered not in one of these camps or the other but in the skate tapes and media history of the sport and community. Popular music, in this game, is not a slippery slope. It is not an element of potential disruption, a chance for narrative distraction, or a sonic space only suitable for ludic endeavors. It is not popular music as we know it from the history of cinema and film music scholarship. In *Tony Hawk's Pro Skater*, punk, hip-hop, and alternative rock are the sound of skateboarding. They are the sounds of *Thrasher*, of the Beastie Boys, and of *720°*. They are even the sounds of Hawk himself whose very image, because of his pivotal role in the mediatization of the culture, brings with it a projection of authenticity, at the very least when a skateboard finds its way onscreen either in a video or a video game. The pivotal role that the music has in these games and the tangents that these songs draw on, therefore, is purposeful and pointed. It is in this vein that we must understand these sounds not as possible disturbances or intrusions but as two-way bridges, pathways between the ongoing media that construct skateboarding's storyworld. Their connections outward from this game draw the players in, and, as they make those links these players become not just viewers but participants in the realizing of the medium's experience, as those familiar with the sport would expect.

Conclusion

In establishing our understanding of any media, early practice and research depends on the forms and frameworks of those structures that have gone before it. This is true for both those that create and those that critique. In one sense, of course media and our reading of it needs to be understood through its audiovisual lineage. Opera to film, film to video games—the idea that those systems have a definable influence on new media is clear and obvious. As practitioners push boundaries, they push the boundaries of older forms. As new technology presents new opportunities, artists use skills and learned abilities from previous media to create new expressions. As scholars map and explore these changes and developments they find frameworks and terminology from previous media to support their assessments, either because practitioners have used those elements, consciously or unconsciously, or because those investigating these arts and media can see clearly the lines of connection. In another sense, there is, or has to be, a moment in which this influence of history changes. It is not that cinema or video games' mediated lineage will be no longer relevant but more that those nodes of influence become part of the medium and the medium itself settles into a position of thinking for itself. Ben Winters highlights such a point in his discussion of music and narrative in cinema.

Winters (2010, 229) contends that, rather than "a troubling element that needs to be assigned to a separate level of narrative," music in the narrative space of cinema is a sign of the "fictional state of the world created on screen, [an] indicator that the universe in which the events we are watching take place is not real." To go further, Winters promotes the idea of "narrative space rather than narrative levels," where "space" projects a three-dimensional text in which the music can be considered as important to the narrative as the film's dialogue and images (236). There is a moment in which cinema becomes distinctly filmic. It is not just a novel with moving images and sounds or a recorded, and much shorter, opera. As Daniel Frampton (2006) proposes with the concept of the "filmind" (7): cinema became a "text that steers its own discourse and has its own intentions and creativities" (5). It does not "merely present objects, but reveals a way of seeing them," a filmic way of hearing and seeing things (49). This duality is inherent in video games as well. The balance between the media influences of this form is important both because they have shaped the medium and because, at some point, they have been consumed by the potentiality of the form too. This transmediality generates, as we have seen above, unique audiovisual relationships which, in this case, echo a particular community and the ways that that community has constructed itself onscreen. It is in that sense, as Lizzie Armanto argued about the *Tony Hawk's Pro Skater* re-release in the chapter's introduction, that the games remain "true to skateboarding culture."

Notes

1. Vert skating, short for vertical, refers to riding your skateboarding on a ramp that is nearly vertical (Red Bull n.d.).
2. Alongside the titular Tony Hawk, the opening montage, and game, includes Bob Burnquist, Kareem Campbell, Rune Gilfberg, Bucky Lasek, Chad Muska, Andrew Reynolds, Geoff Rowley, Elissa Steamer, and Jamie Thomas.
3. The magazine *Skate Boarder* had first been published in 1964. Although it predates both these magazines, it was rebranded in 1980 as *Action Now*, a magazine that focused on a wide variety of action sports and therefore could only have less of an impact on the rise of modern skateboarding (Yochim 2010, 55).
4. Extreme sports, also known as action or alternative sports, are sporting events or pursuits characterized by high speeds and high risks. These may include, but are not necessarily limited to, skateboarding, snowboarding, mountain biking, BMX, and roller skating (Encyclopedia Britannica n.d.).

References

Beastie Boys. 2010. "Beastie Boys—Looking Down the Barrel of a Gun." April 24, 2010. https://www.youtube.com/watch?v=yr1Qe2m8oOA.

Beastie Boys. 2009. "Beastie Boys—Hold It Now, Hit It (Official Music Video)." June 16, 2009. https://www.youtube.com/watch?v=oBoNM6reiRE.

Beastie Boys. 2009. "Beastie Boys—Pass the Mic (Official Music Video)." September 15, 2009. https://www.youtube.com/watch?v=NpsvBvwRufo.

Beastie Boys. 2010. "Beastie Boys—Shake Your Rump." April 23, 2010. https://www.youtube.com/watch?v=NpsvBvwRufo.

Beastie Boys. 2018. "Beastie Boys—Time for Livin'." December 14, 2018. https://www.youtube.com/watch?v=NpsvBvwRufo.

Collins, Karen. 2008. *Game Sound: An Introduction to the History, Theory, and Practice of Video Game Music and Sound Design*. Cambridge, MA: MIT Press.

Davison, Annette. 2004. *Hollywood Theory, Non-Hollywood Practice: Cinema Soundtracks in the 1980s and 1990s*. London: Routledge.

Elleström, Lars. 2019. *Transmedial Narration: Narratives and Stories in Different Media*. Switzerland: Springer.

Encyclopedia Britannica. 2020. "Extreme Sports." February 4, 2020. Accessed June 16, 2022. https://www.britannica.com/sports/extreme-sports.

Fleury, James. 2021. "The Road to Arkham Asylum—Batman: Dark Tomorrow and Transitional Transmedia." In *Comics and Videogames: From Hybrid Medialities to Transmedia Expansions*, edited by Andreas Rauscher, Daniel Stein, and Jan-Noël Thon, 164–185. London: Routledge.

Flinn, Caryl. 1992. *Strains of Utopia: Gender, Nostalgia and Hollywood Film Music*. Princeton: Princeton University Press.

Frampton, Daniel. 2006. *Filmosophy*. London: Wallflower Press.

Gibbons, William. 2010. "Wrap Your Troubles in Dreams: Popular Music, Narrative, and Dystopia in *Bioshock*." *International Journal of Computer Game Research* 10 (3), ISSN: 1604–7982. http://gamestudies.org/1003/articles/gibbons.

Gibbons, William. 2014. "Wandering Tonalities: Silence, Sound, and Morality in *Shadow of the Colossus*." In *Music in Video Games: Studying Play*, edited by K. J. Donnelly, William Gibbons, and Neil Lerner, 122–137. London: Routledge.

Harvey, Colin. 2017. "Video Games, Transmedia, and Cultural Memory." *Media Development* 4: 13–16.

IMDb. n.d. "Brian Bright." Accessed June 29, 2022. https://www.imdb.com/name/nm0109129/.

IMDb. n.d. "Street Sk8ter: Soundtrack." Accessed August 9, 2021. https://www.imdb.com/title/tt5659362/soundtrack.

IMDb. n.d. "Tony Hawk's Pro Skater." Accessed August 9, 2021. https://www.imdb.com/title/tt0271232/.

IMDb. n.d. "Tony Hawk's Pro Skater 1 + 2." Accessed August 9, 2021. https://www.imdb.com/title/tt12316448/.

IMDb. n.d. "Tony Hawk's Pro Skater 2." Accessed August 9, 2021. https://www.imdb.com/title/tt0271233/.

IMDb. n.d. "Tony Hawk's Pro Skater 4." Accessed August 9, 2021. https://www.imdb.com/title/tt0340403/.

IMDb. n.d. "Tony Hawk's Underground." Accessed August 9, 2021. https://www.imdb.com/title/tt0385178/soundtrack.

IMDb. n.d. "Toshiyuki Kakuta." Accessed August 9, 2021. https://www.imdb.com/name/nm1213213/.

IMDb. n.d. "Video Days." Accessed August 9, 2021. https://www.imdb.com/title/tt0375184/.

Kassabian, Anahid. 2001. *Hearing Film: Tracking Identifications in Contemporary Hollywood Film Music*. London: Routledge.

Kudláč, Martin. 2019. "Transmedia Storytelling: The Many Faces of Video Games, Fluid Narratives and Winding Seriality." In *Body and Text: Cultural Transformations in New Media Environments*, edited by David Callahan and Anthony Barker, 191–203. Switzerland: Springer.

Lerner, Neil. 2014. "Mario's Dynamic Leaps: Musical Innovations (and the Specter of Early Cinema) in *Donkey Kong* and *Super Mario Bros*." In *Music in Video Games: Studying Play*, edited by K. J. Donnelly, William Gibbons, and Neil Lerner, 1–29. London: Routledge.

McMahon, James. 2020. "Skate or Die! A Brief History of the Skateboard in Video Games." *NME*, May 26, 2020. https://www.nme.com/features/skate-or-die-a-brief-history-of-the-skateboard-in-video-games-2675770.

Miller, Kiri. 2012. *Playing Along: Digital Games, YouTube, and Virtual Performance*. London: Oxford University Press.

Mullen, Rodney. 2021. "About." Accessed August 9, 2021. https://rodneymullen.com/about.

National Geographic. n.d. "X Games." Resource Library: Encyclopedic Entry. Accessed August 9, 2021. https://www.nationalgeographic.org/encyclopedia/x-games/.

Neo Gamer—The Video Game Archive. 2020. "Behind the Scenes—*Tony Hawk's Pro Skater* 1 + 2." September 5, 2020. https://www.youtube.com/watch?v=sb-X94pX9ks.

Noisey. 2020. "NOISEY & *Tony Hawk's Pro Skater* Showcase Songs off the Game's New Soundtrack | Remastered." July 28, 2020. https://www.youtube.com/watch?v=u4pF9PLeNAc.

Perrot, Lisa, Carol Vernallis, and Holly Rogers, eds. 2019. *Transmedia Directors: Artistry, Industry, and New Audiovisual Aesthetics*. London: Bloomsbury Academic.

Red Bull. n.d. "Vert Skateboarding: What You Should Know." Accessed August 9, 2021. https://www.redbull.com/us-en/vert-skateboarding.

Rogers, Holly. 2013. *Sounding the Gallery: Video and the Rise of Art-Music*. London: Oxford University Press.

Schroeder, David. 2002. *Cinema's Illusions, Opera's Allure: The Operatic Impulse in Film*. London: Bloomsbury.

Sharp, John. 2013. "The Slow Grind: Skateboarding Videogames and the Culture and Practice of Skateboarding." In *Sports Videogames*, edited by Mia Consalvo, Konstantin Mitgutsch, and Abe Stein, 156–174. London: Routledge.

Spratt, Keiran. 2020. "Looking Back at when 'the Birdman' Completed Skateboarding's Holy Grail." *Sportsman*, July 27, 2020. https://www.thesportsman.com/articles/tony-hawk-and-the-legendary-900-landing-at-the-1999-x-games.

Summers, Tim. 2016. *Understanding Video Game Music*. London: Cambridge University Press.

SurferToday. 2020. "720º: The World's First Skateboarding Game." August 21, 2020. https://www.surfertoday.com/skateboarding/720-degrees-the-worlds-first-skateboarding-game.

TED. n.d. "TED Speaker: Rodney Mullen, Skater." Accessed August 9, 2021. https://www.ted.com/speakers/rodney_mullen.

Tessler, Holly. 2008. "The New MTV? Electronic Arts and 'Playing' Music." In *From "Pac-Man" to Pop Music: Interactive Audio in Games and New Media*, edited by Karen Collins, 13–26. Aldershot: Ashgate.

Thomas, Tony. 1973. *Music for the Movies*. New York: A. S. Barnes.

Transworld Skateboarding. 2018. "Video Days: Behind the Blind Video." March 28, 2018. https://skateboarding.transworld.net/videos/video-days-behind-blind-video/.

Willing, Indigo, Ben Green, and Adele Pavlidis. 2020. "The 'Boy Scouts' and 'Bad Boys' of Skateboarding: A Thematic Analysis of The Bones Brigade." *Sports in Society: Cultures, Commerce, Media, Politics* 23 (5): 832–846.

Winters, Ben. 2010. "The Non-Diegetic Fallacy: Film, Music, and Narrative Space." *Music and Letters* 91 (2): 224–244.

Whalen, Zach. 2013. "Film Music vs. Video Game Music: The Case of Silent Hill." In *Music, Sound and Multimedia*, edited by Jamie Sexton, 68–82. Edinburgh: Edinburgh University Press.

X Games. n.d. "Lizzie Armanto." Accessed August 9, 2021. http://www.xgames.com/athletes/3029943/lizzie-armanto.

Yochim, Emily Chivers. 2010. *Skate Life: Re-Imagining White Masculinity*. Michigan: University of Michigan Press.

CHAPTER 30

PLAYING WITH AMERICAN FOLK MUSIC, SUPERNATURAL ENCOUNTERS, AND PERSPECTIVES ON DEATH

PETER SMUCKER

Introduction

My earliest memory of a significant scene in video games involving crossing a supernatural boundary from life to death was probably from *Final Fantasy VI* (1994, as *Final Fantasy III* for the SNES). In a scene necessary to further game, the player learns of a Phantom Train tasked with carrying souls to the "other side." The adventuring party boards the train and attempts to stop it before they "cross over." A character's wife and child board the train (as they had been tragically poisoned) and now must depart on the Phantom Train.[1] The scene sets up two elements common to "crossing-over" myths. First, that there is a means of crossing over. Typically, this involves both a traversable pathway (e.g., a highway, a river, or the air) and some sort of vessel (e.g., a train, boat, or some other vehicle). Second, there is an implicit understanding that the journey is (or should be) a one-way journey.[2]

Around the same time that I was first traveling on the Phantom Train in *Final Fantasy VI*, I was also spending more than several quarters in the local arcade on games like *Street Fighter II* (1991) and the *Star Trek: The Next Generation* (1993) pinball machine, trying to stay alive for as long as possible. Each quarter meant something. It was valuable. Death and loss were frustrating. Yet the loss of life or the failure to achieve victory in video games and the resulting response of the player has changed over time. With the rise of emulators, save-states, free-plays, resurrections, and endless continues, the sting at the loss of your video game character may not be what it was at the height of the arcade era. Still, the changing nature of games to include features like hardcore modes, roguelites, and permadeaths, our relationships with death and failure continues to evolve.[3]

Music and sounds are parts of this evolution. In this chapter I examine the use of American folk songs in video games and explore how interpretations of these songs may enhance player experience. More specifically, I demonstrate how both pre-existing Appalachian folk songs and newly composed American country songs use religious and supernatural tropes to enhance a player's relationships with elements of the game, including social encounters and acceptance of death. The music and lyrics in the games *Kentucky Route Zero* (2013–2020, hereafter *KRZ*) and *The Flame in the Flood* (2016, hereafter *FITF*) support depictions of "crossing over" supernatural boundaries between the real and unreal, or of life and death. Interpreting song lyrics from these games can challenge the player to reconsider the idea of the "loss of a quarter," and especially what happens *after* that loss. No longer is the loss of life without meaning. Or rather, the meaning and perception of that loss changes given an alternate perspective, offering a way to breathe new life into the value of a character's "after-death."

My interest in the songs in *KRZ* and *FTIF* emerges from the potential for multiple interpretations of *text* in many folk songs. Folk *tunes* certainly appear in a variety of ways in video games and can inform cultural significance. American—specifically Appalachian—folk songs carry an abundance of musical meanings, particularly when viewed from certain cultural perspectives. The extramusical meanings of such songs might therefore affect how a player perceives and interacts with elements of the game.[4] Before looking specifically at songs from these two games, I'll first examine some of the rich historical and cultural contexts associated with American folk songs by outlining common tropes that relate to the supernatural, death, and social relationships.

Folk Music in Video Games

There are already abundant discussions on the appearances of folk tunes in video games, generating analyses of contexts and extramusical meanings. Music from *Tetris* (1989) is a common example that highlights the "Russianness" of the popular puzzle game. Dana Plank (2015, 15) points out that the folk tune "'Korobeiniki' was chosen intentionally, to play up the game's Soviet origins, even to those unfamiliar with the original folk song." Other folk tunes serve as source material with little or no direct intentional link to its origins. For example, Konami's *Sexy Parodius* (1996) is a *Gradius*-like, side-scrolling arcade shooter that features the early 20th-century Jewish children's folk dance, "Mayim Mayim." This is at odds with the game's graphics that include near-nude women, flying pigs, and heavily Japanese-inspired characters.[5] Other games draw on instrumentation and aesthetics to elicit a folk-tune-like soundscape. For example, games like *God of War* (2018) and *World of Warcraft: Wrath of the Lich King* (2008) include music inspired by Scandinavian folk styles.[6] Folk and traditional music can also inspire composers to use source materials such as scales, modes, and rhythms.

Liam Hynes-Tawa (2020) shows how composer Koji Kondo may have drawn from the children's tune "Usagi Usagi"—set in the traditional Japanese *miyakobushi* mode—for the "Lost Woods" music cue from *The Legend of Zelda: Ocarina of Time* (1998).

As recording technologies advanced, game composers and sound designers increasingly turned to live folk musicians as a source of authority. Whether as professional musicians on a certain instrument or as consultants on compositional styles, these individuals offer a sense of authenticity to the music—a way to ground the game in cultural tradition from practitioners viewed as experts who are "in the know."[7] This is particularly true in games set in the American West, such as *Red Dead Redemption* (2010); or in rural America like *Fallout 76* (2018), where country, blues, and bluegrass music serve as primary sources for the soundtracks. For the game *Where the Water Tastes Like Wine* (2018), set in early 20th-century America, composer Ryan Ike describes his process for creating the soundtrack, saying that: "If you're tasked with making a soundtrack that 'sounds like America,' bringing in musicians from all over the country seemed like a good way to get there." He goes on to say that "all the musicians I worked with totally ruled, and they added a lot of their own flavour to the stuff I was sending them—I think it all came out sounding very authentic" (Quillfeldt 2018). Similarly, for *Red Dead Redemption 2* (2018), Rockstar Games brought in "renowned old-time musician Eli Smith of the Down Hill Strugglers . . . as a traditional music consultant and arranger. Smith recruited traditional musicians with a deep knowledge of the music's historical roots to bring authentic styles of music to the game" (Leger 2019). While these examples set the stage for musical immersion in the game's environment, my concern is with the content of American folk song lyrics, and how they may inform the game or gameplay. I will first unpack some of the central concepts contained in traditional folk songs, the underlying perspectives of those who perform them, and depictions of a specific subset of an American society, namely Appalachia.

Depictions of Death and the Supernatural in Appalachia

James Crissman devotes an entire chapter to music in his monograph *Death and Dying in Central Appalachia* (1994). He points out that "Central Appalachians had songs for every mood," but a large subset of these songs deals with death, the supernatural, and social encounters (159). Table 30.1 lists common topics that emerge from Crissman's cataloging of folk tunes. More generally, these topics suggest three overarching themes in terms of relationships: (1) social relationships; (2) a relationship with one's surroundings, origins, and homes; and (3) a relationship with beliefs, which encompasses ideas concerning living, dying, and afterlife. Each of these themes translates easily into a gaming world. Relationships with others may include interactions with other players (whether local or remotely), an opposing sports team, nonplayer characters (NPCs) like

TABLE 30.1 Topics in Central Appalachian Songs, from Crissman

Social Relationship	Environmental Relationship	Relationship with Death
• Parents and Family • Social Equality • Prison • Love and Death (Murder Ballads)	• Returning to Home/Mountains • Desire to leave for something better • Prison • Disasters (Mines)	• Judgment Day • Prison • Love and Death (Murder Ballads) • Disasters (Mines) • Loss of family

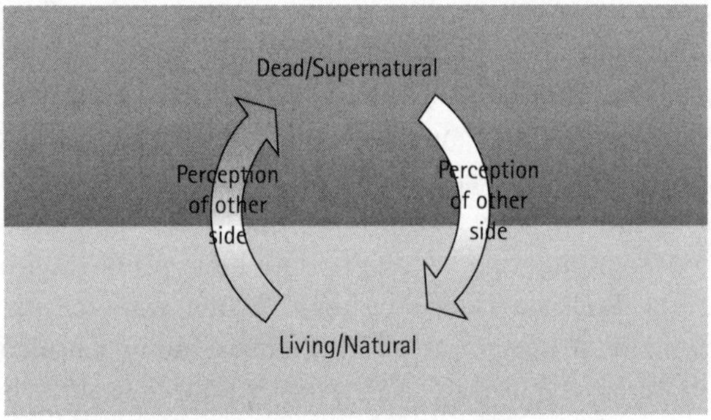

FIGURE 30.1 Perception of the "other side" over the boundary of life and death.

the owner of the shop where you buy items or a quest giver, and so on. A player must always navigate their surroundings (e.g., through an overworld map, a racetrack, or the environmental designs of a level), and players must deal with the potential "end" of a character by loss of life, failure, or completion of the game.

Crissman's focus is on how Central Appalachian society copes with and accepts death and dying. Religious and supernatural undertones of these songs often require the comparison of one's current life against what may happen when one dies. A contentious relationship between life and the "life after" generates at least two viewpoints, or perspectives. One perspective is that life is oppressive, painful, and inevitably sorrowful, and therefore death must be better—that is, an improved, eternal life awaits you. For example, Crissman (1994, 164) offers numerous examples of songs involving young children that might be better off dead: "Orphans in some songs wish for death to release them from their lives of hunger and suffering." An opposing perspective is that one should appreciate life, keep a strong faith, do good in the world, and love your home in the mountains. If not, then death may mean eternal torment.

These seemingly contrasting views create a pair of opposing perceptions of what might be better or worse "on the other side," as shown in Figure 30.1. From the perspective of life, death may be good or bad when compared to your current situation. The opposite perspective, *from death*, is that life was better or worse than your current state of being dead. This dualistic relationship establishes the need for a boundary between life and death, creating two perspectives from which you can perceive and understand the "other side." With the finality of death, however, one can never know for sure until you've crossed that barrier, and you would not be able to return once you're there. With this background on folk songs now in place, I now turn specifically to the music in *KRZ* and *FITF*.

Aural Perspectives in *Kentucky Route Zero*

I'll start with a scene from *KRZ*. After a mysterious encounter at the Márquez farmhouse, Conway must make his way back to his delivery truck. While the sounds of his footsteps and the country evening persist, a new sound fills the air, ever louder as Conway walks down the hill to his truck. The camera pulls back, away from the scene, revealing foregrounded silhouettes of a three-piece band singing the American folk tune "Lonesome Valley."

When I first played through the game, this scene from Act I, shown in Figure 30.2, immediately raised several questions. Who are these people—are they an important part of the game? Why are they singing this quasi-religious folk song about walking alone in a valley—does it have some bearing on the narrative or what I'm supposed to be doing? Why are they silhouetted—is this some sort of "breaking the fourth wall" aspect of

FIGURE 30.2 The Bedquilt Ramblers sing "Lonesome Valley." *Kentucky Route Zero*, Act I (2013).

playing this game? This audiovisual interjection seems novel, although the musicians (Emily, Ben, and Bob, collectively known as the Bedquilt Ramblers) make appearances throughout the remainder of the game.

Before unpacking the scene at the Márquez farmhouse with Conway, his dog, and the Bedquilt Ramblers, a brief overview of the game can help situate this and similar scenes into the larger whole. The point-and-click adventure game's dreamlike logic creates a world in which a linear narrative can give way to an existential and self-reflexive gameplay experience based solely on dialogue choices. Built from Appalachian and Southern Gothic themes, as well as numerous references to art and literature, the player faces questions of life and death, economic ruin, supernatural encounters, and difficult social interactions.[8] *KRZ* opens with a scene at a rural Kentucky gas station with the player controlling Conway, a seemingly lost antiques-delivery man, as he searches for an address for his final delivery. The scene above occurs just after Conway discovers the possible entrance to the mysterious Kentucky Route Zero, a road he must find and travel to reach his destination.

Musically, the game is diverse, consisting of a blend of American folk music, original music by composer Ben Babbitt, taped musical recordings of dead coal miners, a pop song in a dive-bar, and even a Theremin. Performances by the Bedquilt Ramblers stand out for their stark integration into certain moments of the game and have a specific purpose. As Babbitt (2021, 124) explains, Cardboard Computer development team co-collaborators Jake Tamas and Tamas Kemenczy "asked me to record a set of traditional folk songs that they had selected and planned to use in each episode or 'act' of the game to provide a kind of meta-commentary on the events of the story." The trio of musicians in the group, Ben, Emily, and Bob, act as a kind of Greek chorus throughout the game. These three characters are caricatures of real-life musicians Ben Babbitt, Emily Cross, and Bob Buckstaff, thus infusing their performances with an element of authority and a mediated space between the game world and the player.

Using preexisting folk music further strengthens the bond between the real world and the game's environment, which can immediately connect a game with a specific society, locality, or nationality. Lyrics can further enhance these connections as part of a "meta-commentary." In the case of *KRZ*, Babbitt even referenced recordings of bluegrass musician Bill Monroe—a Kentuckian—as he planned the music for the game (Babbitt 2021).[9] The moment of discovering something potentially supernatural in the game coincides with the first time the player encounters the Bedquilt Ramblers singing a folk song—in this case "Lonesome Valley." Table 30.2 provides the lyrics for this piece, along with the song "Long Journey Home" from Act II.[10]

In the natural world Conway seems to be inhabiting at this point, the chorus of "Lonesome Valley"—particularly walking it by oneself—can refer to his isolation as a delivery person. Eventually the player learns that the Kentucky Route Zero is an elusive, strange, and supernatural road. Conway must use his delivery truck as the vessel for crossing the boundary between the natural and supernatural, and one way to do this is through the barn at the Márquez farm. Once the player realizes this, "Lonesome

TABLE 30.2 Lyrics to "Lonesome Valley" and "Long Journey Home" from *Kentucky Route Zero*

"Lonesome Valley"	"Long Journey Home"
V.1	V.1
Hark the voice of Jesus callin'	Black smoke's a-rising and it surely is a train
Come and work for him today	Surely is a train boys, surely is a train
The fearless one, and the heart is fallin'	Black smoke's a-rising and it surely is a train
Come and work for Him today	I'm on my long journey home
Chorus:	V.2
You've got to walk that lonesome valley	Lost all my money but a two dollar bill
You've got to walk it by yourself	Two dollar bill boys, two dollar bill
There's no one here that can go there with you	Lost all my money but a two dollar bill
You've got to go there by yourself	I'm on my long journey home
V.2	V.3
My mother told me when she's dyin'	Homesick and lonesome and I'm feeling kind of blue
Just before her breath was gone	Feeling kind of blue, boys, feeling kind of blue
My darlin' boy, but trust in Jesus,	Homesick and lonesome and I'm feeling kind of blue
For I leave you here alone	I'm on my long journey home
Chorus	V.4
V.3	It's dark and a-raining and I've got to go home
Some people say John was a Baptist,	Got to go home, boys, got to go home
Others say he was a Jew	It's dark and a-raining and I've got to go home
But the Holy Bible tells	I'm on my long journey home
That he was a preacher too	
Chorus	

Valley" creates a new viewpoint, and thus an alternate interpretation. The second half of the chorus, "There's no one here that can go there with you / You've got to go there by yourself," emphasizes a *here* and *there*. For the player, the perception of what "here" and "there" means can shift between the normal/natural and the supernatural worlds. No one *in this natural world* can travel with you to that supernatural place—in this case, Kentucky Route Zero. Alternatively, it could refer to the necessity for Conway to cross over a barrier into the unknown and travel the supernatural road to search for the address for his final delivery, and he can only do this by himself. That is, the "here" might be the *supernatural* route that he must travel alone, and the "there" might be the destination at the end of this journey.

This reading of "Lonesome Valley" in *KRZ* resonates with similar interpretations of country and folk songs like the Carter Family's "Gospel Ship" (1937) and Frank Hitchison's "Hellbound Train" (1930).[11] Both pieces take crossing-over into the afterlife as their framing device, though the destinations seem to be in opposite directions. Depictions of a train or ship heading for the afterlife reinforce the necessity for a supernatural vessel tasked with carrying souls across the boundary of life.[12] The overtly Christian messages in these songs are intertwined with ambiguities regarding the singer's point of view and their perceptions on life and death, offering commentary on more than one level. In video games, Gibbons (2011) similarly points out multiple levels of commentary in *Bioshock*. Referencing the music of Django Reinhardt's instrumental music, Gibbons notes that "players familiar with the lyrics of the song are rewarded for being 'in the know,' catching subtle musical commentary that other gamers might miss."[13] While something similar is happening in *KRZ*, the game provides a way for the player to uncover more than one perspective from the lyrics during gameplay. Conway's discovery of the supernatural path enables the player to retrospectively reinterpret the lyrics of "Lonesome Valley," rather than depending on prior knowledge for a multileveled interpretation.

Now that the cat is out of the bag, so to speak, on the mysterious route and the player's evolving understanding of what may or may not be real in the game, any subsequent appropriation of a folk song is already situated for multiple interpretations. The appearance of another folk song in Act II involves only Ben from the Bedquilt Ramblers playing banjo and singing "Long Journey Home." By this point in the game, the player is accustomed to choosing a variety of dialogue choices and controlling more than one character. Visually, the scene is similar to Act 1 at the first appearance of the singing folk musicians. The silhouetted figure of Ben foregrounds a dense forest. The scene references René Magritte's painting *Le Blanc-Seing* (1965), which creates an occlusion illusion, in which something that should be visually obscured is done so by a seemingly impossible object. The space over an animal's shoulder (a horse in the Magritte painting and a giant eagle in *KRZ*) should be in the background, but instead becomes a "negative object" that occludes something in front of it, thus challenging the perception of foreground and background. As the scene progresses from left to right in *KRZ*, the player controls the young boy Ezra, who encounters Conway and Shannon Márquez (introduced in Act I). Yet Ezra continues to encounter the same individuals as he travels to the right, even though he just saw them immediately behind (to the left) in the woods. The same is true for the silhouetted foreground: Ben continues to emerge from the right side of the screen after having scrolled off the left side of the screen.

As the player watches the scene continuously pan from one side to the other, they experience a phenomenon known as a visual parallax, common to many early side-scrolling platform games. Figure 30.3 depicts how a visual parallax works in the scene. As one person physically moves from viewpoint A to viewpoint B, the object of focus seems to shift against a distant background, changing the observer's relationship between the object and its background. In the forest scene (and nearly all side-scrolling games with multiple background layers), this explains why closer objects appear to move more quickly than distant objects. Ben playing the banjo moves the fastest from right to left, while the distant trees behind the boy Ezra move more slowly. The changing *perspective* of the viewer alters the *perception* of the background and its relationship to an object.

The concept of the parallax was very much on the mind of the game designers, and that the whole idea of altered perceptions based on different perspectives is an important

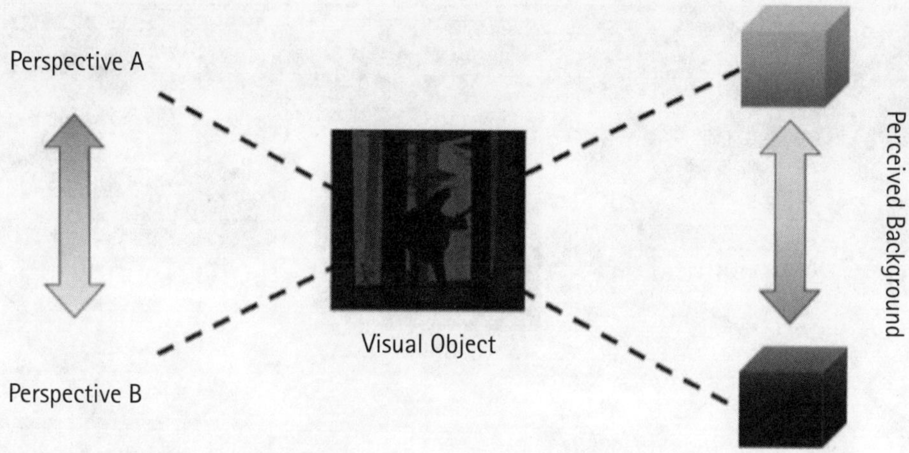

FIGURE 30.3 Visual parallax.

component of the game. Specific to the ideas of relocation and resettlement, developers Jake Elliott and Tamas Kemenczy note:

> For us, this idea of parallax—basically that something can be understood more completely when viewed from two different perspectives alternately/simultaneously—resonates with the issue you identify as "relocation." People are displaced from their homes or places of worship/culture, etc., and then the real tangible & human identity of the place becomes a sort of composite of its former role as a site of life/worship/culture/etc. & its current role as a site of oppression or as a space that tries to be anonymous but still echoes an oppressive trauma. (Filitz 2013)[14]

This concept of alternative perspectives as necessary to perceive something more fully maps onto the tropes of the life and afterlife found in many Appalachian folk songs. By trying to understand death from the perspective of life *and* understand life from the perspective of death, one can draw deeper meaning for both. A change of perspective on a musical performance can similarly alter perceptions of the folk music in *KRZ*. Rather than having a visual object against a perceived background, however, the music (in this case the lyrics) becomes the object of focus. Figure 30.4 overlays Figures 30.1 and 30.3, providing a way to perceive the "other side" through a musical or "aural object." Listeners might produce different interpretations of what the lyrics mean based on their perspectives. That is, rather than observing something from two different physical positions, whoever is listening to the music can alter the meaning of the music through two different "aural" positions.

As an example, I turn to the lyrics of "Long Journey Home" from *KRZ* (see Table 30.2). Instead of focusing on the visual objects of either Ezra, Conway, or Shannon in the forest, or Ben playing banjo in the foreground, the object under consideration is the music and lyrics. Unlike "Lonesome Valley," there is no recurring chorus, but rather the refrain

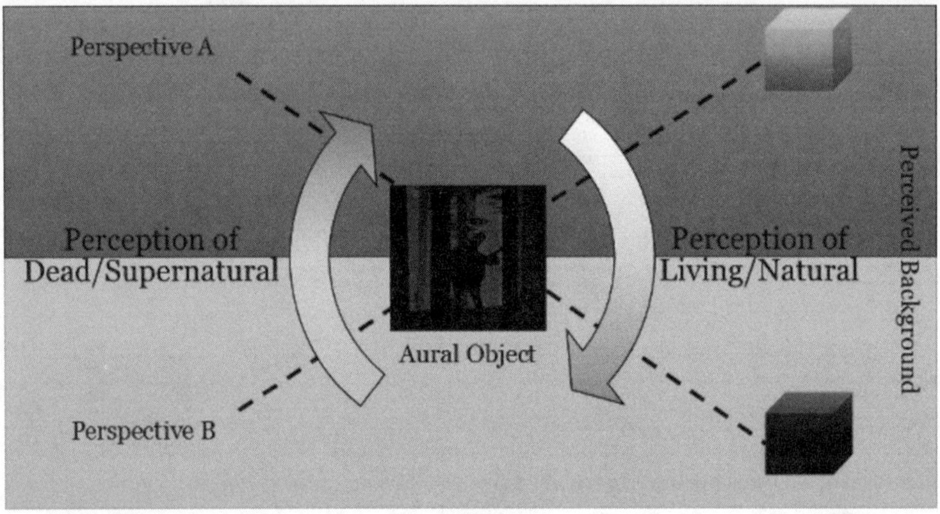

FIGURE 30.4 Perception of "other side" from aural perspectives.

"I'm on my long journey home" at the end of each verse. Once again, some common themes from Crissman emerge. There is a longing for home, there is economic hardship, and there are morose feelings of oppression. As evident in the common themes of either positive or negative associations to life and death in Appalachian folk music, the two perspectives could stand for the two sides of the natural/supernatural barrier. The player may thus interpret the journey home as traveling *from* the natural world *to* the supernatural Route Zero, Conway's ultimate destinate, *and also* interpret the journey home as traveling through the supernatural in order to return to the natural world. The perception of "home" changes dependent on one's viewpoint.[15]

The ambiguity—or perhaps multiplicity—of what is natural and supernatural increases throughout the game, particularly pertaining to uncertainties about life and death. A similar alternating interpretation of "Lonesome Valley" from Act I, and indeed all the songs in *KRZ*, allows players to reinterpret their past decisions while playing the game and what those decisions may mean for future choices. Is Conway caught up in some bizarre, magical realm? Did he actually die in that truck wreck alluded to by the gas station attendant in Act I? Is the player experiencing impressions of Conway's consciousness as he dies? Being able to reinterpret the music from multiple perspectives throughout the game can certainly enhance the enjoyment of replays of the same act or entire game. Because the dialogue choices in *KRZ* offer different ways to "play" the controllable characters, the player's interpretation of each song might influence their interaction of each choice. Another game, the roguelite survival adventure game *The Flame in the Flood* (2016), similarly allows multiple experiences and interpretations of lyrics. In the case of *FITF*, alternative perspectives on life and death may depend on one or more replays of the game.

The Flame in the Flood

Both *KRZ* and *FITF* use various elements of Southern Gothic themes, drawn primarily from literature. In tracing the progression of English to American to the regionally specific Southern Gothic, Thomas Ærvold Bjerre (2017) characterizes Southern Gothic to include "the presence of irrational, horrific, and transgressive thoughts, desires, and impulses; grotesque characters; dark humor, and an overall angst-ridden sense of alienation." From 19th- and early 20th-century authors Edgar Allan Poe, William Faulkner, and Flannery O'Connor, the Southern Gothic "brings to light the extent to which the idyllic vision of the pastoral, agrarian South rests on massive repressions of the region's historical realities: slavery, racism, and patriarchy" (Bjerre 2017). Additional themes of poverty, the grotesque and decrepit, voodoo and spirituality, and repression find their way into later literature and in films such as *Deliverance* (1972), *October Sky* (1999), *O Brother, Where Art Thou?* (2000), and *Songcatcher* (2000). Referring specifically to *KRZ*, Chris Plante's (2019) observation that "someone, or some *thing* haunts this world—some malicious, mysterious force is hidden just beneath the fabric of reality," fits precisely with the Southern Gothic. "Is it a supernatural power," continues Plante, "or is it just the past, which has left these places as empty shadows of themselves." The same can be said of *FITF*, where the player must necessarily confront some of these ideas through the game's narrative and are further highlighted in the music.

In addition to these Southern Gothic themes, *FITF* offers an example of how a game's official soundtrack can generate different perspectives on the supernatural and death. In *KRZ*, these alternating perspectives become apparent while playing through the game for the very first time. The same is likely not the case in *FITF*, however; a complete picture may become apparent only after multiple playthroughs. Singer-songwriter Chuck Ragan composed the game's official soundtrack, described by *New Noise Magazine* music reviewer Dustin (2016) as delivering "exactly what you'd expect from him—brooding Southern Gothic tales set to dark Americana tunes. The songs are the perfect accompaniment to the game, which centers upon a journey through the Deep South, following a character who wanders through the Delta and bayou, faithful dog in tow." Analysis of Ragan's songs will highlight these Southern Gothic themes, including the topics of life, death, the supernatural, and social encounters. To further highlight the interpretations of dual perspectives similar to the music of *KRZ*, the analysis of *FITF* will take the form of two cycles of playing the game. The first cycle portrays a first playthrough of the game, which explains the basic mechanics of the game and interprets two songs from the perspective of nature, survival, and interactions with individuals. The second cycle portrays replaying the game again after completion, this time with a different interpretation of the music based on perspectives from the supernatural, failure, and death.

First Playthrough: Perspective from Life

FITF consists of the player trying to survive in a seemingly postapocalyptic America. Success depends on foraging, hunting, and simply trying to survive the natural elements, all the while trying to maintain life-sustaining resources (food, water, health, rest, and temperature). Gameplay involves guiding the character, Scout, and her dog through two primary types of areas. One type of area involves guiding Scout's raft down a river (see Figure 30.5), which can be treacherous and deadly (e.g., running out of resources or crashing the raft results in serious injury or death). The other primary areas of gameplay involve docking at various points along the river in search of resources to help Scout survive, while also avoiding life-threatening obstacles (e.g., beasts, infections, diseases, etc.). Thus, the entire gameplay involves avoiding death in the wilderness by navigating dangers on both land and water.

The dog, Aesop, is with Scout throughout the game, mostly helping the player find resources and providing visual and aural cues such as barking or growling to help avoid danger.[16] Aside from Scout's faithful companion and various forms of wildlife, there are only a handful of other encounters—six different NPCs—which makes for an overall lonely gaming experience. Each encounter with these NPCs may provide helpful items for Scout as well as some limited dialogue. Due to the game's procedural generation of areas, these characters appear unpredictably, except for two key moments. Scout must necessarily encounter the characters Flimflam and Quincy Collie at the end of regions 4 and 7, respectively.[17] In the typical "campaign mode" of the game, Scout's objective is to first reach a radio tower and activate it (region 4), upon which she is instructed to proceed to another area to be evacuated (region 7). Unfortunately, the treacherous end

FIGURE 30.5 Scout travels down the river. *The Flame in the Flood* (2016).

of region 7 involves an unavoidable crash of Scout's raft. Quincy Collie eventually repairs the raft, allowing Scout to ultimately reach region 10, where she finally survives and escapes the hazards of the river.

The soundtrack for *FITF* consists of 10 original songs by Chuck Ragan. Perhaps more generally identified as alternative-country than folk, Ragan's lyrics and heavy country-rock orchestration provide the player with a soundtrack for the struggles, loneliness, and desperation associated with the game. These mirror some similar topics from Crissman's assessment of Appalachian folk songs as well as the Southern Gothic themes noted by Bjerre. Throughout the game, the music occurs incidentally when leaving or reaching a new region, or occasionally while Scout is navigating the river or foraging through the wilderness. The player hears either instrumental excerpts or Ragan singing through portions of each song, all of which may be disrupted by the player's actions.[18] Two of these songs, "Loup Garou" and "Long Water" appear in Table 30.3.

From the perspective of life—or at least trying to stay alive—Ragan's songs point toward the dangers that exist and the hardship one faces to overcome them. In the verses for "Long Water," Ragan depicts fighting through the "rocks wet with slaughter" and

TABLE 30.3 Lyrics to "Loup Garou" and "Long Water" from *The Flame in the Flood*

Chuck Ragan, "Loup Garou"	Chuck Ragan, "Long Water"
(featuring Adam Faucett)	Chorus:
V.1	Long water carry me
Scan for lights on the brand new banks	Long water humble me
Muddy cars and kitchen sinks	Till I believe in mercy
I need you like I need my health	Know that I'm free
In this world and out of myself	V.1
Pre-Chorus:	Those rocks wet with slaughter
I keep walking to see the next mile	Through the jaws I have fought her
Keep on praying for a stranger's smile	In the midst of the crushing cascades
A hand to hold and a path well-lit	Through the torrent along the levee
A door to close and a place to sit	Chorus
On this earth	V.2
Chorus:	Though the braided channel meanders
These old feet and that old dog	Through the windfall and blowed down timbers
Look to me to make food or fault	Oh I pray to reach the tail water
No one's searching so I'm not lost	Oh unscathed by the force of nature
I don't cry for the paths I've crossed	Chorus
V.2	Know
Pull up the stakes and the weeds	Know
A Loup Garou behind south does sees?	Chorus (altered)
Make some run and make some free	Long water summon me
Make no mistake be afraid of me	Long water humble me
Pre-Chorus	Till I believe
Chorus	I believe
	Unseen sea
	Mm-mm

hoping to emerge "unscathed by the force of nature." The long water of the chorus may be interpreted metaphorically for the journey through life. Traveling down the river of life humbles you and teaches you lessons. The freedom of the sea comes after you emerge from these lessons, all the wiser. I also interpret the pre-chorus lines in "Loup Garou" as the loneliness of someone displaced or oppressed, and in search for a physical place to call home: "A hand to hold and a path well-lit / A door to close and place to sit / On this Earth." There are hints of supernatural content when comparing the pre-chorus and verse two. "These old feet and that old dog / Look to me to make food or fault" refers to Aesop, a life companion in need of nourishment even in the face of failure. But the song's title, "Loup Garou" references a supernatural wolf beast that would be common in Cajun legends and Southern Gothic mythology.[19] Likely referencing the elusive white wolf or elder wolf that Scout may encounter during the game, it also signifies unknown dangers in life, or even punishment on children who misbehave. Even with these metaphors, Ragan's songs can be read as a struggle for survival, fighting against the numerous dangers of life.

Replay: Perspective from Death

If the player manages to guide Scout through all the dangers of the wilderness, she finally escapes the river and reaches the freedom of an open body of water. Despite the likelihood of dying multiple times along the way, the player has "survived" and won the game. Yet the final scene of the game reveals that Scout's journey may not have been what it originally appeared. Scout's final task is to reach "The Kingdom." Upon arriving, Scout finds an apparently abandoned theme park, with plentiful food, domesticated wildlife, and lots of dogs tasked with finding people and bringing them to this location. The final scene brings Scout face-to-face with a giant Spaceship-Earth-like globe, the doors of which swing open.[20] A bright light pours out, and a voice says simply, "Tell us traveler, what's out there?"

This final location of the game challenges the player's understanding of everything that happened up to this point. Rather than trying to survive the entire game, "The Kingdom" seems to suggest that Scout perhaps isn't alive at all but has been guided toward the afterlife by Aesop. From this new perspective, the perceptions of all previous encounters take on new meanings. Furthermore, just as the songs in *KRZ* offer two different perspectives, so too can Ragan's songs. In "Loup Garou," the possibility of an actual supernatural beast supplants the metaphor for life's struggles. Aesop is no longer a dog trying to help Scout *live*, but rather a supernatural hound trying to help Scout *die* and journey safely to the afterlife.[21] Here, importantly, is where the mechanics of the game being a roguelite comes to the fore, elevating Aesop from a support character to a necessary narrative component. Edwin Evans-Thirwell (2015) suggests the dog's role in bringing back items after each of Scout's deaths is "a touching show of how companionship might offer an escape from the cycle of mortality." He goes on to suggest that the dog's role—transcendent of the life & death cycles—enables a meta-commentary on the game due to his namesake: "'Scout' is both a proper name and a generic role, while Aesop's namesake places him outside the confines of the game's fiction."

Once again shifting the listener's perspective from life to death, "Long Water" now becomes a crossing-over song in the same vein as "Gospel Ship," "Hellbound Train," and the songs in *KRZ*. Scout's raft now becomes the vessel necessary to travel down the river, which she must navigate to travel from life to death. Each verse of "Long Water" focuses on elements of nature, but instead of reading these verses as overcoming actual dangers in the wilderness, they become a reflection of experiences of a life now over—a look back on life's hardships that you overcame. In the chorus, the yearning for the long water "carrying me" and "summoning me" is a desire to leave this life of hardship. "Believing in the sea" to "Know that I'm free" stands parallel to trusting one's faith to travel to the "other" side.

Previous encounters of NPCs in the wilderness become supernatural encounters of spirits along the way, which expands the Gothic narratives from merely the downtrodden and grotesque to the supernaturally macabre. For example, an encounter with the grim Cocteau finds him digging a grave with Scout's name on it. He quips, "Don't get too attached. S'all going down river. . . . All yer cares get swept away. Best make ready."[22] Initially, this comes across as a warning to not become too attached to material possessions, because in this disastrous flooding you simply need to let go of anything that you don't need to survive. From the "other side," however, Cocteau is now one of six supernatural guides through the afterlife. From this perspective, the "cares that get swept away" aren't material possessions, but rather the cares of life that you needn't be concerned with now that you're journeying to "The Kingdom." A player's perception of the characters Flimflam and Quincy Collie, whom Scout must encounter in the campaign mode of the game, also likely shift. From the perspective of life, they cast doubt on places like the "Angel Yard" and "The Kingdom" as destinations of a better life in this natural world. "Tall tale, I'd wager. Helps folks sleep at night to think there's a better life," according to Quincy Collie, who further remarks, "Rather stay put. Lead a simple life." Yet as a supernatural encounter en route to the afterlife, what is Quincy's role? Perhaps a gatekeeper of sorts? Or as a decoy to deter the traveler from continuing? Once again, words like those from Cocteau and Quincy, or from Ragan's songs, become the pivot around which one can perceive life or death from the opposing perspectives of death and life.

The After-Death

Kentucky Route Zero and *The Flame in the Flood* capitalize on the deep cultural history of American folk music traditions by highlighting common Appalachian beliefs and Southern Gothic characteristics, both in each game's narratives and their music. Due to each game's relationship with life, death, and the supernatural, song lyrics in each game offer the player a way to consider two perspectives from which they can interpret their actions—one from the side of life, nature, and the real world, and another from death and the supernatural. New perspectives of the "other side" can therefore enrich the player's relationships with a character's mortal cycle of successes and failures. While I have limited this chapter to only looking at American folk and country music, it opens the door for reinterpreting other music and songs of any style and genre. By changing how we view the demise of a character from the perspectives of both death and life *through* music, we can reinterpret our relationship with a game's characters, finding renewed value in their life, death, and after-death.

Notes

1. The Phantom Train dungeon has a unique music cue. There is an optional dungeon later in the game where the player can return to a different version of the Phantom Train, but the music cue is conspicuously absent. I am grateful to Ryan Thompson for his correspondence on the many details of the music in *Final Fantasy VI*.
2. This type of "crossing-over" trope has a long history in mythology, literature, and film, so it should be of little surprise that it has also found its way into games. For example, Charon from Greek mythology carries souls across the River Styx and has made explicit or guised appearances in games such as *Hades* (2018) and *Castlevania II: Simon's Quest* (1987). In J. R. R. Tolkien's *The Lord of the Rings*, the elves eventually board ships at the Grey Havens and travel to the Undying Lands, never to return to Middle Earth, and in the *Pirates of the Caribbean* films, the *Flying Dutchman* was a spectral ship that ferried souls lost at sea to the afterlife. The *Flying Dutchman* itself is a European maritime legend, forming the basis of Richard Wagner's opera *Der fliegende Holländer* (1843).
3. The terms "roguelite" and "roguelike" are often interchangeable, generally referring to games in which there are randomly generated levels and mechanics involving character progression. I will adopt Eric Switzer's (2021) distinction of the two, which states that "roguelites have meta-progression, and roguelikes do not." He refines this distinction, noting that "when you die in a roguelite game, you take something with you into the next run." In contrast, roguelike games mean that "you take nothing with you when you die. There is no [character] progression between each run."
4. Michiel Kamp (2021) identifies three types of hermeneutic approaches with regard to video game analysis: functional, textual, and artistic. For Kamp, "of particular importance in the case of video games is the difference between functional and artistic interpretation" (163). As games continue to include more music with lyrics, textual hermeneutic approaches, such as this current chapter, can also increase in scope. For another example of textual interpretation, see William Gibbons's (2018) discussion of Mozart's Requiem in *BioShock Infinite* (2013), in *Unlimited Replays: Video Games and Classical Music*.
5. For discussion on how the inclusion of "Mayim, Mayim" in *Sexy Parodius* and other aspects of Jewish culture in Japan stems largely from the American occupation of Japan after World War II, see Geselowitz (2017) and Fullwood (2017). For more on music in the *Parodius* series, see Gibbons (2018), especially chapter 6.
6. For more on composer Bear McCreary's use of how folk music inspired his work for *God of War*, see Winkie (2018).

7. The appropriation of folk music for video games, however, is not always met with praise, even as the composers or game companies aim for authenticity. Perhaps even with good intent or reverence for styles of folk music, game designers may be accused of cultural misappropriation. For more on the appropriation of folk music and cultural signifiers, see Austin (2018) and Yee (2021).
8. *Kentucky Route Zero* is an episodic game in five acts, released between 2013 and 2020, with intervening interludes surrounding each main act. The development company Cardboard Computer describes *KRZ* as "a magical realist adventure game about a secret highway running through the caves beneath Kentucky, and the mysterious folks who travel it" (Carboard Computer 2020).
9. Although Babbitt references Bill Monroe recordings, the origins of some songs are unclear and precede Bill Monroe by many decades.
10. According to Russel and Pinson (2008), the first known recording of "Lonesome Valley" was by David Miller in 1927, although the song likely dated back to at least the American Civil War era. "Long Journey Home," also known as "Two Dollar Bill" or "Lost All My Money" was recorded by Bill and Charlie Monroe in 1936—one of their earliest recordings. For more, see Russell and Pinson (2008.)
11. For more on the history of the Carter Family and Frank Hutchison's origins, see Russell (2010). "Hellbound Train" was originally recorded in New York in 1928 and released on Okeh Records in 1930. For more on original recording dates and releases of songs by Hutchison, the Carter Family, and other country artists, see Russell and Pinson (2008).
12. Other similarities and likely influences on country and folk music come from Black spirituals such as "Deep River" and "Michael, Row the Boat Ashore," both of which use crossing the Jordan River as a metaphor for death.
13. Gibbons (2018) later expands his ideas of multiple interpretations of music and lyrics in the *Bioschock* franchise. Andra Ivănescu (2019) also expands on Gibbons about multiple interpretations of pre-existing music in games, saying that "appropriated music works both as part of the whole aesthetic as well as a lyrical commentary on either the action of the game, its spaces, or other narrative elements (130)."
14. The original author of the German language article, Magnus Hildebrandt, also notes the connection to parallax in literature, specifically James Joyce's *Ulysses*, "which describes the same situation from the perspectives of different characters."
15. Jocelyn Neal (2007) defines ideas of belonging to a home or community, as well as the cycle of life and death in country songs as a paradigm that she calls a "Time-Shift narrative." For Neal, this device is typically "interwoven with one of the central tropes in country music, namely the celebration of the human life cycle from birth through death and, finally, spiritual redemption" (42).
16. The default name for the dog is Aesop, although the player has the option to change the name for the dog to Daisy.
17. In the "campaign mode" of the game there are 10 different regions. As Scout travels down the river, she reaches a new region after traveling anywhere from one to six miles. A typical playthrough of the campaign mode includes approximately 40 miles traveling on the river.
18. Additional elements of the sound design come directly from the soundtrack. For example, as Scout crafts items for survival, the player hears one of four different chords: A minor, F major, C major, or E major. Played in succession (when multiple items are crafted in sequence) they form the chord progression of the title song, "Flame in the Flood."

19. Loup garou, or sometimes "rougarou" is typically translated from French as "werewolf." For a brief summary of the history and folklore surrounding the loup garou, see Emily Hingle (2019).
20. Spaceship Earth is a giant globe structure at Disney's Epcot theme park. The reference to "The Kingdom," Scout walking through the entrance to what looks like a theme park, and the visualization of this globe seems to be a clear reference to Walt Disney World Resort.
21. A similar example in television is the 1962 episode of *the Twilight Zone*, called "The Hunt," in which a spirit dog, Rip, helps guide his human master Hyder to Heaven, and warns him against the pathway to Hell. Other similarities exist to the *FITF*, such as Scout's task to reach "The Angel Fields" in region 7 and Hyder's encounter with a spirit who says that only humans, and not dogs, can gain access to the Elysian Fields. This spirit turns out to be the gatekeeper to Hell, and not Heaven.
22. The NPC likely is a reference to French playwright and artist Jean Cocteau, a primary figure in the avant-garde and surrealism. Scout's name also evokes the young protagonist in Harper Lee's *To Kill a Mockingbird*, a primary example of Southern Gothic fiction.

References

Austin, Michael. 2018. "Interfacing with Other Cultures through Video Game Music." Paper presented at Ludo 2018. HMT Leipzig, Germany, April 15, 2018.

Babbitt, Ben. 2021. "Composing for Independent Games: The Music of *Kentucky Route Zero*." In *The Cambridge Companion to Video Game Music*, edited by Melanie Fritsch and Tim Summers, 120–130. Cambridge; New York: Cambridge University Press.

Bjerre, Thomas Ærvold. "Southern Gothic Literature." In *Oxford Research Encyclopedia of Literature*. Accessed January 6, 2024. https://oxfordre.com/literature/view/10.1093/acrefore/9780190201098.001.0001/acrefore-9780190201098-e-304.

Cardboard Computer. 2020. "*Kentucky Route Zero*." Accessed January 10, 2021. http://kentuckyroutezero.com/.

Crissman, James K. 1994. *Death and Dying in Central Appalachia: Changing Attitudes and Practices*. Urbana: University of Illinois Press.

Dustin. 2016. "Review of *The Flame in the Flood*, by Chuck Ragan." *New Noise*, March 4, 2016. Accessed July 10, 2021. https://newnoisemagazine.com/reviews/album-review-chuck-ragan-the-flame-in-the-flood/.

Evans-Thirlwell, Edwin. 2015. "Why Do Video Games Love Killing the Planet?" *Vice*, April 9, 2015. Accessed June 20, 2021. https://www.vice.com/en/article/zngbz3/why-do-video-games-love-killing-the-planet-222.

Filitz, Benjamin. 2013. "Kentucky Fried Zero: Act 2—English Edition." *Superlevel*, July 24, 2013. Accessed September 10, 2021. https://superlevel.rip/spiele/indie-spiele/kentucky-fried-zero-act-2-english-edition/.

Fullwood, Brandi. 2017. "A Jewish Folk Song Is Preserved in a Japanese Video Game." *World*, September 18, 2017. Accessed July 20, 2021. https://www.pri.org/stories/2017-09-18/jewish-folk-song-preserved-japanese-video-game.

Geselowitz, Gabriela. 2017. "How an Israeli Folk Song Became a Hit on Japanese Video Game Soundtracks." *Tablet*, August 8, 2017. Accessed July 20, 2021. https://www.tabletmag.com/sections/news/articles/jewcy-mayim-mayim.

Gibbons, William. 2011. "'Wrap Your Troubles in Dreams': Popular Music, Narrative, and Dystopia in *BioShock*." *Game Studies* 11, no. 3 (December 2011). Accessed June 1, 2022. http://gamestudies.org/1103/articles/gibbons.

Gibbons, William. 2018. *Unlimited Replays: Video Games and Classical Music*. New York: Oxford University Press.

Hingle, Emily. 2019. "The Rougarou Is Gonna Get You: Cajun Folklore." *Where Y'at*, October 29, 2019. Accessed October 10, 2021. https://whereyat.com/the-rougarou-is-gonna-get-you-cajun-folklore.

Hynes-Tawa, Liam. 2020. "Traditional Japanese Modes in Video Game Soundtracks." Paper presented at the North American Conference on Video Game Music. Digital Conference, 2020. Accessed July 16, 2021. https://www.youtube.com/watch?v=4UCSeuiRtUg.

Ivănescu, Andra. 2019. *Popular Music in the Nostalgia Video Game: The Way It Never Sounded*. Cham: Springer International: Imprint: Palgrave Macmillan.

Kamp, Michiel. 2021. "Autoethnography, Phenomenology and Hermeneutics." In *The Cambridge Companion to Video Game Music*, edited by Melanie Fritsch and Tim Summers, 159–175. Cambridge, United Kingdom; New York: Cambridge University Press.

Leger, Devon. 2019. "Roots Music Becomes a Major Player in Video Games." *No Depression*, July 29, 2019. Accessed June 10, 2021. https://www.nodepression.com/roots-music-becomes-a-major-player-in-video-games/.

Neal, Jocelyn. 2007. "Narrative Paradigms, Musical Signifiers, and Form as Function in Country Music." *Music Theory Spectrum* 29 (1): 41–51.

Plank, Dana. 2015. "'From Russia with Fun!': *Tetris*, 'Korobeiniki,' and the Ludic Soviet." *Soundtrack* 8:51–64.

Plante, Chris. 2019. "Why *Kentucky Route Zero* Is the Most Important Game of the Decade." *Polygon*, November 12, 2019. Accessed July 17, 2021. https://www.polygon.com/2019/11/12/20960055/kentucky-route-zero-the-most-important-game-of-the-decade.

Quillfeldt, Thomas. 2018. "*Where the Water Tastes Like Wine* Composer on Soundtracking All the USA." *Laced Records*, March 8, 2018. Accessed June 10, 2021. https://www.lacedrecords.com/blogs/news/where-the-water-tastes-like-wine-composer-on-soundtracking-all-the-usa.

Ragan, Chuck. 2016. *The Flame in the Flood*. Compact Disc. Ten Four Records.

Russell, Tony. 2010. *Country Music Originals: The Legends and the Lost*. New York: Oxford University Press.

Russell, Tony, and Bob Pinson. 2008. *Country Music Records: A Discography, 1921–1942*. Oxford: Oxford University Press.

Switzer, Eric. 2021. "Uh Oh, Everyone Is Mixing Up Roguelikes and Roguelites Again." *Gamer*, April 26, 2021. Accessed May 9, 2022. https://www.thegamer.com/roguelike-roguelite-difference-hades-darkest-dungeon/.

The Lore of the Strings. 2020. "Magic 'Spel': How Scandinavian Folk Music Plays a Role in Video Game Worldbuilding." June 29, 2020. Accessed August 2, 2021. https://loreofthestrings.squarespace.com/ludomusicology/introduction.

Winkie, Luke. 2018. "'God of War': How Viking Folk Music Inspired 'Audacious' New Game's Soundtrack." *Revolver*, April 24, 2018. Accessed August 2, 2021. https://www.revolvermag.com/culture/god-war-how-viking-folk-music-inspired-audacious-new-games-soundtrack.

Yee, Thomas. 2021. "Racialized Fantasy: Authenticity, Appropriation and Stereotype in *Super Mario Odyssey*." Paper presented at the North American Conference on Video Game Music. Digital Conference, June 13, 2021.

CHAPTER 31

TAKING A POP AT LUDONARRATOLOGY

Narrative Perspectives on Popular Music in Video Games

ANDRA IVĂNESCU

Introduction

The application of narratology to both musicology and game studies has a fraught and lengthy history, often riddled with misunderstandings. Espen Aarseth's (2019) first piece of advice for "the aspiring game-studies scholar" was to not "mention the war," referring to the so-called narratology-ludology debate in the early days of game studies. Carolyn Abbate (1991, 14) wrote in her influential work *Unsung Voices* that "critical thinking about music should consider its divergences from language and written texts, as well as differences between criticism in the two domains." Abbate argued that "too often, writing on music and literature, or on musical and literary criticism, posits simple parallels between the two arts or the two critical discourses." Nevertheless, I will not (entirely) heed the warnings of my predecessors here, as the discourses they invoke may be problematic, but are also foundational to the fields at hand—musicology and game studies—and I hope to prove that these hotly debated theories can still enrich our understanding of the use of music (particularly popular music) in video games.

Narrative, Meaning, and Historical Parallels

The "narratology-ludology debate," the commonly used title for this moment in the history of game studies, is itself indicative of a misunderstanding whereby "ludology has been erroneously contrasted with narratology (narrative theory)" (Aarseth 2013, 185). Aarseth's clarification describes the "debate" in terms of three interventions: one critical, which "concerns the viability of storytelling via games and game software"; one methodological, which "concerns the applicability of narratological terminology and concepts to game phenomena"; and a final one which "questions the hermeneutic link between mimetic and mechanical aspects in gameplay" (Aarseth 2013, 186). Parallels to musicology arise here already, as the questions of whether music has narrativity (Nattiez 1990) or whether narratological theories can be applied to music (Abbate 1991), have been asked for decades (and some for significantly longer), and discussions surrounding the narrative functions of music in film and other audiovisual media are also ongoing (e.g., Gorbman 1987; Chion 1994).

Another important parallel exists between the fields themselves, and specifically regarding critical, academic, and fundamentally ontological approaches to both video games and music. In a paper at the UK Ludomusicology Conference, John Vinzant (2020) drew a comparison between the development of ludomusicology as a field and the development of Musikwissenschaft in the 19th century, looking at specific scholars and arguing that the naming of the disciplines was part of their legitimization process in that "beyond simply creating a label for their fields, the connection to academically accepted parlance from an established discipline is evident." Vinzant focused exclusively on the musicology side of the portmanteau, but I argue that the ludology aspect is equally, if not more, telling.[1] Specifically, it emphasizes parallels between approaches in early ludology and early Musikwissenshaft.

If the narratology-ludology debate is an important discussion for early game studies, the debate concerning absolute and program music can be seen as significant to early musicology (as we know it). While the works of many German-language scholars including Friedrich Chrysander, Phillip Spitta, and Guido Adler (to name the founders of the *Vierteljahrsschrift für Musikwissenschaft*) were significant and influential, as Richard Taruskin (2009, 442) argues, "more than any other nineteenth-century academic, Hanslick was a forerunner of today's musicology." Eduard Hanslick's position in favor of absolute music, and the debate itself, is echoed in the ludology-narratology debate in two ways. First, both debates seek the best way to study their media/artforms on their own terms, not necessarily by excluding approaches from other fields (although both debates have been accused of such radicalism, of which they are not entirely innocent) but by finding that which is specific to video games and music respectively. Second, they both concern the issue of narrative. It would certainly be reductive to call program music "narrative," and as Abbate (1991, 24) argues, "nineteenth-century critics . . . seldom use the word 'narrative,' and certainly do not dwell on the meanings that might be ascribed to it." Nevertheless, both debates concern elements of narrative, including events, characters, and plot. Furthermore, approaches against narratology in both fields follow similar arguments: on the one hand, they deny the (inherent) narrativity of video games or music; on the other hand, they argue against the flattening effect of narratology as a methodological perspective. As Abbate (1991, 46) puts it, "a formalist/absolutist could analyze all music as narrative, yet still view music as void of specific expressive, cultural, or moral content" ultimately arguing that "this hints that evocation of literary structuralism is sterile, in the sense that it merely gives us descriptions of one set of structures that can be imperfectly transposed to match descriptions of another set of structures."

Finally, we arrive at the point of this historical detour, which has spanned 19th-century musicology, 1990s musicology, and early 21st-century game studies. My own approach aims to both acknowledge and, in a way, bypass the arguments against narratology, largely through specificity. I do not aim to argue here that either video games or music are narratives, but that music (especially popular music) can serve narrative functions in relation to games, irrespective of whether the games are themselves narrative-driven (for further discussion of ludomusical narrativity see chapter 4 this volume). I thus take a cue from both the interdisciplinary nature of popular music studies and the conclusions of the narratology-ludology debate in game studies, whereby Frasca (2003, 3) argued that this was more an issue of "not favoring narratology as preferred tool for understanding games as a whole" rather than "to completely discard it."

An important aspect of my approach is focus. Popular music in video games is, arguably, most concentrated in two broad genres: rhythm games and sports games (including racing games). These are precisely the genres that I will discount here, as, while they often have elements of narrative, these elements generally remain underdeveloped both inside the game and out, and the functions of popular music here are significantly more ludic than narrative. However, I hesitate to describe the games discussed in this chapter as "story-driven" (although many certainly are), because I also want to address more borderline examples, as their role is entangled with narrative. Therefore, I will outline three related approaches to popular music and narrative in video games: in relation to embedded narrative, in relation to transtextuality, and in relation to nonembedded narrative. The broader function that music plays throughout is one that Summers (2016, 59) refers to as texturing, whereby it "often obviously deploys strategically chosen musical signifiers in order to furnish the game's fictional construct." Summers refers to this as texturing because it "has the result of creating depth, implied detail and rounded context to the surface level of gameplay activity, elaborating beyond the basic frames of the gameplay mechanism" (60). It is also notable that Summers's use of the terms "signifier" and "fictional construct" imply both a semiotic approach and a discussion that is broader than narrative, although much of his work does address narrative directly.

Popular Music and Embedded Narrative

The first approach entails looking at the role popular music plays with regard to the constitutive elements of a game's embedded narrative, drawing on Chatman's (1978) approach to narratology, which synthesizes much of the formalist and structuralist approaches before him. Chatman (1978, 9) broadly divides the structural components into what he describes as "a what and a way"—story and discourse (Figure 31.1), an approach that itself draws on previous narratological work. The story itself is further

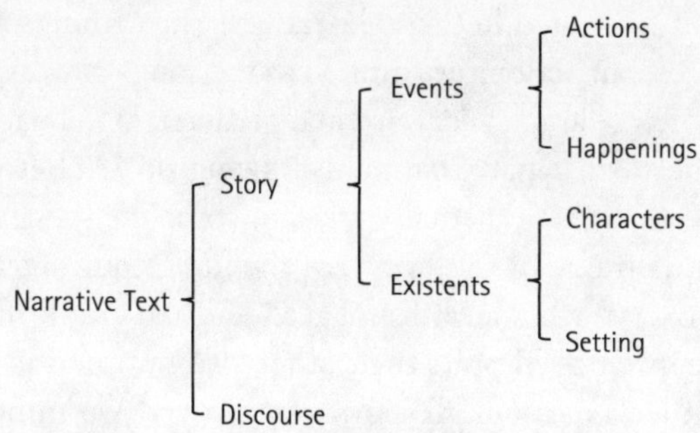

FIGURE 31.1 Chatman's narrative components (1978, 19).

divided into *events* (action and happenings) and *existents* (characters and setting) while the *discourse* refers to the transmission, "the relation of time of story to time of the recounting of story, the source or authority for the story: narrative voice, 'point of view,' and the like" (22), as well as the medium in which the narrative is presented. In applying this model to the analysis of popular music in games, I need to also note where my own approach diverges from Chatman's. First, as Ryan (2006) argues, Chatman's approach to discourse focuses disproportionately on ideas of narration that are most appropriately applied to written narratives; however, I find that these ideas may still be fruitfully applied to the medium of video games to complement the focus on story. Second, my discussion will not focus exclusively on form (as Chatman's approach attempts to do) but will also at times address the content of these games, thus countering some of the flattening effects of this structuralist approach.

Narrative is often reduced to its first set of constituents: its events. Chatman further breaks down his events category into "actions" and "happenings," defined by whether the characters are subject or object in relation to the events. In video games, there are many instances where actions that Chatman (1978, 53) would define as "kernels,"—"narrative moments that give rise to cruxes in the direction taken by events"—are accompanied by popular music.[2] Notable examples include John Marston's crossing into Mexico in *Red Dead Redemption* (2010) to the tune of José González's "Far Away," Snake's ladder climbing to Cynthia Harrell's eponymous "Snake Eater" in *Metal Gear Solid 3: Snake Eater* (2004) and Darren Korb and Ashley Barret's "Setting Sail, Coming Home" as The Kid rescues Zulf in *Bastion* (2011). As Espen Aarseth argues in his exploration of narrative theory in games, "a kernel is what makes us recognize the story; take away the kernel and the story is no longer the same." He also argues that the concept of "kernels" and the associated concept of "satellites" ("what can be replaced or removed while still keeping the story recognizable") are important to understanding "the ways games can contain one or several potential stories" (2012, 131). These particularly musical kernels are notable because they are not only memorable but also similar to one another in how they invite reflection. The three songs play at predefined moments in the games that are significant (traveling into Mexico, having defeated an important boss, and deciding to rescue an important character) and occur multiple hours into gameplay, by which time the player is likely to be invested in these narratives. The action is driven by the player during these sequences, but actions are limited as the songs play, and the player can essentially only move their character forward at a predetermined pace. This is combined with an alignment between what Chatman, drawing on Umberto Eco, describes as "discourse-time" (the time that it actually takes to complete these actions) and "story-time" (the fictional timeframe of the story), or the ludic equivalent of "play time" and "event time" (Juul 2004, 131) which, while not at all unusual for the medium, feels dilated to the player in these instances despite their otherwise common 1:1 time/event relation (133). For instance, it feels particularly slow to take over two minutes of play time to climb a ladder in a game like *Snake Eater*. These songs—all three composed especially for their respective games—thus result in a musical-narrative emphasis created in part through a quasi-suspension of the action otherwise typical of these games.

Other games, however, employ popular music to do the exact opposite, emphasizing the power fantasy typical of many action games by playing songs over action-filled sequences that nonetheless serve as narrative kernels. A perhaps heavy-handed example is *Saints Row: The Third* (2011), in particular the two kernels emphasized by the use of Kanye West's "Power" (2010) and Bonnie Tyler's "Holding Out for a Hero" (1984). Both songs are triggered during important missions in the game—one quite early on (the first main mission following the prologue), and one toward the end of the game (the first in the finale). These songs are not exactly subtle in what they communicate to the player. They are, however, notable in their directness—making the power fantasy literal—and painting the violent massacres the player commits over them in the light of power and heroism respectively, effectively removing any opportunity for reflection the player may have had in these two scenes. Of course, these may be interpreted as ironic, as much of the *Grand Theft Auto* series is (*Saints Row*'s more critically respected bigger brother, gendered language intended), but I would argue the player experience of these moments is not particularly ambiguous. In the final mission, the Bonnie Tyler power ballad also relates to the choice given to the player, whereby they can either eliminate the main antagonist or save a long-standing companion. Here, the song also seems to suggest a correct choice, its validity also confirmed through the narrative continuity with the following installment in the series, *Saints Row IV* (2013). In both cases, popular music again functions as emphasis, underlining the importance of the player's actions within the narrative.

Happenings, on the other hand, those types of events in which the protagonist acts as object rather than subject, are more likely to occur during cutscenes, emphasizing the player-character's lack of influence over the events. A memorable such moment is Dom's death at the end of Act 3 in *Gears of War 3* (2011). In the cutscene, the player watches the team become overwhelmed by enemies, as Dom—the best friend of protagonist Marcus Fenix and an important (and, in cooperative mode, playable) character throughout the franchise—sacrifices himself by driving his vehicle into a fuel tanker. Michael Andrews's instrumental cover of the 1982 Tears for Fears song "Mad World" emphasizes this tragic moment in the game, an impactful one both for the main character and for long-term players. It is also important to note that this cover is almost more famous for its use in one of the game's trailers, which was influential and parodied (the *Battlefield Bad Company* trailer titled "Bad World" is perhaps the most obvious example). It could be argued that the trailer prefigures this significant moment in the narrative, one that is meant to provide the climax for the entire series so far, as the installment provides a conclusion to the story of the first three games. At the same time, because of the sheer fame of the "Mad World" trailer as it would come to be known, the in-game narrative moment may feel more like an echo to those players for whom the ethos of the game did not fully deliver on the promises of the trailer: the player-character's lack of agency is, in this moment, foregrounded.

Moving on from events, Chatman's other major type of narrative component is that of existents: characters and setting. There are quite a few different ways in which popular music is used for characterization, but perhaps the most obvious is characters' diegetic singing. Singing characters are a staple of Supergiant Games titles, for example: Zia in *Bastion* is heard before she is seen, with the player-character following her acousmatic melody until she is discovered; Eurydice and Orpheus both sing in *Hades* (2020); and Red, the protagonist of *Transistor* (2014) is a singer, her voice an important part of the game and her character. Another particularly poignant example occurs in *The Last of Us Part II* (2020), when Joel gifts Ellie (essentially his adoptive daughter) his guitar and they both have emotional (and quasi-interactive) performances. Joel plays Pearl Jam's "Future Days" (2013) when he originally gives her the guitar (and Ellie would echo the performance throughout the game), and Ellie herself plays A-ha's "Take on Me" (1985) for her girlfriend Dina. Both performances say something about the characters themselves as well as the powerful relationships between them.

A-ha's "Take on Me" is, in fact, a popular choice of pre-existing music in games, making an appearance in 2018's *Just Cause 4* (as part of an easter egg paying tribute to the song's famous video), and more importantly in *Saints Row 2* (2008), where an achievement can be gained by listening to "Take on Me" when the player-character sings along—but there are other songs associated with each of the voice actors available, subtly (and retroactively) embedding musical preference as part of the character customization process (the player has three male voices and three female voices to choose from during the initial character design stage). Nonplayer characters (NPCs) also have musical preferences in *Saints Row 2*, as exemplified by Pierce, who sings along to Ne-Yo's "So Sick" (2006) as part of a mission. While the player-character Playa does not sing along here, they do in *Saints Row 3* when Sublime's "What I Got" (1996) plays on the car radio. This sequence is uncharacteristically warm for the series, as the two characters playfully sing together, often getting lyrics wrong and teasing each other.

This type of playfulness is transformed into actual rhythm minigames in the *Yakuza* series (2006–2021) during Karaoke sequences, in which the player's role may change depending on who is performing. At times, these even turn into elaborate (sometimes comedic, sometimes melodramatic) music videos starring the characters. *Disco Elysium* (2019) also features a karaoke scene, which requires several steps to be unlocked as well as a Drama check, which determines how the player-character sings "Smallest Church in Saint-Saëns." If the player succeeds, and sings "well," the Ancient Reptilian Brain voice (one of the parts of the player-character's brain who talk to him) takes over with a gravelly Tom Waits-ian spoken word version of the song, while if the player sings "badly," the Limbic System takes over, and their voice breaks, raw and emotional, uncontrolled, at times painfully high. The different versions express different facets of the character and comments on his masculinity, interestingly framed by the value judgment afforded the performances through the Drama check and subsequent NPC reactions.

Player characterization is, however, not exclusively the domain of embedded narrative, but can become emergent, that is, developed through play. In other words, while developer intentions are not to be underestimated, it is as important to note how players construct narratives and relationships to the characters in the games they play, often through music. This is the focus of Kiri Miller's (2012) work, where she found that most of the respondents in her empirical study associated rap with the player-character CJ in *Grant Theft Auto: San Andreas* (2004). She argued that there are embedded narrative elements that encourage this, like "cut-scene dialogue that establishes CJ's preferences" and that many players would "listen to Radio Los Santos because that's what CJ would do," (2012, 70–71) but that often they would also listen to the radio stations that better reflected their own tastes in a way that would confer their CJ these tastes. As she noted, "rather than listening with the avatar's ears, they preferred to think of the avatar as listening with theirs" (71). The characterization is thus here coconstructed through medium-specific processes of identification.

There are also ways in which popular music plays a dual function as both characterization and setting (and indeed none of the functions outlined here are mutually exclusive). This often happens as part of what Henry Jenkins (2003) describes as "environmental storytelling" in his contribution to the narratology-ludology debate. The music of *San Andreas* is an example; as Miller (2012, 71) argues, irrespective of the way in which they relate the music to the character of CJ or other characters in the game, "nearly all the survey respondents connected the radio with the gameworld's historical setting." Setting in particular has been the focus of many analyses of popular music in games, my own included. On a superficial level, popular music—particularly preexisting popular music—acts as spatial and temporal signifier; in other words, the radios of the *Grand Theft Auto* or *Mafia* games and similar devices provide information about the time and place in which the events of the game take place. The 1980s Miami-like setting of *Grand Theft Auto: Vice City* (2002), the 1960s New Orleans–like setting of *Mafia III* (2016) or the 1990s Pacific Northwest setting of *Gone Home* (2013) are expressed musically through carefully curated and genre-specific diegetic radios and cassette tapes. The role in defining setting does not only apply to the broader game world, however, but also to particular spaces and levels. For instance, particular songs will play in particular spaces in *Bioshock* (2007), similarly acting as temporal and spatial signifier, but thematically narrowing down on specific areas, events, and characters; similarly, in *Vampire: The Masquerade—Bloodlines* (2004) each nightclub in the game world has its own musical identity.

Having discussed Chatman's story elements discretely, it should be pointed out that this separation can only be useful for analytical purposes. Even here it soon becomes obvious that the various elements do not, in practice, operate separately. More than the dual function as characterization and setting already mentioned, evident examples of this occur in the opening cinematics of games. These expositional cutscenes often present opening events while also establishing setting and characters. For instance, all games in the *Borderlands* series (2009–2019) feature opening sequences with morally ambiguous rock songs that hint at the Wild West ethos of the games. From Cage the Elephant's "Ain't No Rest for the Wicked" (2008) in *Borderlands* (2009) to Jungle's "Busy Earnin' " (2014), featured in the first episode of *Tales from the Borderlands* (2014), these up-tempo tracks speak of a rush for monetary gain that does not take into account means or consequences. They feature over heavily edited cutscenes that present the games' settings, the player-characters, and also small humorous vignettes that dictate the tone of the narrative while indicating potential player action. Early cinematics can be quite vague, narratively speaking, but they can also prefigure specific narrative twists, whether they are event- or character-focused. In *Metal Gear Solid V: The Phantom Pain* (2015), for instance, Midge Ure's 1982 version of "The Man Who Sold the World" foreshadows some of the game's narrative while, through its very nature as a cover of David Bowie's more famous original (1970), it hints at issues of identity that are also explored later in the game (see Ivănescu 2020).

Overall, I have outlined how Chatman's elements of story come into play in the analysis of popular music in games, and have hinted at elements of discourse throughout, whether it is a discussion of story- and discourse-time, or medium-specific functions of popular music in relation to diegesis and gameplay. What I have yet to discuss, however, is how popular music can play narrative roles beyond the narrative of the game itself—or rather, across narratives.

Popular Music across Texts and Narratives

Popular music, particularly pre-existing music (that was not composed especially *for* a game but had some form of life before it) inevitably carries what Philip Tagg (2012, 229) describes as "paramusical fields of connotation [that] exist alongside or in connection with the music, as an intrinsic part of musical semiosis in a real cultural context, not as external appendages to the music." In other words, his semiotic approach addresses those meanings that are not purely musical (if such a Hanslickian thing even exists). Many of these meanings are constructed through relationships with other narratives. Because narratives can be considered a type of text, these relationships can be understood as part of Genette's (1992, 81–82) taxonomy of "textual transcendence" that "brings [a text] into relation (manifest or hidden) with other texts," which he broadly deems "transtextuality." The five types of transtextuality that Genette describes are intertextuality, paratextuality, metatextuality, hypertextuality, and architextuality (see Figure 31.2).

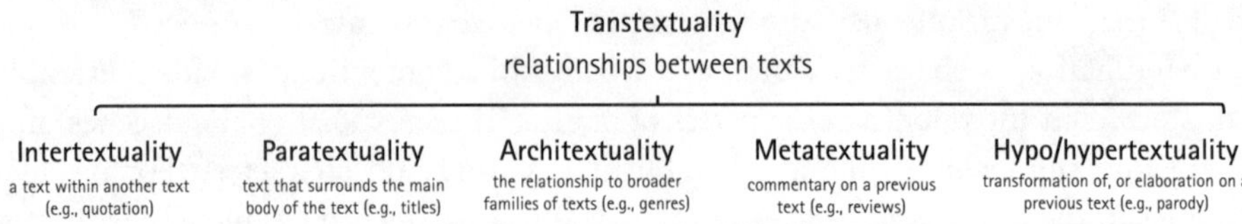

FIGURE 31.2 Summary of Genette's taxonomy.

On a basic level, most relationships between popular music and games fall under the umbrella of intertextuality, which Genette defines as "the literal presence (more or less literal, whether integral or not) of one text within another" (1992, 81). This certainly applies to the inclusion of pre-existing popular music in video games, as texts included in new texts. In this sense, popular music adds texture (to use Summers's term) through its social, cultural, and political connotations. In *Gone Home*, for instance, it builds a connection to third-wave feminism through the Riot Grrrl tapes present throughout the game. More than providing setting, the tapes included here contribute toward an intersectional fourth-wave feminist view (although still fundamentally white) and form an essential part of the narrative about a teenage girl finding herself and finding love, with the musical subculture playing a particularly important role. Music plays similar functions and explores such paramusical connotations in many (if not most) nostalgia games, like the radio stations of the *Fallout* franchise (particularly the games in the series reboot, 2008–2018) which, as Cheng (2014, 35) argues, "resound with fraught ideals" and, as I have argued, evoke the American Dream in many of its forms (Ivănescu 2019, 117).

The previous lives of popular music, however, also make it a nexus *between* narratives. As such, it can be an example of hypertextuality, which Genette (1997, 5) describes as "any relationship uniting a text B (which I shall call the hypertext) to an earlier text A (I shall, of course, call it the hypotext), upon which it is grafted in a manner that is not that of commentary." The *Grand Theft Auto* series, for instance, accomplishes this in both implicit and explicit ways. In *Vice City* (2002) the music in the cutscenes, as well as the playlists associated with the various radio stations, build an image of a particularly mediated version of 1980s Miami, but it also explicitly includes music from the 1980s television program *Miami Vice* (in this case a hypotext) such as Jan Hammer's "Crockett's Theme" or Phil Collins's "In the Air Tonight" (a performance of the song by Phil Collins himself was included in *Vice City Stories* [2006]). While the relationship to the original can be interpreted as either homage or parody, it is indisputable that *Miami Vice* is here an important influence and is also referenced directly in several extramusical ways.

The other types of transtextuality that Genette describes take us outside of the game narratives per se. Paratextuality, "the generally less explicit and more distant relationship that binds the text properly speaking," includes, in this definition, "a title, a subtitle, intertitles; prefaces; postfaces, notices, forewords" and a number of other examples (1997, 3). James Deaville (2017, 242) argues that a film trailer can also be considered paratext, "as a text that imparts significance to a film but is not integral to it." In this context, he adds that "perhaps the most effective appeal mechanism within trailer music is provided by the popular song [whereby] music supervisors count on its intertextual references to create a powerful hook for the audience" (245). Jan Švelch discusses game trailers specifically as paratext and draws a parallel between licensed music in this context and epigraphs (as described by Genette), in that they can "specify or emphasize the meaning of a text by a means of commentary" and "back the text using the authority of a quoted person" (2017, 117). In other words, licensed music not only works as texturing but also brings the musical authority of pop music's history and prior use in other media. Narratively, trailers can prefigure elements of the upcoming game's narrative, act as a bridge between previous games or media and an upcoming game, or transmedially provide new (or rather different) narrative elements. Popular music builds and, at times, subverts these bridges. For instance, "Mad World" was, as already noted, both in the trailer for *Gears of World 3* and the game itself, and the same applies to "Power" in *Saints Row: The Third.* Examples of this reuse are quite frequent, and include the *Fallout* and *Bioshock* franchises, which also provide links between iterations in the series. The *Fallout 3* (2007) trailer's use of The Inkspots' "I Don't Want to Set the World on Fire" (1941) for instance, builds a narrative connection to the opening sequences for *Fallout* (1997) and *Fallout 2* (1998), creating a sense of continuity. Links happen across media as well, as exemplified in the world premiere trailer for *Marvel's Guardians of the Galaxy* (2021) game, which uses Bonnie Tyler's "Holding Out for a Hero" (clearly a popular choice) to create a link to the use of popular music in the *Guardians of the Galaxy* films (2014, 2017). Popular music is also used in trailers for games in which it otherwise does not necessarily feature. The games in the *Assassin's Creed* series, for example, often have cinematic trailers that do not address events in the games but constitute a form of transmedia storytelling by presenting vignettes that introduce setting, characters, and major themes.

While instances of paratextuality tend to use popular music *more* than the games themselves, the opposite is true for metatextuality. Metatextuality, "the relationship most often labeled 'commentary'" (Genette 1997, 3) refers to reviews, commentaries, and analyses of texts. Popular music is rarely used in audio or audiovisual reviews, commentaries (including "Let's Plays" and streams), or video essays—primarily for copyright reasons. If anything, popular music is more likely to be taken out or recorded over when it appears in games than expressly included as part of these metatexts. However, there are videos and streams that address the popular music in these games directly, which act as a clear example of metatexts. Furthermore, extended playlists (on YouTube or Spotify, for instance) that include other popular music in the "style of" songs from the original games (e.g., similar genres) demonstrate a critical understanding of the popular music included in these games and its function in these game worlds. Similarly, there are some official albums that expand game worlds through popular music. Some of these are related to the music included in the games, such as *L.A. Noire Remixed EP* (2011) which, as the title suggests, includes remixes of songs appropriate to the era evoked in the game. Other albums, however, are only indirectly related to in-game music, such as *Batman: Arkham City—The Album* (2011), to which multiple artists contribute songs that are *thematically* related to the game but do not necessarily reflect its soundtrack. While all of these endeavors (official or not) offer some form of commentary, Genette (1997, 397) argues that the metatext is "by essence nonfictional," which would place these contributions in the category of hypertext, which "to some extent functions like a metatext."

Finally, architextual relationships bring us back to the narratives of the games themselves, but also connect to broader families of narratives, indeed "the entire set of general or transcendent categories, types of discourse, modes of enunciation, literary genres—from which emerges each singular text" (Genette 1997, 1). As Švelch (2017, 9) elaborates, "novel, tragedy, prose, poem, essay or first-person shooter are all examples of architexts." The relationship between a game and its architexts is important to players' immersion, so much so that it becomes one of the three main pillars in van Elferen's ALI model of musical immersion—that of literacy—where she argues that "player imagination is not stirred in any random fashion, but in explicit reference to an already-existing audio-visual literacy" (2016, 37), which contributes to the interpretation of tropes and conventions related to broader bodies of narratives. Popular music follows these conventions as much as other types of music, and this can be observed both in broad patterns like the hypermasculine rock anthems which often accompany FPS trailers and in individual instances, like the Bond theme aesthetic of Cynthia Harrell's "Snake Eater." An interesting example in terms of consistency is *L.A. Noire* (2011), which signals its architext paratextually through its title (noir—Noire). Here, the selection of pre-existing popular music employed, and the torch songs especially written for the game build on associations between film noir and jazz as architexts (see chapter 19 this volume). Narratively, this builds on expectations of genre, and can contribute to setting and characterization, as well as prefiguring events, but can also be seen as aspirational, aligning these games with more established traditions.

Popular Music and Nonembedded Narrative

Popular music can serve narrative functions even in less-expected areas, such as in games which align less easily with traditional concepts of narrative: games of emergence. Jesper Juul (2008, 5) describes "two basic ways in which games are structured and provide challenges for players": emergence and progression. The majority of the games described so far in this chapter are games of progression, in that "the player has to perform a predefined set of actions in order to complete the game" and this is also "where we find most games with storytelling ambitions." On the other hand, games of emergence are those whereby "a game is specified as a small number of rules that combine and yield large numbers of game variations for which the players must design strategies to handle" (2008, 5). Juul acknowledges that this is a continuum, and many of the games we discussed have elements of both. However, the two examples I identify in this section fall more clearly on the emergence side, presenting quite different ways of constructing narrative (or rather narratives) using popular music: the first is through transmedia storytelling, while the second is through emergent narrative.

As Jenkins (2006, 95–96) describes, "a transmedia story unfolds across multiple media platforms, with each new text making a distinctive and valuable contribution to the whole." He further contends that "in the ideal form of transmedia storytelling, each medium does what it does best" and that "each franchise entry needs to be self-contained so you don't need to have seen the film to enjoy the game, and vice versa. Any given product is a point of entry into the franchise as a whole." Švelch (2017, 9), however, argues that despite the relative autonomy of various transmedia entries in a franchise, they often "exist in the shadow of a main text." One such text is *League of Legends* (2010) which, as a MOBA (a multiplayer online battle arena) was initially not particularly focused on storytelling until its own "narrative turn," whereby the developers made a conscious decision to change and expand the lore of the game. As developer Tommy Gnox wrote in a well-known 2014 blog post: "At a very broad level, we've decided to push League's story beyond its original focus on explaining in-game action and forge a new narrative path for Runeterra. . . . From champion interactions to bios to events (and beyond), we aim to expand the scope of League's story and pursue a more dynamic and wide-ranging world fit for the outsized capabilities and personalities of our champions."

This perspective illustrates two aspects of this expansion: its transmedial approach, and the centrality of its characters, as evidenced in Riot Games's forays into popular music. These are, of course, also part of their elaborate marketing strategies (see Ivănescu 2021), but also elaborate in interesting ways on the game's narrative, with a particular focus on character. Some of their music videos focus on specific characters, like "Jinxed" (2013), which promotes the new champion Jinx and her personality, or "The Curse of the Sad Mummy" (2015), which tells the story of Amumu. Other videos act as trailers for significant events or upcoming games. Finally, a significant category of Riot Games music videos feature characters as virtual performers, to date grouped in at least three bands: Pentakill (Sona, one of the characters in Pentakill, also has a solo career as DJ Sona), True Damage, and K/DA. Enjoying commercial success beyond the game's fandom, the singles, albums, music videos and live augmented reality performances are an important part of the transmedia storytelling of the franchise alongside comics, short stories, and other cinematics.

While *League of Legends* brings in-game characters into the real world as pop stars, as expressed quite literally in K/DA's debut single *Pop/Stars*, my final example, *The Sims* series, brings popular music and its culture into its game world and possible narratives. I am referring to the famous (or perhaps infamous) Simlish original songs and song covers. Summers (2016, 103) describes the songs in *The Sims* as "derivative, non-memorable music, which sims uncritically consume" and argues that because the covers are in the nonsense language of the game, Simlish, "it is the genre defining musical features that are significant."[3] Like songs in a number of other games (notably the *Grand Theft Auto* and *Saints Row* series), the songs are often grouped by genres on radio stations. Summers reads both the original songs and the re-recorded songs in the later installments as parody, arguing that they paint popular music as "bland and without any individuality" acting as a "sly satiric comment on the vacuousness of the songs' lyrics." He argues that irrespective of this reading, however, the music both connects the player to the real world and simultaneously distances them, but is ultimately "part of the way that the player comes to know and understand the game world, whether through providing information about particular in-game events, describing the temporal properties of the universe, or suggesting the appropriate playing action" (103). Summers here describes three different potential narrative functions of popular music in the game: a specific relationship to elements of the narrative; a relationship to the story- and discourse-time; and a relationship to the gameplay, and, I would argue, the emergent narratives of the game.

Jenkins (2003, 128) describes emergent narratives as "not pre-structured or pre-programmed, taking shape through the game play, yet they are not as unstructured, chaotic, and frustrating as life itself." In *The Sims*, players develop their own narratives *with* and *within* the games, but as Jenkins notes, "unlike Microsoft Word, the game doesn't open on a blank screen" and "most players come away from spending time with The Sims with some degree of narrative satisfaction" (2003, 128). The popular music thus functions differently than in story-driven games, not by adding texture, but by framing affordances and encouraging specific forms of play and the subsequent constructed narratives. There are, for instance, narrative paths that are directly musical like the Fame career in *The Sims: Superstar* (2003), or the Musician career track in *The Sims: Livin' Large* (2000), *The Sims 2: Seasons* (2007), or *The Sims 3* (2009), which also has a Singer career option; all of which link music and characterization. But, beyond the explicitly musical connections, the pop music here frames the narrative experience because it "articulates the player-game world relationship, making manifest in audio the distance and difference between the actual world and the simulated world" (Summers 2016, 104). It thus acts as environmental storytelling in that it can "provide resources for emergent narratives" (Jenkins 2003, 123). Characters, events, and narrative arcs are thus influenced by the often humorous but quite complex role that popular music plays here. Whether original songs or covers of songs by a wide range of performers famously including Katy Perry, Barenaked Ladies, Lily Allen, and My Chemical Romance, the popular music of *The Sims* series shapes the emergent narratives created by the dedicated fans of the games.

The Sims and *League of Legends*, while different games in almost every respect—one is primarily single-player, one multiplayer, one a life simulator, the other a combat-focused strategy game—both employ popular music to construct forms of narrative that expand on those embedded in video games and illustrate how the boundaries of how we explore narrative, video games, and popular music, can be tested.

Conclusions

I began by exploring debates that have been important to the study of video games and to the study of music, and there are two takeaways from those debates that I return to in this conclusion. The first is that the intensity of the debates over narrative only underlines its importance. As Roland Barthes (1978, 237) noted, "there is not, there has never been anywhere, any people without narrative. . . . Like life itself, it is there, international, transhistorical, transcultural." The second is that, in as much as video games borrow and incorporate elements of previous media, and the paramusical connotations of popular music communicate immensely to listeners and players alike, the analysis of their intersection should never ignore that which is specific to the media at hand and to the specific instances at hand. As both Aarseth (2012) and Abbate (1991) warn, drawing simplistic parallels between media can be problematic; that does not, however, mean that all parallels need to be avoided. Quite the contrary—often the most complex and difficult relationships, those which are historically fraught, are the most interesting and fruitful in terms of exploration.

I am certain that many readers of this chapter will by now have their own examples in mind—a pop song that I have not yet addressed, perhaps the humorous *Brütal Legend* (2009) and its heavy metal soundtrack and narrative, the curated soundtrack of the apocalyptic *Death Stranding* (2019), the crossover-building use of Poets of the Fall in Remedy's *Alan Wake* (2010) and *Control* (2019), the J-pop of *Final Fantasy X-2* (2003), or the jazzy battle music of *Bayonetta* (2009). What becomes clear with each example is that the intersections between narrative, popular music, and video games are productive areas for research, which often make visible both the complex intertextual relationships between the media involved and the experiences that these connections can offer players. And each example will, in its own way, continue to reveal how games use popular music to offer players valuable and memorable experiences that are at once narrative, ludic, and musical.

Notes

1. And it is important to note that "ludomusicology," as Moseley argues (2013, 279–318), is explicitly connected to the term "ludology" as coined by Frasca (1999). While ludology is intended to be used as a general term to describe the study of video games, as both Aarseth (2019) and Frasca (2003) note, it was more frequently connected (albeit erroneously) with a particular disciplinary stance and has tellingly been de facto replaced with the term "game studies" today, although it does need to be said that "game studies" itself is not an entirely neutral term, and neither "ludology" nor "game studies" encapsulates (in practice) all theoretical approaches to the study of games.
2. Chatman's concept of "kernels" is roughly equivalent to Roland Barthes's (1975) "cardinal functions."
3. Simlish is a nonsense language and not a constructed language as it does not have a developed grammar and vocabulary, unlike, for example, Tolkien's Elvish, or Klingon from the *Star Trek* universe.

References

Aarseth, Espen. 2012. "A Narrative Theory of Games." In *Proceedings of the International Conference on the Foundations of Digital Games* (FDG '12), 129–133. New York: Association for Computing Machinery.

Aarseth, Espen. 2013. "Ludology." In *The Routledge Companion to Video Game Studies*, edited by Mark J. P. Wolf and Bernard Perron, 185–189. London; New York: Routledge.

Aarseth, Espen. 2019. "Game Studies: How to Play—Ten Play-Tips for the Aspiring Game-Studies Scholar." *Game Studies* 19, no. 2). http://gamestudies.org/1902/articles/howtoplay.

Abbate, Carolyn. 1991. *Unsung Voices: Opera and Musical Narrative in the Nineteenth Century*. Princeton, NJ: Princeton University Press.

Barthes, Roland. 1975. "An Introduction to the Structural Analysis of Narrative." Translated by Lionel Duisit. *New Literary History* 6, no. 2, 237–272.

Chatman, Seymour. 1978. *Story and Discourse*. Ithaca, NY; London: Cornell University Press.

Chion, Michel. 1994. *Audio-Vision: Sound on Screen*. Translated by Claudia Gorbman. New York: Columbia University Press.

Cheng, William. 2014. *Sound Play: Video Games and the Musical Imagination*. Oxford: Oxford University Press.

Deaville, James. 2017. "Trailer or Leader? The Role of Music and Sound in Cinematic Previews." In *The Routledge Companion to Screen Music and Sound*, edited by Miguel Mera, Ronald Sadoff, and Ben Winters, 240–254. New York and London: Routledge.

van Elferen, Isabella. 2016. "Analyzing Game Musical Immersion: The ALI Model." In *Ludomusicology: Approaches to Video Game Music*, edited by Michiel Kampf, Tim Summers, and Mark Sweeney, 32–52. Sheffield: Equinox.

Frasca, Gonzalo. 1999. "Ludology Meets Narratology: Similitude and Differences between (Video)Games and Narrative." *Ludology* (blog). https://ludology.typepad.com/weblog/articles/ludology.htm.

Frasca, Gonzalo. 2003. "Ludologists Love Stories Too: Notes from a Debate That Never Took Place." Proceedings of DiGRA 2003. http://www.ludology.org/articles/frasca_levelUP2003.pdf.

Genette, Gérard. 1992. *The Architext: An Introduction*. Translated by Jane E. Lewin. Berkeley: University of California Press.

Genette, Gérard. 1997. *Palimpsests: Literature in the Second Degree*. Translated by Channa Newman and Claude Doubinsky. Lincoln: University of Nebraska Press.

Gorbman, Claudia. 1987. *Unheard Melodies*. London: BFI Publishing.

Gnox, Tommy. 2014. "Dev Blog: Exploring Runeterra." *MOBAfire* (blog), September 4, 2014. https://www.mobafire.com/league-of-legends/forum/news/dev-blog-exploring-runeterra-31327.

Ivănescu, Andra. 2019. *Popular Music in the Nostalgia Video Game: The Way It Never Sounded*. London: Palgrave Macmillan.

Ivănescu, Andra. 2020. "The Auteur and the 80s Mixtape: Popular Music and Authenticity in *Metal Gear Solid V: The Phantom Pain*." In *History in Games. Contingencies of an Authentic Past*, edited by Martin Lorber and Felix Zimmerman, 157–178. Köln: Transcript.

Ivănescu, Andra. 2021. "Pop Music, Economics and Marketing." In *The Cambridge Companion to Video Game Music*, edited by Tim Summers and Melanie Fritsch, 395–408. Cambridge: Cambridge University Press.

Jenkins, Henry. 2003. "Game Design as Narrative Architecture." In *First Person: New Media as Story, Performance, and Game*, edited by Pat Harrigan and Noah Wardrip-Fruin, 118–130. Cambridge, MA: MIT Press.

Jenkins, Henry. 2006. *Convergence Culture: Where Old and New Media Collide*. New York: New York University Press.

Juul, Jesper. 2004. "Introduction to Game Time." In *First Person: New Media as Story, Performance, and Game*, edited by Noah Wardrip-Fruin and Pat Harrigan, 131–142. Cambridge, MA: MIT Press.

Juul, Jesper. 2008. *Half-Real: Video Games between Real Rules and Fictional Worlds*. Cambridge, MA: MIT Press.

Miller, Kiri. 2012. *Playing along: Digital Games, YouTube, and Virtual Performance*. Oxford: Oxford University Press.

Moseley, Roger. 2013. "Playing Games with Music (and Vice Versa): Ludomusicological Perspectives on *Guitar Hero* and *Rock Band*." In *Taking It to the Bridge: Music as Performance*, edited by Nicholas Cook and Richard Pettengill, 279–318. Ann Arbor: University of Michigan Press.

Nattiez, Jean-Jacques. 1990. *Music and Discourse: Toward a Semiology of Music*. Translated by Carolyn Abbate. Princeton, NJ: Princeton University Press.

Ryan, Marie Laure. 2006. *Avatars of Story*. Minneapolis: University of Minnesota Press.

Summer, Tim. 2016. *Understanding Video Game Music*. Cambridge: Cambridge University Press.

Švelch, Jan. 2017. "Paratexts to Non-Linear Texts: Paratextuality in Video Game Culture." PhD thesis, Praha: Univerzita Karlova.

Tagg, Philip. 2012. *Music's Meanings*. New York; Huddersfield: The Mass Media Music Scholars' Press.

Taruskin, Richard. 2009. *Music in the Nineteenth Century: The Oxford History of Western Music*. Oxford: Oxford University Press.

Vinzant, John. 2020. "Sed Non Eodem Modo: Comparing Ludomusicology to Nineteenth-Century Musikwissenschaft." Paper presented at the Ludomusicology Conference, online, May 2, 2020.

SECTION 7

MUSICAL PERFORMANCE

CHAPTER 32

VIDEO GAMES ALIVE

Ludic Liveness and (Re)Playful Listenings in Video Game Music Concerts

STEFAN GREENFIELD-CASAS

Prelude: Music and Memory

It is—quite literally—a dark and stormy night. The crowd waiting outside the theater huddles as best it can under the building's glass awning, and when security finally opens the doors a few hours before the concert is supposed to start, the concertgoers swarm into the warm foyer of the theater. Rather than immediately finding their seats, however, many—myself included—converge into an hour-long-wait line for the merchandise booth, eager to purchase the video game soundtrack and other limited merchandise related to the concert. I make casual conversation with the concertgoer in front of me—it turns out he has flown across the country to attend the sold-out event, and is flying out early the next day. After making my way through the line and purchasing the orchestral arrangement CD of *NieR: Automata*'s (2017) soundtrack, I take my seat in the concert hall, noticing concertgoers dressed in tuxedos and gowns, cosplay (costumes) of game characters, and everything in between. The lights dim, the conductor walks out on stage, and the concert begins. It has barely been a minute into the first piece on the program before someone in front of me starts to cry; I hear them apologize to their neighbor: "I'm sorry—I'll just never forget my experience of first playing *NieR*."

The preceding anecdote was the prelude to my experience attending the premiere of the 2020 *NieR: Orchestra Concert re: 12018*, a limited concert series of the award-winning soundtracks from the NieR video game series.[1] Such concerts based around video games are gaining popularity, prompting some journalists to ask "are video games the future of live music?" (Ombler 2020), while others wonder if "video games are saving the symphony orchestra" (Needleman 2015).[2] While I do not offer a definite answer to these questions in this chapter, I instead take them as a starting point in exploring how the live event of attending video game music concerts contributes to the aesthetic (re)experience of their source media.

Rather than focusing on ontological questions of the "authenticity" of the music in these concerts, this chapter instead considers video game music concerts from a phenomenological perspective rooted in fandom.[3] That is, what does the experience of attending these concerts entail for these fans? Drawing from existing theoretical work, I build a theory of ludic liveness to consider the politics and play of attending these concerts. In examining fans' relations to these performances, their emotional and material investment in the (live) music, and their personal memories of the multimedia they bring to these concerts, I ultimately argue that especially the live attendance of these concerts leads to an experience of "replaying" the games that these concerts highlight. I will merge two theoretical stances to support this argument: the first takes theories of *liveness* and examines how the event informs the audience's memories; the second considers theoretical models of *listening*, weaving together existing models of listening to revisit and add a new dimension to what Tim Summers (2021) has recently deemed "playful listening."

Ludic Liveness and the Post-Live Provocateur

Though video game music concerts have existed in Japan since the late 1980s (e.g., *Family Classic Concert*, *Final Fantasy Symphonic Suite*), their popularity has dramatically increased in recent years, with concerts now spanning the globe and running the gamut from special, limited shows (e.g., *Undertale Live*, *GAME THEORY: The Indie Game Symphony*) to touring, ongoing concert series (e.g., *Video Games Live*, *Distant Worlds*).[4] Indeed, some devoted fans go so far as to undertake transcontinental trips to attend these concerts as a way of celebrating their favorite video games and their respective soundtracks. The investment in attending these concerts has not gone unnoticed by video game companies, some of which are now adding metacommentary and lore to the games within these concerts as special incentives to attend these live concerts, fueling a convergent transmedia economy (Jenkins 2008).[5]

The *liveness* of these concerts—what I will call ludic liveness—takes a particular dimension with respect to video game music. What does it mean for this music to be performed live, taken from the virtual realm of the games that host this music? Indeed, what does it mean for this music to be performed live on "real" instruments, rather than as synthesized waveforms or samples from a virtual library?[6] Scholars including Karen Collins (2013) and William Cheng (2014), as well as Justin Gagen and Nicholas Cook (2016) have examined the stakes of the performance of (live) music in (virtual) games and the values these players, both ludic and musical, bring to the game. Outside of the ludomusic(ologic)al sphere, Philip Auslander (2008) has problematized what it means for something to be considered "live" at all in our increasingly mediatized and hyperreal world (a point I will return to when discussing different forms of video game music concerts). For Auslander, "liveness" as a category is historically and culturally situated; indeed, as he posits, the idea of "liveness" as we conceive of it today did not exist prior to recording technologies (2008, 158). Paul Sanden (2013), on the other hand, is less interested in the ontological stakes of liveness with which Auslander is preoccupied. Instead, he is more concerned with the audience's *perception* of liveness. To this end, he offers seven categories of liveness: temporal liveness, spatial liveness, liveness of fidelity, liveness of spontaneity, corporeal liveness, interactive liveness, and virtual liveness (31–43, passim). The first six of these categories in some way reflect what Sanden identifies as the "traditional (live) performance paradigm" (32), whereas virtual liveness (which he further theorizes in Sanden 2019) is instead "largely constructed by technological means and conveys a sense of performance that, although meaningful, is not grounded in actuality" (33).[7] These manifold *perceptions* of liveness play into the historical and cultural values Auslander identifies, and further nuance what liveness means in an increasingly digital world.

But just as Auslander claims that the "ideologically engrained sense of television as a live medium makes its historical relationship to the theatre different from that of film, and enabled television to colonize liveness, [as] the one aspect of theatrical presentation that film could not replicate" (13), so too do I argue that the ontological liveness of video games offers a similar conduit for ("classical") musical replication and remediation in a live setting—namely, video game music concerts.

There seems to be something at stake in the live performance of this music, something that drives fans to attend these concerts in droves. Elizabeth Hunt's contribution to this volume, for instance, examines examples of liveness in video game music concerts, though primarily frames them through the *gamification* of these concerts—see chapter 33 this volume (cf. Hunt 2022). For William Gibbons (2018, 161–165), however, at least part of this may have to do with a valorization of game music. That is, in branding this music as "classical"—or, in Michael Long's (2008) framing, we might say in moving it to the classical "register"—there is an aesthetic judgment at stake in this valuation. To put it simply, the music from "low art" video games is "raised" to the level of "high art" classical music. And while I think this framing is at least in part true—that is, that fans bring these cultural values with them—I think an added layer comes about in being able to re-experience, relive, and—in some sense—re*play* these games by way of these concerts.

Julianne Grasso (2020) has suggested a similar phenomenon. In examining "*The Legend of Zelda* 25th Anniversary Medley" (arr. Chad Seiter), she suggests that the music formally "maximizes the affects surrounding the memory of play [with] the melodic materials [acting] as a signifier for *A Link to the Past*" (84). Further still, as Grasso notes, the branding of *The Legend of Zelda* concert series, *Symphony of the Goddesses*, posits a "reliving" of players' respective gaming experiences, with Grasso suggesting that "'Relive' is a term that seems to suggest that the music will allow the listener more than recall: an access to an embodied memory that perhaps enacts something about experiences of play" (84).

And yet, the ability to relive such an experience is ultimately nothing more than a wishful fantasy. The past is the past and cannot *truly* be relived.[8] Yet this technicality does not invalidate the larger points of Grasso's reflection or the *Symphony of the Goddesses* branding. While *truly* reliving the past might be a fantasy, we can still *virtually* "relive" it through our imagination and memories. Here, however, we might opt for a different word instead: *replay*. If to relive is impossibly based in fantasy, then to (mentally) replay is based *in possibility* through our autobiographical memories. Furthermore, replay here has a double meaning, offering both the ability to replay in the mind's eye (and ear) and also having the ability to replay a game. An important element to the "reliving" and replaying of these games, I contend, is the notion of the *event*. Carolyn Abbate (2004) posits in her essay "Music—Drastic or Gnostic?" that for too long music studies has been concerned with clandestine "gnostic" ways of understanding the musical work, rather than a "drastic" understanding of the (live) event. As one example of this, she provides an anecdote of her experience attending two different live performances of Richard Wagner's *Die Meistersinger von Nürnberg*. In the first, the soloist's voice cracked on a high note, very much bringing Abbate into the moment of the live event. In the second performance, just a few days later, she experienced a "momentary optical hallucination, a genuine neurological misfire" wherein the previous performance overrode the performance taking place in front of her (535). As she further muses:

> But what triggered the neurological restaging, the necessary condition for the gnostic mentality to appear as a hallucinatory symbol, was the earlier performance, where, in someone obsessed by Heppner's [the soloist] courage, the drastic attitude had prevailed. The second performance would not have fractured had my experience of the first not been so radically attentive to what was taking place, so inattentive to Wagner's *Meistersinger* and what its music means or conceals. (536)

The marked experience she had attending a previous (live) performance of Wagner's *Meistersinger* surfaced again, and she relived—or, rather, cognitively *replayed*—this experience, informed as she was by the "drastic knowledge" that came with it.

Expanding on Abbate's notion of the drastic, Isabella van Elferen (2020) has argued that both game music as a genre and ludomusicology as a field can lead to what she calls the "New Drastic." Indeed, she cites Abbate's story directly when she claims that the "performative shape of game music, its presence, is unpredictable, which arguably makes it more immediate and more 'live' even than *Die Meistersinger* could ever be. Playing games is making music" (106–107). Van Elferen's attention to the liveness and immediacy of game music further recalls Auslander's (2008, 38) invocation of Walter Benjamin, and the auratic distance we attempt to overcome in the age of mechanical reproduction (see Benjamin 1969, 222–223). But we are now beyond the purely mechanical; instead, we reside in the hyperreal age of the virtual and mediatized (Baudrillard 1994), of which games play a fundamental role (Bown 2017; Juul 2005). But this attempt at overcoming distance to achieve a sense of immediacy remains. The distance to be traversed here is between the virtual and the real, all within a *live* context. As I have argued elsewhere, the arrangement of video game music for the concert hall inherently operates as a world-bridging device, spanning game worlds and the real world (Greenfield-Casas forth.).[9] But to add a new piece to the puzzle, I suggest that the *live performance* of this music as an *event* further links the virtual and real world. This is ludic liveness. But what are these types of liveness and different types of concerts I have hinted at?

Intermission: A Typology of Video Game Music Concerts

As outlined above, Auslander has convincingly argued that liveness should always be situated both historically and culturally. He notes that the traditional or "default definition of live performance is that it is the kind of performance in which the performers and the audience are both physically and temporally co-present to one another" (2008, 60). Auslander immediately problematizes this definition, noting the spatial rupture with live broadcasts, as well as the temporal and spatial disjuncture with that which is "recorded live." Justin Gagen and Nicholas Cook similarly discuss the absence of a singular *now* in *Second Life* due to internet lag: "the present moment is blurred, smeared over a period of several seconds" (2016, 196). And as Paul Sanden has elucidated, perhaps most important in the understanding of liveness is the *perception* of just how live a performance is and how there are various types of liveness which can temper an audience's thoughts on the matter—from the temporal and spatial, to the interactive and virtual. Contemporary understandings of liveness are thus frequently mediated through technology. Following Auslander and Sanden's lead, I add a few additional categories of liveness and proffer a typology of five different forms this liveness takes with video game music concerts (Table 32.1 also summarizes these forms of live concerts).[10] This list is *not*

TABLE 32.1 A Typology of Video Game Concerts

Concert Type	Definition	Examples
Live Concert	A (traditional) concert attended in person with the music being played live in real time	*Undertale Live*; *Journey Live*; *Symphony of the Goddesses*; *Pokémon: Symphonic Evolutions*; *Video Games Live*
Recorded Live Concert	A recording of a Live Concert that fans can purchase and view on their own time	*NieR: Orchestra Concert 12018*; *The Journey of 100: Distant Worlds, Music from Final Fantasy*
Live Recorded Concert	A concert attended in person that plays recordings of music	*FINAL FANTASY VII—A Symphonic Reunion*
Virtual Live Concert	A concert premiered virtually (e.g., over the internet) in real time with an audience watching together	*Sonic 30th Anniversary Symphony* (premiered on YouTube); *Undertale 5th Anniversary Concert* (premiered on Twitch)
Live Virtual Concert	A concert attended virtually (in-game) with the music being played live	Lang Lang's concert in *Second Life*; Travis Scott's shows in *Fortnite*; Open Pit's festivals in *Minecraft*; Lil Nas X's concert in *Roblox*

intended to be comprehensive—there are, I am sure, many examples that fall in liminal spaces between or outside these five examples.

Traditional Live Concerts

A concert that follows Auslander's "default definition" of liveness. There remains the possibility of a ritualistic ceremony here, perhaps more so than with virtual concerts. This form of liveness frequently includes a ceremonial dressing for the concert, whether in cosplay or in formalwear. It also likely includes standing in line at the merch booth to purchase memorabilia with which to remember the concert. Because of the already presumed remembering of the game with the concert, this merchandise acts as a redolent anchor point to a second-order memory: a re-remembering.

Live Recorded Concerts

The pre-E3 *FINAL FANTASY VII—A Symphonic Reunion* concert held in 2019 infamously had a split liveness to it. It was presented live—fans came in person to listen to this music, together—yet much of the concert was *not* performed by a live orchestra. Rather, MIDI recordings of the music were played for a live audience. Fans were unhappy with the concert, commenting that *when* the orchestra was performing, it was an enjoyable experience, but that the MIDI in isolation left something to be desired (Bonthuys 2019). Per Sanden's categories, the liveness of spontaneity here was lost with the recordings. The music was the same—that is, both the MIDI and the orchestral performance came from the *Final Fantasy VII* universe. In fact, the MIDI recordings were in many ways more "authentic" to the original game. Yet attendees felt slighted by this live playing of prerecorded music. I will return to this case study below.

Recorded Live Concerts

Recorded live concerts are concerts that initially occurred under the parameters of the "default definition" of liveness, but which are recorded for documentary (and commercial) purposes. The audience reactions are often captured and exhibited as part of these recordings, providing a kind of metacommentary on the concert: everything from elated smiles to misty eyes are caught live and edited to highlight the (deemed) appropriate feeling the music should convey. These recorded concerts can also become selling points for concert producers.[11] For Abbate, these recorded live concerts do not constitute what she calls "an actual live performance," as she values the "material, present event" (2004, 506); for Auslander, however, this is one form of liveness that has become "another concept [of liveness] we now accept without question" (2008, 60).

Virtual Live Concerts

Virtual concerts take place, well, virtually, and are one example of Sanden's elusive virtual liveness. Here, I especially consider the virtual live concert as a concert that was prerecorded, but which is then *premiered live* virtually, oftentimes as a stream on Twitch or YouTube. These concerts are not always prerecorded, however. With the global pandemic that began in 2020, at the time of writing this type of concert has become one of the default modes of having live video game music concerts. Consider the *Sonic 30th Anniversary Symphony*, which premiered on YouTube on June 23, 2021. Early in the program, approximately four minutes into the premiere, no fewer than 35,000 people were watching the program live. By the end of the concert, over 50,000 people were watching the concert live. These streamed concerts not only open the doors for stadium-sized crowds (rather than the comparatively smaller sphere of the concert hall or the even more intimate recital hall) but they also allow for increased access for persons who might otherwise not be able to travel to attend a concert.[12]

Live Virtual Concerts

The live virtual concert is a concert that takes place *within* the game. As mentioned above, Gagen and Cook have discussed the smearing of "the now" with these concerts, though there is still an emphasis on a shared temporality and virtuality with these concerts. Furthermore, while the above concerts focused on video game music, the most famous examples of virtual concerts often focus on music that was *not* strictly composed for games (e.g., Lang Lang's 2007 classical recital in *Second Life* and, more recently, Lil Nas X's 2020 performance in *Roblox*). As with the virtual live concerts, there was a proliferation of this type of concert in 2020–2021 due to the pandemic.

To immediately reiterate, I am sure there will be (if there are not already) concerts that fall outside of easy categorization, and we might take these categories more as guidelines rather than as strict rules. If a video on demand (VOD) of a virtual live concert is preserved, for instance, it becomes something akin to a recorded live concert. And while both the virtual live concert and its VOD have elements of liveness to them, the experience of this liveness is different for each *event*. A further dimension to consider with these concerts is the inclusion or absence of accompanying moving images. Many of these concert productions include (usually prerecorded) gameplay displayed on a screen behind the performing orchestra (e.g., *Distant Worlds* and *Pokémon: Symphonic Evolutions*).[13] Other concerts intentionally omit this footage so that the audience's sensorial attention is fixed on the music itself (e.g., *A New World* and *Final Symphony*). Concert producer Thomas Böcker (2021), for instance, has been critical of the former model, stating that:

> What I am not convinced about is the way it [video projection] is typically implemented in video game music concerts. It is often similar to a simple clip show. There is no creative approach that would be comparable to what we do with the arrangements, and hence it takes away from the overall experience, at least for me. A concert with equally sophisticated audio and video parts complementing each other would, however, be definitely to my liking; though there would undoubtedly be practical challenges, including gaining the additional support of licensors and investment from promoters. (428–429)

Böcker's concerts lean heavily into the classical music tradition and the traditional model of the live concert. Indeed, his best-known concert production, *Final Symphony*, takes the music from *Final Fantasy VI* (1994), *VII* (1997), and *X* (2001) and arranges them into "proper" classical genres: a symphonic poem, a symphony, and a piano concerto, respectively. Because of this traditional take on musical form and symphonic structure, it follows that his productions would take a conservative stance toward liveness.

Two notable examples of concerts outside of this traditional mold come by way of Chicago's Fifth House Ensemble, wherein the video projection itself was live as well—that is, not prerecorded. In the *Journey Live* concert, premiered at MAGFest in 2016, not only was the music performed live but so too was the gameplay. In performances of *Journey Live*, a special sound-effect-only version of the game is played by an audience member live in front of the audience. They are accompanied by Fifth House Ensemble, who respond to the players actions by playing Patrick O'Malley's arrangement of Austin Wintory's much-lauded score for the game *Journey* (2012). In the *Undertale LIVE* concert, following the mechanics of Toby Fox's original game (2015), the audience determines what route the production (a condensed version of the game) takes by voting in real time. Depending on what the audience votes for, the ensemble responds in kind following conductor Eric Roth's cues.[14]

In many ways, my discussion of ludic liveness is intended to be provocative, offering not definite answers but new ways of considering the relationship between video games, concerts, and liveness. Following van Elferen, we can see that video games and their musics afford a novel type of liveness; following Auslander and Sanden, we can see that liveness is not a static concept—it is one that changes with the times, its cultures, and its technologies. Liveness, more than anything, comes to present a specific type of temporality: an experience, in one way or another, that occurs—at least at one point—in "real time" as Abbate (2004, 511) would frame it. Yet the mediatization of these concerts, whether through recording technologies or streaming latency, often challenges this time's discrete realness; instead, there is a split between real time and virtual time. The audience exists in between these times, within the confines of the event, as Abbate and van Elferen suggest. But in addition to this split virtual and real event, there is also the virtual replaying of each respective audience member's experience playing the game from whence the sounding music came. As van Elferen (2011, 31) notes: "Quantitative research into listening practices shows that the flow of listening to or making music can take us away from the here and now and relocate us into other times and spaces by way of its strong connotations. . . . This musical *mémoire involontaire* destabilizes the fixedness of temporal and spatial referentiality and makes past, present, and future meanings virtually overlap."[15] Abbate's *Meistersinger* anecdote provides one example of this. Listening to this music, especially in the ritualistic setting of a concert space, thus creates a *listening experience* that is a marked event, one linked to the audience's experience of previously hearing this music if they have played the game from which it is taken.[16] For something to be post-live, then, the live must have already occurred. The event is already past. In the context of video game music concerts, the mnemonic *re*playing of the game through its music is what comes after: the playing of the game is the first live event; listening to its music live as another event allows for a post-live replay of what has already come before. The music marks a Barthesian "that has been"-ness, a dead past now relived (or, in my language, replayed) (Barthes 1981, 76–89). But whereas the material photograph that is the object of Barthes's elegy is an ontological object, a perverse signifier of the flatness of Death (and thus the absence of life—the live), the post-live is *at the same time—real* time—also still live. One, after all, can only listen live, as music is notoriously ephemeral (Abbate 2004; Gallope 2017). That is, listening cannot happen *in* the past, even if we can listen *to* the past vis-à-vis recording technologies. It is a mode of being through feeling (literally, considering the physiology of listening). This is perhaps what Jean-Luc Nancy (2008, x) means when he writes of the "sonorous body" in his foreword to Peter Szendy's philosophical treatise, *Listen*.

To summarize what I have suggested so far: with video game music concerts, the supposition is often that attendees have already played the featured game(s). There is a "reliving," perhaps, but there is more specifically a *replaying* inherent to this particular brand of reliving. Certainly, not all concertgoers have played all the games featured. Perhaps a family member or a friend is dragged along to accompany an eager attendee. (I must confess that I myself have not played all the games featured in the concerts I have attended—I will return to this point below.) But in the performance of this music, the *playing* of the instruments, there is a bridge between the virtual and real worlds. Following Auslander's Benjaminian line of reasoning here, attending these concerts provides one way of overcoming the auratic distance of mass media. In the context of video games, this bridge comes by way of the music, now performed live to bridge the experience and entangle the event(s) within each other. Following van Elferen's (2011, 31) hyperrealistic reading of *Guitar Hero*, in which "the rock songs are part of the game but also of the player's cultural memory, evoking in his or her mind emotions, memories, and identifications that are rooted firmly outside the game diegesis," we might further this line of reasoning to consider what kind of hyperreality comes into being with the live performance of video game music. In particular, I will suggest that there is an emergent kind of (re)playful listening.

Re:Playful Listening and the (Non)Ideal Listener

Though the previous section focused explicitly on *liveness*, a perhaps implicit element of the live experience of a concert is the act of *listening* to the music (a point that began to emerge by the previous section's penultimate paragraph). Philosophies and theories of listening abound—oftentimes differentiating active listening against passive hearing—and in recent years a particular vein of scholarship has developed that focuses on modes of listening inherent to music and media.[17] In this section, I would like to further develop a ludic mode of listening based around video game music concerts, expanding Tim Summers's (2021) account of what he calls "playful listening."

For Summers, a playful listening is one which shows how:

> music in its concert, cinematic, and game presentations, can be understood to be implicitly playful, primarily through our awareness of its "potential to be otherwise." That is, we understand that the particular sounding of music that we experience is only one outcome among a range of possibilities within a broader field of potential incarnations of that music. Playful listening is a mode of listening where we consider the alternative possible forms of the musical material. (702)

Summers includes concerts within this mode of listening, though does not fully expand on how they might differ, at least in part, from the source of his study (video games proper). As I argue, this "potential to be otherwise" has two elements in the context of video game music concerts. First, concertgoers experience the remediation of this music outside of the game—it is one *realization* of this potential, an actualization of play which they listen to. Second, there is generally another agent involved in this process of remediation: that of the arranger. As official scores for video games tend not to exist—at least not as traditionally conceived (van Elferen 2020, 106)—arrangers and transcribers are paramount in bringing these concerts to life (Greenfield-Casas 2022, forth.; Thompson 2018).[18] In their arrangements and orchestrations they, along with concert producers, must make decisions on how they will rearrange this music: from pieces that are closer to 1:1 transcriptions of what is heard in the game, to medleys, to free arrangements and paraphrases.[19] For the philosopher Peter Szendy (2008, 36), arrangers are "the only listeners in the history of music to *write down* their listenings, rather than describe them (as critics do)" (emphasis in original). Though this mediating element of the concert is not necessarily "live," it is still very much a playful listening, the arranger's own "projecti[on of] the possible soundings of the music" (Summers 2021, 705).

Indeed, if the concert attendees of the aforementioned *FINAL FANTASY VII—A Symphonic Reunion* concert are any indication, listeners adamantly *do not* want to hear exactly what they would hear in the game. This is not to say that they might not have enjoyed a MIDI arrangement of the music, but the "potential to be otherwise" was not met in this instance. There must be some form of mediation to breathe new life into the work, whether through a particular mode of liveness or an arranger's listening (or a combination of the two). To return briefly to Auslander, we must remember to situate the experience of the concertgoer not only historically but also culturally as well.

One cultural element inherent to video games is the notion of *replay*. William Gibbons (2018) begins his monograph on the relationship between classical music and video games with a discussion of *replay value*, which he suggests is "at the core of the video game experience" (1). He continues, stating that, in replaying a game: "The result is an experience at once familiar and new. Players relive the game, but with their frame of reference and mode of understanding it irrevocably altered—and hopefully enriched—by what they had already accomplished" (1). Such is the presumed experience of the concertgoer and the arranger, who both now have an experience "at once familiar and new" with the music in these concerts. As Masashi Hamauzu says of his arrangement of the *Final Fantasy X* Piano Concerto from the *Final Symphony* program: "There were a few things I couldn't express well enough while I was working originally on the music of FINAL FANTASY X, and I feel like I could express those things this time around."[20] Even as one of the composers on the original soundtrack, Hamauzu still found new ways of (re)playing with the game's score in order to create his new arrangement. Similarly, concertgoers who attend these concerts also will have the chance to (re)playfully listen to these arrangements, understanding them as one realization of the "alternative possible forms of the musical material."

Playful listening, then, becomes *re*playful listening. This is partly simply my own returning and responding to Summers's notion of playful listening and my remediating it from the game world to the real world. It is also, however, one particular way of experiencing playful listening—a specific type of playful listening. Just as replaying a game is still, at base, a way of playing a game, so too is replayful listening simultaneously still also playful listening. But this mode of listening is dependent on a kind of ideal listener, one who has already played through the game, who is culturally situated, and who has personal memories to mediate their experience. At an extreme, they may be a superfan who knows the ins and outs of the game, its lore, its music, and how they are all interconnected together. In listening to this music, whether in isolation (e.g., an orchestra performing without a screen) or in some kind of audiovisual combination, they are able to make sense of this music and what it means. Perhaps they might even encounter a moment of ludomusical dissonance if a scene from the game is displayed that does not actually include the music the orchestra is performing. The nonideal listener, on the other hand, has no relation to the game or its music. Perhaps they are a friend or family member who was dragged along to the concert (perhaps even a season ticket holder), and perhaps they have some disinterested Kantian aesthetic appreciation of the music, but it is (likely) based outside of any preexisting notions of what the music "should" be.[21]

I invite the reader now to engage in a (brief) playful reading with me. If you choose to accept, simply return to the first page of this chapter and reread the opening first paragraph. In this "replay" of sorts, what information is newly brought to your attention that was not before? Perhaps, having read my musings on ludic liveness, you are more attentive to my personal *lived* experience of a specific *event*. Perhaps you picked up on the (re)playful listening the concertgoer (an ideal listener) in front of me had, immediately moved to tears that they were. Indeed, with this opening memory, I hope to illustrate one example of replayful listening mediated through ludic liveness. I remember being distinctly struck by their words, to the point I quickly wrote them down. It was not just a matter of "I'll never forget *NieR*," nor even "I'll never forget my experience with *NieR*," but specifically "I'll just *never* forget my *experience* of *first playing NieR*." Never is a long time, and to cherish memories for a lifetime shows how dear the game was to them. And not only was it their personal experience with *NieR* that came to mind but their *first* playthrough. This implies that they likely replayed the game multiple times. Indeed, both the original *NieR* as well as its sequel, *NieR: Automata*, have a replay system built into the game wherein the "true" ending is only reached if players replay and beat the game multiple times, each time leading to a different ending.[22] That they explicitly mentioned their playthrough of *NieR* suggests a replaying, a re-experiencing of what they had already played, a "that has been"-ness tethering the past and present, real and virtual through the music. But what about the experience of a nonideal listener?

On June 23, 2021—in the midst of writing the first draft of this chapter—I received a message on Discord asking if I was watching the premiere of the *Sonic 30th Anniversary Concert* on YouTube. I quickly saved my work and opened up the concert.[23] As mentioned above, this was an example of what I have called a virtual live concert. It was a prerecorded concert (complete with a clip show playing on a screen behind the orchestra) performed by the FILMharmonic Orchestra, Tomoya Ohtani Band, and Crush 40 that peaked at approximately 50,000 viewers during its premiere. The live chat was filled with fans aggressively expressing their enthusiasm, complimenting the musicians, and reminiscing on their experiences with the franchise. I sat mutely at my table in the coffeeshop I was working in, focusing more on the chat than the music. The reason for this is in no small part because I have little to no attachment to the *Sonic* series. While I vaguely know the premise of the series (somethingsomething blue hedgehog, somethingsomething Eggman, somethingsomething "gotta go fast"), I did not grow up playing this series. In fact, the strongest memory I have of the series is my mother *not* purchasing me *Sonic Adventure 2: Battle* (2002) for my GameCube. The musical performance was stellar—honestly a stronger concert than some other programs I was more personally invested in—but without that connection of having previously played the games within the series, my enjoyment of the concert was severely dampened. William Gibbons and Julianne Grasso (2020, 56) have discussed the (positive) psychology of this repetition in video game music concerts, stating simply that "the themes that are likely to be most familiar to listeners [are] thus most likely to trigger positive reactions. People want to hear the hits." But the opposite is true as well: if the music is unfamiliar to the listener, they are less likely to have a strong reaction to the music. And while it might be stating the obvious, listeners who are not familiar with the game or series cannot have a replayful listening experience.

Coda—Play Again?

In this chapter I have argued that video game music concerts afford a replay experience of the games whose music they feature. A critical element of this experience, I have argued, is the *live event* that is inherent to both playing a game as well as attending a concert. This double experience, both virtual and real, is mediated by listening to the music live—replayful listening—both by the audience in real time and the music's arranger (they who transcribe—that is, to write *across*—media). These concerts, though primarily a phenomenological experience, also ontologically validate the game's music. In the remediation of the music from the half-real game (Juul 2005) to the concert hall, the music fully steps into the real world. But there is one final element in this process. To briefly return to my event which began this chapter (and which, hopefully, you have already reread): upon returning home after the *NieR: Orchestra Concert re: 12018* performance, I turned on my PlayStation 4 and wandered around in *NieR: Automata* for the first time in over a year. The virtual replay of the concert inspired a real (re)play of the game: a re:replay.

Notes

1. The concert tour included performances in Chicago, Los Angeles, London, and Bangkok. Per the "re: 12018" in its title, the concert was a based on a similar four-concert series that occurred in Tokyo in 2018.
2. There are some parallels here with film music concerts, though the structure and content of these concerts is often quite different in practice. On film music concerts (or, as Brooke McCorkle Okazaki has called them, "cine-concerts"), see Audissino (2014), Lehman (2018), and especially McCorkle Okazaki (2020).
3. For the purposes of this chapter, I will focus on officially produced concerts, rather than those produced by fans.
4. The *GAME THEORY: The Indie Game Symphony*, which was supposed to take place on October 5, 2019, at the Ford Amphitheatre in Hollywood, was unfortunately canceled without explanation. It is perhaps worth noting that many officially produced video game music concerts primarily (or solely) feature Triple-A game series, so this was an especially unfortunate occurrence.
5. The *NieR* concert series in particular has incorporated dramatic readings performed by the game's voice actors in order to expand the lore of the games. Square Enix has also premiered trailers of highly anticipated games at some of their concerts, including a trailer that first announced the release date for the long-awaited *Final Fantasy VII Remake* (2020) at the to-be-discussed *FINAL FANTASY VII—A Symphonic Reunion* concert in 2019.
6. Though many AAA ("Triple A") games with large budgets do indeed use orchestras to record their soundtracks.
7. Sanden (2019) further refines this definition to suggest that

   > virtual liveness is a perception of liveness—a perception of performance—that embraces a musical experience's grounding in the various incursions of electronic sound technologies. It involves an extension of the whole concept of performance to include things like the synthesis, samples and simulations that characterise the logics of digital culture, and which would seem to conflict with traditional definitions of what performance is—and, more importantly, is not—while at the same time making room (sometimes through simulation or technological enhancement) for certain elements of those traditional definitions to persist. (183)

8. While I do not explicitly take up nostalgia in this chapter, nostalgia is sometimes defined as a desire to relive or return to the past. Though memory plays a role in nostalgia, I am cautious not to conflate the two or presume the former always leads to the latter. To be sure, nostalgia *can* play a role in these concerts and players *can* attend these concerts to try and "relive" these experiences (Hunt 2022), but here I argue this phenomenon can also happen *involuntarily* through ludic liveness.

9. I first made this claim, in a more directly Auslanderian and Baudrillardian-inspired fashion, when building a theory of a hyperreal mythology that video games (and their musics) afford (Greenfield-Casas 2017, 22–28, esp. 22n36 and 26–27).
10. Cf. Auslander (2008, 61).
11. Perhaps the best example of this is the tetralogy of *NieR* concerts: *NieR Music Concert & Talk Live* (2010), *NieR Music Concert: "The Memories of Puppets"* (2018), *NieR: Orchestra Concert 12018* (2019), and *NieR: Theatrical Orchestra 12020* (2020). Due to the COVID-19 pandemic that began in 2020, the last of these recordings was recorded live, though without an audience.
12. Many concert halls can comfortably seat a few thousand spectators (Carnegie Hall, for instance, is just shy of 3,000 seats in its main auditorium), yet this pales in comparison to the theoretically limitless virtual "seats" that a virtual concert can offer (provided the concert takes place on a site that can handle the bandwidth of a large congregation of virtual bodies).
13. As mentioned in an earlier note, Brooke McCorkle Okazaki (2020) has written at length on the related phenomenon of the "cine-concert," wherein symphony orchestras perform the soundtrack to a film that is screened behind the orchestra. McCorkle Okazaki further interrogates questions of liveness in her analysis, considering especially questions of fidelity in performance as based on different conductors and their respective philosophies about what they believe the cine-concert experience should highlight.
14. When I was interviewing Roth about his experience conducting and arranging for this concert, he said with a laugh that it was "a little nerve-wracking." Personal correspondence, January 19, 2020.
15. Van Elferen is here referencing DeNora (2000).
16. Oftentimes the supposition is that concertgoers will have played the source game before. Julianne Grasso (2020, 84), for instance, points to the language used in the advertisement for the *The Legend of Zelda: Symphony of the Goddesses* concert, suggesting that the concert is for fans of the series. In direct contrast to this stance, however, concert producers like the aforementioned Böcker instead hope to elevate the music to such a degree that it can stand on its own for even those unfamiliar with its source materials.
17. While a complete survey of these modes of listening would warrant a chapter unto itself, some representative texts include Long (2008), Kassabian (2013), Droumeva (2011), and Kamp (2014). Michael Long's notion of "cinematic listening" has become especially influential, spawning a series of related essays (e.g., Lehman [2018] and Cenciarelli [2021]). In the philosophical tradition, we might include Nancy (2007), Szendy (2008), and Drummond (2019). Pertinent to my focus on video game concerts, Milena Droumeva (2011, 145) has suggested one mode that she calls "inter-textual listening," a mode of listening that is the "result of cross-pollination of different media genres, [wherein] this listening position addresses situations where game soundscapes contain radio, telephone, or TV sounds (most famously featured in *Grand Theft Auto*)." She continues, "Conversely, the popular events of *Video Game Concerts* are settings where game sounds live on outside gameworlds and are performed, listened to, and used for other purposes outside of games" (145). I find her writings on nostalgic listening equally fruitful in replayful listening: "An analytical, culturally-critical type of listening that has emerged over time in experienced players who look for iconic game music themes through platforms and generations of a particular game (some notable examples here being the *Final Fantasy*, *Super Mario*, *Zelda* and *Mega Man* series)" (145).

18. Indeed, in my interviews with two professional video game concert arrangers, Eric Roth of AWR Music and Mariam Abounnasr of Procyon Studio, both noted that it was not uncommon for them to have to transcribe the music from the game by ear before they could arrange it for a concert setting.
19. I have discussed this elsewhere, arguing for what I call "political listenings" in how an arranger chooses to end a piece especially (Greenfield-Casas 2022).
20. "FINAL FANTASY X Piano Concerto," *Game Concerts*, n.d. http://www.gameconcerts.com/en/concerts/final-symphony/. Accessed July 18, 2021.
21. To be clear, no concertgoer is a totally a blank slate—we are all indoctrinated with some kind of aesthetic preference based on our upbringing at both a cultural and personal level.
22. For the highly motivated reader who perhaps re-read the entirety of my introduction, they might have caught that this concert was dubbed "re: 12018," as it was a repeat or a return to a concert program that had premiered in Japan two years prior (see n1). Furthermore, the original *NieR* game was recently remastered and re-released as *NieR Replicant ver. 1.22474487139*, offering a further example of replayabilty in the NieR series.
23. The concert can be watched in full (along with a replay of the live chat) on the official Sonic the Hedgehog's YouTube channel at https://www.youtube.com/watch?v=UGTlBHNvjsU. At the time of writing, just a few weeks after the premiere, the concert has already garnered over 1.6 million views on YouTube.

References

Abbate, Carolyn. 2004. "Music—Drastic or Gnostic?" *Critical Inquiry* 30: 505–536.

Audissino, Emilio. 2014. "Overruling a Romantic Prejudice: Forms and Formats of Film Music in Concert Programs." In *Film in Concert, Film Scores and Their Relation to Classical Concert Music*, edited by Sebastian Stoppe, 25–43. Glückstadt: VWH Verlag.

Auslander, Philip. 2008. *Liveness: Performance in a Mediatized Culture*. 2nd ed. New York: Routledge.

Barthes, Roland. 1981. *Camera Lucida: Reflections on Photography*. Translated by Richard Howard. New York: Hill and Wang.

Baudrillard, Jean. [1981] 1994. *Simulacra and Simulation*. Translated by Sheila Faria Glaser. Ann Arbor: University of Michigan Press.

Benjamin, Walter. [1936] 1969. "The Work of Art in the Age of Mechanical Reproduction." In *Illuminations*, edited by Hannah Arendt, translated by Harry Zohn, 217–252. New York: Schocken.

Böcker, Thomas, Melanie Fritsch, and Tim Summers. 2021. "Producing Game Music Concerts." In *The Cambridge Companion to Video Game Music*, edited by Melanie Fritsch and Tim Summers, 424–432. Cambridge: Cambridge University Press.

Bonthuys, Darryn. 2019. "Fans Aren't Happy with a *Final Fantasy VII* Tribute Concert That Used Mostly MIDI Songs Instead of Live Performances." Critical Hit, June 10, 2019. Accessed July 18, 2021. https://www.criticalhit.net/gaming/fans-arent-happy-with-a-final-fantasy-vii-tribute-concert-that-used-mostly-midi-songs-instead-of-live-performances/.

Bown, Alfie. 2017. *The PlayStation Dreamworld*. Cambridge; Malden, MA: Polity.

Cenciarelli, Carlo, ed. 2021. *The Oxford Handbook of Cinematic Listening*. Oxford and New York: Oxford University Press.

Cheng, William. 2014. *Sound Play: Video Games and the Musical Imagination*. Oxford; New York: Oxford University Press.

Collins, Karen. 2013. *Playing with Sound: A Theory of Interacting with Sound and Music in Video Games*. Cambridge, MA: MIT Press.

DeNora, Tia. 2000. *Music in Everyday Life*. Cambridge: Cambridge University Press.

Droumeva, Milena. 2011. "An Acoustic Communication Framework for Game Sound: Fidelity, Verisimilitude, Ecology." In *Game Sound Technology and Player Interaction: Concepts and Developments*, edited by Mark Grimshaw, 131–152. Hershey, PA: Information Science Reference.

Drummond, William J. 2019. "Arrangement, Listening, and the Music of Gérard Pesson." PhD dissertation, Oxford: University of Oxford.

Gagen, Justin, and Nicholas Cook. 2016. "Performing Live in Second Life." In *The Oxford Handbook of Music and Virtuality*, edited by Sheila Whiteley and Shara Rambarran, 191–209. Oxford; New York: Oxford University Press.

Gallope, Michael. 2017. *Deep Refrains: Music, Philosophy, and the Ineffable*. Chicago: University of Chicago Press.

Gibbons, William. 2018. *Unlimited Replays: Video Games and Classical Music*. Oxford; New York: Oxford University Press.

Gibbons, William, and Julianne Grasso. 2020. " 'And So It Goes, On and On': Repetition in the Music of *Final Fantasy*." In *Surpassing the Limit Break: The Psychology of "Final Fantasy,"* edited by Anthony M. Bean, 43–60. Fort Worth, TX: Leyline Publishing, Inc.

Grasso, Julianne. 2020. "On Canons as Music and Muse." *Journal of Sound and Music in Games* 1 (1): 82–86.

Greenfield-Casas, Stefan. 2017. "Between Worlds: Musical Allegory in *Final Fantasy X*." Master's report, University of Texas at Austin.

Greenfield-Casas, Stefan. 2022. "Uematsu's Postgame: The Music of *Final Fantasy* in the Concert Hall (and Beyond)." In *The Music of Nobuo Uematsu in the* Final Fantasy *Series*, edited by Richard Anatone, 291–311. Bristol: Intellect.

Greenfield-Casas, Stefan. Forthcoming. "From the Screen (to the Screen) to the Concert Hall: Arrangement as a World-Building and World-Bridging Device in the *Kingdom Hearts* Series." In *The Oxford Handbook of Arrangement Studies*, edited by Ryan Raul Bañagale. Oxford; New York: Oxford University Press.

Hunt, Elizabeth. 2022. "My Childhood Is in Your Hands: Videogame Concerts as Commodified and Tangible Nostalgic Experiences." In *Nostalgia and Videogame Music: A Primer of Case Studies, Theories, and Analyses for the Player-Academic*, edited by Can Aksoy, Sarah Pozderac-Chenevey, and Vincent E. Rone, 68–84. Bristol; Chicago: Intellect.

Jenkins, Henry. 2008. *Convergence Culture: Where Old and New Media Collide*. Rev. ed. New York: New York University Press.

Juul, Jesper. 2005. *Half-Real: Video Games between Real Rules and Fictional Worlds*. Cambridge, MA: MIT Press.

Kamp, Michiel. 2014. "Four Ways of Hearing Video Game Music." PhD dissertation, Cambridge: University of Cambridge.

Kassabian, Anahid. 2013. *Ubiquitous Listening: Affect, Attention, and Distributed Subjectivity*. Berkeley: University of California Press.

Lehman, Frank. 2018. "Film-as-Concert Music and the Formal Implications of 'Cinematic Listening.'" *Music Analysis* 37 (1): 7–46.

Long, Michael. 2008. *Beautiful Monsters: Imagining the Classic in Musical Media*. Berkeley: University of California Press.

McCorkle Okazaki, Brooke. 2020. "Liveness, Music, Media: The Case of the Cine-Concert." *Music and the Moving Image* 13 (2): 3–24.

Nancy, Jean-Luc. 2007. *Listening*. Translated by Charlotte Mandell. Annotated ed. New York: Fordham University Press.

Needleman, Sarah E. 2015. "How Videogames Are Saving the Symphony Orchestra." *Wall Street Journal*, October 12, 2015. Accessed July 18, 2021. https://www.wsj.com/articles/how-videogames-are-saving-the-symphony-orchestra-1444696737.

Ombler, Mat. 2020. "Are Video Games the Future of Live Music?" *GamesIndustry*, June 10, 2020. Accessed July 18, 2021. https://www.gamesindustry.biz/articles/2020-06-10-are-video-games-the-future-of-live-music.

Sanden, Paul. 2013. *Liveness in Modern Music: Musicians, Technology, and the Perception of Performance*. New York; London: Routledge.

Sanden, Paul. 2019. "Rethinking Liveness in the Digital Age." In *The Cambridge Companion to Music in Digital Culture*, edited by Nicholas Cook, Monique M. Ingalls, and David Trippett, 178–192. Cambridge: Cambridge University Press.

Summers, Tim. 2021. "Fantasias on a Theme by Walt Disney." In *The Oxford Handbook of Cinematic Listening*, edited by Carlo Cenciarelli, 690–711. Oxford; New York: Oxford University Press.

Szendy, Peter, and Jean-Luc Nancy. 2008. *Listen: A History of Our Ears*. Translated by Charlotte Mandell. New York: Fordham University Press.

Thompson, Matthew. 2018. "'There's No Doubt You'll Be Popular after Performing These in Front of Your Friends!': The Pedagogy and Performance of Piano Transcriptions of Video Game Music." *North American Conference on Video Game Music*, University of Michigan, Ann Arbor, January 13–14, 2018.

Van Elferen, Isabella. 2011. "¡Un Forastero! Issues of Virtuality and Diegesis in Videogame Music." *Music and the Moving Image* 4 (2): 30–39.

Van Elferen, Isabella. 2020. "Ludomusicology and the New Drastic." *Journal of Sound and Music in Games* 1 (1): 103–112.

CHAPTER 33

VIDEO GAMES LIVE AND THE GAMIFICATION OF THE ORCHESTRAL CONCERT EXPERIENCE

ELIZABETH HUNT

INTRODUCTION

> With a quick glance to the conductor, the soloist raises her instrument, takes a deep breath and begins: orange, red, red, blue, yellow, yellow, green. As she presses colored buttons on the neck of her plastic guitar controller, the music soars. The soloist slips in and out of the music, astounding the audience with her breathtaking technique. Breaking concert protocol a few minutes later at the cadenza, she jumps to her feet, and with a few tugs of the whammy bar, a flurry of button clicks, and rapid flicks of the strum bar, she totally shreds on the plastic guitar controller.
>
> —Austin (2016, 1)

MICHAEL Austin (2016) opens *Music Video Games: Performance, Politics, and Play* by conjuring the above description of a "preposterous" but "not entirely outside the realm of possibility" orchestral concert that features a video game player as part of the performing ensemble. While the image is supposed to shock the reader, this "preposterous" suggestion is the reality of some video game music concerts. Although Austin does further his discussion by acknowledging *Video Games Live* and other live performances of video game music, it is with a sense that plastic guitars regularly appearing in performances remains an abstract and intangible proposal. In this chapter, I will demonstrate that soloists with plastic guitars are *not* merely a possibility but have been a common occurrence in video game music concerts for over a decade. This will be shown by illustrating the use of *gamification*—the implementation of game mechanics in a nongaming environment—within the context of the concert hall.

Concerts of video game music vary widely in presentation. These can range from "marching band halftime shows, to solo piano concerts, to chamber music" (Gibbons 2018, 157), rock band performances and, as is the focus of this chapter, orchestral concerts featuring symphony orchestras. Most commonly, orchestral video game music concerts feature large screens upon which game footage is projected to accompany the music. Concerts that use this form of presentation include *Pokémon: Symphonic Evolutions* (2014–2017), *The Legend of Zelda: Symphony of the Goddesses* (2012–2017), and *KINGDOM HEARTS Orchestra—World Tour*—(2017–2018). It is also not unusual to see some audience members in costume at such events. In my own attendance at various concerts, I have rubbed shoulders with several video game characters, while similar encounters have been described by both Karen Collins (2008) and Daniel Ross (2015). At the very least, most of the audience come adorned in some sort of video game merchandise, and there is increased activity in the form of clapping and cheering along with what William Cheng has referred to as "performer-audience banter" (2013, 174). Some concerts may even encourage the audience to sing along (Hunt 2022, 81). While this is a generalization of the norm, the presentation of each video game music concert is unique, resulting in an abundance of variety as to the exact experience one will have when attending (see chapter 32 this volume for further on this). Some concerts do not have video screens or costumed audiences and instead are presented with little divergence from the typical, modern orchestral concert experience. Examples of this include the Merregnon Studios produced *Symphonic Odysseys* (2011) and *Final Symphony* (2013–2018). Another nuanced presentation was seen in *rePLAY: A Symphony of Heroes* (2014–2015), which used Joseph Campbell's monomyth as an overarching narrative to tie pieces together throughout the concert. There have also been, on rare occasions, live accompaniment concerts of entire video games. *Journey LIVE* (2016) and *Dear Esther—Live* (2016–2017) feature performers who play the video games *Journey* (2012) and *Dear Esther* (2012), respectively, as part of the concert performance. This gameplay is streamed onto the video screens above the orchestra, who provide a full underscore accompaniment that responds to the player's actions. As video games that feature dynamic music, the choices of the player impact what music will be heard and make every performance unique. For this reason, *Journey LIVE*'s Eric Snoza refers to the player as "actually an instrumentalist within the chamber ensemble" (cited in Sarkar 2016). This concept of the player as performer can also be seen in *Video Games Live*, where volunteering audience members are brought onstage to play various video games, while supported by the orchestra, and thus become an audience-performer.

The focus of this chapter is an analysis of gamification and audience-performers in *Video Games Live* (hereafter, *VGL*). An introduction to the concert illuminates how successful gamification occurs within *VGL*, as *VGL* does not present itself as a typical orchestral concert. First premiering to a sold-out Hollywood Bowl in 2006, *VGL* has toured globally for 15 years. *VGL* is "the longest-running game concert series not dedicated to a specific composer or game franchise" and "has achieved a remarkable level of cultural penetration, performing hundreds of shows to sold-out audiences across six continents" (Gibbons 2020). Although *VGL* is closest in presentation to video game concerts like *Pokémon: Symphonic Evolutions*, there is significant departure from this more typical concert presentation throughout. Produced, hosted, and cocreated by Tommy Tallarico, *VGL* uses a range of extramusical features to enhance the spectacle of the concert. These additions include a rock band that plays alongside the orchestra, light shows, costumed performers, and video effects. This spectacle gives *VGL* the "energy of a rock concert," despite its largely symphonic context and content (Video Games Live 2021). This highly visual and active rock concert atmosphere is in stark contrast to a traditional orchestral concert. Furthermore, it incites Bakhtin's notions of carnival, as discussed by William Gibbons (2016): "[A] time when traditional values are suspended, or reversed" (209). This suspension of traditional values allows for a flexibility of roles and boundaries within *VGL*, which enables the successful transition of audience members to audience-performer. The inciting of carnival and allowance for deviation is supported through the implementation of gaming mechanics to gamify the concert experience.

What Is Gamification?

Gamification is the process of implementing gaming mechanics outside of games, applying game logic and mechanics to real-life contexts. It is not a process that relies solely on video games, but extends to all manners of play, such as boardgames and playground games. The term "gamification" came into use in the early 2000s but gained traction in the business world a decade later, after which gamification techniques have become increasingly common in sectors such as business, health, education, human resources, sustainability, and marketing (see Walz and Deterding 2014; Goethe 2019; Matallaoui, Hanner, and Zarkenow 2017). Nevertheless, Sebastian Deterding (2014) has criticized the way in which the term has often been discussed with a narrow understanding due to scholarship only studying such applications within a software environment. Thus, I seek to take gamification out of this small box by "rethinking the remit of gamification . . . expanding it from the mere re-structuring of activity through (largely software-based) rule systems towards re-framing activity as a specific type of situation (playing games) entailing specific norms, conventions, and understandings" (Deterding 2014, 312). I use *VGL* to investigate gamification techniques found in the new environment of the concert hall. Gameplay mechanics used to promote gamification typically include competition, rules, point scoring, leaderboards, simulated risk, achievement rewards, and artificial narratives. Such mechanics are applied because, in gamification, "the integration of game mechanics into a non-game environment" is with the purpose of creating "a game-like feel" (Matallaoui, Hanner, and Zarkenow 2017, 5). Game mechanics can create this feel by inciting play in social situations where it has previously been inappropriate. Within these situations, "if the situational norms of those non-gaming contexts . . . do not entail 'playing' as appropriate, engaging in play ought to be shunned because it would induce embarrassment" (Deterding 2014, 312), yet the practices of gamification aim to make play a welcome guest in these new environments. It will be demonstrated throughout this chapter that *VGL*'s goal in applying gamification to portions of the concert is to incite this "game-like feel."

It is important, however, not to confuse concert gamification with concert interactivity. These activities should not be treated identically. Gamification is the inciting of a game-like feel of play, and, as such, in this scenario interactivity should be viewed as a gaming mechanic being used to evoke this desired feeling. Thus, when gamification occurs in *VGL* it is highly interactive but game mechanics such as competition, point scoring, risk, rewards, and narratives are also present. Music is also given a supporting background role, as one would expect in a video game, in these gamified moments. In some video game concerts "the music transforms from music designed for gameplay into music designed to remember gameplay" (Grasso 2020). *VGL* does not transform the music to provoke memories but instead transforms the concert hall to a space of play to incite the game-like feel that the music was designed for. Thus, gamification makes *VGL* different from a traditional orchestral concert experience as the process translates the feeling of play from video games to the live environment.

Interactivity, in contrast, promotes action on the part of the consumer yet is not necessarily game-like and is more reminiscent of audience activity. Such activity is common in video game music concerts, described by Ross (2015) as "whooping, hollering and all brands of general concert frippery" (39). Interactivity sets video games apart from other audiovisual media, making it an important element of gamification in video game music concerts. Video games require interaction such as button pressing to be played and progress, while progression triggers new musical gestures. Tim Summers (2016, 25) notes that "in most cases, the musical output of the game is dependent upon the player's engagement with the gameplay." Collins (2013) refers to this tying together of visuals, sound, and player input as a "kinesthetic" occurrence. As a result, players can consider music as "feedback tied to their own . . . actions" (44). Video game music is typically encountered via activity, yet moving video game music to the concert hall relocates the music to an environment where action does not, in most circumstances, elicit a musical reaction.

In contrast to the necessary high levels of activity required by video games, activity is not encouraged at modern orchestral concerts. Indeed, concert halls are governed by "a quite rigid code of conduct" (Wagener 2012, 1). Western concerts of classical music are, since the 19th century, passive experiences which focus on mental and emotional stimulation rather than physical reaction, as ruled by this (often unspoken) code of conduct. At an orchestral concert, "the goal of the audience member/congregant is to become pure of mind" and in doing so "limit bodily activity" (Fonarow 2006, 183). Thus I use the term "passive" here as the intended counterpart to interactivity when describing audiences at more typical orchestral concerts. This does not imply that the classical music concert goer is not an active and stimulated listener, but rather that their bodily output is less noisy and/or physical in their concert attendance than the *VGL* audience members described within this chapter. Nor do I intend to suggest that audiences at other orchestral concerts do not contribute to the event experience, producing different event outcomes based on their actions.

Christopher Small (1998) advocates and argues for the term "musicking," meaning "to take part, in any capacity, in a musical performance, whether by performing, by listening, by rehearsing or practicing, by providing material for performance (what is called composing), or by dancing" (9). In this chapter, I seek to discuss audience member activity in a more specific manner. Although Small's musicking quite rightfully regards all those involved in an event to be active in contributing to its experience, my own discourse on interactivity and gamification here discusses specific gamified activity wherein passive audience members become active participants in the concert performance itself. As outlined in Andreas Wagener's (2012) study, societal norms call for "a clear separation between performing artists and the audience" and enforce the notion that "audiences are to listen seriously and quietly and devote full concentration to the music" (3). Joachim Reiber highlights that this is the expectation of the audience by stating that, in 1841, the Viennese press sought to remind audiences and performers that "the latter commits to sing or play, whereas the former are obliged to listen with attention, with interest" (cited in Wagener). Since the typical modern orchestral concert experience calls for passivity while video games require interactivity, gamification creates moments that break rigid concert-hall expectations to incite feelings of play found in the music's source medium. As the concert hall is an example of somewhere that "engaging in play ought to be shunned because it would induce embarrassment" and break societal norms, that play is integral to the source medium of video games aids *VGL* in "establish[ing] a trusting atmosphere where play is perceived as welcomed and non-embarrassing" (Deterding 2014, 312). By embracing play in an environment previously unwelcoming to it, *VGL* defies the traditional rules of the concert hall and, pushing this further, creates a new type of concert experience which blurs the boundaries between the audience and performers.

Space Invaders, *Frogger*, and the Audience-Performer

It is through *VGL*'s gamification of the concert experience that we see Austin's vision of the plastic guitar wielding soloist come to life. Audience members are invited to become active agents in the concert and, by acting as video game players, they become audience-performers. Audience-performers blur the typically strict divide between audience member and performer by taking on an active and productive role that makes them integral to the successful performance of the pieces in question. For this chapter, audience-performers in the *VGL* segments *Space Invaders*, *Frogger*, and *Guitar Hero* will be examined. These segments function in generally similar ways. In all three segments, members of the audience are invited onstage to play the games (projected onto large screens) while the ensemble plays the accompaniment. While each of these segments could technically appear in *VGL* without audience-performers, the experience would be significantly diminished.

In the *Space Invaders* segment, Tallarico challenges the player to achieve a specific score within two minutes to win a prize. The point scoring and reward incentive are two aspects of gamification, while the fixed length of time for play matches the piece the orchestra performs. The *Space Invaders* segment is not especially sonically interactive; however, it is highly physically interactive as it incorporates the movement of the audience-performer. In the arcade game *Space Invaders* (1978), the player controls a spaceship tasked with fighting off an ever-advancing alien fleet. The player must destroy all alien spaceships and avoid enemy fire to succeed. As such, the core gameplay is simple: evade and shoot. However, *VGL* adds humor and physicality to the performance by asking the audience-performer to wear a motion tracking vest to translate their movements into the video game rather than using traditional joystick wiggling and button pressing to control their direction. The audience-performer must move from side to side across the stage to dodge the incoming missiles. As the alien ships advance, they speed up and become harder to shoot. This, along with their increasing proximity, creates a sense of danger and, gradually, impending doom as they become more evasive of the audience-performer, who in turn must become faster, more evasive, and more accurate.

Despite the fixed nature of early soundtracks (and interestingly so, as the first video game to feature continuous background music), *Space Invaders* features a dynamic soundtrack which reacts to in-game action through the acceleration of a looping melody (Collins 2008). There is also a musical stinger that accompanies the red bonus ship. In *VGL*, the accelerando is facilitated by the conductor's noting of the game state by remaining attentive to the onscreen projection. *Space Invaders*'s feel of a frenetic danger-state is enhanced through its dynamic music. At the beginning of the game, the musical theme is stated clearly—a four-note loop composed of a descending tetrachord. This phrase begins at a slow, plodding pace but soon speeds up. The accelerando occurs gradually and is almost unnoticeable in the first few iterations of the phrase's looping. The steady quickening of the creeping downward melody mirrors the alien ships' downward movement and increasing speed as they near the player in a way reminiscent of the Mickey Mousing technique often found in cartoons.[1] Zach Whalen (2004) argues that Mickey Mousing, where music is synchronized closely with onscreen activity, can "instill objects with even more life" when used both in animated films and in video games. In *Space Invaders*, Mickey Mousing instills life into the dated graphics of the alien invasion and makes the sense of danger with its approach more real, thus providing further immersion and enjoyment. Both the dynamic music and the Mickey Mousing of *Space Invaders* further enhance enjoyment as the changing tempo heightens the frenzy of a player battling off the speedy invaders. In *VGL*, this is much to the amusement of the rest of the audience, who laugh as the audience-performer runs back-and-forth across the stage in an increasingly frantic manner. Although the audience are laughing and interacting, this is not at the expense of the audience-performer. Due to their interactivity, point scoring, and the supporting musical underscore, gamification creates a feeling of play within the concert hall that makes such performance, on the part of the audience-performer, feel welcome within the concert experience.

The audience-performer in *VGL*'s *Space Invaders* fills the role of a soloist. They have the potential to affect the sonic output of the piece by reaching a game-over state before the two-minute timer has elapsed, thus cutting the piece short. More apparent, however, is the audience-performer's impact on the audience's experience of the *Space Invaders* segment. The involvement of the audience-performer enhances the concert experience by placing them in a familiar role to video game players—a hero chosen from the masses for a special quest. This adds significant excitement to the piece. Furthermore, this excitement aids in the audience not experiencing what Winifred Phillips refers to as "repetition fatigue" (2014, 66) for an audience largely composed of individuals whose tastes in music likely align more with homophony and clear melody lines as opposed to *Space Invaders*'s repeating four-note loop. In addition, the audience-performer holds the agency to control this portion of the concert experience; they could, for example, choose to remain static in their movement tracking vest, cutting the segment short. By allowing the music to become the background to extramusical aspects of the concert, such as the added interactivity, audience-performer agency, and reward incentive, the *Space Invaders* segment demonstrates how gamification allows *VGL* to feature pieces otherwise unsuitable for concert performance.

Likewise, in *VGL*'s *Frogger* segment, two volunteering audience members are brought onstage. These audience-performers then take turns playing *Frogger* (1981) for 90 seconds, after which the player with the highest score wins a prize. As with *Space Invaders*, this segment contains a reward incentive, but also adds a competition element. The goal of *Frogger* is to move frogs across a dangerous highway and river to the safety of their home, a highlighted place on the screen. *Frogger*'s implementation of dynamic music is such that a new melody is played as accompaniment for each successive frog that the player controls. Collins's (2007, 219) examination of the "random generation" of *Frogger*'s music identifies that the level reset is the trigger for musical change in the video game. While musical reset is achieved conveniently in video games through the coding of predetermined algorithms, in a live scenario this is much more difficult, because the conductor and performers must react in real time to the actions in the video game. Nonetheless, this is achieved successfully in *VGL*. Here, the conductor is attentive to the audience-performer's gameplay and indicates that the orchestra should halt their playing when a level reset point is reached. The conductor then quickly counts the orchestra in to a new theme as the audience-performer gains control of their next frog. This necessity of attentiveness to their play on the part of other performers demonstrates that the audience-performers are part of the ensemble in *VGL*. As with *Space Invaders*, the success of this live dynamic music is enabled by the technological limitations of early arcade music. The original game has small gaps of silence where the level resets, and a new musical loop does not begin until the player moves their new frog. Mimicking these gaps provides the ensemble with more time to prepare and removes the requirement to blend seamlessly into a new theme. Furthermore, because of the dynamic nature of the music, each performance of *Frogger* at *VGL* will provide a unique experience. Different reset points, different successes, and different failures all accumulate to a wealth of potential for variation in the *Frogger* segment. Thus, the audience-performer's interaction effects the sonic output of the orchestra and the audience experience.

A potential issue with the gamification of the concert experience is highlighted by the presentations of both *Space Invaders* and *Frogger*. In both segments, extramusical features are of greater focus and prominence than the musical experience. The orchestra takes on a background role with the function of supporting the video game and accompanying the audience-performer's play. This is far from the usual modern orchestral concert experience and, while there are potential negative connotations to this disregard of concert etiquette, the lack of passivity due to gamification could be argued to represent a more appropriate concert presentation of music from the gaming medium. "Video game music complements and intensifies the player's perception of virtuality, immersion, and flow" and so, in its primary function, supports play (Lerner 2014, 92–93). By retaining this support function in the live concert environment, *VGL*'s gamified presentation transmutes the music to the live environment while retaining core aspects of the video game form. Thus, while the orchestra and music become background to the concert experience, this is fitting for the music's original implementation as underscore.

Playing the Guitar Hero

Although the *Space Invaders* and *Frogger* segments focus on the interactive experience to a greater extent than the music itself, some *VGL* performances do contain a gamified segment that retains a focus on music. The *Guitar Hero* segment, which appears in select performances of *VGL*, involves an audience member being invited onstage to play a track from the *Guitar Hero* series (2005–2015) with the orchestra. After competing in and winning a preshow *Guitar Hero* contest, an audience member wins the privilege of performing onstage for one final challenge. Tallarico challenges the audience member to achieve a specific score in a performance, together with the ensemble, of "The Pretender" (2007) by Foo Fighters, "Sweet Emotion" (1975) by Aerosmith, or "Jump" (1984) by Van Halen. The orchestra and band perform an arranged accompaniment, with backing harmonies provided, in some cases, by choir (for example, in the chorus of "Sweet Emotion"). The lead vocal melody and the lead guitar line come from the *Guitar Hero* game audio. Once onstage, the audience member is given a *Guitar Hero* controller, which resembles a guitar with the strings replaced by five buttons along the fretboard and a button on the body for strumming. They are then set their challenge and the game begins. The audience-performer must succeed in delivering a sonically complete performance of the assigned song to win a physical prize. To play *Guitar Hero*, one must press the correct buttons on the fretboard and the strum bar in time with the rhythm indicated by the video game screen, which is reminiscent of a downward scrolling instrumental score. As with *Space Invaders* and *Frogger*, the video game is projected above the orchestra for the audience and audience-performer to watch. One could consider the act of playing *Guitar Hero* in *VGL* as reminiscent of a flute solo within a symphony movement. The audience-performer and the flute player must both read the "score" and press the keys on their instrument with as much accuracy as possible to deliver a correct performance. This allusion is supported by the soloistic nature of the lead guitar line which sits separately from the rest of the music produced in the *Guitar Hero* segment.

The interactivity promoted by this segment is particularly well supported by the choice of video game. *Guitar Hero* promotes both performance and spectatorship, as shown by the many party, bar-night, and tournament performances of the game at its peak popularity. Kiri Miller conducted research on participants at such events and examined the varying styles of play that performance context allowed. In tournaments, players were often score oriented. This was evidenced by the way that "competitors focussed on the screen and never indulged in flamboyant rock-star moves" (Miller 2012, 139). Players at recreational *Guitar Hero* functions, however, were found to joke with fellow performers, dance along, and sometimes flaunt cliché rock star moves. The contextual differences are important to the sculpting of these player types and behaviors. In competitions there are serious stakes—merchandise, money, honor—while bar night events are grounded in fun and revelry. Despite the competitive nature of the preshow contest that must be won to be called onstage, *Guitar Hero* performances at *VGL* see both of Miller's performance types. In some performances, the audience-performers adopt a competitive composure and pay serious attention to the screen above the orchestra. In others, audience-performers dance, "head bang" and generally showboat as they enjoy their time in the spotlight. Although the latter audience-performers demonstrate their rock star clichés, generally their performances still maintain a high level of skill. This is probably due to the preshow contest ensuring that only players likely to succeed in the *VGL* performance are permitted to take on the audience-performer role. The contest safeguards the *VGL* concert experience by gatekeeping the role. By making audience-performers earn their role, game literacy and ability ensure that a novice audience-performer is not given control of the concert experience. Thus, although some control of the concert experience is relinquished to the audience-performer, the experience is not completely surrendered through gamifying the concert. However, this method is not always successful in ensuring the *Guitar Hero* segment is performed with success. When giving the audience-performer such control, one cannot always predict the outcome of the performance and, as in all games, there is the potential for the audience-performer to lose.

A mistake in *Guitar Hero* causes the lead guitar line to cut out, which leaves gaps of silence and often elicits a negative audio response from the game in the form of a dissonant "clunk" sound. To perform a piece without these sonic ruptures, the player must play all the notes correctly by pressing and strumming at the right moment. As this is extremely difficult, many *Guitar Hero* performances feature the odd clunk throughout. By recovering from mistakes quickly, players often avoid too much dissonance and salvage the lead guitar line, leaving only small gaps of silence. Several missed notes result in recurring clunks and prolonged silence in the lead guitar line. When too many notes are missed, the player fails: the song ends prematurely, and the player-character is booed by the rowdy in-game audience. Although it is not common for a player to fail in *VGL* due to the preconcert vetting process, when failure does occur the audience-performer is given numerous opportunities to retry the song so that this portion of the concert does not have to be cut short. As *Guitar Hero* is a form of simulation game, "designed to put players in the virtual shoes of live rock-concert performers," continuous failure puts the unfortunate audience-performer in the shoes of a very unpopular musician (Miller 2012, 85). The *VGL* audience tends to grow rowdy and disappointed in the rare cases of continuous failure, booing and jeering the audience-performer. The simulation realized, losing the game here has real-world consequences. Wrong and missed notes in *VGL*'s *Guitar Hero* segment are as important to the piece's performance as they would be, to return to the earlier parallel, if the solo flutist blundered their solo.

With its heavy reliance on the audience-performer for both sonic completeness and audience enjoyment, *Guitar Hero* as performed in *VGL* is without doubt the most gamified element of any video game music concert. By making the *Guitar Hero* segment both physically and sonically interactive, this moment in the concert has real world stakes and implications for everyone in the concert hall. The feeling of play here succeeds in creating an excited atmosphere within the concert hall which greatly adds to the audience's enjoyment of the piece. However, the audience can quickly turn into a raucous crowd should the audience-performer fail. The audience-performer's role in this segment also relates to some contention surrounding music video games like *Guitar Hero*. While some critics have interpreted the video game as an inauthentic substitute for learning to play the guitar, others argue that the goal of the game is to step into the shoes of the titular "guitar hero" and act out being a "rock god" (Miller 2012, 94; Summers 2016, 184). Taking this as *Guitar Hero*'s goal, Dominic Arsenault (2008) proposes that "the game promises to tap into common fantasies of rock superstars playing in front of large audiences more than it guarantees raw simulational fidelity in the act of playing guitar." This is supported through Mario A. Dozal's (2016) analysis of a similar game series, *Rock Band* (2007–2017), which he states is "a video game designed to allow players to fulfil rock star fantasies."

Based on these assessments, through *VGL*'s presentation of *Guitar Hero*, the game has achieved a realization of its simulational goals as the concert allows the audience-performer to act out their rock star fantasies in front of a live audience. *VGL*'s gamification allows *Guitar Hero* to fulfill its purpose insofar as simulation becomes reality through the narrative created for the segment. This is supported through shows where audience-performers display clichéd rock star moves which Summers (2016, 184) identifies as key aspects of this simulation. Not only are these audience-performers supplying a musical performance and competing for a prize but also they are partaking in play by flaunting their rock star fantasy and providing this experience for the concert hall. Throughout the duration of the *Guitar Hero* segment, they *are* a rock star, they are *the* guitar hero. Within this segment, audience-performers are doubly rewarded due to the way gamification is implemented. While those who achieve the high score win a tangible prize, audience-performers are also given the immaterial reward of living out these fantasies. Meanwhile, the audience also benefits as they are given the enhanced experience of the interactive moment where they can clap or jeer and invest in the created narrative of the audience-performer's success or failure. Video games allow players to virtually experience a fantasy. By using gamification to incite play and a "game-like feel," *VGL* invites them to live it.

Conclusion

Through gamification, *VGL* purposely breaks typical modern orchestral concert codes of conduct. Inviting audience members to the stage crosses a liminal boundary. The lines between audience and performer are blurred by inviting audience members to become part of the show. Audience-performers affect sonic output, the performances of their fellow onstage performers, and audience experience. One may argue that this aligns *VGL* with West African music forms as studied by Small as much as it is aligned with concerts of the Western classical tradition. Within his studies, Small found "the line between performer and audience is often . . . blurred" producing "a musical experience where all present are active co-producers of an aesthetic experience" (cited in Fonarow 2006, 23). In the concert segments discussed here, audience members have become coproducers by taking on audience-performer roles and their output has been proven integral to the aesthetic experience of play within the concert. It is through the adaption of game mechanics to the western classical tradition that Small's "participatory spectatorship" has relocated from the West African tradition to the classical music venue. This further brings us back to Bakhtin's notions of carnival and "breaking down the walls between 'high' and 'low' arts" (Gibbons 2016, 209). Yet, in *Space Invaders*, *Frogger*, and *Guitar Hero*, the audience-performer could choose not to partake. *Guitar Hero*'s audience-performer could abstain from pressing their plastic guitar's keys and produce no music, ending the segment prematurely. The *voluntary* nature of this play is, to Deterding (2014), an integral feature of successful gamification. Video games give control of experience to the player, so to take this risk in a live environment truly gamifies the concert experience of *VGL*. However, the familiarity of *Space Invaders* and *Frogger*, and *Guitar Hero*'s preshow contest, reveal an attempt to limit this risk and relinquishing of control. Adapting such parameters and restrictions to a real-world environment, though, is common in gamification and can be seen as game mechanics in themselves. Thus, while the rules we associate with a typical modern orchestral concert experience are somewhat broken, the gamification process brings with it its own set of restrictions. Furthermore, the feel of play in such an alien environment is supported and enabled by other aspects of the *VGL* experience. The additions of the on-stage rock band, the light shows, and even Tallarico's energetic hosting in which he addresses the audience directly, create a relaxed atmosphere. While these features may be seen as unnecessary embellishments which can cheapen or detract from the orchestral music experience by some, including competing video game concert producers Thomas Böcker and Jason Michael Paul (Böcker, Fritsch, and Summers 2021; Gibbons 2018; Hunt 2017), these extramusical touches not only make *VGL* a welcome environment to those who aren't familiar with an orchestral concert but demonstrate a relaxation of upper-class concert hall values to a more accessible, middlebrow presentation of entertainment where one can relax and, perhaps, play.

The performance of *Guitar Hero* in *VGL* acts out Austin's statement regarding the "preposterous" and is a direct realization of video games' infiltration of the concert hall. Through the orchestral presentation of video game music in the concert hall environment, the concert hall has opened itself up to the application of gamification as a means of producing a level of interactivity reminiscent of the music's original medium. As demonstrated by *Space Invaders* and *Frogger*, this gamification risks the musical performance becoming background to the audience-performer. However, the *Guitar Hero* segment shows that gamification can create a new musical focus in the concert hall whereby audience members can become not only more involved but also more aware of their impact on the musical outcome and concert experience. Gamification can even allow for video games to come full circle and reach their simulation goals in the real world.

While *VGL* is not the only video game concert to attempt to gamify the concert experience, the case studies discussed here demonstrate that the implementation of gameplay mechanics in *VGL* has successfully created a "game-like feel" and incited play in an effective manner that has not yet been seen in other video game music concerts. Yet, due to *VGL*'s "remarkable level of cultural penetration" (Gibbons 2020), other concerts may follow this example and similar efforts toward gamifying the concert experience may soon appear, meaning that the regular gamification of the orchestral concert experience could be on the horizon. We may already be seeing the ripples of *VGL*'s impact. Would, for instance, *Journey LIVE* have been even dreamed of without *VGL* first demonstrating that live video game play in the concert hall can be successful? In addition, *VGL* proves that gamification can be successfully implemented outside of the restricted parameters currently discussed by scholars in relation to the topic and that further scholarship examining such varying implementations of gamification would be fruitful. Furthermore, as more video game concerts are produced, there is the potential for each to utilize different game mechanics in the orchestral environment previously constrained by a modern and restrictive code of conduct. Although it is likely that gamification will always be controversial, precisely because of the rules that govern this space, it also provides the potential for a wealth of new and exciting ways of experiencing an orchestral concert of video game music and one day, perhaps, traditional classical music.

Notes

1. The increasing speed of the alien ships which allowed for the dynamic music we hear in *Space Invaders* was in fact a happy accident, as the early game processor's ability to generate speed increased when less aliens were needed to be drawn on the screen (Lerner 2013).

References

Arsenault, Dominic. 2008. "*Guitar Hero*: 'Not Like Playing Guitar at All'?" *Loading* 2, no. 2 (March). https://journals.sfu.ca/loading/index.php/loading/article/view/32.

Austin, Michael. 2016. "Introduction—Taking Note of Music Games." In *Music Video Games: Performance, Politics, and Play*, edited by Michael Austin, 1–22. New York: Bloomsbury Academic.

Böcker, Thomas, Melanie Fritsch, and Tim Summers. 2021. "Producing Game Music Concerts." In *The Cambridge Companion to Video Game Music*, edited by Melanie Fritsch and Tim Summers, 424–432. Cambridge: Cambridge University Press.

Cheng, W. 2013. *Sound Play: Video Games and the Musical Imagination*. New York: Oxford University Press.

Collins, Karen. 2007. "In the Loop: Creativity and Constraint in 8-Bit Video Game Audio." *Twentieth-Century Music* 4, no. 2 (September): 209–227. https://doi.org/10.1017/S147857220 8000510.

Collins, Karen. 2008. *Game Sound: An Introduction to the History, Theory, and Practice of Video Game Music and Sound Design*. London: MIT Press.

Collins, Karen. 2013. *Playing with Sound: A Theory of Interacting with Sound and Music in Video Games*. Cambridge, MA: MIT Press.

Deterding, Sebastian. 2014. "Eudaimonic Design, or: Six Invitations to Rethink Gamification." In *Rethinking Gamification*, edited by Mathias Fuchs, Sonia Fizek, Paolo Rufino, and Niklas Schrape, 305–331. Lüneberg: Meson Press.

Dozal, Mario A. 2016. "Consumerism Hero: The 'Selling Out' of *Guitar Hero* and *Rock Band*." In *Music Video Games: Performance, Politics, and Play*, edited by Michael Austin, 127–152. New York: Bloomsbury Academic.

Fonarow, Wendy. 2006. *Empire of Dirt: The Aesthetics and Rituals of British and Indie Music*. Middletown, CT: Wesleyan University Press.

Gibbons, William. 2016. "Remixed Metaphors: Manipulating Classical Music and Its Meanings in Video Games." In *Ludomusicology: Approaches to Video Game Music*, edited by Michiel Kamp, Tim Summers, and Mark Sweeney, 198–222. Sheffield: Equinox.

Gibbons, William. 2018. *Unlimited Replays: Video Games and Classical Music*. New York: Oxford University Press.

Gibbons, William. 2020. "Rewritable Memory, Concerts, Canons, and Game Music History." *Journal of Sound and Music in Games* 1, no. 1 (January). https://doi.org/10.1525/jsmg.2020.1.1.75.

Goethe, Ole. 2019. *Gamification Mindset*. Cham: Springer. https://doi.org/10.1007/978-3-030-11078-9.

Grasso, Julianne. 2020. "On Canons as Music and Muse." *Journal of Sound and Music in Games* 1, no.1 (January). https://doi.org/10.1525/jsmg.2020.1.1.82.

Hunt, Elizabeth. 2017. "From the Console to the Concert Hall: Interactivity, Nostalgia and Canon in Concerts of Video Game Music." MRes dissertation, University of Liverpool: Liverpool.

Hunt, Elizabeth. 2022. "My Childhood Is in Your Hands: Videogame Concerts as Commodified and Tangible Nostalgic Experiences." In *Nostalgia and Videogame Music: A Primer of Case Studies, Theories, and Analyses for the Player-Academic*, edited by Can Aksoy, Sarah Pozderac-Chenevey, and Vincent E. Rone, 68–84. Bristol: Intellect.

Lerner, Neil. 2013. "The Origins of Musical Style in Video Games, 1977–1983." In *The Oxford Handbook of Film Music Studies*, edited by David Neumeyer, 319–347. Oxford: Oxford University Press.

Lerner, Neil. 2014. "Mario's Dynamic Leaps: Musical Innovations (and the Specter of Early Cinema) in *Donkey Kong* and *Super Mario Bros.*" In *Music in Video Games: Studying Play*, edited by K. J. Donnelly, William Gibbons, and Neil Lerner, 1–29. London: Routledge.

Matalloui, Amir, Nicolai Hanner, and Rüdiger Zarkenow. 2017. "Introduction to Gamification: Foundations and Underlying Theories." In *Gamification: Using Game Elements in Serious Contexts*, edited by Stefan Stieglitz, Christoph Lattemann, Susanne Robra-Bissantz, Rüdiger Zarkenow, and Tobias Brockmann, 3–18. Cham: Springer. https://doi.org/10.1007/978-3-319-45557-0.

Miller, Kiri. 2012. *Playing Along: Digital Games, YouTube and Virtual Performance*. Oxford: Oxford University Press.

Phillips, W. 2014. *A Composer's Guide to Game Music*. Cambridge, MA: MIT Press.

Ross, Daniel. 2015. *Classic FM Handy Guides: Video Game Music*. London: Elliott and Thompson Limited.

Sarkar, Samit. 2016. "How Austin Wintory Brought *Journey LIVE* to Life." *Polygon*, February 16, 2016. https://www.polygon.com/features/2016/2/16/10970474/journey-live-austin-wintory-fifth-house-ensemble-kickstarter.

Small, Christopher. 1998. *Musicking: The Meanings of Performing and Listening*. Hanover, NH: University Press of New England.

Summers, Tim. 2016. *Understanding Video Game Music*. Cambridge: Cambridge University Press.

Video Games Live. n.d. Accessed August 5, 2021. https://www.videogameslive.com.

Wagener, Andreas. 2012. "Why Do People (Not) Cough in Concerts? The Economics of Concert Etiquette." *ACEI Working Paper Series* 2, no. 5 (December). http://www.culturaleconomics.org/wp-content/uploads/2019/01/AWP-05-2012.pdf.

Walz, Stephen, and Sebastian Deterding, eds. 2014. *The Gameful World*. Cambridge, MA: MIT Press.

Whalen, Zach. 2004. "Play Along—An Approach to Videogame Music." *Game Studies* 4, no. 1 (November). http://www.gamestudies.org/0401/whalen/.

Games

Dear Esther. Microsoft Windows et al. Thechineseroom, 2012.

Frogger. Arcade. Konami, 1981.

Guitar Hero III: Legends of Rock. PlayStation 2 et al. Neversoft, 2007.

Guitar Hero: Aerosmith. PlayStation 2 et al. Neversoft, 2008.

Guitar Hero: Van Halen. PlayStation 2 et al. Underground Development, 2009.

Journey. PlayStation 3. Thatgamecompany, 2012.

Rock Band. Xbox 360 et al. Harmonix, 2007.

Space Invaders. Arcade. Taito, 1978.

CHAPTER 34

UNREAL PERFORMANCES

Playing in Games/Playing with Games

JAMES COOK

Introduction

Integral, narrative-driven representations of concert performance—that is, diegetic musical performances—have long been a part of video games. Consider, for example, opera scenes in games ranging from *Final Fantasy VI* (1994) to *Assassin's Creed 3* (2012).[1] This crossing of boundaries is far from one way; concerts of video game music are now well established, with their own complex concert etiquettes and fandoms (see also chapter 32 and chapter 33 this volume).[2] We thus increasingly see representations of concerts in video games, and hear video game music in concerts—but what of the growing practice of using video game technology to produce live, or ostensibly live, concert events?

Music and virtuality constitute a well-worn topic of research,[3] even if, due to evolution of the media, there is always more material which might add to, or challenge, our understanding. But the ludic aspect, play, forms an integral yet often overlooked part of these virtual performances, and so too is gaming culture itself an integral dimension. In this chapter I explore several case studies, from concert performance within online platforms such as *Second Life* (2003) and games such as *Fortnite* (2017), to "live" concert performance by virtual avatars such as Gorillaz and Hatsune Miku, to my own experience of using Virtual Reality to reconstruct lost concert spaces for historically informed performance.[4] Each case study is markedly different—spawned from different impetuses and encompassing different angles of performance using gaming technology. Nonetheless, they are all linked by a ludic—and indeed metaleptic—extension of space into the realm of the virtual, "space" being taken to refer not just to geographical space, but the kind of social space occupied by fans, which crosses between the virtual and the real world.

Live Concert Performances within Game Environments: *Second Life* and the Birth of Virtual Concerts

One of the earliest platforms to exploit the possibilities for concert performance within a game world was *Second Life* (or *SL*). Released in 2003 by Linden Lab, *SL* offers an unscripted open world, allowing "residents" to generate their own content and narratives. They live as avatars—often human, but also a variety of more fantastical options—who interact with a virtual world. During its peak, many real-world locations were programmed into the game, especially educational and arts institutions, which explored activities such as virtual teaching.[5]

SL has a fairly well developed economy. Its currency, the Linden Dollar, is used to buy goods and services but can be converted back into real-world currency. As early as 2006, Ailin Graef (better known by the name of her avatar Anshe Chung) become the first person to have made $1 million via virtual real estate sales (Parloff 2006).[6] Many people run businesses selling virtual goods: buildings, vehicles, devices, even animations and skins, or virtual services such as business management, entertainment, and custom content creation. This developed economic system and the active virtual life of residents made *SL* fertile ground for early experiments in virtual art consumption, including music.

As Gagen and Cook (2016, 191–192) have noted, there was a (brief) heyday in which real-world companies noted the potential for marketization: Sony BMG acquired their own island, which featured concerts from Suzanne Vega, Lang Lang, and the Liverpool Philharmonic, among others. The much-publicized and streamed concert by the pianist Lang Lang was attended by only a handful of avatars; technical constraints would normally have limited an audience to no more than 40 avatars, even if the concert were "sold out." Real-world value for large-scale music industry operators therefore did not lie in the reproducibility of real-world business models, but instead in the fashionableness of virtual events. The 2008 financial crash put an end to much of this experimentation, as corporations began to review their presence in *SL* (2016, 191–192). Nonetheless, music performance has continued unabated in *SL*, in various settings and with various degrees of formality—all divorced from the world of major music labels. It is these more informal, or at least noncorporate musical events that laid the groundwork for the later involvement of Sony (etc.), and they continue to this day, even after *SL* has lost a degree of its shine for the wider world.

The early history of live music performance in *SL* has not yet been told by academics, but it is fairly easily recoverable from blog discussions within the *SL* community (Homeless Martian 2009, January 11). A full discussion of the various milestones is not possible in this chapter, but an outline of important staging posts may be instructive. In general, this history shows live performance moving into *SL* gradually, through the initiative of individual musicians, prior to the involvement of major commercial institutions and increased crossover between the virtual and the real worlds.

The earliest live performance in *SL* was by jazz musician Astrin Few (Sam Hokin) in April 2004, playing guitar. Initially, according to Few, this was "just playing some tunes for friends," rather than any kind of formal performance event (Homeless Martian 2009, January 18). The same month, he played the platform's first in-world, live music event, at a party hosted by Sally Zapata, with tickets purchased through a cancer benefit auction. Nineteen people were present at what was, by default, the largest virtual concert in history. In February 2005, few collaborated with Flaming Moe (Brian Tervo) on the first virtual duet at an event hosted by Drift Monde and Cua Curie. Few, who lived in Wisconsin (USA), had sent his guitar and vocal stream to Flaming Moe, in Florida (USA). Flaming Moe mixed in his own performance on saxophone, and the result was then streamed to *SL* listeners as a ticketed concert entitled "Alone Together" (tickets cost 250 Linden dollars).[7] Part of the concert was recorded by the audience member and host Cua Curie, and could, as of November 2021, still be watched on YouTube.[8] The video reveals that the presentation of the virtual concert is traditional—the guitar- and saxophone-playing avatars sit on stage in front of an audience (albeit with movements that bear no resemblance to their actual playing). Astrin Few thanks the audience for coming while playing softly on the guitar. As the track begins in earnest, our view of the proceedings usefully pans back, allowing us to see the audience: some dance together, others dance alone, while others still sit at tables listening. Overall, the framing experience is practically identical to a similar real-world setting, even if the technology at this point limited opportunities for genuinely live musical interaction between the players.

A month later, in March 2005, the availability of live video streaming expanded the possibilities for performance. In July, *The Lily Pad Lounge* opened, the first music-specific venue that provided a regular music performance spot. Many virtual music venues have since opened, catering to wide tastes; at the time of writing, 53 offer regular live performance (Second Life Live Musician Spots, 2022). Later in 2005, Frogg Marlowe released two CDs of material recorded at *The Lily Pad Lounge*, which were sold in the real world—an unusual crossover of material recorded live in a virtual space being sold in the real world.[9]

Not long after, in 2006, Erik Pasternak founded the first virtual record label, MetaVerse Records. By then, music events had become so ubiquitous in *SL* that a Live Music section was added to the regular events list. In May of that year, the first *SL* festival Celtic Lights Music Fest took place, followed in the same month by Radio One's Big Weekend, which took place in Dundee (Scotland) but was streamed live into an *SL* virtual stage. By this time Suzanne Vega and Duran Duran had become the first well-known, real-world popular musicians to perform in *SL*, triggering a series of bands doing live previews of real-world albums, releasing their material simultaneously in both the real world and *SL*, and/or doing promotional tours of real-world material in-game.

The process of crossing between the real-world and the virtual has been described, in reference to the band Gorillaz, as metalepsis—a term from narratology that refers to the process of transgressing boundaries between narrative levels or distinct worlds (Hofer

2011, 239–242). This may be seen to apply here, especially when concerts by avatars which take place in *SL* are streamed into the real world, or vice versa—though, as we will see below, this process can be taken to more obvious lengths.

Even if the heyday of convergence between major real-world organizations and performers did not last long, performance within *SL* has continued. Nonetheless, one might question its attraction. As noted elsewhere, lag can produce a formidable barrier to liveness, or even vague synchronization between image and sound (Gagen and Cook 2016, 196–200). And it has even been questioned whether music in *SL* is truly performed there—since it generally must be produced in the real world and played back in *SL* (200–206). Streaming music online was nothing new in the early 2000s, and many of the earliest performances in *SL* were not live in the sense that we might generally conceive it. Nonetheless, residents clearly perceived *something* about them which went beyond simply streaming music online. The explosion of live performance events, increasing in complexity, "liveness," and interactivity demonstrates a genuine interest in the exploration of this form of event. Many would point to "presence" in an attempt to explain this widespread interest, but this is a far from simple term, in part since the relationship between a person and their avatar is neither simple nor equivalent for each user. In their work on the "avatar–self" relationship in *SL*, Schultze and Leahy (2009, 4) have usefully divided presence into two categories—"telepresence" and "social presence," suggesting that:

> Telepresence . . . captures the interaction between the communicator and his/her avatar and thus has implications for immersion in virtual spaces, and
>
> Social presence . . . captures the interaction between the communicator, in avatar form, and others and thus has implications for the communicator's (re)presentation of self.

Crucially, they have demonstrated that "communicators in virtual worlds adopt different stances towards their avatar in response to various personal and situational stimuli that emanate from both their real and 'second' life. Furthermore, they cycle through a variety of avatar-self couples, particularly on the telepresence dimension" (Schulze and Leahy 2009, 14).[10] Through a series of interviews with *SL* residents, the authors identified the following stages along a continuum from segmented to augmented interaction between the avatar and the self—in other words, whether the user felt truly at one with their avatar and therefore had maximal presence within *SL*. These stages range, at the level of social presence, from viewing the avatar as "virtual self" (that is, a virtual extension of the self), through a possible/ideal/true self (an extension of the self which might allow the user to explore alternative aspects of their persona), to merely a character which sits entirely separate from their own sense of self. At the dimension of telepresence, there seems to be a greater level of variance, ranging from the invisible avatar (during which the user essentially becomes unaware of the avatar, entirely collapsing the sense of separateness between them and the self), through the avatar as an object of reflection (where they are essentially used for the user to reflect on their real-life selves, often through trying out alternative physical appearances), to the avatar as repository of capital (in which the avatar is seen primarily as an investment of time and money), to the autonomous agent, where the avatar exists entirely separately from the user's sense of self or, as one user put it, that they are "an independent being that **has** an avatar" (11, emphasis original).

Social presence seems to provide much of the attraction for live performance in *SL*. As results from a survey of residents carried out by Gagen and Cook (2016) showed, people certainly felt present as part of the crowd in these events—more so than if they were simply streaming music. Unlike during *SL* events, when streaming, listeners were likely to find themselves "cleaning off the top of a desk, balancing a check book, etc. You aren't completely transported to the event as you are in SL" (196). Others pointed to crowd presence as being somehow more real or more intense than real life: "There is an intimacy and sharing with live performance in SL that I have never seen or felt in RL. . . . I suppose primarily because we can talk without 'interrupting' the performance, even when we talk directly to the performer" (197). Some felt that the crowd's experience was far more positive, noting that, in real life, "crowds can be uncomfortable and oppressive, and it's harder to feel any sense of communal experience when it's impossible—and rude—to communicate in any way" (197).

The various technical limitations of the platform constrain many of the traditional real-world markers of liveness. Gagen and Cook (2016, 205) have instead called for a new "performance ecology"[11] for liveness in virtual reality, noting that an effective approach to creating liveness within virtual reality is not to replicate the conditions of liveness in the real world, but rather to "recontextualize the signifiers of liveness, configuring them anew in light of the affordances and constraints of the new medium" (205). Paul Sanden (2013) has produced a useful overview of the conditions for liveness in modern performance. Many of his characteristics of liveness can helpfully be applied even to virtual performance such as this. "Corporeal liveness" can be extended to the audience through the dancing of an *SL* audience, assuming that the avatar is understood as embodied. "Spatial liveness," although seemingly problematic since performer and audience are explicitly not in the same physical space, is clearly possible if we extend the notion of spatiality to virtual spaces—and indeed there are ways to enhance this feeling of inhabiting shared virtual space. Sanden even offers the category of "virtual liveness," noting that "music can be *live* in a virtual sense even when the conditions for its liveness . . . do not *actually* exist. Virtual liveness, then, depends on the perception of a liveness that is largely created *through* mediatization" (Sanden quoted in Gagen and Cook 2016, 201). That is clearly the case here. The music is construed as live largely because its audience agrees that it is, having reformulated and reconditioned the signifiers of liveness for their own particular musical community.

The key aspect of this musical liveness is social presence and interactivity which elevate *SL* music events beyond simply listening to streamed music—or even, for some, beyond real-life live performances. Trevor Harvey (2016, 184), for instance, suggests a somewhat utopian understanding, noting that, "within musical events, *Second Life* musicians construct [. . .] 'cybersituations,' participatory engagement within sociomusical settings that resist the passivity and alienation inherent within the spectacle of mass-mediated musical culture."[12] Such positive reflections on the relative degree of "activeness" of the audience are clearly mirrored in some of the interview responses noted above.

By the 2010s, the concept of the virtual *SL* performances was well accepted. Nonetheless, even at the heyday of progressively more famous real-world musicians entering into *SL*, the numbers involved remained relatively small. More recent games have propelled the concept of the virtual concert to new heights, though we see many of the same paradigms at work here.

The Virtual Concert Goes Mainstream

The live concert experience within a game world arguably had its watershed moment in early 2018, when the success of *Fortnite*'s (2017) first in-game concert may be seen to have upended traditional assumptions about the viability of game-world concerts. After its release, *Fortnite* quickly came to dominate the emerging market for online, multiplayer third-person shooters. To an extent, music and performance has always been a part of *Fortnite*, and indeed are integral to the broader culture that surrounds it; dancing via the use of "emotes" (dances or movements selected from a menu intended to convey an emotion) is a ubiquitous part of the game. As Marshall (2019) has noted, *Fortnite* dances have a complicated life which crosses boundaries between the virtual and the real (3–15). The majority of the emotes are derived from "grassroots dance culture" (3) in the real world before being co-opted from the game. Key examples include the "Swipe," which began life as the "Milly Rock," popularized by rapper $_2$Milly. This dance began life in a viral video, and quickly gained popularity through rap videos and real-life events. In the virtual world of *Fortnite*, this dance has continued to spread through gamer culture via social media, as memes, and in real life.[13] Music, then, and wider cultures which depend on music, is present both within the game and within the broader culture surrounding it.

The development of in-game concerts should be understood in the context of a gaming culture in which dance and music are tightly enmeshed. In February 2018, Chris Comstock (DJ Marshmello) performed the first live virtual concert in *Fortnite*. It was a roaring success, with 10.7 million active live users watching the 10-minute set (Webster 2019). Many others watched via the livestream service Twitch, and at the time of writing, a YouTube recording of the event has nearly 59 million views.[14] It was successful for DJ Marshmello too; according to Songkick, the event drove a 3,000% increase in page views for the artist, catapulting him to the most visited artist on the platform. He also saw an increase of 62,000 followers on Twitter, a 5,200 growth on Twitch, and two days later he had gained nearly 260,000 followers on Instagram (Stephan 2019). Clearly the lure of the virtual concert was significant for players of the game, but it also was useful to bring the artist to the attention of new fans. That Comstock was a self-confessed fan of the game and sees himself as deeply embedded within gaming culture may also have contributed to the success of the event. This was an insider-event, performed by a fan for fans, making use of the clear adjacency of music to the gaming experience offered by *Fortnite*. The first concert in *Fortnite* might be seen as an extension of the normal behavior of both the players and the game world, exactly as it was in *SL*. It drew on an already accepted social presence within the game world and merely extended wider musical cultures already present.

The way the concert was put together is an example of the blurring between the virtual and real world. The concert was held in the in-game location of Pleasant Park and was gradually teased in the period before it went live. Three "Showtime Challenges" were released in the run-up, which provided in-game, Marshmello-themed material. The first involved finding posters for the virtual concert (see Figure 34.1). Finding one of these provided the "Mello Made It Right" Spray (i.e., graffiti showing DJ Marshmello that players could spray on surfaces in the game world). Visiting the Showtime venue provided the "Keep It Mello" emote. Finally, performing "Keep It Mello" at three different locations would give a "Marshy Smasher" harvesting tool—essentially a giant Marshmello-themed hammer. Completing these challenges has a twofold effect, the player has been forced to collect a poster advertising the gig and, in going to the "showtime location," has seen the erection of the stage (see Figure 34.2); they have also equipped themselves with themed merchandise for the concert itself. The virtual concert deliberately included many of the trappings of a real-world gig. It did not need to be advertised via virtual representations of real-world posters which, as with their real-world counterparts, were simply stuck to walls. Instead, all advertising could have taken place in the real world. Similarly, there was no need to "build" a stage at all for the concert: it was entirely possible to create it in-game immediately.

FIGURE 34.1 A DJ Marshmello concert poster, taken from https://www.gamespot.com/articles/fortnite-showtime-posters-venue-keep-it-mello-loca/1100-6464718/.

FIGURE 34.2 The stage at Pleasant Park, taken from https://www.forbes.com/sites/davidthier/2019/01/30/fortnite-is-already-building-the-stage-for-the-marshmello-concert-at-pleasant-park/?sh=709cfb66776a.

All these activities create an environment as close to the traditional real-world concert as possible—something which the addition of themed "concert merchandise" also helped. Back in the real world, DJ Marshmello added the *Fortnite* location "Pleasant Park" to his tour dates, with nothing to differentiate it from a real-world concert. This seems to be part of a deliberate process of bringing the real world and the virtual into near adjacency, mimicking the real-world set-up of a concert in the virtual world on the one hand and advertising it *as* a real-world concert on the other. This helps to create a liminal space for metalepsis, where performer and audience can transition freely between worlds.

The staging enhances this effect. The stage looks like a real-world stage, replete with plenty of skeuomorphic aspects, such as large speaker stacks and turntable.[15] The lighting effects, from screened text and image, to dancing holographic projections, and beam lighting, are carefully constructed so as to appear entirely plausible within a real-world setting. Light beams emanate from visible light sources; the holographic projections stand over projection boxes; and the screens behave as one would expect backdrop screens at a concert. None of this is required, of course. Lighting can be programmed to appear without lights—and holographic projections can simply appear anywhere they are desired.

Perhaps due to the deliberate trappings of the in-person concert, attendance at the virtual concert largely followed established concert behavior. The use of weapons was banned to avoid the event turning into a bloodbath (which it subsequently did after the concert finished and the enforced peace lifted), and the game allowed automatic respawns in the case of accidental deaths. Both decisions allowed for the concert to be the sole focus of attention for the millions of players who danced and interacted with each other and the DJ, responding to calls for certain dance moves from Marshmello. The two-way interaction between performer and audience encapsulated the sense of liveness (itself somewhat illusory, since Marshmello would not have been able to see more than a selected handful of avatars at any one time) and mirrored real-world expectations. Marshmello began the set with the words "Yo, what is up Fortnite? What's up Pleasant Park? My name is Marshmello and thank you for coming out today and making history with me. You guys ready?"—precisely what we might expect at the start of any real-world concert. After the initial drop, he addressed his audience "let me see everybody moving," later saying "alright, when this song drops, I want to see everyone jump with me, I want to see you jumping. Let's go!"—and jump they did, to great and immediate visual effect. This sense of communal action is of course one of the great attractions of live concert events, as well as helping to increase a sense of presence in the video game. Indeed, this seems to tie most directly to the concept of "social presence"—the players feel part of a community within the game world, with a shared lingua franca, and common actions and aesthetics. As with early concert experiences in *SL*, we again see what Sanden describes as "virtual liveness" through this social presence.

As well as the trappings of real-world concert attendance, and a surprisingly literal approach to copying real-world staging, the game also sought to exploit the various affordances of the virtual world. Those jumping in time with Marshmello's calls found moments where the force of gravity was lessened in time with the music, allowing them to jump much higher than usual. Combined with the stage pyrotechnics, the effect was impressive—and not something possible in real-life. Marshmello's performance style seems to have been modified to take into account the affordances of the staging of the event. If anything, his calls to the crowd for certain actions were more numerous and direct than would be expected at a real-world event, helping to drive a greater sense of participation; in a sense, calling particularly strongly on Sanden's (2013) "interactive liveness" (87–112) to compensate for the perceived absence of some other forms.[16] They were also conspicuously targeted at *Fortnite* players: "I want to see everyone doing your favorite emote right now, when this drops." Nonetheless, we can hardly escape the conclusion that this was in essence a "real-world" concert event, dropped into the virtual space of *Fortnite* with only small changes made to exploit both the physical possibilities offered by the game mechanics and the social contingencies of the game world. In many ways, we might see this as paralleling the early development of live performance in *SL*, drawing on conventions of performance in the real world and pulling them into a newly virtual setting.

Following the overwhelming success of the DJ Marshmello concert, Travis Scott hosted a concert experience, titled "astronomical," in April 2020. This event broke the earlier record with more than 12 million watching opening night (Webster 2020); further dates were launched almost immediately, turning the concert into a miniature tour. In the end, 27.7 million watched the five-night tour live in-game, and over 154 million have since watched on YouTube (Goslin 2020). As with the DJ Marshmello concert, this event began with the trappings of a real-world gig. The stage was gradually built on the in-game location "Sweaty Sands." As players visited the area over the week leading to the concert, they could watch the stage gradually being built. Again, a series of three challenges both drew players' attention toward the stage area (one involved visiting the stage and another jumping on each of five giant "Astro Heads" that formed part of the backdrop to the concert) and also provided themed emotes, sprays, and other merchandise.

Even if this concert started much like DJ Marshmello's, it soon developed into an entirely different experience. It began with similar staging but, if anything, was rather pared-back. The stage was conspicuously empty, showing instead a large circular "video screen" on which a cartoonish planet could be seen floating. Behind this screen, a planet—very much like that on-screen—snuck into view, while the screen revealed itself to be a portal, gradually pulling back to reveal the "real" planet emerging behind it. The planet drew closer, looming over both the stage and the whole island. At the opening of the song "Sicko Mode," an enormous purple meteor left the central speaker-like heart of the planet, and plummeted into the stage, blowing it up and launching the audience into the air (borrowing the reduced-gravity trick from the earlier concert). From this conflagration emerged an enormous, shirtless Travis Scott, who proceeded to roam the island freely. Any expectations of the "normal" concert experience were rapidly obliterated, instead replaced by an extremely creative presentation that made full use of the game world's ability to play with physics. During the concert, the viewer is transported underwater, as well as into space; the entire environment changes to give a fully immersive experience. The audience were able to move and interact with both each other and the performer, as with the Marshmello concert, though this time emotes were restricted, only allowing those which fit with the aesthetic being presented. Travis Scott was transformed into a giant, able to roam across the land, sea, and through space, as reality molded itself to his performance decisions.

As with the virtual concerts in *SL*, those in *Fortnite* appear to have begun as more directly analogous with those in the real world. They seemed to draw on the possibilities for increasing social interaction with a wider range of more distantly located people rather than the possibilities offered with regard to a more malleable reality. In other words, it is the social presence, rather than the telepresence which is initially important. In both examples, successive experiments with the medium begin to explore possibilities of telepresence offered by the platforms. Instead of direct copies of analog concerts, we begin to see deliberate departures from traditional modes of performance, exploring the myriad possibilities offered by the physical malleability of the game world.[17] In other words, we begin to see a new performance ecology as the signifiers of liveness within the *Fortnite* environment evolve. As with *SL*, these appear to have begun as closer to real-world signifiers, but quickly evolved to take account of all the possibilities offered by the virtual world. Initially, these changes seem to throw the illusionary nature of the "liveness" into sharp relief by emphasizing the artificiality of the performer and minimizing the trappings of the real-world concert. Instead, it serves to increase the sense of social presence through revealing shared opportunities offered by the game world as well as increasing the embodied liveness through audience interaction, and the sense of spatial liveness through a sense of spectacle.

Virtual Performers Outside of Game Environments

I wish now to step outside of performances of music by real-world musicians in a virtual game environment and discuss its inverse: virtual performers in real-world settings. This phenomenon has many crossovers with the kind of experience outlined above but is ultimately a quite different prospect. We may still understand this as part of a process of metalepsis, and we might again seek to understand the performers discussed here as avatars—but if we do, we must question if they function in the same way as those seen in *SL* and *Fortnite*. Are they characters, personae, simulacra, or some kind of assemblage?

Gorillaz and the Virtual Band

Arguably the most famous virtual performers are Gorillaz, created in 1998 by Damon Albarn and Jamie Hewlett. The band consists of four animated members: 2-D, Murdoc Niccals, Noodle, and Russel Hobbs. Albarn is the main musical contributor, and he works with a number of collaborators alongside Hewlett's visuals. The virtual band members all have distinct characters and occupy a tightly woven fictional universe. These characters appear in various venues, from music videos, to interviews, and even live virtual performance. According to Hewlett, the initial idea of a virtual band came from watching MTV, as a comment on what they saw as the virtuality of the music industry: "If you watch MTV for too long, it's a bit like hell—there's nothing of substance there. So we got this idea for a virtual band, something that would be a comment on that" (quoted in Gaiman 2005).

Virtuality, then, seems to have been a negative for Albarn and Hewlett—at least initially. Indeed, I would situate this negative outlook within a common trope in popular music scholarship, as well as fan and journalistic writing, of valuing "authenticity." As Moore (2002) has noted, this is always a heavily loaded value term, but one that is not always related to the musical text in question (209–223). To be an authentic popular musician, the artist must "speak the truth of their own situation . . . speak the truth of the situation of (absent) others; and . . . speak the truth of their own culture, thereby representing (present) others" (Moore 2002, 209). We may question, therefore, quite whose truth Gorillaz may be speaking. What is their own situation? And what is their own culture?

Moore's formulation of authenticity within rock discourse seems useful for understanding exactly how Gorillaz functions. Authenticity has come to define a style of writing or performance, associated in particular with the singer/songwriter, in which the attributes of both intimacy and immediacy are highly privileged (Moore 2002, 211). We conspicuously have neither here. The virtual persona sits directly between the artist and the audience, eliding both the intimate and the immediate aspects of the musical performance. Indeed, the other features of the "authentic" rock musician, such as "realism [or] lack of pretense" (211), are similarly lacking in a band who are explicitly both virtual and pretend. But this is, of course, the point. Gorillaz see themselves as a mirror held to the music industry, reflecting the artifice and artificiality they saw at the heart of musicians that presented as real.

This is not the whole story, of course. Gorillaz may have begun life as a sly comment on the music industry, but they have grown beyond that. In many ways, they can be seen as an embodiment of what Lawrence Grossberg (1993), citing the many personas of David Bowie in response to the commoditization of authenticity in the 1960s and early 1970s, has termed the "logic of authentic inauthenticity," in which "the only possible claim to authenticity is derived from the knowledge and admission of your inauthenticity" (205–206). The music that Gorillaz create is not a parody but rather a genuine and serious output, albeit by a fictional band. The band simultaneously present both their fictional identities and the reality of their nature, essentially holding both contradictory positions as true: their website reveals that they were created by Albarn and Hewlett, but also features fictional biographies of each of the animated members; the fictional character Murdoc's house, putatively located in Essex, once featured on an episode of MTV's *Cribs*, while a 2006 "autobiography" of the band was released containing fictional interviews with each of the members (Hofer 2011, 235–236). While there is no effort to hide the reality that these are characters created by Albarn and Hewlett, significant effort is expended on creating real and believable backstories. Hofer (2011, 236) has drawn comparisons between the way that the band is presented and the manner in which actors realize their characters. And to an extent this seems to the point—the virtual avatars are not, in any way, meant to be representations of the "real" personas behind them; they are clearly fictional characters, realized in much the same way as any other cartoon character, via a combination of acting and animation. In other words, these are not avatars of Albarn and Hewlitt, or if they are, they are imagined as standing at the far left of Schulz and Leahy's diagram of the avatar–self relationship: the autonomous agent and the scripted character.

Kelly (2007, 115) argues that "Gorillaz contribute to the demise of the modernist metanarrative of authorial presence in pop performance by making animated images, guest artists, shadow performers and avatars the locus of expression in a performance register that encourages active participation of the spectator in a variety of new ways." In many ways, this mirrors the "cybersituations," mentioned by Harvey (2016, 184) in connection with *SL*, in that it suggests "participatory engagement within sociomusical settings that resists the passivity and alienation inherent within the spectacle of mass-mediated musical culture." Again, there seems to be a suggestion of something almost utopian here in which the extension of space either into or out of the virtual realm invites a degree of participation greater than the real world alone.

In 2005, at the MTV Europe Music Awards in Lisbon, Gorillaz presented what was painted as a true first in music history a 3D hologram concert event. This event involved the band being presented from video projectors onto transparent foil, appearing to step out of the virtual world which they usually inhabited and onto the real-world stage.

The process of metalepsis here is clear; Gorillaz cross the boundary between the fictional animated world they inhabit, and the world of the MTV award stage. The animated cartoon band "transgress[es] from its restricted two-dimensional world into our three-dimensional one" (Hofer 2011, 237). In doing so, they act exactly as one would expect real rock performers—seemingly interacting with the crowd. The entrance of the (nonvirtual) rap-group De La Soul onto the same stage occupied by Gorillaz halfway through the performance further serves to underline this metalepsis. We have both virtual and "in-the-flesh" musicians occupying the same world, the 2D figures transgressing their dimensional boundaries, seemingly becoming 3D and occupying the same performance space as real musicians.[18] In the following year, Gorillaz performed using the same techniques at the Grammy Awards, again with De La Soul. In this performance, however, they were also supported by Madonna, with the performance eventually morphing into her own hit, "Hung Up." This performance doubles down on the metalepsis. The first time we see Madonna, she too is (unbeknownst to the audience) a projection on the foil. This allows her to move closer to the virtual band and to interact with them more directly than would be possible in reality. Later, following a clever change in scenery, she enters the stage in the flesh, transitioning seamlessly from the virtual, cartoon world and into real life. In essence, we have three different positions on a spectrum of real to virtual, all occupying the stage together. Gorillaz exist purely as animation, even if they are projected so as to seem real; Madonna appears real, though she is initially entirely virtual, but then transitions to being present in person; De La Soul, however, are always real—but are able to interact which each of the others through the apparently porous boundaries between the real and the virtual. Just as with *SL* and *Fortnite*, the stage becomes a site of metalepsis where audiences and musicians can travel between reality and virtual reality. In this case, it is the virtual performers who enter our world, rather than vice versa.[19]

Hatsune Miku and the Virtual Popstar

Hatsune Miku is a vocaloid software voicebank, created by Crypton Future Media and represented by their official anthropomorph, a 16-year-old girl with turquoise twintails. She uses (or indeed consists of) singing synthesis technologies, and is modeled on the Japanese voice actress Saki Fujita (Sabo 2019). She has become something of a phenomenon, particularly in Japan, as a virtual idol who has given concerts onstage as an animated projection. Hatsune Miku embodies the idea of unreal performance and virtuality in a number of ways. She is the product not only of multiple creators (the direction of Crypton Future Media, the technology of Yamaha, and the artistic design of manga artist Kei) but also exists in a state of almost perpetual (re)creation by her legion of active fans. In this regard, we might see her as moving a step beyond the virtuality of Gorillaz: this is not a cartoon virtual band, produced by actors under the overall creative control of one or two minds—single, curated personae, albeit virtual ones—but rather a virtual avatar who is continuously cocreated through fan behavior.

Crypton Future Media can tell us a lot about Miku: she is 16 years old, 5ft 2in, and weighs 93 lbs—but she is pure simulacrum. As a vocaloid, she offers the opportunity for the user to control voice samples to a high degree, creating, as Daniel Black (quoted in Sabo 2019, 68) describes, an "entirely new performance independently of the body from which it was originally collected. The words and expression are provided by the owner of the computer software, who turns the generic, mass-produced raw material of the voice to whatever end he or she desires." Hatsune Miku's existence began in 2007 at her official launch. Her name was chosen for its connotations meaning, roughly, "the first sound of the future" (Sabo 2019, 66). She exists simultaneously as voice synthesis software, as a fantasy character, and as a trademark. As noted above, Miku's voice comes from a real Japanese actress—but it is clear that Miku is in no way intended as a replica. As Lam notes, significant work took place to modify the vocal samples for their intended use:

> To develop a human-like singing voice for Miku, the Vocaloid developers digitized separable and transportable fragments of recorded voice and integrated them into a singer library. In the transmission of these fragments to Miku's voice, they were melodically modified and integrated with Miku's bodily expressions. Human voices are decomposed into binary codes and reassembled into the vocals of Hatsune Miku to mimic the naturalness of real human voices. The developers of the singing synthesis technology aim to generate the singing voice that imitates a human singer and to provide what human ones cannot do. (Quoted in Sabo 2019, 67)

The virtual character, too, looks nothing like Saki Fujita, and is purely the creation of an anime artist. Miku can be further distanced from other virtual personae such as *Gorillaz* by the way that persona is created. This is not, like Gorillaz, the product of actors creating animated characters that follow a unified artistic vision, or like Madonna at the Grammy Awards, who appeared as a virtual copy of an existing flesh-and-blood artistic persona into which the virtual copy seamlessly transitioned. As Zaborowski (2016, 111–112) notes, it is difficult to unpack Miku; the traditional understanding which divides between a person, character, and persona does not really pertain here since she is not a person (as she is not human), is not a character (since she transcends narrative boundaries), and is not a persona (since she does not mediate a real person; she does not stand for Saki Fujita). Instead, Miku is continuously cocreated, indeed recreated, by her legion of fans.

Content created for Miku, by fans, is licensed under Creative Commons and uploaded to the official Crypton Future Media website and other video sharing platforms. Combined with 3D animation software, such as *Miku Miku Dance* (Yu Higuchi, 2008), fans can create music videos featuring Miku, to accompany their own musical creations. As Sabo notes, this means she is very much a product of her own fanbase, who are essentially responsible for her creative output and its reception, as an extension of *doujin* culture—a focus on self-published derivative works which is an integral part of Japanese manga and anime fan culture (Sabo 2019, 69). In the case of Miku, the line between producer and consumer is blurred. Fan behavior is very much participatory; as Guga (2015,

40) notes, "participants are granted with a deeply personalized, satisfactory experience of disseminating parts of themselves through these artefacts they took part in making."

In her concert performances, Miku performs fan compositions that have made it to a playlist of her most popular songs. Fans therefore watch their own works back, works that have been shared across fan platforms—dissected, discussed, loved, and responded to—as Miku metaleptically leaps from the realm of the virtual and onto the stage before them. This seems to take the promise of the "participatory" live experience apparently offered by the virtuality of *SL* and *Gorillaz* one step further.

Again, it seems that much of the "liveness" of the event comes from the social presence of the crowd. As with *SL*, but in manifestly different way, the participatory culture is clearly key. There is metalepsis here, but rather than a transition from a world simply of virtual reality into true reality, instead Miku appears to transition between a kind of shared fantasy world, continuously created and recreated in the minds of her legions of fans—and realized in their artwork, songs, and videos—and the stage on which she performs.

Virtual Reality and the Search for "Authenticity"

The examples above have dealt both with metalepsis through the movement of virtual performers into the real world and real-world performances into the virtual. They nonetheless are all explicit about their virtuality, either of the setting or the avatar. At face value, this final section may seem to stand in direct contrast with its focus on an attempt at "authenticity." Nonetheless, it actually shares much in common with the approaches outlined above.

The UK Arts and Humanities Research Council-funded project "Space, Place, Sound and Memory: Immersive Experiences of the Past" and its follow-up "Hearing Historic Scotland"—both of which I led as principal investigator—sought to utilize gaming technology to recreate historical music performances, reconstructing the visual and acoustic environment in which they were initially produced. At face value, this effort uses VR technology only as a technical apparatus that can be deployed in the quest for some kind of historical fidelity. But, of course, this is not really the case. There is still, without a doubt, a degree of "play" and interactivity, for the audience is at the heart of the experience. As with the other examples, the experience is not truly live, but the conditions for liveness, as realized within a virtual performance ecology, act to produce an experience that may have the illusion of liveness, as per Sanden's concept of virtual liveness. What is more, the historical reality it presents is not only virtual but may indeed usefully problematize the very idea of historical "authenticity."

The "Space, Place, Sound, and Memory" project resulted in a full VR experience, available to the public via oculus headsets at Linlithgow Palace in Scotland,[20] as well as an album that was recorded and produced using the virtual acoustics, released by Hyperion Records.[21] Both focused on reconstruction of sacred Renaissance vocal performance.[22] The project sought to utilize the affordances of VR to recapture something of the multimodal or even multimedia experience of Renaissance sacred music. As the historical auditor would have moved through the sacred space—far more open than it is today, unencumbered by pews—they would have been moving through a richly decorated world of wall paintings and sculptures (Kirkman and Weller 2017). Early music performance was a fully immersive, perhaps even overwhelming, multimodal sensory experience. This multimodality is something that is generally lost in early music performance today, either on recordings or in live concerts. But, as we have seen above, virtual worlds often offer a means of transgressing, or at least reconfiguring, modern concert etiquette.

The way the performance space of the past was used was a far cry from our modern experience. Without the pews and other furniture, and further unencumbered by vastly different attitudes and expectations of worship, the auditor had far more agency to explore its bounds than we might otherwise have expected.[23] Again, virtual worlds can offer something of this peripatetic experience—and a sense of participation or play—otherwise impossible when following the conventions of modern concert etiquette or, when simply within the very different domestic setting, listening to recorded performance.

Another vitally important dimension of performance is acoustic. There is broad consensus among early music performers as to the kinds of performance acoustics that work well for this repertoire. Crucially, some scholarly opinions have begun to challenge these (see Zayaruznaya 2017), and the "Space, Place, Sound, and Memory" project has further problematized the assumption that many of the still-extant performance spaces that we might wish to use today have retained configurations that would have been familiar to our musical forebears. Our VR reconstruction, which seeks an accurate reconstruction of the acoustic, carries a markedly different acoustic from what might be considered a "normal" early music performance. It is significantly more intimate—far closer to the performance, and with much less reverb.

The process of virtual reconstruction for this project was complex and multifaceted. There is insufficient space to discuss the process in detail in this chapter, but it is nonetheless important to give a sense of some of the process. It began with the use of LIDAR technology to scan the now-ruined Chapel Royal at Linlithgow Palace. Using this technology, a minutely detailed model of the extant ruins can be produced (see Figure 34.3). This model is too detailed to be functional on anything but the most powerful computers, so it needed to be reduced to a lower-polygon model (see Figure 34.4). The LIDAR scanning also recorded high-resolution photography of the site, which could be overlaid on the structural model, providing a texture skin (see Figure 34.5).

This process gave a virtual reconstruction of the chapel, as it currently stands, which was navigable in both the Unity and Unreal gaming engines. In itself, this is a potentially useful device—it enables access to part of the building which is simply not accessible for those with mobility issues, or indeed those who are unable to travel to a specific part of

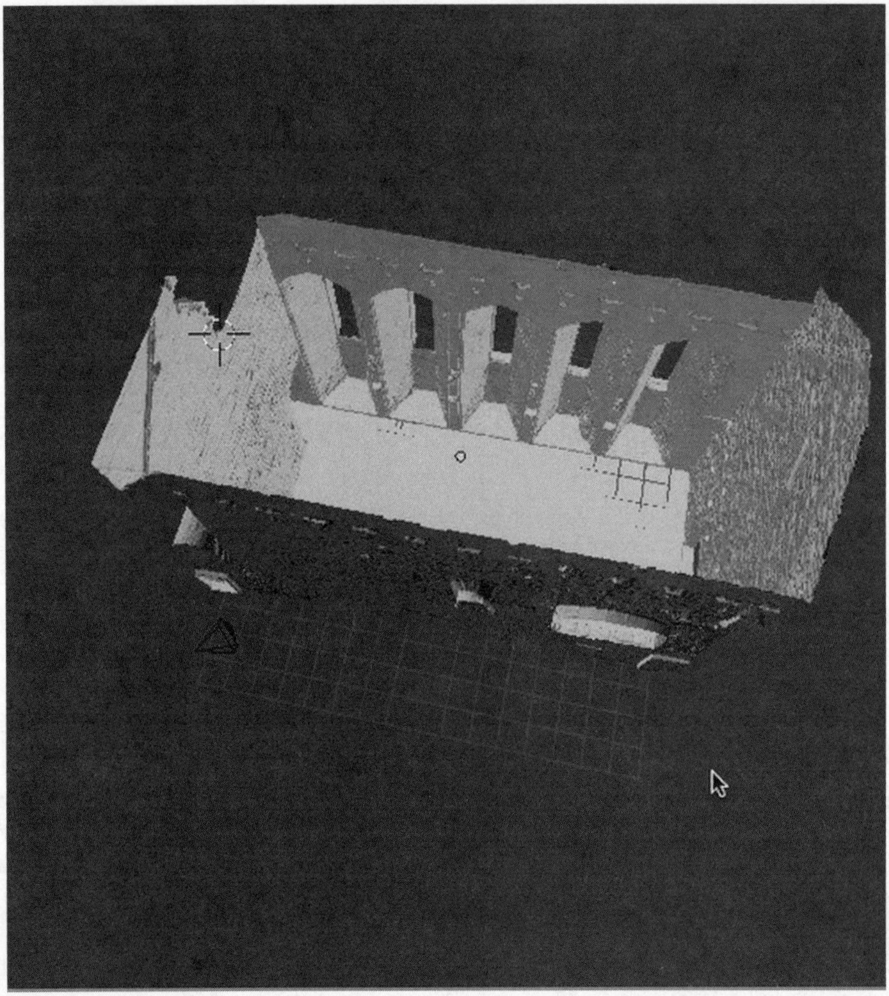

FIGURE 34.3 Lidar scan of Linlithgow Palace.

Scotland.[24] Nonetheless, it is a virtual reconstruction of something which does still exist and which, under normal circumstances, is already accessible. The project also sought to achieve the virtual reconstruction of something which no longer existed and—if we are honest with ourselves—almost certainly never did exist *exactly* in the manner reconstructed.

To produce the historical reconstruction, the team worked with archaeologists, historians, art historians, and archival records to reconstruct the building interior in as complete and historically accurate a manner as possible. Some of these aspects are virtual certainties, but other aspects are the product of intelligent guesswork. The result was then used to produce (initially within Unity but later ported to Unreal) a model that allows the player to move around a reconstruction of the chapel using an oculus headset.

FIGURE 34.4 A lower-polygon version of the model.

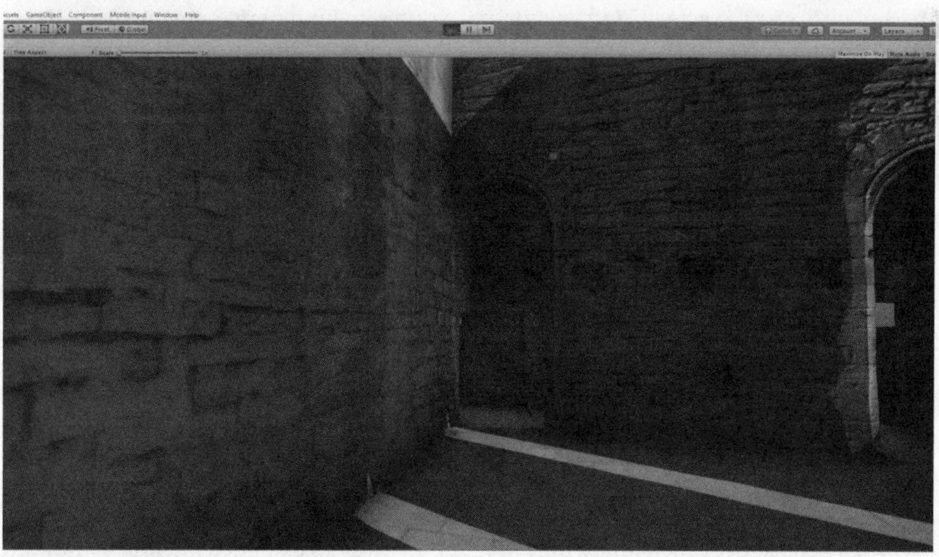

FIGURE 34.5 A virtual reality representation of the palace chapel in the present day.

Using an eye-tracking reticule, the user could transition between past and present to see how the space changed.

Once the visual reconstruction was created, we also worked to replicate the acoustic. All the surface areas of our model—both past and present—had to be tagged with material properties, detailing how certain frequencies were absorbed and scattered by each. This allowed us to produce a model acoustic for our reconstructed space. For our VR experience, we used plug-ins that worked with Unity and Unreal, as our acoustic model had to account for movement of the audience as they traversed the space; for our later album production we were able to use more accurate software (Odeon) since there was no necessity for a moving audience. Once our acoustic model had been derived, we recorded appropriate music in an anechoic chamber—a space with close to no natural acoustic—so that we might impose our reconstructed acoustic on the music, without interference from the acoustic of an intervening recording studio.

So, what might this virtual reconstruction tell us, both about VR and indeed any process of historical reconstruction more generally? What we are offered here, in reconstruction, does not exist without time travel. Beyond even that, even if we were to do the impossible and travel back to the past, what we experienced would not be what we experience in this VR reconstruction. As Hayden White (1988, 1193–1199) has reminded us when outlining the differences between historiography and historiophoty—history as written versus history as represented cinematically/visually—the visual medium may seem at once both too detailed and insufficiently detailed to convey history in the same way as the written word. Through its ability to present *everything* it reminds us of the extent to which all history relies on "filling in the gaps."[25] Nonetheless, I would argue that VR technology conditions a different kind of engagement to more obviously screen-based media, since it collapses the distance—both physical and imaginative—between the audience and the screen, and encourages a different kind of relationship with "presence." The attention to detail regarding the accurate reconstruction of both acoustics and lost multimedia aspects—which, along with the affordances of VR technology, gives an impression of "authenticity"—might somewhat contradictorily remind us of the artificiality of any kind of reconstruction. More broadly, we may agree with the description of virtual reality by McArthur, Steward, and Sandler (2017), as a kind of McLuhanian anti-environment, which serves to make us aware of the ways in which we normally take space for granted (26–40).

As with the other examples discussed above, a concert-like event seems to offer a site for metalepsis in which the viewer transitions into a virtual world. The VR experience is framed by drone footage of the palace, setting out the scientific and historical rationale for the project and offering us a liminal space through which we can step into the virtual performance. This rationale is important for giving a sense of social presence in what is—unlike the other case studies in the chapter—a solitary experience. It connects the experience of watching the performance event to the broader movement of historically informed performance practice and indeed may be seen as an extended attempt at the kind of framing usually used for early music concerts.[26] It therefore does provide at least the illusion of social presence, through the implication of interaction with a broader concert experience, presumably one shared with others, even if the viewer is very much alone in the performance event, with the performing avatars. Alongside this, the VR technology helps to give a sense of being embodied within the performance space, and so too does the ludic ability to move and interact, which helps build the sense of telepresence.

Conclusions

There are a number of themes that tie together the various aspects of "unreal performance" across this chapter. In each instance there is a clear sense of metalepsis, in which concert (or concert-like) events act as liminal space between the virtual and real world, through which audience and performer alike can step. The rituals and social norms of the various discrete performance cultures outlined in this chapter therefore serve as important gateways for this metalepsis. But there is also a sense in which the markers of liveness, and the norms of associated concert etiquettes, have been reconfigured to take account of a new performance ecology. Often this process relies on a sense of social presence, which can be heightened in comparison to the real world—but a sense of spatial liveness, or at least spectacle, is likewise important. Audiences want to feel that they inhabit the performance space, even if that space is virtual. Indeed, I would suggest that the virtual can blur the boundaries between social and spatial presence—sometimes the space being occupied is as much constructed socially and mentally in a virtual realm as it is visually. We certainly see this in the example of Hatsune Miku, through the participatory fan culture, but we arguably also see it in the case of the VR early music performance, where at least some of the enjoyment of the virtual experience seems to be in the pure imaginative potential of experiencing an event "as it really was."

It seems that we today stand at an exciting juncture for virtual performance. Taken together, the examples discussed above focus on the power of virtual realities to reconfigure almost every aspect of performance: the nature of the audience and its relationship to performance events; the performer; and the performance environment. As it currently stands, these explorations have often taken place divorced from one another, but we might ask what could be gained—or lost—from, for instance, a live performance of early music, within a virtually reconstructed historical performance venue, with an audience of multiple people, perhaps some of whom might even be "nonplayer characters."

Notes

1. For more on the use of opera in video games, see Summers (2018).
2. For an exploration of the impact of these music concerts on both canon formation and broader historiography of videogames, see Gibbons (2020); for a discussion of the process of developing game concerts from the perspective of a game concert producer, see Böcker, Fritsch, and Summers (2021).

3. For instance, Whiteley and Rambarran (2016).
4. Throughout this chapter "virtual reality" refers to a reality other than real, while "Virtual Reality" refers to specific headset-based technology which seeks to provide a virtual experience with less obvious mediation via a screen. It should be noted that the designation "concert" is not a contemporaneous description for the kinds of performance event that would have taken place in the space being reconstructed. I use it here for ease of comparison.
5. For an overview of teaching in *Second Life*, which covers the introduction of some of real-world institutions to the virtual world, see Cooke-Plagwitz (2008).
6. That is, USD rather than Linden Dollars.
7. The conversion rate between Linden and US dollars has remained fairly constant over the last decade at c. 240–270 L$ to 1$, see https://www.investopedia.com/terms/l/linden-dollar.asp.
8. The video, found at https://www.youtube.com/watch?v=MDcNoBcY_TE has since been made private.
9. To an extent my own VR project, described below, attempts the same though on a more commercial level.
10. For more on presence, see chapter 47 this volume.
11. For more on this term, see Butler (2014, 93–94).
12. For more on "cybersituations" see Best and Kellner (1999, 129–156).
13. As Marshall (2019) notes, most of these emotes must be bought as one of the many in-game purchases. That they initially seem to have derived from Black culture and to have been co-opted as a way of making vast profits for primarily white game developers continues a problematic discourse that has persisted almost since the start of popular music. That, as Marshall has discussed, many of these *Fortnite* dance trends have then been co-opted in cyber bullying and particularly into white supremacist subcultures adds a further problematic angle (3–5).
14. A recording is available at: https://www.youtube.com/watch?v=NBsCzN-jfvA.
15. It might be argued that most, if not all, visual aspects of this game (and perhaps of games in general) are skeuomorphic, but this is perhaps more pronounced in the above example. Given the acceptance of nondiegetic sound in game contexts, and the various alternative ways in which diegesis could be implied without recourse to the use of so many objects that were functionally useless in-game (but visually redolent of real-world concert production), this choice is striking.
16. We may see parallels here with Mark Butler's (2014) concept of "performing performance" (65–111).
17. There are clear parallels with the history of the music video, developing initially from early promotional videos such as The Beatles's "We Can Work It Out" (1965), which essentially mimicked live performance, toward the more creative and narratively inflected audiovisual experiments such as "Bohemian Rhapsody" (1975) a decade later, and arguably reaching a zenith with the contribution of Hollywood director John Landis to "Thriller" (1984), where the video eclipsed the song in terms of scope, length, and cultural impact.
18. This practice does, of course, have a long history in films such as *Who Framed Roger Rabbit* (1988) and *Cool World* (1992), though here framed as events taking place on screen perhaps helps to situate it still outside of the real world. The relatively recent phenomenon of posthumous performances by artists such as Elvis and Tupac is, of course, a further development of the same processes.

19. As an epilogue to this discussion, and by way of a taster of what is to follow, it is perhaps worth noting that Gorillaz were responsible for one of the earliest VR music videos for "Saturnz barz" (2017). In this, through the affordances of virtual reality, we complete the circle, traveling into the world of Gorillaz in the same manner that they have in the past traveled into ours. For more on this video, see Kamp (2021).
20. The availability is currently limited by closure of the palace to the public.
21. The CD can be purchased, or recordings downloaded, from: https://www.hyperion-records.co.uk/dc.asp?dc=D_CDA68333.
22. The project is also seeking to reconstruct Baroque concert experiences at a reconstruction of St Cecilia's Hall, Scotland's oldest purpose-built concert hall. This aspect of the project has been somewhat delayed by COVID.
23. This nature of the audibility of the music for different people experiencing an act of devotion has been explored by other projects, in more analogic fora, see "The Experience of Worship" project, accessible at www.experienceofworship.org.uk.
24. And it was afforded an unexpected level of usefulness as the COVID pandemic caused lengthy closure of the palace.
25. It is almost inconceivable that the minutiae of the details rendered within this VR experience can be 100% correct. Indeed, even if they were, it would not be the same experience. We are not medieval Christians, participating in an act of worship—we are modern listeners from a different culture and time, who bring entirely different aural baggage with us.
26. For more on this, see Cook (2018, 18–21).

REFERENCES

Böcker, T., Melanie Fritsch, and Tim Summers. 2021. "Producing Game Music Concerts." In *The Cambridge Companion to Video Game Music*, edited by Melanie Fritsch and Tim Summers, 424–432. Cambridge: Cambridge University Press.

Butler, M. 2014. *Playing with Something That Runs: Technology, Improvisation, and Composition in DJ and Laptop Performance*. Oxford: Oxford University Press.

Cook, James. 2018. "Representing Renaissance Rome: Beyond Anachronism in Showtime's *The Borgias* (2011)." In *Recomposing the Past: Representations of Early Music on Stage and Screen*, edited by James Cook, Alexander Kolassa, and Adam Whittaker, 17–31. New York: Routledge.

Cooke-Plagwitz, J. 2008. "New Directions in CALL: An Objective Introduction to Second Life." *CALICO Journal* 25 (3): 547557.

Gagen, J., and Nicholas Cook. 2016. "Performing Live in *Second Life*." In *The Oxford Handbook of Music and Virtuality*, edited by Sheila Whitely and Shara Rambarran, 192–206. New York: Oxford University Press.

Gaiman, N. 2005. "Keeping It (Un)real." *Wired*, July 1, 2005. https://www.wired.com/2005/07/gorillaz-2/.

Gibbons, W. 2020. "Rewritable Memory: Concerts, Canons, and Game Music History." *Journal of Sound and Music in Games* 1 (1): 75–81.

Goslin, A. 2020. "Fortnite's Travis Scott Event Drew over 27 Million Players: It's a New Fortnite Record." *Polygon*, April 24, 2020. https://www.polygon.com/fortnite/2020/4/24/21235017/fortnite-travis-scott-event-concert-astronomical-12-3-million-concurrent-players-record.

Grossberg, L. 1993. “The Media Economy of Rock Culture: Cinema, Post-Modernity, and Authenticity.” In *Sound and Vision: The Music Video Reader*, edited by Simon Frith, Andrew Goodwin, and Lawrence Grossberg, 185–209. New York: Routledge.

Harvey, T. S. 2016. “Avatar Rockstars: Constructing Musical Personae in Virtual Worlds.” In *The Oxford Handbook of Music and Virtuality*, edited by Sheila Whitely and Shara Rambarran, 171–189. New York: Oxford University Press.

Hofer, R. 2011. “Metalepsis in Live Performance: Holographic Projections of the Cartoon Band Gorillaz as a Means of Metalepsis.” In *Metalepsis in Popular Culture*, edited by Karin Kukkonen and Sonja Klimek, 232–251. Berlin and New York: De Gruyter.

Homeless Martian. 2009. “SL Music History: The Time Table.” *Homeless Martian's Blog*. https://homelessmartian.wordpress.com/2009/01/11/sl-music-history-the-time-tabel/.

Kamp, M. 2021. “Old(er) Media and New Musical Affordances in Virtual Reality Experiences.” In *The Oxford Handbook of Cinematic Listening*, edited by Carlo Cenciarelli, 712–731. Oxford: Oxford University Press.

Kelly, J. 2007. “Pop Music, Multimedia, and Live Performance.” In *Music, Sound, and Multimedia: From the Live to the Virtual*, edited by Jamie Sexton, 105–120. Edinburgh: Edinburgh University Press.

Kirkman, A., and Philip Weller. 2017. “Music and Image/Image and Music: The Creation and Meaning of Visual-Aural Force Fields in the Later Middle Ages.” *Early Music* 45 (1): 55–75.

Marshall, W. 2019. “Social Dance in the Age of (Anti-)Social Media: *Fortnite*, Online Video, and the Jook at a Virtual Crossroads.” *Journal of Popular Music Studies* 31 (4): 3–15.

McArthur, A., Rebecca Stewart, and Mark Sandler. 2017. “Sounds Too True to Be Good: Diegetic Infidelity—The Case for Sound in Virtual Reality.” *Journal of Media Practice* 18 (1): 26–40.

Moore, A. 2002. “Authenticity as Authentication.” *Popular Music* 21 (2): 209–223.

Parloff, R. 2006. “Anshe Chung: First Virtual Millionaire.” *Fortune*, November 27, 2006. https://fortune.com/2006/11/27/anshe-chung-first-virtual-millionaire/.

Sabo, A. 2019. “Hatsune Miku: Whose Voice, Whose Body?” *INSAM Journal of Contemporary Music, Art and Technology* 2 (1): 65–80.

Sanden, P. 2013. *Liveness in Modern Music: Musicians, Technology, and the Perception of Performance*. New York: Routledge.

Schultz, U., and Matthew Michael Leahy. 2009. “The Avatar-Self Relationship: Enacting Presence in Second Life.” *International Conference on Information Systems Proceedings* 12. https://aisel.aisnet.org/icis2009/12.

Stephan, B. 2019. “Fortnite Showed Us the Future (and the Past) of Live Music: Ten Million People Tuned in to Marshmello's Concert in Fortnite's Pleasant Park, and It Shows That Music's Next Act Is Virtual.” *Verge*, February 18, 2019. https://www.theverge.com/2019/2/18/18229471/fortnite-marshmello-pleasant-park-live-music-future-past.

Summers, T. 2018. “Opera Scenes in Video Games: Hitmen, Divas and Wagner's Werewolves.” *Cambridge Opera Journal* 29 (3): 253–286.

Webster, A. 2019. “ ‘Fortnite's Marshmello Concert Was the Game's Biggest Event Ever: More Than 10 Million People Watched the Virtual Performance.” *Verge*, February 21, 2019. https://www.theverge.com/2019/2/21/18234980/fortnite-marshmello-concert-viewer-numbers.

Webster, A. 2020. “More Than 12 Million People Attended Travis Scott's Fortnite Concert: A Record Breaking Performance.” *Verge*, March 23, 2020. https://www.theverge.com/2020/4/23/21233946/travis-scott-fortnite-concert-astronomical-record-breaking-player-count.

White, H. 1988. "Historiography and Historiophoty." *American Historical Review* 93 (5): 1193–1199.

Whitely, S., and Shara Rambarran, eds. 2016. *The Oxford Handbook of Music and Virtuality*. New York: Oxford University Press.

Zaborowski, R. 2016. "Hatsune Miku and Japanese Virtual Idols." In *The Oxford Handbook of Music and Virtuality*, edited by Sheila Whiteley and Shara Rambarran, 111–125. New York: Oxford University Press.

Zayaruznaya, A. 2017. "Intelligibility Redux: Motets and the Modern Medieval Sound." *Music Theory Online* 23 (2). https://www.mtosmt.org/ojs/index.php/mto/article/view/386.

CHAPTER 35

OF *GUITAR HEROES* AND *ROCKSMITHS*

Guitars, Games, and Affordance Theory

MARC DUBY

Introduction

This chapter explores guitar-playing and associated games such as *Guitar Hero* (2005) and *Rocksmith* (2011)[1] from the theoretical perspective of J. J. Gibson's ecological psychology, specifically drawing from his theory of affordances. Guitar-playing and guitarist-games are understood as practices informed by motor intentionality, allowing for a basis of comparison between flesh-and-blood and virtual interactions according to the different affordances these provide.

The chapter is structured in three sections. First, I discuss aspects of guitar heroism according to the ways in which innovative guitarists have creatively extended the possibilities the electric guitar affords. It seems apt to bring Gibson's theory of affordances into play, since this theory aims to unearth the tactile and sensorimotor aspects, among others, of engagements within specific environments. The various ways in which musicians interact with their chosen instruments represent to my mind special cases of affordance theory, which Gibson deployed in an open fashion, largely focusing his research on visual affordances. Engaging with such games from the theoretical standpoint of affordance theory seems a logical step.

Second, the electric guitar is considered as part of a network consisting of guitar, pedals, and amplifier technology, a combination that assists guitarists in forging a signature sound. The influence of various technologies in combination is briefly surveyed considering what Steve Waksman (2003b) has termed "the turn to noise."

Finally, I consider scholarship regarding bases for comparison between guitar heroism and its gaming counterparts to discuss questions of authenticity and the role of play with reference to *Guitar Hero* and *Rocksmith*.

What the Electric Guitar Affords the Player (for Good or Ill)

> The turning point in the history of western civilization was reached with the invention of the electric guitar.
>
> —Leni Sinclair cited in Waksman (2003b, 119)

The notion of "affordances" (Gibson 1962, 1968, 2015; Heft 1989, 2001) constitutes a much-debated element of Gibson's ecological psychology. In deploying this neologism, Gibson emphasizes the mutual relations between creature and environment that emerge through interactions within specific ecological niches: "The *affordances* of the environment are what it *offers* the animal, what it *provides* or *furnishes*, either for good or ill. The verb *to afford* is found in the dictionary, but the noun *affordance* is not. I have made it up. I mean by it something that refers to both the environment and the animal in a way that no existing term does. It implies the complementarity of the animal and the environment" (2015, 119, original emphases).

Harry Heft (2001, xvi) describes how the Gibsonian program encompasses sociocultural as well as natural realms with reference to how "the knowledge sustained and elaborated through sociocultural processes are [sic] embodied ecologically in artifacts, tools, and representations, as well as how cognitive functions can be socially distributed. In such public forms, these embodiments of knowing can be aptly referred to as 'ecological knowledge'; and viewed as such, they fit well with Gibson's vision of the environment as being rich in meaning from a psychological standpoint."

Musicologists (Clarke 2005; Krueger 2014; Menin and Schiavio 2012; Duby 2019) have applied the Gibsonian idea of affordances to musical environments as cases of embodied knowledge. Here I argue that the electric guitar, together with its accompanying technologies of sound-transforming pedals and amplifiers,[2] provides a wide range of affordances that have evolved over time. Innovative players such as Charlie Christian, Wes Montgomery, Jimi Hendrix, Frank Zappa, Pat Metheny, Jimmy Page, Tom Verlaine, Steve Tibbetts, Vernon Reid, and many others have extended this range, deploying the available technologies of their time to sculpt new sonic possibilities.[3]

From its earliest incarnation as the 1931 Rickenbacker frying pan (Wendkos 2010) created by George Beauchamp and Adolph Rickenbacker, it took only half a decade till the electric guitar gained wide acceptance so that "[b]y 1936 the electric guitar was firmly established, and players looking for the ability make the voice of their instrument more versatile began using pedals that controlled the volume as well as changed the tone" (Bacon and Wheelwright 2014).

Such affordances include more conventional ones such as legato, chords, counterpoint, bends, vibrato, scordatura, while the strings still sound.[4] The possibilities of such affordances in turn point to various conceptions of embodied knowledge as consisting of "sensorimotor information about potential interactions the objects or events we encounter may allow" (Beilock 2009, 4). Speaking of skilled guitarists, Menin and Schiavio (2012, 210, original emphasis) understand such affordances as based in "*motor knowledge* of the fingers" and propose a conception of affordances as grounded in what they term

> a sub-cognitive, pre-linguistic, intrinsically motor form of intentionality [and a] skilled guitarist might be unable to say where to put her/his finger to perform a solo, but s/he can use the *motor knowledge* of the fingers to reconstruct the actual set of notes played, by just putting the hand on the strings. We believe that this sensory-motor process not only represents the basis of musical understanding but it can also shed light on the notion of musical affordance, relying on a sub-cognitive, pre-linguistic, intrinsically motor form of intentionality.

Such thinking points to a first principle of musicking—for music to sound, motor intentionality plays a crucial role, such that Bashwiner and Bacon (2019, 151) can speak of "the dense interdependence of the auditory and motor systems in music cognition." This also holds true for those who make music without playing an actual instrument. Here I have in mind "singers" of all kinds: humans, birds, whales, dolphins, insects, to name a few (Rothenberg 2017). In some of these cases, the sound-producing mechanisms are concealed from view, but certainly a crucial motor component reveals itself in the ways that vocal cords in humankind, the syrinx in birds, and individually adapted mechanisms for producing sounds for other species, such as insects, vibrate to produce sound. As Marcel Cobussen (2017, 36) argues: "In general, one could state that interaction in music takes place between a body—human or nonhuman—and its environment. This environment—physical or otherwise—can take on many forms and can encompass many different actors, thereby evoking manifold interactions."

In addition to the conventional affordances of fingers and picks, innovative electric guitarists have deployed, for example, their teeth (Hendrix) and a violin bow, as in Page's contribution to "Dazed and Confused" (Wall 2009). Focusing on the neck of the instrument, guitarists use their fingers, glass and steel slides, coordinated tapping, mallets, and so on, leading up to various versions of prepared guitar such as Fred Frith's timbre-altering crocodile clips (Frith 1974), Keith Rowe's lap guitar (Olewnick 2018), and Jonathan Crossley's augmented cyber-guitar. For Crossley (2017, 161), his work in designing and playing the instrument brought about "stimulating new ways of thinking about the cyber-guitar, new relationships with the instrument (both standard and augmented), new concepts of time and texture expressed through both improvisation and composition, and possibly new musics as yet unrealized."

Perhaps the most notorious innovations in rock guitar involve destroying the instrument. Examples include Jimi Hendrix setting his Stratocaster alight—to conclude the Experience's performance of "Wild Thing"—(at the Monterey Pop Festival in 1967), Pete Townshend's record of smashing "more guitars on more stages in more countries the world over than any guitarist in rock 'n' roll history" (Sweetwater 2021), and Matthew Bellamy of Muse's "Guinness record for smashing an astounding 140 guitars on the band's 2004 tour" (Sweetwater 2021).

While such actions in the heat of performance seem to repudiate relationships between guitarist and instrument,[5] Luc Nijs (2017, 49) claims that—under normal circumstances, at least—"the merging of musician and instrument is the condition of possibility to engage in an embodied interaction with music while performing." Musicians might variously understand instruments as prostheses (Crossley 2017), extensions (Ihde 2017), or tools (Duby 2019),[6] but merging with the instrument is grounded in "a sensorimotor experience at a deeper and unconscious level" (Nijs 2017, 49). One of the hallmarks of a virtuoso seems to be the ease with which they arrive at a state of being at one with their instrument.[7]

However, virtuosity is not necessarily what is at stake in this chapter. My field of inquiry also incorporates the tentative, fumbling encounters of the novice, and, in traversing this field, I draw from memories of my own early experience as a beginner guitarist. My first encounter played out on a modest acoustic guitar with steel strings and a high action, whose resistance complicated no end my first attempts at articulating chords. As I recall, the instrument spurned my initial advances for about six weeks. During this time, I could not coordinate the fingers of my left hand sufficiently to sustain a chord, to make all the available notes speak together as one sound.

Suddenly, as if overnight, I grasped the action of simultaneously deploying four fingers together to form a barre chord. I had learned how much coordinated energy was required to overcome the instrument's resistance; I felt that I had somehow acquired this way of knowing in an instant, my understanding transformed, but at the same time it felt like crossing a bridge from which there was no looking back. In short, I had come to know a crucial aspect of the instrument's affordances by way of motor engagement.

Through long hours of practice (Tan, Pfordresher, and Harré 2018b), expert human instrumentalists (as a specialized class of athletes) develop and refine over time a wide range of embodied skills and abilities. For example, musicking draws from coordination (Kelso 2003), hearing (Horowitz 2012), vision (Spence and Soto-Faraco 2010; O'Regan and Noë 2001), fine sensorimotor skills such as touch (Gibson 1962; Eitan and Rothschild 2011; Michaels, Weier, and Harrison 2007), feedback networks (Bamford and Marteniuk 1988), and a degree of physical strength (Large 2010a; 2010b; Loehr, Large, and Palmer 2011; Large et al. 2016), to accumulate and refine the motor knowledge at the heart of instrumental musicking. In this learning process (Tan, Pfordresher, and Harré 2018a), the constituent materials of a musical instrument and its characteristics (its affordances, tout court) shape, direct, and may restrict the musician's embodied material engagement.

So far, the relationship between performer and instrument has been considered in a deliberately restricted environment, as temporarily bracketed off from its wider social circumstances, to limit the field of inquiry to the place where fingers or other interactive devices interact with fretboards. The crucial question: "What's it like *to play an instrument*?" implies the existence of an embodied performer with access only to her own innermost experience.[8] However, as Heft has noted above regarding ecological knowledge (2001, xvi), "cognitive functions can be socially distributed"; hence, wider social circumstances come into play when musicking enters public arenas and is distributed through various media and networks.

The point is that while acquiring musical skills may well be a largely private matter, sharing such skills calls for some kind of audience—direct collaborators, musical peers, or members of a real or virtual audience, who may be fans or detractors. However narrow the focus on the individual musician's learning processes may be, references to broader sociological concerns are unavoidable. The guitar innocently resting on its stand in my studio represents a product of both technology and mythology.

Fans contribute to creating mythologies around apparently superhuman aspects of musical prowess, so that we can marvel at the pinnacle of dexterity exhibited by Sergei Putyatov, reputedly the world's fastest guitarist, who in 2012 managed to play 330 notes in 10 seconds.[9] As Johan Huizinga (1955, 170) argues, "[p]ractically all the known examples of astounding skill called forth by competition belong to mythology, legend and literature rather than to the history of art itself." As for mythological matters of opinion such as the top 10 greatest guitarists of all time, eniGma magazine favors "style, innovation, and signature sounds" over sheer speed, and accordingly ranks Jimi Hendrix as "most skilled and innovative guitar player of all time."[10]

From Silence to Distortion

The greatest recognition for an instrument maker is for their products to be endorsed by a visible and highly rated performer, whose technical prowess and wide range of available choices of instrument become marks of distinction when they settle on a specific maker's instrument. Instruments evolve as new technologies become available, their design and sonic properties intimately dependent on the properties of their constituent materials (Ingold 2013; Malafouris 2013; Ihde and Malafouris 2019).

As regards solid-body electric guitars (Figure 35.1), they require amplification to reveal their full sonic potential, and rock guitarists tend to enhance their available sonic palette by adding various pedals to their arsenal. Combinations of guitar, pedals, and amplifier contribute to establishing a given performer's signature sound and asserting their individuality. Don Ihde (2007, 230) notes how "[t]he sound of rock begins electronically, reproduction and amplification are a part of its very embodiment. Thus the process of electronic reproduction does not get in the way—the music itself is an electronic creation."

The design of the three most influential electric guitars has not fundamentally changed since the 1950s. Bacon and Wheelwright (2014) note how "the Telecaster, the Les Paul, and the Stratocaster—formed the basis for much that was to follow from other electric guitar makers in the United States, Europe, and Japan. Countless copies and variants have been produced since the 1950s and, particularly, following the pop music boom of the early 1960s, which established the electric guitar as the basis of the pop sound."

(a)

FIGURE 35.1A Fender Telecaster.
https://commons.wikimedia.org/wiki/File:Fender_Telecaster_American_Vintage_1952_transparent.png.
https://commons.wikimedia.org/wiki/User:Massimo_Barbier.

While such design features[11] may not have changed substantially in the last seven decades or so, technological developments in electronics such as the vacuum tube, transistor, and integrated circuit in combination with advances in pickup and amplifier design (Dailey 2011) have contributed to shaping distinctive soundscapes. The production of distinctive sonic signatures by individual musicians is subject to the available technologies of the times, so marking in broader terms the ebb and flow of musical genres and eras. From Hendrix to death metal, specific combinations of instruments, electronic circuitry, and production techniques have contributed to the evolution of such guitaristic soundscapes.

As a thought experiment, we might consider how Elvis Presley might sound as produced with the different reverb preferences of the 1980s or using hip-hop's

FIGURE 35.1B Gibson Les Paul.
https://upload.wikimedia.org/wikipedia/commons/b/b8/Gibson_LP_Classic.png.
https://commons.wikimedia.org/wiki/User:Piso17.

production techniques. Arguably, the slapback echo and other sonic characteristics of the 1950s studio are part and parcel of our recognizing Elvis and the sound of his time as coterminous.

Steve Waksman recounts how Willie Kizart's distorted guitar sound on "Rocket 88" by Jackie Brenston and Ike Turner and His Rhythm Kings, recorded at Sam Phillips's studio in Memphis in 1951, resulted from accidental damage to the speaker cone of Kizart's amplifier. Later, the white rockabilly guitarist Paul Burlison discovered the transformational sonic potential wrought by an out-of-place tube in a live performance. Neither guitarist is particularly recognized today for these felicitous accidents, with the advent of distortion as a sound-enhancing potential often attributed to Dave Davies of The Kinks (Kinks 2020). Despite the undoubted popular influence of "You Really Got Me," Waksman's (2003b, 111) remarks attributing "the turn to noise" to US-based musicians make sense in the context of the 1950s, an era which antedated the establishment of the panoply of guitar gods such as Davies, Townshend, Clapton, Hendrix, and others:

(c)

FIGURE 35.1C Fender Stratocaster.
https://commons.wikimedia.org/wiki/File:Howlin%27_Wolf%27s_1963_Fender_Stratocaster_(Rock_and_Roll_Hall_of_Fame,_Cleveland,_OH).jpg.
https://commons.wikimedia.org/wiki/User:ClaudeH.

"The turn to noise among rock and roll guitarists, in the form of fuzz, distortion, and other effects that centered around the creative uses of amplification, was in large part an outgrowth of a two-sided process of adaptation involving, on the one hand, African American musicians who were using the electric guitar to innovate within an existing tradition of sonoric invention, and on the other hand, white Southern musicians who were caught up in the expressive possibilities of African American music."

The Games People Play: *Guitar Hero* and *Rocksmith*

> Many consider *Guitar Hero* to be one of the most influential products of the first decade of the 21st century, attributing it as the spark leading to the growth of the rhythm game market, for boosting music sales for both new and old artists, for introducing more social gaming concepts to the video

> game market, and, in conjunction with the Wii, for improving interactivity with gaming consoles.
>
> —Wendkos (2010)

Guitar Hero's initial promise has not come true. While vastly influential in its day, this rhythm game has not stood the test of time. This may well be because of the vicissitudes of fashion or the nature of its interface, more reminiscent of a toy than a musical instrument (Figure 35.2). This toy-like appearance[12] did not deter Daniel Donato (n.d.), a rising star of the Nashville music scene, who "discovered he had an aptitude for music via the video game *Guitar Hero*." It is perhaps worth noting that he did not develop his skills through continued engagement with the game, but through one of his father's guitars, on which he practiced assiduously.

Scholars such as Dominic Arsenault (2008), Mark Katz (2012), and Kiri Miller (2009, 2012) have raised questions about the differences between guitar-playing and its gaming counterparts. For Arsenault (2008, 2), "[t]he choice of the title *Guitar Hero* marks a choice on the developers' part: the game promises to tap into common fantasies of rock superstars playing in front of large audiences more than it guarantees raw simulational fidelity in the act of playing guitar." Their concerns can broadly be summarized as concerning issues of authenticity and whether the experiences of guitarists and videogame players are comparable.[13]

With respect to *Guitar Hero*, the experiences differ on two principal grounds: as before, *Guitar Hero*'s toy-like interface bears little resemblance to a real guitar fretboard,[14] and second, the gamer guitarist plays along to a track whose details are fixed in advance. In other words, input from the player changes the trajectory of the game against the background of pre-existing musical content, with the outcome (winning or

FIGURE 35.2 *Guitar Hero* controllers (By Itanne99—Own work, CC BY-SA 4.0, https://commons.wikimedia.org/w/index.php?curid=77567999) CC accreditation.

losing, or obtaining a high score) depending on what the game "expects." This activity of reproducing the actions required to correspond with a fixed track is less unusual than it might appear at first glance, because jamming along with pre-recorded material is common practice for some learners in popular music.

Here, I have in mind Lucy Green's (2002, 60) observation that "[b]y far the overriding learning practice for the beginner popular musician, as is already well known, is to copy recordings by ear." This approach will not necessarily develop improvising skills de novo, but the game's purpose is not to develop such skills, but to entertain, to afford opportunities for play.[15] Hence the game correlates more with actual informal learning practices (more the province of budding improvisers) than with refining and developing new creative skills.

For the ludomusicologist Isabella Van Elferen (2020, 104), "[w]e ignore important aspects of the musical experience if we do not recognize music's drastic qualities—that is, without understanding music as an event, in its performed incarnations, experienced as heard and played, rather than over-relying on the secondary, non-sounding materials (scores, recordings, etc.) that have typically been the domain of musicology." Van Elferen calls for the recognition of music's drastic as opposed to its gnostic aspects.[16] This distinction is sketched in very broad strokes, so as perhaps to underestimate the achievements of popular musicology in unsettling the established status quo.[17] For instance, many popular musicians learn by ear and do not initially avail themselves of scores in learning their craft, an aspect of practice that musicologists outside the western art music canon have noted (Green 2002). That said, Van Elferen's emphasis on action as key to understanding musicking afresh agrees with newly emerging theoretical work on embodied and enacted cognition, which has also contributed to fresh debates on musicology's current or former preoccupations.

Van Elferen continues: "More than any other music, game music is an event, not a work; its performance is playful, immediate, and interactive; its sound directly influences the perception and phenomenology of the gaming experience" (106). Understanding music as an event, as she exhorts her readers, shifts attention, as before, to fields of action in which Small's (1998) notion of musicking is realized through individual or collective goal-directed musical action, to become enacted—in short, to become a verb. Questions raised as to how music musicks, how actions become sound, are resolved through the ongoing relationship between musician and instrument, demanding time and devotion to develop to its fullest, but always originating in a form of sensorimotor engagement with an object made of steel or brass or wood (or plastic, for that matter).

The notions of "playing an instrument" or "playing music" (gerund-noun format) always already presuppose a kind of Cartesian duality, a subject–object relationship between player and an inert instrument, obedient servant to the player's intentions, awaiting to be awakened by their touch. This picture does not correlate with Luc Nijs's observations regarding the merging of instrument and player, as noted above.

Cognate terms such as "listening to music," "feeling the music," and so on, tend to reinforce this distinction. This usage may be peculiar to the English language, but while it is true that dancers dance, actors act, writers write, musicians, at least in traditional

English usage, play music. If one is compelled by habit, linguistic convention, or philosophical stance to maintain this distinction, well and good; however, Nijs's research reveals that the potential for merging between musician and instrument seems to dissolve such subject–object distinctions, as the musician is caught up in the flow of playing for its own sake.

Regarding game controllers, the video game researcher Ulrich Wechselberger (2016, 306) refers to natural mapping as "the similarity of actions performed by a player in the real world and their representation within the videogame." The concept of natural mapping suggests that actions which correspond more closely to the properties and responses of musical instruments draw from similar subsets of sensorimotor interactions that a flesh and blood guitarist deploys. Wechselberger's concept provides to my mind a viable theoretical framework for deconstructing debates around authenticity and emphasizes the interactive character of guitar games.

The various interfaces from controllers to actual guitars undoubtedly influence the game's viability and longevity, not to mention the gamer's experience and enjoyment of the pursuit. Whether or not such guitar games provide fresh pathways for musical interactions depends to a large degree on the game's purpose, and Wechselberger (2016, 319) is alert to this possibility, arguing that: "Since a genuine electric guitar . . . exceeds a naturally mapped game controller in both enjoyment and realism, real life tangible mapping in music games could provide both authentic and intrinsically motivating guitar exercise." He suggests that technique-building exercises might become less burdensome for learners once rebooted in a gaming environment and further that the nature of the game allows novices to measure their developing dexterity through the game's scoring capacity.

For Thi Nguyen (2020, 4), games "are a distinctive art form. They offer us access to a unique artistic horizon and a distinctive set of social goods. They are special as an art because they engage with human practicality—with our ability to decide and to do. And they are special as a practical activity precisely because they are an art."

For Graham and Schofield (2018, 66), guitar games create "new modes of musicality" since they draw from "broad and deep reservoirs of existing musical and cultural knowledge," what Harry Heft (2001, xvi) refers to as "embodiments of knowing." The emergent field of ludomusicology may assist in reframing debates about embodied musical knowledge in a fresh disciplinary context, in addition to games providing opportunities for enterprising composers to provide soundtracks to accompany the gaming experience (Phillips 2014). Whether such a context addresses the various affordances guitars and their game counterparts provide and how musicians interact with these various possibilities, ludomusicology addresses issues of culture as evolving and mutable, and, to a degree, exhorts us to look afresh at the canon of traditional musicology. When a guitarist-gamer is fully immersed (Grimshaw 2012) in the game as it unfolds, their lived experience arguably differs in degree rather than kind from the merging between instrument and virtuoso that flesh and blood guitarists experience in the heat of performance.

Conclusion

The Hendrix job-interview joke (Figure 35.3) above puns on the title of his debut album *Are You Experienced?* (1967), in turn referring to the title track and his band of the time, known as the Jimi Hendrix Experience. His early demise in a drug-related incident (September 18, 1970) left many of his musical and technological promises unfulfilled, but the Rock & Roll Hall of Fame regards him as "the most gifted instrumentalist of all time, a self-taught electric guitarist whose fluid, immersive style was perfectly suited to embrace—and then revolutionize—the late '60s psychedelic rock movement." Some five decades later, technological advancements in guitar and amplifier technology together have transformed the range of available sonic resources for contemporary guitarists, and one wonders how Hendrix might have availed himself of current technologies and their affordances and what his music would encompass had he survived into the digital era.

FIGURE 35.3 Jimi Hendrix at a job interview, illustration by Craig Swanson and idea by James Cennamo, via Dangerous Minds, https://laughingsquid.com/.

The early 21st century ushered in a wealth of digitally enabled guitar games, which in some cases (Daniel Donato's, for one, as discussed above) have inspired musicians to engage with the challenges of playing actual musical instruments. To privilege such instrumental encounters as authentic, so valorizing this kind of musical experience over its gaming equivalent, raises the question of musical value-judgments and their appropriateness in a new landscape in which a new discipline, that of ludomusicology, is finding its voice. Perhaps time will be the most appropriate arbiter regarding the musical import of guitar games, and future interactions will uncover new aspects of as yet unheralded musicality.

Disclaimer

This material is based on work supported financially by the National Research Foundation of South Africa. Any opinion, findings and conclusions or recommendations expressed in this material are those of the author(s) and therefore the NRF does not accept any liability thereto.

Notes

1. It's worth noting at the outset that *Guitar Hero* draws from mythologies of simulated rock stardom, while *Rocksmith* (and its successors) is primarily concerned with improving guitar technique for its participants. From ubisoft.com: "We couldn't be prouder of what the original Rocksmith accomplished in the realms of both rhythm gaming and interactive guitar learning, and that first installment taught us an incredible amount about what guitarists and bassists expect from software that lets you play along with your favorite songs on a real instrument" (https://www.ubisoft.com/en-us/game/rocksmith/plus/news-updates/7tWLbSfgXd5YrUVAC4nW6v/original-rocksmith-2011-leaving-stores?isSso=true&refreshStatus=noLoginData, accessed July 19, 2022).
2. An unplugged electric guitar will produce a degree of acoustic sound on its own but comes into its own through various combinations of pedals and amplifiers.
3. Tubes, transistors, integrated circuits, and so on.
4. The physical characteristics of stringed instruments avail string players in general (violinists, double bassists, and so on) differently from pianos, which do not normally allow for modifying the note after it has sounded. Some affordances are specific to the electric guitar and depend in turn on the player's choice of instrument, pedals, and amplification in forging a distinctive sound (Waksman 2003a, 2003b).
5. Townshend claims (2012) that while his initial inspiration to destroy his guitar (Railway Tavern, Harrow, 1964) was accidental, "[t]he smashing guitars thing was epic in a sense. Huge. Then it became ritualistic. Sometimes I felt it very deeply but it was always an artistic statement" (https://harrowonline.org/2019/07/08/harrow-and-music-a-great-track-record/, accessed November 25, 2021).

6. It is perhaps fair to state how Marshall McLuhan's thinking foreshadows at least some of these claims. "To behold, use or perceive any extension of ourselves in technological forms is necessarily to embrace it. By continuously embracing technologies, we relate ourselves to them as servo-mechanisms" (McLuhan 1964, 46). McLuhan's written output emphasizes the notion that *users* are extensions of their technology, thus becoming the servo-mechanisms of their own extensions. I am indebted to my colleague Maurice Azzano for his insights into McLuhan's thought.
7. In Don Ihde's words (2017, 211): "The performer experiences the instrument as taken into his or her bodily activity, and over time and the learning of skills, *feels* the instrument as an extension of his or her body."
8. Nothing mystical intended: I am simply making the point that humans cannot directly access the inner workings of such mechanisms as the autonomic nervous system, for instance.
9. https://www.dailymotion.com/video/x7gphf2, accessed August 4, 2021.
10. https://www.enigma-mag.com/the-top-10-guitarists-o-all-time/, accessed August 4, 2021.
11. "The Stratocaster was designed using both experience from producing the Telecaster and requests from musicians. The result was an instrument that offered improvements in playability, tonal range and ease of manufacture. The slab body of the Telecaster was not always comfortable to play, so the Stratocaster had deep contours cut into the body. Also the top horn was extended to move the front strap button to nearly the 12th fret" (French 2012, 329).
12. Mark Katz's (2012, 472, emphasis added) insights are specially relevant when it comes to comparing the kind of skills called on for guitarists and guitar-video game players: "Certainly both player pianos and guitar controllers are easier to play than the instruments they are modeled on, but they also require actions not demanded of pianists and guitarists—for example, sliding levers and pressing buttons. A distinct type of expertise is thus required to master these. We can see this as a *reconfiguration of skill rather than a simple subtraction of expertise*; such an approach allows us to understand these technologies on their own terms rather than as mere imitations or simulations."
13. Karen Collins, writing in 2013, points to the limited interactivity offered by *Guitar Hero*'s controller: "Current musical game controllers are limited in their expressive abilities: players can lift the neck of the guitar in *Guitar Hero* and to some extent employ the whammy bar, but they cannot employ the nuances of vibrato, palm mutes, bending, slides, or harmonics, and the strength of the button presses makes no difference to the notes produced. The loss of the articulatory, expressive elements of gesture arguably lessens the emotional involvement of the player" (67).
14. However, the first qualification does not hold true for *Rocksmith*, because this game enables the deployment of an acoustic, electric, or bass guitar as the musician's interface of choice (Graham and Schofield 2018).
15. Jan Torge Claussen (2019, 129) observes how: "Musicking with games, like *Rocksmith* or *Guitar Hero*, that require controllers, joysticks, or conventional music instruments is playful. It becomes labourious [sic] when it is expected to teach music in the traditional methods of precise sight-reading and performing."
16. The distinction originates from Carolyn Abbate's 2004 article "Music—Drastic or Gnostic?"
17. Some musicologists might take exception, for instance, to the implication that scores (and recordings) are the only media for their investigations.

References

Abbate, Carolyn. 2004. "Music: Drastic or Gnostic?" *Critical Inquiry* 30 (3): 505–536.

Arsenault, Dominic. 2008. "*Guitar Hero*: 'Not Like Playing Guitar at All'?" *Loading*. . . 2. Accessed December, 26, 2023. https://journals.sfu.ca/loading/index.php/loading/article/view/32.

Bacon, Tony, and Lynn Wheelwright. 2014. "Electric Guitar." In *Grove Music Online* 1:412. https://doi.org/10.1093/gmo/9781561592630.article.A2256412.

Bamford, R. B., and R. G. Marteniuk. 1988. "Visual Feedback, Movement Learning and the Representation of Movement." *Human Movement Science* 7:1–26.

Bashwiner, D., and D. Bacon. 2019. "Musical Creativity and the Motor System." *Current Opinion in Behavioral Sciences* 27:146–153. https://doi.org/10.1016/j.cobeha.2018.12.005.

Beilock, Sian L. 2009. "Grounding Cognition in Action: Expertise, Comprehension, and Judgment." In *Mind and Motion: The Bidirectional Link between Thought and Action*, edited by Markus Raab, Hauke R Heekeren, and Joseph G Johnson, 3–11. Progress in Brain Research 174. Amsterdam: Elsevier.

Clarke, Eric F. 2005. *Ways of Listening: An Ecological Approach to the Perception of Musical Meaning*. Oxford: Oxford University Press.

Cobussen, Marcel. 2017. *The Field of Musical Improvisation*. Leiden: University of Leiden Press.

Collins, Karen. 2013. *Playing with Sound: A Theory of Interacting with Sound and Music in Video Games*. Cambridge, MA: MIT Press.

Crossley, Jonathan. 2017. "The Cyber-Guitar System: A Study in Technologically Enabled Performance Practice." Unpublished PhD Thesis, University of the Witwatersrand.

Dailey, Denton J. 2011. *Electronics for Guitarists*. New York: Springer Science+Business Media, LLC.

Donato, Daniel. n.d. Website. Accessed November 25, 2021. https://danieldonato.com.

Duby, Marc. 2019. "Affordances in Real, Virtual, and Imaginary Musical Performance." In *The Oxford Handbook of Sound and Imagination*, edited by Mark Grimshaw-Aagaard, Mads Walther-Hansen, and Martin Knakkergaard, 97–114. Oxford: Oxford University Press.

Eitan, Zohar, and Inbar Rothschild. 2011. "How Music Touches: Musical Parameters and Listeners' Audio-Tactile Metaphorical Mappings." *Psychology of Music* 39 (4): 449–467. https://doi.org/10.1177/0305735610377592.

Elferen, Isabella van. 2020. "Ludomusicology and the New Drastic." *Journal of Sound and Music in Games* 1 (1): 103–112. https://doi.org/10.1525/jsmg.2020.1.1.103.

French, Richard Mark. 2012. *Technology of the Guitar*. New York: Springer Science+ Business Media.

Frith, Fred. [1974] 2002. *Guitar Solos*. Caroline Records.

Gibson, James J. 1962. "Observations on Active Touch." *Psychological Review* 69 (6): 477–491.

Gibson, James J. 1968. *The Senses Considered as Perceptual Systems*. London: George Allen & Unwin Ltd.

Gibson, James J. 2015. *The Ecological Approach to Visual Perception: Classic Edition*. New York: Psychology Press.

Graham, Kevin, and Damian Schofield. 2018. "Rock God or Game Guru: Using *Rocksmith* to Learn to Play a Guitar." *Journal of Music, Technology and Education* 11 (1): 65–82. https://doi.org/10.1386/jmte.11.1.65_1.

Green, Lucy. 2002. *How Popular Musicians Learn: A Way Ahead for Music Education*. Aldershot: Ashgate.

Grimshaw, Mark. 2012. "Sound and Player Immersion in Digital Games." In *The Oxford Handbook of Sound Studies*, edited by Trevor Pinch and Karin Bijsterveld, 347–366. Oxford: Oxford University Press.

Guitar Hero. 2005. Video game. Harmonix.

Heft, Harry. 1989. "Affordances and the Body: An Intentional Analysis of Gibson's Ecological Approach to Visual Perception." *Journal for the Theory of Social Behaviour* 19 (1): 1–30. https://doi.org/10.1111/j.1468-5914.1989.tb00133.x.

Heft, Harry. 2001. *Ecological Psychology in Context: James Gibson, Roger Barker, and the Legacy of William James's Radical Empiricism*. Mahwah, NJ: Lawrence Erlbaum.

Horowitz, Seth S. 2012. *The Universal Sense: How Hearing Shapes the Mind*. New York: Bloomsbury USA.

Huizinga, Johan. 1955. *Homo Ludens: A Study of the Play-Element in Culture*. Boston: Beacon Press.

Ihde, Don. 2007. *Listening and Voice: Phenomenologies of Sound*. 2nd ed. Albany: State University of New York Press.

Ihde, Don. 2017. "Postphenomenology: Sound beyond Sound." In *The Routledge Companion to Sounding Art*, edited by Barry Truax, Cobussen Marcel, and Meelberg Vincent, 205–212. New York: Routledge.

Ihde, Don, and Lambros Malafouris. 2019. "Homo Faber Revisited: Postphenomenology and Material Engagement Theory." *Philosophy and Technology* 32 (2): 195–214. https://doi.org/10.1007/s13347-018-0321-7.

Ingold, Tim. 2013. *Making: Anthropology, Archaeology, Art and Architecture*. Abingdon: Routledge. http://site.ebrary.com/lib/newschool/docDetail.action?docID=10687189.

Jimi Hendrix Experience. n.d. Accessed November 25, 2021. https://www.rockhall.com/inductees/jimi-hendrix-experience.

Katz, Mark. 2012. "The Amateur in the Age of Mechanical Music." In *The Oxford Handbook of Sound Studies*, edited by Trevor Pinch and Karin Bijsterveld, 459–479. Oxford: Oxford University Press.

Kelso, J. A. Scott. 2003. "Cognitive Coordination Dynamics." In *The Dynamical Systems Approach to Cognition: Concepts and Empirical Paradigms Based on Self-Organization, Embodiment, and Coordination Dynamics*, edited by Wolfgang Tschacher and Jean-Pierre Dauwalder, 45–67. Studies of Nonlinear Phenomena in Life Science. Singapore: World Scientific Publishing. https://doi.org/10.1080/05679320500212114.

"The Kinks: How Dave Davies' Slashed Amp Created Rock Distortion." 2020. https://www.thaliacapos.com/blogs/blog/the-kinks-how-dave-davies-slashed-amp-created-rock-distortion.

Krueger, Joel W. 2014. "Affordances and the Musically Extended Mind." *Frontiers in Psychology* 4 (January): 1–13. https://doi.org/10.3389/fpsyg.2013.01003.

Large, Edward W. 2010a. "A Dynamical Systems Approach to Musical Tonality." In *Nonlinear Dynamics in Human Behavior*, edited by Raoul Huys and Viktor K Jirsa, 193–211. Heidelberg: Springer Berlin. https://doi.org/10.1007/978-3-642-16262-6_9.

Large, Edward W. 2010b. "Neurodynamics of Music." In *Music Perception*, edited by Mari Riess Jones, Richard R Fay, and Arthur N Popper, 201–231. Springer Handbook of Auditory Research 36. Springer New York. https://doi.org/10.1007/978-1-4419-6114-3_7.

Large, Edward W., Ji Chul Kim, Nicole Kristine Flaig, Jamshed J Bharucha, and Carol L. Krumhansl. 2016. "A Neurodynamic Account of Musical Tonality." *Music Perception* 33 (3): 319–331. https://doi.org/10.1525/MP.2016.33.03.319.

Loehr, J. D., E. W. Large, and C. Palmer. 2011. "Temporal Coordination and Adaptation to Rate Change in Music Performance." *Journal of Experimental Psychology: Human Perception and Performance* 37 (4): 1292–1309. https://doi.org/10.1037/a0023102.

Malafouris, Lambros. 2013. *How Things Shape the Mind: A Theory of Material Engagement*. Cambridge, MA: MIT Press.

McLuhan, M. 1964. *Understanding Media: Extensions of Man*. New York: McGraw Hill.

Menin, Damian, and Andrea Schiavio. 2012. "Rethinking Musical Affordances." *Avant* 3 (2): 202–215.

Michaels, Claire F., Zachary Weier, and Steven J. Harrison. 2007. "Using Vision and Dynamic Touch to Perceive the Affordances of Tools." *Perception* 36 (5): 750–772. https://doi.org/10.1068/p5593.

Miller, Kiri. 2009. "Schizophonic Performance: Guitar Hero, Rock Band, and Virtual Virtuosity." *Journal of the Society for American Music* 3 (4). https://doi.org/10.1017/S1752196309990666.

Miller, Kiri. 2012. *Playing Along: Digital Games, YouTube, and Virtual Performance*. New York: Oxford University Press. https://doi.org/10.1093/acprof:oso/9780199753451.001.0001.

Nguyen, C. Thi. 2020. *Games: Agency as Art*. New York: Oxford University Press.

Nijs, Luc. 2017. "The Merging of Musician and Instrument: Incorporation, Presence, and Levels of Embodiment." In *The Routledge Companion to Embodied Music Interaction*, edited by Micheline Lesaffre, Pieter-Jan Maes, and Marc Leman, 49–57. New York: Routledge.

Olewnick, Brian. 2018. *Keith Rowe: The Room Extended*. New York: powerHouse Books.

O'Regan, J. Kevin, and Alva Noë. 2001. "A Sensorimotor Account of Vision and Visual Consciousness." *Behavioral and Brain Sciences* 24:939–1031.

Phillips, Winifred. 2014. *A Composer's Guide to Game Music*. Cambridge, MA: MIT Press.

Rae, Nikki. 2019. "Harrow and Music—A Great Track Record." Accessed November 25, 2021. https://harrowonline.org/2019/07/08/harrow-and-music-a-great-track-record/.

Rocksmith. 2011. Video game. Ubisoft.com.

Rothenberg, David. 2017. "Why I Make Music with Natural Sounds." In *The Routledge Companion to Sounding Art*, edited by Marcel Cobussen, Vincent Meelberg, and Barry Truax, 101–110. Oxfordshire: Routledge.

Small, Christopher. 1998. *Musicking: The Meanings of Performing and Listening*. Middletown, CT: Wesleyan University Press.

Spence, Charles, and Salvador Soto-Faraco. 2010. "Auditory Perception: Interactions with Vision." In *The Oxford Handbook of Auditory Science, Vol. 3: Hearing*, edited by Christopher J. Plack, 271–296. Oxford: Oxford University Press.

Sweetwater. 2021. "A Brief History of Smashing Guitars." *InSync*. March 8, 2021.

Tan, Siu-Lan, Peter Pfordresher, and Rom Harré. 2018a. "Early Musical Development." In *Psychology of Music: From Sound to Significance*, 2nd ed., edited by Siu-Lan Tan, Peter Pfordresher, and Rom Harré, 145–162. Oxfordshire: Routledge.

Tan, Siu-Lan, Peter Pfordresher, and Rom Harré. 2018b. "The Psychology of Music Performance." In *Psychology of Music: From Sound to Significance*, 2nd ed., edited by Siu-Lan Tan, Peter Pfordresher, and Rom Harré, 183–203. Oxfordshire: Routledge.

Torge Claussen, Jan. 2019. "Gaming Musical Instruments." *Digital Culture and Society* 5 (2): 121–130. https://doi.org/10.14361/dcs-2019-0208.

Waksman, Steve. 2003a. "Contesting Virtuosity: Rock Guitar since 1976." In *The Cambridge Companion to the Guitar*, edited by Victor Anand Coelho, 122–132. Cambridge Companions Online.

Waksman, Steve. 2003b. "The Turn to Noise: Rock Guitar from the 1950s to the 1970s." In *The Cambridge Companion to the Guitar*, edited by Victor Anand Coelho, 109–121. Cambridge: Cambridge Companions Online.

Wall, Mick. 2009. *A Biography of Led Zeppelin: When Giants Walked the Earth*. London: Orion Books.

Wechselberger, Ulrich. 2016. "Music Game Enjoyment and Natural Mapping beyond Intuitiveness." *Simulation and Gaming* 47 (3): 304–323. https://doi.org/10.1177/1046878116651024.

Wendkos, Zach. 2010. "The Evolution of the Electric Guitar." May 21, 2010. Accessed December 23, 2023. https://blog.truefire.com/inspiration/first-electric-guitar-evolution/.

CHAPTER 36

MUSICAL REPETITION AND PREDICTIVE GAMEPLAY IN RHYTHM GAMES

STEPHANIE LIND

INTRODUCTION

RISING in popularity during the late 1990s and early 2000s, rhythm games have evolved in format as consoles and controllers have integrated new developments in motion-sensing technology. While the *Guitar Hero* era of the early 2000s brought these games to a peak in popularity, rhythm games continue to be widely enjoyed by both casual and dedicated players. Michael Austin defines rhythm games as video games that require players to match their actions to a given beat and which may involve a variety of interfaces ranging from the player's body, instrument-like peripherals, or motion-sensing controllers (Austin 2021, 140–141). While there are exceptions, the typical structure of rhythm games includes a series of on-screen symbols that tell the player how they must move: this may involve positioning the feet such as in *Dance Dance Revolution* (1998; henceforth abbreviated "*DDR*"), the hands as used in *Samba de Amigo* (1999), the body as demonstrated in *Just Dance* (2009), the fingers or stylus such as in *Elite Beat Agents* (2006), or other combinations. Players learn the mapping of on-screen symbols to physical gesture intuitively through a series of challenges that progressively increase in difficulty, with the eventual goal of reproducing the required gestures as accurately as possible. While players do not need previous music training to succeed at these games, attuning to the music can provide valuable insights about how to structure their gameplay.

Scholars such as Kiri Miller (2017) identify that many rhythm games employ preexisting popular music and as a result adhere to common popular musical structures such as verse/chorus form, a fact that allows a certain amount of predictability to the player in gameplay. As Miller describes in *Playable Bodies: Dance Games and Intimate*

Media (2017, 136–137), players may know the music intimately before even beginning the game, and consequently the required movements sometimes also reference players' previous media experiences of the song such as dance moves from online videos.

Miller presents intriguing analyses of correspondences between musical form and gesture in chapter 4 of *Playable Bodies*. While she approaches analysis from a dance perspective, using the typical language of studio dance instruction, several of her observations hint at musical structuring that might be insightfully approached from a music theory perspective. For instance, Miller alludes to phrase structure upon describing that: "These combinations [of dance moves] were anchored to actual or imagined musical phrase structures through the frequent use of eight-counts or similar verbalized/sung indicators of tempo and meter" (Miller 2017, 119). She also suggests that players experience a form of sight-reading similar to that of musicians, and that players read ahead to better reproduce required gestures (Miller 2017, 121).

As a music theorist, my own experience playing these games has often used a predictive strategy to make up for other shortcomings: I am certainly not going to win a dance competition any time soon, but my knowledge of phrase structure and popular music forms helps me make educated guesses about future moves or gestures. This mindset makes me wonder whether nontheorist players think about musical form in the same way. Miller's work, which takes both an ethnographic approach including participant observation, interviews, and surveys as well as a theoretical approach based on both industry and scholarly materials, suggests that they are consciously aware of these structures (Miller 2017, 16–18; 2009). Building off her work, I will instead take a music theory approach to explore how players use their abilities to recognize patterns in music—that is, an intuitive knowledge of musical structure—to predict future game events, including gestures as well as musical beginnings and endings. Players perform music analysis when playing rhythm games, albeit using different terminology and different levels of awareness depending on the ability of the player. Such pattern recognition is fundamental to producing successful gameplay.

Research in rhythm games to date has focused strongly on the positioning of player as performer, including a flurry of scholarship in the first decade of the 2000s by scholars such as Jacob Smith (2004), Bryan Behrenshausen (2007), Kiri Miller (2009), and Jesper Juul (2010). More recent work from Michael Austin (2021, 152–153) has provided a model for categorization and has also distinguished between procedural (music coupled to game mechanics) versus contextual (music coupled to narrative mechanics) processes for music in rhythm games. However, little has been explored in terms of musical structure and analysis or the link between player gesture and musical events within these games. Miller (2017, 128) is probably the closest in that regard, matching dance moves to specific sections of the verse/chorus structure in her analysis of "Apache," but the overall focus of that analysis is a larger discussion of players' intertextual understanding of race and culture. Peter Shultz (2008) takes a music-theory approach in "Music Theory in Video Games," examining various conceptual similarities between rhythm games and music theory, including reading musical notation and adapting reductive analysis for the creation of nested levels of difficulty. However, his approach takes a broad overview focusing primarily on melodic reduction. This chapter, in contrast, will focus on how musical patterns are taught to players through repetition and/or varied repetition of both sound and gesture, tying together what players hear, what they see, and how they move (see also chapter 37 this volume for an exploration of the player's musicality). This is an implementation of what Karen Collins would term "kinesonic congruence" (the synchronization of gesture and sound), "audiovisual congruence" (the synchronization of visuals and sound), and "kinesonic/audiovisual synchresis" (the new emergent meaning that results via the contextual pairing of sound, gesture, and visuals) (Collins 2013, 35–37).

I will begin this chapter by examining dance-based rhythm game series *Dance Dance Revolution* (1998–2020) and *Just Dance* (2009–2021) to highlight kinesonic congruences and to discuss how players map their recognition of these correspondences to questions of musical phrase structure. The observations made herein will be equally applicable to other forms of rhythm games which employ similar strategies of repetition and musical transformation, and thus the last portion of this chapter will examine *Beat Saber*'s (2018) approach to synchronizing gesture and music with a particular emphasis on variation structure. My analytical approach blends aspects of transformational analysis with analysis of phrase structure, large-scale form, and motivic repetition. Musical transcriptions will help in clarifying some of these properties, but transcriptions need not only focus on melody, rhythm, and form: in rhythm games, the alignment of dance moves or other gestures to phrasing is particularly important. This will provide broader insights into the role that repetition plays in gameplay.

Dance Games as Sight Reading

James Paul Gee (2003, 18) understands game events as semiotic structures that involve learning signs, achieving fluency in interpreting them, and thinking critically about the relationships that are formed therein. Shultz, in his study of video games as music theory (2008, 177, 180), elaborates on Gee's work by stating that music games such as *DDR*, *Guitar Hero* (2005–2015), *and Karaoke Revolution* (2003–2009) act "as a species of pedagogical treatise that reflects interesting concepts of musical space and parses complex musical phenomena into groups of simpler structures." Such a skill is analogous to musical sight-reading: in the same way that musicians receive visual information (the musical score) and must translate it into physical action (performance), players receive on-screen prompts which they must translate into gestures which synchronize with the rhythm of the song.[1] Miller links sight reading to dance games even more explicitly, stating that "Like the *Guitar Hero* and *Rock Band* games, *Just Dance* and *Dance Central* draw on a sight-reading paradigm familiar from the world of Western art music, one that relies on prescriptive notation and the principle that it is possible to 'read ahead' of the actions your body is performing" (Miller 2017, 121).

Parsing music into groups of simpler structures is essential for effective sight-reading; for instance, Auerbach cites research from Michael Rogers explaining that "The eye, ear, and brain find it much simpler to group rhythms together than to jump from individual note to note," and further goes on to explain that "Musicians must be coached to develop two of the behaviors universally exhibited by expert sight readers: chunking notes into groups and using the eyes to scan ahead in the score" (Auerbach 2010, 15). While musicians might cluster individual notes into larger gestural objects such as scales or arpeggios while sight-reading, rhythm game players understand groupings of individual gestures as *combos*.

From the sight-reading perspective, each rhythm game presents its visual information in slightly different ways, but common features include a scrolling field of symbols and positioning on-screen that indicates the required action that players must take. In *DDR*, players step forward, back, left, or right on a dance mat in time to arrows that move toward a line at the top of the screen—in *Just Dance*, players must emulate pictograms that scroll in on the lower right corner of the screen. These symbols act as signs in the semiotic sense, and perceiving groupings of signs allows players to scan ahead for repetitions, groupings of gestures, and, conversely, for deviations from the norm.

Analysis

Since *DDR*'s first release in the late 1990s, avid players have collaborated online to produce practice charts for the games' various levels. Used as study tools to learn new moves and combinations offline, these charts are a useful resource for visually representing the game's required steps—a kind of musical score to serve as a two-dimensional representation for our analysis. Figure 36.1 shows one bar of music from a typical *DDR* step chart. Horizontal bands on the image indicate the four beats of each bar, to which different rhythmic subdivisions are vertically aligned: on-beat steps are aligned to the center of each horizontal band), half-divisions of the beat occur at the border of two bands, and quarter-divisions of the beat are aligned either slightly above or below the middle of

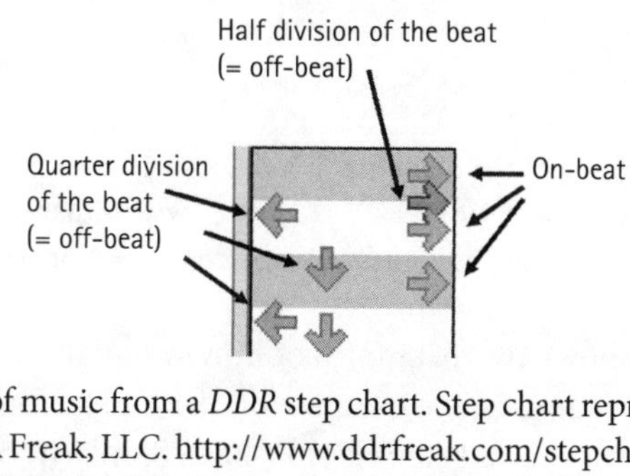

FIGURE 36.1 One bar of music from a *DDR* step chart. Step chart reproduced and adapted with permission of 2003 DDR Freak, LLC. http://www.ddrfreak.com/stepcharts/stepchart.php?song=sakura&mode=Single&difficulty=Maniac&code=Normal&Submit=Submit.

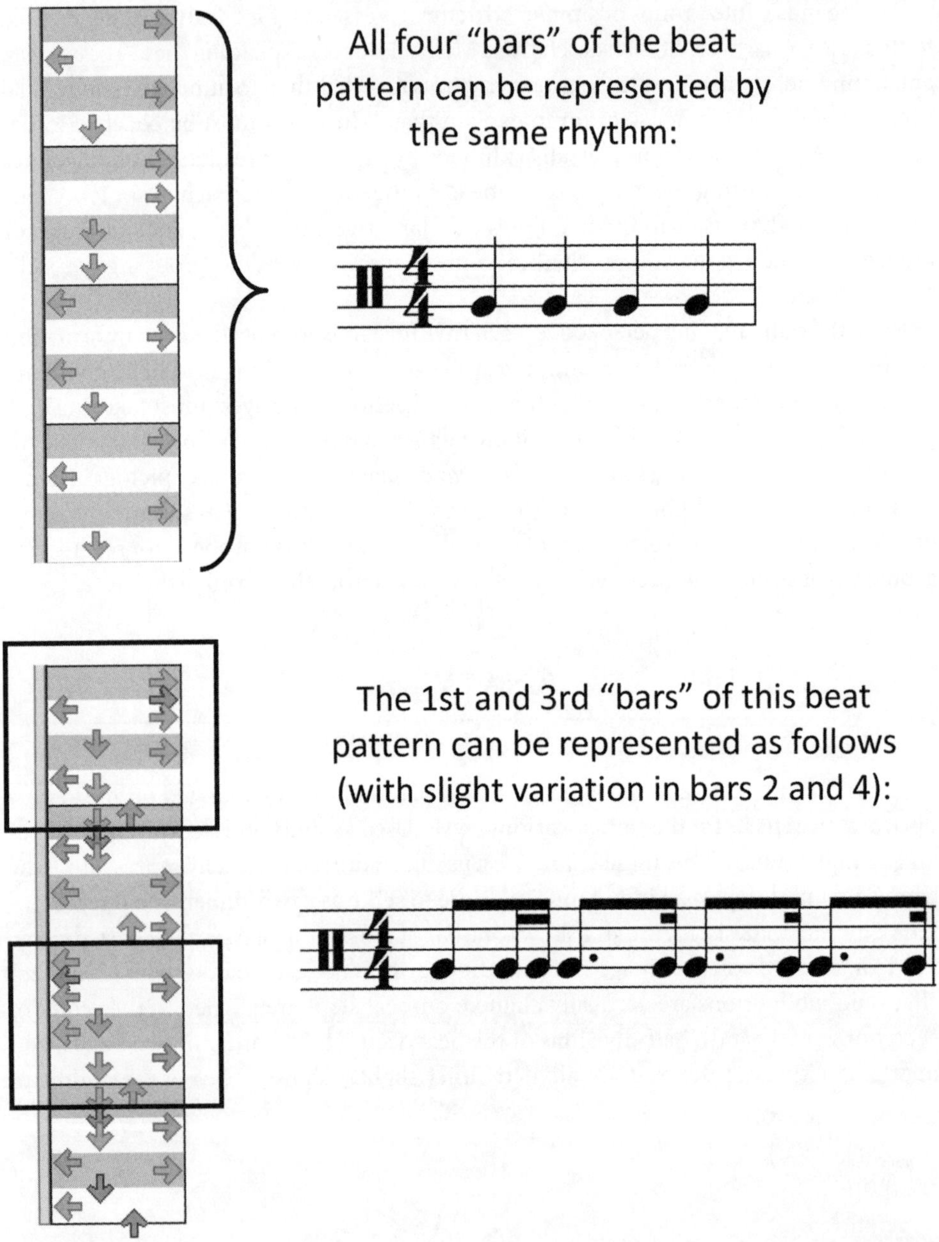

FIGURE 36.2 Some sample rhythms depicted in a *DDR* step chart. Step chart reproduced and adapted with permission of 2003 DDR Freak, LLC. http://www.ddrfreak.com/stepcharts/stepchart.php?song=sakura&mode=Single&difficulty=Maniac&code=Normal&Submit=Submit.

each band. Figure 36.2 shows two examples of how we might translate particular step patterns into musical notation. In the example on the top, all four bars of step patterns produce the same rhythm since all steps are on-beat. Similarly, bars 1 and 3 (boxed) of the example on the bottom share the rhythm notated next to the figure. The required step

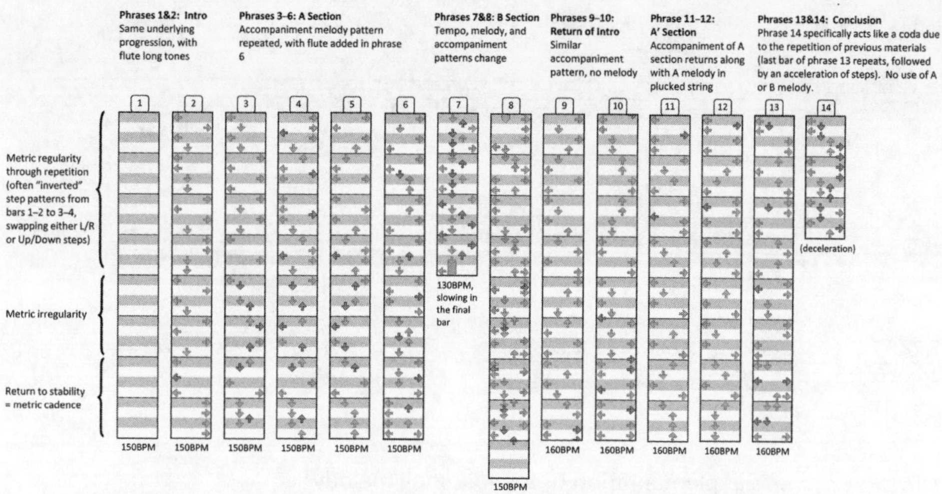

FIGURE 36.3 A basic analysis of step patterns in "Sakura," maniac difficulty. Step chart reproduced and adapted with permission of 2003 DDR Freak, LLC. http://www.ddrfreak.com/stepcharts/stepchart.php?song=sakura&mode=Single&difficulty=Maniac&code=Normal&Submit=Submit.

direction does not explicitly map over to features of rhythm, although, as we will discover shortly, the game designers often choose steps based on predictable patterns that may match elements of musical phrasing and form.

Analyzing a full song will allow us to see some recurring correspondences between steps and sound. Let us use an example from *Dance Dance Revolution Extreme* (2003): "Sakura."[2] Figure 36.3 gives the full step chart for the song: bars are read from top to bottom, and 8-bar groupings are written from left to right.[3] Like the majority of songs in the series, "Sakura" features a regular phrase length of eight bars (with a few minor exceptions; phrases have been numbered on the figure for convenience). Two exceptions to this 8-bar phrase length include phrase 7, which, although it visually appears shorter on the chart, is actually longer than the preceding phrases due to a significant tempo deceleration, and phrase 14, which acts as a short, concluding motive.

Although the same chord progression repeats in each phrase of the song, changes in tempo, melody, and instrumentation suggest a division into different formal sections (indicated above the chart). This mirrors the structure of the original folk song from which this arrangement was derived (given in Figure 36.4; the adaptations to the original melody are shown in part b of the figure).[4] Phrases 1–2 present an introduction with flute long tones and the song's repeating accompaniment progression. Phrases 3–6 form the A section, featuring a plucked string instrument repeating the first phrase of the folk song in the middle register over the same chord progression. Beginning in phrase 7, a change in the plucked string melody and several changes of tempo suggest a new B section: the music and step patterns slow significantly here (the beat lasts twice as long and there is an additional deceleration in the number of beats per minute) before returning to the default tempo at the beginning of phrase 8. This B section also features a change of

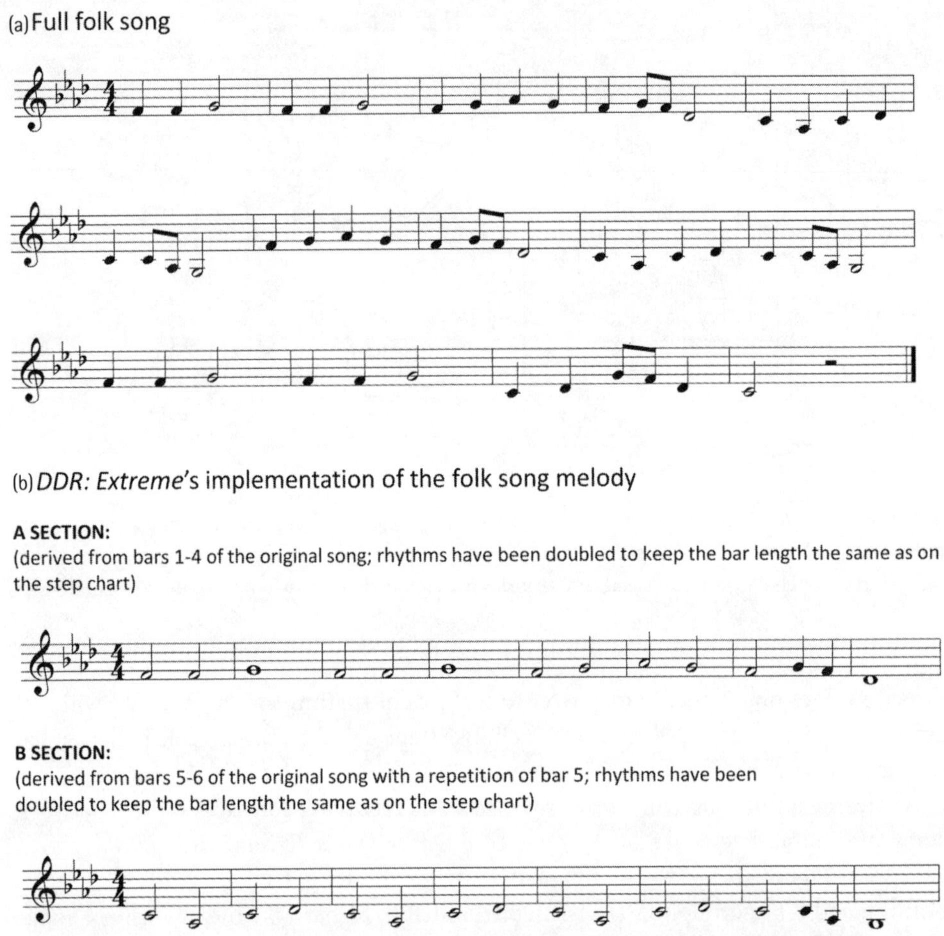

FIGURE 36.4 Melodic source materials and adaptations in "Sakura." Original folk melody transposed from Sakurambo (2006). "Sakura." https://commons.wikimedia.org/wiki/File:Sakura.song.png. Creative Commons Attribution 2.5 Generic (CC BY 2.5).

instrumentation that removes flute and adds a syncopated percussion counter-rhythm. In phrases 9–10, there is a mirroring of the original introduction section with a return to its earlier instrumentation and accompaniment progression at a faster tempo. Phrases 11–12 bring back the original A section melody and accompaniment progression with a modified flute solo (and thus have been labelled A'). Finally, phrases 13–14 abandon the folk song melody, concluding the work with a motive that might be understood analogously to a coda due to its acceleration of steps and repetition (the last bar of steps in phrase 13, for example, repeats as the first bar of phrase 14); indeed, "phrase" 14 might even be perceived as an extension of phrase 13 for the same reasons.

The density of steps mirrors this musical organization. Although the song does feature a gradual acceleration both in the rate of required steps (a common feature in *DDR* levels) and in the musical tempo throughout, the density of required steps is lower in the two A sections (generally requiring one step per beat), allowing us to perceive them as analogous (they also have similar melodies and instrumentation). The acceleration of step rhythm in the B section includes a significant increase in subdivisions of the beat. The extra bar at the end of phrase 8, devoid of any required steps, builds tension and indicates to the player that a section and tempo change is imminent. Thus, the shift from steady tempo to varying tempo and vice-versa provides the players with clues for when repetitions might occur in the song and when to expect a change of steps.

Other components of the music and gameplay also provide hints to the player about future events. The first four bars of phrases 2–3, for example, repeat a continuous quarter-note (i.e., on-beat) rhythm, and phrases 4–6 continue this regular pulse with an occasional off-beat subdivision. The last half of each phrase, however, shifts to a syncopated step pattern with two common recurring rhythms: a long-long-short rhythm, as shown in bar 7 of phrase 2,[5] and a short-long rhythm, which is repeated in bars 5–6 of phrases 3, 4, and 5. The final bar of each phrase returns to emphasize on-beat steps. Conceptually, this functions as a rhythmic cadence: we move from an area of relative stability to one of tension, then back to stability.

Establishing this pattern of stability-tension-stability over five phrases so near the beginning of the piece sets up an expectation of regularity, particularly when coupled with the recurring accompaniment, melody, and chord progression. Players therefore expect to continue the same types of gestures already established until they receive a cue otherwise—in other words, until a significant change occurs in the music. Phrase 7, the start of the B section, provides exactly this change, given that it is the first moment when the music deviates from 150 beats per minute (bpm), and the slowing of the visual arrow also cues the player to get ready for the next phrase. As a result, when the 150 bpm tempo resumes in phrase 8, players are prepared for the increase in complexity—the introduction of sixteenth-note subdivisions.

Repetitions and deviations from established step patterns assist the player in sight-reading the song, but transforming these repetitions is also essential to introducing adequate variety to keep the player interested. Even so, these transformations often occur in consistent ways that still allow for the prediction of future gestures. For example, phrase 2 of "Sakura" begins with the step patterns [left, right, left, down] in bar 1 and [left, left, down, down] in bar 2 (see Figure 36.5). A very common process in dance rhythm games is for the pattern to repeat in mirror-image, with left swapped for right and vice-versa; note that I will term such mirror-imaging processes *inversion* throughout this chapter (abbreviated "I" on analysis figures), a concept pulled from transformational theory.[6] As Miller (2017, 137) describes, "Often a highlighted arm or leg on the card icon cues attention to a particular moving part; players learn to expect that the same motion might immediately be repeated on the opposite side of the body or in the other direction." In "Sakura" this occurs in bars 3–4 of phrase 2, as shown with an arrow on the figure labeled "$I_{L/R}$" (inversion of left and right): all left steps from bars 1–2 are swapped with right steps in bars 3–4, and vice-versa. The pattern recognition Miller identifies suggests a parsing of the music and gesture into mirror-imaged groups, a form of music analysis.

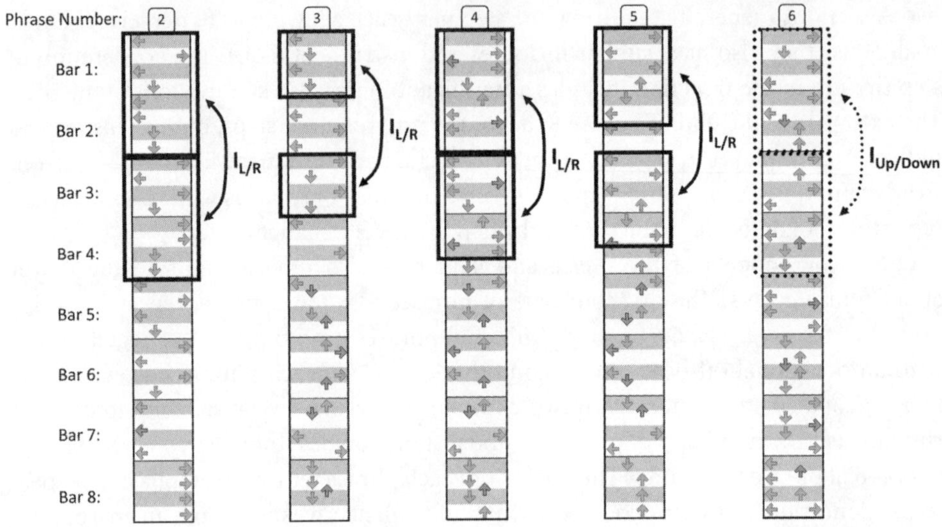

FIGURE 36.5 Examples of step pattern inversion in "Sakura." Step chart reproduced and adapted with permission of 2003 DDR Freak, LLC. http://www.ddrfreak.com/stepcharts/stepchart.php?song=sakura&mode=Single&difficulty=Maniac&code=Normal&Submit=Submit.

Once the player figures out this pattern of transformation in phrase 2, they now have a tool to predict what will happen in future phrases within the same section: phrases 3, 4, and 5 all feature the same mirror-imaging (inversion) in their first four bars, as shown on the figure (although since phrases 3 and 5 present slight variations in their even-numbered bars, I have not included them within the boxes on Figure 36.5). Perhaps not surprisingly, all four of these phrases repeat the same melody in bars 1–4 with slight changes to their accompaniments, further reinforcing that the phrases in this section have the same underlying structure but are transformed. Phrase 6 features a different inversion, swapping up and down steps; the change of process hints that the section is coming to a close.

While the *Dance Dance Revolution* series has waned in popularity in recent years, other dance rhythm games have grown in popularity in conjunction with improvements in motion-sensing controllers, what Collins describes as "a new wave of opportunities for kinesonically congruent sound events" (Collins 2013, 36). The *Just Dance* series, which uses motion-sensing controllers to determine the player's bodily position has, in many ways, acted as the spiritual successor to *DDR*, and employs similar transformations of gesture that allow players to predict future events.

An example from *Just Dance 2020*, "Bad Boy" by Riton & Kah-Lo, will help to illustrate some typical gesture-mapping in the series.[7] Similar to *DDR*, players' intuitive understanding of how dance moves coordinate with musical structure helps them to navigate the game on both macro- and micro-levels, once again suggesting a process of music analysis. However, before delving into this in detail, let us review a few features of how *Just Dance* visually communicates. Figure 36.6 offers a screenshot of gameplay

FIGURE 36.6 Gameplay screenshot, "Bad Boy." Source: Ubisoft, *Just Dance 2020*, Ubisoft, Wii, Nintendo Switch, PlayStation 4, Xbox One, Stadia, 2019.

from "Bad Boy." Several components in the visuals communicate the required dance move to the player. First, the two dancing avatars in the center of the screen reproduce the complete dance in real time. However, in order to give players advance notice of upcoming dance moves, pictograms scroll in from the lower right corner of the screen; the player must begin the dance move when the pictogram is aligned above the highlighted line (seen just underneath the right-most avatar in the figure). The goal of the game is to complete the dance moves as accurately as possible (both in terms of the dance move itself and its alignment with the musical beat) in order to achieve a high score.

Each pictogram displays the intended body position, with additional symbols to indicate what movement is required to create the dance move (for example, arrows at the feet indicate that players must step in that direction, while curved lines indicate that players must shake their bodies along to the beat). In this case, the left-most pictogram in the figure indicates that players should bend forward slightly with arms crossed while shaking their torso to the beat. Previous pictograms remain active—that is, the player should continue the same dance move in synchronization with the beat—until a new pictogram appears above the flashing line within the play area.

Large-scale musical form (the macro level) plays a role in both the required dance moves and the visuals of the gameplay. In "Bad Boy," the background of each section differs significantly in its color palette, with the verse accentuating blue/green, the pre-chorus darker shades such as blue/purple, and the chorus yellow/orange. These visual differences allow the player to quickly understand when a new formal section begins, important to their gameplay because new sections contain new dance moves. The form of "Bad Boy" itself is a clear verse/chorus form, as shown in Table 36.1, framed by an

TABLE 36.1 Formal Sections in "Bad Boy" and Their Visual Color Palette

Formal Section	Color Palette Emphasis
Intro	Orange/pink
Verse	Blue/green
Pre-Chorus	Dark blue/purple
Chorus	Yellow/orange
Verse	Blue/green
Pre-Chorus	Dark blue/purple
Chorus	Yellow/orange
Bridge	Split screen: dark orange, pink/dark blue
Chorus	Yellow/orange
Outro	Orange/pink

FIGURE 36.7 First verse transcription, "Bad Boy." Source: data from Ubisoft, *Just Dance 2020*, Ubisoft, Wii, Nintendo Switch, PlayStation 4, Xbox One, Stadia, 2019 and Riton & Kah-Lo, 2018, "Bad Boy," MNRK Music Group (on behalf of Last Gang).

intro and outro: it features an alternation between verse and chorus with transitional pre-chorus and bridge sections. Each section contains repeating dance moves and there is a clear change to new moves upon beginning each new section. Phrases are also extremely regular, lasting four bars each.

To analyze repetition in the song, I provide transcriptions of the lead melodic line for each section with its accompanying lyrics and dance moves. Figure 36.7 gives a transcription of the first verse. Dance moves, shown on the lower staff, all begin on-beat (e.g., bar 1 of the verse includes new dance moves beginning on beats 1 and 3, whereas the dance moves in bar 8 begin on beats 1 and 4 of the bar). The one-bar repeat symbol does not indicate a musical repetition, but rather will be used in the subsequent figures to indicate a repetition of dance moves at locations where no pictograms are given: players are expected to guess the required moves from their previous context. In the first verse, for example, players have only been introduced to one pair of dance moves thus far (an arm swing above their head that is mirrored in the opposite direction every 2 beats, first performed in bar 1), and therefore this pair should be repeated in bar 2.

The pairing of mirror-image dance moves is a recurring feature that helps players to predict future events throughout the game, but other transformations such as those that swap up and down movements, or that repeat a dance move at a different height, also achieve a similar effect. As shown in Figure 36.8, the mirroring in bars 1 and 2 of the verse swaps left and right, the same transformation previously examined in *DDR*. Bars 3 and 4 also repeat the same gestures from one bar to the next, but instead of a left-to-right inversion the player inverts their body position, leaning frontward with arms in a closed position on beats 1–2 and backward with arms in an open gesture on beats 3–4.

Interestingly, these repetitions and inversions of physical positioning mirror common musical phrase forms. It becomes apparent quite quickly that the first and second half of each phrase create contrast through their different dance moves, with the first half of the phrase engaging the player's arms and the second half of the phrase engaging their torso. Additionally, while the second phrase begins identically to the first, it changes its second half. Specifically, rather than continuing the shake frontward/backward pairing every two beats established in the first phrase, the final bar of the second phrase (and thus the section) shifts the initiation of the dance moves to beats 1 and 4, an irregular spacing. Two new moves—a downward shimmy and an arms-in-the-air gesture—are also introduced. The shift from metric regularity (every two beats) to irregularity (beats 1, 4, and then the next downbeat—an acceleration in the rate of required dance moves) creates a sense of stability, tension, then release that might be understood as a gestural cadence. The structure of these two phrases' dance moves, with their similar openings,

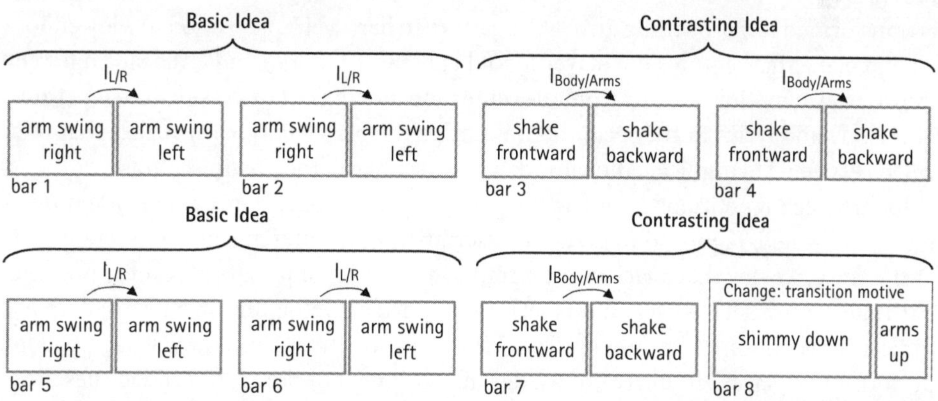

FIGURE 36.8 An analysis of phrase-level form in the dance moves of "Bad Boy," verse. Source: data from Ubisoft, *Just Dance 2020*, Ubisoft, Wii, Nintendo Switch, PlayStation 4, Xbox One, Stadia, 2019 and Riton & Kah-Lo, 2018, "Bad Boy," MNRK Music Group (on behalf of Last Gang).

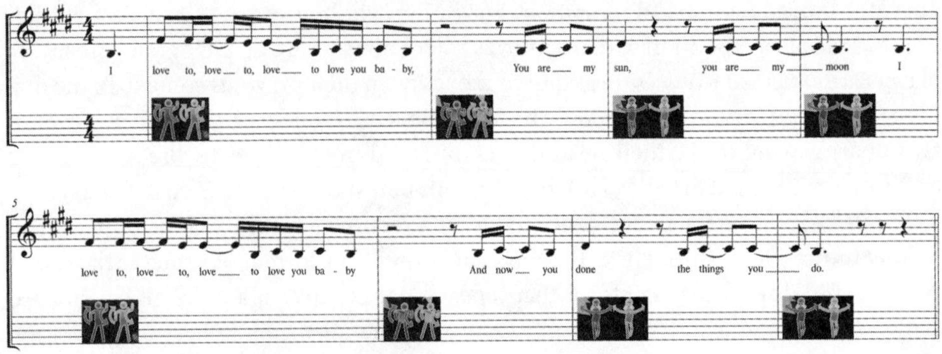

FIGURE 36.9 Chorus transcription, "Bad Boy." Source: data from Ubisoft, *Just Dance 2020*, Ubisoft, Wii, Nintendo Switch, PlayStation 4, Xbox One, Stadia, 2019 and Riton & Kah-Lo, 2018, "Bad Boy," MNRK Music Group (on behalf of Last Gang).

contrasting second half, and a stronger gestural ending in phrase 2 compared to phrase 1 is reminiscent of antecedent/consequent period form even though the melody does not conform to that structure as expected. And from my own perspective as a player, it *feels* musically like an antecedent/consequent phrase pair as the embodied gesture takes priority over the melody, even when I am singing along. This supports Collins's arguments for kinesonic synchresis, where players' musical perceptions merge what they *hear* with what they *embody*; "action and sound can become equally as bound as image and sound and can also lead to an added value in media, where the emergent meaning is thus different from the action or the sound alone" (Collins 2013, 32).[8] A similar phenomenon occurs in sections with stronger melodic repetition such as the chorus (Figure 36.9). As seen in this figure, the chorus repeats the same four-bar phrase twice (both melody and dance moves) with one dance move per bar—a slower rate of change than the verse (a feature that helps players to differentiate this section). Like the verse, however, dance moves are again paired through transformation: the standing arm-wave gesture in bar 1 is transformed to a crouching arm-wave gesture in bar 2, a transposition to a lower horizontal plane that requires the player to fold at the waist. Bars 3 and 4 repeat a different move, an arm motion starting from the center and moving out to the side. The repetition of melody and lyrics in the second phrase helps the player to quickly realize that they will be expected to duplicate the same dance moves like in the previous phrase.

In fact, such repetitions even cue the player in cases where dance moves are not explicitly indicated. Figure 36.10 gives a transcription of the pre-chorus. In a section such as the verse, we saw that a lack of pictograms indicated that players repeat the previous bar's dance moves. However, in this section, the lack of pictograms in bars 5–7 does *not* indicate a repetition of the previous bar. How then does the player know what moves to perform? The player's intuitive knowledge that the previous phrase has ended cues them to look elsewhere for their required dance moves. Because previous sections, such as the verse, featured a parallel phrase pairing—that is, two phrases that begin the same way—players naturally (and correctly) assume that the same will happen here, and that they

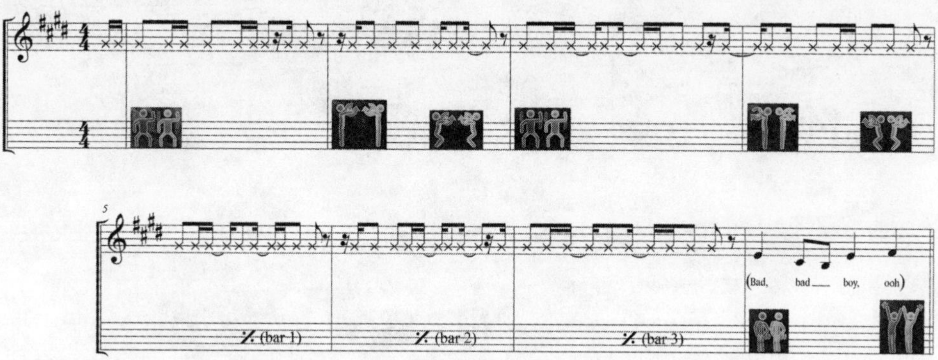

FIGURE 36.10 Pre-chorus transcription, "Bad Boy." Source: data from Ubisoft, *Just Dance 2020*, Ubisoft, Wii, Nintendo Switch, PlayStation 4, Xbox One, Stadia, 2019 and Riton & Kah-Lo, 2018, "Bad Boy," MNRK Music Group (on behalf of Last Gang).

FIGURE 36.11 Intro transcription, "Bad Boy." Source: data from Ubisoft, *Just Dance 2020*, Ubisoft, Wii, Nintendo Switch, PlayStation 4, Xbox One, Stadia, 2019 and Riton & Kah-Lo, 2018, "Bad Boy," MNRK Music Group (on behalf of Last Gang).

can duplicate the dance moves from bars 1, 2, and 3 to fill in the gaps. While players may not know the technical terminology for parallel or period phrase structure, they nevertheless intuit and apply these forms experientially and in real time while performing the song for the first time.

Readers may have noticed that the final bar of the verse and the pre-chorus end with the same melody, dance moves, and lyrics ("Bad, bad boy, ooh"). The intro and bridge sections also end with this motive, as seen in Figures 36.11 and 36.12. While I previously discussed that the accelerated rhythm of this dance move helps to create

FIGURE 36.12 Bridge transcription, "Bad Boy." Source: data from Ubisoft, *Just Dance 2020*, Ubisoft, Wii, Nintendo Switch, PlayStation 4, Xbox One, Stadia, 2019 and Riton & Kah-Lo, 2018, "Bad Boy," MNRK Music Group (on behalf of Last Gang).

a sense of gestural cadence, in the intro and bridge the vocal line's extreme rhythmic regularity (which contrasts with the syncopations of the previous bars) further reinforces the sense of cadence. Paired with the motive's frequent repetition in the same structural position at the final bar of the section, this pattern cues the player that the section is about to end and that they need to prepare for a new selection of dance moves.

Other such comparisons between formal sections of "Bad Boy" allow the player to predict future events. Figure 36.13 presents a transcription of the song's outro section. The sequence of dance moves in this section is similar to those of the intro (Figure 36.11): the second and third phrases of the intro match the first and second phrases of the outro, without the transition motive. Repetition occurs at several levels here, including from bar to bar (dance moves and melodic rhythm) and between two-bar segments (melody). These similarities between the intro and outro rhythm, melody, and dance moves, coupled with the lack of lyrics, mark these sections as functionally related to the player. Bars 5–12 of the intro set up an expectation that bars 1–8 of the outro are a frame for the song. When the player arrives at bar 8 of the outro and the transition motive is missing,

FIGURE 36.13 Outro transcription, "Bad Boy." Source: data from Ubisoft, *Just Dance 2020*, Ubisoft, Wii, Nintendo Switch, PlayStation 4, Xbox One, Stadia, 2019 and Riton & Kah-Lo, 2018, "Bad Boy," MNRK Music Group (on behalf of Last Gang).

this is their cue that the song is about to end, confirmed by the pose-and-hold dance move in the final bar of the song.

Moving beyond Dance Games

As mentioned previously, similar strategies of transformation and repetition appear in nondance rhythm games. However, gestures align differently to the music: while dance games tend to synchronize their gestures with the beat, nondance rhythm games often synchronize gestures to the underlying rhythm of the melody, drums, or guitar. The virtual-reality game *Beat Saber* (2019) offers one such example. The game moves along a fixed path in a manner reminiscent of driving, a genre that Austin (2021, 144) categorizes as a "musical rail shooter game." As seen in Figure 36.14, the player uses two virtual light sabers to hit targets flying toward them. To do so, they must track a variety of parameters: red blocks must be hit by the left light saber and blue by the right, arrows on each block point in the direction the player must swing the light saber, and blocks must be hit at various heights according to their placement within the visual field. Players must also move their bodies to avoid obstacles that appear, on-screen, as shimmering walls. The gestures in *Beat Saber* often match the underlying rhythm of the instrumental accompaniment, and, unlike most of the levels in *Just Dance*, they can include custom-composed

FIGURE 36.14 A gameplay screenshot from *Beat Saber*. Source: Beat Games, *Beat Saber*, Beat Games, PlayStation 4, Microsoft Windows, 2019.

rather than pre-existing music. In one such track, "Legend," gesture rhythm matches the rhythm of the guitar and drums.

To discuss some of the recurring gestural patterns within the song, Figure 36.15 provides a transcription of bars 1–25 of "Legend."[9] Not all gameplay parameters are indicated in the figure, partly because of the difficulty in representing four-dimensional gameplay in a two-dimensional format. The figure furnishes the underlying accompaniment rhythm of the song in standard musical notation, with arrows indicating whether strikes are completed with the right or left hand (light and dark arrows, respectively) and the direction in which the gesture should be made. The placement of the arrows within the gray and white bars represents whether the block appears at a high, middle, or low positioning within the player's visual field. Focusing on these three parameters highlights interesting recurrences in the music.

Like many songs in rhythm games, "Legend" gradually increases in complexity, allowing the player to become familiar with some of the gameplay expectations before facing more advanced challenges. As part of this process, repetition creates a framework for players to practice gestures and to use previous experience to structure future expectations, once again suggesting a process of music analysis. In the portion of the song transcribed in Figure 36.15, three sections occur. The first section (labeled "A1") acts like an introduction, with a simple, repeated one-bar rhythm, which is followed by a section (labeled "B") with a new, repeated rhythm. The section following B may initially appear to be new material due to a change in repeated rhythm; however, as shown in Figure 36.16, the first four bars of A2 actually embed the original rhythm and strikes of A1, adding new strikes on beats 2 and 3 to increase the overall complexity. The result

FIGURE 36.15 Beat patterns in *Beat Saber*'s "Legend," bars 1–25 (dark arrows indicate left-hand strikes while light arrows indicate right-hand strikes). Source: data from Beat Games, *Beat Saber*, Beat Games, PlayStation 4, Microsoft Windows, 2019.

is a tiered learning process that allows the player to build on previous experience in their goal of completing the required gestures as accurately as possible. Miller (2017, 94) identifies this sort of embedded structure between different difficulty levels of a song, functioning as a form of "graded curricula" that is designed to encourage repetition but also to create in-game challenge which is manageable within the player's skillset. Shultz (2008) also examines this sort of nested musical structure—where the gestures of easier levels are embedded inside the more complex gesture sequences of more difficult levels—in his case using melodic reductions to show underlying similarities. But in

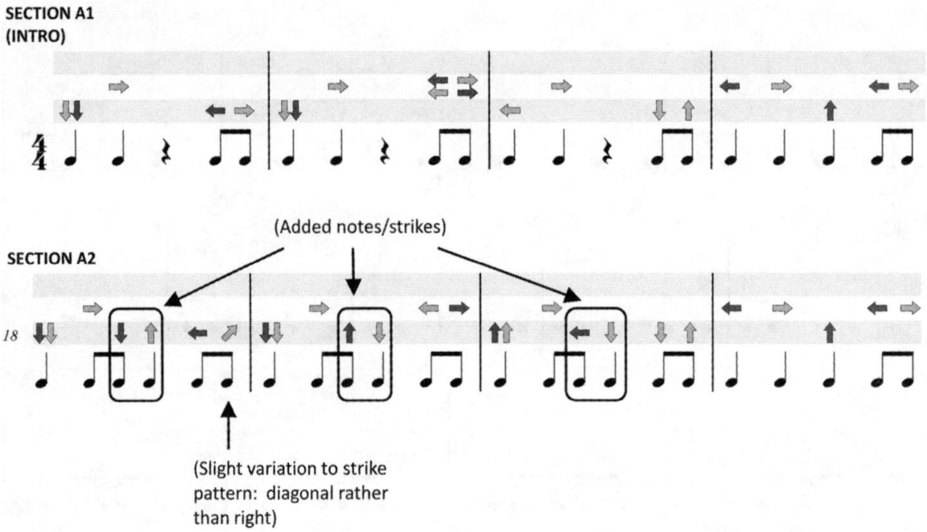

FIGURE 36.16 Comparing sections A1 and A2 of "Legend." Source: data from Beat Games, *Beat Saber*, Beat Games, PlayStation 4, Microsoft Windows, 2019.

"Legend," we are seeing this technique applied *within* a single difficulty level: the player hears the same attack points in the instrumental rhythm, realizes that the first two beats of A2 share the same strike pattern as A1, and makes the connection that the new section will likely be a variation of the first. It therefore still functions, as Miller observed, as a graded curriculum to ease players into more difficult gestural requirements later in the level.

Furthermore, repetition and transition motives also help the player detect phrase groupings. "Legend" groups its music into four-bar phrases, which we can hear because of changes in the repeated rhythmic pattern (such as those seen in bars 10 and 18 of Figure 36.15). A change of rhythm in bars 4 and 8 also cues the player that each phrase is ending: the rate of required strikes increases as a new note/strike is added on beat 3, and a double strike on the next downbeat creates an arrival point or cadence. In section A1, these cadential arrivals match the use of the highest visual field. High strikes are rare in this level: the cadential arrivals in bars 5 and 9, the first two high strikes used in the song, mark these moments as significant. The rhythm and strike pattern of bars 4 and 8 returns in bar 21, creating the same gestural cadence and thus cueing players that the phrase is once again ending, and a new phrase is about to begin.

Other consistencies in the strike patterns also occur, although in *Beat Saber* there are many more exceptions to the established patterns than in either *DDR* or *Just Dance* (perhaps due to the large number of parameters simultaneously in play). Subdivisions of the beat typically retain the same gesture. Eighth notes, for instance, are gesturally articulated by two opposite-direction strikes (see, for example, beat 4 in bars 1–8), and sixteenth notes (such as in bars 22–25) subdivide the eighth-note gesture one step further with a repetition of the eighth gestures in the opposite hand. As an example, compare beats 2 and 4 of bar 24: beat 2, a series of four 16th notes, embeds the 8th-note strike pattern seen in beat 4, but echoes each 8th-note strike with the left hand to produce the 16th notes. Such recurring gesture types are not surprising, as the game requires a certain amount of physical flow from one action to the next, meaning that too many of the same gesture in the same direction would be impossible to perform.

Lastly, mirror-image transformations also occur within "Legend" (see, for example, the swapping of left/right strikes in bars 1–3 and 5–7 of section A1), but with less consistency than in the dance games previously examined. It appears that other processes override a consistent transformation of gesture in *Beat Saber*. For example, in bars 1–8, every bar contains a midfield, right-hand strike to the right on beat 2. In my own gameplay, this is the moment where my actions start to feel like drumming rather than a light-saber battle; the recurring strike creates a steady backbeat and matches the audible drum rhythm of the song. Despite the game presumably not intending to imitate a musical instrument, the player's gestures here embody the rhythm; as Juul explains, "The basic experience of playing these games is that if you do not press the buttons correctly, music appears—it feels as if you *are* making music" (Juul 2010, 115). Jacob Smith similarly observes that "Playing these games can feel like a genuinely musical experience: the controller is no longer a trigger but a percussion instrument, and the player stops thinking in terms of locking on targets and instead tries to feel the groove" (Smith 2004, 65).

Conclusion

While I have focused on outlining specific analytical processes in this chapter—musical repetition, motivic signaling, and consistent forms of gestural transformations—the analytical observations I have made all come down to a single factor: pattern recognition. I believe that such recognition in rhythm games does not occur separately between the aural and gestural domains, but rather is closely intertwined between the two. As Collins might describe it, they are kinesonically congruent. She goes on to identify such congruence as a potential factor affecting player perception, stating that: "Such gestural control over sounds could provide players with useful feedback regarding the strength of gestures, the length of time that an action took, proximity, direction/angle, and so on. This feedback provides more information to the player, and leads to a better sense of control over the character" (Collins 2013, 36). Miller identifies additional benefits to such an approach in her own study, observing that "players also deploy musical listening techniques in the service of aligning these visual and kinesthetic channels; locking into the beat of a song and listening ahead for predictable structural elements reduces the sense of 'kinesthetic lag' that comes along with mirroring an unfamiliar dance in real time" (Miller 2017, 34).[10]

This sense of control obviously assists in creating flow and immersion in gameplay, but, more importantly for rhythm games, it also contributes to an easier learning curve.

Juul, borrowing a term from game designer Chaim Gingold, discusses the use of the "magic crayon effect," a simplification of the game's interface that takes "possibilities from players in order to give a feeling of competence" (Juul 2010, 114–115). He closely links the magic crayon effect to mimetic interface games including rhythm games such as *Guitar Hero*. In the examples I have examined in this chapter, however, a different implementation of the magic crayon effect occurs, with the interface only temporarily simplified, increasing in complexity as the player proceeds from one level to the next and from one section of a song to the next.

The observations presented here also make the argument that music theory and analysis are not only the domain of academics but also of the everyday player. As Miller states:

> Give players patterns to follow and teach them how to anticipate some upcoming moves. Offer them occasional respite from the task of anticipation, creating cycles of suspense and release. Tie these patterns to musical structure; make repeating phrases, verses, and choruses work for you, so that choreographic repetition paints a faithful portrait of a popular song rather than feeling like a tedious technical drill. (Miller 2017, 121)

While Miller views dance games as effective choreography, I would argue that dance games and some other rhythm games like *Beat Saber* also function to effectuate or operationalize music *analysis*. While I am certainly not saying that most players can analyze with specific terminology such as cadence, phrase, and meter, nevertheless they *do* viscerally understand that what they hear and what they embody form particular patterns that create an ebb and flow within the gameplay as well as moments of articulation. Furthermore, there is support for the role that gesture might play in reinforcing our perception of musical regularity: in their study of entrainment across multiple animal species, Margaret Wilson and Peter F. Cook (2016, 1650) state that humans' ability to entrain rhythm is improved when more than one modality is in play (in our case, through dance and music). Rhythm games exemplify this combination, and it would not be misguided to argue that the combination of music and gesture supports and reinforces players' perception of pattern.

Tension and release are key elements in the perception of musical organization and are a fundamental component of musical gestures such as cadence and other forms of resolution. In rhythm games, these are tools to be used by players. Detecting repetitions in motive, phrase, and larger form requires strategic thinking from players, forcing them to listen attentively, think ahead, and plan future moves to optimize gameplay. Reiterative practice via nested levels of difficulty provides a natural, integrated way of reinforcing the scaled learning curve built into the genre. And in the end, while we might discuss these features as creating effective gameplay, they eliminate player frustrations and encouraging participants to return again and again, leading more importantly (in my view) to fun.

Notes

1. As Bret Auerbach explains in his examination of *Dance Dance Revolution* as a pedagogical rhythm tool,

   DDR models the experience of translating a musical score existing in the visual plane into a performance on a simple instrument. The score is oriented vertically and scrolls, allowing only a limited portion of it to be viewed at any time. The "instrument" is the dance pad, a pseudo-keyboard consisting of only four notes that is played with the feet. To extend the analogy being drawn between DDR and meaningful musical activity, we may note that a full gamut of related skills are [sic] monitored and measured by this device. Each score furnished by the DDR software represents the critique of a performance, in which success is determined by one's ability to process beat, read and execute rhythms, and move in time. (Auerbach 2010, 7)

   While Auerbach does not use the term "sight-reading" explicitly in that paragraph, he does go on throughout the remainder of the article to explain "a teaching philosophy and method centered upon the principle of using DDR for the supplemental drilling of rhythm/sight-reading skills" (8), which makes the connection clear.
2. Readers may view the gameplay and hear the music for the song via YouTube at https://www.youtube.com/watch?v=SVjohwtq-kY.
3. Many thanks to Jason Ko of www.ddrfreak.com for permission to use these *DDR* step charts in this chapter.
4. Although English-language information is hard to find on the song, a summary can be found at "Sakura Sakura" (Wikipedia, https://en.wikipedia.org/wiki/Sakura_Sakura, accessed June 21, 2022) and "Sakura" (n.d.). Further information detailing the song's widespread familiarity can be found in (Yamamoto 2002), a study of the song's use in American educational curricula.
5. Or alternately, if measuring in eighth notes, we could express this as a (3+3+2) rhythm.
6. As Dmitri Tymoczko explains, "Geometrically, inversion corresponds to *reflection*: if we were to place a two-sided mirror at [the center-point] . . . then every pitch would be sent to the place where its reflection would be" (2011, 34–35). This definition can be extrapolated beyond pitch to other elements of music and (in the case of this study) to dance moves and other gestures.
7. An official gameplay video is provided by Ubisoft via the official Just Dance YouTube channel at https://youtu.be/dg-IvveN-lw. Note that this video omits the intro and outro sections of the song.
8. Miller also explores this idea in *Playable Bodies*. In linking rhythm games to dance, she explains that:

   Scholars of social dance practices and club cultures have offered ample evidence that when people dance to popular music, they bring techniques of listening, moving, watching, and touching into powerful alignment, generating immersive multisensory experiences and intimate social connections (e.g., Hazzard-Gordon 1990, Thornton 1996, Bollen 2001, Garcia 2011, Salkind 2016). Dance games aim to recreate this kind of experience, building on a fundamental affinity of digital gameplay and club dancing; both practices rely on sensory feedback loops driven by "the interplay, perhaps even tension, between sensation and perception" (Grimshaw 2012, 358). (Miller 2017, 95)

9. Readers may watch and listen to the track at https://youtu.be/64l1tFsbKCM, the YouTube channel of the game's composer, Jaroslav Beck.
10. For those interested, Miller presents an in-depth ethnographic study of this issue in chapters 3 and 4 of *Playable Bodies* (2017); future directions for my own research may include a similar ethnographic approach.

References

Auerbach, Bret. 2010. "Pedagogical Applications of the Video Game *Dance Dance Revolution* to Aural Skills Instruction." *Music Theory Online* 16, no. 1 (January). https://mtosmt.org/issues/mto.10.16.1/mto.10.16.1.auerbach.php.

Austin, Michael. 2021. "Music Games." In *The Cambridge Companion to Video Game Music*, edited by Melanie Frisch and Tim Summers, 140–158. Cambridge: Cambridge University Press.

Beat Games. 2019. *Beat Saber*. PlayStation 4, Microsoft Windows. Beat Games.

Behrenshausen, Bryan G. 2007. "Toward a (Kin)Aesthetic of Video Gaming: The Case of *Dance Dance Revolution*." *Games and Culture* 2, no. 4 (October): 335–354.

Collins, Karen. 2013. *Playing with Sound: A Theory of Interacting with Sound and Music in Video Games*. Cambridge, MA: MIT Press.

Juul, Jesper. 2010. *A Casual Revolution: Reinventing Video Games and Their Players*. Cambridge, MA: MIT Press.

Konami. 2002 (AR), 2003 (JP), 2004 (NA). *Dance Dance Revolution: Extreme*. Arcade, PlayStation 2. Konami.

Miller, Kiri. 2009. "Schizophonic Performance: *Guitar Hero*, *Rock Band*, and Virtual Virtuosity." *Journal of the Society for American Music* 3 (4): 395–429.

Miller, Kiri. 2017. *Playable Bodies: Dance Games and Intimate Media*. New York: Oxford University Press.

"Sakura." n.d. International Shakuhachi Society. Accessed June 21, 2022. http://komuso.com/pieces/pieces.pl?piece=2106.

Shultz, Peter. 2008. "Music Theory in Video Games." In *From "Pac-Man" to Pop Music: Interactive Audio in Games and New Media*, edited by Karen Collins, 177–188. Aldershot, UK: Ashgate Publishing.

Smith, Jacob. 2004. "I Can See Tomorrow in Your Dance: A Study of *Dance Dance Revolution* and Music Video Games." *Journal of Popular Music Studies* 16 (1): 58–84.

Tymoczko, Dmitri. 2011. *A Geometry of Music: Harmony and Counterpoint in the Extended Common Practice*. Oxford: Oxford University Press.

Ubisoft. 2019. *Just Dance 2020*. Wii, Nintendo Switch, PlayStation 4, Xbox One, Stadia. Ubisoft.

Wilson, Margaret, and Peter F. Cook. 2016. "Rhythmic Entrainment: Why Humans Want to, Fireflies Can't Help It, Pet Birds Try, and Sea Lions Have to Be Bribed." *Psychonomic Bulletin and Review* 23 (6): 1647–1659.

Yamamoto, Masako. 2002. "Analysis of American Curricular Materials on Japanese Music, K through 8: Rethinking the Images of the Koto, Sakura, and Kimono." ProQuest Dissertations Publishing.

CHAPTER 37

HOW MUSICAL ARE GAME PLAYERS?

Exploring Musical Situations in Video Games

COSTANTINO OLIVA

Introduction

In this chapter, I intend to expand on the theoretical framings of musical situations, as described by ethnomusicologist John Blacking (1987), by applying the concept to video games. Blacking put the musical situation at the center of his inquiry, considering his discipline "an approach to understanding all musics and music-making in the context of performance and of the ideas and skills that composers, performers and listeners bring to what they define as musical situations" (1987, 3). In parallel with this, my intention is not to prescribe what a musical situation within the context of video games should be, but rather to provide a framework that can be used to position different musical situations, including those determined by music-focused examples like *Rock Band* (Harmonix 2007) and nonmusic-focused ones like *Super Mario Bros.* (Nintendo 1985).

Numerous video games are clearly musical in nature, reenacting familiar and recognizable musical scenarios. In franchises such as *Guitar Hero* (Harmonix/RedOctane 2005–2015), *Rock Band* (Harmonix 2007–2017), and *Dance Dance Revolution* (Konami 1998–2022), players participate in musical performances—"simulations" of rock concerts or dance events. Even this brief list of popular music-oriented video games, often referred to as rhythm games, includes different participation modalities: playing an instrument, singing, and dancing are certainly not identical activities. Still, they all have an evident connection with musicality.

Other "musical" video games do not try to recreate an existing musical scenario. *BIT.TRIP RUNNER* (Gaijin Games 2010), for instance, presents a rather abstract situation, potentially affording even greater musical participation in abstract forms. This "endless runner" game requires players to listen attentively to the musical content to discover that the score contains fundamental cues for traversing the game space. As Reale (2014, 82) notes: "Aligning the map with the score transcription helps to clarify how obstacles combine to create obstacle motives, how the repetitions of the obstacle motives combine to create obstacle phrases, and how the phrases combine to create larger formal structures, complete with a kind of motivic return and development we might expect in a musical passage." *BIT.TRIP RUNNER* loosely maintains the tropes of the music game genre, which features "an intimate and reactive musical bond" (Grimshaw, Tan, and Lipscomb 2013, 291) and "direct engagement with musical sounds as a primary element of gameplay" (Kassabian and Jarman 2016, 124).

Musical content is also abundant in video games that are not immediately related to the music/rhythm genre. Musical compositions of various types (from extensive pieces recorded by a full orchestra to minimalist musical fragments lasting just a few seconds) have been included in a wide variety of video games, constituting an integral part of the media package. Canons of "appropriate" or expected game music have been developed, establishing a connection between popular game genres and highly stylized musical accompaniments. When commenting on the tropes of game music compositions, Phillips (2014, 85) notes that shooter video games such as *Call of Duty: Black Ops* (Treyarch 2010), feature "dark, rhythm-oriented musical scores with the drive of rock and the grandeur of a symphony." A clear trend is also present in platform games, which feature highly eclectic soundtracks (Phillips 2014, 86). For example, the tunes that Koji Kondo composed for *Super Mario Bros.* (Nintendo 1985) have a vast range of musical influences and have been praised for their eclecticism (McAlpine 2019, 115–124). These examples are related to relatively long and complex compositions, but the musical content in video games can also be much shorter. In fact, one of the most distinguishing audio features of *Super Mario Bros.* is the glissando sound of Mario's jumping: "Mario's leap has a pleasant sound (i.e., it does not use minor or diminished intervals), not only because we are supposed to identify favourably with Mario but also because a typical game player will likely hear the same sound repeated hundreds of times" (Whalen 2004).

This sound has musical characteristics (as exemplified by the choice of intervals), but it is arguably not part of the game's "soundtrack"; rather, it is an example of an interactive sound—"sound events occurring in reaction to gameplay, which can respond to the player directly" (Collins 2007, 1). Although interactive sounds in video games are often not explicitly musical, Mario's jumping uses the musical technique of glissando to signify movement in space, pairing a sound ascending in pitch with Mario's agile leaps into the air. While discussing the relationship between the soundtrack and the sound effects part of *Super Mario Bros.*, Kondo remarked how this particular sound has been designed to "complement the music, and vice versa" (NintendoOnline 2010, as cited in Schartmann 2015, 104).

From a musical perspective, the abovementioned video games, and the gameplay occurrences that they potentially generate, differ in nature, yet they all possess an undeniable degree of musicality. It is therefore possible, I argue, to consider these gameplay occurrences as examples of "musical situations" in video games, applying Blacking's ethnomusicological perspective on the nature of musical phenomena. In this conceptualization, music-making activities of various types contribute to multiform musical situations: "[O]ne of the first lessons that ethnomusicologists learn is that music is both a social fact and a multi-media communication: there are many societies that have no word for 'music' and do not isolate it conceptually from dance, drama, ritual, or costume; and even when music is identified as a specific category of thought and action, there are many different ways in which it is defined and in which different characteristics are regarded as significant" (Blacking 1987, 3).

Put succinctly, "it [is] clear that musical things are not always strictly musical" (Blacking 1973, 25)—an understanding echoed by Christopher Small's concept of musicking, which contests the implicit assumption that "musical meaning resides uniquely in music objects" (1998, 5). Expanding on the concept of musicking in contemporary, everyday life contexts, Rautiainen-Keskustalo (2021, 2) noted that although mediated music performances did not explicitly feature in Small's discussion, "nowadays, when the musical experience is inescapably a technological experience (Beer 2010), the mediated aspect in musicking cannot be ignored." This understanding can also be extended to Blacking's findings and, in this chapter, will be applied to the ephemeral, nontotalizing musical situations made possible by video games.

This chapter does not aim to provide tout court an ethnomusicological study of video games' players and communities;[1] rather, the focus here is on Blacking's understanding of ethnomusicology as a method, which has contributed to the contemporary theoretical structure of the discipline. Blacking identifies the prominence given to the "ethnic" element of the field as structurally problematic: "people's musicality and musical interests are not entirely determined by their environment and social background. . . . The widely used label of 'ethnic' music implicitly denies the existence of the individual creative impulse" (Blacking 1987, 2). With this idea in mind, Blacking searches for a theoretical foundation on which to build common ground—a "commonsense view"—for an intercultural understanding of music, emphasizing the individual over sociocultural characterizations.

Extending Blacking's reasoning, the analysis of musical situations in video games should likewise revolve around the individual player's experience and "creative impulse," which are situated within a plethora of shifting cultural contexts (see also chapter 36 this volume). The player's individual experience is indeed a complex and evasive subject. The next section provides a brief selection of theoretical tools from game studies that can be applied to this topic.

Cybermedia: Games as Perspectives

In his analysis of independent video games, Juul (2019, 211–235) warns against normative attitudes in defining video games. He argues that contemporary independent game designers show an experimental attitude toward their craft, creating artifacts that are situated in the context of video games but that lack classic game elements, such as explicit goals or a "rule-based formal system with a variable and quantifiable outcome" (Juul 2005, 6). *Proteus* (Key and Kanaga 2013) is a video game focused on the exploration of an abstract landscape, with no clear goals presented. Although the game retains tropes and conventions typical of popular video games (i.e., a first-person perspective and a focus on exploration), the experience is not directed toward reaching a predetermined game state. Juul (2019, 224) notes that *Proteus* has contributed to changing "our conception of *game*," which is negotiated in a dynamic, changing social ecology involving game creators, players, journalists, academics, and other participants.

This idea is compatible with Aarseth and Calleja's (2015, 2) previous argument that "the phenomenon of games is not a formally definable set but a historically constructed notion," echoing Wittgenstein's ([1953] 2009, 66–67) seminal take on the nature of games. Aarseth and Calleja (2015, 5–6) emphasize the individual player's perspective as a defining element when assessing the nature of player engagement and interactions: "[T]he objects we call digital games are not games in and of themselves. They are software applications that are designed to afford one or several simultaneous game perspectives. . . . What makes any of these systems such is, ultimately, the subjective ludic perspective taken on it."

Taking this approach, Aarseth and Calleja (2015, 6) propose a model intended to facilitate discussions within game studies: "[T]he model we are proposing here frames a more general class of phenomena (cybermedia) to which games belong, and is a matrix constituting four elements: the representational (or surface) sign, the mechanical system, the material medium, and the player."

These cybermedia elements are built on Espen Aarseth's (1997) cybertext framework, which regards video games as objects that can be traversed and reconfigured by means of ergodic effort. The user's individual engagement with a given cybertext is understood not only as a cognitive process but also as a tangible intervention, materially restructuring the medium. Ergodic activity is defined as a form of "non-trivial effort . . . required to allow the reader to traverse the text" (Aarseth 1997, 1). Klevjer elaborates on the meaning of ergodic: "the ergodic signifies the general principle of having to work with the materiality of a text, the need to participate in the construction of its material structure. . . . This means that the user is basically involved as a player (doing ergodic work on the materiality of the text), not as a reader (interpreting on a semantic level)" (2002, 192) . In previous work, I have discussed how the effort described by Aarseth can involve forms of musical participation, determining instances of ergodic musicking (Oliva 2019). This latter concept blends together ergodicity and musicking (Small 1998), focusing on the numerous possible manifestations of musical forms of participation available and practiced during engagement with video games. Although a full discussion of ergodic musicking is beyond the scope of this chapter, I intend here to situate the wide range of musical situations related to video games in a more precise manner by discussing the musical implications that can be identified in relation to the four elements of cybermedia detailed by Aarseth and Calleja.

Sign System

In defining the sign, Aarseth and Calleja (2015, 7) describe this first element of cybermedia as "refer[ring] to the general sense of one or more systems of signification, whether this is alphanumeric text, imagery or sound or other expression types. Our concept of sign . . . refers to the interpretable, 'surface' representational elements that players read/observe in order to be able to use/play the game." The "semiotic layer," or sign system, is a fundamental element of video games. Game designer Steve Swink (2008, 100) describes how "the game's representation and treatment change player expectations about the behavior, movement and interactions of game objects." He considers the possible implications of the sign systems used in different video games, noticing how players' past experiences and notions shape the playing experience: "[W]hat does the thing you're controlling look like, and how do you expect it to behave based on your experience with similar things? If it looks like you're controlling a real car, the expectation is that it will handle like a car, sound like a car and crash like a car" (96).

Game designers use referencing systems to evoke players' existing knowledge, and such references can also point to musical contexts. In fact, certain musical situations in video games are made possible primarily by features of the semiotic layer. An example of this occurrence is *Brütal Legend* (Double Fine Productions 2009), which references heavy metal music culture, including relevant musical works, tropes, and recognized personalities. As van Elferen (2014, 3) has argued, "creating . . . a dichotomy between gaming and musicking is not very fruitful," and the relationship between the two entities should not be limited to only video games that are explicitly musically performative (such as *Rock Band* and *Guitar Hero*). Video games can refer to specific musical genres and cultures, as well as related meanings, without directly engaging with music-making; in fact, *Brütal Legend* is set in "a universe somewhere between Lord of the Rings and Spinal Tap" (Double Fine 2009), where the main character is a roadie for a heavy metal band and brandishes an electric guitar as a weapon. The player must be able to interpret explicit music culture references to grasp the game's musical context. Interestingly, the game features voice acting by actor Jack Black, whose likeness was used for the appearance of the game's protagonist as well. Black is also a recording artist, having released four albums with the band Tenacious D. Moreover, Tenacious D songs have previously been included in the *Guitar Hero* and *Rock Band* franchises, allowing for rich cross-referencing between the semiotic domains of video games and rock music. *Brütal Legend* fits well in this ongoing discourse, as it borrows Tenacious D's characteristic referencing of fantasy literature tropes and exaggerated, comedic tones.

If, as noted by Swink, the sign systems used in video games aim to evoke certain life experiences of the players, in the case of *Brütal Legend* such experiences are connected to a specific "metal" musical context, since in this game "the player engages with the corpus of metal music as well as the subcultural capital pertaining to that genre" (van

Elferen 2014, 3). In the intention of its creators, *Brütal Legend* should therefore realize a musical situation; Blacking (1987, 99) notes how musical situations "resonate with the experiences of people in particular societies," referencing specific social contexts. However, as previously mentioned, individual personal idiosyncrasies are central to this exchange: "music communicates only in so far as individuals choose to listen to it or use it, and not necessarily with any regard to intrinsically musical characteristics" (31). In fact, regardless of the intrinsic characteristics and qualities of *Brütal Legend*'s sign system, the semiotic exchange will only be complete when the fairly complex referencing system is discerned by an actual player, who, during ergodic engagement, will cognitively establish the numerous musical connections determined by the game. This operation is not automatic or obvious but is rather dependent on the specific musical literacy and competence of a given player. The nuances of this particular semiotic exchange have been described by Hart, who notices that "the 'musical experience potentials' in gameplay" (2021, 283) are affected by a number of possible contingencies: "no player is an island . . . friends, birth culture, movies watched in the past, games played in the past, game level, the player's character choice, the darkness of the current in-game scene, and what the player chooses to do next may all inform the player's reception of the game and its elements, forming the contexts in which the player will engage with the game's musical experience potentials" (Hart 2021, 284).

It is already known that game soundtracks are often used to establish musical connections. In his monograph on analyzing video game music, Summers (2016, 141) clarifies how "game music . . . establishes, utilizes and reinforces musical signifiers (interacting with a wider pan-media currency of musical semiotics)." Similarly, van Elferen (2016, 36) notes that "game soundtrack design appeals to a specific game musical literacy . . . through intertextual references to audiovisual idioms from other media." Game musical literacy, however, can also be involved in decoding musical references and values, even when such references are not immediately musical in nature. For example, *Brütal Legend* effectively channels paratextual elements of heavy metal records, having been praised by critics for its "heavy metal fantasy world . . . that a wicked Judas Priest album cover, and the contents within it, might inspire" (Davis 2009). As I have argued elsewhere, players unequipped with the relevant musical literacy would be "unable to competently place the collective imaginary projected . . . in an appropriate semiotic domain, thus missing [out] on a variety of referenced musicking meanings" (Oliva 2021a, 154).

This section has presented a case study in which a musical situation is made possible by the sign system used. Usually, though, video games determine musical situations by using a combination of cybermedia elements. Notably, although the sign systems used by games such as *Rock Band* or *Guitar Hero* present distinct similarities to that of *Brütal Legend* (i.e., a humorous tone and consistent referencing of rock and metal culture), these games also involve very different mechanical systems, which are particularly musical in nature. The next section focuses on the second element of cybermedia, the mechanical system, and the musical situations it makes possible.

Mechanical System

In the original formulation of cybertext, mechanical organization is considered central: "the concept of cybertext focuses on the mechanical organization of the text, by positing the intricacies of the medium as an integral part of the literary exchange" (Aarseth 1997, 1). The defining characteristic of cybermedia is their ability to be manipulated during use: "Machinic operations . . . structure the process, e.g., to switch from one state to another, or simply to change some informational condition, great or small. Any mechanical change that can potentially be recognized as such by an observer with sufficient access to the system's informational sphere will have been effected by the mechanical system" (Aarseth and Calleja 2015, 7).

Video games are commonly designed to include mechanical systems with musical characteristics. Indeed, the most evident and probably the most significant aspect of musical situations in video games is connected to the game's mechanical system, which makes novel forms of musical engagement possible. In the previous section, I mentioned how *Guitar Hero*, *Rock Band*, and *Brütal Legend* have some similarities in their sign systems; however, in contrast to *Brütal Legend*, in *Guitar Hero* and *Rock Band*, overtly musical forms of engagement were clearly prioritized in the design of the mechanical component. These cybermedia are mediated by a simple but rather effective mechanism. Single-instrument tracks (or "stems") from multitrack recordings of featured songs are segmented in sequential fragments and connected with a simplified notation: "The developers . . . have created simplified forms of notation for the instrument controllers, which symbolize specific rhythmic attack points and durations but only relative pitches and pitch contours. . . . What was needed as a basis for interaction with the music was something more than pressing 'play' but something less than complete notated transcriptions of the vocal and instrumental parts" (Biamonte 2010, 135).

Failure to push the right button during gameplay prevents playback of the prerecorded fragment, which is negatively rewarded by the game: if too many notes are missed, the session will end. This highly responsive mechanical system inserts recorded music within the feedback loop that is typical of video games. Kiri Miller (2012, 13) positions the musical interaction of *Guitar Hero* and *Rock Band* within a long history of technological consumption that began with the widespread diffusion of audiorecording and playback technologies: "[E]ver since it became possible to reproduce recorded performances in domestic settings, people have been engaging in musical practices that fall between the poles of passive listening (if there is such a thing) and musica practica." *Guitar Hero* and *Rock Band* have instigated a new phenomenon, letting "players put the performance back in recorded music. . . . Players become live performers of pre-recorded songs, a phenomenon I refer to as "schizophonic performance" (15). "Schizophonia" is a term introduced by Schafer (1994, 273) to indicate "the split between an original sound and its electroacoustic reproduction," and is originally intended with negative connotations, serving to "dramatize the aberrational effect of this twentieth-century development"

(273). In her theorization of the cognitive processes of listening during engagement with video games, Karen Collins (2013) also considered the effects of the technological disembodiment of sound events. Contrary to the negative implications underlined by Schafer, she remarked how "sound is never fully separated from its source in our minds" (22), arguing that "sound in interactive media such as games is multimodal—that is, it involves the interaction of more than one sensory modality and usually contains three (vision, audition, and haptics—action, image, and sound)" (23). Compatibly, Miller emphasizes the positive aspects of schizophonic performances. Notably, the mechanical systems of *Guitar Hero* and *Rock Band* have generated novel musical situations, affording nonmusicians the possibility to engage with a corpus of recorded musical works beyond "simple" listening. "*Guitar Hero* and *Rock Band* are part of a uniquely performative [genre], which creates a new kind of performance space through kinesthetic interaction with musical recordings" (Biamonte 2010, 133).

Kassabian and Jarman (2016, 129) describe examples featuring similar mechanical systems, noting that these "games present music as a task to be achieved, a disciplinary activity in which the player should 'play' again and again until the game (and thereby music) is mastered." It is important to note that cybermedia, including video games, can also feature mechanical systems that do not implement a clear-cut evaluation of players' performances. In these cases, the cybermedia "offer tools to explore the audiovisual possibilities of the digital realm, in which one can make sounds and shapes and colours and patterns and rhythms ad infinitum for very low cost and with very little expertise" (129). A particularly fitting example of this kind of mechanical system is *Electroplankton* (Nintendo 2005). This video game is effectively a collection and expansion of interactive artworks by Japanese media artist Toshio Iwai. For all the works featured in this "miniature museum" (Huhtamo 2016, 92), the system allows for an exploratory, improvisational take. As Collins notes, "with no set objectives, rewards or in-game narratives, these and similar interactive tools—while sold and marketed in the games industry—are arguably not games, but rather musical toys that use game interfaces" (2009, 7). This idea is consistent with the intentions of Iwai, who stated: "[I] always wanted to create creative software played on the game platforms other than game software" (Riley 2006). I have tackled similar topics by designing the research-oriented video game *Otogarden* (Oliva 2021b), which explores cybermedia's improvisational potential through canonic game interfaces (Oliva and Poutiainen 2022).

Cybermedia have contributed to the innovation of possible musickings, in large part thanks to their mechanical systems which allow for the manipulation of musical content. The cybermedia subset of video games is absolutely central in the contemporary musical scenario: "[W]hen we notice that gamers play, and play with, music as they play games, this is not an analogy—players are routinely given agency to prompt and alter musical output of the game. This . . . is part of a modern landscape of musical instrumentation that includes synthesizers, turntables, samplers and virtual instrumentation software" (Summers 2016, 193). The landscape described by Summers can also be expanded to include examples from human-computer interaction research, specifically in the field of new interfaces for musical expression, which has notably experimented with the mechanics of cybermedia to explore novel forms of musicking (Wu and Bryan-Kinns 2019).

Material Medium

Cybermedia are materially instantiated through some form of hardware. The semiotic and mechanical systems of video games are upheld by a variety of platforms, including computers, consoles, tablets, and mobile phones. The materiality of video games has been addressed in an organized fashion in "platform studies," which are "a new focus for the study of digital media, a set of approaches which investigate the underlying computer systems that support creative work" (Bogost and Montfort 2009). Such approaches are considered part of a materialist turn in game studies: Apperley and Jayemane (2012, 15) note that video games are effectively "objects that exist in the world; however much their digital virtuality is celebrated they are enacted and produced in strikingly visceral . . . ways. The noise that a PS3 game makes when it is pushed into the blu-ray drive, the cables over which Xbox LIVE arcade games are downloaded . . . suggest a materiality to gaming that links digital games to the world and demands that they are also understood as objects in the world."

The material medium of video games, manifested as technological, interconnected objects, has determined musical situations of varying breadth and scope. However, Collins (2008, 5) notes that "the relationship between [music] technology and aesthetics in video games is one of mutual influence rather than dominance," arguing that the particular choices of game music composers are the result of personal style as much as of the sonic possibilities afforded by the given hardware. Correspondingly, when commenting on composer Koji Kondo's work on the *Super Mario Bros.* soundtrack, McAlpine (2019, 123) remarks that "his light, open arrangements are as much a function of the need to create a score that tightly integrated with the gameplay as of his love of jazz fusion or the technical constraints of the hardware."

The specific sonic capabilities of the Nintendo Entertainment System hardware have been thoroughly described, emphasizing the compositional tropes to which they contributed (Collins 2008, 24–28; Altice 2015, 249–288; McAlpine 2019, 103–124). In this regard, it is interesting to consider Iwai's first game, *Otocky* (SEDIC 1987), which is often considered a precursor of procedurally generated audio (Collins 2009; Moseley and Saiki 2014; Altice 2015, 270) and of musical improvisation in video games (Oliva 2019, 207–230), in relation to the specific material medium involved. The game, a music-oriented "shoot 'em up," was released in 1987 for the Famicom Disk System, a peripheral for Nintendo's Family Computer console.[2] Among other improvements, the Famicom Disk System added a new, dedicated sound channel: "[T]he Disk System . . . used a rudimentary form of single-cycle wave synthesis that allowed composers to 'draw' custom waveforms to any geometry. . . . Exotic shapes were now at the composer's disposal" (Altice 2015, 268). Iwai used the new audio channel to imitate a variety of instruments' timbres, from electric piano to traditional Japanese percussions. The Famicom Disk System allowed Iwai to realize an aesthetic objective that he had previously pursued in *AV-Game I* (Iwai 1986) and *AV-Game II* (Iwai 1987). Designed to be presented in a gallery space, *AV-Game I* and *AV-Game II* explored game-inspired audiovisual interactions by removing traditional ludic elements, such as competition and point-based systems (Iwai 1994, 22). Similarly, *Otocky* was intended by Iwai as a device that used video game hardware to achieve real-time musical performance (Iwai 1994, 23). As Aarseth and Calleja (2015, 7) note, "different types of hardware also allow for different social contexts in which cybermedia are used." This consideration is particularly meaningful here. In fact, despite the similar elements in the mechanical systems of *AV-Game I*, *AV-Game II*, and *Otocky*, the particular affordances of the Famicom Disk System allowed Iwai to bring his brand of musical interaction out of the gallery setting and into completely different social contexts and cultural scenarios.

As material objects in the world, the material medium of video games has also been significantly manipulated to extend and emphasize its musical implications. In the chiptune scene, video game hardware is repurposed to create new musical situations that extend far beyond the originally intended engagement with the material medium. This is only one aspect of the multifaceted world of chiptune, which cannot be defined solely by the hardware and software used (McAlpine 2019, 2). Chiptune "continues to spread into innumerable musical and media genres, niches and intertextuality" but remains at least "semi-consistent in its microsound or 'bit-crushed' timbres" (Reid 2018, 280). In any case, a modus operandi of chiptune consists of producing specific music-sequencing software for game hardware and accessing the sonic capabilities of the original machine to produce new musical works. The Gameboy sequencer *Little Sound DJ* remains one of the most widely used examples of such software—mechanical systems that repurpose the original material medium solely for music composition and performance objectives.

Whereas sound chips and chiptune music are well-documented aspects of video games' musical materiality, a third aspect has been less thoroughly considered in the relevant literature. Input devices, that is, controllers, are a fundamental part of video games' material medium, and they have often been designed to provide new musical situations. In his analysis of game console controllers, Parisi (2015) argues that, although gamepads have been fairly stable throughout video games' technological evolution, the input devices designed for games such as "*Dance Dance Revolution*, *Rock Band*, *Guitar Hero*, along with capture controllers like Sony's EyeToy, the Wiimote, the Wii Balance Board and, later, the Kinect and Move, each helped interrupt the controller's stability. . . . The paradigm shifted toward interfaces that . . . mobilized a preexisting storehouse of movements performed by the whole body instead of forcing players to assimilate their hands and fingers to the demands of 16-button, dual analog console gamepads" (5, 6).

The affordances of these input devices substantially shaped the musical situations they were involved with. While discussing dance games specifically, (Miller 2012, 13) notes how the Kinect facilitated certain musical styles: "in highlighting the Kinect's affordances, *Dance Central* (Harmonix 2010) privileged particular dance techniques and kinesthetic styles (Foster 2011). . . . The Kinect's innovative potential lay in its capacity to track torso, hip, and shoulder movements, as well as the simultaneous, coordinated motion of different parts of the body—affordances that made it an excellent match for contemporary hip-hop, Latin dance, and related club dance styles."

Within the larger context of music/rhythm games, examples such as the aforementioned *Dance Dance Revolution*, *Rock Band*, and *Guitar Hero*, remain examples of ad hoc (and specifically musical) input device designs. In fact, these controllers' focus is much narrower compared with the canonic gamepads, which were conceived to be used across multiple game genres and applications. Musical input devices are explicitly musical, recreating "a clear instance of musicking: that of performing in a musical context, by using a musical instrument" (Oliva 2019, 162): they are less abstract in nature as they directly mimic an already familiar musical scenario.

The particular musical situation initiated by a video game's input device is also connected to what Alperson (2008, 39) refers to as the "instrumentality of music [considering] the embodied aspect of . . . conventionally understood musical instruments, where the line between body and instrument also frequently blurs. A guitarist playing in the fingerpicking style may consider his fingernails part of the instrument, even to the extent of fashioning his fingernails in particular ways . . . to produce particular sounds on the strings and to facilitate playing."

A similar example can be observed in the practice of ambitious *Taiko no Tatsujin* franchise (Bandai Namco 2001–2021) players. In these arcade games, a large *taiko* drum (a traditional, barrel-shaped Japanese instrument) and proportionately sized drumsticks are prominently featured. It has become common practice, however, to use personalized drumsticks instead of the ones provided with the game. Players modify commercially available drumsticks with extra tape to fit their specific hand grip. The modified stick opens up a variety of techniques imported from snare drum tradition involving swift finger dexterity, including buzz rolls and press rolls, allowing faster movements compared with the game's original sticks.[3] In these and other similar examples, "we need to keep in mind . . . the seamless continuity between the physical instrument and the player's bodily connection with the instrument. . . . Musical instruments are embodied objects" (Alperson 2008, 40). Through mimicking traditionally understood musical situations, video games' input devices create new musical situations of their own and act as embodied objects, forming a continuity between players' bodies and the cybermedia material medium.

Players

Players are the final element of cybermedia. They are involved in a cybernetic feedback loop with the object, realizing and shaping its potential: "for the object or system to become a game, a player needs to think of it as such. That is, she needs to actively interpret the activity as a game for it to be considered a game at all" (Aarseth and Calleja 2015).

Although it is possible for players to actualize a game perspective during engagement with video games, such engagement does not exclude other perspectives that players might be inclined to pursue, including more or less explicitly musical ones. To this point, I have discussed in this chapter obvious musical situations that are manifested through various degrees of tangible musicking. Engagement with video games, however, includes cognitive effort—"a *disposition* and readiness to act, not merely the action of pushing a button or pulling a joystick" (Calleja 2011, 41). Although Blacking (1987, 129) remains primarily focused on music as it is performed, he acknowledges that "listening is as much performance as actually singing and playing." Similarly, Frith (1996, 267) argues that "the music produced by the composer must be distinguished from the music produced by the listener." In this sense, private forms of engagement with video games can be understood as productive in a musical sense, considering that the actual musical output of any given gameplay session is inherently and structurally connected to the players' predispositions and the material affordances of the cybermedia. Considering that engagement with cybermedia involves both a cognitive and a tangible performance, different musical situations are made possible during gameplay. Summers (2016, 193) notes the possible musical affordances of *Super Mario Bros.*: "Mario's jump is musicalized with a rising glissando, collecting coin sounds as a rising fourth, an ascending sequence accompanies a power-up, and so on. . . . Even what is not ostensibly a 'music game,' this is undoubtedly a **musical** [emphasis in original] game . . . bestowing small degrees of musical agency upon the player."

In this example, Summers acknowledges the musical nature of players' engagement; this "musical agency" seems to be particularly visible thanks to the close isomorphic synchronization of action and audiovisual output. Similarly, adaptive audio systems, which are commonly implemented in contemporary video games, manipulate substantial portions of the music in real time, arranging the musical output to match the current game state. In *The Legend of Zelda: Breath of the Wild* (Nintendo 2017), certain musical accompaniments are selected and played by the game system depending on the particular location of the player and the enemies. Although these changes are not as tightly synchronized with the player's input as Mario's jumps, adaptive musical systems dynamically evaluate the player's movements and in-game activities to structure desired musical outputs. Thus, the player's activities, even if they are not immediately musical in nature, are involved in a meaningful musical exchange because the cybernetic feedback loop of video games is permeated by musical features (Oliva 2017; 2019, 258–260).

In the above examples, a number of explicitly musical stored sounds are contained in the cybermedia. Kamp (2021), however, problematizes the musical (or nonmusical) nature of players' inputs and the subsequent aural responses by the cybermedia by considering examples that do not involve explicitly musical sounds. While in examples such as *Guitar Hero* "pressing a button to play a note is a clear musical choice" (173), contemporary games might feature ambiguous musical structures, such as drones, potentially blending players' musical and ludic intentions. Is the players' intervention in such cases "a completely non-musical choice, if soundtrack conventions are so closely intertwined with video game and audiovisual narrative conventions" (174)? In this context, whether players' inputs are musical or nonmusical in nature is not a given, "as in music theory, rules and patterns are historically and culturally contingent" (174). Considering the individual's creative impulse during engagement with cybermedia, the resulting game perspective can be musical in a variety of ways, depending on the contingencies of a given musical situation. As Khan (1999, 68) notes: "Within the history of Western art music, noises were not intrinsically extramusical. . . . The determination of extramusicality rested not in a hard and fast materiality but in the power of musical practice and discourse to negotiate which sonorous materials will be incorporated from a world of sounds . . . and how."

In this sense, actively turning one's attention to sounds during gameplay, perhaps by appreciating the rhythmic nature of a machine gun in a first-person shooter, might amount to a form of musical situation, albeit an extemporaneous and ephemeral one. The nature, scope, and appreciation of this gesture can be largely cognitive, without the manifest observability seen in other examples. However, the musicalization of sound as a sonic technique can reasonably be practiced by game players within the possibility space set out by the cybermedia.

The emergence of similar musical goals can also be much more structured and organized. A unique example of this occurrence involves the official soundtrack for the game *Ape Out* (Cuzzillo, Foddy, and Boch 2019). This game implements a generative system, matching the gameplay with frenetic jazz drumming: the sonic output of *Ape Out* is a creative take on bebop drumming, involving syncopated rhythms and cymbal crashes.[4] The *Ape Out Original Game Soundtrack* (Cuzzillo 2020) is as "an experimental 'LIVE' album, but instead of microphones on stage, we put a controller in the hands of developer Gabe Cuzzillo to drive the performance" (iam8bit 2020). In other words, this soundtrack is an actual recording of one or more play sessions conducted by Cuzzillo. For this particular task, Cuzzillo can reasonably be assumed to have engaged with the cybermedia with a musical perspective because the primary objective was to produce a "live" recording. Here, the musical perspective is not totalizing, as it does not supersede other goals: Cuzzillo still had to play the game in a ludic sense to traverse it and keep the session going. This is compatible with understandings of self-determined goals in video games. Leino (2009, 12) notes that "not all games have goals, and many of those that have, can be played without acknowledging the existence of the goal. . . . The player herself has set the goal to strive for," adding that self-determined goals have to fulfill a general "gameplay condition" set within a given video game. Correspondingly, Cuzzillo met the gameplay condition while trying to achieve a well-established musical goal.

Conclusions

Paraphrasing Aarseth, Hart (2021, 228) describes "texts like video games as 'ergodic,' meaning that work has to be done to them in order to interpret them. . . . Video game music is simultaneously just 'regular old music,' and a relatively new kind of text with potentials for expression and creativity that we have barely started to explore." As Hart suggests, video games have a relatively underexplored potential for musical "expression and creativity." This chapter has situated this topic by providing a framework detailing the manifold instances of musical situations connected to engagement with video games. These situations are not solely present in conjunction with games presenting clearly musical scenarios; rather, musical situations are dependent on the individual user's creative impulse and perspective, which interact with a kernel of musical meaning identifiable in cybermedia. The four elements of cybermedia—"the representational (or surface) sign, the mechanical system, the material medium, and the player" (Aarseth and Calleja 2015, 1)—can present distinct musical features and serve as the basis for the analysis of musical situations in video games. Such musical situations, as discussed by Blacking (1973, 3), are ideally defined by those participating in them, including "composers, performers and listeners." Within the musical situations in video games, participants are intertwined with cybermedia, the larger class of objects that includes video games. These objects are not solely (or even primarily) musical, which is compatible with Blacking's assertion that "it [is] clear that musical things are not always strictly musical" (25).

While I have here focused on the four elements of cybermedia separately, the intention here is not to limit applications. Rather, developments focusing on one or more elements, or their particular interrelations, are possible. For example, I have focused on actual instances of engagement with cybermedia, largely excluding examples of musical situations connected with video games that are outside of ergodic engagement.

The musical situations in video games, as described in this chapter, resonate with the ideals promoted by Blacking in his works: "[I]nherent musical ability is a defining characteristic of being human. This fundamental quality of being human, [Blacking] argued, is systematically stifled in the West by elitist conceptions of music, which arbitrarily set standards of musical competence that inhibit the general participation in artistic creativity of which we are all capable" (Byron 1995, 18). Blacking (1973, 25) also clarified that "music making may be regarded as a form of learned behavior." Indeed, the musical situations in video games create new behaviors of this type, expanding and challenging current musical paradigms while facilitating participation in artistic creativity.

Notes

1. For more on this specific approach, see, for example, Miller's (2012) study of *Guitar Hero* communities.
2. A remodeled version of the console was marketed as the Nintendo Entertainment System in different regions.
3. Multiple examples of this can be observed in YouTube videos; for example, in this video, the YouTuber Mikupi uses modified sticks to enhance her speed: https://youtu.be/cn4RDIiBUfY.
4. This creative design was awarded the 2020 British Academy of Film and Television Arts (BAFTA) Award for Audio Achievement.

REFERENCES

Aarseth, Espen. 1997. *Cybertext*. Baltimore, MD: John Hopkins University Press.

Aarseth, Espen, and Gordon Calleja. 2015. "The Word Game: The Ontology of an Indefinable Object." Paper presented at the 9th International Conference on the Philosophy of Computer Games, Berlin, Germany, October 14–17, 2015.

Alperson, Philip. 2008. "The Instrumentality of Music." *Journal of Aesthetics and Art Criticism* 66, no. 1 (Winter): 37–51.

Altice, Nathan. 2015. *I Am Error: The Nintendo Family Computer / Entertainment System Platform*. Cambridge, MA: MIT Press.

Apperley, Thomas H., and Darshana Jayemane. 2012. "Game Studies' Material Turn." *Westminster Papers in Communication and Culture* 9, no. 1 (October): 5–25.

Bandai Namco. 2001–2021. *Taiko no Tatsujin*. Franchise. Bandai Namco.

Beer, David. 2010. "Mobile Music, Coded Objects and Everyday Spaces." *Mobilities* 5, no. 1 (November): 469–484.

Beverburg Reale, Steven. 2014. "Transcribing Musical Worlds; or, Is *L.A. Noire* a Music Game?" In *Music in Video Games: Studying Play*, edited by K. J. Donnelly, William Gibbons, and Neil Lerner, 77–103. New York. Routledge.

Biamonte, Nicole. 2010. "Musical Representation in the Video Games *Guitar Hero* and *Rock Band*." In *Pop-Culture Pedagogy in the Music Classroom: Teaching Tools from American Idol to YouTube*, edited by Nicole Biamonte, 133–147. Lanham, MD: Scarecrow Press.

Blacking, John. 1973. *How Musical Is Man?* Seattle: University of Washington Press.

Blacking, John. 1987. *A Commonsense View of All Music*. New York: Cambridge University Press.

Bogost, Ian, and Nick Montfort. 2009. "Platform Studies: Frequently Questioned Answers." Paper presented at the UC Irvine Plenaries: After Media—Embodiment and Context, Irvine, CA, December 12–15, 2009.

Byron, Reginald. 1995. "The Ethnomusicology of John Blacking." In *Music, Culture, and Experience: Selected Papers of John Blacking*, edited by Reginald Byron, 1–28. Chicago, IL: University of Chicago Press.

Calleja, Gordon. 2011. *In-Game: From Immersion to Incorporation*. Cambridge, MA: MIT Press.

Collins, Karen. 2007. "An Introduction to the Participatory and Non-Linear Aspects of Video Games Audio." In *Essays on Sound and Vision*, edited by John Richardson and Stan Hawkins, 263–298. Helsinki: Helsinki University Press.

Collins, Karen. 2008. *Game Sound*. Cambridge, MA: MIT Press.

Collins, Karen. 2009. "An Introduction to Procedural Music in Games." *Contemporary Music Review* 28 (1): 5–15.

Collins, Karen. 2013. *Playing with Sound: A Theory of Interacting with Sound and Music in Video Games*. Cambridge, MA: MIT Press.

Cuzzillo, Gabe. 2020. *"Ape Out" Original Game Soundtrack*. Conducted by Gabe Cuzzillo. Composed by Matt Boch.

Cuzzillo, Gabe, Bennett Foddy, and Matt Boch. 2019. *Ape Out*. Devolver Digital.

Davis, Ryan. 2009. "*Brütal Legend* Review." *Giant Bomb*, October 13, 2009. https://www.giantbomb.com/reviews/brutal-legend-review/1900-214/.

Double Fine. 2009. "About *Brütal Legend*." Double Fine Productions, June 24, 2021. http://www.doublefine.com/games/brutal_legend/.

Double Fine Productions. 2009. *Brütal Legend*. Electronic Arts.

Drool. 2016. *Thumper*. Drool.

Foster, Susan Leigh. 2011. *Choreographing Empathy: Kinesthesia in Performance*. New York: Routledge.

Frith, Simon. 1996. *Performing Rites: On the Value of Popular Music*. Cambridge, MA: Harvard University Press.

Gaijin Games. 2010. *BIT.TRIP RUNNER*. Gaijin Games.

Grimshaw, Mark, Siu-Lan Tan, and Scott D. Lipscomb. 2013. "Playing with Sound: The Role of Music and Sound Effects in Gaming." In *The Psychology of Music in Multimedia*, edited by Siu-Lan Tan, Annabel J. Cohen, Scott D. Lipscomb, and Roger A. Kendall, 289–314. New York: Oxford University Press.

Harmonix. 2007. *Rock Band*. MTV Games.

Harmonix. 2010. *Dance Central*. MTV Games.

Harmonix/RedOctane. 2005. *Guitar Hero*. Harmonix/RedOctane.

Hart, Iain. 2021. "Semiotics in Game Music." In *The Cambridge Companion to Video Game Music*, edited by Melanie Fritsch and Tim Summers, 220–237. New York: Cambridge University Press.

Huhtamo, Erkki. 2016. "Art in the Rear-View Mirror." In *A Companion to Digital Art*, edited by Christiane Paul, 69–102. Hoboken, NJ: John Wiley & Sons.

iam8bit. 2020. "*Ape Out* Vinyl Soundtrack." iam8bit. Accessed June 15, 2021. https://www.iam8bit.com/products/ape-out-vinyl-soundtrack.

Iwai, Toshio. 1986. AV-Game I.

Iwai, Toshio. 1987. AV-Game II.

Iwai, Toshio. 1994. "Toshio Iwai by Toshio Iwai." In *Toshio Iwai*, edited by Päivi Talasmaa, 20–29. Exhibition Catalog. Karlsruhe, Germany and Espoo, Finland: Zentrum für Kunst und Medientechnologie Karlsruhe and Galleria OTSO Espoo.

Juul, Jesper. 2005. *Half-Real: Video Games between Real Rules and Fictional Worlds*. Cambridge, MA: MIT Press.

Juul, Jesper. 2007. "Without a Goal: On Open and Expressive Games." In *Videogame/Player/Text*, edited by Barry Atkins and Tanya Kryzwinska, 191–203. Manchester, UK: Manchester University Press.

Juul, Jesper. 2019. *Handmade Pixels: Independent Video Games and the Quest for Authenticity*. Cambridge, MA: MIT Press.

Kaae, Jesper. 2008. "Theoretical Approaches to Composing Dynamic Music for Video Games." In *From "Pac-Man" to Pop Music: Interactive Audio in Games and New Media*, edited by Karen Collins, 75–92. Burlington, VT: Ashgate.

Kahn, Douglas. 1999. *Noise, Water, Meat*. Cambridge, MA: MIT Press.

Kamp, Michiel. 2021. "Autoethnography, Phenomenology and Hermeneutics." In *The Cambridge Companion to Video Game Music*, edited by Melanie Fritsch and Tim Summers, 159–175. New York: Cambridge University Press.

Kassabian, Anahid, and Freya Jarman. 2016. "Game and Play in Music Video Games." In *Ludomusicology: Approaches to Video Game Music*, edited by Michiel Kamp, Tim Summers, and Mark Sweeney, 116–132. Sheffield, UK: Equinox Publishing.

Klevjer, Rune. 2002. "In Defense of Cutscenes." In *Proceedings of Computer Games and Digital Cultures Conference*, 191–202. Tampere, Finland: Tampere University Press.

Key, Ed, and David Kanaga. 2013. *Proteus*. Twisted Tree.

Konami. 1998. *Dance Dance Revolution*. Konami.

Leino, Olli Tapio. 2009. "Understanding Games as Played: Sketch for a First-Person Perspective for Computer Game Analysis." Paper presented at the 7th International Conference on the Philosophy of Computer Games, Oslo, Norway, August 13–15, 2009.

Maxis. 1989. *SimCity*. Maxis.
McAlpine, Kenneth B. 2019. *Bits and Pieces: A History of Chiptunes*. New York: Oxford University Press.
Miller, Kiri. 2012. *Playing Along: Digital Games, YouTube, and Virtual Performance*. New York: Oxford University Press.
Miller, Kiri. 2017. *Playable Bodies: Dance Games and Intimate Media*. New York: Oxford University Press.
Moseley, Roger, and Aya Saiki. 2014. "Nintendo's Art of Musical Play." In *Music in Video Games*, edited by K. J. Donnelly, William Gibbons, and Neil Lerner, 5–76. New York: Routledge.
Nintendo. 1985. *Super Mario Bros*. Nintendo.
Nintendo. 2005. *Electroplankton*. Nintendo.
Nintendo. 2016. *Super Mario Run*. Nintendo.
Nintendo. 2017. *The Legend of Zelda: Breath of the Wild*. Nintendo.
NintendoOnline. 2010. "Interview with Video Game Composer Koji Kondo." Accessed June 20, 2022. https://youtu.be/67Vht-er448.
Oliva, Costantino. 2017. "On the Ontological Status of Musical Actions in Digital Games." Paper presented at the 11th International Conference on the Philosophy of Computer Games, Krakow, Poland, November 28–December 1, 2017.
Oliva, Costantino. 2019. "Musicking with Digital Games." PhD dissertation, University of Malta.
Oliva, Costantino. 2021a. "The Musical Ludo Mix of *Taiko no Tatsujin*." *ToDiGRA: Transactions of the Digital Games Research Association* 5 (2): 131–160.
Oliva, Costantino. 2021b. *Otogarden*. Accessed June 15, 2021. http://otogarden.com.
Oliva, Costantino, and Ari Poutiainen. 2022. "*Otogarden*: Exploring Musical Improvisation in Video Games." *Journal of Sound and Music in Games* 3 (2–3): 28–58.
Parisi, David. 2015. "A Counterrevolution in the Hands: The Console Controller as an Ergonomic Branding Mechanism." *Journal of Games Criticism* 2 (1): 1–23.
Phillips, Winifred. 2014. *A Composer's Guide to Game Music*. Cambridge, MA: MIT Press.
Rautiainen-Keskustalo, Tarja. 2021. "Embodiment through Digital Intangibility: Infrastructures of Musicking." *Journal of New Music Research* 50, no. 2 (March): 1–8.
Reid, George. 2018. "Chiptune: The Ludomusical Shaping of Identity." *Computer Games Journal* 7 (4): 279–290.
Riley, Adam. 2006. "C3 Exclusive Interview: Toshio Iwai on Nintendo, Wii . . and Musical Fish!" *Cubed3.com*. Accessed June 20, 2018. http://www.cubed3.com/news/5724/1/c3-exclusive-interview-toshio-iwai-on-nintendo-wiiand-musical-fish.html.
Saltsman, Adam. 2009. *Canabalt*. Semi Secret Software.
Schafer, R. Murray. 1994. *The Soundscape: The Tuning of the World*. Rochester, VT: Destiny Books.
Schartmann, Andrew. 2015. *Koji Kondo's "Super Mario Bros." Soundtrack*. New York: Bloomsbury Academic.
SEDIC. 1987. *Otocky*. ASCII Corporation.
Small, Christopher. 1998. *Musicking: The Meaning of Performing and Listening*. Middletown, CT: Wesleyan University Press.
Swink, Steve. 2008. *Game Feel: A Game Designer's Guide to Virtual Sensation*. Burlington, MA: Morgan Kaufmann.
Treyarch. 2010. *Call of Duty: Black Ops*. Activision.
United Game Artists. 2001. *Rez*. Sega/Sony Computer Entertainment.
Van Elferen, Isabella. 2014. "Ludomusicology and The New Drastic." Paper presented at Creativity, Circulation and Copyright: Sonic and Visual Media in the Digital Age, Cambridge, UK, March 28–29, 2014.

Van Elferen, Isabella. 2016. "Analyzing Game Musical Immersion." In *Ludomusicology: Approaches to Video Game Music*, edited by Michiel Kamp, Tim Summers, and Mark Sweeney, 32–52. Sheffield: Equinox Publishing.

Whalen, Zach. 2004. "Play Along: An Approach to Videogame Music." *Game Studies* 4, no. 1 (November). Accessed December 29, 2023. https://www.gamestudies.org/0401/whalen/.

Wirman, Hanna. 2009. "On Productivity and Game Fandom." *Transformative Works and Cultures* 3, no. 2 (September). https://doi.org/10.3983/twc.2009.0145.

Wittgenstein, Ludwig. [1953] 2009. *Philosophical Investigations*. Hoboken, NJ: Wiley Blackwell.

Wu, Yongmeng, and Nick Bryan-Kinns. 2019. "Musicking with an Interactive Musical System: The Effects of Task Motivation and User Interface Mode on Non-Musicians' Creative Engagement." *International Journal of Human-Computer Studies* 122: 61–77.

SECTION 8

ACOUSTIC ECOLOGIES

CHAPTER 38

ANALYZING NAVIGABLE NARRATIVES THROUGH MULTIPLE LENSES

ELIZABETH HAMBLETON

Introduction

In 2012, the game publisher The Chinese Room released *Dear Esther*. It had all the trappings of a high-budget video game, such as a photo-realistic environment, a first-person point of view accompanied by narration, an intriguing story, and lovely music. What it lacked was gameplay—*Dear Esther* had no win-loss condition, no ranking system, no puzzles. It became known as the first "walking simulator," a genre that forefronts the narrative through unique blends of linguistic and virtual environmental means at the expense of competitive elements like racing or puzzle-solving (Ballou 2019). These storytelling elements are often centered around sound via diegetic and nondiegetic music, the dynamic soundscape, and the use of voices, often disembodied.

This chapter defines and gives examples of navigable narratives, also commonly known as "walking simulators" or "games without gameplay." In these pages, I will explain how the term "walking simulator" arose and why I choose to rebrand the genre as "navigable narratives," and I present the music and soundscapes of four case studies as examples of navigable-narrative video games.

In the massive catalog of all existing video games, not all games are created equal. For one, according to Roger Caillois (2001), there are two major types of "play," *ludus* and *paidia*, and video games can employ one or both of these types of play. Ludic play[1] is defined by having a win/loss dichotomy and measurable outcomes. Games that tap into ludic play include: competitive games like racing or fighting games (e.g., *F-Zero, Super Smash Bros.*, respectively), where players win or lose and their completion times are measured and ranked; adventure games (e.g., *The Legend of Zelda*), where players gain skills to defeat enemies or be defeated; and logical games like puzzle games (e.g., *Baba*

Is You), in which players must solve puzzles to progress or win. However, not all games, and not all video games, emphasize ludic play. Paidic games use more of a "sandbox" style of play with emphasis on immersive exploration and discovery. These can include creative constructive games (e.g., *Minecraft*), casual and decoration games (e.g., *Animal Crossing*), and our genre featured in this chapter: navigable narratives.

Within the ludic and paidic styles, video games can be social or individualistic, provide heart-pounding excitement or soothing relaxation, offer brain teasers or finger exercises, and a host of other elements that make each game unique and attractive to players. Like books, music, and painting, games tackle various subject matters with a unique blend of artistic, sonic, tactile, and narrative styles. Certain styles of one kind tend to correspond to particular styles of another, and thus multimedia and intermedia tropes are born that are associated with specific sets of genres.

Terminology

The following section establishes working definitions for *video game*, *narrative*, *navigability*, and *navigable narrative*.

Video Game

Video games are a digital art medium. They use any combination of visual components, sonic components, narrative elements, tactile elements (e.g., controller vibration), and interactivity delivered through an electronic medium. As the name suggests, video games emphasize the visual elements and player engagement; they are something to look at, and something to play with. The existence of this handbook, and indeed this entire field of study, confirms that where aural elements are present in video games, they can be as noteworthy and artistic as the video and game components.

Yet, how essential are these video and game aspects? It turns out less essential than one might think. There is a genre of video games designed for blind and low-vision players that have no video programmed into them at all. These audio games, as they are often called, are still built in the video game medium.[2] Similarly, there are many genres of video games that lack game conditions, from task simulators to interactive experiences to visual novels.

What counts as gameplay or game conditions? Games, by definition, involve player participation and a win/loss condition. One of the simplest games, the coin toss, relies on a person to activate the coin, and the game ends when the side is revealed and the win/loss condition is settled. However, video games are not necessarily games in this sense. They require player interactivity, but they do not have to have this condition of beginning and ending, of winning and losing.

Many ludomusicologists adopt ludologist Jesper Juul's definition of "game":

> As an activity, a game is a system that changes state according to a set of rules that are implemented by humans, computers or natural laws. The game is such that its outcome is undetermined, variable, and quantifiable. The players are aware that some outcomes are more desirable than others. The players are able to exert effort in order to influence the outcome. The players feel attached to the eventual outcome. Finally, the consequences of the game *have been* negotiated, ideally before the beginning of the game. (2005, 45)

Juul does not distinguish paidic from ludic play in this definition, though some elements in the definition apply more specifically to ludus than to paidia.

Navigable narratives uphold most of the components in Juul's definition, such as predefining the rules and the player affecting the outcome, thus establishing their "gameness." These rules and outcomes may pertain to a more artistic experience befitting paidic play rather than win/loss conditions typical of ludic play; this is why they are often nicknamed "games without gameplay." In navigable narratives, the rules and environment are set ahead of time. The story is ready to be discovered by the player. The outcome is undefined—the story may or may not be linear, and the musical cues and soundscape have yet to be realized. The player must choose to participate to make the experience (the outcome) happen. It will not be the exact same for every player, nor will it mean the same thing. Narratives offer a more uniquely personal takeaway for the players than the measurable outcomes that Juul prescribes.

Narrative

"Narrative" is complicated to define broadly, as the definition tends to be context-specific. In the field of music, Byron Almén suggests narratives involve "the transvaluation of changing hierarchical relationships and oppositions into culturally meaningful differences" (2008, 41), while Lawrence Kramer considers narrative to be the impulse to communicate, and anything that evinces that impulse is a narrative element (2013, 164). Both definitions are widely adopted in musicology and have applications to ludomusicology and are aligned with similar definitions prevalent in the fields of ludology and narratology.

Juul warns that it is easy to fall into the a priori argument that everything is narrative or everything can be presented as narratives, and that just because something can be presented in narrative form does not mean that it is narrative (2001, 1). He gives the game *Space Invaders* (1977) as an example. The game makers give the player a slice of story as a premise for the game, which boils down to "aliens are evil and should be chased away . . . it is the role of the player to recreate this original positive state [before the invasion]" (2). Yet the player cannot realize this ideal sequence of events by playing the game. What, then, is the narrative of *Space Invaders* if the gameplay has no relationship to the story?

To counteract the circular definitions which he found problematic in previous decades, he offers this anatomy of narratives: "a level of discourse (the telling of the story) and the story (the story told)" (3). These align well with Almén's and Kramer's definitions insofar as they too have composite parts that may be interpreted as the unfolding of the story and the taking in of the story. Kramer's definition explicitly has two parts to it, though both segments seem to place the onus on creating the narrative and have little to do with who interprets it. Almén's definition takes into account relationships and hierarchies in cultural contexts, which are also important facets in how narratives are packaged and how they are interpreted.

For the purposes of this chapter, I submit my own inclusive definition:

> Narrative (or story) is the culturally contextualized creating and packaging of a narrative (a story) by an author that the reader then unpacks in their own cultural context and unique perspective.[3]

Like a piece of music, a narrative has stages of composition (the creation of the narrative), mediation (the physical and situational format, e.g., whether it is read in a book or watched in a movie), and reception (the end-user interpreting the narrative). A narrative-based video game experience, that is, a navigable narrative, consists of a virtual world developed by creators who draw on their own culture and backgrounds to appeal to and communicate with the player, who may have a different culture or background but can find relatable elements and common ground in which to appreciate the story. The communication devices include words (narration and dialog), sound (soundscape and music, both diegetic and nondiegetic), visuals (the virtual space, facial expressions, color palette, and other aesthetics) and haptic feedback in the form of vibrating or pulsating controllers.

Three of my case studies—*Caligo* (Krealit 2017), *What Remains of Edith Finch* (Giant Sparrow 2017), and *Everybody's Gone to the Rapture* (The Chinese Room 2015)—present their stories clearly and overtly and require little imagination from the player to fill in the gaps. Some are multifaceted and modular, and the participant may be unsure of how the threads tie together, as in *Dear Esther* (2012). Some narratives require more mental and explorative legwork on the part of the player, approaching genres like puzzle-exploration or nonviolent action-exploration, like Tonguç Bodur's *Nephise* series (2014–2020).

Navigability

Navigability is a defining feature of video games in one regard and in narratives in another regard. First, navigability can refer to orientation, as in moving through physical or virtual space, whether it entails solving a maze or turning in place. This is standard fare in any video game, no matter the art style. The early text-adventures directed players to choose cardinal directions (e.g., walk north) or landmarks (e.g., approach ladder) and the player had to use their imagination or pen and paper to understand the game map. Puzzle games require a different kind of orientation but also require the player to understand how to move and organize pieces in the provided space.

Navigation can also mean comprehensibility and identifiability, as in drawing connections between clues and solutions and learning to recognize new objects and roles in a fictional context. This type of navigation is more along the lines of learning new semiotic symbols and systems. Each video game brings its own set of new symbols into play. These can include novel symbols, like *Animal Crossing*'s (2001–2021) star on a burlap sack signifying the in-game currency, to color indicators that may or may not have real life connections. For example, many video games employ the symbolic convention that red surfaces are lava and deadly, and players with video game literacy default to this interpretation, but in *Okamiden* (2011), Chibi's red-colored actions pertain to the NPC companion moving without Chibi's input. The red color has no connection to the traditional "danger" meaning and is remapped to a different meaning that players must adopt quickly lest they spend the game confused and anxious about the red actions. Understanding a video game's unique array of symbols and indicators is an important element of video game literacy for genres at large and for specific games, and mentally remapping indices and symbols like colors is a form of symbolic navigation.

Part of the reason navigable narratives were originally called "walking simulators" is because of the emphasis on wandering; the player spends most of their energies moving the avatar through virtual space, often a mod of another game with ludic elements like combat removed (Ballou 2019). The other half is, of course, understanding the narrative, which may involve symbolic navigation. Navigable narratives like Tonguç Bodur's *The Hunting God* (2017) and Stage 2 Studios' *Lifeless Planet* (2014) design lore for the game that may or may not be based on real-life examples but which come to indicate or symbolize specific roles and connotations within the game and the game's narrative. The enormous statues in *The Hunting God* represent the ancient gods the player learns about on their journey through the mountain range. The different plants and colors on the plants in *Lifeless Planet* give the player clues about the environmental dangers and history, and support or cast doubt on details unfolding in the story.

In all these examples, there are ample examples of musical and sonic indicators and symbols. In *Lifeless Planet*, the player becomes accustomed to the gentle hiss of air from the spacesuit's tank and may become anxious when it goes silent. Similarly, musical cues in the otherwise sparse soundscape invoke reactions of anticipation, curiosity, or dread. Scenes in *Firewatch* (2016) and *Everybody's Gone to the Rapture* (2015) are frequently book-ended by musical cues that amplify the emotions in the story. Such transdiegetic sound cues—that is, sound with no source in the game world but which still informs about events in the world (Jørgensen 2007)—are key navigation devices in many video games, especially navigable narratives.

Taking musical symbolism deeper, Jessica Curry's musical score for *Everybody's Gone to the Rapture* features choral songs based on Anglican hymns and orchestral pieces in styles similar to English nationalist composers like Gustav Holst or Ralph Vaughan Williams. On the surface, this fittingly represents the English setting. However, she uses instruments, voices, and synthesized sounds to layer game-specific symbolism pertaining to patriarchy versus feminism and religion versus science over the top of this English, pastoral compositional style. The textures and techniques employed help the player navigate the mystery presented in the story.

It is enough to say that each contributing transdiegetic sound is imbued with purpose and signification. The player may or may not pick up on the meaning consciously and be able to navigate mentally as they try to make sense of the story at hand.

Navigable Narrative

Navigable narratives—or "walking simulators"—put storytelling at the forefront. This genre intersects with interactive stories and digital books, modern soundwalks, and exploration-heavy video games. Although this genre is sometimes framed by the absence of typical ludic elements (e.g., combat), I instead rebrand the genre to embrace what it features.[4] In navigable narratives, the player moves through an intricately designed fictional game world. The game and narrative designers provide signposts and direction, and the narratives are usually quite linear, but the player has freedom to take whatever path they choose and to examine or ignore whatever elements they wish. The purpose of a navigable narrative is to convey a story, rather than to win or achieve a ludic goal, and the kind of storytelling at work is often affective or atmospheric. Navigable narratives employ paidic[5] gameplay and trust the player to embark on the journey in a way that will satisfy themselves.

Dan Pinchbeck, the creative director of The Chinese Room, which produced the navigable narratives *Dear Esther* and *Everybody's Gone to the Rapture*, defends the simplicity of the walking simulator as an asset for the player's experience. In a 2012 conference talk, he stated: "Lack of stimulation is not lack of experience. . . . Lack of stimulation allows different kinds of reflective, emotional experiences. We have to provide space and time for different kinds of experiences and different types of resonances to flourish."[6] Most creators of navigable narratives show a distinct preference for minimizing ludic play and emphasizing paidia and often sanction a slower pace than the average video game for these precise reasons. The experience that navigable narratives offer is not about achievement or prowess, but rather sparking curiosity and creating a mood or atmosphere.

Literary theorist Heidi Ann Colthup suggests that navigable narratives[7] are video games but do not demand the ludic literacy and expertise of a gamer. Yet, they are not interactive novels "because they offer a digital environment familiar to anyone who has played, or watched someone else play a video game" (2018, 122). In this way, navigable narratives offer the most accessible elements of both worlds. One need only be casually familiar with video games and with stories, to be ready to get the full experience of a navigable narrative.

Colthup identifies two overlapping worlds for participants of navigable narratives: the game world and the story world (124). The game world is the coding, the video game conventions, gameplay mechanics, and the onscreen-and-headphones experience—in other words, the digital stage for the scenes to play out. The story world is the narrative the participant interacts with. Colthup goes on to present a diagram of how worlds—realms of experience—map on to one another in concentric circles. The largest world is the real world of the player/reader, within which rests the computer or console, and then the game world inside that and the story world inside the game world.

Expanding on Colthup's theory of concentric worlds, I posit that the soundscape and music of navigable narratives exists in all four worlds (see Figure 38.1). The narrative and soundscape are inextricably linked, and this is a connection between the story world and the game world. The soundscape is spatialized in three-dimensional space, that is, in the console environment and extending into the real world. The fact that the style of play is paidic rather than ludic is not a factor in the soundscape, though it is worth mentioning that it is also a connecting feature between the game world and the story world.

My definition is designed to replace the term "walking simulators" and strengthen the genre definition that the label of navigable narratives tenders: they are not just games lacking another genre's features. I have identified the three core traits of navigable narratives as the following:

> (1) a soundscape spatialized in its three-dimensional space; (2) downplaying or lacking traditional game elements of competition and reward, relying instead on the basic mechanics of movement (walking, running, swimming, flying, etc.) and soundscape for player interactivity; (3) a narrative and soundscape whose pacing and tempo are inextricably linked. (Hambleton 2020, 21)

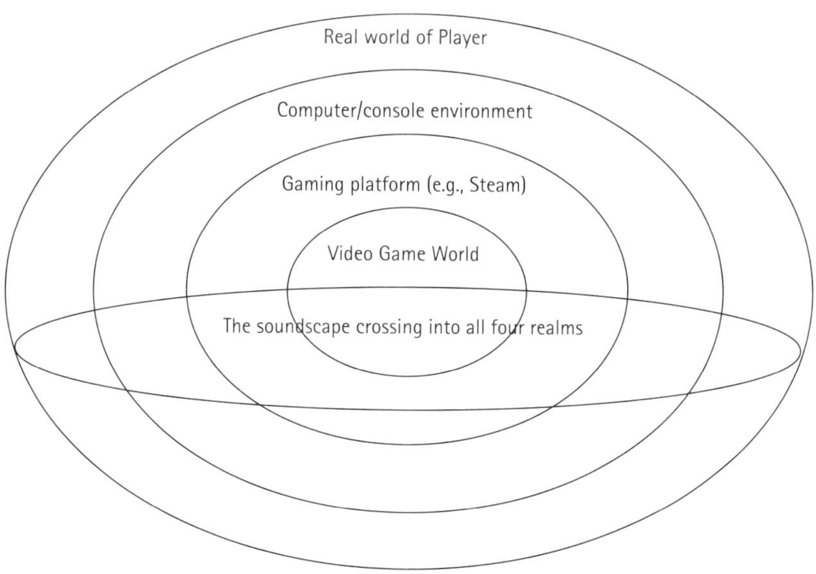

FIGURE 38.1 The concentric worlds of the player, adapted chart from Colthup (2018), with the new addition of the soundscape transcending boundaries.

In short, it must be navigable in a space replete with spatialized sound (and usually 3D visuals, though this is not a hard-and-fast rule), it must have a narrative, the narrative and the navigable space must not be completely separate, and there must be emphasis on paidic rather than ludic play. These traits are more like guidelines and observed commonalities than hard and fast rules, and the genre definition may be more refined as more games are made that join the ranks.

All these traits focus on the sonic realm; for better or for worse, like many video games, the player can still enjoy the experience without sound provided there are ample subtitles or other reading components to tell the story, though their experience will be considered incomplete by the game and/or narrative designer(s). To my knowledge, there are no navigable narratives made without any sonic elements at all, though there are a number made without visuals explicitly for blind players to enjoy. It is in part due to this preference for audibility over visibility that I chose to forefront the sonic components as necessary traits.

The three traits are not necessarily listed in order of importance, but rather in the order a player might recognize them. When a player approaches a new navigable narrative experience, the first trait they can confirm is whether the soundscape is spatialized. A 3D soundscape is often paired with a 3D visual environment, so the visuals of the game can be a tip-off.

For example, iconic navigable narrative *Dear Esther* features a nearly photorealistic 3D world that the player explores, and the soundscape is also three dimensional. Narrative-focused genres like visual novels, such as *The Red Strings Club* (2018), do not spatialize and move sound in the same way, in part because they are usually in a two-dimensional art style and do not afford the same kind of smooth movement through 3D space as navigable narratives.

However, many video games have 3D sound and visuals, so this trait alone is not enough to definitively determine any genre. The second element the player can reveal through experiencing the navigable narrative is what kinds of mechanics and actions the game emphasizes. Video games are often associated with actions like shooting, platforming, or solving puzzles. Navigable narratives may have these elements to some degree, but the primary actions and mechanics will be movement, exploration, and storytelling. *What Remains of Edith Finch*, for instance, has sections that feature leaping as a cat and repetitive chopping in a fish cannery, but these actions directly serve the story by emphasizing narrative points through embodied action.

These gameplay actions are the common dividing line between story-heavy video games that appeal to wide audiences, like *Outer Wilds* (2019), and true navigable narratives, which tend to appeal to a smaller group. Gamers who unwittingly begin a navigable narrative under the assumption it is a standard video game often complain in their reviews that the game was "merely a walking simulator" which is why and how the common parlance for navigable narratives takes on negative connotations.

The third element confirms if the game is indeed a navigable narrative or some other genre of 3D exploration. On the surface, this seems obvious, but this is where one really needs to split hairs. One notable example is David Kanaga and Ed Key's *Proteus* (2013), which is often labeled a walking simulator, yet it cannot be called a navigable narrative because it does not have any narrative or narrative structure at all. Musicologist William O'Hara (2020) has analyzed it as a musical performance, as the unspoken goal of the experience is to explore the island and in doing so create a novel piece of music. Players can post hoc describe the narrative they experienced ("I swam to the island, I chased a rabbit, I watched fireflies until sunset"), but *Proteus* is not designed with any narrative in mind.

Indeed, O'Hara points out that:

> *Proteus*'s lack of a narrative structure . . . is unusual among games, as is its relative dearth of clear goals. Most game spaces and narratives are structured by particular objectives, which may be conceived abstractly (progress from Point A to point B, score as many points as possible, defeat the other players) or in terms of a diegetic narrative (save the princess, win a battle or war, and so forth). (2020, 50–51)

Examples of navigable narratives with overt narratives include *Caligo*, *Dear Esther*, and *What Remains of Edith Finch*. These have been designed around the relationship between movement in space and narrative beats.[8]

Many navigable narratives find a balance between diegetic narrative and nondiegetic narration, as *Everybody's Gone to the Rapture* exemplifies. Unlike the other examples which provide near-constant narration of some kind, *Rapture* relies on the player's curiosity to explore widely and on their obedience in following an ethereal orb to locate the next narrative beat. *Caligo* and *Leaving Lyndow* (2017) reward exploration with bonus scenes and knowledge, but the experience as a whole and the narrative structure are unaffected.

Further Refining the Definition of Navigable Narrative

Navigable narratives tend to possess certain traits that are not in themselves defining features of the genre, but rather are logical or necessary byproducts of other ideations. For instance, most navigable narratives are 3D videogames, rather than 2D. The reason for it is that the creators wanted to craft a 360° immersive environment for the player-character to move through. The fictional worlds they develop and the art and tales they tell do well in a 3D environment that affords realistic vistas and a strong sense of *passing through something* rather than looking down onto the events as would be in the case in most 2D games.

Furthermore, most navigable narratives are first-person, meaning the player has the same point of view as their avatar. The player-character may be entirely embodied by the player if there are no clues as to the avatar's features. This intimate embodiment also plays into the immersiveness of the environment. In some navigable narratives the avatar exhibits bodily features important to the story; for instance, in *What Remains of Edith Finch*, partway through the story the player learns that their avatar is pregnant, and while learning this information through narration the camera pans down and reveals a round belly for the first time. The belly had been invisible before—though not conspicuously so, as there was no real reason for the player to look down. For the remainder of the story the player can choose to tilt their avatar's head down and glimpse her pregnant outline. This bold choice can make or break immersion depending on how connected the player feels to the body they inhabit in the game. Regardless of whether the player viscerally accepts or rejects the proposition that they are pregnant, the startling plot point makes an impact on the virtual embodiment at play.

Some Alternatives and Gray Areas

There are certainly video games that possess traits of navigable narratives that do not fit the label perfectly. I have already discussed *Proteus* above, and there are other games that overemphasize narrative rather than forgo it. For example, literary computer games (also called *interactive books* or *digital books*) are stories told through the medium of a computer platform, and they have interactive elements that readers can play with, like a 21st-century version of a pop-up book. *Unfinished Swan* (2020) is a first-person, explorable interactive storybook. As the player moves through and changes the environment, new areas come into view and the story progresses one small scene at a time, analogous to a book turning pages. The environment is 3D and the sound is spatialized, and the narrative is the foundation of the experience as a whole; however, I would not consider it a navigable narrative because the sound and music are emphatically *secondary* to the story and to the player's painting actions, not "inextricably linked." The game indeed feels like a storybook come to life, but it is not a navigable narrative or walking simulator.

Navigable narratives also overlap with some forms of sound art, particularly virtual soundwalks. Soundwalks are a form of participant-driven sound art. Some modern composed soundwalks take place in virtual-reality (VR) and augmented-reality (AR) environments. For example, the sound artist and sculptor Janet Cardiff's AR and VR soundwalks, such as *City of Forking Paths* (2014) incorporate real-life environments with recorded visual and aural elements, and she acts as an invisible omniscient narrator to guide the participant through physical and virtual spaces. By moving through these spaces and listening to the environment and listening to Cardiff's narration, the participant engages in a soundwalk with a narrative at its foundation. In contrast, composer Fernando Rincón Estrada's mobile soundwalks, such as *Random Is Not That Random* (2017), use only recorded and composed audio to accompany the participant through physical space, but his soundwalks offer more flexibility to take alternate paths or stop for a moment and let the composed sounds decorate the space in a new way. These feel more like physical versions of navigable narratives that support exploration and paidia, though they lack the essential component of a clear narrative.

The purpose of Cardiff's and Estrada's works are to experience art and all that that entails, rather than to play a game either ludically or paidically. However, given the emphasis on narrative and engaging with sound in 3D space in navigable narratives, it is clear to see how the two art forms overlap. The main differences lie in the creators' intentions and the participants' expectations. I would also point out that AR and VR soundwalks often require the participant to do more bodily movement and locomotion than the navigable narratives, which are played at a computer or console, but I have no doubt that in a few years this gap will be made negligible by further advancements in VR technology in games and in art.

All told, there are many works that may bridge genres or blur the line between navigable narratives and other genres. *The Witness* (2016) is often called a walking simulator and it checks many of the boxes of a navigable narrative: it offers a beautiful, 3D world and soundscape, and the player uncovers the underlying narrative by accessing new areas. However, *The Witness* emphasizes ludic play rather than paidic play, as everything hinges around solving hundreds of puzzles and mazes.

Navigable Narratives and Literary Theory

Literary theorist Astrid Ensslin identifies several types of literary video games in her book on the topic. Navigable narratives fit most comfortably into two of her identified categories: auteur games and quasi-literary games. As Bozdog and Galloway (Bozdog and Galloway 2020, 794) state, paraphrasing Ensslin (2014), auteur[9] games are the result of the artistic vision of an individual author (see also chapter 26 this volume), and feature sophisticated linguistic elements such as references to the western literary canon, verbal and audio feedback rather than a visual representation of a cursor, dialog and/or interior monologs, epistolary, and poetic elements, inviting the players to engage in complex processes of interpretation and meaning-making.

Tonguç Bodur's series of navigable narratives (e.g., the *Nephise* series and the *Bottle* [2016–2020] series) exemplify this definition. Bodur's games plaster lines of poetry across the screen when the character arrives at certain locations, so the poem takes the duration of the game to read in full. On the way, the player moves the character through a fitting landscape and witnesses scenes that reflect the line of poetry they have just read or the one that is about to show on the screen.

Quasi-literary games refer to stories and have linear narratives that the player moves through as if reading a book. Ensslin's (2014) example is *The Path* (Tale-of-Tales 2009), which retells the story of Little Red Riding Hood. The player has more interactivity and immersion than when reading a book, but they can only navigate the space in three dimensions, not the narrative, which can only move forward, though the pacing is variable due to the video-game setting. This linear type of narrative is not exclusive to quasi-literary games, and I would argue it is in fact prevalent in video games with narratives. However, Ensslin's definition specifically applies to games that fall under her umbrella of walking simulator, or my umbrella of navigable narrative; there is naught else to do other than engage with the story.

Theorist Adam Ruch (2012, 28) analyzes Juul's modus operandi and suggests that Juul might "claim . . . that there is a very clear division between the activity of gameplay and any consideration of meaning or interpretation." In other words, the actions the player takes or is required to perform to engage in the game have little to no bearing on how the player might understand the story. In the case of adventure video games, the playable actions are a means to an end to progress the storyline, and the storyline is a device to direct the player and inform them the purpose behind their actions, but the two elements do not overlap.

Navigable narratives, on the other hand, do foster overlap between the player's actions and intentions and the story unfolding. This may be a further defining trait that sets them apart from other video games and is an exciting and distinguishing feature all its own. In these examples, the players directly unfold exposition and uncover clues without the mediation of fighting enemies or solving puzzles. Moving through the game world and listening to the diegetic soundscape and nondiegetic narration and music are the primary actions the player can take, and these directly correspond to learning the narrative.

Though navigable narratives are a genre of video game and require the participant to play them, the gameplay is not at the core of the experience. As the name I have given them suggests, the narrative and the movement are at the fore. Both must be explicit, or at least have been a major consideration by the game-maker even if the actual meaning of the narrative is opaque upon reception.

Case Study: *Caligo*

Caligo serves as my model example of a navigable narrative. The provided description in the Steam store reads:

> Caligo is a small atmospheric walking simulator. It's an interactive story where you mainly have to look and listen.
>
> Caligo is the darkness everyone descends into one way or another, and to each of us it's something different. For some it's a short but exciting adventure, some will see it as a place to relax. Yet others will be reminded of their worst nightmare, while for a few, it might come as a revelation. One thing is certain however: everyone will have to answer one big question.

The term *caligo* refers to dimness or obscurity in the sense of proverbial wool pulled over one's eyes. The major theme of the narrative in the game *Caligo* is enlightenment. The protagonist goes on a guided journey through constructed worlds based on his memories. The story unfolds as the protagonist and the devilish guide exchange dialog cued by the player's progress through space. The game should be played at least twice to achieve both possible endings and uncover as much dialog as possible so that the player hears the whole story and the full philosophical argument the guide poses to both the protagonist and the player.

Caligo features a 3D sound environment that realistically matches the area—in other words, the forest is filled with rustling leaves, the beach is backed by roaring waves, and so forth. The player obeys the guide's directions to move through space in order to progress the plot. The guide does not have a physical form in most of the areas, but instead issues commands like "move forward" or "investigate the door" to encourage the player's movement. Following these commands at their own pace, the player thus follows the linear story until faced with a decision at the very end. After playing through once, one choice is more obvious than the other. If this choice is selected, then the player is forced to play through the game again. With the information they learned from the first ending, and from other lore they pick up along the way on their second playthrough, when the player reaches the end again the other choice is now much more obvious, and the player can finally conclude the storyline.

The player moves through space freely. There is a clear path, but they may leave the path or backtrack in the set space of a "memory" at any time. The diegetic dialog between the playable character and the guide is almost constant, filling the sound space with voices and text.

Voice in *Caligo*

Voices provide narration through dialog. The first voice the player encounters is their own. The player-character engages in almost constant conversation throughout the game. The first conversation is with the interim guide who presents as an imposing Anubis figure but has an old, raspy voice and prefers to teleport rather than walk. The rest of the game has the protagonist in dialog with the Devil figure, who is visible upon first meeting and at the very end but remains invisible through the rest of the story as the protagonist moves through abstracted memories of their life.

The guide reveals his true form in the first ending, and the protagonist reveals his appearance in the second ending. Thus, the player is expected to play the game twice to achieve both endings and hear all the dialog and see the big reveal at the end. This also presumes the player will experience the two playthroughs differently, despite presenting identically until the final chapter, because of the knowledge they gained from the first ending.

A common topic I will discuss for each of these case studies is the notion of the disembodied voice, as each game hosts a number of bodiless or faceless narrators and characters. Theorist Steven Connor, in his book on ventriloquism and voice (2000), asserts that omniscient narrators only exist as a voice and have no source, or even a body, and their entire identity is wrapped in their voice. In video games, players may be inclined to understand disembodied voices in video games, whether diegetic or nondiegetic, as narrators and, by extension, likely omniscient, though they may not necessarily seem trustworthy. *Caligo* subverts this reading by presenting the omnipresent deep voice as the Devil manifested, and then makes him invisible and omniscient after the introduction. The Devil's voice is spatialized to position him just out of frame at all times, confirming his supernatural power.[10]

The player may be shocked, then, when in the second ending of the game they trade places with the Devil. In a cinematic cut scene set to music thumping like an anxious heartbeat, the protagonist approaches the now empty throne that the Devil has abandoned, looks down at themselves and suddenly has the body of the Devil, and, upon sitting in the throne, opens a portal and casts the player's point of view into it and out of himself. However, while the protagonist's character becomes embodied, we do not hear his voice again, and cannot know if he retained his voice and presumably his self, or if he has adopted the Devil's voice and become a new character altogether. Eschewing voice altogether gives the ending a dark ambiguity, as the player has witnessed a terrifying transformation but cannot confirm if the transformation is skin-deep or complete without hearing the characters' voices.

CASE STUDY: *EVERYBODY'S GONE TO THE RAPTURE*

Everybody's Gone to the Rapture is another prime example of a navigable narrative. The narrative is not uncovered linearly but rather modularly, and the player's movements and choices have somewhat more lasting effects than in *Caligo*. Memory events are missable, paths are back-trackable, and by the end of the experience the player may have a variety of takeaways and lessons learned from their experiences walking through the fictional English town of Yaughton, Shropshire, where everyone has mysteriously vanished and all that remains are their voices and some unusual floating lights.

The narrative unfolds like clues in a mystery, told through memory events of conversations and by physical remnants like a bloody tissue on a pillow.[11] The other major element exists in the chosen sounds and music. Composer Jessica Curry relates different cultural aspects of the town, and personalities of the characters, to musical and sonic parameters that also map to parameters of patriarchy versus feminism and religion versus science.

Types of Guidance

The player is free to move wherever they wish in the game environment, which is the size of a small town. The player may want to solve the mystery of what happened to the townsfolk, but the game will not explicitly reward the player for reaching a conclusion, nor will it punish a player who remains in the dark. The two main guiding forces are the mysterious, crackling orb of light, and sound transmission devices like radios and telephones hidden in houses and telephone booths.

The orb is an active guide for the player, and it is easy to track in the enormous environment because it is both bright and noisy. In a practical sense, the orb gives the player purpose and guidance in their paidic play. If the player were plopped into this huge and intricate village environment and required to explore until scenes are unearthed, the game would last for days.[12] Instead, the orb leads the player down certain paths, sometimes doubling back or crisscrossing, but the signposting helps the player feel more confident moving through the space, and the landing zones often trigger new memory events.

Radios and telephones offer another kind of guidance. Unlike the orb, these are stationary and usually require the player to venture off the beaten path. The first thing the player learns upon starting the game is to listen for radio static and telephones ringing, as the radio is the first guide before the orb of light appears. After that first radio, these become optional encounters. Some telephones, such as ones in booths, are easy to locate, while others may be located out of the way, such as in houses that are difficult to enter. The player must keep a keen ear out to listen for the tell-tale sounds, and then find a way to access them to trigger the memory event. Many players delight in hunting for secrets like these, and tracking a sound is less straightforward and more interesting than following a visual clue. The reward for curiosity is a deeper understanding of the Yaughton lore—or, in some cases, more mysteries to puzzle over, like spoken strings of numbers that players have (to my knowledge) still not deciphered to this day.

Parameters in the Music and Story

Curry's composed score borrows melodies and styles from Anglican hymns to accompany the player's walk through Yaughton, which is presented as a close-knit, patriarchal and devoutly religious community. The songs feature choirs and appropriately religious lyrics, with the occasional clarinet or oboe solo and piano accompaniment. The town's soundscape is filled with birds and wind rustling in the trees; there are no cars driving, no factories running (or present at all), and no people filling the soundscape at all except during memory events, when the player witnesses past conversations shown by the orb. This allows the player, then, to hear the unexpected technological sounds mixed in: the radios and telephones, as mentioned before, and also the electric crackling of the mysterious orb of light that serves as the player's guide.

Curry's score and soundscape take on further connotations of opposing sides. The Anglican and folk music represents Yaughton and its conservative populace, who had refused to accept into the community Dr. Kate Collins, a Black American scientist who, in this story, stands for feminism and scientific thought. Each character with a dedicated chapter also has musical characteristics associated more directly with them, such as hymns affiliated with Father Jeremy. Rather than having her own musical style or theme, Dr. Collins becomes associated with the technological sounds of radios, telephones, and the orb, as well as a subversion of the patriarchal structure of Yaughton's society. The meaning of the memory events deepens when including sonic cues from the accompanying music and sound effects.

The plot is divided into five chapters which correspond directly to a specific character and roughly map onto a subregion of Yaughton.[13] The order of these chapters is fixed, and the beginning and ending scenes are fixed. The rest of the segments are modular, meaning they can be found and revealed in any order, though the guiding orb may suggest a particular order. Each chapter begins with a pastoral song from Curry's soundtrack. After the song concludes, the soundscape is built by generative audio; the birds chirping will never quite be the same as a previous playthrough, for example. This, on top of the player's own pacing and organization of memory events, ensures that every playthrough features a uniquely realized soundscape and organization of narrative beats.

The use of generative audio and modular narrative beats makes *Everybody's Gone to the Rapture* a wonderfully creative take on my third requirement for defining navigable narratives, which is that the tempos of narrative and sound are inextricably linked.

Another point of interest with *Everybody's Gone to the Rapture*, as is the case with most of these navigable narratives, is the implementation of disembodied voice. *Rapture* has no living characters, and all their voices are, in the truest sense of the meaning, disembodied. They exist inside the electronic devices that are traditionally used for vocal communication: radios and telephones. The voices presented in the devices are crackly and low fidelity, as one might expect from a staticky radio or old telephone. The memory events are clearer but are still slightly masked by the crackling of the orb's light. In short, the characters' voices can only exist in the present time through modern technological means, or in the past when the orb shows a memory. Curry's soundscape generally aligns human voices (the sung hymns) with religion and distortion (the electric crackling) with science, but each scene blends both as the player (and thus the protagonist) try to understand if the rapture was a divine act or an event that can be explained logically.

Case Study: *Dear Esther*

BAFTA-winning *Dear Esther* was one of the first games to be called a walking simulator (Ballou 2019) and sparked the invention of what I call navigable narratives. The Steam store description reads:

> *Dear Esther* immerses you in a stunningly realised world, a remote and desolate island somewhere in the Outer Hebrides. As you step forwards, a voice begins to read fragments of a letter: "Dear Esther . . ."—and so begins a journey through one of the most original first-person games in recent years. *Abandoning traditional gameplay for a pure story-driven experience,* Dear Esther *fuses its beautiful environments with a breathtaking soundtrack to tell a powerful story* of love, loss, guilt and redemption. (emphasis mine)

This description illustrates how it checks all the boxes of being a navigable narrative, and it contextualizes the kind of story and gameplay (or rather lack of ludic gameplay) that players can expect.

Modularity

Like *Everybody's Gone to the Rapture*, *Dear Esther* relies on the player to go to certain areas in order to trigger certain events, and only a handful of events and plot points are nonmissable. There is no external guide in this one, only the hiking paths that the player can choose to traverse or ignore. The island is large, and players can enjoy getting lost in it, but it is smaller than a town like Yaughton, and the player will eventually always end up at the other end of the island, where the story ends.

Whereas *Caligo* and *Everybody's Gone to the Rapture* exposit via dialog, *Dear Esther* exposits through a monolog of written letters to the protagonist and moments of pensive narration. The protagonist dives into a new monolog segment when he sees something he recognizes or finds a new trace of Esther. In this way, the story is modular. Jessica Curry, who also wrote the music for *Dear Esther*, composed an equally modular soundtrack to accompany the narrative beats. The larger soundscape, including the sound effects of ocean waves and so forth, is made up of generative sounds. Having this modular story and generated score, not to mention four separate endings, makes each playthrough a unique experience, and it will likely take players multiple playthroughs to encounter all the story fragments and hear all the possible sounds and musical modules.

Narration and Pronouns

Here, too, voice has an interesting purpose in the video game narrative. *Dear Esther* has only the one voice, the narrator who is also the player's avatar. The voice is not disembodied because it is coming from the first-person point of view; in a sense, it is coming from the player. The narrator-player continually addresses "you," who, depending on context, may be inferred to be Esther, themselves, or the player specifically. In this way, the use of second-person address entwines the player with the identity of the narrator and playable character, making the ending scene all the more startling and poignant.[14]

Heidi Ann Colthup's article on the use of second-person address in *Dear Esther* explains how the game hearkens back to text adventures of the 1970s and 1980s that use lines like, "You are standing at the end of a road" in order to "position the reader within the onscreen game as an apparently active participant of the storyworld" (2018, 121). Before computers could support game graphics, they relied on this form of address to give the player an identity within the game. Nowadays, computers can provide realistic graphics on large screens or VR headsets, and the second-person address is just as powerful as ever when used in a navigable narrative. In *Dear Esther*, the "you" used can be interpreted in multiple ways, either as addressing the player or addressing Esther, and the game intentionally blurs the possible interpretations.

Case Study: *What Remains of Edith Finch*

What Remains of Edith Finch (hereafter, *Edith Finch*) takes place in an old, meandering house tucked in the coastal woods of Washington State. The player enters the environment as the eponymous Edith, who has returned to her family home and is confronted by old family lore as well as memories from her childhood. Throughout the game, the player experiences the life and mysterious death of each of Edith's family members. Each narrative module uses a unique style of gameplay, ranging from platforming to point-and-click visual novel to sailing a boat through a sea of stories. Like *Dear Esther*, the story unfolds using second-person pronouns, and, until the very end, it remains ambiguous whether the "you" refers to the player or to the family member being remembered in each scene.[15]

Ludus Embedded in Paidia

The major narrative beats come from monolog narration by the protagonist. This is positioned as her narrativizing events to write down in her diary later. Within these "chapters," the player inhabits the body of another character and engages with a different play style for the duration of the chapter. Some of the chapters verge on ludic gameplay; at times, the player has to run from danger, find hidden objects, or make choices that affect the story within that chapter.

However, the stakes only apply to that chapter, and the player will find they cannot make a wrong move or wrong choice. When platforming, the player cannot fall; the character will only jump when the next platform is within reach. When running from danger, the music and atmosphere is intense, but the enemy never harms the character. Thus, there are no win-loss conditions applicable to the holistic narrative. In this way, *Edith Finch* maintains the player's attention by frequently changing the style of gameplay and the rules of engagement, so to speak, without affecting the overarching paidic nature of the game.

Linear Story Line

The narrative in *Edith Finch* is purely linear, and no events are missable. Some navigable narratives with this attribute receive lower scores on platforms like Steam because they are deemed boring and not engaging. Two of the case studies above have modular stories and inherent replay value through missable events and vast exploration, and the other, *Caligo*, uses near-constant dialog while traversing unique environments to hold the player's attention for the duration of the story. Yet *Edith Finch*, with its linear story, is one of the longest navigable narratives on the market (three hours per session) and one of the highest rated with an 8.4 user score on Metacritic (for the PC version). I believe it is the use of frame narrative as well as the variety of ludic gameplay throughout the chapters that keeps the player engaged for the entire playthrough.

"Frame narrative" is a literary technique of developing stories within a story within a yet broader story (Bozdog and Galloway 2020, 797). The first frame is established on the ferry, as the protagonist (controlled by the player) is setting off to Orcas Island to visit the old Finch house. The avatar opens the diary and enters the story of Edith, and the player now inhabits Edith as she returns to the Finch house on a previous excursion and begins logging her story in the diary. This second layer is "simultaneously narration and narrated time, the story within a story that hosts other distinctive stories within it" (797). As Edith enters rooms and finds traces of her family, the protagonist is transported into other characters to control for the duration of each chapter, and, in so doing, the player experiences first-hand these second-hand accounts Edith learns about or narrates. At the end of the game, the diary closes and the player recalls that the past three hours were themselves a long memory, and the main character is actually Edith's son making his own pilgrimage to the Finch house.

This frame narrative of *Edith Finch* allows the player to be in control of every part of the story rather than merely reading about them or having Edith or Edith's son do a lot of narration. Each layer of the text is interactive and engaging. Furthermore, by positioning the player as the protagonist of each story with fully voiced characters and unique visual and ludic styles, the chapters become uniquely immersive.

Conclusion

Navigable narratives are so much more than "walking simulators." They are a unique genre that exemplifies the intersection of literature, games, and virtual worlds. They are equally paidia-heavy video games and play-heavy narratives. The music and sound design are core features in establishing the realm of the game world and binding together the disparate elements into a cohesive work of multimedia art and experience.

In the four case studies of this chapter, I have assessed four games that exemplify the genre and have explored many different ways how music and sound design function uniquely in the paradigm of a navigable narrative. For example, composers contrast realistic versus imaginative sound to build a virtual world, embed lore, produce and support exposition, and otherwise propel the narrative. Timbre distinguishes the familiar from the strange. Disembodied voices are a given in the video game medium, and, in navigable narratives, the way voices address the player or interact with diegetic and nondiegetic sounds and follow the player's paidic exploration allows for new ways to exposit and experience narratives. The four games feature different mechanics and narrative types and showcase the power of the sonic elements in the game genre.

Notes

1. The term "ludic" is used inconsistently across video game literature. Many writers use it to mean any kind of "play," opting to use "ludus" as a catch-all term instead of distinguishing it from paidia.
2. For example, see https://www.audiogames.net/list-games/.
3. Throughout this chapter, I often use "narrative" and "story" as synonyms. When examined in their own right, there are nuances between the definitions. For the purpose of this chapter as it focuses on video game sound and music and its relationship with narratives and stories, I find it sufficient to use the terms interchangeably, and I do not mean to offend any narratologists!
4. Many game communities have chosen to reclaim the term "walking simulator" to expunge the original derisive connotations. I support the spirit of this notion; my preference to rebrand comes primarily from my desire to focus on the positives, as I say above. Furthermore, there are some exceptions that cannot be called navigable narratives because they lack a narrative, but they fit well under a more general term like "walking simulator," so perhaps there is a place for both.
5. That is "sandbox" or "open-world."
6. Pinchbeck 2012, interview.
7. She uses the term "walking simulator" throughout her article.
8. Narrative beat: a narrative unit smaller than a scene but larger than a moment (Velikosvky 2016, 218).
9. This term is incredibly fraught and polemic, yet it is the term Ensslin (2014) and Bozdog and Galloway (2020) use in their works, and I would be remiss to alter their language in this case.
10. The player's character is also invisible, but this is less disconcerting, as many video game protagonists and narrative protagonists are set in first-person.
11. These visual-only clues are also missable, while the memory events and most of the telephone and radio segments are not.
12. Or worse, the player would abandon the game altogether!
13. Though all the areas can be reached at all times if the player has the patience to walk all the way away from the prescribed zone.
14. Spoiler: in the end, the player-character dramatically leaps off the cliff and, quite unexpectedly, flies away over the sea.
15. Spoiler: in the end, it turns out the "you" referred to Edith's unborn son.

References

Almén, Byron. 2004. "Narrative and Topic." *Indiana Theory Review* 25: 1–38.

Almén, Byron. 2008. *A Theory of Musical Narrative*. Bloomington: Indiana University Press.

Ballou, Elizabeth. 2019. "The Walking Sim Is a Genuinely New Genre, and No One Fully Understands It." *Vice*, December 23, 2019. Accessed May 18, 2022. https://www.vice.com/en/article/wxeqzw/the-walking-sim-is-a-genuinely-new-genre-and-no-one-fully-understands-it.

Bozdog, Mona, and Dayna Galloway. 2020. "Worlds at Our Fingertips: Reading (in) *What Remains of Edith Finch*." *Games and Culture* 15 (7): 789–808.

Caillois, Roger. 2001. *Man, Play, and Games*. Translated by Meyer Barash. Urbana; Chicago: University of Illinois Press.

Calleja, Gordon. 2011. *In-Game from Immersion to Incorporation*. Cambridge, MA: MIT Press.

Cardiff, Janet. n.d. "Walks." Janet Cardiff; George Bures Miller. Accessed October 29, 2017. http://www.cardiffmiller.com/artworks/walks/.

Cheng, William. 2014. *Sound Play: Video Games and the Musical Imagination*. New York: Oxford University Press.

Christov-Bakargiev, Carolyn. 2004. *Janet Cardiff* [Exhibition catalog]. Long Island City, NY: P.S. 1 Contemporary Art Center.

Collins, Karen. 2008. *Game Sound: An Introduction to the History, Theory, and Practice of Video Game Music and Sound Design*. Cambridge, MA: MIT Press.

Colthup, Heidi Ann. 2018. "'You Were All the World Like a Beach to Me': The Use of Second Person Address to Create Multiple Storyworlds in Literary Video Games: *Dear Esther*, a Case Study." *International Journal of Transmedia Literacy* 4: 117–136. https://doi.org/10.7358/ijtl-2018-005-colt.

Connor, Steven. 2000. *Dumbstruck: A Cultural History of Ventriloquism*. New York: Oxford University Press.

Eden, Meg. 2019. "The History of Walking Simulators." *Super Magfest*, April 26, 2019. Accessed August 20, 2019. https://super.magfest.org/mages-blog/the-history-of-walking-simulators/.

Ensslin, Astrid. 2014. *Literary Gaming*. Cambridge, MA: MIT Press.

Escapist Magazine. 2015. "Should Walking Simulators Be Considered Games?" *Escapist Magazine Forum*, July 19, 2015. Accessed August 7, 2017. http://www.escapistmagazine.com/forums/read/663.878629-Should-walking-simulators-be-considered-games.

Hambleton, Elizabeth. 2020. "Gray Areas: Analyzing Navigable Narratives in the Not-So-Uncanny Valley between Soundwalks, Video Games, and Literary Computer Games." *Journal of Sound and Music in Games* 1 (1): 20–43.

Jørgensen, Kristine. 2007. "On Transdiegetic Sounds in Computer Games." *Northern Lights: Film and Media Studies Yearbook* 5 (1): 105–117.

Juul, Jesper. 2001. "Games Telling Stories? A Brief Note on Games and Narratives." *Game Studies Journal* 1 (1): 1–19.

Kayali, Fares. 2008. "Playing Music: Design, Theory, and Practice of Music-Based Games." MA dissertation, Vienna University of Technology.

Kill Screen Staff. 2016. "Is It Time to Stop Using the Term 'Walking Simulator'?" *Kill Screen*, September 30, 2016. Accessed August 7, 2017. https://killscreen.com/articles/time-stop-using-term-walking-simulator/.

"*Leaving Lyndow*." n.d. Eastshade Studios. Accessed August 25, 2019. https://www.eastshade.com/leaving-lyndow.

McCartney, Andra. 2010. "Soundwalking: Creating Moving Environmental Sound Narratives." *Soundwalking Interactions*, September 27, 2010. Accessed August 7, 2017. https://soundwalkinginteractions.wordpress.com/2010/09/27/soundwalking-creating-moving-environmental-sound-narratives/.

McGookin, David, and Stephen Brewster. 2011. "Earcons." In *The Sonification Handbook*, edited by Thomas Hermann, Andy Hunt, and John G. Neuhoff, 339–361. Berlin: Logos.

Medina-Gray, Elizabeth. 2014. "Modular Structure and Function in Early 21st-Century Video Game Music." PhD dissertation, Yale University.

Medina-Gray, Elizabeth. 2014. "Meaningful Modular Combinations." In *Music and Video Games: Studying Play*, edited by K. J. Donnelly, William Gibbons, and Neil Lerner, 104–121. New York: Routledge.

Medina-Gray, Elizabeth. 2016. "Modularity in Video Game Music." In *Ludomusicology*, edited by Michiel Kamp, Tim Summers, and Mark Sweeney, 53–72. Sheffield, UK: Equinox.

Murray, Janet H. 1997. *Hamlet on the Holodeck: The Future of Narrative in Cyberspace*. Cambridge, MA: MIT Press.

Myers, David. 2009. "The Video Game Aesthetic: Play as Form." In *The Video Game Theory Reader 2*, edited by Bernard Perron and Mark J. P. Wolf, 45–64. New York: Routledge.

O'Hara, William. 2020. "Mapping Sound: Play, Performance, and Analysis in Proteus." *Journal of Sound and Music in Games* 1 (3): 35–66.

Pinchbeck, Dan. "Ambiguity and Abstraction in Game Writing: Lessons from 'Dear Esther,'" Game Developers Conference Europe [recorded conference talk]. Cologne, Germany. Accessed March 16, 2021. https://www.gdcvault.com/play/1016695/Ambiguity-and-Abstraction-in-Game.

Porteous, J. Douglas, and Jane F. Mastin. 1985. "Soundscape." *Journal of Architectural and Planning Research* 2 (3): 169–186.

Reale, Steven. 2014. "Transcribing Musical Worlds; or, Is *L.A. Noire* a Music Game?" In *Music in Video Games: Studying Play*, edited by K. J. Donnelly, William Gibbons, and Neil Lerner, 77–103. New York: Routledge.

Ruch, Adam. 2012. "Understanding Videogames: 3 Perspectives for Criticism." PhD dissertation, Macquarie University.

Summers, Tim. 2016. "Analysing Video Game Music: Sources, Methods, and a Case Study." In *Ludomusicology*, edited by Michiel Kamp, Tim Summers, and Mark Sweeney, 8–31. Sheffield, UK: Equinox.

Summers, Tim. 2016. *Understanding Video Game Music*. Cambridge, UK: Cambridge University Press.

Van Elferen, Isabella. 2016. "Analysing Game Musical Immersion: The ALI Model." In *Ludomusicology*, edited by Michiel Kamp, Tim Summers, and Mark Sweeney, 32–52. Sheffield, UK: Equinox.

Velikovsky, J. T. 2016. "The HOLON/Parton Theory of the Unit of Culture (or the Meme, and Narreme): In Science, Media, Entertainment and the Arts." In *Creative Technologies for Multidisciplinary Applications*, edited by A. Connor and S. Marks, 208–246. Hershey, PA: IGI Global. https://doi.org/10.4018/978-1-5225-0016-2.ch009.

Warren, Alicyn. 1992. "Levels of Reality in Dramatic Music." PhD dissertation, Princeton University.

Westerkamp, Hildegard. 1974. "Soundwalking." *Sound Heritage* 3 (4): 18–27.

Ludography

35MM. 2016. Носков Сергей. Russian/English, PC.

The Beginner's Guide. 2015. Everything Unlimited Ltd. English, PC.

Bottle. 2016. Tonguç Bodur. Turkish/English, PC.

Bottle: Pilgrim. 2017. Tonguç Bodur. Turkish/English, PC.

Caligo. 2017. Krealit. English, PC.

Chionophile. 2020. Tonguç Bodur. Turkish/English, PC.

Dear Esther. 2012. The Chinese Room. English, PC.

Dr. Langeskov, The Tiger, and The Terribly Cursed Emerald: A Whirlwind Heist. 2015. Crows Crows Crows. English, PC.

Drizzlepath. 2015. Tonguç Bodur. Turkish/English, PC.

Drizzlepath: Déjà vu. 2018. Tonguç Bodur. Turkish/English, PC.
Drizzlepath: Genie. 2016. Tonguç Bodur. Turkish/English, PC.
Drizzlepath: Glass. 2017. Tonguç Bodur. Turkish/English, PC.
Everybody's Gone to the Rapture. 2015. The Chinese Room/SCE Santa Monica Studio. English, PlayStation 4.
Firewatch. 2016. Campo Santo/Panic. English, PC.
Gone Home. 2013. Fullbright. English, PC.
Hearing. 2017. skrimm8. English, PC.
The Hunting God. 2017. Tonguç Bodur. Turkish/English, PC.
Leaving Lyndow. 2017. Eastshade Studios. English, PC.
Lifeless Planet. 2014. Stage 2 Studios/KISS Ltd. English/Russian, PC.
MIND: Path to the Thalamus. 2015. Pantumaca Barcelona/Talking About Media. Spanish/English, PC.
The Moon Sliver. 2014. David Szymanski. English, PC.
Myst. 1993. Brøderbund. English, PC.
Nephise. 2017. Tonguç Bodur. Turkish/English, PC.
Nephise: Ascension. 2018. Tonguç Bodur. Turkish/English, PC.
Nephise Begins. 2017. Tonguç Bodur. Turkish/English, PC.
Okamiden. 2011. Capcom. English, Nintendo DS.
Oracle. 2017. Watercolor Games. English, PC.
The Stanley Parable. 2013. Galactic Café. English, PC.
Quern. 2016. Zadbox Entertainment. English, PC.
The Red Strings Club. 2018. Devolver Digital. English, PC.
Tacoma. 2017. Fullbright. English, PlayStation 4.
TIMEFrame. 2015. Random Seed Games. English, PC.
Unfinished Swan. 2020. Annapurna Interactive. English, PC.
What Remains of Edith Finch. 2017. Giant Sparrow/Annapurna Interactive. English, PC.
The Witness. 2016. Thekla Inc. English, PC.

CHAPTER 39

AMBIENT ECOLOGIES

Environmental Music in Video Games

MICHIEL KAMP

Introduction

My dynasty in *Crusader Kings III* (2020) could use some security. My leader, Petty King Murchad mac Donnchad of Munster, has but one son, whose spouse particularly despises him, and who has yet to bear him a child. I pause my game and my conquest of Ireland to weigh my options. Going through the options in the menus, I wonder if I should send her a gift, or choose the cheaper option and devise a murder scheme against the poor woman. She is from the house of Haro, whom I have never heard of (let us hope my leader has a better grasp of medieval European aristocracy), so I zoom out on the game map in order to look for her family's lands. Momentarily, the constant sounds of the rolling seas, rushing wind, and distant bird song are interrupted, and only Andreas Waldetoft and Philip Wareborn's score can be heard. The music hangs on a low string drone on A. Slow but brief melodic lines in the natural minor play over the top in different solo instruments: fiddles, flutes, and textless mezzo-soprano or choir, occasionally answered by distant drums. This is not so much music to scheme along to as it is music that is just *there*, as the sounds of nature were a minute ago before zooming out. Having found my daughter-in-law's estate in Castille, I zoom back in and continue playing.

My kitchen in *The Sims 4* (2014) could use some renovation. My sim, by now a successful freelance artist making more than 3,000 simoleons per day, can surely afford better than the used blue BlandCo counters and YumCooker stove (some of the cheapest kitchen items the game provides). I interrupt my sim's daily activities and switch to the game's Build Mode. Immediately, the diegetic scribbling sounds of virtual stylus on virtual sketchpad and the street noises in the background make way for a nondiegetic cue. Ilan Eshkeri's music is an extravagant combination of orchestra, textless choir, and a variety of solo instruments from flute to electric guitar, all anchored by the steady beat of a rock rhythm section. As a whole, regardless of its timbral, melodic, and rhythmic variety, the score maintains a relentlessly upbeat mood throughout that resembles (and probably satirizes) the corporate genre of library music, a kind of modern-day Muzak. But I am not so much concerned with these aspects as I am with trying out new color palettes for my kitchen counters. There is nothing in the music that explicitly suggests I perform certain actions, and there is nothing in the music to play along—more specifically, interior design along—to. The three-to-four-minute cues are just *there*, as I am, until my kitchen is ready, and I can continue playing.

When writing about the functions of game music, it is easy to focus on dynamic soundtracks and the adaptive transitions between cues (Collins 2008, 125–127), instead of music that is "just *there*" in the player's experience, as it was in my two examples. It is usually those transitions that provide ludic signals to players (van Elferen 2011; Summers 2016, chap. 5), information on how to proceed, or on the possible presence and threat level of enemies. Especially when taking an ecological approach to listening, as Julianne Grasso (2020), Mark Grimshaw (2008), and I (2014, 2021) have done, it is in the dynamic transitions that the musical affordances of a game can be found. But what does the ambient music in *Crusader Kings III* (*CK3*) afford? And what about the build mode cues in *The Sims 4*? How can these nondynamic cues be conceived of as part of the game's acoustic ecology, and how do we listen to them?

Nondynamic music is more ubiquitous in video games than it may seem. In fact, music that changes according to player input is fairly rare, particularly in certain genres and earlier eras. Even contemporary avatar-driven videogames such as *Red Dead Redemption 2* (2018), whose music systems adapt to the presence of enemies or player location, feature long periods of gameplay that are accompanied by cues that just loop or fade in and out, often referred to as "ambient cues." But long, nondynamic periods of music can more often be found in games without player avatars who are followed from a third-person over-the-shoulder view or inhabited from a first-person perspective. Puzzle games like *Tetris* (1989) for the Nintendo Game Boy, strategy games like *CK3* or *StarCraft* (1998), simulation games like *SimCity 2000* (1993) or *Frostpunk* (2018), and indeed the build mode in *The Sims* are examples of games where music is omnipresent but does not seem to indicate anything specific to the player.

In this chapter, I would like to apply an ecological approach to these nondynamic musical situations. Before that, I consider the concept of ambient music and the listening positions this is said to elicit, both in video games and beyond—specifically according to Brian Eno, the originator of the term. The kinds of cues mentioned are often termed "ambient" and analyzing the usage of this term in the discourse of developers and composers, critics, and players can uncover different ways of understanding and listening to this music. The ecological approach I then adopt focuses on three features of ambient music that are found in these discourses. The first addresses the question of what a game environment consists of, and how music can be a part of this or aid in its construction. Second, I consider the idea that ambient music is static or has a global stability to it. Finally, I discuss the multiple listening positions that ambient music is said to afford, distinguishing the concept from background music. First, though, I briefly outline James Gibson's (1979) ecological approach to perception and especially the role that the environment plays in it.

Sound and Environments from an Ecological Perspective

Central to Gibson's ecological approach to the psychology of perception is the mutuality (1979, 8) of animals (including humans) and environment. An animal's perceptual systems have evolved to pick up information from the world around it, which is useful for survival. In other words, animals perceive their environment in terms of what it affords, or its affordances. These are relational properties, dependent on the shape and anatomy of the observer and the environment, but they can be perceived because their perceptual information remains constant, or invariant, under change (of perspective, for example).

Affordances can be good (fire affords warmth) or bad (fire also affords burning), and they relate to actions as well (stairs afford climbing). This affordance-based approach also means that the environment as perceived does not consist of physical entities like atoms or galaxies (Gibson 1979, 9), but of surfaces like the ground and objects like trees and rocks. Temporally, animals perceive events, cycles, and changes like falling rocks and rippling waves, but not the erosion of mountains. This means that in an ecological approach, the environment is a relatively stable, permanent ground against which events and change can take place. Because it is possible for environments to change (e.g., due to weather and seasons), Gibson speaks of environmental stability as persistence rather than permanence.

Gibson's most in-depth elaboration of his ecological approach concerned visual perception (1979), but there have been adoptions of his approach to sound (Gaver 1993a; 1993b) and music (Clarke 2005; Windsor and de Bézenac 2012). In their ecologies of music listening, Luke Windsor, Christophe de Bézenac, and Eric Clarke focus primarily on Gibson's theory of affordances, inquiring about the relationships between music and action in different situations, with a particular focus on questions of movement and synchronization. But even when it comes to questions of listening and mood (e.g., Windsor and de Bézenac 2012, 114–115), musical affordances are seen as sound events that occur *within* an environment, rather than the idea that music can be a sonic *part* of an environment. William Gaver's (1993a, 5) approach to everyday listening offers more insights, suggesting that "[r]everberant sound is informative about the size and layout of the surrounding environment." Still, Gaver is addressing the environmental information in sound events, rather than the idea that there is a sonic aspect of the environment against which those events are heard. The latter is an idea I will develop below in pursuit of an ecological understanding of environmental music.

What Game Music Is Ambient?

We may ask to what extent the musical situations I described in my opening anecdotes are examples of ambient music. When surveying the use of the word "ambient" in game music discourse, multiple meanings of the term start to become apparent. One could start with the game score compilations that YouTube is filled with. These videos that are often many hours long and titled "Ambient music & Ambience" or "Atmospheric music" feature whole soundtracks pulled from open world games and RPGs like *Red Dead Redemption*, *Assassin's Creed*, and *The Elder Scrolls*. When discussing the music in games, critics connect the term "ambient" to game scores from the lush orchestral score for *Abzu* ([2016] Slackie 2016) to the low synth pads and energetic syncopated drum rhythms in *Mortal Kombat: Deception* ([2004] Kasavin 2005). Composers tend to use the term in slightly more specific ways than players and critics, but not unambiguously either. Most often, ambient music is contrasted to action music. This is most clearly stated by composer Winifred Phillips in her *Composer's Guide to Game Music* (2014, 151), who suggests that: "Ambient tracks set the emotional atmosphere during lower energy periods" and "establish a mood that adds layers of meaning to a game's environment." Here, ambient music is used in relation to a specific kind of soundtrack, usually for an avatar-based open-world game (although Phillips also discusses puzzle games); and Phillips' conception is echoed by Russell Shaw in relation to *Fable III* ([2010] Tong 2011a), Inon Zur to *Fallout 3* ([2008] Aihoshi 2008), and Joris de Man talking about *Killzone 2* ([2009] Van Zelfdan 2009). Ambient music is generally understood in this manner in academia as well, such as Richard Stevens's (2020, 85) discussion of narrative scoring during gameplay. The contrast with action music is crucial here, and it echoes other game-musical binaries such as exploration and combat cues, or Zach Whalen's (2004) "safety" and "danger state" music.

Uses of the term "ambient music" by other composers suggest that ambient music is not limited to "lower energy periods" but can accompany more active periods of gameplay as well, as long as it is not too closely synchronized with player actions, and as long as it does not draw too much attention to itself. For instance, in a Gamasutra piece about the score for *Ori and the Will of the Wisps* (2020), composer Gareth Coker refers to the 3–5 minute linear cues that are "almost omnipresent" in certain gameplay sequences but that are not stem-based and do not respond to the player's actions as "ambient tracks" (Kerr 2020).[1] The first criterion, that of loose synchronization, can be related to K. J. Donnelly's (2021, 101–102) idea of *plesiochrony*, which "aims not to match all dynamic changes of gameplay, but instead to provide a general ambience, making a unity of sound and image, and thus an immersive environment for gameplay." Donnelly emphasizes this environmental, atmospheric, and mood-related function of plesiochronic music. While he finds this function in what Phillips would call lower-energy games like *The Old City: Leviathan* (2014),[2] they occur in action sequences in shooters like *Quake* (1996) as well. The second criterion, that of audibility, is related to a long tradition of game and film music discourse that is best summed up by Claudia Gorbman's (1987) *inaudibility* or *unheard melodies* thesis regarding the film soundtrack. This thesis holds that, at least in the classic Hollywood era, film scores were generally composed and implemented in such a way that they did not draw the spectator's attention. In other words, they were meant to go unheard, so that they could do their psychological and semiotic work on the audience subliminally.

Other composers put the term "ambient music" in closer relation to ambient sounds. Dan Licht distinguishes his work on *Silent Hill: Downpour* (2012) from sound design by suggesting that "In certain sections it may be hard to tell what's sound design and what's music, so I'm doing some kind of ambient, washy, tension sounds" (cited in Turi 2011). This close relationship of ambient music to sound effects is also mentioned by Piotr Musiał when discussing his work on *Frostpunk* (Wandzel 2020) and Jeff Broadbent for *I Am Alive* ([2012] Leo 2012). Musiał, in particular, emphasizes the musical properties of ambient cues: "I took a sound, or even fully arranged parts of my sketches and tracks, and I stretched them over time, so that a 5 second sound would play over about 2 minutes. It turned out that if I produce them accordingly, these sounds create an incredibly interesting background which works perfectly as ambient for the game, like a glue" (cited in Wandzel 2020). These musical properties are also emphasized and put in a historical context by Bear McCreary (Tong 2011b). He suggests that technological developments facilitated the possibility of less melodic composition than in the 8-bit era, with an emphasis on sound (timbral) variety. Axel Berndt (2019, 200) connects these musical features to the ambient listening aesthetic as a "mode of subconscious perception" that can be achieved by "an interplay of several musical characteristics such as a low density of musical events, soft amplitude envelopes of the sounds, and a less memorable formal structure."

The musical features of ambient game music mentioned by composers and writers like Musiał and Berndt point toward an understanding of the term beyond game music. A term coined by Brian Eno, "ambient music" has been a genre of album and concert hall music since the 1970s. From its very beginnings, ambient music has had both a particular style and a particular intended function. In the liner notes to *Ambient 1: Music for Airports*, Eno (1978) says that: "My intention is to produce original pieces ostensibly (but not exclusively) for particular times and situations with a view to building up a small but versatile catalogue of environmental music suited to a wide variety of moods and atmospheres." The style of these pieces is best described by Victor Szabo (2017, 316) as having "a global sense of stability (through use of a limited range of melodic gestures, a narrow dynamic range, etc.), while remaining inconstant on the local level (through unpredictable entrances, shifts in color, changes in harmonic quality, and so on)." The relationship between Eno's intended functions and listening attitudes and the musical features of his compositions can be considered in terms of Gibsonian ecological psychology. In the manner that Eric Clarke (2005) approaches music, we may ask how this global sense of stability and local inconstancy affords an environmental way of listening, a question that I will return to in later sections.

Interestingly, in the same liner notes where Eno outlines ambient music's environmental function, he stipulates that it "must be able to accommodate many levels of listening attention without enforcing one in particular; it must be as ignorable as it is interesting"—as opposed to canned music like Muzak, which is only ignorable, background music. We may ask if this multifarious affordance is an essential aspect of the environmental function, and I will return to this issue in the final section. First, however, there is the question whether ambient music in video games works in the same way as Eno's pieces. The many different uses of the term in video game discourse suggest two conceptions that do not always overlap: music that is composed in an ambient style, and music that is (meant to be) perceived as ambient. Musiał and Licht's descriptions suggest an ambient style like that of Eno, as does my opening example of *CK3*; Greg Kasavin's review of *Mortal Kombat Deception* and Gareth Coker's soundtrack for *Ori and the Will of the Wisps* suggest a kind of ambient listening to music that is not necessarily composed in an ambient style, as my opening example of *The Sims 4* attempted to illustrate. As Szabo asserts, the term "ambient" has become ubiquitous in musical discourse. Mark Prendergast's ambitious volume *Ambient Century* proudly lumps everything "from Mahler to Moby" under the term, and ambient musician Keith Fullerton Whitman asks "what music isn't ambient in the 21st century?" (both cited in Szabo 2018, 144). We may take from this the suggestion that even beyond video game music, the ambient listening attitude has been somewhat emancipated from the ambient genre or style: even cues with strong rhythmic developments and melodicity like those in *The Sims 4*, or clear melodic, harmonic and structural teleology in *Ori and the Will of the Wisps* (over global stability) can be heard as ambient depending on the listening context.

All of the features implied or explicitly connected to ambient music in video game discourse can, however, to some extent be traced back to Eno's intentions: the close relatedness of ambient cues to ambient sounds echoes ambient music's surrounding influence, the relative indifference of the music to our actions, its ability to accommodate "many levels of listening attention without enforcing one in particular," and the contrast with action music to its intent "to induce calm and a space to think" (Eno 1978). Exactly how Eno's style, let alone such a wide variety of music labeled ambient by producers and consumers alike, can carry these affordances will be addressed in the following sections.

Musical Environments

We may ask to what extent ambient game music functions in the same way as environmental sound in relation to an environment. Game composers like Licht and Musiał, like Eno himself, suggest there are important similarities between ambient music and ambient sounds that make it worthwhile to unpack the meaning and functions of ambient sound before turning to music. Ambient sounds are usually referred to as sounds that are not directly attached to events or objects that are important for a player's decision making, but that say something about the location or space that is visually represented. There is some important ambiguity, however, as to whether ambient sounds can be synchronized with and refer to visual objects or events in the diegesis, or whether their source should be invisible or, as Michel Chion (1994, 32) would say, *acousmatic*. Consider this hypothetical example of a game in a medieval setting (something like an *Elder Scrolls: Skyrim* [2011] or a *Kingdom Come: Deliverance* [2018]): the sound of a hammer on an anvil can be seen as ambient, but to a player looking to repair their armor, it very much affords turning in a certain direction; unless this sound is part of a track of sound effects that loops intermittently to represent the (imagined) soundscape of a medieval village, and there is no actual smithy present.

Grimshaw (2008, 111–112) connects these two types of sound to *signal sounds* and *keynote sounds* in R. Murray Schafer's theory of soundscapes, respectively, suggesting a link between keynote sounds and ambient sounds in the case of first-person shooters. For both Grimshaw and Schafer, keynote sounds are pervasive, ubiquitous, and their source is often unseen. We would, however, be equally likely to find keynote sounds in a game without an avatar, where spatial audio plays less of an important ludic role; think of a medieval city builder like *Anno 1404* (2009). Schafer's idea of keynote sounds not only includes singular sounds like the sound of a hammer on an anvil but also applies to another category of ambient sounds, sounds that are more continuously present like the rustling of leaves, traffic noises, or chatter at a cocktail party. These can have a directionality to them, but they can be independent of player (camera) movement as well, giving the sense that they are far-off sounds that continuously envelop the player's avatar or camera position. The sounds of nature in my opening example of *CK3* are an example of this. In the case of noninteractive audiovisual media like film, Chion (1994) distinguishes singular from continuous ambient or keynote sounds with the term *elements of auditory setting*: "E.A.S.," like the sound of a hammer on an anvil or the "faraway bark of a dog" (49) "inhabit and define a space, unlike a 'permanent' sound such as the continuous chirping of birds or the noise of ocean surf that is the space itself" (55). This gives E.A.S. a more temporal role within that space, one that Chion terms as punctuation in audiovisual editing. Of course, in video games, editing usually plays a different role, but there is a temporal significance to ambient sound and music that I will return to below.

As Grimshaw (2008, 99–104) argues, sound can create *resonating spaces* that define the space and shape of the player-avatar's environment. They also create *paraspaces* (104–106) that establish a certain time period and location, creating a place in addition to a space. Ambient sounds play an important role in this, both as elements of auditory setting and spatial sounds. In film music terminology, we might call these diegetic sounds, and while nondiegetic music does not necessarily create resonating spaces, it can aid in the creation of paraspaces. Taking a cue again from classic film music theory, in the words of Aaron Copland (2004, 107), music can create "a more convincing atmosphere of time and place." For instance, a score to a desert environment can either suggest that the desert is African or Middle Eastern through the use of augmented second intervals (a common Orientalizing cliché), or North American through the use of instrumentation (harmonicas and electric guitars with heavy reverb and pentatonic scales), something that graphics or sound effects do not necessarily do.[3] Especially in avatar-based open world video games, music can serve to distinguish different places, affording what Julianne Grasso (2020, 60) calls "affective zones."

The term "environmental music" denotes a music that surrounds, deriving its etymology from the Old French *environner*, just as ambient is derived from the Latin *ambientem*, a "going around." It seems logical, then, that a 3D space lends itself better to environmental music: but music can have an environmental, paraspatial function in a 2D environment as well, functioning much like Schafer's keynote sounds, as long as there is a player avatar. Although we look down on Link in *The Legend of Zelda* (1986), the camera hovering over the space he inhabits, we perceive the environment through him. In Gibsonian terms, both the music and our avatar are part of the organism that perceives its environment, as a kind of prosthesis (Kamp 2014, 243). We do not literally perceive the world through Link's eyes and ears as we would in a first-person shooter, but we connect the meaning and structure of the music to the way Link experiences his situation and environment. The situation becomes more complicated if there is no singular avatar present. In a top down, real-time strategy game like *StarCraft*, the player controls individual units in an army, but does not perceive the game world through any particular one of them. The musical cues, in the case of *StarCraft*, are connected to the game's three factions—the Terran, Protoss, and Zerg—and relate to their distinct traits: the southern United States–inspired Terrans are accompanied by twangy electric guitars; the creepy Zerg by numerous distortion, phaser, and flanger effects and chromatic melodic material; and the spiritual Protoss by long drawn out chords and textless (synthesized) choral sounds. If this music has an environmental function, it is the environment of the player's faction. This is commensurate with Gibson's (1979, 43) definition of environments as an animal's relation to the world and not the physical world itself—both a single animal and a set of observers with the same relation to that environment, such as a species or, indeed, a faction. Thus, the same world or game map would be a different environment for the Protoss player than for the Terran player that they are fighting, a difference that is coconstructed by the unique soundtrack for each player.

This environmental musical function of establishing paraspaces can be extended to other strategy games like *CK3* and to simulation games as well, if there is a representational space created by the game's graphics. *CK3*'s score features stereotypical examples of musical medievalism in contemporary audiovisual media, from the omnipresent drones (Troyer 2020, 594), to the wordless vocals that are "subtly linked to plainchant" (Cook 2019), to the distant bass drums that answer some of the melodic phrases in a manner reminiscent of James Horner's score to *Braveheart* (1995). This paraspatial function is somewhat complicated if the space is nonrepresentational, such as in puzzle games like *Tetris* or *Bejeweled* (2001). But in my example of *The Sims 4*, too, there is no clear paraspace that is created by the music. Because Build Mode can be turned on in any game space—from houses, to nightclubs, to national parks—its music does not seem to be related to any particular one. In this case, we might take a cue from Kristine Jørgensen (2008) and Isabella van Elferen (2011) that game music can exceed its diegesis in order to play an environmental role in the physical space in which we play a game. It can have a *metadiegetic* function to sonically block out the real-world environment like a "wall of sound" (Munday 2007, 57), much like arcade cabinets use music to block out the sounds of competing cabinets in an arcade environment (Collins 2008, 9). Here, the environmental function is purely to be ambient: to envelop and to persist, to provide sonic stability against which events—signal sounds—can take place.

Ambient Stability

Another aspect of ambient music postulated by Eno is its stability or stasis—what Szabo calls the idea of global stability and what I, in my introductory anecdotes, called being "just *there*." We can identify two distinct hermeneutic approaches in the study of video game music thus far. The first is a consideration of the meaning of the soundtrack as a whole. For instance, Karen Cook's (2014) work on the *Civilization* series asks how the choices of pre-existing music relate to the setting and gameplay options. Likewise, K. J. Donnelly (2014) interprets the meaning of the nondynamic implementation of the music in *Plants vs. Zombies* (2009). The second approach considers music in terms of the player's moment-to-moment actions and experiences, usually through their avatar's eyes and ears. We can think of very close readings of those experiences, such as the autoethnographic accounts of William Cheng (2014), Kate Galloway (2019), and Mark Sweeney and myself (Kamp and Sweeney 2019), or music-analytical approaches like those of Grasso (2020). There is, overall, a bias in the latter approach toward avatar-driven games with dynamic music systems. Underlying this is perhaps the assumption that when it comes to the ambient soundtracks of games like *Civilization*, *Plants vs. Zombies*, or *CK3*, or indeed the build mode music in *The Sims 4*, there is little to say about music-in-the-gameplay-moment, to paraphrase Jerrold Levinson (1997). This can be attributed to the idea of stability: if the music is not heard as changing from moment to moment, for the purposes of interpreting its meanings, it can be taken as a whole. This is also commensurate with Elizabeth Hellmuth-Margulis's (2014, 7–9) idea that repetition "broadens [the musical] now." But this means that this broad interpretation is afforded by moment-to-moment listening, and Levinson's ideas are a good place to start understanding this.

In *Music in the Moment*, Levinson introduces a conception of musical listening that he terms *concatenationism*. Building on the late 19th-century philosophy of Edmund Gurney, his interests are, in the first place, aesthetic, suggesting that when listening to a piece of music we enjoy the parts and not the whole. Against aesthetic approaches that argue a piece must be appreciated as an architectonic whole (think of theorists like Schenker), Levinson puts forward his concatenational approach. In addition to making this aesthetic point, Levinson offers a number of important phenomenological insights into musical listening when developing this approach. For instance, the parts that he and Gurney discuss are not infinitesimally small. Of importance is the idea of a melody, whose individual notes only make sense in relation to those that came before them, and those that (we expect to) follow them. This prompts the phenomenological questions how long a musical moment can be; whether this length is (solely) dependent on musical features encountered in this moment; and, if so, what musical features can make a moment. These questions are especially pertinent in the case of ambient compositions, whose individual moments are not often deemed aesthetically significant, and which are not often deemed to rely primarily on melody.

Here, it is interesting to note that Levinson's concatenational approach applies to Gurney's *definite* listening. The definite listener, much like Adorno's structural listener (see Leppert 2005), "attends to the specific features of the melodic and harmonic motion of the music as it passes, registers the individuality of what he hears, and has some recognition or recollection capacity for those bits of form as a result" (Levinson 1997, 11). By contrast, the indefinite listener is only aware of "successions of agreeably-toned and harmonious sounds" (Gurney cited in Levinson 1997, 11), undertaking an aesthetically lesser mode of listening that Levinson does not address further in his book. This is unfortunate, because the definite and indefinite listening positions seem to correspond well to the two listening positions that Eno foresaw for his ambient music. I will return to this in the next section. We can, however, find some answers about these listening positions if we compare the question of the length of a Levinsonian concatenational moment with Szabo's idea that ambient music combines global stability with local inconstancy. When playing a game and hearing music as ambient, are we hearing inconstancy, or are we hearing stability?

In a sense, we are hearing both, and this is what not only allows ambient compositions to be ambient but other compositions, such as *The Sims 4*'s build mode music, as well. In a concatenational approach, there cannot really be such a thing as global stability. We hear music as stable if we find no significant difference between the moment that we heard before and the moment we hear now. *CK3*'s score illustrates this rather well: we hear the previous melodic phrase as not significantly different from the phrase we are hearing now. The music has not moved on; it is static. The many concatenational similarities between subsequent phrases are reinforced throughout by the continuous drone on A and the steady, slow tempo. This combination affords hearing those melodic phrases as local inconstancies in a globally stable environment instead of a developing progression of variations that build on each other.

While seemingly much livelier and more dynamic than the music in *CK3*, the music in *The Sims 4* can be heard similarly. Even though there are differences in tempo, instrumentation, harmonic rhythm and development, and meter and rhythms, all of these can be heard as static depending on how we interpret the local and the global, and the stable and the inconstant of ambient music. One of six different cues can be heard at any point while in Build Mode. These all have moderate tempos and duple or triple meters and are all in major keys. For instance, the cue titled "Beatrix" on the soundtrack album has a laid back, 90 bpm tempo, with alternating bass and snare drums, but an active (albeit quiet) hi-hat playing 16th notes. A IV-vi-I-V pop progression in G major with a steady harmonic tempo of one chord per measure is clearly indicated in the rhythm section of a bass playing the root notes on the beat, and a piano, harp, and acoustic guitar playing lightly syncopated broken chords.[4] Over this, a flute and oboe exchange short melodic statements. This forms the A section, which adds more layers of orchestral instruments playing longer notes as the cue progresses. The B section introduces a contrasting melody over a ii-IV-ii-V progression, and this structure is repeated a set number of times. The near constant change of instruments and accompanying layers every section and every four bars mean that it is possible to hear local inconstancies concatenationally. Literal repetition is absent. But the regular repeating AB form means that is possible to hear global stability as well. In other words, both of Eno's listening positions are afforded by "Beatrix" and *The Sims 4*'s other build mode cues: there is variation for Levinson's definite listener, and stability for the indefinite listener.

The limits of the interpretation of stability and inconstancy seem quite broad as well, given Gareth Coker's example of *Ori and the Will of the Wisps* as ambient music. The cue that he discusses—"Separated by the Storm" on the soundtrack album—has a structure that is more developmental than stable, with minimal sectional repetition. It starts with a long-held, root note drone over which a piano plays a simple melody in C# minor with chordal accompaniment. It is then joined by a cello for a B-section melody, followed by a C section which features a viola playing another melody with only scant material from the earlier sections. Only after two minutes does the first piano melody return, this time taken up by a larger orchestral section with the piano playing arpeggiated accompaniment. But this is followed by more sections with large textural variation in relation to the previous sections. Now, it is completely possible to find global stability by looking at invariants between the sections. The C# minor key is never left behind, and the tempo remains constant throughout. Another explanation of the ambient quality of this piece would be from the perspective of Coker's intended listener: this is the first moment in the game where Ori can freely explore the game world. Players might interpret the developing structure of the cue as analogous to their exploration: the new sections line up with the new features of the environment that reveal themselves to players as they move around.

My examples here show that cues can be heard and interpreted in different ways, stable and ambient being just one of them. The cue from *Ori* seems to almost resist interpretation as static and ambient, and it requires a very particular player attitude to not hear the cue as developing or progressing from one section to the next. The *Sims 4*, while relying on repetition in structure, melodic material, and harmony throughout, features constant change and variation in terms of instrumentation and texture. Even *CK3*, whose elements correspond most closely to the compositional style of ambient music, could be heard as a series of developing variations that move from instrument to instrument, and phrase to phrase. But the possibility of different listening attitudes is another central tenet for ambient music according to Eno. In the final section I will address this idea.

Listening Positions

Eno distinguishes ambient music from other types of music in another manner as well: "Most music chooses its own position in terms of your listening to it. Muzak wants to be back there. Punk wants to be up front. Classical wants to be another place. I wanted to make something you could slip in and out of. You could pay attention or you could choose not to be distracted by it if you wanted to do something while it was on" (cited in Grant 1982). This idea about listening attitudes suggests that the main difference between ambient music and Muzak (as a brand of commercial background music) is that the latter only affords inattentive or indefinite listening, while ambient music affords both. In my examples in the previous section, I have suggested that it is possible to hear ambient cues both as static and as developing. Here, I want to speculate from an ecological perspective why this multifarious affordance is crucial for ambient music's environmental function in games.

The most difficult part of Eno's quote is the idea that "Muzak wants to be back there," meaning that it not only affords indefinite listening but that it does *not* afford definite listening, unlike ambient music. Starting from the idea that ambient compositions feature inconstant foreground events like *CK3*'s melodic phrases against a constant background like a drone, one might suggest that background music or Muzak only features drones. But it very much does not. Drones, like ostinato patterns, tend to carry with them an air of expectation (see, e.g., Scruton 1997, 63; Torvinen and Välimäki 2019, 177). They are Gestaltist grounds against which we expect a foreground: a melody or theme in a piece of classical music (e.g., Beethoven's *Ninth Symphony* or Strauss's *Also sprach Zarathustra*), or a jump scare in a horror film.[5] Minimal music, with its maximalized repetition, relies on this constant expectation that works as an anchor to keep our attention, to keep our listening definite and concatenational in order to experience the slowly revolving structures of pieces like Steve Reich's *Piano Phase*. Because music is a temporal medium, a musical ground needs to at some point be followed by some kind of figure in order to maintain its identity as ground—in order to remain "back there." Muzak and other background music, such as the streaming-service music that Paul Allen Anderson (2015) terms *Neo-Muzak*, achieve this by fulfilling every expectation at each possible moment. This can be achieved through extreme familiarity either with the tropes of a musical genre or with a piece itself (in the case of personalized playlists). When turning our attention to a piece of (neo-)Muzak at any moment, there should be nothing interesting to be found in order for it to remain in the background.

Ambient music, instead, *should* have something interesting happening at any possible moment—this is Szabo's local inconstancy. From a concatenational perspective, this means that we should be able to turn our attention toward the music at any point, follow it, and turn away again without difficulty. CK3's soundtrack demonstrates this affordance in the manner in which its melodic phrases come to a beginning and end without requiring a harmonic, melodic, or structural follow-up. While there are certainly phrases that respond to a previous one by using its pitch or rhythmic material, they do not adhere to something like a question-and-answer structure. Each individual phrase can be understood in relation to the rest of the phrases without requiring attention beyond the phrase.

The importance of this can be understood from an ecological perspective when we consider the environment from an acoustic perspective as having a constant background, against which sounds are heard that afford certain actions important to an animal. Whether fleeing in the case of danger, or pursuing in the case of prey, these affordances all amount to some manner of attending to. From a soundscape perspective, the natural environment consists of more continuous keynote sounds such as distant birdsong or the rushing of wind, in which shorter signal sounds are *nested* (to use Gibson's [1979, 12] terminology). But depending on the animal listening, a single cry of a bird could be a signal instead of a keynote sound, as Grimshaw (2008, 110–112) argues. So, whereas a soundscape consists of a series of sounds, from a Gibsonian perspective, any of these need to be able to be picked out by the listener as singular events against a continuous background, which would, from a more objective perspective, consist of very similar sounds to that event (e.g., one birdcall among many).

An ambient soundtrack works in a similar way, consisting of keynote sound events (such as CK3's melodic phrases) nested in a more continuous background, against which signal sounds can at any point be heard. These signals can be ludic music like a dynamic transition that signifies a change in gameplay state, or sound effects that afford some specific gameplay-related action to the player. In a sense, we can say that ambient music mimics the make-up of our sonic ecology in order to blend in with it seamlessly. This is particularly important when ambient music is the sole occupant of the soundtrack and the player's soundscape, such as when zooming out in *CK3* or when in *The Sims 4*'s build mode. Here, local musical inconstancy in the form of melodic phrases or instrumental variation plays the role of Chion's elements of auditory setting that was previously taken up by diegetic sound effects.

Concluding Thoughts

Despite, or perhaps because of, the ubiquity of the term "ambient music" in video game discourse, the concept contains a number of ambiguities. Eno himself is on record as saying that he likes it that way (Grant 1982). But one of Eno's most persistent arguments about ambient music is his attempt to distinguish it from background music. We might dismiss this as a value-judgment: background music like Muzak carries with it too many negative connotations, so, to argue for the value of ambient music, it needs to be distinguished from background music. And perhaps many uses of the term in video game discourse can be characterized as such a distinction as well, made to avoid negative connotations. However, I have attempted to take seriously the differences between ambient music and background music by taking an ecological approach. The features of ambient music that Eno and other writers postulate amount to the affordance of an environment: a stable, persistent space in which one can pursue gameplay goals.

I have deliberately adopted a very broad understanding of environmental music, not just to accommodate the breadth of game scores that have been dubbed "ambient" by composers, critics, and players, but also to shift the discussion away from compositional features to include questions of listening. In a Gibsonian ecological approach, perception is dependent on both animal and environment, whereby one is determined by the other. Thus, what we hear as ambient music in a game is dependent on both the music and our playing. In *Ori and the Will of the Wisps*, we may hear the linear score as ambient, as part of an environment that is gradually revealed to us after we survive a particularly intense storm. In *CK3*, we may hear the melodic phrases against the background drone as ambient because the drone takes the role of the continuous sounds of nature—the rolling of waves and distant birdcalls—when we zoom out from the game map. In *The Sims 4*, we may hear the upbeat, instrumental pop tracks as ambient because they become part of our physical environment outside the game world, like a radio playing in the background. In all these cases, ambient video game music can best be described as "just *there*," seemingly independent and distanced from us, while very much dependent on our listening, and surrounding us as an environment at the same time.

Notes

1. "Stem-based" refers to the technique of splitting a music track into different stems that comprise one or several instrument layers. These stems can then be played or stopped dynamically in response to a player's actions.
2. Also pejoratively called "walking simulators," see Hambleton (2020) and chapter 38 this volume.
3. This paraspatial function can also be connected to Tim Summers's idea of "texturing" (2016, 60) in video games: music points to meanings beyond those immediately visible or audible in the game world or diegesis.
4. This is a variation of the more ubiquitous four-chord pop progressions such as vi-IV-I-V and I-vi-IV-V that, e.g., Scott Murphy (2014) discusses.
5. Even drone music (Demers 2010, 93–97) or *Klangfläche* music (Dahlhaus 1989, 307–309) like Schönberg's Op. 16 No. 3 relies on very slow change rather than pure constancy or repetition to achieve a sense of static or vertical music. This also fits with Robert Fink's idea of repetition as part of a "recombinant teleology" (2005, 42–47).

References

Aihoshi, Richard. 2008. "*Fallout 3* Music Interview." *IGN*, October 20, 2008. https://www.ign.com/articles/2008/10/20/fallout-3-music-interview.

Anderson, Paul Allen. 2015. "Neo-Muzak and the Business of Mood." *Critical Inquiry*, October 2015. http://www.journals.uchicago.edu/doi/abs/10.1086/681787?journalCode=ci.

Berndt, Axel. 2019. "Adaptive Game Scoring with Ambient Music." *In Music Beyond Airports: Appraising Ambient Music*, edited by Monty Adkins and Simon Cummings, 197–226. Huddersfield: University of Huddersfield Press.

Chion, Michel. 1994. *Audio-Vision: Sound on Screen*. Translated by Claudia Gorbman. New York: Columbia University Press.

Cheng, William. 2014. *Sound Play: Video Games and the Musical Imagination*. Oxford: Oxford University Press.

Clarke, Eric. 2005. *Ways of Listening: An Ecological Approach to the Perception of Musical Meaning*. Oxford: Oxford University Press.

Collins, Karen. 2008. *Game Sound: An Introduction to the History, Theory, and Practice of Video Game Music and Sound Design*. Cambridge, MA: MIT Press.

Cook, Karen. 2014. "Music, History, and Progress in Sid Meier's Civilization IV." In *Music in Video Games: Studying Play*, edited by William Gibbons, Neil Lerner, and K. J. Donnelly, 166–182. New York; London: Routledge.

Cook, Karen. 2019. "Medievalism and Emotions in Video Game Music." *Postmedieval* 10 (4): 482–497. https://doi.org/10.1057/s41280-019-00141-z.

Copland, Aaron. 2004. "Tip to Moviegoers: Take off Those Ear-Muffs (1949)." *In Aaron Copland: A Reader: Selected Writings 1923–1972*, edited by Richard Kostelanetz, 104–111. New York; London: Routledge.

Dahlhaus, Carl. 1989. *Nineteenth-Century Music*. Translated by J. Bradford Robinson. Berkeley; Los Angeles; London: University of California Press.

Demers, Joanna. 2010. *Listening through the Noise*. Oxford; New York: Oxford University Press.

Donnelly, K. J. 2014. "Lawn of the Dead: The Indifference of Musical Destiny in Plants vs. Zombies." In *Music in Video Games: Studying Play*, edited by K. J. Donnelly, William Gibbons, and Neil Lerner, 151–165. New York, Abingdon: Routledge.

Elferen, Isabella van. 2011. "¡Un Forastero! Issues of Virtuality and Diegesis in Videogame Music." *Music and the Moving Image* 4 (2): 30–39.

Eno, Brian. 1978. *Music for Airports / Ambient 1*. LP. PVC 7908 (AMB 001).

Fink, Robert. 2005. *Repeating Ourselves: American Minimal Music as Cultural Practice*. Berkeley; Los Angeles; London: University of California Press.

Galloway, Kate. 2019. "Soundwalking and the Aurality of Stardew Valley: An Ethnography of Listening to and Interacting with Environmental Game Audio." In *Music in the Role-Playing Game: Heroes and Harmonies*, edited by William Gibbons and Steven Reale, 159–178. New York: Routledge.

Gaver, William W. 1993a. "What in the World Do We Hear? An Ecological Approach to Auditory Source Perception." *Ecological Psychology* 5 (1): 1–29.

Gaver, William W. 1993b. "How Do We Hear in the World? Explorations in Ecological Acoustics." *Ecological Psychology* 5 (4): 285–313. https://doi.org/10.1207/s15326969ec00504_2.

Gibson, James J. 1979. *The Ecological Approach to Visual Perception*. Boston: Houghton Mifflin.

Gorbman, Claudia. 1987. *Unheard Melodies: Narrative Film Music*. Bloomington: Indiana University Press.

Grant, Steven. 1982. "Brian Eno against Interpretation." 1982. http://www.moredarkthanshark.org/eno_int_tp-aug82.html.

Grasso, Julianne. 2020. "Video Game Music, Meaning, and the Possibilities of Play." PhD dissertation, University of Chicago.

Grimshaw, Mark. 2008. *The Acoustic Ecology of the First-Person Shooter: The Player Experience of Sound in the First-Person Shooter Computer Game*. Saarbrücken: VDM Verlag.

Hambleton, Elizabeth. 2020. "Gray Areas: Analyzing Navigable Narratives in the Not-So-Uncanny Valley between Soundwalks, Video Games, and Literary Computer Games." *Journal of Sound and Music in Games* 1 (1): 20–43.

Hellmuth-Margulis, Elizabeth. 2014. *On Repeat: How Music Plays the Mind*. Oxford; New York: Oxford University Press.

Jørgensen, Kristine. 2008. "Game Studies—Audio and Gameplay: An Analysis of PvP Battlegrounds in *World of Warcraft*." *Game Studies* 8 (2). http://www.gamestudies.org/0802/articles/jorgensen.
Kamp, Michiel. 2014. "Musical Ecologies in Video Games." *Philosophy and Technology* 27 (2): 235–249.
Kamp, Michiel. 2021. "Old(er) Media and New Musical Affordances in Virtual Reality Experiences." In *The Oxford Handbook of Cinematic Listening*, edited by Carlo Cenciarelli, 712–736. Oxford; New York: Oxford University Press.
Kamp, Michiel, and Mark Sweeney. 2019. "Musical Landscapes in *Skyrim*." In *Music in the Role-Playing Game: Heroes and Harmonies*, edited by William Gibbons and Steven Reale, 179–196. New York: Routledge.
Kasavin, Greg. 2005. "*Mortal Kombat*: Deception Review." *GameSpot*, March 2, 2005. https://www.gamespot.com/reviews/mortal-kombat-deception-review/1900-6119566/.
Kerr, Chris. 2020. "In-Depth: Crafting the Score for *Ori and the Will of the Wisps*." *Gamasutra*, September 2, 2020. https://www.gamasutra.com/view/news/368505/Indepth_Crafting_the_score_for_Ori_and_the_Will_of_the_Wisps.php.
Leo, Jon. 2012. "We Talk to the Composer Who Recently Scored the New Survival Action Title *I Am Alive*." *GameSpot*, March 13, 2012. https://www.gamespot.com/articles/sound-byte-meet-the-composer-jeff-broadbent/1100-6364772/.
Leppert, Richard. 2005. "Music 'Pushed to the Edge of Existence' (Adorno, Listening, and the Question of Hope)." *Cultural Critique*, no. 60: 92–133.
Levinson, Jerrold. 1997. *Music in the Moment*. Ithaca, NY: Cornell University Press.
Munday, Rod. 2007. "Music in Video Games." In *Music, Sound and Multimedia: From the Live to the Virtual*, edited by Jamie Sexton, 51–67. Edinburgh: Edinburgh University Press.
Murphy, Scott. 2014. "A Pop Music Progression in Recent Popular Movies and Movie Trailers." *Music, Sound, and the Moving Image* 8 (2): 141–162.
Scruton, Roger. 1997. *The Aesthetics of Music*. Oxford: Clarendon.
Slackie, Kevin. 2016. "Musical Rewind: Looking Back at Some of the Best Game Soundtracks from 2016." *Game Informer*, December 12, 2016. https://www.gameinformer.com/b/features/archive/2016/12/12/musical-rewind-looking-back-at-some-of-the-best-game-soundtracks-from-2016.aspx.
Stevens, Richard. 2020. "The Inherent Conflicts of Musical Interactivity in Video Games." In *The Cambridge Companion to Video Game Music*, edited by Melanie Fritsch and Tim Summers, 74–93. Cambridge: Cambridge University Press.
Summers, Tim. 2016. *Understanding Video Game Music*. Cambridge: Cambridge University Press.
Szabo, Victor. 2018. "'What Music Isn't Ambient in the 21st Century?': A Design-Oriented Approach to Analyzing and Interpreting Ambient Music Recordings." In *The Routledge Companion to Popular Music Analysis*, edited by Ciro Scotto, Kenneth Smith, and John Brackett, 144–158. New York: Routledge.
Tong, Sophia. 2011a. "Sound Byte: Meet the Composer—*Fable III*'s Russell Shaw." *GameSpot*, January 11, 2011. https://www.gamespot.com/articles/sound-byte-meet-the-composer-fable-iiis-russell-shaw/1100-6286164/.
Tong, Sophia. 2011b. "Sound Byte: Meet the Composer—Bear McCreary." *GameSpot*, August 30, 2011. https://www.gamespot.com/articles/sound-byte-meet-the-composer-bear-mccreary/1100-6331889/.

Torvinen, Juha, and Susanna Välimäki. 2019. "Nordic Drone: Pedal Points and Static Textures as Musical Imagery of the Northerly Environment." In *The Nature of Nordic Music*, edited by Tim Howell, 173–192. London: Routledge.

Troyer, Scott R. 2020. "Medievalism and Identity Construction in Pagan Folk Music." In *The Oxford Handbook of Music and Medievalism*, edited by Stephen C. Meyer and Kirsten Yri, 586–603. New York: Oxford University Press. https://doi.org/10.1093/oxfordhb/9780190658441.013.47.

Turi, Tim. 2011. "Interview: Dexter Composer Dan Licht on *Silent Hill: Downpour*." *Game Informer*, January 26, 2011. https://www.gameinformer.com/games/silent_hill_downpour/b/xbox360/archive/2011/01/26/interview-dexter-composer-dan-licht-on-silent-hill-downpour.aspx.

Van Zelfdan, Alex. 2009. "Behind the Music of *Killzone 2*." *IGN*, March 2, 2009. https://www.ign.com/articles/2009/03/02/behind-the-music-of-killzone-2.

Wandzel, Jacek. 2020. "Interview with Composer Piotr Musiał (*Frostpunk*, *This War of Mine*)—Part 1." *Ustatkowany Gracz* (blog), July 21, 2020. https://ustatkowanygracz.pl/piotr-musial-interview-part-1/.

Whalen, Zach. 2004. "Play Along: An Approach to Videogame Music." *Game Studies* 4 (1). http://www.gamestudies.org/0401/whalen/.

Windsor, W. Luke, and Christophe de Bézenac. 2012. "Music and Affordances." *Musicae Scientiae* 16 (1): 102–120.

CHAPTER 40

SEMIOTICS AND THE NEGOTIATION OF MUSICAL COMMUNICATION IN VIDEO GAME MUSIC

An Imprecise and Beautiful Art

IAIN HART

An Infinite Mess

Music fades and silence falls. Alien cricketoids chirp. A human becomes mildly disgruntled. The human adjusts the pattern of twitches they were applying to their controller's thumbsticks. Master Chief's fascination with doing burnouts in a Warthog armored vehicle in an otherwise peaceful dell (the recent repository of several alien corpses) is interrupted. The exit of the dell is located. The structure of gameplay becomes more formal again. Narrative progression resumes. The next open space of the game world approaches. The player's crosshairs seek and find some new dangerous alien foes. And music once again starts to play.

Those familiar with the single-player missions of the *Halo* series, starting with *Halo: Combat Evolved* (Bungie 2001), will also be familiar with scenarios such as these (in proportion to how explorative is their play style). In *Halo* games, musical silence can be a remarkably clear signal from the game that the player is taking too long to get to the next gameplay area once all the difficult enemies in the current area have been defeated. *Halo* composer Martin O'Donnell has described this as a " 'bored now' switch" (Collins 2008, 141); analyses by Karen Collins (2008, 141) and Tim Summers (2016a, 12) have focused on this function's role of preventing musical boredom, while William Gibbons (2014, 125–126) adds to this a deterrent/reward system encouraging gameplay progression. But why set a timeframe on the player's free play at all? What harm to the player or the game if the player wishes to hear the music for longer and does not mind a spot of boredom, or if the player wants to do burnouts in a Warthog for six hours straight? Surely none, other than that the narrative of story-driven action games like the *Halo* series is a dish best served contiguously. So, to maintain the player's interest in the game as its creators intended it to be experienced, and to protect the music's ability to enhance the parts of gameplay that are actually exciting (O'Donnell 2002), the game's music gently fades away to suggest that the player should move along. The player, perhaps semiconsciously aware that doing burnouts in a Warthog for six hours straight may turn out to be less rewarding than taking part in Master Chief's urgent mission to save the galaxy, concedes. The player and the game have negotiated through a point of disagreement (continuing the narrative versus doing more Warthog burnouts) to a point of agreement about how the game will proceed, despite potentially differing attitudes to gameplay and the meanings and experiences each party wants it to contain. At least until the next wide open, burnout-friendly patch of alien world appears.

Jean-Jacques Nattiez (1990, 37) wrote in his book *Music and Discourse* that interpreting meaning in music is "always hazardous." Music (and, as *Halo* demonstrates, the absence of music) can evoke thoughts and emotions and invoke cultures and contexts that well exceed its ostensible scope, producing "a complex and infinite web of interpretants" (37). So, too, is instilling meaning into music a hazardous activity with potentially infinite outcomes—some foreseeable, but many not. These infinite potentials of signification and meaning may provoke in the scholar some measure of alarm. As communicative beings, we may become cautious when meanings are not neatly definable and bias our analyses toward a return to safety. After all, if the scope of possible meanings is infinite, how is it ever possible to communicate—to produce a semiosis that is, in the words of Charles Sanders Peirce (1998, 403), shared "between two minds"?

I suggest that there are two keys to maintaining hope when faced with the beautiful mess of the potentially infinite imprecision of musical communication in video games. Firstly, to cope with the imprecision of communication, one must recognize that both *mis*communication (interpreting an entirely different meaning from the signs of an intended communication) and missed communication (not observing the signs of an intended communication at all) are just as important as successful communication (a meaning interpreted by the player that corresponds with the intended meaning of the composer[1]) from a semiotic point of view. They are not failures of *meaning*, because they still bear meaning; they are merely alternative meaningful outcomes that vary from the composer's intent. As such, they are both eminently analyzable by the ludomusicologist and important for understanding how the player hears and interacts with game music. Secondly, to cope with the potentially infinite scope of meaning requires an understanding that communication (and/or missed/miscommunication) is not a chance alignment of the spheres but the outcome of a negotiation that occurs as a normal part of gameplay. The negotiation of communication distills the infinite potentials of signification in gameplay into a messy yet meaningful and tangible experience that the human player or ludomusicologist can comprehend without despair.

In earlier writing (Hart 2014, 2021), I have developed a framework for the semiotic analysis of video game music that conceives of two semiotic domains: the first encompassing the composer's initial composition of the music, and the second the player's instantiation and experience of the music during interactive gameplay. The meanings of video game music that are understood by the player are the outcome, in essence, of the semiosis of gameplay working on the products of the semiosis of initial composition. Because video games aim to provide the player with a specific set of experiences, it is reasonable to conceive of the composer's initial composition as producing not a set of static signs that the player may stumble over, but instead a set of signs that are purposeful and directed toward the player, and with which the player has to actively contend as part of gameplay (Aarseth 1997, 1). Following a brief summary of the semioses of video game music, I will describe how the player negotiates the communication of game music's meanings with the composer.

The Semiotics of Video Game Music

There are two domains—two distinct contexts of time and situation—in which semiotic activity occurs in relation to video game music. The first is the video game music's creation. This is the context in which ideas about how the music should sound and how it should operate within the game are distilled through processes of composition, recording, and/or programming into musical objects that form part of a video game (note that ideas are themselves signs according to Peirce [1998, 402]). The second is gameplay, or the context in which the player's computer transforms digital elements into an analogue experience of lights, sounds, music, touch, and/or narrative with which the player can interact. These contexts are distinct in that gameplay usually occurs sometime after the game's creation, most often in a separate physical location, and with the involvement of different sets of people. They are linked through the game text, which, rather than being a deific tome with an inviolable prescribed meaning, is a set of signs chosen to present a specific set of "meaning potentials" (van Leeuwen 1998, 26) to the player such that they may create their own meaning-filled experiences from it (a process not unique to video games, but perhaps more strongly evident in video games than many other types of text due to their interactive nature). The experiences of any given player have the same set of potentials as their basis, and the meanings the players perceive are therefore traceable back to that game, yet they are unique to each player due to the constrained yet infinite variability of interactive gameplay and the influence of the player's own self on what the player experiences.

The initial composition of video game music, the first of the semiotic domains, occurs during the creation of the video game (see Figure 40.1). The music is composed to work with the other game elements in providing future players with a particular gameplay experience as envisioned by all the game's artists, writers, programmers, composers, marketers, executives, and so on. Note that each of these other creators is also creating

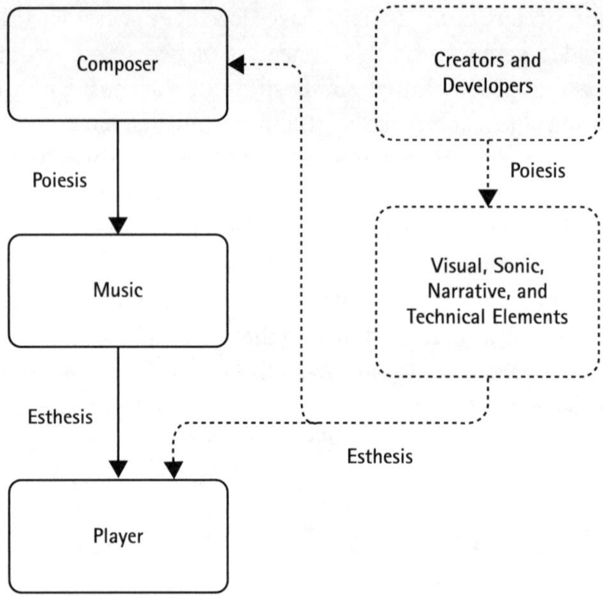

FIGURE 40.1 The semiosis of initial composition.

their own elements with the same goal in mind. The result of these collective processes of creation is a unified collection of elements that may all be experienced concurrently, or at least cocontextually, by future players during gameplay. The primary process of the semiotic domain of initial composition is *poiesis*, or creation. The process of *esthesis*, or reception, typically occurs later during gameplay, but is included here because it is the motivator for poiesis—the game is made to be played.

The second semiotic domain is gameplay (see Figure 40.2). This is the realization of the esthesis of the semiotic domain of initial composition, but it is a vastly more complex process than simply "reception" of a set of signs. This complexity arises due to the interactivity of the player, which modifies and adds to the significations the player experiences in multiple ways. Specifically, interacting with game music during gameplay involves three primary semiotic processes: ergodesis, interactive poiesis, and esthesis.

Ergodesis derives from Espen Aarseth's (1997, 1) conception of "ergodic literature," which require work to be done on them in order to interpret them. The process of ergodesis involves the player making a choice (though not necessarily consciously) about how to engage with the signs in a text. Aarseth suggests there are four "user functions" available to users of ergodic texts pertaining to the kinds of work interpretation requires—in increasing complexity of work, these are the *interpretive*, the *explorative*, the *configurative*, and the *textonic* user functions (64). However, the approach I take here is to conceive of Aarseth's "user functions" as conflations of the user's *decisions* and *actions*, and then to use Aarseth's categories to examine the user's decisions while examining their actions separately. The simplest of the decisions a user makes during ergodesis is the *interpretive*, to simply read the meaning of the sign as though by reflex or

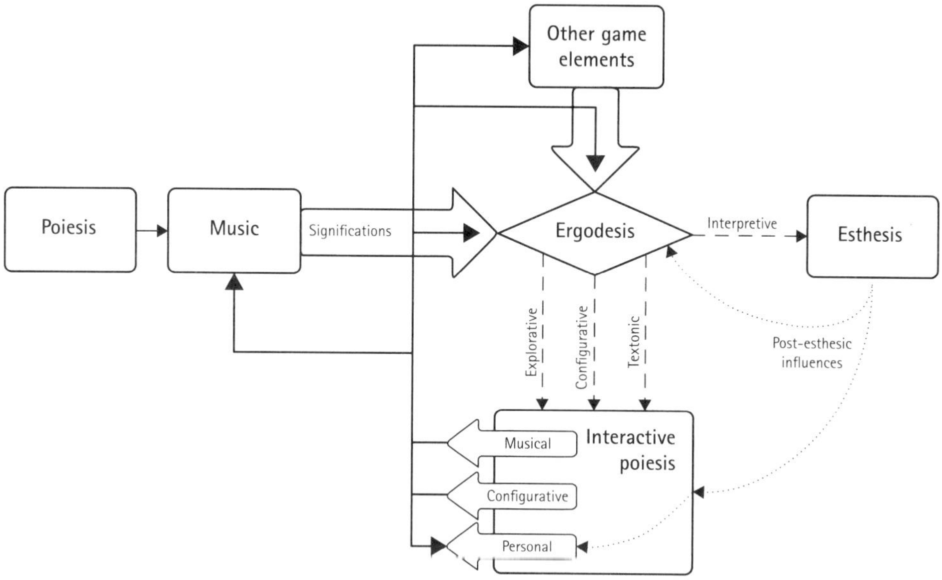

FIGURE 40.2 The semiosis of gameplay.

by convention, such as hearing a bird chirping and interpreting the sound to have come from a nearby bird in a tree. Should the user require a little bit more exploration of the sign before they can understand its meaning, such as listening to a sound a few more times to determine its qualities and its relationships to other game elements, they make an *explorative* decision. If they need to reconfigure the surrounding signs of the text in some way to understand the sign, such as moving to a different location in the game map to hear the sound from a different angle, they make a *configurative* decision. And if the user needs to add signs to the game to understand a sign, such as looking up an online resource to inform their gameplay perception and interpretation, they make a *textonic* decision. These decisions follow Aarseth's categories closely, but their separation from actions allows us to acknowledge and address the differences that may exist between the player's decisions about how to engage with the text and the player's ability to enact their desired form of engagement. The player's decisions are entirely dependent on the player (though constantly variable due to the player being a human), while the player's actions also depend on the game's feedback (in some cases, perhaps, resistance) to the player's attempted engagements.

The player's actions engage with the game through *interactive poiesis*, the process of the player creating the experience of the game text during gameplay. Interactive poiesis follows directly from the explorative, configurative, and textonic ergodic decisions and results in the player engaging with the game music through either musical signs (for example, fragments of music, tempo changes, or entire songs), configurative signs (for example, differences in timing of the start or end of music due to gameplay progress, skipping music due to choices made in response to gameplay narrative, or interruptions to the music when the player ends a session of gameplay), or personal signs (for example, responses to music due to personal musical preferences, choices of external music to play as an alternative soundtrack, or familiarity with music from previous playthroughs of the game). The player may add to, remove, and manipulate these kinds of signs in their interaction with the set of signs presented to them by the game, resulting in the creation of a gameplay experience that is unique to the player and to the gameplay instance.

Meanwhile, the interpretive choice of ergodesis results in the process of esthesis, which is here the process of reading simple or conventional meanings from the sign without manipulation. It should be noted, however, that once the player has interpreted a meaning from a sign, it forms part of the context in which they interpret or interact with all future signs they encounter. Within the semiosis of gameplay, this is called *postesthesic influence*. Interpreted meanings influence how the player makes subsequent choices in ergodesis, and they also influence the signs the player puts into the gameplay experience through interactive poiesis.

The player's semiotic processes, making choices about the text in ergodesis and engaging directly with the manipulation and creation of signs in interactive poiesis, have an important role during gameplay, since they produce a gameplay experience that is both derived from the game text and unique to the player. However, the magnitude of this importance varies by game, by player, and even from moment to moment. The player's choices and the signs they add to gameplay do not negate the signs presented to them by the game, but they can add to, remove from, and manipulate the flow of these signs. As such, the signs and meanings modified by and created by the player must contend with the signs and meanings of the game music as produced by the composer's initial composition. Or, to recast from the other direction, for the composer to communicate meanings to the player during gameplay, they must contend with the influences the player will have over the game's signs during gameplay. It is useful to conceptualize this contention as a negotiation of communication.

Defining Negotiation

For the purposes of the current discussion, I will define negotiation as *a structured, potentially formalized activity that attempts to reach an agreement about the meaning of a set of signs between two or more parties*. To apply this conceptualization of negotiation to the context of video game music, each aspect of this definition needs examination.

A Structured, Potentially Formalized Activity

Firstly, the negotiation of communication in game music is a structured activity, which may or may not be formalized. Negotiation of communication occurs during gameplay, which is itself an activity built of mechanisms for interactivity between the player and the game. Some meanings may be communicated in formal ways, such as leitmotifs that are associated with characters through the coincidence of music with their visual or narrative presence. The leitmotif is a well-established musical form employed in many Western media for its strong denotative powers, easily understood by listeners familiar with Western texts. For example, the opening video for *Left 4 Dead* (Valve 2008) shows the game's more difficult zombie types, such as the fast-jumping Hunter or the exploding Boomer, accompanied by the leitmotifs associated with each type; the video initiates new players to the leitmotifs' meanings and allows the leitmotifs to be used during gameplay as an early aural warning of the presence of these zombies. Others may be less formal, such as the subsets of music cues played for various location types in many open-world games, where contextual association allows musical connotations to saturate the interactive experience. For example, in *The Elder Scrolls V: Skyrim* (Bethesda 2011), music that accompanies walled town environments employs noticeably different stylistic tropes to the open countryside to give an "impression ... of quiet and resolute optimism, encouraging the player to explore in safety" (Lamb and Smith 2018, 82).

Whether the parties involved are aware of the structure behind the negotiation of communication is not terribly important (though such an awareness may itself affect the negotiation); similarly, the structure itself is less important than its existence, in the sense that observing the many ways communication can happen is a more productive activity for the academic than trying to prescribe how communication should happen. It is more important to recognize that communication, when it occurs, is rarely an accidental alignment of the universe, and that its structure stems from both the deliberate actions of the composer and player, and the purpose of the game text as a text to be played.

Aiming for Agreement about Meaning

This goal, secondly, is the "agreement about the meaning of a set of signs." The successful result of the negotiation discussed here is the occurrence of a communication, or in other words, a successful transference of the meaning of a set of signs such that the same idea is shared between two minds. When a game displays an image of a building on the screen, and the image prompts the idea of a building in the player's mind, that is a communication. Similarly, when game music denotes the presence of a particular enemy, and the music prompts the idea of that enemy in the player's mind, the idea of that enemy has been communicated between the game's creators and the player. The *Left 4 Dead* player who hears the leitmotif for a Hunter can capitalize on the information the game is communicating to them by quickly looking around for that zombie to avoid its deadly pounce.

At the risk of making assumptions, it seems fairly safe to hypothesize that games are generally created to be experienced in accordance with the gameplay style, mechanisms, narrative, soundscape, and possibly even marketing strategy envisioned by their creators. This requires agreement about meanings, successful communications that draw the player along with the flow of gameplay like tavern patrons enthralled by a bard in song. A corollary of this hypothesis is that for many negotiations about meaning in game music, the instigator of the negotiation is the composer; the created game attempts to draw the player through the interactive experience envisioned by the game's creators. This should not be understood to mean a diminution of the importance of interactivity; rather, the envisioned experience is interactive gameplay molded to the game's particular form, in which the default semiotic goal is for the player to recognize, within that form, the game the creators sought to make.

Not Always Achieving Agreement

Thirdly, negotiation attempts to reach the aforementioned result of communication, but it may fail. It is vitally important to include in the present definition the possibility that communication (that is, the idea shared between two minds) will not be achieved, and a miscommunication or missed communication may result. Nattiez (1990, 17) notes that communication through music is not guaranteed, as the meanings ascribed to the text by both creative and receptive processes may diverge. He describes as "hazardous" the interpretation of meanings and emotions from the musical text, as "the looseness of the associations between music and what it evokes" requires understanding musical symbolism as a phenomenon of infinite possibility rather than precise definition (37). It is entirely possible that the composer and the player will interpret markedly different meanings from the same musical signs; for example, the inclusion of the Garbage song "As Heaven Is Wide" in the export version of *Gran Turismo* (Polyphony Digital 1997), and particularly the song's chorus lyrics "As far from God / as heaven is wide," may bring a range of unintended emotions into gameplay if the player is currently experiencing a crisis of religious faith. It is also possible that the player will not encounter certain signs and meanings created by the composer during the branching paths of gameplay; for example, the *Fallout 3* (Bethesda 2008) player who doesn't turn on their Pip-Boy 3000's radio will not hear the music from the radio stations broadcast across the Capital Wasteland.

However, miscommunication and missed communication are not necessarily detrimental to the value of the game nor to gameplay. A missed meaning can be a nexus between the game creators' ideated trajectory of the gameplay experience and the full scope of experience potentials, a site of ingress of human experiences such as frustration, amusement, panic, or familiarity into the mechanisms and meanings of gameplay. Jesper Juul (2013, 14) shows that video games are sites of failure by design and that gameplay regularly includes moments in which the player fails to achieve the goals set for them by the game. A failed communication about meaning in game music may form a motivator for increased engagement and redoubled effort against the game's challenges (11–12).

Between Two or More Parties

Finally, negotiation occurs "between two or more parties." In this context, the parties at the table include (at minimum) the player, the composer(s) of the game's music, and the programmers, writers, and artists who construct the other elements of the video game. This may require relinquishing the notion of the author's semiotic irrelevance in the act of gameplay and the hearing of game music. Roland Barthes (1977) famously pronounced the death of the author, a concept that has become so popular amongst academics that challenging it within academia or even hinting at the relevance of authorial intent has become fraught. Yet, outside our universities and schools, the author lives on unperturbed. The popular celebrity, criticism, and/or censorship of authors, directors, composers, artists, and creators is unabated, and copyright law protects (and, in many instances, fails to protect) authorial rights over created works in much the same ways as it always has, notwithstanding the challenges of the digital age.

Silvija Jestrovic (2020, 1–5) notes that Barthes's pronouncement formed part of widespread artistic and cultural upheaval in the late 1960s, led in part by several notable authors and auteurs such as Jean-Paul Sartre, Jean-Luc Godard, and François Truffaut. The author, though pronounced dead by this movement, underwent an "almost immediate resurrection" as the performatively present and engaged revolutionaries at the movement's head (Jestrovic 2020, 4). Jestrovic argues for the necessity of the "resurrection" of the author, in part arguing that the author's removal from the frame of reception may obfuscate the task of analyzing the author's work in light of social and ethical questions arising from the author's biography (21–26, 29). When a composer is accused of inappropriate conduct, what avenues remain for reappraising the impact of their conduct on their work and its place in society if the author is divorced from the work's reception? We may try to resurrect the author and the significance of their biography strictly within the context of ethical (re)analyses, but that is at best a lazy attempt to deal with a theoretical shortcoming, and at worst canonical protectionism. It is better to recognize from the outset that the author has never been either socially or semiotically irrelevant to the reception of their texts. Barthes has helped us to see that the listener has a critical role in determining the received meaning of texts, but we can now progress beyond the falsity of the author's irrelevance. Both the game music composer and the game player have important roles in the negotiation of a text's meaning, and we need not pretend that the composer's seat at the negotiating table is a rather noisy pot plant.

The continued relevance of the composer is one of the fundamental elements of the framework for ludomusicological semiotics. The first semiotic domain of initial composition is focused on the composer's work in creating meanings to be encountered by the player within the context of gameplay. These meanings subsequently form the input for the second semiotic domain of interactive poiesis, where the player's meaning creations involve the interpretation, addition, subtraction, and modification of meanings from that original set of meanings. It is convenient at times to separate the two semiotic domains and analyze one or the other depending on the scope of the analysis at hand, but they always need to be addressed with the other in mind, even if not explicitly. The composer of video game music writes the music to form part of an audiovisual text, forming part of a vast set of signs that work together during gameplay to provide a more-or-less unified experience. Whether these signs successfully transmit the composer's and the game creators' intended meanings and experiences to the player is not terribly important; as above, missed/miscommunication can still be an experience full of meaning that is significant to gameplay. What is important is that the signs were included in the game for a purpose. They have intended meanings that, whether successfully communicated or not, form the starting point of the negotiation of communication, on which the player's interactive poiesis works to weave a uniquely meaningful gameplay experience.

The Negotiation

Defining negotiation in this way helps us to investigate the complexities of the player's interaction with game music and the effect of this interaction on gameplay and the meanings the player finds there. Interactive gameplay is not filled with meaning in the sense of a dictionary being full of prescriptive definitions, a set of the only allowable meanings. Nor is it filled with meaning in the sense of a choose-your-own-adventure book, allowable meanings from which the player can make a constrained choice. Yet neither is it a blank canvas on which the player can cast their own meanings to have them form the complete text; nor is it a box of building blocks from which the player can take predefined parts to be reassembled in any form they choose. Rather, it is something akin to all of these things at once, in tension with each other, yet not in contradiction.

There are times, during gameplay, when the game will attempt to define the meanings of the experience quite strictly. Noninteractive video cutscenes, for example, attempt a much more fully defined experience than may be attempted during more interactive phases of gameplay. At other times, the path through the text is much more within the player's control as they can choose to explore the game world and interact with objects and characters at will. Yet both scenarios are experienced by the player within the context of their own self, their personality and experiences being the determinant of their tendencies of decision making and interpretation. Therefore, the set of meaning potentials composed into the text at its creation (prescriptive and otherwise) is always in tension with the player's personal tendencies to interpret and create meanings in their own way. The video game and its music are works of art, engineering, and narrative crafted by many human minds and hands. Their work of spinning threads of meaning in and around the game starts with the ideation and composition of the video game text, and extends forward through time indefinitely, as each gameplay session instantiates new experiences, and as the memories of past experiences reverberate through the player's future actions. Nattiez (1990, 6) indicates that interpretants of an object generate new interpretants "ad infinitum." Let us, however, maintain a focus on the acts of gameplay, the domain in which the threads of meaning are negotiated into weaving the most tangible fabric.

The *Halo* scene described above centers on a moment of gameplay in which the player's adherence to the game's narrative flow has loosened, and the absence of music is used as a tool to ask them back into the story. This negotiation has a relatively well-defined structure:

1. Gameplay proceeds in alignment with narrative flow
2. Player takes a series of exploratory actions that slow and eventually interrupt the flow of narrative
3. Music ends noticeably
4. Player chooses to realign their gameplay with the narrative, and narrative flow resumes.

This structure is more easily observable than many negotiations of meaning in gameplay because it is repeatable at many points throughout *Halo*. It is a slightly unusual structure to find in screen media because it depends on the player noticing the nondiegetic music's absence, whereas nondiegetic music's functions are often subconscious (Summers 2016b, 154). It is not a particularly formal structure, and it is not initialized by an explicit demonstration early in gameplay. Its duration is dependent almost entirely on the player and when they choose to realign play with narrative. It is also optional, as the player may avoid this kind of negotiation entirely if their play style adheres closely to the narrative flow. This negotiation is structured, but it is an open structure in which the player retains a significant amount of agency.

Yet, despite the player's agency and their power over the duration of the negotiation in particular, it is clearly the game that starts this negotiation. The game's parameters determine the length of time after the most difficult enemies have been defeated at which to cut the music and suggest that the player move along; composer Martin O'Donnell states that this timeframe is five minutes (Collins 2008, 141). The suggestion may be paraphrased as such:

> "You have been doing this too long. Shall we get on with it?"

The aim of this negotiation, therefore, is for the player to think:

> "I have been doing this too long. I had better get on with it."

If the player thinks this thought, the meaning of the cessation of the music is shared between two minds, the two minds being those of the composer who envisioned the music and its parameters nudging the player along in this way, and of course the player. If this happens, the game music and the player have successfully navigated the hazards of musical semiotics and produced a communication.

Of course, throughout this negotiation, music acts in parallel to other game elements. It is almost trivial to mention that the absence of further combat enemies to slay is a significant motivator of gameplay progression in a combat game like *Halo*. The absence of (living) aliens within the scene deprives the player's senses of the exciting and engaging visual and sound effect cues on which the game's primary activities are built. The absence of music accords with, amplifies, and makes explicit the implicit visual and sonic suggestion that gameplay progression is more fun than continued play in the empty-of-enemies scene. Similarly, when the player progresses to the next battle, the return of the visual and aural cues of combat work together with the musical cues of combat music encourage this forward-moving style of gameplay and engagement with the story (Gibbons 2014, 125–126). In this context, deprivation and return of music have substantially more denotative capability than they would alone, allowing such explicit meanings to be communicated through music's otherwise volatile significations (see van Leeuwen 1998, 26).

It may not always be so simple to produce such a communication, however. The player's agency in the negotiation may mean that the length of the negotiation is indeterminate, and agreement (if it is reached at all) is not reached for quite some time. Furthermore, there may be nuances of the player's emotional reaction to the musical signs and to the suggestion to get a move on that make the apparent agreement in the player's realignment with the game's narrative only superficial. If the player starts to resent the game's interference in their free play, for example, then the thought of "I had better get on with it" may be shared, but the underlying motivation for the negotiation, perhaps paraphrased as: "This game is best experienced by following the narrative," may well not be shared or may even be rebelled against. This would be a miscommunication, as only part of the intended meaning ends up being shared between two minds. And that is a perfectly acceptable semiotic result in the real world, where players and game composers are human, and where emotion and circumstance play as perpetually upon the senses as things touched, seen, and heard.

Meaning as a Beautiful Mess

We can now make some observations. Firstly, this is a rather basic example of the negotiation of meaning in game music. Its mechanisms are simple and easily followed. Other negotiations may be more subtle, more complex, or even more basic. Any negotiations about meanings that involve emotions rather than actions will almost necessarily be more complex. Secondly, despite its simplicity, it is still somewhat messy. It has vague input parameters, and its expected results are highly variable if looking beyond the most basic core actions. Each player plays their own way and may respond idiosyncratically to the silent suggestion toward progress, and they may respond differently on the next play-through or even to another instance within the same gameplay session. Negotiation of meaning between the player and game music is fraught with the pitfalls of human cognitive variability. This is to be expected as humans are not optional in the process. I posited above that understanding communication through game music as a negotiation of meaning was a way to deal with the potentially infinite imprecision of musical meaning in games; we see here that although the negotiation between the player and the game has helpfully distilled the infinite potentials of meaning into a discrete meaningful experience, it does so as part of an ongoing conversation.

Finally, though imprecise, there is something beautiful about what the negotiation achieves and how it works. There is considerable technical elegance to an artform that can take musical significations and their semantic volatility and imbue them with the capability to communicate with a broad, uninitiated human audience with any semblance of reliability. There is also a social spark present, an appeal to the heart inherent in all examples of human communication and collaboration, including those mediated by technology and distanced by asynchronicity. Human engagement with humanity and the world in which we find ourselves is foundational to the substance and purpose of art, to our works of beauty and theory and invention and relevance. A call to "Get on with it" in *Halo* may seem inconsequential, but what are the composer and the game creators asking the player to get on with? Engaging with a projection of our achievements and anxieties onto an imagined future; playing out a story about humanity's space exploration that will, over the course of the series, feature physical and cognitive challenges, ethical dilemmas, shifted allegiances, existential questions at the human/technology interface, explorations of comradeship, and loyalty in extremis (all couched in a palatable-to-the-masses coating of alien blood and gore). While *Halo* is not ground-breaking, high-brow, or visionary in this regard, and neither is its story especially deep or nuanced, it is nonetheless a captivating engagement of humans with their existence. Beauty and elegance are perhaps not the usual stuff of semiotics, and the scintillation of human interaction may not be at the forefront of the ludomusicologist's mind when analyzing a game score, but these are symbols (in the Peircean sense) present in all gameplay and small, though powerful, motivators of the negotiation of meaning.

Note

1. I use the term "composer" throughout as shorthand for the person or people responsible for choosing the musical signs to be included in the video game and arranging for their inclusion. This may include composers of musical scores or cues, creators, editors, arrangers, and performers. Video games that use pre-existing music may not have a composer per se, but the people responsible for choosing pre-existing music are filling much the same semiotic role as far as the current discussion is concerned.

References

Aarseth, Espen J. 1997. *Cybertext: Perspectives on Ergodic Literature*. Baltimore: Johns Hopkins University Press.

Barthes, Roland. 1977. "The Death of the Author." In *Image, Music, Text*, translated by Stephen Heath, 142–149. London: Fontana Press.
Bethesda Game Studios. 2008. *Fallout 3*. Video Game. Bethesda Softworks.
Bethesda Game Studios. 2011. *The Elder Scrolls V: Skyrim*. Video Game. Bethesda Softworks.
Bungie. 2001. *Halo: Combat Evolved*. Video Game. Microsoft Game Studios.
Collins, Karen. 2008. *Game Sound: An Introduction to the History, Theory, and Practice of Video Game Music and Sound Design*. Cambridge, MA: MIT Press.
Gibbons, William. 2014. "Wandering Tonalities: Silence, Sound, and Morality in *Shadow of the Colossus*." In *Music in Video Games: Studying Play*, edited by K. J. Donnelly, William Gibbons, and Neil Lerner, 122–137. New York: Routledge.
Polyphony Digital. 1997. *Gran Turismo*. Video Game. Sony Computer Entertainment.
Hart, Iain. 2014. "Meaningful Play: Performativity, Interactivity and Semiotics in Video Game Music." *Musicology Australia* 36 (2): 273–290.
Hart, Iain. 2021. "Semiotics in Game Music." In *The Cambridge Companion to Video Game Music*, edited by Melanie Fritsch and Tim Summers, 220–237. Cambridge: Cambridge University Press.
Jestrovic, Silvija. 2020. *Performances of Authorial Presence and Absence: The Author Dies Hard*. Cham: Palgrave Macmillan.
Juul, Jesper. 2013. *The Art of Failure: An Essay on the Pain of Playing Video Games*. Cambridge, MA: MIT Press.
Lamb, Brendan, and Barnabas Smith. 2018. "From Skyrim to Skellige: Fantasy Video Game Music within a Neo-Mediaevalist Paradigm." *Musicology Australia* 40 (2): 79–100.
Nattiez, Jean-Jacques. 1990. *Music and Discourse: Toward a Semiology of Music*. Translated by Carolyn Abbate. Princeton, NJ: Princeton University Press.
O'Donnell, Martin. 2002. "Producing Audio for Halo." halo.bungie.org. Fan website. Accessed November 30, 2021. http://halo.bungie.org/misc/gdc.2002.music/.
Peirce, Charles Sanders. [1907] 1998. "Pragmatism." In *The Essential Peirce: Selected Philosophical Writings*, edited by Peirce Edition Project, 2: 398–433. Bloomington: Indiana University Press.
Summers, Tim. 2016a. "Analysing Video Game Music: Sources, Methods and a Case Study." In *Ludomusicology: Approaches to Video Game Music*, edited by Michiel Kamp, Tim Summers, and Mark Sweeney, 8–31. Sheffield, UK: Equinox.
Summers, Tim. 2016b. *Understanding Video Game Music*. Cambridge: Cambridge University Press.
Valve. 2008. *Left 4 Dead*. Video Game. Valve.
van Leeuwen, Theo. 1998. "Music and Ideology: Notes toward a Sociosemiotics of Mass Media Music." *Popular Music and Society* 22 (4): 25–54.

CHAPTER 41

ABSTRACT REPRESENTATIONS OF VOICES IN VIDEO GAMES

ELIZABETH MEDINA-GRAY

Introduction

Voice acting is a common feature of many video games, and recent research has begun to illuminate the various functions of voices in games (see Stingel-Voigt 2020; Smith 2021; Stockburger 2010).[1] Recordings of human performers speaking (or singing) lines of text often convey linguistic meaning, for instance, which in turn can advance a game's story or provide functional information related to gameplay; and voice acting can tap into players' experiences with voices in the world outside of the game (both listening to voices and producing them) to yield additional layers of meaning, including emotion or affect, cultural or social identity (Smith 2021, 47), and so on. While voice acting is an important component of many video games, other sonic approaches to dialogue in games also exist, and such sounds are as yet relatively unexplored. In particular, a significant subset of video games include abstract representations of voices as audio components of dialogue. By an "abstract representation" of a voice, I mean a nonrealistic sound that stands in for a voice in the sonic domain; and these sounds can be quite abstract indeed. For example, in *Dragon Quest* (1986, released in North America in 1989 as *Dragon Warrior*), King Lorik opens the game by saying to the player's character: "Descendent of Erdrick, listen now to my words" (see Figure 41.1).[2] But King Lorik's words are conveyed through visual text, and the only sound attached to his dialogue (the only component of his words to which a player might listen) is a repeated pulse-wave tone on the pitch A5, which plays as long as the king's dialogue text is gradually appearing on the screen (see ▶ Video 1).[3] In the more recent game *Celeste* (2018), when the player's character Madeline speaks with an old woman at the beginning of her mountainous trek, animated portraits show these characters' mouths moving and their dialogue appears

FIGURE 41.1 Screenshot of opening dialogue in *Dragon Quest* (*Dragon Warrior*).

gradually as text, but the sounds that accompany this dialogue are an assortment of voice-like timbres that do not replicate the text's messages (see Figure 41.2 and ▶ Video 2). Such abstract representations of voices first arose in the early history of video games, when technical limitations meant that games were not able to include realistic recordings of human voices; other audio strategies for dialogue in early games included speech synthesis (for example, in the arcade game *Berzerk* [1980]) or simply silence (for example, in *Super Mario Bros.* [1985]). While the available sonic options for voices have expanded over the years, abstract representations of voices have continued to appear in certain games, becoming a repeated and recognizable component of video game sound (Stoeber 2020).

This chapter turns a critical ear toward abstract representations of voices in video games, and considers a wide variety of such sounds. Since many sounds in games are in some way representational (indeed, even voice acting involves a degree of representation, composed as it is of recorded sounds that are transposed onto characters that did not actually originate those sounds), it will be helpful to clarify the scope of this chapter from the outset. This chapter focuses on sounds that reasonably serve as audible components of characters' dialogue and that have both of the following two characteristics that make these sounds particularly abstract: (1) these sounds contain no comprehensible linguistic meaning (no recognizable words or phrases); and (2) these

FIGURE 41.2 Screenshot of opening dialogue in *Celeste*.

sounds are not realistic recordings of human voices—they do not sound like they could be directly produced by a human performer, and instead they involve some audibly mechanical or technological quality or qualities. (Note that realistic, voice-acted gibberish speech—as in *The Sims*, for example—is not abstract enough to fit into the purview of this chapter.)

I am particularly interested in how these abstract representations of voices explore spaces that are both human and mechanical. While "human" and "machine" (or "voice" and "technology") may seem to be antithetical, voices more broadly—beyond just video games—are one area where both human and mechanical aspects frequently come into play, for instance when human voices are recorded and processed, or when new voices are synthesized through technological means (Young 2015, 5–6; Malawey 2020, 129–130). Video games seem to present an especially rich arena for experiments in human together with machine, since video games frequently portray interactable human or anthropomorphic characters through a fundamentally technological framework of hardware and software. And while "human" and "machine" may not form an exclusive binary, human voices and mechanical sounds bear some fundamental differences. For instance, human voices are complex sonic and physical productions, involving airflow and produced using tissue with relatively irregular material properties that can moreover change even within a single individual, depending on factors such as time of day, emotional state, food and drug intake, and so on (Titze 2000, 24). By contrast, machine-produced voices—while also complex—are highly regular, predictable, and re-producible; in one sense, mechanical voices are able to reach a degree of purity unavailable to human voices (Young 2015, 77). In considering abstract representations of voices in video games, I focus on a few core questions: what mechanical elements appear in these sounds, and what (if any) elements gesture toward human voices? And in what ways might abstract representations of voices in video games convey human or social meanings—like identity or emotion or affect—despite their overtly mechanical qualities?

In this chapter, I aim to provide a solid foundation for discussing and examining abstract representations of voices in video games. First, I highlight some recurring characteristics of these sounds in a broad survey, and consider ways in which these characteristics are similar to either human voices or the output of machines. Then, I suggest two frameworks—social semiotics and music analysis—that can be useful in analyzing abstract representations of voices and their potential meanings.

To be clear, this chapter has limits in both scope and perspective: I consider a sizable corpus of games encompassing a wide array of sounds, but this corpus does not include every existing game with abstract representations of voices, and I have not examined every instance of dialogue in each game; moreover, I consider the sounds themselves and some potential meanings, but this chapter does not undertake ethnographic research into these sounds' production and reception. (Further research in that direction might ask, for example: Why have designers included these sounds in games? How have players reacted to these sounds and why?) To examine the large number of games in this chapter, I have relied heavily on fan-produced material, especially videos of gameplay footage on YouTube (some of which was recorded using emulators) and, in some cases, sounds extracted from games. I have checked multiple sources to confirm the information in this chapter as best as possible, but because I did not engage firsthand with every game in this corpus on its contemporary hardware, it is feasible that there could be errors among my descriptions of the sounds in these games. Finally, it is important to clarify that I am approaching these sounds and their game contexts from my own perspective as a native English speaker from North America, and I am primarily considering the North American versions of these games, many of which were originally developed in Japan; it is worth emphasizing that this perspective is only one context in which these games might be viewed, and additional or alternate meanings will arise when these sounds and games are considered from, say, the perspective of a native Japanese speaker interacting with the Japanese versions of games.[4] In short, this chapter provides some initial groundwork regarding these intriguing sounds, and there remains much to explore.

Describing Abstract Representations of Voices

The abstract representations of voices in this chapter divide readily into two types: (1) abstract sounds that use voice-like timbres and include multiple phones[5]—and are therefore at least vaguely similar to speech—as in *Celeste*, for example; and (2) abstract sounds that do not include multiple phones and whose timbres might not resemble voices at all, as in *Dragon Quest*. In this section of the chapter, I examine a corpus of 10 games (Group 1) that use sounds of the first type, and a corpus of 20 games (Group 2) that use sounds of the second type. I selected the games in each of these two corpora with an aim to encompass a wide variety of sound characteristics, years of release, developers, and platforms. Since the games in these corpora are only a portion of the games that use these types of sound, I do not make claims here about trends of these sounds' use across time or about the prevalence of particular sonic characteristics in the larger field of video games overall. Rather, these corpora provide a basis in which to examine recurring characteristics of these abstract sounds as well as some specific examples. For each group, I identify some recurring characteristics in terms of timbre, time, and pitch, highlighting these sounds' ability to mix human-like and machine-like qualities to varying degrees. Moreover, although I have initially distinguished these two types of abstract sounds based on the presence or absence of multiple voice-like phones, we will see that these two types often differ in other characteristics as well.

Group 1: Abstract Sounds with Multiple Phones and Voice-Like Timbres

Abstract representations of voices that use multiple phones and voice-like timbres form a relatively small niche in the video game landscape, but this niche includes some prominent games. *Q*bert* (1982) provides an especially early and quirky example of this type of sound, where jumbles of speech-synthesis audio accompany nonlinguistic, visual text symbols, so that the main character's dialogue is given abstract representation in both auditory and visual domains. More commonly in games with this type of sound, specific linguistic messages are conveyed through gradually appearing text while the abstract sounds play; the dialogue of the anthropomorphic animal pilots during the main gameplay levels of *Star Fox* (1993) is an early example of this type of approach. Table 41.1 lists the 10 games that make up Group 1, the corpus for the current examination of abstract representations of voices of this first type, and Table 41.2 summarizes some recurring characteristics of the abstract sounds under consideration here in these 10 games.

In the process of compiling Table 41.2, spectrograms have proven to be a useful tool for considering how these sounds resemble or diverge from realistic human voices (particularly in terms of timbre, but spectrograms can help to visualize other aspects of these sounds as well). Spectrograms are widely used to study voices in various fields, including phonetics.[6] For one comparison, Figure 41.3 shows a wideband spectrogram and a narrowband spectrogram of a recording of realistic speech (see [▶] Audio 1), and Figure 41.4 shows a wideband spectrogram and a narrowband spectrogram of a recording of abstract dialogue sounds from *Celeste* (see [▶] Audio 2).[7] Each of the spectrograms in Figures 41.3 and 41.4 shows time (in seconds) on the X axis, and frequency (in Hz) on the Y axis. Component frequencies—the multiple frequencies that together make up the

TABLE 41.1 List of Games in Group 1: Sample Games That Include Abstract Representations of Voices with Multiple Phones and Voice-Like Timbres

Title	Developer	Year	Platform
*Q*bert*	Gottlieb	1982	Arcade
Star Fox	Nintendo, Argonaut Software	1993	SNES
Banjo-Kazooie	Rare	1998	Nintendo 64
Chibi-Robo!	Skip Ltd., Bandai	2005	GameCube
Ōkami	Clover Studio	2006	PS2
The Legend of Zelda: Twilight Princess (one character: Midna)	Nintendo	2006	GameCube, Wii
The Legend of Zelda: Skyward Sword (one character: Fi)	Nintendo	2011	Wii
Splatoon	Nintendo	2015	Wii U
Celeste	Extremely OK Games	2018	Windows, Switch, PS4, etc.
Animal Crossing: New Horizons	Nintendo	2020	Switch

audio in the recording—appear as gray areas on the spectrogram, with darker shading for relatively stronger frequencies. Wideband spectrograms show finer detail in time, while narrowband spectrograms show finer detail in frequency.

Several basic timbral features of human voices—particularly of vowel sounds—are apparent in both Figures 41.3 and 41.4, and these basic timbral features are present in all of the games in Group 1 (in Table 41.2, this is the first entry in the "human-like characteristics" column). These vowel sounds feature a fundamental frequency—F_0, the lowest frequency in the narrowband spectrogram—and, above that, several evenly spaced harmonics, at frequencies that are multiples of F_0. Critically, these vowel sounds also feature formants, areas of relatively strong harmonics that are most easily visible as dark bands in a wideband spectrogram. Formants are the amplifications of certain frequencies that in human voices occur through resonance in the vocal tract; formants in the range below about 5,000 Hz are what create the sounds of vowels. Compare, for example, the shapes of various vowels in Figure 41.3, and notice the presence of various formants in similar frequency ranges in Figure 41.4. While all 10 games in Group 1 contain these basic human-like qualities in vowel timbres, some games also modify these qualities with machine-like characteristics:[8] for example, *Celeste* includes some strong and changing bands of harmonics at very high frequencies (see the bands at around 6,000–10,000 Hz in Figure 41.4), and Midna's audio in *The Legend of Zelda: Twilight Princess* (2006) features mechanical echo effects. All the games in Group 1 use abstract sounds that involve multiple phones, and so the timbre of these

TABLE 41.2 Some Recurring Human-Like and Machine-Like Characteristics of Abstract Representations of Voices with Multiple Phones and Voice-Like Timbres

Category	Human-Like Characteristics	Machine-Like Characteristics
Timbre	Fundamental frequency (F_0), evenly spaced harmonics, and formants (areas of relatively strong harmonics) Multiple phones (changing timbre) Includes fricatives (see, for example, *Q*bert, Chibi-Robo!, Twilight Princess*)	Includes timbral qualities that are unlike realistic human voices (see, for example, *Star Fox, Celeste, Twilight Princess*) Lacks fricatives (see, for example, *Star Fox, Banjo-Kazooie, Celeste, Ōkami*)
Time	Pauses/silence delineate phrases No regular temporal grid; time between onsets of adjacent phones or syllables varies from each onset to the next Speed of successive phones is similar to human speech (see, for example, *Twilight Princess, Skyward Sword, Celeste*)	Exact repetition of sounds Nonrealistic qualities in concatenation of sounds (see, for example, *Banjo-Kazooie, Ōkami, Chibi-Robo!, Splatoon*) Speed of successive phones is faster than typical human speech (see, for example, *Splatoon, Animal Crossing: New Horizons*)
Pitch	Frequencies fall into feasible registers for human speech (see, for example, *Chibi-Robo!, Twilight Princess, Skyward Sword*) Pitch slides occur Wide array of frequencies (rather than a limited set of discrete pitches)	Frequencies for at least some characters fall outside of feasible registers for human speech (see, for example, *Q*bert, Star Fox, Celeste*)

Note: Characteristics that occur in all or nearly all of the games in Group 1 are listed without specific examples. Characteristics that occur in only some games are listed with examples. Rare characteristics (exceptions) are not listed here.

sounds changes frequently within a single character's audio stream; such timbral changes mark these sounds as similar to human voices.[9] However, some games use a machine-like reduction in the array of available timbres; in particular, multiple games in Group 1 avoid fricatives, the noisy consonants that in human speech are produced by forcing air through narrow passages—compare the heavy noise of the [s] in Figure 41.3's realistic speech with the absence of any such noise in Figure 41.4's audio from *Celeste*.

The abstract sounds in the Group 1 games feature additional recurring characteristics in the domain of time. As with actual human speech, these abstract sounds include pauses (that is, silence) that delineate phrases of dialogue. Also similar to human speech, the time between onsets of adjacent phones or syllables—the inter-onset interval, or IOI—varies from each onset to the next (for example, the first few IOIs in Figure 41.4 are: 137 ms, 163 ms, 173 ms, 202 ms, and so on).[10] On the machine-like side, these games all feature exact repetition of sounds, to varying degrees for various games. *Chibi-Robo!*

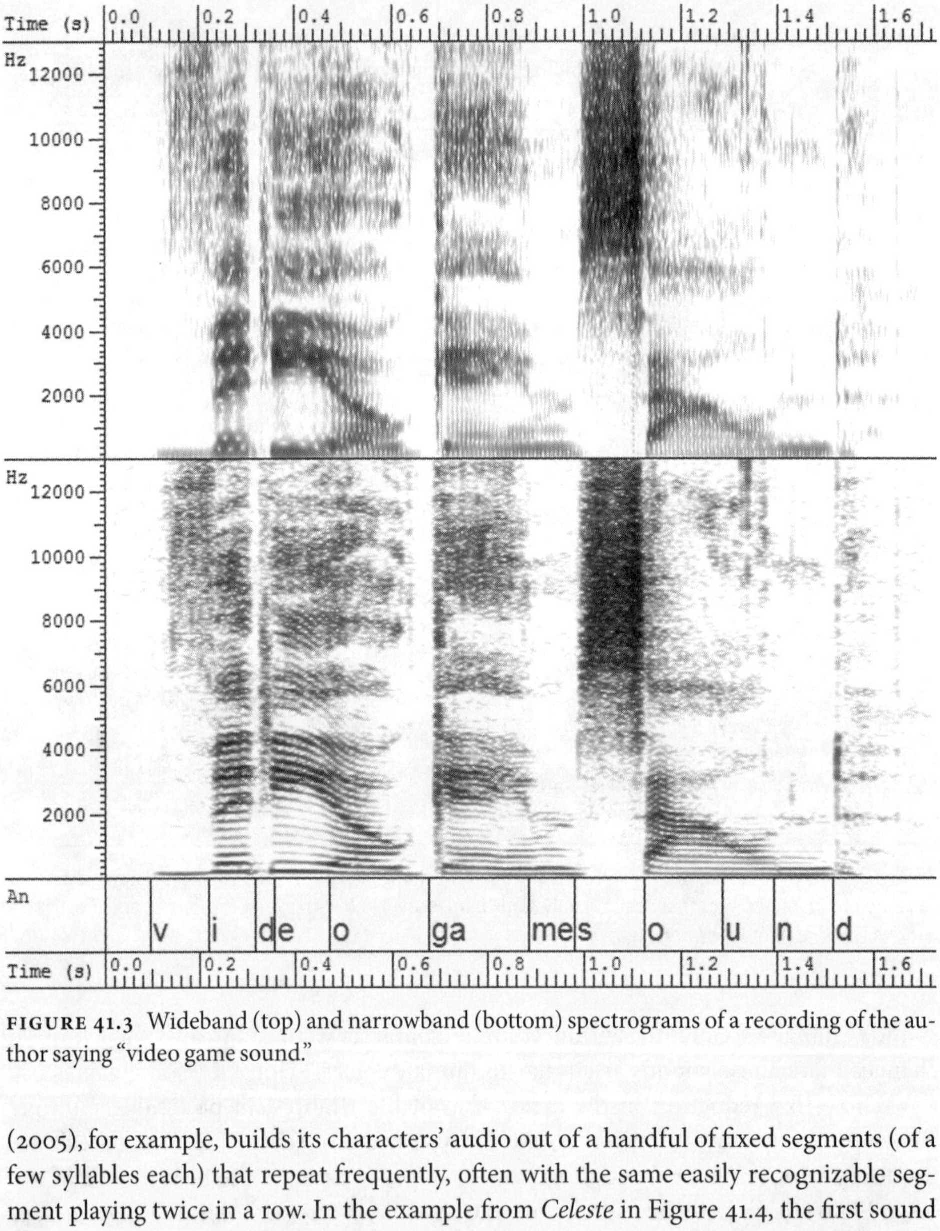

FIGURE 41.3 Wideband (top) and narrowband (bottom) spectrograms of a recording of the author saying "video game sound."

(2005), for example, builds its characters' audio out of a handful of fixed segments (of a few syllables each) that repeat frequently, often with the same easily recognizable segment playing twice in a row. In the example from *Celeste* in Figure 41.4, the first sound and the third-to-last sound are exact duplicates, but several other sounds play in between. Even such a low degree of repetition, however, displays a machine-like quality of perfect replication, as opposed to the imperfect plasticity of human voices. Some games include nonrealistic qualities in the concatenation of sounds—in *Banjo-Kazooie* (1998), for example, the beginning of a syllable often sounds as if it cuts off the previous one. Finally, the speed of phones in several of these games is similar to human speech, while some games use a speed that is faster than typical speech, and may be faster than is feasible for human voices.

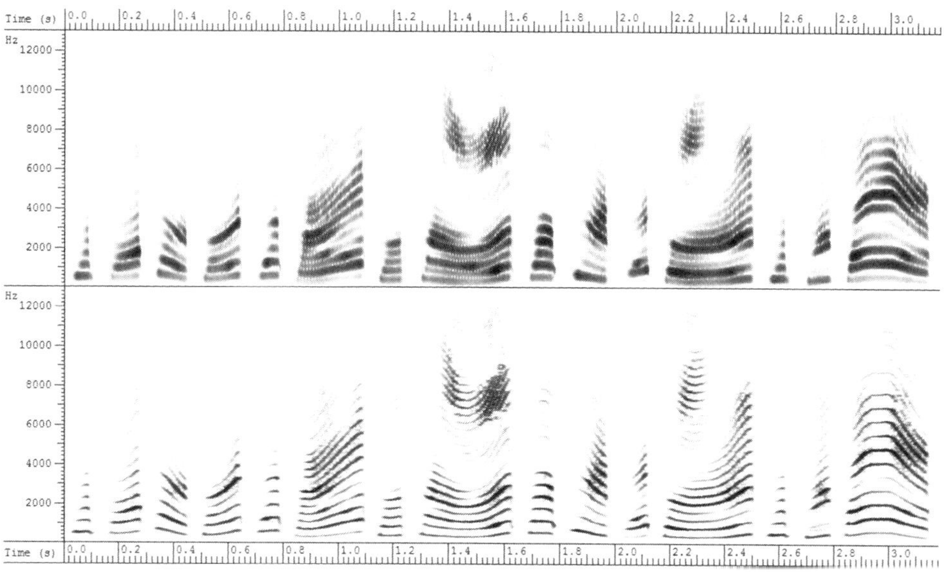

FIGURE 41.4 Wideband (top) and narrowband (bottom) spectrograms of a recorded sample of Madeline's normal audio in *Celeste*.

Recurring characteristics in pitch across the games in Group 1 tend to show affinities with human speech: the abstract sounds in all of these games include pitch slides—visible in the narrowband spectrogram in Figure 41.4 as continuous ascending and descending frequency lines—as well as a wide array of frequencies rather than a limited set of discrete pitches.[11] All of these games also include sounds that fall into feasible registers for human speech, for at least some characters. Those games that include frequencies either too high or too low for realistic human speech—for example, some very low speech-synthesis sounds in *Q*bert*—veer reasonably into machine-like qualities in the realm of pitch.

Overall, these dialogue sounds in the Group 1 games are reaffirmed as abstract through various characteristics that are unlike realistic human voices; but the multiple human-like characteristics also make it relatively easy to hear these sounds in the broad category of voice. In other words, the representational leap from abstract sounds to voice is fairly easy to make here. The situation is different with the next type of abstract sounds.

Group 2: Abstract Sounds without Multiple Phones and Potentially without Voice-Like Timbres

Compared to the first type of abstract representations of voices treated above, a greater number of video games include abstract representations of voices that do *not* include multiple phones and may not even use voice-like timbres.[12] Instead, these games use pitched sounds and/or noise along with gradually appearing text that can reasonably be viewed as spoken dialogue—that is, as words emanating as directly as possible from an in-game character, through speech; such text-understood-as-spoken-dialogue is what allows the attached sounds, abstract as they are, to represent voices. (By contrast, some games frame their text as an overtly mechanical mode of communication, through visible cues like an on-screen typewriter or computer cursor; such explicitly mechanical situations are not considered here.[13])

Table 41.3 lists 20 games that make up Group 2, the corpus for the current examination of abstract sounds of the second type. (*Twilight Princess* and *Animal Crossing: New Horizons* [2020] appear in Group 1 as well as Group 2 because these games each use the first type of abstract sounds with the dialogue of certain characters and the second type of abstract sounds with the dialogue of certain other characters.) Table 41.4 summarizes some recurring characteristics of these abstract representations of voices in the Group 2 games.

TABLE 41.3 List of Games in Group 2: Sample Games That Include Abstract Representations of Voices without Multiple Phones and Potentially without Voice-Like Timbres

Title	Developer	Year	Platform
Portopia Renzoku Satsujin Jiken	Chunsoft	1985	NES (Famicom only)
The Legend of Zelda	Nintendo	1986	NES
Dragon Quest/Dragon Warrior	Chunsoft	1986	NES
Mike Tyson's Punch Out!!	Nintendo	1987	NES
Faxanadu	Hudson Soft	1987	NES
Snatcher	Konami	1988	NEC PC-8801
Soul Blazer	Quintet	1992	SNES
Mega Man X	Capcom	1993	SNES
The Twisted Tales of Spike McFang	Red Company	1993	SNES
EarthBound	Ape, HAL Laboratory	1994	SNES
Terranigma	Quintet	1995	SNES
Harvest Moon 64	Victor Interactive Software	1999	Nintendo 64
Katamari Damacy	Namco	2004	PS2
Phoenix Wright: Ace Attorney	Capcom	2005	Nintendo DS
The Legend of Zelda: Twilight Princess	Nintendo	2006	GameCube, Wii
Ni no Kuni: Wrath of the White Witch	Level-5	2011	PS3
Undertale	Toby Fox	2015	Windows, OS X
Stardew Valley	ConcernedApe (Eric Barone)	2016	Windows
Dragon Quest XI: Echoes of an Elusive Age	Square Enix	2017	PS4
Animal Crossing: New Horizons	Nintendo	2020	Switch

TABLE 41.4 Some Recurring Human-Like and Machine-Like Characteristics of Abstract Representations of Voices without Multiple Phones and Potentially without Voice-Like Timbres

Category	Human-Like Characteristics	Machine-Like Characteristics
Timbre	Fundamental frequency, evenly spaced harmonics, and bands of strong upper-frequency harmonics in a manner similar to formants (see, for example, *The Twisted Tales of Spike McFang*, *Undertale*)	Consistent timbre throughout a given character's audio Fundamental frequency and limited or highly patterned harmonics (see, for example, *Ni no Kuni*, *The Legend of Zelda*, *EarthBound*) Composed mainly or entirely of noise (see, for example, *Faxanadu*, *Katamari Damacy*)
Time	Pauses/silence delineate phrases	Exact repetition of sounds, either with other sounds intervening (see, for example, *Mike Tyson's Punch Out!!*, *Snatcher*, *Katamari Damacy*) or a single sound repeating exactly several times in a row (see, for example, the remaining games in Group 2) Regular temporal grid for multiple sounds in a row; time between onsets of adjacent sounds is often a consistent value
Pitch	Frequencies for at least some characters fall into feasible registers for human speech (see, for example, *Mike Tyson's Punch Out!!*, *Twilight Princess*, *Undertale*) Pitch slides occur (see, for example, *Snatcher*, *Terranigma*) Variety of pitches in a given character's audio (see, for example, *Mike Tyson's Punch Out!!*, *Snatcher*)	Frequencies fall outside of feasible registers for human speech (see, for example, *Dragon Quest*, *EarthBound*, *Harvest Moon 64*) Discrete pitches only (see, for example, *The Legend of Zelda*, *Phoenix Wright: Ace Attorney*, *Dragon Quest XI*) Monotone (see, for example, *Portopia Renzoku Satsujin Jiken*, *Mega Man X*, *Harvest Moon 64*, *Stardew Valley*) Pitch slides are too wide and too quick to resemble human sounds (see, for example, *Katamari Damacy*, *Animal Crossing: New Horizons*)

Note: Characteristics that occur in all or nearly all of the games in Group 2 are listed without specific examples. Characteristics that occur in only some games are listed with examples. Rare characteristics (exceptions) are not listed here.

Some of the abstract sounds in the Group 2 games feature timbres that resemble human voices—they include a fundamental frequency, evenly spaced harmonics, and bands of strong upper harmonics in the manner of formants. However, even those sounds with voice-like timbres also have a decidedly machine-like characteristic that is shared by all of the examples in this Group 2 corpus: a consistent use of that singular timbre throughout a given character's audio. In *Undertale* (2015), for example, the character Toriel's dialogue text is accompanied by what sounds like a somewhat breathy "ah" vowel throughout. Instead of voice-like timbres, most of the games in Group 2 use timbres that are machine-like in that their harmonics are very limited or highly patterned. *Ni no Kuni: Wrath of the White Witch* (2011), for example, uses a sound with only a single frequency and no upper harmonics (a sine wave); several of the early games in Group 2 use square waves, which produce odd harmonics only. For another example, Figure 41.5 shows a wideband and narrowband spectrogram of abstract sounds recorded during dialogue in *Phoenix Wright: Ace Attorney* (2005) (see ▶ Audio 3).[14] Ten instances of the same sound occur in Figure 41.5, and each instance comprises a quick sequence of three pitches, with strong fundamental frequencies at 922 Hz (corresponding to the pitch B♭5), 3638 Hz (B♭7), and 2979 Hz (G♭7). Aside from a missing harmonic in the first pitch, each of these pitches also includes equally spaced harmonics, and the harmonics above each fundamental frequency have roughly equal strengths. (Note that the three pitches are played so quickly that they are not audibly distinguishable as separate sequential events.) In another machine-like option, some games use sounds with a strong noise component (as in *Katamari Damacy* [2004], where the King of All Cosmos's dialogue is accompanied by a sound similar to record-scratching), or the abstract sound might be made entirely of noise (as in *Faxanadu* [1987]).

In the domain of time, a basic human-like characteristic—shared with Group 1—is that phrases of dialogue in Group 2's games are often delineated by silence. However, other characteristics of these abstract sounds across time align them more closely with the sounds of machines. Sounds in Group 2's games repeat exactly—again, as in Group 1—but in this corpus this repetition is often taken to a mechanical extreme, with a single sound repeating exactly several times in a row (see Figure 41.5, for example). Additionally, in most of the games in Group 2, stretches of abstract sounds fall into a regular grid, so that the time between onsets of adjacent sounds (the IOI) is a consistent value for multiple sounds in a row. Many of these games also include occasional, irregularly placed IOIs of a somewhat longer length, yielding a degree of temporal variety, but the short frequently recurring IOIs reflect the precision and regularity of machines. For example, in Figure 41.5, the short IOIs are all 68 ms, with two longer IOIs of 99 ms. (The only games in Group 2 that do not use a consistent IOI for multiple sounds in a row are *Katamari Damacy*, whose abstract sounds do not follow any immediately recurring spacing, and *Soul Blazer* (1992), which instead consistently alternates between IOIs of 32 ms and 64 ms.)

In the domain of pitch, some games in Group 2 employ characteristics that gesture toward human voices, while other games feature more machine-like characteristics. Some of these games' sounds use frequencies that fall within feasible registers for human speech, while many games' sounds fall outside (often above) a feasible register. On the human-like side, a few games in Group 2 use abstract sounds that include pitch slides, while, on the machine-like side, many games use discrete pitches only. In a quality shared with human speech, some games include a variety of pitches in a single characters' abstract audio, either through pitch slides or through multiple discrete pitches; by contrast, in some games the audio with a given character's dialogue is entirely monotone. Finally, some games in Group 2 feature pitch slides that are so wide and so quickly executed that they resemble mechanical rather than human sounds; this is the case with

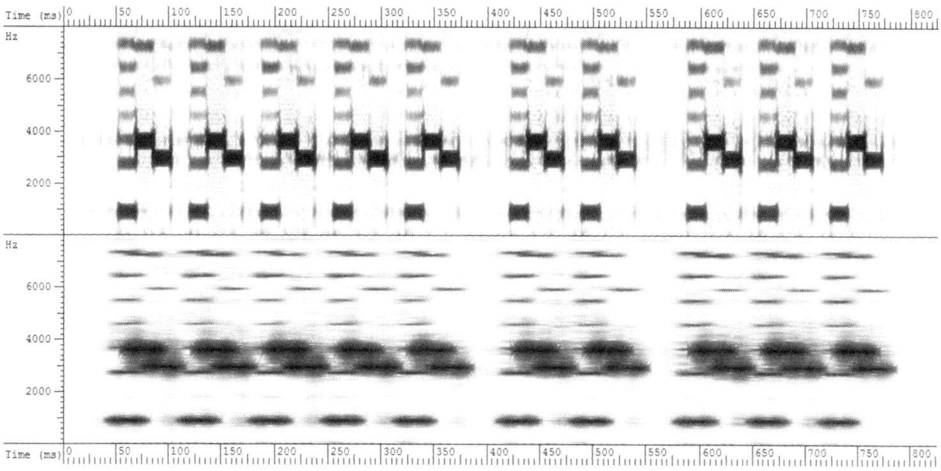

FIGURE 41.5 Wideband (top) and narrowband (bottom) spectrograms of a recorded sample of Mia's audio in *Phoenix Wright: Ace Attorney*.

Katamari Damacy's sounds that resemble record-scratching and the bubble-like sounds that accompany the player character's dialogue text in *Animal Crossing: New Horizons*.

Overall, many of the characteristics of these abstract sounds in Group 2's games are machine-like rather than human-like. Even when particular games include unusually human-like qualities in their abstract sounds (for example, voice-like timbre in *Undertale*, a variety of pitches in *Mike Tyson's Punch Out!!* [1987], and pitch slides that variously ascend and descend in *Snatcher* [1988]), many other characteristics still cast these sounds as overwhelmingly machine-like. With such a preponderance of machine-like characteristics, the representative leap from abstract sound to voice is somewhat larger here than in the examples in Group 1, and indeed, some listeners/players interpret these sounds—and their in-game framing—instead as purely mechanical, representing communication through some sort of text-based technology rather than through speech.[15] The representational connection between sound and voice remains available, however, through the sound's association with dialogue—we will return to consider these intriguing interpretive options later in this chapter.

Analyzing Abstract Representations of Voices

The first part of this chapter described abstract representations of voices in video games, and suggested some basic language and tools (for instance, spectrograms) for discussing these sounds. The rest of this chapter considers some ways in which these abstract sounds might produce meaning, and how we might approach these sounds in an analytical light. As a reminder, the meanings I suggest here primarily relate to my own perspective as a native English speaker considering the North American versions of these games. In analyzing abstract representations of voices, I will first take an approach influenced by social semiotics. Then, I will briefly consider how a music analytical lens might help to highlight further potential meanings in these abstract sounds.

Social Semiotics

Broadly, social semiotics is "an approach to communication that seeks to understand how people communicate by a variety of means in particular social settings" (Machin 2012). Like all semiotics, social semiotics is concerned with meaning, but here the emphasis is more specifically on potential meanings of signs (actions, objects, etc.) in particular social contexts. Social semiotics initially arose in the field of linguistics as a framework for examining meaning in language (Halliday 1978), and it has since expanded to consider meaning in images, sounds, and other modes of communication, as well as communication of meaning in multiple modes at once. Here, I draw inspiration in particular from Theo Van Leeuwen's *Speech, Music, Sound*, in which Van Leeuwen takes a social semiotics approach to sound across areas of (as the title suggests) speech, music, and other sounds (Van Leeuwen 1999).

One of the first aims of a semiotics of sound, according to Van Leeuwen, is to describe the "semiotic resources" of sound, the options available in various domains—such as time, pitch, and so on—that provide a "rich array of semiotic choices" with which users of the semiotic system might create and/or understand meaning (6). Tables 41.2 and 41.4 in this chapter have already listed some semiotic resources available with abstract representations of voices in video games: for example, these sounds might use timbres that are voice-like or not; these sounds' pitches might be high or low, their speeds fast or slow, and so on. Another important aspect of a social semiotics approach is to consider the social and historical context of the sound in question, since such contexts also influence meaning (8). Those contexts might include an individual user's culture and preferences, as well as the setting in which the particular sound occurs—in video games, this would include the genre or style of game, other game components like images and actions, and the category in which the sound is understood, for example, as a mechanical sound, or as voice, or as music. Van Leeuwen also raises another concept that has a bearing on the potential meanings of sounds in this chapter: *modality*. In social semiotics, modality is the concept of how true/factual/real something is *meant to be taken as*. In language, modality can be expressed and understood through modal words like "might," "probably," "certainly," and so on; modality expresses "the truth as seen by the speaker: speakers or writers assign modality to their assertions to express *as how true* they would like these representations to be taken" (156). In a visual mode of communication, modality can be expressed through the amount of detail in an image, among other qualities; for example, in the context of a newspaper, cartoons—with reduced articulation of details in background, depth, shade, and so forth—"are taken as visual 'opinions' and hence as less factual than news photographs," which feature more details in those same dimensions (Van Leeuwen 1999, 159–160; see also Kress and Van Leeuwen 1996). Context is important for modality, because the same type of information might be judged to indicate low levels of truth in one context but high levels of truth in another context; for example, reduced articulations of details in a line-drawn cartoon in a newspaper can indicate low modality (fiction, opinion), whereas reduced articulations of details in a scientific line drawing can indicate high modality (truth, accuracy). In the realm of sound, similarly, Van Leeuwen suggests that a variety of sonic details can affect modality and, again, that context is important (Van Leeuwen 1999, 170).[16] For the sounds that are the focus of this chapter, then, modality depends on the context in which listeners understand these sounds: either somewhat directly as the sounds of machines (perhaps especially readily available for examples in Group 2) or as sounds that represent voices (perhaps an easier leap for examples in Group 1, but available for all examples in both groups). If a player understands these sounds to be the sounds of machines, then the machine-like qualities in Tables 41.2 and 41.4 are realistic qualities, and these can reinforce a high modality (high levels of truth/fact/realism) of these sounds. By contrast, if a player hears these sounds as representations of voices, then the same machine-like qualities can reinforce a degree of abstraction and lower modality; in other words, part of a player's understanding of these sounds (part of the meaning that these sounds produce) would be that they are not meant to be heard as realistic. When these sounds are understood as abstract in this way, considerable imaginative and interpretive space opens up.

A full social semiotic analysis of abstract representations of voices in video games—from creator intention through player reception—is outside the scope of this chapter, but it is a promising prospect. Such an approach could help to illuminate the options (semiotic resources) available to game developers when representing voices (such resources might be influenced by technology or style, for example), why developers might choose some options over others in order to convey meaning, and how and whether players have received meanings (and whether these were the meanings the creators intended). Instead, for the purposes of this chapter, I want to highlight two specific ways in which abstract representations of voices might produce meaning, with a framework of semiotic resources, social context, and modality in mind.

First, in cases where the abstract sounds include some human-like characteristics—that is, where some of the semiotic resources overlap with real-life experiences with speech—as long as a listener understands those sounds in the context of voice, then those specific human-like characteristics could potentially produce meaning in a somewhat realistic way (even though the sounds are still abstract, with relatively low modality, in at least some respects). For example, if a game's abstract representations of voices use frequencies that are feasible for human speech, then high pitch levels could produce a variety of meanings similar to high pitch levels in real-world speech, including high effort, or dominance, or small size, and so on (Van Leeuwen 1999, 107–109). A meaning of "small size," for instance, realistically arises through the high pitch levels in the audio for Telly Vision, the hovering miniature-television character who accompanies the player's character in *Chibi Robo!*, as well as the bouncing, insect-like Issun who accompanies the player's character in *Ōkami* (2006). Similar levels of meaning might also arise through realistic voice-like timbral qualities, or speeds of speech, and so on.

A second way in which abstract representations of voices might produce meaning is by using a range of semiotic resources and establishing what amounts to a game's own interior social contexts; this option is available even with the most abstract sounds—the sounds with the fewest human-like characteristics. In these cases, comparisons and relationships between different instances of abstract sounds within the same game can yield meaning, perhaps more so than comparisons and relationships between the game's abstract sounds and qualities of real-world human voices. In several games in Group 2, for example, different abstract sounds are assigned to different groups of characters in the game, so that some aspect of a character's identity becomes incorporated into the potential meanings of the abstract sound. For instance, *Portopia Renzoku Satsujin Jiken* (1985), *Phoenix Wright: Ace Attorney*, and *Ni no Kuni* each assign relatively higher pitches to female and/or younger characters and lower pitches to male and/or older characters. In each of those three games, all of the characters' pitches are higher than feasible registers for human speech (this is a machine-like characteristic rather than a human-like characteristic), but a relatively higher pitch in the context of the game's own established pitch ranges is able to produce meaning (such as "small" or "female").

To explore how a single game with especially abstract representations of voices can use varying semiotic resources to provide meanings related to identity as well as emotion, I will take a close look at a scene from the beginning of *Phoenix Wright: Ace Attorney*. This case study will close the current consideration of meaning through a social semiotics framework.

Originally released in Japan (as *Gyakuten Saiban*) on the Game Boy Advance in 2001, *Phoenix Wright: Ace Attorney* was first released in North America on the Nintendo DS in 2005, and it is the first entry in a series of several games. (For this case study, I exclusively examine the North American Nintendo DS version of this game.) *Phoenix Wright: Ace Attorney* is a story-centric game whose tone is by turns serious and comedic. The player plays as Phoenix Wright, an initially inexperienced defense attorney in some future, accelerated law system. As Phoenix, the player talks with other characters, examines crime scenes, and works to uncover contradictions in courtroom testimonies in order to ultimately reveal the truth of a case, thereby defending innocent clients and unmasking guilty parties. Visually, the game's illustrations employ Japanese manga or anime styles, and a portrait of a character—mainly static, with subtle or brief animations—often occupies the center of the screen; this visual style together with conversation-heavy gameplay aligns this game with the visual novel genre. The majority of the text in this game is dialogue that is accompanied by this chapter's second type of abstract representations of voices (see Figure 41.5, for example).

Table 41.5 transcribes three portions from a scene near the beginning of *Phoenix Wright: Ace Attorney*. This scene introduces the player's character Phoenix (through text and audio only, since Phoenix's portrait does not appear on screen until later in the game), the smart and more experienced attorney Mia Fey, and Phoenix's client in this first case, Larry Butz (characters in *Phoenix Wright: Ace Attorney* often have humorous and/or wordplay-based names). This scene also includes the first dialogue with audio in the game. (A preceding cutscene featured music and visual dialogue text, but no audio with that text.) For each character's box of dialogue text, Table 41.5 lists two details about the repeated abstract sound that accompanies this text—the sound's three very quick pitches, and the basic IOIs that occur between most neighboring instances of the sound—along with some additional visual and audio components that might contribute meaning.

The opening dialogue between Phoenix and Mia establishes pitch as a basic carrier of meaning related to identity (along with the visible name of the currently speaking character), since Mia's sound is higher than Phoenix's sound by a minor third. Phoenix's opening line, "(Boy am I nervous!)," is reasonably internal monologue, indicated by the parentheses and the text's blue color, rather than most later dialogue's white text. The entire screen shakes during this first line, as well as during Phoenix's next line of dialogue, which could suggest an embodied nervousness, or more generally a heightened tension or emotion. Brief white flashes when Mia arrives might suggest suddenness or jumpiness (nerves again?). An additional bell-like sound (composed of G6 and G7 pitches) might add an inflection of surprise or heightened interest; this sound plays when Phoenix says: "Oh" after Mia first addresses him, and again when Mia says: "A favor?" after Phoenix reveals a prior connection between himself and his client.

A bit later in this scene, a new character begins speaking; parentheses and a green text color suggest that this character is speaking from a different space, or perhaps that the character is speaking to themselves rather than to Phoenix and Mia. Although this new character (who turns out to be Larry) is identified only with "???" in the usual place for a character's name on the screen, the pitch content of the abstract sound with their dialogue text suggests that some aspect of this character's identity is similar to Phoenix rather than to Mia (in this case, male, rather than female). A crash-like sound (together with white screen flashes and screen shakes) could suggest physical crashing in a realistic way (perhaps this unseen character is actually smashing into things in the lobby?), or this could be an abstract sound that adds an element of drama, high emotion, forcefulness, or even loudness to this character's represented voice (Mia says, "Isn't that your client screaming over there?").

Toward the end of this scene, Phoenix and Larry talk one-on-one about Larry's situation. White screen flashes, screen shakes, and the crash-like sound continue to inflect some of Larry's dialogue. Whereas earlier dialogue in this scene all occurred at a single speed (63 or 68 ms for the smallest basic IOIs between abstract sounds)—suggesting an even manner, and perhaps also seriousness or straightforwardness—Larry's dialogue speed in this latter part of the scene fluctuates quite a bit, ranging among slower and faster speeds that suggest the depths of Larry's emotions and unstable mood. Larry's dialogue sometimes even switches speeds partway through a box of text, as in the morosely slower "Oh, it's all over . . . I . . . I'm finished," followed by a quick, forceful "Finished!" Phoenix's final lines in Table 41.5 also use a slower-than-usual speed, perhaps emphasizing the especially serious nature of these internal (in parentheses, with blue text) thoughts. When

TABLE 41.5 Transcription of Three Portions of the Courthouse Lobby Scene at the Beginning of Episode 1, "The First Turnabout," in *Phoenix Wright: Ace Attorney*

Character	Dialogue Text	Pitches of Abstract Sound	Basic IOIs for Abstract Sound	Visual Components	Other Sounds
				Courthouse lobby scene	Musical score; Brief sound (F5-C6-G6) whenever player presses a button to progress to the next text box
Phoenix	(Boy am I nervous!)	G5-G7-E♭7	63/68 ms	Blue text, screen shake during beginning	
Mia	Wright!	B♭5-B♭7-G♭7	63/68 ms	White screen flash before text appears; white text Mia appears	
Phoenix	Oh, h-hiya, Chief.	G5-G7-E♭7	63/68 ms	White screen flash before text appears; white text, screen shake partway through	Bell-like sound (G6-G7) at beginning, tail continues during text
Mia	Whew, I'm glad I made it on time.	B♭5-B♭7-G♭7	63/68 ms	White text	
Mia	Well, I have to say Phoenix, I'm impressed!	B♭5-B♭7-G♭7	63/68 ms	White text	
Mia	Not everyone takes on a murder trial right off the bat like this.	B♭5-B♭7-G♭7	63/68 ms	White text	
Mia	It says a lot about you . . . and your client as well.	B♭5-B♭7-G♭7	63/68 ms	White text	
Phoenix	Um . . . thanks.	G5-G7-E♭7	63/68 ms	White text	

Phoenix	Actually, it's because I owe him a favor.	G5-G7-E♭7	63/68 ms	White text	
Mia	A favor?	B♭5-B♭7-G♭7	63/68 ms	White screen flash before text appears; Mia's portrait changes; white text	Bell-like sound (G6-G7) at beginning, tail continues during text
[. . .]					
???	(It's over!)	G5-G7-E♭7	63/68 ms	White screen flash before text appears; screen shake at beginning; green text; Mia's portrait changes	Crash-like sound (noise) at beginning; music stops (silence)
???	(My life, everything, it's all over!)	G5-G7-E♭7	63/68 ms	White screen flash before text appears; screen shake at beginning; green text	Crash-like sound (noise) at beginning
Mia	. . .	B♭5-B♭7-G♭7	63/68 ms	White text	
Mia	Isn't that your client screaming over there?	B♭5-B♭7-G♭7	63/68 ms	White text	
[. . .]					
Phoenix	What!? What's wrong, Larry?	G5-G7-E♭7	63/68 ms	White text	
Larry	Oh, it's all over . . . I . . . I'm finished. Finished!	G5-G7-E♭7	99/103 ms, then 48/52 ms during "Finished!"	Larry's portrait changes; white screen flash before text appears; screen shake at beginning; white text	
Larry	I can't live in a world without her! I can't!	G5-G7-E♭7	48/52 ms	White text	

(continued)

TABLE 41.5 Continued

Character	Dialogue Text	Pitches of Abstract Sound	Basic IOIs for Abstract Sound	Visual Components	Other Sounds
Larry	Who . . . who took her away from me, Nick? Who did this!?	G5-G7-E♭7	130/135 ms during "Who . . .", then 63/68 ms	White text	
Larry	Aww, Nick, ya gotta tell me! Who took my baby away!?	G5-G7-E♭7	63/68 ms	White screen flash before text appears; screen shake at beginning; white text	Crash-like sound (noise) at beginning
Phoenix	(Hmm. . . . The person responsible for your girlfriend's death?)	G5-G7-E♭7	130/135 ms during "Hmm . . .", then 99/103 ms	Blue text	
Phoenix	(The newspapers say it was you . . .)	G5-G7-E♭7	99/103 ms	Blue text, but "you" in red	Arpeggiated chiming sound (G4-B♭4-D♭5-E5 doubled at two octaves above) at "you"

Phoenix identifies Larry as the current suspect for murder (with the word "you"), red text color and an arpeggiated chiming sound highlight this idea, perhaps adding a meaning of weight or importance in terms of emotion and/or story.

These abstract sounds and visual components in this early scene in *Phoenix Wright: Ace Attorney* thus use a variety of semiotic resources that allow for a range of productive meanings, including identity, emotion, and drama, all without relying on voice acting. Although I have not considered details of the musical score and characters' illustrations in the above analysis, those components certainly contribute meaning throughout this scene as well. The rest of *Phoenix Wright: Ace Attorney*—and later games in the series—continue to use and build on these abstract semiotic resources, developing further meaning out of the game's specific social context.

Music Analysis

The abstract sounds that are the focus of this chapter are not thoroughly or obviously music, but many of these sounds do bear some select semimusical qualities—discrete pitches, for example—that at least potentially invite a musical framework in which to hear and consider these sounds. Indeed, many of the machine-like characteristics listed in Tables 41.2 and 41.4 are also characteristics that we might expect to find in (at least some types of) music: exact repetition of sounds, frequencies and speeds not limited by human voice capabilities, consistent timbre, frequently recurring IOIs, and discrete pitches.

Elsewhere, I have suggested that agreement (smoothness) between a musical score and another simultaneous sound, especially in terms of pitch and/or meter, can emphasize the semimusical quality of that sound or even bring the sound fully into the realm of music (Medina-Gray 2021, 185). This is the case, for example, in *Dragon Quest*, where the abstract sound that accompanies dialogue text (a pulse wave tone on the pitch A5) often agrees with the game's simultaneous score in terms of pitch; moreover, this abstract sound bears a strong tonal relationship with the music of castle and town locations (the former in the key of A minor and the latter in the key of F major), where nearly all dialogue in the game takes place (185–186). With such musical context, this abstract sound that accompanies dialogue text can access a wealth of additional meanings: for instance (I am drawing here from western musical conventions), frequent agreement in pitch between sound and score might suggest that the sound is cooperative and coordinated; a strong tonal relationship (especially as the tonic pitch in an A minor context) could suggest meanings of importance or privilege; the monotone repetition of this single sound bears similarities to a musical drone or pedal-tone, which in turn could suggest meanings of simple, as well as grounded, stable, or referential; and the nonmetrical rhythms in this sound's repetition, in a musical context, might yield meanings of disorganization, or perhaps complexity, or improvisation. When these sounds are understood as representations of voices, then meanings that emerge from a musical context could potentially apply more broadly to the characters' speech as well. In other words, these in-game characters might be understood to speak in ways that are cooperative (with the player, or with the gameplay environment), important, complex, improvisational, and so on.

In addition to *Dragon Quest*, certain other games in Group 2 allow for similarly musical considerations of their abstract representations of voices through smoothness with simultaneous score (see, for example, portions of *Phoenix Wright: Ace Attorney*). By contrast, *The Twisted Tales of Spike McFang* (1993) seems to try to negate a musical framing of its abstract dialogue sounds by using pitches for these sounds that are significantly detuned compared to the pitches of its western tonal score. Across both Group 1 and Group 2, when abstract sounds representing voices cross fully into the realm of music—into song rather than speech—the games in these corpora make this shift obvious by using sounds with both pitches and meters that agree with the simultaneous musical accompaniment, and by explicitly framing the scene as a musical performance (this happens, for example, with Fi in *Skyward Sword*, Telly Vision in *Chibi Robo!*, Mettaton in *Undertale*, and K.K. Slider in *Animal Crossing: New Horizons*).

More broadly, when a musical score plays at the same time as any of the abstract sounds in Groups 1 or 2, the game's varying musical context (varying pitches, harmonies, meters and rhythms, etc.) might allow even a single abstract sound to seem varied, because it sounds different against different musical contexts. Musical context, in other words, might provide an element of human-like variety for even highly machine-like sounds. Overall, a music-analytic approach can sometimes provide an intriguing perspective on potential meanings of these abstract sounds.

Conclusion

Abstract representations of voices in video games are a peculiar confluence of machine-like and human-like qualities. Throughout this chapter, I have described these sounds as "abstract," but we have also seen ways in which these sounds are sometimes understood as realistic (as the sounds of technology) and ways in which certain realistic qualities in these sounds can evoke meaning from similar qualities in real-life human voices. And the contextualizations of these sounds can become even more complex. For instance, what meanings or effects might arise when a quality that is almost always abstract in a game suddenly becomes realistic, as in *Celeste* when the character Theo ends a phrase of dialogue with both a visible and audible "yeah" (see the beginning of the scene at a cable car), or when a character begins to sing with clearly specific (rather than abstract) pitches and rhythms? What layers of meaning might video games evoke (and how might we untangle these layers) when abstract sounds represent machine voices rather than human voices—that is, when a video game uses abstract sounds to represent the voice of an overtly machine-like character who is themselves presumably approximating a human voice? This type of situation happens, for example, with Fi in *Skyward Sword*, and with robot characters in *Snatcher* and *Undertale*.

In considering the ways in which some musical instruments are sometimes understood to have voice-like qualities, Cornelia Fales (2019, 263) suggests that listeners employ interpretive imagination to find such voiceness in these nonhuman sounds; such imagination "allows listeners to fabricate an extra resonance of humanness that may be powerfully experienced, even while understood as entirely fictional." Perhaps abstract representations of voices in video games provide another channel for the imagination that players must employ in order to "find" human—or human-like—characters within the mechanical framework of a game.

Notes

1. See also Cheng (2014, 59–63) and Gibbons (2019) for some historically informed consideration of voice acting (including singing) in video games.
2. Throughout this chapter, I draw examples from the North American (English) versions of games where available.
3. For further details and interpretation of this particular sound in *Dragon Quest*, including a suggestion that this sound might represent characters' voices, see Medina-Gray (2021, 184–187). William Gibbons (2018, 139) has highlighted this same opening dialogue in *Dragon Quest* to point out that while players cannot listen to King Lorik's words, they might instead listen to the game's prominent music.
4. Some of these abstract sounds differ between different localized versions of the same game (see, for example, Stoeber [2020]), while some games' abstract sounds remain consistent across localizations; the aspect of localization is not thoroughly examined here.
5. In phonetics, phones are any speech sounds—for instance, consonants or vowels—that can be discussed with respect to their physical and/or perceptual properties, without regard to these sounds' contributions to meaning in a specific language. By contrast, phonemes are speech sounds that are moreover considered in the context of a specific language.
6. For more on the acoustics of human voices and spectrograms of voices, see, for example, Johnson (2012); Hagiwara (2009).
7. The spectrograms in this chapter were produced using the free software WASP (Version 1.80, (c) 2020 Mark Huckvale, http://www.phon.ucl.ac.uk/resource/sfs/wasp/). This recording of dialogue audio in *Celeste* was made using the game's FMOD Studio project, which is publicly available for educational purposes; see https://fmod.com/resources/documentation-studio?version=2.00&page=appendix-a-celeste.html. Most characters in *Celeste* have multiple, aurally distinct categories of dialogue audio that correspond with the characters' states. Madeline's available audio categories—as labeled in the game's FMOD Studio project—are "normal," "distracted," "sad," "deadpan," "determined," "surprised," "upset," "angry," and "panic."
8. Some of the characteristics I identify as "machine-like" in this chapter might also be more broadly viewed as "nonhuman"; for instance, animals or other nonhuman sources might also be able to produce sounds with some of the characteristics identified in the right-hand columns of Tables 41.2 and 41.4. I focus on the "machine-like" qualifier here in order to examine video games' mixture of human and mechanical aspects, but this current focus does not preclude the possibility that these nonhuman characteristics might also yield other meanings in some game situations.

9. Similarly, changing timbre—with formants—is one source of perceived voice-like qualities in certain musical instruments (Fales 2019). Put another way, speech is "fundamentally a system of organized timbral contrasts" and "the human voice is the supreme instrument of timbral contrast" (Patel 2008, 51).
10. The measurements of time in this chapter are my best approximation using digital tools, and they are reasonably accurate to within a couple ms of error.
11. Fi's audio in *The Legend of Zelda: Skyward Sword* (2011) is a near exception here, since many of the abstract sounds for this overtly machine-like character's dialogue fall into a diatonic set of discrete pitches, but slides outside of these discrete pitches also sometimes occur.
12. As of June 2022, I am aware of over 100 games that include abstract representations of voices of this second type.
13. Examples of explicitly mechanical text with sound appear, for example, in *Where in the World Is Carmen Sandiego* (Broderbund, 1985) and *Super Metroid* (Nintendo, 1994).
14. This recording of dialogue audio in *Phoenix Wright: Ace Attorney* was made using a cable connecting a Nintendo DS's headphone output to a laptop's audio input. A resulting noise artifact was removed using Audacity's noise removal function. This recorded audio corresponds with Mia's dialogue text "[. . .] screaming over there?" which is part of the scene that is transcribed later in this chapter.
15. In one of the few academic studies of game audio that mentions this type of abstract sound at all, Kate Galloway interprets the sounds and framing of dialogue in *Stardew Valley* as thoroughly mechanical: Galloway (2019, 173) describes these sounds as "the data beep-boops as each word is typed into the textbox to reveal [the character's] response." While Jenna Stoeber (2020) discusses this type of sound as standing in for voices, several YouTube commenters have responded to Stoeber to share their contrasting technology-based understanding of these sounds: for example, "I never thought of beeps as speech in old games. I assumed they were just a sound effect for typing." (user Cosmodious, 105 thumbs up, accessed July 20, 2021).
16. For more on modality in the context of representations of voices by musical instruments, see also Van Leeuwen (2010).

References

Cheng, William. 2014. *Sound Play: Video Games and the Musical Imagination*. Oxford: Oxford University Press.

Fales, Cornelia. 2019. "Voiceness in Musical Instruments." In *The Oxford Handbook of Voice Studies*, edited by Nina Sun Eidsheim and Katherine Meizel, 237–268. New York: Oxford University Press.

Galloway, Kate. 2019. "Soundwalking and the Aurality of Stardew Valley: An Ethnography of Listening to and Interacting with Environmental Game Audio." In *Music in the Role-Playing Game: Heroes and Harmonies*, edited by William Gibbons and Steven Reale, 159–178. New York: Routledge.

Gibbons, William. 2018. "Little Harmonic Labyrinths: Baroque Musical Style on the Nintendo Entertainment System." In *Recomposing the Past: Representations of Early Music on Stage and Screen*, edited by James Cook, Alexander Kolassa, and Adam Whittaker, 139–152. Oxfordshire: Routledge.

Gibbons, William. 2019. "Song and the Transition to 'Part-Talkie' Japanese Role-Playing Games." In *Music in the Role-Playing Game: Heroes and Harmonies*, edited by William Gibbons and Steven Reale, 9–20. New York: Routledge.

Hagiwara, Rob. 2009. "How to Read a Spectrogram." Accessed November 27, 2021. http://home.cc.umanitoba.ca/~robh/howto.html.

Halliday, M. A. K. 1978. *Language as Social Semiotic: The Social Interpretation of Language and Meaning*. London: Edward Arnold.

Johnson, Keith. 2012. *Acoustic and Auditory Phonetics*. 3rd ed. Chichester: Wiley-Blackwell.

Kress, Gunther, and Theo Van Leeuwen. 1996. *Reading Images: The Grammar of Visual Design*. London: Routledge.

Machin, David. 2012. "Social Semiotics." In *Glossary of Multimodal Terms*, edited by Diane Mavers and MODE. Accessed November 27, 2021. https://multimodalityglossary.wordpress.com/social-semiotics/.

Malawey, Victoria. 2020. *A Blaze of Light in Every Word: Analyzing the Popular Singing Voice*. New York: Oxford University Press.

Medina-Gray, Elizabeth. 2021. "Interacting with Soundscapes: Music, Sound Effects and Dialogue in Video Games." In *The Cambridge Companion to Video Game Music*, edited by Melanie Fritsch and Tim Summers, 176–192. Cambridge: Cambridge University Press.

Patel, Anniruddh D. 2008. *Music, Language, and the Brain*. Oxford: Oxford University Press.

Smith, Jennifer. 2021. "Voices, Combat, and Music: Identity, Camaraderie, and Relationships in *Final Fantasy XV*." *Journal of Sound and Music in Games* 2 (2): 42–62. https://doi.org/10.1525/jsmg.2021.2.2.42.

Stingel-Voigt, Yvonne. 2020. "Functions and Meanings of Vocal Sound in Video Games." *Journal of Sound and Music in Games* 1 (2): 25–43. https://doi.org/10.1525/jsmg.2020.1.2.25.

Stockburger, Axel. 2010. "The Play of the Voice: The Role of the Voice in Contemporary Video and Computer Games." In *Voice: Vocal Aesthetics in Digital Arts and Media*, edited by Norie Neumark, Ross Gibson, and Theo Van Leeuwen, 281–299. Cambridge, MA: MIT Press.

Stoeber, Jenna. 2020. "*Animal Crossing*'s Fake Language Is Different in Japan, and Here's Why." *Polygon*, March 22, 2020. Accessed November 27, 2021. https://youtu.be/xYZMWkmXX3k.

Titze, Ingo R. 2000. *Principles of Voice Production*. 2nd printing. Iowa City: National Center for Voice and Speech.

Van Leeuwen, Theo. 1999. *Speech, Music, Sound*. New York: St. Martin's.

Van Leeuwen, Theo. 2010. "Vox Humana: The Instrumental Representation of the Human Voice." In *Voice: Vocal Aesthetics in Digital Arts and Media*, edited by Norie Neumark, Ross Gibson, and Theo van Leeuwen, 5–15. Cambridge, MA: MIT Press.

Young, Miriama. 2015. *Singing the Body Electric: The Human Voice and Sound Technology*. New York: Routledge.

CHAPTER 42

SIMULATING SOUNDS OF SPECTATORS

On the Structure, Function, and Realism of Spectator Sounds in a Sports Video Game

NICOLAI JØRGENSGAARD GRAAKJÆR

Introduction

As part of the precautionary measures to help prevent the spread of the COVID-19 virus in 2020 and 2021, spectators' access to professional football (aka soccer) matches was suspended around the world. This situation presented a challenge for broadcasters and television executives, who expressed "a serious concern over what that [people seeing banks of empty seats and people hearing no noise and no audio effects] would do for people's enjoyment of the matches," and the situation was seen to "probably devalue the product" (according to a senior Sky source in Edwards 2020); arguably, the lack of spectator sounds could result in an "eerie silence" which would "make games seem more like training exercises" (Macgregor 2020). The absence of spectator sounds was considered particularly challenging, as it has been suggested that "the crowd's roars, chants and cheers are crucial to the experience and atmosphere of the game" (Lury 2005, 82); more specifically, the sounds have been said to "cover up all the swearing" by the performers (Macgregor 2020) and to act as an indicator of "the excitement and intensity of a sell-out crowd" so that the viewer "can instantly sense by audio alone the importance of any event" (Deninger 2012, 111; see also Graakjær 2020a).

Consequently, to help avoid offering viewers a devalued product, in some settings broadcasters would add prerecorded spectator sounds to the televised broadcast to simulate the soundscape that would otherwise have been produced by the attending spectators. Accordingly, when the English Premier League (EPL) resumed in June 2020 after a period of complete suspension of matches, EPL broadcaster Sky Sports (among others) offered its viewers a soundtrack of spectator sounds supplied by EA Sports (Electronic Arts; the producer of the football simulation video game series of FIFA since 1993): "In partnership with *EA SPORTS FIFA*, Sky Sports has created a range of bespoke and team-specific crowd noises and chants to bring the vibrant atmosphere of the Premier League to the restart" (Sky Sports 2020). The sounds, which were distributed exclusively through the televised broadcast and therefore not available to the players in the stadium setting, were produced from previous recordings—used in the game series of *FIFA*—of spectators at previous, pre-COVID-19 pandemic matches between the involved teams. The process of collecting recordings of spectator sounds began with the creation of *FIFA 15*, when the FIFA team gained "exclusive access to Premier League clubs" allowing not only for the construction of "detailed photography of all 20 stadiums so they could be authentically recreated" but also for "realistic audio to goal reactions, misses, whistles and over two hours of crowd-specific songs" based on recordings of "cheers, chants and sounds of more than 20 Premier League matches" (EA Sports 2014).

The televised broadcast offered both an "audio carpet of flat crowd noise" and "special sounds for penalties, goals and fouls" (Yusha 2020) drawn from a collection of more than 800 different sound clips. According to an EA Sports sounds producer and designer, "[t]here is nothing simulated or generic. It is all club-specific content. You are hearing everything that has been captured from home fans," and, during matches, a sound operator would control "a mix board and sound board where he can hit the button for reaction from a tackle from an away player or a shot from the home team" (Andrew Vance in Associated Press 2020); similar processes of added spectator sounds have been reported in the context of, e.g., American football and baseball (see Baccellieri 2020 and Roehl 2021, respectively).

This particular case exemplifies a mutual influence between the sounds of a video game and the sounds of the televised broadcast. By examining how the video game sounds textually compare to the sounds of the televised broadcast, I will show how sound plays a pivotal role in offering a sense of realism to players, and I will indicate how this ultimately can be considered as an example of how the boundaries between the two media blur (for more on sound and realism, see chapter 43 and chapter 44 this volume).

Situating the Approach

While these developments and procedures indicate that spectator sounds are highly important to the televised broadcast of football (for an examination focused on this importance, see Graakjær 2020a), they also suggest that spectator sounds have a role to play in the video game of *FIFA*. They furthermore suggest that there exists a mutually influencing relationship between the in-game sounds and the sounds of the televised broadcast. However, apart from an initial foray into the subject matter (see Graakjær 2020b), the role of in-game spectator sounds and their relationship to the televised broadcast has not been addressed in scholarly contributions. Previous studies in game audio have merely hinted at this particular type of sound. For example, without further examinations, references have been made to "crowds cheering" (Newman 2015, 40), "the cheering crowd singing songs apt for the teams on the court" (Kayali and Purgathofer 2008, 105) and an "in-game crowd that boos or cheers the player depending on the player's success" (Collins 2013, 64). Arguably, this reflects a more general scarcity of research. Thus, if it is (still) the case, that there exists "very limited work . . . on the sports video game" (Baerg 2014, 272; see also Crawford 2015, 573; Oates and Brookey 2015, 3ff), this seems to hold especially true of the sounds of sports video games (exemplified by the only marginal interest for sound in Consalvo, Mitgutsch, and Stein 2013). Also, spectator sounds represent a type of sound—that is, diegetic, (largely) nonmusical, in-game sounds—which has not been part of the increased interest for (especially nondiegetic) music in video games in recent years (see, e.g., Aska 2017; Donnelly, Gibbons, and Lerner 2014; Kamp, Summers, and Sweeney 2016; Moormann 2013; Summers 2016).

By focusing on spectator sounds, I aim to make contributions also to the subject of game simulation and realism. In general terms, a simulation models "a (source) system through a different system which maintains to somebody some of the behaviors of the original system" (Frasca cited in Bagley and Summers 2015). The resemblance between a video game and the "original system" is often evaluated from the perspective of realism, that is, the degree to which the various aspects or behaviors of a simulation actually "would be, could be, or might have been" (Wolf cited in Giddings 2014, 261)—bearing in mind, that, normally, a video game will not be able to replicate all aspects of the original system while innovative aspects (that is, not included in the original system) will be introduced in the video game. Sports games are viewed as particularly successful when it comes to offering a high degree of realism. It might (still) be the general case that "[g]ames are rarely set in realistic worlds" (Collins 2008, 134), but, if so, sports games appear to represent an obvious exception as, for example, the sports games by EA "aspire to high realism" (129). Moreover, it has been suggested that "[u]nlike most videogame genres, the ongoing quest for more realistic representations causes sports games to become more like the 'real thing'" (Kayali and Purgathofer 2008, 105).

Certainly, a focus on simulation and realism based on the original system of the televised broadcast is not the only possible approach. *FIFA* thus offers "much more than just a simulated television viewership experience" (Bogost 2013, 62) and includes simulated aspects of both playing, watching, and managing football. From the perspective of available typologies of sports games, depending on which aspect(s) of the game are seen as most significant, *FIFA* can be considered to represent a "team sports simulation" (Kayali and Purgathofer 2008, 108). Additionally, the game can be viewed as representative of "the televisual," which is suggested to represent a subgenre of football (or soccer) games (Conway and Finn 2015, 223) and/or as an "action simulation," in which users "guide athletes on virtual playing fields" while the "[a]ction simulations are committed to a visual fidelity" when it comes to modeling athletes, their respective uniforms and equipment, and the stadia in which they play (Bogost 2013, 62). Accordingly, playing or watching football in the stadium setting could serve as (parts of) the original system. Not only can the televised broadcast of a football match be approached as a live simulation of attending a football match in the stadium setting (see, e.g., Sandvoss 2003, 144ff) but the football video game could similarly be considered as a simulation of the live, physical activity of attending or playing football in the physical stadium setting. For example, when asserting that "sports videogames actually are nearly a perfect replica of reality regarding their audiovisual appearance" (Kayali and Purgathofer 2008, 105), "reality" apparently comprises aspects of football both as a *sport-as-mediated* and a *sport-as-played* (inspired by the terminology offered in Conway and Finn 2015, 219) including the following four categories of consideration: implementation of the rules, presentation, course of action, and control. Similarly, when Sicart (2013) examines to what extent the game of *FIFA* offers a realistic simulation of the actual game of football in terms of the rules, tactics, and the individual star players, the sport of football is approached as a sport-as-played.

However, a focus on simulation and realism from the perspective of sport-as-mediated—here with a specific focus on the televised broadcast—seems particularly relevant for an understanding of playing matches in the video game of *FIFA*. The simulated model of the televised broadcast might not be exclusive to *FIFA*. For example, based on qualitative interviews with developers of (the broader category of) sports video games, Stein (2013, 129) claims that "the aesthetics of the game are purposefully designed to reflect the production of sports broadcasts"—and to provide a specific example other than *FIFA*: "*F1 Grand Prix* copies television broadcast aesthetics to assert that the game world has a high degree of realism" (Summers 2016, 114). But *FIFA* is one of the most obvious and referred-to cases when it comes to exemplifying a highly realistic simulation of the structure and aesthetics of the televised broadcast of sports: "simulations of televised sports" is "clearly the case for some games, including the most popular sports franchise annuals like FIFA and Madden" which constructs a "considerable similarity" by "recreating the familiar visual style and technique of television broadcast" (Bogost 2013, 53 and 62). Arguably: "Given side-by-side screen captures from a PlayStation 3 match of EA FIFA and an HDTV airing of a FIFA World Cup match, could you tell which one is 'real' and which one is 'simulated?' I doubt it" (58), and, in a similar vein, "[o]ne can watch the computer play *FIFA*, and it will be only marginally distinguishable from watching a proper football match" (Sicart 2013, 33).

Inspired by these circumstances, my examination will address spectator sounds from the perspective of simulation and realism. In addition, to provide typologies of football sounds and spectator sounds, I will discuss to what extent the simulated sounds can be real(istic). Here, I seek to expand the available insights' almost exclusive focus on the visuals when examining aspects of simulation from a textual perspective—exemplified by the previous quotes' references to visual fidelity, visual style and technique, screen captures, and watch/watching. Furthermore, although some observers have indeed acknowledged a mutual influence between the broadcast and the game—for example, "[t]he relationship between sports videogames and television is not that of 'new' borrowing from an obsolescing 'old.' It's a far more nuanced and bi-directional affair" (Stein 2013, 117)—the structure and significance of sounds have previously been largely neglected.

As stated above, I consider spectator sounds as part of the game's aesthetics seen as the games "visual and auditory production" (Stein 2013, 118). Whereas a textual analysis of the sounds of sports video games seems a relatively rare approach—for example, "textual analyses of sports video games continue to be few and far between" (Baerg 2014, 268)—my focus on spectator sounds during the active gameplay of matches is in line with most previous studies: "While there has been some effort to understand the sport video game by certain scholars, all investigations of the text focus upon the diegetic space of the video game, the game *as played*" (Conway 2009, 68 italics in original). Consequently, the examination does not consider the sounds outside the "diegetic space" of playing actual matches—for an examination of "the nondiegetic space of the soccer video game" including a focus on *FIFA*, see Conway (2009, 68ff; see also Holyoak 2018; Kamp 2016).

The examination of the video game spectator sounds will be based on observations from my own gameplay of *FIFA 19*, acknowledging the necessity (as identified by Summers 2016, 10) of studying video games based on one's own gameplay observations. The playing mode I adopted for the examination was kick-off (off-line), classic match (Premier League), and single-player. All matches studied have included Tottenham Hotspurs in one of four roles: playing with or against as either the away or home team. Limiting the study to a single team created consistency that facilitated comparison of spectator sounds across the match settings (for a similar approach see Sicart 2013). Correspondingly, I relied empirically on pre-COVID-19 televised matches including Tottenham Hotspurs (see Graakjær 2020a) as well as the match between Tottenham Hotspurs and Liverpool (January 28, 2021) played during COVID-19 precautions in front of an empty stadium and broadcast with added spectator sounds.

I begin by specifying spectator sounds from the perspectives of the broad typology of *football sounds* and the more specific category of *sounds at football*. Next, I examine the structure and functions of spectator sounds in *FIFA 19* before I discuss the sounds from the perspective of simulation.

Sounds of Spectators at Football

Figure 42.1 presents an overview of what I suggest to term "football sounds" including three subtypes.

First, the subtype *sounds of football* designates the sounds that originate from the actual playing of a match of football. These are the practically inevitable sounds which emerge from the physical (inter)actions of performers—that is, players, referee(s), and coaches—and their handling of objects, for example, kicking the ball and blowing the whistle. Second, *sounds at football* additionally refer to those sounds which are normally part of the execution of an elite, professional football match. This subtype appears in two forms. In one form (see Box 1 "Physical Setting" in Figure 42.2), the sounds are approached as distributed throughout the physical setting of the stadium. Here, the sounds from the performers are supplemented by organizer sounds (e.g.,

FIGURE 42.1 Overview of subtypes of football sounds.

2. Mediated setting

Sound creators	Television production team(s)	
	Commentators	Sound designers
Examples	Speech	Music (sonic signals)

1. Physical setting

Sound creators	Participants at the venue		
	Performers	Spectators	Organizers (PA system)
Examples	Speech and object sounds	Music, speech, and object sounds	Speech and music

FIGURE 42.2 Overview of the origin of sounds at football in the physical setting and the mediated setting.

announcements over the stadium's PA system) and the sounds of spectators. In another form (see Box 2 "Mediated Setting" in Figure 42.2) the sounds from the stadium setting are mediated through, for example, radio and television broadcast or through playing matches in *FIFA*. In addition to providing the audience and user with a particular version of the sounds from the physical setting, the mediated setting will normally include additional sounds such as, most significantly, commentary and, occasionally, sounds to accompany visual effects.

Whereas sounds of and at football emerge during the here and now of the approximately 90 minutes of an actual football match, thirdly, *sounds for football* refer additionally to sounds that stand for or relate to football in settings outside the execution

Subtypes of sounds of spectators at football	Speech	Musical speech sounds	Music	Musical object sounds	Object sounds
Distinctive examples	Talk (chatter) and shouting interjections	Rhythmic shouting	Melodic and rhythmic singing	Rhythmic clapping	Arrhythmic clapping

FIGURE 42.3 Overview of subtypes of the sounds of spectators at football.

of an actual match. Examples include (but are far from limited to) football talk shows, music for/on football (see, e.g., https://45football.com), title tunes for football programming (see, e.g., Graakjær 2021), and, as hinted at previously, the nondiegetic music of the video game—all of which might contain excerpts of spectator sounds which are, however, not part of the present interest for the structure and significance of spectator sounds during gameplay and televised broadcast of matches.

Figure 42.3 2 offers a further specification of spectator sounds. The figure presents an overview of five main subtypes inspired by a conventional tripartite distinction between music (sounds characterized by defined rhythms, harmonics and/or melodies), speech (here broadly defined as sounds produced by the human vocal tract including talk and interjections), and object sounds (a term I propose to designate sounds produced by—or designed to simulate the sounds from—the motion and interaction of physical objects).

The differentiation of types of spectator sounds is based on, on the one hand, whether the sounds are produced by the human vocal tract (see the left-most column of the five columns representing subtypes in Figure 42.3) or not (see the right-most column), and, on the other hand, whether the sounds are musical (see the middle three columns) or not. The figure thereby indicates that, while some examples of spectator sound unambiguously represent the characteristics of either speech, music, or object sounds, there exist two intermediate or overlapping types of sound indicated by dotted lines between the columns in Figure 42.3. The following section examines how these sounds are structured in *FIFA 19*.

Spectator Sounds in *FIFA 19*

When listening to the soundscape of *FIFA 19*, its resemblance to the televised broadcast is evident. Spectator sounds emerge throughout the match supplemented by the foregrounded commentary and the sporadic organizer sounds (e.g., in the form of in-game announcements of added extra time). However, unlike a regular feature of television broadcasts (when several matches in the league are sometimes played at the same time), there are no sonic signals to announce the scoring of goals in concurrent matches since the adopted play mode implies that no such matches exist. When it comes to the sounds of the performers, every ball stroke is accompanied by a thumping sound event. This sound event is more characteristic of the soundscape of playing the video game of football than of watching the game on television, where such sounds are registered only occasionally by use the sound recording equipment of shotgun microphones (occasionally paired with parabolic reflectors, Wittek 2013) capable of capturing and isolating sounds even when the sound source is far away (thus representing the auditory equivalent to the visual close-up shot).

As in the televised broadcast, the home team supporters are usually the predominant suppliers of in-game spectator sounds. For example, in my own gameplay when playing as Tottenham at home (incidentally defeating Arsenal 3–0), the club's current signature anthem—a version of *When the Saints Go Marching in* with a lyrical substitution of *Saints* for *Spurs*—emerged at the beginning of the match and on five more occasions throughout the rest of the match. In addition to the signature anthem, the spectator sounds are marked mostly by chatter and a variety of outbursts in relation to specific match incidents thereby representing the subtypes of speech (collective interjections) and object sounds (arhythmic clapping). A similar structure of spectator sounds emerged in my own gameplay against Tottenham. For example, when playing as Liverpool away at Tottenham (incidentally losing by 5–3), the signature anthem was likewise heard on several occasions throughout the match. However, when playing as Tottenham away at Liverpool (drawing 3–3), the signature anthem for Tottenham did not clearly transpire. Instead, the signature anthem for Liverpool (*You'll Never Walk Alone*) emerged at the beginning of the match and on several additional occasions throughout the match.

When considering their introduction during gameplay, spectator sounds seem to occupy a composite or overlapping position between so-called player-generated sounds—initiated by, for example, "pressing a controller button"—and game-generated sounds initiated more generally and indirectly by the game's algorithms such as "the control of a nonplaying character, a timer-related action" (Collins 2013, 32). From this perspective, chants can be seen as game-generated, and they hold the potential to play the role of "ambient sounds" which are "not triggered by game or player events (other than that the player enters that particular space in the game world)" (Grimshaw 2014, 120). By comparison, outbursts gravitate toward representing player-generated sounds as they often emerge as a reaction to a specific player input (for example, the striking of the ball into the goalmouth). The performer sounds from striking the ball exemplify more unambiguously a player-generated sound, which acts as a direct and immediate auditory receipt to confirm the player's input. These sounds can therefore also be coined "sound effects" given that they are "typically diegetic" and "triggered by events occurring during gameplay"—examples include "balls being kicked or hit, flesh being punched, and referees' whistles" (Grimshaw 2014, 199).

In contrast to the frequently changing viewpoints of the televised broadcast, the visuals remain constant throughout the actual playing time. The camera operates from a relatively high perspective at one of the side-line grandstands, from where it travels parallel to the position of the ball without getting closer or farther away. The perspective could be termed a "third-person [or: ball] trailing view" (Collins 2013, 49). Although not pertinent during the actual playing time (where no visual shifts occur), spectators sounds can perform a continuity function when the player skips certain elements, for example, slow motion replays and celebrations of scoring a goal (which is included in the game's simulation of the televised broadcast). When doing so, the spectator sounds help to smooth the shifts between shots as the shifts imply both a change from one locational perspective to another and a journey (forward) in playing time. The spectator sounds thereby principally act to anchor the player to the stadium setting of the game. Furthermore, this possible modification to the progression of time indicates how liveness is only partly relevant when it comes to the video game experience. If liveness has to do with making available an experience of presence, immediacy, actuality, and essentially of *being there* (at a distance), *right now, as it happens* (Scannell 2014), the video game arguably offers a more suggestive sense of being *there* compared to *right now*. Apart from the possible time journey during the game, an unrealistic sense of time is produced by the digital time indicator in the top left corner of the screen, which runs significantly faster than real time when the ball is in play during the match (one minute of play time equals approximately eight seconds of real time).

The sense of being *there*—in the setting of the game—is furthered by the sounds in relation to what is arguably a double positioning of the player. On the one hand, the player is positioned as a viewer of the match, which resembles the position of the television viewer. However, although the spectator sounds in the video game are similar to the sounds from the televised broadcast, they *look* different and arguably, somewhat paradoxically, more realistic, as the unchanging point-of-audition (POA) is mirrored by an unchanging point-of-vision in the video game. The traveling camera seems to simulate an eye tracking the ball by someone situated at the stadium, although no spectator would, of course, move so fast and consistently along the sideline. On the other hand, in the video game, the player is positioned as a character or rather as several characters (the chosen team's football players) between which the player can shift during the match. This position is essentially related to the player's ability to control the actions of the characters, but it is advanced also by the active POA provided by the performer sounds of, for example, striking the ball. The performer sounds thus allow the player to experience a sense of proximity to the actions that occur at a physical stadium, specified (indirectly) by the spectator sounds' inclusion of the home team's signature chant.

When assessing the sounds' communicative functions (inspired by Jakobson 1960) in the setting of the video game, immersion is particularly important in creating nuance within the phatic function, which Jakobson suggests primarily serves "to establish, to prolong, or to discontinue communication, to check whether the channel works" (1960, 356). The player is continuously in close contact with the game because the player is in control of the character's actions and is accountable for the outcome of the game. The player is not likely to feel, for example, that nothing much is going on, and the sounds do not perform the role of summoning the attention of the player or presenting a lifeline to the event (which is an important function of the sounds in the televised broadcast). This also indicates that the referential function of the sounds—implying a focus on "the referent, an orientation toward the context" (Jakobson 1960, 353)—is less pronounced within the video game. Although the sounds might be considered to add a sense of atmosphere, the player is normally well-aware of how the game is progressing and would not (in contrast to the potentially, visually distracted television viewer) rely on the spectator sounds for this information. Rather, the spectator sounds potentially add to the immersive quality of the game as the sounds can, for example, overpower the auditory inputs from the real world and provide the opportunity to use one's imagination and to empathize with the characters (Ermi and Mäyrä cited in Collins 2008, 134). Specifically, spectator sounds contribute to the immersive quality of the game as they are arguably able to generate envelopment; that is, "the sensation of being surrounded by sound or the feeling of being inside a physical space" (Collins 2013, 54). Compared with television viewing, the setting of the video game also implies that the emotive and conative functions of the spectator sounds—respectively serving as a "direct expression of the speaker's attitude toward what he is speaking about" and as "an orientation towards the addressee" through "the vocative and imperative" (Jakobson 1960, 354 and 355)—emerge differently since the player is indeed playing and not merely viewing. The player is therefore disposed to experience all game design elements as a resource and call for action (more or less explicitly and consciously).

The understanding of the functions of spectator sounds can be furthered by likening the sounds to "one of the most distinctive aspects of television sound": namely "the audible inclusion of an audience" (Lury 2005, 82). The sounds from an internal audience have long been deployed on television and, before that, on radio. For example, so-called laugh tracks have been organized to guide viewers' responses and promote the illusion of sociability during sitcoms. Reportedly, in the context of television programming, the use of laugh tracks is "falling out of use in recent years, due in no small part to the fact that the 'liveness' of television is increasingly being de-emphasized" (Birdsall and Enns 2012). Leaving aside the question of the relevance of liveness in television, in the context of the video game, the deployment of spectator sounds resembles the use of a laugh track. The sounds can thus generally be considered to promote sociability and guide the player's responses to the game. However, compared with the traditional, televised laugh track, spectator sounds include a more dynamic variety of sounds which allow for a diversified guidance of player responses. For example, the sounds can act both *for* (to encourage and empower) and *against* (to discourage and frustrate) the player based on the general trajectory of the match as well as specific match incidents (for an elaboration of the potential disruptive role of spectator sounds, see Graakjær 2020b).

The Realism of the Simulation

In *FIFA 19*, spectator sounds are positioned among several design features that aspire to realism. For example, in the adopted playing mode, *FIFA 19* includes "official team names, colours and rosters, the various competition's structures and insignia and the modelling of player appearance and stadium settings, which (re)creates the meaning of professional, international football" (Crawford, Muriel, and Conway 2019, 940). Moreover, *FIFA 19* includes existing commentators in form of the voices of Martin Tyler and Adam Smith, who also appear as commentators on Sky Sports' televised broadcasts of matches—an inclusion that arguably illustrates a general trend: "Sports broadcasters and journalists are a major part of mediated sports, and it is no surprise that they play a key role in the remediation of the televisual in sports videogames" (Stein 2013, 124). The game's introduction of the actual matches—for example, the graphics and the music which accompany the presentation of the line-up for the upcoming match—is furthermore identical to the one presented through the televised broadcast. However, if it is reasonable to suggest that the soundscape of the video game during active gameplay is only marginally distinguishable from that of the televised broadcast, it is necessary to stress that those margins matter significantly, especially when interacting with the game (following a similar argument in Sicart 2013, 33).

Generally, while there are some obvious similarities between the televised broadcast and the video game, the two do not entirely overlap. As mentioned previously, the video game will usually include new, innovative aspects compared to the televised broadcast—for example, a notion of *broadcast plus* is used by Stein to designate the game design of an experience that carries "all the signification and representation of the televisual while affording players an additional experience of engagement through interactivity" (2013, 129). Similarly, other scholars have suggested that the "[t]he sports-themed video game simulates the fan's experience but seeks to enhance this through the perception of even greater levels of control and involvement in the experience" (Crawford, Muriel, and Conway 2019, 948). However, while the game provides greater levels of control and interactivity, it does not offer the player the same degree and experience of collectivity; that is, a "now, as it happens"-experience of the match with the awareness of a simultaneously engaged, large crowd and audience. Following this argument, the video game offers less—a sort of *broadcast minus*—by comparison with the televised broadcast.

A limitation of the video game also seems to transpire when assessing the realism of the in-game spectator sounds with the televised broadcasts which have influenced their design. Admittedly, there is nothing from the available sound quality and included types of spectator sounds that indicates that these sounds are unreal in the sense that they would not be, could not be, or might not have been (to paraphrase the previously mentioned quote by Wolf) part of an actual televised broadcast of a match. Therefore, the sounds' authenticity as maintained by producers—that is, that the sounds originate from actual televised football spectators and represent "nothing simulated"—seems warranted, whereas observers' usual characterizations of the sounds as "fake" or as "artificial crowd noise" (see, e.g., Hughes 2020; Mobayed 2021) could appear, at least partly, misleading. However, in attempting to specify the "genealogy" of the sounds, it soon becomes clear how, generally, a distinction between the "fake sounds" and the "real sounds" is quite elusive. Most significantly, the sounds of spectators in the regular televised broadcasts (from which the sounds deployed in FIFA have been captured) were never "real" to begin with. The sounds thus appear as the result of an intervention and reproduction of the soundscape compared to its manifestation and origin in the stands of the stadium setting (for an elaboration of this perspective, see Graakjær 2023). From the perspective of the gaming experience, like sound effects, the spectator sounds can "conform to a realism of action" so that when the player performs and acts (e.g., scores a goal), the action will be accompanied by sound (e.g., cheering), which, on many occasions, "will be authentic (actual recordings of the sounds produced by those events)" (Grimshaw 2014, 119). The sounds need not necessarily be real in the sense of embodying recorded, unmixed sounds of actual spectators. What matters is whether the sounds are verisimilitudinous; that is, they have the appearance or semblance of something real (for a similar argument, see Grimshaw [2014, 199] and Sanden cited in Collins [2013, 95]). If the causal mode of listening—that is, listening for the cause of the sounds or the source from which the sounds emerge—is indeed the "most easily influenced and deceptive mode of listening" (Chion 1994, 26), this holds particularly true of sounds in mediated settings, where the production of the sounds does not necessarily coincide with the distribution of the sound.

However, whereas the existing sounds of spectators appear real in terms of what is there (in the game), the sounds are not unambiguously realistic assessed against the introduction, variety, and progression of the sounds that would also have normally been there in the televised broadcast. In addition to rather abrupt changes in the level of spectator sounds resulting from specific actions on the pitch (which is realistically simulated in the video game), the televised broadcast will normally include prolonged periods of time with an increased or decreased level of spectator sounds. For example, a period with a decreased level of spectator sounds will often appear during the approximately 90 minutes of a match, as, often, "there will be stretches of time when nothing much seems to be going on" (Scannell 2014, 168). By comparison, the soundscape of the video game tends to appear condensed and densified as no such prolonged periods seem to emerge. Arguably, this reflects a more fast-moving execution of the video game (including the unrealistic time frame), where significant actions and events appear more frequently while the player is in control and accountable and not disposed to drowsiness (as indicated previously).

More specifically, a limitation of the video game's inclusion of spectator sounds transpires as some types of spectator sounds, which usually emerge during televised broadcast, are not represented. As far as could be assessed from my own playing, this includes rhythmic shouts and clapping (see Figure 42.3). Furthermore, whereas specific chants other than the signature anthem for each team occasionally transpire during the televised broadcast, such chants are absent when playing the video game. Consequently, the spectator's singing—represented predominantly by signature anthems—does not refer to specific match incidents or contextual aspects, like, for example, the history of previous matches between the two clubs or the career of specific players and managers. Also, there are no chants (or shouts) including swearing, taunting, humor, and abuse, which are otherwise regular features of the sound production of spectators at football—certainly, the football crowd can be "funny and filthy and senseless and racist" (Liew 2020; see, e.g., the categorization of chants in Morris 1981; and for more recent examples, see Holland 1997 and Luhrs 2014).

With respect to the televised broadcast of matches with no spectators during the COVID-19 precautions, the sounds are still real in the sense of representing recordings of authentic (although anonymous, apart from their partisanship) spectators. Additionally, the soundscape represents a wider variety of types of spectator sound, and from that perspective it resembles the normal (including actual spectators) televised broadcast to a greater extent than does the video game—although the filtering or sanitizing of the (verbal content of the) sounds in the video game are maintained in the televised broadcast. However, the introduction of the sounds appears highly unrealistic. Whereas the sound reaction of spectators in the normal televised broadcast can be likened to a meticulously match-monitoring "auditory seismometer" (Graakjær 2020a, 153), the live-operated sounds of the televised broadcast are characterized by occasional mishaps as when, for example, a "routine save . . . saw a huge roar generated that felt incredibly out of place" (Marland 2020), and when the sound operator "mistook a near-miss . . . for a goal and let off the 'goal' sound, before quickly switching to 'miss'" (Allen 2020). Additionally, and consistently, the sounds are not timed and tempered in detail to the action on the pitch. For example, in the observed match between Tottenham and Liverpool, when the home team goal is scored (in a 1–3 defeat), the action is accompanied by cheering only after approximately half a second of delay, while rough tackles against home team players are not accompanied by strong outbursts of displeasure. Therefore, when it comes to the introduction of the sounds, the video game appears more realistic than the televised broadcast—the game's algorithms produce a much more reliable and realistic in-synch introduction of sounds compared to the live, human sound operator.

Although the editorial manipulation of sounds during live sports broadcasting is nothing exceptional, prior examples include practices that aim to uphold a sense of reality and authenticity from the perspective of the viewer. For example, when working on the television production of sounds for American car racing (NASCAR), the sound designer Dennis Baxter was faced with the problem that the cheering crowd could not be heard, because "the noise from the engines bounced around and masked pretty much every other sound" (Andrews 2012). Consequently, Baxter "went to his sound library and found a suitable recording of crowd swell," and the next time the race would come to an end, he "snuck in this pre-recorded crowd, mixing it to sound just right against everything else" (Andrews 2012). In the televised broadcast, the absence of spectators is obvious. Rather than making available (a simulation of) the sounds of what you see—arguably conforming to the mantra of film sound designers: "see a sound, hear a sound" (Grimshaw 2014, 119)—the televised broadcast transparently sacrifices this appeal to authenticity by making available sounds that you cannot see and know could not possibly be there. Arguably, the televised broadcast thereby offers a radicalized version of the video game environment. While a suspension of disbelief is encouraged visually in the video game by the realism of the simulated fans in the in-game grandstands, the televised broadcast offers no such encouragement, which has been largely accepted by viewers (see, e.g., Hughes 2020). The sounds of spectators in this form of televised broadcast can thus appear to represent a nuanced—that is, unceasing and authenticated (by allegedly representing the sounds from actual spectators)—version of the conventional laugh track. The situation reminds us that "live TV sport is a confection processed just like any BBC, HBO or Netflix drama" (Rowe 2020). The sanitized sounds of spectators from the video game of *FIFA* have appeared as an important ingredient.

Conclusions

In this chapter, I have presented insights into aspects of the understudied subject of the sounds of sports video games. I offered an overview of various forms of football sounds and, more specifically, spectator sounds, and have illustrated the structure and functions of spectator sounds in the case of *FIFA 19*. The typologies and case examination are offered for further research initiatives, as the approach should be applicable for the textual study of other sports-themed video games, where the relation between, and significance of, different types, structures, and functions of sounds, as expected, differ markedly (e.g., American football, golf, motorsport).

Furthermore, I have examined spectator sounds from the perspective of simulation. While the sounds of spectators might be received as real (in the sense of representing excerpts of sounds from televised recordings), their appearance in the video game is not realistic: the game includes a reduced and sanitized variety of sounds. However, the sounds in the game do not merely constitute a simulation of the televised broadcast, as they have themselves been the subject of simulation through the televised broadcast during the COVID-19 pandemic. This illustrates concretely how "[t]he producers of videogames borrow and remediate the televisual, while producers of sports broadcasts keep an eye on sports videogames, looking for opportunities to reinvigorate their medium with a game-like aesthetic" (Stein 2013, 118). Certainly, if it is the general case, that the "boundaries between the two media blur" (Stein 2013, 134), simulating spectator sounds in the televised and video game football offers a case in point. During this process, the video game might be considered to play the role of an auditory membrane which allows certain examples of spectator sounds to pass onto the televised broadcast while others are filtered out. Although the televised production's sprinkling of sanitized spectator sounds throughout the broadcast lack precise synchronization and seem to sacrifice appeals to authenticity, it meets the audience's expectation of an internal audience when watching football on television—inspired by the suggestion that the stadium can be seen as a "huge television studio" (Penz 1990, 164) where spectators play "their roles as screen actors who pay to be seen" (Rowe 2020) or, perhaps more relevantly, *heard*. Contrary to what has been previously suggested—for example: "Television will notice our absence, one day. In the end, however much they mike up the crowd, they will be unable to create any atmosphere whatsoever, because there will be nobody there" (Hornby 1992, 189) and, more recently, "a crowd cannot, as yet, be simulated and then banished [because the] spectacle . . . still needs a real crowd in a real stadium" (Goldblatt 2020)—actual spectators appear to be dispensable when the "show must go on." The sounds apparently serve sufficiently to uphold a sense of normalcy, familiarity, and tolerability which trumps the appeal to "authenticity" from the perspective of the television audience. More generally, the distribution of spectator sounds across the included media settings seem to illustrate that "[w]hereas mediatized performance derives its authority from its reference to the live or the real, the live now derives its authority from its reference to the mediatized, which derives its authority from its reference to the live, etc." (Auslander 1999, 39). Additionally, the interaction between the video game and the televised broadcast might be considered as a case of hyperrealism as the soundscapes embody "the generation by models of a real without origin or reality" (Baudrillard [1981] 1994, 1). Game players and television audiences are offered copies (of copies) of sounds with no identifiable original. The mediated sounds could thus be seen to embody a creation which represents something that does not actually exist.

References

Allen, Ben. 2020. "Meet the Man Who Plays Crowd Noise Sounds on a Drum Machine for Sky Sports Football." *GQMagazine*. Accessed August 11, 2021. https://www.gqmagazine.co.uk/sport/article/artificial-crowd-noises.

Andrews, Peregrine. 2012. "The Sound of Sport: What Is Real?" *Acoustics Bulletin* 37 (4): 30–33.

Aska, Alyssa. 2017. "Introduction to the Study of Video Game Music." Lulu.com.

Auslander, Philip. 1999. *Liveness: Performance in a Mediatized Culture*. London: Routledge.

Baccellieri, Emma. 2020. "What's behind MLB's Fake Crowd Noise? A Conductor with an iPad." *SI*. Accessed August 11, 2021. https://www.si.com/mlb/2020/09/05/baseball-fake-crowd-nosie.

Baerg, Andrew. 2014. "Sports." In *The Routledge Companion to Video Games Studies*, edited by Mark Wolf and Bernard Perron, 267–274. New York: Routledge.

Bagley, Meredith M., and Ian Summers. 2015. "Ideology, It's in the Game: Selective Simulation in EA Sports' NCCA Football." In *Playing to Win: Sports Video Games and the Culture of Play*, edited by Robert Allan Brookey and Thomas P. Oates, 191–216. Bloomington: Indiana University Press.

Baudrillard, Jean. [1981] 1994. *Simulacra and Simulation*. Ann Arbor: University of Michigan Press.

Birdsall, Carolyn, and Anthony Enns. 2012. "Editorial: Rethinking Theories of Television Sounds." *Journal of Sonic Studies* 3 (1). Accessed August 11, 2021. https://www.researchcatalogue.net/view/262391/262392.

Bogost, Ian. 2013. "What Are Sports Videogames?" In *Sports Videogames*, edited by Mia Consalvo, Konstantin Mitgutsch, and Abe Stein, 50–66. New York: Routledge.

Chion, Michel. 1994. *Audio-vision: Sound on Screen*. New York: Columbia University Press.

Collins, Karen. 2008. *Game Sound: An Introduction to the History, Theory, and Practice of Video Game Music and Sound Design*. Cambridge, MA: MIT Press.

Collins, Karen. 2013. *Playing with Sound: A Theory of Interacting with Sound and Music in Video Games*. Cambridge, MA: MIT Press

Consalvo, Mia, Konstantin Mitgutsch, and Abe Stein. 2013. *Sports Videogames*. New York: Routledge.

Conway, Steven. 2009. "Starting at 'Start': An Exploration of the Nondiegetic in Soccer Video Games." *Sociology of Sport Journal* 26:67–88.

Conway, Steven, and Mark Finn. 2015. "Carnival Mirrors: Sport and Digital Games." In *Digital Media Sport: Technology, Power and Culture in the Network Society*, edited by Brett Hutchins et al., 221–234. London: Taylor & Francis.

Crawford, Garry. 2015. "Is It in the Game? Reconsidering Play, Spaces, Game Definitions, Theming and Sports Videogames." *Games and Culture* 10 (6): 571–592.

Crawford, Garry, Daniel Muriel, and Steven Conway. 2019. "A Feel for the Game: Exploring Gaming 'Experience' through the Case of Sports-Themed Video Games." *Convergence: The International Journal of Research into New Media Technologies* 25 (5–6): 937–952.

Deninger, Dennis. 2012. *Sports on Television*. New York: Routledge.

Donnelly, K. J., William Gibbons, and Neil Lerner. 2014. *Music in Video Games: Studying Play*. New York: Routledge.

EA Sports. 2014. "FIFA 15—Barclays Premier League—Stadiums." Accessed August 11, 2021. https://web.archive.org/web/20180910133136/https://www.easports.com/fifa/news/2014/fifa-15-barclays-premier-league-stadiums.

Edwards, Richard. 2020. "Sky Sports Considers Using CGI Fans if Premier League Returns Behind-Closed-Doors." Accessed August 11, 2021. https://inews.co.uk/sport/football/premier-league-project-restart-sky-bt-sport-tv-crowds-cgi-behind-closed-doors-423576.

Giddings, Seth. 2014. "Simulation." In *The Routledge Companion to Video Games Studies*, edited by Mark Wolf and Bernard Perron, 276–274. New York: Routledge.

Goldblatt, David. 2020. *The Age of Football: The Global Game in the Twenty-First Century*. London: Picador.

Grimshaw, Mark. 2014. "Sound." In *The Routledge Companion to Video Games Studies*, edited by Mark Wolf and Bernard Perron, 117–124. New York: Routledge.

Graakjær, Nicolai J. 2020a. "Sounds of Soccer On-Screen: A Critical Re-Evaluation of the Role of Spectator Sounds. *Journal of Popular Television* 8 (2): 143–158.

Graakjær, Nicolai J. 2020b. "'Listen to the Atmosphere!': On Spectator Sounds and Their Potentially Disruptive Role in a Football Simulation Video Game." *Soundtrack* 11 (1–2): 39–55.

Graakjær, Nicolai J. 2021. "*Club Foot* for Football—On the (Re)Construction of Meanings of Music and Football through a Television Title Sequence." *Sport in Society* 24 (1): 22–37.

Graakjær, Nicolai J. 2023. *The Sounds of Spectators at Football*. New York: Bloomsbury Academic.

Holland, Brian L. 1997. "Surviving Leisure Time Racism: The Burden of Racial Harassment on Britain's Black Footballers." *Leisure Studies* 16 (4): 261–277.

Holyoak, Matt. 2018. "*FIFA 19* Soundtrack Revealed." Accessed August 11, 2021. https://www.dailyesports.gg/fifa-19-soundtrack-song-list/.

Hornby, Nick. 1992. *Fever Pitch: A Fan's Life*. London: Gollancz.

Hughes, Matt. 2020. "Sky's Fake Crowd Noise with Chanting and Celebrations from *FIFA 20* Video Game Wins the Restart with 75 PER CENT of Fans Choosing to Watch the Premier League with the New Soundtrack." Accessed August 11, 2021. https://www.dailymail.co.uk/sport/football/article-8436219/Three-quarters-fans-choose-watch-Premier-Leagues-return-fake-crowd-noise.html.

Jakobson, Roman. 1960. "Closing Statement: Linguistics and Poetics." In *Style and Language*, edited by Thomas Sebeok, 350–377. Cambridge, MA: MIT Press.

Kamp, Michiel. 2016. "Suture and Peritexts: Music beyond Gameplay and Diegesis." In *Ludomusicology: Approaches to Video Game Music*, edited by Michiel Kamp, Tim Summers, and Mark Sweeney, 73–91. Bristol: Equinox Publishers.

Kamp, Michiel, Tim Summers, and Mark Sweeney, eds. 2016. *Ludomusicology: Approaches to Video Game Music*. Bristol: Equinox Publishers.

Kayali, Fares, and Peter Purgathofer. 2008. "Two Halves of Play: Simulation versus Abstraction and Transformation in Sports Videogames Design." *Eludamos* 2 (1): 105–127.

Liew, Jonathan. 2020. "Football Is Back and We Are Grateful but a Crowd Is Not a Sound Effect." https://www.theguardian.com/football/blog/2020/jun/30/football-is-back-and-we-are-grateful-but-a-crowd-is-not-a-sound-effect.

Luhrs, Joanne. 2014. "Blason Populaire, Football Chants and the Construction of Masculinity." *Tradition Today* 4:46–59.

Lury, Karen. 2005. *Interpreting Television*. London: Bloomsbury Publishing.

Macgregor, Jody. 2020. "EA Sports Will Provide Crowd Noise for Premier League Matches in the Absence of Live Crowds." Accessed August 11, 2021. https://www.pcgamer.com/ea-sports-will-provide-crowd-noise-for-premier-league-matches-in-the-absence-of-live-crowds/.

Marland, Daniel. 2020. "Premier League Returns with Fake Crowd Noise and Fans Aren't Sure about It." Accessed August 11, 2021. https://www.sportbible.com/football/football-news-reactions-premier-league-returns-with-fake-crowd-noise-20200617.

Mobayed, Tamim. 2021. "The Psychology of Fake Crowd Noise." *Blog*. Accessed August 11, 2021. https://blogs.lse.ac.uk/psychologylse/2021/01/28/the-psychology-of-fake-crowd-noise/

Moormann, Peter. 2013. *Music and Game: Perspectives on a Popular Alliance*. Springer: Wiesbaden.

Morris, Desmond. 1981. *The Soccer Tribe*. London: Jonathan Cape.

Newman, Michael Z. 2015. "The Name of the Game is Jocktronics: Sport and Masculinity in Early Video Games." In *Playing to Win: Sports Video Games and the Culture of Play*, edited by Robert Allan Brookey and Thomas P. Oates, 23–44. Bloomington: Indiana University Press.

Oates, Thomas P., and Robert A. Brookey. 2015. "Introduction." In *Playing to Win: Sports Video Games and the Culture of Play*, edited by Robert Allan Brookey and Thomas P. Oates, 1–20. Bloomington: Indiana University Press.

Penz, Otto. 1990. "Sport and Speed." *International Review for Sociology of Sport* 25 (2): 157–167.

Roehl, Alexander. 2021. "Superbowl Artificial Crowd Noise." Accessed August 11, 2021. https://www.acentech.com/blog/superbowl-artificial-crowd-noise/.

Rowe, David. 2020. "And the Winner Is . . . TELEVISION! Spectacle and Sport in a Pandemic." *IdrottsForum*. Accessed August 11, 2021. https://idrottsforum.org/forumbloggen/and-the-winner-is-television-spectacle-and-sport-in-a-pandemic/.

Sandvoss, Cornel. 2003. *A Game of Two Halves: Football, Fandom, Television and Globalisation*. London: Routledge.

Scannell, Paddy. 2014. *Television and the Meaning of*live: *An Enquiry into the Human Situation*. Cambridge: Polity Press.

Sicart, Miguel. 2013. "A Tale of Two Games: Football and *FIFA 12*." In *Sports Videogames*, edited by Mia Consalvo, Konstantin Mitgutsch, and Abe Stein, 32–49. New York: Routledge.

Sky Sports. 2020. "Crowd Noise Available for Sky Sports Premier League Games: How It Works."Accessed August 11, 2021. https://www.skysports.com/football/news/11661/12004035/crowd-noise-available-for-sky-sports-premier-league-games-how-it-works.

Stein, Abe. 2013. "Playing the Game on Television." In *Sports Videogames*, edited by Mia Consalvo, Konstantin Mitgutsch, and Abe Stein, 115–137. New York: Routledge.

Summers, Tim. 2016. *Understanding Video Game Music*. Cambridge: Cambridge University Press.

Wittek, Helmut. 2013. "Microphone Usage for Sports Broadcasting." Accessed August 11, 2021. https://www.live-production.tv/case-studies/production-facilities/microphone-usage-sports-broadcasting.html.

Yusha, Azwad. 2020. "How 'Crowd Noise' Works in Premier League." Accessed August 11, 2021. https://www.tbsnews.net/splash/how-crowd-noise-works-premier-league-107857.

SECTION 9

VIRTUALITY/ REALITY

CHAPTER 43

AUDITORY REALITY AND VIRTUALITY

Is Space the Final Audio Frontier for Games?

KC COLLINS AND BILL KAPRALOS

Introduction

For the past few years, coinciding with an escalation of interest in virtual reality (VR), there has been a rapid increase in the amount of attention paid to spatial audio (sometimes referred to as "3D" or "virtual audio"). Spatial audio allows a listener using headphones or loudspeakers to perceive the three-dimensional position of a virtual sound source as if it were coming from a particular location in space. *VentureBeat* promised us that "3D audio is the next big step for virtual reality" (Wesemann 2017), and *Engadget* explained: "For VR to be truly immersive, it needs convincing sound to match: Personalized 3D audio delivers the best results" (Lalwani 2016). With most advances in the computer and gaming realm, press emphasis is placed on the visuals, so the fact that many popular tech magazines and journals were emphasizing the role of audio in VR is notable. The initial commercial hype around VR led many in the audio world to turn their attention toward the technical issues of rendering spatial audio for these environments. Perhaps, as a consequence of both the interest in spatial audio for consumer VR and the rise of object-based audio systems such as Dolby Atmos and THX Spatial Audio, spatial audio is also now being touted as the "next big thing" for music as well (e.g., Gordon 2020). Zoom meetings are also being spatialized, promising us less ear fatigue and an increased ability to determine who is speaking (see, for instance, Rosedale 2020).

This rise in interest in spatial audio has captivated the audio engineering world, with several dedicated conferences having now been held around the world (such as the Audio Engineering Society's International Conference on Audio for Virtual and Augmented Reality, or AVAR), and a growing body of research touting new ways to solve some of the technical issues of spatial audio (for instance, head locking or head tracking? How do we effectively cancel crosstalk for presentation over loudspeakers? Do we need custom head-related transfer functions (HRTFs)? What pathfinding methods are the best to use? What are the most efficient and realistic rendering methods? And so on.).[1] Indeed, there are still some important technical problems to overcome when it comes to highly accurate and computationally efficient spatial audio. However, we contend that this pervasive focus on the technical difficulties and needs of spatial audio reproduction has deflected attention away from some foundational questions we should be asking regarding audio in VR and virtual environments. Here, we outline some ideas and questions that have emerged from our recent research work on audio for virtual reality. These views fall under two main umbrellas. First, that we do not yet have a comprehensive understanding of human perception and how that perception is or is not different in a virtual space. Second, that we are missing the creative, artistic aesthetic in the pursuit of physical realism. We argue that the fetishization of technological advancement in the audio realm has come at the expense of creative and artistic advancement.

Human Perception in Spatial Audio Rendering

When we attempt to mimic real-world sound with spatial audio, there are two main considerations we must take into account: the way humans hear and localize sound in space, and the way that sound propagates in space. In other words, we must account for both the human listener and the environment (the room acoustics). The combination of these two considerations results in significant computational complexity, requiring substantial processing power (which, when not available, prevents real-time rendering), which is why various shortcuts or trade-offs have been built into existing rendering systems.

Humans, of course, have two ears, and it is the use of these two ears together that allows us to determine where sounds are occurring in space.[2] The fact that we have two ears, separated on each side of our head, implies that there are differences between when and how the sound reaches and interacts with each of our ears, and how our brain processes the subtle differences between the sound signal at each ear to localize the sound. More specifically, there is a slight time delay from when the sound arrives at the ear closest to the sound versus the further ear, known as the interaural time difference (ITD). There is also a slight difference in volume level (intensity) in the sound reaching the ear closest to the sound source versus the further ear, called the interaural level difference (ILD) or interaural intensity difference. Collectively, the ITD and ILD cues form the duplex theory of hearing, which explains sound localization on the horizontal plane. However, there are aspects of human sound localization which the duplex theory does not account for. More specifically, we cannot differentiate the placement of a sound source directly in front, in back, above, and below the listener since both ITD and ILD cues are the same, and thus we rely on visual cues or moving our heads to localize these sounds. In fact, the duplex theory is ambiguous for sound sources positioned in the cone of confusion, an imaginary cone centered on the interaural axis with the center of the head as its apex: a sound source positioned at any point on the surface of the "cone of confusion" will have the same ITD values (Blauert 1996), and the larger the ITD, the larger the cone. During the 1960s, it was observed that sounds reaching the ears interact with the listener's head, shoulders, upper torso, and, most notably, the pinna of each ear in a direction- and distance-dependent manner, and that this can be used to determine the distance and direction to a sound source while overcoming the limitations associated with the duplex theory. Collectively, these interactions are characterized by a complex response known as the head-related transfer function (HRTF) and encompass various sound localization cues including ITDs, ILDs, and changes in the spectral shape (frequency distribution) of the sound reaching a listener. Each of us experiences sound slightly differently, since we are shaped as unique reflecting and absorbing bodies, with individual hearing abilities, and differently shaped pinnae (resulting in different frequencies being reflected differently into our auditory canal).

The generation of effective spatial audio generally relies on the incorporation of HRTFs. The process of measuring HRTFs is a highly complex and time-consuming process requiring specialized equipment and facilities. Although best results are achieved when an individual's own HRTFs are measured and used for that individual, measuring the HRTFs for each user of a spatial audio system is not feasible. Therefore, generic nonindividualized HRTFs obtained using a variety of methods, such as measuring the HRTFs of an anthropomorphic dummy head or of an above-average human localizer or the averaging of the HRTFs measured from several different individuals (and/or dummy heads).

Modeling accurate HRTFs helps us to identify a sound's direction, but there are also some other cues in the real world that we use to determine a sound's location and distance. Louder sounds are perceptually closer to us, for instance, and to some extent we determine a sound's proximity based on past experiences of similar related sounds (for example, we hear whispered voices as being perceptually closer, even at louder volumes—see Dalton and Hughes 2014). When we are indoors or outside with reflective surfaces around us, there will be a delay from when the initial sound reaches our ears to when we hear the reflections and reverberation, called the initial time delay. This delay is also used to determine proximity. How much of the original signal we hear versus how much reverberation we hear (the wet/dry mix) also determines how far we perceive a signal to be. The velocity of a moving sound source (motion parallax) can also influence where we perceive a signal to be located. Since high frequencies are absorbed by air more quickly than lower frequencies, the amount of high-frequency attenuation also influences the perceived distance. All of these are calculated instantaneously by our brains but, in virtual environments, must be calculated and processed in real time to send the correct signal to our ears.

Finally, we have the position of the head itself. If you've ever strained to listen for something, you have probably tilted and turned your head to try to obtain a better sense of where the sound was coming from. When we tilt our head, there are changes in how the sound hits our ears, particularly with respect to higher frequency sounds. Therefore, even if we process all the perceptual influences on our ability to localize sound in space, if we fail to consider the position of the listener's head, it will result in good but not *great* localization. When we are wearing headphones, unless we are tracking not just head location but the head's angle and position, we are missing some of these important cues.

As mentioned, in addition to how people localize sounds, we also must take into consideration how sound propagates in space—that is, how sound moves around in the air and water, how it interacts with objects it may encounter—and recreate that propagation and potential interaction in the engine in real time. The most obvious element of propagation is reverberation. Sound usually reflects off smooth surfaces and is usually absorbed or diffused by porous, soft surfaces. The type of interaction (reflection or diffusion) is a matter of how the signal is changed by the surface: when sound bounces off hard, smooth surfaces, the sound wave is discretely reflected, with most of the wave intact, resulting in distinct echoes. Diffusion scatters the sound wave in many directions, maintaining the sound's energy in the room (unlike absorption). Because we know how sound behaves on different surfaces, we can model such reverberation. However, the potentially large number of interactions, and the complexity of many surfaces that a sound encounters, implies that some frequencies may be absorbed or diffused by the surface, while others may be reflected, so there is considerable computation involved. In addition, frequencies are being absorbed by the air in a frequency-dependent manner (higher frequencies are absorbed more) as they move, and, therefore, the reverberation will die out over time, rather than continue to propagate, at different rates for different frequencies.

In our natural environment, the direct path between a sound source and a listener is often occluded due to the presence of an occluding object/obstacle in the direct path between the sound source and the listener. However, due to the phenomenon of diffraction, sound is still able to reach the listener by bending (refracting) around the occluder. We can think of diffraction approximately as the behavior of sound: that is, what happens when sound meets something in space. Sound waves bend when they hit barriers. We can hear sounds through doors, for instance, even if we are not standing directly in front of the doorway—they propagate outward from the barrier source. They can also be completely or partially obstructed by solid surfaces, and how much of the original sound we hear and how much of the reflections is quite complicated in complex three-dimensional environments. Formally, diffraction can be defined as the "bending mode" of sound propagation whereby sound waves move (bend) around an obstacle that lies directly in the line of straight propagation allowing us to hear sounds around corners and around barriers (Cremer and Muller 1978).

On top of processing how sounds are propagating around the environment (the surfaces and absorption coefficients), and on top of how the player is hearing sounds, in virtual environments we must account for moving sounds and, potentially, moving listeners as well. All these data need to be processed in real time, and any delay, even in the millisecond range, can be picked up by the human brain and skew the accuracy of our perception. Spatial audio rendering is, in other words, a highly complex process. There are a great many different spatial-audio rendering methods that, in an attempt to find a computationally efficient, yet physically accurate simulation of real-world physics, involve, for instance, different algorithms to pathfind (that is, to trace the reflection of a sound wave off a surface and its path toward the listener), along with different approaches to preprocessing or real-time processing of the propagation, different occlusion processors (determining how much sound should travel through or be blocked by a surface), different means of calculating diffusion and reflections, and further aspects that are being and have been explored. These approaches have been the subject of a growing and considerable body of research (see Beig et al. 2019 for an overview).

However, one question that is seemingly missing from the research into the most effective method to render spatial audio is simply, do users of the system notice any discrepancy in accuracy or prefer a particular method of spatial audio rendering? Our own research found that different methods did have some impact when it came to performance on one particular task. In one study, 23 participants completed a navigation task using different rendering methods in a 3D game (amplitude panning, amplitude panning using FMOD's raycast occlusion method, and our own 3D graph-based audio rendering system). The players had to locate sounding objects in a virtual space by tracking their sounds. Although we found that there was a statistically significant difference in task performance between the rendering methods, we also found that some expert players expected audio to behave as it had in previous games with which they were familiar (Cowan, Kapralos, and Collins 2020a). However, these tests involved a small group of participants, and the task involved may not have rendered the results as accurately as necessary to allow for a blanket statement that any one method is an improvement over another.

Moreover, when performing a specific task, such as the one assigned in our own study, it may be preferred to have a method that is not highly accurate, but which may bleed a sound through walls and floors to more quickly locate a particular sound. In addition, as noted, one important finding was that players came to the task with assumptions based not on real-world acoustics but on past media consumption. Expert gamers who had previously become accustomed to one means of three-dimensional audio rendering in games expected the audio to behave as audio in other recent games had behaved, not as the real world behaves. How long does it take for a listener to adapt before these differences between the real and the virtual world become habituated and part of a set of expectations? Furthermore, how long does it take to break that habit and reaccustom a user to a new system? We simply do not know.

Perhaps most importantly, in thinking through the design of a follow-up study that will compare the perceptual performance of different rendering methods, it became clear to us that, in fact, we have no knowledge of how well non-visually impaired, non-hearing-impaired people may be able to accurately wayfind an audio signal in the real world, let alone the virtual world! Without any knowledge of how much we rely on our ears in the real world when presented with visual cues (or, as well, in the absence of visual cues), how can we make any assumptions about what method is preferable in the virtual world? How can we test for the perceptual abilities in a virtual environment if we have little understanding of those perceptions in the real world? There is, clearly, a need for some basic, fundamental research into human auditory perception in real-world environments before we can make claims as to what is the best method to render audio in a virtual environment. With the many years of efforts put into accurate spatial audio rendering, it seems strange that the human perception of sound localization in real and virtual space is so underexplored.

What is clear from the existing auditory perceptual research is that there are some localization errors that we experience as humans that are not, to our knowledge, accounted for in current systems. Indeed, it is sometimes as if our perception is meant to become superhuman once we enter the virtual realm. There are some factors that make localization of sound sources in space difficult, including reverb, occluders, sound source frequency, hearing ability of the listener, and the loudness of the sound.[3] We also have difficulty localizing sounds in specific locations due to the binaural nature of our heads: Sounds directly in front or behind get confused, because of the lack of difference in interaural time delay, level delay, and so on, leading to the cone of confusion mentioned above. Moreover, when dealing with sounds propagated in space, if there is a sound source that is not traveling along a direct path, but is reflected before reaching a listener, the listener may incorrectly perceive the source direction. Are such occlusion errors necessary to account for in a virtual world? Is the addition of such errors into a system a gimmick, and do people even hear and perceive the difference?

As described, accurate spatial audio rendering requires considerable computational processing power. Often, this audio processing need conflicts with the simultaneous need to process the graphics and, more recently, the artificial intelligence in the game, and thus various trade-offs must be made to reduce the computational load. These trade-offs inherently involve some reduction in the fidelity (level of realism) to real-world physics. Which trade-offs can be ignored, and which influence the listener's perception of sound in space? What should be prioritized in terms of sound rendering in spatial audio systems for VR? For instance, is anything beyond a first-order reflection in a reverb tail superfluous? Should sounds most important to the simulation be rendered most accurately with HRTFs, while others be given generic reverbs to save processing needs? How can we leverage perceptual-based rendering, whereby the rendering parameters (typically of the visuals/graphics) are adjusted based on the perceptual system (see Hulusić et al. 2011), to limit computational processing while maximizing the effectiveness of the overall rendering system to the listener? Although prior work has demonstrated a strong influence between sound and the visual scene (see Kapralos et al. 2017), what, if any, consequence(s) does such perceptual-based rendering have within different kinds of interactive virtual environments?

We do not know whether people can hear a difference between different rendering methods and the real world under different circumstances or whether highly accurate audio rendering matters. We believe there is a lot of room in this space for user studies to be undertaken, not just in spatial audio rendering but also in the ways that humans process and localize auditory information in the real world, and the role that such localization plays for sighted people in particular. We know, for instance, that humans are better at localizing certain *types* of sounds (e.g., low frequencies are harder to accurately localize), but our knowledge of localization when it comes to important sounds in games (such as footsteps, gunshots, etc.) is incredibly incomplete. If we had a better understanding of psychoacoustics we could perhaps build perceptual-based spatial audio rendering systems that prioritize and emphasize the sounds that are difficult to localize, and make those more accurate, and prerender the rest as needed. We might, in other words, be wasting our time building highly accurate rendering systems that may provide no benefit to the listener. We have entered a rabbit-hole of technical details to build what we believe are ever-more robust and accurate systems while ignoring the needs of the users.

Those researchers and companies who have tended to build spatial audio systems have generally worked in the audio domain for a large amount of time and are particularly attuned to sound. Are these researchers special-case expert listeners with more attuned hearing, and not the average listeners/game players? We know that some people who have been visually impaired for a lengthy time can train themselves to echolocate (see Thaler et al. 2011).[4] Some degree of expertise is likely to come from those who have spent long periods of time listening to and training themselves to focus on sounds in their environment: how do we account for these differences in our understanding of spatial audio rendering?[5] Are personalized or individualized HRTFs necessary for certain people (e.g., "expert" listeners) or are generic HRTFs enough for everyone? Or should everyone be customizing their HRTFs to have the most accurate audio—will users even notice any difference with such customized HRTFs, and if so, do the effects of customized HRTFs change over time?

There are so many auditory confusions that occur when we are using recorded audio samples, as well. We know that past experience can influence our perception of sound—as described above, prior experience tells us that a whisper is up close, and a yell is usually distant (see Zahorik et al. 2005), but when we are dealing with replicated (recorded) audio that may be close or distant-miked, and therefore have all the sonic properties of being close or distant in terms of their spectral differences and frequency performance, how does that experience translate into the virtual realm? Are we confusing our perception of distance in the way in which we are miking different sounding objects? There are no standards for microphone distance in recording samples, but should there be, so that we might learn a new set of expectations for the virtual realm? There are a great many factors at play in why we place microphones to record different sounds at different distances (loudness, the potential mess an object might make with debris, liquids, the amount of detail desired, etc.), so it seems highly unrealistic to suggest such standards, and yet, our knowledge of the impact of this distancing on listeners is almost nonexistent.

Another important aspect to perception of sound in a virtual world is the multimodal interactions that occur. In the natural environment, sound is experienced in conjunction with our other senses, notably the visual and haptic (touch-based) senses (see Collins and Kapralos 2019). Our language to describe sound is littered with references to our other senses: "high, low, deep, warm, cold, bright, dark, rough, smooth, big, small, soft, edgy, round, flat, sharp, dull," and so forth (Görne 2019, 18). We very often use metaphors referring to our other senses to talk about sound, so ingrained is this synesthetic experience. When we translate the real into the virtual, we must (at this time) abandon several of these other senses—notably touch, but also scent, and taste. How does the absence of any one of these critical other senses impact our reception of the sound? We know that it is possible to leverage some of the cross-modal interactions to invoke a pseudo-haptic relationship, yet this research remains incredibly underexplored (see Collins and Kapralos 2019 for a review).

Perhaps the most important question that seems to be so often missed (notably with respect to the new spatial audio rendering of music as well): do consumers *want* realistic virtual world audio? (See chapter 44 this volume on the fetish of realism for further discussion of this topic and chapter 42 this volume.) And do they need it? Intuitively we may believe that such accuracy is more important for training and real-life simulation, but is that the case when it comes to most types of video games? Are there times when different rendering methods in the same simulation or virtual world may be more fruitful than a single method? What are the benefits and drawbacks of switching between methods based on listener preference?

Attention and Focus in Perceptual Audio Rendering

When it comes to our perception of sound, there are some important aspects that our rendering engines do not take into account, perhaps the most important of which is the role of attention and focus on what we hear. Just as with sight, what we are focused on in terms of our soundscape alters the ways in which we experience that sound. This focus of our attention on sound and the ability to simultaneously filter out unwanted sounds in the same environment is known as the cocktail party effect (see Arons 1992). That is, when we focus on sound, as on a speaker at a cocktail party, we can exclude other sounds that get in the way of our focus, prioritizing what we want to hear. Similarly, the "Invisible Gorilla" experiment, where focus is drawn to some visual object on a screen while a man in a gorilla suit jumps about, usually unnoticed, shows how inattentional blindness—that is, the ability to completely ignore a stimulus in our visual field—has been replicated in terms of auditory perception (see Dalton and Hughes 2014), although studies are still lacking in how to best simulate such a feature in terms of a virtual world. Should we be able to focus our auditory perception on an object in a scene and prioritize that sound in the mix depending on where our gaze is fixed, to replicate this real-world phenomenon, or is it even possible to carry our ability from the real world into a virtual space (and should visuals also adapt)?

Similarly, Walter Murch (2005) defined for film what has since been referred to as the "five layer law," where, in a film mix, there are only five layers of sound that are reasonable for the audience to process at any one time, but that this can be altered depending on the positioning of the sound (panning), as well as the context in terms of the action and visuals of the film. Does a similar rule of thumb apply to the real world or to virtual worlds, which can have three-dimensional audio spatialized around us? How many simultaneous sounds are reasonable for a listener to process in a virtual space, and does that change if they are spatialized? How does that change according to our focus and attention? We do not have the answers to these questions, but they seem to be important to our understanding of how best to deliver audio to listeners in a virtual world.

There are clearly many perceptual aspects to virtual audio rendering that are still unresolved and may differ for individuals and/or depend on the believability or realism involved in the simulation itself—after all, what does a monster or an alien world sound like? We are likely to accept more deviations from our world physics in such scenarios. The approach up to now, to focus on recreating real-world physics into a virtual realm, is all well and good but, we have argued, may not be the most fruitful use of our time and most importantly may not result in the best user experiences. As described above, we know there are some perceptual differences between the ways in which we hear sound in virtual space and how we hear sound in reality. There are expectations based on their previous consumption of media that a user brings to a virtual world that are not present in reality. Simply put, reality, when presented virtually, just does not live up to the hyperreal virtual experience: real-world physics can sound less than realistic when presented in the virtual world. A user, for instance, expects sounds in outer space, as experienced in film and games. What happens when the believable collides with the realistic? And which is more important to replicate—the believable, or the realistic? The answer of course depends on the genre of game, but so, too, should how we spatialize audio in virtual worlds: realism is not always the best choice.

Psychological Uses of Sound

There is a saying in the game audio world, by *Halo* (2001) composer Marty O'Donnell: "Sound makes it real, music makes you feel" (cited in Collins 2016, 80). Game audio has often off-loaded the emotional properties of audio onto music, rather than sound design. This decision—conscious or not—has sublimated much of game sound design to a secondary role of merely supporting the believability of the spatial realm being presented, rather than supporting what we might argue is one of the more important roles of emotional, psychological connection to, and immersion in, that virtual world. We do not debate the importance of the suspension of disbelief and that this suspension can be tied to a believable sonic atmosphere, but games are not about *realism*. We are willing to accept deviations from real-world accuracy in our consumption of media, particularly when we are emotionally engaged in that media. A few examples from film sound design will illustrate our point.

There are some films where the sound design overwhelms the senses, where sound plays a primary role in driving the story, rather than merely supporting the story, a role that is very rare in games. Two examples that come to mind are Shinya Tsukamoto's *Tetsuo: The Iron Man* (1989) and *Eraserhead* (Lynch 1977). It is interesting that both these films are primarily shot in black and white, both have little dialogue, and both have significant levels of surrealism and symbolism, lending themselves, perhaps, to more mysterious and creative uses of sound. *Eraserhead* (sound design by Alan Splet) makes sound a character in the film, the constant industrial drones providing an oppressive, atmospheric score in every scene. Ambiguous sounds disturb and play with the audience's ears: we hear rats squealing but then see puppies, for instance. Some sounds are missing from the soundtrack, such as protagonist Henry's stepping into a puddle: the audience senses that the missing sounds highlight such scenes and reinforce their surreal worlds. The confusion between sound effects and music in *Eraserhead*, and the primacy of industrial atmospheric sound, is not just found but pushed further in *Tetsuo: The Iron Man*. Here, the main character is gradually turned into a machine. As with *Eraserhead*, some sounds are notably absent, while others are overemphasized. Rather than detract from the believability of the world, the absence of some sounds lends credence to the surreal, dream-state nature of the films. We struggle to find a similar example in the world of games: while many games skirt the boundaries of surrealism, there are very few where sound is given the kind of emotional and central role found in such films.

At the other end of the sonic spectrum of the constant-noise of *Eraserhead* and *Tetsuo* is the use of silence or near-silence. Many games find themselves in a constant battle to be louder than the last, using a cacophony of noise to carry the energy to their audience. But without silence, there can be no loudness: it is dynamic range that carries the energy, not loudness alone. One of the most notable cinematic uses of silence is in Sam Mendes's *Jarhead* (2005). In one scene, as explosions are going off all around, we hear almost nothing, just the delicate spray of sand onto the face of main character Anthony Swofford. Described by supervising sound editor Pat Jackson:

> [Mendes] has a lot of ideas of his own about sound, and he's also very decisive, so you quickly learn the types of things that he likes and doesn't like. But when he says he wants silence, he means *no audio*. For example, there's a place in the movie where there's incoming artillery for the first time, Sam wanted it to be absolutely silent as all these bombs are going off—yet the visual is really great because there's this rain of grit and sand debris. The first time I saw it, I thought, "You want to hear that [rain of grit] because this whole movie is from Anthony Swofford's point of view." It was that way in how it was shot and the way it was edited. So I wondered, "Could we have that sound?" And initially he said, "No, I want it silent." Then, when you see the final version, it's quite wonderful: The explosions start and they get distant and muffled and

> then it goes to absolute quiet and then there's a subtle rain of grit. It's a profoundly moving moment in the film because you really sense something about what it's like to be there. (cited in Jennings-X 2005)

Indeed, had Mendes chosen to rely on the usual explosions or bombs of most war films, the scene would have had far less impact. The constant battle for louder sounds and for more sounds, has numbed the audience to the power that sound could have. It is the near silence of the grains of sand heard in an explosive scene in *Jarhead* that gives us room to breathe and take in the moment, before returning us to the brash blasts of war: just as light needs darkness to show contrast, so does noise need silence.

Other examples that come to mind are the symbolic use of sound in Tarkovsky's *Stalker* (1979), notably the infamous handcar scene where the sound carries the scene for nearly four and a half minutes as the visuals offer us little to hold onto, cutting back and forth between the faces of two characters. The gradually increasing use of effects on the sound takes us from the known, natural world into the unknown world, from the land of the mundane into the mysterious "Zone." The transition is told through the sound, rather than the visuals, and it is the subtlety of the sound that, we would argue, gives the film its power.

It is difficult to imagine a spatial-audio-rendering engine that considers such artful or evocative uses of sound. The power of the sound in these films are creative decisions that are not driven by technically accurate renderings of an imagined three-dimensional space, enslaved to the modeling of that space, but are emotionally driven, psychologically driven. As Walter Murch stated in reference to using the sound of the desert in *The English Patient* (Minghella 1996): "The problem is that if you record the actual sound that goes with that space, it has nothing to do with the *emotion* of being there. . . . So the trick . . . was to evoke, with sound, a space that is silent" (cited in Ondaatje 2002, 118). A sound designer's job is to determine which sounds belong in the mix, which do not, and how to best support the story, not to create a *realistic* space, but to create a believable yet expressive space.

Conclusions

As shown, sound effects do carry emotion. They tell of psychological states of characters, draw us into the story and its emotions; they can be symbolic or metaphoric, can act as a stand-in for visuals, and can do so much more than make things "realistic." It is unfortunate that sound design has been given the short straw and treated as a tool of realism, rather than exploited for what it could be. In fact, we have argued that nonrealistic sound is often far more impactful than realism. While realistic simulation of physical space is an interesting scientific goal, for creative media, we would argue that expending resources on such a task is futile without more basic research into the human auditory and multimodal perceptual system. Sound design would, in other words, be better served if audio researchers would turn their attention toward creative aspects of sound design, and a deeper understanding of multimodality and sound.

Our argument here is that the focus on technological advancement and sophistication in game audio tools is fundamentally flawed. The drive toward physical modeling is well suited to some forms of simulations that require a high degree of real-world accuracy: for instance, in training simulations for medical professionals. However, very little media outside of such simulations requires—or should even *want*—such accuracy. The focus on realism in spatial audio has driven attention away from what sound could really achieve. Nowhere is this more evident than in the tools for spatial audio rendering. When we compare the game and VR audio tools to those of linear digital audio workstations or visual creation tools, the current game and VR tools often require significant training and do not lend themselves well to creativity. We posit that thinking through how to make such tools more likely to support creative uses might be a better use of our time than tiny incremental improvements in technical sophistication.

Our drive to realism also implies a hyperrealism, where simulation can match and surpass reality, where every detail is captured and rendered for our enjoyment. However, such detail ends up being *hypo*real, not *hyper*real: Though highly detailed, hyperreality becomes anemic in its ability to capture our imagination. Just as the book is nearly always better than the movie, it is what is *not* present, the gaps left to our imagination, that are just as interesting—if not more interesting—and believable as realism. What is not sounded is as important as what is sounded. Our realism-geared tools are not allowing more creative approaches to mixing in spatial audio, and the intent has shifted focus to physical simulation not on experience or emotion. In a talk at the Game Developers' Conference, Kevin Bolen, Damian Kastbauer, and Bill Rudolph (2018) describe some of the challenges of using game audio tools to develop sound for an artistic VR experience conceived by Alejandro G. Iñárritu, *Carne y Arena*, and come to the conclusion that "you need to assess your balance between *artistically* correct and *technically* correct." We encourage the audio community to refocus our attention on these artistic needs, rather than the technical needs.

NOTES

1. For an overview of the recent state of rendering engines, see Beig et al. (2019).
2. It is technically possible to localize audio with one ear, but more difficult and complex. See, for example, Kumpik and King (2019).
3. For an overview of how we attempted to account for some of these discrepancies, see Cowan, Kapralos, and Collins (2020b).
4. We differentiated between sighted and visually impaired for this concept because visually impaired people would have a lot more practice wayfinding using audio cues, whereas those who tend to rely on sight, of course will have less developed listening skills. Another experiment could easily be done to compare visually impaired and unimpaired listening skills in auditory wayfinding tasks.
5. For a critique of expert listeners as they relate to evaluation panels, see Grimshaw-Aagaard (2019).

References

Arons, Barry. 1992. "A Review of the Cocktail Party Effect." *Journal of the American Voice I/O Society* 12 (7): 35–50.

Beig, Mirza, Bill Kapralos, Karen Collins, and Pejman Mirza-Babaei. 2019. "An Introduction to Spatial Sound Rendering in Virtual Environments and Games." *Computer Games Journal* 8 (4): 199–214.

Blauert, Jens. 1996. *The Psychophysics of Human Sound Localization*. Cambridge, MA: MIT Press.

Bolen, Kevin, Damian Kastbauer, and Bill Rudolph. 2018. "*Carne y Arena*: Uncompromising Audio for Narrative VR." VRDC, Game Developers' Conference Vault. https://www.gdcvault.com/play/1024859/-Carne-y-Arena-Uncompromising.

Bungie. 2001. *Halo*. Xbox. Xbox Game Studios.

Collins, Karen. 2016. *The Beep Book, Vol. 2*. Waterloo: Ehtonal.

Collins. Karen, and Bill Kapralos. 2019. "Pseudo-Haptics: A Review of Leveraging Cross-Modal Perception in Virtual Environments." *Senses and Society* 14 (3): 313–329.

Cowan, Brent, Bill Kapralos, and Karen Collins. 2020a. "Does Improved Sound Rendering Increase Player Performance? A Graph-Based Spatial Sound Framework." *IEEE Transactions on Games*. https://doi.org/10.1109/TG.2020.3000261.

Cowan, Brent, Bill Kapralos, and Karen Collins. 2020b. "Realistic Audio AI: Spatial Sound Modelling to Provide NPCs with Sound Perception." Audio Engineering Society International Conference on Audio for Virtual and Augmented Reality, Redmond, WA, August 17–19, 2020.

Cremer, Lothar, and Helmut A. Muller. 1978. *Principles and Applications of Room Acoustics*. Barking, UK: Applied Science Publishers.

Dalton, Polly, and Robert W. Hughes. 2014. "Auditory Attentional Capture: Implicit and Explicit Approaches." *Psychological Research* 78 (3): 313–320.

Görne, Thomas. 2019. "The Emotional Impact of Sound: A Short Theory of Film Sound Design." In *EPiC Series in Technology klingt gut! 2017 International Symposium on Sound*, Vol. 1: 17–30. https://doi.org/10.29007/jk8h.

Gordon, Whitson. 2020. "Surround Sound Music Is Back, and Now It's in Dolby Atmos." *Inventory*, August 31, 2020. https://theinventory.com/best-5-1-dolby-atmos-music-albums-1844545261.

Grimshaw-Aagaard, Mark. 2019. "The Necessity of Vagueness and Ambiguity to the Imagining of Sound." In *The Oxford Handbook of Sound and Imagination*, edited by Mark Grimshaw-Aagaard, Mads Walther-Hansen, and Martin Knakkergaard, Vol. 1, 104–113. New York: Oxford University Press.

Hulusić, Vedad, Kurt Debattista, Vibhor Aggarwal, and Alan Chalmers. 2011. "Maintaining Frame Rate Perception in Interactive Environments by Exploiting Audio-Visual Cross-Modal Interaction." *Visual Computer* 27 (1): 57–66.

Huttunen, Tomi, Antti Vanne, Sstine Harder, Rasmus Reinhold Paulsen, Sam King, Lee Perry-Smith, and Leo Kärkkäinen. 2014. "Rapid Generation of Personalized HRTFs." Audio Engineering Society Conference: 55th International Conference: Spatial Audio.

Jennings-X, Steve, 2005. "The Interior Life of Jarhead." *Mix Online*, December 1, 2005. https://www.mixonline.com/sfp/interior-life-jarhead-369124.

Kapralos, Bill, Fuad Moussa, Karen Collins, and Adam Dubrowski. 2017. "Levels of Fidelity and Multimodal Interactions." In *Techniques to Improve the Effectiveness of Serious Games*, edited by P. Wouters and H. van Oostendorp, 79–101. Springer Advances in Game-Based Learning Book Series. Basel: Springer International Publishing AG.

Kumpik, Daniel P., and Andrew J. King. 2019. "A Review of the Effects of Unilateral Hearing Loss on Spatial Hearing." *Hearing Research* 372:17–28.

Lalwani, Mona. 2016. "For VR to Be Truly Immersive, It Needs Convincing Sound to Match." *Engadget*, January 22, 2016. https://www.engadget.com/2016-01-22-vr-needs-3d-audio.html.

Lynch, David. 1977. *Eraserhead*. Libra Films. Criterion Collection, 2014. DVD.

Mendes, Sam. 2005. *Jarhead*. Universal Pictures, 2005. DVD.

Minghella, Anthony. 1996. *The English Patient*. Miramax Films. DVD.

Murch, Walter. 2005. "Dense Clarity—Clear Density." *Transom Review*. https://transom.org/2005/walter-murch/#part-2.

Ondaatje, Michael. 2002. *The Conversations: Walter Murch and the Art of Editing Film*. London: Bloomsbury.

Rosedale, Philip. 2020. "What if Zoom Had Spatial Audio?" *High Fidelity*, December 10, 2020. https://www.highfidelity.com/blog/what-if-zoom-had-spatial-audio.

Tarkovsky, Andrei. 1979. *Stalker*. Soviet Union: Mosfilm. Criterion Collection, 2017. DVD.

Thaler, Lore, Stephen R. Arnott, and Melvyn A. Goodale. 2011. "Neural Correlates of Natural Human Echolocation in Early and Late Blind Echolocation Experts." *PLoS One* 6 (5): e20162.

Tsukamoto, Shinya. 1989. *Tetsuo: The Iron Man*. Kaijyu Theatres. Image Entertainment, 1998. DVD.

Wesemann, Eva. 2017. "Why 3D Audio Is the Next Big Step for Virtual Reality." *VentureBeat*, July 21, 2017. https://venturebeat.com/2017/07/21/3d-audio-is-the-next-big-step-for-virtual-reality/.

Zahorik, Pavel, Douglas S. Brungart, and Adelbert W. Brokhorst. 2005. "Auditory Distance Perception in Humans: A Summary of Past and Present Research." *Acta Acustica* 91 (3): 409–420.

CHAPTER 44

VIDEO GAME SOUND DESIGN AND THE FETISH OF REALISM

MARK GRIMSHAW-AAGAARD

Introduction

> Special attention was put to the realism and amount of details in our Navigation Sounds.
>
> —Dion (2017)

> Our main goal with the audio for the settlements was to make them feel alive, dynamic and responsive to certain in-game conditions for an added level of realism.
>
> McCaren and Goellner (2019)

There is a fetishistic regard for realism in some video games that infects the sound design of the games: it is unnecessary, a waste of resources and processing power, and represents nothing less than the lazy picking of the low-hanging fruit rather than the intelligent, thoughtful sound design that video games and their consumers deserve. Such a statement might represent the more extreme and unforgiving view of video game sound design, and, while it might contain more than a grain of truth, in its barbed, stark unequivocality it masks a complex picture that deals with the often tense intersection between philosophy, psychology, phenomenology, and the natural sciences as they converge on video games. This complexity covers terms and concepts such as reality, realism, fidelity, authenticity, precision, verisimilitude, imagination, experience, to name a few.

In this essay, I examine the trope of realism in video game sound design: the use of realism as a marketing device, the reality of realism in the actual sound design of games, and players' boredom with overly realistic games (see also chapter 42 and chapter 43 this volume). I begin by discussing notions of reality and realism in general within simulation and emulation media, showing that an appeal to realism has long been used for marketing purposes regardless of, with hindsight, the weaknesses of the technology. Following this, I briefly discuss and differentiate fidelity, authenticity, and verisimilitude, before I present the notions of realism of form and realism of content with regard to video game sound suggesting that it is form that is paramount in persuading players of the verisimilitude of the game experience.

Reality and Realism

Elsewhere in this handbook (chapter 47 this volume), I make the point that reality is the experience of an environment, which environment is the dynamic perceptual modeling of a salient externality which deals with that potential external to our selves which is available to be actualized as sensation because it lies within our salient horizon. The salient horizon marks the limits of our sensory abilities: this differs from species to species and from individual to individual and is the result of a complex and largely indeterminable mix of many factors including the capacity of sensory apparatuses, proximity to external potential, interference from other potential and external materiality, focus, the often attenuating and dissolving effects on potential of the medium, and so on. Regarding auditory potential, viz. sound waves, for humans, our auditory system is theoretically capable of actualizing potential up to 20 kHz in frequency and down to $20x10^{-6}$ Pa in pressure, although this greatly differs between individuals. In our everyday externality, other factors influencing our abilities to sense sound waves include energy absorption over distance in air, terrain and occluding features such as buildings, clothing, and, especially today, decisions to focus on other auditory potential such as the sound waves emanating from earphones. We all inhabit our own individual spatiotemporality in relation to externality, and, along with our unique cognitive understandings and knowledge of externality, this makes for very individualized realities.

If one makes the initial assumption that claims for realism in the virtual externality of some video games are claims to emulate material externality, typically described in the field as reality, and that the potential provided by video games is actualized as sensations, and ultimately as perceptions, in the same manner as occurs in material externality, then there are problems that must be dealt with. To start with, such an emulation, for many of the reasons pointed out above, would be different for each individual. Our sensory abilities differ, and our spatiotemporal position in relation to salient externality differs. The perceptions that form as sounds in our environments, with cognition using understanding and knowledge to form percepts such as "car" or "bird," differ because our experiences differ. This is no less the case when the potential of our salient externality is sourced from digital software and hardware as when playing a video game. Where the claims for realism as an emulation of externality fail, it is because the range and presentation of potential in video games is severely limited on several bases. For instance, with few exceptions, even the games making claims for realism use only two of the several modalities normally available to human beings: vision and hearing. Additionally, the synchronization of audio to graphics in a video game is tempered according to player expectations. As an example, the delay between perception of a sound and the accompanying image of the source action is a reasonably reliable cue to distance between perceiver and source, and, in an enclosed space with perceptible reflections, the size of the space. Where reverberation is used in video games to manipulate the perception of spatial volume in the game world, delays between arrival at the body of sound and light potential are not. While technically trivial to accomplish, the reason for this lapse in realism is to account for our acculturated expectations from a thoroughly mediated life and to immediately provide the player with necessary, uncomplicated information about the game state. It would be reasonable to assume that the typical gamer is an urban dweller having spent much of their life exposed to audiovisual media where synchronicity between aural and visual events is paramount. As Denis Zlobin, a sound designer at Ubisoft, puts it:

> Distances, proportions and movement speeds in video games look believable, but they are nearly always unrealistic. Introducing a realistic speed of sound parameter will not work in such context. . . . Modern people who live in the cities are rarely exposed to sound being noticeably delayed compared to the image, except for the thunder. We are used to temporal synchrony in films and games, violation of synchrony in audiovisual media feels weird and unnatural. We are generally working not to represent the real world phenomena, but to meet the player's expectations. . . . Especially in real-time, action-based games sound is responsible for informing the player about the events that happen in the offscreen space. Providing that information with a delay (even though close-by sounds will have no delay) is also potentially damaging for the experience.[1]

And not just video game sound designers are playing with natural physics in order to fool us into accepting the video game's artifice. Even our own modeling of salient externality is playing tricks on us, organizing and reorganizing the apparent spatiotemporality of such potential in order to make an environment that is a meaningful and utilitarian interface between our selves and externality. Keetels and Vroomen (2012, 147–148) state it thus:

> to perceive synchrony, the brain has to deal with differences in *physical* (outside the body) and *neural* (inside the body) transmission times. Sounds, for example, travel through air much slower than visual information does (i.e., 300,000,000 m/s for vision vs. 330 m/s for audition), whereas no physical transmission time through air is involved for tactile stimulation as it is presented directly at the body surface. The *neural* processing time also differs between the senses, and it is typically slower for visual than it is for auditory stimuli (approximately 50 vs. 10 ms, respectively). . . . Because of these differences, one might expect that for audiovisual events, only those occurring at the so-called "horizon of simultaneity" . . . a distance of approximately 10 to 15 m from the observer—will result in the approximate synchronous arrival

> of auditory and visual information at the primary sensory cortices. Sounds will arrive before visual stimuli if the audiovisual event is within 15 m from the observer, whereas vision will arrive before sounds for events farther away.

Sound is to do with action as it takes place over time. It is not possible to have sounds displayed on our living-room walls; we use images for that purpose because images, fundamentally, are still and actionless. As noted above, because differences in light-wave speed and sound-wave speed and differences in the speed of assembly of the sensation of such potential into perceptions, it is the sound perception that forms first from any event taking place within front of us that is within about 15 m. To form the percept, then, from two sets of potential in our salient externality, sound provides the basis to which image is glued (contrary to those who mistakenly suppose that sound's purpose is to confirm the meaning of that which we see). In watching a cartoon or playing a video game (behaviors typically taking place within 15 m. of a screen and loudspeakers),[2] the sound is already there in our modeling of externality—the environment—changing over time as the environment is remodeled from new sensation as the sound wave develops. Being already there, it provides a ready-made form into which visual perception can be poured. As action, to us as a species, it is a necessity for verisimilitude that the sound then, as a form, conforms to some expectation drawn from experience, and so the visual perception more quickly finds the form in which to be molded to a percept and strung together with other images to form a visual narrative. If the sound we perceive matches our experience of the sound, a sharp metal object being slashed violently into something soft and organic (and who, having experience of a kitchen, has not done this?), then we accept the reality of Tom slicing Jerry[3] with the meat cleaver despite the irreality of the image because it is the sound that provides form, and it is the form that provides the realism (see more on this below).

Thus, one must conclude that claims for realism as an emulation of externality are without foundation. That is, the potential supplied to us by game technology is lacking in at least two respects: it provides no means of sensing mass and temperature and no chemicals enabling smell and taste, and only rarely and primitively is the tactile modality available; and the spatiotemporal relationship between those modalities that are available is greatly simplified and manipulated in the service of other objectives (player experience) than survival and competence in a material externality for which, presumably, our auditory system has developed.

Realism, though, remains a strong trope in many areas of media design and marketing and we certainly have a strong sense of the real as opposed to the not real. Furthermore, what is sensed and accepted as real, conforming to our standards for reality, shifts over time as our shared human experience is subjected to an almost overwhelming onslaught of new combinations of potential. The term "lifelike" has connotations of realism, especially the invocation and appeal of "life" that must, by definition, be real. Even today, the 18th-century automata of Jaquet-Droz are described as lifelike,[4] although anyone who has witnessed them in action, while undoubtedly not failing to marvel at the ingenuity of their construction, could not now with all honestly describe their image and actions as lifelike: particularly after a lifetime of exposure to increasingly sophisticated computer-generated imagery and animations.

So too have claims for realism been used for marketing purposes and long before the existence of video games. In terms of sound wave recording and reproduction, one can go back to advertisements of over 100 years ago for Edison's New Phonograph, which touted the benefits of experiencing Edison's Realism Test. Part of the advertisement states (with the accompanying image shown in Figure 44.1):

> Certainly you'll come and try Mr. Edison's Realism Test. People all over the country are talking about Mr. Edison's Realism Test. It has astonished them with

FIGURE 44.1 Mr. Edison's Realism Test.

> a new insight into the New Edison's marvelous Realism. Try this interesting test for yourself. The Realism test will help you to determine whether the New Edison causes you the same emotions as the voice of the living singer—the sound of an actual instrument—or the strains of an entire orchestra. (Gazette Times, August 15, 1920, cited in Levy 2020)

No-one today, listening to the output of such a device, could fail to note the faults, the lack of fidelity to an acoustic singing voice—the tinniness, the crackling, the smallness of the sound—and this comes about because (a) we are no longer astonished at the then relatively recent marvelous invention of audio recording and so our judgement is not clouded and (b) we have become accustomed to increased audio quality and fidelity through advances in technology.

There are parallels here to the Uncanny Valley hypothesis (Mori 2012) where a robot's lifelike appearance and similarity to humans (and this hypothesis has since been extended to computer-generated characters) can only advance so far before human comfort with, and acceptance of, the robot's appearance and movements dramatically diminishes, and the robot becomes uncanny and threatening. Theoretically, according to this hypothesis, there is a point where the artificial generation of lifelike/human appearance and movement is so accomplished that the robot crosses the depths of the valley to the sunlit other side to become accepted as human. However, as noted above with regard to Edison's Realism Test, improvements in the faithfulness of technological reproduction or simulation of aspects of externality mean that, before long, such acceptable robots (and computer-generated characters) slip back down the valley as we begin to notice the imperfections wrought by the technology of the time in relation to what the current technology is capable of. Thus, the Uncanny Valley hypothesis fails and is better reformulated as the Uncanny Wall whereby "technological discernment on the part of the audience generally keeps pace with technological developments used in the attempt to create realistic, human-like characters such that, ultimately, the perception of uncanniness for such characters is inevitable" (Tinwell, Grimshaw, and Williams 2011, 339).

Also related to this is the belief that presence in virtual worlds[5] increases in direct proportion to the fidelity of the technology's simulation of potential from salient externality (for example, photorealism of graphics or precise spatial disposition of audio). This is a claim made by Slater and many others working in the context of virtual reality whereby the level of immersion vis-à-vis sensory stimuli depends on the preservation of "fidelity in relation to their equivalent real-world sensory modalities [while] presence is a human reaction to immersion" (Slater 2003, 1–2). Thus, the better the immersive capabilities of the technology, viz. the better it is at emulating potential found in externality, the greater the presence, and "[o]ne way to induce presence is to increase realism" (4). Leaving aside more philosophical (but no less necessary for it) questions such as *is presence an on/off state or really a sliding scale according to immersion whereby one can be just a little bit present?* which I have dealt with elsewhere (Grimshaw-Aagaard 2019), much of the writing from this period of virtual reality design (about 20–30 years ago) reflects a positivist optimism toward an attainable objective and measurable equation between fidelity to "real-world sensory modalities" delivered by the system and presence. Experience and engagement are utterly distinct from presence (and the right experience and engagement comes with the highest level of immersion): "Separate from presence are aspects of an experience such as involvement, interest and emotion. These are to do with the content of the experience. Presence is the form" (Slater 2003, 4). This lack of concern with any relationship of experience to presence is probably the reason why video game design pursuing too much realism in terms of, for instance, graphical fidelity and historical accuracy leaves players unimpressed as this user review makes clear:

> There are too many mundane, small tasks *Red Dead Redemption 2* forces players to complete. In order to maintain the efficacy of their guns, players must routinely clean and inspect them, otherwise, they'll get a notification on their screen informing them their gun is poor quality. Players also have to go to their horse in order to change weapons, something that's easy to forget especially when players are about to start a mission. The main problem is that while, yes, individuals would have to do these sorts of things if they were an outlaw in real-life, it's annoying to be forced to do it mid-game. Many folks play video games to escape from reality, as a way to relieve stress or tension. (Sakellariou 2020)

No matter how much one might try to emulate externality's potential with immersive technology, ignore the perception and cognitive use of such sensory stimuli and one is left with nothing worthwhile. Presence, if it is indeed mere form, cannot be attained without consummate attention to the end experience.

Fidelity

There are several terms that come into play when discussing realism in the context of media such as cinema, television, virtual reality, and video games. One mentioned above is "fidelity." As the object or action under scrutiny must, by definition, have fidelity to something, in this context, the referent is externality or what is commonly referred to as the real world as opposed to the virtual worlds of video games and other similar media. Certainly, as noted above, there is a significant trend in virtual reality design to create the conditions for presence (as the sense of being in a place and being able to act within and on that place) through the fidelity of delivered sensory stimuli to their real-world referents.

Attempts to deliver fidelity for sound typically involve recording the sound waves of the target source—there are attempts to achieve the same effect through advanced forms of synthesis, but this is fraught with difficulty, and, when marketing a video game on the basis of realism, it does not carry quite the same cachet to say *the audio was carefully synthesized to match their real-world equivalents* as claiming *no expense was spared in recording real sound for every action in the game*. Nevertheless, the latter, despite claims to the contrary, is impossible. No two sound waves are ever the same.[6] Differences come about through a variety of factors that include variations in production of the sound wave (intensity and volume, for instance), the surroundings (sounding in an open space or in a concrete-lined enclosure), conditions of the medium (moist, warm air or dry, cold air or even underwater), and so on, and this is before the recording (effects of equipment used such as the specifications of the microphone, distance it is placed from the source) or playback (the characteristics and placement and surroundings of loudspeakers, differences between headphones, amplifiers, and sound cards) even takes place. Finally, recording every single variation of the sounding of a source, in every conceivable context, is likewise impossible for a number of reasons such as time and storage capacity for the audio files. Fidelity is an unachievable ideal.

Authenticity

Closely related to fidelity is the concept of authenticity. The two are often treated as synonyms, but a more subtle use of the latter is that perceptions of authenticity are subject to interpretation. As Gilbert (2016, 323) states, "immersion is the system-based factor that influences presence . . . authenticity is the human-based factor that influences presence" and:

> A VE with higher immersion, so the argument goes, should lead to higher fidelity, and generate a greater sense of presence, the subjective experience felt by the user. But if I put you in a highly immersive environment and give you badly designed content to experience, will you perceive the VE as realistic and experience presence? Probably not. What's missing from this dichotomy of immersion (objective, system-focused) and presence (subjective, user-focused) is a computational theory about the extent to which the VE reflects the expected regularities of world that it is attempting to represent—its authenticity. Authenticity draws on two streams of thought: expectations and motivations. (322)

In this sense, perceived authenticity is dependent upon user expectation and user motivation: in the context of this video game and my knowledge of the conventions of video games (my motivations for playing being engaging fun, a quick action fix, and "to relieve stress or tension"), does this sound meet my expectations, in that it serves the purpose of allowing me to be present in the game world and to proceed with the aims and objectives of the game? Yes, if the purpose is to kill all my enemies in a first-person shooter, and the sound I hear conforms to the expectations aroused by the depiction of a shotgun in my character's hands on the screen in front of me. No, if I hear a duck quacking. The absurdity of providing a duck quack to the action of firing a virtual shotgun is likely, at first experience,[7] to be disruptive to expectation and motivation.

Verisimilitude

While the concept of authenticity in some uses (particularly popular usage) is synonymous with fidelity to source, where the concept changes to perception, as in an assessment, it is more closely related to the concept of verisimilitude or believability. As Droumeva (2011, 137) writes, in relation to the sounds of video games: "If fidelity refers to the faithfulness of sound quality in computer games, verisimilitude concerns itself with the experience and nature of truthfulness and authenticity in a game context, as conveyed through the game soundscape," and she relates the notion of verisimilitude to "the cultural emergence of authenticity, immersion and suspension of disbelief in cinema" (132). Droumeva goes on to state: "In its traditional literary/theatrical definition, verisimilitude reflects the extent to which a work of fiction exhibits realism or authenticity, or otherwise conforms to our sense of reality. In film, the notion of verisimilitude signifies the relative success of cinematography at creating an immersive, engaging fictional world of hyper-realistic proportions both in terms of image and sound but also of intensity of emotion and experience" (137).

What is being referred to here is the construction of the cinematic soundscape, much of the process for which, and especially the created audience expectations arising from, have followed through into video game sound design. In particular, as Droumeva points out, this is derived from the practice of Foley design, whereby sounds that, for one reason or another, are difficult if not impossible to record are substituted by recording sounds from other sources. Thus, footsteps on rice grains synced to image become footsteps in the snowy landscape depicted on screen, a fist rammed into the side of a pig's carcass becomes the sickening punch to a protagonist's jaw. For intensity of emotion and visceral reaction, maintaining fidelity to source regarding the Terminator shotgun does not suffice: the sound crafted[8] must be hyperreal, conforming to the Hollywood "law of enlarged firearm calibre" (Palmer 2002, 9), and, now, audiences would no doubt find it underwhelming were the authentic recording to be used, true to source though it might be—such crafted sounds become "our reference for reality itself" (Chion 1994, 108). Thus, the boundaries of realism, of what is perceived to be authentic, what is verisimilitudinous, are stretched and distorted "to conform to our sense of reality while at the same time it has constructed a sense of reality, particular to games, that we now expect" (Droumeva 2011, 137). Or, as Bowker and Star (2000, 49) put it, "the system's description of reality becomes true."

The review excerpt above, complaining about the excessive pursuit of realism in the design of *Red Dead Redemption 2*, shows that it is the experience that trumps designs on realism, so much so that too much realism can ruin the experience. This is borne out by several commentators and researchers such as Poole (2000, 99–100), who writes that attempting to make a character's movements too realistic in the game might lead to the expectation, and subsequent frustration, on the part of the player that other movements are possible when they are not. Realism, it appears, is a double-edged blade when applied to game design: excessive realism can easily bore by dragging players away from fantasy; and it can set up expectations that, if unfulfilled, bring the entire illusion crashing to the ground.

Form and Content

Several researchers make the point that realism of the medium—the photorealism of the graphics or fidelity of audio to external source—is less important than the perception of realism brought about by coherence with expectation, and this holds true whether the topic of discussion is presence in virtual reality or the experience of video games. For example, with regard to video games, Poole (2000, 95) states that "it is lack of coherence rather than unrealism which ruins a gameplaying experience" while Ribbens and Malliet (2010, 586) note that "whether a media text is perceived as realistic . . . is important because research suggests that user perceptions can be better predictors of behavioral outcomes than the features of the medium itself." This view is further reinforced by Flach and Holden (1998, 94) writing on presence in virtual reality: "The experience depends more on what can be "done" than on the quality of visual or acoustic images," and Lee (2004) who claims that a high quality of image is not necessary to presence because most of what we see in externality is actually from peripheral vision and thus out of focus. Similar arguments can be made that we do not perceive all sound waves impinging on our auditory apparatus, and so, to provide every potential sound wave source in any virtual world scene with a sounding audio file would likewise be a waste of time and resources.

What is clear from some of the comments above is that careful distinctions should be made on the basis of content and form when it comes to realism: the presentation and potential the design of the video game provides, and the perception and experience derived from the potential. It is about frameworks set up by experience. Expectation arises from knowledge of the medium's framework, its form, which framework itself exists within a larger experiential framework. Experience arises from action within that framework and is judged to be consistent or not with expectation—what is inconsistent, cognitively dissonant with our expectation, is contested and often rejected. This, in essence, is what lies behind arguments about fidelity, authenticity, verisimilitude, and the reported boredom and frustration of playing *Red Dead Redemption 2*: the form must be acceptable within the broader framework of our life experience, our conception that is the world, because it is this that allows us to model externality and make sense of it (see chapter 47 this volume). Within this form, the content itself is quite flexible. This is why cartoons work and we can make sense of them: what is on the screen is not a mouse, is not a cat, it is the reflection of patterned light cast through designs on a celluloid strip. We know that a mouse is somewhat different, cannot carry a heavy-looking object, and cannot attack a cat with it, and we know that a diced-up cat cannot be reconstituted. For a few minutes of delirious fun, though, the shared components of our worlds allow us all to fashion a common scenario from the image on screen—Tom slicing Jerry with a meat cleaver—and this, in part, is greatly aided by the sound wave whose importance is not its content but rather its form.

What then is the form of a sound wave as opposed to its content? Form can be approximately equated to the mundane labels we give sound waves, the description of the sound perception, and, as Risset and Wessel (1999) point out in an analysis of the timbre of musical tones, in the main, one instrument is distinguished from another by temporal factors. That is, how the amplitude of the sound wave and its frequency spectrum change over sound. This distinguishing quality of timbre is not so surprising given that a sound wave is nothing without time, but it points to the importance of change over time in our perception of form. Not for nothing is change in sound wave amplitude referred to as the amplitude envelope while change in frequency spectrum is called the spectral envelope (although the latter can only be a great approximation).

The importance of these envelopes to establishing the form of the sound perceptions, and thus distinguishing them from each other, applies too to nonmusical sound. But other factors are also important such as pitch and relative loudness—think of the sound of an elephant compared to a mouse; using a mouse squeak to accompany the image of an elephant trumpeting a warning would be absurd. There is another audio envelope that is important when it comes to form, and this is the frequency or pitch envelope. This can be used to illustrate the action seen on screen as in Mickey-Mousing (or isomorphism [viz. same-shape]), where the direction of the fundamental frequency change over the duration of the sound wave follows the direction of the displayed action (e.g., a cartoon character tumbles down some stairs).

Within this form of the sound wave, there is a great deal of flexibility as to content of the sound wave. That is, the frequency components poured into the mold can be quite variable in their frequency, relative amplitudes, and number. We recognize a piano sound because its various envelopes conform to established piano norms (mainly of amplitude envelope), not because we are capable of finding the common "pianoness" from the vast range of differing frequency characteristics offered by Fazioli, Steinway, Bechstein, Bösendorfer, Kawai, Yamaha, Pearl River, and so on. Take two recordings of a piano and a violin playing a tone of the same amplitude and pitch, replace the attack portion of the violin tone with that of the piano, and, because the amplitude envelope has now changed,[9] that violin tone will now be perceived as a piano. It is form, rather than content, that gives meaning, and form governs our assessment of realism. This is what verisimilitude delivers.

This is why the Terminator shotgun, referred to above, works regardless of the content of the audio: its form, particularly its amplitude envelope, meets our expectations. In an otherwise self-serving paeon to the *Gran Turismo* (1997–2022) video game series, representatives of Mazda and Polyphony Digital (developers of the series) discuss the "incredible vehicle realism" of the games in a web article entitled *Gran Turismo: Realism Redefined* (Melville 2020). Of interest here, in the context of reality and verisimilitude, is the reference to vehicle sounds: "The illusion of reality that Gran Turismo achieves is fragile, and relies on perfection in every aspect of the game's execution. One crucial element in maintaining this illusion is vehicle sound." While there is much to chew over and critique in this statement, what is wonderfully illustrated here, in the title, and elsewhere in the article, is the fetish of realism in some video games combined with the lack of fidelity to source when it comes to audio (i.e., the sound wave source of the car in externality that is represented in the game). This last is illustrated by the admission that: "The sound of the RX-VISION GT3 CONCEPT is different from most other in-game vehicles in that it is created using audio recorded from another vehicle, in this case Mazda's Le Mans winning 787B race car." The illusion of reality is delivered by a realism achieved not by the game's fidelity to external source but by its verisimilitude of form.

Concluding Thoughts

Where realism is equated with emulations of externality and the concept of fidelity to source, attempts to import this process to video games typically fail because players wish for something else that sidesteps the humdrum reality of everyday life. More successful is game and sound design in which tropes of realism become subservient to player experience; fidelity to source evolves into verisimilitude, where form is paramount over content.

Why then, do some game developers and sound designers, in appealing to fans, push the notion of fidelity when it counts for so little in the players' perception of the game's realism, its verisimilitude? The easy answer would be that it provides purchase for marketing hype or that it is easier to record a sample than to create and design audio from scratch, with attention paid to affect and function rather than sound levels and type of microphone. But I think the answer lies in (a) misconceptions of realism, mistaking fidelity to source for it, and a denial of the role of individual experience in shaping reality, and, (b), the pursuit of objectivity as a surrogate for truth, the belief that there are only facts, that the world can be utterly measured and, in so doing, described in its entirety: once thus described, it is precisely reproducible in digital worlds. This present-at-hand approach is disdainful of the player's concern and rightly merits the player's disdain in return.

Notes

1. Personal communication September 19, 2020.
2. The wearing of headphones *over* the ears (and so the sound wave source is even closer than the light wave source) merely lends further credence to my claim.
3. I refer to the animated series.
4. See, for example, https://www.flipscience.ph/technology/jaquet-drozs-automata-eerily-lifelike-18th-century-robots-that-still-work-today/ and https://www.magzter.com/stories/Lifestyle/WOW-Singapore/Lifelike-Machines.

5. There is some confusion around the terms "immersion" and "presence." They are typically distinct but related concepts in virtual reality but usually synonyms in the field of video games.
6. One could make the argument that it is perfectly possible to reproduce exactly the direct output of a preset on a synthesizer in a video game and so claim fidelity to source, but such sounds are already artificial, and produced in a carefully controlled environment, with very little of the complexity of natural sounds such as bird calls and whale song or even human-made sounds such as pianos and gunfire, which sounds are mediated by their physical materials and proportions and their surroundings.
7. Given enough time and exposure, though, the absurdity becomes mundane.
8. https://www.youtube.com/watch?v=tiq-oBeEn1M.
9. The attack portion of an amplitude envelope is of particular importance because it is here that the spectral envelope of the sound wave is most unstable but moving toward the relative stability to be found in the sustain portion of the amplitude envelope.

References

Bowker, Geoffrey C., and Susan Leigh Star. 2000. *Sorting Things Out: Classification and Its Consequences*. Cambridge, MA: MIT Press.

Chion, Michel. 1994. *Audio-Vision: Sound on Screen*. Edited by Claudia Gorbman. Translated by Claudia Gorbman. New York: Columbia University Press.

Dion, Louis Philippe. 2017. "Game Design Deep Dive: Dynamic Audio in Destructible Levels in *Rainbow Six: Siege*." *Gamasutra*. Accessed December 3, 2021. https://www.gamasutra.com/view/news/288565/Game_Design_Deep_Dive_Dynamic_audio_in_destructible_levels_in_Rainbow_Six_Siege.php.

Droumeva, Milena. 2011. "An Acoustic Communication Framework for Game Sound: Fidelity, Verisimilitude, Ecology." In *Game Sound Technology and Player Interaction: Concepts and Developments*, edited by Mark Grimshaw, 131–152. Hershey, PA: IGI.

Flach, John M., and John G. Holden. 1998. "The Reality of Experience: Gibson's Way." *Presence: Teleoperators and Virtual Environments* 7 (1): 90–95.

Gilbert, Stephen B. 2016. "Perceived Realism of Virtual Environments Depends on Authenticity." *Presence: Teleoperators and Virtual Environments* 25 (4): 322–324. https://dx.doi.org/10.1162/PRES_a_00276.

Grimshaw-Aagaard, Mark Nicholas. 2019. "Presence and Biofeedback in First-Person Perspective Computer Games: The Potential of Sound." In *Foundations in Sound Design for Interactive Media*, edited by Michael Filimowicz, 78–94. New York: Routledge.

Keetels, Mirjam, and Jean Vroomen. 2012. "Perception of Synchrony between the Senses." In *The Neural Bases of Multisensory Processes*, edited by M. M. Murray and M. T. Wallace, 147–177. Boca Raton, FL: CRC Press/Taylor & Francis.

Lee, Kwan Min. 2004. "Why Presence Occurs: Evolutionary Psychology, Media Equation, and Presence." *Presence: Teleoperators and Virtual Environments* 13 (4): 494–505. https://dx.doi.org/10.1162/1054746041944830.

Levy, Lauren Fay. 2020. "The Edison Realism Test: Early Experiments in Capturing the Soul of Live Music in a Recording." Accessed December 3, 2021. https://insheepsclothinghifi.com/edison-realism-test/.

McCaren, Tom, and Valentin Goellner. 2019. "Behind the Audio of *Total War: Three Kingdoms*." *Gamasutra*. Accessed December 3, 2021. https://www.gamasutra.com/view/news/345905/Behind_the_audio_of_Total_War_Three_Kingdoms.php.

Melville, Tommy. 2020. "*Gran Turismo*: Realism Redefined." Accessed December 3, 2021. https://www.mazda.com.au/beyond-the-drive/Summer-2020/gran-turismo-realism-redefined/.

Mori, Masahiro. 2012. "The Uncanny Valley." *IEEE Robotics and Automation Magazine*: 1–4. https://dx.doi.org/10.1109/MRA.2012.2192811.

Palmer, Ian J. 2002. "How Realistic Is the Sound Design in the D-Day Landing Sequence in *Saving Private Ryan?*" Master's thesis, Bournemouth University.

Poole, Steven. 2000. *Trigger Happy: Videogames and the Entertainment Revolution*. New York: Arcade.

Ribbens, Wannes, and Steven Malliet. 2010. "Perceived Digital Game Realism: A Quantitative Exploration of Its Structure." *Presence: Teleoperators and Virtual Environments* 19 (6): 585–600. https://dx.doi.org/10.1162/pres_a_00024.

Risset, Jean-Claude, and David L. Wessel. 1999. "Exploration of Timbre by Analysis and Synthesis." In *The Psychology of Music*, edited by Diana Deutsch, 113–169. San Diego: Academic Press.

Sakellariou, Alexandra. 2020. "How RDR2 Prioritizes Realism at the Expense of Playability." Accessed December 3, 2021. https://screenrant.com/red-dead-redemption-2-realism-extreme-boring-controls/.

"Shotgun Sound Design Deconstructed from *Terminator 2*." June 21, 2018. Accessed December 3, 2021. https://www.youtube.com/watch?v=tiq-oBeEn1M.

Slater, Mel. 2003. "A Note on Presence Terminology." *Presence Connect* 3 (3): 1–5.

Tinwell, Angela, Mark Grimshaw, and Andrew Williams. 2011. "The Uncanny Wall." *International Journal of Arts and Technology* 4 (3): 326–341.

CHAPTER 45

MUSIC AND MOTION IN FIRST-PERSON VIRTUAL REALITY GAMES

KATE MANCEY

Introduction

In many ways, music fulfills the same roles in virtual reality (VR) games as in non-VR games. We can think of these as both functional and aesthetic roles, such as providing emotional cues or progressing the narrative, and these two categories need not be mutually exclusive.[1] However, VR marks a distinct change in player experience, which highlights the importance of the manipulation of the perception of motion in music when building a virtual world engaging enough to pass the all-important immersion threshold and enable players to feel as if they are in the game (see chapter 47 this volume for more on immersion/presence). Technological advances have improved computer graphics cards, sound cards, game pads, loading speeds, and so on, but the physical reality of playing a video game—player removed from screen—has stayed relatively consistent, whether in the arcade hall or in your living room. The introduction of motion controllers brought an increased level of bodily participation—player movements now mirrored by their on-screen counterparts—but still physically distanced from the screen. These controllers can be stand-ins for their real-world correlates in specific game franchises, such as the guitar-shaped controllers for Harmonix's *Guitar Hero* (2005), or they can be multigame controllers that act as extensions of a player's hands, such as Nintendo's "Wii Remote." In reducing the distance between player and screen through head-mounted displays, virtual reality alters the relationship between player and game by scaling the player down and the game world up. This change in scale can lead to these virtual game worlds feeling more real than their non-VR game cousins. Slater (2009) argues that two orthogonal components contribute to this experience of people responding realistically to—or feeling—situations and events portrayed in immersive

VR systems. These components are *place illusion*, defined as "the strong illusion of being in a place in spite of the sure knowledge that you are not there," and *plausibility illusion*, defined as "the illusion that what is apparently happening is really happening," where the VR environment provides "correlations between external events not directly caused by the participant and his/her own sensations (both exteroceptive and interoceptive)" (3549–3553).

Music contributes to place illusion in its ability to generate the impression that a world of activity exists beyond a player's immediate field of vision, so that the player feels as if they are just one actor in a world full of potential actors and activity. It can also contribute to plausibility illusion in offering cues for events external to the player's direct actions, such as musical cues for a lurking enemy threat, reinforcing the illusion that a digital enemy is a real threat to the player. Supported by concepts in music and embodied cognition, and concepts in music production, we can think of motion as a significant factor in music's contribution to place and plausibility illusions. Unlike diegetic sound sources, music is not tied to a player's head position; it has greater freedom to move around the sound space. This freedom invites the player to imagine the existence of something other than what can be immediately seen and can support a player's sense of the depth of the virtual world. Looking to Valve's *Half-Life: Alyx* (2020), we can analyze the ways in which motion is constructed in its music and consider how this contributes to the VR experience.

Virtual Reality Gaming

In 1838, Charles Wheatstone invented the stereoscope, which demonstrated that two two-dimensional images side by side (one for each eye) can be processed by the brain to make one three-dimensional image. It proved to be a popular (albeit gimmicky) technology, with thousands of stereographic photo cards produced in the 19th century,[2] and the publishing of guides on how to draft your own pair of stereoscopic drawings. This stereoscopic principle is still used in contemporary VR headsets, with screens and pixels replacing image slides, working alongside the addition of audio and haptic feedback to create three-dimensional virtual worlds. The recent growth in consumer-grade VR headsets at progressively lower costs, accompanied by an increase in VR game releases, has brought the experience of VR gaming to a broader audience. Headsets such as the HTC Vive, which interfaces with gaming PCs; the PSVR, which interfaces with the PlayStation 4 and PlayStation 5; and the Oculus Quest, which operates as a standalone unit, have opened up the VR market to a range of players at different hardware buy-in levels. Each headset comes with its own benefits and trade-offs,[3] with platform-exclusive game releases and nongaming VR content serving as hardware purchase incentives.[4] However, the general hardware layout of these systems is similar: a stereoscopic headset worn over the eyes and fitted to the face with elasticated/adjustable straps, built-in speakers and/or the option to plug headphones into the headset, a motion controller for each hand, and either a physical tether to a console or a PC, or a wireless connection making the headset a standalone unit. Room-scale technology is growing in popularity, which allows a player to walk around a predesignated play area mapped by cameras so that their motion is reflected in the game. However, as this requires a designated VR gaming space (not everybody can donate their living rooms), it is more common for players to experience VR either seated or in relatively stationary standing; truly free motion is still limited. For some game styles this is less noticeable, such as third-person games like Cortopia Studio's *Down the Rabbit Hole* (2020), a story-book puzzle game, or for games where the player's character is seated such as Drool's *Thumper* (2016), a rhythm game set on rails. For many first-person games, in-game mechanics, such as teleport posts or zero gravity environments, allow for player movement through the virtual world without needing the same physical distance to be covered by the player themselves, circumventing some of the limitations of stationary VR.

In dramatically reducing the distance between the player and the screen, the player's relationship to the virtual world is fundamentally altered. Jaron Lanier (2021)—dubbed by some as a "founding father" of modern VR[5]—notes that the change in scale of player to environment drastically alters the psychology of the gaming experience: "Whatever the [non-VR] game, it exists on a screen that's not as big as you. You're the master of a little world. Virtual reality is the opposite, you're inside of it. It's a different situation emotionally, you feel small because you are small."[6]

This change in scale is central in both the place illusion and plausibility illusion of VR games; you feel you are both the actor and acted upon. If only for a moment, the virtual informs your physiological reality. As Lanier (2017, 54) writes: "The nervous system is holistic, so it chooses one external world at a time to believe in. A virtual reality system's task is to sway the nervous system over a threshold so that the brain believes in the virtual world instead of the physical one for a while." The fantastical worlds of video games don't need to be plausible within the confines of our physical reality to have a psychological or physical effect on a player. Rather, the audio, visual, and haptic cues afforded by VR hardware must create a space which pushes players over the threshold of our reality so that they feel as if they can exist in the virtual world. In this process, sound is as important as image.

With speakers built into VR headsets and players encouraged to wear headphones, small changes in sound qualities become easier to hear. This is important in localizing the sounds of objects within the virtual space. Binaural audio algorithms—modeled on the ways in which humans hear sounds, "bi" referring to the use of two ears—process sounds in real time in relation to a player's head position. In modeling how the sounds of objects behave in the real world, and how we listen to and process sound, binaural audio is vital in concretizing a player's sense of place in a game world. Music and other sounds that are not localized do not need to be processed by the game engine in the same way. Instead, stereophonic (stereo) sound is more commonly used here, offering a left and right track, which can be implemented dynamically and mixed in real time, without the need to be tied to a location in the same fashion as either a stationary object or something moving through the game world. Both stereo and binaural sound sources contribute to the believability of the virtual world in supporting the illusion that the virtual world is full of life, of sounding bodies.

Music and Motion in VR Games

What Is Diegetic in a VR World?

Before we consider how motion in music can impact the VR experience, we should first consider what might fall under the category of music in first-person VR games. Drawing the distinction between music and other sound in games is not always easy: as Medina-Gray (2021, 192) suggests, "music, sound effects and dialogue each bring a wide variety of effects to video games, and the potential for innovative and engaging experiences with players only expands when the boundaries between these three sonic categories blur." Moreover, I (2017) have previously used the term *warping diegesis* to describe the effect of employing similar nondiegetic and diegetic timbres in VR game scoring, blurring the lines between the game world and our real world. However, in thinking about music in VR, the application of this terminology from film studies seems less appropriate. There is a strange duality needed for successful VR experiences; the player is, in theory, inhabiting the game character and inhabiting the game world, but they also need to sit slightly outside of the character perspective to engage with the various game mechanisms which support the building of narratives and the creation of mood. The player is both actor and audience. Therefore, I'm proposing we move away from the film terms "diegetic" and "nondiegetic" and think instead in terms of sound which adheres to *player positional tracking* (PTT), and sound which does not adhere to player positional tracking, *nonpositional tracking* sound (NPT). By PPT, I mean sound that is processed in relation to the player's head position. This can be music, sound effects, and dialogue. For example, a player might switch on a radio directly in front of them and then turn around and walk away. As the player turns, the sound from the radio seems to move behind them, becoming fainter and changing in sound quality as the player walks away. For PPT sound, the player's head position in relation to objects in the game world has direct impact on sound quality, especially its spatialization. By NPT, I mean sound which is not processed in relation to a player's head position, regardless of whether it is triggered by player actions. For example, as a player approaches an enemy, "danger state music" (Whalen 2004) might kick in to let the player know of the imminent threat. The music might be triggered dynamically by the player's movement, but the player's head position as they approach the combat area does not change the quality or spatialization of the sound. The music here is distinct from PPT sound because its position in the stereo field is not determined by the player's head position. This is not entirely different from the concepts of diegetic and nondiegetic music: in many ways NPT music is nondiegetic as it sits outside of the binaural audio processing which goes some way to mimic the character's ear. However, it is also possible to have diegetic sound that is NPT, such as room tone and generically atmospheric sounds, or singular narrative sound events such as an explosion far in the distance. Therefore, the distinction is not whether a sound could plausibly come from the game world, or whether "nonmusical" sound is repurposed as music, but whether a sound (musical or not) is processed in relation to a player's head position. The difference between diegetic/nondiegetic and PPT/NPT is a difference of degree, not kind.[7] However, it is an important distinction in thinking about the role of music in VR games; NPT music is free to move through the sound space and it is this freedom that enables it to support the building of virtual environments through working both as a narrative and emotive cue, and in offering a vehicle for motion and activity.

Music and Motion

The perception of motion in NPT music supports the illusions of place and plausibility in a VR game, the believability that draws a player into the virtual world in such a way that the virtual space can have an emotional and physical impact on them. In not being tied to the player's head position, NPT music can expand the virtual world through the manipulation of sonic motion. This motion acts as a metaphor for the movement and activity of nonplayer characters (human or not) which sit outside of the player's field of view. This effect can be manipulated to suggest that the player is one actor in a sea of nonplayer characters, as seen in the Gotham City setting of Rocksteady Studio's *Batman: Arkham VR* (2016). Similarly, a relative lack of musical motion, or fluctuating levels of motion, can support the narrative that a player is alone in a vast emptiness, as seen in the space station setting for Ready at Dawn's *Lone Echo* (2017), or momentarily shut-off from the rest of the virtual world, as seen in the desert setting for Vertigo Games' *Arizona Sunshine* (2016).

Looking to research from the field of music and embodied cognition supports an understanding of how motion might be embodied and perceived in music. As Cox (2011) writes, we can conceive of motion in music in various ways, both actual motion and metaphorical motion. He suggests, "concepts of musical space and motion originate in embodied metaphoric reasoning [and that this] accounts for the feel of . . . spatial and locomotive concepts." This is supported by the idea that "motion and space seem to be literal properties of time because our experiences of temporality in general and in the specific case of locomotion have a shared phenomenology" and, subsequently, that "musical motion *seems* or *feels* like actual motion because the phenomenology of anticipation-presence-memory is shared by both domains" (Cox 2017, 121–124). Therefore, our perception of musical events creates a simulacrum of actual motion because our lived experiences of spatiotemporal events follow a similar anticipation-presence-memory model to that of music. This is not limited to acoustic sounds. As Peters (2012, 18) argues, despite the disembodied nature of electronic music, and the "undoing of the spatial, temporal, and qualitative ties between maker of sound and occurring sound [there still exists] a residue of bodily presence in the sound we hear [therefore] our listening experience is embodied . . . as a consequence of active participation." In creating the possibility for people to feel space and motion through mimetic motor imagery, NPT music contributes to the believability of the virtual world by increasing the types of motion perceived by the player. An interpretation indebted to embodied-cognitive approaches would determine that this is happening both in the bodily participations engendered by music (acoustic and electronic) and in the ways in which we map this music to spatial and locomotive concepts.

When considering the ways in which motion can be constructed in music, we can think about various musical agents as existing within a sound sphere,[8] affected by locomotive forces as the sounds move around the space and through time. The location of a sound, whether PPT or NPT, can be determined relative to a player's head by considering the imagined azimuth value (along the horizontal plane) the imagined elevation value (along the median plane), and the imagined distance from the player.[9] Although this is based in how we process real-world sound binaurally, thinking about the imagined values of these three coordinates for instruments in NPT music offers a way of understanding how motion might be perceived in music. As Lennox (2009, 264) notes: "Using dynamic combinations of panning, alteration of dry-reverb balance, change in amplitude, and filtering, one can give the impression that some items in the soundstage are moving and others are not." The perception of movement as facilitated by audio processing works alongside perceptions of abstracted metaphors of movement in music, such as metaphors of pitch space, to create a sound environment rich in activity. When coupled with the visual and haptic experience of a VR game, this sound sphere can be thought of as a constituent part of the game world's atmosphere. When a player puts on their headset and enters the VR environment, they are also entering this sound sphere. Figure 45.1 offers a graphic representation of a few ways in which transformations of sounds might impact our perception of motion within this sphere. These various audio features do not exist in isolation from one another. However, separating them out for the purpose of this diagram allows for an overview of various ways in which musical sound might be perceived as moving. In Figure 45.1a, sound A is panned in a central position; sound B is panned further right and is therefore perceived as generated by a source further to the right of the player than the source of sound A, moving along the horizontal plane. In Figure 45.1b, sound C has a lower fundamental pitch than sound D, this pitch space can be mapped to visual space (as per Cox's understanding of pitch space and metaphor) with sound D interpreted as coming from further above the player, moving along the median plane. In Figure 45.1c, sound E has a band-pass filter applied which is removed in sound F, creating the impression of an expanse across the median plane as more frequencies are now heard. In Figure 45.1d, reverb manipulation of sound G gives the impression that it is further away than sound H, which is a drier sound, as we can hear less of sound G's dry signal and more of its reflections.

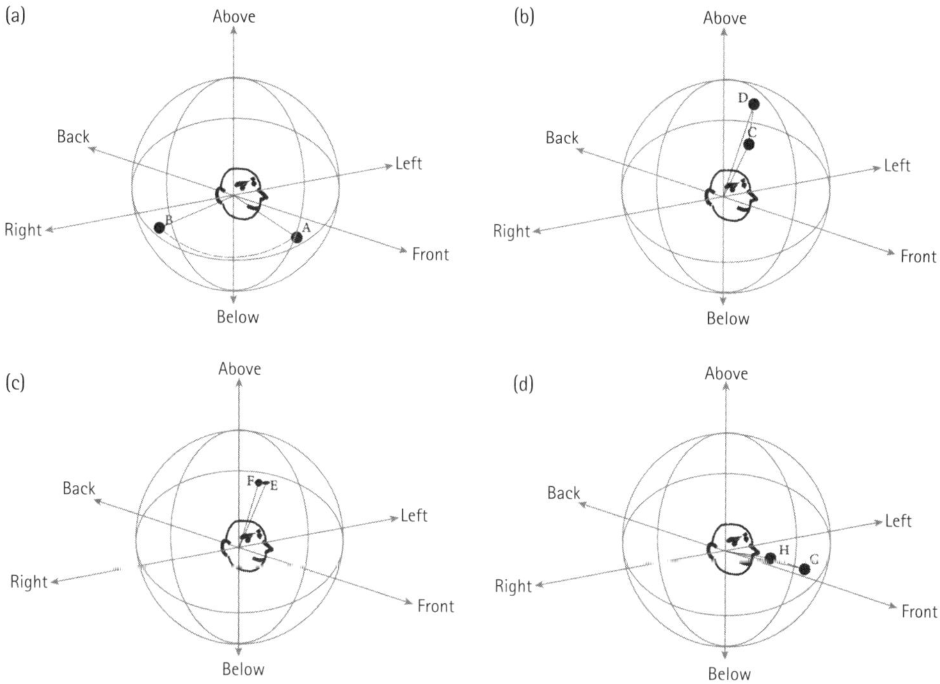

FIGURE 45.1 Diagrams of audio motion perception for individual audio processes when wearing a VR headset.

Approaches to Analyzing Motion in Video Game Soundtracks

Dynamic music implementation, with its potential for a plethora of realizations through various combinations and lengths of audio modules, poses challenges for music analysis in its undefined musical work. As Born (2005, 26) argues: "The ontology of the musical work envisions hierarchical assemblage: the composer-hero stands over the interpreter, conductor over instrumentalist, interpreter over listener, just as the work ideal authorizes and supervises the score, which supervises performance, which supervises reception." When the "composer-hero" hands control of the unfolding of the piece to the player, this hierarchy begins to break down. There is no singular way to experience a game soundtrack, and even precomposed events, such as cutscenes, can be bookended and nested within a wide variety of game audio experiences. Even when separated from nonmusic sound events for analysis (whether arbitrarily or not), each player's in-game decisions will alter the resulting piece to some degree. In an attempt to combat some of the difficulties of analyzing a transient work, the approach I have chosen for analyzing NPT music takes into account a combination of my experiences with the soundtrack to

Valve's *Half-Life: Alyx* both in and outside of the VR environment. Undertaking multiple playthroughs, alongside watching others' gaming content, provides an understanding of what triggers the onset and ending of the various sections of NPT music and the audio, visual, and haptic context in which these are heard in-game. Taking into consideration the official soundtrack as released by Valve provides a secondary source of material for analysis and a foundation for creating tables and diagrams of sounds within the music. Its abstraction from the game also provides a marker against which I can compare my own in-game experiences of the soundtrack, and those of other players I have seen/heard, to build a more general understanding of how the soundtrack can be experienced.

Four audio processing techniques: panning, the manipulation of reverb, changes in amplitude, and the addition of filters, will be my primary focus in analyzing the ways in which motion is conveyed in NPT music. Rather than considering game music as a cousin to the film score—as a score-based music—treating video game music as recorded sound recognizes that, despite the various ways in which the music may be implemented, the sounds and sound qualities are somewhat fixed across different playthroughs. It is these combinations of recorded sounds (whether the original instrument source is acoustic or electronic), including how they have been processed, that constitute the music. This understanding of the score opens potential avenues for analysis outside of what can be notated and considers the role of the audio producer alongside that of the composer. However, focusing this analysis on how motion is conveyed in video game music, achieved through the layering of multiple smaller recorded sonic events, does not necessarily rely on considering the game's soundtrack as a singular linear event or singular recorded text in the same fashion as a recorded pop song. Instead, it considers how motion is layered across different instruments within a piece of NPT music. This relieves some of the pressure on naming a definitive, primary, or even ideal, player encounter with the music, and allows for thinking separated from a traditional linear score or fixed text, while still considering the significance of this music as recorded sound. This approach draws inspiration from Smalley's (2007) discussion of soundscapes, where he notes that space can be more significant than time, despite the ways in which time contributes to the articulation and shaping of spectral and perspectival space of sounds. Time remains a significant factor in the unfolding of a dynamic game score, but the way we think about video game music need not be bound by the formal constraints of predetermined linear scores.

Case Study: Valve's *Half-Life: Alyx* (2020)

Valve's VR game *Half-Life: Alyx* (2020) is the latest installment in the *Half-Life* series, falling narratively in the time between the events of *Half Life* (1998) and *Half-Life*

2 (2004). You play as Alyx Vance, a member of the human resistance fighting to end the rule of the alien Combine police state on Earth. Although billed as a first-person shooter, the game also includes horror elements, such as the zombies and aliens, and puzzle elements. It has proven popular for a VR game, receiving a Metascore of 93/100 on Metacritic[10] and surpassing two million downloads on Steam in December 2020.[11] The NPT music in *Half-Life: Alyx* is not wall-to-wall, it comes into the sound space to support specific moments in the game. However, music and sound, both PPT and NPT, are not easily separated using the game settings, as is more common in video games. Players have the option to control master volume, game (game sound), combat music, and character voice levels. Notably, not all music is considered combat music. In these instances, NPT and PPT sounds are being treated as equally important components of the game's sound world. This analysis will explore the music of two levels from different chapters of the game, "Coetaneous Entanglement" and "Quantum Cubicles." In these examples, the volume of the NPT music cannot be controlled separately from the other sounds in the game. The titles, "Coetaneous Entanglement" and "Quantum Cubicles," are also the titles used for these two pieces of music in the official soundtrack.

"Coetaneous Entanglement"

The NPT music of "Coetaneous Entanglement" brings you from the sterile, white box waiting room of the title screen to the hazy dystopian world of City 17. As shown in Figure 45.2, your vantage point from the balcony of Alyx's hideout affords a long view of the cityscape that draws your eye up to the Citadel. This is your first glimpse of the game world. The NPT music helps to ground the player in the game by creating a sense of activity and motion through manipulations of sound position and quality, supporting the notion that City 17 is a large city of many moving parts. It also helps the player to understand the scale of the city, with the lack of rigid tonal form contributing to a sense of vastness, suggesting that this soundscape—and, therefore, the game world—has no definitive beginning or end in time, it is not unfolding toward a particular harmonic goal. The mixture of timbres, both electronic in origin and heavily processed acoustic instruments, mirror the juxtaposition of the Citadel, with its long-reaching cables, helicopters and drones flying around, and bright blue shots of electricity running through them all, against the older city buildings, with their rusting railings and tired facades. We are hearing a snapshot of life in the dystopian city.

Table 45.1 offers an overview of the various instruments in "Coetaneous Entanglement," with codenames used in this analysis and timestamps for when they can first be heard in the official soundtrack. Sounds that are identifiable as PPT in game-play but are also included in the official soundtrack are marked with an asterisk. The NPT music fades out once the player has left the balcony, moving into a greenhouse. S4 continues inside the greenhouse, once the other instruments in this scene have disappeared, but is not tied to the player's head position. Instead, it offers the sound of destructive activity in the distance, offering an auditory continuation of the opening

FIGURE 45.2 The view of City 17 from Alyx's balcony, *Half-Life: Alyx* (2020).

gameplay. It is also important to note that the master volume of the NPT music drops dramatically after the first two minutes of gameplay, if the player has not already moved to the greenhouse by that point.

The various instruments work together to create a general impression of motion throughout the city. One way this is achieved is through sound synthesis. Two audio processes I will focus on here are dynamic shaping and the use of reverb. As Schmidt Horning (2012) notes, studies have shown that reverb conjures the sense of physical space for listeners. This is particularly true of perception of a sound source's distance from the listener, as explored by Mershon and King (1975) and Mershon and Bowers (1979). These two processes work in conjunction to create the impression that a sound is moving either toward or away from the player. Figures 45.3a and 45.3b provide a diagram of the ways in which reverb and dynamic shaping alter the perception of an instrument's distance from the player for the instruments in "Coetaneous Entanglement."

TABLE 45.1 Table of Instruments Heard in "Coetaneous Entanglement" from *Half-Life: Alyx* (2020)

Name	Label	Timestamp
S1	Bass synth	0'00
S2	Electronic buzzing synth	0'03"
S3	Electronic whisper synth	0'10"
S4	Bubbling sound-bomb	0'12"
S5	Metallic synth	0'20"
S6	Low rumbling toms	0'30"
S7	Airy synth pad	0'47"
S8	Affected helicopter	0'50"
S9	Synthesized string pad	0'57"
S10	Synthesized voice pad	0'57"
S11	Synthesized chimes	3'42"
S12	Motorbike revving	4'37"

As shown in Figures 45.3a and 45.3b, S1 provides a wavering base with a largely consistent rate of movement from the moment the player sees City 17 for the first time, at 0'51" in the soundtrack recording, until the onset of the more extreme forward-back motion of S12. The combination of its forward position in the sound sphere and its low but moving frequency (pitch) creates a pocket of sound close to the ear against which the other instruments can be positioned. These other instruments don't adhere to the rate or pulse of S1's motion. Instead, they move through the front-back space at their own individual pace, except for S9 and S10, which are spaced apart but move in tandem. This front-back motion helps to individuate the instruments, considered in this context as sonic representations of actors within the game world, and supports the visual depth in Alyx's long view across the city, with its mass of familiar city dwellings, alien Citadel, and Combine creatures. In this sense, the application of reverb and the dynamic shaping of these instrument lines in the opening of the game supports the genesis of the player's sense of place by offering a sonic reflection of both the movement of actors seen by the player and the movement of actors out of view.

We can also consider the movement of sound across the horizontal plane, created through stereo panning. Stereo panning aims to control the perception of (phantom) sound source direction, and the application of stereo panning, in conjunction with the application of reverb, dynamic shaping, and sound filtering, can create the impression of separating out the various instruments so that they take up their own space, supporting the idea that these instruments are real objects (Lennox 2009). Figure 45.4 provides a histogram of pan position per frequency in "Coetaneous Entanglement."[12]

As shown in Figure 45.4, there is a wealth of audio information spread across the horizontal plane and across the audible frequency spectrum. The left-right position of the sounds extends beyond the player's field of vision from 0 Hz up to 15,000 Hz,

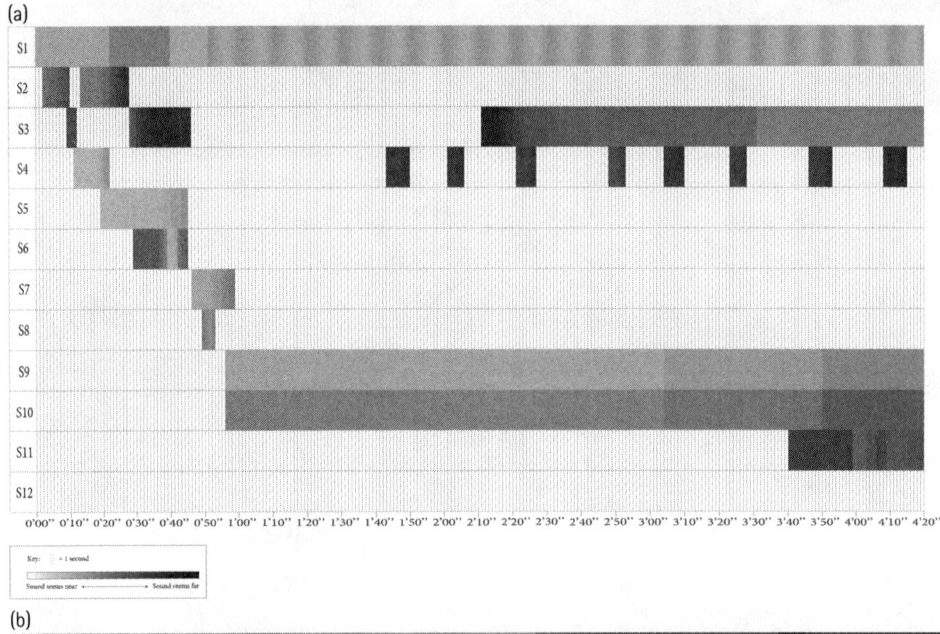

FIGURE 45.3 (a and 3b) Diagram of front-back motion in "Coetaneous Entanglement" from Valve's *Half-Life: Alyx* (2020).

reflecting the player's position on the balcony, where they can see both the streets below and the various Combine biochemical war machines that tower over the buildings. This creates the impression of a full and active game world. We can combine the construction of front-back and horizontal motion to visualize where each instrument moves within the game's sound sphere. As shown in Figure 45.5, there is

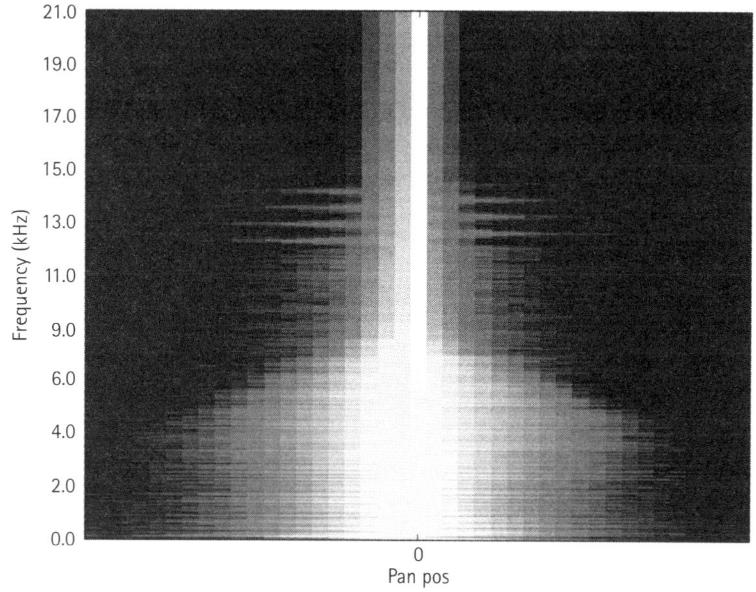

FIGURE 45.4 Histogram of pan positions per frequency in "Coetaneous Entanglement" from Valve's *Half-Life: Alyx* (2020).

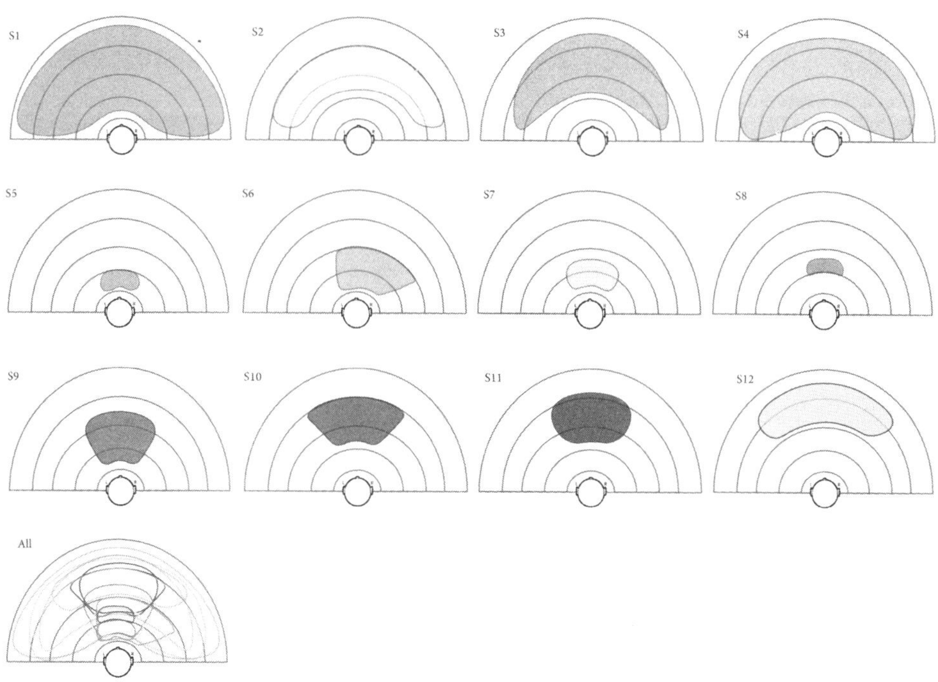

FIGURE 45.5 Left-right and front-back mapping for each instrument in "Coetaneous Entanglement" from Valve's *Half-Life: Alyx* (2020)

reasonable overlap in the paths traced by the various instruments in their distance and horizontal movement. This helps to concretize the space of the game world by suggesting a boundary, however large, which the instruments can move within, offering an audio realization of the city—a bounded place—with its many human and alien inhabitants. In this sense, the use of NPT music in the opening of the game is contributing to Slater's illusion of place by supporting the player in developing an understanding of the VR world.

"Quantum Cubicles"

Away from the open skies of Alyx's balcony, "Quantum Cubicles" kicks in as you attempt to pry a shotgun from a dead zombie's hand in the Drainage Tunnels, as depicted in Figure 45.6. Before you have had time to load your newly acquired shotgun, reanimated zombies burst through the bricked-up tunnels. Here, music's efficacy in representing movement creates the sonic image that something—or, more importantly, something alive—exists beyond the player's immediate surroundings, to tell you that, despite what you can see, you are not alone. Table 45.2 summarizes the various instruments in "Quantum Cubicles," with codenames used in this analysis and timestamps for when they can first be heard in the official soundtrack. As with "Coetaneous Entanglement," we can consider the ways in which the application and manipulation of reverb, in conjunction with dynamic shaping, can impact how near or far a sound seems to the player. Figures 45.7a and 45.7b provide a diagram of the perceived distance from the player for each instrument in "Quantum Cubicles."

In an interview with The Sound Test (2020), *Half-Life: Alyx* composer Mike Morasky notes: "One of the things I explored a little bit was different time signatures on top of each other or switching back and forth in ways that are . . . really uncomfortable."[13] Although not explicitly stated by Morasky, this exploration of multiple time signatures, and lack of a singular pulse, is made more prominent in "Quantum Cubicles" by the manipulation of reverb. The various amounts, and shaping, of reverb for S3 and S4 heighten the rhythmic tension between the two instruments by pulling them closer to or pushing them away from the player, making it more difficult to find and hold onto either pulse; heavy reverb pushes the sound away from you, drier sounds create the impression that the instrument is closer to you than before, long tails keep the impression of the sound lingering in the mix. The effect created by separate reverb manipulation for S3 and S4 also suggests to us that they are both on their own trajectory around the sound sphere, jumping forward and fading backward, or growing in intensity before suddenly disappearing. They offer musical metaphors for the creatures hidden from sight, contributing to the uneasy atmosphere of the game level in being unpredictable, supporting the notion that something alive (or undead) is waiting for the player behind the walls. However, despite these largely independent trajectories, there is still interplay between the two instruments. As seen in Figures 45.7a and 45.7b, they don't occupy the same space along the horizontal plane at the same time. However, it is not

FIGURE 45.6 View of the Drainage Tunnels from the "Quantum Cubicles" level, *Half-Life: Alyx* (2020).

TABLE 45.2 Table of Instruments Heard in "Quantum Cubicles" from *Half-Life: Alyx* (2020)

Name	Instrument	Timestamp
S1	Dark synth bass	0'00"
S2	Synthesized strings	0'00"
S3	Floor tom	0'09"
S4	Snare	0'11"
S5	Synthesized horn solo	0'42"
S6	Synthesized brass bass	0'33"
S7	Sweeping synth	0'52"

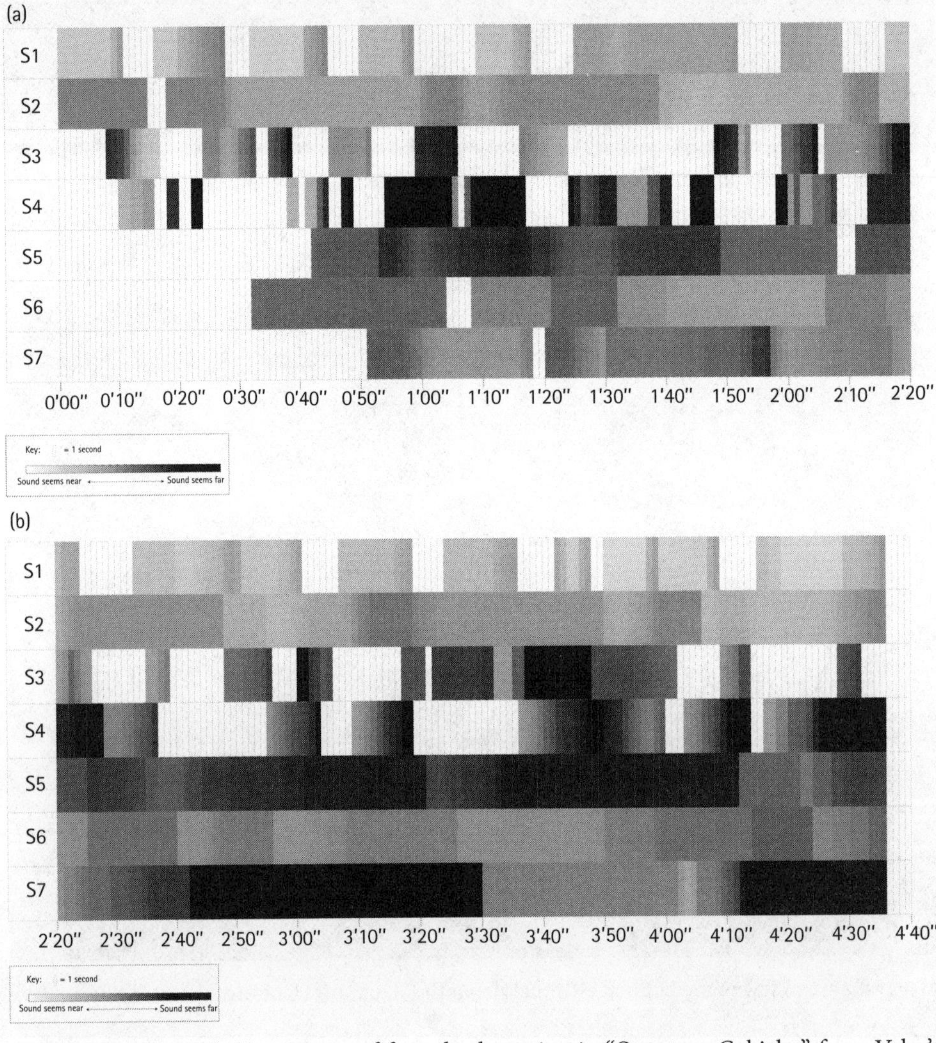

FIGURE 45.7 (a and 7b) Diagram of front-back motion in "Quantum Cubicles" from Valve's *Half-Life: Alyx* (2020).

as straightforward as a space swap, with one coming forward as the other moves back. Instead, there is tension building in the smaller interplay in the mid-far area of the horizontal plane, you become unsure of whether the sound is going to disappear entirely, or if you are due another moment of sound jumping closer to the ear. This is supported by the forward-back spacing of the other instruments which, although generally more stable than S3 and S4, create the impression of an alive, breathing space through their limited movement. Again, it is difficult to place a singular, strong pulse, but there is uniform harmonic movement that hovers around C minor, C# minor, and C# diminished chords, binding the instruments together in harmonic space despite their lack of rhythmic synchronicity.

We can also consider the left-right movement created in this piece through the manipulation of stereo panning. Figure 45.8 provides a histogram of pan position per frequency in "Quantum Cubicles."

In "Coetaneous Entanglement," NPT music underpins the player's first encounter with the entire game world. A plethora of sounds moving across the sound space at a range of perceived distances from the player help to establish the game world, supporting the development of an illusion of place. In contrast, the music of "Quantum Cubicles" is more keenly developing the illusion of plausibility in the sonification of actors which will have a more immediate interaction with the player. This can be seen in the use of the available panning space. Figure 45.8 shows bands of extreme panning throughout the lower end of the frequency range. When combined with pitch metaphors mapped onto the median plane, (as discussed by Cox 2017) this helps to conceptually expand the size of the tunnel setting beyond what can be seen, pushing the sound floor to the edges of the space, allowing it to seem as far reaching as possible. The mass of sound sits closer to the center, which helps to shape the overall impression of left-right movement; the instruments are not fighting for space which increases the impact of pushing an audio source to hard left or right as it moves into a previously empty space. We can consider how this works in tandem with the use of reverb to create an overall image of

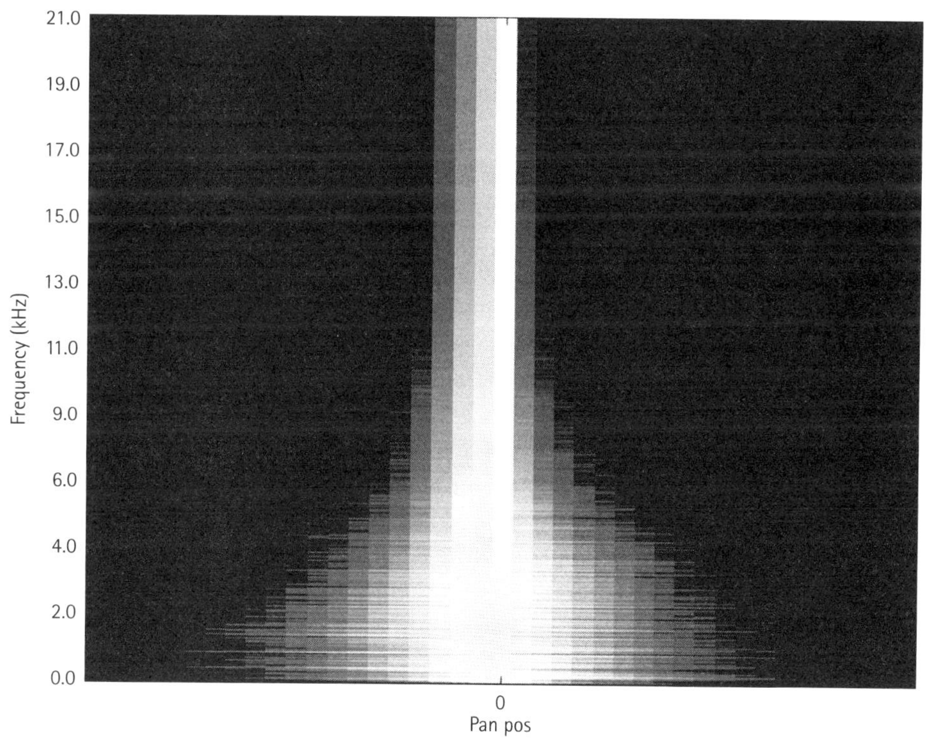

FIGURE 45.8 Histogram of pan positions per frequency in "Quantum Cubicles" from Valve's *Half-Life: Alyx* (2020).

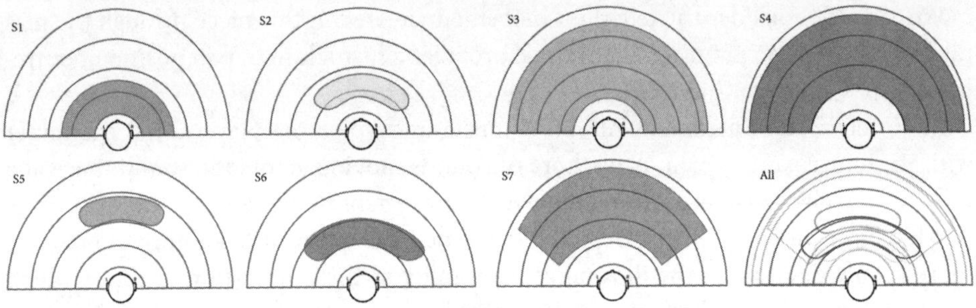

FIGURE 45.9 Left-right and front-back mapping for each instrument in "Quantum Cubicles" from *Half-Life: Alyx* (2020).

the horizontal plane and distance from the player. Figure 45.9 provides a diagram which traces the individual instrument lines in "Quantum Cubicles" through left-right and front-back sound spaces in relation to the player's head.

As seen in Figure 45.9, S1 creates a solid platform from the very beginning of "Quantum Cubicles" against which the rest of the instruments can be placed in the player's mental image of the sound sphere. It has a stable position, sitting closer to the player, and seems to envelop the ear in taking up the full stereo width available. S6, S2, and S5 stack on top of S1. They are also stationary in their stereo position, sitting more centrally, but are not as far reaching as S1. This creates pockets of empty space into which S3, S4, and S7 can move. The independence of each line's position helps to create the illusion of a multitude of moving parts at varying distances from the player. As previously discussed, this separating of the various instruments through panning, dynamic shaping, and the manipulation of reverb reinforces the impression that these instruments are objects in the game world, and therefore capable of being a real threat in the zombie-horror scene of the Drainage Tunnels.

The evolving filter of S7 contributes median plane movement to "Quantum Cubicles." As the upper partials are amplified, and the lower partials and fundamental are filtered out, the sound gives the impression of a rising electronic growl. Similarly, as these upper partials are cut, and the lower partials are allowed back in, the sound seems to move underground, as if it is sitting beneath something dense. As with S3 and S4, there is no discernible pulse to the filter sweeping of S7, going underground before suddenly jumping up then disappearing as quickly as it arrived. The unpredictability of the filtering supports the idea that this sound is a sonic representation of a living thing within the game world and contributes to the perceptual creation of the virtual world. It works alongside the other parameters of motion to create a more comprehensive understanding of the Drainage Tunnels, laden with zombies and headcrabs, out of sight, but not out of mind (or ear). As the player moves through the space, they cannot resolve the musical tension by locating any of the sound sources individually, they continue to be out of reach. Instead, the tension is resolved once they have killed all the reanimated zombies and there is no longer anything alive hiding in the tunnels. Considering this in tandem with an embodied cognition of music offers a way for us to understand this motion as being felt by the player, and therefore the threat it stands for to be felt by the player too, a threat of whatever is lurking just beyond their line of sight. In the first-person, shooter-horror hybrid of *Half-Life: Alyx*, this works to heighten the emotional and physiological impact of the Drainage Tunnel environment.

Conclusion

As seen in *Half-Life: Alyx*, NPT music can offer a simulacrum of motion in a virtual world. The manipulation of reverb, amplitude, stereo panning, and sound filtering, creates a perceptual sound space through which the various instruments seem to move. This works in conjunction with metaphors of motion in music to generate a dimension of activity which exists beyond the limitations of what can be seen by a player in any given moment. Considering this sonic motion as felt motion helps to broaden our understanding of the ways in which a virtual world can feel real through using music as metaphor for living creatures in a VR game. This felt motion supports the creation of a virtual world believable enough to become a temporary reality, one which can have an immediate physiological and psychological impact on the player. When we put on a VR headset, we become the creator of that world, we give life to an otherwise static digital space. When we remove the headset, we effectively deaden the virtual world. This could pose issues for the believability of game worlds, particularly in Slater's plausibility illusion. However, the manipulation of motion in NPT music can also aid in generating the impression that the game world will continue to exist beyond the player's time spent within it; it can support the notion that the player is one actor and not *the* actor, despite building on a narrative that is centered around player actions. This continuation, kindled by music, is a life force for the virtual world.

Notes

1. Much has been written about the various roles played by music in video games, and there are many chapters in this volume that explore these applications of music.
2. As discussed on http://lookingglassvr.com, Looking Glass VR's eponymous application (2017) allows the user to view stereoscopic images from Keystone View Company's "Tour of the World."
3. For example, Facebook bought Oculus in 2014. The release of the Oculus Quest 2 in 2020, which promised high-spec VR gaming and other VR content at a reasonably low price and without the need for a separate VR ready gaming PC, came with the caveat that you must have a Facebook account to use the headset.
4. Note, there are many workarounds to access content only available on a separate platform, including linking headsets to PCs remotely or with cable tethers.
5. See Firth (2013) and Mack (2019).
6. Lanier quoted in the *Washington Post* (Smith 2021).

7. As mentioned, I had previously thought in terms of "warping diegesis," of the breaking down of actor–audience barriers through the introduction of diegetic timbres in the nondiegetic score. However, this still places the emphasis on the actor–audience divide in thinking about what could and could not conceivably come from the game world. In thinking about PPT/NPT instead, the focus shifts to the concerns about audio processing in the game, particularly what is processed binaurally in real time, which in turn sets us up for thinking about how music can make use of this freedom from this real-time binaural processing and offer a vehicle for motion and activity.
8. The image of a perfectly round sphere is a simplification. There are many compounding factors that alter our perception of sound, but thinking about the three dimensions in this way can help us to understand how we might perceive sound as moving through space.
9. See Plack (2005, 174) for a more detailed explanation of this concept.
10. The Metacritic page for *Half-Life: Alyx* provides a breakdown of the various review categories, available at: https://www.metacritic.com/game/pc/half-life-alyx. The Matescore is correct as of July 17, 2021.
11. See Baker (2020). Steam is a video game digital distribution platformed owned by Valve, and Steam Spy is one of many Steam data reporting sites. Valve are said to be working on their own Steam data tracking/publishing platform, but, for now, third-party sites like Steam Spy offer some data insights using Valve's Web API.
12. Computer-generated histogram based on Dan Stowell's stereoscope.py script, code repository available at: https://gist.github.com/danstowell/8872466.
13. See: Sound Test (2020). Quote begins at 45'29".

References

Baker, H. 2020. "*Half-Life: Alyx* Surpasses 2 Million Owners on Steam, Steam Spy Suggests." *Upload VR*, December 4, 2020. https://uploadvr.com/half-life-alyx-2-million/.

Born, G. 2005. "On Musical Mediation: Ontology, Technology and Creativity." *Twentieth Century Music* 2 (1): 7–36.

Cox, A. 2011. "Embodying Music: Principles of the Mimetic Hypothesis." *Music Theory Online* 17 (2). https://mtosmt.org/issues/mto.11.17.2/mto.11.17.2.cox.html.

Cox, A. 2017. *Music and Embodied Cognition*. Bloomington: Indiana University Press.

Firth, N. 2013. "Virtual Reality: Meet Founding Father Jaron Lanier." *New Scientist*, June 19, 2013. https://www.newscientist.com/article/mg21829226-000-virtual-reality-meet-found ing-father-jaron-lanier/.

Lanier, J. 2017. *Dawn of the New Everything: A Journey through Virtual Reality*. London: Bodley Head.

Lennox, P. 2009. "Spatialization and Computer Music." In *Oxford Handbook of Computer Music*, edited by R. Dean, 258–273. New York: Oxford University Press.

Mack, Z. 2019. "Jaron Lanier's Ideas for the Future of Profiting from Your Own Data." *Verge*, April 9th 2019. https://www.theverge.com/2019/4/9/18302076/data-monetization-control-manipulation-economy-jaron-laniers-virtual-reality-vr-vergecast.

Medina-Gray, E. 2021. "Interacting with Soundscapes: Music, Sound Effects and Dialogue in Video Games." In *The Cambridge Companion to Video Game Music*, edited by M. Fritsch, and T. Summers, 176–192. Cambridge Companions to Music. Cambridge: Cambridge University Press.

Mershon, D. H., and J. N. Bower. 1979. "Absolute and Relative Cues for the Auditory Perception of Egocentric Distance." *Perception* 8 (3): 311–322. https://doi.org/10.1068/p080311.
Mershon, D. H., and L. E. King. 1975. "Intensity and Reverberation as Factors in the Auditory Perception of Egocentric Distance." *Perception and Psychophysics* 18 (6): 409–415. https://doi.org/10.3758/BF03204113.
Peters, D. 2012. "Touch: Real, Apparent, and Absent—On Bodily Expression in Electronic Music." In *Bodily Expression in Electronic Music: Perspectives on Reclaiming Performativity*, edited by D. Peters, G. Eckel, and A. Dorschel, 17–34. London: Routledge.
Plack, C. J. 2005. *The Sense of Hearing*. Mahwah, NJ: Lawrence Erlbaum.
Schmidt Horning, S. 2012. "The Sounds of Space: The Studio as Instrument in the Era of High Fidelity." In *The Art of Record Production*, edited by S. Frith and S. Zagorski-Thomas, 29–42. Burlington: Ashgate.
Slater M. 2009. "Place Illusion and Plausibility Can Lead to Realistic Behaviour in Immersive Virtual Environments." *Philosophical Transactions of the Royal Society of London. Series B, Biological Sciences* 364 (1535): 3549–3557. https://doi.org/10.1098/rstb.2009.0138.
Smalley, D. 2007. "Space-Form and the Acousmatic Image." *Organised Sound: An International Journal of Music Technology* 12 (1): 35–58.
Smith, N. 2021. "Virtual Reality Is Starting to See Actual Gains in Gaming." *Washington Post*, February 4, 2021. https://www.washingtonpost.com/video-games/2021/02/04/virtual-reality-future-games/.
The Sound Test. 2020. "THE SOUND TEST Bonus—Mike Morasky Interview (*Half-Life: Alyx*)." YouTube. https://www.youtube.com/watch?v=TIzL_ixOm-A.
Whalen, Z. 2004. "Play Along: An Approach to Videogame Music." *Game Studies* 4 (1). http://gamestudies.org/0401/whalen/.

Ludology

Arizona Sunshine. 2016. Vertigo Games. Valve Index, HTC Vive, Oculus Rift, Oculus Quest, Oculus Quest 2, Windows Mixed Reality. Rotterdam: Vertigo Games.
Batman: Arkham VR. 2016. Rocksteady. PlayStation 4, Microsoft Windows. Burbank, USA: Warner Brothers Interactive Entertainment.
Down the Rabbit Hole. 2020. Cortopia Studios. Valve Index, HTC Vive, Oculus Rift, Oculus Quest, Oculus Quest 2, Windows Mixed Reality. Stockholm, Cortopia Studios.
Guitar Hero. 2005. Harmonix. PlayStation 2. USA: Activision.
Half-Life: Alyx. 2020. Valve. Valve Index, HTC Vive, Oculus Rift, Windows Mixed Reality. Washington: Valve.
Lone Echo. 2017. Ready at Dawn. Oculus Rift, Oculus Quest, Oculus Quest 2. California: Oculus Studios.
Thumper. 2016. Drool. PSVR/PlayStation 4, Oculus/Microsoft Windows. USA: Drool.

CHAPTER 46

INTRINSICALLY UNPLEASANT SOUNDS AND PLAYER EXPERIENCE

DENIS ZLOBIN

Introduction

This chapter explores how game audio designers can modulate player experience with unpleasant sound effects. There are sounds that every human finds unpleasant to hear, probably because of the visceral reaction they trigger. In the video game context, such sounds can help guide and motivate the players, control their cognitive load, or elicit a specific emotional response. Following the ideas of intentional sound design (Alves and Roque 2010), I see game sound design not as an act of designing sounds for video games, but rather as an act of designing video games via sound. Authoring sounds is a crucial part of our craft, but the craft needs to extend further. And there are times when we should stop thinking about sound as an object we design, and start treating it as a tool to create something bigger—a video game.

Game developers primarily associate psychological aspects of player experience—such as attention, motivation, and cognitive load—with the disciplines of game- and UX-design. A very few would say that sound does not influence those aspects, but, in any case, sound is rarely the main area of concern. We are so used to thinking of sight as our primary sense that we forget that the aural modality has many strengths to leverage when designing the player experience. This text describes some of those strengths and demonstrates how we can consider them when working in game audio.

In this chapter, I focus on sound's ability to help the player deal with gameplay challenges and achieve their goals—its ludic function (Stevens and Raybould 2015; Zlobin 2021). Being well understood by professional sound designers, this functional dimension of game audio remains somewhat underexplored in literature. At the same time, I believe that most sounds in a game serve both gameplay and narrative, so many ideas I describe also synergize with narrative design.

The famous thought experiment asks: "If a tree falls in a forest and no one is around to hear it, does it make a sound?" The answer depends on what we think sound is—a purely physical phenomenon or a human perception of such phenomenon. In this chapter, I opt for the second definition—understanding sound not just as a soundwave, but as a soundwave as perceived by a human being. Sound quality thus depends on a combination of the acoustic properties of a soundwave; the physiological and neurophysiological properties of the human auditory system; and far less measurable factors like current context, our mental state, or experience.

The focus of this chapter is *intrinsically* unpleasant sounds—the ones humans tend to dislike in every context, such as fingernails scratching over a chalkboard (Halpern, Blake, and Hillenbrand 1986). It is difficult to imagine a situation when hearing such sound will not cause a strong aversive reaction. Since the reaction is not linked to the context where the sound is heard, it must be elicited by some acoustic properties of the sound itself. Understanding and controlling these properties allows sound designers to target specific emotional and cognitive reactions in players of any origin, background, and life experience.

The topic of unpleasant sound may appear too narrow, but when we speak about the player experience, we rarely discuss unidirectional approaches. Once we know what makes a sound intrinsically unpleasant, and when such sound is instrumental, we are better equipped to deal with sounds that disrupt the experience. Some ideas I express in this chapter are easy to apply in reverse to *reduce* unpleasantness, which is arguably a more common goal for sound designers.

First, based on the existing research in cognitive psychology and psychoacoustics, I analyze the common acoustic factors that make most people experience unpleasant sensations. Following that, I propose a simple framework to evaluate the appropriateness of unpleasant sound in a game using three different lenses. Finally, reflecting on my personal experience as a practicing sound designer, I provide some contexts and examples when unpleasant sounds serve the game, and how we can use them to create synergies with our colleagues from other game development departments.

Factors of Auditory Unpleasantness

Hearing is an important survival mechanism that helps humans sense distant motion and vibration.[1] Unlike sight, hearing covers 360 degrees, and does not require a direct unobstructed pathway between the emitter and the listener. We can hear in the dark. Auditory reaction time is faster than visual (Solanki et al. 2012; Jain et al. 2015). The auditory system is constantly monitoring our surroundings even when we sleep. Our ears have no earlids to interrupt the stream of auditory information. Thanks to these features, the sense of hearing has ensured the survival of thousands of species over millions of years.

Because humans constantly process a massive amount of auditory information, our hearing is fine-tuned to prioritize survival-related signals. Threat detection happens at an early stage of auditory processing (Pannese, Grandjean, and Frühholz 2016; Kumar et al. 2012). The brain detects a potential threat by analyzing the fine structure of the soundwave way before we recognize what we have heard or understand where the sound came from. And this implies there are acoustic features we unconsciously associate with direct or indirect threats. The features we can measure and manipulate in the sound design process.

Threat-related stimuli naturally trigger reactions like fear, annoyance, uneasiness, and disgust. I use "unpleasantness" as an umbrella term, describing a spectrum of arousing, negative-valence emotions. Sounds associated with an immediate threat will likely cause a strong reaction like fear. Others could indicate that we are in a vulnerable state and should be vigilant toward our surroundings. The sensations we experience on hearing those are closer to anxiety or disorientation. Russell's circumplex model (see Figure 46.1) allows mapping different emotions on a circle on the two-dimensional plane, where the horizontal axis is valence, and the vertical axis is arousal (Russell 1980). The sounds that I call "intrinsically unpleasant" typically elicit the emotions from the upper-left quadrant of this plane—the neutral-to-arousing sounds with a neutral-to-negative valence.

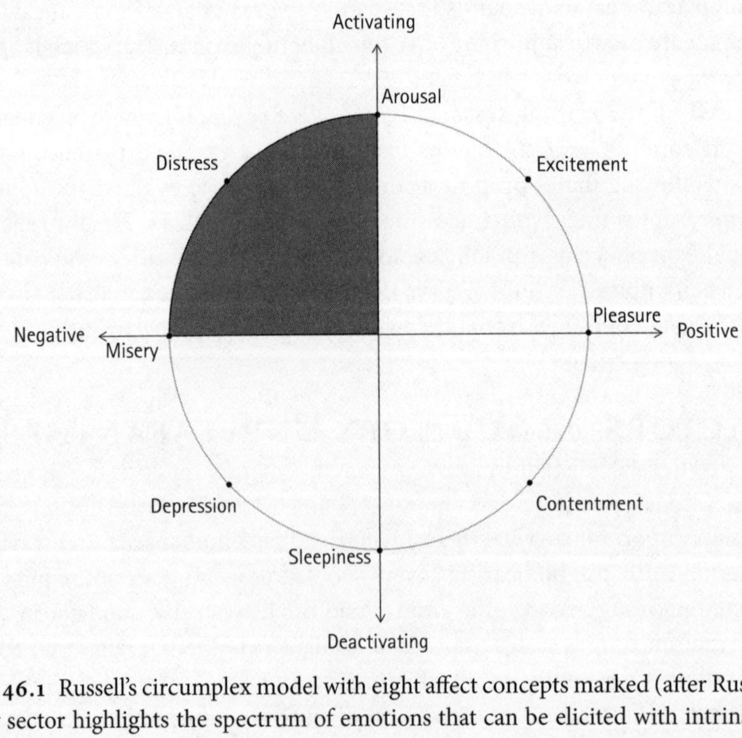

FIGURE 46.1 Russell's circumplex model with eight affect concepts marked (after Russell 1980). The gray sector highlights the spectrum of emotions that can be elicited with intrinsically unpleasant audio.

The emotions that belong to the lower-left quadrant are also unpleasant; however, I did not find any evidence they can be elicited with the properties of a soundwave, neither was I able to imagine a context-agnostic sound to trigger them.

Linking a sound to a specific negative emotion is problematic, because the same sound can trigger different reactions depending on the context. The sound of the neighbor's hammer drill easily scares us for a fraction of a second when we hear it unexpectedly. But once we realize what it is, we feel annoyance rather than fear when the neighbor starts drilling again. In both cases the acoustic structure of the sound could tell us it is coming from a dangerous object. But when the survival mechanism puts us in an alert state for the second time, we know we are safe and feel annoyed for being falsely alarmed and having our afternoon nap disturbed. Still, both emotions remain unpleasant, and it is hard to imagine a scenario when the neighbor's drill makes us experience positive sensations.

Academic sources mention a few acoustic features responsible for the intrinsic auditory unpleasantness. Psychoacoustic experiments are often done with purposefully decontextualized, and thus sterile and unnatural audio. Although the results of such experiments appear difficult to extrapolate to sound in media, the absence of context is essential to understand whether the sound is intrinsically unpleasant. If the sound is rated as unpleasant under the laboratory conditions, it will likely remain unpleasant in the game.

The experiments often contradict each other, labeling certain features as irrelevant or insignificant. Being a sound designer, I approach this from a pragmatic perspective. My goal is not to fully answer which features indeed cause unpleasant sensations and which do not, but to find the best option to create the intended effect. In that sense, anything reliable enough is useful for my craft. The contents of this section are rooted in academic research, but I add a personal view on the appropriateness of using certain features in the game-development context based on my professional experience.

Loudness

Loudness is the most apparent sensation we associate with unpleasantness, and many sources identify it as a significant factor in disliking a sound (Skagerstrand, Köbler, and Stenfelt 2017; Steel and Chon 2007; Cho, Yi, and Cho 2001; Hall et al. 2013). Evolution has taught us to sense distant movement via our ears. Loudness, as the subjective perception of sound intensity, tells us about either the large scale or the proximity of such motion, forcing us to pay immediate attention to the source of the sound. A harmless source might emit a loud noise which masks other sounds that we need for survival, leaving us more vulnerable and thus making us feel anxious or uneasy.

However, the data from one experiment (Garner, Grimshaw, and Nabi 2010) shows no significant correlation between the audio playback volume and the players' emotional-response intensity, and other evidence (Ellermeier, Mader, and Daniel 2004) suggests that loudness is not the most critical factor of unpleasantness. In both experiments, loudness stayed within the reasonably safe levels, comparable to how the players usually experience the game. Its influence increases as sound pressure levels approach the threshold of pain, but, fortunately, this does not apply to our medium.

There are other reasons why sound designers should not rely on loudness to make things sound less pleasant. When working on a game, we operate in a limited dynamic range and need to respect the loudness standards. In addition to that, the player usually has complete control over the playback volume. If we make something uncomfortably loud, they will simply adjust the volume to a more comfortable level. Still, it is helpful to remember that a sound needs to be loud enough to feel unpleasant. On top of that, loudness influences our perception of some other factors of auditory unpleasantness like sharpness and roughness (both described below) that seem to have a more substantial effect (Fastl and Zwicker 2007, 245).

Duration and Temporal Envelope

The intensity of unpleasant sensations from hearing a sound depends on how long we hear it. This factor is rarely mentioned in academic literature, mainly because researchers aim to select stimuli with similar duration when conducting experiments. However, many game sound designers know from experience that longer sound effects tend to be more irritating, especially after dozens of repetitions.

In one experiment, participants said that the duration of one second was not enough to make the sound feel annoying (Steel and Chon 2007). Another study demonstrated a significant difference in judgment on unpleasantness depending on the temporal evolution (the way sound changes in time), not just the duration of the signals. Sounds with the longer attack time were perceived as more unpleasant than the shorter ones (Geissner and Parizet 2007). Bach and others (2007, 2009) suggest that increasing sound intensity is an intrinsic warning cue: a steadily growing sound tells us that something is approaching from a distance.

At the same time, most of us experience a startle reaction to a sudden, fast sound. A short attack time makes the sound feel more urgent (Edworthy, Loxley, and Dennis 1991), probably because it indicates a sudden change in our surroundings. According to Farnell (2010, 105), such sounds can cause immediate sensations of fear and vigilance. Impulsive sounds usually annoy us more than a steady-state noise (Rajala and Hongisto 2020).

When it comes to the relation between unpleasantness and onset time, both short and long attack ideas seem logical. But given the wide variety of mundane sounds falling under one of the two categories, this is hardly the most critical factor that game sound designers should pay attention to. Since we usually aim for temporal congruity with visuals, controlling unpleasantness by adjusting the duration of a sound is mainly applicable to nonsynchronized sounds. However, thanks to the auditory dominance in temporal processing (Repp and Penel 2002), we usually accept some mismatch in the duration of the visual and auditory events, prioritizing the duration of a sound.

In my practice, making frequently repeating sound effects shorter than their visual counterparts sometimes helps to reduce annoyance from repetition.

Temporal Fine Structure

Auditory unpleasantness depends on the power and frequency of temporal modulations (both amplitude and frequency). The main features associated with temporal modulations are roughness, nonlinearity, and fluctuation strength. Roughness reflects the power of temporal modulations that occur in the range[2] between 15 and 300 Hz (Fastl and Zwicker 2007, 257). The notion that such modulations influence auditory unpleasantness parallels Helmholtz's (1863) view on dissonance resulting from beating harmonics (Helmholtz and Ellis 2009).

Arnal and colleagues (2015) found that roughness in the range between 30 and 150 Hz engages subcortical structures critical to rapidly appraising danger. They mention that modulations in that range are prominent in artificial alarm signals and human screams. Screams are the natural alarm signals that humans use, often involuntarily, and thus it makes perfect sense for the human auditory system to prioritize them as critical for survival. Taffou, Suied, and Delmon (2021) have confirmed that roughness elicits defensive responses in humans. Film sound designers, intentionally or intuitively, use scream-like sounds to manipulate our emotional responses (Blumstein, Davitian, and Kaye 2010). The temporal fine structure of terrifying film music, such as the infamous shrieking violins in Hitchcock's *Psycho* (1960), also often demonstrates a similar pattern (Trevor, Arnal, and Frühholz 2020).

When writing about the scream-like acoustic structure, some authors refer to nonlinearity (Blumstein, Davitian, and Kaye 2010; Blesdoe and Blumstein 2014). If roughness describes the salience of temporal modulations in the specific frequency range, nonlinearity points at the random character of modulations. It emerges from desynchronized, chaotic, and unpredictable changes in signal intensity, common for mammalian distress signals. Horowitz (2013, 119) calls such sounds "pseudo-random," using the following example: "[W]hen someone screeches uncontrollably as if in pain or a panic and the normally harmonic structure of the voice becomes ragged and out of control." The sound can be rough and nonlinear at the same time.

Farnell (2010) calls roughness "the doom tone," though he refers to a different frequency range. He describes roughness as "an interference rhythm composed of cycles in the 4Hz to 8Hz range resulting from a dangerous high-energy phenomenon like stampeding animals and high-speed wind. When it modulates higher frequency components, the resulting critical band ambiguity leads to an unsettling effect" (Farnell 2010, 89). Zwicker and Fastl propose a different term for this acoustic feature: "fluctuation strength." The principal difference between the two is that we perceive roughness as timbral quality, while we can still hear individual beatings in the case of fluctuation strength. However, the authors mention that there is no clear border between the two sensations (Fastl and Zwicker 2007, 247).

A study by Kumar and others (2008) strongly links unpleasantness with the same modulation range. The researchers examined some commonly hated sounds, such as scratching glass with forks and knives, dragging a spade, scraping a piece of chalk along the blackboard, and screaming. As a result, they found out that the most unpleasant sounds shared two acoustic features: they show much energy between 2,400 and 5,500 Hz and intense temporal modulations between 1 and 16 Hz. A different study identified fluctuation strength among the strongest predictors of the unpleasantness of an urban soundscape, alongside sharpness and loudness (Hall et al. 2013).

Some studies challenge the influence of roughness (Kurakata, Mizunami, and Matsushita 2013) and fluctuation strength (Kurakata, Mizunami, and Matsushita 2013; Ellermeier, Mader, and Daniel 2004) in the sensation of auditory unpleasantness. In day-to-day work, we often introduce temporal modulations and nonlinearities when we use distortion or similar effects. Sound designers might intuitively use such effects to increase the unpleasantness of a sound, but they rarely consciously target the specific modulation ranges.

Spectral Factors

Scholarly literature identifies three key spectral regions related to unpleasantness: the high end (4–20 kHz), the upper midrange between roughly 2 and 4 kHz, and the low end (20–250 Hz). Sharpness is a distinct sensation that correlates with the amount of high-frequency content in sound (Fastl and Zwicker 2007, 239–240). Humans show faster reaction time to high-pitched (and low-pitched) sounds on low-intensity levels compared to a 1,000 kHz tone (Santee and Kohfeld 1977). The quicker reaction time suggests that our hearing is fine-tuned to detect such sounds; high frequencies have a shorter wavelength and get easily absorbed by the air, meaning that in nature, we would not hear them unless the source is particularly close to us and deserves some attention.

Multiple studies confirm the role of sharpness in acoustic unpleasantness. Garner and Grimshaw (2013) conducted an experiment suggesting that sharp sounds can elevate players' sensations of fear. Outside of a video game context, there is evidence both supporting (Fastl and Zwicker 2007, 239; Cho, Yi, and Cho 2001; Weber and Eilers 2007; Hall et al. 2013) and challenging (Kurakata, Mizunami, and Matsushita 2013; Halpern, Blake, and Hillenbrand 1986) the prominent role of sharpness in the sensation of unpleasantness.

Equal loudness contours show that our ears are most sensitive to the region between 2 and 4 kHz. The popular explanation describes this frequency range as prominent in baby cries, making us especially attentive to it. Gustafson and Green suggest that baby cries with more energy between 3 and 4 kHz are the most aversive (1989). This is also true for adult cries (Hansen, Nandwana, and Shokouhi 2017). Unsurprisingly, some authors mention this region as a separate factor of unpleasantness (Kumar et al. 2008; Reuter, Oehler, and Mühlhans 2014). The region is high enough to cause the sensation of sharpness but limited at the high end, so it is easy to mistake one for another.

The opposite of sharpness is the measure of low-frequency content, sometimes called "boominess." As mentioned above, humans are quick to react to low-pitched sounds (Santee and Kohfeld 1977). In the wild, such sounds often come from large predator growls or dangerous natural events like earthquakes. Horowitz mentions that loud and low-pitched often mean large and scary (2013, 114). In one experiment, the traffic noise with prominent low frequencies was named comfortably loud but annoying (Skagerstrand, Köbler, and Stenfelt 2017). A study focused on low-frequency pure tones found a meaningful correlation between annoyance and prominent low-end components (Subedi et al. 2005).

Sound designers can easily control the spectral properties of sound effects both during the authoring process and in runtime. Even though, at least to my knowledge, there is a lack of easily accessible tools to measure sharpness as it is defined in the psychoacoustic literature, we could manipulate the high end of the frequency spectrum according to our subjective judgment. The low end is a bit more complicated because this range is harder to control, so we often reserve it for the most important sounds in the mix.

Perceptual Fluency

Zwicker and Fastl (2007) name tonality as a factor of sensory pleasantness, describing it as a feature distinguishing noise versus tone quality of sounds. According to them, sensory pleasantness increases with tonality and decreases if the signal becomes noisier (244). In that sense, noisiness is the opposite of tonality, and makes sounds less pleasant to hear.[3]

There is evidence that broadband noise and broadband tone-based complex sounds are more unpleasant than pink noise[4] and narrow-band stimuli (Steel and Chon 2007). At the same time, another study suggests that narrow-band noise is less unpleasant than pure tones with the same central frequency and sound pressure level (Kurakata, Mizunami, and Matsushita 2013).

Trying to make sense of a noisy recording is hardly a pleasant auditory experience. If we hear a sound and cannot easily extract meaningful information from it, our mental model of surroundings becomes incomplete, making us vulnerable. Noisy sounds lack perceptual fluency; they carry redundant information, and the human brain needs to filter it out. This parallels the processing fluency theory of aesthetic pleasure (Reber, Winkielman, and Schwarz 1998), which states that the very concept of beauty depends on how efficiently our brain can process incoming information. A competing idea suggests that perceptual fluency is not the mechanism that drives positive affect but an amplification factor that strengthens any kind of stimuli (Landwehr and Eckmann 2020). If this interpretation is accurate, noisiness could be a neutralizing factor for both pleasant and unpleasant signals rather than a separate factor of auditory unpleasantness.

Noisiness is not the only feature that makes the sound difficult to process. The human auditory system seems to be particularly sensitive to ambiguity and unpredictability (Gwilliams et al. 2018; Whalen 2007), probably for the reasons outlined above. In that sense, we can think that noisiness is one specific case of ambiguity, but sound in a game can be ambiguous in many ways (see also chapter 13 this volume). Most of them are contextual—for example, it may be incongruent with what the source object does or direct the player's attention to a nonexistent entity. In some cases, the player may be unsure whether the sound is diegetic or a part of background music (Bridgett 2021, 84–91). The location of the sound in the acoustic field may be ambiguous because of both contextual and acoustic factors. For instance, one small-scale experiment showed that players perceive hard-to-localize sounds as more scary (Ekman and Kajastila 2009). Another larger-scale study did not show an effect of binaural processing on the sensation of fear (Garner, Grimshaw, and Nabi 2010).

I see perceptual fluency (at least, in terms of the mix clarity and balance) mainly as a factor of auditory pleasantness that is not very reliable when applied in reverse. But of course, one could think of cases when noisiness, clutter, or muffling become a creative choice to illustrate that the player-character is in some abnormal, morbid state or to make the player feel anxiety, disorientation, or terror.

Nonacoustic Factors

The contents of the previous subsections are mainly based on psychoacoustic experiments, designed to be devoid as possible of any context. This is the strength of intrinsic unpleasantness: if the stimulus already works on its own, the congruently unpleasant context will only enhance its effect. For that reason, although this chapter focuses on the context-agnostic acoustic features, I cannot omit some contextual factors relevant to sound design.

Nonacoustic factors influence the experiment results, especially when the test subjects recognize the sounds (Ellermeier, Zeitler, and Fastl 2004; Skagerstrand, Köbler, and Stenfelt 2017). During our lives, we memorize sounds that accompany unpleasant events and incorporate them into mental models. The threatening sounds of the technology-driven world are not necessarily the same as in the primal era, and evolution has not yet taught us to recognize them. Any sound can become irritating when it is repetitive and we cannot shut it down. A sound can feel disorienting because it comes from an unknown source (Horowitz 2013, 225) or annoying when out of sync with the image we see on the screen. There are also unpleasant sounds like vomiting that do not show any of the acoustic features listed above (Reuter, Oehler, and Mühlhans 2014). Such sounds are universally, but not intrinsically, unpleasant.

A very effective nonacoustic factor for auditory unpleasantness is unexpectedness. Even a pleasant sound can scare us if we hear it at the wrong time—imagine being woken up by your favorite song in the middle of the night or hearing a voice calling your name in an empty room. The absence of expected sound is also an unexpected sound because we hear and react to it. Good understanding of the context and mastery of unexpectedness (like preceding a loud sound with a period of silence) is crucial to make audio appear more unpleasant and to make already unpleasant audio more efficient.

Models of Auditory Unpleasantness

The influence of nonacoustic factors and the many contradictions in the results of the experiments suggest that auditory unpleasantness cannot be reduced to acoustic factors alone. Hence, they are insufficient to build a model that explains auditory unpleasantness. But understanding the acoustic factors could still help us develop a reliable technique to design intrinsically unpleasant sounds that elicit the cognitive and emotional responses we need. A model that fails to explain everything but delivers predictable outcomes is good enough for practical use.

However, even this goal is nontrivial. Most of the listed features are very common for both video game sound effects and our natural soundscape. Still, most of the time, we are not disgusted, irritated, or scared of the sounds we hear—most likely because auditory unpleasantness emerges from the interplay of several factors. For instance, many studies referenced above mention screams as universally, intrinsically unpleasant sounds. By mimicking the acoustic structure of scream-like signals, we could reliably trigger unpleasant sensations in humans. But "scream-likeness" is a complex characteristic, seemingly dependent on roughness, nonlinearity, and spectral prominence of the frequency range between 2 and 4 kHz.

Fastl and Zwicker (2007, 243–246, 327–329) describe two models that could help better understand the intrinsic auditory unpleasantness. The model of sensory pleasantness, as the name suggests, describes how humans would judge the sound based on the perceptions of sharpness, roughness, loudness, and tonality (the only factor with positive correlation). The psychoacoustic annoyance model uses nearly the same set of parameters, having fluctuation strength instead of tonality.

With mathematical models available, we could build a tool to measure intrinsic unpleasantness. And if its outputs happen to be reliable, it could evolve into a real-time effect to control the unpleasantness of in-game sounds based on higher-level integrated parameters like narrative tension or threat level. The effect could either "horrifize" a familiar sound to scare the player or drastically neutralize an aggressive soundscape when they struggle with a tough challenge, similar to the "emotioneering" system proposed by Garner, Grimshaw, and Nabi (2010).

Three Lenses of Game Audio Design

Assume we know how to design an intrinsically unpleasant sound: how appropriate is it, then, in a video game? In order to aid in answering this question, I have devised a framework to assess sound, as an immediate product of sound design, from three perspectives. The framework has been inspired by Schell's *The Art of Game Design: A Book of Lenses* (2008) and Bridgett's proposition (2021, 94–96) that sound is designed for three audiences: player, spectator, and creator.

The Narrative Lens

Video games are interactive narrative[5] experiences. Non-story-focused games often have a narrative wrapper, and even very abstract games generate a narrative in the player's mind (Post 2009). From this perspective, unpleasant sounds are not just acceptable but often desired. First, to sonically represent the real-life objects that make unpleasant sounds—for example, police sirens, electric drills, or turbo engines. A fictional world with no unpleasant sounds would be hard to believe. Second, to modulate the player's emotional response, inducing the negative emotions we want them to experience. Strong negative emotions elicited by sound can help the player feel empathy toward their character and increase immersion. In horror games, such emotions lie at the core of the experience (Garner and Grimshaw 2011; Graja, Lopes, and Chanel 2020).

The Ludic Lens

Video games require active participation from the player. Unpleasant sounds can help and guide participation in a few ways, described in the next subsection. At the same time, there is a risk that these sounds become distracting, annoying, or cognitively demanding to the point when the sound itself adds an extra challenge to the overall experience. Dealing with unpleasant noise is rarely a fun challenge, and so, from the ludic perspective, unpleasant sounds are situational. They are helpful to reach specific design goals but should be avoided when there is no gameplay-relevant purpose.

The Product Lens

A commercially released video game is a digital entertainment product, something people interact with in their leisure time. People may dislike a product because of the unpleasant noise it makes.[6] A horrible-sounding game is no different, unless the audience expects it to sound horrible because of the genre, setting, or other attributes. Very few would complain about unsettling noises in a horror game. But the same sounds could shock or frustrate the players in a meditative puzzle.

The Product lens has another layer. Developers usually aim to provide a good experience specifically for the player, but we should not forget about others who share that player's sonic experience—friends, family members, cohabitants, or the audience on a streaming platform. Even if narratively appropriate or expected by the player, a sudden unpleasant noise may become a rather painful surprise for the spectators who did not consent to experience it. From the pure product perspective, unpleasant sounds are undesirable, except for the cases where product strategy or the audience expectations somehow justify their use.

The three lenses represent different points of view on this topic, suggesting we need to look for compromises. Depending on the game, we might prefer one lens over the other. In a story-driven horror game, we favor the Narrative lens, inducing fear in our audience. If we work on a casual puzzle game, we would better follow the Product lens, ensuring we do not stress out the players and whoever else hears the sounds we design. The Ludic lens could work best for competitive multiplayer games. At the same time, I advise against focusing on one lens to the extent that the other two are ignored. When we forget about the narrative lens, we end up with a sterile, soulless soundscape. Omit the ludic perspective, and the audio can become subversive for the gameplay experience. Ignoring the product perspective may result in an alienating soundscape.

Practical Applications

From the gameplay perspective, the intentional use of unpleasant sounds is situational. This section describes a few typical cases when intrinsically unpleasant sounds become synergetic with game design.

Attention Control

Human attentional resources are scarce. As game developers, we often need to control the player's attention to make them experience the game as intended. Hodent (2018, 56) writes: "You must direct players' attention to relevant information while minding their cognitive load to avoid overwhelming their working memory."

We have two modes of attention: top-down (goal-oriented) and bottom-up (stimulus-driven) (Katsuki and Constantinidis 2013). When we actively listen to something, we use top-down attention. If someone calls us by name, we notice it using the bottom-up attention and redirect our top-down attention to a different goal. Being a 360°, always-active sense, hearing is a perfect driver for bottom-up attention, especially when we hear a sound that triggers a visceral response. Threat-related stimuli generally cause strong and quick reactions (March, Gaertner, and Olson 2017). Thus, sounds we subconsciously associate with threats provide good means to attract the player's attention and ensure a faster reaction time.

The novel and significant sound can trigger an orienting reflex, forcing us to immediately focus our active attention on the source (Westman and Walters 1981; Bradley 2009). This response is useful when we want the player to turn or move their camera toward some object outside their field of view. We can also utilize an intrinsically unpleasant nondiegetic sound to alert the player about the state of their character's health or to make them notice a new notification on the screen. A snappy, alarming sound will cause the players to react faster than any other stimulus, which is vital in fast-paced competitive games.

When authored carefully, intrinsically unpleasant sounds are acceptable without a narrative justification: they do not need to signify something negative to be efficient. Since threat detection happens before we realize what the sound is (Kumar et al. 2012; Horowitz 2013, 114), the visceral reaction will drag the player's attention to the source of an intrinsically unpleasant sound before they decode the message it carries. The use of unpleasant sounds for attention control should be limited to the most important signs and notifications from the gameplay systems, especially when there is a risk that the player may miss them. If their value to the player is subjectively lower than their noticeability, they will distract the player from a more important goal, disrupting the gameplay experience. We also do not want feedback sounds to be intrinsically unpleasant unless we want to punish the player for their mistakes. The player is already tuned in to the sonic feedback from their actions, so extra noticeability via unpleasantness is excessive.

Learning and Motivation

Attention and memory are interconnected. People memorize things they pay more attention to, and paying attention costs memory resources. Since we pay more attention to unpleasant things, we see them as more impactful, memorize them better, and learn from them more efficiently. This effect is called "negativity bias." As Baumeister and others (2001) summarize it: "Bad is stronger than good." One way to use the negativity bias in game development is through teaching the players by punishing their mistakes. It is up to game designers to decide when to punish or reward the player, but, when needed, sound designers can support them, using unpleasant sound effects to teach the players to avoid specific actions. For instance, a sound can reinforce the existing punishment, like the loud impact that plays when the player-character is getting damage in *World of Tanks* (Wargaming 2010). Repetitive beeping noises, signifying low health state in game series like *The Legend of Zelda* (Nintendo 1986–present) or *Halo* (Xbox Game Studios 2001–present), act both as a warning and a punishment that irritates the player, incentivizing them to take action. In music-based rhythm games like *Rock Band* (MTV Games, Mad Catz, Harmonix 2007–2017) the sound that plays when the player makes a mistake becomes a punishment of its own.

In general, we use punishments to teach the player, not to make them feel miserable. Hence, punishing the player with sound works best to highlight the easy-to-avoid mistakes, but not failures or lack of skill. Punishing sounds are often the direct feedback to the player's (in)actions. The notorious exception is the aforementioned continuous warning sound that motivates the player to stop long-lasting effects like injury or poisoning. In this case, the desire to shut down the sound and "fix" the soundscape can push the player to deal with the problem faster.

Cognitive Load Management

The soundscape has a significant effect on task performance (Westman and Walters 1981). Since unpleasant sounds are cognitively demanding on their own, there is a risk of overwhelming the player with them. Too much unpleasant audio may massively increase the extraneous cognitive load the player experiences. Moreover, once the player realizes that the soundscape affects their ability to solve a difficult challenge or get to the goal, they may turn down the volume or switch the sound off. I could imagine some niche cases when adding extraneous cognitive load is good for the game, like a single challenge to decipher a hidden message in a heavily distorted audio signal. Still, scenarios in which this might be entertaining are relatively uncommon.

Instead of using unpleasant sounds to overwhelm the player, designers could put some effort into reducing or neutralizing them in cognitively demanding scenes. Think of an intense car chase in an action video game. Should the police sirens stay equally loud throughout the sequence, or could we bring them down to reduce the player's cognitive load? The answer depends on the design goal, but we cannot make a rational choice unless we ask this question.

Modulating Emotional Response

So far, I've described how we can use unpleasant sounds to trigger particular behavior via quick emotional responses. But the emotional response is often a design goal of its own. We might want the player to feel fear, discomfort, or disgust not because we want them to do something in the game but because these emotions are the part of the experience we design. Many horror games like the *Resident Evil* series (Capcom 1996–present) capitalize on unpleasant sounds being one of the key drivers of the horror experience. The connection between sound and emotional reactions is a large topic that stretches beyond the scope of this chapter. Garner, Grimshaw, and others carefully explored the relationship between sound, emotion (especially fear), and immersion in games, and I recommend reading their works for a deeper view on this topic (Grimshaw 2009; Garner, Grimshaw, and Nabi 2010; Garner and Grimshaw 2011; Garner and Grimshaw 2013; Garner 2016).

Intrinsically unpleasant audio is useful to elicit generally unpleasant emotions, but not necessarily *specific* emotional reactions. The influence of nonacoustic factors and the complexity of our cognitive processes prevent us from having straightforward recipes in the format of "Do X to make them feel Y." But we can still look at the broader principles and notorious exceptions. The sounds that communicate a direct threat can trigger the fight-or-flight reaction and defensive response. When unexpected and loud enough, such sounds can startle us. Both the startle and the defensive responses are psychophysiological reactions that arouse us and elicit the sensation of fear (Westman and Walters 1981). Horror games that heavily rely on jump scares[7] often use sound to trigger the startle response in players. The defensive response may depend on prior conditioning (teaching the player that this specific sound means danger) but can also be elicited with acoustic factors like roughness (Taffou, Suied, and Viaud-Delmon 2021).

The *Silent Hill* series (Konami 1999–2024) masterfully elicits emotions like anxiety and apprehension with ambiguous, difficult to recognize sounds. *Amnesia: The Dark Descent* (Frictional Games 2010) disorients the players with loud, persistent and unpredictable noise. Annoyance is easy to trigger with steady or repetitive sounds the player cannot control. Unexpected sonic feedback or lack of expected sound may confuse and alert the player. An unexpected sound that comes from an obscure source is likely to be alarming or scary. And all of those sounds will likely become more effective when they are intrinsically unpleasant.

Sometimes we need to avoid intrinsically unpleasant sounds even when they are narratively appropriate. A perfect example is a clean, soft, and almost soothing bomb explosion sound, commonly used in modern casual puzzle games like *Homescapes* (Playrix 2017). The developers of these games usually want the player to feel safe and relaxed. But an explosion is a loud, boomy, noisy, and rough event that could put the player in a different emotional state. To prevent this, sound designers address the acoustic properties that make the explosion intrinsically unpleasant and turn it into a much softer, though still contextually valid, sound.

Conclusion

The chapter assumes that we perceive sounds as intrinsically unpleasant when something in their acoustic structure communicates a threat, disorients us, or indicates our vulnerability. We cannot reduce auditory unpleasantness to acoustic factors alone, but evidence shows that some features can reliably trigger unpleasant sensations. Even though the precise model of intrinsic auditory unpleasantness does not yet exist (or is not accessible to game audio professionals), there is enough evidence about individual acoustic features that could serve as its foundation.

Not all acoustic features are easy to control in the video game context, and not all of them may trigger the right kind of unpleasantness for a particular scene or a gameplay event. Through the lens of my own experience, I see the scream-like acoustic structure as the most reliable (but not the only) predictor that the sound will be intrinsically unpleasant in a video game context. "Scream-likeness" is typical for notoriously scary video game sound effects, such as Stalker's vocalizations in *Dead Space 2* (Electronic Arts 2011), or the "Terror meter" sound that plays when the player is chased by a monster in *Amnesia: The Dark Descent* (Frictional Games 2010). The scream-like acoustic structure seemingly results from an interplay of roughness, nonlinearity, and spectral prominence of the region between 2 and 4 kHz. Other features mentioned in the chapter could contribute to the sensation.

I have constructed this chapter in such a way that the solution (how to design an unpleasant sound?) precedes the problem (why do we need unpleasant sound in a game?), but I need to explicitly say that the "why" should always come first. The mere appropriateness of unpleasant audio in a game is easy to question; its presence should solve a meaningful ludic or narrative goal, if not both.

From the gameplay perspective, unpleasant audio is helpful to attract and control the player's attention, trigger an immediate reaction, help the players learn game rules and mechanics, or elicit emotional responses like fear and anxiety. Many more use cases could be specific to particular genres and projects. In an open-world RPG, we could use unpleasant sounds to indirectly communicate that enemies in the new area are too tough for the current character level. In a high-risk/reward action game, an annoying sound can taunt a player, provoking them to make a reckless move. And there could be many other cases that lie beyond my knowledge and experience.

Since unpleasant sounds are often narratively appropriate, their presence may sometimes disrupt the gameplay experience. On such occasions, sound designers could deliberately attempt to neutralize the negative effects. As a result, they could reduce the number of distractions, get rid of unfair punishments, decrease the cognitive load the player experiences, and better support the emotional state the game has been designed for.

The approach to sound design I demonstrate in this essay is oriented toward effective collaboration and synergies with other development departments. Even though the chapter focuses on a narrow topic, it illustrates how audio designers can do more than support visuals on the screen. When we use sound to solve player-experience problems, we ensure that audio becomes an integral part of the game, not a service that can be "applied" on top of a ready product. This way, we can influence the recognition of our craft in the game industry and improve the quality of the games we develop.

Notes

1. This section is heavily grounded in an earlier article I wrote on a similar topic for my blog (Zlobin 2020).
2. The 15–300 Hz range is defined for modulation frequency, not the lower end of the acoustic spectrum that audio professionals typically deal with.
3. "Less pleasant" doesn't automatically mean "more unpleasant." In a way, a noisier spectrum could just make otherwise pleasant sounds appear more neutral.
4. Type of noise that has equal energy per octave, so the signal intensity is inversely proportional to the frequency.
5. There are many definitions of "video game narrative." In this chapter, I follow the one given by Thomas Grip (2014) who defines it as "the totality of the experience" and "the player's subjective journey through the game."
6. Alongside a variety of noisy children's toys that drive adults mad, there was a notorious case of a very loud package of potato chips that led to a flood of complaints from the customers and a decline in sales (Wilburn and Wilburn 2015)
7. Sudden audiovisual changes, introduced to scare the audience by surprise.

References

Alves, Valter, and Licínio Roque. 2010. "Guidelines for Sound Design in Computer Games." In *Game Sound Technology and Player Interaction*, edited by Mark Grimshaw, 362–383. https://doi.org/10.4018/978-1-61692-828-5.ch017.

Arnal, Luc H., Adeen Flinker, Andreas Kleinschmidt, Anne-Lise Giraud, and David Poeppel. 2015. "Human Screams Occupy a Privileged Niche in the Communication Soundscape." *Current Biology* 25 (15): 2051–2056. https://doi.org/10.1016/j.cub.2015.06.043.

Bach, Dominik R., John G. Neuhoff, Walter Perrig, and Erich Seifritz. 2009. "Looming Sounds as Warning Signals: The Function of Motion Cues." *International Journal of Psychophysiology* 74 (1): 28–33. https://doi.org/10.1016/j.ijpsycho.2009.06.004.

Bach, Dominik R., Hartmut Schachinger, John G. Neuhoff, Fabrizio Esposito, Francesco Di Salle, Christoph Lehmann, Marcus Herdener, Klaus Scheffler, and Erich Seifritz. 2007. "Rising Sound Intensity: An Intrinsic Warning Cue Activating the Amygdala." *Cerebral Cortex* 18 (1): 145–150. https://doi.org/10.1093/cercor/bhm040.

Baumeister, Roy F., Ellen Bratslavsky, Catrin Finkenauer, and Kathleen D. Vohs. 2001. "Bad Is Stronger Than Good." *Review of General Psychology* 5 (4): 323–370. https://doi.org/10.1037/1089-2680.5.4.323.

Blesdoe, Ellen K., and Daniel T. Blumstein. 2014. "What Is the Sound of Fear? Behavioral Responses of White-Crowned Sparrows *Zonotrichia Leucophrys* to Synthesized Nonlinear Acoustic Phenomena." *Current Zoology* 60 (4): 534–541. https://doi.org/10.1093/czoolo/60.4.534.

Blumstein, Daniel T., Richard Davitian, and Peter D. Kaye. 2010. "Do Film Soundtracks Contain Nonlinear Analogues to Influence Emotion?" *Biology Letters* 6 (6): 751–754. https://doi.org/10.1098/rsbl.2010.0333.

Bradley, Margaret M. 2009. "Natural Selective Attention: Orienting and Emotion." *Psychophysiology* 46 (1): 1–11. https://doi.org/10.1111/j.1469-8986.2008.00702.x.

Bridgett, Rob. 2021. *Leading with Sound*. Kindle ed. Abingdon: Taylor and Francis.

Cho, Jayoung, Eunjou Yi, and Gilsoo Cho. 2001. "Physiological Responses Evoked by Fabric Sounds and Related Mechanical and Acoustical Properties." *Textile Research Journal* 71 (12): 1068–1073. https://doi.org/10.1177/004051750107101206.

Edworthy, Judy, Sarah Loxley, and Ian Dennis. 1991. "Improving Auditory Warning Design: Relationship between Warning Sound Parameters and Perceived Urgency." *Human Factors: The Journal of the Human Factors and Ergonomics Society* 33 (2): 205–231. https://doi.org/10.1177/001872089103300206.

Ekman, Inger, and Raine Kajastila. 2009. "Localization Cues Affect Emotional Judgments—Results from a User Study on Scary Sound." In *AES 35th International Conference: Audio for Games*. AES E-Library. http://www.aes.org/e-lib/browse.cfm?elib=15177.

Ellermeier, Wolfgang, Alfred Zeitler, and Hugo Fastl. 2004. "Predicting Annoyance Judgments from Psychoacoustic Metrics: Identifiable versus Neutralized Sounds." In *INTER-NOISE and NOISE-CON Congress and Conference Proceedings*, 1322–1327. https://www.ingentaconnect.com/contentone/ince/incecp/2004/00002004/00000007/art00093.

Ellermeier, Wolfgang, Markus Mader, and Peter Daniel. 2004. "Scaling the Unpleasantness of Sounds According to the BTL Model: Ratio-Scale Representation and Psychoacoustical Analysis." *Acustica United with Acta Acustica* 90 (1): 101–107.

Farnell, Andy. 2010. *Designing Sound*. Cambridge, MA: MIT Press.

Fastl, Hugo, and Eberhard Zwicker. 2007. *Psychoacoustics: Facts and Models*. 3rd ed. Berlin; Heidelberg: Springer.

Garner, Tom A. 2016. "From Sinewaves to Physiologically-Adaptive Soundscapes: The Evolving Relationship between Sound and Emotion in Video Games." *Emotion in Games*, 197–214. https://doi.org/10.1007/978-3-319-41316-7_12.

Garner, Tom, and Mark Grimshaw. 2011. "A Climate of Fear." Proceedings of the 6th Audio Mostly Conference. New York: ACM. https://doi.org/10.1145/2095667.2095672.

Garner, Tom Alexander, and Mark Grimshaw. 2013. "Psychophysiological Assessment of Fear Experience in Response to Sound during Computer Video Gameplay." In *International Conference Interfaces and Human Computer Interaction*, 45–53. Prague: International Association for Development, IADIS.

Garner, Tom, Mark Grimshaw, and Debbie Abdel Nabi. 2010. "A Preliminary Experiment to Assess the Fear Value of Preselected Sound Parameters in a Survival Horror Game." *Proceedings of the 5th Audio Mostly Conference*. New York: ACM. https://doi.org/10.1145/1859799.1859809.

Geissner, Emilie, and Etienne Parizet. 2007. "Continuous Assessment of the Unpleasantness of a Sound." *Acta Acustica United with Acustica* 93 (3): 469–476.

Graja, Sarra, Phil Lopes, and Guillaume Chanel. 2020. "Impact of Visual and Sound Orchestration on Physiological Arousal and Tension in a Horror Game." *IEEE Transactions on Games* 13 (3): 287–299. https://doi.org/10.1109/tg.2020.3006053.

Grimshaw, Mark. 2009. "The Audio Uncanny Valley: Sound, Fear and the Horror Game." In *Audio Mostly 4th Conference on Interaction with Sound*.

Grip, Thomas. 2014. "4-Layers, a Narrative Design Approach." *Game Developer*. https://www.gamedeveloper.com/design/4-layers-a-narrative-design-approach.

Gwilliams, Laura, Tal Linzen, David Poeppel, and Alec Marantz. 2018. "In Spoken Word Recognition, the Future Predicts the Past." *Journal of Neuroscience* 38 (35): 7585–7599. https://doi.org/10.1523/jneurosci.0065-18.2018.

Hall, Deborah A., Amy Irwin, Mark Edmondson-Jones, Scott Phillips, and John E. W. Poxon. 2013. "An Exploratory Evaluation of Perceptual, Psychoacoustic and Acoustical Properties of Urban Soundscapes." *Applied Acoustics* 74 (2): 248–254. https://doi.org/10.1016/j.apacoust.2011.03.006.

Halpern, D. Lynn, Randolph Blake, and James Hillenbrand. 1986. "Psychoacoustics of a Chilling Sound." *Perception and Psychophysics* 39 (2): 77–80. https://doi.org/10.3758/bf03211488.

Hansen, John H. L., Mahesh Kumar Nandwana, and Navid Shokouhi. 2017. "Analysis of Human Scream and Its Impact on Text-Independent Speaker Verification." *Journal of the Acoustical Society of America* 141 (4): 2957–2967. https://doi.org/10.1121/1.4979337.

Helmholtz, Hermann L. F. 2009/1875. *On the Sensations of Tone as a Physiological Basis for the Theory of Music*. Translated by Alexander J. Ellis. Cambridge: Cambridge University Press.

Hodent, Celia. 2018. *The Gamer's Brain*. Boca Raton: CRC Press.

Horowitz, Seth. 2013. *The Universal Sense*. Kindle ed. Bloomsbury: Bloomsbury Publishing.

Jain, Aditya, Ramta Bansal, Avnish Kumar, and K. D. Singh. 2015. "A Comparative Study of Visual and Auditory Reaction Times on the Basis of Gender and Physical Activity Levels of Medical First Year Students." *International Journal of Applied and Basic Medical Research* 5 (2): 124–127. https://doi.org/10.4103/2229-516X.157168.

Katsuki, F., and Constantinidis, C. 2013. "Bottom-Up and Top-Down Attention." *Neuroscientist* 20 (5): 509–521.

Kumar, Sukhbinder, Helen M. Forster, Peter Bailey, and Timothy D. Griffiths. 2008. "Mapping Unpleasantness of Sounds to Their Auditory Representation." *Journal of the Acoustical Society of America* 124 (6): 3810–3817. https://doi.org/10.1121/1.3006380.

Kumar, Sukhbinder, Katharina von Kriegstein, Karl Friston, and Timothy D. Griffiths. 2012. "Features versus Feelings: Dissociable Representations of the Acoustic Features and Valence of Aversive Sounds." *Journal of Neuroscience* 32 (41): 14184–14192. https://doi.org/10.1523/jneurosci.1759-12.2012.

Kurakata, Kenji, Tazu Mizunami, and Kazuma Matsushita. 2013. "Sensory Unpleasantness of High-Frequency Sounds." *Acoustical Science and Technology* 34 (1): 26–33. https://doi.org/0.1250/ast.34.26.

Landwehr, Jan R., and Lisa Eckmann. 2020. "The Nature of Processing Fluency: Amplification versus Hedonic Marking." *Journal of Experimental Social Psychology* 90:103997. https://doi.org/10.1016/j.jesp.2020.103997.

March, David S., Lowell Gaertner, and Michael A. Olson. 2017. "In Harm's Way: On Preferential Response to Threatening Stimuli." *Personality and Social Psychology Bulletin* 43 (11): 1519–1529. https://doi.org/10.1177/0146167217722558.

Pannese, Alessia, Didier Grandjean, and Sascha Frühholz. 2016. "Amygdala and Auditory Cortex Exhibit Distinct Sensitivity to Relevant Acoustic Features of Auditory Emotions." *Cortex* 85:116–125. https://doi.org/10.1016/j.cortex.2016.10.013.

Post, Jack. 2009. "Bridging the Narratology-Ludology Divide: The *Tetris* Case." *Computer Games between Text and Practice* III (5): 31–36.

Reber, Rolf, Piotr Winkielman, and Norbert Schwarz. 1998. "Effects of Perceptual Fluency on Affective Judgments." *Psychological Science* 9 (1): 45–48. https://doi.org/10.1111/1467-9280.00008.

Repp, Bruno H., and Amandine Penel. 2002. "Auditory Dominance in Temporal Processing: New Evidence from Synchronization with Simultaneous Visual and Auditory Sequences." *Journal of Experimental Psychology: Human Perception and Performance* 28 (5): 1085–1099. https://doi.org/10.1037/0096-1523.28.5.1085.

Reuter, Christoph, Michael Oehler, and Jörg Helmut Mühlhans. 2014. "Physiological and Acoustical Correlates of Unpleasant Sounds." In *Joint Conference ICMPC13-APSCOM5*. http://dx.doi.org/10.13140/2.1.2914.6249.

Russell, James A. 1980. "A Circumplex Model of Affect." *Journal of Personality and Social Psychology* 39 (6): 1161–1178. https://doi.org/10.1037/h0077714.

Santee, Jeffrey L., and David L. Kohfeld. 1977. "Auditory Reaction Time as a Function of Stimulus Intensity, Frequency, and Rise Time." *Bulletin of the Psychonomic Society* 10 (5): 393–396. https://doi.org/10.3758/bf03329370.

Schell, Jesse. 2008. *The Art of Game Design: A Book of Lenses*. Amsterdam: Elsevier/Morgan Kaufmann.

Skagerstrand, Åsa, Susanne Köbler, and Stefan Stenfelt. 2017. "Loudness and Annoyance of Disturbing Sounds: Perception by Normal Hearing Subjects." *International Journal of Audiology* 56 (10): 775–783. https://doi.org/10.1080/14992027.2017.1321790.

Solanki, Jayesh, Naisargi Joshi, Chinmay Shah, H. B. Mehta, and P. A. Gokhle. 2012. "A Study of Correlation between Auditory and Visual Reaction Time in Healthy Adults." *International Journal of Medicine and Public Health* 2 (2): 36–38. https://doi.org/10.5530/ijmedph.2.2.8.

Steel, Daniel, and Song Hui Chon. 2007. "A Perceptual Study of Sound Annoyance." In *Audio Mostly 2007—2nd Conference on Interaction with Sound*, 19–24.

Stevens, Richard, and Dave Raybould. 2015. "The Reality Paradox: Authenticity, Fidelity and the Real in *Battlefield 4*." *Soundtrack* 8 (1): 57–65. https://doi.org/10.1386/st.8.1-2.57_1.

Subedi, Jishnu K., Hiroki Yamaguchi, Yasunao Matsumoto, and Mitsutaka Ishihara. 2005. "Annoyance of Low Frequency Tones and Objective Evaluation Methods." *Journal of Low Frequency Noise, Vibration and Active Control* 24 (2): 81–95. https://doi.org/10.1260/0263092054531000.

Taffou, Marine, Clara Suied, and Isabelle Viaud-Delmon. 2021. "Auditory Roughness Elicits Defense Reactions." *Scientific Reports* 11 (1). https://doi.org/10.1038/s41598-020-79767-0.

Trevor, Caitlyn, Luc H. Arnal, and Sascha Frühholz. 2020. "Terrifying Film Music Mimics Alarming Acoustic Feature of Human Screams." *Journal of the Acoustical Society of America* 147 (6): EL540-EL545. https://doi.org/10.1121/10.0001459.

Weber, Reinhard, and Reef Eilers. 2007. "Combined Contribution of Roughness and Sharpness to the Unpleasantness of Modulated Band Pass Noise." In *DAGA '07*, 565–566. Stuttgart: Deutsche Gesellschaft für Akustik.

Westman, Jack C., and James R. Walters. 1981. "Noise and Stress: A Comprehensive Approach." *Environmental Health Perspectives* 41: 291–309. https://doi.org/10.1289/ehp.8141291.

Whalen, Paul J. 2007. "The Uncertainty of It All." *Trends in Cognitive Sciences* 11 (12): 499–500. https://doi.org/10.1016/j.tics.2007.08.016.

Wilburn, Kathleen, and Wilburn, Ralph. 2015. "Social Purpose in a Social Media World." *Journal of Global Responsibility* 6 (2): 163–177.

Zlobin, Denis. 2020. "Deconstructing Unpleasantness in Videogame Sound Effects: Part 1: Theory." https://uxdesign.cc/deconstructing-unpleasantness-in-videogame-sound-effects-part-1-theory-191b660b1a2b.

Zlobin, Denis. 2021. "Ludic and Narrative Sound in Games." https://uxdesign.cc/ludic-and-narrative-sound-in-games-3fc52dbbfee1.

Ludology

Amnesia: The Dark Descent. 2010. Frictional Games.
Dead Space 2. 2011. Electronic Arts.
Halo. 2001–present. Xbox Game Studios.
Homescapes. 2017. Playrix.
Resident Evil. 1996–present. Capcom.
Rock Band. 2007–2017. MTV Games, Mad Catz, Harmonix.
Silent Hill. 1999–2024. Konami.
The Legend of Zelda. 1986–present. Nintendo.
World of Tanks. 2010. Wargaming.

CHAPTER 47

THE IMPORTANCE OF SOUND TO THE FORMATION OF PRESENCE

MARK GRIMSHAW-AAGAARD

INTRODUCTION

THIS essay constitutes a certain tying together of various strands in my past research that have often separately covered sound (its definition and perception) and presence (and the part sound plays in its formation). The implicit aim in this past research has been a thoroughgoing understanding and conceptualization of the phenomenon of presence in both of what are colloquially termed virtual worlds and the real world. As I show here, the term and concept of "presence" are both contested and subject to various interpretations and splintering depending on the field of enquiry in which they are used. My ultimate aim is to provide clarity and discipline to the field of presence; I am aware that this is a somewhat quixotic endeavor, but the journey is interesting nonetheless.

The purpose of this chapter is to highlight the role of sound and hearing in the formation of presence, a role that, hitherto, has suffered in comparison to image and sight. I begin by defining some terminology and limits to my inquiry that provide the framework within which to proceed. In some of this terminology, I follow common usage; elsewhere, because of conflicting usage and confusion, I make and justify decisions as to which form I decide on. The terminology I define and explain in this section includes: *first-person perspective games* and the presentation of audio within them; *externality* and *self*, allowing me to set up conceptions of *environment*, *potential*, and *reality* as a means to explicate presence; and *sound* as opposed to a sound wave. Following this, I briefly survey past and current conceptions of presence ending that section by focusing on the concepts as used in virtual reality and video games (in which it is often conflated with the concept of immersion). Finally, I state the case for my contention that sound warrants more attention when designing virtual worlds such as first-person perspective video games than it has previously been given.

Terminology

Audio and the First-Person-Perspective Video Game

For the purposes of this essay, I focus on first-person-perspective video games. Such games, most prominently first-person shooter games, provide the player with a view on the game world that encodes western artistic perspective and tricks of parallax in the arrangement of pixels presented on the flat, 2-dimensionality of the computer monitor or television screen. The 3-dimensionality is presented as the view the player would have were they physically in the game world, an illusory perspective often aided by the presentation of the player's avatar's arms receding into the screen from the bottom of the monitor. Notably, there is no representation of nose or eye superstructure that a human can see, presumably because these would interfere with the action taking place on the screen. Importantly, unlike a platform scroller game, for example, the player in a first-person-perspective game typically has a great deal of latitude in moving his or her character around the game world, and it is here that the concept of first-person audition comes into play.

While the positioning of the apparent sound wave source in the 3-dimensionality of the game world is fairly primitive compared to the case for the real world—and this primitivity is further compounded by the use of loudspeakers (stereo or surround systems) or headphones—it does provide a good degree of localization of sound wave source within the game world, and importantly, it expands that world beyond what can be seen on the screen. While the player is free to explore the game world in any lateral direction (and often vertical too, depending on the design of the game world), this is often done in response to the perceived location of a sound wave source. The programming of the audio shifts around the player's character as the player moves or rotates, giving the illusion that the player is moving in space as in the real world. Sound wave sources might be perceived as being off-screen to the left, right, out of sight in the distance, or even behind the player's character, and it is this centering of the character (and, by extension, the player themself) within the game world's audio field, this first-person audition, that, more so than first-person perspective which merely places the player in front of an unfolding visual tableau, allows the player to perceive their conception of self as being at the center of, and thus within, the game world.

Despite all its sensorial shortcomings in comparison—lack of smell, taste, sense of gravity and temperature, a primitive visual sensory field, and no tactility or little to speak of—the first-person-perspective video game, through its first-person audition, provides the framework that is somewhat analogous to hearing in the real world, and with which we are able to bootstrap our sense of presence in the game world.

Externality and Self

How I make use of sensations from audio in the first-person perspective video game is clearly important to an understanding of the role sound has in the formation of the feeling of presence. If I am present, I am present somewhere and at some present time, and, along with other sensations (in this context, mainly visual), I leverage the spatiotemporality of sound and derive meaning from it with which to form a construct of space and time in which to be present. Figure 47.1 provides a simple schematic of a framework for understanding this process. Space does not allow me to go into greater detail—for a deeper explanation, I direct the reader to previous work where, with my colleague Mads Walther-Hansen, an early version of the schematic was explicated (Walther-Hansen and Grimshaw-Aagaard 2020).

On the left of Figure 47.1 is *externality*. This comprises *potential* of which some, but by no means all, is available to be sensed by sensing organisms. This *sensable externality* differs from species to species—for example, while electromagnetism is sensable to some creatures, humans are not able naturally to sense it, nor, in terms of audition, are they able to sense anthropocentrically defined infrasound and ultrasound. From

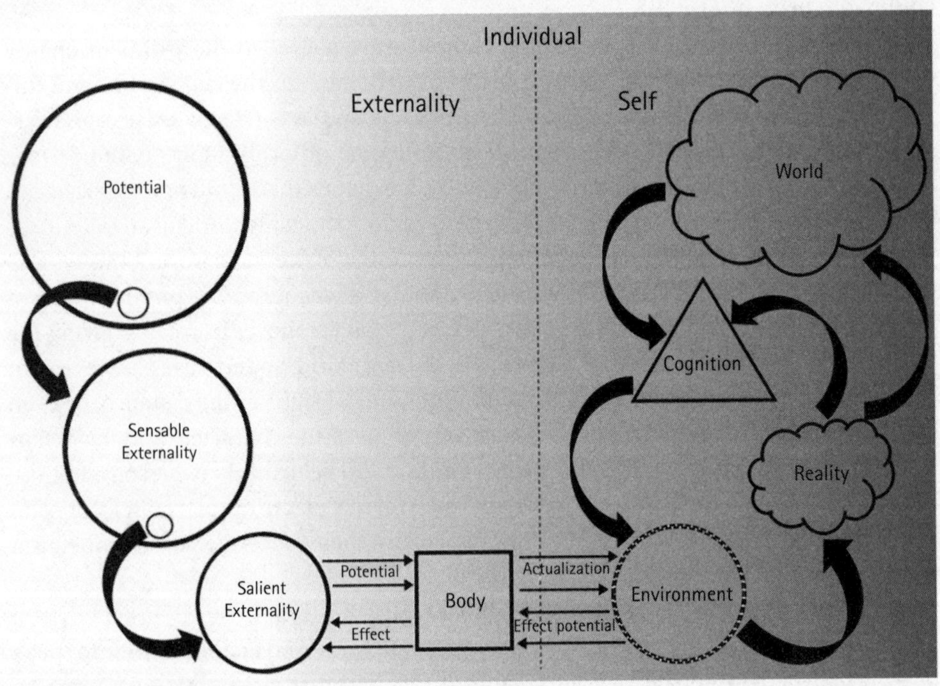

FIGURE 47.1 Externality and self.

within the highly constrained subset that is sensable externality, we are able to sense a small set of potential that I define as *salient externality*. Some of this we are consciously aware of, and so are perceptually able to label and categorize it—that part of salient externality that we are able to define as a car passing by in the street, for example. Other aspects of salient externality we are only subconsciously aware of. That is to say, we do not need to choose to be aware of, or be made to focus on, all such potential, but our brain is still processing it and utilizing it. An example might be the particular spatial acoustic quality of a space that we become consciously aware of only when it is brought to our attention or we pause to assess it, but which, nevertheless, our brain is always using to aid in the forming of presence. While sensable externality is what *can* be sensed, salient externality is that which *is* sensed—I cannot see what is behind me but could do so should I choose to turn around. Finally, our material body provides the means to *actualize* potential as sensation—the pathway from acoustic energy to electrical energy that is in our auditory physiology, for example—and, in turn, if it derives from salient externality, this actualized potential forms part of my conception of self because it defines nonself.

On the right of Figure 47.1 is the *self*. The self is everything that externality is not. Its source is the brain's knowledge and understanding and the cognitive processing of salient externality which, as noted above, might be conscious or subconscious. The *environment* is a dynamic working model of salient externality formed by the interplay between cognition and the actualization of potential. Cognition, as the use of knowledge and understanding, is brought to bear on actualized potential, sensation, to form the model of salient externality in which we are present, and thus I am then able to use my body to then operate on salient externality and beyond. *Reality* is my conscious experience of the environment. It is a highly filtered and mediated view of externality. As my environment is dynamic—always shifting as my cognition acts on new sensation—so too is my reality. Reality is by no means static and is, like the environment, emergent. As the experience of the environment, reality is conscious and, in terms of the self's time, present. The reflex action of turning my head toward a sudden and loud sound wave source (of which I only later become aware of the experience) is not a part of my reality, but it does require an environment in which to reflexively act. But directed action in the environment is a part of my reality as I am conscious of the experience of it. The *world* I define as a selected store of experience from past realities (gained through direct experience or vicariously through, for instance, reading a newspaper). This is my store of facts and knowledge about how to do things—my understanding. It does not need to come from my present salient externality for me to know that a certain thing is going on in externality—the sun setting somewhere while I write this on a sunny morning here, for example. This store drives cognition, which is the directed (consciously or not) use of knowledge and understanding contained in the world. Cognition makes use of past realities (the world) but also makes use of present reality to create the model of salient externality (the environment), and this allows the self to act within this environment. This action can affect salient externality (mine and other's) and is effected through my body as when I lift a coffee cup toward my mouth—I need to understand *about* coffee and cups, but I also need to have the *experience* in the present that the coffee cup is sitting there before me for me to be able to reach out and grasp its handle.

Sound

As should be clear by now, I carefully make a distinction between a sound wave and a sound. Although the official (i.e., natural sciences) definition of sound is: "(a) Oscillation in pressure, stress, particle displacement, particle velocity etc., propagated in a medium with internal forces (e.g. elastic or viscous) or the superposition of such propagated oscillation" or the "(b) Auditory sensation evoked by the oscillation described in (a)" (Accredited Standards Committee S1, Acoustics 2013, 1), I have elsewhere argued against this (Grimshaw 2015; Grimshaw and Garner 2015) as have others (Pasnau 1999; O'Callaghan 2007). Accordingly, I will be brief here.

While the standard dictionary definition of sound follows definition (a) above (sound is a sound wave), our everyday usage of the term "sound" is quite different and is a result of the actualization of sound wave potential and its cognitive processing based on our world store. It is a perception that can form part of a percept; both contribute to my environment, and I have an *experience* of both as part of my reality—*your* ultimate experience of the same sound wave might well be quite different.[1] As Heidegger notes (see below), this percept is usually related to the general sound wave source in externality (a wagon, a motorcycle, and so forth),[2] and our *description* of the sound as perception (part of our experience of the environment as our reality) sometimes points to the sound wave source (e.g., a mechanical sound—it is artificial to describe a sound by its sound wave properties of frequency, intensity, and so on) and sometimes toward the affective quality of the sound (e.g., a dark sound or a sharp sound). This latter, in particular, illustrates the multimodal nature of sound in its recourse to descriptive language drawn from other modalities (sensory-perceptual channels)—here, vision and touch. The McGurk Effect is another example of the multimodality of sound; in this case, how vision affects our hearing. In this so-called auditory illusion, two different articulations of the speaker's mouth in a video effect the sound we hear, even though the same audio recording (and thus the same sound wave) is used over the two clips of video. Of particular interest here is the cognitive challenge presented to my self in forming the ultimate percept of a syllable which, in regard to the sound wave at least, is in one case utterly wrong.

My localization of sound, according to the framework of sonic virtuality (Garner and Grimshaw 2014), plays a large part in the spatial foundation of my environment. Within the fields of acoustics and psychoacoustics, the localization of sound is the process of locating the actual source in externality of a sound wave. Were this to really be the case, and my stereophonic auditory apparatus the sole means, then a large part of externality would simply not make sense. Rather, as sonic virtuality has it, the localization of sound is the directed placement of sound in the environment according to where it might best be placed to form an adequate, working model of salient externality.

Take the case of playing a first-person-perspective video game such as a first-person shooter. In externality, sound wave sources are the vibrating diaphragms of headphones or loudspeakers. If I were to localize sound on such sources, it is highly unlikely that I would be able to play the game at all, much less design such a video game with current technology. Rather, in modeling salient externality as an environment, I place sound as perception within my environment, to which are matched the perceptions of graphical events and objects and perspectival space that I see on the flat screen before me. Thus, the sharp, percussive sound wave emanating from a loudspeaker diaphragm to my front left in externality, forms the basis of the percept of an enemy rushing toward me and firing a gun in my direction. The coding of the game, my salient externality, and the cognitive leveraging of my world provide the means to locate sound where it gives the best meaning, where it makes sense to place it in the environment, allowing for a more efficient attainment of presence. Thus, the environment is not just a model of salient externality, but it is also a reordering of it in order to provide a more commodious and meaningful reality.

Presence

A working definition of presence is that it is the sense or feeling of being in a place and the ability to act within and upon that place. This, at least, is the essence of presence as used in telepresence and virtual reality (e.g., Minsky 1980; IJsselsteijn, Freeman, and de Ridder 2001; Slater 2003), and such a definition feeds through to the design of video games—particularly first-person-perspective games, where the term is often conflated with "immersion" (see Grimshaw 2012; Calleja 2014, for example). Immersion, as an analog to presence, is an important marketing device for developers of first-person perspective games and is the term most often used by reviewers and players themselves.[3] However, in common with Slater (2003) discussing the concepts of immersion and presence in virtual reality, I have more recently preferred to make a distinction: presence is the psychological effect (as in the working definition above) that is delivered by the immersive potential of the technology. In other words, immersion is an objective measure, and the more immersive the technology is, the more likely that the user of that technology (viz. the player of video games) will experience presence. While there are problems with this distinction that I have discussed elsewhere (Walther-Hansen and Grimshaw-Aagaard 2020), it is a useful one. Here, then, I am discussing presence as a psychological experience created by immersive technology, and the reader should subsume the term "immersion" (as found in video game literature both popular and academic) under the general term "presence."

If we take it as a given that the player in a first-person perspective game is indeed able to act within and on that place—that is, that the player, via their character, can navigate the game world, open doors, shoot enemies, and so on in the same way that a user can navigate and edit a computer document or operate a remote robot on Mars—then I must briefly deal with the question: *How does the player attain the feeling part of the presence definition?*

If one answer is that the feeling of presence in so-called virtual worlds is enabled by the immersive technology delivering the same potential as that found in the externality of the so-called real world—in other words, presence in virtual worlds is the same as presence in the real world—then this is a good first step. However, that still leaves one wondering how we can experience such presence when the potential delivered by video game technology is so impoverished in comparison? There is only light wave and sound wave potential; with few exceptions there is no tactility, and no potential to actualize sensations of smell or taste let alone sensations of mass and temperature.

The answer, according to Lee (2004, 39), is that "imagination and other information-processing mechanisms simulate the remaining sensory cues and create a compelling sense of reality." This is how it is in the real world, too. I do not need to see my neighbor to be able to picture his actions (currently vacuuming) and to place him in various rooms of his apartment from the sounds of footsteps in the ceiling above me. The cleverly and artificially crafted photographs of restaurant dishes on a menu stimulate me to imagine the taste, smell, and texture of the dishes—even words alone are capable of this if the words are well chosen. As I jump from the top of a building in a video game, I do not need to feel the pressure on my joints and the pain in my body: imagining my mass hitting the concrete is enabled through a well-crafted sound effect.

Imagination is essential to crafting a sufficiently workable environment in which to be present, filling in the gaps that are there in actualized potential. The dynamic model of externality, virtual or actual, is where my self is present rather than in externality itself. Reality, in its everyday usage, is simply not real enough, and imagination, making use of our concept of the world, is necessary to the model of externality in which to be present.[4]

The above definition and description of presence is one that I term "self-presence": how my self attains the feeling of presence in the environment in order to control my body in acting within and on externality. My body is physically in externality, but my self is present in the environment. This is a concept of the environment as a metonym of salient externality—as my body, like the player's character, operates in externality, that externality is remodeled in the dynamic environment. But it is not just my self that is present in the environment; the environment itself comprises other-presences that manifest as percepts. A distinction should be made between self-presence (the "presence" of the definition above) and other-presence (what forms the "place" of the definition above), and the role of other-presence in the formation of self-presence should not be neglected.

As a model of salient externality, the environment must perforce comprise models of aspects of externality in order to provide the perceptual space in which my self can attain self-presence. I must feel present in a model of somewhere to be able to act within and on that somewhere. The environment comprises percepts that are other-present to my self—self-presence cannot be achieved without the perception of other-presence. As Heidegger (1962, 207) puts it: "What we 'first' hear is never noises or complexes of sounds but the creaking waggon, the motor-cycle," and thus the percept has other-presence within my environment.

This is one of the few examples in *Being and Time* where Heidegger mentions hearing—all else is based on vision. This betrays a visual and temporal bias to the foundation of other-presence as a concept that is found in other philosophers' works, and thus finds its way into the technology and conception of virtual reality. Gumbrecht (2004, 17), for example, states that: "What is 'present' to us . . . is in front of us," while Heidegger (1962, 47) claims that: "Entities are grasped in their Being as 'presence'; this means they are understood with regard to a definite mode of time–the 'Present.'" In other words, to be other-present to us, entities must be seen—and vision, the result of the essentially instantaneous passage of light waves from an object to my eyes, operates in the present tense. Other-presence is here (seen in front of me) and now (in the present). A few examples are enough to refute this conception. My neighbor is not in front of me, there to be seen sweeping his vacuum-cleaner across his floor, yet his actions through their sound alone—and my understanding of them—provide other-presence. My perception of the sounds forms part of a percept in my environment that, through the process of imagination, includes a rough image of his face, how he moves, his gripping of the machine's handle, the shoes on his feet, and so on. The whistling I simultaneously hear also forms part of the resultant percept because this neighbor is an example of someone who really does whistle while he works. On the matter of the present, it must make way for the past, because the passage of potential from source in externality through to sensation and ultimately perception, percept, and other-presence in my environment is like a handicapped race. If we accept that the speed of light waves is, for practical purposes, instantaneous at c. 300,000 km/s, the speed of sound waves in air is not (c. 341 m/s): we may well see the present, but we hear the past. As a counterweight to this, the time taken for actualization of sound wave potential to sensation through to the perception of sound is about 40 msec faster than the same process for light waves, such that a simultaneous production of light wave and sound wave potential in externality must be about 10–15 m away from us in order that a perception of image and a perception of sound occur in consciousness at the same time (Keetels and Vroomen 2012, 147–148; Westerhoff 2011, 67). Closer to or further away from us, the perceptions arise at different times—within certain limits, the light wave and sound wave will be perceived as one percept if cognition judges it so. And this is just vision and hearing.

If other-presence can also be derived as I claim from sensable potential other than light waves, then the inexorable conclusion is that there is no external, absolute present time, and that our perception of the present, my self's present, is an illusion. It is a necessary illusion, though, because we need a model of salient externality in which to be self-present and for our survival and flourishing in externality at large; but the environment is a model of past events. If it were not so, there would be no sport to be had in boxing, for example, as boxers would always dodge the advancing fist with ease.

In terms of the visual bias to presence, which I claim is endemic in virtual reality and the development of immersive technology, descriptions of virtual reality devices such as head-mounted displays (HMDs) tend to favor the visual and graphics capabilities over the audio. Regarding HMDs, described as "sealing off the physical environment and presenting the senses with an inclusive virtual environment" (IJsselsteijn 2003, 34), this may well be the case for the visual sense, but is not a claim that can be made for any other sense. Anyone who has tried an HMD will know that not only do its audio capabilities *not* fully block any sound waves from nearby (among many reasons, sound waves are transmitted through our skulls) but one still smells and tastes from outside, and one still feels the ground beneath the feet, the clothes one is wearing, the temperature in the room, and so on. Or take this early description of what leads to presence in immersive virtual environments (viz. virtual reality): "It is immersive since it immerses a representation of the person's body . . . in the computer-generated environment. . . . Immersion can lead to presence" (Slater, Usoh, and Steed 1994, 131). Once more, the concentration on the visual, in this case, a third-person representation of the user.

While video game technology and approaches bear some parallels to those of virtual reality, it developed separately. Here too, there is an overwhelming bias to the visual over the auditory (the first video games had no audio), and discussions of immersion favor graphics technology and reproduction over the audio. The review of "most immersive first-person games" I provided earlier states: "Games can be immersive because of their polished graphics, remarkable storytelling, or intuitive controls." There is praise for graphics, animations, resolution and framerate, ray tracing and texture shading, but nothing about audio or sound. None of this is to say that there is no use of audio by developers of virtual reality and video games, far from it, but there is clearly a visual bias in these fields toward perceptions of what presence is and how it is achieved. It appears, in the main, that graphics lead to presence while audio plays a supportive role and is designed as effect.

Waterworth and Waterworth (2014, 589) further describe (self-)presence as the feeling that "distinguishes self from nonself" where "nonself" may be equated to my concept of externality (that which is not self). But I disagree with this, preferring instead to turn that statement on its head. Thus, it is self-presence that itself arises from the process of individuating self from externality (Walther-Hansen and Grimshaw 2016; Grimshaw-Aagaard 2019). The construction of the environment, as a metonym for salient externality, is a process of continual modeling and remodeling of salient externality—this is similar to Clark's (2013) description of the generation and selection of perceptual hypotheses. If self-presence is indeed the feeling of being in a place, then there must perforce be a place in which to be present, and this is my reason to disagree with Waterworth and Waterworth. The environment is where my self is present, and the environment is formed due to the fundamental imperative to distinguish my self from nonself, to arrive at self-presence as a distinction to the other-presences that form the basis for the environment. Other-presences manifest as percepts (the confluence of cognition and typically multimodal perception such as "a car," "coffee," "my wife," for instance) in the environment, mapped out as a model of salient externality, and my experience of self in that environment forms my reality.[5]

The Importance of Sound to Presence

How then does presence arise in the context of the first-person-perspective video game, and what is the role of sound in the attainment of it? I start from the premise that presence in video games is the same feeling as presence attained elsewhere. That is, the feeling that I am in a place and able to act within and on that place (right now, sitting in my living room on a wet, early summer morning putting pen to paper) is the same regardless of the source of the potential that is actualized. It makes no difference to presence whether the instigator of potential is computer code, the sun, or electricity driving a ventilation motor. We engage with and use the potential in the same manner, and, in this, I make no distinction between so-called virtual worlds and the so-called real-world—it is all externality. What *is* different is the manner of presentation of potential and mode of engagement with externality. Whereas I can direct my body through a doorway to pass from one room to another, I must guide a proxy in order to approach achieving the same in a video game. I might be physically in externality, where that externality is the material externality of direct potential, but cannot be so in the video game, where the externality is composed of indirect potential that attempts to cover up and misdirect as to its digital provenance. This attempt at obfuscation is one reason why some scholars describe presence (in digital worlds) as a perceptual illusion of nonmediation (Green and McAllister 2020).

Presence works in the first-person-perspective video game because the potential available for sensory actualization does not depend for its actualization on its instigating source. We use such potential in the same way regardless of that source. That we attain presence in such games despite their many and manifest shortcomings (little if any touch and no smell, taste, temperature, gravity) is witness to my self's need to be present somewhere, to derive meaning from externality whatever the source of potential in externality. The ability to derive meaning from externality's potential is something learned as we grow and develop from dependent babies to functioning individuals. We learn to connect potential, to construct the presence habitat that is our environment, in a way that makes sense because acting within and on the environment is the proxy enabler for acting within and on externality, to survive and thrive in it.

All the evidence suggests that sound, early on, is the catalyst for the formation of self. This is beautifully put by Anzieu (1989, 167) when he states that "the Self forms as a sound envelope through the experience of a bath of sounds" and that, citing a number of studies of babies, "mental capacities operate first on acoustic material [, and] feedback loops with the environment [i.e., externality] [are] audio-phonological in nature" (164–165). In other words, early in life, humans form a conception of self that is driven by sound wave potential from externality. This sound wave potential becomes other-presence in our environment, and this provides two things: it provides the experience of nonself that, in its existence, provides the means to form the concept of self; and it provides the place in which that self can attain self-presence.

As I noted earlier, the derivation of perception from actualized potential in salient externality occurs faster for sound than for image within a roughly 15 m horizon. Take the typical video-gaming set-up: both screen and loudspeakers are easily within that horizon. Thus, perceptions of sound are formed first—even more so in the case of headphone usage—and so it is from these perceptions that the experience of other-presence arises, and thus the space in which the self can be present.

Notes

1. I like to play my students the recording of a Geiger counter and ask them what they hear. Answers do include the correct one (for those who do have the requisite worldly experience [usually vicarious]), but also include ones such as "popcorn cooking" or "hailstones on a skylight." Their realities, as the experience of the environment, are, as I play the recording, quite different to mine.
2. The wagon itself is not the source of the sound wave; the composite sound wave, foundational to what is heard, results from movements of and friction between components of the wagon, its interactions with the immediate surroundings, even peripherals such as the shouting drover and neighing horses.
3. For example, https://www.thegamer.com/first-person-video-games-best-most-immersive/ (accessed May 2, 2021).
4. In the case of presence in dream worlds, I might even say that imagination is necessary and sufficient. But that is another essay.
5. Although it does not form fully part of this discussion, I should note the conclusion to be derived from reflex action. If I lunge away from the teetering wine glass at the dinner table, this is a reflex and requires no self-presence. Indeed, I am only aware of the action *after* it has happened. To do this requires what I term a *protoenvironment*; I must, after all, possess some basic model of salient externality, in which my reflex can respond, because I do not lurch *toward* the spilling wine. Consequently, again I must conclude that the place in which to feel present has already been formed and so is not itself the result of self-presence.

References

Accredited Standards Committee S1, Acoustics. 2013. *Acoustic Terminology: ANSI/ASA S1.1-2013*. ANSI. Melville, NY: Acoustical Society of America.

Anzieu, Didier. 1989. *The Skin Ego: A Psychoanalytical Approach to the Self*. Translated by Chris Turner. New Haven; London: Yale University Press.

Calleja, Gordon. 2014. "Immersion in Virtual Worlds." In *The Oxford Handbook of Virtuality*, edited by Mark Grimshaw, 222–236. New York: Oxford University Press.

Clark, Andy. 2013. "Expecting the World: Perception, Prediction, and the Origins of Human Knowledge." *Journal of Philosophy* 110 (9): 469–496.

Garner, Tom Alexander, and Mark Grimshaw. 2014. "Sonic Virtuality: Understanding Audio in a Virtual World." In *The Oxford Handbook of Virtuality*, edited by Mark Grimshaw, 364–377. New York: Oxford University Press.

Green, Melanie C., and Cass A. McAllister. 2020. "Presence." *International Encyclopedia of Media Psychology*. Accessed December 7, 2020. https://onlinelibrary.wiley.com/doi/10.1002/9781119011071.iemp0058.

Grimshaw, Mark. 2012. "Sound and Player Immersion in Digital Games." In *The Oxford Handbook of Sound Studies*, edited by Trevor Pinch and Karin Bijsterveld, 347–366. New York: Oxford University Press.

Grimshaw, Mark. 2015. "A Brief Argument for, and Summary of, the Concept of Sonic Virtuality." *Danish Musicology Online*, special edition, 81–98.

Grimshaw-Aagaard, Mark. 2019. "Presence, Environment, and Sound and the Role of Imagination." In *The Oxford Handbook of Sound and Imagination*, edited by Mark Grimshaw-Aagaard, Mads Walther-Hansen, and Martin Knakkergaard, 669–681. New York: Oxford University Press.

Grimshaw, Mark, and Tom Alexander Garner. 2015. *Sonic Virtuality: Sound as Emergent Perception*. New York: Oxford University Press.

Gumbrecht, Hans Ulrich. 2004. *Production of Presence: What Meaning Cannot Convey*. Stanford, CA: Stanford University Press.

Heidegger, Martin. 1962. *Being and Time*. Translated by John Macquarrie and Edward Robinson. Oxford: Blackwell.

IJsselsteijn, Wijnand A., Jonathan Freeman, and Huib de Ridder. 2001. "Presence: Where Are We?" *Cyberpsychology and Behavior* 4 (2): 179–182. https://dx.doi.org/10.1089/109493101300117875.

IJsselsteijn, Wijnand. 2003. "Presence in the Past: What Can We Learn from Media History?" In *Being There: Concepts, Effects and Measurements of User Presence in Synthetic Environments*, edited by Giuseppe Riva, Fabrizio Davide, and Wijnand A. IJsselsteijn, 17–40. Amsterdam: IOS Press.

Keetels, Mirjam, and Jean Vroomen. 2012. "Perception of Synchrony between the Senses." In *The Neural Bases of Multisensory Processes*, edited by M. M. Murray and M. T. Wallace, 147–177. Boca Raton, FL: CRC Press/Taylor & Francis.

Lee, Kwan Min. 2004. "Presence, Explicated." *Communication Theory* 14 (1): 27–50. https://dx.doi.org/10.1111/j.1468-2885.2004.tb00302.x.

Minsky, Marvin. 1980. "Telepresence." *Omni*, 45–51.

O'Callaghan, Casey. 2007. *Sounds*. Oxford: Oxford University Press.

Pasnau, Robert. 1999. "What Is Sound?" *Philosophical Quarterly* 49 (196): 309–324.

Slater, Mel, Martin Usoh, and Anthony Steed. 1994. "Depth of Presence in Virtual Environments." *Presence: Teleoperators and Virtual Environments* 3 (2): 130–144. https://dx.doi.org/10.1162/pres.1994.3.2.130.

Slater, Mel. 2003. "A Note on Presence Terminology." *Presence Connect* 3 (3): 1–5.

Walther-Hansen, Mads, and Mark Grimshaw. 2016. "Being in a Virtual World: Presence, Environment, Salience, Sound." In *Audio Mostly 2016*, 77–84. Piteå, Sweden: Interactive Institute. http://dl.acm.org/citation.cfm?id=2986425.

Walther-Hansen, Mads, and Mark Grimshaw-Aagaard. 2020. "Don't Extend! Reduce! The Sound Approach to Reality." In *The 15th International Conference on Audio Mostly*, edited by Katharina Groß-Vogt and Robert Höldrich, 8–15. https://dl.acm.org/doi/proceedings/10.1145/3411109.

Waterworth, John A., and Eva L. Waterworth. 2014. "Distributed Embodiment: Real Presence in Virtual Bodies." In *The Oxford Handbook of Virtuality*, edited by Mark Grimshaw, 589–601. New York: Oxford University Press.

Westerhoff, Jan. 2011. *Reality: A Very Short Introduction*. Oxford: Oxford University Press.

Index

For the benefit of digital users, indexed terms that span two pages (e.g., 52–53) may, on occasion, appear on only one of those pages.

Note: Tables and figures are indicated by an italic t and f following the page number.